The Statute of the International Criminal Court:
A Documentary History

Compiled by
M. Cherif Bassiouni

Transnational Publishers, Inc.
Ardsley, New York

Library of Congress Catalog Card Number: 98-61370

The statute of the international criminal court: a documentary history /
compiled by M. Cherif Bassiouni.
ISBN 1-57105-095-7

TABLE OF CONTENTS

About the Author

Chairman of the Drafting Committee of the United Nations Diplomatic Conference on the Establishment of an International Criminal Court, Rome, Italy, June 15-July 17, 1998; Vice-Chairman of the General Assembly's Preparatory Committee on the Establishment of an International Criminal Court (1996-1998); Vice-Chairman of the General Assembly's *Ad Hoc* Committee on the Establishment of an International Criminal Court (1995).

Chairman of the United Nations Commission of Experts Established Pursuant to Security Council 780 (1992) to Investigate Violations of International Humanitarian Law in the Former Yugoslavia and Special Rapporteur on Gathering and Analysis of the Facts, 1992-1994.

For over thirty years he worked for the establishment of an international criminal court. During that period he prepared for the Commission on Human Rights the "Study on Ways and Means of Ensuring the Implementation of International Instruments Such as the International Convention on the Suppression and Punishment of the Crime of Apartheid, Including the Establishment of the International Jurisdiction Envisaged by the Convention."

In 1977 he also served as co-chair of the Committee of Experts that prepared the first draft of the United Nations Convention on the Prevention and Suppression of Torture.

His many writings and numerous activities to promote international criminal justice and to establish a permanent international criminal court have earned him worldwide recognition

A Professor of Law at DePaul University since 1964, he is the author and editor of 41 books on International and Comparative Criminal Law and Human Rights and 165 law review articles in Arabic, English, French, Italian and Spanish. Some of these publications have been cited by the International Court of Justice, the United States Supreme Court, United States Appellate and Federal District Courts, and State Supreme Courts.

He was elected President of the International Association of Penal Law in 1989 after having served as Secretary-General from 1974 to 1988. Since 1988 he also is President of the International Institute of Higher Studies in Criminal Sciences in Siracusa, Italy, after having served as Dean from 1979-1988.

In 1998 he was appointed by the Commission on Human Rights as Special Rapporteur on the Right to Restitution, Compensation, and Rehabilitation for Victims of Grave Violations of Human Rights and Fundamental Freedoms.

Author's Preface

For most of this century many individuals have played an important role in sustaining the idea of establishing a permanent international criminal court (ICC). Vespasian V. Pella, Henri Donnedieu de Vabres, Hans Kelsen, Ricardo Alfaro, Jean Spiropoulos, Stefan Glaser, Robert Jackson, Jean Graven, Pierre Carjeu, Quintiliano Saldana, and Anthony Sottile, to name only the most prominent, are now a part of history. In the last thirty years, a succeeding generation took over, and its most prominent personalities include: Giuliano Vassalli, Hans-Heinrich Jescheck, Benjamin Ferencz, Gerhard O.W. Mueller, Julius Stone, and Robert K. Woetzel. Then in the late 1980s, a highly distinguished group of the ICC's proponents emerged. Among the most notable are: Arthur N.R. Robinson, Emma Bonino, Robert Badinter, Jimmy Carter, Abdou Diouf, Abdula Omar, Jacques Baudin, Aryeh Neier, and Richard Goldstone. Each succeeding group of leaders picked up the baton of history's relay, but there are also many others in academia, public life, and non-governmental organizations (NGOs) that provided the necessary support for the idea of an ICC to become one of the goals of international civil society. They all merit our recognition and appreciation.

Between 1920 and 1980 there were very few organizations whose mission was the establishment of an ICC. The Association International de Droit Pénal (AIDP), a pioneer non-governmental organization (NGO), along with the International Law Association (ILA) and the Inter-Parliamentary Union (which is not an NGO), were the first to propose, in 1926, the idea of a permanent ICC. Until the late 1980s, however, the AIDP was virtually the only major scholarly organization to consistently advocate the establishment of an ICC. It was joined during the 1970s by the International Institute of Higher Studies in Criminal Studies (ISISC). No other organizations have done as much and for as long as these two organizations have in support of an ICC, and credit must be given to them, even though it may appear self-fulfilling since I have the honor to preside both organizations. During the 1980s, a number of other NGOs became active and took the lead on this issue. They are mentioned with due credit and appreciation below.

The efforts aimed at establishing an ICC entered into a new phase in the 1990s and a positive outcome became at last foreseeable. During this phase an idea and an ideal were converted into a political reality. It began in 1989 when the International Law Commission (ILC) received a cautious and limited mandate from the General Assembly concerning drugs. The credit for that initiative goes to Arthur N.R. Robinson, now President of Trinidad and Tobago. The ILC had long concerned itself with the question of the codification of Crimes Against the Peace and Security of Mankind but only peripherally with the establishment of an ICC. Early on in the ILC's work on these questions, the most active ILC members on the subject of the Draft Code from 1947 to 1954 were: Ricardo Alfaro, and Jean Spiropoulos. Then in the 1990s, the ILC's most active members on the questions of the Draft Code and the Draft Statute were: James R. Crawford, Christian Tomuschat, Alain Pellet and Doudou Thiam. It was the ILC who in 1994 completed the Draft ICC Statute and on that basis in 1995 the General Assembly established the *Ad Hoc* Committee on the Establishment of a Permanent International Criminal Court (*Ad Hoc* Committee) which was followed in 1996 by the Preparatory Committee on an International Criminal Court (PrepCom). The latter completed its work in 1998 in view of the Diplomatic Conference called by the General Assembly for the period June 15-July 17, 1998 to convene in Rome at the generous invitation of the Italian Government.

During 1989 to 1998, a great deal happened that changed the attitudes of governments. First, and possibly foremost, was the end of the "cold war." Then the Yugoslavia and Rwanda experiences and the resulting establishment by the Security Council of the International Criminal Tribunal for the Former Yugoslavia and International Criminal Tribuanl for Rwanda. It was during this time that the ICC was finally conceived and then in Rome on July 17, 1998, it was born.

At the meetings of the *Ad Hoc* Committee and PrepCom between 1995-1998 a new coalition of "like-minded states" emerged that became the driving force of the ICC. These states and the NGOs who organized a coalition of some 300 organizations were very effective throughout the three and a half year process. NGO contributions were so effective at the *Ad Hoc* Committee meetings and the PrepCom that they were given unprecedented access to the proceedings of the Rome Diplomatic Conference. Several of these NGOs deserve special recognition for their contribution. They include: the American Bar Association, Amnesty International, the Carter Center, the European Law Students Association, Human Rights Watch, the International Commission of Jurists, the Lawyers Committee for Human Rights, No Peace Without Justice, Parliamentarians for Global Action, the Women's Caucus, the World Federalist Association, and the Washington Working Group on the International Criminal Court. I would be remiss not to recognize the exceptional contribututions of three persons whose untiring work and dedication deserve our highest appreciation. They are: William Pace, Coordinator of the NGO Coalition for an International Criminal Court; Christopher Hall, Amnesty International; and Richard Dicker, Human Rights Watch.

During the course of this process several inter-governmental organizations also played an active role. The International Committee of the Red Cross made valuable scientific contributions to the definition of war crimes, the European Union was politically supportive at the level of Heads of States, Ministers of Foreign Affairs and Commissioners, and the African-Asian Legal Consultative Council and the League of Arab States were also active in the process.

Within the United Nations system, there were many who have consistently supported the establishment of an ICC and a system of international criminal justice, particularly Secretary-General Kofi Annan. Hans Correll, Under-Secretary General and Legal Counsel, was also consistently supportive, and since she took office, Mary Robinson, High Commission for Human Rights has also been a strong supporter of the ICC. The Secretariat of the *Ad Hoc* Committee, the PrepCom, and the Diplomatic Conference was provided from the legal staff of the Codification Division which must be praised for their dedication, competence, and hard work that significantly contributed to the success of the Diplomatic Conference.

Many academics have also worked for the establishment of an ICC and their scholarly writings, cited in *Historical Survey 1919-1998,* made it possible for the idea to gain international recognition and national support.

The Italian Ministry of Foreign Affairs, who carried the responsibility for the Diplomatic Conference, must be congratulated for their hard work, diligence, and commitment to the success of the Treaty of Rome. The leadership of Foreign Minister Lamberto Dini, the support of Ambassador Vattani, Secretary General of the Italian Ministry of Foreign Affairs,

Ambassador Fulci, Professor Leanza, Professor Mauro Politi and Councellor Umberto Colessanti, merit our highest praise.

Recognition should also be given to the John D. & Catherine T. MacArthur Foundation whose support for the establishment of an international criminal court has been very important, particularly in their funding of a special project for Least Developed Countries undertaken by the International Criminal Justice and Weapons Control Center of DePaul University. The Foundation helped bring several LDC's to the December 1997 and March-April 1998 sessions of the PrepCom and 21 delegates to the Diplomatic Conference in Rome. These delegates were from Bangladesh, Benin, Burkina Faso, Burundi, Cameroon, Cape Verde, Comoros, Djibouti, Ethiopia, Gabon, Guinea, Guinea-Bissau, Haiti, Lesotho, Malawi , Mozambique, Nepal, Niger, South Africa, Tanzania, and Yemen to the Diplomatic Conference in Rome

During the process of the establishment of the ICC many individuals also played a leading role that must be recognized, for without them, the accomplishment in Rome would have been impossible. Most of them are mentioned in *Historical Survey: 1919 - 1998*, but three deserve special recognition. They are: Giovanni Conso, Chairman of the Conference; Phillipe Kirsch, Chairman of the Committee of the Whole; and Adriaan Bos, who chaired the *Ad Hoc* Committee and PrepCom.

My hope is that the efforts of all these individuals, and the others that I have not mentioned, shall not be forgotten and that those who will one day look back at this period will realize how difficult it was to bring about this result.

It was my privilege to have been part of those who brought about this big step forward for justice and peace. For me, it is the end of a thirty year journey. But, I know that it is only the beginning of a new momentum, that of bringing about the effective operation of the ICC. The next stage of bringing the ICC into operational reality is likely to be as arduous as the previous. It will also be a more critical stage.

As succeeding generations add their contribution to the overall enterprise, we must be confident in the ultimate result, just as we must feel comforted in the belief that this enterprise is part of the building of civilization. In so doing, no one's task is too small to be insignificant, for each one of us is a part of the whole.

M. Cherif Bassiouni

PREFACE

THE SECRETARY-GENERAL

STATUTE OF THE INTERNATIONAL CRIMINAL COURT:
A DOCUMENTARY HISTORY
October 1998

This book is being published at an auspicious time in the history of international law. Rarely, if ever, have we witnessed such genuine promise of achieving a world where the interests of peace and justice will no longer be seen as contradictory. For in this 50th anniversary year of the Universal Declaration of Human Rights, the international community has passed two historic landmarks.

In Arusha, the International Criminal Tribunal for Rwanda announced the first judgement ever given by an international court in a case of genocide. This precedent-setting case was born out of one of the darkest hours of the late 20th century. But as we stand on the eve of the 21st, it also provides us with one of the brightest rays of hope. For the work of the two United Nations criminal tribunals, for Rwanda and the former Yugoslavia, though still incomplete, has been a milestone in the struggle to end the "culture of impunity"; the culture in which it has been easier to bring someone to justice for killing one person than for killing 100,000. It has been a milestone in the quest to prove that, when crimes occur of such magnitude that they are rightly dubbed "crimes against humanity", humanity is not without recourse.

Above all, we might claim it as a milestone on the road to Rome - an essential step towards the adoption on 17 July this year of the Rome Statute of the International Criminal Court. The adoption of the Rome Statute followed more than 50 years of hope alternated with despair. In 1947, the United Nations first addressed the issue of an international criminal court through the work of the International Law Commission. In subsequent efforts, repeatedly hampered by the realities of the Cold War, Professor Bassiouni played an indefatigable part - as he later did in the creation of the International Criminal Tribunal for the former Yugoslavia.

If the establishment of the tribunals for the former Yugoslavia and Rwanda helped bring home to Governments the feasibility of a permanent international criminal court, the role of international civil society was equally vital.

The NGO Coalition for an International Criminal Court brought together a broad-based network of NGOs and international law experts to develop strategies and foster awareness. Hundreds of non-governmental organizations took part in the conference itself -- an unprecedented level of participation by civil society in a law-making conference.

There were also many individuals, including distinguished scholars, civic leaders and government officials, who advocated and supported the establishment of an international criminal court. Among them, the leading role played by Professor Bassiouni for over 30 years culminated in his contribution as Chairman of the Drafting Committee of the Rome Diplomatic Conference.

It gives me great pleasure, therefore, to welcome the publication of this book, which provides a legislative history of the ICC as well as a record of the work of the United Nations in support of its establishment. I hope that as the Court is established and as its jurisdiction continues to evolve, this record will be of use to government officials, researchers and historian everywhere.

INTRODUCTION

The Honorable Jimmy Carter,
Former President of the United States of America,
Chair, The Carter Center

United Nations efforts to establish a permanent International Criminal Court (ICC) began in the aftermath of World War II when, in 1951, a special committee of the General Assembly prepared the first draft statute. However, the Cold War overshadowed and paralyzed any concerted efforts to advance the process. Now, in 1998, an overwhelming number of the nations of the world finally have agreed on a statute establishing the Court.

The statute resulting from the Diplomatic Conference in Rome is an imperfect text, as are most treaties negotiated amid diverse political pressures and priorities. Nevertheless, the delicate compromise in Rome gives the world an unprecedented opportunity to deter crimes and to hold accountable the worst criminals and eliminate impunity resulting in endless cycles of violence in many countries. Governments and citizens of every nation should reflect on this historic achievement and firmly support the Court.

The previous edition of these texts compiled by Professor Bassiouni during the drafting process of the ICC was a useful reference for delegates of governments and non-governmental organizations during the intensive negotiations in Rome. I also hope that the statute itself, which appears in this updated edition, will be broadly ratified in the near future so that perpetrators of the crimes covered by it will never again escape justice.

I congratulate him on his life-long commitment to the ICC.

**Ceremony for the Opening of Signature of the Treaty on the
Establishment of an International Criminal Court
"Il Campidoglio," Rome, July 18, 1998**

H.E. Kofi Annan, Secretary-General of the United Nations

Your Excellency,
Ladies and Gentlemen,

This is indeed a historic moment.

Two millennia ago one of this city's most famous sons Marcus Tullius Cicero, declared that "in the midst of arms, law stands mute."

As a result of what we are doing here today, there is real hope that that bleak statement will be less true in the future than it has been in the past.

Until now, when powerful men committed crimes against humanity, they knew that as long as they remained powerful no earthly court could judge them.

Even when they *were* judged—as happily some of the worst criminals were in 1945—they could claim that this is happening only because others have proved more powerful, and so are able to sit in judgement over them. Verdicts intended to uphold the rights of the weak and helpless can be impugned as "victors' justice."

Such accusations can also be made, however unjustly, when courts are set up only *ad hoc*, like the Tribunals in the Hague and in Arusha, to deal with crimes committed in specific conflicts or by specific regimes. Such procedures seem to imply that the same crimes, committed by different people, or at different times and places, will go unpunished.

Now at last, thanks to the hard work of the States that participated in the United Nations Conference over the last five weeks—and indeed for many more months before that—we shall have a permanent court to judge the most serious crimes of concern to the international community as a whole: genocide, crimes against humanity and war crimes.

Other crimes, wherever and whenever they may be committed, may be included in the future. The crime of aggression is already mentioned in the Statute.

For the United Nations, this decision has special significance. We never forget that our Organization has its origins in a global struggle against régimes which were guilty of mass murder on a horrendous scale. And unhappily we have had to deal all to recently, in Rwanda and the Former Yugoslavia, with new crimes of the same appalling nature, if not quite of the same magnitude.

By adopting this Statute, participants in the Conference have overcome many legal and political problems, which kept this question on the United Nations agenda almost throughout the Organization's history.

No doubt, many of us would have liked a Court vested with even more far-reaching powers, but that should not lead us to minimize the breakthrough you have achieved. The establishment of the Court is still a gift of hope to future generations, and a giant step forward in the march towards universal human rights and the rule of law

It is an achievement which, only a few years ago, nobody would have thought possible.

It therefore gives me great pleasure to be here in person; to place in your custody the Final Act of the Conference; and to transmit to you the Rome Statute of the International Criminal Court adopted yesterday. From now on the Statute will bear the name of this Eternal City, in fitting tribute to the people of Rome and of Italy who have hosted this Conference, and to their Government which worked tirelessly for its successful conclusion.

The Statute was opened yesterday for signature. Some States have already signed it, and more will do so during this ceremony. It will remain in your hands until 17 October 1998. After that it will be deposited with me, as Secretary-General of the United Nations, and will stay open for signature in New York until 31 December 2000.

It is my fervent hope that by then a large majority of United Nations Member States will have signed and ratified it, so that the Court will have unquestioned authority and the widest possible jurisdiction.

Ceremony for the Opening of Signature of the Treaty on the Establishment of an International Criminal Court "Il Campidoglio," Rome, July 18, 1998

H.E. Lamberto Dini, Minister of Foreign Affairs of the Republic of Italy

Mr. Secretary-General, Distinguished Colleagues, Distinguished Delegates,

An intense round of resolute, patient negotiating has now been concluded, just in time, with the adoption of the Final Act and the opening for signature of the Rome Statute of the International Criminal Court. Italy is honoured to have hosted such an important event to lay down the rules that will govern the international community and to define the instruments to be used to guarantee their enforcement. The government and the City of Rome are also honoured to provide this solemn venue to celebrate the conclusion of the Conference.

None of us can fail to perceive the significance of this ceremony. None of us can fail to appreciate the expectations of international public opinion, clamouring around these ancient walls, but which will not be disappointed thanks to the farsightedness shown by all of you and the countries you represent. This success would not have been possible without the pressure of civil society in our countries expressed by the Non-Governmental Organisations that have so passionately backed the word of governments.

Inevitably, these negotiations have been difficult, at times even acrimonious. But this was to be expected. The Statute of the Court introduces radically important innovations into relations between States, affecting their sovereign prerogatives, and establishing a new relationship between the national courts and international jurisdiction. It complements that Declaration of Human Rights which, fifty years on, still remains one of the defining moments in the history of the United Nations. And thanks to this Court, UN credibility has now been further enhanced. Every country has played a part in drafting the Statute, including those which have declared their unwillingness to sign it. And we can understand their reasons. But we earnestly hope that once the nature and the operation of the Court has been more carefully appraised, they will come to a different determination in the not to distant future, and will accede to the new Institution.

Not everything that some of us had hoped for has been put into the Statute. This was inevitable in such a complex exercise, carried through by such a large number of countries, with the aim of attracting the broadest possible support for the future. I nevertheless believe that we must acknowledge that the International Court that is being instituted here in Rome today is vested with the qualities of effectiveness, independence and authority commensurate to the tasks that lie ahead of it.

It is not over-optimistic to say that the Court will help us to feel that our individual rights are now more safely guaranteed, and will render coexistence between peoples less precarious, reducing recourse to arbitrary conduct and violence on a large scale. In other words, it will mark not only a political but a moral stride forward by international society.

I would therefore like to express my gratitude for the work of the delegations, for the constructive attitude adopted by your governments, for the commitment of the United Nations and particularly its Secretary-General, Kofi Annan, whom I wish to thank for being here in person, and for the hospitality of the Mayor of Rome, Francesco Rutelli.

It is with these sentiments in mind that I take custody of the Final Act of the Conference and the Text of the Rome Statute for three months, which I shall now sign and invite everyone present with the powers to do so to sign it with me.

Ceremony for the Opening of Signature of the Treaty on the Establishment of an International Criminal Court "Il Campidoglio," Rome, July 18, 1998

H.E. Professor Giovanni Conso, President of the Diplomatic Conference

I am truly happy and honored to be alongside UN Secretary-General Kofi Annan in this prestigious hall for the solemn celebration of an extraordinary event, the opening of signature of the Rome Treaty establishing an international criminal court.

I would like to thank one more time all those who participated in the work of the Conference and whose constant dedication and commitment were absolute. In particular, my gratitude to the President of the Committee of the Whole, Ambassador Philippe Kirsch, for his determined contribution which brought about the success of this endeavor. The same also goes to Ambassador Adriaan Bos for the preceding preparatory work which took place under his enlightened direction and without which the desired result would not have been achieved. Equally, I extend my gratitude to the President of the Drafting Committee, Professor Cherif Bassiouni, who was able to ensure that the drafting of the texts submitted to him were done, and were done within the limited time available. Finally, my special thanks to Hans Corell and Roy Lee who ensured that the organization of the work proceeded in an admirable manner.

The satisfaction we all feel is great because we have all contributed to a page of history. This is truly an event without precedent, an event which will achieve a radical change in the course of a long voyage to protect the fundamental values of humanity.

After fifty years of the Universal Declaration of Human Rights approval by the General Assembly of the United Nations, there is a new message that now comes from Rome, which is also a very specific notice; the international community will no longer tolerate the horrors that chill the conscience of every individual nor will it tolerate impunity for the perpetrators of those atrocities.

As we enter this third millennium, the result of this Conference allows us to affirm that we can walk into it with our head high, and that is precisely because we have succeeded in our endeavor which millions of persons of every part of the world looked forward to with hope. This endeavor provides an irreversible basis on which the international criminal court shall be established. It seemed that it was an unreachable dream, now it has become a reality.

**Ceremony for the Opening of Signature of the Treatyon the
Establishment of an International Criminal Court
"Il Campidoglio," Rome, July 18, 1998**

H.E. Ambassador Philippe Kirsch, Chairman of the Committee of the Whole

Ladies and gentlemen,

Yesterday, with the adoption of the Rome Statute of the International Criminal Court, we were witness to an historic moment. At the end of a century that has seen untold horrors, and where impunity has become commonplace, the world community took a stand last night and began the difficult but essential task of building a permanent international criminal court.

The foundations have been established for an institution that will have a profound impact on the lives of ordinary people. A clarion call has gone out to potential perpetrators of unspeakable atrocities, that the world is not going to stand by silently and watch the commission of outrageous violations of international law, such as genocide or crimes against humanity. The world has decided that "enough is enough."

The step that we have taken was a very big step, but equally large steps remain.

The Court will not begin its important work until sixty States have ratified the Statute. Thus, it is imperative that those States who have supported this Court continue to do so by ratifying the Statute as soon as possible, and by giving their continued political support to the creation of this Court. The sooner this is done, the sooner the Court can begin protecting victims by acting as a deterrent and by redressing impunity.

It is also hoped that those States with concerns about the Court will carefully consider the contents of the Statute. This Statute contains numerous checks and balances which will ensure that the Court operates in a credible and responsible manner, consistent with its role in upholding the rule of law. This Court is not a threat to any State which is committed to the security and well-bing of individual human beings. The Court will serve the objectives of such States by contributing to long-term stability.

My dear friends and colleagues, it was an honour to work with you. I know that difficult decisions have been made by all participants in this Conference. Agreement on the form and function of this institution was only possible with the spirit of cooperation which I believe has been demonstrated by every delegation. In addition, we are all indebted to the Italian government and to the Secretary-General of the United Nations for the indispensable support they have provided. I would like to say in closing how profoundly grateful I am to all of you whose contributions and efforts have brought about this great step forward in international law.

Thank you.

Ceremony for the Opening of Signature of the Treaty on the
Establishment of an International Criminal Court
"Il Campidoglio," Rome, July 18, 1998

Professor M. Cherif Bassiouni, Chairman of the Drafting Committee

The world will never be the same after the establishment of the international criminal court. Yesterday's adoption of the Final Act of the United Nations Diplomatic Conference and today's opening of the Convention for signature marks both the end of a historical process that started after World War I as well as the beginning of a new phase in the history of international criminal justice. The establishment of the ICC symbolizes and embodies certain fundamental values and expectations shared by all peoples of the world and is, therefore, a triumph for all peoples of the world.

The ICC reminds governments that *realpolitik,* which sacrifices justice at the altar of political settlements, is no longer accepted. It asserts that impunity for the perpetrators of "genocide," "crimes against humanity" and "war crimes" is no longer tolerated. In that respect it fulfils what Prophet Mohammad said, that "wrongs must be righted." It affirms that justice is an integral part of peace and thus reflects what Pope Paul VI once said, "If you want peace, work for justice." These values are clearly reflected in the ICC's Preamble.

The ICC will not be a panacea for all the ills of humankind. It will not eliminate conflicts, nor return victims to life, or restore survivors to their prior conditions of well-being and it will not bring all perpetrators of major crimes to justice. But it can help avoid some conflicts, prevent some victimization and bring to justice some of the perpetrators of these crimes. In so doing, the ICC will strengthen world order and contribute to world peace and security. As such, the ICC, like other international and national legal institutions, will add its contribution to the humanization of our civilization.

The ICC also symbolizes human solidarity, for as John Donne so eloquently stated, "No man is an island, entire of itself; each man is a piece of the continent, a part of the main . . . Any man's death diminishes me because I am involved in mankind."

Lastly, the ICC will remind us not to forget these terrible crimes so that we can heed the admonishment so aptly recorded by George Santayana, that those who forget the lessons of the past are condemned to repeat their mistakes.

Ultimately, if the ICC saves but one life, as it is said in the *Talmud,* it will be as if it saved the whole of humanity.

From Versailles to Rwanda, and now to the "Treaty of Rome," many have arduously labored for the establishment of a system of international criminal justice. Today our generation proudly, yet humbly, passes that torch on to future generations. Thus, the long relay of history goes on, with each generation incrementally adding on to the accomplishments of its predecessors.

But today, I can say to those who brought about this historic result, the government delegates in Rome, those who preceded them in New York since 1995, the United Nations staff, members of the Legal Office, the non-governmental organizations and here in Rome the staff of the Italian Ministry of Foreign Affairs, what Winston Churchill once said about heroes of another time, "Never have so many, owed so much, to so few."

Thank you.

Historical Survey: 1919-1998

M. Cherif Bassiouni[*]

Introduction

The purposes and functions of a permanent international criminal court combine humanistic values and policy considerations which are not only essential to the attainment of justice, redress and prevention, but also to the preservation, restoration and maintenance of peace.[1]

The history of civilization reveals that any polity, no matter how structured or unstructured, developed judicial institutions whose purposes were to mediate, resolve and impose settlements to conflicts that disrupted the social order.[2] The mere existence and effective operation of judicial institutions alone cannot create conditions and outcomes of order, lawfulness, rectitude, redress, prevention, justice and peace.[3] But without such institutions, these conditions and outcomes could not occur, even when imposed by forceful means. Force is never a satisfactory means to obtain such conditions and outcomes other than for a short duration, and even then it frequently brings about more harm than ultimate good. Furthermore, imposed conditions lack legitimacy.

Judicial institutions, along with other social, political, and economic institutions, are indispensable to the attainment of conditions and outcomes of order, lawfulness, rectitude, redress, prevention, justice and peace in national societies. And that also applies with respect to the international society.

In order to accomplish these value-oriented goals, the International Criminal Court (ICC) must be capable of translating moral values commonly shared by the international polity into applied precepts that engender positive reactions within the collectivity.

The ICC, which is the international polity's counterpart of national judicial institutions but with broader purposes, must be an effective and credible theater on which the private drama of a given case or series of cases can evolve publicly and project internationally. Like a Greek drama, it must at times fulfill the role of the *Theos ek mechanes* or, in Latin, the *Deus ex machina*, which appears at the scene of a crisis to provide a solution or diversion, albeit artificial, in respect to the causes of the conflict.[4] The transferral of the conflict's venue from the battlefield to the courtroom, not only changes the scenery, but helps freeze the harmful consequences of conflict while setting in motion a new cycle of highly visible impressionistic events that can bring about the end of the conflict's violent interaction. In that respect, the ICC is a necessary, *voire*, even an indispensable mechanism which can contribute to ending conflicts, restoring order, bringing about peace and preserving it.

The purposes of the ICC include: dispensing exemplary and retributive justice; providing victim redress; recording history; reinforcing social values; strengthening individual rectitude;

---

[*] Portions of this article derive from: M. Cherif Bassiouni, *Establishing an International Criminal Court: Historical Survey*, 149 MIL. L. REV. 49-63 (1995); and M. Cherif Bassiouni, *From Versailles to Rwanda in Seventy-Five Years: The Need to Establish a Permanent International Criminal Court*, 10 HARV. HUM. RTS. J. 11-62 (1997).

[1] *See* M. Cherif Bassiouni, *Searching for Peace and Achieving Justice: The Need for Accountability*, 59 LAW & CONTEMP. PROB. 9 (1996). *See also* W. Michael Reisman, *Institutions and Practices for Restoring and Maintaining Public Order*, 6 DUKE J. COMP. & INT'L L. 175 (1995).

[2] HISTOIRE DES INSTITUTIONS ET DES FAITS SOCIAUX (2 vols. 1957). *See also, The Philosophy of Law in Histou el Pesfective* (Carl Joechum Frudrich ed., 2d ed., 1963), Henry Wigmore, *A Panorama of World Legal Systems* 1206 (3 Vol.xxxi, 1928).

[3] W. Michael Reisman, *Stopping Wars and Making Peace: Reflections on the Ideology of Conflict Termination in Contemporary World Politics,"* 6 TULANE J. INT'L L. & COMP. L. 5, 46-52 (1998).

[4] *Id.* at 29.

educating present and future generations, and, more importantly, deterring and preventing future human depredations.[5] To accomplish these results, the ICC must act with predictability, consistency and publicly perceived fairness, and, when appropriate it must have the courage and wisdom to temper the harshness of the law with understanding and compassion.

The success of the ICC, like all human institutions, will depend on those who will be part of it. But they will need the resources and political support of many states to make this important institution work effectively. Only time will tell whether these expectations will be met. But judging from the ground swell of the international community's support, the prospects are favorable.

World War I was dubbed as "the war to end all wars," but no sooner had it ended when the winds of World War II started blowing. As World War II emptied its horrors, a new promise emerged, "never again." Yet since then, some 250 conflicts of an international and non-international character occurred, which, along with tyrannical regime victimizations produced an estimated 170 million casualties and other inestimable harmful consequences.[6] The "never again" promise was never redeemed. Governments and individuals went about the pursuit of power and wealth and the tragic events which succeeded and which caused such terrible devastation went by with limited attention and even lesser action by those governments who were in a position to prevent their occurrences or pursue restorative and retributive justice.

Whether the nature of contemporary democratic forms of governments is such as to make it difficult to obtain institutional responses[7] and to induce leadership action, or whether the humanistic values that most people share do not transcend individual interests or public apathy, the devastating results have been a neglect of prevention and control of these terrible occurrences, disregard of a victims' need for redress and justice and of the national and international community's needs for accountability and justice. This is particularly shocking in view of the extraordinarily high level of victimization that has occurred and the fact that most of that victimization falls under the proscriptive norms of genocide, crimes against humanity and war crimes, to name only the three major *jus cogens* international crimes.[8] As a result, the worst perpetrators of these crimes, including decision-makers and senior executors, have seldom been

---

[5]   *See* Mark J. Osiel, *Ever Again, Legal Remembrance of Administrative Massacre*, 144 U. PA. L. REV. 463 (1995). *See also* articles contained within *Accountability for International Crimes and Serious Violations of Fundamental Human Rights*, 59 LAW & CONTEMP. PROB. (1996) and *infra* note 9.

[6]   *See* Bassiouni, *supra* note 1. *See also* Jennifer L. Balint, *An Empirical Study of Conflict, Conflict Victimization and Legal Redress*, 14 NOUVELLES ÉTUDES PÉNALES 101 (Christopher C. Joyner, Special Ed. & M. Cherif Bassiouni, General Ed., 1998). *See generally* SIPRI YEARBOOKS 1975-1996. There were two reported studies in the PIOOM newsletter and progress report in 1994 and 1995: A.J. Jongman & A.P. Schmid, *Contemporary Conflicts: A Global Survey of High- and Lower Intensity Conflicts and Serious Disputes*, 7 PIOOM NEWSLETTER AND PROGRESS REPORT 14 (Winter 1995) (Interdisciplinary Research Program on Causes of Human Rights Violations, Leiden, Netherlands), and *Study*, 6 PIOOM NEWSLETTER 17 (1994); *see also* Alex P. Schmid, *Early Warning of Violent Conflicts: Causal Approaches*, in VIOLENT CRIME & CONFLICTS 47 (ISPAC 1997); *PIOOM World Conflict Map 1994-1995*, 7 PIOOM NEWSLETTER, *supra*.

[7]   *See* DEMOCRACY: ITS PRINCIPLES AND ACHIEVEMENT (Inter-Parliamentary Union 1998). *See* particularly M. Cherif Bassiouni, *Toward a Universal Declaration on the Basic Principles of Democracy: From Principles to Realization*, in DEMOCRACY: ITS PRINCIPLES AND ACHIEVEMENT, *supra*.

[8]   *See* M. Cherif Bassiouni, *International Crimes: Jus Cogens and Obligatio Erga Omnes*, 59 LAW & CONTEMP. PROB. 63 (1996).

brought to account for their misdeeds.[9] They have benefitted from impunity.[10] But, international civil society has finally reached the limits of its tolerance with the practice of impunity and now demands some *modicum* of justice. The ICC can fulfill the purposes of a symbol of justice as well as an effective judicial reality that can fairly mete out some retributive and restorative justice.

What follows is a history of the international community's quest for international criminal justice and, in particular, the establishment of a permanent international criminal court. It begins with the aftermath of World War I in 1919 and concludes with the opening for signature on July 18, 1998, of the Treaty of Rome containing the Statute for the International Criminal Court.[11]

International Investigative and Prosecutorial Bodies from 1919-1994

Since the end of World War I (1919), the world community has sought to establish a permanent international criminal court.[12] The attainment of that goal has been slow and

---

[9]   *See* Diane F. Orentlicher, *Settling Accounts: The Duty to Prosecute Human Rights Violations of a Prior Regime*, 100 YALE L.J. 2537 (1991). *See also* STEVEN R. RATNER & JASON S. ABRAMS, ACCOUNTABILITY FOR HUMAN RIGHTS ATROCITIES IN INTERNATIONAL LAW: BEYOND THE NUREMBERG LEGACY (1997).

[10]   *See e.g.*, articles contained within REINING IN IMPUNITY FOR INTERNATIONAL CRIMES AND SERIOUS VIOLATIONS OF FUNDAMENTAL HUMAN RIGHTS: PROCEEDINGS OF THE SIRACUSA CONFERENCE 17-21 SEPTEMBER 1997, 14 NOUVELLES ÉTUDES PÉNALES (Christopher C. Joyner, Special Ed. & M. Cherif Bassiouni, General Ed., 1998).

[11]   Adopted by the United Nations Diplomatic Conference of Plenipotentiaries on the Establishment of an International Criminal Court (A/Conf. 183/9, 1998).

[12]   *See generally* GUILIANO VASSALLI, LAGIUSTIZIA INTERNAZIONALE PENALE (1995); INTERNATIONAL COURTS FOR THE TWENTY-FIRST CENTURY (Mark W. Janis ed. 1992); FARHAD MALEKIAN, INTERNATIONAL CRIMINAL LAW: THE LEGAL AND CRITICAL ANALYSES OF INTERNATIONAL CRIMES (1991); M. CHERIF BASSIOUNI, AN INTERNATIONAL CRIMINAL CODE AND DRAFT STATUTE FOR AN INTERNATIONAL CRIMINAL TRIBUNAL (1987); BENJAMIN FERENCZ, AN INTERNATIONAL CRIMINAL COURT (2 vols. 1980); JULIUS STONE & ROBERT WOETZEL, TOWARD A FEASIBLE INTERNATIONAL CRIMINAL COURT (1970); PIERRE CARJEU, PROJET D'UNE JURIDICTION PÉNALE INTERNATIONALE (1953); A. SOTTILE, THE PROBLEM OF THE CREATION OF A PERMANENT INTERNATIONAL CRIMINAL COURT (1951); L'UNION INTERPARLIAMENTAIRE, COMPTE RENDU DE LA XXVII CONFERENCE TENUE A ROME EN 1948 (1949); UNITED NATIONS WAR CRIMES COMMISSION, HISTORY OF THE UNITED NATIONS WAR CRIMES COMMISSION AND THE DEVELOPMENT OF THE LAWS OF WAR 443-50 (1949) (discussing a project for the establishment of a convention for the creation of a United Nations Tribunal for War Crimes); U.N. SECRETARY GENERAL, HISTORICAL SURVEY OF THE QUESTION OF INTERNATIONAL CRIMINAL JURISDICTION, U.N. Doc. A/AC.4/7/Rev.1, U.N. Sales No. V.8 (1949); THE INTERNATIONAL LAW ASSOCIATION, REPORT OF THE 34TH CONFERENCE, VIENNA, AUGUST 5-11, 1926 (1927) (adopting the Projet d'une Cour Criminelle Internationales); COMPTE RENDU DE LA XXIII CONFERENCE TENUE A WASHINGTON ET A OTTAWA EN 1925 (1926); REPORT OF THE TASK FORCE ON AN INTERNATIONAL CRIMINAL COURT OF THE AMERICAN BAR ASSOCIATION (Alaire Bretz Rieffel ed. 1994); *The International Criminal Court: Observations and Issues before the 1997-98 Preparatory Committee; and Administrative and Financial Implications*, 13 NOUVELLES ÉTUDES PÉNALES (M. Cherif Bassiouni ed. 1997); *Observations on the Consolidated ICC Text before the Final Session of the Preparatory Committee*, 13*bis* NOUVELLES ÉTUDES PÉNALES (Leila Sadat Wexler ed. 1998); *Model Draft Statute for the International Criminal Court Based on the Preparatory Committee's Text to the Diplomatic Conference, Rome, June 15-July 17, 1998*, 13*ter* NOUVELLES ÉTUDES PÉNALES (Leila Sadat Wexler ed. 1998); *Report of the Preparatory Committee on the Establishment of an International Criminal Court*, Vols. I &II, U.N. GAOR, 51st Sess., Supp. No. 22, A/51/22 [hereinafter *1996 PrepCom Report*]; *1995 Summary of the Proceedings of the Preparatory Committee during the Period 25 March-12 April 1996*, U.N. Doc. A/AC.249/1 (1996); *Report of the Ad Hoc Committee on the Establishment of an International Criminal Court*, U.N. GAOR, 50th Sess., Supp. No. 22, U.N. Doc. A/50/22 (1995) [hereinafter *1995 Ad Hoc Committee Report*]; *See Report of the International Law Commission*, 46th Sees., U.N. GAOR, 49th Sess., Supp. No. 10, U.N. Doc. A/49/10 (1994); M. Cherif Bassiouni, *International Criminal Investigations and Prosecutions: From Versailles to Rwanda*, *in* 3 INTERNATIONAL CRIMINAL LAW [hereinafter BASSIOUNI, ICL] (M. Cherif Bassiouni ed., 2d ed. forthcoming in 1998); Giorgio Bosco, *Verso l'istituzione di una Corte Penale Internazionale*, 250 RIVISTA DI STUDI POLITICI INTERNAZIONALI 223 (1998); VERSO UN TRIBUNALE PERMANENTE INTERNAZIONALE SUI CRIMINI L'UMANITÀ. PRECEDENTI STORICI E PROSPETTIVE DI ISTITUZIONE (P. Ungari & M.P. Pietrosanti Malintoppi eds. 1998) Hans-Peter Kaul, *Towards a Permanent International Criminal Court: Some Observations of a Negotiator*, 18 HUM. RTS. L.J. 169 (1997); Benjamin B. Ferencz, *International Criminal Courts: The Legacy of Nuremberg*, 10 PACE INT'L L. REV. 201 (1997); Daniel B. Pickard, *Proposed Sentencing Guidelines for the International Criminal Court*, 20 LOY. L.A. INT'L &COMP. L.J. 123 (1997); Bruce Broomhall, *Looking Forward to the Establishment of an International Criminal Court: Between State Consent and the Rule of Law*, 8 CRIM. L.

FORUM 317 (1997); Christopher L. Blakesley, *Comparing the Ad Hoc Tribunal for Crimes Against Humanitarian Law in the Former Yugoslavia and the Project for an International Criminal Court: An Appraisal,* 67 REVUE INTERNATIONALE DE DROIT PENAL 139 (1996); M. Cherif Bassiouni, *Recent United Nations Activities in Connection with the Establishment of a Permanent International Criminal Court and the Role of the Association Internationale de Droit Penal (AIDP) and the Istituto Superiore Internazionale di Scienze Criminali (ISISC),* 67 INTERNATIONAL REVIEW OF PENAL LAW (1996); Leila Sadat Wexler, *The Proposed International Criminal Court: An Appraisal,* 29 CORNELL INT'L L.J. 665 (1996); M. Cherif Bassiouni, *Establishing an International Criminal Court: Historical Survey,* 149 MIL. L. REV. 49 (1995); Henri D. Bosly, *Actualité du Tribunal International Penal,* 1-2 ANNALES DE DROIT DE LOUVAIN 3 (1995); William C. Gilmore, *The Proposed International Criminal Court: Recent Developments,* 5 TRANSNAT'L L. & CONTEMP. PROBS. 263 (1995); Daniel H. Derby, *An International Criminal Court for the Future,* 5 TRANSNAT'L L. & CONTEMP. PROBS. 307 (1995); Sandra L. Jamison, *A Permanent International Criminal Court: A Proposal that Overcomes Past Objections,* 23 DENV. J. INT'L L. & POL'Y 2 (1995); James Crawford, *Prospects for an International Criminal Court,* 48 CURRENT LEGAL PROBS. 303 (1995); Sandra L. Jamison, *A Permanent International Criminal Court: A Proposal that Overcomes Past Objections,* 23 DENV. J. INT'L L. & POL'Y 419 (1995); Matthew Lippman, *Towards an International Criminal Court,* 3 SAN DIEGO JUST. 1 (1995); Paul D. Marquardt, *Law Without Borders: The Constitutionality of an International Criminal Court,* 33 COLUM. J. TRANSNAT'L L. 73 (1995); Timothy L. H. McCormack & Gerry J. Simpson, *A New International Criminal Law Regime,* 42 NETH. INT'L L. REV. 177 (1995); Manuel Rama-Montaldo, *Acerca de Algunos Conceptos Basicos Relativas al Derecho Penal Internacional y a una Jurisdiction Penal Internacional,* in EL DERECHO INTERNACIONAL EN UN MUNDO EN TRANSFORMACION (Manuel Rama-Montaldo ed. 1995); Brigitte Stern, *La Cour Criminelle Internationale dans le projet de la Commission du Droit International,* in INTERNATIONAL LEGAL ISSUES ARISING UNDER THE UNITED NATIONS DECADE OF INTERNATIONAL LAW 739-60 (1995); Peter Burns, *An International Criminal Tribunal: The Difficult Union of Principles and Politics,* 5 CRIM. L. F. 341 (1994); James Crawford, *The ILC's Draft Statute for an International Criminal Tribunal,* 88 AM J. INT'L L. 140 (1940); Timothy C. Evered, *An International Criminal Court: Recent Proposals and American Concerns,* 6 PACE INT'L L. REV. 121 (1994); M. Cherif Bassiouni, *Investigating Violations of International Humanitarian Law and Establishing an International Criminal Tribunal,* 25 SEC. DIALOGUE 409 (1994); Alfred P. Rubin, *An International Criminal Tribunal for the Former Yugoslavia,* 6 PACE INT'L L. REV. 7 (1994); Michael P. Scharf, *Getting Serious About an International Criminal Court,* 6 PACE INT'L L. REV. 103 (1994); *American Bar Association Task Force on an International Criminal Court, New York Bar Association Joint Report with Recommendations to the House of Delegates: Establishment of an International Criminal Court,* 27 INT'L L. 270 (1993); M. Cherif Bassiouni, *Draft Statute International Criminal Tribunal,* 8 NOUVELLES ÉTUDES PÉNALES 1 (1993); M. Cherif Bassiouni, *Draft Statute International Criminal Tribunal* (French and Spanish translations) 10 NOUVELLES ÉTUDES PÉNALES 1 (1993); William N. Gianaris, *The New World Order and the Need for an International Court,* 16 FORDHAM INT'L L. J. 88 (1992-93); M. Cherif Bassiouni & Christopher Blakesley, *The Need for an International Criminal Court in the New International Order,* 25 VAND. J. TRANSNAT'L L. 151 (1992); Joel Cavicchia, *The Prospects for an International Criminal Court in the 1990s,* 10 DICK. J. INT'L L. 223 (1992); John W. Rolph, *Perfecting an International Code of Crimes,* 39 Fed. B. News & J. 528 (1992); Christopher L. Blakesley, *Obstacles to the Creation of a Permanent War Crimes Tribunal,* 18 FLETCHER FORUM WORLD AFF. 77 (1992); Benjamin J. Ferencz, *An International Criminal Code and Court: Where They Stand and Where They're Going,* 30 COLUM. J. TRANSNAT'L L. 375 (1992); James A. Leach, *The Case for Establishing an International Criminal Court* (Occasional Paper No. 1, Parliamentarians for Global Action 1992); Bryan F. MacPherson, *An International Criminal Court: Applying World Law to Individuals* (The Center for U.N. Reform Education 1992); M. Cherif Bassiouni, *A Comprehensive Strategic Approach on International Cooperation for the Prevention, Control and Suppression of International and Transnational Criminality, Including the Establishment of an International Criminal Court,* 15 NOVA L. REV. 353 (1991); M. Cherif Bassiouni, *The Time Has Come for an International Criminal Court,* 1 IND. INT'L & COMP. L. REV. 1 (1991); Michael Scharf, *The Jury is Still Out on the Need for an International Criminal Court,* 1 DUKE J. COMP. & INT'L L. 135 (1991); *Draft Statute for an International Commission of Criminal Inquiry and a Draft Statute for an International Criminal Court,* in REPORT OF THE 60TH CONFERENCE OF THE INTERNATIONAL LAW ASSOCIATION (1983); M. Cherif Bassiouni & Daniel Derby, *Final Report on the Establishment of an International Criminal Court for the Implementation of the Apartheid Convention and Other Relevant International Instruments,* 9 HOFSTRA L. REV. 523 (1981); Louis Kos-Rabcewicz-Zubkowski, *La Création d'une Cour Pénal Internationale et L'Administration International de la Justice,* 1977 CAN. Y.B. INT'L L. 253; Louis Kos-Rabcewicz-Zubkowski, *The Creation of an International Criminal Court,* in INTERNATIONAL TERRORISM AND POLITICAL CRIMES 519 (M. Cherif Bassiouni ed. 1975); *La Création d'une Jurisdiction Pénale Internationale et la Cooperation Internationale en Matiére Pénale,* 45 REVUE INTERNATIONALES DE DROIT PÉNALE 435 (1974); Jean Y. Dautricourt, *The Concept of International Criminal Court Jurisdiction–Definition and Limitations of the Subject,* in II A TREATISE ON INTERNATIONAL CRIMINAL COURT 636 (M. Cherif Bassiouni & V. P. Nanda eds., 1973); *Draft Statute for am International Criminal Court,* in Work Paper, Abidjan World Conference on World Peace Through Law, Aug. 26-31 (1973); Richard I. Miller, *Far Beyond Nuremberg: Steps Toward International Criminal Jurisdiction,* 61 KY. L. J. 925 (1973); *Draft Statute for an International Criminal Court,* Foundation for the Establishment of an International Criminal Court (Wingspread Conference, Sept. 1971); Fannie Klein & Daniel Wilkes, *United Nations Draft Statute for an International Criminal Court: An American Evaluation,* in INTERNATIONAL CRIMINAL LAW 526 (Gerhard O. W. Mueller & Edward M. Wise eds., 1965); George A. Finch, *Draft Statute for an*

painstaking. But finally it was achieved.[13]

In the course of the last 50 years, as the world's major political powers saw fit, four *ad hoc* tribunals and five investigatory commissions have been established.[14] The four tribunals are: (1) The International Military Tribunal (IMT) sitting at Nuremberg,[15] (2) the International Military Tribunal for the Far East (IMTFE) sitting at Tokyo,[16] (3) the International Criminal Tribunal for

---

International Criminal Court, 46 AM. J. INT'L L. 89 (1952); Yeun-Li Liang, *The Establishment of an International Criminal Jurisdiction: The First Phase*, 46 AM. J. INT'L L. 73 (1952); John J. Parker, *An International Criminal Court: The Case for its Adoption*, 38 A.B.A. J. 641 (1952); Quincy Wright, *Proposal for an International Criminal Court*, 46 AM. J. INT'L L. 60 (1952); George A. Finch, *An International Criminal Court: The Case Against Its Adoption*, 38 A.B.A. J. 644 (1952); *Comments Received from Governments Regarding the Report of the Committee on International Criminal Jurisdiction*, U.N. GAOR, 7th Sess., Annex 2, Agenda Item 52, at 1, U.N. Doc. A/2186 and Add.1 (1952); Vespasian V. Pella, *Towards an International Criminal Court*, 44 AM. J. INT'L L. 37 (1950); Bienvenido C. Ambion, *Organization of a Court of International Criminal Jurisdiction*, 29 PHILIPPINE L.J. 345 (1950); Bienvenido C. Ambion, *Establishment of the Proposed International Criminal Court*, 30 PHILIPPINE L.J. 370 (1955); *Constitution et Procédure d'un Tribunal Approprié pour Juger de la Responsabilitié des Auteurs des Crimes de Guerre, Presenté a la Conference Preliminaire de Paix par la Commission de Responsabilites des Auteurs de la Guerre et Sanctions*, III LA PAIX DE VERSAILLES (1930); Vespasian V. Pella, *Plan d'un Code Repressif Mondial*, 6 REVUE INTERNATIONALE DE DROIT PÉNAL (1928) (presented by the International Association of Penal Law to the League of Nations in 1927); *Projet de Statut pour la Création d'une Chambre Criminelle au Sein de la Cour Permanente de Justice Internationale*, 5 REVUE INTERNATIONLAE DE DROIT PENAL (1928) (presented by the International Association of Penal Law to the League of Nations in 1927); *Project of an International Criminal Court of the International Association of Penal Law, in* ACTES DE PREMIER CONGRÉS INTERNATIONAL DE DROIT PÉNAL, BRUXELLES, 26-29 JUNE 1926 (1927); Vespasian V. Pella, *An International Criminal Court, in* L'UNION INTERPARLIAMENTAIRE COMPTE RENDU DE LA XXII CONFERENCE TENUE A BERNE ET A GENÈVE EN 1924 (1924).

[13]   *See supra* note 11.

[14]   A commission called The Commission on the Truth was established under the peace agreements between the government of El Salvador and the Frente Farabundo Marti para la Liberación Nacional (FMLN). This Commission was, therefore, established pursuant to an agreement between a government and an internal insurgency movement. Nevertheless, the three Commission members were designated by the Secretary-General of the United Nations. It is unclear whether this Commission can be deemed an international commission as in the case of the others mentioned herein. For the report of the Commission see *Letter dated 29 March 1993 from the Secretary-General addressed to the President of the Security Council*, U.N. SCOR, 48th Sess., U.N. Doc. S/25500 (1993).
    There has also been one non-governmental investigatory commission that rises to the level of a quasi-official one: The Carnegie Endowment for International Peace established a commission to investigate alleged atrocities committed against civilians and prisoners of war during the First Balkan War of 1912 and the Second Balkan War of 1913. *See Report of the International Commission on the Causes and Conduct of the Balkan Wars, reprinted in* CARNEGIE ENDOWMENT FOR INTERNATIONAL PEACE, THE OTHER BALKAN WARS: A 1913 CARNEGIE ENDOWMENT INQUIRY IN RETROSPECT WITH A NEW INTRODUCTION AND REFLECTIONS ON THE PRESENT CONFLICT BY GEORGE F. KENNAN (1993).

[15]   Prosecution and Punishment of Major War Criminals of the European Axis, Aug. 8, 1945, 82 U.N.T.S. 279, 59 Stat. 1544, 3 Bevans 1238 [hereinafter London Agreement]; Agreement for the Prosecution and Punishment of the Major War Criminals of the European Axis, Aug. 8, 1945, Charter of the International Military Tribunal, 59 Stat. 1544, 1546, 82 U.N.T.S. 279, 284 [hereinafter London Charter]. *See also* DAVID IRVING, NUREMBERG: THE LAST BATTLE (1996); JOSEPH E. PERSICO, NUREMBERG: INFAMY ON TRIAL (1994); TELFORD TAYLOR, THE ANATOMY OF THE NUREMBERG TRIALS 16 (1992); M. CHERIF BASSIOUNI, CRIMES AGAINST HUMANITY IN INTERNATIONAL CRIMINAL LAW 18-32 (1992) [hereinafter BASSIOUNI, CRIMES AGAINST HUMANITY]; ANN TUSA & JOHN TUSA, THE NUREMBERG TRIAL 22 (1984); BRADLEY F. SMITH, REACHING JUDGEMENT AT NUREMBERG (1977); John F. Murphy, *Norms of Criminal Procedure at the International Military Tribunal, in* THE NUREMBERG TRIAL AND INTERNATIONAL LAW 61 (George Ginsburgs & Vladimir N. Kudriavtsev eds., 1990); Roger Clark, *Crimes against Humanity at Nuremberg, in* THE NUREMBERG TRIAL AND INTERNATIONAL LAW 177 (George Ginsburgs & Vladimir N. Kudriavtsev eds., 1990); M. Cherif Bassiouni, *Das Vermächtnis von Nurnberg: Eine historische Bewertung funzig Jahre danach in*, STRAFGERICHTE GEGEN MENSCHHEITSVERBRECHEN (Gerd Hankel & Gerhard Stuby eds., 1995) [hereinafter *Nuremberg Fifty Years Later*].

[16]   Special Proclamation: Establishment of an International Military Tribunal for the Far East, Jan. 19, 1946, T.I.A.S. No. 1589, at 3, 4 Bevans 20; Charter for the International Military Tribunal for the Far East, *approved* Apr. 26, 1946, T.I.A.S. No. 1589, at 11, 4 Bevans 27. *See Activities of the Far Eastern Commission, Report by the Secretary General, February 26-July 10, 1947*, 16 DEP'T ST. BULL. 804-06 (1947) [hereinafter *Far Eastern Commission Report*]. *See also* PHILIP R. PICCIGALLOS, THE JAPANESE ON TRIAL (1979); ARNOLD C. BRACKMAN, THE OTHER NUREMBERG: THE UNTOLD STORY OF THE TOKYO WAR CRIMES TRIALS (1987); RICHARD H. MINEAR, VICTORS' JUSTICE: THE TOKYO WAR CRIMES TRIALS (1971); BERNARD V.A. ROLING, THE TOKYO TRIALS AND BEYOND: REFLECTIONS OF A

the former Yugoslavia (ICTY) sitting at The Hague,[17] and (4) the International Criminal Tribunal for Rwanda (ICTR) sitting at Arusha.[18] The five investigatory commissions are: (1) the 1919 Commission on the Responsibilities of the Authors of War and on Enforcement of Penalties, investigating crimes occurring during World War I;[19] (2) the 1943 United Nations War Crime Commission, which investigated German war crimes during World War II;[20] (3) the 1946 Far Eastern Commission,[21] which investigated Japanese war crimes during World War II; (4) the Commission of Experts Established Pursuant to Security Council Resolution 780, to investigate violations of international humanitarian law in the former Yugoslavia;[22] and (5) the Independent Commission of Experts Established in accordance with Security Council Resolution 935, the Rwandan Commission, to investigate violations committed during the Rwandan civil war.[23]

After World War I, the Treaty of Versailles provided for *ad hoc* tribunals,[24] but none were established. Article 227 of that treaty provided for the prosecution of Kaiser Wilhelm II for "a

---

PEACEMONGER (Antonio Cassese ed. 1993); THE TOKYO JUDGEMENT (Bernard V.A. Roling & Fritz Reuter eds., 1977); THE TOKYO WAR CRIMES TRIAL: THE COMPLETE TRANSCRIPTS OF THE INTERNATIONAL MILITARY TRIBUNAL FOR THE FAR EAST (22 vols., R. John Pritchard & Sonia M. Zaide eds., 1981); THE TOKYO WAR CRIMES TRIALS: THE COMPREHENSIVE INDEX & GUIDE TO THE PROCEEDINGS OF THE INTERNATIONAL MILITARY TRIBUNAL FOR THE FAR EAST (R. John Pritchard ed. 1981-87); THE TOKYO WAR CRIMES TRIAL: AN INTERNATIONAL SYMPOSIUM (C. Hosoya et al., eds., 1986). *See generally* N.E. TUTOROW, WAR CRIMES, WAR CRIMINALS, AND WAR CRIMES TRIALS 259-82 (1986) (providing a comprehensive bibliographic listing of works on the IMT and IMTFE). The constitutionality of the Tribunal was challenged before the United States Supreme Court and upheld in *Hirota v. MacArthur*, 388 U.S. 197 (1948).

[17]   S.C. Res. 827, U.N. SCOR, 48th Sess., 3217th mtg., U.N. Doc. S/RES/827 (1993) [hereinafter ICTY Statute]. *See* M. CHERIF BASSIOUNI (WITH THE COLLABORATION OF PETER MANIKAS), THE LAW OF THE INTERNATIONAL CRIMINAL TRIBUNAL FOR THE FORMER YUGOSLAVIA (1996).

[18]   S.C. Res. 955, U.N. SCOR, 49th Sess., U.N. Doc. S/RES/955 (1994) [hereinafter ICTR Statute]. *See* VIRGINIA MORRIS & MICHAEL P. SCHARF, THE INTERNATIONAL CRIMINAL TRIBUNAL FOR RWANDA (2 vols. 1998).

[19]   CARNEGIE ENDOWMENT FOR INTERNATIONAL PEACE, PAMPHLET No. 32, VIOLATIONS OF THE LAWS AND CUSTOMS OF WAR 1 (1919), *reprinted in* 14 AM. J. INT'L L. 95 (1920); *Memorandum of Reservations Presented by the Representatives of the United States to the Report of the Commission on Responsibilities*, Annex II (4 Apr. 1919), *reprinted in* 14 AM. J. INT'L L. 127 (1920); *Reservations by the Japanese Delegation*, Annex III (4 Apr. 1919), *reprinted in* 14 AM. J. INT'L L. 151 (1920); Treaty of Peace with Turkey, July 24, 1923 (Treaty of Lausanne), *reprinted in* 18 AM. J. INT'L L. 1 (Supp. 1924); Vahakn N. Dadrian, *Genocide as a Problem of National and International Law: The World War I Armenian Case and its Contemporary Legal Ramifications*, 14 AM. J. INT'L L. 127 (1989); BASSIOUNI, CRIMES AGAINST HUMANITY, *supra* note 15, at 200.

[20]   The Inter-Allied Declaration, Jan. 13, 1942, *reprinted in* PUNISHMENT FOR WAR CRIMES: THE INTER-ALLIED DECLARATION SIGNED AT ST. JAMES' PALACE, LONDON, ON 13 JANUARY 1942, AND RELATIVE DOCUMENTS (Inter-Allied Information Committee, London, undated). HISTORY OF THE UNWCC, *supra* note 12, at 433-50; TUSA & TUSA, *supra* note 15, at 22.

[21]   *Far Eastern Commission Report*, *supra* note 16, at 804-06.

[22]   S.C. Res. 780, U.N. SCOR, 47th Sess., U.N. Doc. S/RES/780 (1992). *See Final Report of the Commission of Experts Established pursuant to Security Council Resolution 780 (1992)*, U.N. SCOR, 47th Sess., Annex, U.N. Doc. S/1994/674 (1994); *Annexes to the Final Report*, U.N. SCOR, 47th Sess., U.N. Doc. S/1994/674/Add.2 (1994). *See also* M. Cherif Bassiouni, *The United Nations Commission of Experts Established Pursuant to Security Council Resolution 780 (1992)*, 88 AM. J. INT'L L. 784 (1994). M. Cherif Bassiouni, *The Commission of Experts Established pursuant to Security Council Resolution 780: Investigating Violations of International Humanitarian Law in the Former Yugoslavia*, 5 CRIM. L. F. 1 (1994); M. Cherif Bassiouni, *Former Yugoslavia: Investigating Violations of International Humanitarian Law and Establishing an International Criminal Tribunal*, 25 SECURITY DIALOGUE 411 (1994).

[23]   S.C. Res. 935 U.N. SCOR, 49th Sess., 3400th mtg. at 1, U.N. Doc. S/RES/935 (1994); *See Preliminary Report of the Independent Commission of Experts Established in accordance with Security Council Resolution 935 (1994)*, U.N. SCOR, U.N. Doc. S/1994/1125 (1994); *Final Report of the Commission of Experts Established pursuant to Security Council Resolution 935 (1994)*, and *Annex*, U.N. SCOR, U.N. Doc. S/1994/1405 (1994) (available in U.N. Gopher/Current Information/Secretary-General's Reports/Dec. 1994).

[24]   Treaty of Peace Between the Allied and Associated Powers and Germany (Treaty of Versailles), 28 June 1919, art. 227, 11 Martens (3d) 323, *reprinted in* 2 Bevans 43; 1 Friedman 417 [hereinafter Treaty of Versailles].

supreme offense against international morality and the sanctity of treaties."[25] Additionally, Articles 228 and 229 provided for tribunals to prosecute "persons accused of having committed acts in violation of the laws and customs of war."[26] But, no international tribunals came into existence. Instead, with the consent of the Allies who included these provisions in the Treaty of Versailles, token national prosecutions took place in Germany.[27] This compromise demonstrates that the political will of the world's major powers is paramount over all else.

Throughout the 75 years since 1919, the world's major powers, selective as they have been in establishing *ad hoc* bodies to investigate certain international crimes have, nevertheless, progressively recognized the aspirations of international civil society for the establishment of a permanent system of international criminal justice. But in the course of the historical evolution that took place, only the concept of individual criminal responsibility was recognized,[28] with the exception of the criminal responsibility of organizations in the Nuremberg trials.[29] The concept of state criminal responsibility has, so far, not been applied.[30]

In the aftermath of World War II, the IMT,[31] and the IMTFE,[32] were established to prosecute individuals for "crimes against peace," "war crimes," and "crimes against humanity." In occupied Germany, the four major Allies, pursuant to CCL 10,[33] prosecuted, in their respective zones of occupation, the same crimes as did the IMT,[34] while some of the Allies in the Pacific Theater prosecuted the Japanese for "war crimes" under their respective military laws.[35] These two post-war experiences with international prosecutions started with the establishment of international commissions, though, as described below, in neither case was their work particularly relevant to the subsequent prosecutions.

---

[25] *Id.* at art. 227.

[26] *Id.* at arts. 228, 229.

[27] CLAUD MULLINS, THE LEIPZIG TRIALS: AN ACCOUNT OF THE WAR CRIMINALS' TRIALS AND A STUDY OF GERMAN MENTALITY 98-112 (1921).

[28] S. Prakash Sinha, *The Position of the Individual in an International Criminal Law*, *in* 1 A TREATISE ON INTERNATIONAL CRIMINAL LAW 122-34 (M. Cherif Bassiouni & Ved P. Nanda eds., 1973).

[29] M. Cherif Bassiouni, *The Sources and Content of International Criminal Law: A Theoretical Framework*, *in* 1 BASSIOUNI, ICL, *supra* note 12, (M. Cherif Bassiouni ed., 2d ed. forthcoming in 1998).

[30] Fritz Munch, *Criminal Responsibility of States*, *in* BASSIOUNI, ICL, *supra* note 12, at 123-29 (M. Cherif Bassiouni ed. 1986); FARHAD MALEKIAN, INTERNATIONAL CRIMINAL RESPONSIBILITY OF STATES (1985). For individual and group criminal responsibility, see Bassiouni, *supra* note 29, at section 6.

[31] *See* London Agreement and London Charter, *supra* note 15. For the Proceedings Before the IMT, see International Military Tribunal sitting at Nuremberg, *reported in* TRIAL OF THE MAJOR WAR CRIMINALS BEFORE THE INTERNATIONAL MILITARY TRIBUNAL (1949) (commonly known as the "Blue Series"). For the Subsequent Proceedings of the IMT see TRIALS OF WAR CRIMINALS BEFORE THE NUREMBERG MILITARY TRIBUNALS UNDER CONTROL COUNCIL LAW NO. 10 (1949) (commonly known as the "Green Series").

[32] *See supra* note 16.

[33] Allied Control Council Law No. 10, Punishment of Persons Guilty of War Crimes, Crimes against Peace and against Humanity, 20 Dec. 1945, Official Gazette of the Control Council for Germany, No. 3, 31 Jan. 1946, *reprinted in* FERENCZ, *supra* note 12 [hereinafter CCL 10]. For the United States prosecution, see FRANK M. BUSCHER, THE U.S. WAR CRIMES TRIAL PROGRAM IN GERMANY, 1946-1955 (1989).

[34] *See generally* JEAN PIERRE MAUNOIR, LA REPRESSION DES CRIMES DE GUERRE DEVANT LES TRIBUNAUX FRANCAIS ET ALLIES (1956); HENRI MEYROWITZ, LA REPRESSION PAR LES TRIBUNAUX ALLEMANDS DES CRIMES CONTRE L'HUMANITE ET DE L'APPARTENANCE A UNE ORGANIZATION CRIMINELLE (1960); Remigiusz Bierzanek, *War Crimes: History and Definition*, *in* 3 BASSIOUNI, ICL, *supra* note 12, at 29 (M. Cherif Bassiouni ed., 2d ed. forthcoming in 1998); BASSIOUNI, CRIMES AGAINST HUMANITY, *supra* note 15, at 470-527.

[35] *See* RICHARD LAEL, THE YAMASHITA PRECEDENT: WAR CRIMES AND COMMAND RESPONSIBILITY (1982); A. FRANK REEL, THE CASE OF GENERAL YAMASHITA (1949); R. John Pritchard, *War Crimes Trials in the Far East*, *in* CAMBRIDGE ENCYCLOPEDIA OF JAPAN 107 (Richard Bowring & Peter Kornick eds., 1993); and R. John Pritchard, *International Military Tribunal for the Far East and the Allied National War Crimes Trials in Asia*, *in* 3 BASSIOUNI, ICL, *supra* note 12 (M. Cherif Bassiouni ed., 2d ed. forthcoming in 1998). *See also* R. John Pritchard, *The Gift of Clemency Following British War Crimes Trials in the Far East, 1946-1947*, 7 CRIM. L.F. 15 (1996).

The post-World War I experience showed the extent to which international justice can be compromised for the sake of political expedience. Conversely, the post-World War II experience revealed how effective international justice could be when there is political will to support it and the necessary resources to render it effective. Whether fully realized or not, these sets of experiences were one sided, as they imposed "victors" justice over the defeated;[36] however, they were not unjust. Among all historic precedents, the IMT, whatever its shortcomings may have been, stands as the epitome of international justice and fairness.[37]

Subsequent to World War II, national prosecutions occurred in the Federal Republic of Germany[38] and other countries, such as Canada,[39] France,[40] and Israel.[41] Australia[42] and the

---

[36]   During World War II, the German *Wehrmacht* had organized a special office to record violations of international law committed against the German peoples. But, the Allies disregarded these claims. *See* ALFRED M. DE ZAYAS, THE WEHRMACHT BUREAU (1989). For a critical comment see IRVING, *supra* note 15. The IMTFE prosecutions and some of the Far East Allies prosecutions—like the Yamashita trial in the Philippines—revealed procedural infirmities and a substantive lack of fairness. *See In re Yamashita*, 327 U.S. 1, 67-125 (Rutledge & Murphy JJ., dissenting); *see also* REEL, *supra* note 35.

[37]   *See* M. Cherif Bassiouni, *The "Nuremberg Legacy"*, in 3 BASSIOUNI, ICL, *supra* note 12 (M. Cherif Bassiouni ed., 2d ed. forthcoming in 1998).

[38]   Nicholas R. Doman, *Aftermath of Nuremberg: The Trial of Klaus Barbie*, 60 COLO. L. REV. 449 (1989).

[39]   Regina v. Finta, 61 D.L.R. 4th 85 (1989); Regina v. Finta, 50 C.C.C. 3d. 236; Regina v. Finta, [1994] 1 S.C.R. 701; Regina v. Finta, 112 D.L.R. 4th 13 (1994). *See generally* Irwin Cotler, *Bringing Nazi War Criminals in Canada to Justice: A Case Study*, in ASIL PROCEEDINGS 262-69 (1997). *See also* Sharon A. Williams, *Laudable Principles Lacking Application: The Prosecution of War Criminals in Canada*, in THE LAW OF WAR CRIMES 151 (T.L.H. McCormack & G.J. Simpson eds., 1997); PATRICK BRODE, CASUAL SLAUGHTERS AND ACCIDENTAL JUDGMENTS: CANADIAN WAR CRIMES PROSECUTIONS, 1944-1948 (1997); Leslie C. Green, *Canadian Law and the Punishment of War Crimes*, 28 CHITTY'S LAW J. 249 (1980); Leslie C. Green, *Canadian Law, War Crimes and Crimes against Humanity*, 1988 BRIT. Y.B. INT'L L. 217; Michele Jacquart, *La Notion de Crime Contre l'Humanite en Droit International Contemporain et en Droit Canadien*, 21 REVUE GENERALE DE DROIT 607 (1990), and Christopher Amerasinghe, *The Canadian Experience*, in 3 BASSIOUNI, ICL, *supra* note 12 (M. Cherif Bassiouni ed., 2d ed. forthcoming in 1998).

[40]   The Touvier judgments: Judgment of Feb. 6, 1975, Cass. Crim., 1975 D.S. Jur. 386, 387 (Report of Counselor Chapan), 1975 Gaz. Pal. Nos. 124-26 (May 4-6, 1975); Judgment of Oct. 27, 1975 Chambre d'accusation de la cour d'appel de Paris, 1976 D.S. Jur. 260 (Note Coste-Floret), 1976 Gaz. Pal. Nos. 154-55, at 382; Judgment of June 30, 1976, Cass. Crim., 1977 D.S. Jur. 1, 1976 Gaz. Pal. Nos. 322, 323, 1976 J.C.P. II G, No. 18,435; Judgment of Nov. 27, 1992, Cass. Crim., 1993 J.C.P. II G, No. 21,977; Judgment of Apr. 13, 1992, Cour d'appel de Paris, Première chambre d'accusation, at 133-62, *reprinted in part* in 1992 Gaz. Pal. 387, 387-417; Judgment of June 2, 1993, Cour d'appel de Versailles, Première chambre d'accusation 31; Judgment of June 1, 1995, Cour de Cassation, Bull. crim. n°42, p.113.

The Barbie judgments: Matter of Barbie, GAZ. PAL. JUR. 710 (Cass. Crim. Oct. 6, 1983); Judgment of Oct. 6, 1983, Cass. Crim., 1984 D.S. Jur. 113, Gaz. Pal. Nos. 352-54 (Dec. 18-20, 1983), 1983 J.C.P. II G, No. 20,107, J.D.I. 779 (1983); Judgment of Jan. 26, 1984, Cass. Crim., 1984 J.C.P. II G, No. 20,197 (Note Ruzié), J.D.I. 308 (1984); Judgment of Dec. 20, 1985, Cass. Crim., 1986 J.C.P. II G, No. 20,655, 1986 J.D.I.; Judgment of June 3, 1988, Cass. Crim., 1988 J.C.P. II G, No. 21,149 (Report of Counselor Angevin).

The Papon judgments: Papon was indicted on September 18, 1996; the indictment was confirmed on January 23, 1997; Judgment of Sept. 18, 1996, Chambre d'accusation de la cour d'appel de Bordeaux (unpublished), affirmed Judgment of Jan. 23, 1997, Cass. Crim., 1997 J.C.P. II G, No. 22,812. In April 1998 Maurice Papon was convicted for "crimes against humanity" and sentenced to 10 years imprisonment. *See* Craig R. Whitney, *Ex-Vichy Aide Is Convicted and Reaction Ranges Wide*, NEW YORK TIMES, Apr. 3, 1998, at sec. A, p.1; Craig R. Whitney, *Vichy Official Found Guilty of Helping Deport Jews*, NEW YORK TIMES, Apr. 2, 1998, at sec. A, p.8; and Charles Trueheart, *Verdict Nears in Trial of Vichy Official*, WASH. POST, Apr. 1, 1998, at sec. A, p.21.

For information on the Touvier case see generally ÉRIC CONAN & HENRY ROUSSO, VICHY, UN PASSÉ QUI NE PASSE PAS (1994); ALAIN JAKUBOWICZ & RENÉ RAFFIN, TOUVIER HISTOIRE DU PROCÈS (1995); ARNO KLARSFELD, TOUVIER UN CRIME FRANCAIS (1994); JACQUES TRÉMOLET DE VILLERS, L'AFFAIRE TOUVIER, CHRONIQUE D'UN PROCÈS EN IDÉOLOGIE (1994).

For information on the Barbie case see generally LADISLAS DE HOYAS, KLAUS BARBIE (Nicholas Courtin trans., 1985); BRENDAN MURPHY, THE BUTCHER OF LYON (1983); Angevin, *Enseignements de l'Affaire Barbie en Matiere de Crimes Contre l'Humanite*, LA SEMAIRE JURIDIQUE, 62e annee. No. 5, 14 Dec. 1988, 2149; Doman, *supra* note 27; Le Gunehec, *Affaire Barbie*, GAZETTE DU PALAIS, No. 127-28, 106e anneè, Mercredi 7-Jeudi 8 Mai, 1985; Ponceler, *L'Humanité, une Victime Peu Présentable*, 1991, No. 34, 1987 REVUE DES SCIENCES CRIMINELLES 275.

United Kingdom[43] passed national legislation enabling prosecution, similar to the corresponding Canadian law,[44] but so far only one person has been brought to trial.

The International Military Tribunal at Nuremberg, the International Military Tribunal in the Far East, and subsequent prosecutions by the Allies were significant precedents in the efforts to establish an effective system of international criminal justice.[45] These historical precedents have developed new legal norms and standards of responsibility which have advanced the international rule of law, for example the elimination of the defense of "obedience to superior orders," and the accountability of heads of state.[46] With the passage of time, these precedents, notwithstanding their shortcomings, acquired more perceived legitimacy and precedential value. Indeed, time and the unfulfilled quest for international criminal justice have put a favorable gloss over the infirmities and flaws of these proceedings. The symbolic significance which emerged from these experiences is their moral legacy, now heralded by those who seek a permanent, effective, and politically uncompromised system of international criminal justice.[47]

For information on the Papon case see generally Laurent Greilsamer, *Mauricer Papon, la vie masquée*, LE MONDE, Dec. 19, 1995, *available in* LEXIS, Nexis Library, Monde File; Barry James, *The Final Trial for Vichy? A Model French Bureaucrat Accused*, INT'L HERALD TRIB., Jan. 6-7, 1996, at 2.

For additional information on these cases and French prosecution of war criminals in general see generally Leila Sadat Wexler, *National Prosecutions for International Crimes: The French Experience, in* 3 INTERNATIONAL CRIMINAL LAW (M. Cherif Bassiouni ed., 2d ed. forthcoming in 1998); Leila Sadat Wexler, *Prosecutions for Crimes Against Humanity in French Municipal Law: International Implications, in* ASIL PROCEEDINGS 270-76 (1997); Leila Sadat Wexler, *The Interpretation of the Nuremberg Principles by the French Court of Cassation: From Touvier to Barbie and Back Again*, 32 COLUM. J. TRANSNAT'L L. 289 (1994); Leila Sadat Wexler, *Reflections on the Trial of Vichy Collaborator Paul Touvier for Crimes Against Humanity in France*, 20 J. L. & SOC. INQUIRY 191 (1995); Leila Sadat Wexler, *Prosecutions for Crimes Against Humanity in French Municipal Law: International Implications* (Working Paper No. 97-4-3, Washington University School of Law, 1997); Jacques Francillon, *Crimes de guerre, Crimes contra l'humanité*, JURIS-CLASSEUR, DROIT INT'L, FASCICULE 410 (1993); Mireille Delmas-Marty, *Le crime contra l'humanité, les droits de l'homme, et l'irréductible humain*, 3 REV. SC. CRIM. 477 (1994); Catherine Grynfogel, *Le crime contre l'humanité: notion et régime juridique*, TOULOUSE-1 727 (1991); Michel Masse, *Les crimes contre l'humanité dans le nouveau code pénal français*, 2 REV. SC. CRIM. 376 (1994); Claude Lombois, *Un crime international en droit positif français: l'apport de l'affaire Barbie à la théorie française du crime contre l'humanité*, MÉLANGES VITU, 367 (1989); Pierre Truche, *La notion de crime contre l'humanité: bilan et propositions*, 181 REV. ESPRIT 67 (1992); Elizabeth Zoller, *La définition des crimes contre l'humanité*, J.D.I. 549 (1993); and P. Truche & P. Biriretz, *Crimes de guerre - crimes contra l'humanité*, 2 ENCLOPEDIA DALLOZ, DROIT PÉNAL (1993).

[41] *See Attorney General of Israel v. Eichmann*, 36 I.L.R. 5 (Dis. Ct. 1962) (Isr.); *Attorney General of Israel v. Eichmann*, 36 I.L.R. 277 (Sup. Ct. 1962) (Isr.) (dismissing appeal). *See generally* GIDEON HAUSNER, JUSTICE IN JERUSALEM (1966); PETER PAPADATOS, LE PROCES D'EICHMANN (1964); Leslie C. Green, *Legal Issues of the Eichmann Trial*, 37 TUL. L. REV. 641 (1962).

[42] War Crimes Amendment Act 1988, No. 3 (1989) (Austl.); Graham T. Blewitt, *The Australian Experience, in* 3 BASSIOUNI, ICL, *supra* note 12 (M. Cherif Bassiouni ed., 2d ed. forthcoming in 1998).

[43] War Crimes Act 1991, at ch. 13 (U.K.); *see* WAR CRIMES: REPORT OF THE WAR CRIMES INQUIRY (Sir Thomas Hetherington & William Chalmers, members 1988); Jane Garwood-Cutler, *The British Experience, in* 3 BASSIOUNI, ICL, *supra* note 12 (M. Cherif Bassiouni ed., 2d ed. forthcoming in 1998).

[44] Criminal Code, R.S.C. 1927, ch. c 36, s. 7 3.71-3.77 (Can.); *see supra* note 39.

[45] *See generally Individual Criminal Responsibility and International Prosecutions, in* BASSIOUNI, CRIMES AGAINST HUMANITY, *supra* note 15, at 192-234.

[46] BASSIOUNI, CRIMES AGAINST HUMANITY, *supra* note 15, at 368-96; Hayes Parks, *Command Responsibility for War Crimes*, 62 MIL. L. REV. 1 (1973); LESLIE GREEN, SUPERIOR ORDERS IN NATIONAL AND INTERNATIONAL LAW 15-242 (1976); E. MULLER-RAPPARD, L'ORDRE SUPERIEUR MILITAIRE ET LA RESPONSIBILITE DU SUBORDONNÉ 185-251 (1965); YORAM DINSTEIN, THE DEFENSE OF "OBEDIENCE TO SUPERIOR ORDERS" IN INTERNATIONAL LAW 5-20 (1965); N. KEIZJER, MILITARY OBEDIENCE (1978).

[47] Matthew Lippman, *Nuremberg: Forty-Five Years Later*, 7 CONN. J. INT'L L. 1 (1991); M. Cherif Bassiouni, *Nuremberg Forty Years After: An Introduction*, 18 CASE W. RES. J. INT'L L. 261 (1986); *Forty Years After the Nuremberg and Tokyo Tribunals: The Impact of the War Crimes Trials on International and National Law, in* PROCEEDINGS OF THE EIGHTIETH ANNUAL MEETING OF THE AMERICAN SOCIETY OF INTERNATIONAL LAW (Apr. 1986) (containing comments by Telford Taylor, Jordan Paust, Richard Falk, and M. Cherif Bassiouni); Hans Kelsen, *Will the Nuremberg Trial Constitute a Precedent in International Law?*, 1 INT'L L.Q. 153 (1947); *Nuremberg Fifty Years Later,*

The conflict in the former Yugoslavia provided another opportunity for advancing international criminal justice. The United Nations Security Council saw fit to establish an *ad hoc* international criminal tribunal to prosecute those responsible for violations of international humanitarian law and the laws and customs of war.[48] In so doing, the Security Council added another important precedent to the history of international criminal law. Like prior experiences, it started with the establishment of an investigatory commission followed by the establishment of a tribunal. Unlike prior experiences, however, it sought to create a continuum between the investigatory and prosecutorial aspects of the pursuit of justice.[49] Then, on the strength of this experience, the Security Council repeated the process in connection with the civil war in Rwanda.[50]

After the decision to create the Rwanda Tribunal, which took much time and effort to establish and function, the Security Council reached a point of "tribunal fatigue."[51] Indeed, the logistics of setting up the *ad hoc* tribunals for the former Yugoslavia and for Rwanda have strained the capabilities and resources of the United Nations and consumed the Security Council's time. This stage of *ad hoc* tribunals coincided with renewed efforts for establishing a permanent international criminal court, thus enhancing its prospects.

Establishing an International Criminal Court: 1937-1989

The efforts to establish a permanent ICC started with the League of Nations and were continued by the United Nations.[52] The League of Nations's efforts were linked to a permanent international criminal court whose jurisdiction was limited only to enforcement of the 1937 Terrorism Convention, but regrettably failed owing to the world crisis that followed the Spanish

---

supra note 15. *See also* Bassiouni, *The "Nuremberg Legacy," supra* note 37.

    [48]   The Security Council decided to establish an international criminal tribunal to prosecute those responsible for violations of international humanitarian law in the former Yugoslavia in Resolution 808, S.C. Res. 808, U.N. SCOR, 48th Sess., 3175th mts. at 1, U.N. Doc. S/RES/808 (1993). Pursuant to Security Council Resolution 808, the Secretary-General prepared a report containing comments on the articles of the statute of the tribunal. The tribunal's statute appears in an Annex to the Secretary-General's report. *Report of the Secretary-General pursuant to paragraph 2 of Security Council Resolution 808 (1993)*, U.N. SCOR, 48th Sess., U.N. Doc. S/2507 (1993). The Security Council adopted the Secretary-General's draft of the statute without change in resolution 827, *supra* note 17. *See supra* note 22.

    [49]   Resolution 808, *supra* note 48, at para. 10; Bassiouni, *The Commission of Experts Established pursuant to Security Council Resolution 780: Investigating Violations of International Humanitarian Law in the Former Yugoslavia, supra* note 22.

    [50]   In July 1994, the Security Council passed resolution 935, using the precedent of the former Yugoslavia as a model, to establish a commission of experts to investigate violations committed during the Rwandan civil war, *supra* note 23. The Rwandan commission lasted only four months which was not long enough for it to effectively perform its task. On 1 October 1994, the Rwandan commission submitted its preliminary report to the Secretary-General, and submitted a final report on 9 December 1994. *See Preliminary Report of the Independent Commission of Experts Established in accordance with Security Council Resolution 935 (1994), supra* note 23; *Final Report of the Commission of Experts Established pursuant to Security Council Resolution 935 (1994), supra* note 23. The statute and judicial mechanism for the Rwandan tribunal were adopted in Security Council resolution 955, *supra* note 18. Even though the statutes for the Rwandan tribunal and the tribunal for the former Yugoslavia differ, the tribunals share a common Prosecutor and a common Appellate chamber. This is a curious formula for separate *ad hoc* tribunals, but perhaps demonstrating the need for a permanent body to administer international criminal justice. The seat of the Rwandan tribunal is in Arusha, Tanzania. *See* Larry Johnson, *The International Criminal Tribunal for Rwanda, in* 3 BASSIOUNI, ICL, *supra* note 12 (M. Cherif Bassiouni ed., 2d ed. forthcoming in 1998); Madeline H. Morris, *The Trials of Concurrent Jurisdiction: The Case of Rwanda*, 7 DUKE J. COMP. & INT'L L. 349 (1997); and MORRIS & SCHARF, *supra* note 18.

    [51]   A term aptly coined by David Scheffer, Senior Counsel and Advisor to the United States Permanent Representative to the United Nations, in a speech at the 1994 International Law Weekend at the New York City Association of the Bar. Mr. Scheffer is presently Ambassador at large for War Crimes Issues in the Office of Secretary of State Albright.

    [52]   For the history of this endeavor, see *supra* note 12.

civil war, Italy's invasion of Abbyssinia, and Germany's aggressive and militaristic policies in the years that preceded World War II.[53]

The United Nations goal was, however, more encompassing than that of the League of Nations as it aimed at establishing a permanent international criminal court. These efforts can be traced along two separate tracts: codification of international crimes[54] and the elaboration of a draft statute for the establishment of an international court.[55] Curiously, however, the two tracts evolved separately, though logic would have required that they be integrated. But the history of these two tracts reveals the lack of political will by the world's major powers to join them in a coordinated endeavor. This is evidenced in the separate courses that the various United Nations institutions have taken between 1947 and 1998.

In 1947, the General Assembly mandated the Committee on the Codification of International Law, the International Law Commission's (ILC) predecessor, to:

(1) formulate the principles of international law recognized in the Charter of the Nuremberg Tribunal and in the Judgement of the Tribunal, and
(2) prepare a draft code of offences against the peace and security of mankind, indicating clearly the place to be accorded to the principles mentioned in sub-paragraph (a) above.[56]

Two years later, in compliance with that resolution, the ILC started to "[formulate] the principles recognized in the Charter of the Nuremberg Tribunal" and to "[prepare] a draft code

---

[53] Convention for the Creation of an International Criminal Court, opened for signature at Geneva, 16 Nov. 1937, League of Nations O.J. Spec. in Supp. No. 156 (1938), League of Nations Doc. C.547(I).M.384(I).1937.v (1938) (never entered into force).

[54] G.A. Res. 174(II), U.N. Doc. A/519, at 105-10 (1946). For a history of these efforts, see M. Cherif Bassiouni, *The History of the Draft Code of Crimes Against the Peace and Security of Mankind*, 27 ISR. L. REV. 1-21 (1993), *reprinted in* COMMENTARIES ON THE INTERNATIONAL LAW COMMISSION'S 1991 DRAFT CODE OF CRIMES AGAINST THE PEACE AND SECURITY OF MANKIND, 11 NOUVELLES ÉTUDES PÉNALES 1 (1993); M. CHERIF BASSIOUNI, A DRAFT INTERNATIONAL CRIMINAL CODE AND DRAFT STATUTE FOR AN INTERNATIONAL CRIMINAL TRIBUNAL (1987); M. CHERIF BASSIOUNI, INTERNATIONAL CRIMINAL LAW: A DRAFT INTERNATIONAL CRIMINAL CODE (1980); FARHAD MALEKIAN, INTERNATIONAL CRIMINAL LAW: THE LEGAL AND CRITICAL ANALYSIS OF INTERNATIONAL CRIMES (2 vols. 1991); Daniel Derby, *A Framework for International Criminal Law*, *in* 1 BASSIOUNI, ICL, *supra* note 12, at 33 (M. Cherif Bassiouni ed. 1986); Yoram Dinstein, *International Criminal Law*, 1981 ISR. Y.B. INT'L L. 9; Robert Friedlander, *The Foundations of International Criminal Law: A Present Day Inquiry*, 15 CASE W. RES. J. INT'L L. 13 (1983); Robert Friedlander, *The Enforcement of International Criminal Law: Fact or Fiction*, 17 CASE W. RES. J. INT'L L. 79 (1985); Leslie C. Green, *An International Criminal Code—Now?*, 3 DALHOUSIE L.J. 560 (1976); Leslie C. Green, *Is There an International Criminal Law?*, 21 ALBERTA L. REV. 251 (1983); Leslie C. Green, *New Trends in International Criminal Law*, 1981 ISR. Y.B. INT'L L. 9; Gerhard O.W. Mueller & Douglas J. Besharov, *Evolution and Enforcement of International Criminal Law*, *in* BASSIOUNI, ICL, *supra* note 12, at 59 (M. Cherif Bassiouni ed. 1986); Georg Schwarzenberger, *The Problem of International Criminal Law*, 3 CURRENT LEGAL PROBS. 263 (1950), *reprinted in* INTERNATIONAL CRIMINAL LAW 3-36 (Gerhard O.W. Mueller & Edward M. Wise eds., 1965); Quincy Wright, *The Scope of International Criminal Law*, 15 VA. J. INT'L L. 562 (1975). *See also* 52 REVUE INTERNATIONALE DE DROIT PENAL (1984), symposium issue on Draft International Criminal Court: Pierre Bouzat, *Introduction*, 331; Hans-Heinrich Jescheck, *Development, Present State and Future Prospects of International Criminal Law*, 377; John Decker, *A Critique of the Draft International Criminal Code*, 365; Valeri Shupilov, *General Comments on the Draft International Criminal Code*, 373; Reynald Ottenhof, *Considerations sur la Forme le Style, et la Methode d'Elaboration du Projet de Code Penal International*, 385; Robert Friedlander, *Some Observations Relating to the Draft International Criminal Code Project*, 393; Dietrich Oehler, *Perspectives on the Contents of the Special Part of the Draft International Criminal Code*, 407. For a more detailed discussion see Bassiouni, *The Sources and Content of International Criminal Law: A Theoretical Framework*, *supra* note 29.

[55] *See supra* note 12.

[56] G.A Res. 174, U.N. GAOR, 2d Sess., U.N. Doc. A/519 (1947).

of the offences against the peace and security of mankind."[57] A subcommittee was formed and a special rapporteur was appointed to prepare a Draft Code of Offences Against the Peace and Security of Mankind.[58] That title was changed in 1988 to Draft Code of Crimes Against the Peace and Security of Mankind.[59]

Concurrently, the task of formulating a draft statute for the establishment of an international criminal court was assigned to another special rapporteur, who submitted his first report to the ILC in March of 1950.[60] That report argued that a substantive criminal code and a statute for an international criminal court should complement one another.[61] Contrary to logic and rational drafting policy, these two codification projects remained purposely separated.[62] In 1950, another rapporteur was appointed to study the further development of an international criminal court.[63] The two rapporteurs differed on whether the time was ripe for an international criminal court.[64] Jean Spiropoulos was moved by idealism while Emil Sandstrom espoused political realism. Their clashing perspectives represented the two trends in a world that just emerged from the terrifying experience of World War II, and the reality of the new post World War II "cold war."

While certain governments believed the establishment of an international criminal court was desirable in theory, they were always skeptical about its success in view of the absence of consensus among the world's major powers.[65] These positions can be summarized as follows:

---

[57]   1 Y.B. INT'L L. COMM'N vi (1949), referring to Resolution 174, *supra* note 56 and G.A. Res. 95, U.N. GAOR, 1st Sess., U.N. Doc. A/64/Add.1 (1946).

[58]   The first report was completed in 1950. *Report of the International Law Commission*, U.N. GAOR, 5th Sess., U.N. Doc. A/CN.4/25 (1950).

[59]   *See Report of the International Law Commission*, U.N. GAOR, 40th Sess., Supp. No. 10, at 145, U.N. Doc. A/43/10 (1988). The Draft Code of Offences, subsequently the Draft Code of Crimes, was never intended to codify all international crimes. The number of crimes included within the code has fluctuated from a current high of 25 to a low of five. *Draft Code of Crimes Against the Peace and Security of Mankind: Titles and Articles on the Draft Code of Crimes Against the Peace and Security of Mankind, adopted by the International Law Commission on its forty-eight session*, U.N. GAOR, 51st Sess., U.N. Doc. A/CN.4L.532 (1996), *rev'd by* U.N. Doc. A/CN.4L.532/Corr. 1 *and* U.N. Doc. A/CN.4L.532/Corr. 3 [hereinafter *1996 Draft Code of Crimes*]. As of 1998, the categories of international crimes are: aggression, genocide, crimes against humanity, war crimes, crimes against United Nations and associated personnel, unlawful possession of, use or emplacement of weapons, theft of nuclear materials, mercenarism, *apartheid*, slavery and slave related practices, torture and other forms of cruel, inhuman or degrading treatment or punishment, unlawful human experimentation, piracy, aircraft hijacking and unlawful acts against international air safety, unlawful acts against the safety of maritime navigation and the safety of platforms on the high seas, threat and use of force against internationally protected persons, taking of civilian hostages, unlawful use of the mail, unlawful traffic in drugs and related drug offenses, destruction and/or theft of national treasures, unlawful acts against certain internationally-protected elements of the environment, international traffic in obscene publications, falsification and counterfeiting, unlawful interference with international submarine cables, and bribery of foreign public officials. The three crimes most-recently included are: crimes against United Nations and associated personnel, mercenarism, and unlawful acts against the safety of maritime navigation and the safety of platforms on the high seas. *See* M. CHERIF BASSIOUNI, INTERNATIONAL CRIMES: DIGEST/INDEX OF INTERNATIONAL INSTRUMENTS 1815-1985 (2 vols., 1985) [hereinafter BASSIOUNI, DIGEST/INDEX]; and 1 INTERNATIONAL CRIMINAL LAW CONVENTIONS (M. Cherif Bassiouni ed. 1998).

[60]   *Report of the International Law Commission on Question of International Criminal Jurisdiction*, U.N. GAOR, 5th Sess., U.N. Doc. A/CN.4/15 (1950).

[61]   *Id. See also Report of the International Law Commission*, U.N. GAOR, 5th Sess., Supp. No. 12, U.N. Doc. A/1316 (1950), and discussions on this report by the Sixth Committee of the General Assembly, *reprinted in* 2 FERENCZ, *supra* note 12.

[62]   That situation continued in part because of political considerations, and later, in part because the ILC's 1991 Draft Code of Crimes was not well received. *Commentaries on the International Law Commission's 1991 Draft Code of Crimes Against the Peace and Security of Mankind*, 11 NOUVELLES ÉTUDES PÉNALES (M. Cherif Bassiouni ed. 1993) [hereinafter *Commentaries on 1991 Draft Code*].

[63]   *Report of the International Law Commission*, U.N. GAOR, 5th Sess., U.N. A/CN.4/20 (1950).

[64]   *Id.; Report of the Sixth Committee to the General Assembly*, U.N. GAOR, 5th Sess., U.N. Doc. A/1639 (1950), *reprinted in* FERENCZ, *supra* note 12, at 306-11.

[65]   *Id.* at 26-31.

the Soviet Union believed its sovereignty would be affected by the establishment of such a tribunal;[66] the United States was not prepared to accept the establishment of such a court at the height of the "cold war;" France expressed support for the establishment of a permanent international criminal court, but did not throw its weight to further the process; and the United Kingdom regarded the idea as politically premature.[67]

Nevertheless, a Special Committee of the General Assembly was established in 1950, composed of representatives of 17 states, for the purpose of drafting a convention for the establishment of an international criminal court.[68] The Special Committee appointed to draft the statute for the formulation of an international criminal court finished its task in 1951, modeling the statute in part after that of the International Court of Justice.[69] The discussions and written comments, particularly those of major powers, clearly indicated that the project had no chance of acceptance and was politically premature.[70] Because these states did not want to assume political responsibility for the demise of a permanent international criminal court within only five and six years respectively, of the IMTFE and IMT's judgements,[71] the Committee's mandate was extended, with some membership changes, and in 1953 it produced a revised text.[72]

The reason for the 1953 revision of the 1951 Draft Statute stemmed, for the most part, from political pressure. In 1951 the committee appeared to work from an optimistic base, creating what they felt was the best possible structure for an international criminal court. However, by 1953 the committee had become a little less optimistic and bowed to political pressure by adding provisions that limited jurisdiction and allowed state parties to retain more control. For example, the article on attribution of jurisdiction was modified to specify that "jurisdiction of the Court is not to be presumed," and stated precisely that acceptance of the Court's jurisdiction did not bind a state to bring specific cases before the Court but only permitted a state to do so. The new draft also included an express provision on the powers of states to withdraw jurisdiction once

---

[66]   *Id.*

[67]   *Id.* Currently, while no state openly opposes the establishment of such a court, some extend the debate as a way of delaying the drafting of a statute. If, despite these tactics, a compromise statute is adopted, it is likely that it will contain certain provisions that will reduce its effectiveness. *See 1995 Ad Hoc Committee Report, supra* note 12. The writing is already on the wall with insistence by some states on "complementary." *See id.* at 6-7. The proposals that came out of the Second Session of the Preparatory Committee on "international cooperation," in effect would require the ICC to be subject to national laws and procedures on surrender of accused, and legal assistance to obtain evidence. *See 1996 PrepCom Report, supra* note 12.

[68]   *See Report of the Sixth Committee, reprinted in* FERENCZ, *supra* note 12, at 298-305; *1995 Ad Hoc Committee Report, supra* note 12; M. Cherif Bassiouni, *Recent United Nations Activities in Connection With the Establishment of a Permanent International Criminal Court and the Role of the Association Internationale de Droit Pénal and the Instituto Superiore Internazionale di Scienze Criminali*, 67 REVUE INTERNATIONALE DE DROIT PÉNALE 127 (1996).

[69]   *Report of the Committee on International Criminal Court Jurisdiction*, U.N. GAOR, 7th Sess., Supp. No. 11, at 21-25, U.N. Doc. A/2136 (1952) [hereinafter *1951 Draft Statute*]. *See also Comments Received from Governments Regarding the Report of the Committee on International Criminal Jurisdiction*, U.N. GAOR, 7th Sess., U.N. Doc. A/2186 and U.N. Doc. A/2186/Add.1. *See also Historical Survey of the Question of International Criminal Jurisdiction, Memorandum by the Secretary-General*, U.N. GAOR, 4th Sess., U.N. Doc. A/CN.4/7/Rev. 1 (1949), *reprinted in* FERENCZ, *supra* note 12, at 399.

[70]   *See Report of the Sixth Committee*, U.N. GAOR, 7th Sess., U.N. Doc. A/2275 (1952) and discussions on this report by the Sixth Committee, *reprinted in* FERENCZ, *supra* note 12, at 424-28.

[71]   In 1952 the Allies were still holding trials in Germany under CCL 10, *supra* note 33, and in the Far East.

[72]   *Report of the Committee on International Criminal Jurisdiction*, U.N. GAOR, 7th Sess., Supp. No. 12, at 21, U.N. Doc. A/26645 (1954). The revised statute made a number of changes to the 1951 Draft Statute in order to encourage more states to accept such a proposal, mostly softening the compulsory jurisdiction of the court by allowing more flexibility and voluntary participation on the part of states, including the opportunity for states to withdraw from the court's jurisdiction upon one year's notice. The Special Committee was eager to develop a project that was politically acceptable to the major powers, but even so, the political climate was still not ripe.

conferred on the Court, and deleted the requirement that jurisdiction be approved by the General Assembly.[73]

The 1953 revised Draft Statute was submitted to the General Assembly, which found it necessary to first consider the ILC's work on the Draft Code of Offences, which had not yet been completed. The statute for an international criminal court was, therefore, tabled until the Draft Code of Offences was finalized in 1954.[74] The ILC's approved text of the Draft Code of Offences, consisting of five articles listing 13 separate international crimes, was submitted to the General Assembly in 1954.[75] But, the 1954 Draft Code was tabled until such a time as "aggression" could be defined.[76] The reason for this incongruent situation was that the General Assembly in 1950 had removed "aggression" from the ILC's mandate to elaborate a Draft Code of Offences, and gave that task to a special committee of the General Assembly. That committee was remandated in 1952, and then again in 1954; and it took 20 years for the committee to define "aggression."[77]

The definition of aggression in 1974 thus removed the reason for tabling the 1954 Draft Code of Offences. But between 1974 and 1978, the General Assembly did not take up the subject of the Draft Code of Offences, which it had previously tabled. In 1978, efforts by a number of governments and non-governmental organizations (NGOs) forced the issue and the General Assembly placed the matter back on its agenda. However, it was only two years later that it mandated the ILC to work on that question. In 1982, a new rapporteur of the ILC produced his first report on the Draft Code,[78] which contained a variety of generalities concerning international criminal law, individual and state responsibility, and observations on the eventual contents of such a code.[79] The new rapporteur was starting his work on the project

---

[73]   These political considerations that figured so prominent in the 1950's were revisited at the PrepCom and the Diplomatic Conference. Many of them were included in the statute adopted in Rome. *See* Rome Statute of the International Criminal Court, A/Conf.183/9 (1998) at Part 2, Arts. 5 to 21.

[74]   G.A. Res. 898 (IX), U.N. GAOR, 9th Sess., Supp No. 21, at 50, U.N. Doc. A/2890 (1954) [hereinafter Resolution 898 (IX)].

[75]   *See Third Report Relating to a Draft Code of Offenses Against the Peace and Security of Mankind,* U.N. GAOR, 6th Sess., U.N. Doc. A/CN.4/85 (1954). *See also* D.H.N. Johnson, *The Draft Code of Offenses Against the Peace and Security of Mankind,* 4 INT'L COMP. L.Q. 445 (1955).

[76]   *See* U.N. G.A. Res. 898 (IX) (14 Dec. 1954) (tabling the Draft Code of Offences until aggression was defined); U.N. G.A. Res. 1187 (XII) (11 Dec. 1957) (tabling the Draft Code of Offences for a second time).

[77]   There were four committees on the question of defining aggression. The last committee finished its work in 1974, finally defining aggression after 20 years of debating the issue. The General Assembly adopted the definition by a consensus resolution. U.N. G.A. Res. 3314 (XXIX), 29 U.N. GAOR Supp. No. 31, at 142, U.N. Doc. A/9631 (1974). For a history of the committee on aggression's work, see BENJAMIN FERENCZ, DEFINING INTERNATIONAL AGGRESSION (1975). In 1998, the question of aggression was still not ripe for definition in the ICC Statute. The political compromise in the Statute was to include aggression within the jurisdiction of the Court but suspending its application until it could be defined. *See* Article 5, paragraph 2 of the ICC Statute. It states "The Court shall exercise jurisdiction over the crime of aggression once a provision is adopted in accordance with articles 121 and 123 defining the crime and setting out the conditions under which the Court shall exercise jurisdiction with respect to this crime. Such a provision shall be consistent with the relevant provisions of the Charter of the United Nations."

[78]   *See Report of the International Law Commission on the work of its thirty-fifth session,* U.N. GAOR, 38th Sess., Supp. No. 10, at 11-28, U.N. Doc. A/38/10 (1983).

[79]   It should be noted that the new rapporteur, like his predecessors, confined criminal responsibility to individuals, excluding organizations and states. *But see* FARHAD MALEKIAN, INTERNATIONAL CRIMINAL RESPONSIBILITY OF STATES (1985). The enunciation of the principles of state responsibility have, however, since 1976 contained the notion of state criminal responsibility. *See* 1976 Y.B. INT'L L. COMM'N, U.N. GAOR, 31st Sess., U.N. Doc A/CN/SER.A/1976 (1976); *Report of the International Law Commission,* U.N. GAOR, 36th Sess., Supp. No. 10, U.N. Doc. A/36/10 (1984). Commenting on this concept, see IAN BROWNLIE, SYSTEM OF THE LAW OF NATIONS: STATE RESPONSIBILITY 32-33 (1983); YEARBOOK OF THE INTERNATIONAL LAW COMMISSION, *supra,* at 26-54 (containing Special Rapporteur Ago's approach): Virginia Morris & M. Christiane Bourloyannis-Vrailas, *Current Development: The Work of the Sixth Committee at the Fiftieth Session of the U.N. General Assembly,* 90 AM. J. INT'L L. 491, 494

ab initio, and it took him until 1991 to produce what was intended to be a final text.[80] Because the report was criticized by governments and scholars[81] it was revised and adopted by the ILC in 1996.[82]

As stated above, during the period in which the General Assembly had mandated the ILC to prepare the Draft Code of Offences, later renamed the Draft Code of Crimes, it also gave a mandate to another special committee to prepare a draft statute for an international criminal court. That committee produced a text in 1951[83] which was revised in 1953.[84] The 1953 Draft Statute of the court was tabled because the Draft Code of Offences was not completed, and when it was completed in 1954, the Draft Code of Offences was tabled because the definition of aggression, which had been entrusted to another body, was not completed. That result was expected since there were different bodies working separately at different venues (Geneva and New York), and producing different texts at different times. It was, therefore, easy for the General Assembly to table each text successively because the one or the other was not then ready. That lack of synchronization was not entirely fortuitous: it was the result of a political will to delay the establishment of an international criminal court because that was a time when the world was sharply divided and frequently at risk of war.

Changing Times: 1989 to 1998

Since World War II, only two international conventions referred to an international criminal jurisdiction: Article 6 of the 1948 Genocide Convention[85] and Article 5 of the 1973 *Apartheid* Convention.[86] The former, however, only referred to the jurisdiction over genocide of an eventual international criminal court.[87] The latter referred to the establishment of an international criminal jurisdiction to prosecute *apartheid,* but none was established. In 1979, the United Nations *ad hoc* Committee for Southern Africa requested this writer to prepare a draft statute for the establishment of an international criminal jurisdiction to prosecute violators of the

---

(1996).

[80]   *Report of the International Law Commission,* U.N. GAOR, 46th Sess. Supp. No. 10, U.N. Doc. A/46/10 (1991) [hereinafter *1991 Draft Code of Crimes*].

[81]   *Commentaries on 1991 Draft Code, supra* note 62.

[82]   *1996 Draft Code of Crimes, supra* note 59.

[83]   *1951 Draft Statute, supra* note 69.

[84]   *Revised Draft Statute for an International Criminal Court* (Annex to the Report of the Committee on International Criminal Jurisdiction, 20 Aug. 1953), GAOR, 9th Sess., Supp. 12, at 21, U.N. Doc. A/2645 (1954); *see also Report of the Sixth Committee to the U.N. General Assembly considering the (Final) Report of the 1953 Committee on International Criminal Jurisdiction,* U.N. GAOR, 9th Sess., Supp., U.N. Doc. A/2827/Corr.1 (1954); *Report of the 1953 Committee on International Criminal Jurisdiction to the Sixth Committee,* U.N. GAOR, 9th Sess., Supp. No. 12, at 23, U.N. Doc. A/2645 (1953).

[85]   Convention on the Prevention and Punishment of the Crime of Genocide, 9 Dec. 1948, 78 U.N.T.S. 277, *reprinted in* 45 AM. J. INT'L L. 7 (1951) (Supp.).

[86]   Convention on the Suppression and Punishment of the Crime of Apartheid, 30 Nov. 1973 G.A. Res. 3068 (XXVIII), 28th Sess., Supp. No. 30, at 75, U.N. Doc. A/9030, *reprinted in* 13 I.L.M. 50.

[87]   *See* Louis René Beres, *Genocide and Genocide-Like Crimes in,* 1 BASSIOUNI, ICL, *supra* note 12, at 271 (M. Cherif Bassiouni ed. 1986); M. Cherif Bassiouni, *Introduction to the Genocide Convention, in* BASSIOUNI, ICL, *supra* note 12, at 281 (M. Cherif Bassiouni ed. 1986); Matthew Lippman, *The Drafting of the 1948 Convention on the Prevention and Punishment of the Crime of Genocide,* 3 B.U. INT'L L.J. 1 (1984); *The 1948 Convention on the Prevention and Punishment of the Crime of Genocide: Forty-Five Years Later,* 8 TEMP. INT'L & COMP. L.J. 1 (1994); PIETER N. DROST, THE CRIME OF STATE: BOOK II, GENOCIDE (1959); LEO KUPER, GENOCIDE (1981). *See also generally* BASSIOUNI, CRIMES AGAINST HUMANITY, *supra* note 15 (1992); Matthew Lippman, *The Convention on the Prevention and Punishment of the Crime of Genocide, in* 1 BASSIOUNI, ICL, *supra* note 12 (M. Cherif Bassiouni ed., 2d ed. forthcoming in 1998).

Apartheid Convention, but there was no further action on the proposal for obvious political reasons.[88]

The question of an international criminal court came back to the United Nations by an unexpected route in 1989 after a hiatus of 26 years.[89] In 1989, the General Assembly held a special session on the problem of drug trafficking and Trinidad and Tobago suggested that a specialized international criminal court be established. Following that, the General Assembly requested that the ILC prepare a report on the establishment of an international criminal court for the prosecution of persons engaged in drug trafficking.[90] Contemporaneously, an NGO committee of experts,[91] chaired by this author, prepared a draft statute in June 1990[92] for an international criminal court that would have jurisdiction over all international crimes. The draft was modeled on the 1981 text prepared for the implementation of the *Apartheid* Convention mentioned above. The 1990 unofficial text was submitted to the Eighth United Nations Congress on Crime Prevention and the Treatment of Offenders[93] which recognized the need for an international criminal court and recommended that the ILC take up the matter.[94]

In response to the General Assembly's mandate arising out of the 1989 special session on drugs, the ILC in 1990 completed a report which was submitted to the 45th session of the General Assembly.[95] Though that report was not limited to the drug trafficking question it was, nonetheless, favorably received by the General Assembly, which encouraged the ILC to

---

[88]   *Study on Ways and Means of Insuring the Implementation of International Instruments such as the International Convention on the Suppression and Punishment of the Crime of Apartheid, Including the Establishment of the International Jurisdiction Envisaged by the Convention*, U.N. Doc. E/CN.4/1426 (1981) [hereinafter *Study on the Suppression and Punishment of the Crime of Apartheid*]. *See generally* Bassiouni & Derby, *supra* note 12. The draft has never been acted upon, and it is not likely to be in view of the recent changes in South Africa. *See* Internal Memorandum, Ministry of Justice of South Africa, *Promotion of National Unity and Reconciliation Bill 011094JE*, Act Number 30 of 1995; Ziyad Motala, *The Promotion of National Unity and Reconciliation Act: The Constitution and International Law*, 28 COMP. & INT'L L.J. S. AFRICA 338 (1995).
        That text, however, served as a model to the ILC in its formulation of the 1993 Draft Statute for an ICC. *See International Law Commission Revised Report of the Working Group on the Draft Statute for an International Criminal Court*, ILC, 45th Sess., U.N. Doc. A/CN.4/L.490 (1993) [hereinafter 1993 Draft Statute].
[89]   *See Revised Draft Statute for an International Criminal Court*, U.N. GAOR, 9th Sess., Supp. No. 12, Annex, U.N. Doc. A/2645 (1954).
[90]   G.A. Res. 43/164 (1988) and 44/39 (1989). In particular, see Agenda item 152, *International Criminal Responsibility of Individuals and Entities Engaged in Illicit Trafficking of Narcotic Drugs Across National Frontiers and Other Transnational Criminal Activities Establishment of an International Criminal Court with Jurisdiction Over Such Crimes, Report of the Sixth Committee to the General Assembly*, U.N. Doc. A/44/770 (1989). The proposal made by Trinidad and Tobago was the brainchild of President A.N.R. Robinson, who has been a consistent supporter of the ICC.
[91]   The committee of experts was assembled by the International Institute of Higher Studies in Criminal Sciences (Siracusa, Italy), in cooperation with the United Nations Crime Prevention Branch and the Italian Ministry of Justice. *See* M. Cherif Bassiouni, *Draft Statute International Tribunal*, 9 NOUVELLES ÉTUDES PÉNALES 1 (1993); M. Cherif Bassiouni, *Draft Statute International Tribunal*, 10 NOUVELLES ÉTUDES PÉNALES (1993) (containing French and Spanish translations of the statute).
[92]   This draft statute was based on this author's proposal to the United Nations to prosecute *apartheid* violators. *See Study on the Suppression and Punishment of the Crime of Apartheid, supra* note 88. Subsequently, the draft statute was amended and published in M. CHERIF BASSIOUNI, A DRAFT INTERNATIONAL CRIMINAL CODE AND DRAFT STATUTE FOR AN INTERNATIONAL TRIBUNAL (1987).
[93]   U.N. Doc. A/Conf. 144/NGO.7, DRAFT STATUTE: INTERNATIONAL CRIMINAL TRIBUNAL (1990), Item 5, *reprinted in* 15 NOVA L. REV. 375 (1991). *See also* M. Cherif Bassiouni, *A Comprehensive Strategic Approach on International Cooperation for the Prevention, Control and Suppression of International and Transnational Criminality, Including the Establishment of an International Criminal Court*, 15 NOVA L. REV. 353 (1991).
[94]   *Report of the Eighth United Nations Congress on the Prevention of Crime and the Treatment of Offenders*, U.N. Doc. A/Conf. 144/28, at 277 (1990).
[95]   *Report of the International Law Commission on the Work of its forty-second session*, U.N. GAOR, 45th Sess., Supp. No. 10, A/45/10 (1990).

continue its work. Thus, without a clear and specific mandate, the ILC went from a mandate limited to drug trafficking to an all-encompassing project of preparing a comprehensive statute for an international criminal court. Wisely, the ILC started with a preliminary report in 1992,[96] and when that report was favorably received by the General Assembly, the ILC produced a comprehensive text in 1993,[97] which it modified in 1994.[98] The changes made in 1994 were intended to answer the political concerns of some of the world's major powers,[99] and as a result the draft was ideally less satisfactory than its earlier 1993 text.[100] Still, the ILC's perseverance and ingenuity in developing the limited mandate it received from the General Assembly in 1989 into the 1994 Draft Statute for an International Criminal Court merits high praise.

The 1994 ILC report on the draft statute for an international criminal court was submitted to the 49th Session of the General Assembly, which resolved to consider it at its 50th session, but first it set up an *ad hoc* committee to discuss the proposal. This committee, referred to as the 1995 *Ad Hoc* Committee for the Establishment of an International Criminal Court, met inter-sessionally for two sessions of two weeks each from April through August 1995.[101] In the resolution establishing the *Ad Hoc* Committee the General Assembly, however, decoupled the

---

[96]   *Report of the International Law Commission on the work of its 44th Session*, 4 May-24 July 1992, U.N. GAOR, 47th Sess., Supp. No. 10, U.N. Doc. A/47/10 (1992).

[97]   *See Revised Report of the Working Group on the Draft Statute for an International Criminal Court*, ILC, 45th Sess., 3 May-23 July 1993, A/CN.4/L.490 (1993); *Revised Report of the Working Group on the Draft Statute for an International Criminal Court: Addendum*, ILC, 45th Sess., 3 May-23 July 1993, A/CN.4/L.490/Add.1 (1993); *Report of the International Law Commission*, U.N. GAOR, 47th Sess., Supp. No. 10, U.N. Doc. A/47/10 (1992); *Report of the International Law Commission*, U.N. GAOR, 44th Sess., Supp. No. 10, at 255, U.N. Doc. A/46/10 (1991). An NGO committee of experts was convened under the chairmanship of this writer by the International Institute of Higher Studies in Criminal Sciences (Siracusa, Italy), in cooperation with the United Nations Crime Prevention Branch and the Italian Ministry of Justice and prepared the text of a substitute based on the 1981 *Study of Ways and Means of Insuring the Implementation of International Instruments such as the International Convention on the Suppression and Punishment of the Crime of Apartheid, Including the Establishment of the International Criminal Court Envisaged by the Convention. See Study on the Suppression and Punishment of the Crime of Apartheid, supra* note 88. The new text was published as M. Cherif Bassiouni, *Draft Statute International Tribunal*, 9 NOUVELLES ÉTUDES PÉNALES 1 (1993); M. Cherif Bassiouni, *Draft Statute International Tribunal*, 10 NOUVELLES ÉTUDES PÉNALES 1 (1993) (containing French and Spanish translations of the statute).

[98]   *Report of the International Law Commission*, 46th Sess., 2 May-22 July 1994, U.N. GAOR, 49th Sess., Supp. No. 10, U.N. Doc. A/49/10 (1994). Timothy C. Evered, *An International Criminal Court: Recent Proposals and American Concerns*, 6 PACE INT'L L. REV. 121 (1994); Michael P. Scharf, *Getting Serious about an International Criminal Court*, 6 PACE INT'L L. REV. 103 (1994).

[99]   The process was reminiscent of the same reaction that occurred in 1953 when the Revised Draft Statute for an International Criminal Court amended the Report of the Committee on International Criminal Court Jurisdiction to placate political opposition. *See* the 1951 and 1953 drafts, *supra* notes 69 and 72 respectively, and corresponding text.

[100]   *Report of the International Law Commission, 46th Sess.*, U.N. GAOR, 49th Sess., Supp. No. 10, U.N. Doc. A/49/10 (1994). For example, the 1994 Draft does not define the crimes within the "inherent"jurisdiction of the Court; draws an incorrect distance between the "laws and customs of war" and the Geneva Conventions of 19 August 1949, which are deemed in that text "treaty crimes," when these conventions are well recognized as having become part of the customary laws of armed conflict. Since this article is not intended to be a critique of the 1994 text which has, otherwise, great merit, no discussion is presented on its weaknesses. M. Cherif Bassiouni, *The Time Has Come for an International Criminal Court*, 1 IND. INT'L & COMP. L. REV. 1 (1991); and M. Cherif Bassiouni & Christopher Blakesley, *The Need for an International Criminal Court in the New International World Order*, 25 VAND. J. TRANSNAT'L L. 151 (1992). Timothy C. Evered, *An International Criminal Court: Recent Proposals and American Concerns*, 6 PACE INT'L L. REV. 121 (1994); Michael P. Scharf, *Getting Serious about an International Criminal Court*, 6 PACE INT'L L. REV. 103 (1994).

[101]   U.N. GAOR 6th Comm., 49th Sess., U.N. Doc. A/C.6/49/L.24 (23 Nov. 1994).

ILC's 1994 Draft Statute for an International Criminal Court from its 1991 Draft Code of Crimes Against the Peace and Security of Mankind.[102]

In late 1995, the *Ad Hoc* Committee produced its report which became the basis for the General Assembly to establish the 1996 Preparatory Committee on the Establishment of an International Criminal Court (PrepCom). The 1996 PrepCom also relied on the ILC's 1994 Draft Statute and proceeded to modify it.[103] The 1996 PrepCom Report was then submitted to the General Assembly's 51st session on October 28, 1996, with a recommendation that the General Assembly extend the PrepCom term with a specific mandate to negotiate proposals with a view to producing a consolidated text of a convention, statute, and annexed instruments by 1998.[104] The General Assembly thereupon extended the PrepCom's mandate from 1996 to April 1998.[105] During that period (1994-1997) many governments changed their position on the ICC and in December 1997 the General Assembly called for the convening of a diplomatic conference in Rome, June 15 -July 17, 1998, to adopt a Convention on the Establishment of an International Criminal Court.[106] This meant that the PrepCom had to produce a consolidated text in time for the Diplomatic Conference.

The change in the political climate and in the attitude by governments towards an ICC was extraordinary. While there was little hope for the prospects of an ICC between 1989 and 1992, a chain of events was set in motion when the Security Council, in Resolution 780,[107] established a Commission of Experts to investigate violations of international humanitarian law in the former Yugoslavia. This was the first time since World War II that the international community provided for the investigation of violators of international humanitarian law. In its first interim report, the Commission of Experts stated that the establishment of an *ad hoc* international criminal tribunal would be "consistent with the direction of its work."[108] Recalling that report, the Security Council, in Resolution 808, proceeded to establish the International Criminal Tribunal for the former Yugoslavia.[109] The resolution stated that the Security Council:

> *[d]ecide[d]* that an international criminal tribunal shall be established for the prosecution of persons responsible for serious violations of international humanitarian law committed in the territory of the former Yugoslavia since 1991[.][110]

---

[102]   *See 1991 Draft Code of Crimes, supra* note 80. This text was subsequently redrafted by the ILC, see *1996 Draft Code of Crimes, supra* note 59. The latter however was not completed by the ILC until 1996, and took into account the experiences of the ICTY and the ICTR, as well as the debates of the *Ad Hoc* Committee and of the Preparatory Committee on the International Criminal Court which the General Assembly set up after the *Ad Hoc* Committee completed its mandate.

[103]   GA Res. 50/46, U.N. GAOR, 50th Sess., U.N. Doc. A/RES/50/46 (1995). *See also Summary of the Proceedings of the Preparatory Committee on the Establishment of an International Criminal Court*, U.N. GAOR, 50th Sess., Supp. No. 22, U.N. Doc. A/50/22 (1995).

[104]   *1996 PrepCom Report, supra* note 12. M. Cherif Bassiouni, *Recent United Nations Activities in Connection with the Establishment of a Permanent International Criminal Court and the Role of the Association Internationals de Droit Pénal and the Instituto Superiore Internazionale di Scienze Criminali*, 67 REVUE INTERNATIONALE DE DROIT PÉNAL 127 (1996).

[105]   G.A. Res. 207, U.N. GAOR, 51st Sess., U.N. Doc. A/RES/51/207 (1997).

[106]   G.A. Res. 160, U.N. GAOR, 52d Sess., U.N. Doc. A/RES/52/160 (1997).

[107]   *See* Resolution 780, *supra* note 22.

[108]   *Letter from the Secretary-General to the President of the Security Council*, Feb. 9, 1993, U.N. Doc. S/25274 (1993), *transmitting Interim Report of the Commission of Experts Established pursuant to Security Council Resolution 780 (1992)*, para. 74.

[109]   Resolution 808, *supra* note 48.

[110]   *Id.* at para. 1.

The Security Council followed the same procedure in 1994 in connection with the events in Rwanda, and established the International Criminal Tribunal for Rwanda.

The events in Yugoslavia and Rwanda shocked the world out of its complacency and the idea of prosecuting those who committed international crimes acquired a broad based support in world public opinion and in many governments.

The experience with the two *ad hoc* tribunals was mixed and included, *inter alia*, the following:

(1) The ICTY on the whole worked better than the ICTR and started functioning at high capacity much before the ICTR. The latter was crippled by inefficiency and neglect for its first three years;

(2) The Security Council, as the organ that created both tribunals, found itself frequently seized with issues and problems concerning these tribunals and their administration, and as a result became less inclined to establish other similar organs;

(3) The two tribunals gained on the whole world wide recognition and credibility and thus gave support to the need for the establishment of a permanent international criminal court;

(4) The international community gave strong support to the two tribunals and became more vocal about a permanent institution with universal recognition that would not suffer from the problems of *ad hoc* institutions.

These and other factors combined to create a new international climate that compelled governments to support the establishment of a permanent international criminal court. Among these other factors was the rising influence of international civil society, which was no longer willing to tolerate that perpetrators of major international crimes go unpunished. It was believed that a permanent international criminal court would help put an end to impunity for international crimes and serious violations of fundamental human rights.[111]

Assessing the Progress from 1989 to 1998

The General Assembly, in 1994, established an *Ad Hoc* Committee to review the ILC's 1994 Draft Statute.[112] According to General Assembly resolution 49/53 of 9 December 1994, the mandate of the *Ad Hoc* Committee was:

to review the major substantive and administrative issues arising out of the draft statute prepared by the International Law Commission and, in the light of that review, to consider arrangements for the convening of an international conference of plenipotentiaries.[113]

The General Assembly hoped that the *Ad Hoc* Committee would resolve the differences between states favoring the establishment of an ICC and those who were opposed or reluctant to see this result in the short term. The *Ad Hoc* Committee met for two sessions in 1995,[114] but

---

[111] See the articles contained within *Accountability for International Crimes and Serious Violations of Fundamental Human Rights*, 59 LAW & CONTEMP. PROBS. (M. Cherif Bassiouni, Special Ed., 1996) and REINING IN IMPUNITY FOR INTERNATIONAL CRIMES AND SERIOUS VIOLATIONS OF FUNDAMENTAL HUMAN RIGHTS: PROCEEDINGS OF THE SIRACUSA CONFERENCE 17-21 SEPTEMBER 1997, 14 NOUVELLES ÉTUDES PÉNALES (Christopher C. Joyner, Special Ed. & M. Cherif Bassiouni, General Ed., 1998).

[112] U.N. Doc. A/RES/49/53.

[113] U.N. Doc. A/RES/50/46.

[114] The two sessions were held from 3 to 13 April and from 14 to 25 August 1995.

failed to come to sufficient agreement to call a conference of plenipotentiaries. However, these meetings had the positive effect of allowing states to familiarize themselves with the issues involved in the creation of an International Criminal Court. The educational value produced by the work of the *Ad Hoc* Committee served a beneficial purpose and led to the establishment of a Preparatory Committee in 1996.[115] The mandate of the 1996 PrepCom was explicit and goal-oriented. But the fact that most of the delegates at the PrepCom had been delegates at the *Ad Hoc* Committee and that the same persons remained engaged in the process between 1996-98 was invaluable,[116] and that lead to a consolidated text.[117] The benefits of the 1995 *Ad Hoc* Committee must be tempered, however, with the acknowledgment of the difficulties that still confronted the PrepCom. Proponents of the ICC have had to face many difficulties that prevented the process from moving forward. The process was slow due to the unfamiliarity of some delegates with the technical issues involved, and the desire of some to cast a court which would be most responsive to the political concerns of their governments. Furthermore, the large number of proposals made by states at the PrepCom made it difficult to deal with them efficiently in the time available, namely 12 weeks of working sessions between 1996-98. It would be unfair, however, to say that a purposeful war of attrition was being waged by opponents of the court though there were certainly some delaying tactics. Lastly, the costs that governments had to bear in sending experts from capitals to these meetings in New York was felt by many delegations, and that may have caused more limited participation of Developing and Least Developed Countries at the *Ad Hoc* Committee and PrepCom meetings.[118]

Building on the work of the *Ad Hoc* Committee, the 1996 PrepCom was mandated by the General Assembly:

> to discuss further the major substantive and administrative issues arising out of the draft statute prepared by the International Law Commission and, taking into account the different views expressed during the meetings, to draft texts, with a view to preparing a widely acceptable consolidated text of a convention for an international criminal court as a next step towards consideration by a conference of plenipotentiaries, and [it was] also decide[ed] that the work of the Preparatory Committee should be based on the draft statute prepared by the International Law Commission and should take into account the report of the *Ad Hoc* Committee and written comments submitted by States . . . and, as appropriate, contributions of relevant organizations.[119]

As stated above, this mandate had a more specific, goal oriented character and it signified a progression from the earlier mandate of the *Ad Hoc* Committee. The 1996 PrepCom did not, however produce a "consolidated" text of a draft statute, and only succeeded in creating a report

---

[115]   The two sessions were held from 25 March to 12 April and from 12 to 30 August 1996.

[116]   The four sessions of the 1997-98 PrepCom were held from 11 to 21 February 1997, from 4 to 15 August 1997, from 1 to 12 December 1997 and from 16 March to 3 April 1998.

[117]   *Report of the Preparatory Committee on the Establishment of an International Criminal Court,* A/Conf.183/2/Add.1 (1998).

[118]   This is why the United Nations established a trust fund to assist Least Developed Countries (LDC's) in having one delegate per applying country. A similar program was developed by the International Criminal Justice and Weapons Control Center of DePaul University, funded by the John D. and Catherine T. MacArthur Foundation, helped bring several LDC's to the December 1997 and March-April 1998 sessions of the PrepCom. These programs also helped to bring LDC delegates to the Diplomatic Conference in Rome. Specifically, the United Nations program brought 45 delegates to Rome and the DePaul program brought 23 delegates to Rome.

[119]   U.N. Doc. A/RES/50/46 at para.2.

which compiled various proposals. On the basis on this work, the 1996 PrepCom proposed to the General Assembly to continue it's work with an enhanced mandate and meet for another nine weeks in 1997-98 before a diplomatic conference could be held. With all of this in mind, the 1996 PrepCom, in its report to the Sixth Committee stated:

> recognizing that this is a matter for the General Assembly, . . . on the basis of its scheme of work, considers that it is realistic to regard the holding of a diplomatic conference of plenipotentiaries in 1998 as feasible.[120]

Some of the language in this recommendation was troubling, in particular, the insistence by some delegations on the inclusion of a footnote in the recommendations of the 1996 PrepCom reserving their positions on its findings and its decision to move towards a Diplomatic Conference in 1998 necessitates caution. The footnote states that:

> [s]ome delegations expressed reservations on the conclusions of the Preparatory Committee and felt that these conclusions do not prejudge the position of the States in the General Assembly.[121]

The lack of an imperative to complete it's work by April 1998 in the language of the recommendation to the PrepCom raised concerns that the 1997-98 work could delay the convening of the conference in June 1998, and the wording of the 1996 PrepCom Report may not have been sufficiently peremptory. But the General Assembly's resolution was quite specific.[122] It mandated the 1997-98 PrepCom to:

> (a)   to meet three or four times up to a total of 9 weeks before the diplomatic conference. To organize its work so that it will finalize its work in April of 1998 and so as to allow the widest possible participation of States. The work should be done in the form of open-ended working groups, concentrating on the negotiation of proposals with a view of producing a widely acceptable draft consolidated text of a convention, to be submitted to the diplomatic conference. No simultaneous meetings of the working groups were to be held in order to not handicap smaller delegations. The working groups were to work with complete transparency and should be by general agreement to secure the universality of the convention. Submission of reports of its debates was not be required. Interpretation and translation services were however made available to some of the working groups.
> (b)   the subjects to be dealt with by the Preparatory Committee were:
>   1.   List and definition and elements of crimes
>   2.   Principles of criminal law and penalties
>   3.   Organization of the court
>   4.   Procedures
>   5.   Complementarity and trigger mechanism
>   6.   Cooperation with states
>   7.   Establishment of the ICC and relationship with the UN

---

[120]   *1996 PrepCom Report*, *supra* note 12, at Vol. 1, para.370.
[121]   *Id.* at p.77, note 12.
[122]   U.N. Doc. A/51/627. This resolution was adopted by the U.N. General Assembly on December 17, 1996.

8. Final clauses and financial matters
9. Other matters

The renewed mandate of the 1997-98 PrepCom was a more positive, goal oriented statement than that of the 1996 PrepCom, and it engendered a successful progression to the negotiation stage of the process which occurred during the 1997-98 PrepCom.[123]

The 1997-98 PrepCom attained its goal, and the draft report of the PrepCom[124] stated:

1.   The General Assembly, in its resolution 50/46 of 11 December 1995, decided to establish a preparatory committee for the establishment of an international criminal court to discuss the major substantive and administrative issues arising out of the draft statute prepared by the International Law Commission in 1994 and to draft texts with a view to preparing a widely acceptable consolidated text of a convention for an international criminal court as a next step towards consideration by a conference of plenipotentiaries.

2.   The Preparatory Committee on the Establishment of an International Criminal Court met from 25 March to 12 April and from 12 to 30 August 1996, during which time it discussed further the issues arising out of the draft statute and began preparing a widely acceptable consolidated text of a convention for an international criminal court.[125]

3.   In its resolution 51/207 of 17 December 1996, the General Assembly decided that the Preparatory Committee would meet in 1997 and 1998 in order to complete the drafting of a text for submission to the diplomatic conference of plenipotentiaries.

4.   The Preparatory Committee met from 11 to 21 February, from 4 to 15 August and from 1 to 12 December 1997, during which time it continued to prepare a widely acceptable consolidated text of a convention for an international criminal court.[126]

5.   The General Assembly, in its resolution 52/160 of 15 December 1997, accepted with deep appreciation the generous offer of the Government of Italy to act as host to the United Nations Diplomatic Conference of Plenipotentiaries on the Establishment of an International Criminal Court and decided to hold the Conference in Rome from 15 June to 17 July 1998.

6.   In the same resolution, the General Assembly requested the Preparatory Committee to continue its work in accordance with Assembly resolution 51/207 and, at the end of its sessions, to transmit to the Conference the text of a draft convention on the establishment of an international criminal court prepared in accordance with its mandate.

7.   The Preparatory Committee met from 16 March to 3 April 1998 and had before it a consolidated text compiled by the Bureau and coordinators on the basis of all the texts that it had worked out or that had been submitted to it (A/AC.249/1998/L.13). The compilation was the product of an informal meeting held in Zutphen, the Netherlands, from 19 to 30 January 1998 and was used as a basis for the work of the Committee at that session.

---

[123]   *Id.*

[124]   *Draft Report of the Preparatory Committee*, A/AC.249/1998/L.16, 1998.

[125]   *See Official Records of the General Assembly, Fifty-first Session, Supplement No. 22* (A/51/22) [This is an original footnote from document A/AC.249/1998/L.16].

[126]   *See Decisions Taken by the Preparatory Committee at its Session Held from 11 to 21 July 1997* (A/AC.249/1997/L.5); *Decisions Taken by the Preparatory Committee at its Session Held from 4 to 15 August 1997* (A/AC.249/1997/L.8/Rev.1); and *Decisions Taken by the Preparatory Committee at its Session Held from 1 to 12 December 1997* (A/AC.249/1997/L.9/Rev.1) [This is an original footnote from document A/AC.249/1998/L.16].

8.   At its 56th meeting, on 16 March, the Preparatory Committee decided to conduct its work through working groups on the following subjects: procedural matters (chaired by Ms. Silvia Fernádndez de Gurmendi); composition and administration of the court (chaired by Mr. Lionel Yee); establishment of the court and relationship with the United Nations (chaired by Mr. Rama Rao); applicable law (chaired by Mr. Per Saland); on *non bis in idem* (chaired by Mr. John Holmes); jurisdictional issues (chaired by Mr. Erkki Kourula), and enforcement (chaired by Mrs. Molly Warlow). The final clauses were considered at the informal meetings under the chairmanship of Mr. Adriaan Bos.

9.   At its 57th meeting, on 1 April, the Preparatory Committee adopted the reports of the working groups mentioned above.

10.   At its --meeting, on 3 April, the Preparatory Committee adopted the text of a draft statute on the establishment of an international criminal court (A/AC.249/CRP.6-18) and the draft final act (A/AC.249/1998/CRP. 19).

11.   In its resolution 52/160, the General Assembly requested the Secretary-General to prepare the text of the draft rules of procedure of the Conference, to be submitted to the Preparatory Committee for its consideration and recommendations to the Conference, with a, view to the adoption of such rules by the Conference in accordance with the rules of procedure of the General Assembly, and to provide for consultations on the organization and methods of work of the Conference, including rules of procedure, prior to the convening of the last session of the Committee. At its --th meeting, on 3 April, the Preparatory Committee adopted the draft provisional rules of procedure of the Conference prepared by the Secretary-General (A/AC.249/1998/CRP.3) pursuant to resolution 52/160.

12.   At its --th meeting, on --April, the Preparatory Committee took note of the draft organization of work prepared by the Secretariat and decided to transmit it to the Conference.

13.   At its --th meeting, on --April, the Preparatory Committee agreed to transmit to the Conference the following documents:

    (a)   Draft statute for the establishment of an international criminal court;

    (b)   Draft final act,

    (c)   Draft provisional rules of procedure of the Conference;

    (d)   Draft organization of work.

14.   In its resolution 52/160, the General Assembly requested the Secretary-General to invite non-governmental organizations, accredited by the Preparatory Committee with due regard to the provisions of section VII of Economic and Social Council resolution 1996/3 1 of 25 July 1996, and in particular to the relevance of their activities to the work of the Conference, to participate in the Conference, along the lines followed in the Committee, on the understanding that participation meant attending meetings of its plenary and, unless otherwise decided by the Conference in specific situations, formal meetings of its subsidiary bodies except the drafting group, receiving copies of the official documents, making available their materials to delegates and addressing, through a limited number of their representatives, its opening and/or closing sessions, as appropriate, in accordance with the rules of procedure to be adopted by the Conference. On the basis of the list of non-governmental organizations compiled by the Secretariat with the assistance of the NGO Coalition for the Establishment of an International Criminal Court A (A/AC.249/1998/CRP.22), the Preparatory Committee decided that the non-governmental

organizations listed therein should be invited to participate in the Conference in the manner set out in resolution 52/160.

15. At the 57th meeting, on 1 April, the representative of the Netherlands announced his country's candidacy of The Hague for the seat of the international criminal court.

16. Pursuant to paragraph 7 of resolution 51/207, the Secretary-General established a trust fund for the participation of the least developed countries in the work of the Preparatory Committee and the Conference. Guidelines were established for the administration of the fund. The Committee noted that the following Governments had made contributions to the fund: Belgium, Canada, Denmark, Finland, Netherlands, Norway, Sweden and United Kingdom of Great Britain and Northern Ireland. Thirty-three representatives from 18 States had thus far utilized the trust fund to facilitate their participation in the meetings of the Preparatory Committee during 1997 and 1998. The European Commission had awarded a grant to the trust fund, but owing to procedural difficulties, the transfer of the contribution had been delayed.

17. Pursuant to paragraph 7 of resolution 52/160, the Secretary-General also established a trust fund for the participation of other developing countries in the work of the Preparatory Committee and in the Conference. The Government of the Netherlands had made a contribution, which would be available to those developing countries requesting assistance to facilitate their participation in the Conference.

18. The Preparatory Committee expressed its deep appreciation to the Governments that had made contributions and to the European Commission for its award to the above-mentioned trust funds. The Committee noted that the General Assembly, in its resolution 52/160, called upon States to contribute voluntarily to the trust funds.

The 1997-98 PrepCom completed its work on 3 April 1998 with a consolidated text of 173 pages, containing 116 articles, but which had some 1300 words in brackets.[127] This was the text that the Diplomatic Conference was going to deal with in its five weeks in Rome.

Informal Inter-sessional Meetings
A number of delegations met inter-sessionally during the *Ad Hoc* Committee in 1995, the 1996 PrepCom sessions, as well as during the 1997-98 PrepCom sessions. Four inter-sessional meetings took place at the International Institute of Higher Studies in Criminal Sciences (ISISC), producing the Siracusa Draft, in a meeting from December 3-8, 1995; the Updated Siracusa Draft, during the July 10-14, 1996 meeting; the Abbreviated Compilation of Proposals on Rules of Procedure and Evidence, during the May 29 to June 4, 1997 meeting;[128] and the Abbreviated Compilation of Proposals on International Cooperation and Judicial Assistance and Enforcement, during the November 17-21, 1997 meeting.[129] Another informal inter-sessional meeting took place in Zutphen, The Netherlands, consisting of members of the Bureau and working group coordinators. This meeting resulted in the Report of the Inter-Sessional Meeting From 19 to 30 January 1998 in Zutphen, The Netherlands.[130]

---

[127]   *See supra* note 117.
[128]   U.N Doc. A/AC.249/L.2, 1996, presented by the Netherlands and Australia.
[129]   A/AC.249/1997/WG.5/CRP.1, 1997, presented by South Africa.
[130]   *Report of the Inter-Sessional Meeting From 19 to 30 January 1998 in Zutphen, The Netherlands*, U.N. Doc. A/AC.249/1998/L.13 (1998).

These inter-sessional meetings proved very useful to the work of the *Ad Hoc* Committee and to the PrepCom, they were open to all interested delegations and NGOs, except for the Zutphen meeting.

The "Like-Minded States"

A group of delegations known as the "like-minded states" have been a significant driving force behind the ICC's momentum. Their contributions have been effective and constructive. This group, which has benefitted from the coordination and hospitality of the U.N. Canadian mission, has grown in number. By April 1998, it included: Australia, Austria, Argentina, Belgium, Canada, Chile, Croatia, Denmark, Egypt, Finland, Germany, Greece, Guatemala, Hungary, Ireland, Italy, Lesotho, Netherlands, New Zealand, Norway, Portugal, Samoa, Slovakia, South Africa, Sweden, Switzerland, Trinidad and Tobago (representing 12 Caricon states), Uruguay and Venezuela.

The NGO Community

Non-governmental organizations, and particularly the 'NGO Coalition for an ICC'[131] played an important and useful part in the process. Their contributions took the form of aiding the PrepCom through publishing expert NGO papers which contributed to a deeper understanding

---

[131]   The NGO Coalition for an ICC had some 300 participating organizations including: African Law Students, Young Lawyers Association; All Saints Newman Center; ALTERLAW; American Bar Association; Amnesty International; Advocats Sans Frontieres; B'nai B'rith International; Baha'i International Community; Campaign for Tibet; Canadian Network for an International Criminal Court; The Carter Center; Center for Civil Human Rights; Center for Development of International Law; Center for Reproductive Law and Policy; Center for U.N. Reform Education; Center for Women's Global Leadership; Coordinating Board of Jewish Organizations; Counseling and Mediation Center; Crusade Against Violence; Drug Free Society; Egyptian Organization for Human Rights; Equality Now; European Law Students Association; European Peace Movement; Evangelical Lutheran Church in America; Federation Internationale des Ligues Droits de l'Hommes; FN-Forbundet/Danish UNA; Global Policy Forum; Guatemala Human Rights Commission/USA; Helsinki Citizens Assembly; Human Rights Internet; Human Rights Watch; Humanitarian Law Center; International Law Association (U.S. Branch) Committee on an International Criminal Court; International Association of Penal Law; Institute for the study of Genocide; Instituto Superiore Internazionale di Scienze Criminali; Interkeekelyk Vredesberaad; International Bar Association; International Commission of Jurists; International Human Rights Law Group; International Human Rights Law Institute, DePaul University School of Law; International Indian Treaty Council; International League for Human Rights; International Service for Human Rights; International Society for Human Rights; International Society for Traumatic Stress Studies; International Committee for the Convention against Microwave Weapons; Lawyers Committee for Human Rights; Lawyers Committee on Nuclear Policy; League of Human Rights; Legal Aid for Women and Environmental Development; Leo Kuper Foundation; Manobik Unnayan Parishad; Maryknol Society Justice and Peace Office; Medecins Sans Frontieres; Morgan, Lewis & Bockius LLP; No Peace Without Justice (TRP); Nuclear Age Peace Foundation; Nurnberger Menschenrechtszentrum; Ordre des Avocats a la Cour de Paris; Organization for Defending Victims of Violence; Pace Peace Centre, Pace Law School; Parliamentarians for Global Action; Procedural Aspects of International Law Institute; Quaker U.N. Office; Redress; Robert F. Kennedy Memorial Center for Human Rights; SOS Balkanes; Syracuse University; The People's Decade of Human Rights Education; Transnational Radical Party; United Church Board for World Ministries; United Nations Association; Urban Morgan Institute for Human Rights; War & Peace Foundation; Washington Office on Latin America; World Federalist Association; World Federalist Movement, Institute for Global Policy; Womens' Environment and Development Organization; World Order Models Project; World Organization of Building Officials. A list of the NGOs who participated at the Diplomatic Conference is contained in Annex IV of A/Conf.183/9 (1998).

Many organizations and individuals deserve recognition, but some truly stand out for their hard work and commitment and for the effectiveness of their contribution. They are: Harry Barnes, The Carter Center; Bill Butler, International Commission of Jurists; Rhonda Copeland, Women's Caucus; Richard Dicker, Human Rights Watch; Adama Dieng, International Commission of Jurists; Steven Gerber, Washington Working Group on the International Criminal Court; Christopher Hall, Amnesty International; Jelena Pejic, Lawyers Committee for Human Rights; Michael Posner, Lawyers Committee for Human Rights; Shazia Z. Rafi, Parliamentarians for Global Action; Mona Rishmawi, International Commission of Jurists; Ken Roth, Human Rights Watch; and the team of No Peace Without Justice which includes many but those who must be mentioned include Gianfranco Dell'Alba; Sergio Stanzani, and Marino Busdachin.

of the issues and creating opportunities for generating ideas, and for informal meetings with delegates through which NGO experts could offer advice to the delegates. Equally, the close attention which NGOs have paid to the proceedings of the PrepCom, the meetings which the NGO Coalition has held during the PrepCom with various states, groups of states, and other influential persons inside the ICC process, and the lobbying which has gone on at the United Nations, have all served to sustain and strengthen the momentum of the process. At a broader level, outside of the PrepCom, efforts were undertaken by NGOs to influence political leaders, create worldwide awareness of the Court issue, and hence support for the Court has been crucial, and should be acknowledged as such.

The Rome Diplomatic Conference of June 15 - July 17, 1998

From 1995 to the middle of 1998 two committees set up by the General Assembly worked 13 weeks at U.N. Headquarters in New York to produce a consolidated text of a Draft Statute for the establishment of an international criminal court.[132]

The Draft Statute and Draft Final Act submitted to the Diplomatic Conference were completed on April 3, 1998 at the last session of the PrepCom. The Draft Statute consisted of 116 articles which were contained in 173 pages of text with some 1,300 words in brackets, representing multiple options to entire provisions or only to some words contained in certain provisions.[133] The Draft Statute and Draft Final Act[134] were made available to the U.N. missions in New York at the end of April and this left only six weeks for the text to make its way from the U.N. Missions in New York to the respective ministries of foreign affairs, and then from there to ministries of justice and in some cases to ministries of defense. Thus, by the time the text reached those officials who later joined their government's delegations in Rome, there was very little time available for them to study the complex Draft Statute.[135]

To follow such a text was not easy even for those who participated in the three and a half years work of the *Ad Hoc* Committee and the PrepCom, and more so for those delegates who saw it for the first time just before coming to Rome, or who perhaps even saw it for the first time in Rome.

Experience taught that the Rome delegates who had not participated in the discussions of the *Ad Hoc* Committee or the PrepCom would probably represent two-thirds of those in attendance. That meant that a new learning curve period could be anticipated in Rome and thus slow down the discussions. Anticipating some of the difficulties, particularly because of the

---

[132]   The *Ad Hoc* Committee worked in 1995 and was followed by the Preparatory Committee from 1996-1998. For the *Ad Hoc* Committee's Report, see *1995 Ad Hoc Committee Report*, *supra* note 12. For the Preparatory Committee's Report, see *1996 PrepCom Report*, *supra* note 12.

[133]   Report of the Preparatory Committee on the Establishment of an International Criminal Court, *Draft Statute and Draft Final Act*, A/Conf.183/2/Add.1, 1998.

[134]   *Id.*

[135]   It should be noted that throughout the process, from the *Ad Hoc* Committee to the Diplomatic Conference many NGO's played a significant role in discussing the issues and proposing options to government delegations. Among the leading ones were: Amnesty International, Human Rights Watch, The Lawyers Committee for Human Rights, the International Commission of Jurists, the International Institute of Higher Studies in Criminal Sciences (ISISC), the Women's Caucus and No Peace Without Justice. The work of 238 NGO's at the Diplomatic Conference was coordinated by the Coalition for an ICC. The NGO's work has been recognized by all concerned as productive and professional and as having significantly contributed to the positive outcome in Rome.

Diplomatic Conference's relatively short period,[136] the PrepCom's Bureau decided at its last session in March-April '98 that it would be useful to hold an organizational meeting before the beginning of the Diplomatic Conference with the three elected chairs (conference, committee of the whole and drafting), the coordinators of the working groups that had worked so effectively during the PrepCom and who were also very familiar with the text and the Secretariat. However, a legal problem arose in that the PrepCom's mandate from the General Assembly ended on April 3,[137] and therefore the Bureau and the coordinators of the working groups no longer had any official capacity after that date. As to the three persons who were nominated by the PrepCom as chairs of the Diplomatic Conference,[138] they would not be formally elected until June 15, the Conference's opening day, and thus had no legal capacity before their formal election in Rome. Consequently, no formal meetings could take place. The pragmatic solution was to have an informal meeting, but that still left the problem of who was to convene that meeting and how it was to be funded. Two NGO's offered to assume that responsibility in cooperation with the Italian Ministry of Foreign Affairs[139] and the meeting took place May 4-8, at Courmayeur, Italy, with all of the above-mentioned participants, the designated Executive Secretary of the conference,[140] other members of the United Nations Secretariat and officials of the Italian Ministry of Foreign Affairs representing the host country.

The purposes of the Courmayeur meeting were: to discuss the implementation of the organizational plan for the Diplomatic Conference's work proposed by the PrepCom;[141] a

---

[136]   While it may appear that five weeks is a long time for a Diplomatic Conference, the fact is that there were only 24 working days of six hours a day with simultaneous interpretation for the Committee of the Whole, the Working Group of the Committee of the Whole, and the Drafting Committee. During that period of time the delegates had to cover 116 articles, including reaching political compromises on the definitions of crimes, jurisdiction, triggering mechanisms, the role of the Security Council and the prosecutor, and other difficult political issues that the PrepCom had not resolved. If one considers the fact that the articles of a legal technical nature require significant drafting attention, and approximately 30 articles involve sensitive political judgments, it is quite clear that 24 working days would simply not be enough. The participation of 161 delegations and some 2,000 delegates compounded the difficulty of achieving consensus in such a limited period of time.

[137]   G.A. Res. 51/207, 17 Dec. 1996.

[138]   Professor Giovanni Conso (Italy), Ambassador Adrian Bos (Netherlands) and Professor M. Cherif Bassiouni (Egypt). *See* Report of the Preparatory Committee on the Establishment of an International Criminal Court, *Draft Rules of Procedure*, A/Conf.183/2/Add.2, 1998.

[139]   The meeting was organized by International Scientific and Professional Advisory Council (ISPAC) and International Institute of Higher Studies in Criminal Sciences (ISISC). The latter had already hosted several informal meetings in Siracusa of working groups of the PrepCom and the work produced by the delegates who participated in these meetings proved quite useful to the PrepCom.

[140]   Mr. Roy Lee, Director, Codification Division, OLA.

[141]   The PrepCom's *Draft Organization of Work*, A/AC.249/1998/CRP.21, 1998, provided that:
1.   As mandated by the General Assembly in its resolution 52/160, of 15 December 1997, the task of the Conference is to finalize and adopt a convention on the establishment of an international criminal court. The Conference should move promptly to the consideration of substantive matters after a short session on organizational matters.
2.   After the opening of the Conference by the Secretary-General of the United Nations, the Conference will meet to elect the President, adopt the agenda and the rules of procedure and elect other officers.
3.   The General Committee will meet immediately following the election of its members. Its work will include, *inter alia*, assisting the President in the general conduct of business and making recommendations with respect to the election of members of the Drafting Committee.
4.   The plenary, on the recommendations of the General Committee will then elect the members of the Drafting Committee and adopt the programme of work of the Conference.
5.   The plenary will then proceed to hear statements from States in accordance with an established list of speakers prepared on a first-come-first-served basis. The Conference will also hear statements from a limited number of intergovernmental organizations and non-governmental organizations. The list of speakers will be opened for inscription on 15 April 1998.
6.   With a view to the efficient and expeditious discharge of the work of the plenary, a time limit may be established for statements by States on the one hand (e.g., 10 minutes) and intergovernmental organizations and non-governmental

tactical approach to the order of discussion of the various parts of the Draft Statute; and to establish the manner in which the flow of work would proceed between the Plenary, the Committee of the Whole, the Working Group, and the Drafting Committee.[142] Among the tactical decisions made at that meeting, it was agreed that the Plenary would only convene the first week,[143] but as of June 17th, the Committee of the Whole and the Drafting Committee would start their meetings. It was also agreed that Parts I and III of the Draft Statute would be discussed first by the Committee of the Whole and the Working Group, since they were more likely to be readily accepted. These parts would then be sent to the Drafting Committee, which would rapidly complete them in order to create a positive momentum likely to lead into a rapid pace of accomplishment by the Committee of the Whole.

The Courmayeur plan was sound, and the PrepCom's working group coordinators, subsequently reappointed at the Conference to serve in that capacity, were very knowledgeable of their tasks. Leadership, continuity and expertise, it was felt, were very important for the Conference's success in only five weeks, particularly because of the anticipated large number of delegates that would come to the Conference without having previously been involved in the process.

Shortly after that meeting, however, Ambassador Adrian Bos, Chairman of the *Ad Hoc* Committee and PrepCom, and who was the Chairman designate of the Committee of the Whole of the Diplomatic Conference, underwent emergency surgery. His wise leadership of three and one half years was going to be missing at the Diplomatic Conference, particularly because, as stated above, the time available at the Conference was so limited.[144]

Adrian Bos suggested Ambassador Phillip Kirsh of Canada as his replacement and the choice was readily accepted. Kirsh, a skilled and decided diplomat, proved to be most effective at the Conference. But at that time in May, Kirsh was representing his government in a fisheries dispute before the International Court of Justice in the Hague. He came from the Hague to Rome on June 13, two days before the Conference started, and went directly from the fisheries case to the International Criminal Court, making his subsequent success at the Conference all the more meritorious. To coordinate the planning of the Conference's work with the new chairman of the Committee of the Whole, a meeting was arranged on Sunday, June 14, in Rome to pick up from the Courmayeur meeting, with the three designated chairpersons[145] and the former

---

organizations on the other. In principle, States should be given more time than intergovernmental organizations and non-governmental organizations. A total of eight meetings may be allotted for this purpose.

7.   The Committee of the Whole should concentrate on the substantive work and should begin its work on 16 June. It may hold up to four meetings (with full interpretation) per day throughout the Conference, i.e., two bodies may meet concurrently, both morning and afternoon. The Committee of the Whole will report to the plenary upon the completion of its work.

8.   A working group of the Committee of the Whole will begin its work on the afternoon of 17 June.

9.   The Drafting Committee may begin its work on 19 June; two meetings (with full interpretation) per day may be allotted to it throughout the Conference. The Drafting Committee will receive its work from the Committee of the Whole and report to it. Time constraints might make it necessary to allow the Drafting Committee to report on the last portion of its work directly to die plenary.

10.   The Credentials Committee will meet sometime during the second or third week of the Conference. One meeting has been allotted for that purpose.

11.   The last day of the Conference is reserved for the signature of the Final Act and of the Statute of the Court and for the closure of the Conference.

[142]   These were the official structures established in the Conference's rules, *see supra* note 138.

[143]   To maximize the use of time, Heads of Delegations were each given 5-7 minutes for their opening remarks and Inter-governmental and some NGO's 3-5 minutes.

[144]   *See supra* note 136.

[145]   Conso, Kirsch (who replaced Bos) and Bassiouni, *see supra* note 138.

coordinators of the PrepCom's working groups (that Kirsh was to reappoint at the Conference) as well as the United Nations Secretariat staff, representatives of the Italian Ministry of Foreign Affairs and the Secretary General's Representative, Hans Corell. Kirsh accepted the Courmayeur plan urging, however, flexibility in the allotted time that had been established for the discussions of the various parts of the Draft Statute by the Committee of the Whole and the Working Group of the Committee of the Whole.

Kirsh's request of June 14 for flexibility did not have to be proven right. In fact, no sooner did the Committee of the Whole meet on June 17, than it became clear that the Courmayeur schedule could not be maintained. Owing to the large number of delegates who dealt with this question for the first time, the Committee of the Whole and its Working Group, which consisted of all interested delegations in the Committee of the Whole, found themselves bogged down in the same discussions that the *Ad Hoc* Committee and PrepCom had previously gone through for over three years. Thus, the delegates fell into two categories: those who were veterans of the *Ad Hoc* Committee and PrepCom, or had participated in some of the sessions along with the few who had studied the Draft Statute, and those who had either scant or no knowledge of the text. The former were optimistic, the latter, were not and their initial reaction was to express concerns and raise questions that had been previously debated, and, in some cases, even settled by the PrepCom. With this beginning, a positive outcome of the Conference was not promising, and some delegates started to float the idea of a second Diplomatic Conference.

This situation made the first two weeks of the Conference very tenuous. To accelerate the pace of the discussions, several "informal working groups" were established. These "informal working groups" then broke down into smaller "informal-informal working groups" as they were called. At times, there were as many as a dozen "informal working groups" and "informal-informal working groups" convening simultaneously, while delegations were consulting amongst themselves and while regional and political groups were holding their meetings.[146] As a result, most of the delegates' daily schedule after the second week consisted of 10 to 12 working hours, including Saturdays, and many delegates who assumed leading roles worked even longer hours. The pace was hectic, but the mood was still not turning to the positive.

The breakdown into smaller groups and the extensive work schedule was to the detriment of the smaller delegations which consisted of two or three delegates and who could not cover all the meetings.[147] It was also particularly detrimental to non-English-speaking delegations who had difficulties attending informal meetings conducted in English only.[148]

Nevertheless, as a result of this technique, the process moved faster even though only a few delegates had a grasp of the entire picture. In fact, most delegates saw some of the trees, but not

---

[146] Among the most active for example was the Arab Group which met frequently and adopted common positions.

[147] Delegations with 10 delegates could adequately cover all of the proceedings, and even so, at that working pace, it was a grueling experience. But not so for smaller ones. The pressure on the Secretariat however was even more intense. The extraordinary performance of the leading Secretariat staff deserves recognition and praise. This includes Hans Corell, Representative of the Secretary-General; Roy Lee, Executive Secretary of the Diplomatic Conference; Mahnoush Arsanjani, Secretary of the Committee of the Whole and Christiane Bourloyannis-Vrailas and Virginia Morris, who assisted her; Manuel Rama-Montaldo, Secretary of the Drafting Committee, who was assisted by Vladimir Rudnitsky and Renan Villacis; and Mpazi Sinjela, who was the special assistant to Mr. Correll and Secretary of the Credentials Committee.

[148] One of the difficulties with the work of these groups was the absence of simultaneous interpretation in six languages which, for obvious reasons of personnel, logistics and costs could not be afforded. Since the dominant language was English, delegates from non-English-speaking countries were at a disadvantage, while delegations without English-speaking delegates, or with only a few of them, were in fact shut out of that aspect of the process.

the forest, and there was no time in the hectic pace of the Conference to take stock of the overall progress. Things moved both too slowly and too fast, but mostly in a way that left most delegates uncertain about the overall progress.

The breakdown of the working groups into "informal working groups" and "informal-informal working groups" also meant that the various articles in the various parts of the Draft Statute were dealt piece-meal. Consequently, only parts of draft articles were sent to the Drafting Committee after their *pro forma* approval by the Committee of the Whole.[149] Thus, the Drafting Committee, as of the second week, received an average of 10 to 15 articles a day concerning different parts of the Draft Statute, but more frequently it only received some of the provisions of the articles referred to it and not the entire articles, let alone entire parts, which would have been the optimum if time would have permitted it. This meant that the Drafting Committee received on a daily basis pieces of a large jigsaw puzzle without knowing precisely where a given piece might fit and what its connection to another piece might entail. Furthermore, the disparity in language, approach and technique of the various groups that worked on these texts was evident in many of the referred articles. That led to the need for these articles to be redrafted by the Drafting Committee at least twice and sometimes even three times before they were completed.[150] But this piece-meal referral process also caused the Drafting Committee significant difficulties in maintaining consistency in form and style, making sure that the same words had the same meaning in the different articles and in providing cross-references to other related articles. Considering also that the Drafting Committee worked in six languages simultaneously and that it did corrections on all the translated articles, the task was most burdensome for the 25 elected delegations on the Drafting Committee.[151] But the members of the Drafting Committee performed extraordinarily well and worked in an excellent spirit of friendly cooperation and by Wednesday, July 15, the Drafting Committee had completed all 111 articles referred to it by the Committee of the Whole. But, the Drafting Committee had not been referred the 17 articles contained in Part 2, Articles 5-21 and some of the articles in the "Final Clauses."

---

[149]   The Committee of the Whole essentially approved in a *pro-forma* way the work product of the various working groups which were presented to it as a report of the Coordinator of that working group. This led to some criticism because it precluded the opportunity for the delegations to review a larger number of articles and to discuss their connection to other articles. But there was no time for that for reasons discussed above.

[150]   Rule 49 of the Conference, Report of the Preparatory Committee on the Establishment of an International Criminal Court, *Draft Rules of Procedure, supra* note 138, provided that the Drafting Committee would not deal with substantive issues. The drafting issues however became more difficult in the third and fourth week when the working groups, eager to move on at a faster pace, became less concerned with the way the texts were drafted and more reliant on the Drafting Committee to do that. The Drafting Committee had therefore much to do in terms of clarification.

[151]   Cameroon, China, Dominican Republic, Egypt, France, Germany, Ghana, India, Jamaica, Lebanon, Mexico, Morocco, Philippines, Poland, Republic of Korea, Russian Federation, Slovenia, South Africa, Spain, Sudan, Switzerland, Syrian Arab Republic, United Kingdom of Great Britain and Northern Ireland, United States of America and Venezuela. The members of these delegations were not always the same throughout the five weeks. Since there was no official roster of delegates representing these delegations, the following names are those that I recorded, though other delegates also occasionally participated. Thus, the following list is incomplete. Cameroon: Maurice Kamto, Victor Tchatchouwo; China: Xu Hong; Dominican Republic: Christina Aguiar; Egypt: M. Cherif Bassiouni; France: François Alabrune, Pierre-André Lageze; Germany: Hans-Joerg Behrens; Ghana: Immanuel Akwei Addo; India: S. Rama Rao; Republic of Korea: Sung-Kyu Lee; Lebanon: Hicham Hamdan; Jamaica: Wayne McCook, Cheryl Thompson-Barrow; Mexico: Socorro Rovirosa, Jorge Palacios Treviño, Luis Fernández Doblado; Morocco: Amal Belcaid, Fakhr Eddine Essaaidi; Philippines: Antonio Morales, Jose Tomas Syquia; Poland: Maria D. Frankowska, Kirill G. Gevorgyan; Russian Federation: Alexei Dronov; Slovenia: Mirjam Skrk; South Africa: Sabelo Sivuyile Maqungo; Spain: Juan Antonio Yañez-Barnuevo, Julio Montesino Ramos; Sudan: Awad El-Hassan El-Noor, Abdalla Ahmed Mahdi; Switzerland: Lucius Caflisch, Jürg Lindenmann; Syrian Arab Republic: Mohammad Said Al-Bounni; United Kingdom: Susan Dickson, Franklin Berman; United States: Clifton Johnson, Michele Klein Solomon, Jamison S. Borek; Venezuela: Victor Rodríguez Cedeño, Milagros C. Betancourt, Norman L. Monagas.

It was truly a tribute to the Drafting Committee that on July 15, the Committee of the Whole in less than two hours approved the Drafting Committee's proposed text, save for Part 2, Articles 5-21 and some of the "Final Clauses," which the Chairman of the Committee of the Whole presented on behalf of the Bureau on the last day of the Conference.

Part 2 contained, *inter alia,* the definition of crimes, jurisdiction, triggering mechanisms, some aspects of the role of the prosecutor, the role of the Security Council and the prospective application of the substantive provisions of the Statute. In other words, it contained all of the political issues that have not been fully addressed by governments at the PrepCom. While the Conference delegates were heavily involved in all of the technical legal issues, as well as other political issues of a lesser significance, the big issues contained in Part 2 were characteristically left for last moment political compromises. By the third week, however, the Chairman of the Committee of the Whole saw the necessity of producing a Chairman's text that identified the points on which agreement had been reached and those on which it appeared possible to reach a compromise. He and members of the Bureau held extensive meetings and consultations for the remaining two weeks of the Conference, and, on the last day of the Conference a Bureau text was presented to the Committee of the Whole on a take it or leave it basis. The reason for that approach was that whatever text was presented, if left open for further discussions by the Committee of the Whole at that late stage of the Conference, it would have meant the collapse of the Conference. Thus, it was both a tactical political judgment by the Chairman, and a gamble, since some delegations could have opposed the approach and blocked it procedurally in the few remaining hours of the Conference.

The Bureau's text was completed in all 6 languages at 2 a.m. on Friday, July 17, while the Conference was officially supposed to end at 1800 hours on that day or at the latest at midnight. To allow delegations to study the Part 2 "package," the Committee of the Whole convened after 1800 hours on that last Friday to adopt the Bureau's proposal which was by then, thanks to the extraordinary efficiency of the Secretariat and staff of the Conference, integrated with the remaining parts of the Statute that had been completed by the Drafting Committee and which the Committee of the Whole had previously adopted on Wednesday, the 15th.[152] At that late hour in the Conference, with the clock ticking to the midnight call, two delegations, namely India and the United States, sought to introduce last minute amendments to the proposed "package." For reasons stated above, to reopen discussions at that late stage would have meant the collapse of the Conference. Thus, the Chairman of the Committee of the Whole acted boldly and decisively in arranging a "no action" vote on these two proposals. Norway introduced with respect to each of the two proposed amendments a "no action" motion, which is the same as a motion to table. The vote of the "no action" motion on India's proposal was 114 in favor, 16 against and 20 abstentions. The vote on the "no action" motion on the U.S.'s proposal was 113 in favor, 17 against and 25 abstentions. That represented 155 present and voting delegations out of 161 registered for the Conference. After this second vote, which was final,[153] the delegates burst into a spontaneous standing ovation which turned into rhythmic applause that lasted close to 10 minutes, while some delegates embraced one another, others had tears in their eyes. It was one of the most extraordinary emotional scenes ever to take place at a diplomatic conference. The prevailing feeling was that the long historic journey that started after World War I had finally

---

[152] Unlike the other parts of the Statute, Part 2, Articles 5 to 21, was not, because of time constraints, referred to the Drafting Committee.

[153] Draft Statute for the International Criminal Court, A/Conf.183/C.1/L. 76; A/Conf. 183/C.I/L. 76/Add.1-Add.14, 1998.

reached its destination. It was truly a historic moment of great significance for all who had worked so hard to bring about the momentous result. But it was also a moment of release from the tensions and pressures of the previous five weeks of intensive work.

The Committee of the Whole adjourned at about 2100 hours and shortly thereafter the final session of the Plenary was convened. It was to be a quick formal session, but, to everyone's surprise, the U.S. asked for another vote.[154] This time 120 delegations voted for the adoption of the Statute, the Final Act of the Diplomatic Conference[155] and for the opening of the Convention for signature on the next day, while 7 voted against[156] and 21 abstained. This overwhelmingly positive vote was followed by explanations of their votes by some delegations as well as general statements by delegations which went on past 2 a.m. of the following day. The clock was, however, figuratively stopped at one minute before midnight so that the Plenary could be said to have completed its work within the General Assembly's mandate which was that the Conference should end on July 17.

The next day the Convention was open for signature at "Il Campidoglio" in Rome. In order to permit the Secretariat and the translators to put the final touches to the text of the Convention, the ceremony started at 1600. The United Nations protocol sheet of that Ceremony describes it as follows:[157]

> There will be a head table in the room and a small side-table on which the Statute will be placed for signature. Seated at the head table will be the minister for Foreign Affairs of Italy, the Representative of the Secretary-General, the President of the Conference, the Mayor of Rome, the Chairman of the Committee of the Whole, the Chairman of the Drafting Committee, the Chairman of the Credentials Committee and the Executive Secretary of the Conference. The flags of the United Nations, the Republic of Italy and the City of Rome will be displayed behind the head table - UN flag in the center, Italian flag to its right and the City flag to its left. Visual medial will be present to record the event.
>
> The ceremony starts. The Mayor of Rome makes a statement of welcome. The Executive Secretary hands over the Final Act to the Minister for Foreign Affairs of Italy. The Representative of the Secretary-General, the Legal Counsel, hands over the Statute to the

---

[154]　This was an unrecorded vote.

[155]　Rome Statute of the International Criminal Court, A/Conf.183/9, 1998. As a result of the limited time available between the adoption of the Statute and the treaty's opening for signature ceremony, the adopted Statute required a few corrections. The United Nations Office of Legal Affairs is in the process, as of September 9, 1998, of bringing about these corrections. The procedure established by the Treaty Section of the office of Legal Affairs is called "non-Objection Procedure." It is based on Article 79 of the 1969 Vienna Convention on the Law of Treaties. It has been resorted to with respect to a number of multi-lateral conventions. This procedure is essentially designed to correct non-substantive errors such as typographical errors, punctuation errors, errors in cross-referencing which refer only to numbering, numbering of paragraphs and the like. Corrections having a substantive significance are: Article 8, paragraph 4; Article 121, paragraph 5; and Article 124. The Office of Legal Affairs is expected to obtain the "Non-Objection" of the states that signed the treaty as well as the 161 states that participated in the Diplomatic Conference. It is unknown at this time how this "Non-Objection" will be obtained. The translation of the English text was the one submitted for signature in Rome. The text will not be translated into the other official United Nations languages (Arabic, Chinese, French, Russian and Spanish) until such time as the "Non-Objection" procedure has been completed. Thus, until such time as other language texts are available, the English one is the only authoritative text.

[156]　Regrettably the United States, China and India did not join in the vote for the establishment of the ICC, and because of the importance of these states, it is hoped that they will see fit to join at a later date. The Preparatory Commission whish is to be established by the General Assembly based on the Diplomatic Conference's resolution contained in Annex I, F of the Final Act may be the vehicle through which these major governments and others could explore possibilities of finding solutions to their concerns.

[157]　Text available in the author's files.

Minister for Foreign Affairs of Italy and reads a message from the Secretary-General. The President of the Conference makes a statement. The Chairman of the Committee of the Whole makes a statement followed by a statement by the Chairman of the Drafting Committee. The Minister for Foreign Affairs of Italy makes a statement and then declares that those States that are in a position to sign but did not do so on 17 July may sign the Statute. Representatives of those States are called upon to sign. An Italian official will assist in calling the States and also in the signing ceremony. The duration of each statement is expected to be not more than three minutes. The ceremony is concluded.

By 1800 of 18 July 1998, 26 governments had signed the treaty, which will remain in Rome at the Italian Ministry of Foreign Affairs where states can sign it until 30 October 1998. The number of signatures as of 19 October 1998 totaled 53. It will thereafter be transferred to the Secretary-General as its official depository and remain open for signature until 31 December 2000. By then, it is hoped that the 60 required ratifications will have occurred, and the treaty will enter into force. In the meantime, a Preparatory Commission will be established by the General Assembly to prepare the way for the Court to function without delay as soon as the treaty enters into force.[158]

---

[158] Final Act of the United Nations Diplomatic Conference of Plenipotentiaries on the Establishment of an International Criminal Court, A/Conf.183/9, 1998, at Annex I (F). The text of Annex I (F) follows:

F.

The United Nations Conference of Plenipotentiaries on the Establishment of an International Criminal Court,
Having adopted the Statute of the International Criminal Court,
Having decided to take all possible measures to ensure the coming into operation of the International Criminal Court without undue delay and to make the necessary arrangements for the commencement of its functions,
Having decided that a preparatory commission should be established for the fulfilment of these purposes,
Decides as follows:
1   There is hereby established the Preparatory Commission for the International Criminal Court. The Secretary-General of the United Nations shall convene the Commission as early as possible at a date to be decided by the General Assembly of the United Nations.
2.   The Commission shall consist of representatives of States which have signed the Final Act of the United Nations Diplomatic Conference of Plenipotentiaries on the Establishment of an International Criminal Court and other States which have been invited to participate in the Conference.
3.   The Commission shall elect its Chairman and other officers, adopt its rules of procedure and decide on its programme of work. These elections shall take place at the first meeting of the Commission.
4.   The official and working languages of the Preparatory Commission shall be those of the General Assembly of the United Nations.
5.   The Commission shall prepare proposals for practical arrangements for the establishment and coming into operation of the Court, including the draft texts of:
    (a)   Rules of Procedure and Evidence;
    (b)   Elements of Crimes;
    (c)   A relationship agreement between the Court and the United Nations;
    (d)   Basic principles governing a headquarters agreement to be negotiated between the Court and the host country;
    (e)   Financial regulations and rules;
    (f)   An agreement on the privileges and immunities of the Court;
    (g)   A budget for the first financial year;
    (h)   The rules of procedure of the Assembly of States Parties.
6.   The draft texts of the Rules of Procedure and Evidence and of the Elements of Crimes shall be finalized before 30 June 2000.
7.   The Commission shall prepare proposals for a provision on aggression, including the definition and Elements of Crimes of aggression and the conditions under which the International Criminal Court shall exercise its jurisdiction with regard to this crime. The Commission shall submit such proposals to the Assembly of States Parties at a Review Conference, with a view to arriving at an acceptable provision on the crime of aggression for inclusion in this Statute. The provisions relating to the crime of aggression shall enter into force for the States Parties in accordance with the relevant provisions of this Statute.
8.   The Commission shall remain in existence until the *conclusion* of the first meeting of the Assembly of States

This writer's speech at the Rome Ceremony on July 18 and reproduced at page xxi of this book expresses the moral, ethical and policy significance of this historical journey.[159]

Conclusion

The establishment of *ad hoc* tribunals in the former Yugoslavia and Rwanda were important steps, though grudgingly undertaken by the Security Council. Even if they have not yet produced a sufficient record on which to be judged, these tribunals' establishment is a major accomplishment as is much of their work so far. But, their existence depends on the will of the Security Council which created them and whose authority is to deal with threats to peace and security and the maintenance of peace and security. Once peace and security is restored, the Council loses its competence and the tribunals it created must come to a close unless the Council finds that their continued existence is necessary to maintain peace and security.

Unless we have a permanent judicial institution to continue the work begun, and proceed with the work to come, we will not be able to put an end to the practice of impunity, and

---

9.   The Commission shall prepare a report on all matters within its mandate and submit it to the first meeting of the Assembly of States Parties.
10.   The Commission shall meet at the Headquarters of the United Nations. The Secretary-General of the United Nations is requested to provide to the Commission such secretariat services as it may require, subject to the approval of the General Assembly of the United Nations.
11.   The Secretary-General of the United Nations shall bring the present resolution to the attention of the General Assembly for any necessary action.
    [159]   In that speech I refer to the few to which so many owe their thanks. Among those who were delegates and who merit special recognition for their commitment, hard work and dedication to the success of this endeavor are: François Alabrune, France; Zeid Ra'ad Zeid Al-Hussein, Jordan; Hans-Joerg Behrens, Germany; Franklin Berman, UK; Trevor Chimimba, Malawi; Jamison S. Borek, US; Adriaan Bos, The Netherlands; Lucius Caflisch, Switzerland; Delia Chatoor, Trinidad and Tobago; Roger Clark, Samoa; Harvey Dalton, US; Phani Daskalopoulou-Livada, Greece; Susan J. Dickson, UK; Paula Escarameia, Portugal; Sylvia Alejandra Ferandez de Gurmendi, Argentina; Rolf Einar Fife, Norway; Charles Garraway, UK; Fabricio Guariglia, Argentina; Gerhard Hafner, Austria; John Holmes, Canada; Mark B. Jennings, Australia; Hans-Peter Kaul, Germany; Philippe Kirsch, Canada; Erkki Kourula, Finland; Sung-Kyu Lee, Korea; Beatrice Le Fraper du Hellen, France; Lamia Mekheimer, Egypt; Phakiso Mochochoko, Lesotho; Christopher Muttukumaru, UK; Yasumasa Nagamine, Japan; Hisashi Owada, Japan; Marc Perrin de Brichambaut, France; Donald Piragoff, Canada; Mauro Politi, Italy; Rama Rao, India; Medard R. Rwelamira, South Africa; Waleed Sadi, Jordan; Per Saland, Sweden; David Scheffer, US; Joanna Scott, France; Cathrine Lisa Steans, Australia; Peter Tomka, Slovakia, Peter Vallance, UK; Hermann Von Hebel, The Netherlands; Mary Ellen Warlow, US; Elizabeth Wilmhurst, UK; Felicity Wong, New Zealand; Lionel Yee, Singapore.
    The responsibility for the Diplomatic Conference rested on the Italian Ministry of Foreign Affairs, and more particularly on Ambassador Umberto Vattani, Secretary-General of the Ministry; Professor Umberto Leanza, Director of Legal Affairs and his Deputy Counselor, Umberto Colesanti; and at the Italian Mission to the U.N., Ambassador Francesco Paolo Fulci and Professor Mauro Politi. Last, but not least, is Professor Giovanni Conso, Former Minister of Justice and Honorary President of the Constitutional Court, who was the President of the Diplomatic Conference.
    Many academics have worked for the establishment of the ICC and their scholarly reports made it possible for the idea to gain international recognition and national support. They include in addition to those mentioned above: Christopher Blakesley, U.S.; Peter Burns, Canada; Bartram Brown, U.S.; Lucius Caflisch, Switzerland; Roger Clark, New Zealand; Jean Dautricourt, Belgium; Yoram Dinstein, Israel; John Dugard, South Africa; Feliz Ermacora, Austria; Albin Eser, Germany; Benjamin Ferencz, U.S.; Guilermo Fiero, Argentina; Hans-Heinrich Jescheck, Germany; Otto Lagodny, Germany; Claude Lambois, France; Haidong Li, China; Farhad Malekian, Iran/Sweden; Timothy I.H. McCormack, Australia; Theodore Meron, U.S.; Gerhard Mueller, U.S.; Rein Müllerson, Estonia; Ved P. Nanda, India; Diana Orentlicher, U.S.; Stanislaw Plawksi, Poland; A. Quintanno Rippolles, Spain; Nigel Rodley, U.K.; Herwig Rogemann, Germany; William Schabas, Canada; Michael Scharf, U.S.; Wolfgang Schomburg, Germany; Shaping Shao, China; Gerry J. Simpson, Australia; Brigitte Stern, France; Julius Stone, Australia; Otto Triffterer, Austria; Abdel Azim Wazir, Egypt; Herbert Wechsler, U.S.; Ruth Wedgewood, U.S.; Burns Weston, U.S.; Leila Sadat Wexler, U.S.; Edward M. Wise, U.S.; Robert K. Woetzel, U.S.; Quincy Wright, U.S.; Christine Van den Wyngaert, Belgium; Giuliano Vassalli, Italy; Manuel Viera, Uruguay.
    As with all such developments, it takes dedicated, knowledgeable and capable persons to transform ideals into reality. Throughout this process there have been many, and I expect many more will join. But the leadership of the few who can make a difference will always be needed.

perpetrators will go free, deterrence will dissipate, justice will be discredited, and the chances for peace will be reduced. That is why we need a permanent international criminal court, free from political manipulations and with the capability of prosecuting victors and defeated, soldiers and generals, effectively and fairly.

Victims are entitled to justice, offenders deserve punishment and the world needs to establish a historic record of major international crimes, if for no other reason than to know the truth and educate future generations. Maybe then we can deter potential criminals and avoid the repetition of those crimes. Otherwise we are condemned to repeat the terrible mistakes of the past.

This is an idea whose time has not only come, but which is long overdue. Hopefully all major governments will support it, and many states will join it so that it can attain a level of universality that will give it credence and moral authority. Our civil society demands no less than a system of international criminal justice to sustain peace, for in the final analysis there is no peace without justice, and no justice without peace. If nothing else, the ICC represents a symbol of justice and embodies the values of a culture of legality. This is what the new world order requires in this global age.

UNITED NATIONS DOCUMENTS

ROME STATUTE FOR THE INTERNATIONAL CRIMINAL COURT*

Adopted by the United Nations Diplomatic Conference of Plenipotentiaries on the Establishment of an International Criminal Court on 17 July 1998

PREAMBLE

The States Parties to this Statute,

Conscious that all peoples are united by common bonds, their cultures pieced together in a shared heritage, and concerned that this delicate mosaic may be shattered at any time,

Mindful that during this century millions of children, women and men have been victims of unimaginable atrocities that deeply shock the conscience of humanity,

Recognizing that such grave crimes threaten the peace, security and well-being of the world,

Affirming that the most serious crimes of concern to the international community as a whole must not go unpunished and that their effective prosecution must be ensured by taking measures at the national level and by enhancing international cooperation,

Determined to put an end to impunity for the perpetrators of these crimes and thus to contribute to the prevention of such crimes,

Recalling that it is the duty of every State to exercise its criminal jurisdiction over those responsible for international crimes,

Reaffirming the Purposes and Principles of the Charter of the United Nations, and in particular that all States shall refrain from the threat or use of force against the territorial integrity or political independence of any State, or in any other manner inconsistent with the Purposes of the United Nations,

Emphasizing in this connection that nothing in this Statute shall be taken as authorizing any State Party to intervene in an armed conflict in the internal affairs of any State,

Determined to these ends and for the sake of present and future generations, to establish an independent permanent International Criminal Court in relationship with the United Nations system, with jurisdiction over the most serious crimes of concern to the international community as a whole,

Emphasizing that the International Criminal Court established under this Statute shall be complementary to national criminal jurisdictions,

Resolved to guarantee lasting respect for the enforcement of international justice,

Have agreed as follows:

PART 1. ESTABLISHMENT OF THE COURT
Article 1
The Court

An International Criminal Court ("the Court") is hereby established. It shall be a permanent institution and shall have the power to exercise its jurisdiction over persons for the most serious crimes of international concern, as referred to in this Statute, and shall be complementary to national criminal jurisdictions. The jurisdiction and functioning of the Court shall be governed by the provisions of this Statute.

Article 2
Relationship of the Court with the United Nations

The Court shall be brought into relationship with the United Nations through an agreement to be approved by the Assembly of States Parties to this Statute and thereafter concluded by the President of the Court on its behalf.

Article 3
Seat of the Court

1.   The seat of the Court shall be established at The Hague in the Netherlands ("the host State").
2.   The Court shall enter into a headquarters agreement with the host State, to be approved by the Assembly of States Parties and thereafter concluded by the President of the Court on its behalf.
3.   The Court may sit elsewhere, whenever it considers it desirable, as provided in this Statute.

Article 4
Legal status and powers of the Court

1.   The Court shall have international legal personality. It shall also have such legal capacity as may be necessary for the exercise of its functions and the fulfilment of its purposes.
2.   The Court may exercise its functions and powers, as provided in this Statute, on the territory of any State Party and, by special agreement, on the territory of any other State.

PART 2. JURISDICTION, ADMISSIBILITY AND APPLICABLE LAW
Article 5
Crimes within the jurisdiction of the Court

1.   The jurisdiction of the Court shall be limited to the most serious crimes of concern to the international community as a whole. The Court has jurisdiction in accordance with this Statute with respect to the following crimes:
  (a)   The crime of genocide;
  (b)   Crimes against humanity;
  (c)   War crimes;
  (d)   The crime of aggression.
2.   The Court shall exercise jurisdiction over the crime of aggression once a provision is adopted in accordance with articles 121 and 123 defining the crime and setting out the conditions under which the Court shall exercise jurisdiction with respect to this crime. Such a provision shall be consistent with the relevant provisions of the Charter of the United Nations.

Article 6
Genocide

For the purpose of this Statute, "genocide" means any of the following acts committed with intent to destroy, in whole or in part, a national, ethnical, racial or religious group, as such:
  (a)   Killing members of the group;
  (b)   Causing serious bodily or mental harm to members of the group;
  (c)   Deliberately inflicting on the group conditions of life calculated to bring about its physical destruction in whole or in part;

(d) Imposing measures intended to prevent births within the group;

(e) Forcibly transferring children of the group to another group.

Article 7
Crimes against humanity

1.   For the purpose of this Statute, "crime against humanity" means any of the following acts when committed as part of a widespread or systematic attack directed against any civilian population, with knowledge of the attack:

(a) Murder;

(b) Extermination;

(c) Enslavement;

(d) Deportation or forcible transfer of population;

(e) Imprisonment or other severe deprivation of physical liberty in violation of fundamental rules of international law;

(f) Torture;

(g) Rape, sexual slavery, enforced prostitution, forced pregnancy, enforced sterilization, or any other form of sexual violence of comparable gravity;

(h) Persecution against any identifiable group or collectivity on political, racial, national, ethnic, cultural, religious, gender as defined in paragraph 3, or other grounds that are universally recognized as impermissible under international law, in connection with any act referred to in this paragraph or any crime within the jurisdiction of the Court;

(i) Enforced disappearance of persons;

(j) The crime of apartheid;

(k) Other inhumane acts of a similar character intentionally causing great suffering, or serious injury to body or to mental or physical health.

2.   For the purpose of paragraph 1:

(a) "Attack directed against any civilian population" means a course of conduct involving the multiple commission of acts referred to in paragraph 1 against any civilian population, pursuant to or in furtherance of a State or organizational policy to commit such attack;

(b) "Extermination" includes the intentional infliction of conditions of life, inter alia the deprivation of access to food and medicine, calculated to bring about the destruction of part of a population;

(c) "Enslavement" means the exercise of any or all of the powers attaching to the right of ownership over a person and includes the exercise of such power in the course of trafficking in persons, in particular women and children;

(d) "Deportation or forcible transfer of population" means forced displacement of the persons concerned by expulsion or other coercive acts from the area in which they are lawfully present, without grounds permitted under international law;

(e) "Torture" means the intentional infliction of severe pain or suffering, whether physical or mental, upon a person in the custody or under the control of the accused; except that torture shall not include pain or suffering arising only from, inherent in or incidental to, lawful sanctions;

(f) "Forced pregnancy" means the unlawful confinement, of a woman forcibly made pregnant, with the intent of affecting the ethnic composition of any population or carrying out other grave violations of international law. This definition shall not in any way be interpreted as affecting national laws relating to pregnancy;

(g) "Persecution" means the intentional and severe deprivation of fundamental rights contrary to international law by reason of the identity of the group or collectivity;

(h) "The crime of apartheid" means inhumane acts of a character similar to those referred to in paragraph 1, committed in the context of an institutionalized regime of systematic oppression and domination by one racial group over any other racial group or groups and committed with the intention of maintaining that regime;

(i) "Enforced disappearance of persons" means the arrest, detention or abduction of persons by, or with the authorization, support or acquiescence of, a State or a political organization, followed by a refusal to acknowledge that deprivation of freedom or to give information on the fate or whereabouts of those persons, with the intention of removing them from the protection of the law for a prolonged period of time.

3.   For the purpose of this Statute, it is understood that the term "gender" refers to the two sexes, male and female, within the context of society. The term "gender" does not indicate any meaning different from the above.

Article 8
War crimes

1.   The Court shall have jurisdiction in respect of war crimes in particular when committed as part of a plan or policy or as part of a large-scale commission of such crimes.

2.   For the purpose of this Statute, "war crimes" means:

(a)   Grave breaches of the Geneva Conventions of 12 August 1949, namely, any of the following acts against persons or property protected under the provisions of the relevant Geneva Convention:

(i)   Wilful killing;

(ii) Torture or inhuman treatment, including biological experiments;

(iii) Wilfully causing great suffering, or serious injury to body or health;

(iv) Extensive destruction and appropriation of property, not justified by military necessity and carried out unlawfully and wantonly;

(v)   Compelling a prisoner of war or other protected person to serve in the forces of a hostile Power;

(vi) Wilfully depriving a prisoner of war or other protected person of the rights of fair and regular trial;

(vii) Unlawful deportation or transfer or unlawful confinement;

(viii) Taking of hostages.

(b)   Other serious violations of the laws and customs applicable in international armed conflict, within the established framework of international law, namely, any of the following acts:

(i)   Intentionally directing attacks against the civilian population as such or against individual civilians not taking direct part in hostilities;

(ii) Intentionally directing attacks against civilian objects, that is, objects which are not military objectives;

(iii) Intentionally directing attacks against personnel, installations, material, units or vehicles involved in a humanitarian assistance or peacekeeping mission in accordance with the

Charter of the United Nations, as long as they are entitled to the protection given to civilians or civilian objects under the international law of armed conflict;

(iv) Intentionally launching an attack in the knowledge that such attack will cause incidental loss of life or injury to civilians or damage to civilian objects or widespread, long-term and severe damage to the natural environment which would be clearly excessive in relation to the concrete and direct overall military advantage anticipated;

(v) Attacking or bombarding, by whatever means, towns, villages, dwellings or buildings which are undefended and which are not military objectives;

(vi) Killing or wounding a combatant who, having laid down his arms or having no longer means of defence, has surrendered at discretion;

(vii) Making improper use of a flag of truce, of the flag or of the military insignia and uniform of the enemy or of the United Nations, as well as of the distinctive emblems of the Geneva Conventions, resulting in death or serious personal injury;

(viii) The transfer, directly or indirectly, by the Occupying Power of parts of its own civilian population into the territory it occupies, or the deportation or transfer of all or parts of the population of the occupied territory within or outside this territory;

(ix) Intentionally directing attacks against buildings dedicated to religion, education, art, science or charitable purposes, historic monuments, hospitals and places where the sick and wounded are collected, provided they are not military objectives;

(x) Subjecting persons who are in the power of an adverse party to physical mutilation or to medical or scientific experiments of any kind which are neither justified by the medical, dental or hospital treatment of the person concerned nor carried out in his or her interest, and which cause death to or seriously endanger the health of such person or persons;

(xi) Killing or wounding treacherously individuals belonging to the hostile nation or army;

(xii) Declaring that no quarter will be given;

(xiii) Destroying or seizing the enemy's property unless such destruction or seizure be imperatively demanded by the necessities of war;

(xiv) Declaring abolished, suspended or inadmissible in a court of law the rights and actions of the nationals of the hostile party;

(xv) Compelling the nationals of the hostile party to take part in the operations of war directed against their own country, even if they were in the belligerent's service before the commencement of the war;

(xvi) Pillaging a town or place, even when taken by assault;

(xvii) Employing poison or poisoned weapons;

(xviii) Employing asphyxiating, poisonous or other gases, and all analogous liquids, materials or devices;

(xix) Employing bullets which expand or flatten easily in the human body, such as bullets with a hard envelope which does not entirely cover the core or is pierced with incisions;

(xx) Employing weapons, projectiles and material and methods of warfare which are of a nature to cause superfluous injury or unnecessary suffering or which are inherently indiscriminate in violation of the international law of armed conflict, provided that such weapons, projectiles and material and methods of warfare are the subject of a comprehensive prohibition and are included in an annex to this Statute, by an amendment in accordance with the relevant provisions set forth in articles 121 and 123;

(xxi) Committing outrages upon personal dignity, in particular humiliating and degrading treatment;

(xxii) Committing rape, sexual slavery, enforced prostitution, forced pregnancy, as defined in article 7, paragraph 2 (f), enforced sterilization, or any other form of sexual violence also constituting a grave breach of the Geneva Conventions;

(xxiii) Utilizing the presence of a civilian or other protected person to render certain points, areas or military forces immune from military operations;

(xxiv) Intentionally directing attacks against buildings, material, medical units and transport, and personnel using the distinctive emblems of the Geneva Conventions in conformity with international law;

(xxv) Intentionally using starvation of civilians as a method of warfare by depriving them of objects indispensable to their survival, including wilfully impeding relief supplies as provided for under the Geneva Conventions;

(xxvi) Conscripting or enlisting children under the age of fifteen years into the national armed forces or using them to participate actively in hostilities.

(c) In the case of an armed conflict not of an international character, serious violations of article 3 common to the four Geneva Conventions of 12 August 1949, namely, any of the following acts committed against persons taking no active part in the hostilities, including members of armed forces who have laid down their arms and those placed hors de combat by sickness, wounds, detention or any other cause:

(i)   Violence to life and person, in particular murder of all kinds, mutilation, cruel treatment and torture;

(ii) Committing outrages upon personal dignity, in particular humiliating and degrading treatment;

(iii) Taking of hostages;

(iv) The passing of sentences and the carrying out of executions without previous judgement pronounced by a regularly constituted court, affording all judicial guarantees which are generally recognized as indispensable.

(d) Paragraph 2 (c) applies to armed conflicts not of an international character and thus does not apply to situations of internal disturbances and tensions, such as riots, isolated and sporadic acts of violence or other acts of a similar nature.

(e) Other serious violations of the laws and customs applicable in armed conflicts not of an international character, within the established framework of international law, namely, any of the following acts:

(i)   Intentionally directing attacks against the civilian population as such or against individual civilians not taking direct part in hostilities;

(ii) Intentionally directing attacks against buildings, material, medical units and transport, and personnel using the distinctive emblems of the Geneva Conventions in conformity with international law;

(iii) Intentionally directing attacks against personnel, installations, material, units or vehicles involved in a humanitarian assistance or peacekeeping mission in accordance with the Charter of the United Nations, as long as they are entitled to the protection given to civilians or civilian objects under the international law of armed conflict;

(iv) Intentionally directing attacks against buildings dedicated to religion, education, art, science or charitable purposes, historic monuments, hospitals and places where the sick and wounded are collected, provided they are not military objectives;

(v) Pillaging a town or place, even when taken by assault;

(vi) Committing rape, sexual slavery, enforced prostitution, forced pregnancy, as defined in article 7, paragraph 2 (f), enforced sterilization, and any other form of sexual violence also constituting a serious violation of article 3 common to the four Geneva Conventions;

(vii) Conscripting or enlisting children under the age of fifteen years into armed forces or groups or using them to participate actively in hostilities;

(viii) Ordering the displacement of the civilian population for reasons related to the conflict, unless the security of the civilians involved or imperative military reasons so demand;

(ix) Killing or wounding treacherously a combatant adversary;

(x) Declaring that no quarter will be given;

(xi) Subjecting persons who are in the power of another party to the conflict to physical mutilation or to medical or scientific experiments of any kind which are neither justified by the medical, dental or hospital treatment of the person concerned nor carried out in his or her interest, and which cause death to or seriously endanger the health of such person or persons;

(xii) Destroying or seizing the property of an adversary unless such destruction or seizure be imperatively demanded by the necessities of the conflict;

(f) Paragraph 2 (e) applies to armed conflicts not of an international character and thus does not apply to situations of internal disturbances and tensions, such as riots, isolated and sporadic acts of violence or other acts of a similar nature. It applies to armed conflicts that take place in the territory of a State when there is protracted armed conflict between governmental authorities and organized armed groups or between such groups.

3. Nothing in paragraphs 2 (c) and (e) shall affect the responsibility of a Government to maintain or re-establish law and order in the State or to defend the unity and territorial integrity of the State, by all legitimate means.

Article 9
Elements of Crimes

1. Elements of Crimes shall assist the Court in the interpretation and application of articles 6, 7 and 8. They shall be adopted by a two-thirds majority of the members of the Assembly of States Parties.

2. Amendments to the Elements of Crimes may be proposed by:

(a) Any State Party;

(b) The judges acting by an absolute majority;

(c) The Prosecutor.

Such amendments shall be adopted by a two-thirds majority of the members of the Assembly of States Parties.

3. The Elements of Crimes and amendments thereto shall be consistent with this Statute.

Article 10

Nothing in this Part shall be interpreted as limiting or prejudicing in any way existing or developing rules of international law for purposes other than this Statute.

Article 11
Jurisdiction ratione temporis

1.   The Court has jurisdiction only with respect to crimes committed after the entry into force of this Statute.

2.   If a State becomes a Party to this Statute after its entry into force, the Court may exercise its jurisdiction only with respect to crimes committed after the entry into force of this Statute for that State, unless that State has made a declaration under article 12, paragraph 3.

Article 12
Preconditions to the exercise of jurisdiction

1.   A State which becomes a Party to this Statute thereby accepts the jurisdiction of the Court with respect to the crimes referred to in article 5.

2.   In the case of article 13, paragraph (a) or (c), the Court may exercise its jurisdiction if one or more of the following States are Parties to this Statute or have accepted the jurisdiction of the Court in accordance with paragraph 3:

    (a)   The State on the territory of which the conduct in question occurred or, if the crime was committed on board a vessel or aircraft, the State of registration of that vessel or aircraft;

    (b)   The State of which the person accused of the crime is a national.

3.   If the acceptance of a State which is not a Party to this Statute is required under paragraph 2, that State may, by declaration lodged with the Registrar, accept the exercise of jurisdiction by the Court with respect to the crime in question. The accepting State shall cooperate with the Court without any delay or exception in accordance with Part 9.

Article 13
Exercise of jurisdiction

    The Court may exercise its jurisdiction with respect to a crime referred to in article 5 in accordance with the provisions of this Statute if:

    (a)   A situation in which one or more of such crimes appears to have been committed is referred to the Prosecutor by a State Party in accordance with article 14;

    (b)   A situation in which one or more of such crimes appears to have been committed is referred to the Prosecutor by the Security Council acting under Chapter VII of the Charter of the United Nations; or

    (c)   The Prosecutor has initiated an investigation in respect of such a crime in accordance with article 15.

Article 14
Referral of a situation by a State Party

1.   A State Party may refer to the Prosecutor a situation in which one or more crimes within the jurisdiction of the Court appear to have been committed requesting the Prosecutor to investigate the situation for the purpose of determining whether one or more specific persons should be charged with the commission of such crimes.

2.   As far as possible, a referral shall specify the relevant circumstances and be accompanied by such supporting documentation as is available to the State referring the situation.

Article 15
Prosecutor

1.   The Prosecutor may initiate investigations proprio motu on the basis of information on crimes within the jurisdiction of the Court.

2.   The Prosecutor shall analyse the seriousness of the information received. For this purpose, he or she may seek additional information from States, organs of the United Nations, intergovernmental or non-governmental organizations, or other reliable sources that he or she deems appropriate, and may receive written or oral testimony at the seat of the Court.

3.   If the Prosecutor concludes that there is a reasonable basis to proceed with an investigation, he or she shall submit to the Pre-Trial Chamber a request for authorization of an investigation, together with any supporting material collected. Victims may make representations to the Pre-Trial Chamber, in accordance with the Rules of Procedure and Evidence.

4.   If the Pre-Trial Chamber, upon examination of the request and the supporting material, considers that there is a reasonable basis to proceed with an investigation, and that the case appears to fall within the jurisdiction of the Court, it shall authorize the commencement of the investigation, without prejudice to subsequent determinations by the Court with regard to the jurisdiction and admissibility of a case.

5.   The refusal of the Pre-Trial Chamber to authorize the investigation shall not preclude the presentation of a subsequent request by the Prosecutor based on new facts or evidence regarding the same situation.

6.   If, after the preliminary examination referred to in paragraphs 1 and 2, the Prosecutor concludes that the information provided does not constitute a reasonable basis for an investigation, he or she shall inform those who provided the information. This shall not preclude the Prosecutor from considering further information submitted to him or her regarding the same situation in the light of new facts or evidence.

Article 16
Deferral of investigation or prosecution

No investigation or prosecution may be commenced or proceeded with under this Statute for a period of 12 months after the Security Council, in a resolution adopted under Chapter VII of the Charter of the United Nations, has requested the Court to that effect; that request may be renewed by the Council under the same conditions.

Article 17
Issues of admissibility

1.   Having regard to paragraph 10 of the Preamble and article 1, the Court shall determine that a case is inadmissible where:

(a)   The case is being investigated or prosecuted by a State which has jurisdiction over it, unless the State is unwilling or unable genuinely to carry out the investigation or prosecution;

(b)   The case has been investigated by a State which has jurisdiction over it and the State has decided not to prosecute the person concerned, unless the decision resulted from the unwillingness or inability of the State genuinely to prosecute;

(c)   The person concerned has already been tried for conduct which is the subject of the complaint, and a trial by the Court is not permitted under article 20, paragraph 3;

(d)   The case is not of sufficient gravity to justify further action by the Court.

2.   In order to determine unwillingness in a particular case, the Court shall consider, having regard to the principles of due process recognized by international law, whether one or more of the following exist, as applicable:

(a) The proceedings were or are being undertaken or the national decision was made for the purpose of shielding the person concerned from criminal responsibility for crimes within the jurisdiction of the Court referred to in article 5;

(b) There has been an unjustified delay in the proceedings which in the circumstances is inconsistent with an intent to bring the person concerned to justice;

(c) The proceedings were not or are not being conducted independently or impartially, and they were or are being conducted in a manner which, in the circumstances, is inconsistent with an intent to bring the person concerned to justice.

3.   In order to determine inability in a particular case, the Court shall consider whether, due to a total or substantial collapse or unavailability of its national judicial system, the State is unable to obtain the accused or the necessary evidence and testimony or otherwise unable to carry out its proceedings.

Article 18
Preliminary rulings regarding admissibility

1.   When a situation has been referred to the Court pursuant to article 13 (a) and the Prosecutor has determined that there would be a reasonable basis to commence an investigation, or the Prosecutor initiates an investigation pursuant to articles 13 (c) and 15, the Prosecutor shall notify all States Parties and those States which, taking into account the information available, would normally exercise jurisdiction over the crimes concerned. The Prosecutor may notify such States on a confidential basis and, where the Prosecutor believes it necessary to protect persons, prevent destruction of evidence or prevent the absconding of persons, may limit the scope of the information provided to States.

2.   Within one month of receipt of that notice, a State may inform the Court that it is investigating or has investigated its nationals or others within its jurisdiction with respect to criminal acts which may constitute crimes referred to in article 5 and which relate to the information provided in the notification to States. At the request of that State, the Prosecutor shall defer to the State's investigation of those persons unless the Pre-Trial Chamber, on the application of the Prosecutor, decides to authorize the investigation.

3.   The Prosecutor's deferral to a State's investigation shall be open to review by the Prosecutor six months after the date of deferral or at any time when there has been a significant change of circumstances based on the State's unwillingness or inability genuinely to carry out the investigation.

4.   The State concerned or the Prosecutor may appeal to the Appeals Chamber against a ruling of the Pre-Trial Chamber, in accordance with article 82. The appeal may be heard on an expedited basis.

5.   When the Prosecutor has deferred an investigation in accordance with paragraph 2, the Prosecutor may request that the State concerned periodically inform the Prosecutor of the progress of its investigations and any subsequent prosecutions. States Parties shall respond to such requests without undue delay.

6.   Pending a ruling by the Pre-Trial Chamber, or at any time when the Prosecutor has deferred an investigation under this article, the Prosecutor may, on an exceptional basis, seek authority

from the Pre-Trial Chamber to pursue necessary investigative steps for the purpose of preserving evidence where there is a unique opportunity to obtain important evidence or there is a significant risk that such evidence may not be subsequently available.

7.   A State which has challenged a ruling of the Pre-Trial Chamber under this article may challenge the admissibility of a case under article 19 on the grounds of additional significant facts or significant change of circumstances.

Article 19
Challenges to the jurisdiction of the Court
or the admissibility of a case

1.   The Court shall satisfy itself that it has jurisdiction in any case brought before it. The Court may, on its own motion, determine the admissibility of a case in accordance with article 17.

2.   Challenges to the admissibility of a case on the grounds referred to in article 17 or challenges to the jurisdiction of the Court may be made by:

(a) An accused or a person for whom a warrant of arrest or a summons to appear has been issued under article 58;

(b) A State which has jurisdiction over a case, on the ground that it is investigating or prosecuting the case or has investigated or prosecuted; or

(c) A State from which acceptance of jurisdiction is required under article 12.

3.   The Prosecutor may seek a ruling from the Court regarding a question of jurisdiction or admissibility. In proceedings with respect to jurisdiction or admissibility, those who have referred the situation under article 13, as well as victims, may also submit observations to the Court.

4.   The admissibility of a case or the jurisdiction of the Court may be challenged only once by any person or State referred to in paragraph 2. The challenge shall take place prior to or at the commencement of the trial. In exceptional circumstances, the Court may grant leave for a challenge to be brought more than once or at a time later than the commencement of the trial. Challenges to the admissibility of a case, at the commencement of a trial, or subsequently with the leave of the Court, may be based only on article 17, paragraph 1 (c).

5.   A State referred to in paragraph 2 (b) and (c) shall make a challenge at the earliest opportunity.

6.   Prior to the confirmation of the charges, challenges to the admissibility of a case or challenges to the jurisdiction of the Court shall be referred to the Pre-Trial Chamber. After confirmation of the charges, they shall be referred to the Trial Chamber. Decisions with respect to jurisdiction or admissibility may be appealed to the Appeals Chamber in accordance with article 82.

7.   If a challenge is made by a State referred to in paragraph 2 (b) or (c), the Prosecutor shall suspend the investigation until such time as the Court makes a determination in accordance with article 17.

8.   Pending a ruling by the Court, the Prosecutor may seek authority from the Court:

(a) To pursue necessary investigative steps of the kind referred to in article 18, paragraph 6;

(b) To take a statement or testimony from a witness or complete the collection and examination of evidence which had begun prior to the making of the challenge; and

(c) In cooperation with the relevant States, to prevent the absconding of persons in respect of whom the Prosecutor has already requested a warrant of arrest under article 58.

9. The making of a challenge shall not affect the validity of any act performed by the Prosecutor or any order or warrant issued by the Court prior to the making of the challenge.

10. If the Court has decided that a case is inadmissible under article 17, the Prosecutor may submit a request for a review of the decision when he or she is fully satisfied that new facts have arisen which negate the basis on which the case had previously been found inadmissible under article 17.

11. If the Prosecutor, having regard to the matters referred to in article 17, defers an investigation, the Prosecutor may request that the relevant State make available to the Prosecutor information on the proceedings. That information shall, at the request of the State concerned, be confidential. If the Prosecutor thereafter decides to proceed with an investigation, he or she shall notify the State to which deferral of the proceedings has taken place.

Article 20
Ne bis in idem

1. Except as provided in this Statute, no person shall be tried before the Court with respect to conduct which formed the basis of crimes for which the person has been convicted or acquitted by the Court.

2. No person shall be tried by another court for a crime referred to in article 5 for which that person has already been convicted or acquitted by the Court.

3. No person who has been tried by another court for conduct also proscribed under articles 6, 7 or 8 shall be tried by the Court with respect to the same conduct unless the proceedings in the other court:

(a) Were for the purpose of shielding the person concerned from criminal responsibility for crimes within the jurisdiction of the Court; or

(b) Otherwise were not conducted independently or impartially in accordance with the norms of due process recognized by international law and were conducted in a manner which, in the circumstances, was inconsistent with an intent to bring the person concerned to justice.

Article 21
Applicable law

1. The Court shall apply:

(a) In the first place, this Statute, Elements of Crimes and its Rules of Procedure and Evidence;

(b) In the second place, where appropriate, applicable treaties and the principles and rules of international law, including the established principles of the international law of armed conflict;

(c) Failing that, general principles of law derived by the Court from national laws of legal systems of the world including, as appropriate, the national laws of States that would normally exercise jurisdiction over the crime, provided that those principles are not inconsistent with this Statute and with international law and internationally recognized norms and standards.

2. The Court may apply principles and rules of law as interpreted in its previous decisions.

3. The application and interpretation of law pursuant to this article must be consistent with internationally recognized human rights, and be without any adverse distinction founded on

grounds such as gender as defined in article 7, paragraph 3, age, race, colour, language, religion or belief, political or other opinion, national, ethnic or social origin, wealth, birth or other status.

PART 3. GENERAL PRINCIPLES OF CRIMINAL LAW
Article 22
Nullum crimen sine lege

1.   A person shall not be criminally responsible under this Statute unless the conduct in question constitutes, at the time it takes place, a crime within the jurisdiction of the Court.

2.   The definition of a crime shall be strictly construed and shall not be extended by analogy. In case of ambiguity, the definition shall be interpreted in favour of the person being investigated, prosecuted or convicted.

3.   This article shall not affect the characterization of any conduct as criminal under international law independently of this Statute.

Article 23
Nulla poena sine lege

A person convicted by the Court may be punished only in accordance with this Statute.

Article 24
Non-retroactivity ratione personae

1.   No person shall be criminally responsible under this Statute for conduct prior to the entry into force of the Statute.

2.   In the event of a change in the law applicable to a given case prior to a final judgement, the law more favourable to the person being investigated, prosecuted or convicted shall apply.

Article 25
Individual criminal responsibility

1.   The Court shall have jurisdiction over natural persons pursuant to this Statute.

2.   A person who commits a crime within the jurisdiction of the Court shall be individually responsible and liable for punishment in accordance with this Statute.

3.   In accordance with this Statute, a person shall be criminally responsible and liable for punishment for a crime within the jurisdiction of the Court if that person:

    (a) Commits such a crime, whether as an individual, jointly with another or through another person, regardless of whether that other person is criminally responsible;

    (b) Orders, solicits or induces the commission of such a crime which in fact occurs or is attempted;

    (c) For the purpose of facilitating the commission of such a crime, aids, abets or otherwise assists in its commission or its attempted commission, including providing the means for its commission;

    (d) In any other way contributes to the commission or attempted commission of such a crime by a group of persons acting with a common purpose. Such contribution shall be intentional and shall either:

        (i) Be made with the aim of furthering the criminal activity or criminal purpose of the group, where such activity or purpose involves the commission of a crime within the jurisdiction of the Court; or

(ii) Be made in the knowledge of the intention of the group to commit the crime;

(e) In respect of the crime of genocide, directly and publicly incites others to commit genocide;

(f) Attempts to commit such a crime by taking action that commences its execution by means of a substantial step, but the crime does not occur because of circumstances independent of the person's intentions. However, a person who abandons the effort to commit the crime or otherwise prevents the completion of the crime shall not be liable for punishment under this Statute for the attempt to commit that crime if that person completely and voluntarily gave up the criminal purpose.

4. No provision in this Statute relating to individual criminal responsibility shall affect the responsibility of States under international law.

Article 26
Exclusion of jurisdiction over persons under eighteen

The Court shall have no jurisdiction over any person who was under the age of 18 at the time of the alleged commission of a crime.

Article 27
Irrelevance of official capacity

1.   This Statute shall apply equally to all persons without any distinction based on official capacity. In particular, official capacity as a Head of State or Government, a member of a Government or parliament, an elected representative or a government official shall in no case exempt a person from criminal responsibility under this Statute, nor shall it, in and of itself, constitute a ground for reduction of sentence.

2.   Immunities or special procedural rules which may attach to the official capacity of a person, whether under national or international law, shall not bar the Court from exercising its jurisdiction over such a person.

Article 28
Responsibility of commanders and other superiors

In addition to other grounds of criminal responsibility under this Statute for crimes within the jurisdiction of the Court:

1. A military commander or person effectively acting as a military commander shall be criminally responsible for crimes within the jurisdiction of the Court committed by forces under his or her effective command and control, or effective authority and control as the case may be, as a result of his or her failure to exercise control properly over such forces, where:

(i) That military commander or person either knew or, owing to the circumstances at the time, should have known that the forces were committing or about to commit such crimes; and

(ii) That military commander or person failed to take all necessary and reasonable measures within his or her power to prevent or repress their commission or to submit the matter to the competent authorities for investigation and prosecution.

2. With respect to superior and subordinate relationships not described in paragraph (a), a superior shall be criminally responsible for crimes within the jurisdiction of the Court committed by subordinates under his or her effective authority and control, as a result of his or her failure to exercise control properly over such subordinates, where:

(i) The superior either knew, or consciously disregarded information which clearly indicated, that the subordinates were committing or about to commit such crimes;

(ii) The crimes concerned activities that were within the effective responsibility and control of the superior; and

(iii) The superior failed to take all necessary and reasonable measures within his or her power to prevent or repress their commission or to submit the matter to the competent authorities for investigation and prosecution.

Article 29
Non-applicability of statute of limitations

The crimes within the jurisdiction of the Court shall not be subject to any statute of limitations.

Article 30
Mental element

1.   Unless otherwise provided, a person shall be criminally responsible and liable for punishment for a crime within the jurisdiction of the Court only if the material elements are committed with intent and knowledge.

2.   For the purposes of this article, a person has intent where:

(a) In relation to conduct, that person means to engage in the conduct;

(b) In relation to a consequence, that person means to cause that consequence or is aware that it will occur in the ordinary course of events.

3.   For the purposes of this article, "knowledge" means awareness that a circumstance exists or a consequence will occur in the ordinary course of events. "Know" and "knowingly" shall be construed accordingly.

Article 31
Grounds for excluding criminal responsibility

1.   In addition to other grounds for excluding criminal responsibility provided for in this Statute, a person shall not be criminally responsible if, at the time of that person's conduct:

(a) The person suffers from a mental disease or defect that destroys that person's capacity to appreciate the unlawfulness or nature of his or her conduct, or capacity to control his or her conduct to conform to the requirements of law;

(b) The person is in a state of intoxication that destroys that person's capacity to appreciate the unlawfulness or nature of his or her conduct, or capacity to control his or her conduct to conform to the requirements of law, unless the person has become voluntarily intoxicated under such circumstances that the person knew, or disregarded the risk, that, as a result of the intoxication, he or she was likely to engage in conduct constituting a crime within the jurisdiction of the Court;

(c) The person acts reasonably to defend himself or herself or another person or, in the case of war crimes, property which is essential for the survival of the person or another person or property which is essential for accomplishing a military mission, against an imminent and unlawful use of force in a manner proportionate to the degree of danger to the person or the other person or property protected. The fact that the person was involved in a defensive operation conducted by forces shall not in itself constitute a ground for excluding criminal responsibility under this subparagraph;

(d) The conduct which is alleged to constitute a crime within the jurisdiction of the Court has been caused by duress resulting from a threat of imminent death or of continuing or imminent serious bodily harm against that person or another person, and the person acts necessarily and reasonably to avoid this threat, provided that the person does not intend to cause a greater harm than the one sought to be avoided. Such a threat may either be:

(i) Made by other persons; or

(ii) Constituted by other circumstances beyond that person's control.

2. The Court shall determine the applicability of the grounds for excluding criminal responsibility provided for in this Statute to the case before it.

3. At trial, the Court may consider a ground for excluding criminal responsibility other than those referred to in paragraph 1 where such a ground is derived from applicable law as set forth in article 21. The procedures relating to the consideration of such a ground shall be provided for in the Rules of Procedure and Evidence.

Article 32
Mistake of fact or mistake of law

1. A mistake of fact shall be a ground for excluding criminal responsibility only if it negates the mental element required by the crime.

2. A mistake of law as to whether a particular type of conduct is a crime within the jurisdiction of the Court shall not be a ground for excluding criminal responsibility. A mistake of law may, however, be a ground for excluding criminal responsibility if it negates the mental element required by such a crime, or as provided for in article 33.

Article 33
Superior orders and prescription of law

1. The fact that a crime within the jurisdiction of the Court has been committed by a person pursuant to an order of a Government or of a superior, whether military or civilian, shall not relieve that person of criminal responsibility unless:

(a) The person was under a legal obligation to obey orders of the Government or the superior in question;

(b) The person did not know that the order was unlawful; and

(c) The order was not manifestly unlawful.

2. For the purposes of this article, orders to commit genocide or crimes against humanity are manifestly unlawful.

PART 4. COMPOSITION AND ADMINISTRATION OF THE COURT
Article 34
Organs of the Court

The Court shall be composed of the following organs:

(a) The Presidency;

(b) An Appeals Division, a Trial Division and a Pre-Trial Division;

(c) The Office of the Prosecutor;

(d) The Registry.

Article 35
Service of judges

1. All judges shall be elected as full-time members of the Court and shall be available to serve on that basis from the commencement of their terms of office.
2. The judges composing the Presidency shall serve on a full-time basis as soon as they are elected.
3. The Presidency may, on the basis of the workload of the Court and in consultation with its members, decide from time to time to what extent the remaining judges shall be required to serve on a full-time basis. Any such arrangement shall be without prejudice to the provisions of article 40.
4. The financial arrangements for judges not required to serve on a full-time basis shall be made in accordance with article 49.

Article 36
Qualifications, nomination and election of judges

1. Subject to the provisions of paragraph 2, there shall be 18 judges of the Court.
2. (a) The Presidency, acting on behalf of the Court, may propose an increase in the number of judges specified in paragraph 1, indicating the reasons why this is considered necessary and appropriate. The Registrar shall promptly circulate any such proposal to all States Parties.

(b) Any such proposal shall then be considered at a meeting of the Assembly of States Parties to be convened in accordance with article 112. The proposal shall be considered adopted if approved at the meeting by a vote of two thirds of the members of the Assembly of States Parties and shall enter into force at such time as decided by the Assembly of States Parties.

(c) (i) Once a proposal for an increase in the number of judges has been adopted under subparagraph (b), the election of the additional judges shall take place at the next session of the Assembly of States Parties in accordance with paragraphs 3 to 8, and article 37, paragraph 2;

(ii) Once a proposal for an increase in the number of judges has been adopted and brought into effect under subparagraphs (b) and (c) (i), it shall be open to the Presidency at any time thereafter, if the workload of the Court justifies it, to propose a reduction in the number of judges, provided that the number of judges shall not be reduced below that specified in paragraph 1. The proposal shall be dealt with in accordance with the procedure laid down in subparagraphs (a) and (b). In the event that the proposal is adopted, the number of judges shall be progressively decreased as the terms of office of serving judges expire, until the necessary number has been reached.
3. (a) The judges shall be chosen from among persons of high moral character, impartiality and integrity who possess the qualifications required in their respective States for appointment to the highest judicial offices.

(b) Every candidate for election to the Court shall:

(i) Have established competence in criminal law and procedure, and the necessary relevant experience, whether as judge, prosecutor, advocate or in other similar capacity, in criminal proceedings; or

(ii) Have established competence in relevant areas of international law such as international humanitarian law and the law of human rights, and extensive experience in a professional legal capacity which is of relevance to the judicial work of the Court;

(c) Every candidate for election to the Court shall have an excellent knowledge of and be fluent in at least one of the working languages of the Court.

4.   (a) Nominations of candidates for election to the Court may be made by any State Party to this Statute, and shall be made either:

(i) By the procedure for the nomination of candidates for appointment to the highest judicial offices in the State in question; or

(ii) By the procedure provided for the nomination of candidates for the International Court of Justice in the Statute of that Court.

Nominations shall be accompanied by a statement in the necessary detail specifying how the candidate fulfils the requirements of paragraph 3.

(b) Each State Party may put forward one candidate for any given election who need not necessarily be a national of that State Party but shall in any case be a national of a State Party.

(c) The Assembly of States Parties may decide to establish, if appropriate, an Advisory Committee on nominations. In that event, the Committee's composition and mandate shall be established by the Assembly of States Parties.

5.   For the purposes of the election, there shall be two lists of candidates:

List A containing the names of candidates with the qualifications specified in paragraph 3 (b) (i); and

List B containing the names of candidates with the qualifications specified in paragraph 3 (b) (ii).

A candidate with sufficient qualifications for both lists may choose on which list to appear. At the first election to the Court, at least nine judges shall be elected from list A and at least five judges from list B. Subsequent elections shall be so organized as to maintain the equivalent proportion on the Court of judges qualified on the two lists.

6.   (a) The judges shall be elected by secret ballot at a meeting of the Assembly of States Parties convened for that purpose under article 112. Subject to paragraph 7, the persons elected to the Court shall be the 18 candidates who obtain the highest number of votes and a two-thirds majority of the States Parties present and voting.

(b) In the event that a sufficient number of judges is not elected on the first ballot, successive ballots shall be held in accordance with the procedures laid down in subparagraph (a) until the remaining places have been filled.

7.   No two judges may be nationals of the same State. A person who, for the purposes of membership of the Court, could be regarded as a national of more than one State shall be deemed to be a national of the State in which that person ordinarily exercises civil and political rights.

8. (a) The States Parties shall, in the selection of judges, take into account the need, within the membership of the Court, for:

(i)   The representation of the principal legal systems of the world;

(ii) Equitable geographical representation; and

(iii) A fair representation of female and male judges.

(b) States Parties shall also take into account the need to include judges with legal expertise on specific issues, including, but not limited to, violence against women or children.

9.   (a) Subject to subparagraph (b), judges shall hold office for a term of nine years and, subject to subparagraph (c) and to article 37, paragraph 2, shall not be eligible for re-election.

(b) At the first election, one third of the judges elected shall be selected by lot to serve for a term of three years; one third of the judges elected shall be selected by lot to serve for a term of six years; and the remainder shall serve for a term of nine years.

(c) A judge who is selected to serve for a term of three years under subparagraph (b) shall be eligible for re-election for a full term.

10. Notwithstanding paragraph 9, a judge assigned to a Trial or Appeals Chamber in accordance with article 39 shall continue in office to complete any trial or appeal the hearing of which has already commenced before that Chamber.

Article 37
Judicial vacancies

1. In the event of a vacancy, an election shall be held in accordance with article 36 to fill the vacancy.

2. A judge elected to fill a vacancy shall serve for the remainder of the predecessor's term and, if that period is three years or less, shall be eligible for re-election for a full term under article 36.

Article 38
The Presidency

1. The President and the First and Second Vice-Presidents shall be elected by an absolute majority of the judges. They shall each serve for a term of three years or until the end of their respective terms of office as judges, whichever expires earlier. They shall be eligible for re-election once.

2. The First Vice-President shall act in place of the President in the event that the President is unavailable or disqualified. The Second Vice-President shall act in place of the President in the event that both the President and the First Vice-President are unavailable or disqualified.

3. The President, together with the First and Second Vice-Presidents, shall constitute the Presidency, which shall be responsible for:

(a) The proper administration of the Court, with the exception of the Office of the Prosecutor; and

(b) The other functions conferred upon it in accordance with this Statute.

4. In discharging its responsibility under paragraph 3 (a), the Presidency shall coordinate with and seek the concurrence of the Prosecutor on all matters of mutual concern.

Article 39
Chambers

1. As soon as possible after the election of the judges, the Court shall organize itself into the divisions specified in article 34, paragraph (b). The Appeals Division shall be composed of the President and four other judges, the Trial Division of not less than six judges and the Pre-Trial Division of not less than six judges. The assignment of judges to divisions shall be based on the nature of the functions to be performed by each division and the qualifications and experience of the judges elected to the Court, in such a way that each division shall contain an appropriate combination of expertise in criminal law and procedure and in international law. The Trial and Pre-Trial Divisions shall be composed predominantly of judges with criminal trial experience.

2. (a) The judicial functions of the Court shall be carried out in each division by Chambers.

(b) (i) The Appeals Chamber shall be composed of all the judges of the Appeals Division;

(ii) The functions of the Trial Chamber shall be carried out by three judges of the Trial Division;

(iii) The functions of the Pre-Trial Chamber shall be carried out either by three judges of the Pre-Trial Division or by a single judge of that division in accordance with this Statute and the Rules of Procedure and Evidence;

(c) Nothing in this paragraph shall preclude the simultaneous constitution of more than one Trial Chamber or Pre-Trial Chamber when the efficient management of the Court's workload so requires.

3.   (a) Judges assigned to the Trial and Pre-Trial Divisions shall serve in those divisions for a period of three years, and thereafter until the completion of any case the hearing of which has already commenced in the division concerned.

(b) Judges assigned to the Appeals Division shall serve in that division for their entire term of office.

4.   Judges assigned to the Appeals Division shall serve only in that division. Nothing in this article shall, however, preclude the temporary attachment of judges from the Trial Division to the Pre-Trial Division or vice versa, if the Presidency considers that the efficient management of the Court's workload so requires, provided that under no circumstances shall a judge who has participated in the pre-trial phase of a case be eligible to sit on the Trial Chamber hearing that case.

Article 40
Independence of the judges

1.   The judges shall be independent in the performance of their functions.

2.   Judges shall not engage in any activity which is likely to interfere with their judicial functions or to affect confidence in their independence.

3.   Judges required to serve on a full-time basis at the seat of the Court shall not engage in any other occupation of a professional nature.

4.   Any question regarding the application of paragraphs 2 and 3 shall be decided by an absolute majority of the judges. Where any such question concerns an individual judge, that judge shall not take part in the decision.

Article 41
Excusing and disqualification of judges

1.   The Presidency may, at the request of a judge, excuse that judge from the exercise of a function under this Statute, in accordance with the Rules of Procedure and Evidence.

2.   (a) A judge shall not participate in any case in which his or her impartiality might reasonably be doubted on any ground. A judge shall be disqualified from a case in accordance with this paragraph if, inter alia, that judge has previously been involved in any capacity in that case before the Court or in a related criminal case at the national level involving the person being investigated or prosecuted. A judge shall also be disqualified on such other grounds as may be provided for in the Rules of Procedure and Evidence.

(b) The Prosecutor or the person being investigated or prosecuted may request the disqualification of a judge under this paragraph.

(c) Any question as to the disqualification of a judge shall be decided by an absolute majority of the judges. The challenged judge shall be entitled to present his or her comments on the matter, but shall not take part in the decision.

Article 42
The Office of the Prosecutor

1. The Office of the Prosecutor shall act independently as a separate organ of the Court. It shall be responsible for receiving referrals and any substantiated information on crimes within the jurisdiction of the Court, for examining them and for conducting investigations and prosecutions before the Court. A member of the Office shall not seek or act on instructions from any external source.

2. The Office shall be headed by the Prosecutor. The Prosecutor shall have full authority over the management and administration of the Office, including the staff, facilities and other resources thereof. The Prosecutor shall be assisted by one or more Deputy Prosecutors, who shall be entitled to carry out any of the acts required of the Prosecutor under this Statute. The Prosecutor and the Deputy Prosecutors shall be of different nationalities. They shall serve on a full-time basis.

3. The Prosecutor and the Deputy Prosecutors shall be persons of high moral character, be highly competent in and have extensive practical experience in the prosecution or trial of criminal cases. They shall have an excellent knowledge of and be fluent in at least one of the working languages of the Court.

4. The Prosecutor shall be elected by secret ballot by an absolute majority of the members of the Assembly of States Parties. The Deputy Prosecutors shall be elected in the same way from a list of candidates provided by the Prosecutor. The Prosecutor shall nominate three candidates for each position of Deputy Prosecutor to be filled. Unless a shorter term is decided upon at the time of their election, the Prosecutor and the Deputy Prosecutors shall hold office for a term of nine years and shall not be eligible for re-election.

5. Neither the Prosecutor nor a Deputy Prosecutor shall engage in any activity which is likely to interfere with his or her prosecutorial functions or to affect confidence in his or her independence. They shall not engage in any other occupation of a professional nature.

6. The Presidency may excuse the Prosecutor or a Deputy Prosecutor, at his or her request, from acting in a particular case.

7. Neither the Prosecutor nor a Deputy Prosecutor shall participate in any matter in which their impartiality might reasonably be doubted on any ground. They shall be disqualified from a case in accordance with this paragraph if, inter alia, they have previously been involved in any capacity in that case before the Court or in a related criminal case at the national level involving the person being investigated or prosecuted.

8. Any question as to the disqualification of the Prosecutor or a Deputy Prosecutor shall be decided by the Appeals Chamber.

(a) The person being investigated or prosecuted may at any time request the disqualification of the Prosecutor or a Deputy Prosecutor on the grounds set out in this article;

(b) The Prosecutor or the Deputy Prosecutor, as appropriate, shall be entitled to present his or her comments on the matter;

9. The Prosecutor shall appoint advisers with legal expertise on specific issues, including, but not limited to, sexual and gender violence and violence against children.

Article 43
The Registry

1.   The Registry shall be responsible for the non-judicial aspects of the administration and servicing of the Court, without prejudice to the functions and powers of the Prosecutor in accordance with article 42.

2.   The Registry shall be headed by the Registrar, who shall be the principal administrative officer of the Court. The Registrar shall exercise his or her functions under the authority of the President of the Court.

3.   The Registrar and the Deputy Registrar shall be persons of high moral character, be highly competent and have an excellent knowledge of and be fluent in at least one of the working languages of the Court.

4.   The judges shall elect the Registrar by an absolute majority by secret ballot, taking into account any recommendation by the Assembly of States Parties. If the need arises and upon the recommendation of the Registrar, the judges shall elect, in the same manner, a Deputy Registrar.

5.   The Registrar shall hold office for a term of five years, shall be eligible for re-election once and shall serve on a full-time basis. The Deputy Registrar shall hold office for a term of five years or such shorter term as may be decided upon by an absolute majority of the judges, and may be elected on the basis that the Deputy Registrar shall be called upon to serve as required.

6.   The Registrar shall set up a Victims and Witnesses Unit within the Registry. This Unit shall provide, in consultation with the Office of the Prosecutor, protective measures and security arrangements, counselling and other appropriate assistance for witnesses, victims who appear before the Court and others who are at risk on account of testimony given by such witnesses. The Unit shall include staff with expertise in trauma, including trauma related to crimes of sexual violence.

Article 44
Staff

1.   The Prosecutor and the Registrar shall appoint such qualified staff as may be required to their respective offices. In the case of the Prosecutor, this shall include the appointment of investigators.

2.   In the employment of staff, the Prosecutor and the Registrar shall ensure the highest standards of efficiency, competency and integrity, and shall have regard, mutatis mutandis, to the criteria set forth in article 36, paragraph 8.

3.   The Registrar, with the agreement of the Presidency and the Prosecutor, shall propose Staff Regulations which include the terms and conditions upon which the staff of the Court shall be appointed, remunerated and dismissed. The Staff Regulations shall be approved by the Assembly of States Parties.

4.   The Court may, in exceptional circumstances, employ the expertise of gratis personnel offered by States Parties, intergovernmental organizations or non-governmental organizations to assist with the work of any of the organs of the Court. The Prosecutor may accept any such offer on behalf of the Office of the Prosecutor. Such gratis personnel shall be employed in accordance with guidelines to be established by the Assembly of States Parties.

Article 45
Solemn undertaking

Before taking up their respective duties under this Statute, the judges, the Prosecutor, the Deputy Prosecutors, the Registrar and the Deputy Registrar shall each make a solemn undertaking in open court to exercise his or her respective functions impartially and conscientiously.

Article 46
Removal from office

1.   A judge, the Prosecutor, a Deputy Prosecutor, the Registrar or the Deputy Registrar shall be removed from office if a decision to this effect is made in accordance with paragraph 2, in cases where that person:

(a)   Is found to have committed serious misconduct or a serious breach of his or her duties under this Statute, as provided for in the Rules of Procedure and Evidence; or

(b)   Is unable to exercise the functions required by this Statute.

2.   A decision as to the removal from office of a judge, the Prosecutor or a Deputy Prosecutor under paragraph 1 shall be made by the Assembly of States Parties, by secret ballot:

(a)   In the case of a judge, by a two-thirds majority of the States Parties upon a recommendation adopted by a two-thirds majority of the other judges;

(b)   In the case of the Prosecutor, by an absolute majority of the States Parties;

(c)   In the case of a Deputy Prosecutor, by an absolute majority of the States Parties upon the recommendation of the Prosecutor.

3.   A decision as to the removal from office of the Registrar or Deputy Registrar shall be made by an absolute majority of the judges.

4.   A judge, Prosecutor, Deputy Prosecutor, Registrar or Deputy Registrar whose conduct or ability to exercise the functions of the office as required by this Statute is challenged under this article shall have full opportunity to present and receive evidence and to make submissions in accordance with the Rules of Procedure and Evidence. The person in question shall not otherwise participate in the consideration of the matter.

Article 47
Disciplinary measures

A judge, Prosecutor, Deputy Prosecutor, Registrar or Deputy Registrar who has committed misconduct of a less serious nature than that set out in article 46, paragraph 1, shall be subject to disciplinary measures, in accordance with the Rules of Procedure and Evidence.

Article 48
Privileges and immunities

1.   The Court shall enjoy in the territory of each State Party such privileges and immunities as are necessary for the fulfilment of its purposes.

2.   The judges, the Prosecutor, the Deputy Prosecutors and the Registrar shall, when engaged on or with respect to the business of the Court, enjoy the same privileges and immunities as are accorded to heads of diplomatic missions and shall, after the expiry of their terms of office, continue to be accorded immunity from legal process of every kind in respect of words spoken or written and acts performed by them in their official capacity.

3.   The Deputy Registrar, the staff of the Office of the Prosecutor and the staff of the Registry shall enjoy the privileges and immunities and facilities necessary for the performance of their functions, in accordance with the agreement on the privileges and immunities of the Court.

4.   Counsel, experts, witnesses or any other person required to be present at the seat of the Court shall be accorded such treatment as is necessary for the proper functioning of the Court, in accordance with the agreement on the privileges and immunities of the Court.

5.   The privileges and immunities of:

(a) A judge or the Prosecutor may be waived by an absolute majority of the judges;

(b) The Registrar may be waived by the Presidency;

(c) The Deputy Prosecutors and staff of the Office of the Prosecutor may be waived by the Prosecutor;

(d) The Deputy Registrar and staff of the Registry may be waived by the Registrar.

Article 49
Salaries, allowances and expenses

The judges, the Prosecutor, the Deputy Prosecutors, the Registrar and the Deputy Registrar shall receive such salaries, allowances and expenses as may be decided upon by the Assembly of States Parties. These salaries and allowances shall not be reduced during their terms of office.

Article 50
Official and working languages

1.   The official languages of the Court shall be Arabic, Chinese, English, French, Russian and Spanish. The judgements of the Court, as well as other decisions resolving fundamental issues before the Court, shall be published in the official languages. The Presidency shall, in accordance with the criteria established by the Rules of Procedure and Evidence, determine which decisions may be considered as resolving fundamental issues for the purposes of this paragraph.

2.   The working languages of the Court shall be English and French. The Rules of Procedure and Evidence shall determine the cases in which other official languages may be used as working languages.

3.   At the request of any party to a proceeding or a State allowed to intervene in a proceeding, the Court shall authorize a language other than English or French to be used by such a party or State, provided that the Court considers such authorization to be adequately justified.

Article 51
Rules of Procedure and Evidence

1.   The Rules of Procedure and Evidence shall enter into force upon adoption by a two-thirds majority of the members of the Assembly of States Parties.

2.   Amendments to the Rules of Procedure and Evidence may be proposed by:

(a) Any State Party;

(b) The judges acting by an absolute majority; or

(c) The Prosecutor.

Such amendments shall enter into force upon adoption by a two-thirds majority of the members of the Assembly of States Parties.

3.　After the adoption of the Rules of Procedure and Evidence, in urgent cases where the Rules do not provide for a specific situation before the Court, the judges may, by a two-thirds majority, draw up provisional Rules to be applied until adopted, amended or rejected at the next ordinary or special session of the Assembly of States Parties.

4.　The Rules of Procedure and Evidence, amendments thereto and any provisional Rule shall be consistent with this Statute. Amendments to the Rules of Procedure and Evidence as well as provisional Rules shall not be applied retroactively to the detriment of the person who is being investigated or prosecuted or who has been convicted.

5.　In the event of conflict between the Statute and the Rules of Procedure and Evidence, the Statute shall prevail.

Article 52
Regulations of the Court

1.　The judges shall, in accordance with this Statute and the Rules of Procedure and Evidence, adopt, by an absolute majority, the Regulations of the Court necessary for its routine functioning.

2.　The Prosecutor and the Registrar shall be consulted in the elaboration of the Regulations and any amendments thereto.

3.　The Regulations and any amendments thereto shall take effect upon adoption unless otherwise decided by the judges. Immediately upon adoption, they shall be circulated to States Parties for comments. If within six months there are no objections from a majority of States Parties, they shall remain in force.

PART 5. INVESTIGATION AND PROSECUTION
Article 53
Initiation of an investigation

1.　The Prosecutor shall, having evaluated the information made available to him or her, initiate an investigation unless he or she determines that there is no reasonable basis to proceed under this Statute. In deciding whether to initiate an investigation, the Prosecutor shall consider whether:

　　(a)　The information available to the Prosecutor provides a reasonable basis to believe that a crime within the jurisdiction of the Court has been or is being committed;

　　(b)　The case is or would be admissible under article 17; and

　　(c)　Taking into account the gravity of the crime and the interests of victims, there are nonetheless substantial reasons to believe that an investigation would not serve the interests of justice.

If the Prosecutor determines that there is no reasonable basis to proceed and his or her determination is based solely on subparagraph (c) above, he or she shall inform the Pre-Trial Chamber.

2.　If, upon investigation, the Prosecutor concludes that there is not a sufficient basis for a prosecution because:

　　(a)　There is not a sufficient legal or factual basis to seek a warrant or summons under article 58;

　　(b)　The case is inadmissible under article 17; or

(c) A prosecution is not in the interests of justice, taking into account all the circumstances, including the gravity of the crime, the interests of victims and the age or infirmity of the alleged perpetrator, and his or her role in the alleged crime;

the Prosecutor shall inform the Pre-Trial Chamber and the State making a referral under article 14 or the Security Council in a case under article 13, paragraph (b), of his or her conclusion and the reasons for the conclusion.

3.   (a) At the request of the State making a referral under article 14 or the Security Council under article 13, paragraph (b), the Pre-Trial Chamber may review a decision of the Prosecutor under paragraph 1 or 2 not to proceed and may request the Prosecutor to reconsider that decision.

(b) In addition, the Pre-Trial Chamber may, on its own initiative, review a decision of the Prosecutor not to proceed if it is based solely on paragraph 1 (c) or 2 (c). In such a case, the decision of the Prosecutor shall be effective only if confirmed by the Pre-Trial Chamber.

4.   The Prosecutor may, at any time, reconsider a decision whether to initiate an investigation or prosecution based on new facts or information.

Article 54
Duties and powers of the Prosecutor with respect to investigations

1.   The Prosecutor shall:

(a) In order to establish the truth, extend the investigation to cover all facts and evidence relevant to an assessment of whether there is criminal responsibility under this Statute, and, in doing so, investigate incriminating and exonerating circumstances equally;

(b) Take appropriate measures to ensure the effective investigation and prosecution of crimes within the jurisdiction of the Court, and in doing so, respect the interests and personal circumstances of victims and witnesses, including age, gender as defined in article 7, paragraph 3, and health, and take into account the nature of the crime, in particular where it involves sexual violence, gender violence or violence against children; and

(c) Fully respect the rights of persons arising under this Statute.

2.   The Prosecutor may conduct investigations on the territory of a State:

(a) In accordance with the provisions of Part 9; or

(b) As authorized by the Pre-Trial Chamber under article 57, paragraph 3 (d).

3.   The Prosecutor may:

(a) Collect and examine evidence;

(b) Request the presence of and question persons being investigated, victims and witnesses;

(c) Seek the cooperation of any State or intergovernmental organization or arrangement in accordance with its respective competence and/or mandate;

(d) Enter into such arrangements or agreements, not inconsistent with this Statute, as may be necessary to facilitate the cooperation of a State, intergovernmental organization or person;

(e) Agree not to disclose, at any stage of the proceedings, documents or information that the Prosecutor obtains on the condition of confidentiality and solely for the purpose of generating new evidence, unless the provider of the information consents; and

(f) Take necessary measures, or request that necessary measures be taken, to ensure the confidentiality of information, the protection of any person or the preservation of evidence.

Article 55
Rights of persons during an investigation

1. In respect of an investigation under this Statute, a person:

   (a) Shall not be compelled to incriminate himself or herself or to confess guilt;

   (b) Shall not be subjected to any form of coercion, duress or threat, to torture or to any other form of cruel, inhuman or degrading treatment or punishment; and

   (c) Shall, if questioned in a language other than a language the person fully understands and speaks, have, free of any cost, the assistance of a competent interpreter and such translations as are necessary to meet the requirements of fairness;

   (d) Shall not be subjected to arbitrary arrest or detention, and shall not be deprived of his or her liberty except on such grounds and in accordance with such procedures as are established in this Statute.

2. Where there are grounds to believe that a person has committed a crime within the jurisdiction of the Court and that person is about to be questioned either by the Prosecutor, or by national authorities pursuant to a request made under Part 9, that person shall also have the following rights of which he or she shall be informed prior to being questioned:

   (a) To be informed, prior to being questioned, that there are grounds to believe that he or she has committed a crime within the jurisdiction of the Court;

   (b) To remain silent, without such silence being a consideration in the determination of guilt or innocence;

   (c) To have legal assistance of the person's choosing, or, if the person does not have legal assistance, to have legal assistance assigned to him or her, in any case where the interests of justice so require, and without payment by the person in any such case if the person does not have sufficient means to pay for it;

   (d) To be questioned in the presence of counsel unless the person has voluntarily waived his or her right to counsel.

Article 56
Role of the Pre-Trial Chamber in relation to a unique investigative opportunity

1. (a) Where the Prosecutor considers an investigation to present a unique opportunity to take testimony or a statement from a witness or to examine, collect or test evidence, which may not be available subsequently for the purposes of a trial, the Prosecutor shall so inform the Pre-Trial Chamber.

   (b) In that case, the Pre-Trial Chamber may, upon request of the Prosecutor, take such measures as may be necessary to ensure the efficiency and integrity of the proceedings and, in particular, to protect the rights of the defence.

   (c) Unless the Pre-Trial Chamber orders otherwise, the Prosecutor shall provide the relevant information to the person who has been arrested or appeared in response to a summons in connection with the investigation referred to in subparagraph (a), in order that he or she may be heard on the matter.

2. The measures referred to in paragraph 1 (b) may include:

   (a) Making recommendations or orders regarding procedures to be followed;

   (b) Directing that a record be made of the proceedings;

   (c) Appointing an expert to assist;

(d) Authorizing counsel for a person who has been arrested, or appeared before the Court in response to a summons, to participate, or where there has not yet been such an arrest or appearance or counsel has not been designated, appointing another counsel to attend and represent the interests of the defence;

(e) Naming one of its members or, if necessary, another available judge of the Pre-Trial or Trial Division to observe and make recommendations or orders regarding the collection and preservation of evidence and the questioning of persons;

(f) Taking such other action as may be necessary to collect or preserve evidence.

3. (a) Where the Prosecutor has not sought measures pursuant to this article but the Pre-Trial Chamber considers that such measures are required to preserve evidence that it deems would be essential for the defence at trial, it shall consult with the Prosecutor as to whether there is good reason for the Prosecutor's failure to request the measures. If upon consultation, the Pre-Trial Chamber concludes that the Prosecutor's failure to request such measures is unjustified, the Pre-Trial Chamber may take such measures on its own initiative.

(b) A decision of the Pre-Trial Chamber to act on its own initiative under this paragraph may be appealed by the Prosecutor. The appeal shall be heard on an expedited basis.

4. The admissibility of evidence preserved or collected for trial pursuant to this article, or the record thereof, shall be governed at trial by article 69, and given such weight as determined by the Trial Chamber.

Article 57
Functions and powers of the Pre-Trial Chamber

1. Unless otherwise provided in this Statute, the Pre-Trial Chamber shall exercise its functions in accordance with the provisions of this article.

2. (a) Orders or rulings of the Pre-Trial Chamber issued under articles 15, 18, 19, 54, paragraph 2, 61, paragraph 7, and 72 must be concurred in by a majority of its judges.

(b) In all other cases, a single judge of the Pre-Trial Chamber may exercise the functions provided for in this Statute, unless otherwise provided for in the Rules of Procedure and Evidence or by a majority of the Pre-Trial Chamber.

3. In addition to its other functions under this Statute, the Pre-Trial Chamber may:

(a) At the request of the Prosecutor, issue such orders and warrants as may be required for the purposes of an investigation;

(b) Upon the request of a person who has been arrested or has appeared pursuant to a summons under article 58, issue such orders, including measures such as those described in article 56, or seek such cooperation pursuant to Part 9 as may be necessary to assist the person in the preparation of his or her defence;

(c) Where necessary, provide for the protection and privacy of victims and witnesses, the preservation of evidence, the protection of persons who have been arrested or appeared in response to a summons, and the protection of national security information;

(d) Authorize the Prosecutor to take specific investigative steps within the territory of a State Party without having secured the cooperation of that State under Part 9 if, whenever possible having regard to the views of the State concerned, the Pre-Trial Chamber has determined in that case that the State is clearly unable to execute a request for cooperation due to the unavailability of any authority or any component of its judicial system competent to execute the request for cooperation under Part 9.

(e)   Where a warrant of arrest or a summons has been issued under article 58, and having due regard to the strength of the evidence and the rights of the parties concerned, as provided for in this Statute and the Rules of Procedure and Evidence, seek the cooperation of States pursuant to article 93, paragraph 1 (j), to take protective measures for the purpose of forfeiture, in particular for the ultimate benefit of victims.

Article 58
Issuance by the Pre-Trial Chamber of a warrant
of arrest or a summons to appear

1.   At any time after the initiation of an investigation, the Pre-Trial Chamber shall, on the application of the Prosecutor, issue a warrant of arrest of a person if, having examined the application and the evidence or other information submitted by the Prosecutor, it is satisfied that:

(a)   There are reasonable grounds to believe that the person has committed a crime within the jurisdiction of the Court; and

(b)   The arrest of the person appears necessary:

(i)   To ensure the person's appearance at trial,

(ii)   To ensure that the person does not obstruct or endanger the investigation or the court proceedings, or

(iii)   Where applicable, to prevent the person from continuing with the commission of that crime or a related crime which is within the jurisdiction of the Court and which arises out of the same circumstances.

2.   The application of the Prosecutor shall contain:

(a)   The name of the person and any other relevant identifying information;

(b)   A specific reference to the crimes within the jurisdiction of the Court which the person is alleged to have committed;

(c)   A concise statement of the facts which are alleged to constitute those crimes;

(d)   A summary of the evidence and any other information which establish reasonable grounds to believe that the person committed those crimes; and

(e)   The reason why the Prosecutor believes that the arrest of the person is necessary.

3.   The warrant of arrest shall contain:

(a)   The name of the person and any other relevant identifying information;

(b)   A specific reference to the crimes within the jurisdiction of the Court for which the person's arrest is sought; and

(c)   A concise statement of the facts which are alleged to constitute those crimes.

4.   The warrant of arrest shall remain in effect until otherwise ordered by the Court.

5.   On the basis of the warrant of arrest, the Court may request the provisional arrest or the arrest and surrender of the person under Part 9.

6.   The Prosecutor may request the Pre-Trial Chamber to amend the warrant of arrest by modifying or adding to the crimes specified therein. The Pre-Trial Chamber shall so amend the warrant if it is satisfied that there are reasonable grounds to believe that the person committed the modified or additional crimes.

7.   As an alternative to seeking a warrant of arrest, the Prosecutor may submit an application requesting that the Pre-Trial Chamber issue a summons for the person to appear. If the Pre-Trial Chamber is satisfied that there are reasonable grounds to believe that the person committed the crime alleged and that a summons is sufficient to ensure the person's appearance, it shall issue

the summons, with or without conditions restricting liberty (other than detention) if provided for by national law, for the person to appear. The summons shall contain:

(a) The name of the person and any other relevant identifying information;

(b) The specified date on which the person is to appear;

(c) A specific reference to the crimes within the jurisdiction of the Court which the person is alleged to have committed; and

(d) A concise statement of the facts which are alleged to constitute the crime.

The summons shall be served on the person.

Article 59
Arrest proceedings in the custodial State

1.   A State Party which has received a request for provisional arrest or for arrest and surrender shall immediately take steps to arrest the person in question in accordance with its laws and the provisions of Part 9.

2.   A person arrested shall be brought promptly before the competent judicial authority in the custodial State which shall determine, in accordance with the law of that State, that:

(a) The warrant applies to that person;

(b) The person has been arrested in accordance with the proper process; and

(c) The person's rights have been respected.

3.   The person arrested shall have the right to apply to the competent authority in the custodial State for interim release pending surrender.

4.   In reaching a decision on any such application, the competent authority in the custodial State shall consider whether, given the gravity of the alleged crimes, there are urgent and exceptional circumstances to justify interim release and whether necessary safeguards exist to ensure that the custodial State can fulfil its duty to surrender the person to the Court. It shall not be open to the competent authority of the custodial State to consider whether the warrant of arrest was properly issued in accordance with article 58, paragraph 1 (a) and (b).

5.   The Pre-Trial Chamber shall be notified of any request for interim release and shall make recommendations to the competent authority in the custodial State. The competent authority in the custodial State shall give full consideration to such recommendations, including any recommendations on measures to prevent the escape of the person, before rendering its decision.

6.   If the person is granted interim release, the Pre-Trial Chamber may request periodic reports on the status of the interim release.

7.   Once ordered to be surrendered by the custodial State, the person shall be delivered to the Court as soon as possible.

Article 60
Initial proceedings before the Court

1.   Upon the surrender of the person to the Court, or the person's appearance before the Court voluntarily or pursuant to a summons, the Pre-Trial Chamber shall satisfy itself that the person has been informed of the crimes which he or she is alleged to have committed, and of his or her rights under this Statute, including the right to apply for interim release pending trial.

2.   A person subject to a warrant of arrest may apply for interim release pending trial. If the Pre-Trial Chamber is satisfied that the conditions set forth in article 58, paragraph 1, are met,

the person shall continue to be detained. If it is not so satisfied, the Pre-Trial Chamber shall release the person, with or without conditions.

3.   The Pre-Trial Chamber shall periodically review its ruling on the release or detention of the person, and may do so at any time on the request of the Prosecutor or the person. Upon such review, it may modify its ruling as to detention, release or conditions of release, if it is satisfied that changed circumstances so require.

4.   The Pre-Trial Chamber shall ensure that a person is not detained for an unreasonable period prior to trial due to inexcusable delay by the Prosecutor. If such delay occurs, the Court shall consider releasing the person, with or without conditions.

5.   If necessary, the Pre-Trial Chamber may issue a warrant of arrest to secure the presence of a person who has been released.

Article 61
Confirmation of the charges before trial

1.   Subject to the provisions of paragraph 2, within a reasonable time after the person's surrender or voluntary appearance before the Court, the Pre-Trial Chamber shall hold a hearing to confirm the charges on which the Prosecutor intends to seek trial. The hearing shall be held in the presence of the Prosecutor and the person charged, as well as his or her counsel.

2.   The Pre-Trial Chamber may, upon request of the Prosecutor or on its own motion, hold a hearing in the absence of the person charged to confirm the charges on which the Prosecutor intends to seek trial when the person has:

(a) Waived his or her right to be present; or

(b) Fled or cannot be found and all reasonable steps have been taken to secure his or her appearance before the Court and to inform the person of the charges and that a hearing to confirm those charges will be held.

In that case, the person shall be represented by counsel where the Pre-Trial Chamber determines that it is in the interests of justice.

3.   Within a reasonable time before the hearing, the person shall:

(a) Be provided with a copy of the document containing the charges on which the Prosecutor intends to bring the person to trial; and

(b) Be informed of the evidence on which the Prosecutor intends to rely at the hearing.

The Pre-Trial Chamber may issue orders regarding the disclosure of information for the purposes of the hearing.

4.   Before the hearing, the Prosecutor may continue the investigation and may amend or withdraw any charges. The person shall be given reasonable notice before the hearing of any amendment to or withdrawal of charges. In case of a withdrawal of charges, the Prosecutor shall notify the Pre-Trial Chamber of the reasons for the withdrawal.

5. At the hearing, the Prosecutor shall support each charge with sufficient evidence to establish substantial grounds to believe that the person committed the crime charged. The Prosecutor may rely on documentary or summary evidence and need not call the witnesses expected to testify at the trial.

6.   At the hearing, the person may:

(a) Object to the charges;

(b) Challenge the evidence presented by the Prosecutor; and

(c) Present evidence.

7.   The Pre-Trial Chamber shall, on the basis of the hearing, determine whether there is sufficient evidence to establish substantial grounds to believe that the person committed each of the crimes charged. Based on its determination, the Pre-Trial Chamber shall:

(a) Confirm those charges in relation to which it has determined that there is sufficient evidence, and commit the person to a Trial Chamber for trial on the charges as confirmed;

(b) Decline to confirm those charges in relation to which it has determined that there is insufficient evidence;

(c) Adjourn the hearing and request the Prosecutor to consider:

(i) Providing further evidence or conducting further investigation with respect to a particular charge; or

(ii) Amending a charge because the evidence submitted appears to establish a different crime within the jurisdiction of the Court.

8.   Where the Pre-Trial Chamber declines to confirm a charge, the Prosecutor shall not be precluded from subsequently requesting its confirmation if the request is supported by additional evidence.

9.   After the charges are confirmed and before the trial has begun, the Prosecutor may, with the permission of the Pre-Trial Chamber and after notice to the accused, amend the charges. If the Prosecutor seeks to add additional charges or to substitute more serious charges, a hearing under this article to confirm those charges must be held. After commencement of the trial, the Prosecutor may, with the permission of the Trial Chamber, withdraw the charges.

10. Any warrant previously issued shall cease to have effect with respect to any charges which have not been confirmed by the Pre-Trial Chamber or which have been withdrawn by the Prosecutor.

11. Once the charges have been confirmed in accordance with this article, the Presidency shall constitute a Trial Chamber which, subject to paragraph 8 and to article 64, paragraph 4, shall be responsible for the conduct of subsequent proceedings and may exercise any function of the Pre-Trial Chamber that is relevant and capable of application in those proceedings.

PART 6. THE TRIAL
Article 62
Place of trial

Unless otherwise decided, the place of the trial shall be the seat of the Court.

Article 63
Trial in the presence of the accused

1.   The accused shall be present during the trial.

2.   If the accused, being present before the Court, continues to disrupt the trial, the Trial Chamber may remove the accused and shall make provision for him or her to observe the trial and instruct counsel from outside the courtroom, through the use of communications technology, if required. Such measures shall be taken only in exceptional circumstances after other reasonable alternatives have proved inadequate, and only for such duration as is strictly required.

Article 64
Functions and powers of the Trial Chamber

1.   The functions and powers of the Trial Chamber set out in this article shall be exercised in accordance with this Statute and the Rules of Procedure and Evidence.

2.   The Trial Chamber shall ensure that a trial is fair and expeditious and is conducted with full respect for the rights of the accused and due regard for the protection of victims and witnesses.

3.   Upon assignment of a case for trial in accordance with this Statute, the Trial Chamber assigned to deal with the case shall:

(a)   Confer with the parties and adopt such procedures as are necessary to facilitate the fair and expeditious conduct of the proceedings;

(b)   Determine the language or languages to be used at trial; and

(c)   Subject to any other relevant provisions of this Statute, provide for disclosure of documents or information not previously disclosed, sufficiently in advance of the commencement of the trial to enable adequate preparation for trial.

4.   The Trial Chamber may, if necessary for its effective and fair functioning, refer preliminary issues to the Pre-Trial Chamber or, if necessary, to another available judge of the Pre-Trial Division.

5.   Upon notice to the parties, the Trial Chamber may, as appropriate, direct that there be joinder or severance in respect of charges against more than one accused.

6.   In performing its functions prior to trial or during the course of a trial, the Trial Chamber may, as necessary:

(a)   Exercise any functions of the Pre-Trial Chamber referred to in article 61, paragraph 11;

(b)   Require the attendance and testimony of witnesses and production of documents and other evidence by obtaining, if necessary, the assistance of States as provided in this Statute;

(c)   Provide for the protection of confidential information;

(d)   Order the production of evidence in addition to that already collected prior to the trial or presented during the trial by the parties;

(e)   Provide for the protection of the accused, witnesses and victims; and

(f)   Rule on any other relevant matters.

7.   The trial shall be held in public. The Trial Chamber may, however, determine that special circumstances require that certain proceedings be in closed session for the purposes set forth in article 68, or to protect confidential or sensitive information to be given in evidence.

8.   (a)   At the commencement of the trial, the Trial Chamber shall have read to the accused the charges previously confirmed by the Pre-Trial Chamber. The Trial Chamber shall satisfy itself that the accused understands the nature of the charges. It shall afford him or her the opportunity to make an admission of guilt in accordance with article 65 or to plead not guilty.

(b)   At the trial, the presiding judge may give directions for the conduct of proceedings, including to ensure that they are conducted in a fair and impartial manner. Subject to any directions of the presiding judge, the parties may submit evidence in accordance with the provisions of this Statute.

9.   The Trial Chamber shall have, inter alia, the power on application of a party or on its own motion to:

(a)   Rule on the admissibility or relevance of evidence; and

(b)   Take all necessary steps to maintain order in the course of a hearing.

10. The Trial Chamber shall ensure that a complete record of the trial, which accurately reflects the proceedings, is made and that it is maintained and preserved by the Registrar.

Article 65
Proceedings on an admission of guilt

1. Where the accused makes an admission of guilt pursuant to article 64, paragraph 8 (a), the Trial Chamber shall determine whether:

(a) The accused understands the nature and consequences of the admission of guilt;

(b) The admission is voluntarily made by the accused after sufficient consultation with defence counsel; and

(c) The admission of guilt is supported by the facts of the case that are contained in:

(i) The charges brought by the Prosecutor and admitted by the accused;

(ii) Any materials presented by the Prosecutor which supplement the charges and which the accused accepts; and

(iii) Any other evidence, such as the testimony of witnesses, presented by the Prosecutor or the accused.

2. Where the Trial Chamber is satisfied that the matters referred to in paragraph 1 are established, it shall consider the admission of guilt, together with any additional evidence presented, as establishing all the essential facts that are required to prove the crime to which the admission of guilt relates, and may convict the accused of that crime.

3. Where the Trial Chamber is not satisfied that the matters referred to in paragraph 1 are established, it shall consider the admission of guilt as not having been made, in which case it shall order that the trial be continued under the ordinary trial procedures provided by this Statute and may remit the case to another Trial Chamber.

4. Where the Trial Chamber is of the opinion that a more complete presentation of the facts of the case is required in the interests of justice, in particular the interests of the victims, the Trial Chamber may:

(a) Request the Prosecutor to present additional evidence, including the testimony of witnesses; or

(b) Order that the trial be continued under the ordinary trial procedures provided by this Statute, in which case it shall consider the admission of guilt as not having been made and may remit the case to another Trial Chamber.

5. Any discussions between the Prosecutor and the defence regarding modification of the charges, the admission of guilt or the penalty to be imposed shall not be binding on the Court.

Article 66
Presumption of innocence

1. Everyone shall be presumed innocent until proved guilty before the Court in accordance with the applicable law.

2. The onus is on the Prosecutor to prove the guilt of the accused.

3. In order to convict the accused, the Court must be convinced of the guilt of the accused beyond reasonable doubt.

Article 67
Rights of the accused

1.   In the determination of any charge, the accused shall be entitled to a public hearing, having regard to the provisions of this Statute, to a fair hearing conducted impartially, and to the following minimum guarantees, in full equality:

(a)   To be informed promptly and in detail of the nature, cause and content of the charge, in a language which the accused fully understands and speaks;

(b)   To have adequate time and facilities for the preparation of the defence and to communicate freely with counsel of the accused's choosing in confidence;

(c)   To be tried without undue delay;

(d)   Subject to article 63, paragraph 2, to be present at the trial, to conduct the defence in person or through legal assistance of the accused's choosing, to be informed, if the accused does not have legal assistance, of this right and to have legal assistance assigned by the Court in any case where the interests of justice so require, and without payment if the accused lacks sufficient means to pay for it;

(e)   To examine, or have examined, the witnesses against him or her and to obtain the attendance and examination of witnesses on his or her behalf under the same conditions as witnesses against him or her. The accused shall also be entitled to raise defences and to present other evidence admissible under this Statute;

(f)   To have, free of any cost, the assistance of a competent interpreter and such translations as are necessary to meet the requirements of fairness, if any of the proceedings of or documents presented to the Court are not in a language which the accused fully understands and speaks;

(g)   Not to be compelled to testify or to confess guilt and to remain silent, without such silence being a consideration in the determination of guilt or innocence;

(h)   To make an unsworn oral or written statement in his or her defence; and

(i)   Not to have imposed on him or her any reversal of the burden of proof or any onus of rebuttal.

2.   In addition to any other disclosure provided for in this Statute, the Prosecutor shall, as soon as practicable, disclose to the defence evidence in the Prosecutor's possession or control which he or she believes shows or tends to show the innocence of the accused, or to mitigate the guilt of the accused, or which may affect the credibility of prosecution evidence. In case of doubt as to the application of this paragraph, the Court shall decide.

Article 68
Protection of the victims and witnesses and their participation in the proceedings

1.   The Court shall take appropriate measures to protect the safety, physical and psychological well-being, dignity and privacy of victims and witnesses. In so doing, the Court shall have regard to all relevant factors, including age, gender as defined in article 7, paragraph 3, and health, and the nature of the crime, in particular, but not limited to, where the crime involves sexual or gender violence or violence against children. The Prosecutor shall take such measures particularly during the investigation and prosecution of such crimes. These measures shall not be prejudicial to or inconsistent with the rights of the accused and a fair and impartial trial.

2.   As an exception to the principle of public hearings provided for in article 67, the Chambers of the Court may, to protect victims and witnesses or an accused, conduct any part of the proceedings in camera or allow the presentation of evidence by electronic or other special

means. In particular, such measures shall be implemented in the case of a victim of sexual violence or a child who is a victim or a witness, unless otherwise ordered by the Court, having regard to all the circumstances, particularly the views of the victim or witness.

3.   Where the personal interests of the victims are affected, the Court shall permit their views and concerns to be presented and considered at stages of the proceedings determined to be appropriate by the Court and in a manner which is not prejudicial to or inconsistent with the rights of the accused and a fair and impartial trial. Such views and concerns may be presented by the legal representatives of the victims where the Court considers it appropriate, in accordance with the Rules of Procedure and Evidence.

4.   The Victims and Witnesses Unit may advise the Prosecutor and the Court on appropriate protective measures, security arrangements, counselling and assistance as referred to in article 43, paragraph 6.

5.   Where the disclosure of evidence or information pursuant to this Statute may lead to the grave endangerment of the security of a witness or his or her family, the Prosecutor may, for the purposes of any proceedings conducted prior to the commencement of the trial, withhold such evidence or information and instead submit a summary thereof. Such measures shall be exercised in a manner which is not prejudicial to or inconsistent with the rights of the accused and a fair and impartial trial.

6.   A State may make an application for necessary measures to be taken in respect of the protection of its servants or agents and the protection of confidential or sensitive information.

Article 69
Evidence

1.   Before testifying, each witness shall, in accordance with the Rules of Procedure and Evidence, give an undertaking as to the truthfulness of the evidence to be given by that witness.

2.   The testimony of a witness at trial shall be given in person, except to the extent provided by the measures set forth in article 68 or in the Rules of Procedure and Evidence. The Court may also permit the giving of viva voce (oral) or recorded testimony of a witness by means of video or audio technology, as well as the introduction of documents or written transcripts, subject to this Statute and in accordance with the Rules of Procedure and Evidence. These measures shall not be prejudicial to or inconsistent with the rights of the accused.

3.   The parties may submit evidence relevant to the case, in accordance with article 64. The Court shall have the authority to request the submission of all evidence that it considers necessary for the determination of the truth.

4.   The Court may rule on the relevance or admissibility of any evidence, taking into account, inter alia, the probative value of the evidence and any prejudice that such evidence may cause to a fair trial or to a fair evaluation of the testimony of a witness, in accordance with the Rules of Procedure and Evidence.

5.   The Court shall respect and observe privileges on confidentiality as provided for in the Rules of Procedure and Evidence.

6.   The Court shall not require proof of facts of common knowledge but may take judicial notice of them.

7.   Evidence obtained by means of a violation of this Statute or internationally recognized human rights shall not be admissible if:

     (a)   The violation casts substantial doubt on the reliability of the evidence; or

(b) The admission of the evidence would be antithetical to and would seriously damage the integrity of the proceedings.

8. When deciding on the relevance or admissibility of evidence collected by a State, the Court shall not rule on the application of the State's national law.

Article 70
Offences against the administration of justice

1. The Court shall have jurisdiction over the following offences against its administration of justice when committed intentionally:

(a) Giving false testimony when under an obligation pursuant to article 69, paragraph 1, to tell the truth;

(b) Presenting evidence that the party knows is false or forged;

(c) Corruptly influencing a witness, obstructing or interfering with the attendance or testimony of a witness, retaliating against a witness for giving testimony or destroying, tampering with or interfering with the collection of evidence;

(d) Impeding, intimidating or corruptly influencing an official of the Court for the purpose of forcing or persuading the official not to perform, or to perform improperly, his or her duties;

(e) Retaliating against an official of the Court on account of duties performed by that or another official;

(f) Soliciting or accepting a bribe as an official of the Court in conjunction with his or her official duties.

2. The principles and procedures governing the Court's exercise of jurisdiction over offences under this article shall be those provided for in the Rules of Procedure and Evidence. The conditions for providing international cooperation to the Court with respect to its proceedings under this article shall be governed by the domestic laws of the requested State.

3. In the event of conviction, the Court may impose a term of imprisonment not exceeding five years, or a fine in accordance with the Rules of Procedure and Evidence, or both.

4. (a) Each State Party shall extend its criminal laws penalizing offences against the integrity of its own investigative or judicial process to offences against the administration of justice referred to in this article, committed on its territory, or by one of its nationals;

(b) Upon request by the Court, whenever it deems it proper, the State Party shall submit the case to its competent authorities for the purpose of prosecution. Those authorities shall treat such cases with diligence and devote sufficient resources to enable them to be conducted effectively.

Article 71
Sanctions for misconduct before the Court

1. The Court may sanction persons present before it who commit misconduct, including disruption of its proceedings or deliberate refusal to comply with its directions, by administrative measures other than imprisonment, such as temporary or permanent removal from the courtroom, a fine or other similar measures provided for in the Rules of Procedure and Evidence.

2. The procedures governing the imposition of the measures set forth in paragraph 1 shall be those provided for in the Rules of Procedure and Evidence.

Article 72
Protection of national security information

1.   This article applies in any case where the disclosure of the information or documents of a State would, in the opinion of that State, prejudice its national security interests. Such cases include those falling within the scope of article 56, paragraphs 2 and 3, article 61, paragraph 3, article 64, paragraph 3, article 67, paragraph 2, article 68, paragraph 6, article 87, paragraph 6 and article 93, as well as cases arising at any other stage of the proceedings where such disclosure may be at issue.

2.   This article shall also apply when a person who has been requested to give information or evidence has refused to do so or has referred the matter to the State on the ground that disclosure would prejudice the national security interests of a State and the State concerned confirms that it is of the opinion that disclosure would prejudice its national security interests.

3.   Nothing in this article shall prejudice the requirements of confidentiality applicable under article 54, paragraph 3 (e) and (f), or the application of article 73.

4.   If a State learns that information or documents of the State are being, or are likely to be, disclosed at any stage of the proceedings, and it is of the opinion that disclosure would prejudice its national security interests, that State shall have the right to intervene in order to obtain resolution of the issue in accordance with this article.

5.   If, in the opinion of a State, disclosure of information would prejudice its national security interests, all reasonable steps will be taken by the State, acting in conjunction with the Prosecutor, the defence or the Pre-Trial Chamber or Trial Chamber, as the case may be, to seek to resolve the matter by cooperative means. Such steps may include:

(a) Modification or clarification of the request;

(b) A determination by the Court regarding the relevance of the information or evidence sought, or a determination as to whether the evidence, though relevant, could be or has been obtained from a source other than the requested State;

(c) Obtaining the information or evidence from a different source or in a different form; or

(d) Agreement on conditions under which the assistance could be provided including, among other things, providing summaries or redactions, limitations on disclosure, use of in camera or ex parte proceedings, or other protective measures permissible under the Statute and the Rules.

6.   Once all reasonable steps have been taken to resolve the matter through cooperative means, and if the State considers that there are no means or conditions under which the information or documents could be provided or disclosed without prejudice to its national security interests, it shall so notify the Prosecutor or the Court of the specific reasons for its decision, unless a specific description of the reasons would itself necessarily result in such prejudice to the State's national security interests.

7.   Thereafter, if the Court determines that the evidence is relevant and necessary for the establishment of the guilt or innocence of the accused, the Court may undertake the following actions:

(a) Where disclosure of the information or document is sought pursuant to a request for cooperation under Part 9 or the circumstances described in paragraph 2, and the State has invoked the ground for refusal referred to in article 93, paragraph 4:

(i)   The Court may, before making any conclusion referred to in subparagraph 7 (a) (ii), request further consultations for the purpose of considering the State's representations, which may include, as appropriate, hearings in camera and ex parte;

(ii)   If the Court concludes that, by invoking the ground for refusal under article 93, paragraph 4, in the circumstances of the case, the requested State is not acting in accordance with its obligations under this Statute, the Court may refer the matter in accordance with article 87, paragraph 7, specifying the reasons for its conclusion; and

(iii)   The Court may make such inference in the trial of the accused as to the existence or non-existence of a fact, as may be appropriate in the circumstances; or

(b)   In all other circumstances:

(i)   Order disclosure; or

(ii)   To the extent it does not order disclosure, make such inference in the trial of the accused as to the existence or non-existence of a fact, as may be appropriate in the circumstances.

Article 73
Third-party information or documents

If a State Party is requested by the Court to provide a document or information in its custody, possession or control, which was disclosed to it in confidence by a State, intergovernmental organization or international organization, it shall seek the consent of the originator to disclose that document or information. If the originator is a State Party, it shall either consent to disclosure of the information or document or undertake to resolve the issue of disclosure with the Court, subject to the provisions of article 72. If the originator is not a State Party and refuses to consent to disclosure, the requested State shall inform the Court that it is unable to provide the document or information because of a pre-existing obligation of confidentiality to the originator.

Article 74
Requirements for the decision

1.   All the judges of the Trial Chamber shall be present at each stage of the trial and throughout their deliberations. The Presidency may, on a case-by-case basis, designate, as available, one or more alternate judges to be present at each stage of the trial and to replace a member of the Trial Chamber if that member is unable to continue attending.

2.   The Trial Chamber's decision shall be based on its evaluation of the evidence and the entire proceedings. The decision shall not exceed the facts and circumstances described in the charges and any amendments to the charges. The Court may base its decision only on evidence submitted and discussed before it at the trial.

3.   The judges shall attempt to achieve unanimity in their decision, failing which the decision shall be taken by a majority of the judges.

4.   The deliberations of the Trial Chamber shall remain secret.

5.   The decision shall be in writing and shall contain a full and reasoned statement of the Trial Chamber's findings on the evidence and conclusions. The Trial Chamber shall issue one decision. When there is no unanimity, the Trial Chamber's decision shall contain the views of the majority and the minority. The decision or a summary thereof shall be delivered in open court.

Article 75
Reparations to victims

1.   The Court shall establish principles relating to reparations to, or in respect of, victims, including restitution, compensation and rehabilitation. On this basis, in its decision the Court may, either upon request or on its own motion in exceptional circumstances, determine the scope and extent of any damage, loss and injury to, or in respect of, victims and will state the principles on which it is acting.

2.   The Court may make an order directly against a convicted person specifying appropriate reparations to, or in respect of, victims, including restitution, compensation and rehabilitation. Where appropriate, the Court may order that the award for reparations be made through the Trust Fund provided for in article 79.

3.   Before making an order under this article, the Court may invite and shall take account of representations from or on behalf of the convicted person, victims, other interested persons or interested States.

4.   In exercising its power under this article, the Court may, after a person is convicted of a crime within the jurisdiction of the Court, determine whether, in order to give effect to an order which it may make under this article, it is necessary to seek measures under article 93, paragraph 1.

5.   A State Party shall give effect to a decision under this article as if the provisions of article 109 were applicable to this article.

6.   Nothing in this article shall be interpreted as prejudicing the rights of victims under national or international law.

Article 76
Sentencing

1.   In the event of a conviction, the Trial Chamber shall consider the appropriate sentence to be imposed and shall take into account the evidence presented and submissions made during the trial that are relevant to the sentence.

2.   Except where article 65 applies and before the completion of the trial, the Trial Chamber may on its own motion and shall, at the request of the Prosecutor or the accused, hold a further hearing to hear any additional evidence or submissions relevant to the sentence, in accordance with the Rules of Procedure and Evidence.

3.   Where paragraph 2 applies, any representations under article 75 shall be heard during the further hearing referred to in paragraph 2 and, if necessary, during any additional hearing.

4.   The sentence shall be pronounced in public and, wherever possible, in the presence of the accused.

PART 7. PENALTIES
Article 77
Applicable penalties

1.   Subject to article 110, the Court may impose one of the following penalties on a person convicted of a crime referred to in article 5 of this Statute:

    (a)   Imprisonment for a specified number of years, which may not exceed a maximum of 30 years; or

(b) A term of life imprisonment when justified by the extreme gravity of the crime and the individual circumstances of the convicted person.

2. In addition to imprisonment, the Court may order:

(a) A fine under the criteria provided for in the Rules of Procedure and Evidence;

(b) A forfeiture of proceeds, property and assets derived directly or indirectly from that crime, without prejudice to the rights of bona fide third parties.

Article 78
Determination of the sentence

1. In determining the sentence, the Court shall, in accordance with the Rules of Procedure and Evidence, take into account such factors as the gravity of the crime and the individual circumstances of the convicted person.

2. In imposing a sentence of imprisonment, the Court shall deduct the time, if any, previously spent in detention in accordance with an order of the Court. The Court may deduct any time otherwise spent in detention in connection with conduct underlying the crime.

3. When a person has been convicted of more than one crime, the Court shall pronounce a sentence for each crime and a joint sentence specifying the total period of imprisonment. This period shall be no less than the highest individual sentence pronounced and shall not exceed 30 years' imprisonment or a sentence of life imprisonment in conformity with article 77, paragraph 1 (b).

Article 79
Trust Fund

1. A Trust Fund shall be established by decision of the Assembly of States Parties for the benefit of victims of crimes within the jurisdiction of the Court, and of the families of such victims.

2. The Court may order money and other property collected through fines or forfeiture to be transferred, by order of the Court, to the Trust Fund.

3. The Trust Fund shall be managed according to criteria to be determined by the Assembly of States Parties.

Article 80
Non-prejudice to national application of
penalties and national laws

Nothing in this Part affects the application by States of penalties prescribed by their national law, nor the law of States which do not provide for penalties prescribed in this Part.

PART 8. APPEAL AND REVISION
Article 81
Appeal against decision of acquittal or conviction
or against sentence

1. A decision under article 74 may be appealed in accordance with the Rules of Procedure and Evidence as follows:

(a) The Prosecutor may make an appeal on any of the following grounds:

(i) Procedural error,

  (ii) Error of fact, or

  (iii) Error of law;

 (b) The convicted person, or the Prosecutor on that person's behalf, may make an appeal on any of the following grounds:

  (i) Procedural error,

  (ii) Error of fact,

  (iii) Error of law, or

  (iv) Any other ground that affects the fairness or reliability of the proceedings or decision.

2. (a) A sentence may be appealed, in accordance with the Rules of Procedure and Evidence, by the Prosecutor or the convicted person on the ground of disproportion between the crime and the sentence;

 (b) If on an appeal against sentence the Court considers that there are grounds on which the conviction might be set aside, wholly or in part, it may invite the Prosecutor and the convicted person to submit grounds under article 81, paragraph 1 (a) or (b), and may render a decision on conviction in accordance with article 83;

 (c) The same procedure applies when the Court, on an appeal against conviction only, considers that there are grounds to reduce the sentence under paragraph 2 (a).

3. (a) Unless the Trial Chamber orders otherwise, a convicted person shall remain in custody pending an appeal;

 (b) When a convicted person's time in custody exceeds the sentence of imprisonment imposed, that person shall be released, except that if the Prosecutor is also appealing, the release may be subject to the conditions under subparagraph (c) below;

 (c) In case of an acquittal, the accused shall be released immediately, subject to the following:

  (i) Under exceptional circumstances, and having regard, inter alia, to the concrete risk of flight, the seriousness of the offence charged and the probability of success on appeal, the Trial Chamber, at the request of the Prosecutor, may maintain the detention of the person pending appeal;

  (ii) A decision by the Trial Chamber under subparagraph (c) (i) may be appealed in accordance with the Rules of Procedure and Evidence.

4. Subject to the provisions of paragraph 3 (a) and (b), execution of the decision or sentence shall be suspended during the period allowed for appeal and for the duration of the appeal proceedings.

Article 82
Appeal against other decisions

1. Either party may appeal any of the following decisions in accordance with the Rules of Procedure and Evidence:

 (a) A decision with respect to jurisdiction or admissibility;

 (b) A decision granting or denying release of the person being investigated or prosecuted;

 (c) A decision of the Pre-Trial Chamber to act on its own initiative under article 56, paragraph 3;

 (d) A decision that involves an issue that would significantly affect the fair and expeditious conduct of the proceedings or the outcome of the trial, and for which, in the opinion of the

Pre-Trial or Trial Chamber, an immediate resolution by the Appeals Chamber may materially advance the proceedings.

2.   A decision of the Pre-Trial Chamber under article 57, paragraph 3 (d), may be appealed against by the State concerned or by the Prosecutor, with the leave of the Pre-Trial Chamber. The appeal shall be heard on an expedited basis.

3.   An appeal shall not of itself have suspensive effect unless the Appeals Chamber so orders, upon request, in accordance with the Rules of Procedure and Evidence.

4.   A legal representative of the victims, the convicted person or a bona fide owner of property adversely affected by an order under article 75 may appeal against the order for reparations, as provided in the Rules of Procedure and Evidence.

Article 83
Proceedings on appeal

1.   For the purposes of proceedings under article 81 and this article, the Appeals Chamber shall have all the powers of the Trial Chamber.

2.   If the Appeals Chamber finds that the proceedings appealed from were unfair in a way that affected the reliability of the decision or sentence, or that the decision or sentence appealed from was materially affected by error of fact or law or procedural error, it may:

(a)   Reverse or amend the decision or sentence; or

(b)   Order a new trial before a different Trial Chamber.

For these purposes, the Appeals Chamber may remand a factual issue to the original Trial Chamber for it to determine the issue and to report back accordingly, or may itself call evidence to determine the issue. When the decision or sentence has been appealed only by the person convicted, or the Prosecutor on that person's behalf, it cannot be amended to his or her detriment.

3.   If in an appeal against sentence the Appeals Chamber finds that the sentence is disproportionate to the crime, it may vary the sentence in accordance with Part 7.

4.   The judgement of the Appeals Chamber shall be taken by a majority of the judges and shall be delivered in open court. The judgement shall state the reasons on which it is based. When there is no unanimity, the judgement of the Appeals Chamber shall contain the views of the majority and the minority, but a judge may deliver a separate or dissenting opinion on a question of law.

5.   The Appeals Chamber may deliver its judgement in the absence of the person acquitted or convicted.

Article 84
Revision of conviction or sentence

1.   The convicted person or, after death, spouses, children, parents or one person alive at the time of the accused's death who has been given express written instructions from the accused to bring such a claim, or the Prosecutor on the person's behalf, may apply to the Appeals Chamber to revise the final judgement of conviction or sentence on the grounds that:

(a)   New evidence has been discovered that:

(i)   Was not available at the time of trial, and such unavailability was not wholly or partially attributable to the party making application; and

(ii) Is sufficiently important that had it been proved at trial it would have been likely to have resulted in a different verdict;

(b) It has been newly discovered that decisive evidence, taken into account at trial and upon which the conviction depends, was false, forged or falsified;

(c) One or more of the judges who participated in conviction or confirmation of the charges has committed, in that case, an act of serious misconduct or serious breach of duty of sufficient gravity to justify the removal of that judge or those judges from office under article 46.

2.   The Appeals Chamber shall reject the application if it considers it to be unfounded. If it determines that the application is meritorious, it may, as appropriate:

(a) Reconvene the original Trial Chamber;

(b) Constitute a new Trial Chamber; or

(c) Retain jurisdiction over the matter,

with a view to, after hearing the parties in the manner set forth in the Rules of Procedure and Evidence, arriving at a determination on whether the judgement should be revised.

Article 85
Compensation to an arrested or convicted person

1.   Anyone who has been the victim of unlawful arrest or detention shall have an enforceable right to compensation.

2.   When a person has by a final decision been convicted of a criminal offence, and when subsequently his or her conviction has been reversed on the ground that a new or newly discovered fact shows conclusively that there has been a miscarriage of justice, the person who has suffered punishment as a result of such conviction shall be compensated according to law, unless it is proved that the non-disclosure of the unknown fact in time is wholly or partly attributable to him or her.

3.   In exceptional circumstances, where the Court finds conclusive facts showing that there has been a grave and manifest miscarriage of justice, it may in its discretion award compensation, according to the criteria provided in the Rules of Procedure and Evidence, to a person who has been released from detention following a final decision of acquittal or a termination of the proceedings for that reason.

PART 9. INTERNATIONAL COOPERATION AND JUDICIAL ASSISTANCE
Article 86
General obligation to cooperate

States Parties shall, in accordance with the provisions of this Statute, cooperate fully with the Court in its investigation and prosecution of crimes within the jurisdiction of the Court.

Article 87
Requests for cooperation: general provisions

1.   (a) The Court shall have the authority to make requests to States Parties for cooperation. The requests shall be transmitted through the diplomatic channel or any other appropriate channel as may be designated by each State Party upon ratification, acceptance, approval or accession.

Subsequent changes to the designation shall be made by each State Party in accordance with the Rules of Procedure and Evidence.

(b) When appropriate, without prejudice to the provisions of subparagraph (a), requests may also be transmitted through the International Criminal Police Organization or any appropriate regional organization.

2. Requests for cooperation and any documents supporting the request shall either be in or be accompanied by a translation into an official language of the requested State or in one of the working languages of the Court, in accordance with the choice made by that State upon ratification, acceptance, approval or accession.

Subsequent changes to this choice shall be made in accordance with the Rules of Procedure and Evidence.

3. The requested State shall keep confidential a request for cooperation and any documents supporting the request, except to the extent that the disclosure is necessary for execution of the request.

4. In relation to any request for assistance presented under Part 9, the Court may take such measures, including measures related to the protection of information, as may be necessary to ensure the safety or physical or psychological well-being of any victims, potential witnesses and their families. The Court may request that any information that is made available under Part 9 shall be provided and handled in a manner that protects the safety and physical or psychological well-being of any victims, potential witnesses and their families.

5. (a) The Court may invite any State not party to this Statute to provide assistance under this Part on the basis of an ad hoc arrangement, an agreement with such State or any other appropriate basis.

(b) Where a State not party to this Statute, which has entered into an ad hoc arrangement or an agreement with the Court, fails to cooperate with requests pursuant to any such arrangement or agreement, the Court may so inform the Assembly of States Parties or, where the Security Council referred the matter to the Court, the Security Council.

6. The Court may ask any intergovernmental organization to provide information or documents. The Court may also ask for other forms of cooperation and assistance which may be agreed upon with such an organization and which are in accordance with its competence or mandate.

7. Where a State Party fails to comply with a request to cooperate by the Court contrary to the provisions of this Statute, thereby preventing the Court from exercising its functions and powers under this Statute, the Court may make a finding to that effect and refer the matter to the Assembly of States Parties or, where the Security Council referred the matter to the Court, to the Security Council.

Article 88
Availability of procedures under national law

States Parties shall ensure that there are procedures available under their national law for all of the forms of cooperation which are specified under this Part.

Article 89
Surrender of persons to the Court

1.   The Court may transmit a request for the arrest and surrender of a person, together with the material supporting the request outlined in article 91, to any State on the territory of which that person may be found and shall request the cooperation of that State in the arrest and surrender of such a person. States Parties shall, in accordance with the provisions of this Part and the procedure under their national law, comply with requests for arrest and surrender.

2.   Where the person sought for surrender brings a challenge before a national court on the basis of the principle of ne bis in idem as provided in article 20, the requested State shall immediately consult with the Court to determine if there has been a relevant ruling on admissibility. If the case is admissible, the requested State shall proceed with the execution of the request. If an admissibility ruling is pending, the requested State may postpone the execution of the request for surrender of the person until the Court makes a determination on admissibility.

3.   (a) A State Party shall authorize, in accordance with its national procedural law, transportation through its territory of a person being surrendered to the Court by another State, except where transit through that State would impede or delay the surrender.

    (b) A request by the Court for transit shall be transmitted in accordance with article 87. The request for transit shall contain:

        (i) A description of the person being transported;

        (ii) A brief statement of the facts of the case and their legal characterization; and

        (iii) The warrant for arrest and surrender;

    (c) A person being transported shall be detained in custody during the period of transit;

    (d) No authorization is required if the person is transported by air and no landing is scheduled on the territory of the transit State;

    (e) If an unscheduled landing occurs on the territory of the transit State, that State may require a request for transit from the Court as provided for in subparagraph (b). The transit State shall detain the person being transported until the request for transit is received and the transit is effected, provided that detention for purposes of this subparagraph may not be extended beyond 96 hours from the unscheduled landing unless the request is received within that time.

4.   If the person sought is being proceeded against or is serving a sentence in the requested State for a crime different from that for which surrender to the Court is sought, the requested State, after making its decision to grant the request, shall consult with the Court.

Article 90
Competing requests

1.   A State Party which receives a request from the Court for the surrender of a person under article 89 shall, if it also receives a request from any other State for the extradition of the same person for the same conduct which forms the basis of the crime for which the Court seeks the person's surrender, notify the Court and the requesting State of that fact.

2.   Where the requesting State is a State Party, the requested State shall give priority to the request from the Court if:

    (a) The Court has, pursuant to articles 18 and 19, made a determination that the case in respect of which surrender is sought is admissible and that determination takes into account the investigation or prosecution conducted by the requesting State in respect of its request for extradition; or

(b) The Court makes the determination described in subparagraph (a) pursuant to the requested State's notification under paragraph 1.

3.   Where a determination under paragraph 2 (a) has not been made, the requested State may, at its discretion, pending the determination of the Court under paragraph 2 (b), proceed to deal with the request for extradition from the requesting State but shall not extradite the person until the Court has determined that the case is inadmissible. The Court's determination shall be made on an expedited basis.

4.   If the requesting State is a State not Party to this Statute the requested State, if it is not under an international obligation to extradite the person to the requesting State, shall give priority to the request for surrender from the Court, if the Court has determined that the case is admissible.

5.   Where a case under paragraph 4 has not been determined to be admissible by the Court, the requested State may, at its discretion, proceed to deal with the request for extradition from the requesting State.

6.   In cases where paragraph 4 applies except that the requested State is under an existing international obligation to extradite the person to the requesting State not Party to this Statute, the requested State shall determine whether to surrender the person to the Court or extradite the person to the requesting State. In making its decision, the requested State shall consider all the relevant factors, including but not limited to:

(a) The respective dates of the requests;

(b) The interests of the requesting State including, where relevant, whether the crime was committed in its territory and the nationality of the victims and of the person sought; and

(c) The possibility of subsequent surrender between the Court and the requesting State.

7.   Where a State Party which receives a request from the Court for the surrender of a person also receives a request from any State for the extradition of the same person for conduct other than that which constitutes the crime for which the Court seeks the person's surrender:

(a) The requested State shall, if it is not under an existing international obligation to extradite the person to the requesting State, give priority to the request from the Court;

(b) The requested State shall, if it is under an existing international obligation to extradite the person to the requesting State, determine whether to surrender the person to the Court or to extradite the person to the requesting State. In making its decision, the requested State shall consider all the relevant factors, including but not limited to those set out in paragraph 6, but shall give special consideration to the relative nature and gravity of the conduct in question.

8.   Where pursuant to a notification under this article, the Court has determined a case to be inadmissible, and subsequently extradition to the requesting State is refused, the requested State shall notify the Court of this decision.

Article 91
Contents of request for arrest and surrender

1.   A request for arrest and surrender shall be made in writing. In urgent cases, a request may be made by any medium capable of delivering a written record, provided that the request shall be confirmed through the channel provided for in article 87, paragraph 1 (a).

2.   In the case of a request for the arrest and surrender of a person for whom a warrant of arrest has been issued by the Pre-Trial Chamber under article 58, the request shall contain or be supported by:

(a) Information describing the person sought, sufficient to identify the person, and information as to that person's probable location;

(b) A copy of the warrant of arrest; and

(c) Such documents, statements or information as may be necessary to meet the requirements for the surrender process in the requested State, except that those requirements should not be more burdensome than those applicable to requests for extradition pursuant to treaties or arrangements between the requested State and other States and should, if possible, be less burdensome, taking into account the distinct nature of the Court.

3.   In the case of a request for the arrest and surrender of a person already convicted, the request shall contain or be supported by:

(a) A copy of any warrant of arrest for that person;

(b) A copy of the judgement of conviction;

(c) Information to demonstrate that the person sought is the one referred to in the judgement of conviction; and

(d) If the person sought has been sentenced, a copy of the sentence imposed and, in the case of a sentence for imprisonment, a statement of any time already served and the time remaining to be served.

4.   Upon the request of the Court, a State Party shall consult with the Court, either generally or with respect to a specific matter, regarding any requirements under its national law that may apply under paragraph 2 (c). During the consultations, the State Party shall advise the Court of the specific requirements of its national law.

Article 92
Provisional arrest

1.   In urgent cases, the Court may request the provisional arrest of the person sought, pending presentation of the request for surrender and the documents supporting the request as specified in article 91.

2.   The request for provisional arrest shall be made by any medium capable of delivering a written record and shall contain:

(a) Information describing the person sought, sufficient to identify the person, and information as to that person's probable location;

(b) A concise statement of the crimes for which the person's arrest is sought and of the facts which are alleged to constitute those crimes, including, where possible, the date and location of the crime;

(c) A statement of the existence of a warrant of arrest or a judgement of conviction against the person sought; and

(d) A statement that a request for surrender of the person sought will follow.

3.   A person who is provisionally arrested may be released from custody if the requested State has not received the request for surrender and the documents supporting the request as specified in article 91 within the time limits specified in the Rules of Procedure and Evidence. However, the person may consent to surrender before the expiration of this period if permitted by the law of the requested State. In such a case, the requested State shall proceed to surrender the person to the Court as soon as possible.

4. The fact that the person sought has been released from custody pursuant to paragraph 3 shall not prejudice the subsequent arrest and surrender of that person if the request for surrender and the documents supporting the request are delivered at a later date.

Article 93
Other forms of cooperation

1. States Parties shall, in accordance with the provisions of this Part and under procedures of national law, comply with requests by the Court to provide the following assistance in relation to investigations or prosecutions:

    (a) The identification and whereabouts of persons or the location of items;

    (b) The taking of evidence, including testimony under oath, and the production of evidence, including expert opinions and reports necessary to the Court;

    (c) The questioning of any person being investigated or prosecuted;

    (d) The service of documents, including judicial documents;

    (e) Facilitating the voluntary appearance of persons as witnesses or experts before the Court;

    (f) The temporary transfer of persons as provided in paragraph 7;

    (g) The examination of places or sites, including the exhumation and examination of grave sites;

    (h) The execution of searches and seizures;

    (i) The provision of records and documents, including official records and documents;

    (j) The protection of victims and witnesses and the preservation of evidence;

    (k) The identification, tracing and freezing or seizure of proceeds, property and assets and instrumentalities of crimes for the purpose of eventual forfeiture, without prejudice to the rights of bona fide third parties; and

    (l) Any other type of assistance which is not prohibited by the law of the requested State, with a view to facilitating the investigation and prosecution of crimes within the jurisdiction of the Court.

2. The Court shall have the authority to provide an assurance to a witness or an expert appearing before the Court that he or she will not be prosecuted, detained or subjected to any restriction of personal freedom by the Court in respect of any act or omission that preceded the departure of that person from the requested State.

3. Where execution of a particular measure of assistance detailed in a request presented under paragraph 1, is prohibited in the requested State on the basis of an existing fundamental legal principle of general application, the requested State shall promptly consult with the Court to try to resolve the matter. In the consultations, consideration should be given to whether the assistance can be rendered in another manner or subject to conditions. If after consultations the matter cannot be resolved, the Court shall modify the request as necessary.

4. In accordance with article 72, a State Party may deny a request for assistance, in whole or in part, only if the request concerns the production of any documents or disclosure of evidence which relates to its national security.

5. Before denying a request for assistance under paragraph 1 (l), the requested State shall consider whether the assistance can be provided subject to specified conditions, or whether the assistance can be provided at a later date or in an alternative manner, provided that if the Court

or the Prosecutor accepts the assistance subject to conditions, the Court or the Prosecutor shall abide by them.

6.   If a request for assistance is denied, the requested State Party shall promptly inform the Court or the Prosecutor of the reasons for such denial.

7.   (a) The Court may request the temporary transfer of a person in custody for purposes of identification or for obtaining testimony or other assistance. The person may be transferred if the following conditions are fulfilled:

   (i)   The person freely gives his or her informed consent to the transfer; and

   (ii) The requested State agrees to the transfer, subject to such conditions as that State and the Court may agree.

   (b) The person being transferred shall remain in custody. When the purposes of the transfer have been fulfilled, the Court shall return the person without delay to the requested State.

8.   (a) The Court shall ensure the confidentiality of documents and information, except as required for the investigation and proceedings described in the request.

   (b) The requested State may, when necessary, transmit documents or information to the Prosecutor on a confidential basis. The Prosecutor may then use them solely for the purpose of generating new evidence.

   (c) The requested State may, on its own motion or at the request of the Prosecutor, subsequently consent to the disclosure of such documents or information. They may then be used as evidence pursuant to the provisions of Parts 5 and 6 and in accordance with the Rules of Procedure and Evidence.

9.   (a) (i) In the event that a State Party receives competing requests, other than for surrender or extradition, from the Court and from another State pursuant to an international obligation, the State Party shall endeavour, in consultation with the Court and the other State, to meet both requests, if necessary by postponing or attaching conditions to one or the other request.

   (ii) Failing that, competing requests shall be resolved in accordance with the principles established in article 90.

   (b) Where, however, the request from the Court concerns information, property or persons which are subject to the control of a third State or an international organization by virtue of an international agreement, the requested States shall so inform the Court and the Court shall direct its request to the third State or international organization.

10. (a) The Court may, upon request, cooperate with and provide assistance to a State Party conducting an investigation into or trial in respect of conduct which constitutes a crime within the jurisdiction of the Court or which constitutes a serious crime under the national law of the requesting State.

   (b) (i) The assistance provided under subparagraph (a) shall include, inter alia:

   (a) The transmission of statements, documents or other types of evidence obtained in the course of an investigation or a trial conducted by the Court; and

   (b) The questioning of any person detained by order of the Court;

   (ii) In the case of assistance under subparagraph (b) (i) (a):

   (a) If the documents or other types of evidence have been obtained with the assistance of a State, such transmission shall require the consent of that State;

   (b) If the statements, documents or other types of evidence have been provided by a witness or expert, such transmission shall be subject to the provisions of article 68.

(c) The Court may, under the conditions set out in this paragraph, grant a request for assistance under this paragraph from a State which is not a Party to this Statute.

Article 94
Postponement of execution of a request in respect
of ongoing investigation or prosecution

1. If the immediate execution of a request would interfere with an ongoing investigation or prosecution of a case different from that to which the request relates, the requested State may postpone the execution of the request for a period of time agreed upon with the Court. However, the postponement shall be no longer than is necessary to complete the relevant investigation or prosecution in the requested State. Before making a decision to postpone, the requested State should consider whether the assistance may be immediately provided subject to certain conditions.
2. If a decision to postpone is taken pursuant to paragraph 1, the Prosecutor may, however, seek measures to preserve evidence, pursuant to article 93, paragraph 1 (j).

Article 95
Postponement of execution of a request in
respect of an admissibility challenge

Without prejudice to article 53, paragraph 2, where there is an admissibility challenge under consideration by the Court pursuant to articles 18 or 19, the requested State may postpone the execution of a request under this Part pending a determination by the Court, unless the Court has specifically ordered that the Prosecutor may pursue the collection of such evidence pursuant to article 18 or 19.

Article 96
Contents of request for other forms of
assistance under article 93

1. A request for other forms of assistance referred to in article 93 shall be made in writing. In urgent cases, a request may be made by any medium capable of delivering a written record, provided that the request shall be confirmed through the channel provided for in article 87, paragraph 1 (a).
2. The request shall, as applicable, contain or be supported by the following:

(a) A concise statement of the purpose of the request and the assistance sought, including the legal basis and the grounds for the request;

(b) As much detailed information as possible about the location or identification of any person or place that must be found or identified in order for the assistance sought to be provided;

(c) A concise statement of the essential facts underlying the request;

(d) The reasons for and details of any procedure or requirement to be followed;

(e) Such information as may be required under the law of the requested State in order to execute the request; and

(f) Any other information relevant in order for the assistance sought to be provided.

3. Upon the request of the Court, a State Party shall consult with the Court, either generally or with respect to a specific matter, regarding any requirements under its national law that may

apply under paragraph 2 (e). During the consultations, the State Party shall advise the Court of the specific requirements of its national law.

4.   The provisions of this article shall, where applicable, also apply in respect of a request for assistance made to the Court.

Article 97
Consultations

Where a State Party receives a request under this Part in relation to which it identifies problems which may impede or prevent the execution of the request, that State shall consult with the Court without delay in order to resolve the matter. Such problems may include, inter alia:

(a) Insufficient information to execute the request;

(b) In the case of a request for surrender, the fact that despite best efforts, the person sought cannot be located or that the investigation conducted has determined that the person in the requested State is clearly not the person named in the warrant; or

(c) The fact that execution of the request in its current form would require the requested State to breach a pre-existing treaty obligation undertaken with respect to another State.

Article 98
Cooperation with respect to waiver of immunity
and consent to surrender

1.   The Court may not proceed with a request for surrender or assistance which would require the requested State to act inconsistently with its obligations under international law with respect to the State or diplomatic immunity of a person or property of a third State, unless the Court can first obtain the cooperation of that third State for the waiver of the immunity.

2.   The Court may not proceed with a request for surrender which would require the requested State to act inconsistently with its obligations under international agreements pursuant to which the consent of a sending State is required to surrender a person of that State to the Court, unless the Court can first obtain the cooperation of the sending State for the giving of consent for the surrender.

Article 99
Execution of requests under articles 93 and 96

1.   Requests for assistance shall be executed in accordance with the relevant procedure under the law of the requested State and, unless prohibited by such law, in the manner specified in the request, including following any procedure outlined therein or permitting persons specified in the request to be present at and assist in the execution process.

2.   In the case of an urgent request, the documents or evidence produced in response shall, at the request of the Court, be sent urgently.

3.   Replies from the requested State shall be transmitted in their original language and form.

4.   Without prejudice to other articles in this Part, where it is necessary for the successful execution of a request which can be executed without any compulsory measures, including specifically the interview of or taking evidence from a person on a voluntary basis, including doing so without the presence of the authorities of the requested State Party if it is essential for the request to be executed, and the examination without modification of a public site or other

public place, the Prosecutor may execute such request directly on the territory of a State as follows:

(a)   When the State Party requested is a State on the territory of which the crime is alleged to have been committed, and there has been a determination of admissibility pursuant to article 18 or 19, the Prosecutor may directly execute such request following all possible consultations with the requested State Party;

(b)   In other cases, the Prosecutor may execute such request following consultations with the requested State Party and subject to any reasonable conditions or concerns raised by that State Party. Where the requested State Party identifies problems with the execution of a request pursuant to this subparagraph it shall, without delay, consult with the Court to resolve the matter.

5.   Provisions allowing a person heard or examined by the Court under article 72 to invoke restrictions designed to prevent disclosure of confidential information connected with national defence or security shall also apply to the execution of requests for assistance under this article.

Article 100
Costs

1.   The ordinary costs for execution of requests in the territory of the requested State shall be borne by that State, except for the following, which shall be borne by the Court:

(a)   Costs associated with the travel and security of witnesses and experts or the transfer under article 93 of persons in custody;

(b)   Costs of translation, interpretation and transcription;

(c)   Travel and subsistence costs of the judges, the Prosecutor, the Deputy Prosecutors, the Registrar, the Deputy Registrar and staff of any organ of the Court;

(d)   Costs of any expert opinion or report requested by the Court;

(e)   Costs associated with the transport of a person being surrendered to the Court by a custodial State; and

(f)   Following consultations, any extraordinary costs that may result from the execution of a request.

2.   The provisions of paragraph 1 shall, as appropriate, apply to requests from States Parties to the Court. In that case, the Court shall bear the ordinary costs of execution.

Article 101
Rule of speciality

1.   A person surrendered to the Court under this Statute shall not be proceeded against, punished or detained for any conduct committed prior to surrender, other than the conduct or course of conduct which forms the basis of the crimes for which that person has been surrendered.

2.   The Court may request a waiver of the requirements of paragraph 1 from the State which surrendered the person to the Court and, if necessary, the Court shall provide additional information in accordance with article 91. States Parties shall have the authority to provide a waiver to the Court and should endeavour to do so.

Article 102
Use of terms

For the purposes of this Statute:

(a) "surrender" means the delivering up of a person by a State to the Court, pursuant to this Statute.

(b) "extradition" means the delivering up of a person by one State to another as provided by treaty, convention or national legislation.

PART 10. ENFORCEMENT
Article 103
Role of States in enforcement of
sentences of imprisonment

1.   (a) A sentence of imprisonment shall be served in a State designated by the Court from a list of States which have indicated to the Court their willingness to accept sentenced persons.

(b) At the time of declaring its willingness to accept sentenced persons, a State may attach conditions to its acceptance as agreed by the Court and in accordance with this Part.

(c) A State designated in a particular case shall promptly inform the Court whether it accepts the Court's designation.

2.   (a) The State of enforcement shall notify the Court of any circumstances, including the exercise of any conditions agreed under paragraph 1, which could materially affect the terms or extent of the imprisonment. The Court shall be given at least 45 days' notice of any such known or foreseeable circumstances. During this period, the State of enforcement shall take no action that might prejudice its obligations under article 110.

(b) Where the Court cannot agree to the circumstances referred to in subparagraph (a), it shall notify the State of enforcement and proceed in accordance with article 104, paragraph 1.

3.   In exercising its discretion to make a designation under paragraph 1, the Court shall take into account the following:

(a) The principle that States Parties should share the responsibility for enforcing sentences of imprisonment, in accordance with principles of equitable distribution, as provided in the Rules of Procedure and Evidence;

(b) The application of widely accepted international treaty standards governing the treatment of prisoners;

(c) The views of the sentenced person;

(d) The nationality of the sentenced person;

(e) Such other factors regarding the circumstances of the crime or the person sentenced, or the effective enforcement of the sentence, as may be appropriate in designating the State of enforcement.

4.   If no State is designated under paragraph 1, the sentence of imprisonment shall be served in a prison facility made available by the host State, in accordance with the conditions set out in the headquarters agreement referred to in article 3, paragraph 2. In such a case, the costs arising out of the enforcement of a sentence of imprisonment shall be borne by the Court.

Article 104
Change in designation of State of enforcement

1. The Court may, at any time, decide to transfer a sentenced person to a prison of another State.

2. A sentenced person may, at any time, apply to the Court to be transferred from the State of enforcement.

Article 105
Enforcement of the sentence

1. Subject to conditions which a State may have specified in accordance with article 103, paragraph 1 (b), the sentence of imprisonment shall be binding on the States Parties, which shall in no case modify it.

2. The Court alone shall have the right to decide any application for appeal and revision. The State of enforcement shall not impede the making of any such application by a sentenced person.

Article 106
Supervision of enforcement of sentences and conditions of imprisonment

1. The enforcement of a sentence of imprisonment shall be subject to the supervision of the Court and shall be consistent with widely accepted international treaty standards governing treatment of prisoners.

2. The conditions of imprisonment shall be governed by the law of the State of enforcement and shall be consistent with widely accepted international treaty standards governing treatment of prisoners; in no case shall such conditions be more or less favourable than those available to prisoners convicted of similar offences in the State of enforcement.

3. Communications between a sentenced person and the Court shall be unimpeded and confidential.

Article 107
Transfer of the person upon completion of sentence

1. Following completion of the sentence, a person who is not a national of the State of enforcement may, in accordance with the law of the State of enforcement, be transferred to a State which is obliged to receive him or her, or to another State which agrees to receive him or her, taking into account any wishes of the person to be transferred to that State, unless the State of enforcement authorizes the person to remain in its territory.

2. If no State bears the costs arising out of transferring the person to another State pursuant to paragraph 1, such costs shall be borne by the Court.

3. Subject to the provisions of article 108, the State of enforcement may also, in accordance with its national law, extradite or otherwise surrender the person to the State which has requested the extradition or surrender of the person for purposes of trial or enforcement of a sentence.

Article 108
Limitation on the prosecution or punishment of other offences

1. A sentenced person in the custody of the State of enforcement shall not be subject to prosecution or punishment or to extradition to a third State for any conduct engaged in prior to

that person's delivery to the State of enforcement, unless such prosecution, punishment or extradition has been approved by the Court at the request of the State of enforcement.

2.   The Court shall decide the matter after having heard the views of the sentenced person.

3.   Paragraph 1 shall cease to apply if the sentenced person remains voluntarily for more than 30 days in the territory of the State of enforcement after having served the full sentence imposed by the Court, or returns to the territory of that State after having left it.

Article 109
Enforcement of fines and forfeiture measures

1.   States Parties shall give effect to fines or forfeitures ordered by the Court under Part 7, without prejudice to the rights of bona fide third parties, and in accordance with the procedure of their national law.

2.   If a State Party is unable to give effect to an order for forfeiture, it shall take measures to recover the value of the proceeds, property or assets ordered by the Court to be forfeited, without prejudice to the rights of bona fide third parties.

3.   Property, or the proceeds of the sale of real property or, where appropriate, the sale of other property, which is obtained by a State Party as a result of its enforcement of a judgement of the Court shall be transferred to the Court.

Article 110
Review by the Court concerning reduction of sentence

1.   The State of enforcement shall not release the person before expiry of the sentence pronounced by the Court.

2.   The Court alone shall have the right to decide any reduction of sentence, and shall rule on the matter after having heard the person.

3.   When the person has served two thirds of the sentence, or 25 years in the case of life imprisonment, the Court shall review the sentence to determine whether it should be reduced. Such a review shall not be conducted before that time.

4.   In its review under paragraph 3, the Court may reduce the sentence if it finds that one or more of the following factors are present:

   (a) The early and continuing willingness of the person to cooperate with the Court in its investigations and prosecutions;

   (b) The voluntary assistance of the person in enabling the enforcement of the judgements and orders of the Court in other cases, and in particular providing assistance in locating assets subject to orders of fine, forfeiture or reparation which may be used for the benefit of victims; or

   (c) Other factors establishing a clear and significant change of circumstances sufficient to justify the reduction of sentence, as provided in the Rules of Procedure and Evidence.

5.   If the Court determines in its initial review under paragraph 3 that it is not appropriate to reduce the sentence, it shall thereafter review the question of reduction of sentence at such intervals and applying such criteria as provided for in the Rules of Procedure and Evidence.

Article 111
Escape

If a convicted person escapes from custody and flees the State of enforcement, that State may, after consultation with the Court, request the person's surrender from the State in which the person is located pursuant to existing bilateral or multilateral arrangements, or may request that the Court seek the person's surrender. It may direct that the person be delivered to the State in which he or she was serving the sentence or to another State designated by the Court.

PART 11. ASSEMBLY OF STATES PARTIES
Article 112
Assembly of States Parties

1.   An Assembly of States Parties to this Statute is hereby established. Each State Party shall have one representative in the Assembly who may be accompanied by alternates and advisers. Other States which have signed this Statute or the Final Act may be observers in the Assembly.

2.   The Assembly shall:

(a) Consider and adopt, as appropriate, recommendations of the Preparatory Commission;

(b) Provide management oversight to the Presidency, the Prosecutor and the Registrar regarding the administration of the Court;

(c) Consider the reports and activities of the Bureau established under paragraph 3 and take appropriate action in regard thereto;

(d) Consider and decide the budget for the Court;

(e) Decide whether to alter, in accordance with article 37, the number of judges;

(f) Consider pursuant to article 87, paragraphs 5 and 7, any question relating to non-cooperation;

(g) Perform any other function consistent with this Statute or the Rules of Procedure and Evidence.

3.   (a) The Assembly shall have a Bureau consisting of a President, two Vice-Presidents and 18 members elected by the Assembly for three-year terms.

(b) The Bureau shall have a representative character, taking into account, in particular, equitable geographical distribution and the adequate representation of the principal legal systems of the world.

(c) The Bureau shall meet as often as necessary, but at least once a year. It shall assist the Assembly in the discharge of its responsibilities.

4.   The Assembly may establish such subsidiary bodies as may be necessary, including an independent oversight mechanism for inspection, evaluation and investigation of the Court, in order to enhance its efficiency and economy.

5.   The President of the Court, the Prosecutor and the Registrar or their representatives may participate, as appropriate, in meetings of the Assembly and of the Bureau.

6.   The Assembly shall meet at the seat of the Court or at the Headquarters of the United Nations once a year and, when circumstances so require, hold special sessions. Except as otherwise specified in this Statute, special sessions shall be convened by the Bureau on its own initiative or at the request of one third of the States Parties.

7.   Each State Party shall have one vote. Every effort shall be made to reach decisions by consensus in the Assembly and in the Bureau. If consensus cannot be reached, except as otherwise provided in the Statute:

(a) Decisions on matters of substance must be approved by a two-thirds majority of those present and voting provided that an absolute majority of States Parties constitutes the quorum for voting;

(b) Decisions on matters of procedure shall be taken by a simple majority of States Parties present and voting.

8.   A State Party which is in arrears in the payment of its financial contributions towards the costs of the Court shall have no vote in the Assembly and in the Bureau if the amount of its arrears equals or exceeds the amount of the contributions due from it for the preceding two full years. The Assembly may, nevertheless, permit such a State Party to vote in the Assembly and in the Bureau if it is satisfied that the failure to pay is due to conditions beyond the control of the State Party.

9.   The Assembly shall adopt its own rules of procedure.

10. The official and working languages of the Assembly shall be those of the General Assembly of the United Nations.

PART 12. FINANCING
Article 113
Financial Regulations

Except as otherwise specifically provided, all financial matters related to the Court and the meetings of the Assembly of States Parties, including its Bureau and subsidiary bodies, shall be governed by this Statute and the Financial Regulations and Rules adopted by the Assembly of States Parties.

Article 114
Payment of expenses

Expenses of the Court and the Assembly of States Parties, including its Bureau and subsidiary bodies, shall be paid from the funds of the Court.

Article 115
Funds of the Court and of the Assembly of States Parties

The expenses of the Court and the Assembly of States Parties, including its Bureau and subsidiary bodies, as provided for in the budget decided by the Assembly of States Parties, shall be provided by the following sources:

(a) Assessed contributions made by States Parties;

(b) Funds provided by the United Nations, subject to the approval of the General Assembly, in particular in relation to the expenses incurred due to referrals by the Security Council.

Article 116
Voluntary contributions

Without prejudice to article 115, the Court may receive and utilize, as additional funds, voluntary contributions from Governments, international organizations, individuals, corporations and other entities, in accordance with relevant criteria adopted by the Assembly of States Parties.

Article 117
Assessment of contributions

The contributions of States Parties shall be assessed in accordance with an agreed scale of assessment, based on the scale adopted by the United Nations for its regular budget and adjusted in accordance with the principles on which that scale is based.

Article 118
Annual audit

The records, books and accounts of the Court, including its annual financial statements, shall be audited annually by an independent auditor.

PART 13. FINAL CLAUSES
Article 119
Settlement of disputes

1.   Any dispute concerning the judicial functions of the Court shall be settled by the decision of the Court.

2.   Any other dispute between two or more States Parties relating to the interpretation or application of this Statute which is not settled through negotiations within three months of their commencement shall be referred to the Assembly of States Parties. The Assembly may itself seek to settle the dispute or may make recommendations on further means of settlement of the dispute, including referral to the International Court of Justice in conformity with the Statute of that Court.

Article 120
Reservations

No reservations may be made to this Statute.

Article 121
Amendments

1.   After the expiry of seven years from the entry into force of this Statute, any State Party may propose amendments thereto. The text of any proposed amendment shall be submitted to the Secretary-General of the United Nations, who shall promptly circulate it to all States Parties.

2.   No sooner than three months from the date of notification, the next Assembly of States Parties shall, by a majority of those present and voting, decide whether to take up the proposal. The Assembly may deal with the proposal directly or convene a Review Conference if the issue involved so warrants.

3.   The adoption of an amendment at a meeting of the Assembly of States Parties or at a Review Conference on which consensus cannot be reached shall require a two-thirds majority of States Parties.

4.   Except as provided in paragraph 5, an amendment shall enter into force for all States Parties one year after instruments of ratification or acceptance have been deposited with the Secretary-General of the United Nations by seven-eighths of them.

5.   Any amendment to article 5, 6, 7 and 8 of this Statute shall enter into force for those States Parties which have accepted the amendment one year after the deposit of their instruments of ratification or acceptance. In respect of a State Party which has not accepted the amendment, the

Court shall not exercise its jurisdiction regarding a crime covered by the amendment when committed by that State Party's nationals or on its territory.

6.   If an amendment has been accepted by seven-eighths of States Parties in accordance with paragraph 4, any State Party which has not accepted the amendment may withdraw from this Statute with immediate effect, notwithstanding article 127, paragraph 1, but subject to paragraph article 127, paragraph 2 by giving notice no later than one year after the entry into force of such amendment.

7.   The Secretary-General of the United Nations shall circulate to all States Parties any amendment adopted at a meeting of the Assembly of States Parties or at a Review Conference.

Article 122
Amendments to provisions of an institutional nature

1.   Amendments to provisions of this Statute which are of an exclusively institutional nature, namely, article 35, article 36, paragraphs 8 and 9, article 37, article 38, article 39, paragraphs 1 (first two sentences), 2 and 4, article 42, paragraphs 4 to 9, article 43, paragraphs 2 and 3, and articles 44, 46, 47 and 49, may be proposed at any time, notwithstanding article 121, paragraph 1, by any State Party. The text of any proposed amendment shall be submitted to the Secretary-General of the United Nations or such other person designated by the Assembly of States Parties who shall promptly circulate it to all States Parties and to others participating in the Assembly.

2.   Amendments under this article on which consensus cannot be reached shall be adopted by the Assembly of States Parties or by a Review Conference, by a two-thirds majority of States Parties. Such amendments shall enter into force for all States Parties six months after their adoption by the Assembly or, as the case may be, by the Conference.

Article 123
Review of the Statute

1.   Seven years after the entry into force of this Statute the Secretary-General of the United Nations shall convene a Review Conference to consider any amendments to this Statute. Such review may include, but is not limited to, the list of crimes contained in article 5. The Conference shall be open to those participating in the Assembly of States Parties and on the same conditions.

2.   At any time thereafter, at the request of a State Party and for the purposes set out in paragraph 1, the Secretary-General of the United Nations shall, upon approval by a majority of States Parties, convene a Review Conference.

3.   The provisions of article 121, paragraphs 3 to 7, shall apply to the adoption and entry into force of any amendment to the Statute considered at a Review Conference.

Article 124
Transitional Provision

Notwithstanding article 12, paragraph 1 and 2, a State, on becoming a party to this Statute, may declare that, for a period of seven years after the entry into force of this Statute for the State concerned, it does not accept the jurisdiction of the Court with respect to the category of crimes referred to in article 8 when a crime is alleged to have been committed by its nationals or on its territory. A declaration under this article may be withdrawn at any time. The provisions of this article shall be reviewed at the Review Conference convened in accordance with article 123, paragraph 1.

Article 125
Signature, ratification, acceptance, approval or accession

1.   This Statute shall be open for signature by all States in Rome, at the headquarters of the Food and Agriculture Organization of the United Nations, on 17 July 1998. Thereafter, it shall remain open for signature in Rome at the Ministry of Foreign Affairs of Italy until 17 October 1998. After that date, the Statute shall remain open for signature in New York, at United Nations Headquarters, until 31 December 2000.
2.   This Statute is subject to ratification, acceptance or approval by signatory States. Instruments of ratification, acceptance or approval shall be deposited with the Secretary-General of the United Nations.
3.   This Statute shall be open to accession by all States. Instruments of accession shall be deposited with the Secretary-General of the United Nations.

Article 126
Entry into force

1.   This Statute shall enter into force on the first day of the month after the 60th day following the date of the deposit of the 60th instrument of ratification, acceptance, approval or accession with the Secretary-General of the United Nations.
2.   For each State ratifying, accepting, approving or acceding to this Statute after the deposit of the 60th instrument of ratification, acceptance, approval or accession, the Statute shall enter into force on the first day of the month after the 60th day following the deposit by such State of its instrument of ratification, acceptance, approval or accession.

Article 127
Withdrawal

1.   A State Party may, by written notification addressed to the Secretary-General of the United Nations, withdraw from this Statute. The withdrawal shall take effect one year after the date of receipt of the notification, unless the notification specifies a later date.
2.   A State shall not be discharged, by reason of its withdrawal, from the obligations arising from this Statute while it was a Party to the Statute, including any financial obligations which may have accrued. Its withdrawal shall not affect any cooperation with the Court in connection with criminal investigations and proceedings in relation to which the withdrawing State had a duty to cooperate and which were commenced prior to the date on which the withdrawal became effective, nor shall it prejudice in any way the continued consideration of any matter which was already under consideration by the Court prior to the date on which the withdrawal became effective.

Article 128
Authentic texts

The original of this Statute, of which the Arabic, Chinese, English, French, Russian and Spanish texts are equally authentic, shall be deposited with the Secretary-General of the United Nations, who shall send certified copies thereof to all States.

IN WITNESS WHEREOF, the undersigned, being duly authorized thereto by their respective Governments, have signed this Statute.

DONE at Rome, this 17th day of July 1998.

Addendum

FINAL ACT OF THE UNITED NATIONS DIPLOMATIC CONFERENCE OF PLENIPOTENTIARIES ON THE ESTABLISHMENT OF AN INTERNATIONAL CRIMINAL COURT

1.   The General Assembly of the United Nations, in its resolution 51/207 of 17 December 1996, decided to hold a diplomatic conference of plenipotentiaries in 1998 with a view to finalizing and adopting a convention on the establishment of an international criminal court.

2.   The General Assembly, in its resolution 52/160 of 15 December 1997, accepted with deep appreciation the generous offer of the Government of Italy to act as host to the conference and decided to hold the United Nations Diplomatic Conference of Plenipotentiaries on the Establishment of an International Criminal Court in Rome from 15 June to 17 July 1998.

3.   Previously, the General Assembly, in its resolution 44/39 of 4 December 1989, had requested the International Law Commission to address the question of establishing an international criminal court; in resolutions 45/41 of 28 November 1990 and 46/54 of 9 December 1991, invited the Commission to consider further and analyse the issues concerning the question of an international criminal jurisdiction, including the question of establishing an international criminal court; and in resolutions 47/33 of 25 November 1992 and 48/31 of 9 December 1993, requested the Commission to elaborate the draft statute for such a court as a matter of priority.

4.   The International Law Commission considered the question of establishing an international criminal court from its forty-second session, in 1990, to its forty-sixth session, in 1994. At the latter session, the Commission completed a draft statute for an international criminal court, which was submitted to the General Assembly.

5.   The General Assembly, in its resolution 49/53 of 9 December 1994, decided to establish an ad hoc committee to review the major substantive and administrative issues arising out of the draft statute prepared by the International Law Commission and, in light of that review, to consider arrangements for the convening of an international conference of plenipotentiaries.

6.   The Ad Hoc Committee on the Establishment of an International Criminal Court met from 3 to 13 April and from 14 to 25 August 1995, during which time the Committee reviewed the issues arising out of the draft statute prepared by the International Law Commission and considered arrangements for the convening of an international conference.

7.   The General Assembly, in its resolution 50/46 of 11 December 1995, decided to establish a preparatory committee to discuss further the major substantive and administrative issues arising out of the draft statute prepared by the International Law Commission and, taking into

account the different views expressed during the meetings, to draft texts with a view to preparing a widely acceptable consolidated text of a convention for an international criminal court as a next step towards consideration by a conference of plenipotentiaries.

8.   The Preparatory Committee on the Establishment of an International Criminal Court met from 25 March to 12 April and from 12 to 30 August 1996, during which time the Committee discussed further the issues arising out of the draft statute and began preparing a widely acceptable consolidated text of a convention for an international criminal court.

9.   The General Assembly, in its resolution 51/207 of 17 December 1996, decided that the Preparatory Committee would meet in 1997 and 1998 in order to complete the drafting of the text for submission to the Conference.

10.   The Preparatory Committee met from 11 to 21 February, from 4 to 15 August and from 1 to 12 December 1997, during which time the Committee continued to prepare a widely acceptable consolidated text of a convention for an international criminal court.

11.   The General Assembly, in its resolution 52/160 of 15 December 1997, requested the Preparatory Committee to continue its work in accordance with General Assembly resolution 51/207 and, at the end of its sessions, to transmit to the Conference the text of a draft convention on the establishment

of an international criminal court prepared in accordance with its mandate.

12.   The Preparatory Committee met from 16 March to 3 April 1998, during which time the Committee completed the preparation of the draft Convention on the Establishment of an International Criminal Court, which was transmitted to the Conference.

13.   The Conference met at the headquarters of the Food and Agriculture Organization of the United Nations in Rome from 15 June to 17 July 1998.

14.   The General Assembly, in its resolution 52/160, requested the Secretary-General to invite all States Members of the United Nations or members of specialized agencies or of the International Atomic Energy Agency to participate in the Conference. The delegations of 160 States participated in the Conference. The list of participating States is contained in annex II.

15.   The General Assembly, in the same resolution, requested the Secretary-General to invite representatives of organizations and other entities that had received a standing invitation from the Assembly pursuant to its relevant resolutions to participate as observers in its sessions and work, on the understanding that such representatives would participate in that capacity, and to invite, as observers to the Conference, representatives of interested regional intergovernmental organizations and other interested international bodies, including the International Tribunals for the Former Yugoslavia and for Rwanda. The list of such organizations which were represented at the Conference by an observer is contained in annex III

16.   The Secretary-General, pursuant to the same resolution, invited non-governmental organizations accredited by the Preparatory Committee with due regard to the provisions of section VII of Economic and Social Council resolution 1996/31 of 25 July 1996, and in particular to the relevance of their activities to the work of the Conference, to participate in the Conference, along the lines followed in the Preparatory Committee and in accordance with the resolution, as well as the rules of procedure to be adopted by the Conference. The list of non-governmental organizations represented at the Conference by an observer is contained in annex IV.

17.   The Conference elected Mr. Giovanni Conso (Italy) as President.

18. The Conference elected as Vice-Presidents the representatives of the following States: Algeria, Austria, Bangladesh, Burkina Faso, China, Chile, Colombia, Costa Rica, Egypt, France, Gabon, Germany, India, Iran (Islamic Republic of), Japan, Kenya, Latvia, Malawi, Nepal, Nigeria, Pakistan, Russian Federation, Samoa, Slovakia, Sweden, the former Yugoslav Republic of Macedonia, Trinidad and Tobago, United Kingdom of Great Britain and Northern Ireland, United Republic of Tanzania, United States of America and Uruguay.

19. The following committees were set up by the Conference:

General Committee

Chairman:	The President of the Conference
Members:	The President and Vice-Presidents of the Conference, the Chairman of the Committee of the Whole and the Chairman of the Drafting Committee

Committee of the Whole

Chairman:	Mr. Philippe Kirsch (Canada)
Vice-Chairmen:	Ms. Silvia Fernandez de Gurmendi (Argentina), Mr. Constantin Virgil Ivan (Romania) and Mr. Phakiso Mochochoko (Lesotho)
Rapporteur:	Mr. Yasumasa Nagamine (Japan)

Drafting Committee

Chairman:	Mr. M. Cherif Bassiouni (Egypt)
Members:	Cameroon, China, Dominican Republic, France, Germany, Ghana, India, Jamaica, Lebanon, Mexico, Morocco, Philippines, Poland, Republic of Korea, Russian Federation, Slovenia, South Africa, Spain, Sudan, Switzerland, Syrian Arab Republic, United Kingdom of Great Britain and Northern Ireland, United States of America and Venezuela.

The Rapporteur of the Committee of the Whole participated *ex officio* in the work of the Drafting Committee in accordance with rule 49 of the rules of procedure of the Conference.

Credentials Committee

Chairman:	Ms. Hannelore Benjamin (Dominica)
Members:	Argentina, China, Côte d'Ivoire, Dominica, Nepal, Norway, Russian Federation, United States of America and Zambia.

20. The Secretary-General was represented by Mr. Hans Corell, Under-Secretary-General, the Legal Counsel. Mr. Roy S. Lee, Director of the Codification Division of the Office of Legal Affairs, acted as Executive Secretary. The secretariat was further composed as follows: Mr. Manuel Rama-Montaldo, Secretary, Drafting Committee; Ms. Mahnoush H. Arsanjani, Secretary, Committee of the Whole; Mr. Mpazi Sinjela, Secretary, Credentials Committee; Assistant Secretaries of the Conference: Ms. Christiane Bourloyannis-Vrailas, Ms. Virginia Morris, Mr. Vladimir Rudnitsky, Mr. Renan Villacis.

21. The Conference had before it a draft Statute on the Establishment of an International Criminal Court transmitted by the Preparatory Committee in accordance with its mandate (A/CONF.183/2/Add.1).

22. The Conference assigned to the Committee of the Whole the consideration of the draft Convention on the Establishment of an International Criminal Court adopted by the Preparatory Committee. The Conference entrusted the Drafting Committee, without reopening substantive discussion on any matter, with coordinating and refining the drafting of all texts referred to it without altering their substance, formulating drafts and giving advice on drafting as requested by the Conference or by the Committee of the Whole and reporting to the Conference or to the Committee of the Whole as appropriate.

23. On the basis of the deliberations recorded in the records of the Conference (A/CONF.183/SR.1 to SR. ...) and of the Committee of the whole (A/CONF.183/C.1/SR.1 to SR ...) and the reports of the Committee of the Whole (A/CONF.183/8) and of the Drafting Committee (A/CONF.183/C.1/L.64, L.65/Rev.1, L.66 and Add.1, L.67/Rev.1, L.68/Rev.2, L.82-L.88 and 91), the Conference drew up the *Rome Statute of the International Criminal Court.*

24. The foregoing Statute, which is subject to ratification, acceptance or approval, was adopted by the Conference on .. July 1998 and opened for signature on .. July 1998, in accordance with its provisions, until 17 October 1998 at the Ministry of Foreign Affairs of Italy and, subsequently, until 31 December 2000, at United Nations Headquarters in New York. The same instrument was also opened for accession in accordance with its provisions.

25. After 17 October 1998, the closing date for signature at the ministry of Foreign Affairs of Italy, the Statute will be deposited with the Secretary-General of the United Nations.

26. The Conference also adopted the following resolutions, which are annexed to the present Final Act:

> *Tribute to the International Law Commission*
>
> *Tribute to the participants at the Preparatory Committee on the Establishment of an International Criminal court and its Chairman*
>
> *Tribute to the President of the Conference, to the Chairman of the Committee of the Whole and to the Chairman of the Drafting Committee*
>
> *Tribute to the People and the Government of Italy*
>
> *Resolution on treaty crimes*
>
> *Resolution on the Establishment of the Preparatory Commission for the International Criminal Court*

IN WITNESS WHEREOF the representatives have signed this Final Act.

DONE at Rome this ..th day of July, one thousand nine hundred and ninety-eight, in a single copy in the Arabic, Chinese, English, French, Russian and Spanish languages, each text being equally authentic.

By unanimous decision of the Conference, the original of this Final Act shall be deposited in the archives of the ministry of Foreign Affairs of Italy.

ANNEX I

*Resolutions adopted by the United Nations Diplomatic
Conference of Plenipotentiaries on the Establishment
of an International Criminal Court*

A.

The United Nations Diplomatic Conference of Plenipotentiaries on the Establishment of an International Criminal Court,

Resolves to express its deep gratitude to the International Law Commission for its outstanding contribution in the preparation of the original draft of the Statute, which constituted the basis for the work of the Preparatory Committee.

B.

The United Nations Diplomatic Conference of Plenipotentiaries on the Establishment of an International Criminal Court,

Pays tribute to the participants of the Preparatory Committee on the Establishment of an International Criminal Court and its Chairman, Mr. Adriaan Bos, for their outstanding and hard work, commitment and dedication.

C.

The United Nations Diplomatic Conference of Plenipotentiaries on the Establishment of an International Criminal Court,

Expresses its deep appreciation and gratitude to the People and the Government of Italy for making the necessary arrangements for the holding of the Conference in Rome, for their generous hospitality and for their contribution to the successful completion of the work of the Conference.

D.

The United Nations Diplomatic Conference of Plenipotentiaries on the Establishment of an International Criminal Court,

Expresses its appreciation and thanks to Mr. Giovanni Conso, President of the Conference, Mr. Philippe Kirsch, Chairman of the Committee of the Whole, and Mr. M. Cherif Bassiouni, Chairman of the Drafting Committee, who, through their experience, skilful efforts and wisdom in steering the work of the Conference, contributed greatly to the success of the Conference.

E.

The United Nations Diplomatic Conference of Plenipotentiaries on the Establishment of an International Criminal Court,

Having adopted the Statute of an International Criminal Court,

Recognizing that terrorist acts, by whomever and wherever perpetrated and whatever their forms, methods or motives, are serious crimes of concern to the international community,

Recognizing that the international trafficking of illicit drugs is a very serious crime, sometimes destabilizing the political and social and economic order in states,

Deeply alarmed at the persistence of these scourges, which pose serious threats to international peace and security,

Regretting that no generally acceptable definition of the crimes of terrorism and drug crimes could be agreed upon for the inclusion, within the jurisdiction of the Court,

Affirming that the Statute of the International Criminal Court provides for a review mechanism, which allows for an expansion in future of the jurisdiction of the Court,

Recommends that a Review Conference pursuant to article 111 of the Statute of the International Criminal Court consider the crimes of terrorism and drug crimes with a view to arriving at an acceptable definition and their inclusion in the list of crimes within the jurisdiction of the Court.

F.

The United Nations Conference of Plenipotentiaries on the Establishment of an International Criminal Court,

Having adopted the Statute of the International Criminal Court,

Having decided to take all possible measures to ensure the coming into operation of the International Criminal Court without undue delay and to make the necessary arrangements for the commencement of its functions,

Having decided that a preparatory commission should be established for the fulfilment of these purposes,

Decides as follows:

1. There is hereby established the Preparatory Commission for the International Criminal Court. The Secretary-General of the United Nations shall convene the Commission as early as possible at a date to be decided by the General Assembly of the United Nations.

2. The Commission shall consist of representatives of States which have signed the Final Act of the United Nations Diplomatic Conference of Plenipotentiaries on the Establishment of an International Criminal Court and other States which have been invited to participate in the Conference.

3. The Commission shall elect its Chairman and other officers, adopt its rules of procedure and decide on its programme of work. These elections shall take place at the first meeting of the Commission.

4. The official and working languages of the Preparatory Commission shall be those of the General Assembly of the United Nations.

5. The Commission shall prepare proposals for practical arrangements for the establishment and coming into operation of the Court, including the draft texts of:

    (a) Rules of Procedure and Evidence;

    (b) Elements of Crimes;

    (c) A relationship agreement between the Court and the United Nations;

    (d) Basic principles governing a headquarters agreement to be negotiated between the Court and the host country;

    (e) Financial regulations and rules;

    (f) An agreement on the privileges and immunities of the Court;

    (g) A budget for the first financial year;

    (h) The rules of procedure of the Assembly of States Parties.

6. The draft texts of the Rules of Procedure and Evidence and of the Elements of Crimes shall be finalized before 30 June 2000.

7. The Commission shall prepare proposals for a provision on aggression, including the definition and Elements of Crimes of aggression and the conditions under which the International Criminal Court shall exercise its jurisdiction with regard to this crime. The Commission shall submit such proposals to the Assembly of States Parties at a Review Conference, with a view to arriving at an acceptable provision on the crime of aggression for inclusion in this Statute. The provisions relating to the crime of aggression shall enter into force for the States Parties in accordance with the relevant provisions of this Statute.

8. The Commission shall remain in existence until the *conclusion* of the first meeting of the Assembly of States Parties.

9. The Commission shall prepare a report on all matters within its mandate and submit it to the first meeting of the Assembly of States Parties.

10. The Commission shall meet at the Headquarters of the United Nations. The Secretary-General of the United Nations is requested to provide to the Commission such secretariat services as it may require, subject to the approval of the General Assembly of the United Nations.

11. The Secretary-General of the United Nations shall bring the present resolution to the attention of the General Assembly for any necessary action.

ANNEX II

LIST OF STATES PARTICIPATING IN THE UNITED NATIONS DIPLOMATIC CONFERENCE OF PLENIPOTENTIARIES ON THE ESTABLISHMENT OF AN INTERNATIONAL CRIMINAL COURT

Afghanistan
Albania
Algeria
Andorra
Angola
Argentina
Armenia
Australia
Austria
Azerbaijan
Bahrain
Bangladesh
Barbados
Belarus
Belgium
Benin
Bolivia
Bosnia and Herzegovina
Botswana
Brazil

Brunei Darussalam
Bulgaria
Burkina Faso
Burundi
Cameroon
Canada
Cape Verde
Central African Republic
Chad
Chile
China
Colombia
Comoros
Congo
Costa Rica
Côte d'Ivoire
Croatia
Cuba
Cyprus
Czech Republic

Democratic Republic of the Congo
Denmark
Djibouti
Dominica
Dominican Republic
Ecuador
Egypt
El Salvador
Eritrea
Estonia
Ethiopia
Finland
France
Gabon
Georgia
Germany
Ghana
Greece
Guatemala
Guinea
Guinea-Bissau
Haiti
Holy See
Honduras
Hungary
Iceland
India
Indonesia
Iran (Islamic Republic of)
Iraq
Ireland
Israel
Italy
Jamaica
Japan
Jordan
Kazakhstan
Kenya
Kuwait
Kyrgyzstan
Lao Peoples Democratic Republic
Latvia
Lebanon
Lesotho
Liberia

Libyan Arab Jamahiriya
Liechtenstein
Lithuania
Luxembourg
Madagascar
Malawi
Malaysia
Mali
Malta
Mauritania
Mauritius
Mexico
Monaco
Morocco
Mozambique
Namibia
Nepal
Netherlands
New Zealand
Nicaragua
Niger
Nigeria
Norway
Oman
Pakistan
Panama
Paraguay
Peru
Philippines
Poland
Portugal
Qatar
Republic of Korea
Republic of Moldova
Romania
Russian Federation
Rwanda
Samoa
San Marino
Sao Tome and Principe
Saudi Arabia
Senegal
Sierra Leone
Singapore
Slovakia

Slovenia
Solomon Islands
South Africa
Spain
Sri Lanka
Sudan
Swaziland
Sweden
Switzerland
Syrian Arab Republic
Tajikistan
Thailand
The former Yugoslav Republic of
   Macedonia
Togo
Trinidad and Tobago
Tunisia

Turkey
Uganda
Ukraine
United Arab Emirates
United Kingdom of Great Britain and
   Northern Ireland
United Republic of Tanzania
United States of America
Uruguay
Uzbekistan
Venezuela
Viet Nam
Yemen
Zambia
Zimbabwe

ANNEX III

LIST OF ORGANIZATIONS AND OTHER ENTITIES REPRESENTED AT THE CONFERENCE BY AN OBSERVER

Organizations

Palestine

Intergovernmental organizations and other entities

Agence de Coopération Culturelle et Technique (A.C.C.T.)
Asian-African Legal Consultative Committee (AALCC)
Council of Europe
European Community
European Court of Human Rights
Humanitarian Fact-Finding Commission
Inter-American Institute of Human Rights
International Committee of the Red Cross (ICRC)
International Criminal Police Organization (INTERPOL)
International Federation of Red Cross and Red Crescent Societies
Inter-Parliamentary Union
League of Arab States
Organization of African Unity
Organization of American States
Organization of the Islamic Conference (OIC)
Sovereign Military Order of Malta

Specialized agencies and related organizations

International Labour organization (ILO)
Food and Agriculture Organization of the United Nations (FAO)

United Nations Educational, Scientific and Cultural organization (UNESCO)
International Fund for Agricultural Development (IFAD)
International Atomic Energy Agency (IAEA)
United Nations programmes and bodies
United Nations Children's Fund (UNICEF)
Office of the United Nations High Commissioner for Refugees (UNHCR)
United Nations Commission on Crime Prevention and Criminal Justice
United Nations Office of the High Commissioner for Human Rights
United Nations Office at Vienna, Office for Drug Control and Crime Prevention
International Criminal Tribunal for Rwanda
International Tribunal for the Former Yugoslavia
International Law Commission (ILC)
World Food Programme

ANNEX IV

LIST OF NON-GOVERNMENTAL ORGANIZATIONS REPRESENTED AT THE CONFERENCE BY AN OBSERVER

Agir ensemble pour les droits de l'homme (Working Together for Human Rights)
American Association for the International Commission of Jurists
American Association of Jurists
American Bar Association
Amnesty International
Arab Lawyers Union
Asia Pacific Forum on Women, Law and Development
Asian Center for Women's Human Rights
Asian Women's Human Rights Council
Asociación por Derechos Humanos (APRODEH; Association for Human Rights)
Australian Lawyers for Human Rights
Baha'i International Community
Bangladesh Legal Aid and Services Trust
Bar Human Rights Committee of England and Wales
Cairo Institute for Human Rights Studies
Canadian Network for an ICC/World Federalists of Canada
Carter Center
Center for Civil Human Rights
Center for Development of International Law
Center for Human Rights and Rehabilitation
Center for Reproductive Law and Policy
Children's Fund of Canada, Inc.
Colombian Commission of Jurists
Comité de Defensa do los Derechos Humanos y del Pueblo (Committee for the Defence of Human Rights and of the People)
Coalition for International Justice

Comité Latinoamericano y del Caribe para la Defensa de los Derechos de la Mujer (CLADEM; Latin American and Caribbean Committee for the Defence of Women's Rights)
Commission of Churches on International Affairs of the World Council of Churches
Committee of Former Nuremberg Prosecutors
Community Law Centre
Conseil national des barreaux (National Bar Council)
Coordinating Board of Jewish organizations
Corporación Coiectivo de Abogados "José Alvear Restrepo" (José Alvear Restrepo Lawyers Collective Association)
Corporación de Desarrollo de la Mujer (La Morada; Association for the Development of Women)
Croatian Law Centre
Deutscher Juristinnenbund (German Women Lawyers Association)
Droits et devoirs en démocratie (3D; Rights and Duties in Democracy)
Egyptian Organization for Human Rights
European Law Students Association
Federación de Asociaciones de Defensa y Promoción de los Derechos Humanos (Federation of Associations for the Defence and Promotion of Human Rights)
Fédération Internationale de l'action des Chrétiens pour l'abolition de la torture (FIACAT; International Federation of Christian Action to Abolish Torture)
Foundation for Human Rights Initiative
Foundation for the Establishment of an International Criminal Court and International Law Commission
Friends World Committee for Consultation
Fundación Ecuménica Para el Desarollo y la Paz (FEDEPAZ; Ecumenical Foundation for Development and Peace)
General Board of Church and Society of the United Methodist Church
Human Rights Advocates
Human Rights Watch
ICAR Foundation
Information Workers for Peace
Instituto Latinoamericano de Servicios Legales Alternativos (TLSA; Latin American Institute of Alternative Legal Services)
Inter Press Service
Interafrican Union for Human Rights
Interamerican Concertation of Women's Human Rights Activists (CIMA)
Inter-American Legal Services Association
International Association of Latin American Lawyers
Interights
Intermedia
International Association for Religious Freedom
International Association of Democratic Lawyers
International Association of Lawyers
International Association of Lawyers against Nuclear Arms (IALANA)
International Association of Penal Law

International Bar Association
International Centre for Criminal Law Reform and Criminal Justice Policy
International Centre for Human Rights and Democratic Development
International Commission of Jurists
International Court of the Environment
International Criminal Defense Attorneys Association
International Federation of Human Rights Leagues
International Federation of Women Lawyers, Kenya
International Human Rights Law Group
International Institute of Higher Studies in Criminal Sciences
International Law Association Committee on a Permanent ICC
International League for Human Rights
International Peace Bureau
International Right to Life Federation
International Scientific and Professional Advisory Council of the United Nations Crime Prevention and Criminal Justice Programme
International Service for Human Rights
International Society for Human Rights, Gambia
International Society for Human Rights, Germany
International Society for Traumatic Stress Studies
Japan Federation of Bar Associations
Juristes sans frontières (Lawyers without Borders)
Lama Gangchen World Peace Foundation
Law Projects Center, Yugoslavia
Lawyers Committee for Human Rights
Lawyers Committee on Nuclear Policy
Lawyers without Borders
Legal Research and Resource Development Centre
Leo Kuper Foundation
Lutheran world Federation
Médecins du monde (Doctors of the World)
Médecins sans frontières/Doctors without Borders
Minnesota Advocates for Human Rights
Movimento Nacional de Direitos Humanos (National Movement for Human Rights)
Movimiento por la Paz, Desarme y Libertad (National Movement for Peace, Disarmament and Freedom)
MOVIMONDO (Italy)
National Institute for Public Interest Law and Research
Netherlands Institute of Human Rights
No Peace Without Justice
Norwegian Helsinki Committee
Observatoire international des prisons, section du Cameroun (International Monitoring Centre for Prisons, Cameroon Branch)
Observatorio para la Paz (Peace Monitoring Centre)
One World Trust

OXFAM (United Kingdom and Ireland)
Pace Peace Center
Parliamentarians for Global Action
Plural - Centro de Estudios Constitutionales (Plural - Centre for Constitutional Studies)
Real Women of Canada
Redress
Rencontre africaine pour la défense des droits de l'homme (RADDHO; African Meeting for the Defence of Human Rights)
Save the Children Fund
South Asia Human Rights Documentation Centre
Tamilandu United Nations Association
Terre des Hommes Foundation
Terre des Hommes, Germany
Transnational Radical Party
Unión Nacional de Juristas de Cuba (National Union of Cuban Lawyers)
Unitarian Universalist Association
United Nations Association, USA
Volunteers for Prison Inmates
Washington Working Group on the ICC/World Federalist Association
Woman and Men Engaged in Advocacy, Research and Education (WEARE) for Human Rights
Women's Caucus for Gender Justice and the ICC/MADRE
Women's Consortium of Nigeria
Women's Information Consultative Center
Women's International League for Peace and Freedom
Women's League of Lithuania
World Conference on Religion and Peace
World Federalist Association
World Federalist Movement/IGP
Young European Federalists
ZIMRIGHTS (Zimbabwe Human Rights Association)

Editor's Note:
On 25 September 1998 the United Nations Office of Legal Affairs issued "No Objection Letter" pursuant to Article 79 of the Vienna Convention on the Law of Treaty (1969) with respect to a number of corrections to the text approved by the Diplomatic Conference on 17 July 1998. These changes have been incorporated in the text of the Statute as it appears in this volume. What follows are the correction to the Rome Statute which were circulated by the Office of Legal Affairs to the member states through their New York missions.

**PROPOSED CORRECTIONS TO THE ROME STATUTE OF THE
INTERNATIONAL CRIMINAL COURT**

[-A- ORIGINAL TEXT]	[-B- PROPOSED CORRECTIONS]
Preamble First parpagraph	Preamble Before the first paragraph, add: <u>The States Parties to this Statute,</u>
Article 8 (1) ...when committed <u>as a part</u> of a plan	Article 8 (1) ...when committed <u>as part of</u> a plan

Article 8 (2) (e) (iii)
...under the law of armed conflict...

Article 8 (2) (e) (iii)
...under the <u>international</u> law of armed conflict...

Article 8 (3)
3. Nothing in paragraph 2 (c) and (<u>d</u>) shall affect...

Article 8 (3)
3. Nothing in paragraph 2 (c) and (<u>e</u>) shall affect...

Article 18 (4)
...in accordance with article 82, <u>paragraph 2</u>.

Article 18 (4)
...in accordance with article 82.

Article 19 (9)
9. The making <u>of challenge</u> shall...

Article 19 (9)
9. The making <u>of a challenge</u> shall...

Article 19 (11)
...shall notify the State <u>in respect of the proceedings of</u>
<u>which deferral</u> has taken place.

Article 19 (11)
...shall notify the State <u>to which deferral of the</u>
<u>proceedings</u> has taken place.

Article 20 (2)
2. No person shall be tried <u>before</u> another court...

Article 20 (2)
2. No person shall be tried <u>by</u> another court...

Article 21 (3)
...such as gender, as defined in...

Article 21 (3)
...such as gender as defined in... (delete comma)

Article 28: Numbering of paragraphs reads as follows:
1.
    (a)
    (b)
2.
    (a)
    (b)
    (c)

Article 28: Numbering of paragraphs reads as follows:
(a)
    (i)
    (ii)
(b)
    (i)
    (ii)
    (iii)

Article 28 (2)
...not described in paragraph <u>1</u>, a superior...

Article 28 (2)
...not described in paragraph <u>(a)</u>, a superior...

Article 38 (2) (b)
...<u>two-thirds</u> of the members...

Article 38 (2) (b)
...<u>two thirds</u> of the members...

Article 36 (2) (c) (i)
...paragraphs 3 to 8 <u>inclusive</u>, and...

Article 36 (2) (c) (i)
...paragraphs 3 to 8, and...

Article 36 (7)
...membership <u>in</u> the Court...

Article 36 (7)
...membership <u>of</u> the Court...

Article 53 (2) (c)
The Prosecutor...

Article 53 (2) (c)
the Prosecutor...

Article 55 (1) (d)
...arrest or detention; and shall...

Article 55 (1) (d)
...arrest or detention, and shall... (replace ";" by ",")

Article 55 (1) (d)
...are established in <u>the</u> Statute.

Article 55 (1) (d)
...are established in <u>this</u> Statute.

Article 55 (2)
...made under Part 9 <u>of this Statute</u>, that person...

Article 55 (2)
...made under Part 9, that person...

Article 57 (1)
1. Unless otherwise provided <u>for</u> in this Statute...

Article 57 (1)
1. Unless otherwise provided in this Statute...

Article 57 (3) (e)
...forfeiture in particular...

Article 57 (3) (e)
...forfeiture, in particular... (add comma)

Article 61 (7) (a)
...there is sufficient evidence; and...

Article 61 (7) (a)
...there is sufficient evidence, and... (replace ";" by ",")

Article 68 (1)
...as defined in article <u>2</u>, paragraph 3...

Article 68 (1)
...as defined in article <u>7</u>, paragraph 3...

Article 72 (5)
...the Prosecutor, the <u>D</u>efinse or...

Article 72 (5)
...the Prosecutor, the <u>d</u>efinse or...

Article 72 (7) (a) (ii)
...its obligations under the Statute...

Article 72 (7) (a) (ii)
...its obligations under <u>this</u> Statute...

Article 73
...and refused consent...

Article 73
...and refused <u>to</u> consent...

Article 77 (1)
...of a crime <u>under</u> article 5...

Article 77 (1)
...of a crime <u>referred to in</u> article 5...

Article 80
Nothing in this Part <u>of the Statute</u> affects...

Article 80
Nothing in this Part affects...

(b) The convicted person, or the Prosecutor on that person's behalf may... (add comma after "person", delete comma after "behalf")

Article 82 (4)
...under article 75...

Article 87 (5)
Add (a) at the beginning of first paragraph starting with "The Court..."
Add (b) at the beginning of second paragraph starting with "Where a State..."

Article 89 (3) (e)
...effected, provided... (replace ";" by ",")

Article 90 (7) (b)
...to the Court or to extradite the person...

Article 93 (5)
...the Court or the Prosecutor...

Article 93 (8) (b)
...for the purpose of generating new evidence. (replace ";" by ".")

Article 93 (10) (b): Numbering of subparagraphs should read:
(b) (i)
    a.
    b.
    (ii)
    a.
    b.

Article 93 (10) (b) (ii)
In the case of assistance under subparagraph (b) (i) a:

Article 93 (10) (c)
...a Party to this Statute.

Article 95
...article 18 or 19...

Article 97 (b)
...in the requested State...

Article 99 (4) (a)
...pursuant to article 18 or 19...

Article 103 (3) (c)
(c) The views of the sentenced person;

Article 112 (1)
...Other States which have signed this Statute...

Article 119 (2)
...dispute or may recommendations...

Article 121 (5)
5. Any amendments to article 5, 6, 7, and 8 of this Statute...

Article 121 (6)
...article 127, paragraph 1, but subject to article 127, paragraph 2...

Article 122 (1)
1. Amendments to provision of this Statute...

Article 122 (1)
...paragraphs 8 and 9, article 37... (add comma)

Article 124
Notwithstanding article 12 paragraphs 1 and 2, a State...

Article 82 (4)
...under article 73...

Article 87 (5): subparagraphs are not identified

Article 89 (3) (e)
...effected; provided...

Article 90 (7) (b)
...to the Court or extradite the person...

Article 93 (5)
...the Court of the Prosecutor...

Article 93 (8) (b)
...for the purpose of generating new evidence;

Article 93 (10) (b): Numbering of subparagraphs reads as follows:
(b) (i)
    (1)
    (2)
    (ii)
    (1)
    (2)

Article 93 (10) (b) (ii)
In the case of assistance under subparagraph (b) (1) (1):

Article 93 (10) (c)
...a Party to the Statute.

Article 95
...articles 18 or 19...

Article 97 (b)
...in the custodial State...

Article 99 (4) (a)
...pursuant to articles 18 or 19...

Article 103 (3) (c)
(c) The views of the sentenced person; and

Article 112 (1)
...Other States which have signed the Statute...

Article 119 (2)
...dispute or make recommendations...

Article 121 (5)
5. Any amendments to article 5 of this Statute...

Article 121 (6)
...paragraph 1 of article 127, but subject to paragraph 2 of article 127...

Article 122 (1)
1. Amendments to provision of the Statute...

Article 122 (1)
...paragraphs 8 and 9 article 37...

Article 124
Notwithstanding article 12 paragraph 1, a State...

Article 126
...approving or acceding to the Statute...

**REPORT OF THE PREPARATORY COMMITTEE ON THE ESTABLISHMENT
OF AN INTERNATIONAL CRIMINAL COURT**

[Editorial Note - the U.N. page numbers of this document are indicated in bolded brackets [*] in the text].

[*2] INTRODUCTION

1.   The General Assembly, in its resolution 50/46 of 11 December 1995, decided to establish a preparatory committee for the establishment of an international criminal court to discuss the major substantive and administrative issues arising out of the draft statute prepared by the International Law Commission in 1994 and to draft texts with a view to preparing a widely acceptable consolidated text of a convention for an international criminal court as a next step towards consideration by a conference of plenipotentiaries.

2.   The Preparatory Committee on the Establishment of an International Criminal Court met from 25 March to 12 April and from 12 to 30 August 1996, during which time it discussed further the issues arising out of the draft statute and began preparing a widely acceptable consolidated text of a convention for an international criminal court./1

3.   Pursuant to paragraph 2 of General Assembly resolution 50/46, the Preparatory Committee was open to all States Members of the United Nations or members of the specialized agencies or of the International Atomic Energy Agency.

4.   Mr. Hans Corell, Under-Secretary-General, the Legal Counsel, opened the session and represented the Secretary-General. Mr. Roy S. Lee, Director of the Codification Division of the Office of Legal Affairs, acted as Secretary of the Preparatory Committee. The Codification Division provided substantive servicing for the Preparatory Committee.

5.   The Bureau of the Preparatory Committee comprised the following:

Chairman:	Mr. Adriaan Bos (Netherlands)
Vice-Chairmen:	Mr. Cherif Bassiouni (Egypt)
	Mrs. Silvia A. Fernçndez de Gurmendi (Argentina)
	Mr. Marek Madej (Poland) (1996-1997);
	Mr. Peter Tomka (Slovakia) (1998)
Rapporteur:	Mr. Juan Yoshida (Japan) (1996);
	Mr. Masataka Okano (Japan) (1997-1998)

6.   By paragraphs 3 and 4 of its resolution 51/207 of 17 December 1996, the General Assembly reaffirmed the mandate of the Preparatory Committee and decided that it should meet from 11 to 21 February, 4 to 15 August and 1 to 12 December 1997, and from 16 March to 3 April 1998, in order to complete the drafting of a widely acceptable consolidated text of a convention, to be submitted to the diplomatic conference of plenipotentiaries, and requested the Secretary-General to provide the necessary facilities for the performance of its work.

7.   The General Assembly, in its resolution 52/160 of 15 December 1997, accepted with deep appreciation the generous offer of the Government of Italy to act as host to the United Nations Diplomatic Conference of Plenipotentiaries on [*3] the Establishment of an International Criminal Court and decided to hold the Conference in Rome from 15 June to 17 July 1998.

8.   In the same resolution, the General Assembly requested the Preparatory Committee to continue its work in accordance with Assembly resolution 51/207 and, at the end of its sessions, to transmit to the Conference the text of a draft convention on the establishment of an international criminal court prepared in accordance with its mandate.

9.   The Preparatory Committee held its sessions at United Nations Headquarters./2 At its last session, held from 16 March to 3 April 1998, the Preparatory Committee had before it a consolidated text/3 prepared by its Bureau and coordinators on the basis of all the texts that it had elaborated or that had been submitted to it. The compilation was used as a basis for the work of the Committee at that session.

10.   At its 56th meeting, on 16 March 1998, the Preparatory Committee decided to conduct its work through working groups on the following subjects: procedural matters (chaired by Ms. Silvia Fernçndez

de Gurmendi); composition and administration of the court (chaired by Mr. Lionel Yee); establishment of the court and its relationship with the United Nations (chaired by Mr. Sankurathripati Rama Rao); applicable law (chaired by Mr. Per Saland); ne bis in idem (chaired by Mr. John Holmes); jurisdictional issues (chaired by Mr. Erkki Kourula); and enforcement (chaired by Mrs. Molly Warlow). The final clauses were considered at the informal meetings under the chairmanship of Mr. Adriaan Bos.

11. At its 57th meeting, on 1 April 1998, the Preparatory Committee adopted the reports of the working groups mentioned above.

12. At its 60th meeting, on 3 April 1998, the Preparatory Committee adopted the text of a draft statute on the establishment of an international criminal court/4 and the draft final act./5

13. In its resolution 52/160, the General Assembly had requested the Secretary-General to prepare the text of the draft rules of procedure of the Conference, to be submitted to the Preparatory Committee for its consideration and recommendations to the Conference, with a view to the adoption of such rules by the Conference in accordance with the rules of procedure of the General Assembly, and to provide for consultations on the organization and methods of work of the Conference, including rules of procedure, prior to the convening of the last session of the Committee. At its 61st meeting, on 3 April 1998, the Preparatory Committee adopted for recommendation to the Conference the draft rules of procedure of the Conference,/6 as amended orally, pursuant to resolution 52/160.

14. At its 61st meeting, on 3 April 1998, the Preparatory Committee took note of the draft organization of work prepared by the Secretariat and decided to transmit it to the Conference.

15. At the same meeting, the Preparatory Committee agreed to transmit to the Conference the following:

[*4] •   Draft statute for the International Criminal Court (part one of the present report; see A/CONF.183/2/Add.1);

•   Draft Final Act of the United Nations Diplomatic Conference of Plenipotentiaries on the Establishment of an International Criminal Court (part two of the present report; see A/CONF.183/2/Add.1);

•   Draft rules of procedure for the United Nations Diplomatic Conference of Plenipotentiaries on the Establishment of an International Criminal Court (part three of the present report; see A/CONF.183/2/Add.2);

•   Draft organization of work of the United Nations Diplomatic Conference of Plenipotentiaries on the Establishment of an International Criminal Court (part four of the present report; see below).

16. In its resolution 52/160, the General Assembly requested the Secretary-General to invite non-governmental organizations, accredited by the Preparatory Committee with due regard to the provisions of section VII of Economic and Social Council resolution 1996/31 of 25 July 1996, and in particular to the relevance of their activities to the work of the Conference, to participate in the Conference, along the lines followed in the Committee, on the understanding that participation meant attending meetings of its plenary and, unless otherwise decided by the Conference in specific situations, formal meetings of its subsidiary bodies except the drafting group, receiving copies of the official documents, making available their materials to delegates and addressing, through a limited number of their representatives, its opening and/or closing sessions, as appropriate, in accordance with the rules of procedure to be adopted by the Conference. On the basis of the lists of non-governmental organizations compiled by the Secretariat with the assistance of the NGO Coalition for the Establishment of an International Criminal Court,/7 the preparatory Committee decided that the non-governmental organizations listed therein should be invited to participate in the Conference in the manner set out in resolution 52/160.

17. At the 57th meeting, on 1 April 1998, the representative of the Netherlands announced his country's candidacy of The Hague for the seat of the international criminal court.

18. Pursuant to paragraph 7 of resolution 51/207, the Secretary-General established a trust fund for the participation of the least developed countries in the work of the Preparatory Committee and the Conference. Guidelines were established for the administration of the fund. The Committee noted that the following Governments had made contributions to the fund: Belgium, Canada, Denmark, Finland, Netherlands, Norway, Sweden and United Kingdom of Great Britain and Northern Ireland. Thirty-three

representatives from 18 States had thus far utilized the trust fund to facilitate their participation in the meetings of the Preparatory Committee during 1997 and 1998. The European Commission had awarded a grant to the trust fund, but owing to procedural difficulties, the transfer of the contribution had been delayed.

19. Furthermore, pursuant to paragraph 7 of resolution 52/160, the Secretary-General also established a trust fund for the participation of other developing countries in the work of the Preparatory Committee and in the Conference. The [*5] Government of the Netherlands had made a contribution, which would be available to those developing countries requesting assistance to facilitate their participation in the Conference.

20. The Preparatory Committee expressed its deep appreciation to the Governments that had made contributions and to the European Commission for its award to the above-mentioned trust funds. The Committee noted that the General Assembly, in its resolution 52/160, had called upon States to contribute voluntarily to the trust funds.

21. At its 61st meeting, on 3 April 1998, the Preparatory Committee took note of the following nominations for officers of the Conference:

President:	Mr. Giovanni Conso (Italy);
Chairman of the Committee of the Whole:	Mr. Adriaan Bos (Netherlands);
Chairman of the Drafting Committee:	Mr. Cherif Bassiouni (Egypt).

Notes

1/ See Official Records of the General Assembly, Fifty-first Session, Supplement No. 22 (A/51/22).

2/ See the decisions taken by the Preparatory Committee at its session held from 11 to 21 February 1997 (A/AC.249/1997/L.5); decisions taken by the Preparatory Committee at its session held from 4 to 15 August 1997 (A/AC.249/1997/L.8/Rev.1); and decisions taken by the Preparatory Committee at its session held from 1 to 12 December 1997 (A/AC.249/1997/L.9/Rev.1).

3/ A/AC.249/1998/L.13.

4/ A/AC.249/1998/CRP.6-18 and corrigenda.

5/ A/AC.249/1998/CRP.19.

6/ A/AC.249/1998/CRP.3/Rev.1.

7/ A/AC.249/1998/CRP.22.

[*6] Part One. Draft Statute for the International Criminal Court (See A/CONF.183/2/Add.1)

Part Two. Draft Final Act of the United Nations Diplomatic Conference of Plenipotentiaries on the Establishment of an International Criminal Court (See A/CONF.183/2/Add.1)

Part Three. Draft rules of procedure for the United Nations Diplomatic Conference of Plenipotentiaries on the Establishment of an International Criminal Court (See A/CONF.183/2/Add.2)

PART FOUR
Draft organization of work of the United Nations Diplomatic Conference of Plenipotentiaries on the Establishment of an International Criminal Court

1. As mandated by the General Assembly in its resolution 52/160, of 15 December 1997, the task of the Conference is to finalize and adopt a convention on the establishment of an international criminal court. The Conference should move promptly to the consideration of substantive matters after a short session on organizational matters.

2. After the opening of the Conference by the Secretary-General of the United Nations, the Conference will meet to elect the President, adopt the agenda and the rules of procedure and elect other officers.

3. The General Committee will meet immediately following the election of its members. Its work will include, inter alia, assisting the President in the general conduct of business and making recommendations with respect to the election of members of the Drafting Committee.

4. The plenary, on the recommendations of the General Committee will then elect the members of the Drafting Committee and adopt the programme of work of the Conference.

5.   The plenary will then proceed to hear statements from States in accordance with an established list of speakers prepared on a first-come-first-served basis. The Conference will also hear statements from a limited number of intergovernmental organizations and non-governmental organizations. The list of speakers will be opened for inscription on 15 April 1998.

6.   With a view to the efficient and expeditious discharge of the work of the plenary, a time limit may be established for statements by States on the one hand (e.g., seven (7) minutes) and intergovernmental organizations and non-governmental organizations on the other (e.g., five (5) minutes). In principle, States should be given more time than intergovernmental organizations and non-governmental organizations. A total of seven meetings may be allotted for this purpose.

7.   The Committee of the Whole should concentrate on the substantive work and should begin its work on 16 June. It may hold up to four meetings (with full interpretation) per day throughout the Conference, i.e., two bodies may meet concurrently, both morning and afternoon. The Committee of the Whole will report to the plenary upon the completion of its work.

8.   A working group of the Committee of the Whole will begin its work on the afternoon of 17 June.

9.   The Drafting Committee may begin its work on 19 June; two meetings (with full interpretation) per day may be allotted to it throughout the Conference. The Drafting Committee will receive its work from the Committee of the Whole and report to it. Time constraints might make it necessary to allow the Drafting Committee to report on the last portion of its work directly to the plenary.

10.   The Credentials Committee will meet sometime during the second or third week of the Conference. One meeting has been allotted for that purpose.

11.   The last day of the Conference is reserved for the signature of the Final Act and of the Statute of the Court and for the closure of the Conference.

REPORT OF THE PREPARATORY COMMITTEE ON THE ESTABLISHMENT OF AN INTERNATIONAL CRIMINAL COURT

[Editorial Note - The U.N. page numbers of this document are indicated in bolded brackets [*] in the text].

[*1] Addendum

[*10] PREAMBLE[1]

The States Parties to this Statute,

Desiring to further international cooperation to enhance the effective prosecution and suppression of crimes of international concern, and for that purpose to establish an international criminal court;

Emphasizing that such a court is intended to exercise jurisdiction only over the most serious crimes of concern to the international community as a whole;

Emphasizing further that such a court is intended to be complementary to national criminal justice systems in cases where such trial procedures may not be available or may be ineffective;[2]

Have agreed as follows:

[*11] PART 1. ESTABLISHMENT OF THE COURT
Article 1
The Court

There is established an International Criminal Court ("the Court"), which shall have the power to bring persons to justice for the most serious crimes of international concern, and which shall be complementary to national criminal jurisdictions. Its jurisdiction and functioning shall be governed by the provisions of this Statute.

N.B. Attention should be paid to using the term "Court" throughout the Statute in a consistent manner.

Article 2
Relationship of the Court with the United Nations

The Court shall be brought into relationship with the United Nations by an agreement to be approved by the States Parties to this Statute and concluded by the President on behalf of the Court.

Article 3
Seat of the Court

1. The seat of the Court shall be established at ... in ... ("the host State").
2. The President, with the approval of the Assembly of States Parties, may conclude an agreement with the host State, establishing the relationship between that State and the Court.
3. The Court may exercise its powers and functions on the territory of any State Party and, by special agreement, on the territory of any other State.

Article 4
[*12] Status and legal capacity

1. The Court is a permanent institution open to States Parties in accordance with this Statute. It shall act when required to consider a case submitted to it.
2. The Court shall have international legal personality and such legal capacity as may be necessary for the exercise of its functions and the fulfilment of its purposes.

---

[1]   In this connection, there was a proposal contained in document A/AC.249/1998/DP.6.

[2]   Delegations have expressed their opposition to the wording of the third paragraph of the preamble and have asked that this paragraph be made consistent with article 1 of the Statute so as to read as follows:

"**Emphasizing further** that such a court shall be complementary to national criminal jurisdictions;"

PART 2. JURISDICTION, ADMISSIBILITY AND APPLICABLE LAW
Article 5
Crimes within the jurisdiction of the Court
The Court has jurisdiction in accordance with this Statute with respect to the following crimes:

(a) the crime of genocide;

(b) the crime of aggression;

(c) war crimes;

(d) crimes against humanity;

(e) ...

N.B. Once a decision is made as to which crimes should be included in the draft Statute, the paragraphs of this introductory article should be adjusted and the subsequent provisions placed in separate articles and numbered accordingly.

Crime of genocide
[*13] For the purpose of the present Statute, the crime of genocide means any of the following acts committed with intent[1] to destroy, in whole or in part, a national, ethnical, racial or religious group,[2] as such:

(a) killing members of the group;

(b) causing serious bodily or mental harm[3] to members of the group;

(c) deliberately inflicting on the group conditions of life calculated to bring about its physical destruction in whole or in part;

(d) imposing measures intended to prevent births within the group;

(e) forcibly transferring children of the group to another group;

[The following acts shall be punishable:

(a) genocide;

(b) conspiracy to commit genocide;

(c) direct and public incitement to commit genocide;

(d) attempt to commit genocide;

[*14] (e) complicity in genocide.][4]

[5Crime of aggression6
Note: This draft is without prejudice to the discussion of the issue of the relationship of the Security Council with the International Criminal Court with respect to aggression as dealt with in article 10.

Option 1
[For the purpose of the present Statute, the crime [of aggression] [against peace] means any of the following acts committed by an individual [who is in a position of exercising control or capable of directing political/military action in a State]:

(a) planning,

---

[1]   The reference to "intent to destroy, in whole or in part ... a group, as such" was understood to refer to the specific intention to destroy more than a small number of individuals who are members of a group.

[2]   The Preparatory Committee took note of the suggestion to examine the possibility of addressing "social and political" groups in the context of crimes against humanity.
N.B. The need for this footnote should be reviewed in the light of the discussions that have taken place in respect of crimes against humanity.

[3]   The reference to "mental harm" is understood to mean more than the minor or temporary impairment of mental faculties.

[4]   The Working Group will return to the question of the placement of article III of the Genocide Convention once the Working Group on general principles of criminal law has considered this issue in the context of its work.
N.B. See also article 23 (Individual criminal responsibility).

[5]   This square bracket closes at the end of paragraph 2.

[6]   The proposal reflects the view held by a large number of delegations that the crime of aggression should be included in the Statute.
The Preparatory Committee considered this crime without prejudice to a final decision on its inclusion in the Statute.

(b)   preparing,

(c)   ordering,

(d)   initiating, or

(e)   carrying out

[an armed attack] [the use of armed force] [a war of aggression,] [a war of aggression, or a war in violation of international treaties, agreements or assurances, or participation in a common plan or conspiracy for the [*15] accomplishment of any of the foregoing] by a State against the [sovereignty,] territorial integrity [or political independence] of another State [when this] [armed attack] [use of force] [is] [in contravention of the Charter of the United Nations] [[in contravention of the Charter of the United Nations as determined by the Security Council].]

Option 2

1.   [For the purposes of this Statute, the crime of aggression is committed by a person who is in a position of exercising control or capable of directing political/military actions in his State, against another State, in contravention to the Charter of the United Nations, by resorting to armed force, to threaten or violate the sovereignty, territorial integrity or political independence of that State.]

[2.   [Acts constituting [aggression] [armed attack] include the following:][7]

[Provided that the acts concerned or their consequences are of sufficient gravity, acts constituting aggression [are] [include] the following:]

(a)   the invasion or attack by the armed forces of a State of the territory of another State, or any military occupation, however temporary, resulting from such invasion or attack, or any annexation by the use of force of the territory of another State or part thereof;

(b)   bombardment by the armed forces of a State against the territory of another State [, or the use of any weapons by a State against the territory of another State];

(c)   the blockade of the ports or coasts of a State by the armed forces of another State;

(d)   an attack by the armed forces of a State on the land, sea or air forces, or marine and air fleets of another State;

(e)   the use of armed forces of one State which are within the territory of another State with the agreement of the receiving State in contravention of the [*16] conditions provided for in the agreement, or any extension of their presence in such territory beyond their termination of the agreement;

(f)   the action of a State in allowing its territory, which it has placed at the disposal of another State, to be used by that other State for perpetrating an act of aggression against a third State;

(g)   the sending by or on behalf of a State of armed bands, groups, irregulars or mercenaries, which carry out acts of armed force against another State of such gravity as to amount to the acts listed above, or its substantial involvement therein.]]

Option 3

[1.   For the purpose of the present Statute [and subject to a determination by the Security Council referred to in article 10, paragraph 2, regarding the act of a State], the crime of aggression means either of the following acts committed by an individual who is in a position of exercising control or capable of directing the political or military action of a State:

(a)   initiating, or

(b)   carrying out an armed attack directed by a State against the territorial integrity or political independence of another State when this armed attack was undertaken in [manifest] contravention of the Charter of the United Nations [with the object or result of establishing a [military] occupation of, or annexing, the territory of such other State or part thereof by armed forces of the attacking State.]

2.   Where an attack under paragraph 1 has been committed, the

(a)   planning,

(b)   preparing, or

(c)   ordering

---

[7]   Paragraph 2 of the text reflects the view held by some delegations that the definition should include an enumeration of the acts constituting aggression.

thereof by an individual who is in a position of exercising control or capable of directing the political or military action of a State shall also constitute a crime of aggression.]

[*17] War crimes[8]

For the purpose of the present Statute, war crimes means:

A.   Grave breaches of the Geneva Conventions of 12 August 1949, namely, any of the following acts against persons or property protected under the provisions of the relevant Geneva Convention:

(a)   wilful killing;

(b)   torture or inhuman treatment, including biological experiments;

(c)   wilfully causing great suffering, or serious injury to body or health;

(d)   extensive destruction and appropriation of property, not justified by military necessity and carried out unlawfully and wantonly;

(e)   compelling a prisoner of war or other protected person to serve in the forces of a hostile Power;

(f)   wilfully depriving a prisoner of war or other protected person of the rights of fair and regular trial;

(g)   unlawful deportation or transfer or unlawful confinement;

(h)   taking of hostages.

B.   Other serious violations of the laws and customs applicable in international armed conflict within the established framework of international law, namely, any of the following acts:

(a)

Option 1

[*18] intentionally directing attacks against the civilian population as such, as well as individual civilians not taking direct part in hostilities;

Option 2   No paragraph (a).

(a bis)

Option 1

intentionally directing attacks against civilian objects which are not military objectives;

Option 2

No paragraph (a bis).

(b)

Option 1

intentionally launching an attack in the knowledge that such attack will cause incidental loss of life or injury to civilians or damage to civilian objects or widespread, long-term and severe damage to the natural environment which is not justified by military necessity;[9]

Option 2

[*19] intentionally launching an attack in the knowledge that such attack will cause incidental loss of life or injury to civilians or damage to civilian objects or widespread, long-term and severe damage to the natural environment which would be excessive in relation to the concrete and direct overall military advantage anticipated;[10]

---

[8]   Views were expressed that certain provisions should be placed within square brackets. The relative placement of the various options does not indicate in any way the measure of support for such options. Some options commanded very limited support.

[9]   It has been accepted that it will be necessary to insert a provision, probably in the general principles section, which sets out the elements of knowledge and intent which must be found to have existed for an accused to be convicted of a war crime. For example: "in order to conclude that an accused had the knowledge and criminal intention required to be convicted of a crime, the Court must first determine that, taking account of the relevant circumstances of, and information available to, the accused at the time, the accused had the requisite knowledge and intent to commit the crime."

N.B. With respect to this footnote see, however, articles 29 (Mens rea (mental elements)) and 30 (Mistake of fact or of law), which deal with similar issues.

[10]   Ibid.

Option 3

intentionally launching an attack in the knowledge that such attack will cause incidental loss of life or injury to civilians or damage to civilian objects or widespread, long-term and severe damage to the natural environment;[11]

Option 4

No paragraph (b).

(b bis)

Option 1

intentionally launching an attack against works or installations containing dangerous forces in the knowledge that such attack will cause excessive loss of life, injury to civilians or damage to civilian objects which would be excessive in relation to the concrete and direct military advantage anticipated;

Option 2

No paragraph (b bis).

(c)

Option 1

attacking or bombarding, by whatever means, towns, villages, dwellings or buildings which are undefended;

Option 2

[*20] making non-defended localities and demilitarized zones the objects of attack;

(d) killing or wounding a combatant who, having laid down his arms or having no longer means of defence, has surrendered at discretion;

(e) making improper use of flag of truce, of the flag or of the military insignia and uniform of the enemy or of the United Nations, as well as of the distinctive emblems of the Geneva Conventions, resulting in death or serious personal injury;

(f)

Option 1

the transfer by the Occupying Power of parts of its own civilian population into the territory it occupies;

Option 2

the transfer by the Occupying Power of parts of its own civilian population into the territory it occupies, or the deportation or transfer of all or parts of the population of the occupied territory within or outside this territory;

Option 3

(i) the establishment of settlers in an occupied territory and changes to the demographic composition of an occupied territory;

(ii) the transfer by the Occupying Power of parts of its own civilian population into the territory it occupies, or the deportation or transfer of all or parts of the population of the occupied territory within or outside this territory;

Option 4

No paragraph (f).

[*21] (g)

Option 1

intentionally directing attacks against buildings dedicated to religion, art, science or charitable purposes, historic monuments, hospitals and places where the sick and wounded are collected, provided they are not being used at the time for military purposes;

Option 2

intentionally directing attacks against buildings dedicated to religion, education, art, science or charitable purposes, historic monuments, hospitals and places where the sick and wounded are collected, provided they are not being used at the time for military purposes;

---

[11] Ibid.

(h)   subjecting persons who are in the power of an adverse Party to physical mutilation or to medical or scientific experiments of any kind which are neither justified by the medical, dental or hospital treatment of the person concerned nor carried out in his interest, and which cause death to or seriously endanger the health of such person or persons;

(i)   killing or wounding treacherously individuals belonging to the hostile nation or army;

(j)   declaring that no quarter will be given;

(k)   destroying or seizing the enemy's property unless such destruction or seizure be imperatively demanded by the necessities of war;

(l)   declaring abolished, suspended or inadmissible in a court of law the rights and actions of the nationals of the hostile party;

(m)   compelling the nationals of the hostile party to take part in the operations of war directed against their own country, even if they were in the belligerent's service before the commencement of the war;

(n)   pillaging a town or place, even when taken by assault;

(o)

Option 1

[*22] employing the following weapons, projectiles and material and methods of warfare which are calculated to cause superfluous injury or unnecessary suffering:

(i)   poison or poisoned weapons,

(ii)   asphyxiating, poisonous or other gases, and all analogous liquids, materials or devices,

(iii)   bullets which expand or flatten easily in the human body, such as bullets with a hard envelope which does not entirely cover the core or is pierced with incisions,

(iv)   bacteriological (biological) agents or toxins for hostile purposes or in armed conflict,

(v)   chemical weapons as defined in and prohibited by the 1993 Convention on the Prohibition of the Development, Production, Stockpiling and Use of Chemical Weapons and On Their Destruction;

Option 2

employing the following weapons, projectiles and material and methods of warfare which are of a nature to cause superfluous injury or unnecessary suffering:

(i)   poison or poisoned weapons,

(ii)   asphyxiating, poisonous or other gases, and all analogous liquids, materials or devices,

(iii)   bullets which expand or flatten easily in the human body, such as bullets with a hard envelope which does not entirely cover the core or is pierced with incisions,

(iv)   bacteriological (biological) agents or toxins for hostile purposes or in armed conflict.

(v)   chemical weapons as defined in and prohibited by the 1993 Convention on the Prohibition of the Development, Production, Stockpiling and Use of Chemical Weapons and On Their Destruction,

[*23]   (vi)   such other weapons or weapons systems as become the subject of a comprehensive prohibition pursuant to customary or conventional international law;

Option 3

employing weapons, projectiles and material and methods of warfare which are of a nature to cause superfluous injury or unnecessary suffering or which are inherently indiscriminate;

Option 4

employing the following weapons, projectiles and material and methods of warfare which are of a nature to cause superfluous injury or unnecessary suffering or which are inherently indiscriminate:

or

employing weapons, projectiles and material and methods of warfare which are of a nature to cause superfluous injury or unnecessary suffering or which are inherently indiscriminate, such as but not limited to:

(i)   poison or poisoned weapons,

(ii)   asphyxiating, poisonous or other gases, and all analogous liquids, materials or devices,

(iii)   bullets which expand or flatten easily in the human body, such as bullets with a hard envelope which does not entirely cover the core or is pierced with incisions,

(iv)   bacteriological (biological) agents or toxins for hostile purposes or in armed conflict,

(v)   chemical weapons as defined in and prohibited by the 1993 Convention on the Prohibition of the Development, Production, Stockpiling and Use of Chemical Weapons and On Their Destruction,

(vi)   nuclear weapons,

(vii) anti-personnel mines,

[*24]   (viii)   blinding laser weapons,

(ix)   such other weapons or weapons systems as become the subject of a comprehensive prohibition pursuant to customary or conventional international law;

(p)

Option 1

committing outrages upon personal dignity, in particular humiliating and degrading treatment;

Option 2

committing outrages upon personal dignity, in particular humiliating and degrading treatment as well as practices of apartheid and other inhuman and degrading practices involving outrages upon personal dignity based on racial discrimination;

(p bis) committing rape, sexual slavery, enforced prostitution, enforced pregnancy, enforced sterilization, and any other form of sexual violence also constituting a grave breach of the Geneva Conventions;

(q)   utilizing the presence of a civilian or other protected person to render certain points, areas or military forces immune from military operations;

(r)   intentionally directing attacks against buildings, material, medical units and transport, and personnel using, in conformity with international law, the distinctive emblems of the Geneva Conventions;

(s)   intentionally using starvation of civilians as a method of warfare by depriving them of objects indispensable to their survival, including wilfully impeding relief supplies as provided for under the Geneva Conventions;

(t)

Option 1

forcing children under the age of fifteen years to take direct part in hostilities.

[*25] Option 2

recruiting children under the age of fifteen years into armed forces or using them to participate actively in hostilities.[12]

Option 3

(i)   recruiting children under the age of fifteen years into armed forces or groups; or

(ii)   allowing them to take part in hostilities;

Option 4

No paragraph (t).

* * *

OPTION I

Sections C and D of this article apply to armed conflicts not of an international character and thus do not apply to situations of internal disturbances and tensions, such as riots, isolated and sporadic acts of violence or other acts of a similar nature.

[*26] C. In the case of an armed conflict not of an international character, serious violations of article 3 common to the four Geneva Conventions of 12 August 1949, namely, any of the following acts committed

---

[12]   This option seeks to incorporate the essential principles contained under accepted international law while using language suitable for individual criminal responsibility as opposed to State responsibility.

The words "using" and "participate" have been adopted in order to cover both direct participation in combat and also active participation in military activities linked to combat such as scouting, spying, sabotage and the use of children as decoys, couriers or at military checkpoints. It would not cover activities clearly unrelated to the hostilities such as food deliveries to an airbase of the use of domestic staff in an officer's married accommodation. However, use of children in a direct support function such as acting as bearers to take supplies to the front line, or activities at the front line itself, would be included within the terminology.

against persons taking no active part in the hostilities, including members of armed forces who have laid down their arms and those placed hors de combat by sickness, wounds, detention or any other cause:

(a)   violence to life and person, in particular murder of all kinds, mutilation, cruel treatment and torture;

(b)   committing outrages upon personal dignity, in particular humiliating and degrading treatment;

(c)   taking of hostages;

(d)   the passing of sentences and the carrying out of executions without previous judgement pronounced by a regularly constituted court, affording all judicial guarantees which are generally recognized as indispensable.

D.   Other serious violations of the laws and customs applicable in armed conflicts not of an international character, within the established framework of international law, namely, any of the following acts: (a)

Option 1

intentionally directing attacks against the civilian population as such, as well as individual civilians not taking direct part in hostilities;

Option 2

No paragraph (a).

(b)   intentionally directing attacks against buildings, material, medical units and transport, and personnel using, in conformity with international law, the distinctive emblems of the Geneva Conventions;

(c)

Option 1

[*27] intentionally directing attacks against buildings dedicated to religion, art, science or charitable purposes, historic monuments, hospitals and places where the sick and wounded are collected, provided they are not being used at the time for military purposes;

Option 2

intentionally directing attacks against buildings dedicated to religion, education, art, science or charitable purposes, historic monuments, hospitals and places where the sick and wounded are collected, provided they are not being used at the time for military purposes;

(d)   pillaging a town or place, even when taken by assault;

(e)   committing outrages upon personal dignity, in particular humiliating and degrading treatment;

(e *bis*) committing rape, sexual slavery, enforced prostitution, enforced pregnancy, enforced sterilization, and any other form of sexual violence also constituting a serious violation of article 3 common to the four Geneva Conventions;

(f)

Option 1

forcing children under the age of fifteen years to take direct part in hostilities;

Option 2

recruiting children under the age of fifteen years into armed forces or groups or using them to participate actively in hostilities;

Option 3

(i)   recruiting children under the age of fifteen years into armed forces or groups; or

(ii)   allowing them to take part in hostilities;

[*28] Option 4

No paragraph (f).

(g)   ordering the displacement of the civilian population for reasons related to the conflict, unless the security of the civilians involved or imperative military reasons so demand;

(h)   killing or wounding treacherously a combatant adversary;

(i)   declaring that no quarter will be given;

(j)   subjecting persons who are in the power of another Party to the conflict to physical mutilation or to medical or scientific experiments of any kind which are neither justified by the medical, dental or hospital treatment of the person concerned nor carried out in his interest, and which cause death to or seriously endanger the health of such person or persons;

(k) destroying or seizing the property of an adversary unless such destruction or seizure be imperatively demanded by the necessities of the conflict;

(l)

Option 1

No provision on prohibited weapons.

Option 2

A reference to arms, in the light of the discussions on paragraph B(o).

OPTION II

Insert the following provisions in section D:

- intentionally using starvation of civilians as a method of warfare by depriving them of objects indispensable to their survival, including wilfully impeding relief supplies as provided for under the Geneva Conventions;

- intentionally launching an attack in the knowledge that such attack will cause incidental loss of life or injury to civilians or damage to [*29] civilian objects or widespread, long-term and severe damage to the natural environment;

- intentionally launching an attack against works or installations containing dangerous forces in the knowledge that such attack will cause excessive loss of life, injury to civilians or damage to civilian objects which would be excessive in relation to the concrete and direct military advantage anticipated;

- slavery and the slave trade in all their forms;

OPTION III

Delete the opening clause of sections C and D.

OPTION IV

Delete section D.

OPTION V

Delete sections C and D.

* * *

Elsewhere in the Statute:

Option 1

The jurisdiction of the Court shall extend to the most serious crimes of concern to the international community as a whole. The Court shall have jurisdiction in respect of the crimes listed in article X (war crimes) only when committed as part of a plan or policy or as part of a large-scale commission of such crimes.[13]

[*30] Option 2

The jurisdiction of the Court shall be limited to the most serious crimes of concern to the international community as a whole. The Court shall have jurisdiction in respect of the crimes listed in article X (war crimes) in particular when committed as a part of a plan or policy or as part of a large-scale commission of such crimes.[2]

Option 3

No provision on threshold.

* * *

Article Y

(relating to the part of the Statute dealing with the definition of crimes)

Without prejudice to the application of the provisions of this Statute, nothing in this part of the Statute shall be interpreted as limiting or prejudicing in any way existing or developing rules of international law.

N.B.

- Article Y could constitute a separate article or could be placed in article 5 (Crimes within the jurisdiction of the Court).

---

[13] The view was expressed that the substance and placement of this proposal should be considered.

-   Article 21, paragraph 3 (<u>Nullum crimen sine lege</u>) and article 20 (Applicable law) deal with related issues.

Crimes against humanity

1.   For the purpose of the present Statute, a crime against humanity means any of the following acts when committed

[as part of a widespread [and] [or] systematic commission of such acts against any population]:

[as part of a widespread [and] [or] systematic attack against any [civilian] population] [committed on a massive scale] [in armed conflict] [on political, philosophical, racial, ethnic or religious grounds or any other arbitrarily defined grounds]:

[*31] N.B. In case the second alternative is retained, its relationship with paragraph 1 (h) should be considered.

   (a)   murder;
   (b)   extermination;
   (c)   enslavement;
   (d)   deportation or forcible transfer of population;
   (e)   [detention or] [imprisonment] [deprivation of liberty] [in flagrant violation of international law] [in violation of fundamental legal norms];[14]
   (f)   torture;
   (g)   rape or other sexual abuse [of comparable gravity,] or enforced prostitution;
   (h)   persecution against any identifiable group or collectivity on political, racial, national, ethnic, cultural or religious [or gender] [or other similar] grounds[15] [and in connection with other crimes within the jurisdiction of the Court];
   (i)   enforced disappearance of persons;[16]
   (j)   other inhumane acts [of a similar character] [intentionally] causing [great suffering,] or serious injury to body or to mental or physical health.[17]

[*32] [2.   For the purpose of paragraph 1:

   (a)   extermination includes the [wilful, intentional] infliction of conditions of life calculated to bring about the destruction of part of a population;
   (b)   "deportation or forcible transfer of population" means the movement of [persons] [populations] from the area in which the [persons] [populations] are [lawfully present] [present] [resident] [under national or international law] [for a purpose contrary to international law] [without legitimate and compelling reasons] [without lawful justification];
   (c)   ["torture" means the intentional infliction of severe pain or suffering, whether physical or mental, upon a person [in the custody or physical control of the accused] [deprived of liberty]; except that torture shall not include pain or suffering arising only from, inherent in or incidental to, lawful sanctions [in conformity with international law]]
   ["torture" as defined in the Convention against Torture and Other Cruel, Inhuman or Degrading Treatment or Punishment of 10 December 1984];
   (d)   persecution means the wilful and severe deprivation of fundamental rights contrary to international law [carried out with the intent to persecute on specified grounds];
   (e)   ["enforced disappearance of persons" means when persons are arrested, detained or abducted against their will by or with the authorization, support or acquiescence of the State or a political organization, followed by a refusal to acknowledge that deprivation of freedom or to give information on the fate or whereabouts of those persons, thereby placing them outside the protection of the law]

---

[14]   It was suggested that this subparagraph does not include freedom of speech and that it includes the unilateral blockade of populations.
[15]   This also includes, for example, social, economic and mental or physical disability grounds.
[16]   It was suggested that some more time was needed to reflect upon the inclusion of this subparagraph.
[17]   It was suggested that the inclusion of this paragraph should be subject to further clarification. It was also suggested that the list of acts should include institutionalized discrimination.

*18

[*33] [Crimes of terrorism

For the purposes of the present Statute, crimes of terrorism means:

(1) Undertaking, organizing, sponsoring, ordering, facilitating, financing, encouraging or tolerating acts of violence against another State directed at persons or property and of such a nature as to create terror, fear or insecurity in the minds of public figures, groups of persons, the general public or populations, for whatever considerations and purposes of a political, philosophical, ideological, racial, ethnic, religious or such other nature that may be invoked to justify them;

(2) An offence under the following Conventions:

(a) Convention for the Suppression of Unlawful Acts against the Safety of Civil Aviation;

(b) Convention for the Suppression of Unlawful Seizure of Aircraft;

(c) Convention on the Prevention and Punishment of Crimes against Internationally Protected Persons, including Diplomatic Agents;

(d) International Convention against the Taking of Hostages;

(e) Convention for the Suppression of Unlawful Acts against the Safety of Maritime Navigation;

(f) Protocol for the Suppression of Unlawful Acts against the Safety of Fixed Platforms located on the Continental Shelf;

(3) An offence involving use of firearms, weapons, explosives and dangerous substances when used as a means to perpetrate indiscriminate violence involving death or serious bodily injury to persons or groups of persons or populations or serious damage to property.]

[Crimes against United Nations and associated personnel

1. For the purpose of the present Statute, "crimes against United Nations and associated personnel" means any of the following acts [when committed intentionally and in a systematic manner or on a large scale against United Nations and associated personnel involved in a United Nations operation with a view to preventing or impeding that operation from fulfilling its mandate]:

[*34] (a) murder, kidnapping or other attack upon the person or liberty of any such personnel;

(b) violent attack upon the official premises, the private accommodation or the means of transportation of any such personnel likely to endanger his or her person or liberty.

2. This article shall not apply to a United Nations operation authorized by the Security Council as an enforcement action under Chapter VII of the Charter of the United Nations in which any of the personnel are engaged as combatants against organized armed forces and to which the law of international armed conflict applies.]

[[19]Crimes involving the illicit traffic in narcotic drugs and psychotropic substances

For the purposes of the present Statute, crimes involving the illicit traffic in narcotic drugs and psychotropic substances means any of the following acts committed on a large scale and in a transboundary context:

(a) (i) The production, manufacture, extraction, preparation, offering, offering for sale, distribution, sale, delivery on any terms whatsoever, brokerage, dispatch, dispatch in transit, transport, importation or exportation of any narcotic drug or any psychotropic substance contrary to the provisions of the 1961 Convention, the 1961 Convention as amended or the 1971 Convention;

---

[18] The Preparatory Committee considered the following three crimes (crimes of terrorism, crimes against United Nations and associated personnel and crimes involving the illicit traffic in narcotic drugs and psychotropic substances) without prejudice to a final decision on their inclusion in the Statute. The Preparatory Committee also discussed these three crimes only in a general manner and did not have time to examine them as thoroughly as the other crimes.

[19] This square bracket ends at the end of the article.

(ii)   The cultivation of opium poppy, coca bush or cannabis plant for the purpose of the production of narcotic drugs contrary to the provisions of the 1961 Convention and the 1961 Convention as amended;

(iii)   The possession or purchase of any narcotic drug or psychotropic substance for the purpose of any of the activities enumerated in subparagraph (i) above;

(iv)   The manufacture, transport or distribution of equipment, materials or of substances listed in Table I and Table II of the [*35] annex to the 1988 United Nations Convention against Illicit Traffic in Narcotic Drugs and Psychotropic Substances knowing that they are to be used in or for the illicit cultivation, production or manufacture of narcotic drugs or psychotropic substances;

(v)   The organization, management or financing of any of the offences enumerated in subparagraphs (i), (ii), (iii) or (iv) above;

(b) (i)   The conversion or transfer of property, knowing that such property is derived from any offence or offences established in accordance with subparagraph (a) of this paragraph, or from an act of participation in such offence or offences, for the purpose of concealing or disguising the illicit origin of the property or of assisting any person who is involved in the commission of such an offence to evade the legal consequences of his or her actions;

(ii)   The concealment or disguise of the true nature, source, location, disposition, movement, rights with respect to, or ownership of property, knowing that such property is derived from an offence or offences established in accordance with subparagraph (a) of this paragraph or from an act of participation in such an offence or offences.

N.B. The Court's jurisdiction with regard to these crimes will only apply to States parties to the Statute which have accepted the jurisdiction of the Court with respect to those crimes. Refer to article 9, option 1, paragraph 2, or option 2, paragraph 1.]

Article 6
[Exercise of jurisdiction] [Preconditions
to the exercise of jurisdiction]

1.   The Court [may exercise its] [shall have] jurisdiction [over a person] with respect to a crime referred to in article 5, paragraph [(a) to (e), or any combination thereof] [and in accordance with the provisions of this Statute] if:

[(a) the [matter] [situation] is referred to the Court by the Security Council, [in accordance with article 10] [acting under Chapter VII of the Charter];]

[*36] (b) a complaint is lodged by a State Party [two State Parties] [or a non-State Party] in accordance with article 11;

[(c) the matter is brought by the Prosecutor, in accordance with article 12.]

[2.   [In the case of paragraphs 1 (b) [and (c)],] the Court [may exercise its] [shall have] jurisdiction [only if the States which have jurisdiction over the case in question have accepted the jurisdiction of the Court in accordance with article 9 and] [if national jurisdiction is either not available or ineffective] [in accordance with article 15] or if [an interested State] [interested States] [those States] have deferred the matter to the Court.]

[[20]Article 7
Preconditions to the exercise of jurisdiction

Opening clause of paragraph 1
Option 1[21]

---

[20]   This square bracket ends at the end of article 7.

[21]   Options are not put in square brackets because they are alternatives supported by only some delegations. Some other delegations suggested the deletion of one or more of the options or have suggested other changes within the options.

[In the case of article 6, paragraphs 1 (b) [and (c)],] The Court [may exercise its] [shall have] jurisdiction [over a person] if the following State(s) has/have accepted [the exercise of] the jurisdiction of the Court over the crimes referred to in [article 5, paragraphs (a) to (e), or any combination thereof] in accordance with article 9:
Option 2
[In the case of article 6, paragraphs 1 (b) [and (c)],] the Court [may exercise its] [shall have] jurisdiction [over a person] if the following State(s) has/have accepted the exercise of the jurisdiction of the Court with respect to a case in question which is the subject of a complaint lodged by a State:
[*37] [(a)   [the State that has custody of the suspect with respect to the crime ("custodial State")] [by the State on whose territory the person is resident at the time the complaint is lodged] [in accordance with international law];]
[(b)   the State on the territory of which the act [or omission] in question occurred [or if the crime was committed on board a vessel or aircraft, the State of registration of that vessel or aircraft;]
[(c)   if applicable, the State that has requested, under an international agreement, the custodial State to surrender a suspect for the purposes of prosecution, [unless the request is rejected];]
[(d)   the State of which the victim is a national;]
[(e)   the State of which the [accused] [suspect] of the crime is a national;]
[2.   If a State whose acceptance is required for the exercise of the jurisdiction by the Court rejects such acceptance, that State shall so inform the Court [giving reasons thereof].][22]
[3.   Notwithstanding paragraph 1, if a State whose acceptance is required has not indicated whether it gives such acceptance or not within a period of (...), then the Court [may] [may not] exercise its jurisdiction accordingly.][23]
[4.   When a State that is not a Party to the Statute has an interest in the acts mentioned in the complaint, this State may, by an express declaration deposited with the Registrar of the Court, agree that the Court shall exercise jurisdiction in respect of the acts specified in the declaration.]]

[*38] [[24]Article 8[25]
Temporal jurisdiction
1.   The Court has jurisdiction only in respect of crimes committed after the date of entry into force of this Statute.
[When a State becomes a Party to this Statute after its entry into force, the Court cannot be seized in respect of crimes committed by its nationals or on its territory or against its nationals, unless those crimes have been committed after the deposit by that State of its instrument of ratification or accession.]
[2.   The Court has no jurisdiction in respect of crimes for which, even if they have been committed after the entry into force of this Statute, the Security Council, acting under Chapter VII of the Charter of the United Nations, has decided before the entry into force of this Statute to establish an ad hoc international criminal tribunal. The Security Council may, however, decide otherwise.]]
N.B. There is an interrelationship between this article and article 22 (Non-retroactivity).

[[26]Article 9
Acceptance of the jurisdiction of the Court
Option 1[27]
1.   A State that becomes a Party to this Statute thereby accepts the [inherent] jurisdiction of the Court with respect to the crimes referred to in article 5, paragraphs [(a) to (d), or any combination thereof].

---

[22]   This paragraph is relevant only to option 2 of the opening clause to paragraph 1.
[23]   Ibid.
[24]   This square bracket ends at the end of article 8.
[25]   The issues raised in this article deserve further reflection as to its place in the Statute.
[26]   The square bracket ends at the end of paragraph 5 of this article.
[27]   Options 1 and 2 are not mutually exclusive and could be combined in such a way that option 1 may be used in respect of some crimes and option 2 in respect of other crimes.

[*39] 2.   With regard to the crimes referred to in article 5 other than those mentioned in paragraph 1, a State Party to this Statute may declare:

(a)   at the time it expresses its consent to be bound by the Statute; or

(b)   at a later time that it accepts the jurisdiction of the Court with respect to such of the crimes as it specifies in the declaration.

3.   If under article 7 the acceptance of a State that is not a Party to this Statute is required, that State may, by declaration lodged with the Registrar, consent to the exercise of jurisdiction by the Court with respect to the crime. [The accepting State will cooperate with the Court without any delay or exception, in accordance with Part 9 of the Statute.]

Option 2

1.   A State Party to this Statute may:

(a)   at the time it expresses its consent to be bound by the Statute, by declaration lodged with the depositary; or

(b)   at a later time, by declaration lodged with the Registrar; accept the jurisdiction of the Court with respect to [such of] the crimes referred to in [article 5, paragraphs (a) to (e), or any combination thereof] as it specifies in the declaration.

2.   A declaration may be of general application, or may be limited to [particular conduct or to conduct] [one or more of the crimes referred to in article 5, paragraphs (a) to (e),] committed during a particular period of time.[28]

3.   A declaration may be made for a specified period, in which case it may not be withdrawn before the end of that period, or for an unspecified period, in which case it may be withdrawn only upon giving a six month's notice of withdrawal to the Registrar. Withdrawal does not affect proceedings already commenced under this Statute.[29]

[*40] 4.   If under article 7 the acceptance of a State that is not a Party to this Statute is required, that State may, by declaration lodged with the Registrar, consent to the exercise of jurisdiction by the Court with respect to the crime. [The accepting State will cooperate with the Court without any delay or exception, in accordance with Part 9 of the Statute.]

[5.   A declaration referred to in paragraphs 1 to 3 may not contain other limitations than those mentioned in paragraphs 1 to 3.]]

Further option

Acceptance of the jurisdiction of the Court:

1.   A State which becomes a Party to the Statute thereby accepts the jurisdiction of the Court with respect to the crimes referred to in article 5, [paragraphs (a) to (d)].

[2.   A State that is not a Party to this Statute may, by declaration lodged with the Registrar, accept the obligation to cooperate with the Court with respect to the prosecution of any crime referred to in article 5. The accepting State shall then cooperate with the Court without any delay or exception in accordance with Part 9 of this Statute.]

[[30]Article 10

[[Action by] [Role of] The Security Council] [Relationship between the Security Council and the International Criminal Court]

1.   [Notwithstanding article 6, [7] [and [9], the Court has jurisdiction in accordance with this Statute with respect to crimes [referred to] [specified] in article 5 [as a consequence of the referral of] [on the basis of a [formal] decision to refer] a [matter] [situation] in which one or more crimes appear to have been committed to [the Prosecutor of] the Court by the Security Council [acting under Chapter VII of the Charter of the United Nations] [in accordance with the terms of such referral].

---

[28]   This paragraph may also apply to option 1.

[29]   Ibid.

[30]   This square bracket ends at the end of option 2 of paragraph 7.

[*41] 2. [Notification of] [A letter from the President of the Security Council conveying] the Security Council decision to the Prosecutor of the Court shall be accompanied by all supporting material available to the Council.]

3.   The Security Council, on the basis of a formal decision under Chapter VI of the Charter of the United Nations, may lodge a complaint with the Prosecutor specifying that crimes referred to in article 5 appear to have been committed.]

4.

Option 1

[A complaint of or directly related to [an act] [a crime] of aggression [referred to in article 5] may [not] be brought [under this Statute] unless the Security Council has [first] [determined] [formally decided] that the act of a State that is the subject of the complaint, [is] [is not] an act of aggression [in accordance with Chapter VII of the Charter of the United Nations].

Option 2

[The determination [under Article 39 of the Charter of the United Nations] of the Security Council that a State has committed an act of aggression shall be binding on the deliberation of the Court in respect of a complaint, the subject matter of which is the act of aggression.]

5.   [A referral of a matter to the Court or] [A determination] [A formal decision] by the Security Council [under paragraph 4 above] shall not be interpreted as in any way affecting the independence of the Court in its determination of the criminal responsibility of the person concerned.

6.   [A complaint of or directly related to an act of aggression brought under this Statute and the findings of the Court in such cases is without prejudice to the powers of the Security Council under Chapter VII of the Charter.]

[³¹7. Option 1

No prosecution may be commenced under this Statute arising from a [dispute or] situation [[pertaining to international peace and security or an act of aggression] which [is being dealt with] [actively] by the Security Council] [*42] [as a threat to or breach of the peace or an act of aggression] [under Chapter VII of the Charter], [where the Security Council has decided that there is a threat to or breach of the peace and for which it is exercising its functions under Chapter VII of the Charter of the United Nations], [unless the Security Council otherwise decides] [without the prior consent of the Security Council].

Option 2

1.   [Subject to paragraph 4 of this article], no prosecution may be commenced [or proceeded with] under this Statute [for a period of twelve months] where the Security Council has [decided that there is a threat to or breach of the peace or an act of aggression and], acting under Chapter VII of the Charter of the United Nations, [given a direction] [taken a [formal and specific] decision] to that effect.

2.   [Notification] [A formal decision of the Security Council to the effect] that the Security Council is continuing to act may be renewed at intervals of twelve months [by a subsequent decision].]

3.   [Should no action be taken by the Security Council in accordance with Chapter VII of the Charter of the United Nations within a reasonable time, the Court may exercise its jurisdiction in respect of the situation referred to in paragraph 1 of this article.]]]

Article 11³²
Complaint by State

1.

Option 1

[[A State Party which is also a Contracting Party to the Convention on the Prevention and Punishment of the Crime of Genocide of 9 December 1948] [A State Party [which accepts the jurisdiction of the Court under article 9 with respect to a crime]] may lodge a complaint [referring a [matter] [situation] in which

---

³¹   This square bracket ends at the end of paragraph 3 of option 2.

³²   This article was moved here from Part 5.

one or more crimes within the jurisdiction of the Court appear to have been committed to] [with] the Prosecutor [alleging that [a crime of genocide] [such a crime] [a crime under article 5, paragraphs [(a) to (d), or any combination [*43] thereof]] appears to have been committed] [and requesting that the Prosecutor investigate the situation for the purpose of determining whether one or more specific persons should be charged with the commission of such crimes.]]

Option 2

[A State Party [which accepts the jurisdiction of the Court under article 9 with respect to a crime] [that has a direct interest] listed under (a) to (d) below may lodge a complaint with the Prosecutor alleging that [such a crime] [a crime under article 5, paragraphs [(a) to (d), or any combination thereof]] appears to have been committed:

    (a)   a State on the territory of which the act [or omission] in question occurred;

    (b)   a State of the custody;

    (c)   a State of the nationality of a suspect;

    (d)   a State of the nationality of victims.]

[2.   A State Party, which, for a crime under article 5, paragraph (e), has accepted the jurisdiction of the Court pursuant to article 9 and is a party to the treaty concerned may lodge a complaint with the Prosecutor alleging that such a crime appears to have been committed.][33]

[3.   As far as possible, a complaint shall specify the relevant circumstances and be accompanied by such supporting documentation as is available to the complainant State.][34]

[4.   The Prosecutor shall notify the Security Council of all complaints lodged under article 11.]

[*44] [Article 12[35]

Prosecutor

The Prosecutor [may] [shall] initiate investigations [ex officio] [proprio motu] [or] on the basis of information [obtained] [he may seek] from any source, in particular from Governments, United Nations organs [and intergovernmental and non-governmental organizations]. The Prosecutor shall assess the information received or obtained and decide whether there is sufficient basis to proceed. [The Prosecutor may, for the purpose of initiating an investigation, receive information on alleged crimes under article 5, paragraphs (a) to (d), from Governments, intergovernmental and non-governmental organizations, victims and associations representing them, or other reliable sources.]][36]

N.B. The terms "sufficient basis" used in this article (if retained) and "reasonable basis" in article 54, paragraph 1, should be harmonized.

[Article 13

Information submitted to the Prosecutor

1.   Upon receipt of information relating to the commission of a crime under article 5, submitted by victims, associations on their behalf, regional or international organizations or any other reliable source, the Prosecutor shall analyse the seriousness of the information. For this purpose, he or she may seek additional information from States, organs of the United Nations, non-governmental organizations, victims or their representatives or other sources that he or she deems appropriate, and may receive written or oral testimony at the seat of the Court. If the Prosecutor concludes that there is a reasonable basis to proceed with an investigation, he or she shall submit to the Pre-Trial Chamber a request for authorization of an investigation, together with any supporting material collected. Victims may make representations to the Pre-Trial Chamber, in accordance with the Rules.

---

[33]   This provision is without any prejudice to the position of delegations with regard to "treaty crimes".

[34]   Further discussion on the content of a complaint may be necessary in the context of matters dealing with procedures.

[35]   This article was moved here from Part 5.

[36]   The procedure to be followed by the Prosecutor in relation to this article may be discussed further.

2.   If the Pre-Trial Chamber, upon examination of the request and the accompanying material, considers that there is a reasonable basis to proceed [*45] with an investigation, and that the case appears to fall within the jurisdiction of the Court, having regard to article 15, it shall authorize the commencement of the investigation. This shall be without prejudice to subsequent determinations by the Court as to the jurisdiction and admissibility of the case pursuant to article 17.

The refusal of the Pre-Trial Chamber to authorize the investigation shall not preclude the presentation of a subsequent request by the Prosecutor based on new facts or evidence pertaining to the same situation.
3.   If, after the preliminary examination referred to in paragraph 1, the Prosecutor concludes that the information provided does not constitute a reasonable basis for an investigation, he or she shall inform those who provided the information. This shall not preclude the Prosecutor from considering further information submitted in accordance with paragraph 1 pertaining to the same situation in the light of new facts or evidence.]

Further option for articles 6, 7, 10 and 11[37]

[Article 6
Exercise of jurisdiction

The Court may exercise its jurisdiction with respect to a crime referred to in article 5 in accordance with the provisions of this Statute if:
(a)   a situation in which one or more of such crimes appears to have been committed is referred to the Prosecutor by a State Party in accordance with article 11;
[(b) the Prosecutor has initiated an investigation in respect of such a crime in accordance with article 12]; or
(b)   a situation in which one or more of such crimes appears to have been committed is referred to the Prosecutor by the Security Council [acting under Chapter VII of the Charter of the United Nations]].

[*46] [Article 7
Acceptance of jurisdiction

1.   A State which becomes a Party to the Statute thereby accepts the jurisdiction of the Court with respect to the crimes referred to in article 5.
2.   Where a situation has been referred to the Court by a State Party [or where the Prosecutor has initiated an investigation], the Court may exercise its jurisdiction with respect to a crime referred to in article 5 provided that [one of] the following States [are Parties] [is Party] to the Statute or [has] [have] accepted the jurisdiction of the Court with respect to the crime in question in accordance with paragraph 3 below:
[(a)   the State that has custody of the suspect with respect to the crime ("custodial State")] [the State of the nationality of the suspect];
(b)   the State on the territory of which the act or omission in question occurred or, if the crime was committed on board a vessel or aircraft, the State of registration of that vessel or aircraft.
3.   If the acceptance of a State that is not a Party to this Statute is required under paragraph 2 above, that State may, by declaration lodged with the Registrar, consent to the exercise of jurisdiction by the Court with respect to the crime in question. The accepting State shall cooperate with the Court without any delay or exception in accordance with Part 9 of this Statute.]

[Article 10
Role of the Security Council

[1.   The Court may not exercise its jurisdiction with respect to a crime of aggression unless the Security Council has first determined under Chapter VII of the Charter of the United Nations that the State

---

[37]   It was mentioned that although the approach taken in this option merited consideration, strong reservations were expressed with regard to the references to the Security Council; the view was also expressed that the Court should not exercise jurisdiction unless States Parties gave their express consent.

concerned has committed an act of aggression. A determination by the Security Council shall not be interpreted as in any way affecting the independence of the Court in its determination of the criminal responsibility of any person concerned.]

2.   No investigation or prosecution may be commenced or proceeded with under this Statute [for a period of twelve months] after the Security Council[, acting under Chapter VII of the Charter of the United Nations,] has requested the Court [*47] to that effect; that request may be renewed by the Council under the same conditions.]

[Article 11
Referral of a situation by a State

1.   A State Party may refer to the Prosecutor a situation in which one or more crimes within the jurisdiction of the Court appear to have been committed, requesting the Prosecutor to investigate the situation for the purpose of determining whether one or more specific persons should be charged with the commission of such crimes.

2.   As far as possible, a referral shall specify the relevant circumstances and be accompanied by such supporting documentation as is available to the complainant State.

3.   The Prosecutor shall notify the Security Council of all situations referred under this article.]

Article 14
Duty of the Court as to jurisdiction

The Court shall satisfy itself that it has jurisdiction in any case brought before it.

N.B. This article seems to be unnecessary in view of a similar text in paragraph 1 of article 17 (Challenges to the jurisdiction of the Court or the admissibility of a case) and could therefore be deleted.

[*48] Article 15
Issues of admissibility[38]

> The following draft text represents the results of informal consultations on article 15 and is intended to facilitate the work towards the elaboration of the Statute of the Court. The content of the text represents a possible way to address the issue of complementarity and is without prejudice to the views of any delegation. The text does not represent agreement on the eventual content or approach to be included in this article.

1.   Having regard to paragraph 3 of the preamble,[39] the Court shall determine that a case is inadmissible where:

(a)   the case is being investigated or prosecuted by a State which has jurisdiction over it, unless the State is unwilling or unable genuinely to carry out the investigation or prosecution; [*40]

(b)   the case has been investigated by a State which has jurisdiction over it and the State has decided not to prosecute the person concerned, unless the decision resulted from the unwillingness or inability of the State genuinely to prosecute;

---

[38]   The present text of article 15 is without prejudice to the question whether complementarity-related admissibility requirements of this article may be waived by the State or States concerned.

[39]   Suggestions were made that the principle of complementarity should be further clarified either in this article or elsewhere in the Statute.

[40]   The proposal on extradition or international cooperation is not included in the text, subject to the determination of whether the relevant State would be able to present arguments in the procedure on admissibility.

N.B. In the context of this footnote, see also article 17, paragraph 2 (Challenges to the jurisdiction of the Court or the admissibility of a case).

[*49] (c) the person concerned has already been tried for conduct which is the subject of the complaint,[41] and a trial by the Court is not permitted under paragraph 2 of article 18;[42]
***[43]

(d) the case is not of sufficient gravity to justify further action by the Court.[44]

2. In order to determine unwillingness in a particular case, the Court shall consider whether one or more of the following exist, as applicable:

(a) the proceedings[45] were or are being undertaken or the national decision was made for the purpose of shielding the person concerned from criminal responsibility for crimes within the jurisdiction of the Court as set out in article 5;

[*50] (b) there has been an undue delay in the proceedings which in the circumstances is inconsistent with an intent to bring the person concerned to justice;

(c) the proceedings were not or are not being conducted independently or impartially and they were or are being conducted in a manner which, in the circumstances, is inconsistent with an intent to bring the person concerned to justice.

3. In order to determine inability in a particular case, the Court shall consider whether, due to a total or partial collapse or unavailability of its national judicial system, the State is unable to obtain the accused or the necessary evidence and testimony or otherwise unable to carry out its proceedings.

* * *

An alternative approach, which needs further discussion, is that the Court shall not have the power to intervene when a national decision has been taken in a particular case. That approach could be reflected as follows:

"The Court has no jurisdiction where the case in question is being investigated or prosecuted, or has been prosecuted, by a State which has jurisdiction over it."

[Article 16
Preliminary rulings regarding admissibility

1. When a matter has been referred to the Court pursuant to article 6 and the Prosecutor has determined that there would be a sufficient basis to commence an investigation of the matter, the Prosecutor shall make such referral known by public announcement and by notification to all States Parties.

2. Within [ ] days of the public announcement of such referral, a State may inform the Court that it is investigating its nationals or others within its jurisdiction with respect to criminal acts that allegedly were committed in the context of the matter referred to the Court and that may constitute offences described in article 5. At the request of that State, the Prosecutor shall defer to the State's investigation of such persons unless the Prosecutor determines that there has been a total or partial collapse or unavailability of the State's national judicial system, or the State is unwilling or unable [*51] genuinely to carry out the investigation and prosecutions. Before the Prosecutor may commence investigation of such persons, the Prosecutor must obtain a preliminary ruling from a Pre-Trial Chamber confirming the Prosecutor's

---

[41] If the Security Council can refer situations to the Court or the Prosecutor can initiate investigations, then the appropriate wording may be considered.

[42] It was noted that article 15 should also address, directly or indirectly, cases in which there was a prosecution resulting in conviction or acquittal, as well as discontinuance of prosecutions and possibly also pardons and amnesties. A number of delegations expressed the view that article 18, as currently worded, did not adequately address these situations for purposes of complementarity. It was agreed that these questions should be revisited in light of further revisions to article 18 to determine whether the reference to article 18 was sufficient or whether additional language was needed in article 15 to address these situations.

[43] Some delegations preferred the inclusion of the following subparagraph: "the accused is not liable under article 92 (Rule of speciality) to be prosecuted before or punished by the Court".
N.B. In the light of the text of article 92 (Rule of speciality), consideration should be given as to whether this footnote is still necessary.

[44] Some delegations believed that this subparagraph should be included elsewhere in the Statute or deleted.

[45] The term "proceedings" covers both investigations and prosecutions.

determination. The Prosecutor's deferral to the State's investigation shall be open for review by the Prosecutor [six months] [one year] after the date of deferral.

3.   A preliminary ruling of the Pre-Trial Chamber confirming the Prosecutor's determination may be appealed to the Appeals Chamber by the State concerned. If the preliminary ruling is appealed by the State, [two thirds] [all] of the judges of the Appeals Chamber must confirm that ruling before the Prosecutor may commence the investigation and seek indictments.

4.   When the Prosecutor has deferred an investigation pursuant to section 2, the Prosecutor may request that the State concerned report periodically on the progress of its investigations and any subsequent prosecutions. States Parties shall respond to such requests without undue delay.

5.   That a State has challenged a preliminary ruling under the present article shall not prejudice its right to challenge admissibility of a case under article 17[46] [or to withhold its consent to the exercise of jurisdiction under article 7].]

Article 17
Challenges to the jurisdiction of the Court
or the admissibility of a case

1.   At all stages of the proceedings, the Court (a) shall satisfy itself as to its jurisdiction over a case and (b) may, on its own motion, determine the admissibility of the case pursuant to article 15.[47]

2.   Challenges to the admissibility of the case, pursuant to article 15, or challenges to the jurisdiction of the Court may be made by:

[*52] (a) an accused [or a suspect];[48]

(b) [A State] [[An interested] State Party] which has jurisdiction over the crime on the ground that it is investigating or prosecuting the case or has investigated or prosecuted[49]

[a State [State Party] of nationality of a person referred to in paragraph 2 (a) [on the ground that it is investigating or prosecuting the case or has investigated or prosecuted]]

[and a State [State Party] which has received a request for cooperation];

The Prosecutor may seek a ruling from the Court regarding a question of jurisdiction or admissibility.

In proceedings with respect to jurisdiction or admissibility, those having submitted the case pursuant to article 6,[50] [those non-States parties which have jurisdiction over the crimes][51] as well as victims, may also submit observations to the Court.

3.[52] The admissibility of a case or the jurisdiction of the Court may be challenged only once by any person or State referred to in paragraph 2.

The challenge must take place prior to or at the commencement of the trial.

[*53] In exceptional circumstances, the Court may grant leave for a challenge to be brought more than once or at a time later than the commencement of the trial.

Challenges to the admissibility of a case, at the commencement of a trial, or subsequently with the leave of the Court as provided in the preceding subparagraph, may only be based on article 15, paragraph 1 (c).[53]

---

[46]   Article 17, paragraph 5, should be revised to require a vote by two thirds of the judges of the Appeals Chamber to decide that a case is admissible.

[47]   In the light of the wording to be adopted for article 17, several draft provisions of the Statute may have to be re-examined including article 54, paragraph 6, and article 58, paragraph 2 (b).

[48]   The term "suspect" includes a person who is the subject to an investigation. Another option is to limit the right to challenge to a suspect arrested on the basis of a pre-indictment arrest warrant.

[49]   The final wording of this subparagraph will depend on the content of article 15.

[50]   The final wording (States, Security Council, Prosecutor) will depend on the content of article 6.

[51]   This provision would apply to the option where only States parties can challenge the jurisdiction of the Court or the admissibility of a case.

[52]   It was suggested that if several States have jurisdiction over a case and one of those States has already challenged the jurisdiction of the Court, the remaining States should not bring additional challenges except on different grounds.

[53]   The final wording of this subparagraph will depend on the content of article 15.

4.   A State referred to in paragraph 2 (b) of the present article shall make a challenge at the earliest opportunity.[54]

5.   Prior to the confirmation of the indictment, challenges to the admissibility of a case or challenges to the jurisdiction of the Court, shall be referred to the Pre-Trial Chamber. After confirmation of the indictment, they shall be referred to the Trial Chamber.

Decisions with respect to jurisdiction or admissibility may be appealed to the Appeals Chamber.[55]

[6.   If the Court has decided that a case is inadmissible pursuant to article 15, the Prosecutor, may, at any time, submit a request for a review of the decision, on the grounds that conditions required under article 15 to render the case inadmissible no longer exist or that new facts arose.]

Article 18
Ne bis in idem

1.   Except as provided in this Statute,[56] no person shall be tried before the Court with respect to conduct which formed the basis of crimes for which the person has been convicted or acquitted by the Court.

[*54] 2.   No person shall be tried before another court for a crime[57] referred to in article 5 for which that person has already been convicted or acquitted by the Court.

3.[58]   No person who has been tried by another court for conduct also proscribed under article 5 shall be tried by the Court unless the proceedings in the other court:
...[59]

(a)   were for the purpose of shielding the person concerned from criminal responsibility for crimes within the jurisdiction of the Court; or

(b)   otherwise were not conducted independently or impartially and were conducted in a manner which, in the circumstances, was inconsistent with an intent to bring the person concerned to justice.
...[60]

* * *

An alternative approach, which needs further discussion, is that the Court shall not have the power to intervene when a national decision has been taken in a particular case. That approach could be reflected as follows:

[*55] "The Court has no jurisdiction where the case in question is being investigated or prosecuted, or has been prosecuted, by a State which has jurisdiction over it."

[Article 19[61]

Without prejudice to article 18, a person who has been tried by another court for conduct also proscribed under article 5 may be tried by the Court if a manifestly unfounded decision on the suspension of the enforcement of a sentence or on a pardon, a parole or a commutation of the sentence excludes the application of any appropriate form of penalty.]

---

[54]   The question arises as to what consequences, if any, should flow from the failure of a State to make a timely challenge.

[55]   The question concerning the suspension of the trial proceeding in case of appeal should be addressed in the Rules of Procedure and Evidence.

[56]   The phrase "Except as provided in this Statute" should be reviewed in the light of the final text of article 83.

[57]   It was noted that further consideration might be necessary on whether this paragraph should apply to conduct constituting a crime or a similar notion.

[58]   Further consideration might be necessary in the light of the final text of article 15.

[59]   It was noted that further consideration might be necessary on whether there should be additional exceptions to the principle of ne bis in idem, such as failure to take account of the grave nature of the crime, at either the trial or the sentencing stage.

[60]   The principle in article 77 that the Court may deduct time previously served in connection with conduct underlying the crime should be reviewed, as it was pointed out that the Court should, in principle, be obliged to deduct any such time.

[61]   It was noted that further consideration of this article, in particular its content and placement, is needed.

Article 20
Applicable law

1.   The Court shall apply:

   (a)   in the first place, this Statute and its Rules of Procedure and Evidence;

   (b)   if necessary, applicable treaties and the principles and rules of general international law [, including the established principles of the law of armed conflict];

   (c)[62]

Option 1

failing that, general principles of law derived by the Court from national laws of legal systems of the world [, where those national laws are not inconsistent with this Statute and with international law and internationally recognized norms and standards].

Option 2

[*56] failing that, and only insofar as it is consistent with the objectives and purpose of this Statute:

   (i)   the national law of the State where the crime was committed or, if the crime was committed in the territories of more than one State, the national law of the State where the substantial part of the crime was committed;

   (ii)   if the laws of the State or States mentioned in subparagraph (i) do not exist, the national law of the State of nationality of the accused or, if the accused does not have a nationality, the national law of the State of his or her permanent residence; or

   (iii)   if the laws of the States mentioned in subparagraphs (i) and (ii) do not exist, the national law of the State which has custody of the accused.

2.   The Court may apply principles and rules of law as interpreted in its previous decisions.

3.   The application and interpretation of law pursuant to this article must be consistent with internationally recognized human rights, which include the prohibition on any adverse distinction founded on gender, age, race, colour, language, religion or belief, political or other opinion, national, ethnic or social origin, wealth, birth or other status, or on any other similar criteria.[63]

[*57] PART 3. GENERAL PRINCIPLES OF CRIMINAL LAW
Article 21
Nullum crimen sine lege

1.   Provided that this Statute is applicable in accordance with article 6, 7, 8, 9 or 10 a person shall not be criminally responsible under this Statute:

   (a)   in the case of a prosecution with respect to a crime referred to in article 5, paragraphs [(a) to (d)], unless the conduct in question constitutes a crime that is defined in this Statute;

   (b)   in the case of a prosecution with respect to a crime referred to in article [5, paragraph (e)], unless the treaty in question was applicable to the conduct of the person at the time that the conduct occurred.

[2.   Conduct shall not be construed as criminal and sanctions shall not be applied under this Statute by a process of analogy.]

3.   Paragraph 1 shall not affect the character of such conduct as being crimes under international law, apart from this Statute.

---

[62]   There was broad support for option 1. Some delegations, however, favoured the approach taken in option 2.

[63]   It was generally agreed that consistency with internationally recognized human rights would require that interpretation by the Court be consistent with the principle of nullum crimen sine lege. A view was also expressed that this should be explicitly stated in this article or be made clearer in article 21. For example, article 21, paragraph 2, could be reformulated as follows:

"The provisions of article 5 shall be strictly construed and shall not be extended by analogy to, or be interpreted to proscribe, conduct not clearly criminal under it."

Article 22
Non-retroactivity

1.   Provided that this Statute is applicable in accordance with article 21, a person shall not be criminally responsible under this Statute for conduct committed prior to its entry into force.

[2.   If the law as it appeared at the commission of the crime is amended prior to the final judgement in the case, the most lenient law shall be applied.][1]

Article 23
[*58] Individual criminal responsibility

1.   The Court shall have jurisdiction over natural persons pursuant to the present Statute.

2.   A person who commits a crime under this Statute is individually responsible and liable for punishment.

[3.   Criminal responsibility is individual and cannot go beyond the person and the person's possessions.][2]

4.   The fact that the present Statute provides criminal responsibility for individuals does not affect the responsibility of States under international law.

[5.   The Court shall also have jurisdiction over legal persons, with the exception of States, when the crimes committed were committed on behalf of such legal persons or by their agencies or representatives.

6.   The criminal responsibility of legal persons shall not exclude the criminal responsibility of natural persons who are perpetrators or accomplices in the same crimes.][3]

N.B. In the context of paragraphs 5 and 6, see also articles 76 (Penalties applicable to legal persons) and 99 (Enforcement of fines and forfeiture measures).

7.   [Subject to the provisions of articles 25, 28 and 29,] a person is criminally responsible and liable for punishment for a crime defined [in article 5] [in this Statute] if that person:

[*59] (a)   commits such a crime, whether as an individual, jointly with another, or through another person regardless of whether that person is criminally responsible;

    (b)   orders, solicits or induces the commission of such a crime which in fact occurs or is attempted;

    [(c)   fails to prevent or repress the commission of such a crime in the circumstances set out in article 25;]

    (d)   [with [intent] [knowledge] to facilitate the commission of such a crime,] aids, abets or otherwise assists in the commission [or attempted commission] of that crime, including providing the means for its commission;[4]

    (e)   either:

        (i)   [intentionally] [participates in planning] [plans] to commit such a crime which in fact occurs or is attempted; or

---

[1]   This provision raises issues relating to non-retroactivity, amendment of the Statute and penalties. Accordingly, further consideration of this issue is required.

[2]   This proposal deals mainly with the limits of civil liability and should be further discussed in connection with penalties, forfeiture and compensation to victims of crimes.

[3]   There is a deep divergence of views as to the advisability of including criminal responsibility of legal persons in the Statute. Many delegations are strongly opposed, whereas some strongly favour its inclusion. Others have an open mind. Some delegations hold the view that providing for only the civil or administrative responsibility/liability of legal persons could provide a middle ground. This avenue, however, has not been thoroughly discussed. Some delegations, who favour the inclusion of legal persons, hold the view that this expression should be extended to organizations lacking legal status.

[4]   It was pointed out that the commentary to the ILC Draft Code of Crimes (A/51/10, p. 24, para. (12)) implicitly also includes aiding, abetting or assisting ex post facto. This presumption was questioned in the context of the ICC. If aiding, etc., ex post facto were deemed necessary to be criminalized, an explicit provision would be needed.

[(ii)   agrees with another person or persons that such a crime be committed and an overt act in furtherance of the agreement is committed by any of these persons that manifests their intent [and such a crime in fact occurs or is attempted];][5] [6]

(f) [directly and publicly] incites the commission of [such a crime] [genocide] [which in fact occurs], [with the intent that such crime be committed];

[*60] (g)[7] [with the intent to commit such a crime,] attempts to commit that crime by taking action that commences its execution by means of a substantial step, but that crime does not occur because of circumstances independent of the person's intentions.[8]

N.B. This article should be re-examined as to the references to the mental element in view of article 29 (<u>Mens rea</u> (mental elements)).

Article 24
Irrelevance of official position

1.   This Statute shall be applied to all persons without any discrimination whatsoever: official capacity, either as Head of State or Government, or as a member of a Government or parliament, or as an elected representative, or as a government official, shall in no case exempt a person from his criminal responsibility under this Statute, nor shall it [per se] constitute a ground for reduction of the sentence.

2.   Any immunities or special procedural rules attached to the official capacity of a person, whether under national or international law, may not be relied upon to prevent the Court from exercising its jurisdiction in relation to that person.[9]

Article 25
[*61] Responsibility of [commanders] [superiors][10] for acts of
[forces under their command] [subordinates][11]

[In addition to other forms of responsibility for crimes under this Statute, a [commander] [superior] is criminally responsible] [A [commander] [superior] is not relieved of responsibility][12] for crimes under this Statute committed by [forces] [subordinates] under his or her command [or authority] and effective control as a result of the [commander's] [superior's] failure to exercise properly this control where:

(a)   the [commander] [superior] either knew, or [owing to the widespread commission of the offences] [owing to the circumstances at the time] should have known, that the [forces] [subordinates] were committing or intending to commit such crimes; and

(b)   the [commander] [superior] failed to take all necessary and reasonable measures within his or her power to prevent or repress their commission [or punish the perpetrators thereof].

---

[5]   In addition to the two types of conduct described in paragraph (e), there is a third type of criminal association that may be considered. One formulation of this third category would be to refer to the conduct of a person who "participates in an organization which aims at the realization of such a crime by engaging in an activity that furthers or promotes that realization".

[6]   The inclusion of this subparagraph gave rise to divergent views.

[7]   Questions pertaining to voluntary abandonment or repentance should be further discussed in connection with grounds for excluding criminal responsibility.

[8]   A view was expressed that it would be preferable that issues connected with attempt be taken up in a separate article rather than in the framework of individual responsibility. In that view, the article on individual responsibility should only refer to the way in which the person takes part in the commission of a crime, regardless of whether it deals with a completed crime or an attempted crime.

[9]   Further discussion of paragraph 2 would be required in connection with international judicial cooperation.

[10]   Most delegations were in favour of extending the principle of command responsibility to any superior.

[11]   One delegation held the view that this principle should be dealt with in connection with the definitions of the crimes.

[12]   The alternatives highlight the question whether command responsibility is a form of criminal responsibility in addition to others or whether it is a principle that commanders are not immune for the acts of their subordinates.

Article 26
Age of responsibility
N.B. In the context of this article, see also article 75, paragraph (a) (Applicable penalties).
Proposal 1
1.   A person under the age of [twelve, thirteen, fourteen, sixteen, eighteen] at the time of the commission of a crime [shall be deemed not to know the wrongfulness of his or her conduct and] shall not be criminally responsible [*62] under this Statute [, unless the Prosecutor proves that the person knew the wrongfulness of his or her conduct at that time].
[2.   A person who is between the age of [sixteen] and [twenty-one] at the time of the [alleged] commission of a crime shall be evaluated [by the Court] as to his or her maturity to determine whether the person is responsible under this Statute.]
Proposal 2
[Persons aged 13 to 18 years at the time of the facts shall be criminally responsible but their prosecution, trial and sentence and the regime under which they serve their sentence may give rise to the application of special modalities specified in the Statute.][13]

Article 27
Statute of limitations
[*63] Proposal 1
[1.   The period of limitations shall be completed upon the lapse of xx years for the offence of ..., and yy years for the offence of ...
2.   The period of limitations shall commence to run at the time when criminal conduct has ceased.
3.   The period of limitations shall cease to run on the institution of the prosecution against the case concerned to this Court or to a national court of any State that has jurisdiction on such case. The period of limitations begins to run when the decision of the national court becomes final, where this Court has jurisdiction over the case concerned.]
Proposal 2
[There is no statute of limitations for those crimes within the [inherent] jurisdiction of the Court.]
Proposal 3
[There is no statute of limitations for those crimes within the [inherent] jurisdiction of the Court; but [for those crimes not within the Court's inherent jurisdiction] the Court may decline to exercise jurisdiction if, owing to the lapse of time, a person would be denied a fair trial.]
Proposal 4
[Crimes not subject to limitation
The crimes referred to in article 5, paragraphs (a), (b) and (d), shall not be subject to limitation.

---

[13]   Different views exist among States as to a specific age of responsibility.

It was observed that many international conventions (such as the International Covenant on Civil and Political Rights, the European Convention on Human Rights, the Inter-American Convention on Human Rights) prohibit the punishment of minors.

The question arising from the draft proposals was whether an absolute age of responsibility should be mandated or whether a presumptive age should be included with a means to rebut the presumption.

It was observed that a consistent approach (in terms of either an evaluation by the Court or proof by the Prosecutor) should be taken in paragraphs 1 and 2 of proposal 1 in respect of both of the age groups mentioned.

A question was raised as to what would be the criteria of the evaluation process, and should this be left for the Court to develop in supplementary rules or by jurisprudence?

It was observed that, in its article 1, the Convention on the Rights of the Child defines as a child every human being younger than eighteen years of age and that, in its article 37, it lays down a series of limitations as regards the applicable penalties, ruling out the death penalty and life imprisonment without parole.

Crimes subject to limitation

1.   Proceedings before the Court in respect of the crimes referred to in article 5, paragraph (c), shall be subject to a period of limitation of 10 full years from the date on which the crime was committed, provided that during this period no prosecution has been brought.

[*64] 2.   If a prosecution has been initiated during this period, either before the Court or in a State competent to bring a prosecution under its internal law, the proceedings before the Court shall not be subject to limitation until 10 full years have elapsed from the date of the most recent prosecution.]

Proposal 5

[1.   The statute of limitations as established hereunder shall extinguish the criminal prosecution and the punishment.

2.   The statute of limitations will be [ ] years and shall commence to run as follows:

(a)   in case of instantaneous crime, from the moment of its perpetration;

(b)   in case of attempt, from the moment the last act of execution was performed or the due conduct was omitted;

(c)   in case of permanent crime, from the moment of the cessation of the criminal conduct.

3.   The statute of limitations may be interrupted by the actions taken in the investigation of the crime and its perpetrators. If those actions were stopped, the statute of limitations will run again as of the day the last act of investigation was carried out.

4.   The statute of limitations for definitive sanctions will run as of the moment the condemned person escaped and will be interrupted with its detention.]

N.B. The proposals under this article have not been consolidated.

[Article 28
Actus reus (act and/or omission)

1.   Conduct for which a person may be criminally responsible and liable for punishment as a crime can constitute either an act or an omission, or a combination thereof.

2.   Unless otherwise provided and for the purposes of paragraph 1, a person may be criminally responsible and liable for punishment for an omission where the person [could] [has the ability], [without unreasonable risk of danger to [*65] him/herself or others,] but intentionally [with the intention to facilitate a crime] or knowingly fails to avoid the result of an offence where:

(a)   the omission is specified in the definition of the crime under this Statute; or

(b)   in the circumstances, [the result of the omission corresponds to the result of a crime committed by means of an act] [the degree of unlawfulness realized by such omission corresponds to the degree of unlawfulness to be realized by the commission of such act], and the person is [either] under a pre-existing [legal] obligation under this Statute[14] to avoid the result of such crime [or creates a particular risk or danger that subsequently leads to the commission of such crime].[15]

[3.   A person is only criminally responsible under this Statute for committing a crime if the harm required for the commission of the crime is caused by and [accountable] [attributable] to his or her act or omission.][16]][17]

Article 29
Mens rea (mental elements)

1.   Unless otherwise provided, a person is only criminally responsible and liable for punishment for a crime under this Statute if the physical elements are committed with intent and knowledge.

---

[14]   Some delegations questioned whether the source of this obligation is wider than the Statute.

[15]   Some delegations had concerns about including this clause which referred to the creation of a risk. Other delegations thought that, in the context of the offences of the Statute, breach of an obligation under the Statute to avoid the result of a crime was sufficient.

[16]   Some delegations thought that a provision on causation was not necessary.

[17]   These brackets reflect the view expressed that, although much progress has been made on the definition of omission, the question whether omission should be inserted in the Statute depends upon the final drafting of this article.

[*66] 2. For the purposes of this Statute and unless otherwise provided, a person has intent where:

   (a)   in relation to conduct, that person means to engage in the act [or omission];

   (b)   in relation to a consequence, that person means to cause that consequence or is aware that it will occur in the ordinary course of events.

3.   For the purposes of this Statute and unless otherwise provided, "know", "knowingly" or "knowledge" means to be aware that a circumstance exists or a consequence will occur.

[4.[18] [19] For the purposes of this Statute and unless otherwise provided, where this Statute provides that a crime may be committed recklessly, a person is reckless with respect to a circumstance or a consequence if:

   (a)   the person is aware of a risk that the circumstance exists or that the consequence will occur;

   (b)   the person is aware that the risk is highly unreasonable to take;

   [and]

   [(c)   the person is indifferent to the possibility that the circumstance exists or that the consequence will occur.]]

N.B. The inclusion of the notion of recklessness should be re-examined in view of the definition of crimes.

[*67] Article 30[20]
Mistake of fact[21] or of law

Option 1

   Unavoidable mistake of fact or of law shall be a ground for excluding criminal responsibility provided that the mistake is not inconsistent with the nature of the alleged crime. Avoidable mistake of fact or of law may be considered in mitigation of punishment.

Option 2

1.   A mistake of fact shall be a ground for excluding criminal responsibility only if it negates the mental element required by the crime [charged provided that said mistake is not inconsistent with the nature of the crime or its elements] [, and provided that the circumstances he reasonably believed to be true would have been lawful].

2.   Mistake of law may not be cited as a ground for excluding criminal responsibility [, except where specifically provided for in this Statute].[22]

[*68] Article 31
Grounds for excluding criminal responsibility

1.   In addition to other grounds for excluding criminal responsibility permitted by this Statute, a person is not criminally responsible if at the time of that person's conduct:[23]

   (a)   the person suffers from a mental disease or defect that destroys that person's capacity to appreciate the unlawfulness or nature of his or her conduct, or capacity to control his or her conduct to conform to the requirements of law;

---

[18]   Further discussion is needed on this paragraph.

[19]   A view was expressed to the effect that there was no reason for rejecting the concept of commission of an offence also through negligence, in which case the offender shall be liable only when so prescribed by the Statute.

[20]   There were widely divergent views on this article.

[21]   Some delegations were of the view that mistake of fact was not necessary because it was covered by mens rea.

[22]   Some delegations felt that paragraph 2 of option 2 still left some ambiguity, and an alternative approach could read as follows:

   "Mistake of law as to whether a particular type of conduct is a crime under this Statute, or whether a crime is within the jurisdiction of the Court, is not a ground for excluding criminal responsibility. However, a [reasonable] mistake of law may be a ground for excluding criminal responsibility if it negates the mental element required by such crime."

[23]   The link between the opening clause of paragraph 1 and paragraph 2 may need to be further considered.

[(b) the person is in a state of [involuntary] intoxication [by alcohol, drugs or other means] that destroys that person's capacity to appreciate the unlawfulness or nature of his or her conduct, or capacity to control his or her conduct to conform to the requirements of law; [provided, however, that if the person has voluntarily become intoxicated [[with the pre-existing intent to commit the crime] [or knowing that the circumstances would arise that led him or her to commit the crime and that those circumstances could have that effect]],[24] the person shall remain criminally responsible;]

(c) the person [, provided that he or she did not put himself or herself voluntarily into a position causing the situation to which that ground for excluding criminal responsibility would apply,] acts [swiftly and] reasonably [*69] [, or in the reasonable belief that force is necessary,] to defend himself or herself or another person [or property] against an [imminent ...[25] use of force] [immediate ...[26] threat of force] [impending ...[27] use of force] and [[unlawful] [and] [unjustified]] use of force in a [not excessive] manner[.] [[not disproportionate] [reasonably proportionate] to the degree of danger to the person [or liberty] [or property] protected];

(d) [the person reasonably believes that][28] there is a threat of [imminent] death or serious bodily harm against that person or another person [or against his or her liberty] [or property or property interests] and the person acts reasonably to avoid this threat, provided that the person's action[29] [causes] [was not intended to cause] [n]either death [n]or a greater harm than the one sought to be avoided;[30] [however, if the person has [knowingly] [recklessly] exposed him or herself to a situation which was likely to lead to the threat, the person shall remain responsible];

(e) [the person reasonably believes that there are][31] [there are] [the person necessarily acts in response to] circumstances beyond that person's control which constitute a [threat of [imminent] death or serious bodily harm] [danger] to that person or another person [or property or property rights][32] and the person acts reasonably to avoid the [threat] [danger], [provided that the [*70] person intended to prevent a greater harm [and did not intend to cause] [and did not cause] death][33] and provided that there exists no other way to avoid such threat].

2. The Court may[34] determine the applicability of the grounds for exclusion of criminal responsibility [listed in paragraph 1] [permitted by this Statute] [to the case before it].[35]

---

[24]   There are two approaches to the question of voluntary intoxication: If it is decided that voluntary intoxication should in no case be an acceptable ground for excluding criminal responsibility, the text within brackets "[with the pre-existing intent to commit the crime] [or knowing that the circumstances would arise that led him or her to commit the crime and that those circumstances could have that effect]" would have to be deleted. In that case, however, provision should be made for mitigation of punishment with regard to persons who were not able to form a specific intent, where required, towards the crime committed due to their intoxication. If this text were to be retained, the ground for excluding criminal responsibility would apply in all cases of voluntary intoxication except for those in which the person became intoxicated in order to commit the crime in an intoxicated condition (actio libera in causa). This would probably lead to a great number of war crimes and crimes against humanity going unpunished.

[25]   Dots inserted so as not to repeat "[[unlawful] [and] [unjustified]]" in all three alternatives.

[26]   Ibid.

[27]   Ibid.

[28]   This should be considered together with article 30.

[29]   A proposal was made to replace the rest of the first sentence by "is under the circumstances not reasonably more excessive than the threat or perceived threat".

[30]   A proposal was made to replace "provided that the person's action [causes] [was not intended to cause] [n]either death [n]or a greater harm than the one sought to be avoided" with "employing means which are not disproportionate to the risk faced".

[31]   This should be considered together with article 30.

[32]   It was suggested that a mere reference to the law of necessity would suffice in place of the first part of the sentence.

[33]   This applies more to a military situation.

[34]   The issue of the extent to which the facts underlying these grounds, for excluding criminal responsibility, if not sufficient to exclude criminal responsibility, should instead be considered in mitigation of punishment will be dealt with in Part 7.

[35]   The link between the opening clause of paragraph 1 and paragraph 2 may need to be reconsidered.

Article 32
Superior orders and prescription of law

1.　The fact that a person's conduct was pursuant to an order of a Government or of a superior [whether military or civilian] shall [not] relieve the person of criminal responsibility [[if] [unless] the order [was known to be unlawful or] appeared to be manifestly unlawful].[36]

[2.　The perpetrator of or an accomplice in a crime of genocide [or a crime against humanity] [or a ...] shall not be exempted from criminal responsibility on the sole ground that the person's conduct was pursuant to an order of a Government or a superior, or pursuant to national legislation or regulations.][37][38]

[*71] [Article 33][39]
[Possible grounds for excluding criminal responsibility
specifically referring to war crimes]

...

Article 34
Other grounds for excluding criminal responsibility

1.　At trial the Court may consider a ground for excluding criminal responsibility not specifically enumerated in this part if the ground:

(a)　is recognized [in general principles of criminal law common to civilized nations] [in the State with the most significant contacts to the crime] with respect to the type of conduct charged; and

(b)　deals with a principle clearly beyond the scope of the grounds for excluding criminal responsibility enumerated in this part and is not otherwise inconsistent with those or any other provisions of the Statute.

2.　The procedure for asserting such a ground for excluding criminal responsibility shall be set forth in the Rules of Procedure and Evidence.[40]

[*72] PART 4.　COMPOSITION AND ADMINISTRATION OF THE COURT
Article 35
Organs of the Court

The Court consists of the following organs:

(a)　a Presidency;
(b)　an Appeals Chamber, Trial Chambers and [a Pre-Trial Chamber] [Pre-Trial Chambers];
(c)　the Office of the Prosecutor;
(d)　a Registry.

Article 36
Judges serving on a full-time basis

The judges composing the Presidency[41] shall serve on a full-time basis as soon as they are elected. [The judges composing [the] [a] Pre-Trial Chamber shall serve on a full-time basis [once the Court[42] is seized of a matter] [when required in the view of the President].] [On the recommendation of the Presidency, the States Parties] [The Presidency] may [by a two-thirds majority] decide that the workload of the Court requires that the judges [composing any of the other Chambers] should serve on a full-time [or part-time] basis.

---

[36]　An unlawful or manifestly unlawful order must be understood as an order in conflict with the rules of international law applicable in armed conflict.

[37]　This subparagraph should be considered together with article 31, paragraph 2.

[38]　For the question of mitigating circumstances, see Part 7.

[39]　It was questioned whether such grounds as military necessity could be dealt with in connection with the definition of war crimes.

[40]　This article needs to be further considered together with article 31, paragraph 2, and article 20.

[41]　The view was expressed that reference should be made here to the "President" rather than the "Presidency".

[42]　Delegations agreed that this reference to "the Court" means the whole Court, as set out in article 35.

Article 37
Qualification and election of judges

[*73] 1.   Subject to the provisions in paragraph 2, there shall be [...] judges of the Court.

[There shall be no fewer than [...][43] judges from each geographical group as established by the General Assembly of the United Nations.]

2.   (a) The President, acting on behalf of the Court, [as well as any State Party] may propose an increase [or decrease] in the number of judges, indicating the reasons why this is considered necessary and appropriate. Any such proposal shall be submitted to the Registrar, who shall promptly circulate it to all States Parties;[44]

(b) Any such proposal shall then be considered at a meeting of States Parties to be convened in accordance with article [...].[45] The adoption and entry into force of any such proposal shall require a [two-thirds] majority of States Parties [present and voting at that meeting];[46]

(c) The election of additional judges shall then take place at the next session of the Assembly of States Parties. [Any decrease in the number of judges shall however only be given effect as and when the terms of office of the relevant number of existing judges end.][47]

3.   The judges of the Court shall:

(a) be persons of high moral character and impartiality [who possess all the qualifications required in their respective States for appointment to the highest judicial offices]; [and]

[*74] (b) have:

(i)   [at least ten years'] [extensive] criminal [law] [trial] experience [as a judge, prosecutor or defending counsel]; [or] [and, where possible]

(ii)   recognized competence in international law [in particular international criminal law, international humanitarian law and human rights law] [; and

(c) possess an excellent knowledge of and be fluent in at least one of the working languages referred to in article 51].

4.   Option 1

Each [State Party] [national group appointed for the purpose by a State [Party]] may nominate for election not more than three persons [, all of whom must be nationals of different [States] [States Parties],] [who possess the qualification(s) referred to in paragraph 3] [and who are willing to serve as may be required on the Court].

[The [State Party] [national group] shall indicate which of the qualifications referred to in paragraph 3 (b) the candidate possesses.]

Option 2

(a)   When an election is required, the Nominating Committee shall develop a list of candidates, equal in number to the number of positions to be filled.

(b)   The Nominating Committee shall be composed by the Assembly of States Parties.

(c)   Once the Nominating Committee is established, the Registrar shall provide the Committee, upon request, with any necessary facilities and administrative and staff support.

5.   The judges of the Court shall be elected by secret ballot by [an absolute] [a two-thirds] majority vote of the [Assembly of the [States Parties present and [*75] voting] [General Assembly of the United Nations] [and the Security Council] from a list of persons nominated in accordance with paragraph 4.[48]

---

[43]   The number is dependent on the total number of judges.

[44]   The relationship between this provision and the provisions on amendments to the Statute needs to be borne in mind.

[45]   The article dealing with the convening of regular and extraordinary meetings of the Assembly of States Parties.

[46]   Consideration could be given to the quorum required for extraordinary meetings of the Assembly of States Parties in the appropriate article dealing with the convening of such meetings.

[47]   This provision is conditional upon the acceptance of the words "or decrease" in paragraph 2 (a).

[48]   Matters relating to the mode by which votes would be cast and the compilation and announcement of results could be dealt with by the Rules of Procedure and Evidence.

[[Two thirds] [One half] of the States Parties shall constitute a quorum at the meeting of the Assembly of States Parties for this purpose.]

[In the event that a sufficient number of judges is not elected, the Nominating Committee shall provide a further list of candidates and there shall be another election.][49]

6.   No two judges may be nationals of the same State.

[7.   [A sufficient number of the judges to constitute the Pre-Trial Chamber and Trial Chambers] [[Two thirds] [A majority] of the judges] shall be elected from among candidates having criminal [trial] [law] experience.]

8.   [States Parties] [The General Assembly of the United Nations][50] shall, in the election of the judges, [bear in mind] [take into account the need for]:

    (a)   the representation of the principal legal systems of the world;

    [(b) the representation of the main forms of civilization;]

    (c)   equitable geographical distribution;

    [(d) gender balance;]

    [(e) the need, within the membership of the Court, for expertise on issues related to sexual and gender violence, violence against children and other similar matters].

[9.   A judge may not be over the age of 65 at the time of election.]

10.   Judges shall hold office for a term of [five] [nine] years and [are eligible for re-election [for a further term of five years]] [, subject to [*76] article 38, paragraph 2, are not eligible for re-election]. At the first election, one third of the judges chosen by lot shall serve for a term of [three] years [and are eligible for re-election]; one third of the judges chosen by lot shall serve for a term of [six] years; and the remainder shall serve for a term of [nine] years.[51]

11.   Notwithstanding paragraph 10, a judge shall continue in office in order to complete any case the hearing of which has commenced.

Article 38
Judicial vacancies

1.   In the event of a vacancy, a replacement judge shall be elected in accordance with article 37.

2.   A judge elected to fill a vacancy shall serve for the remainder of the predecessor's term[, and [if that period is less than three years] is eligible for re-election for a further term].

Article 39
The Presidency

1.   The President and the First and Second Vice-Presidents shall be elected by an absolute majority of the judges. They shall serve for a term of three years or until the end of their term of office as judges, whichever is earlier. They shall be eligible for re-election only once.

2.   The First Vice-President shall act in place of the President in the event that the President is unavailable or disqualified. The Second Vice-President shall act in place of the President in the event that both the President and the First Vice-President are unavailable or disqualified.

3.   The President and the First and Second Vice-Presidents shall constitute the Presidency, which shall be responsible for:

[*77] (a) the due administration of the Court [, including the supervision and direction of the Registrar and staff of the Registry and the Court,][52] with the exception of the Office of the Prosecutor; and

    (b)   the other functions conferred on it by this Statute.

---

[49]   This provision is linked to option 2 in paragraph 4.

[50]   These options reflect the different entities which may elect the judges.

[51]   The need for staggering in the event of a change of number of judges can be addressed in the Rules of Procedure and Evidence.

[52]   Detailed administrative arrangements on, e.g., consultation with the Prosecutor for specific matters of mutual concern, could be dealt with in the Rules.

[4.   In discharging its responsibility under paragraph 3 (a), the Presidency shall coordinate with and seek the concurrence of the Prosecutor on all matters of mutual concern including, for example, the functioning of the Registry and security arrangements for defendants, witnesses and the Court.]

Article 40
Chambers

1.   The Appeals Chamber [shall be established as soon as possible after the election of the judges. It] shall consist of [three] [five] [seven] judges to be elected by an absolute majority of the judges of the Court.[53] [At least one third of the judges must possess the qualifications set out in paragraph 3 (b) [(i)] [(ii)] of article 37.]

2.   Judges of the Appeals Chamber shall serve [for a period of three years [and may be re-elected]] [until the end of their terms of office as judges of the Court]. They may, however, continue to sit on the Chamber in order to complete any case the hearing of which has commenced.

3.   The Presidency shall assign judges who are not members of the Appeals Chamber to Trial Chambers and [Pre-Trial Chambers] [the Pre-Trial Chamber] in [*78] accordance with the [Rules of Procedure and Evidence] [Regulations of the Court].[54]

[4.   Judges of the Pre-Trial Chamber or the Trial Chambers, as the case may be, shall serve in their respective Chambers for a period of three years. They may, however, continue to sit on the Chamber in order to complete any case the hearing of which has commenced.]

5.   A Trial Chamber shall consist of [three] [five] judges. [[At least one of] [A majority of] [All] the judges must possess the qualifications set out in paragraph 3 (b) (i) of article 37.]

6.   [A] [The] Pre-Trial Chamber shall consist of [one judge] [three judges] and shall perform such pre-trial functions as are assigned to it by this Statute. [The number of judges may be [increased to three] [reduced to one][55] in accordance with the Rules of Procedure and Evidence]. [[The judge] [At least two judges] must possess the qualifications set out in paragraph 3 (b) (i) of article 37.]

[7.   At the time a Chamber is constituted, alternate judges [may] [shall] be nominated by the Presidency to attend the proceedings of that Chamber and, provided that an alternate judge has been present throughout the proceedings, that judge may act as a member of that Chamber in the event that a judge of ·that Chamber dies, is disqualified or otherwise becomes unavailable during the course of the proceedings.][56]

Article 41
Independence of the judges

[*79] 1.   In performing their functions, the judges shall be independent.

2.   Judges shall not engage in any activity which is likely to interfere with their judicial functions or to affect confidence in their independence.

3.   Judges serving on a full-time basis shall not engage in any other occupation of a professional nature.

4.   Any doubt on the points raised in paragraphs 2 and 3 shall be decided by an absolute majority of the judges of the Court. Where any question concerns an individual judge, that judge shall not take part in the decision.

---

[53]   Consideration needs to be given to whether the members of the Presidency of the Court should be members of the Appeals Chamber.

[54]   Mechanisms that could be adopted for this purpose could include the assignment of judges to specific Chambers by lot, the rotation of judges, judges assigned to specific Chambers for a fixed term or fixed teams of judges with a team assigned to be the Trial Chamber and another team assigned to be the Pre-Trial Chamber for a given case.

[55]   These options are linked to the earlier provision on the number of judges for the Chamber.

[56]   This paragraph needs to be harmonized with paragraph 1 of article 72 and other provisions, if any, dealing with alternate judges for judicial proceedings other than trial proceedings.

Article 42
Excusing and disqualification of judges

1.   The Presidency may at the request of a judge excuse that judge from the exercise of a function under this Statute, in accordance with the [Rules of Procedure and Evidence] [Regulations of the Court].

2.   Judges shall not participate in any case in which their impartiality might reasonably be doubted on any ground. A judge shall be excluded from a case in accordance with this paragraph if, inter alia, he or she has previously been involved in any capacity in that case before the Court or in a related criminal case involving the accused at the national level [, or is a national of a complainant State, [of the State on whose territory the offence is alleged to have been committed] or of a State of which the accused is a national].

3.   The Prosecutor [or] the accused [or an interested State] may request the disqualification of a judge under paragraph 2.

4.   Any question as to the disqualification of a judge shall be decided by an absolute majority of the judges of the Court.[57] The challenged judge shall be entitled to present his or her comments on the matter, but shall not take part in the decision.

[*80] Article 43
The Office of the Prosecutor

1.   The Office of the Prosecutor shall act independently as a separate organ of the Court. It shall be responsible for receiving [complaints] [or] [referrals] [or any substantiated information related to the alleged commission of a crime under the jurisdiction of the Court], for examining them and for conducting investigations and prosecutions before the Court. A member of the Office of the Prosecutor shall not seek or act on instructions from any external source.

2.   The Office of the Prosecutor shall be headed by the Prosecutor. [Without prejudice to article 47, the] [The] Prosecutor shall have full authority over the management and administration of the Office of the Prosecutor, including the staff, facilities and other resources thereof. The Prosecutor shall be assisted by one or more Deputy Prosecutors, who are entitled to carry out any of the acts required of the Prosecutor under this Statute. The Prosecutor and the Deputy Prosecutors shall be of different nationalities [and represent different legal systems]. They shall [be available to] serve on a full-time basis.

3.   The Prosecutor and Deputy Prosecutors shall be persons of high moral character, be highly competent in and have [at least ten years] [extensive] practical experience in the prosecution [or trial][58] of criminal cases. They shall, furthermore, have an excellent knowledge of and be fluent in at least one of the working languages of the Court.

4.   The Prosecutor [and the Deputy Prosecutors] shall be elected by secret ballot by an absolute majority of the States Parties.[59] [The Deputy Prosecutors shall be appointed by the Prosecutor.[60]] Unless a shorter term is otherwise [*81] decided on at the time of their election [or appointment], they shall hold office for a term of [five] [seven] [nine] years and are [not] eligible for re-election. The Prosecutor and Deputy Prosecutors may not be over 65 years of age at the time of election [or appointment].

5.   The Prosecutor and Deputy Prosecutors shall not engage in any activity which is likely to interfere with their prosecutorial functions or to affect confidence in their independence. [When serving on a full-time basis, they] [They] shall not engage in any other occupation of a professional nature.

---

[57]   Some delegations expressed the view that questions of disqualification should be decided by an absolute majority of the members of the Chamber concerned.

[58]   Most delegations thought that both prosecutorial and judicial experience in criminal trials should be regarded as practical experience in that sense, but as some delegations felt that prosecutorial experience should be of paramount importance, the reference to "trial experience" was kept in square brackets.

[59]   There ought to be a procedure for the Assembly to have a list of candidates rather than to have nominations put to the election directly, but it was felt that this was a matter for the rules of the Assembly.

[60]   If this option is kept, there should be some system of involvement for the States parties, either by way of drawing up a list for the candidates or by having a possibility to object to an appointment by a certain number of States parties.

6.   The Presidency may excuse the Prosecutor or a Deputy Prosecutor at his or her request from acting in a particular case.

7.   [Neither the Prosecutor nor the Deputy Prosecutors shall participate in any matter in which their impartiality might reasonably be doubted on any ground.][61] They shall be excluded from a case in accordance with this paragraph if, <u>inter alia</u>, they have previously been involved in any capacity in that case before the Court or in a related criminal case involving the accused at the national level [, or are a national of a complainant State[, of the State on whose territory the offence is alleged to have been committed] or of a State of which the accused is a national].

8.   Any question as to the disqualification of the Prosecutor or a Deputy Prosecutor shall be decided by [the Presidency] [the Appeals Chamber] [the Judges of the Court]. The accused may at any time request the disqualification of the Prosecutor or a Deputy Prosecutor on the grounds set out in this paragraph. The Prosecutor or Deputy Prosecutor, as appropriate, shall be entitled to present his or her comments on the matter.

[9.   The Prosecutor shall appoint advisers with legal expertise on specific issues, including, but not limited to, sexual and gender violence and violence against children.][62]

[10.   The Office of the Prosecutor shall be responsible for providing protective measures to witnesses to be called by the Prosecution. The Office of the [*82] Prosecutor shall include staff with expertise in trauma, including trauma related to crimes of sexual violence.][63]

Article 44
The Registry

1.   Subject to article 43, the Registry shall be responsible for the non-judicial aspects of the administration and servicing of the Court.

2.   [The judges] [The States Parties] by an absolute majority by secret ballot shall elect a Registrar, who [, under the authority of the President of the Court,] shall be the principal administrative officer of the Court. They may [in the same manner elect] [appoint] a Deputy Registrar if the need arises.

3.   The Registrar shall hold office for a term of [five] [nine] years, is [not] eligible for re-election [once] and shall serve on a full-time basis. The Deputy Registrar shall hold office for a term of five years or such shorter term as may be decided on by an absolute majority of the judges, and may be [elected] [appointed] on the basis that the Deputy Registrar is willing to serve as required. [Their term shall end in all cases when they reach 65 years of age.] The Registrar and the Deputy Registrar shall have an excellent knowledge of and be fluent in at least one of the working languages of the Court.

[4.   The Registrar shall set up a Victims and Witnesses Unit within the Registry. This Unit shall provide counselling and other assistance to victims, [defence][64] witnesses, their family members and others at risk on account of testimony given by such witnesses and shall advise the organs of the Court on appropriate measures of protection and other matters affecting the rights and [*83] the well-being of such persons. The unit shall include staff with expertise in trauma, including trauma related to crimes of sexual violence.][65]

---

[61]   Views were expressed that the reasons for doubts should be set out specifically.

[62]   Many delegations preferred this to be in the Rules of Procedure and Evidence.

[63]   Such staff could be available in the Victims and Witnesses Unit under article 44, paragraph 4, but some delegations felt that there was a need for such staff in the Office of the Prosecutor, too. Some delegations felt that at least the first sentence was already covered in article 68.

[64]   Some delegations were of the view that there should be a separate unit for prosecution witnesses in the Office of the Prosecutor, as reflected in the bracketed language in article 43, paragraph 9; others were of the view that there should be only one unit located in the Registry.

[65]   The relationship with paragraph 5 of article 68 was considered. Views were expressed that parts of paragraph 4 should appear in article 68.

Article 45
Staff

1.   The Registrar and the Prosecutor shall appoint such qualified staff of their respective offices, including investigators in case of the Prosecutor, as may be required.

2.   In the employment of the staff, the Registrar and the Prosecutor shall ensure the highest standards of efficiency, competence and integrity and shall have regard to the criteria set forth in article 37, paragraph 8.

3.   The staff regulations, which shall apply to the staff of all organs of the Court, shall be proposed by the Registrar with the agreement of the Presidency and the Prosecutor. Such regulations shall be circulated to the States Parties for comment, before they take effect. The Registrar shall take into account the comments made by States Parties.[66]

[4.   Any State Party, intergovernmental organization [or non-governmental organization] may offer to detail personnel to assist with the work of any of the organs of the Court and to be considered for such work. The Prosecutor may accept any such offer for the Office of the Prosecutor. In any other case, the Presidency, in consultation with the Registrar, may accept the offer.][67]

[*84] Article 46
Solemn undertaking

Before first exercising their functions under the present Statute, judges, the Prosecutor, Deputy Prosecutors, the Registrar and the Deputy Registrar shall make a public and solemn undertaking to do so impartially and conscientiously.

Article 47[68]
Removal from office

1.   A judge, Prosecutor, Deputy Prosecutor, Registrar or Deputy Registrar who is found to have committed serious misconduct or a serious breach of his or her duties under this Statute [or the [Rules of Procedure and Evidence] [Regulations of the Court]], or to be unable to exercise the functions required by this Statute,[69] shall cease to hold office if a decision to this effect is made in accordance with paragraph 2.

2.   A decision as to the loss of office under paragraph 1 shall be made by secret ballot:

   (a)   in the case of a judge, by an [absolute] [two-thirds] majority of the States Parties further to a recommendation adopted by a two-thirds majority of the other judges of the Court;

   (b)   in the case of the Prosecutor [or a Deputy Prosecutor], by an absolute majority of the States Parties;

[*85] [(c) in the case of a Deputy Prosecutor, by the Prosecutor or by an absolute majority of the States Parties;]

   [(c)] [(d)] in the case of the Registrar or Deputy Registrar, by a majority vote of the [judges] [or the] [States Parties].

3.   The judge, Prosecutor, Deputy Prosecutor, Registrar or Deputy Registrar whose conduct or ability otherwise to hold office is challenged under this article shall have full opportunity to present and receive

---

[66]   Some delegations wanted an approval procedure for the States parties to be set out in the Statute, whereas other delegations felt that circulation should be just for information.

[67]   Some delegations felt that this was already covered under the part dealing with cooperation or that it should be addressed in that part.

[68]   Several delegations expressed the view that a separate article is required in the Statute to deal with the general issue of expiry of terms of office. It was suggested that such an article should be drafted along the following lines:

   "The term of office of a judge, Prosecutor, Deputy Prosecutor, Registrar or Deputy Registrar ends upon the expiry of their term of office, death, resignation or removal from office in accordance with article 47."

[69]   A number of delegations expressed the view that a separate procedure for removal of office in the case of an inability to exercise the functions required (through, for example, long-term illness or disability) should be set out in the Regulations of the Court.

evidence and to make submissions in accordance with the [Rules of Procedure and Evidence] [Regulations of the Court], but shall not otherwise participate in the consideration of the matter.

Article 48
Disciplinary measures

A judge, Prosecutor, Deputy Prosecutor, Registrar or Deputy Registrar who has committed misconduct of a less serious nature than that set out in paragraph 1 shall be subject to disciplinary measures, in accordance with the [Rules of Procedure and Evidence] [Regulations of the Court].[70]

Article 49
Privileges and immunities

1.   The judges, the Prosecutor, [the Deputy Prosecutors,] [the Registrar] [and the Deputy Registrar] shall [, when engaged in the business of the Court,] enjoy diplomatic privileges and immunities.

2.   The [Deputy Prosecutors,] [the Registrar,] [the Deputy Registrar] [and] staff of the Office of the Prosecutor and the Registry shall enjoy the privileges, immunities and facilities necessary for the performance of their functions [in accordance with the Rules of Procedure and Evidence].

3.   Counsel, experts, witnesses or any other person required at the seat of the Court shall be accorded such treatment as is necessary for the proper [*86] functioning of the Court. [In particular and without prejudice to article 70, they shall, in respect of the words spoken or written and acts done by them in the discharge of their functions, be immune from legal process of every kind. This immunity from legal process shall continue to be accorded notwithstanding that the persons concerned are no longer discharging their functions.][71]

4.   The privileges and immunities of:

(a)   [a judge] [the members of the Presidency] and the Prosecutor may be waived by an absolute majority of the judges;

[(b)   the other judges may be waived by the Presidency;]

(c)   the Registrar may be waived by the Presidency;

(d)   the Deputy Prosecutors and staff of the Office of the Prosecutor may be waived by the Prosecutor; and

(e)   the Deputy Registrar and staff of the Registry may be waived by the Registrar.[72]

Article 50
Salaries, allowances and expenses

The judges, the Prosecutor, the Deputy Prosecutors, the Registrar and the Deputy Registrar shall receive such salaries, allowances and expenses as may be decided upon by the Assembly of States Parties [in the Rules of Procedure and Evidence]. These salaries and allowances may not be decreased during their terms of office.

[*87] Article 51
Working languages

1.   The working languages of the Court shall be English and French, pursuant to the Rules of Procedure and Evidence.

---

[70]   Several delegations expressed the view that this provision relating to disciplinary measures should be contained in the Rules.

[71]   Some delegations felt that the principle set out in the first sentence was sufficient for the Statute and that any elaboration of that principle could be left for the Rules of Procedure and Evidence or the Host Country Agreement. Views were also expressed that this paragraph should be placed in article 68.

[72]   A view was expressed that the President should be given the power to waive the privileges and immunities of the staff of the Registry and that the Prosecutor's privileges and immunities should be waived by the Deputy Prosecutors.

2.   The Court shall, at the request of any Party, authorize a language other than English or French to be used by that Party.

Article 52
Rules of Procedure and Evidence[73]

1.   [Option 1

The Rules of Procedure and Evidence, including an elaboration of the elements of offenses that must be proven, annexed at ____, shall be an integral part of this Statute.]

[Option 2:

The Rules of Procedure and Evidence shall enter into force [upon adoption by the Assembly of States Parties by [an absolute majority] [a two-thirds majority of those present and voting]] [together with this Statute]. They shall be consistent with the Statute.]

2.   Amendments to the Rules of Procedure and Evidence may be proposed by:

    (a)   any State Party;

    (b)   the judges acting by an absolute majority;

    [(c)   the Prosecutor].

They shall enter into force upon adoption by the Assembly of States Parties [by a [...] majority]. Any modification shall be consistent with this Statute.

[*88] [3. In urgent cases, the judges may by [consensus] [a two-thirds majority] draw up a rule to be applied provisionally until the Assembly of States Parties adopts, amends or rejects it.]

Article 53
Regulations of the Court[74]

1.   As far as provided in this Statute or the Rules of Procedure and Evidence or otherwise necessary for the routine functioning of the Court, the judges shall by [a two-thirds] [an absolute] majority adopt the Regulations of the Court. The Regulations of the Court shall be consistent with the Statute and the Rules of Procedure and Evidence. [In the event of conflict, the Statute or the Rules of Procedure and Evidence shall prevail.]

2.   The Prosecutor [and the Registrar] shall be consulted in the elaboration of the Regulations and any amendments thereto. [The Regulations of the Court and any amendments thereto shall be circulated to the States Parties for comment. The judges shall take into account the comments made by States Parties.]

3.   The Regulations and any amendments thereto shall take effect immediately upon adoption by the judges, unless otherwise decided by the judges, and shall remain in effect unless a majority of States Parties objects to them.[75]

[*89] PART 5. INVESTIGATION AND PROSECUTION
Article 54
Investigation of alleged crimes

1.   On receiving a complaint [or upon notification of a decision of the Security Council referred to in article 10, paragraph 1,] [or ex officio upon any other substantiated information], the Prosecutor shall [subject to paragraphs 2 and 3] initiate an investigation unless the Prosecutor concludes that there is no reasonable basis for a prosecution under this Statute and decides not to initiate an investigation, in which case the Prosecutor shall so inform the [Presidency] [Pre-Trial Chamber].

---

[73]   References to the Rules in the Statute will have to be revisited and adjusted to the language used in this article (see also footnote 34 below).

[74]   It was suggested that these provisions might be called "Rules of the Court" so as to enable a reference to the "Rules" in the Statute to refer to either of the sets of provisions, as appropriate.

[75]   Some delegations wanted to see the procedure for objections to be clarified in the Rules of Procedure and Evidence.

N.B. The term "reasonable basis" in the opening clause is also used in the criteria listed in paragraph 2 (i). If the latter is retained, a broader term in the opening clause might be necessary in order to cover all the criteria listed under paragraph 2.

[2. Prior to initiating investigation the Prosecutor shall:

(a)   [notify the States Parties of any complaint [or any decision of the Security Council referred to in article 10, paragraph 1], and those States Parties shall so inform the persons within their jurisdiction who are referred to by name in the submission; and]

(b)   determine whether:

(i)   the complaint provides or is likely to provide a reasonable basis [in law or on the facts] for proceeding with a prosecution under this Statute; and

(ii)   the case is or would be admissible under article 15; and

[(ii) <u>bis</u> a prosecution under this Statute would be [in the interests of justice] [taking into account the gravity of the offences] [and the interests of victims];

(iii)   [an investigation would be consistent with the terms of any relevant Security Council decision]; and

[*90]   (iv)   to seek a preliminary ruling from the Court regarding the Court's jurisdiction if the case could later be challenged under article 17.]

[3.   The Prosecutor shall not initiate an investigation where the submission of the case to the Court is challenged under article 15 within one month of notification under article 54, paragraph 2 (a) until the final ruling of the Court.]

4.   The Prosecutor may:[1]

(a)   request the presence of and question suspects, victims and witnesses;

(b)   collect documentary and other evidence [documents, records and articles of evidence];

(c)

Option 1

conduct on-site investigations;

Option 2

(i)   Except as provided for in this paragraph, when evidence is in the territory of a State, the Prosecutor shall, as necessary, seek the cooperation of that State in order to obtain that evidence. The Prosecutor may conduct investigations on the territory of a State only:

a.   [with the consent of its competent authorities] [upon notification of and where necessary with the consent of its competent authorities] [in accordance with Part 9] [subject to the waiver by the competent authorities of the requirement of consent];

[*91] [b. When the Pre-Trial Chamber is satisfied that competent authorities to whom a request for assistance under Part 9 can be transmitted are not available [or not functioning].]

[(ii)   In the case of paragraph (i) (b) above, [such investigations] [investigations of a non-compulsory nature[2]] shall be conducted with the [concurrence] [approval] of the Pre-Trial Chamber [which shall have regard to the views of [interested States]]. [Notification shall be given to the State in question, in particular for the purpose of the State obtaining an extension of the period for execution of a relevant request for judicial assistance.]

[(iii)   In the case of paragraph (i) (b) above, the Prosecutor may use compulsory measures for collecting evidence (such as search and seizure and compelling the attendance of witnesses) based upon a valid warrant issued by the Pre-Trial Chamber.]

(d)   take necessary measures to ensure the confidentiality of information or the protection of any person [, including victims];

---

[1]   It was proposed that the following text be included as the first line of article 54, paragraph 4:

"When evidence is in the territory of a State Party whose competent authority is functioning properly, the Prosecutor shall request, as necessary, the Pre-Trial Chamber to seek the cooperation of a State Party pursuant to Part 9 of this Statute."

[2]   This set of square brackets will apply if paragraph (iii) is accepted.

[(e) The Prosecutor shall take appropriate measures to ensure the effective investigation and prosecution of crimes within the jurisdiction of the Court, and in so doing, respect the interests and personal circumstances of victims and witnesses, including age, gender and health, and take into account the nature of the crime, in particular, but not limited to, where it involves sexual or gender violence or violence against children;]

N.B. See also article 68, paragraph 2 (Protection of the [accused], victims and witnesses [and their participation in the proceedings]).

(f) as appropriate, seek the cooperation of any State or of the United Nations, [or of any peacekeeping force that may be present in the territory where an investigation is to be undertaken];

[(g) where documents or information have been obtained by the Prosecutor upon a condition as to their confidentiality, which are, or are intended to be, used solely for the purposes of generating new evidence, agree that such documents or information will not be disclosed at any stage of the proceedings unless the provider of the information consents.]

[*92] N.B. This paragraph, as well as articles 58, paragraph 10 (d) and (f) (Commencement of prosecution), 61, paragraph 2 (Notification of the indictment), 67, paragraph 2, 68, paragraph 9 (Protection of the [accused], victims and witnesses [and their participation in the proceedings]), 71 (Confidential information), 90, paragraphs 2 and 6 (Other forms of cooperation [and judicial and legal [mutual] assistance]) all relate to confidentiality and they should be examined with a view to avoiding any duplication or contradiction.

[(h) enter into such arrangements or agreements, not otherwise inconsistent with this Statute, as may be necessary to secure the cooperation or assistance of a State or person in the investigation.]

N.B. In the final drafting of paragraph 4, attention should be given to harmonizing the use of the words "shall" and "may".

5. The [Presidency] [Pre-Trial Chamber] may, at the request of the Prosecutor, issue such subpoenas [, orders] and warrants as may be required for the purposes of an investigation, including a warrant under article 59, paragraph 1, for the pre-indictment arrest of a suspect.

6. If, upon investigation and having regard, inter alia, to the matters referred to in article 15, the Prosecutor concludes that [a case is inadmissible under article 15 or] there is [not a sufficient basis for a prosecution] [no prima facie case] under this Statute [or a prosecution would not be in the interests of justice] [taking into account the interests of victims] and decides not to file an indictment, the Prosecutor shall so inform the [Presidency] [Pre-Trial Chamber], as well as the complainant State [or the Security Council, in a case to which article 10, paragraph 1, applies], giving details of the nature and basis of the complaint and of the reasons for not filing an indictment.

[7. A decision referred to in paragraph 6 based on considerations of the interests of justice shall only become effective upon its having been confirmed by the [Presidency] [Pre-Trial Chamber] under paragraph 8 of this article.]

8. At the request of a complainant State [or, in a case to which article 10, paragraph 1, applies, at the request of the Security Council,] the [Presidency] [Pre-Trial Chamber] [shall] [may] review a decision of the Prosecutor not to initiate an investigation or not to file an indictment, and may request the Prosecutor to reconsider the decision [but it may do so only once] [: provided that the Prosecutor, any suspect and the complainant State [or the Security Council (as the case may be)] shall be informed of such review proceedings or confirmation proceedings within the contemplation of paragraph 6 of this article [*93] which involves a decision based on considerations of the interests of justice and shall be entitled to submit his/her/their/its viewpoints with regard thereto, which viewpoints shall be considered by the [Presidency] [Pre-Trial Chamber] in coming to its decision].

[When new information is brought to his/her attention regarding the facts in respect of which he or she decided not to initiate an investigation or not to institute proceedings, the Prosecutor may reconsider his/her decision.]

[9. After a determination to initiate an investigation in accordance with article 54, paragraph 4, and prior to the commencement of a trial, a State requested by the Prosecutor to carry out investigations or a State on the territory of which the Prosecutor intends to conduct investigations may challenge the decision of

the Prosecutor to initiate an investigation before the Pre-Trial Chamber on the grounds of lack of sufficient basis for a prosecution under this Statute.]
10.   A person suspected of a crime under this Statute shall have the right:
     (a)   prior to being questioned, to be informed that the person is a suspect [, of the conduct that the person is alleged to have committed which may constitute a crime under this Statute] and of the rights under (b) to (d) hereafter;
     (b)   to remain silent, without such silence being a consideration in the determination of guilt or innocence;
     (c)   to have [at all times] [in connection with questioning] the [prompt] [competent] legal assistance of the person's choosing; [or, if the person does not have legal assistance, to have legal assistance assigned by the Court in any case where the interests of justice so require, including where the person is unable to secure counsel, and without payment if the person lacks sufficient means to pay for such assistance];
     [(d)   to be questioned in the presence of counsel unless the suspect has voluntarily waived his or her right to counsel;]
     (e)   not to be compelled to testify or to confess guilt nor to be subjected to any form of coercion, duress or threat;
     (f)   if questioned in a language other than [a language the person understands and speaks] [his or her own language], to have, free of any cost, [*94] the assistance of a competent interpreter and a translation of any document on which the person is to be questioned;
     (g)   not to be subjected to torture, or to cruel, inhuman or degrading treatment or punishment.
[11. Evidence obtained during questioning in violation of these rights shall under no circumstances be used in the trial unless they are favourable to the suspect.][3]
[12. (a) The Prosecutor shall fully respect the rights of suspects under the Statute and the Rules of Procedure and Evidence.
     (b)   [To establish the truth the Prosecutor shall [ex officio] extend the investigation to cover all facts and evidence that are relevant to an assessment of the charge and to the legal consequences that may follow. The Prosecutor shall investigate equally incriminating and exonerating circumstances.]
     (c)   [If the Prosecutor concludes that there is a basis for prosecution under this Statute, he shall, in accordance with the Rules of Procedure and Evidence, investigate the case by seeking the cooperation of the States concerned or by himself, and such investigation shall be conducted in conformity with international law and fully respecting the sovereignty of the States concerned.]][4]
[13. (a)   A person suspected of committing a crime within the meaning of this Statute:
         (i)   shall, as soon as he is involved in an investigation or prosecuted under this Statute, be entitled to collect all of the evidence that he deems necessary for his defence;
         (ii)   may either collect this evidence himself or request the Pre-Trial Chamber of the Court to accomplish certain acts, seeking, where necessary, cooperation from any State Party.
     The Pre-Trial Chamber may reject the request.
[*95] (b) If the suspect elects to collect the evidence himself in accordance with this paragraph, he may apply to the [Presidency] [Pre-Trial Chamber] for the following orders and subpoenas: [list to be inserted]]
N.B.
     -    In view of the length of the article, consideration may be given to placing some of its elements in a separate article.
     -    The drafting of this article might need revision in the light of the decisions to be taken in respect of article 57 (Functions of the Pre-Trial Chamber in relation with investigation).

---

[3]   This paragraph will be discussed in connection with article 69.
[4]   This paragraph will be discussed in connection with article 43.

[Article 55
Information on national investigations or proceedings
1.   [A State Party shall promptly inform the Prosecutor] [At any time, a State Party may inform the Prosecutor] [Where the Court has jurisdiction over a crime pursuant to articles 6 and 7, the Court may request a State Party to inform it] about national investigations or proceedings as soon as it considers that any such investigations or proceedings involve the commission of a crime within the jurisdiction of the Court. Such information shall, at the request of the State Party concerned, be confidential and shall include a concise statement of the circumstances of the alleged crime, the status of the investigation or proceeding concerned and, where possible, the identity and whereabouts of any suspect or accused.
The Prosecutor may subsequently request the State Party to provide additional information about the national investigations or proceedings.
2.   The Prosecutor may, after examining the information received from a State Party under paragraph 1 and having regard to the matters referred to in article 15, decide to initiate an investigation pursuant to articles 12 and 54. For that purpose, he may seek a ruling from the Pre-Trial Chamber in accordance with article 17.]

[Article 56
[*96] Deferral of an investigation by the Prosecutor[5]
1.   In the event that the Prosecutor, having regard to the matters referred to in article 15, defers an investigation, the Prosecutor may request that the relevant State make available to the Prosecutor information on the proceedings. Such information shall, at the request of the State concerned, be confidential.
2.   If the Prosecutor thereafter decides to proceed with an investigation, he or she shall notify the State in respect of whose proceedings deferral has taken place.]

[*97] [Article 57][6]
Functions of the Pre-Trial Chamber in relation with investigation[7]
1.   [Where the Prosecutor intends to take an investigative action which may] [When the Prosecutor considers an investigation to] present a unique opportunity, which may not be available subsequently for the purposes of a trial, to take testimony or a statement from a witness, or to examine, collect or test evidence, [the Prosecutor shall] [, if the suspect/accused has not been identified or is not available] inform the Pre-Trial Chamber; and] the Pre-Trial Chamber, on the request of the Prosecutor, [or a suspect,] [or on its own initiative,] may take such measures as may be necessary to assure the efficiency and integrity of the proceedings, and in particular to protect the rights of the defence.
2.   These measures may include the power:

---

[5]   A view was expressed that article 56 could be examined in the context of article 54.

[6]   Article 57 was tabled by some 15 interested delegations at the August 1997 meeting of the Preparatory Committee. It was written de novo and did not derive from any particular delegation's proposal.

The proposal contemplates that, in exceptional circumstances in which a unique opportunity appears to exist for the taking or collection of evidence, the Pre-Trial Chamber may be involved in order to assure a fair trial/protect the interests of the defence.

Some delegations believed that the authority of the Pre-Trial Chamber set out in the proposal should be exercised only to collect and preserve evidence for the defence. In relation to the Prosecutor's investigation, the Pre-Trial Chamber should only intervene for the purpose of checking on the lawfulness of the Prosecutor's conduct.

The alternative options reflect differing views as to the balance to be struck between the need to ensure the Prosecutor's independence and the desirability of conferring a limited role on the Pre-Trial Chamber.

If this proposal is adopted, it seems likely that other proposals in relation to article 54 could be deleted or may need revision. Consideration would need to be given to article 54, paragraphs 1, 4 (a), (b), (c), (f) and (h), 5, 6, 7, 8, 9 and 13.

[7]   The powers contemplated by this draft provision include the power for the Pre-Trial Chamber to seek judicial assistance from a State.

[*98] (a) to make [orders] [recommendations] [orders and recommendations] regarding procedures to be followed;

    (b) to direct that a record be made of the proceedings;

    (c) to appoint an expert to assist;

    (d) to authorize counsel for a suspect to assist, or where suspects have not been identified or have not designated counsel, appoint a lawyer to attend and represent the interest of the defence;

    (e) to name one of its members [or an available judge of the Court]:

        (i) to observe and make [orders] [recommendations] [orders and recommendations] regarding the collection and preservation of evidence or the questioning of persons;

        (ii) to decide on questions of law; or

        (iii) to take such other actions as may be necessary to collect or preserve evidence [favourable to the defence] [relevant to the case].

Option: [When in the course of a proceeding a unique opportunity presents itself to collect evidence, the Pre-Trial Chamber may, at the request of the Prosecutor or of the suspect, name one of its members or an available judge of the Court to take necessary measures to collect or preserve evidence, while respecting the rights of the defence.]

3.   [If any [order] [recommendation] [order and recommendation] of the Pre-Trial Chamber is breached or is not complied with, the Pre-Trial Chamber may:

    (a) reject the admissibility of any evidence obtained as a result or consequence of such a breach or non-compliance; or

    (b) consider such breach or non-compliance in respect of whether any weight should be attached to any evidence obtained as a result or consequence of such breach or non-compliance.]

Article 58

Commencement of prosecution

[*99] 1. If upon investigation [in the course of an investigation] the Prosecutor, having regard to the matters referred to in article 15, concludes that [the case is admissible, and] [a case does exist against one or more persons named,] [there is a prima facie case] [there is sufficient evidence that could justify a conviction of a suspect, if the evidence were not contradicted at trial,] [which the accused could be called on to answer and that is desirable in the interests of justice that the case should proceed], the Prosecutor shall file with the Registrar an indictment containing a concise statement of the allegations of fact and of the crime or crimes with which the suspect is charged in respect of each of the persons referred to, their name and particulars, a statement of the allegations of fact against them, and the characterization of these facts within the jurisdiction of the Court and shall be accompanied by [relevant] [sufficient] evidence collected by the Prosecutor for the purposes of confirmation [of the indictment] by the [Presidency] [Pre-Trial Chamber].

[2. The [Presidency] [Pre-Trial Chamber] shall examine the indictment, any amendment and any supporting material and determine whether:

    (a) [a prima facie case exists] [there is sufficient evidence that could justify a conviction of a suspect, if the evidence were not contradicted at trial] [there is strong evidence against the accused] with respect to a crime within the jurisdiction of the Court; and

    (b) having regard, <u>inter alia</u>, to the matters referred to in article 15, the case should on the information available be heard by the Court [if the Court has not yet ruled on this issue];

    [(c) it is desirable in the interests of justice that the case should proceed;]

If so, it shall [by majority/consensus] confirm the indictment and establish a trial chamber in accordance with article 40 [, and inform the Presidency].]

[3. Any State concerned may challenge the decision of the Prosecutor to file an indictment before the Pre-Trial Chamber on grounds of inconsistency with this Statute.]

[4. After the filing of an indictment, the Pre-Trial Chamber shall [in any case] [if the accused is in custody or has been judicially released by the Court pending trial] notify the indictment to the accused, [set a deadline prior to the confirmation hearing, until which the [*100] Prosecutor and the defence may add new evidence [for purposes of such confirmation hearing]], and set a date for the review of the indictment. The hearing shall be held in the presence of the Prosecutor and the accused, as well as his/her counsel, subject to the provisions of paragraph 8. In the hearing, the accused shall be allowed to object to the indictment and criticize the material on which it is based.

Following the hearing, the Pre-Trial Chamber may:

    (a) confirm the indictment in its entirety;

    (b) confirm only part of the indictment [and amend it], by giving a different qualification to the facts;

    [(c) order further investigation];

    (d) refuse to confirm the indictment.

When it confirms the indictment in its entirety or in part, the Pre-Trial Chamber shall commit the accused to the Trial Chamber for trial on the indictment as confirmed. Confirmation of indictment shall uphold the warrants issued earlier, except if the Court decides otherwise.]

5.   If, after any adjournment that may be necessary to allow additional material to be produced, the [Presidency] [Pre-Trial Chamber] decides not to confirm the indictment, it shall so inform the complainant State [or, in a case to which article 10, paragraph 1, applies, the Security Council].

[If it does not confirm the indictment, all the warrants issued prior to the decision of non-confirmation shall cease immediately to have effect.]

[6.   The dismissal of a count in an indictment shall not preclude the Prosecutor from subsequently bringing a new indictment based on the acts underlying that count if supported by additional evidence.]

[7.

Option 1

The [Presidency] [Pre-Trial Chamber] may [, on its own or] at the request of the Prosecutor amend the indictment [, in which case it shall make any necessary orders to ensure that the accused is notified of the amendment and has adequate time to prepare a defence] [after hearing the accused, provided that the Trial Chamber is satisfied that the accused is not prejudiced in his rights to defend himself].]

Option 2

[*101] Prior to the confirmation of the indictment by the Pre-Trial Chamber, the Prosecutor may amend or withdraw the indictment. [The accused shall be informed of the withdrawal as well as of any amendment. In the event of withdrawal, the Pre-Trial Chamber may, under the provisions provided for in article 54, ask the Prosecutor to reconsider his/her decision.]

After the confirmation of the indictment, the Prosecutor may amend the indictment only with the permission of the Pre-Trial Chamber, and after notice to the accused. If the Prosecutor is seeking to add additional charges or to substitute more serious charges for those in the confirmed indictment, the new or amended charges must be confirmed by the Pre-Trial Chamber in accordance with the procedures for confirmation of the indictment set out in paragraph [...].

After the commencement of the trial, the Prosecutor may withdraw the indictment or certain charges within the indictment only with the permission of the Trial Chamber].

[In case of withdrawal of the indictment after the confirmation thereof, new prosecution may be instituted for the same offence only based upon a newly discovered material evidence which was not available to the Prosecutor at the time of the withdrawal in the interest of the defence.]

N.B. Consideration may be given to limiting paragraph 7 to the main principles regarding amendment and withdrawal of the indictment while addressing the details in the Rules of Procedure and Evidence.

[8.[x] When one or more of the accused has fled or cannot be found, and when all reasonable steps have been taken to inform the accused, the Pre-Trial Chamber may still hold a hearing in order to examine whether it shall confirm the indictment. In that case, the accused cannot be represented by counsel.

---

    [x]   The Preparatory Committee decided to defer the consideration of paragraph 8 of article 58 for such time as article 63 is considered.

When it confirms the indictment, in its entirety or in part, against an accused who has fled or cannot be found, the Pre-Trial Chamber shall issue a warrant to search for, arrest and transfer the accused, which is tantamount to committing him to the Trial Chamber for trial.]

[9. Anyone who has [personally] suffered [direct] injury caused by a crime submitted to the Court, [the legal representatives of victims, victims' relatives, successors and assigns,] may inform the [Prosecutor] [and the] [*102] [Pre-Trial Chamber] in writing of the acts having caused injury to him/her/them and the nature and amount of the losses which he/she/they has/have sustained.

When it confirms the indictment, in its entirety or in part, the Pre-Trial Chamber may order provisional measures which may be necessary [in order to enable a Trial Chamber, upon a subsequent conviction,] to compensate the victim designated in the above paragraph. For that purpose, the Pre-Trial Chamber shall seek the cooperation of the interested States.

    · Such provisions shall also apply when the accused has fled or cannot be found.]

N.B. Paragraph 9 should be reviewed in the light of article 73 (Reparations to victims).

10. The [Presidency] [Pre-Trial Chamber] [Trial Chamber] may make any further orders required for the conduct of the trial, including an order:

    (a) determining the language or languages to be used during the trial;

    (b)

Option 1

    requiring the disclosure to the defence [of the relevant evidence that the defence requests] within a sufficient time before the trial to enable the preparation of the defence, of [relevant] documentary or other evidence available to the Prosecutor [, whether or not the Prosecutor intends to rely on that evidence] [which the Prosecutor intends to rely upon]; [if the Prosecutor fails to comply with an order under this subparagraph, the evidence in question will be inadmissible at the trial;]

Option 2

    save in respect of documents or information referred to in article 54, paragraph 4 (g), and subject to subparagraph (f) below, requiring the disclosure to the defence of documents or information which are either considered [material] [relevant] to the preparation of the defence, or are intended for use by the Prosecutor at trial or were obtained from the accused;[9]

[*103] (c)   providing for the exchange of information between the Prosecutor and the defence, so that both parties are sufficiently aware of the issues to be decided at the trial;

    (d) providing [, at the request of either party or a State, or at the instance of the Court on its own volition,] for the protection of the accused, victims and witnesses and of confidential information;

    (e) providing [, at the request of either party or a State, or at the instance of the Court on its own volition,] for the protection and privacy of victims and witnesses;

    [(f) providing, at the request of either party or a State, or at the instance of the Court of its own volition, for the non-disclosure or protection of documents or information provided by a State the disclosure of which would [endanger] [prejudice] the national security or national defence interests of a State in accordance with criteria to be specified in rules made pursuant to this Statute.]

N.B. Subparagraphs (d), (e) and (f) of paragraph 10 could be consolidated further.

Article 59

Arrest

1. At any time after an investigation has been initiated, the [Presidency] [Pre-Trial Chamber] may at the request of the Prosecutor issue a warrant for the pre-indictment arrest of a suspect if there are reasonable grounds[10] [11] to believe that:

    (a) the suspect has committed a crime within the jurisdiction of the Court; and

    (b) taking the suspect into custody is necessary to ensure that the suspect does not:

---

    [9]   [Quaere: definition of "relevant" for the Rules of Procedure and Evidence?]
    [10]   The term "reasonable grounds" was understood to embody objective criteria.
    [11]   Some delegations preferred other terms such as "serious reasons".

[*104] (i)   fail to appear for trial;

[(ii)   [interfere with or destroy evidence;][12]

[(iii) [intimidate] [influence] witnesses or victims;]

[(iv)   engage in collusion with accomplices;] or

[(v)   [continue to commit a crime within the jurisdiction of the Court.][13]

[The Pre-Trial Chamber may also issue a warrant of judicial supervision in order to place a person under restrictions of liberty other than arrest.][14]

[*107] [No person shall be subjected to arbitrary arrest or detention. Nor shall any person be deprived of his liberty except on such grounds and in accordance with such procedures as are established by the rules of the Court.][15]

2.   (a)   The warrant for the pre-indictment arrest shall be deemed to have lapsed and the request for the pre-indictment arrest of a suspect shall be deemed to have been withdrawn if [the indictment has not been confirmed] [a post-indictment warrant has not been served] within [30] [60] [90] days of the arrest, or in exceptional circumstances such longer time up to a total of [60] [90] days as the [Presidency] [Pre-Trial Chamber] may allow.

(b)   In the case of a State Party which has notified the Court under article 88, paragraph 2, that it can surrender pre-indictment, the warrant for the pre-indictment arrest of a suspect shall be deemed to have been withdrawn if [the indictment has not been confirmed] [a post-indictment warrant has not been confirmed] [a post-indictment warrant has not been served] within [30] [60] [90] [*105] days of the surrender, or in exceptional circumstances such longer time up to a total of [60] [90] days as the [Presidency] [Pre-Trial Chamber] may allow.

If the Prosecutor decides not to indict the suspect or the [Presidency] [Pre-Trial Chamber] decides not to [confirm the indictment] [not to issue a post-indictment warrant], the Prosecutor shall immediately advise the custodial State of that fact.[16]

3."Opening clause":

Option 1

[In the case where no pre-indictment warrant has been obtained,] [Prior to the confirmation hearing,] [As soon as practicable] [after the confirmation of the indictment], the Prosecutor shall seek from the [Presidency] [Pre-Trial Chamber] a [post-indictment] warrant for the arrest and transfer of the accused. The [Presidency] [Pre-Trial Chamber] shall issue such a warrant unless it is satisfied that:

Option 2

Upon confirmation of the indictment, a warrant for the arrest of the accused shall be issued by the Pre-Trial Chamber, unless, having heard the views of the Prosecutor, it is satisfied that:

(a)   the accused will voluntarily appear for trial and none of the other factors in paragraph 1 (b) are present]; or

(b)   there are special circumstances making it unnecessary for the time being to issue the warrant.

4.   The Court[17] shall transmit the warrant to any State where the person may be located, along with a request for the provisional arrest, or arrest and [surrender, transfer, extradition] of the person under Part 9.

5.   [Pre-indictment and post-indictment warrants may also be issued when the accused is a fugitive. In this case, the post-indictment warrant issued by the [*106] Pre-Trial Chamber shall have the effect of an

---

[12]   Some delegations suggested that subparagraphs (ii), (iii) and (iv) could be merged under a more general formulation such as "obstructing or endangering the investigation or the court proceedings".

[13]   Some delegations favoured addressing situations in which the accused may be harmed or at risk. Other delegations stated that the accused could be adequately protected under article 68.

[14]   It was suggested that this provision could be deleted because it is addressed in article 60, paragraph 6.

[15]   It was suggested that this provision could be moved to article 54, paragraph 10.

[16]   It was suggested that the questions of release and re-arrest could be addressed in another provision of this Statute.

[17]   The term "Court" is understood to include its constituent organs, including the Prosecutor, as defined in article 35.

international warrant and shall be disseminated by all appropriate means. When the accused is apprehended, the authorities shall proceed as provided for in Part 9.]

6.   [A post-indictment warrant shall remain in effect until the date of the judgement. The effects of the warrant delivered by the Pre-Trial Chamber shall not be interrupted by the actions challenging the submission of cases to the Court.]

Article 60
Pre-trial detention or release

1.   [The States [Parties] [in which the person is located] [and in which the crime was committed] shall be notified of a warrant issued by the Pre-Trial Chamber.] The State that has received a pre- or post-indictment warrant and a request for the arrest of a person under article 59, paragraph 5, shall immediately [in accordance with its laws][18] [[and] in accordance with the provisions of Part 9 of this Statute] take steps to arrest the suspect [on the basis of the warrant issued by the Court or by obtaining a domestic warrant for arrest based on the Court's warrant and request].[19]

[2.   The Prosecutor may, with the consent of the Pre-Trial Chamber, execute a warrant for arrest by him or herself only in cases where the competent authority of the State Party concerned may not be available or may be ineffective.][20]

[*107] 3. A person arrested shall be brought promptly before a competent judicial authority in the custodial State who shall determine, in accordance with the law of that State, that the warrant applies to that person and the person has been arrested in accordance with the proper process and that the person's rights have been respected.

4.   The person shall have the right to apply to [the competent judicial authority in the custodial State] [the Pre-Trial Chamber] for interim release pending [surrender] [transfer] [extradition] [in accordance with its national law]. [The custodial State shall take into account the views of the Prosecutor [and Court] on interim release.]

N.B. The term "Court", if retained in this paragraph, should be clarified.

5.   After the [decision to] [surrender] [transfer] [extradite] to the Court, the person may apply to the [Presidency] [Pre-Trial Chamber] for interim release pending trial.

6.   The person shall be detained unless the [Presidency] [Pre-Trial Chamber] is satisfied that the person will voluntarily appear for trial and none of the other factors in article 59, paragraph 1 (b), are present. If it decides to release the person, it may do so with or without conditions [or may issue a warrant of judicial supervision restricting the person's liberty other than by arrest]. [The [Presidency] [Pre-Trial Chamber] shall also, on its own initiative, review its ruling periodically. If satisfied that changed circumstances require that the ruling be modified, it may order any measure provided for in paragraph 5.]

N.B. Reference to "any measure provided for in paragraph 5" should be revised in the light of the current language of paragraph 5.

7.   (a)   The [Presidency] [Pre-Trial Chamber] may, either of its own initiative or at the request of the person concerned or the Prosecutor, modify its ruling as to detention [, judicial supervision] or conditional release in effect at that time.

[(b) The person may be detained prior to trial for a maximum of one year; however, this period may be extended up to an additional year by the [Presidency] [Pre-Trial Chamber] if the Prosecutor

---

[18]   Under article 59, paragraph 5, a warrant for pre-indictment arrest is forwarded to the State in which the individual sought may be located, along with a request for provisional arrest or transfer/surrender under Part 9. If Part 9 specifies the extent to which national laws apply to requests for provisional arrest or transfer/surrender, it will be unnecessary to treat this issue here as well.

[19]   The issue of whether a State can decline to arrest and detain a person, pending resolution of a challenge under article 17, could be dealt with in that article.

[20]   This provision raises a host of issues, including under what conditions the Prosecutor should be able to exercise such authority, whether the Prosecutor would have adequate resources to do so, and whether such issues should be addressed elsewhere in the Statute.

can demonstrate that he or she will be ready for trial within that period and can show good cause for the delay.]

[*108] (c) The person and the Prosecutor may appeal the [Presidency's] [Pre-Trial Chamber's] determination regarding release or detention to the Appeals Chamber.

8. If necessary, the [Presidency] [Pre-Trial Chamber] may issue a warrant of arrest to secure the presence of an accused who has been released.

9. A person arrested may apply to the [Presidency] [Pre-Trial Chamber] for a determination of the lawfulness under this Statute of any arrest warrant or order of detention issued by the Court. If the [Presidency] [Pre-Trial Chamber] decides that the arrest or detention was unlawful under the Statute, it shall order the release of the person, [and may award compensation] [in accordance with article ...].[21]

10. [A person arrested shall be held, pending trial or release on bail, in an appropriate place of detention in the arresting State, in the State in which the trial is to be held, or if necessary in the host State.] [Once ordered [surrendered] [transferred] [extradited] by the custodial State, the person shall be delivered to the Court as soon as possible, and shall be held in an appropriate place of detention in the host State or other State in which the trial is to be held.]

Article 61[22]
Notification of the indictment

N.B. It might be necessary to broaden the title of this article to cover the whole of its content.

1. The [Prosecutor] [Registrar] shall ensure, where necessary with the cooperation of national authorities, that a person who has been arrested is personally served, as soon as possible after being taken into custody, with certified copies of the following documents, [in a language that the accused understands] [in his own language]:

(a) in the case of the pre-indictment arrest of a suspect, [a statement of the grounds for the arrest] [the warrant of arrest or restriction of liberty];

[*109] (b)   in any other case, the confirmed indictment;

(c) a statement of the [accused's] [arrested person's] rights under [articles 54 or 67 of] this Statute and the Rules [, as applicable].

[2. An indictment shall be made public, except in the following situations:

(a)   The [Presidency] [Pre-Trial Chamber] may, at the request of the Prosecutor, order that there be no public disclosure of the indictment until it is served on the accused, or in the case of joint accused, on all the accused. In exercising its discretion, the [Presidency] [Pre-Trial Chamber] shall take account of all relevant factors, including the potential for pre-arrest flight of an accused, destruction of evidence and harm to victims or witnesses if the indictment is made public;

(b)[23] The [Presidency] [Pre-Trial Chamber] may, at the request of the Prosecutor, also order that there be no disclosure of an indictment, or part thereof, or of all or any part of any particular document or information, if satisfied that the making of such an order is required to give effect to a provision of the Rules, to protect confidential information obtained by the Prosecutor, or is otherwise in the interests of justice.]

3. In any case to which paragraph 1 (a) applies, the indictment shall be served on the accused as soon as possible after it has been confirmed.

4. If, 60[24] days after the indictment has been confirmed, the accused is not in custody pursuant to a warrant issued under article 59, paragraph 3, or for some reason the requirements of paragraph 1 cannot be complied with, the [Presidency] [Pre-Trial Chamber] [the Registrar] [may] [shall] on the application of the Prosecutor prescribe some other manner of bringing the indictment to the attention of the accused.

---

[21]   This paragraph should be reviewed in the light of the text of article 84.

[22]   The wording of this article might be modified in the light of the decisions to be taken as regards the question of hearing of the confirmation of an indictment.

[23]   The contents of this subparagraph could become the subject matter of the provision being negotiated on questions of confidentiality, disclosure and protection of information.

[24]   The matter concerning a specific deadline may be more appropriate for the rules of procedure.

[5.   [The accused] [Anyone suspected of committing a crime within the meaning of this Statute] shall be entitled:

[*110] (a)   to be informed promptly of the nature and cause of the charge against him or her [and be questioned in a language which he understands, and, to this end, to have the free assistance of a competent interpreter, and to be provided free of charge with a translation of the documents on the basis of which he is being questioned or that show why a measure infringing upon his liberty or property has been proposed];

(b)   [to have adequate time and facilities for the preparation of his or her defence and to communicate with counsel;] [to be assisted promptly by a lawyer of his own choosing, or, if he does not have sufficient means to pay for one, by a lawyer appointed by the [Pre-Trial Chamber of the] Court;]

(c)   [before being questioned, or when a measure infringing upon his liberty or property has been proposed and brought to his attention, to be fully informed of the charges against him and the rights to which he is entitled under paragraph 1 of this article.]]

[*111] Further option for articles 58 to 61[25] [26]

Article 58
Issuance by the Pre-Trial Chamber of an arrest warrant or a summons to appear[27]

1.   At any time after an investigation has been initiated, the Pre-Trial Chamber may, at the application of the Prosecutor, issue a warrant for the arrest for a person if:

(a)   there are reasonable grounds to believe that the person has committed a crime within the jurisdiction of the Court; and

[*112] (b)   it appears that the arrest of the person is necessary to assure the person's appearance at trial, to assure that the person does not obstruct or endanger the investigation or the court proceedings, [or to prevent the person from continuing to commit a crime within the jurisdiction of the Court].

2.   The application shall specify:

(a)   the name of the person or persons, and any other relevant identifying information;

(b)   the specific crimes within the jurisdiction of the Court which the person is alleged to have committed;

(c)   a concise statement of the facts which are alleged to constitute those crimes;

(d)   a summary of the evidence and any other information which form reasonable grounds to believe the person committed those crimes; and

(e)   the reason why the Prosecutor believes the arrest of the person is necessary.

3.   The Pre-Trial Chamber shall examine the application and the evidence or other information submitted by the Prosecutor and, if satisfied that there are reasonable grounds to believe that the person named committed the crimes alleged and that the arrest of the person appears necessary, shall issue a warrant for the arrest of the person. The warrant of arrest shall identify the person to be arrested and the crimes for

---

[25]   The proposal represents a simplified and somewhat restructured text for articles 58 through 61. This simplified version of these articles has been achieved as a result of adoption of the framework outlined in A/AC.249/1998/WG.4/DP.36 and the withdrawal or abbreviation by many delegations of their proposals currently contained in A/AC.249/1998/L.13. This reflects a decision by many of the authors to move away from national positions towards a single, straightforward procedural approach, acceptable to delegations representing different national legal systems.

The proposal does not attempt to resolve issues such as the trigger mechanism or powers of the Prosecutor. Similarly, it does not attempt to incorporate at this time procedures relating to challenges to admissibility or jurisdiction.

The purpose of the proposed text, if delegations agree, is to provide a basis for a more focused and efficient discussion in Rome of the procedural stages addressed in the above articles 58 through 61.

[26]   A view was expressed that the proposal for articles 58 to 61 under this option omits procedures of substantive nature which have been included in the text of the same articles above.

[27]   Provisions in the option for article 59 presented on page 87 ("[No person shall be subjected to arbitrary arrest or detention. Nor shall any person be deprived of his liberty except on such grounds and in accordance with such procedures as are established by the rules of the Court.]") should be moved to article 54.

which the person's arrest is sought, and shall contain a concise statement of the facts which are alleged to constitute those crimes. The warrant of arrest shall remain in effect until otherwise ordered by the Court.
4.   Based on the arrest warrant, the Court may request the provisional arrest, or the arrest and [surrender][extradition] of the person under Part 9.
[5.   Prior to the [surrender][extradition] of the person, the Prosecutor may request that the Pre-Trial Chamber amend the warrant of arrest by modifying or adding to the crimes specified therein. The Pre-Trial Chamber shall so amend [*113] the warrant if it is satisfied that there are reasonable grounds to believe the person committed the modified or additional crimes.][28]
6.   As an alternative to seeking a warrant of arrest, the Prosecutor may submit an application requesting that the Pre-Trial Chamber issue a summons for the person to appear. If the Pre-Trial Chamber finds that there are reasonable grounds to believe that the person committed the crime alleged, and that a summons is sufficient to assure the person's appearance, it shall issue the summons for the person to appear on a specified date. The summons shall identify the person summoned and the crimes which the person is alleged to have committed, and shall contain a concise statement of the facts which are alleged to constitute the crime. The summons shall be served on the person. [The Pre-Trial Chamber may request the State that serves the summons to place the person under restrictions of liberty, if permitted by the law of that State.][29]

Article 59
Arrest proceedings in the custodial State
1.   A State Party which has received a request for provisional arrest or for arrest and [surrender][extradition] shall immediately take steps to arrest the suspect in accordance with its laws and the provisions of Part 9.[30]
2.   A person arrested shall be brought promptly before a competent judicial authority in the custodial State who shall determine, in accordance with the law of that State, that the warrant applies to that person, that the person has been arrested in accordance with the proper process, and that the person's rights have been respected.
[*114] 3.   The person arrested shall have the right to apply for interim release pending [surrender][extradition] to [the Pre-Trial Chamber][the competent judicial authority in the custodial State in accordance with its national law. The custodial State shall take into account the views of the Prosecutor and the Court regarding the interim release.]
[4.   Pending a decision on [surrender][extradition], a person may apply to the Pre-Trial Chamber for a determination of the lawfulness under this Statute of any arrest warrant issued by the Court. If the Pre-Trial Chamber decides that the arrest warrant was unlawful under the Statute, it shall order the release of the person.][31]
5.   Once ordered to be [surrendered][extradited] by the custodial State, the person shall be delivered to the Court as soon as possible.

Article 60
Initial proceedings before the Court
1.   Upon the [surrender][extradition] of the person to the Court, or the person's appearance before the Court voluntarily or pursuant to a summons, the Pre-Trial Chamber shall satisfy itself that the person has

---

[28]   Such a provision may be necessary, particularly if a strict rule of specialty were adopted.
[29]   The question whether the Pre-Trial Chamber shall have the possibility to request the State that serves the summons to place the person under restrictions of liberty, despite the fact that it found that a summons is sufficient to assure the person's appearance, will have to be examined.
[30]   It is contemplated that, in unusual circumstances, for example of grave illness, the State might, if permitted by its law, place the person under judicial supervision rather than arrest the person and take him into custody.
[31]   Serious questions were raised about on what grounds such a challenge would be based and whether this provision was needed at all in light of the procedures for judicial review of the arrest warrant and judicial confirmation of the charges for trial.

been informed of the crimes he or she is alleged to have committed, and of his or her rights under the Statute, including the right to apply for interim release pending trial.

2.   A person subject to a warrant of arrest may apply for interim release pending trial. However, the person shall be detained unless the Pre-Trial Chamber is satisfied that the person, if released, will appear for trial, will not obstruct or endanger the investigation or the Court's proceedings[, or will not continue to commit crimes within the jurisdiction of the Court]. If it decides to release the person, the Pre-Trial Chamber may do so with or without conditions, including conditions restricting the person's liberty.

3.   The Pre-Trial Chamber shall periodically review its ruling on the release or detention of the person, and may do so at any time on the request of [*115] the Prosecutor or accused.[32] Upon such review, it may modify its ruling as to detention, release, or conditions of release, if it is satisfied that changed circumstances so require.

4.   The Pre-Trial Chamber shall assure that a person is not detained for an unreasonable period prior to trial due to unexcusable delay by the Prosecutor. If such delay has occurred, the Court shall consider releasing the person pursuant to conditions.

5.   If necessary, the Pre-Trial Chamber may issue a warrant of arrest to secure the presence of an accused who has been released.

Article 61
Confirmation of the charges before trial[33]

1.   Within a reasonable time after the person's surrender or voluntary appearance before the Court, the Pre-Trial Chamber shall hold a hearing to confirm the charges on which the Prosecutor intends to seek trial. The hearing shall be held in the presence of the Prosecutor and the accused, as well as his or her counsel[, unless -

(a)   the person has waived his right to be present; or

(b)   the person has fled or cannot be found and all reasonable steps have been made to inform the person of the proposed charges and that a hearing to confirm those charges will be held, in which case the person shall not be represented by counsel].

2.   A reasonable time before the hearing, the person shall be provided with a copy of the charges on which the Prosecutor intends to seek trial, and be informed of the evidence on which the Prosecutor intends to rely at the hearing. The Pre-Trial Chamber may make orders regarding the disclosure of information [*116] for purposes of the hearing as may be appropriate under the Statute and the Rules.

3.   Before the hearing, the Prosecutor may continue the investigation and may amend or withdraw any proposed charges. The accused shall be given reasonable notice before the hearing of any amendment or withdrawal of proposed charges.

4.   At the hearing, the Prosecutor shall have the burden of presenting, for each charge on which he seeks trial, sufficient evidence to establish substantial grounds to believe that the person committed the crime charged. The Prosecutor may rely on documentary or summary evidence and need not call the witnesses expected to testify at the trial.

5.   At the hearing, the accused person may object to the proposed charges, criticize the evidence presented by the Prosecutor and present evidence on his or her own behalf.

---

[32]   A view was expressed that there should be a specific time limit in the Statute within which the Pre-Trial Chamber must review a detention decision.

[33]   Paragraph 9 of the option for article 58 presented on page 85 referred to the power of the Pre-Trial Chamber to order provisional measures to preserve the Court's ability to order compensation to victims. It is suggested that this concept be moved to article 57, paragraph 2, and be among the general powers of the Pre-Trial Chamber and not only exercisable at the time of confirmation.

6. The Pre-Trial Chamber shall determine whether, considering the presentations by both the Prosecutor and the accused, there is sufficient evidence to establish substantial grounds to believe that the person committed each of the crimes charged.[34] Based on its determinations, the Pre-Trial Chamber may:[35]

(a) confirm those proposed charges as to which it has determined there is sufficient evidence, and commit the person to a Trial Chamber for trial on the charges as confirmed;

(b) refuse to confirm those proposed charges as to which it has determined there is insufficient evidence;

(c) adjourn the hearing and request the Prosecutor to consider -

(i) providing further evidence or conduct further investigation with respect to a particular charge; or

[*117] (ii) amending a proposed charge because the evidence submitted appears to establish a different crime within the jurisdiction of the Court.[36]

7. After the charges are confirmed and before the trial has begun, the Prosecutor may amend the charges, but only with the permission of the Pre-Trial Chamber and after notice to the accused. If the Prosecutor seeks to add additional charges or to substitute more serious charges, a hearing under this Article to confirm those charges must be held. After commencement of the trial, the Prosecutor may withdraw the charges only with the permission of the Trial Chamber.

8. A previously issued warrant shall cease to have effect with respect to any charges which have not been confirmed by the Pre-Trial Chamber or which have been withdrawn by the Prosecutor.

[*118] PART 6. THE TRIAL
Article 62
Place of trial

1. Unless otherwise decided in accordance with paragraph 2, the place of the trial will be the seat of the Court.

2. The [Presidency] [Assembly of the State parties] may authorize the Court to exercise its functions at a place other than its seat [where it will ensure the efficient conduct of the trial and is in the interest of justice] [or] [when trial by the members of the Court is likely to make the proceedings simpler and less costly]

3. [(a) The Presidency of the Court shall make inquiries with the State Party that appears likely to receive the Court.

[(b) After the State Party likely to receive the Court has agreed, the decision [under the preceding paragraph] to hold a session away from the Court's seat shall be taken by the Assembly of the States Parties, which shall be informed either by one of its members, the Presidency, the Prosecutor or the Assembly of the Judges of the Court.]

4. [With the express agreement of the State Party receiving the Court], the privileges, immunities and facilities provided for in _____ shall continue to be effective when the Court holds a session pursuant to paragraph 2.

5. [The provisions of this article shall also apply to non-States Parties which, after inquiries by the Presidency, state that they agree to receive the Court and to grant the privileges, immunities and facilities provided for in _____.]

N.B. Some of the issues raised in the proposals may be dealt with in the Rules of Procedure and Evidence.

---

[34] A decision needs to be made whether any hearing on admissibility will be held separately, or whether admissibility issues raised by the accused should also be considered at this hearing.

[35] The question remains whether the decisions of the Pre-Trial Chamber on confirmation of the charges should be unanimous or by majority vote.

[36] Amending the charge may have implications under a rule of speciality provision.

Article 63
Trial in presence of the accused

[*119] Comment: There appear, in essence, to be three options regarding trials in absentia which have emerged to date, in addition to the ILC draft (A/51/22, vol. II). The ILC text and the proposed options are set out below:

N.B. The ILC text as such could be deleted since it seems to have been superseded by the options that were developed as a consequence of the discussions at the Preparatory Committee.

ILC draft

1.   As a general rule, the accused should be present during the trial.
2.   The Trial Chamber may order that the trial proceed in the absence of the accused if:
    (a)   the accused is in custody, or has been released pending trial, and for reasons of security or the ill-health of the accused it is undesirable for the accused to be present;
    (b)   the accused is continuing to disrupt the trial; or
    (c)   the accused has escaped from lawful custody under this Statute or has broken bail.
3.   The Chamber shall, if it makes an order under paragraph 2, ensure that the rights of the accused under this Statute are respected, and in particular:
    (a)   that all reasonable steps have been taken to inform the accused of the charge; and
    (b)   that the accused is legally represented, if necessary by a lawyer appointed by the Court.
4.[1]   In cases where a trial cannot be held because of the deliberate absence of an accused, the Court may establish, in accordance with the Rules, an Indictment Chamber for the purpose of:
[*120] (a)   recording the evidence;
    (b)   considering whether the evidence establishes a prima facie case of a crime within the jurisdiction of the Court; and
    (c)   issuing and publishing a warrant of arrest in respect of an accused against whom a prima facie case is established.
5.   If the accused is subsequently tried under this Statute:
    (a)   the record of evidence before the Indictment Chamber shall be admissible;
    (b)   any judge who was a member of the Indictment Chamber may not be a member of the Trial Chamber.

* * *

Option 1
    The trial shall not be held if the accused is not present.[2]
Option 2
General rule
1.   As a general rule, the accused shall be present during the trial.
Exceptions
2.   In exceptional circumstances, the Trial Chamber may order that the trial proceed in the absence of the accused, if the accused, having been present at the commencement of the trial thereafter:
    (a) has escaped from lawful custody or has broken bail; or
[*121] [(b)   is continuing to disrupt the trial.][3]

---

[1]   The questions addressed in paragraphs 4 and 5 may be better dealt with in the context of the pre-trial proceedings.
[2]   Option 1 prohibits trial in absentia without any exception; like option 2, it would deal with procedures needed to preserve evidence for trial as a matter separate from trial in absentia.
[3]   Some proponents of option 2 do not agree that this should necessarily be a basis for a trial in absentia.

Rights of the accused

3.   The Trial Chamber shall, if it makes an order under paragraph 2, ensure that the rights of the accused under this Statute are respected, and in particular that the accused is legally represented, if necessary by a lawyer appointed by the Court.[4]

Proceedings to preserve evidence[5]

Subsequent trial[6]

Option 3

1.   As a general rule, the accused should be present during the trial.

2.   In exceptional circumstances, the Trial Chamber may, in the interests of justice [at the request of the Prosecutor] [proprio motu or at the request of one of the parties] order that the trial proceed in the absence of the accused, if the latter, having been duly informed of the opening of the trial:

    (a)   Requests to be excused from appearing for reasons of serious ill-health;

    (b)   Disrupts the trial;

[*122] (c)   Does not appear on the day of the hearing;

    (d)   under detention has, when summoned for the date of the trial, refused to appear without good reason, and made it particularly difficult to bring him to the Court; or

In the event that the accused is convicted following a trial held in his absence, the Trial Chamber may issue a warrant for the arrest and transfer of the accused for the purposes of executing the judgement. The decision taken under the provisions of this paragraph shall be communicated to the accused and may be appealed.

3.   The Trial Chamber shall, if it makes an order under paragraph 2, ensure that the rights of the accused under this Statute are respected, and in particular:

    (a)   that all reasonable steps have been taken to inform the accused of the charge; and

    (b)   that the accused is legally represented, if necessary by a lawyer appointed by the Court.

4.   When the accused has not been duly informed of the opening of the trial and when all reasonable steps have been taken to inform the accused of the charges, the Trial Chamber may also, in very exceptional circumstances, [at the request of the Prosecutor] [proprio motu or at the request of one of the parties], order that the trial proceed in the absence of the accused when required in the interests of justice or the interests of the victims.

The accused may not then be represented by a lawyer of the accused's choosing, but the judge presiding over the Trial Chamber may appoint a lawyer on his own motion.

When the accused, having been judged in accordance with the above provisions, is taken prisoner or is arrested, the decisions taken in his absence by the Trial Chamber shall be null and void in all their provisions. The evidence submitted during the trial held in the absence of the accused may not be used, during the second trial, to establish the charges levelled against the accused, except where it is impossible for the depositions to be made a second time or where the evidence cannot again be produced.

Nevertheless, the accused may agree to the decision if the sentence pronounced in his absence is less than or equal to 10 years of imprisonment.

[*123] Option 4

1.   The accused shall have the right to be present at the trial, unless the Trial Chamber, having heard such submissions and evidence as it deems necessary, concludes that the absence of the accused is deliberate.

2.[7]   The Trial Chamber shall, if it makes an order under (paragraph 2), ensure that the rights of the accused under this Statute are respected, and in particular:

---

[4]   This provision follows paragraph 3 of the ILC draft, except that it omits subparagraph (a), regarding steps to inform the accused of the charges. This is unnecessary under this option since a trial in absentia is permitted only if the accused was present at the commencement of the trial, a stage at which the indictment is to be read out.

[5]   There is no separate proposal to preserve evidence for trial. This could be dealt with as part of pre-trial proceedings, and would not necessarily be confined to situations where the accused is absent.

[6]   Under this option, there would be no second trial following a trial in absentia.

[7]   This is paragraph 3 of the ILC text, which requires consequential adjustments to be harmonized with the text of this Option.

(a)   that all reasonable steps have been taken to inform the accused of the charge; and

(b)   that the accused is legally represented, if necessary by a lawyer appointed by the Court.

Article 64
Functions and powers of the Trial Chamber

1.   At the commencement of the trial, the Trial Chamber shall:

(a)   have the indictment read;

(b)   ensure that articles 58, paragraph 10 (b), and 61 have been complied with sufficiently in advance of the trial to enable adequate preparation of the defence;

(c)   satisfy itself that the other rights of the accused under this Statute and the Rules have been respected;

(d)   allow the accused to enter a plea of not guilty or to make an admission of guilt before the Trial Chamber [and should the accused fail to do so, enter a plea of not guilty on his or her behalf].

2.   The Chamber shall ensure that a trial is fair and expeditious and is conducted in accordance with this Statute and the Rules, with full respect for [*124] the rights of the accused and due regard for the protection of victims and witnesses.

[3.   The President of the Trial Chamber shall control and direct the hearing, and decide upon the manner by which evidence shall be produced by the parties. In all circumstances, the President shall have the duty to remain impartial.]

N.B. It was suggested that the beginning of the paragraph should refer to the person presiding over the Trial Chamber.

4.   The Trial Chamber may, subject to the Rules, hear charges against more than one accused arising out of the same factual situation.

5.   The trial shall be held in public, unless the Trial Chamber determines that certain proceedings be in closed session in accordance with article 68, or for the purpose of protecting confidential or sensitive information which is to be given in evidence.

The deliberations of the Court shall remain confidential.

6.   The Trial Chamber shall, subject to this Statute and the Rules of Procedure and Evidence, have, inter alia, the power on the application of a party or of its own motion to:

(a)   issue a warrant for the arrest and transfer of an accused who is not already in the custody of the Court;

(b)   exercise the same powers as the Pre-Trial Chamber regarding measures that restrict the liberty of a person;

(c)   terminate or modify any warrants issued by the Pre-Trial Chamber;

(d)   rule on any preliminary motions.

N.B. See the last paragraph of article 17, paragraph 5 (Challenges to the jurisdiction of the Court or the admissibility of a case) for any possible inconsistency with paragraph 6 (d) and article 81.

(b)   require the attendance and testimony of witnesses, and the production of documents and other evidentiary materials by obtaining, if necessary, the assistance of States as provided in this Statute;

[(b) bis order the production of further evidence to that already collected prior to the trial or presented during the trial by the parties;]

[*125] (c)   rule on the admissibility or relevance of evidence;

(d)   protect confidential information; and

(e)   maintain order in the course of a hearing.

The provisions of article 58, paragraph 10 (f), will apply mutatis mutandis for the purposes of orders sought under subparagraph (d) above.

7.   [The Trial Chamber may refer pre-trial issues under this article to the Pre-Trial Chamber for resolution.]

8.   The Trial Chamber shall ensure that a complete record of the trial, which accurately reflects the proceedings, is maintained and preserved by the Registrar.

Article 65
Proceedings on an admission of guilt
1.   Where the accused makes an admission of guilt under article 64, paragraph 1 (d), the Trial Chamber shall determine whether:

(a)   the accused understands the nature and consequences of the admission of guilt and whether the admission is voluntarily made after sufficient consultation with defence counsel; and

(b)   the admission of guilt is [firmly] supported by the facts of the case that are contained in:

(i)   the indictment and in any supplementary materials presented by the Prosecutor, and which the accused admits; and

(ii)   any other evidence, including the testimony of witnesses, presented by the Prosecutor or the accused.

2.   Where the Trial Chamber is satisfied that the matters referred to in paragraph 1 are established, the Trial Chamber shall consider the admission of guilt, together with any additional evidence presented and admitted, as an admission of all the essential facts that are required to prove the crime to which the admission of guilt relates, and [may] [shall] convict the accused of that crime.

[*126] 3.   Where the Trial Chamber is not satisfied that the matters referred to in paragraph 1 are established, the Trial Chamber shall order that the trial be continued under the ordinary trial procedures provided by this Statute, and shall consider the admission of guilt not to have been made [and shall [may] remit the case to another Trial Chamber].

4.   Where the Trial Chamber is of the opinion that a more complete presentation of the facts of the case is otherwise required in the interests of justice, in particular the interests of the victims, the Trial Chamber may request that the Prosecutor present additional evidence, including the testimony of witnesses, or may order that the trial be continued under the ordinary trial procedures provided by this Statute and, in the latter situation, shall consider the admission of guilt not to have been made [and shall [may] remit the case to another Trial Chamber].

5.   Discussions between the Prosecutor and the defence regarding modification of the charges in the indictment, acceptance of the admission of guilt by the accused, or the penalty to be imposed shall not be legally binding on the Chamber.[8]

Article 66
Presumption of innocence
Everyone shall be presumed innocent until proved guilty in accordance with law. The onus is on the Prosecutor to establish the guilt of the accused beyond a reasonable doubt.[9]

Article 67
Rights of the accused
1.   In the determination of any charge under this Statute, the accused is entitled [, in addition to any rights afforded to a suspect under this Statute,] to a public hearing, having regard to [article 64 and] article 68, and to a fair [*127] hearing by an independent and impartial tribunal, and to the following minimum guarantees in full equality:[10]

(a)   to be informed promptly and in detail, [in a language that the accused understands] [in his own language], of the nature, cause and content of the charge;

(b)   to have adequate time and facilities for the preparation of the defence, and to communicate freely with counsel of the accused's choosing, in confidence;[11]

(c)   to be tried without [undue] [unreasonable] delay and to enjoy a speedy trial;

---

[8]   Concerns were expressed about this paragraph and it was suggested that its formulation should continue to be examined.

[9]   Reservations were expressed regarding the phrases "in accordance with law" and "beyond a reasonable doubt".

[10]   A proposal was made that the wording of subparagraphs (a) to (g) of paragraph 3 of article 14 of the International Covenant on Civil and Political Rights should be used as such.

[11]   The question of privileged communications could be addressed in the context of article 69.

(d) subject to article 63, paragraph 2, to be present at the trial, to conduct the defence in person or through legal assistance of the accused's choosing, to be informed, if the accused does not have legal assistance, of this right and to have legal assistance assigned by the Court in any case where the interests of justice so require, including where the person is unable to secure counsel, and without payment if the accused lacks sufficient means to pay for such assistance;

(e) to examine, or have examined, the prosecution witnesses and to obtain the attendance and examination of witnesses for the defence under the same conditions as witnesses for the prosecution; [In addition the accused shall also be entitled to present any other evidence;]

(f) if any of the proceedings of or documents presented to the Court are not in a language the accused understands and speaks, to have, free of any cost, the assistance of a competent interpreter and such translations as are necessary to meet the requirements of fairness;

· (g) not to be compelled to testify or to confess guilt and to remain silent, without such silence being a consideration in the determination of guilt or innocence;

[*128] [[(h) to make an unsworn statement in his or her defence, if desired] [to declare in his or her defence, but [need] [shall] not take an oath to speak the truth]];

[(i) to request the Pre-Trial Chamber or, after the commencement of the trial, the Trial Chamber to seek the cooperation of a State Party pursuant to Part 9 [7] of this Statute to collect evidence for him/her;]

[(j) no reverse onus or duty of rebuttal shall be imposed on the accused.]

N.B. See also article 68, paragraph 2 (Protection of the [accused], victims and witnesses [and their participation in the proceedings]) for any possible inconsistency with subparagraph 1.

2. [Exculpatory evidence] [Evidence which shows or tends to show the innocence] [or mitigate the guilt] of the accused or may affect the credibility of prosecution evidence that becomes available to the Procuracy prior to the conclusion of the trial shall be [made available] [disclosed] to the defence. In case of doubt as to the application of this paragraph or as to the admissibility of the evidence, the Trial Chamber shall decide. [The provisions of article 58, paragraph 10 (f), will apply mutatis mutandis for the purposes of a decision made under this subparagraph.]

[3. The right of all persons to be secure in their homes and to secure their papers and effects against entries, searches and seizures shall not be impaired by the Court except upon warrant issued by the [Court] [Pre-Trial Chamber], on the request of the Prosecutor, in accordance with Part 9 or the Rules of the Court, for adequate cause and particularly describing the place to be searched and things to be seized, or except on such grounds and in accordance with such procedures as are established by the Rules of the Court.]

[4. No person shall be deprived of life or liberty, nor shall any other criminal penalty be imposed, without due process of law.][12]

Article 68
Protection of the [accused], victims and witnesses
[*129] [and their participation in the proceedings]

1. The Court shall take the necessary measures available to it to protect the accused, victims and witnesses. Notwithstanding the principle of public hearings, the Court may to that end conduct closed proceedings or allow the presentation of evidence by electronic or other special means. [In camera hearings are mandatory when they are requested by an accused who was a minor at the time of the commission of the acts or by a victim of sexual violence.]

2. [The Prosecutor shall, in ensuring the effective investigation and prosecution of crimes, respect and take appropriate measures to protect the privacy, physical and psychological well-being, dignity and security of victims and witnesses, having regard to all relevant factors, including age, gender and health, and the nature of the crime, in particular, whether the crime involves sexual or gender violence. These measures will be consistent with the rights of the accused.]

N.B. See also article 54, paragraph 4 (e) (Investigation of alleged crimes).

---

[12] The rights addressed in paragraphs 3 and 4, which are of a general nature, should perhaps be located in another part of the Statute. In addition, paragraph 4 could be reformulated.

3.   The Court shall take such measures as are necessary to ensure the safety, physical and psychological well-being, dignity and privacy of victims and witnesses, at all stages of the process, including, but not limited to, victims and witnesses of sexual and gender violence. However, these measures [may not] [shall not] be [inconsistent with] [prejudicial to] the rights of the accused.

4.   [The Court [shall] [may] permit the views and concerns of the victim to be presented and considered at appropriate stages of the proceedings where their personal interests are affected in a manner which is consistent with the rights of the accused and a fair and impartial trial.]

[5.   The Victims and Witnesses Unit, established under article 44 of this Statute, shall provide counselling and other assistance to victims and witnesses and advise the Prosecutor and the Court on appropriate measures of protection and other matters affecting their rights. These measures may extend to family members and others at risk on account of testimony given by such witnesses.]

N.B. See article 44, paragraph 4.

[6.   Notwithstanding paragraph 1 of article 58, if disclosure of any evidence and/or any of the particulars referred to in that paragraph will probably lead to the security of any witness or his/her family being gravely endangered, the Prosecutor may, for purposes of these proceedings, withhold such particulars and [*130] submit a summary of such evidence. Such a summary shall, for purposes of any later trial proceedings before the Court, be deemed to form part of the particulars of the indictment.]

[7.   The rules of procedure shall include provisions giving effect to the United Nations Declaration of Basic Principles of Justice for Victims of Crime and Abuse of Power.]

[8.   Legal representatives of victims of crimes have the right to participate in the proceedings with a view to presenting additional evidence needed to establish the basis of criminal responsibility as a foundation for their right to pursue civil compensation.]

N.B. This paragraph should be reviewed in the light of the text on article 73 (Reparations to victims).

9.   A State may make an application for necessary measures to be taken in respect of the protection of its servants or agents and the protection of sensitive information.

Article 69
Evidence

1.   Before testifying, each witness shall, in accordance with [or as excepted by] the Rules of Procedure and Evidence, give an undertaking as to the truthfulness of the evidence to be given by that witness.[13]

2.   The testimony of a witness at trial shall be given in person, except to the extent provided by the measures set forth in article 68 or in the Rules of Procedure and Evidence. The Court may also permit the giving of <u>viva voce</u> (oral) or recorded testimony of a witness by means of video or audio technology, as well as the introduction of documents or written transcripts, subject to this Statute and in accordance with the Rules of Procedure and Evidence.[14] These [*131] measures shall not be [prejudicial to] [inconsistent with] the rights of the accused.

3.   The Court has the authority to call all evidence that it considers necessary for the determination of the truth.

4.   The Court may rule on the relevance or admissibility of any evidence in accordance with the Rules of Procedure and Evidence.[15]

---

[13]   Many delegations were of the view that it would be more appropriate to deal with the subject matter of this paragraph in the Rules of Procedure and Evidence.

[14]   A proposal was made that the Rules of Procedure and Evidence could permit the use of video or audio technology when the witness is not able to attend the Court due to illness, injury, age or other justifiable reason.

[15]   A proposal was made, supported by a number of delegations, to add the following paragraph to the Statute: "The Court may decide not to admit evidence where its probative value is substantially outweighed by its prejudice to a fair trial of an accused or to a fair evaluation of the testimony of a witness, including any prejudice caused by discriminatory beliefs or bias." Other delegations supported a proposal that the Statute or Rules of Procedure and Evidence also make reference to the exclusion of evidence of prior sexual conduct of a witness, evidence protected by the lawyer-client privilege, as well as other grounds of exclusion. It was finally proposed that these matters should be addressed in the Rules of Procedure and Evidence, as opposed to in the Statute. Many delegations also felt that the Rules

5.   The Court shall not require proof of facts of common knowledge but may take judicial notice of them.[16]

6.   Evidence obtained by means of a violation of this Statute[17] or internationally recognized human rights [or other relevant rules of international law], and which either casts substantial doubt on its reliability or the admission of which is antithetical to and would seriously damage the integrity of the proceedings, shall not be admissible.

7.   [With regard to defences open to the accused under the general principles of criminal law in the present Statute, the onus of proof shall be on the [*132] accused, subject to a preponderance of probability as applicable in civil cases.][18]

8.   When deciding on the relevance or admissibility of evidence collected by a State, the Court shall not rule on [, but may have regard to,] the application of the State's national law.

Article 70
Offenses or acts against the integrity of the Court

1.   The Court shall have jurisdiction over the following offenses and acts against its integrity when committed intentionally, as defined below:

   (a)   giving false testimony when under an obligation pursuant to article 69, paragraph 1, to tell the truth;

   (b)   presenting evidence that the party knows is false or forged;

Option 1

   [(c)   obstructing or disrupting the conduct of the Court's proceedings by disorderly or offensive conduct;]

   [(d)   disobeying an order made by or under the authority of the Court in connection with the conduct of its proceedings;]

Option 2

   [The Court may, by [fine] or other sanction, punish misbehaviour of persons committed during its proceedings, to the extent provided for in the Rules.]

   (e)   corruptly influencing a witness, obstructing or interfering with the attendance or testimony of a witness, retaliating against a witness for giving testimony or destroying, tampering with or interfering with the collection of evidence;

[*133] (f)   impeding, intimidating or corruptly influencing an official of the Court for the purpose of forcing or persuading the official not to perform, or to perform improperly, his or her duties;

   (g)   retaliating against an official of the Court on account of duties performed by that or another official.

2.   The offenses referred to in the present article shall be tried before a Chamber other than the Chamber in which the alleged offenses were committed in accordance with the Rules of Procedure and Evidence.

3.   The Court may, in the event of conviction, impose a term of imprisonment not exceeding [X months/years] [or a fine, or both].

N.B. It is not contemplated that all the provisions of the Statute and Rules, whether substantive or procedural, regarding the Court's exercise of jurisdiction over article 5 crimes would apply equally to these offenses. Further work to clarify this issue will be essential. Moreover, similar thought must be given to States parties' obligation to surrender persons charged with these offenses, especially when the State Party is pursuing prosecution itself.

---

should provide sufficient flexibility to enable the Court to rule on the relevance and admissibility of evidence where no other rule provides guidance on the standards to be applied.

[16]   It was questioned whether this provision was strictly necessary.

[17]   The question as to whether a violation of the Rules of Procedure and Evidence should also be considered in the context of the application of article 69, paragraph 5, or whether such violation should be addressed by a separate provision in the Statute or Rules of Procedure and Evidence, needs to be determined in the context of the consideration of articles 20 and 52.

[18]   Such a provision might better be discussed in the context of articles 66, 67 or 31.

[Article 71
Sensitive national security information

N.B. This title is suggested.

Option 1

1.   Any person requested to give information or evidence to the Court may refuse to do so on the ground that they are of a confidential nature and that their disclosure would seriously prejudice the national defence or security interest of the State party concerned.

2.   The Court may ask the State party concerned whether it confirms that the disclosure of these information or evidence would seriously prejudice its national defence or security interest.

If the State so confirms, the provision of article 90 (2) (c) and article [...] apply.

Option 2

[*134] 1.   This article applies in any case [falling within the scope of articles [54, paragraph 4 (g),] 58, paragraph 10 (d) and (f), 67, paragraph 2; 68, paragraph 9; 71 and 90, paragraph 2] where the disclosure of the information or documents of a State would, in the opinion of that State, prejudice its national security interests.

2.   If, in the opinion of a State, disclosure of documents or information would prejudice its national security interests, all reasonable steps will be taken by the State, acting in conjunction with the Prosecutor or the Defence (as the case may be), to seek to resolve the matter by cooperative means. In appropriate circumstances, this may include the possibility of seeking a determination of the Court as to:

    (a)   Whether the request might be modified or clarified;

    (b)   The relevance of the information or documents sought;

    (c)   Whether there might be agreement on the conditions under which disclosure might be given by providing summaries or redactions, by the use of in camera and/or ex parte proceedings or by means of other protective measures permissible under this Statute or the Rules.

3.   Without prejudice to article 54, paragraph 4 (g), the Pre-Trial Chamber or the Trial Chamber shall not make a determination that disclosure should be made except in accordance with the provisions set out below.

4.   The Court may hold a hearing for the purposes of hearing the State's representations on non-disclosure. If so, notice to the State will be given in accordance with the Rules.[19] The Pre-Trial Chamber or Trial Chamber shall, if so [*135] requested by the State, hold in camera and ex parte hearings, and may make other special arrangements, including, as appropriate:

-    Designating a single judge to examine documents or hear submissions;

-    Allowing documents to be submitted in redacted form, accompanied by an affidavit signed by a senior State official explaining the reasons for the redaction;

-    Allowing the State to provide its own interpreters for the hearing and its own translations of sensitive documents; and

-    Ordering that no transcripts be made of such proceedings, and that documents not required by the Pre-Trial Chamber or Trial Chamber be returned directly to the State without being deposited or filed in the registry of the Court.

5.   The Pre-Trial Chamber or Trial Chamber shall not make a determination to which this article applies unless:

    (a)   It is clear from the State's actions that it is not acting in good faith towards the Court; and, in determining the State's bona fides, the Pre-Trial Chamber or Trial Chamber shall have regard to the following factors:

---

[19]   The provisions on notice to States might read as follows:

"(a) Subject to subparagraph (b) below, a determination will not be made unless [x days'] notice of the matter has been given to the State concerned and that State has been given an opportunity to make representations to the Court;

(b) If, having regard to all the circumstances, the Pre-Trial Chamber or the Trial Chamber decides that there are substantial reasons for not giving the State notice of the matter, a determination to which this article applies shall not take effect until [x] days after it has been served on that State and the State has been given the opportunity to make representations to the Court."

(i)   Whether efforts have been made to secure the State's assistance through cooperative means and without recourse to measures of compulsion;

(ii)   Whether the State has expressly refused to cooperate;

(iii)   Whether there is clear evidence that the State does not intend to cooperate either because there has been excessive delay in complying with a request for assistance or because there are other circumstances clearly indicating an absence of good faith on its part;

(b)   The information or evidence is relevant to an issue before the Court and is necessary for the efficient and fair conduct of the proceedings; and

[*136] (c)   Having regard to the State's claim that its national security interests would be prejudiced by disclosure, the Pre-Trial Chamber or the Trial Chamber is satisfied that the claim is manifestly without foundation.

6.   Where a State makes a claim falling within paragraph 2 (c) above, it shall submit a reasoned case, orally or in writing, in support of its claim that its national security interests would be so prejudiced.

Option 3

1.   Article 90, paragraph 2, option 2, subparagraphs (c) and (d), which now permits a State Party to deny assistance where "execution of the request would seriously prejudice its national security, ordre public or other essential interests" or where "the request concerns the production of any documents or disclosure of evidence which relates to its national [security] [defence]", would be deleted and replaced by a narrower formulation for subparagraph (c), to read as follows:

Article 90, paragraph 2 (c)

"A State Party may deny a request for assistance, in whole or in part, only if:

"...

"(c) having complied with the provisions of article [see new article below], it determines that there are no conditions under which it can comply with the request, including request for information or evidence arising under article 64, without seriously prejudicing its national security interests."

2.   A new article, perhaps following current article 90, would set out procedures to be followed before a State party could deny assistance on national security grounds:

"Article [ ]

"1.   If a State Party receives a request for information or evidence from the Prosecutor or the Court, the disclosure of which would, in the opinion of the State, seriously prejudice its national security interests, the State shall without delay notify the Prosecutor or the Court of its concerns and request consultations to determine whether there are means whereby its concerns may be addressed, which may include, among other things, the following:

[*137] "(a)   modification or clarification of the request;

"(b) a determination by the Pre-Trial or Trial Chamber regarding the relevance of the information or evidence sought;

"(c) obtaining the information or evidence from a different source or in a different form; or

"(d) agreement on conditions under which the assistance could be provided, including, among other things, providing summaries or redactions, limitations on disclosure, use of in camera and/or ex parte proceedings, or other protective measures permissible under the Statute and the Rules.

"2.   For purposes of hearing the State's concerns regarding disclosure or facilitating consultations to address those concerns, the Pre-Trial Chamber or Trial Chamber shall, if so requested by the State, hold in camera and/or ex parte hearings, and make other special arrangements, as appropriate.

"3.   If, following such consultations, the Prosecutor or Court reaffirms the request for the information or evidence and the State determines there are no means or conditions under which it could provide that information or evidence without serious prejudice to its national security interests, it shall so notify the Prosecutor or the Court of its determination and the specific reasons therefor, unless a specific description of the reasons would itself necessarily result in such a serious prejudice to the State's national security interests.

"4.   If a State has complied with the provisions of paragraphs 1 and 3, it may then deny the request for assistance under article 90, paragraph 2 (c).

"5.   If the Court is of the view that information or evidence sought from a State is important to the resolution of a critical issue in the case and that the State has manifestly acted in bad faith in denying a request for that information or evidence under article 90, paragraph 2 (c), the Court shall communicate its views to the Assembly of States Parties, and, in an appropriate case, to the Security Council, for such further action as may be necessary and appropriate."]

[*138] Article 72
Quorum and judgement

1.   A quorum consists of [at least four] [all] members of the Trial Chamber. The judgement shall be given only by judges who have been present at each stage of the trial before the Trial Chamber and throughout its deliberations.

[All of the judges of the Trial Chamber shall be present at each stage of the trial and throughout their deliberations, provided, however, that the trial or deliberation may proceed with four judges, if one, for a good cause, is unable to attend.]

2.   The Trial Chamber's judgement shall be based on its evaluation of the evidence and the entire proceedings. The judgement shall not exceed the facts and circumstances described in the indictment or its amendment, if any.[20] The Court may base its judgement only on evidence submitted and discussed before it at the trial.

3.   Option 1

The judges shall attempt to achieve unanimity in their judgement, failing which it shall be taken by a majority of the judges.

Option 2

All judges must concur in a decision as to conviction and at least three judges must concur as to the sentence to be imposed.

4.   If the required majority for a decision as to conviction or the sentence to be imposed cannot be reached, the opinion which is more favourable to the accused shall prevail.[21]

5.   The deliberations of the Trial Chamber shall remain secret.

6.   The judgement shall be in writing and shall contain a full and reasoned statement of the findings on the evidence and conclusions. [It shall be the [*139] sole judgement issued.] [It may contain dissenting opinions [, one dissent covering all dissenting opinions].] The judgement or a summary thereof shall be delivered in open court.

[Article 73
Reparations to victims

1.   The Court [shall] [may] establish principles relating to reparations to, or in respect of,[22] victims, including restitution, compensation and [compensation for the purposes of] rehabilitation. The Court may, upon request, [or upon its own motion if the interests of justice so require,] determine, in its judgement, the scope and extent of any damage, loss and injury to, or in respect of, victims.

2.   In accordance with the principles established by the Court:

---

[20]   It was suggested that this sentence could be included in the Rules of Procedure and Evidence.

[21]   This paragraph would only be necessary if majority decisions are allowed and a quorum could consist of an even number of judges.

[22]   Such a provision refers to the possibility for appropriate reparations to be granted not only to victims but also to others such as the victim's families and successors (in French, "ayant-droit"). For the purposes of defining "victims" and "reparations", reference may be made to the Declaration of Basic Principles of Justice for Victims of Crime and Abuse of Power (General Assembly resolution 40/34 of 29 November 1985, annex) and the revised draft basic principles and guidelines on the right to reparation for victims of gross violations of human rights and humanitarian law (E/CN.4/Sub.2/1996/17).

(a)   The Court may make an order directly against a convicted person for an appropriate form of reparations to, or in respect of, victims, including restitution, compensation and rehabilitation.[23] [An award by way of compensation may comprise:

      (i)   an exemplary element;

      (ii)   a compensatory element;

      (iii)   both]

[*140] [Where appropriate, the Court may order that the award for reparations be made into the trust fund provided for in article 79];

(b)   [The Court may also [make an order] [recommend] that an appropriate form of reparations to, or in respect of, victims, including restitution, compensation and rehabilitation, be made by a State]:

    [- if the convicted person is unable to do so himself/herself; [and

    -   if the convicted person was, in committing the offence, acting on behalf of that State in an official capacity, and within the course and scope of his/her authority]];

(c)   [In any case other than those referred to in subparagraph (b), the Court may also recommend that States grant an appropriate form of reparations to, or in respect of, victims, including restitution, compensation and rehabilitation].

3.   In exercising its power under the present article, the Court may determine whether, in order to give effect to any order it may make, it is necessary to request protective measures under article 90, paragraph 1.[24]

4.   Before making a decision under the present article, the Court shall take account of and may invite any written or oral representations from or on behalf of the convicted person, victims [, other interested persons] or interested States.

5.   Victims or their successors or assigns may seek enforcement of an order [or judgement] under the present article by competent national authorities. In this regard, they may ask the Court to seek enforcement of the orders [or judgement] under [Part 9 and] Part 10 of the Statute. [To that end, States Parties shall take the necessary measures to assist them].

6.   Nothing in the present article shall be interpreted as prejudicing the rights of victims [not covered by the judgement of the Court] under national or international law.

[*141] 7. [Victims or any person acting on their behalf, the convicted person [or any interested State] [or other interested persons] may appeal against judgement under this article, in accordance [with [Part 8 of the Statute and] the Rules].

8.   [Rules necessary to give effect to the provisions of the present article shall be made in accordance with article 52].]

N.B. The following provision has been considered by the Preparatory Committee and it was deemed that it would be appropriate for the Rules: "The judgement of the Court under this article will be transmitted by the Registrar to the competent authorities of the State or States with which the convicted person appears to have direct connection by reason of either nationality, domicile or habitual residence or by virtue of the location of the convicted person's assets and property or with which the victim has such connection".

Article 74
Sentencing

1.   In the event of a conviction, the Trial Chamber shall consider the appropriate sentence to be imposed and shall take into account the evidence presented and submissions made during the trial that are relevant to sentence.

---

[23]   It was suggested that since, under the present article, the national courts could render a decision with respect to reparations in conflict with an order of the Court, there should, in the interests of legal certainty, be safeguards to prevent any such conflict.

[24]   As regards the reference to article 90 and to Part 10 of the Statute in general, the view was expressed that it would be necessary to clarify whether the property and assets referred to in that article includes both crime and non-crime related property and assets.

2.   Except where article 65 applies, the Trial Chamber may on its own motion, and shall at the request of the Prosecutor or the accused, made before the completion of the trial, hold a further hearing to hear any additional evidence or submissions relevant to sentence, in accordance with the Rules.

3.   Where paragraph 2 applies, any representations under article 73 shall be heard during the hearing referred to in paragraph 2.

4.   The sentence shall be pronounced in public [and in the presence of the accused].[25]

[*142] PART 7. PENALTIES
Article 75
Applicable penalties

The Court may impose on a person convicted under this Statute [one or more of the following penalties] [the following penalty]:

(a)[1] [a term of life imprisonment or imprisonment for a specified number of years;]

[a maximum term of imprisonment of [30] years;]

[a definite term of imprisonment between [20] and [40] years [, unless this is reduced according to the provisions of this Statute][2];]

[The Court may attach to the sentence of imprisonment a minimum period during which the convicted person may not be granted any [release under relevant provisions of Part 10 of the Statute].]

[In the case of a convicted person under the age of 18 years at the time of the commission of the crime, a specified term of imprisonment of no more than 20 years];

[*143] [When imposing a penalty on a person under the age of 18 years [at the time of the commission of the crime], the Court shall determine the appropriate measures to ensure the rehabilitation of the offender][3]

N.B. The two preceding paragraphs should be harmonized with article 26 (Age of responsibility).

[(b) A fine [in addition to a sentence of imprisonment on conviction of a crime under article 5]];[4]

[(c)

(i)   [[disqualification from seeking public office for the person's term of imprisonment and any further period of time that may be imposed] [in the modality and to the extent that the penalty could be imposed in accordance with the laws of the State in which such a penalty is to be enforced];][5]

(ii)   a forfeiture of [instrumentalities of crime and] proceeds, property and assets obtained by criminal conduct, without prejudice to the rights of bona fide third parties. [When the whole or part of the

---

[25]   The bracketed portion of the text requires further consideration in the light of the decision to be taken concerning trials in absentia.

[1]   To meet the concerns of several delegations regarding the severity of a life sentence or a long sentence of imprisonment, it was suggested that Part 10, article 100, should provide a mandatory mechanism by which the prisoner's sentence would be re-examined by the Court after a certain period of time, in order to determine whether he or she should be released. In this way, the Court could also ensure the uniform treatment of prisoners regardless of the State where they served their sentence.

[2]   The view was expressed that if such a provision providing for minimum sentencing is included, there should be a reference to factors that may reduce the minimum sentence. In such a case, the list of relevant factors should be exhaustive. It was suggested that among those factors could be the following: (i) diminished mental capacity that falls short of exclusion of criminal responsibility; (ii) the age of the convicted person; (iii) as appropriate, duress; and (iv) the subsequent conduct of the convicted person.

[3]   The following proposals were made which should be treated either under age of responsibility or the jurisdiction of the Court:

"[The Court shall have no jurisdiction over those who were under the age of 18 years at the time they are alleged to have committed a crime which would otherwise come within the jurisdiction of the Court] [; however, under exceptional circumstances, the Court may exercise jurisdiction and impose a penalty on a person aged 16 to 18 years, provided it has determined that the person was capable of understanding the unlawfulness of his or her conduct at the time the crime was committed]."

[4]   Some delegations held the view that such a provision would give rise to difficult issues of enforcement.

[5]   The terms in this provision should be brought into line with similar terms used elsewhere in this Statute once those provisions are finalized.

[instrumentalities of crime or] proceeds, [*144] property, assets mentioned in ... cannot be forfeited, a sum of money equivalent thereto may be collected.];[6]]

[(d) Appropriate forms of reparation]

[[without prejudice to the obligation on every State to provide reparation in respect of conduct engaging the responsibility of the State][7] [or reparation through any other international arrangement], appropriate forms of reparation [, [including] [such as] restitution, compensation and rehabilitation]].[8]

N.B. If retained, subparagraph (d) should be examined in the context of the discussions on article 73 (Reparations to victims).

[(e) (Death penalty)]

Option 1

[death penalty, as an option, in case of aggravating circumstances and when the Trial Chamber finds it necessary in the light of the gravity of the crime, the number of victims and the severity of the damage.]

Option 2

No provision on death penalty.

[*145] [Article 76[9] [10]

Penalties applicable to legal persons

A legal person shall incur one or more of the following penalties:

(i) fines;

[(ii) dissolution;]

[(iii) prohibition, for such period as determined by the Court, of the exercise of activities of any kind;]

[(iv) closure, for such a period as determined by the Court, of the premises used in the commission of the crime;]

[(v) forfeiture of [instrumentalities of crime and] proceeds, property and assets obtained by criminal conduct;[11]] [and]

[(vi) appropriate forms of reparation.][12]

N.B. Subparagraph (vi) should be examined in the context of reparation to victims.

---

[6] It was suggested that forfeiture not be included as a penalty, but instead be included as a mechanism which the Court would request States to use with regard to execution of an order for reparations. According to this view, a provision on forfeiture could be considered as a separate paragraph of this article or elsewhere in the Statute.

[7] It was suggested that there was no need for such a clause relating to State responsibility, since it was already dealt with in the context of rules on individual criminal responsibility.

[8] A number of delegations suggested that the Statute should address the issue of reparations to victims and their families. Opinions were divided as to whether this issue should be dealt with in the context of penalties. It was suggested that it could usefully be dealt with within the framework of the Working Group on Procedural Matters. It was also noted that the issue of reparations had a bearing on rules of enforcement in Part 10. A number of delegations expressed the view that there mights be merit in dealing with these issues in a unified way focusing on all the issues related to compensation.

[9] Inclusion of a provision on such penalties would depend on the outcome of considerations in the context of individual criminal responsibility for legal persons.

[10] It was suggested that such provisions may give rise to issues of enforcement in the context of Part 10.

[11] See footnote 6 concerning forfeiture for natural persons. There may be merit in adopting a unified approach in both provisions, including all relevant qualifications.

[12] See footnote 6 concerning reparation in the context of natural persons. There may be merit in adopting a unified approach in both provisions, including all relevant qualifications.

[*146] Article 77
Determination of the sentence
1.   In determining the sentence, the Court shall, in accordance with the Rules of Procedure and Evidence, take into account such factors as the gravity of the crime and the individual circumstances of the convicted person.[13]
2.   In imposing a sentence of imprisonment, the Court shall deduct the time, if any, previously spent in detention in accordance with an order of the Court. The Court may deduct any time otherwise spent in detention in connection with conduct underlying the crime.
3.   When a person had been convicted of more than one crime, the Court shall:
Option 1
    [pronounce a single sentence of imprisonment [not exceeding the maximum sentence prescribed for the gravest crime] [, increased by half]]
Option 2
    [indicate whether multiple sentences of imprisonment shall be served consecutively or concurrently.]

[*147] [Article 78[14]
Applicable national legal standards
Option 1
    In determining the length of a term of imprisonment or the amount of a fine to be imposed, [or property to be forfeited,] the Court [may have regard to the penalties provided for by law of] [shall impose the highest penalty provided for by the law of either]:
    (a)   [the State of which the convicted person is a national];
    (b)   [the State where the crime was committed;] [or]
    (c)   [the State which had custody of and jurisdiction over the accused.]
[In cases where national law does not regulate a specific crime, the Court will apply penalties ascribed to analogous crimes in the same national law.]
Option 2
    No provision on national legal standards.][15]

[Article 79[16]
Fines [and assets] collected by the Court
    Fines [and assets] collected by the Court may be transferred, by order of the Court, to one or more of the following:
[*148] [(a) [as a matter of priority,] a trust fund [established by the Secretary-General of the United Nations] or [administered by the Court] for the benefit of victims of the crime [and their families];]
    [(b) a State the nationals of which were the victims of the crime;]

---

[13]   It may be impossible to foresee all of the relevant aggravating and mitigating circumstances at this stage. Many delegations felt that factors should be elaborated and developed in the Rules of Procedure and Evidence, while several other delegations expressed the view that a final decision on this approach would depend upon the mechanism agreed for adopting the Rules. Among the factors suggested by various delegations as having relevance were: the impact of the crime on the victims and their families; the extent of damage caused or the danger posed by the convicted person's conduct; the degree of participation of the convicted person in the commission of the crime; the circumstances falling short of exclusion of criminal responsibility such as substantially diminished mental capacity or, as appropriate, duress; the age of the convicted person; the social and economic condition of the convicted person; the motive for the commission of the crime; the subsequent conduct of the person who committed the crime; superior orders; the use of minors in the commission of the crime.

[14]   It was suggested that this issue should be dealt with only in the context of article 20 on applicable national laws. Another suggestion was to move this issue to article 77, paragraph 1. Moreover, the view was held that this kind of provision should be avoided altogether.

[15]   Consideration could be given to inserting an express provision to this effect.

[16]   It was suggested that there may be options other than (a) and (b) as to the manner in which fines or assets collected by the Court could be distributed to victims.

[(c) the Registrar, to defray the costs of the trial.]]
N.B. This article should be examined in the context of reparations to victims.

[*149] PART 8. APPEAL AND REVIEW
Article 80
Appeal against judgement or sentence

1.   A [decision] [conviction] under article 72 may be appealed, in accordance with the Rules of Procedure and Evidence, as provided for below:

(a)   The Prosecutor may make such an appeal on the following grounds:

(i)   procedural error,

(ii)   error of fact, or

(iii)   error of law;

(b)   The convicted person or the Prosecutor on that person's behalf may make such an appeal on the following grounds:

(i)   procedural error,

(ii)   error of fact,

(iii)   error of law, or

(iv) any other ground that affects the fairness or reliability of the proceedings or decision.

[(c) The Prosecutor shall not be entitled to appeal against the conviction but he or she shall be entitled to draw the attention of the Appeals Chamber to a point of law, which in his or her opinion requires interpretation or clarification.]

2.   (a)   A sentence may be appealed, in accordance with the Rules of Procedure and Evidence, by the Prosecutor or the convicted person on the ground of [significant] disproportion between the crime and the sentence;

(b)   If on an appeal against sentence, the Court considers that there are grounds on which the conviction might be set aside, wholly or in part, it may invite the Prosecutor and the convicted person to submit grounds under [*150] article 80, paragraph 1 (a) or (b), and may render a decision on conviction in accordance with article 82.

The same procedure applies when the Court, on an appeal against conviction only, considers that there are grounds to reduce the sentence under article 80, paragraph 2 (a).

[3.

Option 1

The Prosecutor or the convicted person may, in accordance with the Rules of Procedure and Evidence, appeal [to the Appeals Chamber] against a decision rendered in absentia under article 63.

Option 2

The Prosecutor or the convicted person may not appeal against a decision rendered in absentia under article 63 except that an appeal against judgement given on the merits in the absence of the accused shall be allowed if the accused accepts the judgement or was represented during the trial before the Trial Chamber by Defence Counsel appointed by the accused.]

4.   (1)   Unless the Trail Chamber otherwise orders, a convicted person shall remain in custody pending an appeal.

When his time in custody exceeds the sentence of imprisonment imposed, he shall be released, but if the Prosecutor is also appealing, his release may be subject to the conditions under (2) below.

(2)   In case of an acquittal, the accused shall be released immediately, subject to the following:

(a)   Under exceptional circumstances, and having regard, inter alia, to the concrete risk of flight, the seriousness of the offence charged and the probability of success on appeal, the Trial Chamber, at the request of the Prosecutor, may maintain the detention of the person pending appeal;

(b)   A decision by the Trial Chamber under (a) above may be appealed in accordance with the Rules of Procedure and Evidence.

[*151] 5. Subject to the provisions of paragraph 4 (1), execution of the judgement shall be suspended during the period allowed for appeal and for the duration of the appeal proceedings.

Article 81
Appeal against interlocutory decisions[1]
1.   Either party may appeal any of the following interlocutory decisions in accordance with the Rules of Procedure and Evidence:
  (a)   A decision with respect to jurisdiction or admissibility;
  (b)   An order granting or denying release of the defendant on bail;
  [(c)   An order that confirms or denies, wholly or in part, the indictment;]
  [(d)   An order of exclusion of evidence;]
  [(e)   When the majority of members of a Trial Chamber shall be of the opinion that the order involves a controlling issue as to which there is substantial ground for difference of opinion and that immediate appeal from the order may materially advance the ultimate conclusion of the trial and a majority of the judges of the Appeals Chamber, at their discretion, agree to hear the appeal.]
2.   An interlocutory appeal shall not of itself have suspensive effect unless the Appeals Chamber so orders upon request in accordance with the rules.

Article 82
Proceedings on appeal[2]
1.   For the purposes of proceedings under articles 80 and 82, the Appeals Chamber also has all the powers of the Trial Chamber.
[*152] 2. If the Appeals Chamber finds that the proceedings appealed from were unfair in a way that affected the reliability of the decision, judgement or sentence, or that the decision, judgement or sentence appealed from was materially affected by error of fact or law or procedural error, it may:
  (a)   Reverse or amend the decision, judgement or sentence; or
  (b)   Order a new trial before a different Trial Chamber.
For these purposes, the Appeals Chamber may remand a factual issue to the original Trial Chamber for it to determine and to report back accordingly, or may itself call evidence to determine the issue. When the decision has been appealed only by the accused, it cannot be amended to his or her detriment.
[Those defences shall be admissible only if already raised in the Trial Chamber or if resulting from the proceedings in that Chamber.]
3.   If in an appeal against sentence the Chamber finds that the sentence is [significantly] disproportionate to the crime, it may vary the sentence in accordance with Part 7.[3]
4.   The decision of the Chamber shall be taken by a majority of the judges and shall be delivered in open court. [[Six] [Four] judges constitute a quorum.] [The judges shall attempt to achieve unanimity in their judgement, failing which it shall be taken by a majority of the judges.]
The judgement shall state the reasons on which it is based. [If the judgement does not represent in whole or in part the unanimous opinion of the judges, any judge shall be entitled to deliver a separate or dissenting opinion.]
5.   The Appeals Chamber may deliver its judgement in the absence of the accused.

Article 83
Revision of conviction or sentence
Option 1 (two-step process)
[*153] 1. The convicted person or, after death, the person's spouse, [successors or assigns] [children, relatives or any persons having express instructions] [, the State of the person's nationality], or the Prosecutor on the person's behalf, may apply to the [Presidency] [Appeals Chamber] to revise the final judgement of conviction or sentence on the grounds that:
  (a)   New evidence has been discovered that

---

  [1]   Further consideration should be given to the question of what decisions could be appealed under this article.
  [2]   In Part 10 the question of what constitutes a final decision or judgement will be discussed.
  [3]   To be revised in conjunction with article 81.

(i)   was not available at the time of trial, and such unavailability was not wholly or partially attributable to the party making application; and

(ii)   is sufficiently important that had it been proven at trial it likely would have resulted in a different verdict;

(b)   It has been newly discovered that decisive evidence, taken into account at trial and upon which the conviction depends, was false, forged or falsified;

(c)   One or more of the judges who participated in a conviction or in its confirmation has committed in that case a serious breach of his or her duties;

[(d) The conduct upon which the conviction was based no longer constitutes a crime under the Statute or the sentence being served exceeds the maximum penalty currently provided in the Statute;]

[(e) The Court[, or where applicable, the court of a State Party,] rendered a decision that necessarily also invalidates the judgement in this case.]

[2.   The Prosecutor may apply for revision of a final judgement of acquittal on the grounds that, within five years after pronouncement of the final judgement, new evidence of the kind referred to in paragraph 1 (a) or 1 (b) is discovered [or the acquitted person has confessed guilt with respect to the crime concerned].]

3.   The [Presidency] [Appeals Chamber] shall reject the application if it considers it to be unfounded. If it determines that there is a [significant possibility] [probability] that the application is meritorious, it: [may, as appropriate:

(a)   Reconvene the original Trial Chamber;

[*154] (b)   Constitute a new Trial Chamber; or

(c) [Refer the matter to the Appeals Chamber][4] [retain jurisdiction over the matter][5]
with a view to, after hearing the parties in the manner set forth in the Rules of Procedure and Evidence, arriving at a determination on whether the judgement should be revised.]

[OR
[shall annul the conviction and refer the accused to a Chamber at the same level as, but having composition different from, that of the Chamber that handed down the annulled decision.]

[4.   The decision of the Presidency or of a Trial Chamber disposing of the application may be appealed by either party to the Appeals Chamber.]

<u>Option 2 (one-step process)</u>

1.   The convicted person or, after death, the person's spouse, [successors or assigns] [children, relatives or any persons having express instructions] [, the State of the person's nationality], or the Prosecutor on the person's behalf, may apply to [the original or, if unavailable or if relief is sought on the basis of paragraph 1 (c), another] [a] Trial Chamber to revise the final judgement of conviction or sentence on the grounds that:

1 (a)-(e) [same as in option 1]

2.   [same as in option 1]

3.   The Chamber shall hear the parties in the manner set forth in the Rules of Procedure and Evidence. It shall reject the application if it considers it to be unfounded. If it agrees with the application, it may, as appropriate:

(a) Enter a corrected judgement;

[*155] (b)   Order a new trial; or

(c) Refer the matter to the Appeals Chamber.

[4.   The decision of the Trial Chamber disposing of the application may be appealed by either party to the Appeals Chamber.]

---

⁴   This bracketed text would be used if the Presidency makes the initial review of the application for revision.

⁵   This bracketed text would be used if the Appeals Chamber makes the initial review of the application for revision.

[Article 84
Compensation to a suspect/accused/convicted person
1.   Anyone who has been subject to arrest or detention in violation of the Statute, [the Rules] or internationally recognized human rights law shall have a right to compensation from the Court, in accordance with the Rules.
2.   When a person has, by a final decision, been convicted of a criminal offence, and when subsequently his or her conviction has been reversed, or he or she has been pardoned on the ground that a new or newly discovered fact shows conclusively that there has been a miscarriage of justice, the person who has suffered punishment as a result of such conviction shall be compensated in accordance with the Rules, unless it is proved that the non-disclosure of the unknown fact in time is wholly or partly attributable to him or her.
[3.   The Court may also award compensation to a person who was held in detention, based on the prejudice caused to him by such detention, when the proceedings against him have concluded with a decision to release him because of insufficient charges against him or because of a final decision of acquittal.]]

[*156] PART 9.   INTERNATIONAL COOPERATION AND JUDICIAL ASSISTANCE[1]
N.B. Consideration should be given to interchanging parts 9 and 10.

Article 85
General obligation to cooperate
States Parties shall, in accordance with the provisions of this [Part] [Statute], fully cooperate with the Court[2] in its investigation and prosecution of crimes under this Statute. States Parties shall so cooperate without [undue] delay.

Article 86[3]
[Requests for cooperation: general provisions]
[*157] 1. Authorities competent to make and receive requests/Channels for communication of requests
    (a)   The Court shall have the authority to make requests to States Parties for cooperation. The requests shall be transmitted through the diplomatic channel or any other appropriate channel as may be designated by each State Party upon ratification, accession or approval. Such designation and subsequent changes shall be done in accordance with the Rules of Procedure and Evidence.
    (b)   When appropriate, without prejudice to the provisions of paragraph 1 (a), requests may also be transmitted through the International Criminal Police Organization or any appropriate regional organization.

---

[1]   Articles 86, 88, 89 and 90 contain virtually identical provisions, some of which should be harmonized.
[2]   "Court" throughout this Part is understood to include its constituent organs, including the Prosecutor, as defined in article 35. Such a provision could be inserted elsewhere in the Statute.
N.B. See N.B. on article 35 (Organs of the Court).
[3]   It was suggested that the provisions of article 88, paragraph 4, and article 90, paragraph 8, concerning the protection of witnesses and victims should be combined in a single paragraph in article 86, which would read:
    "The Court may withhold, in accordance with article 68, from the requested State [or a State making a request to the Court under article 90, paragraph 7], specific information about any victims, potential witnesses and their families if it considers that this is necessary to ensure their safety or physical and psychological well-being. Any information that is made available to a State under this part shall be provided and handled in a manner that protects the safety or physical or psychological well-being of any victims, potential witnesses or their families."
    It was also suggested that the content of such a provision should be considered further.

2.   Language of requests[4]

Requests for cooperation [and supporting documents] shall be [either] in [an official language of the requested State [unless otherwise agreed]] [or in] [one of the working languages reflected in article 51, in accordance with the choice made by that State upon ratification, accession or approval].

[The legal effect of such request shall not be diminished if any supporting document is not in such working language provided that a brief summary of any such document in that working language is also submitted.]

3.   Confidentiality of requests from the Court

The requested State shall keep confidential a request and any supporting documents, except to the extent that the disclosure is necessary for execution of the request.

4.   Cooperation by non-States Parties[5]

[(a) The Court may [call on] [invite] any State not party to this Statute to provide assistance under this part on the basis of [comity,] an ad hoc arrangement, an agreement with such State [or any other appropriate basis].]

[*158] [(b) Where a State not party to this Statute [which has entered into an ad hoc arrangement or an agreement with the Court],[6] fails to cooperate with requests under paragraph (a), thereby preventing the Court from performing its duties under this Statute, the Court may make a finding to that effect and refer the matter to [the General Assembly of States Parties][7] [or] [the United Nations General Assembly] [or, where the Security Council referred the matter to the Court,] [to the Security Council] [so that necessary measures may be taken to enable the Court to exercise its jurisdiction].[8]]

5.   Cooperation of intergovernmental organizations

The Court may ask any intergovernmental organizations to provide information or documents. The Court may also ask for other forms of cooperation and assistance as may be agreed upon with such organizations and in accordance with their respective competencies and/or mandates.

6.[9] States Parties' failure to cooperate [comply]

Where a State Party fails to comply with a request by the Court contrary to the provisions of the Statute, thereby preventing the Court from performing its duties under this Statute, the Court may make a finding to that effect and refer the matter to [the Assembly of States Parties][10] [or] [the General Assembly of the United Nations] [or, where the Security Council referred the matter to the Court] [to the Security Council] [so that necessary measures may be taken to enable the Court to exercise its jurisdiction].[11]

[*159] **N.B. In view of the length of the article, the headings of the paragraphs are retained pending a decision on the text of the article. Consideration may be given to dividing the article into three as follows:**

- **paragraphs 1 to 3;**
- **paragraphs 4 and 5;**
- **paragraph 6.**

---

[4]   The language to be used by States in their replies to the Court is dealt with under article 91.

[5]   It was suggested that the issue of non-States Parties should be addressed in a separate article 85.

[6]   It was suggested that a reference to paragraph (a) would cover this concern.

[7]   It was suggested that the referral be made to a standing committee of the General Assembly of States Parties. This issue needs to be further addressed in Part 4.

[8]   The question of "necessary measures" has to be further examined.

[9]   It was suggested that this paragraph should be inserted in article 85.

[10]   It was suggested that the referral be made to a standing committee of the Council of States Parties. This issue needs to be further addressed in the organization of the Court.

[11]   The question of "necessary measures" has to be further examined.

Article 87
[Surrender] [Transfer] [Extradition] of persons[12] to the Court

1.   The Court may transmit a request for the arrest and [surrender] [transfer] [extradition] of a person, along with the supporting material outlined in article 88, to any State on the territory of which that person may be found, and shall request the cooperation of that State in the arrest and [surrender] [transfer] [extradition] of such person. States Parties shall, in accordance with the provisions of this Part [and the procedure under their national law], comply with requests for arrest and [surrender] [transfer] [extradition] without [undue] delay.

[2.   The national law of a requested State shall govern the [conditions] [procedure] for granting or denying a request for [surrender] [transfer] [extradition] [except as otherwise provided in this Part].]

3.

[Option 1: No grounds for refusal.]

[Option 2: A State Party may deny a request for [surrender] [transfer] [extradition] only if:[13]

      (a) with respect to a crime under [article 5 (b) through (e)] [article 5 (e)], it has not accepted the jurisdiction of the Court;

[*160] [(b) the person is a national of the requested State;][14]

      (c) the person has been investigated or has been proceeded against, convicted or acquitted in the requested State or another State for the offence for which his [surrender] [transfer] [extradition] is sought [, except that a request may not be denied if the Court has determined that the case is admissible under article 15];

      [(d) the information submitted in support of the request does not meet the minimum evidentiary requirements of the requested State, as set forth in article 88, paragraph 1 (c);]

      (e) compliance with the request would put it in breach of an existing obligation that arises from [a peremptory norm of] general international law [treaty] obligation undertaken to another State.][15]

N.B. The options in this subparagraph are not clear.

[4.   If a request for [surrender] [transfer] [extradition] is denied, the requested State Party shall promptly inform the Court of the reasons for such denial.]

5.   Application to the Court to set aside [surrender] [transfer] [extradition]

      A State Party [having received a request under paragraph 1 may, in accordance with the Rules of Procedure and Evidence[16]] [may, in [...] days of receiving a request under paragraph 1], file a written application with the [*161] Court to [set aside] [withdraw] the request on specified grounds [including those mentioned in articles 15 and 18]. Pending a decision of the Court on the application, the State concerned may delay complying with the request but shall take appropriate measures [as may be available] to ensure the compliance with the request after a decision of the Court to reject the application.

6.   Parallel requests from the Court and State(s)

Option 1

      (a) A State Party [which has accepted the jurisdiction of the Court] [, if it is a party to the treaty covered by [article 5, paragraph (e),] with respect to the crime,] shall [, as far as possible,] give priority to a request from the Court under paragraph 1 over requests for extradition from other States [Parties].

---

[12]   The term "persons" is understood to include "suspects", "accused" and "convicted persons". [The term "suspect" means a person who is the subject of a pre-indictment arrest warrant.]

[13]   There is no agreement on the list of grounds contained in this option.

[14]   It was suggested that even if a person is a national of the requested State, this does not prevent that State from [transferring] [surrendering] [extraditing] the person to the Court if the latter guarantees that the national in question shall be returned to the requested State to serve the sentence pronounced by the Court (cf. article 94, paragraph 1).

[15]   It was suggested that the following ground for refusal should be included: when the imposition or the execution of punishment for the offence for which surrender is requested would be barred by reasons prescribed under the law of the requested State if the requested State were to have jurisdiction over the offence.

[16]   Questions dealing with the consequences of lapse of time will be addressed in the Rules of Procedure and Evidence.

(b)   If the requested State also receives a request from a non-State Party to which it is bound by an extradition agreement for the extradition of the same person, either for the same offence or for a different offence for which the Court is seeking the person's [surrender] [transfer] [extradition], the requested State shall determine whether to [surrender] [transfer] [extradite] the person to the Court or to extradite the person to the State. In making its decision the requested State shall consider all relevant factors, including but not limited to:

   (i)   the respective dates of the requests;
   (ii)   if the offences are different, the nature and gravity of the offences;
   (iii)   the interests of the State requesting extradition, including, where relevant, whether the offence was committed in its territory and the nationality of the victims of the offence; and
   (iv)   the possibility of subsequent [surrender] [transfer] [extradition] or extradition between the Court and the State requesting extradition.

Option 2

(a)   If the requested State also receives a request from a [State] [State Party] [to which it is bound by an extradition agreement] for the extradition of the same person, either for the same offence or for a different offence for which the Court is seeking the person's [surrender] [transfer] [extradition], the appropriate authority of the requested State shall determine whether to [**162] [surrender] [transfer] [extradite] the person to the Court or to extradite the person to the State. In making its decision the requested State shall consider all relevant factors, including but not limited to:

   (i)   whether the extradition request was made pursuant to a treaty;
   (ii)   the respective dates of the requests;
   (iii)   if the offences are different, the nature and gravity of the offences;
   (iv)   the interests of the State requesting extradition, including, where relevant, whether the offence was committed in its territory and the nationality of the victims of the offence; and
   (v)   the possibility of subsequent [surrender] [transfer] or extradition between the Court and the State requesting extradition.

(b)   The requested State may not, however, deny a request for the [surrender] [transfer] [extradition] made under this article in deference to another State's request for extradition of the same person for the same offence if the State requesting extradition is a State Party and the Court has ruled the case before it is admissible, and its decision took into consideration the proceedings in that State which gave rise to its extradition request.

Option 3

(a)   Subject to paragraph (b), a State Party [shall] [may] accord priority to a request by a State over a request by the Court for the extradition, transfer or surrender of a person to the requesting State under the provisions of any existing bilateral or multilateral agreement.

(b)   A State Party shall however accord priority to requests from the Court over a request by a State where the Court has [positively] determined pursuant to article 15 that the requesting State is unwilling or unable genuinely to carry out the investigation or prosecution of the case for which extradition, transfer or surrender is sought.

[7.   Proceeding in requested State

Where the law of the requested State so requires, the person whose [surrender] [transfer] [extradition] is sought shall be entitled to challenge the request for arrest and [surrender] [transfer] [extradition] in the court of the requested State on [only] the following grounds:

[**163] [(a)   lack of jurisdiction of the Court;]

   [(b)   non bis in idem; or]

   [(c)   the evidence submitted in support of the request does not meet the evidentiary requirements of the requested State as set forth in article 88, paragraph 1 (b) (v) and (c) (ii).]]

8.   Delayed or temporary [surrender] [transfer] [extradition]

If the person sought is being proceeded against or is serving a sentence in the requested State for an offence different from that for which [surrender] [transfer] [extradition] to the Court is sought, the requested State, after making its decision to grant the request, may:

(a)   temporarily [surrender] [transfer] [extradite] the person to the Court and in that case, the Court shall return the person to that State after the completion of the trial or as otherwise agreed; or

(b)   [with the consent of the [Court] [Pre-Trial Chamber] which shall rule after having heard the Prosecutor] postpone the [surrender] [transfer] [extradition] of the person until the completion or abandonment of the prosecution [or completion of service of the sentence].[17]

[9.   Extradite or prosecute obligation[18]

(a)   In the case of a crime to which article 5, paragraph (e), applies, the requested State [, if it is a party to the treaty in question but has not accepted the Court's jurisdiction with respect to that crime,] shall, where it decides not to [surrender] [transfer] [extradite] the accused to the Court, promptly take all necessary steps to extradite the accused to a State having requested extradition or [at the request of the Court] refer the case [through proceedings in accordance with national laws] to its competent authorities for the purpose of prosecution.

[*164] [(b) In any other case, the requested State Party shall [consider whether it can], in accordance with its legal procedures, take steps to arrest and [surrender] [transfer] [extradite] the accused to the Court, or [whether it should take steps to extradite the accused to a State having requested extradition or [at the request of the Court] refer the case to its competent authorities for the purpose of prosecution.]

[(c)   The [surrender] [transfer] [extradition] of an accused to the Court will constitute, as between States Parties which accept the jurisdiction of the Court with respect to the crime in question, compliance with a provision of any treaty requiring that a suspect be extradited or that the case be referred to the competent authorities of the requested State for the purpose of prosecution.]]

[10.   Provision of evidence irrespective of [surrender] [transfer] [extradition]

[To the extent permitted under the law of the requested State and] without prejudice to the rights of third parties, all items found in the requested State [that have been acquired as a result of the alleged crime or] that may be required as evidence shall, upon request, be transmitted to the Court [if the [surrender] [transfer] [extradition] is granted on conditions to be determined by the Court] [even if the [surrender] [transfer] [extradition] of the person cannot be carried out]. [Any rights which third parties may have acquired in the said items shall be preserved where these rights exist. The property shall be returned without charge to the requested State as soon as possible after the trial.]]

N.B.

-   **It would be more appropriate to deal with the issues raised in this paragraph in the context of article 90 (Other forms of cooperation [and judicial and legal [mutual] assistance]).**

-   **Consideration may be given to dealing with some of the details in this paragraph in the Rules of Procedure and Evidence.**

[*165] 11.   Transit of [surrendered] [transferred] [extradited] person[19]

(a)   A State Party shall authorize transportation under its national procedural law through its territory of a person being [surrendered] [transferred] [extradited] to the Court by another State. A request by the Court for transit shall be transmitted in accordance with article 86. The request for transit shall contain a description of the person being transported, a brief statement of the facts of the case and the legal characterization and the warrant for arrest and [transfer] [surrender] [extradition]. A person in transit shall be detained in custody during the period of transit.

[(b)   No authorization is required where air transportation is used and no landing is scheduled on the territory of the State of transit.]

(c)   If an unscheduled landing occurs on the territory of the State of transit, it may require a request for transit as provided for in subparagraph (a). The State of transit shall detain the person to be transported

---

[17]   If it is agreed that consent of the Court will be required for postponement, then the last set of brackets can be removed.

[18]   The text of paragraph 9 (a) and (b) applies if there is a consent regime. If the Court has jurisdiction over core crimes and there is no consent regime, these provisions could be deleted.

[19]   It has been suggested that this or other provisions could form the basis for a separate article. In addition, some felt that a number of details set forth in this text would be more appropriately regulated in the Rules of Procedure and Evidence.

until the request for transit is received and the transit is effected, so long as the request is received within 96 hours of the unscheduled landing.

12. Costs

The costs associated with the [surrender] [transfer] [extradition] of a person shall be borne by the [Court] [requested State] [Court or the requested State depending upon where the cost concerned arises].

N.B. In view of the length of the article, the headings of the paragraphs are retained. Consideration may be given to dividing the article into shorter articles, without prejudice to their retention, as follows:

- **paragraphs 1 and 2;**
- **paragraphs 3 and 4;**
- **paragraph 5;**

[*166]- **paragraph 6;**
- **paragraph 7;**
- **paragraph 8;**
- **paragraph 9;**
- **paragraph 10;**
- **paragraph 11;**
- **paragraph 12.**

Article 88

Contents of request for [surrender] [transfer] [extradition][20]

1. A request for arrest and [surrender] [transfer] [extradition] shall be made in writing. In urgent cases a request may be made by any medium capable of delivering a written record,[21] provided that a request shall be confirmed [if necessary] through the channel provided for in article 86. The request shall contain or be supported by:

(a) information describing the person sought, sufficient to identify the person and information as to that person's probable location;

(b) in the case of a request for pre-indictment arrest and [surrender] [transfer] [extradition]:

(i) a copy of warrant for arrest;[22]

[*167] (ii) a statement of the reasons to believe the suspect may have committed a crime within the jurisdiction of the Court and that the Prosecutor expects to seek an indictment within [90] days;

(iii) a brief summary of the [essential] facts of the case;

(iv) a statement as to why pre-indictment arrest is urgent and necessary;[23]

(v) [such documents, statements, or other types of information regarding the commission of the offence and the person's role therein, which may be required by the laws of the requested State;] [however, in no event may the requested State's requirements be more burdensome than those applicable to requests for extradition pursuant to treaties with other States;]

(c) in the case of a request for post-indictment arrest and [surrender] [transfer] [extradition]:

(i) a copy of the warrant of arrest and indictment;

[(ii) such documents, statements, or other types of information regarding the commission of the offence and the accused's role therein which may be required by the laws of the requested State; [however, in no event may the requested State's requirements be more burdensome than those applicable to requests for extradition pursuant to treaties or other arrangements with other States];]

---

[20] Portions of this article might also be provided for in the Rules of Procedure and Evidence rather than in the Statute.

[21] Issues relating to the security of this type of transmission will have to be discussed.

[22] The question of authentication of a warrant of arrest will be dealt with in the Rules of Procedure and Evidence.

[23] Article 59 covers pre-indictment arrest, while this paragraph also addresses the form of a request for pre-indictment arrest. The text of these two provisions must be examined together to ensure that there are no inconsistencies or duplications.

(d)   in the case of a request for the arrest and [surrender] [transfer] [extradition] of a person already convicted:[24]

(i)   a copy of any warrant of arrest for that person;

(ii)   a copy of the judgement of conviction;

[*168]   (iii)   information to demonstrate that the person sought is the one referred to in the judgement of conviction;

(iv)   [if the person sought has been sentenced,] a copy of the sentence imposed and a statement of any time already served and that remaining.

2.   A State Party shall notify the Court at the time of ratification, accession or approval whether it can [surrender] [transfer] [extradite] on the basis of a pre-indictment warrant and the information specified in paragraph 1 (b) or it can only [surrender] [transfer] [extradite] following [confirmation of indictment] [issuance of a post-indictment warrant] on the basis of the information in paragraph 1 (c).

[3.   Where the requested State Party considers the information provided insufficient to allow it to comply with the request, it shall seek, without delay, additional information and may fix a reasonable time limit for the receipt thereof. [Any proceedings in the requested State may be continued, and the person sought may be detained, for such period as may be necessary to enable the Court to provide the additional information requested.] If the additional information is not provided within the reasonable time limit fixed by the requested State, the person may be released.]

[4.   The Court may in accordance with article 68 withhold from the requested State specific information about any victims, potential witnesses and their families if it considers that it is necessary to ensure their safety or physical or psychological well-being. Any information that is made available under this article shall be provided and handled in a manner that protects the safety or physical or psychological well-being of any victims, potential witnesses and their families.][25]

N.B. This provision is similar to the text in articles 89, paragraph 3, (Provisional arrest) and 90, paragraph 8 (b) (Other forms of cooperation [and judicial and legal [mutual] assistance]). Consideration may be given to combining them in a single article.

[*169] Article 89
Provisional arrest[26]

1.   In case of urgency, the Court may request the provisional arrest of the person sought pending presentation of the request for [surrender] [transfer] [extradition] and supporting documents under article 88.

2.   The request for provisional arrest shall [be made by any medium capable of delivering a written record and shall] contain:

(i)   a description of the person sought and information regarding the probable location of such person;

(ii)   a brief statement of the essential facts of the case, including, if possible, the time and location of the offence;

(iii)   a statement of the existence of a warrant of arrest or a judgement of conviction against the person sought, and, if applicable, a description of the specific offence or offences with which the person has been charged or for which he has been convicted; and

(iv)   a statement that a request for [surrender] [transfer] [extradition] of the person sought will follow.

3.   The Court may withhold from the requested State specific information about any victims, potential witnesses and their families or close associates if it considers that it is necessary to ensure their safety or

---

[24]   It was suggested that this paragraph is an enforcement-of-sentence issue to be treated in Part 10.

[25]   This paragraph could also be included under article 86.

[26]   ILC article 52 (1) (a) addresses provisional arrest, as well as search and seizure and other measures pertaining to mutual assistance. In order to present all proposals in a clear fashion, the present document treats provisional arrest in this article and the other matters in article 90.

well-being. Any information that is provided under this article to the requested State shall be provided in a manner that protects the safety or well-being of any victims, potential witnesses and their families or close associates.

N.B. See the N.B. in article 88, paragraph 4 (Contents of request for [surrender] [transfer] [extradition]).

[*170] 4. A person who is provisionally arrested may be discharged from custody upon the expiration of [ ]²⁷ days from the date of provisional arrest if the requested State has not received the request for [surrender] [transfer] [extradition] and the supporting documents specified under article 88. However, the person may consent to [surrender] [transfer] [extradition] before the expiration of this period if the legislation of the requested State allows, in which case that State shall proceed to [surrender] [transfer] [extradite] the person to the Court as soon as possible.²⁸

5. The fact that the person sought has been discharged from custody pursuant to paragraph 4 shall not prejudice the subsequent rearrest and [surrender] [transfer] [extradition] of that person if the request for [surrender] [transfer] [extradition] and supporting documents are delivered at a later date.

Article 90
Other forms of cooperation [and judicial and
legal [mutual] assistance]²⁹

1. States Parties shall, in accordance with the provisions of this Part [and their national [procedural] law], comply with requests for assistance by the Court for:

    (a) the identification and whereabouts of persons or the location of items;

    (b) the taking of evidence, including testimony under oath, and the production of evidence, including expert opinions or reports necessary to the Court;

    (c) the questioning of any suspect or accused;

[*171] (d) the service of documents, including judicial documents;

    (e) facilitating the appearance of persons before the Court;

    [(f) the temporary transfer of persons in custody, with their consent [which cannot be withdrawn], in order to provide testimony [or other assistance] to the Court;]

    [(g) the conduct of on-site investigations and inspections³⁰ [with the consent of the requested State];]

    [(h) the conduct of proceedings of the Court in its territory with the consent of the requested State;]³¹

    (i) the execution of searches and seizures;

    (j) the provision of records and documents, including official records and documents;

    (k) the protection of victims and witnesses and the integrity of evidence;

    (l) the identification, tracing and freezing or seizure of proceeds, property and assets and instrumentalities of crimes for the purpose of eventual forfeiture without prejudice to the rights of bona fide third parties;³² and

    (m) any other types of assistance [not prohibited by the law of the requested State].

[2. Grounds for refusal

Option 1

A State Party shall not deny a request for assistance from the Court.

[*172] Option 2

A State Party may deny a request for assistance, in whole or in part, only if:³³

---

²⁷ Some delegations have proposed a 30-day period, some a 40-day period and some a 60-day time period.

²⁸ It was suggested that the simplified surrender procedure should be the object of a separate paragraph, since it applies to both the provisional arrest stage and after a full surrender request has been submitted. This paragraph could also be included in article 86.

²⁹ This issue has to be revisited after the title of Part 9 is confirmed.

³⁰ This issue is also addressed in article 54, paragraph 4 (c).

³¹ The relationship between subparagraphs (g) and (h) and article 91, paragraph 4, needs to be examined.

³² The issue of whether the Court is to be vested with such powers is linked with article 75 in Part 7 on Penalties.

³³ The list of possible grounds for refusal is not an agreed list.

(a)   with respect to a crime [under [article 5, paragraphs (b) through (e)] [article 5, paragraph (e)], it has not accepted the jurisdiction of the Court;

(b)   the authorities of the requested State would be prohibited by its national laws from carrying out the action requested with regard to the investigation or prosecution of a similar offence in that State;

(c)   execution of the request would seriously prejudice its national security, ordre public or other essential interests;

(d)   the request concerns the production of any documents or disclosure of evidence which relates to its national [security] [defence];

(e)   execution of the request would interfere with an ongoing investigation or prosecution in the requested State or in another State [or with a completed investigation or prosecution that might have led to an acquittal or conviction, except that a request may not be denied if the investigation or prosecution relates to the same matter which is the subject of the request and the Court has determined that the case is admissible under article 15];

(f)   compliance with the request would put it in breach of an existing [international law] [treaty] obligation undertaken to another [State] [non-State Party].]

[3.   Before denying a request for assistance, the requested State shall consider whether the requested assistance can be provided subject to specified conditions, or whether the assistance can be provided at a later time or in an alternative manner, provided that if the Court or the Prosecutor accepts the assistance subject to conditions, it shall abide by them.]

4.   If a request for assistance is denied, the requested State Party shall promptly inform the Court or the Prosecutor of the reasons for such denial.

[5.   If a requested State does not produce a document or disclose evidence under paragraph 2 (d) on the ground that it relates to its national defence, the Trial [*173] Chamber shall only make such inferences that relate to the guilt or innocence of the accused.]

N.B. See article 71.

6.   Confidentiality[34]

(a)   The Court shall ensure the confidentiality of documents and information except as required for the investigation and proceedings described in the request.

(b)   The requested State may, when necessary, transmit documents or information to the Prosecutor on a confidential basis. The Prosecutor may then use them solely for the purpose of generating new evidence.

(c)   The requested State may, on its own motion or at the request of the Prosecutor, subsequently consent to the disclosure of such documents or information. They may then be used as evidence pursuant to the provisions of Parts 5 and 6 of the Statute and related Rules of Procedure and Evidence.

7.   Assistance by the Court

(a)   The Court [may] [shall], upon request, cooperate with and provide assistance [within its competence] to a State Party conducting an investigation into or trial in respect of acts which constitute a crime under this Statute [or which constitute a serious crime under the national law of the requesting State].

(b)[35]

(i)   The assistance provided under subparagraph (a) shall include, among others:

(1)   the transmission of statements, documents or other types of evidence obtained in the course of an investigation or a trial conducted by the Court; and

[*174]   (2)   the questioning of any person detained by the Court;

(ii)   In the case of assistance under subparagraph (b) (i) (1):

---

[34]   Views have also been expressed that subparagraphs (b) and (c) should be addressed in the Rules of Procedure and Evidence.

[35]   Views have been expressed that this subparagraph should be addressed in the Rules of Procedure and Evidence.

(1)   If the documents or other types of evidence have been obtained with the assistance of a State, such transmission shall require the consent of that State;[36]

(2)   If the statements, documents or other types of evidence have been provided by a witness or expert, such transmission shall be subject to the provisions of article 68[37] [and shall require the consent of that witness or expert];

(c)   The Court may, under the conditions set out in this paragraph, grant a request for assistance under this paragraph from a non-State party.

8.   Form and contents of the request

(a)   Requests for [judicial and legal] [mutual] assistance shall:

(i)   be made in writing. In urgent cases, a request may be made by any medium capable of delivering a written record, provided that it shall be confirmed [, if necessary,] through the channel provided for in article 86; and

(ii)   contain the following, as applicable:

(1)   a brief statement of the purpose of the request and the assistance sought, including the legal basis and grounds for the request;

(2)   as much detailed information as possible about the location or identification of any person or place that must be found or identified in order for the assistance sought to be provided;

(3)   a brief description of the essential facts underlying the request;

[*175]   (4)   the reasons for and details of any procedure or requirement to be followed;

[(5)   such information as may be required under the law of the requested State in order to execute the request;]

(6)   any other information relevant to the assistance being sought.

(b)   The Court may withhold, in accordance with article 68, from the requested State [or a State making a request under paragraph 6] specific information about any victims, potential witnesses and their families if it considers that this is necessary to ensure their safety or physical and psychological well-being. Any information that is made available under this article to the requested State shall be provided and handled in a manner that protects the safety or physical or psychological well-being of any victims, potential witnesses and their families.

N.B. See the N.B. in article 88, paragraph 4 (Contents of request for [surrender] [transfer] [extradition]).

N.B. Consideration may be given to dividing this article into shorter articles, without prejudice to their retention, as follows:

- **paragraph 1;**
- **paragraphs 2 to 5;**
- **paragraph 6;**
- **paragraph 7;**
- **paragraph 8.**

Article 91
Execution of requests under article 90

1.   Requests for assistance shall be executed in accordance with the law of the requested State [and, unless prohibited by such law, in the manner specified in the request, including following any procedures outlined therein or permitting [*176] persons specified in the request to be present at and assist in the execution process[38] [by its competent authorities]].

2.   In the case of an urgent request, the documents or evidence produced in response shall, at the request of the Court, be sent urgently.[39]

---

[36]   The relationship with article 92 needs to be considered.

[37]   This relates to the provisions on the protection of victims and witnesses.

[38]   There is a link between this provision and the empowerment provisions of paragraph 4.

[39]   Views have been expressed that this should be addressed in the Rules of Procedure and Evidence.

3.   Replies from States Parties, including any accompanying documents, [may be in the language of the requested State] [shall be in accordance with paragraph 2 of article 86. The Court may also request the transmission of documents in their original language].

[4.   The [Prosecutor] [Court] may [, if requested,] assist the authorities of the requested State with the execution of the request for judicial assistance [and may, with the consent of the requested State, carry out certain inquiries on its territory].][40]

[5.   [For the purposes of paragraph 4,] the requested State shall, upon request, inform the Court of the time and place of execution of the request for assistance.][41]

6.   (a)   The ordinary costs for execution of requests in the territory of the requested State shall be borne by the requested State except for the following which should be borne by the Court:

(i)   Costs associated with the travel and security of witnesses and experts or the transfer of persons in custody;

(ii)   Costs of translation, interpretation and transcription;

(iii)   The travel and subsistence costs of the Prosecutor, members of his office or any other member of the Court; and

[*177]   (iv)   The costs of any expert opinion or report requested by the Court.

(b)   Where the execution of a request will result in extraordinary costs, [there shall be consultations to determine how those costs will be met] [those costs shall be met by the Court].

(c)   The provisions in this paragraph shall apply with appropriate modifications to requests made to the Court for assistance.[42]

N.B.

-   Consideration may be given to whether this provision should constitute a separate article where all the provisions dealing with costs would be combined. See also article 87, paragraph 12 ([Surrender] [Transfer] [Extradition] of persons to the Court).

-   Consideration may also be given to dealing with some of the details relating to the costs in the Rules of Procedure and Evidence.

[7.   (a)   Witnesses or experts may not be compelled to testify at the seat of the Court.

[(b)   If they do not wish to travel to the seat of the Court, their evidence shall be taken in the country in which they reside or in such other place as they may agree upon with the Court [in accordance with national requirements [and in compliance with international law standards][43]].

(c)   In order to guarantee the safety of witnesses and experts, any means of communication may be used to take their evidence while preserving their anonymity.[44]][45]

[*178]   [(d) No witness or expert who appears before the Court may be prosecuted, detained or submitted to any restriction of personal freedom by the Court in respect of any acts [or omissions] that preceded the departure of that person from the requested State.]

8.   Provisions allowing a person heard or examined by the Court under article [...] to invoke restrictions designed to prevent disclosure of confidential information connected with national defence or security also apply to the execution of requests for assistance under this article.

[Article 92
Rule of speciality
1.   Limit on other proceedings against [surrendered] [transferred] [extradited] person

---

[40]   Views have been expressed that paragraph 1 is an alternative to this paragraph.

[41]   Views have been expressed that this should be addressed in the Rules.

[42]   Similar provisions may have to be inserted elsewhere to address the situation where the Court renders assistance to States or States Parties.

[43]   The exact formulation will depend on the formulation adopted for article 69.

[44]   The protection of witnesses is also addressed in articles 54 and 68.

[45]   Views have been expressed on the relationship between subparagraphs (b) and (c) and article 63 on trial in the presence of the accused.

A person [surrendered] [transferred] [extradited] to the Court under this Statute shall not be:

(a) proceeded against, punished or detained for any criminal act other than that for which the person has been [surrendered] [transferred] [extradited];

(b) [surrendered] [transferred] [extradited] to another State in respect of any criminal act[46] [except when he or she commits the criminal act after [extradition] [surrender] [transfer]].

2. Limit on other uses of evidence

Evidence provided by a State Party under this Statute shall [, if that State Party so requests,] not be used as evidence for any purpose other than that for which it was provided [unless this is necessary to preserve a right of the accused under article 67, paragraph 2].

3. Waiver of rule by the requested State

[*179] The Court may request the State concerned to waive the requirements of paragraphs 1 or 2, for the reasons and purposes to be specified in the request. In the case of paragraph 1, this request shall be accompanied by an additional warrant of arrest and by a legal record of any statement made by the accused with respect to the offence.][47]

N.B. The headings of the paragraphs are retained pending a decision on the text of the article.

[*180] PART 10. ENFORCEMENT[1]
Article 93
General obligation regarding recognition
[and enforcement] of judgements

States Parties [shall] [undertake to recognize] [[and to] enforce directly on their territory] [give effect to] the judgements of the Court [, in accordance with the provisions of this part].

[The judgements of the Court shall be binding on the national jurisdictions of every State Party as regards the criminal liability of the person convicted and the principles relating to compensation for damage caused to victims and the restitution of property acquired by the person convicted and other forms of reparation ordered by the Court, such as restitution, compensation and rehabilitation.][2]

N.B. This article should also be considered in the context of the discussions on article 73 (Reparations to victims).

Article 94
Role of States in enforcement [and supervision]
of sentences of imprisonment

[3]1.

Option 1

[*181] A sentence of imprisonment shall be served in a State designated by the [Court] [Presidency].

Option 2

(a) A sentence of imprisonment shall be served in a State designated by the [Court] [Presidency] from a list of States which have indicated to the Court their willingness to accept sentenced persons. The State so designated shall promptly inform the [Court] [Presidency] whether it accepts the request.

(b)[4] A State may make its consent conditional. [When a State makes its consent conditional, on the applicability of its domestic laws relating to pardon, conditional release and commutation of sentence, and

---

[46] The issue of transfer, etc., from the State of enforcement of a sentence of imprisonment to a third State is addressed in article 97.

[47] These square brackets reflect the view that there should be no rule of speciality in the Statute.

[1] One delegation was of the view that this part deals with issues also relevant to judicial assistance and that there might be grounds for non-recognition or non-enforcement of judgements.

[2] There was a question whether this sort of provision should be in article 72, Part 7 or in Part 10.

[3] The issue arises as to whether provision should be made concerning whether non-States Parties should accept sentenced persons for imprisonment.

[4] If retained, this provision will need to conform with provisions of article 100.

on its administration of the sentence, the consent of the Court is not required to subsequent actions by that State in conformity with those laws, but the Court shall be given at least 45 days' notice of any decision which might materially affect the terms or extent of the imprisonment].

2.

(a) The [Court's] [Presidency's] designation of a State under paragraph 1 shall be governed by principles of [equitable distribution] [burden sharing] to be elaborated [in the Rules.] [However, no such designation shall be made with respect to the State where or against which the crime was committed or the State of which the convicted person or the victim is a national [, unless the [Court] [Presidency] explicitly decides otherwise for reasons of social rehabilitation].]

(b) In making a designation under paragraph 1, the [Court] [Presidency] shall allow the person sentenced to provide views on any concerns as to personal security or rehabilitation. However, the consent of the person is not required for the [Court] [Presidency] to designate a particular State for enforcement of the sentence.

[(c) In making a designation under paragraph 1, the [Court] [Presidency] shall take into account reasonable compliance with international standards governing treatment of prisoners.]

3.

[*182] If no State is designated under paragraph 1, the sentence of imprisonment shall be served in the prison facility made available by the host State, in conformity with and under the conditions as set out in the Host State Agreement as referred to in article 3, paragraph 2.

Article 95
Enforcement of the sentence

1. [Subject to conditions it may have specified in paragraph (b) of option 2 of article 94,][5] the sentence of imprisonment shall be binding on the States Parties, which may in no case modify it.

2. The Court alone shall have the right to decide any application for review of the judgement or sentence. The State of enforcement shall not impede the sentenced person from making any such application.

Article 96
Supervision and administration of sentence

1. The enforcement of a sentence of imprisonment shall be subject to the supervision of the [Court] [Presidency] [, and consistent with internationally recognized standards governing treatment of prisoners.]

2.

Option 1

The conditions of detention shall be governed by the law of the State of enforcement and consistent with internationally recognized standards governing treatment of prisoners. [However, the [Court] [Presidency] may, on its own motion or at the request of the sentenced person, modify the conditions of detention of the sentenced person. The State of enforcement shall enforce the modified conditions of detention. The [Court] [Presidency] may also on its own motion, or at the request of the sentenced person or the State of enforcement, decide that the sentenced person be transferred to another State for the continued serving of the sentence [provided that State agrees].

[*183] Option 2

The conditions of detention shall be governed by the law of the State of enforcement, consistent with internationally recognized minimum standards, but in any case not more or less favourable than those available to prisoners convicted of similar offenses in the State of enforcement.

3. Communications between persons sentenced and the Court shall be unimpeded [and confidential].

---

[5] The text in square brackets will be retained in the event option 2 of article 94 is adopted.

Article 97
Transfer of the person upon completion of sentence

1.   Unless the State of enforcement agrees to permit the prisoner to remain in its territory following completion of sentence, the prisoner shall be released into the custody of the State of the person's nationality or another State that has agreed to receive the person.

2.   The costs involved in transporting the prisoner to another State under article 94 shall be borne by the Court, unless the State of enforcement or the receiving State agree otherwise.

3.   [Unless prohibited by the provisions of article 92] [with the consent of the Court as provided in article 98],[6] the State of enforcement may also, in accordance with its national law, extradite or otherwise surrender the prisoner to the State which has requested the extradition or surrender of the prisoner for purposes of trial or enforcement of a sentence.

[Article 98
Limitation of prosecution/punishment for other offences[7]

[*184] 1. A sentenced person in the custody of the State of enforcement shall not be subjected to prosecution or punishment [or extradition to a third State] for any conduct committed prior to delivery to the State of detention, unless such prosecution or punishment [or extradition] has been approved by the [Court] [Presidency] [at the request of the State of detention].

2.   The [Court] [Presidency] shall rule on the matter after having heard the prisoner.

3.   Paragraph 1 of this article shall cease to apply if the sentenced person remains more than 30 days on the territory of the State of enforcement after having served the full sentence imposed by the Court.]

[Article 99
Enforcement of fines and forfeiture measures

1.   States Parties shall [, in accordance with their national law,] enforce fines and forfeiture measures [and measures relating to compensation or [restitution] [reparation]][8] as fines and forfeiture measures [and measures relating to compensation or [restitution] [reparation]] rendered by their national authorities.

[For the purpose of enforcement of fines, the [Court] [Presidency] may order the forced sale of any property of the person sentenced which is on the territory of a State Party. For the same purposes, the [Court] [Presidency] may order the forfeiture of proceeds, property and assets and instrumentalities of crimes belonging to the person sentenced.][9] [10]

[*185] [Decisions by the Presidency are implemented by States Parties in conformity with their domestic laws.

[The provisions of this article shall apply to legal persons.]]

2.   Property, including the proceeds of the sale thereof, which is obtained by a State Party as a result of its enforcement of a judgement of the Court shall be handed over to the [Court] [Presidency] [which will dispose of that property in accordance with the provisions of article 79 [paragraph 5 of article 54].]

---

[6]   There is a question as to whether the permissibility of re-extradition of the prisoner should be addressed in article 92 (Rule of speciality) or in article 98.

[7]   Consideration should be given to the relationship of this article to the rule of speciality, as found in article 92. This article is also related to article 87, paragraph 8, regarding temporary or delayed surrender.

[8]   References to fines, forfeiture, restitution or compensation, or similar terms, will depend on the range of sanctions and compensatory measures ultimately provided for in Part 7 [article 76].

N.B. This footnote should be reviewed in the context of the discussions on article 73 (Reparations to victims)

[9]   There is a question whether this provision concerns enforcement of sentences, or rather the powers of the Court to order particular measures relating to enforcement of fines or confiscation. If it is meant to refer to States enforcing specific orders relating to fines or confiscation, then paragraph 1 might be amended to make clear that that enforcement by States Parties would include "giving effect to orders of the Court relating to enforcement of fines or forfeitures, such as the seizure of particular property or the forced sale of property of the convicted person to satisfy a fine".

[10]   There was a suggestion that this paragraph should be placed first.

Article 100[11]
Pardon,[12] parole and commutation of sentences [early release]

Option 1

1. The prisoner may apply to the [Court] [Presidency] for a [decision on] [ruling regarding the appropriateness of] [pardon,] parole or commutation of sentence, if under a generally applicable law of the State of enforcement, a person in the same circumstances who had been convicted for the same conduct by a court of that State would be eligible for [pardon,] parole or commutation of sentence.

[*186] Option 2

1. (a)   The State of enforcement shall not release the prisoner before the expiry of the sentence as pronounced by the Court.

(b)   The [Court] [Presidency] alone shall have the right to decide any application for [commutation of the sentence] [commutation of the sentence or parole] [commutation of the sentence, parole or [pardon]]. [If appropriate in the circumstances, parole may be granted after the prisoner has served:

(i)   not less than 20 years in case of life imprisonment;

(ii)   not less than two thirds of the term in case of imprisonment for a definite term.

Parole may be revoked when the parolee is convicted of having committed an offence while on parole, or has violated any condition of his parole.]

2.   Procedures regarding an application for commutation of sentence [or parole [or pardon]] and the [Court's] [Presidency's] decision on such an application shall be governed by the Rules of Procedure and Evidence.

N.B. Consideration should be given to whether this article should be placed in Part 7.

[Article 101
Escape

In the event of an escape, the sentenced person shall, as soon as he has been arrested pursuant to a request of the Court under article 88, paragraph 1 (d), be delivered to the State in which he was serving his sentence or to another place determined by the Court.]

[*187] PART 11. ASSEMBLY OF STATES PARTIES
Article 102
Assembly of States Parties

1.   There is hereby established an Assembly of States Parties to this Statute. Each State Party shall have one representative in the Assembly who may be accompanied by alternates and advisers. The signatories of the [Statute] [Final Act] may be [observers] [members] in the Assembly.[1]

2.   The Assembly shall:

[(a) consider and adopt recommendations of the preparatory commission;]

(b) provide management oversight to the Presidency, Prosecutor and Registrar regarding the administration of the Court;

(c) consider the reports and activities of the Bureau and take appropriate action in regard thereto;

(d) consider and approve the budget for the Court [in consultation with the Registrar] [and rule on any financial issue];

---

[11]   In the discussion on penalties in the Preparatory Committee, it was suggested that, to meet concerns of several delegations regarding the severity of a life sentence or a long sentence of imprisonment, article 100 should provide a mandatory mechanism by which the prisoner's sentence would be re-examined by the Court after a certain period of time, in order to determine whether he or she should be released. In this way, the Court could also ensure the uniform treatment of prisoners regardless of the State where they served their sentence.

[12]   A concern was expressed that pardon might involve political considerations which would not be appropriate for determination by the Court, so that the authority to decide on an application for pardon might better be vested in the Assembly of States Parties.

[1]   Delegations expressed the view that this could be dealt with in the Rules of Procedure of the Assembly.

(e)   determine whether to alter, as appropriate, the number of judges [or members of the Office of the Prosecutor or the Registry], serving on a full- or part-time basis, for such period as it shall determine;

[(f)   consider, upon recommendation [of the Court] [of the Bureau], any question relating to non-cooperation by States Parties [and non-States Parties] and take [necessary] [appropriate] measures, including referring the matter to [the Security Council] [the United Nations General Assembly] as provided in article 86.]²

(g)   perform any other function or take any other action as specified in this Statute or the Rules of Procedure and Evidence [including consideration of [*188] requests for a review of these instruments] [including consideration of applications relating to pardon submitted to it.]³

3.   (a)   The Assembly shall have a Bureau consisting of a President, a Vice-President and [18]⁴ members elected by the Assembly for three-year terms.⁵ The President of the Court, the Prosecutor and the Registrar or their representatives may, as appropriate, participate as [observers] [members] in meetings of the Bureau.⁶

(b)   The Bureau shall [have a representative character] [be elected on the basis of ensuring its representative character], taking into account, in particular, equitable geographical distribution and bearing in mind the adequate representation of the principal legal systems of the world [as far as possible].

The Bureau shall meet as often as necessary, but at least once a year, and shall assist the Assembly in the discharge of its responsibilities.

(c)   The Assembly may also establish other subsidiary bodies as may be necessary, including an independent oversight mechanism for inspection, evaluation and investigation in order to enhance the efficiency and economy of [non-judicial administration] [operations] of the Court.

4.   The Assembly shall meet at the seat of the Court or at the Headquarters of the United Nations [or in any other place as it may decide] once a year and, when circumstances so require, hold special sessions. Except as otherwise specified in the Statute, special sessions shall be convened [by the Bureau on its own initiative or] at the request of one third of the States Parties.

[*189] 5. Each State Party shall have one vote. Every effort shall be made to reach decisions on matters of substance by consensus in the Assembly and in the Bureau. If consensus cannot be reached, decisions on matters of substance must be approved by [a two-thirds majority of those present and voting, representing the absolute majority of States Parties] [a two-thirds majority of those present and voting] [an absolute majority of States Parties] except as otherwise provided in the Statute.

6.   [A State Party that is in arrears in the payment of its financial contributions to the costs of the Court shall have no vote in the Assembly and in the Bureau if the amount of its arrears equals or exceeds the amount of the contributions due from it for the preceding [two full] [three] [five] years. The Assembly may, nevertheless, permit such a State Party to vote in the Assembly and in the Bureau if it is satisfied that the failure to pay is due to conditions beyond the control of the State Party].⁷

7.   The Assembly shall adopt its own Rules of Procedure.

[*190] PART 12. FINANCING OF THE COURT
Article 103
Payment of expenses of the Court

Expenses of the Court as assessed by the States Parties shall be paid from the funds of the Court, in accordance with the Statute and the Financial Regulations and Rules adopted by the States Parties.

---

²   It will be necessary to ensure consistency between this provision and the content of article 86.
³   The final wording will depend on the outcome of the discussions on article 100. Mention was also made in this context of a possible role of the Assembly in dispute resolution.
⁴   It was suggested that the possibility of having a procedure for increasing the number of members of the Bureau could be considered. It was also suggested that there should be more than one Vice-President.
⁵   It was suggested that the elections should be staggered. This could be dealt with in the Rules of Procedure of the Assembly.
⁶   Delegations expressed the view that this could be dealt with in the Rules of Procedure of the Assembly.
⁷   This is subject to the finalization of the provisions on financing of the Court.

Article 104
Funds of the Court

Option 1

The funds of the Court shall comprise assessed contributions made by States Parties.

Option 2

The expenses of the Court shall be borne by the United Nations, subject to the approval of the General Assembly of the United Nations.[1]

Option 3

1. The funds of the Court shall include:
    (a)   Assessed contributions of States Parties;
    (b)   Funds provided by the United Nations.[2]

[*191] 2. However, during the initial phase,[3] the expenses of the Court shall be borne by the United Nations, subject to the approval of the General Assembly of the United Nations.

Article 105
Voluntary contributions

Without prejudice to article 104, the Court may utilize voluntary contributions from Governments, international organizations, individuals, corporations and other entities, in accordance with relevant criteria adopted by the States Parties.

Article 106
Assessment of contributions

The contributions of States [Parties] shall be assessed in accordance with an agreed scale of assessment [based upon [the scale used for the regular budget of the United Nations] [a multi-unit class system along the lines of that used in the International Telecommunication Union or the Universal Postal Union]].

Article 107
Annual audit

The records, books and accounts of the Court, including its annual financial statements, shall be audited annually by an independent auditor.

[*192] PART 13. FINAL CLAUSES
Article 108
Settlement of disputes

Option 1

[Except as otherwise provided in the Statute] [,a] [A]ny dispute concerning the interpretation or application of this Statute shall be settled by the decision of the Court.

Option 2

Without prejudice to the competence of the Court concerning disputes relating to its judicial activities as is established in accordance with this Statute, any dispute between two or more States Parties relating to interpretation or application of this Statute which is not resolved through negotiations [within a

---

[1]   This would require a decision of the General Assembly.
[2]   The view was expressed that, in the case of a referral by the Security Council, the relevant expenses of the Court should be borne by the United Nations.
[3]   The duration of the "initial phase" has to be determined.

reasonable time] [within ... months] shall be referred to the Assembly of States Parties which shall make recommendations on further means of settlement of the dispute.[1]

Option 3

Any dispute concerning the judicial functions of the Court shall be settled by the decision of the Court.

Option 4

No article on dispute settlement.

Article 109
[*193] Reservations

Option 1

· No reservations may be made to this Statute.

Option 2

Paragraphs 1 and 2

Option A

1. No reservations other than those made in accordance with paragraph 2 of the present article shall be permitted.

2. Any State may at the time of signature, ratification, acceptance, approval or accession make reservations in respect of the following ...

Option B

1. No reservations to this Statute shall be permitted unless expressly provided for in specific articles of the Statute.

2. No paragraph 2.

3.   A State which has made reservations may at any time by notification in writing to the Secretary-General withdraw all or part of its reservations.

4.

Option A

In the event of a dispute or legal question arising in connection with the admissibility of reservations made by a State under paragraph 2, the Court shall be competent to decide the admissibility of such reservations.

Option B

No paragraph 4.

[*194] Option 3

1. At the time of signature, ratification, acceptance, approval or accession, any State may make reservations to articles of this Statute except [those in Parts ...] [articles ...].

2. A State which has made reservations may at any time by notification in writing to the Secretary-General of the United Nations withdraw all or part of its reservation.

Option 4

No article on reservations.

Article 110
Amendments

1.   After the expiry of [...] years from the entry into force of this Statute, any State Party may propose amendments thereto. The text of any proposed amendment shall be submitted to [the Secretary-General of the United Nations,] who shall promptly circulate it to all States Parties.

---

[1]   The view was expressed that the same procedure may be used for resolving disputes relating to the admissibility of reservations.

It was also observed a cross reference in this article should be made to article 102 (Assembly of States Parties).

2.   A proposed amendment to this Statute shall be considered at the next [meeting of the Assembly of States Parties] [Review Conference], provided that no consideration shall take place until three months after its circulation pursuant to paragraph 1.

3.

Option 1

The adoption of an amendment at a meeting of the Assembly of States Parties shall be by consensus.

Option 2

The adoption of an amendment at a meeting of the Assembly of States Parties shall require a [2/3] [3/4] majority of [all the States Parties] [those present and voting].

[*195] 4. [The Secretary-General of the United Nations] shall circulate any amendment adopted at a meeting of the Assembly of States Parties to all States Parties.

5.   An amendment adopted at a meeting of the Assembly of States Parties shall enter into force for all States Parties one year after instruments of ratification or acceptance have been deposited with the Secretary-General of the United Nations by [2/3] [3/4] of [all the States Parties].[2]

6.   Any State Party that has not ratified or accepted the amendment may withdraw from the Statute with immediate effect, notwithstanding paragraph 1 of article 115, by giving notice no later than one year after the entry into force of such amendment.

Article 111[3]
Review of the Statute

Option 1

1.   After the expiry of [...] years from the entry into force of this Statute, the meeting of the Assembly of States Parties may decide, by a two-thirds majority of [States Parties] [those present and voting], to convene a special meeting of the Assembly of States Parties to review the Statute.

[Such a meeting shall not be held more frequently than [...] years from the previous such meeting.]

2.   The provisions of paragraphs 3 to 6 of article 110 shall apply to any amendment to the Statute proposed at such a meeting of the Assembly of States Parties.

[*196] Option 2

1.   [Five] years after the entry into force of this Statute the Depositary shall convene a meeting of the Assembly of States Parties to review the list of crimes within the jurisdiction of the Court contained in article 5, in order to consider additions to the list. Any amendment to that effect shall be subject to paragraphs 3 and 4 of article 110 and shall enter into force with regard to those States Parties which have deposited their instrument of acceptance on the [thirteenth] day following the deposit of the [tenth] instrument of acceptance. For each State whose instrument of acceptance is deposited after the entry into force of the amendment, the amendment shall enter into force on the [thirtieth] day after the deposit by such State of its instrument of acceptance. If an amendment has not entered into force for a State, the Court shall not exercise its jurisdiction with respect to a crime covered by the amendment when committed on the territory of that State or by its nationals. Subsequently, at the request of a State Party, the Depositary shall, upon approval by a majority of States Parties, convene a meeting of the Assembly of States Parties in order to consider additions to the list of crimes within the jurisdiction of the Court.

2.   Without prejudice to paragraph 1, the meeting of the Assembly of State Parties may at any time after the entry into force of this Statute decide, by a two-thirds majority of [Sates Parties] [those present and voting], to convene a special meeting of the Assembly of States Parties to review the Statute. Any amendment to the Statute proposed at such a meeting of the Assembly of States Parties shall be subject to paragraphs 3 to 6 of article 110.

---

[2]   It was observed that consideration should also be given to requiring a qualified majority for amendments relating to institutional matters and to acceptance by all States Parties for matters of substance.

[3]   Some delegations proposed that articles 110 and 111 be merged.

Article 112
Signature, ratification, acceptance, approval or accession
1.   This Statute shall be open for signature by all States [without any kind of discrimination] in Rome, at the headquarters of the Food and Agriculture Organization of the United Nations, on [17 July 1998]. Thereafter, it will remain open for signature in Rome at the Ministry of Foreign Affairs of Italy until [17 October 1998]. After that date, the Statute shall remain open for signature in New York, at United Nations Headquarters, until 31 December 2000.
2.   This Statute is subject to ratification, acceptance or approval by signatory States. Instruments of ratification, acceptance or approval shall be deposited with the Secretary-General of the United Nations. [*197] 3. This Statute shall be open to accession by all States. Instruments of accession shall be deposited with the Secretary-General of the United Nations.

[Article 113
Early activation of principles and rules of the Statute
Pending the entry into force of the Statute, States that have signed the Statute shall, in accordance with applicable principles of international law, refrain from acts that would defeat the object and purpose of the Statute. To this end, in ensuring the international prosecution and suppression of crimes of international concern, States should pay due regard to the relevant principles and provisions contained in the Statute, including in the performance of their responsibilities in competent organs of the United Nations, with a view to accelerating the achievement of the shared goal of establishing the Court.]

Article 114
Entry into force
1.   This Statute shall enter into force [following the completion of the Rules of Procedure and Evidence] on the [60th] day following the date of the deposit of the [...] instrument of ratification, acceptance, approval or accession with the Secretary-General of the United Nations [provided that such instruments have been deposited by no fewer than [one] [two] [four] members from each geographical group as established by the General Assembly of the United Nations].
2.   For each State ratifying, accepting, approving or acceding to the Statute after the deposit of the [...] instrument of ratification, acceptance, approval or accession, the Statute shall enter into force on the [60th] day after the deposit by such State of its instrument of ratification, acceptance, approval or accession.

Article 115
Withdrawal
1.   A State Party may, by written notification addressed to the Secretary-General of the United Nations, withdraw from this Statute. The withdrawal shall [*198] take effect one year after the date of receipt of the notification, unless the notification specifies a later date.
2.   A State shall not be discharged by reason of its withdrawal from the financial obligations which accrued while it was a Party to this Statute. Nor shall the withdrawal affect the duty of that State to cooperate with the Court in connection with criminal investigations and proceedings commenced under this Statute prior to its termination for that State; nor shall it prejudice in any way the continued consideration of any matter which is already under consideration by the Court prior to the date at which the withdrawal becomes effective.
[A State shall not be discharged by reason of its withdrawal from the obligations arising from the Statute while it was a Party to this Statute. Nor shall the withdrawal prejudice in any way the continued consideration of any matter which is already under consideration by the Court prior to the date at which the withdrawal becomes effective.]

Article 116
Authentic texts

The original of this Statute, of which the Arabic, Chinese, English, French, Russian and Spanish texts are equally authentic, shall be deposited with the Secretary-General of the United Nations, who shall send certified copies thereof to all States.

IN WITNESS WHEREOF, the undersigned, being duly authorized thereto by their respective Governments, have signed this Statute.

DONE at Rome, this 17th day of July 1998.

[*199] PART TWO
DRAFT FINAL ACT OF THE UNITED NATIONS DIPLOMATIC CONFERENCE OF PLENIPOTENTIARIES ON THE ESTABLISHMENT OF AN INTERNATIONAL CRIMINAL COURT

1.   The General Assembly, in its resolution 51/207 of 17 December 1996, decided to hold a diplomatic conference of plenipotentiaries in 1998 with a view to finalizing and adopting a convention on the establishment of an international criminal court.

2.   The General Assembly, in its resolution 52/160 of 15 December 1997, accepted with deep appreciation the generous offer of the Government of Italy to act as host to the conference and decided to hold the United Nations Diplomatic Conference of Plenipotentiaries on the Establishment of an International Criminal Court in Rome from 15 June to 17 July 1998.

3.   Previously, the General Assembly, in its resolution 44/39 of 4 December 1989, had requested the International Law Commission to address the question of establishing an international criminal court; in resolutions 45/41 of 28 November 1990 and 46/54 of 9 December 1991, invited the Commission to consider further and analyse the issues concerning the question of an international criminal jurisdiction, including the question of establishing an international criminal court; and in resolutions 47/33 of 25 November 1992 and 48/31 of 9 December 1993, requested the Commission to elaborate the draft statute for such a court as a matter of priority.

4.   The International Law Commission considered the question of establishing an international criminal court from its forty-second session, in 1990, to its forty-sixth session, in 1994. At that session, the Commission completed a draft statute for an international criminal court, which was submitted to the General Assembly.

5.   The General Assembly, in its resolution 49/53 of 9 December 1994, decided to establish an ad hoc committee to review the major substantive and administrative issues arising out of the draft statute prepared by the International Law Commission and, in the light of that review, to consider arrangements for the convening of an international conference of plenipotentiaries.

6.   The Ad Hoc Committee on the Establishment of an International Criminal Court met from 3 to 13 April and from 14 to 25 August 1995, during which time [*200] the Committee reviewed the issues arising out of the draft statute prepared by the International Law Commission and considered arrangements for the convening of an international conference.

7.   The General Assembly, in its resolution 50/46 of 11 December 1995, decided to establish a preparatory committee to discuss further the major substantive and administrative issues arising out of the draft statute prepared by the International Law Commission and, taking into account the different views expressed during the meetings, to draft texts with a view to preparing a widely acceptable consolidated text of a convention for an international criminal court as a next step towards consideration by a conference of plenipotentiaries.

8.   The Preparatory Committee on the Establishment of an International Criminal Court met from 25 March to 12 April and from 12 to 30 August 1996, during which time the Committee discussed further the issues arising out of the draft statute and began preparing a widely acceptable consolidated text of a convention for an international criminal court.

9.   By its resolution 51/207 of 17 December 1996, the General Assembly decided that the Preparatory Committee would meet in 1997 and 1998 in order to complete the drafting of the text for submission to the Conference.

10.   The Preparatory Committee met from 11 to 21 February, from 4 to 15 August and from 1 to 12 December 1997, during which time the Committee continued to prepare a widely acceptable consolidated text of a convention for an international criminal court.

11.   In its resolution 52/160 of 15 December 1997, the General Assembly requested the Preparatory Committee to continue its work in accordance with General Assembly resolution 51/207 and, at the end of its sessions, to transmit to the Conference the text of a draft convention on the establishment of an international criminal court prepared in accordance with its mandate.

12.   The Preparatory Committee met from 16 March to 3 April 1998, during which time the Committee completed the preparation of the draft Convention on the Establishment of an International Criminal Court, which was transmitted to the Conference.

13.   The Conference met at the headquarters of the Food and Agriculture Organization of the United Nations in Rome from 15 June to 17 July 1998.

14.   The General Assembly, in its resolution 52/160, requested the Secretary-General to invite all States Members of the United Nations or members of [*201] specialized agencies or of the International Atomic Energy Agency to participate in the Conference. The delegations of ... States participated in the Conference, as follows: ...

15.   In the same resolution, the General Assembly requested the Secretary-General to invite representatives of organizations and other entities that had received a standing invitation from the Assembly pursuant to its relevant resolutions to participate as observers in its sessions and work on the understanding that such representatives would participate in that capacity, and to invite, as observers to the Conference, representatives of interested regional intergovernmental organizations and other interested international bodies, including the International Tribunals for the Former Yugoslavia and for Rwanda. The following organizations were represented at the Conference by an observer: ...

16.   Pursuant to the same resolution, the Secretary-General invited non-governmental organizations accredited by the Preparatory Committee with due regard to the provisions of section VII of Economic and Social Council resolution 1996/31 of 25 July 1996, and in particular to the relevance of their activities to the work of the Conference, to participate in the Conference, along the lines followed in the Preparatory Committee and in accordance with the resolution as well as the rules of procedure to be adopted by the Conference. The following non-governmental organizations were represented at the Conference by an observer: ...

17.   The Conference elected ... as President.

18.   The Conference elected as Vice-Presidents the representatives of the following States: ...

19.   The following committees were set up by the Conference:

General Committee
   Chairman: ...
   Members: ...
Committee of the Whole
   Chairman: ...
   Vice-Chairmen: ...
[*202] Rapporteur: ...
Drafting Committee
   Chairman: ...
   Members: ...
   The Rapporteur of the Committee of the Whole participated ex officio in the work of the Drafting Committee in accordance with rule 49 of the rules of procedure of the Conference.
Credentials Committee
   Chairman: ...
   Members: The representatives of ...

20. The Secretary-General was represented by Mr. Hans Corell, Under-Secretary-General, the Legal Counsel. Mr. Roy S. Lee, Director of the Codification Division of the Office of Legal Affairs, acted as Executive Secretary. The Secretariat was further composed as follows: ...

21. The Conference had before it a draft Convention on the Establishment of an International Criminal Court transmitted by the Preparatory Committee in accordance with its mandate ...

22. The Conference assigned to the Committee of the Whole the consideration of the draft Convention on the Establishment of an International Criminal Court adopted by the Preparatory Committee. The Conference entrusted the Drafting Committee, without reopening substantive discussion on any matter, with coordinating and refining the drafting of all texts referred to it without altering their substance, formulating drafts and giving advice on drafting as requested by the Conference or by the Committee of the Whole and reporting to the Conference or to the Committee of the Whole as appropriate.

23. On the basis of the deliberations recorded in the records of the Conference (A/CONF. ...) and of the Committee of the Whole (A/CONF. ...) and the reports of the Committee of the Whole and the Drafting Committee (A/CONF. ...), the Conference drew up the following [Convention]:

[Rome Convention on the Establishment of an
[*203] International Criminal Court]

24. The foregoing Convention, which is subject to ratification, was adopted by the Conference on ... July 1998 and opened for signature on [17 July 1998], in accordance with its provisions, until [17 October 1998] at the Ministry of Foreign Affairs of Italy and, subsequently, until 31 December 2000, at United Nations Headquarters in New York. The same instrument was also opened for accession in accordance with its provisions.

25. After 17 October 1998, the closing date for signature at the Ministry of Foreign Affairs of Italy, the Convention will be deposited with the Secretary-General of the United Nations.

26. The Conference also adopted the following resolutions, which are annexed to the present Final Act:

Tribute to the International Law Commission

Tribute to the President of the Conference, to the Chairman of the Committee of the Whole and to the Chairman of the Drafting Committee

Tribute to the People and the Government of Italy

[Resolution on the Establishment of the Preparatory Commission for the International Criminal Court]

...

IN WITNESS WHEREOF the representatives have signed this Final Act.

DONE at Rome this seventeenth day of July, one thousand nine hundred and ninety-eight, in a single copy in the Arabic, Chinese, English, French, Russian and Spanish languages, each text being equally authentic.

By unanimous decision of the Conference, the original of this Final Act shall be deposited in the archives of the Ministry of Foreign Affairs of Italy.

[*204] ANNEX
Resolutions adopted by the United Nations Diplomatic Conference
of Plenipotentiaries on the Establishment of an International
Criminal Court

...

The United Nations Conference on the Establishment of an International Criminal Court,

Having adopted the Statute of the International Criminal Court,

Having decided to take all possible measures to ensure the coming into operation of the International Criminal Court without undue delay and to make the necessary arrangements for the commencement of its functions,

Having decided that a preparatory commission should be established for the fulfilment of these purposes,

Decides as follows:

1.   There is hereby established the Preparatory Commission for the International Criminal Court. The Secretary-General of the United Nations shall convene the Commission [as early as possible at a date to be decided by [the General Assembly of the United Nations] [the Secretary-General]] [upon signature of or accession to the Statute by ... States].[1]

2.   The Commission shall consist of representatives of States which have signed the Final Act of the United Nations Diplomatic Conference of Plenipotentiaries on the Establishment of an International Criminal Court and other States which have been invited to participate in the Conference.

[*205] 3. The Commission shall elect its Chairman and other officers, adopt its rules of procedure and decide on its programme of work. These elections shall take place at the first meeting of the Commission.

4.   The Commission shall prepare proposals for practical arrangements for the establishment and coming into operation of the Court, including the draft texts of:

    (a)   Rules of Procedure and Evidence [including elements of offences][2] on a priority basis;

    (b)   a relationship agreement between the Court and the United Nations;

    (c)   basic principles governing a headquarters agreement to be negotiated between the Court and the host country;

    [(d)   staff regulations;][3]

    (e)   financial regulations and rules;

    [(f)   an agreement on the privileges and immunities of the Court;]

    (g)   a budget for the first financial year;

    (h)   the rules of procedure of the Assembly of States Parties.

5.   The Commission shall remain in existence until the conclusion of the first meeting of the Assembly of States Parties. [It shall convene the first meeting of the Assembly of States Parties.]

6.   The Commission shall prepare a report on all matters within its mandate and submit it to the first meeting of the Assembly of States Parties.

7.   The Commission shall meet at the Headquarters of the United Nations. The Secretary-General of the United Nations is requested to provide to the [*206] Commission such secretariat services as it may require, subject to the approval of the General Assembly of the United Nations.

8.   The Secretary-General of the United Nations shall bring this resolution to the attention of the General Assembly for any necessary action.

---

[1]   With regard to these alternatives, a proposal was also made that the Rules of Procedure and Evidence of the Court, including an elaboration of the elements of the offences that must be proved, shall be prepared and adopted by a conference of participating States immediately following the conclusion of the present Statute. Such rules shall be consistent with the provisions of the Statute. The Statute shall be open for signature once the Rules of Procedure and Evidence have been finally adopted.

[2]   The view was expressed that the Preparatory Commission may decide to make use of the expertise and experience of the International Tribunals for the Former Yugoslavia and for Rwanda, particularly in drafting the Rules of Procedure and Evidence. To this end, representatives of the Tribunals may be invited to participate as observers in the work of the Commission.

[3]   This subparagraph should be in conformity with article 45 of the Statute.

REPORT OF THE PREPARATORY COMMITTEE ON THE ESTABLISHMENT OF AN INTERNATIONAL CRIMINAL COURT

[Editorial Note - the U.N. page numbers of this document are indicated in bolded brackets [*] in the text].

[*1] Addendum

PART THREE

DRAFT RULES OF PROCEDURE FOR THE UNITED NATIONS DIPLOMATIC CONFERENCE OF PLENIPOTENTIARIES ON THE ESTABLISHMENT OF AN INTERNATIONAL CRIMINAL COURT

[*4] DRAFT PROVISIONAL RULES OF PROCEDURE

CHAPTER I

Representation and credentials

Rule 1.   Composition of delegations

The delegation of each State participating in the Conference shall consist of a head of delegation and such other accredited representatives, alternate representatives and advisers as may be required. Unless otherwise specified, the term "representative" in chapters I to X and XII refers to a representative of a State.

Rule 2.   Alternates and advisers

The head of delegation may designate an alternate representative or an adviser to act as a representative.

Rule 3.   Submission of credentials

The credentials of representatives and the names of alternate representatives and advisers shall be submitted early to the Executive Secretary and, if possible, not later than 24 hours after the opening of the Conference. Any later change in the composition of delegations shall also be submitted to the Executive Secretary. The credentials shall be issued either by the Head of State or Government or by the Minister for Foreign Affairs.

Rule 4.   Credentials Committee

A Credentials Committee shall be appointed at the beginning of the Conference. It shall consist of nine members, who shall be appointed by the Conference on the proposal of the President. It shall examine the credentials of representatives and report to the Conference without delay.

Rule 5.   Provisional participation in the Conference

Pending a decision of the Conference upon their credentials, representatives shall be entitled to participate provisionally in the Conference.

[*5] CHAPTER II

Officers

Rule 6.   Elections

The Conference shall elect the following officers: a President and [22] Vice-Presidents, as well as the Chairman of the Committee of the Whole provided for in rule 48 and the Chairman of the Drafting Committee provided for in rule 49. These officers shall be elected on the basis of ensuring the representative character of the General Committee, taking into account in particular equitable geographical distribution and bearing in mind the adequate representation of the principal legal systems of the world. The Conference may also elect such other officers as it deems necessary for the performance of its functions.

Rule 7.   General powers of the President

1.   In addition to exercising the powers conferred upon him or her elsewhere by these rules, the President shall preside at the plenary meetings of the Conference, declare the opening and closing of each meeting,

direct the discussion, ensure observance of these rules, accord the right to speak, promote the achievement of general agreement, put questions to the Conference for decision and announce decisions. The President shall rule on points of order and, subject to these rules, shall have complete control of the proceedings and over the maintenance of order thereat. The President may propose to the Conference the closure of the list of speakers, a limitation on the time to be allowed to speakers and on the number of times each representative may speak on a question, the adjournment or the closure of the debate and the suspension or the adjournment of a meeting.

2.   The President, in the exercise of his or her functions, remains under the authority of the Conference.

Rule 8.   Acting President

1.   If the President finds it necessary to be absent from a meeting or any part thereof, he or she shall designate the Vice-President to take his or her place.

2.   A Vice-President acting as President shall have the powers and duties of the President.

Rule 9.   Replacement of the President

If the President is unable to perform his or her functions, a new President shall be elected.

[*6] *Rule 10.   Voting rights of the President*

The President, or Vice-President acting as President, shall not vote in the Conference, but may appoint another member of his or her delegation to vote in his or her place.

CHAPTER III

General Committee

Rule 11.   Composition

There shall be a General Committee consisting of [25] members, which shall comprise the President and Vice-Presidents, the Chairman of the Committee of the Whole and the Chairman of the Drafting Committee. The President, or in his or her absence, one of the Vice-Presidents designated by him or her, shall serve as Chairman of the General Committee.

Rule 12.   Substitute members

If the President or a Vice-President finds it necessary to be absent during a meeting of the General Committee, he or she may designate a member of his or her delegation to sit and vote in the Committee. In the case of absence, the Chairman of the Committee of the Whole shall designate a Vice-Chairman of that Committee as his or her substitute and the Chairman of the Drafting Committee shall designate a member of the Drafting Committee. When serving on the General Committee, a Vice-Chairman of the Committee of the Whole or member of the Drafting Committee shall not have the right to vote if he or she is of the same delegation as another member of the General Committee.

Rule 13.   Functions

The General Committee shall assist the President in the general conduct of the business of the Conference and, subject to the decisions of the Conference, shall ensure the coordination of its work. It shall also exercise the powers conferred upon it by rule 34.

CHAPTER IV

Secretariat

Rule 14.   Duties of the Secretary-General

1.   The Secretary-General of the United Nations shall be the Secretary-General of the Conference. He, or his representative, shall act in that capacity in all meetings of the Conference and its subsidiary bodies.

[*7] 2. The Secretary-General shall appoint an Executive Secretary of the Conference and shall provide and direct the staff required by the Conference and its subsidiary bodies.

Rule 15.   Duties of the secretariat

The secretariat of the Conference shall, in accordance with these rules:

(a)   Interpret speeches made at meetings;

(b)   Receive, translate, reproduce and distribute the documents of the Conference;

(c)   Publish and circulate the official documents of the Conference;

(d)   Prepare and circulate records of public meetings;

(e) Make and arrange for the keeping of sound recordings of meetings;

(f) Arrange for the custody and preservation of the documents of the Conference in the archives of the United Nations; and

(g) Generally perform all other work that the Conference may require.

Rule 16. Statements by the secretariat

The Secretary-General or any other member of the staff of the secretariat who may be designated for that purpose may, at any time, make either oral or written statements concerning any question under consideration.

CHAPTER V

Opening of the Conference

Rule 17. Temporary President

The Secretary-General shall open the first meeting of the Conference and preside until the Conference has elected its President.

Rule 18. Decisions concerning organization

The Conference shall, to the extent possible, at its first meeting:

(a) Adopt its rules of procedure, the draft of which shall, until such adoption, be the provisional rules of procedure of the Conference;

(b) Elect its officers and constitute its committees;

[*8] (c) Adopt its agenda, the draft of which shall, until such adoption, be the provisional agenda of the Conference;

(d) Decide on the organization of its work.

CHAPTER VI

Conduct of business

Rule 19. Quorum

[The President may declare a meeting open and permit the debate to proceed when the representatives of at least one third of the States participating in the Conference are present. The presence of representatives of a majority of the States so participating shall be required for any decision to be taken.]

Rule 20. Speeches

1. No one may address the Conference without having previously obtained the permission of the President. Subject to rules 21, 22 and 25 to 27, the President shall call upon speakers in the order in which they signify their desire to speak. The secretariat shall be in charge of drawing up a list of speakers.

2. Debate shall be confined to the question before the Conference and the President may call a speaker to order if his or her remarks are not relevant to the subject under discussion.

3. The Conference may limit the time allowed to each speaker and the number of times each delegation may speak on a question. Before such a decision is taken, two representatives may speak in favour of, and two against, a proposal to set such limits, after which the motion shall be immediately put to the vote. In any event, unless otherwise decided by the Conference, the President shall limit each intervention on procedural matters to three minutes. When the debate is limited and a speaker exceeds the allotted time, the President shall call him or her to order without delay.

Rule 21. Precedence

The chairman or rapporteur of a committee or the representative of a working group may be accorded precedence for the purpose of explaining the conclusions arrived at by that committee or working group.

Rule 22. Points of order

During the discussion of any matter, a representative may at any time raise a point of order, which shall be decided immediately by the President in accordance with these rules. A representative may appeal against the ruling of the [*9] President. The appeal shall be put to the vote immediately and the President's ruling shall stand unless overruled by a majority of the representatives present and voting. A representative may not, in raising a point of order, speak on the substance of the matter under discussion.

Rule 23. Closing of the list of speakers
During the course of a debate, the President may announce the list of speakers and, with the consent of the Conference, declare the list closed.

Rule 24. Right of reply
1. Notwithstanding rule 23, the President shall accord the right of reply to any representative who requests it. A representative referred to in rules 60, 61 or 62 may be granted the opportunity to make a reply.
2. Replies made pursuant to this rule shall normally be made at the end of the last meeting of the day.
3. No delegation may make more than two statements under this rule at a given meeting.
4. The first intervention in the exercise of the right of reply for any delegation at a given meeting shall be limited to five minutes and the second intervention shall be limited to three minutes.

Rule 25. Adjournment of debate
A representative may at any time move the adjournment of the debate on the question under discussion. In addition to the proposer of the motion, two representatives may speak in favour of, and two against, the adjournment, after which the motion shall, subject to rule 28, be put immediately to the vote.

Rule 26. Closure of debate
A representative may at any time move the closure of the debate on the question under discussion, whether or not any other representative has signified his or her wish to speak. Permission to speak on the motion shall be accorded only to two speakers opposing the closure, after which the motion shall, subject to rule 28, be put immediately to the vote.

Rule 27. Suspension or adjournment of the meeting
Subject to rule 39, a representative may at any time move the suspension or the adjournment of the meeting. Such motions shall not be debated, but shall, subject to rule 28, be put immediately to the vote.

[*10] *Rule 28. Order of motions*
Subject to rule 22, the motions indicated below shall have precedence in the following order over all proposals or other motions before the meeting:
    (a) To suspend the meeting;
    (b) To adjourn the meeting;
    (c) To adjourn the debate on the question under discussion;
    (d) To close the debate on the question under discussion.

Rule 29. Basic proposal
The draft convention on the establishment of an international criminal court transmitted by the Preparatory Committee on the Establishment of an International Criminal Court shall constitute the basic proposal for consideration by the Conference.

Rule 30. Other proposals
Other proposals shall normally be submitted in writing to the Executive Secretary, who shall circulate copies to all delegations. As a general rule, no proposal shall be considered at any meeting of the Conference unless copies of it have been circulated to all delegations not later than the day preceding the meeting. The president may, however, permit the consideration of amendments, even though these amendments have not been circulated or have only been circulated on the same day.

Rule 31. Withdrawal of proposals and motions
A proposal or a motion may be withdrawn by its proposer at any time before a decision on it has been taken, provided that it has not been amended. A proposal or a motion that has thus been withdrawn may be reintroduced by any representative.

Rule 32. Decisions on competence
Subject to rules 22 and 28, any motion calling for a decision on the competence of the Conference to discuss any matter or to adopt a proposal submitted to it shall be put to the vote before the matter is discussed or a decision is taken on the proposal in question.

[*11] *Rule 33 Reconsideration of proposals*
When a proposal has been adopted or rejected it may not be reconsidered unless the Conference, by a two-thirds majority of the representatives present and voting, so decides. Permission to speak on a motion

to reconsider shall be accorded only to two speakers opposing the motion, after which it shall be put immediately to the vote.

CHAPTER VII
Decision-taking
Rule 34. General agreement
1. The Conference shall make its best endeavours to ensure that the work of the Conference is accomplished by general agreement.
2. If, in the consideration of any matter of substance, all feasible efforts to reach general agreement have failed, the President of the Conference shall consult the General Committee and recommend the steps to be taken, which may include the matter being put to the vote.
Rule 35. Voting rights
Each State participating in the Conference shall have one vote.
Rule 36. Majority required
[1. Subject to rule 34, decisions of the Conference on all matters of substance shall be taken by a two-thirds majority of the representatives present and voting.
2. Decisions of the Conference on matters of procedure shall be taken by a majority of the representatives present and voting.
3. If the question arises whether a matter is one of procedure or of substance, the President shall rule on the question. An appeal against this ruling shall be put to the vote immediately and the President's ruling shall stand unless overruled by a majority of the representatives present and voting.
4. If a vote is equally divided, the proposal or motion shall be regarded as rejected.]
Rule 37. Meaning of the expression "representatives present and voting"
For the purpose of these rules, the phrase "representatives present and voting" means representatives present and casting an affirmative or negative [*12] vote. Representatives who abstain from voting shall be considered as not voting.
Rule 38. Method of voting
1. Except as provided in rule 45, the Conference shall normally vote by show of hands or by standing, but any representative may request a roll-call. The roll-call shall be taken in the English alphabetical order of the names of the States participating in the Conference, beginning with the delegation whose name is drawn by lot by the President. The name of each State shall be called in all roll-calls and its representative shall reply "yes", "no" or "abstention".
2. When the Conference votes by mechanical means, a non-recorded vote shall replace a vote by show of hands or by standing and a recorded vote shall replace a roll-call. Any representative may request a recorded vote, which shall, unless a representative requests otherwise, be taken without calling out the names of the States participating in the Conference.
Rule 39. Conduct during voting
The President shall announce the commencement of voting, after which no representative shall be permitted to intervene until the result of the vote has been announced, except on a point of order in connection with the process of voting.
Rule 40. Explanation of vote
Representatives may make brief statements, consisting solely of explanations of their votes, before the voting has commenced or after the voting has been completed. The President may limit the time to be allowed for such explanations. The representative of a State sponsoring a proposal or motion shall not speak in explanation of vote thereon, except if it has been amended.
Rule 41. Division of proposals
A representative may move that parts of a proposal be decided on separately. If a representative objects, a decision shall be taken on the motion for division. Permission to speak on the motion shall be accorded only to two representatives in favour of and to two opposing the division. If the motion is carried, those parts of the proposal that are subsequently approved shall be put to the Conference for decision as a whole.

If all operative parts of the proposal have been rejected, the proposal shall be considered to have been rejected as a whole.

[*13] *Rule 42.*   *Amendments*

1.   A proposal is considered an amendment to another proposal if it merely adds to, deletes from or revises part of that proposal.

2.   Unless specified otherwise, the word "proposal" in these rules shall be considered as including amendments.

Rule 43. Decisions on amendments

When an amendment is moved to a proposal, the amendment shall be decided on first. When two or more amendments are moved to a proposal, the Conference shall first decide on the amendment furthest removed in substance from the original proposal and then on the amendment next furthest removed therefrom and so on until all the amendments have been decided on. Where, however, the adoption of one amendment necessarily implies the rejection of another amendment, the latter amendment shall not be put to a decision. If one or more amendments are adopted, a decision shall then be taken on the amended proposal.

Rule 44. Decisions on proposals

1.   If two or more proposals relate to the same question, the Conference shall, unless it decides otherwise, decide on the proposals in the order in which they were submitted. The Conference may, after each decision on a proposal, decide whether to take a decision on the next proposal.

2.   Revised proposals shall be decided on in the order in which the original proposals were submitted, unless the revision substantially departs from the original proposal. In that case, the original proposal shall be considered as withdrawn and the revised proposal shall be treated as a new proposal.

3.   A motion requiring that no decision be taken on a proposal shall be put to a decision before a decision is taken on the proposal in question.

Rule 45. Elections

All elections shall be held by secret ballot unless otherwise decided by the Conference.

Rule 46. Elections

1.   If, when one person or one delegation is to be elected, no candidate obtains in the first ballot a majority of the representatives present and voting, a second ballot restricted to the two candidates obtaining the largest number of votes shall be taken. If in the second ballot the votes are equally divided, the President shall decide between the candidates by drawing lots.

[*14] 2.   In the case of a tie in the first ballot among three or more candidates obtaining the largest number of votes, a second ballot shall be held. If a tie results among more than two candidates, the number shall be reduced to two by lot and the balloting, restricted to them, shall continue in accordance with the preceding paragraph.

Rule 47. Elections

1.   When two or more elective places are to be filled at one time under the same conditions, those candidates, in a number not exceeding the number of such places, obtaining in the first ballot a majority of the votes of the representatives present and voting and the largest number of votes shall be elected.

2.   If the number of candidates obtaining such majority is less than the number of places to be filled, additional ballots shall be held to fill the remaining places, the voting being restricted to the candidates obtaining the greatest number of votes in the previous ballot, to a number not more than twice the places remaining to be filled, provided that, after the third inconclusive ballot, votes may be cast for any eligible person or delegation. If three such unrestricted ballots are inconclusive, the next three ballots shall be restricted to candidates who obtained the greatest number of votes in the third unrestricted ballot, to a number not more than twice the places remaining to be filled, and the following three ballots thereafter shall be unrestricted, and so on until all the places have been filled.

CHAPTER VIII
Subsidiary bodies
Rule 48. Committee of the Whole
The Conference shall establish a Committee of the Whole. Its bureau shall consist of a Chairman, three Vice-Chairmen and a Rapporteur.
Rule 49. Drafting Committee
1.   The Conference shall establish a Drafting Committee consisting of [21] members, including its Chairman who shall be elected by the Conference in accordance with rule 6. The other [20] members of the Committee shall be appointed by the Conference on the proposal of the General Committee, taking into account equitable geographical distribution as well as the need to ensure the representation of the languages of the Conference and to enable the Drafting Committee to fulfil its functions. The Rapporteur of the Committee of the Whole participates ex officio without a vote, in the work of the Drafting Committee.
2.   The Drafting Committee shall, without reopening substantive discussion on any matter, coordinate and refine the drafting of all texts referred to it, without altering their substance, formulate drafts and give advice on drafting [*15] as requested by the Conference or by the Committee of the Whole and report to the Conference or to the Committee of the Whole as appropriate.
Rule 50. Other subsidiary bodies
The Committee of the Whole may set up working groups.
Rule 51. Officers
Except as otherwise provided in rule 6, each subsidiary body shall elect its own officers.
Rule 52. Officers, conduct of business and voting
[The rules contained in chapters II, VI and VII (except rule 34) above and IX and X below shall be applicable, mutatis mutandis, to the proceedings of subsidiary bodies, except that:
    (a)   The Chairmen of the General, Drafting and Credentials Committees may exercise the right to vote;
    (b)   The Chairman of the Committee of the Whole may declare a meeting open and permit the debate to proceed when representatives of at least one quarter of the States participating in the Conference are present. The presence of representatives of a majority of the States so participating shall be required for any decision to be taken;
    (c)   A majority of the representatives of the General, Drafting or Credentials Committee or of any working group shall constitute a quorum;
    (d)   The Committee of the Whole shall make its best endeavours to ensure that its work is accomplished by general agreement. The Chairman of the Committee of the Whole shall keep the President of the Conference informed of the progress of the work of the Committee. If, in the consideration of any matter of substance, all feasible efforts to reach general agreement have failed, the Chairman of the Committee of the Whole shall consult the other members of its bureau and recommend the steps to be taken, which may include the matter being put to the vote;
    (e)   Subject to subparagraph (d), decisions shall be taken by a majority of the representatives present and voting, except that the reconsideration of a proposal shall require the majority established by rule 33.]

[*16] CHAPTER IX
Languages and records
Rule 53. Languages of the Conference
Arabic, Chinese, English, French, Russian and Spanish shall be the languages of the Conference.
Rule 54. Interpretation
1.   Speeches made in a language of the Conference shall be interpreted into the other such languages.
2.   A representative may speak in a language other than a language of the Conference if the delegation concerned provides for interpretation into one such language.
Rule 55. Languages of official documents
Official documents of the Conference shall be made available in the languages of the Conference.

Rule 56. Records and sound recordings of meetings
1.   Summary records of the plenary meetings of the Conference and of the meetings of the Committee of the Whole shall be kept in the languages of the Conference. As a general rule, they shall be circulated as soon as possible, simultaneously in all the languages of the Conference, to all representatives, who shall inform the secretariat within five working days after the circulation of the summary record of any changes they wish to have made.
2.   The secretariat shall make sound recordings of meetings of the Conference, the Committee of the Whole and the Drafting Committee. Such recordings shall be made of meetings of other committees when the body concerned so decides.

CHAPTER X

Public and private meetings
Rule 57. Plenary meetings and meetings of the Committee of the Whole
The plenary meetings of the Conference and the meetings of the Committee of the Whole shall be held in public unless the body concerned decides otherwise. All decisions taken by the plenary of the Conference at a private meeting shall be announced at an early public meeting of the plenary.
[*17] *Rule 58.   Meetings of other subsidiary bodies*
As a general rule, meetings of other subsidiary bodies shall be held in private.
Rule 59. Communiqués on private meetings
At the close of any private meeting, the chairman of the body concerned may issue a communiqué to the press through the Executive Secretary.

CHAPTER XI

Observers
Rule 60. Representatives of organizations and other entities that have received a standing invitation from the General Assembly pursuant to its relevant resolutions to participate, in the capacity of observers, in its sessions and work
Representatives designated by organizations and other entities that have received a standing invitation from the General Assembly pursuant to its relevant resolutions to participate, in the capacity of observers, in its sessions and work have the right to participate as observers, without the right to vote, in the deliberations of the Conference, the Committee of the Whole and subsidiary bodies established under rule 50.
Rule 61. Representatives of other regional intergovernmental organizations
Representatives designated by other regional intergovernmental organizations invited to the Conference may participate as observers, without the right to vote, in the deliberations of the Conference, the Committee of the Whole and subsidiary bodies established under rule 50.
Rule 62. Representatives of other international bodies
Representatives designated by other international bodies invited to the Conference may participate as observers, without the right to vote, in the deliberations of the Conference, the Committee of the Whole and subsidiary bodies established under rule 50.
Rule 63. Representatives of non-governmental organizations
Non-governmental organizations invited to the Conference may participate in the Conference through their designated representatives as follows:
[*18] (a) By attending plenary meetings of the Conference and, unless otherwise decided by the Conference in specific situations, formal meetings of the Committee of the Whole and of subsidiary bodies established under rule 50;
          (b)   By receiving copies of official documents;
          (c)   Upon the invitation of the President and subject to the approval of the Conference, by making, through a limited number of their representatives, oral statements to the opening and closing sessions of the Conference, as appropriate.

Rule 64. Written statements

Written statements submitted by the designated representatives referred to in rules 60 to 63 shall be made available by the secretariat to delegations in the quantities and in the language or languages in which the statements are made available to it at the site of the Conference, provided that a statement submitted on behalf of a non-governmental organization is related to the work of the Conference and is on a subject in which the organization has a special competence. Written statements shall not be made at United Nations expense and shall not be issued as official documents.

CHAPTER XII

Amendments to the Rules of Procedure

Rule 65. Method of amendment

These Rules of Procedure may be amended by a decision of the Conference taken by a two-thirds majority of the representatives present and voting.

DRAFT REPORT OF THE INTERSESSIONAL MEETING
FROM 19 TO 30 JANUARY 1998 IN ZUTPHEN, THE NETHERLANDS

[Editorial Note - The U.N. pages numbers of this document are indicated in bolded brackets [*] in the text].

[*8] I. INTRODUCTION

1.   At the initiative of the Chairman of the Preparatory Committee, Mr. Adriaan Bos, an intersessional meeting took place in Zutphen, the Netherlands, from 19 to 30 January 1998. The members of the Bureau, Chairs of different Working Groups, Coordinators and the Secretariat participated in the meeting.

2.   The purpose of the meeting was to facilitate the work of the last session of the Preparatory Committee scheduled to take place from 16 March to 3 April 1998 (March/April session) by performing the following tasks:

(a)   considering the structure of the Statute and the placement of the articles;

(b)   identifying relationships between articles, including possible overlaps and inconsistencies; and

(c)   considering the required degree of detail in the articles and whether some articles or their more detailed versions could be placed in an instrument other than the Statute.

3.   Thus far, the Preparatory Committee has considered various parts and articles of the Statute separately and at different stages. Therefore, the Group participating in this intersessional meeting (the Group) found it useful to place before the last session of the Preparatory Committee a complete set of articles so as to provide an overview of the Statute as a whole. Thus, the relationship between the articles may be more easily identified. The present document also contains proposals on articles which have not been discussed in the Preparatory Committee in 1997 in an attempt to present a practical working document for the discussions in the March/April session.

4.   The texts of the articles before the Preparatory Committee may be divided into four categories: texts proposed by the Working Groups of the Preparatory Committee; texts proposed in A/AC.249/1998/WG.7/CRP.1 on Composition and administration of the Court and A/AC.249/1998/ L.11 on Final clauses; texts proposed by the International Law Commission (ILC); and texts proposed by delegations during the 1996 sessions (A/51/22, vol.II) and those submitted during the 1997 sessions of the Preparatory Committee. The texts are included as follows:

(a)   text of articles contained in the reports of the Working Groups (A/AC.249/1997/L.5, L.8/Rev.1 and L.9/Rev.1);

(b)   text of articles contained in A/AC.249/1998/L.11 and A/AC.249/1998/WG.7/CRP.1 in the absence of texts contained in (a);

(c)   text of the ILC draft together with the texts proposed by delegations in 1996-1997 (A/51/22, vol. II and DP series) in the absence of texts contained in (a) and (b); and

[*9] (d)   texts proposed by delegations in 1996-1997 (A/51/22, vol.II and DP series) in the absence of any other texts contained in (a), (b) and the ILC draft.

5.   Comments and suggestions by the Group are indicated by a <u>Nota Bene</u> (N.B.) which appears in bold next to the text to which it applies.

6.   The substance of the articles has not been changed. In some places, the wording of the texts has been slightly modified for the purposes of consistency or of reflecting discussions in the Preparatory Committee. Where suggestions for deletions or adjustments affect phrases and sentences, the latter have been retained but stricken through with the Group's suggestion next to them. Some obviously necessary editorial changes have been made. As far as possible, the format of the texts developed by Working Groups has been harmonized. Some footnotes which had become obsolete in the light of subsequent discussions have been deleted.

7.   The Group suggests that the Statute be entitled "Statute for the International Criminal Court" and be divided as follows:

Preamble

Part 1.   Establishment of the Court

Part 2.   Jurisdiction, admissibility and applicable law
Part 3.   General principles of criminal law
Part 4.   Composition and administration of the Court
Part 5.   Investigation and prosecution
Part 6.   The trial
Part 7.   Penalties
Part 8.   Appeal and review
Part 9.   International cooperation and judicial assistance
Part 10.   Enforcement
Part 11.   Final clauses

8.   The Group's suggestions for titles is an attempt to present the articles in an easily identifiable manner to the Preparatory Committee at the March/April session. Once there is agreement on the contents of the parts and the articles, their titles could be reconsidered.

9.   The Group suggests placing "Jurisdiction, admissibility and applicable law" and "General principles of criminal law" as Parts 2 and 3 because of the substantive issues they address. Thereafter follows Part 4 "Composition and administration of the Court" which addresses more structural and procedural issues. The Group, however, recognizes that there may also be reasonable grounds for placing Part 4 before Part 2.

[*10] 10. In reviewing the articles of the Statute, the Group is of the view that it would be useful to attempt, to the extent possible, to have a balanced Statute in terms of the level of detail in the articles of various Parts. The Group believes that in a number of articles, the principles of the issues with which they deal should be placed in the Statute, while details could more usefully be addressed elsewhere, such as in the Rules. In several places the Group has made suggestions to that effect in a N.B.

11.   Where the Group has identified particular links between the articles, possible overlaps or inconsistencies, they have been indicated in a N.B.

12.   The articles have been renumbered and the text and footnotes adjusted accordingly. Throughout the text, the previous numbers of the parts and articles appear in square brackets next to the new numbers.

13.   For ease of reference, the report also includes a draft final act and a draft resolution for the establishment of a Preparatory Commission, contained in document A/AC.249/1998/L.11, for consideration by the Preparatory Committee.

14.   The Group expresses its appreciation to the Government of the Netherlands for its generosity and hospitality in organizing the intersessional meeting in Zutphen.

[*11] DRAFT STATUTE FOR THE INTERNATIONAL CRIMINAL COURT

PREAMBLE
N.B. The Preamble was not considered by the Prep Com in 1997.

ILC Draft

The States Parties to this Statute,

Desiring to further international cooperation to enhance the effective prosecution and suppression of crimes of international concern, and for that purpose to establish an international criminal court;

Emphasizing that such a court is intended to exercise jurisdiction only over the most serious crimes of concern to the international community as a whole;

Emphasizing further that such a court is intended to be complementary to national criminal justice systems in cases where such trial procedures may not be available or may be ineffective;

Have agreed as follows:

Other proposals contained in A/51/22, vol. II[1]

Desiring to further international cooperation ...;

Emphasizing that such a court is intended ...;

[Recognizing that it is the primary duty of States to bring to justice persons responsible for such serious crimes;]

Emphasizing further that such a court is intended to be complementary to national criminal justice systems [in case where such systems may be ineffective and/or in cases where national jurisdiction is unavailable] [in cases where such trial procedures may not be available or may be ineffective];
  or

Emphasizing further that the international criminal court shall complement national criminal justice systems when they are unable or unwilling to fulfil their obligations to bring to trial such persons;

[*12] PART 1. ESTABLISHMENT OF THE COURT
N.B. The articles in Part 1 were not considered by the Prep Com in 1997.
Article 1
The Court
ILC Draft

There is established an International Criminal Court ("the Court"), whose jurisdiction and functioning shall be governed by the provisions of this Statute.

Other proposals contained in A/51/22, vol.II[2]

There is established an International Criminal Court ("the Court") [which shall be complementary to national criminal justice systems. Its jurisdiction and functions] (whose jurisdiction and functioning) shall be governed by the provisions of this Statute.

* * *

A Permanent International Criminal Court ("the Court"), whose jurisdiction and functioning shall be governed by the provisions of this Statute, is hereby established.

N.B. It might be useful to include in Part 1 an additional article on the organs of the Court, since reference to such organs is already made in articles prior to Part 4 where they are listed in article 29|5|. The content of such an article could be decided upon during the discussions on article 29|5| in the March/April session of the Prep Com. In that case, the text of article 29|5| should be harmonized with the new article.

Article 2
Relationship of the Court with the United Nations[3]
ILC Draft

The President, with the approval of the States parties to this Statute ("States parties"), may conclude an agreement establishing an appropriate relationship between the Court and the United Nations.

[*13] Other proposals contained in A/51/22, vol.II[4]

The Court shall, as soon as possible, be brought into relationship with the United Nations. It shall constitute one of the specialized agencies provided for in Article 57 of the Charter of the United Nations. The relationship shall form the subject of an agreement with the United Nations pursuant to Article 63 of the Charter.

The agreement, proposed by the Presidency of the Court, shall be submitted to the General Assembly of the States parties for approval. It shall provide the means for establishing effective cooperation between the Court and the United Nations in the pursuit of their common aims. It shall, at the same time, set forth the autonomy of the Court in its particular field of competence, as defined in this Statute.

---

[1]   Pp. 1-2.
[2]   P. 3.
[3]   See also A/AC.249/1998/L.10.
[4]   P. 4.

N.B. To the extent that articles 2 and 3 refer to the conclusion of agreements respectively with the United Nations and the host State, relevant provisions to this effect could be better placed in the final clauses.

Article 3

Seat of the Court

ILC Draft

1.   The seat of the Court shall be established at ... in ... ("the host State").
2.   The President, with the approval of the States parties, may conclude an agreement with the host State, establishing the relationship between that State and the Court.
3.   The Court may exercise its powers and functions on the territory of any State party and, by special agreement, on the territory of any other State.

Other proposals contained in A/51/22, vol. II[5]

1.   ~~The seat of the Court shall be established at ... in ... ("the host State").~~
        The Presidency of the Court shall submit for the approval of the General Assembly of the States parties an agreement establishing relations between the host State and the Court.
[*14] ~~2.   The Court may also, for a particular case and when travel by the members of the Court is likely to make the proceedings simpler and less costly, sit in a State party other than the host State.~~
~~   The Presidency of the Court shall make inquiries with the State party that appears likely to receive the Court.~~
~~   After the State party likely to receive the Court has agreed, the decision under the preceding paragraph to hold a session away from the Court's seat shall be taken by the General Assembly of the States parties, which shall be informed either by one of its members, the Presidency, the Prosecutor or the General Assembly of Judges of the Court.~~
~~   With the express agreement of the State party receiving the Court, the privileges, immunities and facilities provided for in article x shall continue to be effective when the Court holds a session pursuant to the three preceding subparagraphs.~~
~~3.   The provisions of paragraph 2 of this article shall also apply to non-party States which, after inquiries by the Presidency, state that they agree to receive the Court and to grant the privileges, immunities and facilities provided for in article x.~~
N.B. Article 55[32] (Place of trial), under "Other proposals", contains proposals similar to the deleted texts. Article 55[32] and the Rules might be more appropriate to deal with the issues raised in the deleted texts.

Article 4

Status and legal capacity

ILC Draft

1.   The Court is a permanent institution open to States parties in accordance with this Statute. It shall act when required to consider a case submitted to it.
2.   The Court shall enjoy in the territory of each State party such legal capacity as may be necessary for the exercise of its functions and the fulfilment of its purposes.

Other proposals contained in A/51/22, vol. II[6]

1.   The Court is a permanent institution open to States parties under the conditions set out in this Statute. It shall act when required to consider a case submitted to it.
[*15] 2.   Without prejudice to the provisions of paragraph 1 of this article, the Presidency, the Preliminary Investigations Chambers, the Procuracy and the Registry shall perform their functions at the Court on a permanent basis.

---

⁵   P. 5.
⁶   P. 6.

3.   When the Presidency considers that the Court's case-load requires the permanent presence of all the judges of the Court, it shall so inform the General Assembly of the States parties, which may decide that all judges shall perform their duties full-time, for a period determined by the General Assembly or until further notice.

N.B. A number of issues raised in paragraphs 2 and 3 could more appropriately be considered in connection with Part 4.

[*16] PART 2. JURISDICTION, ADMISSIBILITY AND APPLICABLE LAW
Article 5[20]
Crimes within the jurisdiction of Court

N.B. The text of this introductory article as such was not considered by the Prep Com in 1997.

ILC Draft

The Court has jurisdiction in accordance with this Statute with respect to the following crimes:

(a)   the crime of genocide;

(b)   the crime of aggression;

(c)   serious violations of the laws and customs applicable in armed conflict;

(d)   crimes against humanity;

(e)   crimes, established under or pursuant to the treaty provisions listed in the Annex,[7] which, having regard to the conduct alleged, constitute exceptionally serious crimes of international concern.

Other proposals contained in A/51/22, vol II[8]

The Court has jurisdiction in accordance with this Statute with respect to the following crimes:

(a)   the crime of genocide;

(b)   crimes against humanity;

(c)   the crime of aggression;

(d)   serious violations of the laws and customs applicable in armed conflicts;

(e)   - grave breaches of the four Geneva Conventions of 12 August 1949;

        - grave breaches of article 3 common to the four Geneva Conventions of 12 August 1949.

[*17] N.B.

-        **It might be useful to start this Part with an article listing the crimes within the jurisdiction of the Court along the lines of the ILC draft. In light of subsequent discussions, the reference in paragraph (c) should be changed to "war crimes".**

-        **Once a decision is made as to which crimes should be included in the draft Statute, the paragraphs of this introductory article should be adjusted and the subsequent provisions placed in separate articles and numbered accordingly.**

-        **It might be necessary to have a cross-reference to article 63[44 bis] (Offences against the integrity of the Court) in this Part.**

---

7   See appendix II of the annex to the ILC Draft.

8   P. 55.

Crime of genocide[9]

For the purpose of the present Statute, the crime of genocide means any of the following acts committed with intent[10] to destroy, in whole or in part, a national, ethnical, racial or religious group,[11] as such:[12]

[*18] (a) Killing members of the group;

 (b) Causing serious bodily or mental harm[13] to members of the group;

 (c) Deliberately inflicting on the group conditions of life calculated to bring about its physical destruction in whole or in part;

 (d) Imposing measures intended to prevent births within the group;

 (e) Forcibly transferring children of the group to another group;

[The following acts shall be punishable:

 (a) Genocide;

 (b) Conspiracy to commit genocide;

 (c) Direct and public incitement to commit genocide;

 (d) Attempt to commit genocide;

 (e) Complicity in genocide.][14]

[*19] [[15] Crime of aggression[16] [17]

Note: This draft is without prejudice to the discussion of the issue of the relationship of the Security Council with the International Criminal Court with respect to aggression as dealt with in article 10[23].

1. [For the purpose of the present Statute, the crime [of aggression] [against peace] means any of the following acts committed by an individual [who is in a position of exercising control or capable of directing political/military action in a State]:

---

 [9] See A/AC.249/1997/L.5, p. 3.

 [10] The reference to "intent to destroy, in whole or in part ... a group, as such" was understood to refer to the specific intention to destroy more than a small number of individuals who are members of a group.

 [11] The Working Group took note of the suggestion to examine the possibility of addressing "social and political" groups in the context of crimes against humanity.
N.B. The need for this footnote should be reviewed in the light of the discussions that have taken place in respect of crimes against humanity.

 [12] The Working Group noted that with respect to the interpretation and application of the provisions concerning the crimes within the jurisdiction of the Court, the Court shall apply relevant international conventions and other sources of international law.

In this regard, the Working Group noted that for purposes of interpreting the present article it may be necessary to consider other relevant provisions contained in the Convention on the Prevention and Punishment of the Crime of Genocide, as well as other sources of international law. For example, article I would determine the question of whether the crime of genocide set forth in the present article could be committed in time of peace or in time of war.

~~Furthermore, article IV would determine the question of whether persons committing genocide or other acts enumerated in the present article [article III of the Genocide Convention] shall be punished irrespective of their status as constitutionally responsible rulers, public officials or private individuals.~~
N.B. The issue of irrelevance of official position has been dealt with in article 18[B.e.] (Irrelevance of official position).

The interrelationship between the various articles of the present Statute would need to be examined in the next phase of the work. For example, the matters dealt with in the first to third paragraphs of the present note would need to be considered in relation to article 14[33] (Applicable law) of the Statute and the provisions dealing with principles of criminal law.

 [13] The reference to "mental harm" is understood to mean more than the minor or temporary impairment of mental faculties.

 [14] The Working Group will return to the question of the placement of article III of the Genocide Convention once the Working Group on general principles of criminal law has considered this issue in the context of its work.
N.B. See also article 17[B a.to d.] (Individual criminal responsibility).

 [15] This square bracket closes at the end of paragraph 2.

 [16] A/AC.249/1997/L.5, p.14.

 [17] The proposal reflects the view held by a large number of delegations that the crime of aggression should be included in the statute.

The Working Group considered this crime without prejudice to a final decision on its inclusion in the statute.

(a) planning,

(b) preparing,

(c) ordering,

(d) initiating, or

(e) carrying out

[an armed attack] [the use of armed force] [a war of aggression,] [a war of aggression, or a war in violation of international treaties, agreements or assurances, or participation in a common plan or conspiracy for the accomplishment of any of the foregoing] by a State against the [sovereignty,] territorial integrity [or political independence] of another State [when this] [armed attack] [use of force] [is] [in contravention of the Charter of the United Nations] [[in contravention of the Charter of the United Nations as determined by the Security Council].]

[For the purposes of this Statute, the crime of aggression is committed by a person who is in a position of exercising control or capable of directing political/military actions in his State, against another State, in contravention to the Charter of the United Nations, by resorting to armed force, to threaten or violate the sovereignty, territorial integrity or political independence of that State.]

[*20] [2. [Acts constituting [aggression] [armed attack] include the following:][18]

[Provided that the acts concerned or their consequences are of sufficient gravity, acts constituting aggression [are] [include] the following:]

(a) the invasion or attack by the armed forces of a State of the territory of another State, or any military occupation, however temporary, resulting from such invasion or attack, or any annexation by the use of force of the territory of another State or part thereof;

(b) bombardment by the armed forces of a State against the territory of another State [, or the use of any weapons by a State against the territory of another State];

(c) the blockade of the ports or coasts of a State by the armed forces of another State;

(d) an attack by the armed forces of a State on the land, sea or air forces, or marine and air fleets of another State;

(e) the use of armed forces of one State which are within the territory of another State with the agreement of the receiving State in contravention of the conditions provided for in the agreement, or any extension of their presence in such territory beyond their termination of the agreement;

(f) the action of a State in allowing its territory, which it has placed at the disposal of another State, to be used by that other State for perpetrating an act of aggression against a third State;

(g) the sending by or on behalf of a State of armed bands, groups, irregulars or mercenaries, which carry out acts of armed force against another State of such gravity as to amount to the acts listed above, or its substantial involvement therein.]]

N.B. Since the report of the Working Group (A/AC.249/1997/L.5), there have been consultations among delegations on the crime of aggression; see A/AC.249/1997/WG.1/DP.20.

[*21] <u>War crimes</u>[19] [20]

For the purpose of ~~this~~ the present Statute, war crimes means: ~~the crimes listed in this article.~~

N.B. The opening clause has been harmonized with the opening clauses of the previous provisions.

<u>A</u>.   Grave breaches of the Geneva Conventions of 12 August 1949, namely, any of the following acts against persons or property protected under the provisions of the relevant Geneva Convention:

(a) wilful killing;

(b) torture or inhuman treatment, including biological experiments;

(c) wilfully causing great suffering, or serious injury to body or health;

---

[18]   Paragraph 2 of the text reflects the view held by some delegations that the definition should include an enumeration of the acts constituting aggression.

[19]   A/AC.249/1997/L.9/Rev.1, p.3.

[20]   Views were expressed that certain provisions should be placed within square brackets. The relative placement of the various options does not indicate in any way the measure of support for such options. Some options commanded very limited support.

(d)   extensive destruction and appropriation of property, not justified by military necessity and carried out unlawfully and wantonly;

(e)   compelling a prisoner of war or other protected person to serve in the forces of a hostile Power;

(f)   wilfully depriving a prisoner of war or other protected person of the rights of fair and regular trial;

(g)   unlawful deportation or transfer or unlawful confinement;

(h)   taking of hostages.

B.   Other serious violations of the laws and customs applicable in international armed conflict within the established framework of international law, namely, any of the following acts:

(a)

Option 1

intentionally directing attacks against the civilian population as such, as well as individual civilians not taking direct part in hostilities;

[*22] Option 2

No paragraph (a).

(a bis)

Option 1

intentionally directing attacks against civilian objects which are not military objectives;

Option 2

No paragraph (a bis).

(b)

Option 1

intentionally launching an attack in the knowledge that such attack will cause incidental loss of life or injury to civilians or damage to civilian objects or widespread, long-term and severe damage to the natural environment which is not justified by military necessity;[21]

Option 2

intentionally launching an attack in the knowledge that such attack will cause incidental loss of life or injury to civilians or damage to civilian objects or widespread, long-term and severe damage to the natural environment which would be excessive in relation to the concrete and direct overall military advantage anticipated;[22]

Option 3

intentionally launching an attack in the knowledge that such attack will cause incidental loss of life or injury to civilians or damage to [*23] civilian objects or widespread, long-term and severe damage to the natural environment;[23]

Option 4

No paragraph (b).

(b bis)

Option 1

intentionally launching an attack against works or installations containing dangerous forces in the knowledge that such attack will cause excessive loss of life, injury to civilians or damage to civilian objects which would be excessive in relation to the concrete and direct military advantage anticipated;

---

[21]   It has been accepted that it will be necessary to insert a provision, probably in the general principles section, which sets out the elements of knowledge and intent which must be found to have existed for an accused to be convicted of a war crime. For example: "in order to conclude that an accused had the knowledge and criminal intention required to be convicted of a crime, the Court must first determine that, taking account of the relevant circumstances of, and information available to, the accused at the time, the accused had the requisite knowledge and intent to commit the crime."
N.B. With respect to this footnote see, however, articles 23[H] (Mens rea (mental elements)) and 24[K] (Mistake of fact or of law) which deal with similar issues.

[22]   Ibid.

[23]   Ibid.

Option 2
    No paragraph (b <u>bis</u>).
    (c)
Option 1
    attacking or bombarding, by whatever means, towns, villages, dwellings or buildings which are undefended;
Option 2
    making non-defended localities and demilitarized zones the objects of attack;
    (d) killing or wounding a combatant who, having laid down his arms or having no longer means of defence, has surrendered at discretion;
    (e) making improper use of flag of truce, of the flag or of the military insignia and uniform of the enemy or of the United Nations, as well as of the distinctive emblems of the Geneva Conventions, resulting in death or serious personal injury;
    (f)
Option 1
    the transfer by the Occupying Power of parts of its own civilian population into the territory it occupies;
[*24] Option 2
    the transfer by the Occupying Power of parts of its own civilian population into the territory it occupies, or the deportation or transfer of all or parts of the population of the occupied territory within or outside this territory;
Option 3
    (i)   the establishment of settlers in an occupied territory and changes to the demographic composition of an occupied territory;
    (ii) the transfer by the Occupying Power of parts of its own civilian population into the territory it occupies, or the deportation or transfer of all or parts of the population of the occupied territory within or outside this territory;
Option 4
    No paragraph (f).
    (g)
Option 1
    intentionally directing attacks against buildings dedicated to religion, art, science or charitable purposes, historic monuments, hospitals and places where the sick and wounded are collected, provided they are not being used at the time for military purposes;
Option 2
    intentionally directing attacks against buildings dedicated to religion, education, art, science or charitable purposes, historic monuments, hospitals and places where the sick and wounded are collected, provided they are not being used at the time for military purposes;
    (h) subjecting persons who are in the power of an adverse Party to physical mutilation or to medical or scientific experiments of any kind which are neither justified by the medical, dental or hospital treatment of the person concerned nor carried out in his interest, and which cause death to or seriously endanger the health of such person or person;
    (i)   killing or wounding treacherously individuals belonging to the hostile nation or army;
    (j)   declaring that no quarter will be given;
    (k) destroying or seizing the enemy's property unless such destruction or seizure be imperatively demanded by the necessities of war;
[*25] (l) declaring abolished, suspended or inadmissible in a court of law the rights and actions of the nationals of the hostile party;
    (m) compelling the nationals of the hostile party to take part in the operations of war directed against their own country, even if they were in the belligerent's service before the commencement of the war;
    (n) pillaging a town or place, even when taken by assault;

(o)

Option 1

employing the following weapons, projectiles and material and methods of warfare which are calculated to cause superfluous injury or unnecessary suffering:

    (i)   poison or poisoned weapons,

    (ii) asphyxiating, poisonous or other gases, and all analogous liquids, materials or devices,

    (iii) bullets which expand or flatten easily in the human body, such as bullets with a hard envelope which does not entirely cover the core or is pierced with incisions,

    (iv) bacteriological (biological) agents or toxins for hostile purposes or in armed conflict,

    (v) chemical weapons as defined in and prohibited by the 1993 Convention on the Prohibition of the Development, Production, Stockpiling and Use of Chemical Weapons and On Their Destruction;

Option 2

employing the following weapons, projectiles and material and methods of warfare which are of a nature to cause superfluous injury or unnecessary suffering:

    (i)   poison or poisoned weapons,

    (ii) asphyxiating, poisonous or other gases, and all analogous liquids, materials or devices,

    (iii) bullets which expand or flatten easily in the human body, such as bullets with a hard envelope which does not entirely cover the core or is pierced with incisions,

    (iv) bacteriological (biological) agents or toxins for hostile purposes or in armed conflict,

[*26]   (v) chemical weapons as defined in and prohibited by the 1993 Convention on the Prohibition of the Development, Production, Stockpiling and Use of Chemical Weapons and On Their Destruction,

    (vi) such other weapons or weapons systems as become the subject of a comprehensive prohibition pursuant to customary or conventional international law;

Option 3

employing weapons, projectiles and material and methods of warfare which are of a nature to cause superfluous injury or unnecessary suffering or which are inherently indiscriminate;

Option 4

employing the following weapons, projectiles and material and methods of warfare which are of a nature to cause superfluous injury or unnecessary suffering or which are inherently indiscriminate:

or

employing weapons, projectiles and material and methods of warfare which are of a nature to cause superfluous injury or unnecessary suffering or which are inherently indiscriminate, such as but not limited to:

    (i)   poison or poisoned weapons,

    (ii) asphyxiating, poisonous or other gases, and all analogous liquids, materials or devices,

    (iii) bullets which expand or flatten easily in the human body, such as bullets with a hard envelope which does not entirely cover the core or is pierced with incisions,

    (iv) bacteriological (biological) agents or toxins for hostile purposes or in armed conflict,

    (v) chemical weapons as defined in and prohibited by the 1993 Convention on the Prohibition of the Development, Production, Stockpiling and Use of Chemical Weapons and On Their Destruction,

    (vi) nuclear weapons,

    (vii) anti-personnel mines,

    (viii) blinding laser weapons,

[*27] (ix) such other weapons or weapons systems as become the subject of a comprehensive prohibition pursuant to customary or conventional international law;

(p)

Option 1

committing outrages upon personal dignity, in particular humiliating and degrading treatment;

Option 2

committing outrages upon personal dignity, in particular humiliating and degrading treatment as well as practices of apartheid and other inhuman and degrading practices involving outrages upon personal dignity based on racial discrimination;

(p bis) committing rape, sexual slavery, enforced prostitution, enforced pregnancy, enforced sterilization, and any other form of sexual violence also constituting a grave breach of the Geneva Conventions;

(q) utilizing the presence of a civilian or other protected person to render certain points, areas or military forces immune from military operations;

(r) intentionally directing attacks against buildings, material, medical units and transport, and personnel using, in conformity with international law, the distinctive emblems of the Geneva Conventions;

(s) intentionally using starvation of civilians as a method of warfare by depriving them of objects indispensable to their survival, including wilfully impeding relief supplies as provided for under the Geneva Conventions;

(t)

Option 1

forcing children under the age of fifteen years to take direct part in hostilities.

Option 2

recruiting children under the age of fifteen years into armed forces.

Option 3

allowing children under the age of fifteen years to take direct part in hostilities.

[*28] Option 4

(i) recruiting children under the age of fifteen years into armed forces or groups; or

(ii) allowing them to take part in hostilities;

Option 5

No paragraph (t).

* * *

OPTION I

Sections C and D of this article apply to armed conflicts not of an international character and thus do not apply to situations of internal disturbances and tensions, such as riots, isolated and sporadic acts of violence or other acts of a similar nature.

C.   In the case of an armed conflict not of an international character, serious violations of article 3 common to the four Geneva Conventions of 12 August 1949, namely, any of the following acts committed against persons taking no active part in the hostilities, including members of armed forces who have laid down their arms and those placed *hors de combat* by sickness, wounds, detention or any other cause:

(a) violence to life and person, in particular murder of all kinds, mutilation, cruel treatment and torture;

(b) committing outrages upon personal dignity, in particular humiliating and degrading treatment;

(c) taking of hostages;

(d) the passing of sentences and the carrying out of executions without previous judgement pronounced by a regularly constituted court, affording all judicial guarantees which are generally recognized as indispensable.

D.   Other serious violations of the laws and customs applicable in armed conflicts not of an international character, within the established framework of international law, namely, any of the following acts:

(a)

Option 1

intentionally directing attacks against the civilian population as such, as well as individual civilians not taking direct part in hostilities;

[*29] Option 2

No paragraph (a).

(b)   intentionally directing attacks against buildings, material, medical units and transport, and personnel using, in conformity with international law, the distinctive emblems of the Geneva Conventions;
(c)
Option 1
intentionally directing attacks against buildings dedicated to religion, art, science or charitable purposes, historic monuments, hospitals and places where the sick and wounded are collected, provided they are not being used at the time for military purposes;
Option 2
intentionally directing attacks against buildings dedicated to religion, education, art, science or charitable purposes, historic monuments, hospitals and places where the sick and wounded are collected, provided they are not being used at the time for military purposes;
(d)   pillaging a town or place, even when taken by assault;
(e)   committing outrages upon personal dignity, in particular humiliating and degrading treatment;
(e bis)   committing rape, sexual slavery, enforced prostitution, enforced pregnancy, enforced sterilization, and any other form of sexual violence also constituting a serious violation of article 3 common to the four Geneva Conventions;
(f)
Option 1
forcing children under the age of fifteen years to take direct part in hostilities;
Option 2
recruiting children under the age of fifteen years into armed forces or groups;
Option 3
      (i)   recruiting children under the age of fifteen years into armed forces or groups; or
[*30]   (ii)   allowing them to take part in hostilities;
Option 4
No paragraph (f).
(g)   ordering the displacement of the civilian population for reasons related to the conflict, unless the security of the civilians involved or imperative military reasons so demand;
(h)   killing or wounding treacherously a combatant adversary;
(i)   declaring that no quarter will be given;
(j)   subjecting persons who are in the power of another Party to the conflict to physical mutilation or to medical or scientific experiments of any kind which are neither justified by the medical, dental or hospital treatment of the person concerned nor carried out in his interest, and which cause death to or seriously endanger the health of such person or persons;
(k)   destroying or seizing the property of an adversary unless such destruction or seizure be imperatively demanded by the necessities of the conflict;
(l)
Option 1
No provision on prohibited weapons.
Option 2
A reference to arms, in the light of the discussions on paragraph B(o).
OPTION II
Insert the following provisions in section D:
-   intentionally using starvation of civilians as a method of warfare by depriving them of objects indispensable to their survival, including wilfully impeding relief supplies as provided for under the Geneva Conventions;
-   intentionally launching an attack in the knowledge that such attack will cause incidental loss of life or injury to civilians or damage to civilian objects or widespread, long-term and severe damage to the natural environment;
-   intentionally launching an attack against works or installations containing dangerous forces in the knowledge that such attack will cause excessive loss of life, injury to civilians or damage to [*31]

civilian objects which would be excessive in relation to the concrete and direct military advantage anticipated;

- slavery and the slave trade in all their forms;

OPTION III

Delete the opening clause of sections C and D.

OPTION IV

Delete section D.

OPTION V

Delete sections C and D.

* * *

Elsewhere in the Statute:

Option 1

The jurisdiction of the Court shall extend to the most serious crimes of concern to the international community as a whole. The Court shall have jurisdiction in respect of the crimes listed in article X (war crimes) only when committed as part of a plan or policy or as part of a large-scale commission of such crimes.[24]

Option 2

The jurisdiction of the Court shall be limited to the most serious crimes of concern to the international community as a whole. The Court shall have jurisdiction in respect of the crimes listed in article X (war crimes) in particular when committed as a part of a plan or policy or as part of a large-scale commission of such crimes.[2]

Option 3

No provision on threshold.

* * *

Article Y

(relating to the part of the Statute dealing with the definition of crimes)

[*32] Without prejudice to the application of the provisions of this Statute, nothing in this part of the Statute shall be interpreted as limiting or prejudicing in any way existing or developing rules of international law.

N.B.

- **Article Y could constitute a separate article or could be placed in article 5[20] (Crimes within the jurisdiction of the Court).**

- **Article 15[A] (3) (Nullum crimen sine lege) and article 14[33] (Applicable law) deal with related issues.**

Crimes against humanity[25]

1. For the purpose of the present Statute, ~~any of the following acts constitutes a crime against humanity when committed~~ a crime against humanity means any of the following acts when committed

N.B. This opening clause has been harmonized with the opening clauses of the previous provisions.

[as part of a widespread [and] [or] systematic commission of such acts against any population]:

[as part of a widespread [and] [or] systematic attack against any [civilian] population] [committed on a massive scale] [in armed conflict] [on political, philosophical, racial, ethnic or religious grounds or any other arbitrarily defined grounds]:

N.B. In case the second alternative is retained, its relationship with subparagraph 1(h) should be considered.

    (a) murder;

    (b) extermination;

    (c) enslavement;

---

[24] The view was expressed that the substance and placement of this proposal should be considered.

[25] A/AC.249/1997/L.5, p.4.

(d) deportation or forcible transfer of population;

(e) [detention or] [imprisonment] [deprivation of liberty] [in flagrant violation of international law] [in violation of fundamental legal norms];[26]

(f) torture;

[*33] (g) rape or other sexual abuse [of comparable gravity,] or enforced prostitution;

(h) persecution against any identifiable group or collectivity on political, racial, national, ethnic, cultural or religious [or gender] [or other similar] grounds[27] [and in connection with other crimes within the jurisdiction of the Court];

(i) enforced disappearance of persons;[28]

(j) other inhumane acts [of a similar character] [intentionally] causing [great suffering,] or serious injury to body or to mental or physical health.[29]

[2. For the purpose of paragraph 1:

(a) extermination includes the [wilful, intentional] infliction of conditions of life calculated to bring about the destruction of part of a population;

(b) "deportation or forcible transfer of population" means the movement of [persons] [populations] from the area in which the [persons] [populations] are [lawfully present] [present] [resident] [under national or international law] [for a purpose contrary to international law] [without legitimate and compelling reasons] [without lawful justification];

(c) ["torture" means the intentional infliction of severe pain or suffering, whether physical or mental, upon a person [in the custody or physical control of the accused] [deprived of liberty]; except that torture shall not include pain or suffering arising only from, inherent in or incidental to, lawful sanctions [in conformity with international law]]

["torture" as defined in the Convention against Torture and Other Cruel, Inhuman or Degrading Treatment or Punishment of 10 December 1984];

(d) persecution means the wilful and severe deprivation of fundamental rights contrary to international law [carried out with the intent to persecute on specified grounds];

(e) ["enforced disappearance of persons" means when persons are arrested, detained or abducted against their will by or with the authorization, support or acquiescence of the State or a political organization, followed by a refusal to [*34] acknowledge that deprivation of freedom or to give information on the fate or whereabouts of those persons, thereby placing them outside the protection of the law]

["enforced disappearance of persons" as defined in the Inter-American Convention on the Forced Disappearance of Persons of 9 June 1994, as referred to in the Declaration on the Protection of All Persons from Enforced Disappearance (General Assembly resolution 47/133 of 18 December 1992)].

*30

[Crimes of terrorism[31]

~~The Court has jurisdiction with respect to the following terrorist crimes:~~ For the purposes of the present Statute, crimes of terrorism means:

N.B. This opening clause has been harmonized with the opening clauses of the previous provisions.

---

[26] It was suggested that this subparagraph does not include freedom of speech and that it includes the unilateral blockade of populations.

[27] This also includes, for example, social, economic and mental or physical disability grounds.

[28] It was suggested that some more time was needed to reflect upon the inclusion of this subparagraph.

[29] It was suggested that the inclusion of this paragraph should be subject to further clarification. It was also suggested that the list of acts should include institutionalized discrimination.

[30] The Working Group considered the following three crimes (crimes of terrorism, crimes against United Nations and associated personnel and crimes involving the illicit traffic in narcotic drugs and psychotropic substances) without prejudice to a final decision on their inclusion in the statute. The Working Group also discussed these three crimes only in a general manner and did not have time to examine them as thoroughly as the other crimes.

[31] A/AC.249/1997/L.5, p. 16.

(1)   Undertaking, organizing, sponsoring, ordering, facilitating, financing, encouraging or tolerating acts of violence against another State directed at persons or property and of such a nature as to create terror, fear or insecurity in the minds of public figures, groups of persons, the general public or populations, for whatever considerations and purposes of a political, philosophical, ideological, racial, ethnic, religious or such other nature that may be invoked to justify them;

(2)   An offence under the following Conventions:

    (a)   Convention for the Suppression of Unlawful Acts against the Safety of Civil Aviation;

    (b)   Convention for the Suppression of Unlawful Seizure of Aircraft;

    (c)   Convention on the Prevention and Punishment of Crimes against Internationally Protected Persons, including Diplomatic Agents;

    (d)   International Convention against the Taking of Hostages;

    (e)   Convention for the Suppression of Unlawful Acts against the Safety of Maritime Navigation;

[*35] (f)   Protocol for the Suppression of Unlawful Acts against the Safety of Fixed Platforms located on the Continental Shelf;

(3)   An offence involving use of firearms, weapons, explosives and dangerous substances when used as a means to perpetrate indiscriminate violence involving death or serious bodily injury to persons or groups of persons or populations or serious damage to property.]

[Crimes against United Nations and associated personnel[32]

1.   For the purpose of the present Statute, "crimes against United Nations and associated personnel" means any of the following acts [when committed intentionally and in a systematic manner or on a large scale against United Nations and associated personnel involved in a United Nations operation with a view to preventing or impeding that operation from fulfilling its mandate]:

    (a)   murder, kidnapping or other attack upon the person or liberty of any such personnel;

    (b)   violent attack upon the official premises, the private accommodation or the means of transportation of any such personnel likely to endanger his or her person or liberty.

2.   This article shall not apply to a United Nations operation authorized by the Security Council as an enforcement action under Chapter VII of the Charter of the United Nations in which any of the personnel are engaged as combatants against organized armed forces and to which the law of international armed conflict applies.]

[Crimes involving the illicit traffic in narcotic
drugs and psychotropic substances][33]
Article 6[21][34]
[Exercise of jurisdiction] [Preconditions
to the exercise of jurisdiction]

1.   The Court [may exercise its] [shall have] jurisdiction [over a person] with respect to a crime referred to in article 5[20] [(a) to (e) or any combination thereof] [and in accordance with the provisions of this Statute] if:

[*36] [(a)   the [matter] [situation] is referred to the Court by the Security Council, [in accordance with article 10[23]] [acting under Chapter VII of the Charter];]

    (b)   a complaint is lodged by a State Party [two State Parties] [or a non-State Party] in accordance with article 45[25];

    [(c)   the matter is brought by the Prosecutor, in accordance with article 46[25 bis].]

[2.   [In the case of subparagraphs 1 (b) [and (c)],] the Court [may exercise its] [shall have] jurisdiction [only if the States which have jurisdiction over the case in question have accepted the jurisdiction of the Court in accordance with article 9[22] and] [if national jurisdiction is either not available or ineffective]

---

[32]   A/AC.249/1997/L.5, p. 16.
[33]   A/AC.249/1997/L.5, p. 17.
[34]   A/AC.249/1997/L.8/Rev.1, p. 3.

[in accordance with article 11[35]] or if [an interested State] [interested States] [those States] have deferred the matter to the Court.]

[35 Article 7[21 bis]36
Preconditions to the exercise of jurisdiction

Opening clause of paragraph 1

Option 137

[In the case of article 6[21], subparagraphs 1 (b) [and (c)],] The Court [may exercise its] [shall have] jurisdiction [over a person] if the following State(s) has/have accepted [the exercise of] the jurisdiction of the Court over the crimes referred to in [article 5[20] (a) to (e) or any combination thereof] in accordance with article 9[22]:

Option 2

[In the case of article 6[21], subparagraphs 1 (b) [and (c)],] the Court [may exercise its] [shall have] jurisdiction [over a person] if the following State(s) has/have accepted the exercise of the jurisdiction of the Court with respect to a case in question which is the subject of a complaint lodged by a State:

[*37] [(a) the State that has custody of the suspect with respect to the crime ("custodial State")] [by the State on whose territory the person is resident at the time the complaint is lodged] [in accordance with international law];]

[(b) the State on the territory of which the act [or omission] in question occurred [or if the crime was committed on board a vessel or aircraft, the State of registration of that vessel or aircraft;]

[(c) if applicable, the State that has requested, under an international agreement, the custodial State to surrender a suspect for the purposes of prosecution, [unless the request is rejected];]

[(d) the State of which the victim is a national;]

[(e) the State of which the [accused] [suspect] of the crime is a national;]

[2.   If a State whose acceptance is required for the exercise of the jurisdiction by the Court rejects such acceptance, that State shall so inform the Court [giving reasons thereof].]38

[3.   Notwithstanding paragraph 1, if a State whose acceptance is required has not indicated whether it gives such acceptance or not within a period of (...), then the Court [may] [may not] exercise its jurisdiction accordingly.]39

[4.   When a State that is not a Party to the Statute has an interest in the acts mentioned in the complaint, this State may, by an express declaration deposited with the Registrar of the Court, agree that the Court shall exercise jurisdiction in respect of the acts specified in the declaration.]]

[40 Article 8[21 ter]41 42
Temporal jurisdiction

N.B. This title is suggested if the article is retained.

1.   The Court has jurisdiction only in respect of crimes committed after the date of entry into force of this Statute.

---

35   This square bracket ends at the end of article 7[21 bis].
36   A/AC.249/1997/L.8/Rev.1, p. 3.
37   Options are not put in square brackets because they are alternatives supported by only some delegations. Some other delegations suggested the deletion of one or more of the options or have suggested other changes within the options.
38   This paragraph is relevant only to option 2 of the opening clause to paragraph 1.
39   Ibid.
40   This square bracket ends at the end of article 8[21 ter].
41   The issues raised in this article deserve further reflection as to its place in the Statute.
42   A/AC.249/1997/L.8/Rev.1, p. 5.

[*38] [When a State becomes a Party to this Statute after its entry into force, the Court cannot be seized in respect of crimes committed by its nationals or on its territory or against its nationals, unless those crimes have been committed after the deposit by that State of its instrument of ratification or accession.]
[2.   The Court has no jurisdiction in respect of crimes for which, even if they have been committed after the entry into force of this Statute, the Security Council, acting under Chapter VII of the Charter of the United Nations, has decided before the entry into force of this Statute to establish an ad hoc international criminal tribunal. The Security Council may, however, decide otherwise.]]
N.B. There is an interrelationship between this article and article 16[A bis](Non-retroactivity).

[43 Article 9[22]44
Acceptance of the jurisdiction of the Court

Option 1[45]
1.   A State that becomes a Party to this Statute thereby accepts the [inherent] jurisdiction of the Court with respect to the crimes referred to in article 5[20], paragraphs [(a) to (d) or any combination thereof].
2.   With regard to the crimes referred to in article 5[20] other than those mentioned in paragraph 1, a State Party to this Statute may declare:
    (a)   at the time it expresses its consent to be bound by the Statute; or
    (b)   at a later time that it accepts the jurisdiction of the Court with respect to such of the crimes as it specifies in the declaration.
3.   If under article 7[21 bis] the acceptance of a State that is not a Party to this Statute is required, that State may, by declaration lodged with the Registrar, consent to the exercise of jurisdiction by the Court with respect to the crime. [The accepting State will cooperate with the Court without any delay or exception, in accordance with Part 9[7] of the Statute.]
Option 2
1.   A State Party to this Statute may:
[*39] (a) at the time it expresses its consent to be bound by the Statute, by declaration lodged with the depositary; or
    (b)   at a later time, by declaration lodged with the Registrar;
accept the jurisdiction of the Court with respect to [such of] the crimes referred to in [article 5[20] (a) to (e) or any combination thereof] as it specifies in the declaration.
2.   A declaration may be of general application, or may be limited to [particular conduct or to conduct] [one or more of the crimes referred to in article 5[20] (a) to (e)] committed during a particular period of time.[46]
3.   A declaration may be made for a specified period, in which case it may not be withdrawn before the end of that period, or for an unspecified period, in which case it may be withdrawn only upon giving a six month's notice of withdrawal to the Registrar. Withdrawal does not affect proceedings already commenced under this Statute.[47]
4.   If under article 7[21 bis] the acceptance of a State that is not a Party to this Statute is required, that State may, by declaration lodged with the Registrar, consent to the exercise of jurisdiction by the Court with respect to the crime. [The accepting State will cooperate with the Court without any delay or exception, in accordance with Part 9 [7] of the Statute.]
[5.   A declaration referred to in paragraphs 1 to 3 may not contain other limitations than those mentioned in paragraphs 1 to 3.]]

---

[43]   The square bracket ends at the end of paragraph 5 of this article.
[44]   A/AC.249/1997/L.8/Rev.1, p. 5.
[45]   Options 1 and 2 are not mutually exclusive and could be combined in such a way that option 1 may be used in respect of some crimes and option 2 in respect of other crimes.
[46]   This paragraph may also apply to option 1.
[47]   Ibid.

[[48] Article 10[23][49]

[[Action by] [Role of] The Security Council] [Relationship between the Security Council and the International Criminal Court]

1.   [Notwithstanding article 6[21], [7[21 bis]] [and [9[22]], the Court has jurisdiction in accordance with this Statute with respect to crimes [referred to] [specified] in article 5[20] [as a consequence of the referral of] [on the basis of a [formal] decision to refer] a [matter] [situation] in which one or more crimes appear to have been committed to [the Prosecutor of] the Court by the Security Council [acting under Chapter VII of the Charter of the United Nations] [in accordance with the terms of such referral].

[*40] 1 bis. [Notification of] [A letter from the President of the Security Council conveying] the Security Council decision to the Prosecutor of the Court shall be accompanied by all supporting material available to the Council.]

1 ter. The Security Council, on the basis of a formal decision under Chapter VI of the Charter of the United Nations, may lodge a complaint with the Prosecutor specifying that crimes referred to in article 5[20] appear to have been committed.]

2. Option 1
      [A complaint of or directly related to [an act] [a crime] of aggression [referred to in article 5[20]] may [not] be brought [under this Statute] unless the Security Council has [first] [determined] [formally decided] that the act of a State that is the subject of the complaint, [is] [is not] an act of aggression [in accordance with Chapter VII of the Charter of the United Nations].

Option 2
      [The determination [under Article 39 of the Charter] of the Security Council that a State has committed an act of aggression shall be binding on the deliberation of the Court in respect of a complaint, the subject matter of which is the act of aggression.]

2 bis.[A referral of a matter to the Court or] [A determination] [A formal decision] by the Security Council [under paragraph 2 above] shall not be interpreted as in any way affecting the independence of the Court in its determination of the criminal responsibility of the person concerned.

2 ter. [A complaint of or directly related to an act of aggression brought under this Statute and the findings of the Court in such cases is without prejudice to the powers of the Security Council under Chapter VII of the Charter.]

[[50] 3. Option 1
      No prosecution may be commenced under this Statute arising from a [dispute or] situation [[pertaining to international peace and security or an act of aggression] which [is being dealt with] [actively] by the Security Council] [as a threat to or breach of the peace or an act of aggression] [under Chapter VII of the Charter], [where the Security Council has decided that there is a threat to or breach of the peace and for which it is exercising its functions under Chapter VII of the Charter of the United Nations], [unless the Security Council otherwise decides] [without the prior consent of the Security Council].

[*41] Option 2
1.   [Subject to paragraph 2 of this article], no prosecution may be commenced [or proceeded with] under this Statute [for a period of twelve months] where the Security Council has [decided that there is a threat to or breach of the peace or an act of aggression and], acting under Chapter VII of the Charter of the United Nations, [given a direction] [taken a [formal and specific] decision] to that effect.

2.   [Notification] [A formal decision of the Security Council to the effect] that the Security Council is continuing to act may be renewed at intervals of twelve months [by a subsequent decision].]

3.   [Should no action be taken by the Security Council in accordance with Chapter VII of the Charter of the United Nations within a reasonable time, the Court may exercise its jurisdiction in respect of the situation referred to in paragraph 1 of this article.]]]

---

48   This square bracket ends at the end of option 2 of paragraph 3.
49   A/AC.249/1997/L.8/Rev.1, p. 6.
50   This square bracket ends at the end of paragraph 3 of option 2.

~~Article 0 [24]~~[51]
~~Duty of the Court as to jurisdiction~~
~~The Court shall satisfy itself that it has jurisdiction in any case brought before it.~~

N.B. This article seems to be unnecessary in view of a similar text in paragraph 1 of article 12[36] (Challenges to the jurisdiction of the Court or the admissibility of a case) and could therefore be deleted.

Article 11[35][52]
Issues of admissibility [53]

> The following draft text represents the results of informal consultations on article 11[35] and is intended to facilitate the work towards the elaboration of the Statute of the Court. The content of the text represents a possible way to address the issue of complementarity and is without prejudice to the views of any delegation. The text does not represent agreement on the eventual content or approach to be included in this article.

[*42] ~~1.   [On application of the accused or at the request of [an interested State] [a State which has jurisdiction over the crime] at any time prior to [or at] the commencement of the trial, or of its own motion], the Court shall determine whether a case before it is inadmissible.~~

N.B. This paragraph seems to be unnecessary in view of article 12[36] (Challenges to the jurisdiction of the Court or the admissibility of a case) and could therefore be deleted. Subsequent paragraphs have been renumbered accordingly.

1[2].   Having regard to paragraph 3 of the preamble,[54] the Court shall determine that a case is inadmissible where:

(a)   the case is being investigated or prosecuted by a State which has jurisdiction over it, unless the State is unwilling or unable genuinely to carry out the investigation or prosecution; *[55]

(b)   the case has been investigated by a State which has jurisdiction over it and the State has decided not to prosecute the person concerned, unless the decision resulted from the unwillingness or inability of the State genuinely to prosecute;

(c)   the person concerned has already been tried for conduct which is the subject of the complaint,[56] and a trial by the Court is not permitted under paragraph 2 of article 13[42];[57]

---

[51]   A/AC.249/1997/L.8/Rev.1, p. 8.

[52]   A/AC.249/1997/L.8/Rev.1, p. 10.

[53]   The present text of article 11[35] is without prejudice to the question whether complementarity-related admissibility requirements of this article may be waived by the State or States concerned.

[54]   Suggestions were made that the principle of complementarity should be further clarified either in this article or elsewhere in the Statute.

[55]   The proposal on extradition or international cooperation is not included in the text, subject to the determination of whether the relevant State would be able to present arguments in the procedure on admissibility. **N.B. In the context of this footnote, see also article 12[36](2) (Challenges to the jurisdiction of the Court or the admissibility of a case).**

[56]   If the Security Council can refer situations to the Court or the Prosecutor can initiate investigations, then the appropriate wording may be considered.

[57]   It was noted that article 11[35] should also address, directly or indirectly, cases in which there was a prosecution resulting in conviction or acquittal, as well as discontinuance of prosecutions and possibly also pardons and amnesties. A number of delegations expressed the view that article 13[42], as currently worded, did not adequately address these situations for purposes of complementarity. It was agreed that these questions should be revisited in light of further revisions to article 13[42] to determine whether the reference to article 13[42] was sufficient or whether additional language was needed in article 11[35] to address these situations.

[*43] **[58]

(d)   the case is not of sufficient gravity to justify further action by the Court.[59]

2[3]. In order to determine unwillingness in a particular case, the Court shall consider whether one or more of the following exist, as applicable:

(a)   the proceedings[60] were or are being undertaken or the national decision was made for the purpose of shielding the person concerned from criminal responsibility for crimes within the jurisdiction of the Court as set out in article 5[20];

(b)   there has been an undue delay in the proceedings which in the circumstances is inconsistent with an intent to bring the person concerned to justice;

(c)   the proceedings were not or are not being conducted independently or impartially and they were or are being conducted in a manner which, in the circumstances, is inconsistent with an intent to bring the person concerned to justice.

3[4].   In order to determine inability in a particular case, the Court shall consider whether, due to a total or partial collapse or unavailability of its national judicial system, the State is unable to obtain the accused or the necessary evidence and testimony or otherwise unable to carry out its proceedings.

* * *

An alternative approach, which needs further discussion, is that the Court shall not have the power to intervene when a national decision has been taken in a particular case. That approach could be reflected as follows:

"The Court has no jurisdiction where the case in question is being investigated or prosecuted, or has been prosecuted, by a State which has jurisdiction over it."

[*44] Article 12[36][61]
Challenges to the jurisdiction of the Court
or the admissibility of a case

1.   At all stages of the proceedings, the Court (a) shall satisfy itself as to its jurisdiction over a case pursuant to article 24 and (b) may, on its own motion, determine the admissibility of the case pursuant to article 11[35].[62]

N.B. The words "pursuant to article 24" in the second line have been deleted in view of the proposed deletion of this article (Duty of the Court as to jurisdiction), p.....

2.   Challenges to the admissibility of the case, pursuant to article 11[35], or challenges to the jurisdiction of the Court may be made by:

(a)   an accused [or a suspect];[63]

(b)   [A State] [[An interested] State Party] which has jurisdiction over the crime on the ground that it is investigating or prosecuting the case or has investigated or prosecuted[64]

[a State [State Party] of nationality of a person referred to in paragraph 2 (a) [on the ground that it is investigating or prosecuting the case or has investigated or prosecuted]]

[and a State [State Party] which has received a request for cooperation];

The Prosecutor may seek a ruling from the Court regarding a question of jurisdiction or admissibility.

---

[58]   Some delegations preferred the inclusion of the following subparagraph: "the accused is not liable under article 84[57] (Rule of speciality) to be prosecuted before or punished by the Court".
N.B. In the light of the text of article 84[57] (Rule of speciality), consideration should be given as to whether this footnote is still necessary.

[59]   Some delegations believed that this subparagraph should be included elsewhere in the Statute or deleted.

[60]   The term "proceedings" covers both investigations and prosecutions.

[61]   A/AC.249/1997/L.9/Rev.1, p.28.

[62]   In the light of the wording to be adopted for article 12[36], several draft provisions of the statute may have to be reexamined including article 47[26], paragraph 4, and article 51[27], paragraph 2 (b).

[63]   The term "suspect" includes a person who is the subject to an investigation. Another option is to limit the right to challenge to a suspect arrested on the basis of a pre-indictment arrest warrant.

[64]   The final wording of this subparagraph will depend on the content of article 11[35].

In proceedings with respect to jurisdiction or admissibility, those having submitted the case pursuant to article 6[21],[65] [those non-State parties which [*45] have jurisdiction over the crimes][66] as well as victims, may also submit observations to the Court.

3.[67] The admissibility of a case or the jurisdiction of the Court may be challenged only once by any person or State referred to in paragraph 2.

The challenge must take place prior to or at the commencement of the trial.

In exceptional circumstances, the Court may grant leave for a challenge to be brought more than once or at a time later than the commencement of the trial.

Challenges to the admissibility of a case, at the commencement of a trial, or subsequently with the leave of the Court as provided in the preceding subparagraph, may only be based on article 11[35], paragraph 1[2] (c).[68]

3 bis. A State referred to in paragraph 2 (b) of the present article shall make a challenge at the earliest opportunity.[69]

4. Prior to the confirmation of the indictment, challenges to the admissibility of a case or challenges to the jurisdiction of the Court, shall be referred to the Pre-Trial Chamber. After confirmation of the indictment, they shall be referred to the Trial Chamber.

Decisions with respect to jurisdiction or admissibility may be appealed to the Appeals Chamber.[70] [71]

[5. If the Court has decided that a case is inadmissible pursuant to article 11[35], the Prosecutor, may, at any time, submit a request for a review of the decision, on the grounds that conditions required under article 11[35] to render the case inadmissible no longer exist or that new facts arose.]

[*46] Article 13[42]
Non bis in idem

N.B.
- **This article as such was not considered by the Prep Com in 1997.**
- **Consideration should be given to placing certain portions of this article in a separate article before article 12[36] (Challenges to the jurisdiction of the Court or the admissibility of a case).**

ILC Draft

1. No person shall be tried before any other court for acts constituting a crime of the kind referred to in article 5[20] for which that person has already been tried by the Court.

2. A person who has been tried by another court for acts constituting a crime of the kind referred to in article 5[20] may be tried under this Statute only if:

   (a) the acts in question were characterized by that court as an ordinary crime and not as a crime which is within the jurisdiction of the Court; or

   (b) the proceedings in the other court were not impartial or independent or were designed to shield the accused from international criminal responsibility or the case was not diligently prosecuted.

3. In considering the penalty to be imposed on a person convicted under this Statute, the Court shall take into account the extent to which a penalty imposed by another court on the same person for the same act has already been served.

---

[65] The final wording will depend on the content of article 6[21] (States, Security Council, Prosecutor).

[66] This provision would apply to the option where only States parties can challenge the jurisdiction of the Court or the admissibility of a case.

[67] It was suggested that if several States have jurisdiction over a case and one of those States has already challenged the jurisdiction of the Court, the remaining States should not bring additional challenges except on different grounds.

[68] The final wording of this subparagraph will depend on the content of article 11[35].

[69] The question arises as to what consequences, if any, should flow from the failure of a State to make a timely challenge.

[70] Subject to the final decision or the organization of the Court.

[71] The question concerning the suspension of the trial proceeding in case of appeal should be addressed in the Rules of Procedure.

N.B. Consideration should be given to whether paragraph 3 is already covered by article 70[BCE] (2) (Determination of the sentence).

<u>Other proposals contained A/51/22, vol. II</u>[72]

1.   [No person shall be tried before any other court for acts constituting a crime referred to in article 5[20] for which that person already has been tried by the Court.] [Once convicted or acquitted by a final judgement of the Court] for acts constituting a crime of the kind referred to in article 5[20] a person may no longer be accused on the basis of the same evidence, even for a different offence, either by the organs of the Court or by the judicial authorities of the States Parties, unless new evidence is made known [in which case the Prosecutor of the Court may institute new proceedings].

[*47] 2.   [No person shall be tried before any other court for acts constituting a crime referred to in article 5[20] for which that person already has been tried by the Court.] A person who has been tried by another court for acts constituting a crime of the kind referred to in article 5[20] may be tried under this Statute only if:

(a)   the acts in question were characterized by that court as an ordinary crime and not as a crime which is within the jurisdiction of the Court; or

(b)   the proceedings in the other court were not impartial or independent or were designed to shield the accused from international criminal responsibility or the case was not diligently prosecuted.

[2 <u>bis</u>.   The court has no jurisdiction under this Statute when:

~~(a)   The acts mentioned in the submission to the Court are still being investigated by a State and the investigation is not manifestly intended to relieve the person concerned of criminal responsibility;~~

~~(b)   The acts mentioned in the submission to the Court have already been duly investigated by a State and the decision not to institute proceedings was taken by that State when it had knowledge of all the facts mentioned in the submission and the decision was not motivated by a manifest willingness to relieve the persons concerned of any criminal responsibility;~~

N.B. The above text seems to have been superseded by article 11[35] (Issues of admissibility).

(c)   Any person(s) mentioned in the submission to the Court have already been acquitted or convicted by a final ruling in a State for the acts involved unless the decision failed to take account of all facts contained in the submission or the proceedings were conducted in the State concerned by evading the rule of international law for the manifest purpose of relieving the persons concerned of criminal responsibility.

3.   In considering the penalty to be imposed on a person convicted under this Statute, the Court shall take into account the extent to which a penalty imposed by another court on the same person for the same act has already been served.

N.B. Consideration should be given to whether paragraph 3 is already covered by article 70[BCE] (2) (Determination of the sentence).

N.B. Article 13[42] was moved to this Part because of its relationship to jurisdiction and admissibility.

Article 14[33]

Applicable law

N.B. This article was not considered by the Prep Com in 1997.

[*48] ILC Draft

The Court shall apply:

(a)   this Statute;

(b)   applicable treaties and the principles and rules of general international law; and

(c)   to the extent applicable, any rule of national law.

---

[72]   P. 202.

Other proposals contained in A/51/22, vol. II[73]

Proposal 1

1. The Court shall apply this Statute.
2. When the Court cannot find the necessary provision to be applied, the Court may apply:

    (a) The national law of the State where the crime was committed;

    (b) If the crime was committed in the territories of more than one State, the national law of the State where the substantial part of the crime was committed;

    (c) If the laws of the States mentioned in (a) and (b) do not exist, the national law of the State of nationality of the accused, or if the accused does not have any nationality, the national law of the State of permanent residence of the accused; or

    (d) If the laws of the States mentioned in (a), (b) and (c) do not exist, the national law of the State which had custody of the accused, as far as these laws are consistent with the objectives and purposes of this Statute.

Proposal 2

1. The Court shall apply:

    (a) The Statute, including annexes A and B [A/51/22, vol. II], rules adopted pursuant to article 43[19] and elements of crimes and principles of liability and defence elaborated pursuant to article 20 bis;

    (b) Applicable treaties and the principles and rules of general international law; and

    (c) Principles of law developed by the Court from national law.

[*49] 2. In developing principles of law as referred to in paragraph 1(c), the Court shall [conduct and] take into account [a survey of] the national laws of States representing the major legal systems of the world, where those laws are not inconsistent with international law and internationally recognized norms and standards.

The Court shall only apply paragraph 1(c) to the extent that a matter is not covered by paragraphs 1 (a) or (b).

Proposal 3

The Court shall apply:

    (a) Its Statute, including the annexes thereto;

    (b) The other relevant rules of international law;

    (c) General principles of criminal law identified by it and approved by States parties to the statute;

    (d) Rules of national law, to the extent authorized by the Statute, and

    (e) Its Rules of Procedure and Evidence.

Proposal 4

1. This Statute (and the rules promulgated thereunder) shall be the primary source of law for the Court.
2. To the extent not inconsistent with the above, the Court may apply principles and rules of law that are generally recognized in national legal systems as a subsidiary source of law.
3. To the extent not inconsistent with the above, the Court may apply specific rules of applicable national law, or applicable treaty provisions, where necessary to the determination of a specific question that is governed by such law or treaty, or where the application or interpretation of such specific law or treaty is in fact at issue in the case.

Proposal 5

The Court shall apply:

    (a) In the first place, this Statute and the treaties to which it makes reference;

    (b) If necessary, the principles and rules of general international law;

    (c) Failing that, and provided that such action does not conflict with the provisions mentioned above, the internal law of the State in whose territory the crime has been committed and, on a subsidiary basis, the internal law of the State of which the accused is a national.

---

[73]   Pp.104-107.

[*50] Proposal 6

The Court may apply principles and rules of law enunciated in its previous decisions.

Proposal 7

1.   Subject to paragraphs 2 and 3, the judges may by absolute majority elaborate the elements of the crimes set out in article 5[20] and elaborate principles of liability and defence that are not otherwise set out in, and that are not inconsistent with, the elements and principles in the Statute or in annex B. In elaborating elements and principles, the Court shall not create any new offences or crimes.

2.   The initial elements and principles elaborated by the Court shall be drafted by the judges within six months of the first elections for the Court, and submitted to a conference of States parties for approval. The judges may decide that an element or principle subsequently elaborated under paragraph 1 should also be submitted to a conference of States parties for approval.

3.   In any case to which paragraph 2 does not apply, elements or principles elaborated under paragraph 1 shall be transmitted to States parties and may be confirmed by the Presidency unless, within six months after transmission, a majority of States parties have communicated in writing their objections.

4.   An element or principle may provide for its provisional application in the period prior to its approval or confirmation. An element or principle not approved or confirmed shall lapse.

N.B. This proposal only partly covers the subject of the other proposals under article 14[33]. It has a clear relationship both with the definition of crimes in this Part and the General principles of criminal law in Part 3.

N.B.

-        **Article 14[33] has a bearing on many parts of the Statute which contain specific provisions on this question in particular contexts.**

-        **As regards the placement of the article, either it could be retained here at the end of this Part or be placed between the articles on jurisdiction and those on admissibility.**

-        **See also the first footnote in paragraph 2 of article 25[L] (Grounds for excluding criminal responsibility).**

[*51] PART 3. GENERAL PRINCIPLES OF CRIMINAL LAW
Article 15[A][74]
Nullum crimen sine lege

1.   Provided that this Statute is applicable in accordance with article 6[21], 7[21 bis], 8[21 ter], 9[22] or 10[23] a person shall not be criminally responsible under this Statute:

    (a)   in the case of a prosecution with respect to a crime referred to in article 5[20] [(a) to (d)], unless the conduct in question constitutes a crime that is defined in this Statute;

    (b)   in the case of a prosecution with respect to a crime referred to in article [5[20] (e)], unless the treaty in question was applicable to the conduct of the person at the time that the conduct occurred.

[2.   Conduct shall not be construed as criminal and sanctions shall not be applied under this Statute by a process of analogy.]

3.   Paragraph 1 shall not affect the character of such conduct as being crimes under international law, apart from this Statute.

Article 16[A bis][75]
Non-retroactivity

1.   Provided that this Statute is applicable in accordance with article   15[A], a person shall not be criminally responsible under this Statute for conduct committed prior to its entry into force.

---

74   A/AC.249/1997/L.5, p. 19.
75   Ibid., pp. 19-20.

[2.   If the law as it appeared at the commission of the crime is amended prior to the final judgement in the case, the most lenient law shall be applied.][76]

~~Other proposals that may also relate to, inter alia, issues concerning trigger mechanism and other jurisdictional questions respectively, and which will be debated by the Preparatory Committee at a later session~~

~~[When a State becomes a party to this Statute after its entry into force, the Court has jurisdiction only in respect of acts committed by its nationals or on its territory or against its nationals after the deposit by that State of its [*52] instrument of ratification or accession. A non-party State may, however, by an express declaration deposited with the Registrar of the Court, agree that the Court has jurisdiction in respect of the acts that it specifies in the declaration.~~

~~The Court has no jurisdiction in respect of crimes for which, even if they have been committed after the entry into force of this Statute, the Security Council, acting under Chapter VII of the Charter of the United Nations, has decided before the entry into force of this Statute to establish an ad hoc international criminal tribunal. The Security Council may, however, decide otherwise.]~~

~~[The present Statute shall apply only to acts committed in the territory of a State party to the present Statute or by the nationals of a State party to the present Statute or against the nationals of a State party to the present Statute.]~~

N.B. Other proposals under paragraph 2 could be deleted because the issues with which they dealt are covered under articles 7[21 _bis_] (Preconditions to the exercise of jurisdiction), 8[21 _ter_] (Temporal jurisdiction) and 9[22] (Acceptance of the jurisdiction of the Court).

Article 17[B a.to d.][77]
Individual criminal responsibility

1.   The Court shall have jurisdiction over natural persons pursuant to the present Statute.

2.   A person who commits a crime under this Statute is individually responsible and liable for punishment.

[3.   Criminal responsibility is individual and cannot go beyond the person and the person's possessions.][78]

4.   The fact that the present Statute provides criminal responsibility for individuals does not affect the responsibility of States under international law.

[5.   The Court shall also have jurisdiction over legal persons, with the exception of States, when the crimes committed were committed on behalf of such legal persons or by their agencies or representatives. [*53] 6.   The criminal responsibility of legal persons shall not exclude the criminal responsibility of natural persons who are perpetrators or accomplices in the same crimes.][79]

N.B. In the context of paragraphs 5 and 6, see also articles 69[47 _bis_] (Penalties applicable to legal persons) and 88[59 _ter_] (Enforcement of fines and forfeiture measures).

7.   [Subject to the provisions of articles 19[C], 22[G] and 23[H],] a person is criminally responsible and liable for punishment for a crime defined [in article 5[20]] [in this Statute] if that person:

(a)   commits such a crime, whether as an individual, jointly with another, or through another person regardless of whether that person is criminally responsible;

(b)   orders, solicits or induces the commission of such a crime which in fact occurs or is attempted;

---

[76]   This provision raises issues relating to non-retroactivity, amendment of the statute and penalties. Accordingly, further consideration of this issue is required.

[77]   A/AC.249/1997/L.5, pp. 20-22.

[78]   This proposal deals mainly with the limits of civil liability and should be further discussed in connection with penalties, forfeiture and compensation to victims of crimes.

[79]   There is a deep divergence of views as to the advisability of including criminal responsibility of legal persons in the Statute. Many delegations are strongly opposed, whereas some strongly favour its inclusion. Others have an open mind. Some delegations hold the view that providing for only the civil or administrative responsibility/liability of legal persons could provide a middle ground. This avenue, however, has not been thoroughly discussed. Some delegations, who favour the inclusion of legal persons, hold the view that this expression should be extended to organizations lacking legal status.

[(c) fails to prevent or repress the commission of such a crime in the circumstances set out in article 19[C];]

(d) [with [intent] [knowledge] to facilitate the commission of such a crime,] aids, abets or otherwise assists in the commission [or attempted commission] of that crime, including providing the means for its commission;[80]

(e) either:

(i) [intentionally] [participates in planning] [plans] to commit such a crime which in fact occurs or is attempted; or

[(ii) agrees with another person or persons that such a crime be committed and an overt act in furtherance of the agreement is committed by any [*54] of these persons that manifests their intent [and such a crime in fact occurs or is attempted];[81]][82]

(f) [directly and publicly] incites the commission of [such a crime] [genocide] [which in fact occurs], [with the intent that such crime be committed];

(g)[83] [with the intent to commit such a crime,] attempts to commit that crime by taking action that commences its execution by means of a substantial step, but that crime does not occur because of circumstances independent of the person's intentions.[84]

N.B. This article should be reexamined as to the references to the mental element in view of article 23[H] (**Mens rea** (mental elements)).

Article 18[B.e.][85]
Irrelevance of official position

1. This Statute shall be applied to all persons without any discrimination whatsoever: official capacity, either as Head of State or Government, or as a member of a Government or parliament, or as an elected representative, or as a government official, shall in no case exempt a person from his criminal responsibility under this Statute, nor shall it [per se] constitute a ground for reduction of the sentence.

2. Any immunities or special procedural rules attached to the official capacity of a person, whether under national or international law, may not be [*55] relied upon to prevent the Court from exercising its jurisdiction in relation to that person.[86]

Article 19[C][87]
Responsibility of [commanders] [superiors][88] for acts of
[forces under their command] [subordinates][89]

---

[80] It was pointed out that the commentary to the ILC Draft Code of Crimes (A/51/10, p. 24, para. (12)) implicitly also includes aiding, abetting or assisting ex post facto. This presumption was questioned in the context of the ICC. If aiding, etc., ex post facto were deemed necessary to be criminalized, an explicit provision would be needed.

[81] In addition to the two types of conduct described in para. (e), there is a third type of criminal association that may be considered. One formulation of this third category would be to refer to the conduct of a person who "participates in an organization which aims at the realization of such a crime by engaging in an activity that furthers or promotes that realization".

[82] The inclusion of this subparagraph gave rise to divergent views.

[83] Questions pertaining to voluntary abandonment or repentance should be further discussed in connection with grounds for excluding criminal responsibility.

[84] Questions pertaining to voluntary abandonment or repentance should be further discussed in connection with grounds for excluding criminal responsibility.

[85] A/AC.249/1997/L.5, p. 22.

[86] Further discussion of paragraph 2 would be required in connection with procedure as well as international judicial cooperation.
N.B. The deleted text is no longer relevant in the light of subsequent discussions.

[87] A/AC.249/1997/L.5, p. 23.

[88] Most delegations were in favour of extending the principle of command responsibility to any superior.

[89] Most delegations were in favour of extending the principle of command responsibility to any superior.

[In addition to other forms of responsibility for crimes under this Statute, a [commander] [superior] is criminally responsible] [A [commander] [superior] is not relieved of responsibility][90] for crimes under this Statute committed by [forces] [subordinates] under his or her command [or authority] and effective control as a result of the [commander's] [superior's] failure to exercise properly this control where:

(a) the [commander] [superior] either knew, or [owing to the widespread commission of the offences] [owing to the circumstances at the time] should have known, that the [forces] [subordinates] were committing or intending to commit such crimes; and

(b) the [commander] [superior] failed to take all necessary and reasonable measures within his or her power to prevent or repress their commission [or punish the perpetrators thereof].

[*56] Article 20[E][91]
Age of responsibility

N.B. In the context of this article, see also article 68[A] (a) (Applicable penalties).
Proposal 1

1.　A person under the age of [twelve, thirteen, fourteen, sixteen, eighteen] at the time of the commission of a crime [shall be deemed not to know the wrongfulness of his or her conduct and] shall not be criminally responsible under this Statute[, unless the Prosecutor proves that the person knew the wrongfulness of his or her conduct at that time].

[2.　A person who is between the age of [sixteen] and [twenty-one] at the time of the [alleged] commission of a crime shall be evaluated [by the Court] as to his or her maturity to determine whether the person is responsible under this Statute.]

Proposal 2

[Persons aged 13 to 18 years at the time of the facts shall be criminally responsible but their prosecution, trial and sentence and the regime under which they serve their sentence may give rise to the application of special modalities specified in the Statute.][92]

[*57] Article 21[F][93]
Statute of limitations

Proposal 1

[1.　The period of limitations shall be completed upon the lapse of xx years for the offence of ..., and yy years for the offence of ...

2.　The period of limitations shall commence to run at the time when criminal conduct has ceased.

---

[90]　The alternatives highlight the question whether command responsibility is a form of criminal responsibility in addition to others or whether it is a principle that commanders are not immune for the acts of their subordinates.

[91]　A/AC.249/1997/L.5, pp.23-24.

[92]　Different views exist among States as to a specific age of responsibility.

It was observed that many international conventions (such as the International Covenant on Civil and Political Rights, the European Convention on Human Rights, the Inter-American Convention on Human Rights) prohibit the punishment of minors.

The question arising from the draft proposals was whether an absolute age of responsibility should be mandated or whether a presumptive age should be included with a means to rebut the presumption.

It was observed that a consistent approach (in terms of either an evaluation by the Court or proof by the Prosecutor) should be taken in paragraphs 1 and 2 of proposal 1 in respect of both of the age groups mentioned.

A question was raised as to what would be the criteria of the evaluation process, and should this be left for the Court to develop in supplementary rules or by jurisprudence?

~~It was questioned whether the Statute should specify that mitigation of sentence should or could be appropriate for those minors who were found to be mature enough to be criminally responsible.~~

N.B. This paragraph of the footnote is redundant in the light of article 70[BCE] (Determination of the sentence).

It was observed that, in its article 1, the Convention on the Rights of the Child defines as a child every human being younger than eighteen years of age and that, in its article 37, it lays down a series of limitations as regards the applicable penalties, ruling out the death penalty and life imprisonment without parole.

[93]　A/AC.249/1997/L.5, pp. 24-26.

3.   The period of limitations shall cease to run on the institution of the prosecution against the case concerned to this Court or to a national court of any State that has jurisdiction on such case. The period of limitations begins to run when the decision of the national court becomes final, where this Court has jurisdiction over the case concerned.]

Proposal 2

[There is no statute of limitations for those crimes within the [inherent] jurisdiction of the Court.]

Proposal 3

[There is no statute of limitations for those crimes within the [inherent] jurisdiction of the Court; but [for those crimes not within the Court's inherent jurisdiction] the Court may decline to exercise jurisdiction if, owing to the lapse of time, a person would be denied a fair trial.]

Proposal 4

[Crimes not subject to limitation

The crimes referred to in article 5[20] (a), (b) and (d) shall not be subject to limitation.

[*58] Crimes subject to limitation

1.   Proceedings before the Court in respect of the crimes referred to in article 5[20](c) shall be subject to a period of limitation of 10 full years from the date on which the crime was committed, provided that during this period no prosecution has been brought.

2.   If a prosecution has been initiated during this period, either before the Court or in a State competent to bring a prosecution under its internal law, the proceedings before the Court shall not be subject to limitation until 10 full years have elapsed from the date of the most recent prosecution.]

Proposal 5

[1.   The statute of limitations as established hereunder shall extinguish the criminal prosecution and the punishment.

2.   The statute of limitations will be [ ] years and shall commence to run as follows:

    (a)   in case of instantaneous crime, from the moment of its perpetration;

    (b)   in case of attempt, from the moment the last act of execution was performed or the due conduct was omitted;

    (c)   in case of permanent crime, from the moment of the cessation of the criminal conduct.

3.   The statute of limitations may be interrupted by the actions taken in the investigation of the crime and its perpetrators. If those actions were stopped, the statute of limitations will run again as of the day the last act of investigation was carried out.

4.   The statute of limitations for definitive sanctions will run as of the moment the condemned person escaped and will be interrupted with its detention.]

N.B. The proposals under this article have not been consolidated.

Article 22[G][94]

Actus reus (act and/or omission)

1.   Conduct for which a person may be criminally responsible and liable for punishment as a crime can constitute either an act or an omission, or a combination thereof.

2.   Unless otherwise provided and for the purposes of paragraph 1, a person may be criminally responsible and liable for punishment for an omission where the [*59] person [could] [has the ability], [without unreasonable risk of danger to him/herself or others,] but intentionally [with the intention to facilitate a crime] or knowingly fails to avoid the result of an offence where:

    (a)   the omission is specified in the definition of the crime under this Statute; or

    (b)   in the circumstances, [the result of the omission corresponds to the result of a crime committed by means of an act] [the degree of unlawfulness realized by such omission corresponds to the degree of unlawfulness to be realized by the commission of such act], and the person is [either] under a pre-existing

---

[94]   A/AC.249/1997/L.5, pp. 26-27.

[legal] obligation under this Statute[95] to avoid the result of such crime [or creates a particular risk or danger that subsequently leads to the commission of such crime].[96]

[3. A person is only criminally responsible under this Statute for committing a crime if the harm required for the commission of the crime is caused by and [accountable] [attributable] to his or her act or omission.][97]

Article 23[H][98]
Mens rea (mental elements) ~~of crime~~

1. Unless otherwise provided, a person is only criminally responsible and liable for punishment for a crime under this Statute if the physical elements are committed with intent and knowledge.

2. For the purposes of this Statute and unless otherwise provided, a person has intent where:

    (a) in relation to conduct, that person means to engage in the act or omission;

    (b) in relation to a consequence, that person means to cause that consequence or is aware that it will occur in the ordinary course of events.

[*60] 3. For the purposes of this Statute and unless otherwise provided, "know", "knowingly" or "knowledge" means to be aware that a circumstance exists or a consequence will occur.

[4.[99] [100] For the purposes of this Statute and unless otherwise provided, where this Statute provides that a crime may be committed recklessly, a person is reckless with respect to a circumstance or a consequence if:

    (a) the person is aware of a risk that the circumstance exists or that the consequence will occur;

    (b) the person is aware that the risk is highly unreasonable to take;

    [and]

    [(c) the person is indifferent to the possibility that the circumstance exists or that the consequence will occur.]]

N.B. The inclusion of the notion of recklessness should be reexamined in view of the definition of crimes.

Article 24[K][101] [102]
Mistake of fact[103] or of law

Option 1

    Unavoidable mistake of fact or of law shall be a ground for excluding criminal responsibility provided that the mistake is not inconsistent with the nature of the alleged crime. Avoidable mistake of fact or of law may be considered in mitigation of punishment.

Option 2

1. A mistake of fact shall be a ground for excluding criminal responsibility only if it negates the mental element required by the crime [charged provided that said mistake is not inconsistent with the nature of the crime or its [*61] elements] [, and provided that the circumstances he reasonably believed to be true would have been lawful].

---

[95] Some delegations questioned whether the source of this obligation is wider than the statute.

[96] Some delegations had concerns about including this clause which referred to the creation of a risk. Other delegations thought that, in the context of the offences of the statute, breach of an obligation under the Statute to avoid the result of a crime was sufficient.

[97] Some delegations thought that a provision on causation was not necessary.

[98] A/AC.249/1997/L.5, pp. 27-28.

[99] Further discussion is needed on this paragraph.

[100] A view was expressed to the effect that there was no reason for rejecting the concept of commission of an offence also through negligence, in which case the offender shall be liable only when so prescribed by the statute.

[101] A/AC.249/1997/L.5, p. 28.

[102] There were widely divergent views on this article.

[103] Some delegations were of the view that mistake of fact was not necessary because it was covered by mens rea.

2.   Mistake of law may not be cited as a ground for excluding criminal responsibility [, except where specifically provided for in this Statute].[104]

Article 25[L][105]
Grounds for excluding criminal responsibility

1.   In addition to other grounds for excluding criminal responsibility permitted by this Statute, a person is not criminally responsible if at the time of that person's conduct:[106]

(a)   the person suffers from a mental disease or defect that destroys that person's capacity to appreciate the unlawfulness or nature of his or her conduct, or capacity to control his or her conduct to conform to the requirements of law;

[(b)   the person is in a state of [involuntary] intoxication [by alcohol, drugs or other means] that destroys that person's capacity to appreciate the unlawfulness or nature of his or her conduct, or capacity to control his or her conduct to conform to the requirements of law; [provided, however, that if the person has voluntarily become intoxicated [[with the pre-existing intent to commit the crime] [or knowing that the circumstances would arise that led him or her to commit the crime and that those circumstances could have that effect]],[107] the person shall remain criminally responsible;]

[*62] (c)   the person [, provided that he or she did not put himself or herself voluntarily into a position causing the situation to which that ground for excluding criminal responsibility would apply,] acts [swiftly and] reasonably [, or in the reasonable belief that force is necessary,] to defend himself or herself or another person [or property] against an [imminent ...[108] use of force] [immediate ...[109] threat of force] [impending ...[110] use of force] and [[unlawful] [and] [unjustified]] use of force in a [not excessive] manner[.] [[not disproportionate] [reasonably proportionate] to the degree of danger to the person [or liberty] [or property] protected];

(d)   [the person reasonably believes that][111] there is a threat of [imminent] death or serious bodily harm against that person or another person [or against his or her liberty] [or property or property interests] and the person acts reasonably to avoid this threat, provided that the person's action[112] [causes] [was not intended to cause] [n]either death [n]or a greater harm than the one sought to be avoided;[113] [however, if

---

[104]   Some delegations felt that paragraph 2 of option 2 still left some ambiguity, and an alternative approach could read as follows:

"Mistake of law as to whether a particular type of conduct is a crime under this Statute, or whether a crime is within the jurisdiction of the Court, is not a ground for excluding criminal responsibility. However, a [reasonable] mistake of law may be a ground for excluding criminal responsibility if it negates the mental element required by such crime."

[105]   A/AC.249/1997/L.9/Rev.1, pp. 16-18.

[106]   The link between the opening clause of paragraph 1 and paragraph 2 may need to be further considered.

[107]   There are two approaches to the question of voluntary intoxication: If it is decided that voluntary intoxication should in no case be an acceptable ground for excluding criminal responsibility, the text within brackets "[with the pre-existing intent to commit the crime] [or knowing that the circumstances would arise that led him or her to commit the crime and that those circumstances could have that effect]" would have to be deleted. In that case, however, provision should be made for mitigation of punishment with regard to persons who were not able to form a specific intent, where required, towards the crime committed due to their intoxication. If this text were to be retained, the ground for excluding criminal responsibility would apply in all cases of voluntary intoxication except for those in which the person became intoxicated in order to commit the crime in an intoxicated condition (actio libera in causa). This would probably lead to a great number of war crimes and crimes against humanity going unpunished.

[108]   Dots inserted so as not to repeat "[[unlawful] [and] [unjustified]]" in all three alternatives.

[109]   Ibid.

[110]   Ibid.

[111]   This should be considered together with article 24[K].

[112]   A proposal was made to replace the rest of the first sentence by "is under the circumstances not reasonably more excessive than the threat or perceived threat".

[113]   A proposal was made to replace "provided that the person's action [causes] [was not intended to cause] [n]either death [n]or a greater harm than the one sought to be avoided" with "employing means which are not disproportionate to the risk faced".

the person has [knowingly] [recklessly] exposed him or herself to a situation which was likely to lead to the threat, the person shall remain responsible];

(e) [the person reasonably believes that there are][114] [there are] [the person necessarily acts in response to] circumstances beyond that person's control which constitute a [threat of [imminent] death or serious bodily harm] [*63] [danger] to that person or another person [or property or property rights][115] and the person acts reasonably to avoid the [threat] [danger], [provided that the person intended to prevent a greater harm [and did not intend to cause] [and did not cause] death][116] and provided that there exists no other way to avoid such threat];

2. The Court may[117] determine the applicability of the grounds for exclusion of criminal responsibility[118] [listed in paragraph 1] [permitted by this Statute] [to the case before it].[119]

Article 26[M][120]
Superior orders and prescription of law

1. The fact that a person's conduct was pursuant to an order of a government or of a superior [whether military or civilian] shall [not] relieve the person of criminal responsibility [[if] [unless] the order [was known to be unlawful or] appeared to be manifestly unlawful].[121]

[*64] [The perpetrator of or an accomplice in a crime of genocide [or a crime against humanity] [or a ...] shall not be exempted from criminal responsibility on the sole ground that the person's conduct was pursuant to an order of a government or a superior, or pursuant to national legislation or regulations.][122] [123]

[2. Persons who have carried out acts ordered by the Security Council or in accordance with a mandate issued by it shall not be criminally responsible before the Court.][124]

[Article 27[N]] [125]
Possible grounds for excluding criminal responsibility specifically referring to war crimes]

...

Article 28[O][126]
Other grounds for excluding criminal responsibility

---

[114]   This should be considered together with article 24[K].

[115]   It was suggested that a mere reference to the law of necessity would suffice in place of the first part of the sentence.

[116]   This applies more to a military situation.

[117]   There was support, in principle, for two proposals regarding application of international law and non-discrimination in the interpretation of general principles of criminal law. The first proposal is to insert, after the word "may" the phrase ", in accordance with international law,". The second proposal is to add the following provision: "The application and interpretation of the general sources of law must be consistent with international human rights standards and the progressive development thereof, which encompasses the prohibition on adverse discrimination of any kind, including discrimination based on gender." These proposals relate to both article 14[33] and Part 3. In order to avoid duplication, discussion could take place in the context of those provisions.

[118]   The issue of the extent to which the facts underlying these grounds, for excluding criminal responsibility, if not sufficient to exclude criminal responsibility, should instead be considered in mitigation of punishment will be dealt with in Part 7.

[119]   The link between the opening clause of paragraph 1 and paragraph 2 may need to be reconsidered.

[120]   A/AC.249/1997/L.9/Rev.1, pp. 18-19.

[121]   An unlawful or manifestly unlawful order must be understood as an order in conflict with the rules of international law applicable in armed conflict.

[122]   This subparagraph should be considered together with article 25[L], paragraph 2.

[123]   For the question of mitigating circumstances, see Part 7.

[124]   There were widespread doubts about the contents and the placement of this paragraph.

[125]   It was questioned whether such grounds as military necessity could be dealt with in connection with the definition of war crimes.

[126]   A/AC.249/1997/L.9/Rev.1, p. 19.

1.   At trial the Court may consider a ground for excluding criminal responsibility not specifically enumerated in this ~~chapter~~ Part if the ground:

(a)   is recognized [in general principles of criminal law common to civilized nations] [in the State with the most significant contacts to the crime] with respect to the type of conduct charged; and

(b)   deals with a principle clearly beyond the scope of the grounds for excluding criminal responsibility enumerated in this ~~chapter~~ Part and is not otherwise inconsistent with those or any other provisions of the Statute.

[*65] 2.   The procedure for asserting such a ground for excluding criminal responsibility shall be set forth in the Rules of the Court.[127]

~~Article P~~
~~Presumption of innocence~~

~~Everyone shall be presumed innocent until proved guilty in accordance with law. The onus is on the Prosecutor to establish the guilt of the accused beyond a reasonable doubt.~~

N.B. Article P is proposed for deletion because it is reproduced in article 59[40] (Presumption of innocence).

[*66] PART 4. COMPOSITION AND ADMINISTRATION OF THE COURT

N.B.

-   The articles in Part 4 were not considered by the Prep Com in 1997. Except for article 44[31] (ILC Draft), the articles in this Part are abbreviated compilations of proposals contained in A/51/22, vol. II.

-   During the discussion of this Part at the March/April session of the Prep Com, consideration should be given to whether provisions of a more detailed nature could be placed more appropriately in the Rules.

Article 29[5][128]
Organs of the Court

The Court consists of the following organs:

(a)   [a Presidency,][an Administrative Council] as provided in article 32[8];

[(aa) Pre-Trial Chambers, as provided for in article ...][an Investigative Judge, as provided for in article 47[26](2)(c)];

(b)   an Appeals Chamber, Trial Chambers [and a Remand Chamber] and other Chambers, as provided for in article 33[9];

(c)   a [Procuracy][Prosecutor's Office], as provided for in article 36[12]; and

(d)   a Registry, as provided for in article 37[13].

[(e)   a General Assembly of Judges, consisting of all the judges of the Court.]

[(f)   an Assembly of States Parties, as provided for in article ...]

[*67] **N.B.**

-   This article could also be placed in Part 1.

-   The use of the terms "Procuracy/Prosecutor" should be harmonized throughout the text of the Statute.

-   With respect to the use of the term "Court", consideration may be given to the inclusion in this article of the following provision:

In this Statute, unless a specific organ of the Court is referred to, the Court's powers shall be exercised and its obligations shall be discharged by such organs as may be prescribed by...

---

[127]   This article needs to be further considered together with article 25[L], paragraph 2, and article 14[33].

[128]   A/AC.249/1998/WG.7/CRP.1, p. 1.

Article 30[6][129]
Qualification and election of judges

1.	The judges of the Court shall be persons of [high][the highest] moral character, [independence,][impartiality and integrity] who [possess [all] the qualifications required [in their respective countries] for [appointment to the highest judicial offices]] [are highly competent jurists].

[The judges shall have, in addition][In the composition of the court and its Chamber, due account shall be taken of the experience of the judges in]:

(a)	[at least five years'] [great] [criminal law][criminal trial] experience [as a [judge][member of the judiciary], Prosecutor or [defending attorney][advocate]]; [or][and/or][and, where possible]

(b)	[recognized competence] in [relevant] international [criminal] law [including international humanitarian law and human rights law].

[They shall also possess an excellent knowledge of and be fluent in at least one of the working languages referred to in article ...]

2.	Option 1

Each [State party][national group] may nominate for election not more than [two][three] persons, [of different nationality,] [who possess the qualification[s] referred to in paragraph 1 [(a) or that referred to in paragraph 1 (b)],] and who are willing to serve as may be required on the Court.

Option 2

(a)	When an election is required, the Nominating Committee shall develop a list of candidates, equal in number to the number of positions to be [*68] filled, taking into account such views as may be submitted to it by the [Presidency][Administrative Council], the Procuracy and States Parties and such other sources as the Committee may consult. [In addition to the mandatory requirements set forth in this article, the Committee shall consider as desirable criteria the degree of excellence in meeting the mandatory requirements, technical ability in professional skills and expertise in criminal law.]

(b)	The Nominating Committee shall be composed of the [Secretary-General of the United Nations][General Assembly of States Parties][Chairmen of the Regional Groups] and shall consist of two members from each Regional Group, selected from among nominations by States Parties.

(c)	Once the Nominating Committee is established, the Registrar shall provide the Committee, upon request, with any necessary facilities and administrative and staff support.

3.	[12][18][24][?][130] [The] judges [of the Court] shall be elected by [an absolute majority vote][a two-thirds majority vote][[the General Assembly of] the States Parties] [the General Assembly of the United Nations][the General Assembly and the Security Council from a list of persons nominated by national groups appointed for the purpose by their Governments] [by secret ballot].

[In the event that a sufficient number of judges is not elected, the Nominating Committee shall provide a further list of candidates and there shall be another election.]

[Election may be by diplomatic note, with the results to be compiled and announced by the Depositary or, once the Court is established, the Registrar.]

[Ten judges shall first be elected, from among the persons nominated as having the qualification referred to in paragraph 1 (a). Eight judges shall then be elected, from among the persons nominated as having the qualification referred to in paragraph 1 (b).] [At least two thirds of the candidates should have experience in criminal proceedings.]

4.	No two judges may be nationals of the same State. [The term of office shall end in all cases when the judge reaches 75 years of age.][A judge may not be over the age of [61][66][65][?] at the time of nomination][Judges shall retire at the age of [70][75].

5.	[States Parties][The Nominating Committee] [should bear in mind][shall endeavour][shall take as a basis] in the [election][and/or][appointment] of the judges that the representation of the principal legal systems of the world [and the representation of the main forms of civilization] [should be][is][are] assured

---

[129]	A/AC.249/1998/WG.7/CRP.1, pp. 2-4.

[130]	It was suggested that the number of judges should be made flexible, depending on the volume of the work of the Court. A change in the number of judges should be possible without the need to amend the Statute.

and [should aim for][shall be on the basis of] [[overall balanced][representation of geographic regions][equitable geographic [*69] distribution] [and cultures] and representation of women as well as men][gender balance][gender diversity].

6.   Judges hold office for a term of [nine years and [are eligible for re-election][, subject to paragraph 7 and article 31[7] (2), are not eligible for re-election] [[five][six] years and may be re-elected [only once]].

A judge shall, however, continue in office in order to complete any case the hearing of which has commenced [even beyond the limit fixed by this article] [on the understanding that the matter be concluded within five years].

7.   At the first election, [five][six][eight][?] judges chosen by lot shall serve for a term of [three][two] years and are eligible for re-election; [five][six][eight][?] judges chosen by lot shall serve for a term of [six][four] years; and the remainder shall serve for a term of [nine][six] years. [In the event that the number of judges is increased at any stage, the terms of the additional judges shall be similarly staggered.][131]

[8.   Judges nominated as having the qualification referred to in paragraph 1 (a) or 1 (b), as the case may be, shall be replaced by persons nominated as having the same qualification.]

Article 31[7][132]
Judicial vacancies

1.   In the event of a vacancy, a replacement judge shall be elected in accordance with article 30[6].

2.   A judge elected to fill a vacancy shall serve for the remainder of the predecessor's term, and if that period is less than [three][five] years is eligible for re-election for a further term.

Article 32[8][133]
The [Presidency][Administrative Council]

[0.   The college of judges of the Court shall consist of:

(a)   a [President][Chief Judge];

[*70] (b)   six [Vice-Presidents][Deputy Chief Judges], including a First [Vice-President][Deputy Chief Judge] and a Second [Vice-President][Deputy Chief Judge];

(c)   seventeen judge counsellors.]

[The General Assembly of Judges of the Court shall be convened when one of the posts referred to in paragraph 0 (a) and (b) of this article falls vacant.]

1.   The [President][Chief Judge], the First and Second [Vice-Presidents][Deputy Chief Judges] [and [two][four] alternate [Vice-Presidents][Deputy Chief Judges]] shall be elected by an absolute majority [of the judges][composing the Court]][at a General Assembly of Judges following their first election].

[The [Vice-Presidents][Deputy Chief Judges] and Alternates shall be chosen so as to represent both the appellate and trial judges.]

They shall serve for a term of three years or until the end of their term of office as judges, whichever is earlier. [They shall be eligible for re-election once.]

2.   The First [or Second] [Vice-President][Deputy Chief Judge] [,as the case may be,] [may][shall] act in place of the [President][Chief Judge] in the event that the [President][Chief Judge] is unavailable or disqualified. [The Second [Vice-President][Deputy Chief Judge] shall act in place of the [President][Chief Judge] in the event that both the [President][Chief Judge] and the First [Vice-President][Deputy Chief Judge] are unavailable or disqualified. [The [President][Chief Judge] may appoint][an/An] alternate [Vice-President][Deputy Chief Judge] [who] may act in place of either [Vice-President][Deputy Chief Judge] as required.

3.   The [President and the [First and Second] Vice-Presidents] [Chief and Deputy Chief Judges] shall constitute the [Presidency][Administrative Council], which shall be responsible for:

---

[131]   This allows for a decision to increase the number of judges, but the means by which this decision is made depends on overall administrative arrangements and will be addressed elsewhere.

[132]   A/AC.249/1998/WG.7/CRP.1, p. 5.

[133]   A/AC.249/1998/WG.7/CRP.1, pp. 6-7.

(a)   the due administration of the Court [including the supervision and direction of the Registrar and staff of the Registry and the Court. The [Presidency][Administrative Council] shall consult with the Prosecutor and include the Prosecutor or Deputy in their meetings on all matters of mutual concern including, for example, the functioning of the Registry and security arrangements for defendants, witnesses and the Court][; and

(b)   the other functions conferred on it by this Statute].

[4.   Unless otherwise indicated, pre-trial and other procedural functions conferred on the Court under this Statute may be exercised by the [Presidency][Administrative Council] in any case where a Chamber of the Court is not seized of the matter.]

[4 <u>bis</u>. Decisions of the [Presidency][Administrative Council] shall be taken by [consensus][majority vote] of the members. [The [President][Chief Judge] shall have a casting vote in the event of a tie.]]

[*71] [5.   The [Presidency][Administrative Council] may, in accordance with the Rules, delegate to one or more judges the exercise of a power vested in it under articles 47[26] (3), 51[27] (5), 52[28], 53[29] or 54[30] (3) in relation to a case, during the period before a Trial Chamber is established for that case.]

Article 33[9][134]

Chambers

1.   [As soon as possible after each election of judges to the Court,] [The [Presidency] [Administrative Council] shall in accordance with the Rules, constitute an Appeals Chamber][and a Pre-Trial Chamber].[An Appeals Chamber shall [be constituted of] [consist of] [the [President][Chief Judge] and [six][four][two] other judges][seven judges], [of whom [at least] three shall be judges elected from among the persons nominated as having the qualification referred to in article 30[6] (1) (b)] [and of whom [at least] three shall be judges elected from among the persons nominated as having the qualification referred to in article 30[6] (1) (a)] [to be elected by an absolute majority of the judges of the Court].

[The [President][Chief Judge] shall preside over the Appeals Chamber.]

[The Appeals Chamber shall consist of six judge counsellors and either the First [Vice-President][Deputy Chief Judge] or Second [Vice-President][Deputy Chief Judge], who shall preside over it.]

[2.   The [Indictment Chamber and the] Appeals Chamber shall be constituted for a term of three years. Members of the [Indictment Chamber and the] Appeals Chamber shall, however, continue to sit on the Chamber in order to complete any case the hearing of which has commenced.]

[Judges of the Indictment Chamber shall not serve in the Trial Chambers or in the Appeals Chamber at the same time.][Judges who have served in the Appeals Chamber shall not serve in any other Chamber and judges who have served in a Trial Chamber shall not serve in the Appeals Chamber.][Judges shall serve only once in any of the Chambers established by the Court.]

[(a) No member of the [Presidency][Administrative Council] who has participated in a decision by the [Presidency][Administrative Council] under articles 47[26](3), 51[27](5), 52[28], 53[29] or 54[30](3) of the Statute concerning the case being tried or under appeal may sit as a member of the Trial or Appeals Chamber in that case. No judge who has made a decision under articles 47[26](3), 51[27](5), 52[28], 53[29] or 54[30](3) of the Statute concerning the case being tried or under appeal pursuant to a delegation from the [Presidency][Administrative Council] under article 32[8](5) of the Statute may sit as a member of the Trial or Appeals Chamber in that case.

[*72] (b) A member of the [Presidency][Administrative Council] who participated in the confirmation of the indictment against a suspect under article 51[27](2) of the Statute may not subsequently sit as a member of the Trial Chamber for the trial of that accused or as a member of the Appeals Chamber hearing an appeal in relation to that trial.

(c)   If a judge is disqualified from continuing to sit in a part-heard trial and thereby deprives the Trial Chamber of its required quorum under article 65[45](1) of the Statute, he or she shall be replaced

---

[134]   A/AC.249/1998/WG.7/CRP.1, pp. 8-10.

immediately by an alternate judge if the Trial Chamber has from the start of the trial comprised more than the required number of judges. Otherwise, the [Presidency] [Administrative Council] shall order a retrial.]

N.B. The issues raised in the second indented paragraph and subparagraphs (a) to (c) seem to deal with the disqualification of judges and may be considered in the context of article 35[11] (Excusing and disqualification of judges).

[3.   Judges may be renewed as members of the Appeals Chamber for a second or subsequent term.]

4.   Judges not members of the Appeals Chamber shall be available to serve on Trial Chambers and [other chambers][Pre-Trial Chambers][the Indictment Chamber] as required by this Statute, and to act as substitute members of the Appeals Chamber in the event that a member of that Chamber is unavailable or disqualified.

5.   The [Presidency][Administrative Council] shall nominate [on a rotational basis [and for a fixed period of time] as far as possible and] in accordance with the Rules [and for a period of three years] [five][three] such judges to be members of the [Trial Chamber][two Trial Chambers][Pre-Trial Chamber][Indictment Chamber] for a given case. [A [Trial Chamber][Pre-Trial Chamber] shall include at least [three][two] judges elected from among the persons nominated as having the qualification referred to in article 30[6] (1) (a).]

[A Pre-Trial Chamber shall be responsible in the given case for such functions as prescribed in [articles 47[26](3) and (5), 51[27](2) to (4)and (5)(b), 52[28](1) to (3), 54[30](3), and any other functions concerning the pre-trial process.]

[The Trial Chamber shall consist of four judge counsellors and a [Vice-President][Deputy Chief Judge], who shall preside over it.]

[The members of the Trial Chambers shall continue to sit in order to complete any case the hearing of which has commenced.]

6.   [The Rules may provide for alternate judges to be nominated [to attend a trial and] to act as members of [the Pre-Trial Chamber and] the Trial Chamber [or Indictment Chambers and the Appeals Chamber] in the event that a judge dies or becomes unavailable during the course of the trial.]

[*73] [If a judge sitting as a member of the Trial Chamber is unable to continue sitting in a part-heard trial owing to illness or other incapacity, the Presiding Judge may adjourn the proceedings if the cause of that inability seems likely to be of short duration. Otherwise, or if the cause of the inability is still present ten days after the adjournment, the Presiding Judge shall report to the [Presidency][Administrative Council], which shall order a retrial. If the Trial Chamber has comprised more than the required number of judges from the start of the trial, the judge in question shall be replaced immediately by an alternate judge. This rule shall also apply to cases of death, loss of office or resignation of a judge from the Trial Chamber.]

[6 (a) The [Presidency][Administrative Council] shall nominate in accordance with the Rules five such judges who are not members of the Pre-Trial Chamber for a given case to be members of the Trial Chamber for the same case. A Trial Chamber shall include at least three judges elected from among the persons nominated as having the qualification referred to in article 30[6](1)(a).]

[7.   No judge who is a national of a complainant State or of a State of which the accused is a national shall be a member of a Chamber dealing with the case.]

N.B. This paragraph deals with the disqualification of judges and may be considered in the context of article 35[11] (Excusing and disqualification of judges).

[8.   The Pre-Trial Chambers shall perform pre-trial functions, in accordance with Part 5[4] of this Statute. 8. (a) A Pre-Trial Chamber shall be established for each case by the [President][Chief Judge] of the Court. It shall consist of two [Vice-Presidents][Deputy Chief Judges] and either the First [Vice-President][Deputy Chief Judge] or Second [Vice-President][Deputy Chief Judge], who shall preside over it.]

[9.   The Remand Chamber shall consist of four judge counsellors and either the First [Vice-President][Deputy Chief Judge] or Second [Vice-President][Deputy Chief Judge], who shall preside over it.]

[10. All members of the Chambers referred to in paragraph 1 of this article shall be chosen by lot. Judges drawn by lot may be excluded as a result of incompatibilities under article ... When the membership of a Chamber drawn by lot encounters difficulties owing to incompatibilities under article ..., the First and the

Second [Vice-President] [Deputy Chief Judge] may be replaced by a [Vice-President][Deputy Chief Judge], and a [Vice-President][Deputy Chief Judge] by the most senior judge counsellor in the Court or, failing such a judge, the oldest.

10a. The [President][Chief Judge] of the Court may, if he so wishes, preside over one of the chambers referred to in paragraph 1 of this article, subject to the provisions of article 37[13].

10b. For the membership of each of the Chambers referred to in article ..., the [President][Chief Judge] of the Court may arrange for as many alternate judge [*74] counsellors as he deems necessary to be chosen by lot. They attend hearings of the Chamber for which they have been designated, but do not participate in the deliberations. They are not, in that event, subject to the incompatibilities referred to in article ...

10c. In the course of a hearing, an alternate judge counsellor may be required to replace a member of the Chamber to which he has been designated when that member is temporarily unable to perform his duties, either for medical reasons or for one of the reasons set out in articles ... and ... The judge shall be chosen by lot from among the alternate judge counsellors designated for that Chamber. Incompatibilities under article ... shall apply to alternate judge counsellors required to sit under the conditions referred to in the preceding paragraph.]

[11. For the purposes of ruling on a case, the following functions may not be combined:

...

(b) serving as a member of the Trial Chamber and as a member of the Appeals Chamber.]

N.B. Paragraph 11 deals with disqualification of judges and may be considered in the context of article 35[11] (Excusing and disqualification of judges).

N.B. In the light of discussions on article 51[27] (Commencement of prosecution), the confirmation of the indictment would appear to be vested in either the Presidency or the Pre-Trial Chamber. Consideration should therefore be given to whether references to the "Indictment Chamber" should be retained.

Article 34[10][135]
Independence of the judges

1.   In performing their functions, the judges shall be independent.

2.   Judges shall not engage in any activity which is likely to interfere with their judicial functions or to affect confidence in their independence. In particular they shall not while holding the office of judge be a member of the legislative or executive branches of the Government of a State, or of a body responsible for the investigation or prosecution of crimes.

[Judges should be prohibited from exercising any political or administrative function or engaging in any other occupation of a professional nature.]

[*75] [2 (a) Judges who are required to serve permanently on the Court, pursuant to article ..., may not engage in any other employment or hold any other office.]

3.   Any question as to the application of paragraph 2 shall be decided by [the [Presidency] [Administrative Council] [an absolute majority of the judges of the Court].

4.   [On the recommendation of the [Presidency] [Administrative Council],] [When the [Presidency] [Administrative Council] considers that the Court's caseload requires the permanent presence of all the judges of the Court, it shall so inform], the [General Assembly of] the States parties [which] may [by a two-thirds majority] decide that [the workload of the Court requires that] the judges should serve on a full-time basis [for a period determined by the General Assembly or until further notice]. In that case:

(a) existing judges who elect to serve on a full-time basis shall not hold any other [full-time] office or employment; and

(b) judges subsequently elected shall not hold any other [full-time] office or employment.

---

[135]   A/AC.249/1998/WG.7/CRP.1, p. 11.

Article 35[11][136]
Excusing and disqualification of judges

1.   The [Presidency][Administrative Council] [at the request of][with the agreement of] a judge may excuse that judge from the exercise of a function under this Statute.

2.   [Judges shall not participate in any case [in which they have previously been involved in any capacity][in the event of one of the incompatibilities under article ...] or in which their impartiality might reasonably be doubted on any ground, including an actual, apparent or potential conflict of interest].

[In the following cases a judge shall be excluded from the exercise of his functions under this Statute:

(a)   if he himself is the injured party;

(b)   if he is or was a relative of the accused or the injured party;

(c)   if he is a national of a complainant State or of a State of which the accused is a national;

·   (d)   if he is the legal representative, supervisor of the guardian or curator of the accused or the injured party;

[*76] (e)   if he has acted as a witness or an expert witness in the case involving the accused or the injured party;

(f)   if he has acted as the representative, counsel or assistant of the accused in the case involving that accused;

(g)   if he has exercised the functions of a public prosecutor or a judicial officer in the case involving the accused;

(h)   if he has previously exercised the functions of a judge in the case involving the accused at the national level; or

(i)   if he has participated in the decision mentioned in article 32[8] or 56[37] (4), in the decision by the Court below, in the original judgment of the case which has been sent back in accordance with the provisions of article 75[50] or in the investigations which form the basis of such decisions.]

3.   The [[Presidency][Administrative Council],] Prosecutor or the accused may request the disqualification of a judge under paragraph 2. [Any request for the disqualification of a judge should include detailed reasons for the request.]

4.   Any question as to the disqualification of a judge shall be decided by [an absolute majority of the members of the Chamber concerned][the Appeals Chamber]. The challenged judge shall not take part in the decision [if he forms part of that Chamber; he shall then be replaced by another judge chosen by lot].

[5.   For the purposes of ruling on a case, the following functions may not be combined:

(a)   serving as a member of the Pre-Trial Chamber appointed for a case under article 34[10] and as a member of one of the chambers hearing the same case;

(b)   serving as a member of the Trial Chamber and as a member of the Appeals Chamber.]

[6.   Procedures of the trial subsequent to the change of the judges in accordance with this article shall be prescribed by the rules.]

N.B. See also article 33[9] (2), (7) and (11) (Chambers).

Article 36[12][137]
The Procuracy

1.   The Procuracy is an independent organ of the Court responsible [under this Statute] [for the investigation of complaints brought in accordance with this Statute and for the conduct of prosecutions][for receiving complaints addressed [*77] to the Court, for examining them and for conducting investigations and prosecutions before the Court]. A member of the Procuracy shall not seek or act on instructions from any external source.

2.   The Procuracy shall be headed by the Prosecutor, assisted by [one or more][two] Deputy Prosecutors, who [may act in place of the Prosecutor in the event that the Prosecutor is unavailable][are entitled to carry

---

[136]   A/AC.249/1998/WG.7/CRP.1, pp. 12-13.
[137]   A/AC.249/1998/WG.7/CRP.1, pp. 14-16.

out any of the acts required of the Prosecutor under this Statute]. [The Procuracy is an indivisible body.] The Prosecutor and the Deputy Prosecutors shall be of different nationalities. The Prosecutor may appoint such other qualified staff as may be required.

3.   The Prosecutor and Deputy Prosecutors shall be persons of high moral character, [impartiality and integrity in] and have [high][the highest level of] competence and [practical] experience][in the investigation and] in the prosecution of criminal cases. [They shall, furthermore, have an excellent knowledge of and be fluent in at least one of the working languages referred to in article 45[25].] They [shall][should] be elected by secret ballot by an absolute majority of the [States parties][[States parties, from among candidates nominated by [the members of the Court]][members of the Court, from among candidates nominated by the States Parties]. Unless a shorter term is otherwise decided on at the time of their election, they shall hold office for a term of [five][seven][nine] years and are [not] eligible for re-election.

4.   The States parties may [elect the Prosecutor and Deputy Prosecutors][nominate two persons] on the basis that they are willing to serve as [may be] required [in the Procuracy of the Court].

[4 bis (a) The Prosecutor and Deputy Prosecutors shall be elected by the General Assembly of the States Parties. The election of the Prosecutor shall be held first, followed by that of the two Deputy Prosecutors. No two members of the Procuracy of the Court may be of the same nationality.

(b)   The Prosecutor and Deputy Prosecutors shall hold office for nine years. The term shall end in all cases when the person reaches 70 years of age. They shall not be eligible for re-election.]

[4 ter. The Prosecutor and Deputy Prosecutors shall not engage in any activity which is likely to interfere with their prosecutorial functions or to affect confidence in their independence. In particular they shall not, while holding office, be a member of the legislative or executive branches of the Government of a State [, or of a body responsible for the investigation or prosecution of crimes].]

5.   [The Prosecutor and Deputy Prosecutors shall not act in relation to a complaint [initiated by their State of nationality or] involving a person of their own nationality [or in any case in which they have previously been involved in any capacity]].[They shall not participate in any case in which they are or have previously been involved in any capacity or in which their impartiality might reasonably be doubted on any ground, including an actual, apparent or potential conflict of interest.]

[*78] [The Prosecutor and Deputy Prosecutors shall not act in relation to a complaint falling in the following cases:

(a)   if they themselves are the injured party;

(b)   if they are or were a relative of the accused or the injured party;

(c)   if they are a national of a complainant State or of a State of which the accused is a national;

(d)   if they are the legal representative, supervisor of the guardian or curator of the accused or the injured party;

(e)   if they have acted as a witness or an expert witness in the case involving the accused or the injured party; or

(f)   if they have acted as the representative, counsel or assistant of the accused in the case involving that accused.]

6.   [The [Presidency][Administrative Council] may excuse the Prosecutor or a Deputy Prosecutor at their request from acting in a particular case, and shall decide any question raised in a particular case as to the disqualification of the Prosecutor or a Deputy Prosecutor.]

[The Prosecutor or a Deputy Prosecutor may not participate in a case in which his impartiality might be doubted on any ground, including an actual, apparent or potential conflict of interest. The [Presidency][Administrative Council] of the Court may, on its own motion or at the request of the Prosecutor or of a suspect or accused person, excuse a member of the Procuracy from following a case for one of the reasons set out in the preceding paragraph.]

[In case the Prosecutor or a Deputy Prosecutor falls in the cases prescribed in the preceding paragraph, he may be challenged by the accused. The [Presidency] [Administrative Council] shall decide on challenges against the Prosecutor or a Deputy Prosecutor made before the first day of the public trial. Challenges made afterwards shall be decided by the Trial Chamber concerned.]

7.　The staff of the Procuracy shall be subject to staff regulations drawn up by the Prosecutor. [The paramount consideration in the employment of the staff of the Procuracy and in the drawing up of the Staff Regulations shall be the necessity of securing the highest standards of efficiency, competence and integrity. In the employment of the staff the Prosecutor should bear in mind the criteria set forth in article [30[6](5)]].

[8.　The Prosecutor may choose investigators who shall assist him in his duties and shall be placed under his sole authority. They may carry out any acts for which they have been delegated by the Prosecutor or a Deputy Prosecutor, with the exception of requests for cooperation referred to in Part 9[7] of this Statute. They shall be staff members of the Court within the meaning of this Statute.]

[*79] [9　(a)　The Prosecutor may request a State Party to make persons available to him to assist him in a particular case;

(b)　Such persons shall be under the authority of the Prosecutor for the duration of the case for which they have been made available. They may carry out acts under the conditions established for investigators in article ...]

N.B. See also article 44[31] (Persons made available to assist in a prosecution).

Article 37[13][138]
The Registry

[0.　The Registry shall be responsible for the administration and servicing of the Court.]

1.　[On the proposal of the [Presidency][Administrative Council], the judges][The General Assembly of Judges] by an absolute majority by secret ballot shall elect a Registrar, who shall be the principal administrative officer of the Court [and shall be under the authority of the [President][Chief Judge] of the Court]. They may in the same manner elect a Deputy Registrar.

2.　The Registrar shall hold office for a term of five years, is eligible for re-election [once] and shall be available on a full-time basis. The Deputy Registrar shall hold office for a term of five years or such shorter term as may be decided on [by the judges by consensus][by an absolute majority of the judges], and may be elected on the basis that the Deputy Registrar is willing to serve as required. [Their term shall end in all cases when they reach 65 years of age.]

3.　The [Presidency][Administrative Council] may appoint or authorize the Registrar to appoint such other staff of the Registry as may be necessary.

4.　The staff of the Registry shall be subject to staff regulations drawn up by the Registrar. [Such regulations shall be circulated to the States parties for comment, whenever possible before they take effect.]

[5.　The Registry may be removed by a majority vote of the judges for inadequate performance, malfeasance or other good cause.]

N.B. See also article 39[15] (Loss of office).

N.B. The question of the Victims and Witnesses Unit should also be addressed in this Part. See, in this context, article 61[43] (5) (Protection of the [accused], victims and witnesses [and their participation in the proceedings]).

[*80] Article 38[14][139]
Solemn undertaking

1.　Before first exercising their functions under this Statute, judges and other officers of the Court shall make a public and solemn undertaking [to do so][to perform their duties] impartially and conscientiously.

[2.　In performing their duties, the officers of the Court and the staff of the Court shall not seek or accept instructions from any Government or any authority outside the Court. They shall refrain from any act incompatible with their status and shall be accountable only to the Court.]

---

[138]　A/AC.249/1998/WG.7/CRP.1, p. 17.
[139]　A/AC.249/1998/WG.7/CRP.1, p. 18.

[3. The States Parties undertake to respect the exclusive international character of the duties of the officers of the Court and the staff of the Court and not to seek to influence them in the performance of their duties.]

Article 39[15][140]
Loss of office

1. A judge, the Prosecutor or other officer of the Court who is found to have committed misconduct or a serious breach of [this Statute [such as to jeopardize his independence or his impartiality]][his official duties], or to be unable to exercise the functions required by this Statute because of long-term illness or disability [duly established by at least two experts], [or if he/she has been engaged in delinquency, whether officially or privately, which raises serious doubts in public confidence in his/her capacity as a judge] [shall] [may] [cease to hold office] [be dismissed under the conditions laid down in paragraph 2 of this article].

[A judge, the Prosecutor or a Deputy Prosecutor shall not be removed against his will except by procedures in this article unless judicially declared mentally or physically incompetent to perform his official duties.]

[1 (a) A [judge][Prosecutor or Deputy Prosecutor] who has committed misconduct other than those mentioned in the preceding paragraph shall be subject to disciplinary measures as decided by [a two-thirds majority of the judges excluding himself/herself.][...].]

[1. (b) Discipline, including loss of office against other staff of the Court, shall be governed by the Rules and the Staff Regulations.]

2. A decision as to the loss of office under paragraph 1 shall be made by secret ballot:
[*81] [(a) in the case of the Prosecutor or a Deputy Prosecutor, by an absolute majority of the States Parties;

(b) in any other case, by a two-thirds majority of the judges [excluding himself/herself]].
[further to an assenting opinion of the General Assembly of Judges of the Court, by the General Assembly of States Parties].

[A judge can be removed by a [two-thirds] majority of the States Parties upon request by either [more than three judges][the Presidency][the Administrative Council] or more than one tenth of the States Parties.]

3. The judge, the Prosecutor or any other officer whose conduct or fitness for office is [impugned][challenged under this article] shall have full opportunity to present evidence and to make submissions but shall not otherwise participate in the discussion of the question. [All evidence against him shall be communicated to him.]

4. Discipline, including loss of office against other staff of the Court, shall be governed by the Rules of the Court.

Article 40[16][141]
Privileges and immunities

1. The judges, the Prosecutor, the Deputy Prosecutors and the staff of the Procuracy, the Registrar and the Deputy Registrar shall enjoy the privileges, immunities and facilities of a diplomatic agent within the meaning of the Vienna Convention on Diplomatic Relations of 16 April 1961.

[Members of the Court shall enjoy diplomatic privileges and immunities when engaged in the business of the Court.]

2. The staff of the Registry [and other staff members of the Court] shall enjoy the privileges, immunities and facilities necessary to the [independent] performance of their functions.

---

[140]　A/AC.249/1998/WG.7/CRP.1, p. 19.
[141]　A/AC.249/1998/WG.7/CRP.1, p. 20.

3. Counsel, experts and witnesses before the Court shall enjoy the privileges and immunities necessary to the independent exercise of their duties.
4. [The judges may by an absolute majority decide to revoke a privilege or waive an immunity conferred by this article, other than an immunity of a judge, the Prosecutor or Registrar as such. In the case of other officers and staff of the Procuracy or Registry, they may do so only on the recommendation of the Prosecutor or Registrar, as the case may be.]
[*82] [With the exception of those referred to in paragraph 1 of this article, the privileges, immunities and facilities granted may be revoked or waived by a decision taken by an absolute majority, by secret ballot, of the General Assembly of Judges of the Court.]

Article 41[17][142]
Allowances and expenses

1. [The [President][Chief Judge] shall receive an annual allowance.][All permanent members of the Court, as defined in article 29[5] (2) and (3) shall receive remuneration.]
2. The [Vice-Presidents][Deputy Chief Judges] shall receive a special allowance for each day they exercise the functions of the [President][Chief Judge].
3. [Subject to paragraph 4, the judges shall receive a daily allowance during the period in which they exercise their functions. They may continue to receive a salary payable in respect of another position occupied by them consistently with article 34[10].]
    [All judges should receive a base salary of no less than half of the salary received by judges of the International Court of Justice. Those who are in function should receive additional compensation on a pro-rata basis up to the maximum of the equivalent compensation received by judges of the International Court.]
4. If it is decided under article 34[10] (4) that judges shall thereafter serve on a full-time basis, existing judges who elect to serve on a full-time basis, and all judges subsequently elected, shall be paid a salary.

Article 42[18][143]
Working languages

The working languages of the Court shall be English and French.

[*83] Article 43[19][144]
Rules of the Court

[0. The rules of organization, functioning and procedure of the Court not set out in this Statute shall appear in the Regulations and the Rules of Procedure of the Court.]
1. [Subject to paragraphs 2 and 3, the judges may][The States Parties [may] [shall]] by an absolute majority make rules for the functioning of the Court in accordance with this Statute, including rules regulating:
    (a) the conduct of investigations;
    (b) the procedure to be followed and the rules of evidence to be applied;
    (c) any other matter which is necessary for the implementation of this Statute.
2. The [initial Rules of the Court][draft regulations and rules of procedure of the Court] shall be drafted by the [General Assembly of] judges within six months of the first elections for the Court, and [submitted to][adopted by] [a conference][the General Assembly] of States parties [for approval] [which may amend them]. The judges may decide that a rule subsequently made under paragraph 1 should also be submitted to a conference of States parties for approval. [The rules and regulations adopted in accordance with the preceding paragraph may be amended under the same conditions.]

---

[142]   A/AC.249/1998/WG.7/CRP.1, p. 21.
[143]   A/AC.249/1998/WG.7/CRP.1, p. 22.
[144]   A/AC.249/1998/WG.7/CRP.1, p. 23.

3.   In any case to which paragraph 2 does not apply, rules made under paragraph 1 shall be transmitted to States parties and may be confirmed by the [Presidency] [Administrative Council] unless, within six months after transmission, a majority of States parties have communicated in writing their objections.
[3a. [Any State Party] [Five States Parties] may propose an amendment to the rules of the Court and file it with the [Registrar][Secretary-General of the United Nations]. The judges may decide by an absolute majority to propose an amendment to the rules of the Court. The [Registrar][Secretary-General] shall communicate to States parties the amendment proposed by any State Party or by the judges. The amendment shall be considered adopted unless within [three] months from the date of such communication [a majority] of States Parties have communicated in writing their objection.]
4.   A rule may provide for its provisional application in the period prior to its approval or confirmation. A rule not approved or confirmed shall lapse.
[5.   The judges may by an absolute majority adopt supplementary rules in accordance with the Rules of the Court.]

[*84] Article 44[31]
Persons made available to assist in a prosecution
ILC Draft

1.   The Prosecutor may request a State party to make persons available to assist in a prosecution in accordance with paragraph 2.
2.   Such persons should be available for the duration of the prosecution, unless otherwise agreed. They shall serve at the direction of the Prosecutor, and shall not seek or receive instructions form any Government or source other than the Prosecutor in relation to their exercise of functions under this article.
3.   The terms and conditions on which persons may be made available under this article shall be approved by the Presidency on the recommendation of the Prosecutor.
N.B. Insofar as this article deals with State cooperation, see also article 82[55] (Other forms of cooperation [and judicial and legal [mutual] assistance]).

[*85] PART 5. INVESTIGATION AND PROSECUTION
Article 45[25][145]
Complaint by State

1. Option 1
    [[A State Party which is also a Contracting Party to the Convention on the Prevention and Punishment of the Crime of Genocide of 9 December 1948] [A State Party [which accepts the jurisdiction of the Court under article [22] with respect to a crime]] may lodge a complaint [referring a [matter] [situation] in which one or more crimes within the jurisdiction of the Court appear to have been committed to] [with] the Prosecutor [alleging that [a crime of genocide] [such a crime] [a crime under article 5[20], subparagraphs [(a) to (d) or any combination thereof]] appears to have been committed] [and requesting that the Prosecutor investigate the situation for the purpose of determining whether one or more specific persons should be charged with the commission of such crimes.]]
Option 2
    [A State Party [which accepts the jurisdiction of the Court under article 9[22] with respect to a crime] [that has a direct interest] listed under (a) to (d) below may lodge a complaint with the Prosecutor alleging that [such a crime] [a crime under article 5[20] [(a) to (d) or any combination thereof]] appears to have been committed:
    (a)   a State on the territory of which the act [or omission] in question occurred;
    (b)   a State of the custody;
    (c)   a State of the nationality of a suspect;
    (d)   a State of the nationality of victims.]

---

[145]   A/AC.249/1997/L.8/Rev.1, pp.8-9.

[2.   A State Party, which, for a crime under article 5[20](e), has accepted the jurisdiction of the Court pursuant to article 9[22] and is a party to the treaty concerned may lodge a complaint with the Prosecutor alleging that such a crime appears to have been committed.][146]
[*86] [3. As far as possible, a complaint shall specify the relevant circumstances and be accompanied by such supporting documentation as is available to the complainant State.][147]
[4.   The Prosecutor shall notify the Security Council of all complaints lodged under article 45[25].]

[Article 46[25 bis][148]
Prosecutor

The Prosecutor [may] [shall] initiate investigations [ex officio] [proprio motu] [or] on the basis of information [obtained] [he may seek] from any source, in particular from Governments, United Nations organs [and intergovernmental and non-governmental organizations]. The Prosecutor shall assess the information received or obtained and decide whether there is sufficient basis to proceed. [The Prosecutor may, for the purpose of initiating an investigation, receive information on alleged crimes under article 5[20] (a) to (d) from Governments, intergovernmental and non-governmental organizations, victims and associations representing them, or other reliable sources.]][149]
N.B. The terms "sufficient basis" used in this article (if retained) and "reasonable basis" in article 47[26] (1) should be harmonized.

Article 47[26][150]
Investigation of alleged crimes

1.   On receiving a complaint [or upon notification of a decision of the Security Council referred to in article 10[23], paragraph 1] [or ex officio upon any other substantiated information], the Prosecutor shall [subject to paragraph 1 bis and ter] initiate an investigation unless the Prosecutor concludes that there is no reasonable basis for a prosecution under this Statute and decides not to initiate an investigation, in which case the Prosecutor shall so inform the [Presidency] [Pre-Trial Chamber].
N.B. The term "reasonable basis" in the opening clause is also used in the criteria listed in 1 bis (i). If the latter is retained, a broader term in the [*87] opening clause might be necessary in order to cover all the criteria listed under paragraph 1 bis.
[1 bis. Prior to initiating investigation the Prosecutor shall:
      (a)   [notify the States Parties of any complaint [or any decision of the Security Council referred to in article 10[23], paragraph 1], and those States Parties shall so inform the persons within their jurisdiction who are referred to by name in the submission; and]
      (b)   determine whether:
            (i)   the complaint provides or is likely to provide a reasonable basis [in law or on the facts] for proceeding with a prosecution under this Statute; and
            (ii)   the case is or would be admissible under article 11[35]; and
            [(ii) bis   a prosecution under this Statute would be [in the interests of justice] [taking into account the gravity of the offences] [and the interests of victims];
            (iii) [an investigation would be consistent with the terms of any relevant Security Council decision]; and
            (iv)   to seek a preliminary ruling from the Court regarding the Court's jurisdiction if the case could later be challenged under article 12[36].]

---

[146]   This provision is without any prejudice to the position of delegations with regard to "treaty crimes".
[147]   Further discussion on the content of a complaint may be necessary in the context of matters dealing with procedures. Due regard may be paid to option B on page 110 of A/51/22, vol. II.
[148]   A/AC.249/1997/L.8/Rev.1, pp.9-10.
[149]   The procedure to be followed by the Prosecutor in relation to this article may be discussed further.
[150]   A/AC.249/1997/L.8/Rev.1, pp.14-19.

[1 ter. The Prosecutor shall not initiate an investigation where the submission of the case to the Court is challenged under article 11[35] within one month of notification under article 47[26], paragraph 1 bis (a) until the final ruling of the Court.]

2.   The Prosecutor may:[151]

(a)   request the presence of and question suspects, victims and witnesses;

(b)   collect documentary and other evidence [documents, records and articles of evidence];

[*88] (c)

Option 1

conduct on-site investigations;

Option 2

(i)   Except as provided for in this paragraph, when evidence is in the territory of a State, the Prosecutor shall, as necessary, seek the cooperation of that State in order to obtain that evidence. The Prosecutor may conduct investigations on the territory of a State only:

a.   [with the consent of its competent authorities] [upon notification of and where necessary with the consent of its competent authorities] [in accordance with Part 9[7]] [subject to the waiver by the competent authorities of the requirement of consent];

[b.   When the Pre-Trial Chamber is satisfied that competent authorities to whom a request for assistance under Part 9[7] can be transmitted are not available [or not functioning].]

[(ii) In the case of paragraph (i) (b) above, [such investigations] [investigations of a non-compulsory nature[152]] shall be conducted with the [concurrence] [approval] of the Pre-Trial Chamber [which shall have regard to the views of [interested States]]. [Notification shall be given to the State in question, in particular for the purpose of the State obtaining an extension of the period for execution of a relevant request for judicial assistance.]

[(iii) In the case of paragraph (i) (b) above, the Prosecutor may use compulsory measures for collecting evidence (such as search and seizure and compelling the attendance of witnesses) based upon a valid warrant issued by the Pre-Trial Chamber.]

(d)   take necessary measures to ensure the confidentiality of information or the protection of any person [, including victims];

[(d) bis The Prosecutor shall take appropriate measures to ensure the effective investigation and prosecution of crimes within the jurisdiction of the Court, and in so doing, respect the interests and personal circumstances of victims and witnesses, including age, gender and health, and take into account the nature of the crime, in particular, but not limited to, where it involves sexual or gender violence or violence against children;]

[*89] **N.B. See also article 61[43] (2) (Protection of the [accused], victims and witnesses [and their participation in the proceedings]).**

(e)   as appropriate, seek the cooperation of any State or of the United Nations, [or of any peacekeeping force that may be present in the territory where an investigation is to be undertaken];

[(f)   where documents or information have been obtained by the Prosecutor upon a condition as to their confidentiality, which are, or are intended to be, used solely for the purposes of generating new evidence, agree that such documents or information will not be disclosed at any stage of the proceedings unless the provider of the information consents.]

N.B. This paragraph, as well as articles 51[27] (5) (f) (Commencement of prosecution), 54[30] (1 bis) (Notification of the indictment), 61[43] (9) (Protection of the [accused], victims an witnesses [and their participation in the proceedings]), 64[44 ter] (Confidential information), 65[45] (Quorum and judgement), 79[53] (5) ([Surrender][Transfer][Extradition] of persons to the Court), 82[55] (5) (Other forms of cooperation [and judicial and legal [mutual] assistance]) and 86[59] (3) (c) (Role of

---

[151]   It was proposed that the following text be included as the first line of article 47[26], paragraph 2:

[152]   This set of square brackets will apply if paragraph (iii) is accepted.

States in enforcement [and supervision] of sentences of imprisonment) all relate to confidentiality and they should be examined with a view to avoiding any duplication or contradiction.

[(g) enter into such arrangements or agreements, not otherwise inconsistent with this Statute, as may be necessary to secure the cooperation or assistance of a State or person in the investigation.]

N.B. In the final drafting of paragraph 2, attention should be given to harmonizing the use of the words "shall" and "may".

3. The [Presidency] [Pre-Trial Chamber] may, at the request of the Prosecutor, issue such subpoenas [, orders] and warrants as may be required for the purposes of an investigation, including a warrant under article 52[28], paragraph 1, for the pre-indictment arrest of a suspect.

4. If, upon investigation and having regard, inter alia, to the matters referred to in article 11[35], the Prosecutor concludes that [a case is inadmissible under article 11[35] or] there is [not a sufficient basis for a prosecution] [no prima facie case] under this Statute [or a prosecution would not be in the interests of justice] [taking into account the interests of victims] and decides not to file an indictment, the Prosecutor shall so inform the [Presidency] [Pre-Trial Chamber], as well as the complainant State [or the Security Council, in a case to which article 10[23], paragraph 1, applies], giving details of the nature and basis of the complaint and of the reasons for not filing an indictment.

[4 bis. A decision referred to in paragraph 4 based on considerations of the interests of justice shall only become effective upon its having been confirmed by the [Presidency] [Pre-Trial Chamber] under paragraph 5 of this article.]

[*90] 5. At the request of a complainant State [or, in a case to which article 10[23], paragraph 1, applies, at the request of the Security Council,] the [Presidency] [Pre-Trial Chamber] [shall] [may] review a decision of the Prosecutor not to initiate an investigation or not to file an indictment, and may request the Prosecutor to reconsider the decision [but it may do so only once] [: provided that the Prosecutor, any suspect and the complainant State [or the Security Council (as the case may be)] shall be informed of such review proceedings or confirmation proceedings within the contemplation of paragraph 4 of this article which involves a decision based on considerations of the interests of justice and shall be entitled to submit his/her/their/its viewpoints with regard thereto, which viewpoints shall be considered by the [Presidency] [Pre-Trial Chamber] in coming to its decision].

[When new information is brought to his/her attention regarding the facts in respect of which he or she decided not to initiate an investigation or not to institute proceedings, the Prosecutor may reconsider his/her decision.]

[5 bis. After a determination to initiate an investigation in accordance with article 47[26], paragraph 2, and prior to the commencement of a trial, a State requested by the Prosecutor to carry out investigations or a State on the territory of which the Prosecutor intends to conduct investigations may challenge the decision of the Prosecutor to initiate an investigation before the Pre-Trial Chamber on the grounds of lack of sufficient basis for a prosecution under this Statute.]

6. A person suspected of a crime under this Statute shall have the right:

(a) prior to being questioned, to be informed that the person is a suspect [, of the conduct that the person is alleged to have committed which may constitute a crime under this Statute] and of the rights under (b) to (d) hereafter;

(b) to remain silent, without such silence being a consideration in the determination of guilt or innocence;

(c) to have [at all times] [in connection with questioning] the [prompt] [competent] legal assistance of the person's choosing; [or, if the person does not have legal assistance, to have legal assistance assigned by the Court in any case where the interests of justice so require, including where the person is unable to secure counsel, and without payment if the person lacks sufficient means to pay for such assistance];

[(d) to be questioned in the presence of counsel unless the suspect has voluntarily waived his or her right to counsel;]

(e) not to be compelled to testify or to confess guilt nor to be subjected to any form of coercion, duress or threat;

[*91] (f) if questioned in a language other than [a language the person understands and speaks] [his or her own language], to have, free of any cost, the assistance of a competent interpreter and a translation of any document on which the person is to be questioned;

(g) not to be subjected to torture, or to cruel, inhuman or degrading treatment or punishment.

[6 bis.   Evidence obtained during questioning in violation of these rights shall under no circumstances be used in the trial unless they are favourable to the suspect.][153]

[7. (a) The Prosecutor shall fully respect the rights of suspects under the Statute and the Rules.

(b) [To establish the truth the Prosecutor shall [ex officio] extend the investigation to cover all facts and evidence that are relevant to an assessment of the charge and to the legal consequences that may follow. The Prosecutor shall investigate equally incriminating and exonerating circumstances.]

(c) [If the Prosecutor concludes that there is a basis for prosecution under this Statute, he shall, in accordance with the Rules of the Court, investigate the case by seeking the cooperation of the States concerned or by himself, and such investigation shall be conducted in conformity with international law and fully respecting the sovereignty of the States concerned.]][154]

[8. (a)   A person suspected of committing a crime within the meaning of this Statute:

(i)   shall, as soon as he is involved in an investigation or prosecuted under this Statute, be entitled to collect all of the evidence that he deems necessary for his defence;

(ii)   may either collect this evidence himself or request the Pre-Trial Chamber of the Court to accomplish certain acts, seeking, where necessary, cooperation from any State Party.

The Pre-Trial Chamber may reject the request.

(b) If the suspect elects to collect the evidence himself in accordance with ~~article 26,~~ this paragraph ~~3 (a)~~, he may apply to the Presidency for the following orders and subpoenas: [list to be inserted]]

[*92] N.B.

-    **In view of the length of the article, consideration may be given to placing some of its elements in a separate article.**

-    **The drafting of this article might need revision in the light of the decisions to be taken in respect of article 50[26 quater] (Functions of the Pre-Trial Chamber in relation with investigation).**

[Article 48[26 bis][155]
Information on national investigations or proceedings
N.B. This title is suggested in case the article is retained.

1.   States Parties shall promptly inform the Prosecutor about national investigations or proceedings undertaken with respect to the alleged commission of a crime within the jurisdiction of the Court. Such information shall be confidential to the extent necessary and shall include a concise statement of the circumstances of the alleged crime, the identity and whereabouts of any suspect (or accused), and the progress of the investigation or proceeding concerned.

2.   The Prosecutor shall examine the information received from the State(s) Party(ies) concerned and if he/she believes, having regard to the matters referred to in article 11[35], that the conditions exist for having the Court entertain the case, shall seek a ruling from the Pre-Trial Chamber and inform of his/her decision the State(s) Party(ies) concerned and the suspect (or accused). The Prosecutor may also request the State(s) Party(ies) concerned to provide additional information about the national investigation or proceeding within a given time, and defer a decision until he/she has examined such additional information.

3.   The States Parties to the present Statute undertake to submit periodical reports to the Prosecutor on the measures they have adopted which give effect to the prosecution of crimes falling within the jurisdiction of the Court.]

---

[153]   This set of square brackets will apply if paragraph (iii) is accepted.
[154]   This paragraph will be discussed in connection with article 36[12].
[155]   A/AC.249/1997/L.9/Rev.1, p.21.

[Article 49[26 ter][156]
Deferral of an investigation by the Prosecutor
1.   In the event that the Prosecutor, having regard to the matters in article 11[35], defers an investigation, then the Prosecutor [may request that] [*93] [may seek an order of the Court that] the relevant State make available to the [Prosecutor] [Court] information on the proceedings.[157]
2.   Any information so provided will, to the extent necessary, be kept confidential.
3.   If the Prosecutor thereafter decides to proceed with an investigation, he or she shall notify the State in respect of whose proceedings deferral has taken place.]

[Article 50[26 quater]][158 159]
Functions of the Pre-Trial Chamber in relation with investigation[160]
1.   [Where the Prosecutor intends to take an investigative action which may] [When the Prosecutor considers an investigation to] present a unique [*94] opportunity, which may not be available subsequently for the purposes of a trial, to take testimony or a statement from a witness, or to examine, collect or test evidence, [the Prosecutor shall] [, if the suspect/accused has not been identified or is not available] inform the Pre-Trial Chamber; and] the Pre-Trial Chamber, on the request of the Prosecutor, [or a suspect,] [or on its own initiative,] may take such measures as may be necessary to assure the efficiency and integrity of the proceedings, and in particular to protect the rights of the defence.
2.   These measures may include the power:
    (a)   to make [orders] [recommendations] [orders and recommendations] regarding procedures to be followed;
    (b)   to direct that a record be made of the proceedings;
    (c)   to appoint an expert to assist;
    (d)   to authorize counsel for a suspect to assist, or where suspects have not been identified or have not designated counsel, appoint a lawyer to attend and represent the interest of the defence;
    (e)   to name one of its members [or an available judge of the Court]:
        (i)   to observe and make [orders] [recommendations] [orders and recommendations] regarding the collection and preservation of evidence or the questioning of persons;
        (ii)   to decide on questions of law; or
        (iii) to take such other actions as may be necessary to collect or preserve evidence [favourable to the defence] [relevant to the case].
Option: [When in the course of a proceeding a unique opportunity presents itself to collect evidence, the Pre-Trial Chamber may, at the request of the Prosecutor or of the suspect, name one of its members or an

---

[156]   A/AC.249/1997/L.9/Rev.1, p.22.
[157]   The term "proceedings" covers both investigations and prosecutions (see A/AC.249/1997/L.8/Rev.1, annex I, article 11[35], note 24).
[158]   This article is reproduced from document A/AC.249/1997/L.8/Rev.1, p.20, where it appears as 26 ter. To avoid confusion, it has been renumbered as 50[26 quater].
[159]   Article 50[26 quater] was tabled by some 15 interested delegations at the August 1997 meeting of the Preparatory Committee. It was written de novo and did not derive from any particular delegation's proposal.
      The proposal contemplates that, in exceptional circumstances in which a unique opportunity appears to exist for the taking or collection of evidence, the Pre-Trial Chamber may be involved in order to assure a fair trial/protect the interests of the defence.
      Some delegations believed that the authority of the Pre-Trial Chamber set out in the proposal should be exercised only to collect and preserve evidence for the defence. In relation to the Prosecutor's investigation, the Pre-Trial Chamber should only intervene for the purpose of checking on the lawfulness of the Prosecutor's conduct.
      The alternative options reflect differing views as to the balance to be struck between the need to ensure the Prosecutor's independence and the desirability of conferring a limited role on the Pre-Trial Chamber.
      If this proposal is adopted, it seems likely that other proposals in relation to article 47[26] could be deleted or may need revision. Consideration would need to be given to article 47[26] (1), (2) ((a), (b), (c), (e) and (g)), (3), (4), (4 bis), (5), (5 bis) and (8).
[160]   The powers contemplated by this draft provision include the power for the Pre-Trial Chamber to seek judicial assistance from a State.

available judge of the Court to take necessary measures to collect or preserve evidence, while respecting the rights of the defence.]

3.   [If any [order] [recommendation] [order and recommendation] of the Pre-Trial Chamber is breached or is not complied with, the Pre-Trial Chamber may:

(a)   reject the admissibility of any evidence obtained as a result or consequence of such a breach or non-compliance; or

(b)   consider such breach or non-compliance in respect of whether any weight should be attached to any evidence obtained as a result or consequence of such breach or non-compliance.]

[*95] Article 51[27][161]
Commencement of prosecution

1.   If upon investigation [in the course of an investigation] the Prosecutor, having regard to the matters referred to in article 11[35], concludes that [the case is admissible, and] [a case does exist against one or more persons named,] [there is a prima facie case] [there is sufficient evidence that could justify a conviction of a suspect, if the evidence were not contradicted at trial,] [which the accused could be called on to answer and that is desirable in the interests of justice that the case should proceed], the Prosecutor shall file with the Registrar an indictment containing a concise statement of the allegations of fact and of the crime or crimes with which the suspect is charged in respect of each of the persons referred to, their name and particulars, a statement of the allegations of fact against them, and the characterization of these facts within the jurisdiction of the Court and shall be accompanied by [relevant] [sufficient] evidence collected by the Prosecutor for the purposes of confirmation [of the indictment] by the [Presidency] [Pre-Trial Chamber].

[2.   The [Presidency] [Pre-Trial Chamber] shall examine the indictment, any amendment and any supporting material and determine whether:

(a)   ~~whether~~ [a prima facie case exists] [there is sufficient evidence that could justify a conviction of a suspect, if the evidence were not contradicted at trial] [there is strong evidence against the accused] with respect to a crime within the jurisdiction of the Court; and

(b)   ~~whether,~~ having regard, inter alia, to the matters referred to in article 11[35], the case should on the information available be heard by the Court [if the Court has not yet ruled on this issue];

[(c)   ~~whether~~ it is desirable in the interests of justice that the case should proceed;]

If so, it shall [by majority/consensus] confirm the indictment and establish a trial chamber in accordance with article 33[9] [, and inform the Presidency].]

[2 bis. Any State concerned may challenge the decision of the Prosecutor to file an indictment before the Pre-Trial Chamber on grounds of inconsistency with this Statute.]

[2 ter. After the filing of an indictment, the Pre-Trial Chamber shall [in any case] [if the accused is in custody or has been judicially released by the Court pending trial] notify the indictment to the accused, [set a deadline prior to the confirmation hearing, until which the Prosecutor and the defence may add new evidence [for purposes of such confirmation hearing]], and set a date for the review of the indictment. The hearing shall be held in the presence of the [*96] Prosecutor and the accused, as well as his/her counsel, subject to the provisions of paragraph 4 bis. In the hearing, the accused shall be allowed to object to the indictment and criticize the material on which it is based.

Following the hearing, the Pre-Trial Chamber may:

(a)   confirm the indictment in its entirety;

(b)   confirm only part of the indictment [and amend it], by giving a different qualification to the facts;

[(c)   order further investigation];

(d)   refuse to confirm the indictment.

---

[161]   A/AC.249/1997/L.8/Rev.1, pp.21-25.

When it confirms the indictment in its entirety or in part, the Pre-Trial Chamber shall commit the accused to the Trial Chamber for trial on the indictment as confirmed. Confirmation of indictment shall uphold the warrants issued earlier, except if the Court decides otherwise.]

3.   If, after any adjournment that may be necessary to allow additional material to be produced, the [Presidency] [Pre-Trial Chamber] decides not to confirm the indictment, it shall so inform the complainant State [or, in a case to which article 10[23] (1) applies, the Security Council].

[If it does not confirm the indictment, all the warrants issued prior to the decision of non-confirmation shall cease immediately to have effect.]

[3 bis. The dismissal of a count in an indictment shall not preclude the Prosecutor from subsequently bringing a new indictment based on the acts underlying that count if supported by additional evidence.]

[4.

Option 1

The [Presidency] [Pre-Trial Chamber] may [, on its own or] at the request of the Prosecutor amend the indictment [, in which case it shall make any necessary orders to ensure that the accused is notified of the amendment and has adequate time to prepare a defence] [after hearing the accused, provided that the Trial Chamber is satisfied that the accused is not prejudiced in his rights to defend himself].]

Option 2

Prior to the confirmation of the indictment by the Pre-Trial Chamber, the Prosecutor may amend or withdraw the indictment. [The accused shall be informed of the withdrawal as well as of any amendment. In the event of withdrawal, the Pre-Trial Chamber may, under the provisions provided for in article 26, ask the Prosecutor to reconsider his/her decision.]

[*97] After the confirmation of the indictment, the Prosecutor may amend the indictment only with the permission of the Pre-Trial Chamber, and after notice to the accused. If the Prosecutor is seeking to add additional charges or to substitute more serious charges for those in the confirmed indictment, the new or amended charges must be confirmed by the Pre-Trial Chamber in accordance with the procedures for confirmation of the indictment set out in paragraph [...].

After the commencement of the trial, the Prosecutor may withdraw the indictment or certain charges within the indictment only with the permission of the Trial Chamber].

[In case of withdrawal of the indictment after the confirmation thereof, new prosecution may be instituted for the same offence only based upon a newly discovered material evidence which was not available to the Prosecutor at the time of the withdrawal in the interest of the defence.]

N.B. Consideration may be given to limiting paragraph 4 to the main principles regarding amendment and withdrawal of the indictment while addressing the details in the Rules.

[4 bis.[162] When one or more of the accused has fled or cannot be found, and when all reasonable steps have been taken to inform the accused, the Pre-Trial Chamber may still hold a hearing in order to examine whether it shall confirm the indictment. In that case, the accused cannot be represented by counsel.

When it confirms the indictment, in its entirety or in part, against an accused who has fled or cannot be found, the Pre-Trial Chamber shall issue a warrant to search for, arrest and transfer the accused, which is tantamount to committing him to the Trial Chamber for trial.]

[4 ter. Anyone who has [personally] suffered [direct] injury caused by a crime submitted to the Court, [the legal representatives of victims, victims' relatives, successors and assigns,] may inform the [Prosecutor] [and the] [Pre-Trial Chamber] in writing of the acts having caused injury to him/her/them and the nature and amount of the losses which he/she/they has/have sustained.

When it confirms the indictment, in its entirety or in part, the Pre-Trial Chamber may order provisional measures which may be necessary [in order to enable a Trial Chamber, upon a subsequent conviction,] to compensate the victim designated in the above paragraph. For that purpose, the Pre-Trial Chamber shall seek the cooperation of the interested States.

---

[162]   The Working Group decided to defer the consideration of paragraph 4 bis of article 51[27] for such time as article 56[37] is considered.

Such provisions shall also apply when the accused has fled or cannot be found.]

[*98] **N.B. Paragraph 4 ter should be considered together with article 66[45 bis] (Compensation to victims).**

5.   The [Presidency] [Pre-Trial Chamber] [Trial Chamber] may make any further orders required for the conduct of the trial, including an order:

    (a)   determining the language or languages to be used during the trial;

    (b)

Option 1

requiring the disclosure to the defence [of the relevant evidence that the defence requests] within a sufficient time before the trial to enable the preparation of the defence, of [relevant] documentary or other evidence available to the Prosecutor [, whether or not the Prosecutor intends to rely on that evidence] [which the Prosecutor intends to rely upon]; [if the Prosecutor fails to comply with an order under this subparagraph, the evidence in question will be inadmissible at the trial;]

Option 2

save in respect of documents or information referred to in article 47[26], paragraph 2 (f), and subject to subparagraph (f) below, requiring the disclosure to the defence of documents or information which are either considered [material] [relevant] to the preparation of the defence, or are intended for use by the Prosecutor at trial or were obtained from the accused;[163]

    (c)   providing for the exchange of information between the Prosecutor and the defence, so that both parties are sufficiently aware of the issues to be decided at the trial;

    (d)   providing [, at the request of either party or a State, or at the instance of the Court on its own volition,] for the protection of the accused, victims and witnesses and of confidential information;

    (e)   providing [, at the request of either party or a State, or at the instance of the Court on its own volition,] for the protection and privacy of victims and witnesses;

    [(f)   providing, at the request of either party or a State, or at the instance of the Court of its own volition, for the non-disclosure or protection of documents or information provided by a State the disclosure of which would [endanger] [prejudice] the national security or national defence interests of a State in accordance with criteria to be specified in rules made pursuant to this Statute.]

[*99] **N.B. Subparagraphs (d), (e) and (f) of paragraph 5 could be consolidated further.**

Article 52[28][164]
Arrest

1.   At any time after an investigation has been initiated, the [Presidency] [Pre-Trial Chamber] may at the request of the Prosecutor issue a warrant for the pre-indictment arrest of a suspect if there are reasonable grounds[165] [166] to believe that:

    (a)   the suspect has committed a crime within the jurisdiction of the Court; and

    (b)   taking the suspect into custody is necessary to ensure that the suspect does not:

        (i)   fail to appear for trial;

        [(ii) [interfere with or destroy evidence;][167]

        [(iii) [intimidate] [influence] witnesses or victims;]

        [(iv) engage in collusion with accomplices;] or

        [(v) [continue to commit a crime within the jurisdiction of the Court.][168]

---

[163]   [Quaere: definition of "relevant" for the Rules?]

[164]   A/AC.249/1997/L.9/Rev.1, pp.23-25.

[165]   The term "reasonable grounds" was understood to embody objective criteria.

[166]   Some delegations preferred other terms such as "serious reasons".

[167]   Some delegations suggested that subparagraphs (ii), (iii) and (iv) could be merged under a more general formulation such as "obstructing or endangering the investigation or the court proceedings".

[168]   Some delegations favoured addressing situations in which the accused may be harmed or at risk. Other delegations stated that the accused could be adequately protected under article 61[43].

[The Pre-Trial Chamber may also issue a warrant of judicial supervision in order to place a person under restrictions of liberty other than arrest.][169]

[*100] [No person shall be subjected to arbitrary arrest or detention. Nor shall any person be deprived of his liberty except on such grounds and in accordance with such procedures as are established by the rules of the Court.][170]

2.   (a)   The warrant for the pre-indictment arrest shall be deemed to have lapsed and the request for the pre-indictment arrest of a suspect shall be deemed to have been withdrawn if [the indictment has not been confirmed] [a post-indictment warrant has not been served] within [30] [60] [90] days of the arrest, or in exceptional circumstances such longer time up to a total of [60] [90] days as the [Presidency] [Pre-Trial Chamber] may allow.

(b)   In the case of a State Party which has notified the Court under article 80[53 bis] (1 bis) that it can surrender pre-indictment, the warrant for the pre-indictment arrest of a suspect shall be deemed to have been withdrawn if [the indictment has not been confirmed] [a post-indictment warrant has not been confirmed] [a post-indictment warrant has not been served] within [30] [60] [90] days of the surrender, or in exceptional circumstances such longer time up to a total of [60] [90] days as the [Presidency] [Pre-Trial Chamber] may allow.

If the Prosecutor decides not to indict the suspect or the [Presidency] [Pre-Trial Chamber] decides not to [confirm the indictment] [not to issue a post-indictment warrant], the Prosecutor shall immediately advise the custodial State of that fact.[171]

3.   "Opening clause":

Option 1

[In the case where no pre-indictment warrant has been obtained,] [Prior to the confirmation hearing,] [As soon as practicable] [after the confirmation of the indictment], the Prosecutor shall seek from the [Presidency] [Pre-Trial Chamber] a [post-indictment] warrant for the arrest and transfer of the accused. The [Presidency] [Pre-Trial Chamber] shall issue such a warrant unless it is satisfied that:

Option 2

Upon confirmation of the indictment, a warrant for the arrest of the accused shall be issued by the Pre-Trial Chamber, unless, having heard the views of the Prosecutor, it is satisfied that:

(a)   the accused will voluntarily appear for trial and none of the other factors in paragraph 1 (b) are present]; or

[*101] (b) there are special circumstances making it unnecessary for the time being to issue the warrant.

4.   The Court[172] shall transmit the warrant to any State where the person may be located, along with a request for the provisional arrest, or arrest and [surrender, transfer, extradition] of the person under Part 9[7].

5.   [Pre-indictment and post-indictment warrants may also be issued when the accused is a fugitive. In this case, the post-indictment warrant issued by the Pre-Trial Chamber shall have the effect of an international warrant and shall be disseminated by all appropriate means. When the accused is apprehended, the authorities shall proceed as provided for in Part 9[7].]

6.   [A post-indictment warrant shall remain in effect until the date of the judgement. The effects of the warrant delivered by the Pre-Trial Chamber shall not be interrupted by the actions challenging the submission of cases to the Court.]

---

[169]   It was suggested that this provision could be deleted because it is addressed in article 53[29], paragraph 5.

[170]   It was suggested that this provision could be moved to article 47[26], paragraph 6.

[171]   It was suggested that the questions of release and re-arrest could be addressed in another provision of this Statute.

[172]   The term "Court" is understood to include its constituent organs, including the Prosecutor, as defined in article 29[5].

Article 53[29][173]
Pre-trial detention or release

1. [The States [Parties] [in which the person is located] [and in which the crime was committed] shall be notified of a warrant issued by the Pre-Trial Chamber.] The State that has received a pre- or post-indictment warrant and a request for the arrest of a person under article 52[28] (5) shall immediately [in accordance with its laws][174] [[and] in accordance with the provisions of Part 9[7] of this Statute] take steps to arrest the suspect [on the basis of the warrant issued by the Court or by obtaining a domestic warrant for arrest based on the Court's warrant and request].[175]

[*102] [1 bis. The Prosecutor may, with the consent of the Pre-Trial Chamber, execute a warrant for arrest by him or herself only in cases where the competent authority of the State Party concerned may not be available or may be ineffective.][176]

2. A person arrested shall be brought promptly before a competent judicial authority in the custodial State who shall determine, in accordance with the law of that State, that the warrant applies to that person and the person has been arrested in accordance with the proper process and that the person's rights have been respected.

3. The person shall have the right to apply to [the competent judicial authority in the custodial State] [the Pre-Trial Chamber] for interim release pending [surrender] [transfer] [extradition] [in accordance with its national law]. [The custodial State shall take into account the views of the Prosecutor [and Court] on interim release.]

N.B. The term "Court", if retained in this paragraph, should be clarified.

4. After the [decision to] [surrender] [transfer] [extradite] to the Court, the person may apply to the [Presidency] [Pre-Trial Chamber] for interim release pending trial.

5. The person shall be detained unless the [Presidency] [Pre-Trial Chamber] is satisfied that the person will voluntarily appear for trial and none of the other factors in article 52[28] (1) (b) are present. If it decides to release the person, it may do so with or without conditions [or may issue a warrant of judicial supervision restricting the person's liberty other than by arrest]. [The [Presidency] [Pre-Trial Chamber] shall also, on its own initiative, review its ruling periodically. If satisfied that changed circumstances require that the ruling be modified, it may order any measure provided for in paragraph 4.]

N.B. Reference to "any measure provided for in paragraph 4" should be revised in light of the current language of paragraph 4.

6. (a) The [Presidency] [Pre-Trial Chamber] may, either of its own initiative or at the request of the person concerned or the Prosecutor, modify its ruling as to detention[, judicial supervision] or conditional release in effect at that time.

[(b) The person may be detained prior to trial for a maximum of one year; however, this period may be extended up to an additional year by the [Presidency] [Pre-Trial Chamber] if the Prosecutor can demonstrate that he or [*103] she will be ready for trial within that period and can show good cause for the delay.]

(c) The person and the Prosecutor may appeal the [Presidency's] [Pre-Trial Chamber's] determination regarding release or detention to the Appeals Chamber.

7. If necessary, the [Presidency] [Pre-Trial Chamber] may issue a warrant of arrest to secure the presence of an accused who has been released.

---

[173]   A/AC.249/1997/L.9/Rev.1, pp.26-27.

[174]   Under article 52[28] (5), a warrant for pre-indictment arrest is forwarded to the State in which the individual sought may be located, along with a request for provisional arrest or transfer/surrender under Part 9[7]. If Part 9[7] specifies the extent to which national laws apply to requests for provisional arrest or transfer/surrender, it will be unnecessary to treat this issue here as well.

[175]   The issue of whether a State can decline to arrest and detain a person, pending resolution of a challenge under article 12[36], could be dealt with in that article.

[176]   This provision raises a host of issues, including under what conditions the Prosecutor should be able to exercise such authority, whether the Prosecutor would have adequate resources to do so, and whether such issues should be addressed elsewhere in the Statute.

8.   A person arrested may apply to the [Presidency] [Pre-Trial Chamber] for a determination of the lawfulness under this Statute of any arrest warrant or order of detention issued by the Court. If the [Presidency] [Pre-Trial Chamber] decides that the arrest or detention was unlawful under the Statute, it shall order the release of the person, [and may award compensation] [in accordance with article ...].[177]

9.   [A person arrested shall be held, pending trial or release on bail, in an appropriate place of detention in the arresting State, in the State in which the trial is to be held, or if necessary in the host State.] [Once ordered [surrendered] [transferred] [extradited] by the custodial State, the person shall be delivered to the Court as soon as possible, and shall be held in an appropriate place of detention in the host State or other State in which the trial is to be held.]

Article 54[30][178] [179]
Notification of the indictment

N.B. It might be necessary to broaden the title of this article to cover the whole of its content.

1.   The [Prosecutor] [Registrar] shall ensure, where necessary with the cooperation of national authorities, that a person who has been arrested is personally served, as soon as possible after being taken into custody, with certified copies of the following documents, ~~in a language understood by that person~~ [in a language that the accused understands] [in his own language]:

[*104] (a) in the case of the pre-indictment arrest of a suspect, [a statement of the grounds for the arrest] [the warrant of arrest or restriction of liberty];

(b)   in any other case, the confirmed indictment;

(c)   a statement of the [accused's] [arrested person's] rights under [articles 47[26] or 60[41] of] this Statute and the Rules [, as applicable].

[1 bis. An indictment shall be made public, except in the following situations:

(a)   The [Presidency] [Pre-Trial Chamber] may, at the request of the Prosecutor, order that there be no public disclosure of the indictment until it is served on the accused, or in the case of joint accused, on all the accused. In exercising its discretion, the [Presidency] [Pre-Trial Chamber] shall take account of all relevant factors, including the potential for pre-arrest flight of an accused, destruction of evidence and harm to victims or witnesses if the indictment is made public;

(b)[180] The [Presidency] [Pre-Trial Chamber] may, at the request of the Prosecutor, also order that there be no disclosure of an indictment, or part thereof, or of all or any part of any particular document or information, if satisfied that the making of such an order is required to give effect to a provision of the Rules, to protect confidential information obtained by the Prosecutor, or is otherwise in the interests of justice.]

2.   In any case to which paragraph 1 (a) applies, the indictment shall be served on the accused as soon as possible after it has been confirmed.

3.   If, 60[181] days after the indictment has been confirmed, the accused is not in custody pursuant to a warrant issued under article 52[28] (3), or for some reason the requirements of paragraph 1 cannot be complied with, the [Presidency] [Pre-Trial Chamber] [the Registrar] [may] [shall] on the application of the Prosecutor prescribe some other manner of bringing the indictment to the attention of the accused.

---

[177]   A number of issues were raised regarding compensation, including whether it should be mandatory or discretionary, whether it should be granted even when the Prosecutor acted in good faith, whether such determination is not appropriate until the judgement becomes final and whether granting compensation may prevent the Prosecutor from diligently carrying out his or her duties.

[178]   A/AC.249/1997/L.8/Rev.1, pp.25-27.

[179]   The wording of this article might be modified in the light of the decisions to be taken as regards the question of hearing of the confirmation of an indictment.

[180]   The contents of this subparagraph could become the subject matter of the provision being negotiated on questions of confidentiality, disclosure and protection of information.

[181]   The matter concerning a specific deadline may be more appropriate for the rules of procedure.

[4.][182]

[*105] [5. [The accused is] [Anyone suspected of committing a crime within the meaning of this Statute shall be] shall be entitled:

(a) to be informed promptly of the nature and cause of the charge against him or her [and be questioned in a language which he understands, and, to this end, to have the free assistance of a competent interpreter, and to be provided free of charge with a translation of the documents on the basis of which he is being questioned or that show why a measure infringing upon his liberty or property has been proposed];

(b) [to have adequate time and facilities for the preparation of his or her defence and to communicate with counsel;] [to be assisted promptly by a lawyer of his own choosing, or, if he does not have sufficient means to pay for one, by a lawyer appointed by the [Pre-Trial Chamber of the] Court;]

(c) [before being questioned, or when a measure infringing upon his liberty or property has been proposed and brought to his attention, to be fully informed of the charges against him and the rights to which he is entitled under paragraph 1 of this article.]]

[*106] PART 6. THE TRIAL
Article 55[32]
Place of trial
N.B. This article was not considered by the Prep Com in 1997.
ILC Draft
Unless otherwise decided by the Presidency, the place of the trial will be the seat of the Court.
Other proposals contained in A/51/22, vol. II[183]
Competent organ and criteria to decide the place of the trial

1.   Unless otherwise decided in accordance with paragraph 2, the place of the trial will be the seat of the Court.

2.   The [Presidency] [General Assembly of the States parties] may authorize the [Trial Chamber][Court] to [exercise its functions at a place other than the seat of the Court] [sit in a State Party other than the host State][for a particular case][where it will ensure the efficient conduct of the trial and is in the interests of justice] [or] [when travel by the members of the Court is likely to make the proceedings simpler and less costly].[184]

3.   [(a) The Presidency of the Court shall make inquiries with the State Party that appears likely to receive the Court.

[(b) After the State Party likely to receive the Court has agreed, the decision [under the preceding paragraph] to hold a session away from the Court's seat shall be taken by the General Assembly of the States Parties, which shall be informed either by one of its members, the Presidency, the Prosecutor or the General Assembly of the Judges of the Court.]

4.   With the express agreement of the State Party receiving he Court, the privileges, immunities and facilities provided for in article [10[23]?] shall continue to be effective when the Court holds a session pursuant to [this article] [the three preceding paragraphs].

[*107] 5. The provisions of this article shall also apply to non-party States which, after inquiries by the Presidency, state that they agree to receive the Court and to grant the privileges, immunities and facilities provided for in article [10[23]?].

N.B. Some of the issues raised in the proposals may be dealt with in the Rules.

---

[182]   Former paragraph 4 of the abbreviated compilation of proposals on procedural matters (4 August 1997) (hereinafter abbreviated compilation) could become a subject matter for the rules of procedure.

[183]   P. 150.

[184]   This raises a number of issues, including the need for agreement of States Parties or the host State for a trial chamber to exercise its function away from the seat of the Court and whether authority to initiate such a step should rest with the President or the trial chamber.

Article 56[37][185]
Trial in presence of the accused

Comment: There appear, in essence, to be three options regarding trials *in absentia* which have emerged to date, in addition to the ILC draft, that appear in the Report, volume II. The ILC text and the proposed options are set out below:

N.B. The ILC text as such could be deleted since it seems to have been superseded by the options that were developed as a consequence of the discussions at the Prep Com.

ILC Draft

1.   As a general rule, the accused should be present during the trial.

2.   The Trial Chamber may order that the trial proceed in the absence of the accused if:

(a)   the accused is in custody, or has been released pending trial, and for reasons of security or the ill-health of the accused it is undesirable for the accused to be present;

(b)   the accused is continuing to disrupt the trial; or

(c)   the accused has escaped from lawful custody under this Statute or has broken bail.

3.   The Chamber shall, if it makes an order under paragraph 2, ensure that the rights of the accused under this Statute are respected, and in particular:

(a)   that all reasonable steps have been taken to inform the accused of the charge; and

(b)   that the accused is legally represented, if necessary by a lawyer appointed by the Court.

[*108] 4.[186] In cases where a trial cannot be held because of the deliberate absence of an accused, the Court may establish, in accordance with the Rules, an Indictment Chamber for the purpose of:

(a)   recording the evidence;

(b)   considering whether the evidence establishes a prima facie case of a crime within the jurisdiction of the Court; and

(c)   issuing and publishing a warrant of arrest in respect of an accused against whom a prima facie case is established.

5.   If the accused is subsequently tried under this Statute:

(a)   the record of evidence before the Indictment Chamber shall be admissible;

(b)   any judge who was a member of the Indictment Chamber may not be a member of the Trial Chamber.

* * *

Option 1
The trial shall not be held if the accused is not present.[187]

Option 2
General rule
1.   As a general rule, the accused shall be present during the trial.

Exceptions
2.   In exceptional circumstances, the Trial Chamber may order that the trial proceed in the absence of the accused, if the accused, having been present at the commencement of the trial thereafter:

(a)   has escaped from lawful custody or has broken bail; or

[(b)   is continuing to disrupt the trial.][188]

---

[185]   A/AC.249/1997/L.8. Rev.1, p. 27.

[186]   The questions addressed in paragraphs 4 and 5 may be better dealt with in the context of the pre-trial proceedings.

[187]   Option 1 prohibits trial *in absentia* without any exception; like option 2, it would deal with procedures needed to preserve evidence for trial as a matter separate from trial *in absentia*.

[188]   Some proponents of option 2 do not agree that this should necessarily be a basis for a trial *in absentia*.

[*109] Rights of the accused

3.   The Trial Chamber shall, if it makes an order under paragraph 2, ensure that the rights of the accused under this Statute are respected, and in particular that the accused is legally represented, if necessary by a lawyer appointed by the Court.[189]

Proceedings to preserve evidence[190]

Subsequent trial[191]

Option 3

1.   As a general rule, the accused should be present during the trial.

2.   In exceptional circumstances, the Trial Chamber may, in the interests of justice [at the request of the Prosecutor] [proprio motu or at the request of one of the parties] order that the trial proceed in the absence of the accused, if the latter, having been duly informed of the opening of the trial:

    (a)   Requests to be excused from appearing for reasons of serious ill-health;

    (b)   Disrupts the trial;

    (c)   Does not appear on the day of the hearing;

    (d)   under detention has, when summoned for the date of the trial, refused to appear without good reason, and made it particularly difficult to bring him to the Court; or

In the event that the accused is convicted following a trial held in his absence, the Trial Chamber may issue a warrant for the arrest and transfer of the accused for the purposes of executing the judgement. The decision taken under the provisions of this paragraph shall be communicated to the accused and may be appealed.

[*110] 3. The Trial Chamber shall, if it makes an order under paragraph 2, ensure that the rights of the accused under this Statute are respected, and in particular:

    (a)   that all reasonable steps have been taken to inform the accused of the charge; and

    (b)   that the accused is legally represented, if necessary by a lawyer appointed by the Court.

4.   When the accused has not been duly informed of the opening of the trial and when all reasonable steps have been taken to inform the accused of the charges, the Trial Chamber may also, in very exceptional circumstances, [at the request of the Prosecutor] [proprio motu or at the request of one of the parties], order that the trial proceed in the absence of the accused when required in the interests of justice or the interests of the victims.

The accused may not then be represented by a lawyer of the accused's choosing, but the judge presiding over the Trial Chamber may appoint a lawyer on his own motion.

When the accused, having been judged in accordance with the above provisions, is taken prisoner or is arrested, the decisions taken in his absence by the Trial Chamber shall be null and void in all their provisions. The evidence submitted during the trial held in the absence of the accused may not be used, during the second trial, to establish the charges levelled against the accused, except where it is impossible for the depositions to be made a second time or where the evidence cannot again be produced.

Nevertheless, the accused may agree to the decision if the sentence pronounced in his absence is less than or equal to 10 years of imprisonment.

Option 4

1.   The accused shall have the right to be present at the trial, unless the Trial Chamber, having heard such submissions and evidence as it deems necessary, concludes that the absence of the accused is deliberate.

---

[189]   This provision follows paragraph 3 of the ILC draft, except that it omits subparagraph (a), regarding steps to inform the accused of the charges. This is unnecessary under this option since a trial in absentia is permitted only if the accused was present at the commencement of the trial, a stage at which the indictment is to be read out.

[190]   There is no separate proposal to preserve evidence for trial. This could be dealt with as part of pre-trial proceedings, and would not necessarily be confined to situations where the accused is absent.

[191]   Under this option, there would be no second trial following a trial in absentia.

2.[192] The Trial Chamber shall, if it makes an order under (paragraph 2), ensure that the rights of the accused under this Statute are respected, and in particular:
  (a) that all reasonable steps have been taken to inform the accused of the charge; and
  (b) that the accused is legally represented, if necessary by a lawyer appointed by the Court.

[*111] Article 57[38][193]
Functions and powers of the Trial Chamber

1.   At the commencement of the trial, the Trial Chamber shall:
  (a) have the indictment read;
  (b) ensure that articles 51[27] (5) (b) and 54[30] have been complied with sufficiently in advance of the trial to enable adequate preparation of the defence;
  ·   (c) satisfy itself that the other rights of the accused under this Statute and the Rules have been respected;
  (d) allow the accused to enter a plea of not guilty or to make an admission of guilt before the Trial Chamber [and should the accused fail to do so, enter a plea of not guilty on his or her behalf].
2.   The Chamber shall ensure that a trial is fair and expeditious and is conducted in accordance with this Statute and the Rules, with full respect for the rights of the accused and due regard for the protection of victims and witnesses.
[2 bis. The President of the Trial Chamber shall control and direct the hearing, and decide upon the manner by which evidence shall be produced by the parties. In all circumstances, the President shall have the duty to remain impartial.]
3.   The Trial Chamber may, subject to the Rules, hear charges against more than one accused arising out of the same factual situation.
4.   The trial shall be held in public, unless the Trial Chamber determines that certain proceedings be in closed session in accordance with article 43, or for the purpose of protecting confidential or sensitive information which is to be given in evidence. The deliberations of the Court shall remain confidential.
5.   The Trial Chamber shall, subject to this Statute and the Rules, have, inter alia, the power on the application of a party or of its own motion to:
  (a) issue a warrant for the arrest and transfer of an accused who is not already in the custody of the Court;
  (a) bis exercise the same powers as the Pre-Trial Chamber regarding measures that restrict the liberty of a person;
  (a) ter terminate or modify any warrants issued by the Pre-Trial Chamber;
  [*112] (a) quater rule on any preliminary motions, and such ruling shall not be subject to interlocutory appeal except as provided for in the Rules;
N.B. See the last paragraph of article 12[36] (4)(Challenges to the jurisdiction of the Court or the admissibility of a case) for any possible inconsistency with subparagraph 5 (a) quater.
  (b) require the attendance and testimony of witnesses, and the production of documents and other evidentiary materials by obtaining, if necessary, the assistance of States as provided in this Statute;
  [(b) bis order the production of further evidence to that already collected prior to the trial or presented during the trial by the parties;]
  (c) rule on the admissibility or relevance of evidence;
  (d) protect confidential information; and
  (e) maintain order in the course of a hearing.
The provisions of article 51[27], paragraph 5 (f), will apply mutatis mutandis for the purposes of orders sought under subparagraph (d) above.

---

  [192]   This is paragraph 3 of the ILC text, which requires consequential adjustments to be harmonized with the text of this Option.
  [193]   A/AC.249/1997/L.8. Rev.1, p.32

5 bis. [The Trial Chamber may refer pre-trial issues under this article to the Pre-Trial Chamber for resolution.]

6.   The Trial Chamber shall ensure that a complete record of the trial, which accurately reflects the proceedings, is maintained and preserved by the Registrar.

Article 58[38 bis][194]
Proceedings on an admission of guilt

1.   Where the accused makes an admission of guilt under article 57[38], paragraph 1 (d), the Trial Chamber shall determine whether:

(a)   the accused understands the nature and consequences of the admission of guilt and whether the admission is voluntarily made after sufficient consultation with defence counsel; and

(b)   the admission of guilt is [firmly] supported by the facts of the case that are contained in:

(i)   the indictment and in any supplementary materials presented by the Prosecutor, and which the accused admits; and

[*113]   (ii)   any other evidence, including the testimony of witnesses, presented by the Prosecutor or the accused.

2.   Where the Trial Chamber is satisfied that the matters referred to in paragraph 1 are established, the Trial Chamber shall consider the admission of guilt, together with any additional evidence presented and admitted, as an admission of all the essential facts that are required to prove the crime to which the admission of guilt relates, and [may] [shall] convict the accused of that crime.

3.   Where the Trial Chamber is not satisfied that the matters referred to in paragraph 1 are established, the Trial Chamber shall order that the trial be continued under the ordinary trial procedures provided by this Statute, and shall consider the admission of guilt not to have been made [and shall [may] remit the case to another Trial Chamber].

4.   Where the Trial Chamber is of the opinion that a more complete presentation of the facts of the case is otherwise required in the interests of justice, in particular the interests of the victims, the Trial Chamber may request that the Prosecutor present additional evidence, including the testimony of witnesses, or may order that the trial be continued under the ordinary trial procedures provided by this Statute and, in the latter situation, shall consider the admission of guilt not to have been made [and shall [may] remit the case to another Trial Chamber].

5.   Discussions between the Prosecutor and the defence regarding modification of the charges in the indictment, acceptance of the admission of guilt by the accused, or the penalty to be imposed shall not be legally binding on the Chamber.[195]

Article 59[40][196]
Presumption of innocence[197]

Everyone shall be presumed innocent until proved guilty in accordance with law. The onus is on the Prosecutor to establish the guilt of the accused beyond a reasonable doubt.[198]

[*114] Article 60[41][199]
Rights of the accused

---

[194]   A/AC.249/1997/L.8. Rev.1, p.32.
[195]   Concerns were expressed about this paragraph and it was suggested that its formulation should continue to be examined.
[196]   A/AC.249/1997/L.8. Rev.1, p.33.
[197]   The final provision of A/51/22, vol. II, p. 194, requiring a finding of guilt by a majority of the Trial Chamber, could be addressed in article 65[45].
[198]   Reservations were expressed regarding the phrases "in accordance with law" and "beyond a reasonable doubt" contained in the ILC text.
[199]   A/AC.249/1997/L.8. Rev.1, p. 34.

1.   In the determination of any charge under this Statute, the accused is entitled [, in addition to any rights afforded to a suspect under this Statute,] to a public hearing, having regard to [article 57[38] and] article 61[43],[200] and to a fair hearing by an independent and impartial tribunal, and to the following minimum guarantees in full equality:[201]

(a)   to be informed promptly and in detail, [in a language that the accused understands] [in his own language], of the nature, cause and content of the charge;

(b)   to have adequate time and facilities for the preparation of the defence, and to communicate freely with counsel of the accused's choosing, in confidence;[202]

(c)   to be tried without [undue] [unreasonable] delay and to enjoy a speedy trial;

(d)   subject to article 56[37] (2), to be present at the trial, to conduct the defence in person or through legal assistance of the accused's choosing, to be informed, if the accused does not have legal assistance, of this right and to have legal assistance assigned by the Court in any case where the interests of justice so require, including where the person is unable to secure counsel, and without payment if the accused lacks sufficient means to pay for such assistance;

(e)   to examine, or have examined, the prosecution witnesses and to obtain the attendance and examination of witnesses for the defence under the same conditions as witnesses for the prosecution; [In addition the accused shall also be entitled to present any other evidence;]

(f)   if any of the proceedings of or documents presented to the Court are not in a language the accused understands and speaks, to have, free of any cost, [*115] the assistance of a competent interpreter and such translations as are necessary to meet the requirements of fairness;

(g)   not to be compelled to testify or to confess guilt and to remain silent, without such silence being a consideration in the determination of guilt or innocence;

[[(h)   to make an unsworn statement in his or her defence, if desired] [to declare in his or her defence, but [need] [shall] not take an oath to speak the truth]];

[(i)   to request the Pre-Trial Chamber or, after the commencement of the trial, the Trial Chamber to seek the cooperation of a State Party pursuant to Part 9 [7] of this Statute to collect evidence for him/her;]

[(j)   no reverse onus or duty of rebuttal shall be imposed on the accused.]

N.B. See also the second paragraph of article 61[43] (5) (Protection of the [accused], victims and witnesses [and their participation in the proceedings]) for any possible inconsistency with subparagraph 1 (j).

2.   [Exculpatory evidence] [Evidence which shows or tends to show the innocence] [or mitigate the guilt] of the accused or may affect the credibility of prosecution evidence that becomes available to the Procuracy prior to the conclusion of the trial shall be [made available] [disclosed] to the defence. In case of doubt as to the application of this paragraph or as to the admissibility of the evidence, the Trial Chamber shall decide. [The provisions of article 51[27], paragraph 5 (f), will apply <u>mutatis mutandis</u> for the purposes of a decision made under this subparagraph.]

[3. The right of all persons to be secure in their homes and to secure their papers and effects against entries, searches and seizures shall not be impaired by the Court except upon warrant issued by the [Court] [Pre-Trial Chamber], on the request of the Prosecutor, in accordance with Part 9[7] or the Rules of the Court, for adequate cause and particularly describing the place to be searched and things to be seized, or except on such grounds and in accordance with such procedures as are established by the Rules of the Court.]

---

[200]   The matters relating to the exceptions concerning a public hearing could be addressed in article 57[38]. The matters in section A on pp. 195 and 196 of A/51/22, vol. II, could be considered under article 57[38].

[201]   A proposal was made that, as to subparagraphs (a)-(g) of paragraph (1) of article 60[41] in the abbreviated compilation the wording of subparagraphs (a)-(g) of paragraph (3) of article 14 of the International Covenant on Civil and Political Rights should be used as such.

[202]   The question of privileged communications could be addressed in the context of article 62[44].

[4. No person shall be deprived of life or liberty, nor shall any other criminal penalty be imposed, without due process of law.][203]

[*116] Article 61[43][204]
Protection of the [accused], victims and witnesses
[and their participation in the proceedings]

1.   The Court shall take the necessary measures available to it to protect the accused, victims and witnesses and may to that end conduct closed proceedings or allow the presentation of evidence by electronic or other special means.

Notwithstanding the principle of public hearings, the Court may order that the proceedings be closed, in the interest of the accused, the victims or the witnesses. [In camera hearings are mandatory when they are requested by an accused who was a minor at the time of the commission of the acts or at the request of a victim of sexual violence.]

N.B. To avoid repetition, the proposals under this paragraph may be merged to read as follows:
1.   The Court shall take the necessary measures available to it to protect the accused, victims and witnesses. Notwithstanding the principle of public hearings, the Court may to that end conduct closed proceedings or allow the presentation of evidence by electronic or other special means. [In camera hearings are mandatory when they are requested by an accused who was a minor at the time of the commission of the acts or by a victim of sexual violence.]

2.   [The Prosecutor shall, in ensuring the effective investigation and prosecution of crimes, respect and take appropriate measures to protect the privacy, physical and psychological well-being, dignity and security of victims and witnesses, having regard to all relevant factors, including age, gender and health, and the nature of the crime, in particular, whether the crime involves sexual or gender violence. These measures will be consistent with the rights of the accused.]

N.B. See also article 47[26] (2) (d bis) (Investigation of alleged crimes).

3.   The Court shall take such measures as are necessary to ensure the safety, physical and psychological well-being, dignity and privacy of victims and witnesses, at all stages of the process, including, but not limited to, victims and witnesses of sexual and gender violence. However, these measures [may not] [shall not] be [inconsistent with] [prejudicial to] the rights of the accused.

4.   [The Court [shall] [may] permit the views and concerns of the victim to be presented and considered at appropriate stages of the proceedings where their personal interests are affected in a manner which is consistent with the rights of the accused and a fair and impartial trial.][205]

[*117] [5.   The Victims and Witnesses Unit, established under article 37[13] of this Statute, shall provide counselling and other assistance to victims and witnesses and advise the Prosecutor and the Court on appropriate measures of protection and other matters affecting their rights. These measures may extend to family members and others at risk on account of testimony given by such witnesses.][206]

[6.   Notwithstanding paragraph 1 of article 51[27], if disclosure of any evidence and/or any of the particulars referred to in that paragraph will probably lead to the security of any witness or his/her family being gravely endangered, the Prosecutor may, for purposes of these proceedings, withhold such particulars and submit a summary of such evidence. Such a summary shall, for purposes of any later trial proceedings before the Court, be deemed to form part of the particulars of the indictment.]

[7.   The rules of procedure shall include provisions giving effect to the United Nations Declaration of Basic Principles of Justice for Victims of Crime and Abuse of Power.]

---

[203]   The rights addressed in paragraphs 3 and 4, which are of a general nature, should perhaps be located in another part of the Statute. In addition, paragraph 4 could be reformulated.
[204]   A/AC.249/1997/L.8. Rev.1, p. 36.
[205]   Some delegations thought that there should be further reflection on the paragraph.
[206]   This issue will be addressed in the context of the organization of the Court.

[8. Legal representatives of victims of crimes have the right to participate in the proceedings with a view to presenting additional evidence needed to establish the basis of criminal responsibility as a foundation for their right to pursue civil compensation.]
N.B. This paragraph should be reviewed in the light of the discussions on article 66[45 bis] (Compensation to victims).
9. A State may make an application for necessary measures to be taken in respect of the protection of its servants or agents and the protection of sensitive information.

Article 62[44][207]
Evidence

1. Before testifying, each witness shall, in accordance with [or as excepted by] the Rules, give an undertaking as to the truthfulness of the evidence to be given by that witness.[208]
2. 1. bis The testimony of witness at trial shall be given in person, except to the extent provided by the measures set forth in article 61[43] or in the rules [*118] of evidence. These measures shall not be [prejudicial to] [inconsistent with] the rights of the accused.[209] [210]
3. [The Court has the authority and duty to call all evidence that it considers necessary for the determination of the truth.][211] [It] The Court may [also] require to be informed of the nature of any evidence before it is offered so that it may rule on its relevance or admissibility [after hearing the parties to the case]. [The Court may base its decision only on evidence submitted and discussed before it at the trial.][212]
4. The Court shall not require proof of facts of common knowledge but may take judicial notice of them.[213]
5. Evidence obtained by means of a serious violation of this Statute or of other rules of international law [or by means which cast substantial doubt on its reliability] [or whose admission is antithetical to, and would seriously damage, the integrity of the proceedings] [or by means which constitute a serious violation of internationally protected human rights] [or which have been collected in violation of the rights of the defence] shall not be admissible.[214]
[*119] [With regard to defences open to the accused under the general principles of criminal law in this Statute, the onus of proof shall be on the accused, subject to a preponderance of probability as applicable in civil cases.][215]
N.B. See also article 60[41] (1) (j) (Rights of the accused) for any possible inconsistency with the second indent of paragraph 5.

---

[207] A/AC.249/1997/L.9./Rev.1, p. 30. There was no time to discuss in the Working Group paragraphs 3 to 6 of this article.
[208] Many delegations were of the view that the subject matter of this paragraph was more appropriate to be dealt with in the Rules of Procedure.
[209] It was suggested that article 61[43] could be drafted in a more detailed or descriptive manner.
[210] Some delegations expressed their concern about the possibility of allowing witnesses to testify without revealing personal data.
[211] This provision is meant to indicate that the relevant evidence cannot be determined by the parties alone, but has also to be determined by the Court's evaluation of the necessary depth of investigation and determination of the facts. This is, of course, basically a civil law concept, but delegations should bear in mind the additional historical dimension and truth-finding mission of the Court.
[212] These provisions might be better placed in article 65[45].
[213] It was questioned whether this provision was strictly necessary.
[214] This is an attempt to merge the additional proposals (paragraph 5, subparagraphs 2 to 5) concerning the admissibility of evidence with the ILC draft. It was felt that it would be better to refer to "rules of international law" than to single out the International Covenant on Civil and Political Rights, although this will of course be the main focus of this rule. The formula "internationally protected human rights" is intended to cover non-treaty standards as well and would therefore be broader than "international law".
[215] Such a provision might be better placed either under article 59[40] or in the context of "Grounds for excluding criminal responsibility" in the part dealing with general principles of criminal law.

[6. The Court has, in case of evidence obtained by national authorities, to presume irrebuttably that the national authorities acted in accordance with the domestic provisions. The Rules of Court shall address the admissible motions against this presumption.]

Article 63[44 bis][216] [217] [218]
Offences against the integrity of the Court
1. The Court shall have jurisdiction over the following offences against the integrity of the Court:
   (a) perjury committed during the course of its proceedings;
   (b) influencing, impeding or retaliating against officials of the Court;
   (c) obstructing the functions of the Court; and
   (d) contempt committed during the course of its proceedings.
2. The Court may impose a term of imprisonment not exceeding [X months/years] [or a fine, or both].
3. The offences referred to in this article shall be tried before a Chamber other than the Chamber in which the alleged offences were committed. The rules shall determine the applicable procedure for these offences.

N.B. See the N.B. on article 5[20] (Crimes within the jurisdiction of the Court).

[*120] [Article 64[44 ter][219] [220]
Confidential information
N.B. This title is suggested in case the article is retained.
1. Any person heard or examined by the Trial Chamber may invoke restrictions provided for in his national law and designed to prevent the disclosure of confidential information connected with national defence or national security.
2. The Trial Chamber may ask the State of which the persons being heard or examined are nationals whether it confirms their claim to be bound to secrecy.

If the State confirms to the Trial Chamber that an obligation of secrecy exists, the Chamber shall note this fact.
3. The provisions of the preceding paragraphs shall also apply to execution of a request for judicial assistance made under Part 9[7] of this Statute.]

Article 65[45][221]
Quorum and judgement[222] [223]
1. A quorum consists of [at least four] [all] members of the Trial Chamber. [The judgement shall be given only by judges who have been present at each stage of the trial before the Trial Chamber and throughout its deliberations.]

---

[216] Delegations favoured the options that the Court shall have jurisdiction over offences against its integrity but the precise formulation of this article must be further reflected upon. There was a view that these offences required further definition in the Statute. Some previous proposals in this respect may be found on pages 44 to 46 of the abbreviated compilation of August 1997.
[217] A/AC.249/1997/L.9./Rev.1, p.31.
[218] Additional discussions are needed on this article.
[219] A/AC.249/1997/L.9. Rev.1, p. 32
[220] Additional discussions are needed on this article.
[221] A/AC.249/1997/L.9. Rev.1, p. 32
[222] The present text was put forward by individual delegations in order to simplify the existing text and to show more clearly which are the various options. The proposal does not constitute as such a new substantive proposal.
[223] Throughout this article, "Court" has been replaced with "Trial Chamber". Decisions by the Pre-Trial Chamber (as well as its composition) and by the Appeals Chamber are dealt with elsewhere. Furthermore, it is questionable whether this article should only address judgements or whether it should also cover other (procedural) decisions. As currently drafted, it only deals with judgements.

[*121] [1 <u>bis</u> [The Trial Chamber's judgement shall be based on its evaluation of the evidence and the entire proceedings.] [The judgement shall not exceed the facts and circumstances described in the indictment or its amendment, if any.]][224]

2.

Option 1

The [decision] [judgement] shall be taken by [a majority] [at least three] of the judges.

Option 2

All judges must concur in a decision as to conviction [or acquittal] and at least three judges must concur as to the sentence to be imposed.

Option 3

All judges must concur in a decision as to conviction [or acquittal] as well as to the sentence to be imposed.

3.[225]

Option 1

If after a sufficient time for deliberation a Chamber which has been reduced to four judges is unable to agree on a decision, it may order a new trial.

Option 2

If the required majority for a decision as to conviction or the sentence to be imposed cannot be reached, the opinion which is more favourable to the accused shall prevail.

[3 <u>bis</u>. The Trial Chamber shall pronounce its findings separately for each charge in the indictment. If several accused are tried together, the Chamber shall rule separately on the case of each of them.]

4.   The deliberations of the Trial Chamber shall remain [secret] [confidential].

5.   The judgement shall be in writing and shall contain a full and reasoned statement of the findings [on the evidence] and conclusions. [It shall be the [*122] sole judgement issued] [It may contain dissenting opinions], and shall be delivered in open court.

[Article 66[45 bis]
Compensation to victims]

N.B. This title is suggested in case the article is retained.

N.B. The following provisions of the draft Statute are also related to this issue:

Article 51[27] (4 <u>ter</u>) (Commencement of prosecution).

Article 61[43] (8) (Protection of the [accused], victims and witnesses [and their participation in the proceedings]).

Article 68[A] (d) (Applicable penalties).

Article 69[47 <u>bis</u>] (vi) (Penalties applicable to legal persons).

Article 72[47 <u>ter</u>] (c) (Fines [and assets] collected by the Court).

Article 85[58] (second paragraph) (General obligation regarding recognition [and enforcement] of judgments).

Article 86[59 <u>ter</u>] (1) (Enforcement of fines and forfeiture measures).

Proposals contained in A/51/22, vol. II and in DPs (1997)

N.B. At the request of the Chair of the Working Group on Procedural Matters during the last session (December), the delegations which submitted the proposals below agreed to consolidate them and submit a revised text for consideration by the Working Group at the March/April session.

Proposal 1

~~Compensation for the victims~~[226]

---

[224]   This is a new paragraph addressing two proposals which are moved here from article 65[45](5) in the abbreviated compilation and from the revised article 62[44](3).

[225]   This paragraph would only be necessary if majority decisions are allowed and a quorum could consist of an even number of judges.

[226]   A/51/22, vol. II, p. 224.

1.   The Registrar shall transmit to the competent authorities of the States concerned the judgment by which the accused was found guilty of an offence which caused damage to the victim.

2.   The victims or his successors and assigns may, in accordance with the applicable national law, institute proceedings in a national jurisdiction or any other competent institution in order to obtain compensation for the prejudice caused to them.

[*123] 3. The judgement of the Court shall be binding on the national jurisdictions of every State party as regards the criminal liability of the person convicted and the principles relating to compensation for damage caused to victims and the restitution of property unlawfully acquired by the person convicted.

Proposal 2

~~Compensation to victims~~[227]

1.   Where necessary, the Trial Chamber shall also determine the scope and extent of the victimization and establish principles relating to compensation for damage caused to the victims and to restitution of property unlawfully acquired by the person convicted, in order to allow victims to rely on that judgement for the pursuit of appropriate forms of reparation, such as restitution, compensation and rehabilitation, either in national courts or through their governments, in accordance with national law.

2.   If the national competent authorities are no longer able, due to their total or partial collapse or unavailability, to proceed upon the judgement, the Court shall do so directly.

Proposal 3

~~Reparations~~[228]

1.

(a)   The Trial Chamber shall, in accordance with this Statute and the Rules of the Court, determine whether a monetary award, or any other award by way of reparations, should be made against a convicted person to a victim or victims of a crime in respect of which that person has been convicted.

(b)   A monetary award may be comprised of:
  (i)   a punitive element;
  (ii) a compensatory element;
  (iii) both.

(c)   An order for reparations may include:
  (i)   an order for restitution of property by the convicted person to a victim of the crime(s) in question;
  (ii) any other order which the Court considers appropriate.

2.   In making an order under this Article, the Trial Chamber shall also determine whether, in order to give effect to its order, it is necessary to [*124] request protective measures, including the tracing, freezing or seizure of proceeds, property and assets and instrumentalities of the person convicted, or of any assignee of his assets where the Trial Chamber is satisfied that there is prima facie evidence that the assignment was made in order to defeat any protective order which the Court might request.

3.   Before making any award or orders under this Article, the Court shall take account of any written or oral representations made:

(a)   by or on behalf of the convicted person;

(b)   by or on behalf of any person directly affected by any order which the Trial Chamber may wish to make;

(c)   by or on behalf of the victim or victims.

4.   In appropriate cases, the Trial Chamber may, in accordance with the Rules of Court, require a victim to describe the basis on which compensation or any other order under this Article is sought.

5.   The judgements of the Trial Chamber making awards or orders under this Article will be transmitted by the Registrar to the competent authorities of the State or States with which the convicted person appears

---

[227]   A/AC.249/1997/WG.4/DP.3.
[228]   A/AC.249/1997/WG.4/DP.13.

to have a direct connection either by reason of nationality or domicile or habitual residence or by virtue of the location of the convicted person's assets.

6. A victim, or his successors or his assigns, may, in accordance with applicable national law, pursue their remedies under the relevant law. To that end, States parties shall take the necessary measures to ensure that judgements of the Trial Chamber have binding force.

Article 67[46]

Sentencing

N.B. This article as such was not considered by the Prep Com in 1997.

ILC Draft

1. In the event of a conviction, the Trial Chamber shall hold a further hearing to hear any evidence relevant to sentence, to allow the Prosecutor and the defence to make submissions and to consider the appropriate sentence to be imposed.

2. ~~In imposing sentence, the Trial Chamber should take into account such factors as the gravity of the crime and the individual circumstances of the convicted person.~~

[*125] Other proposals contained in A/51/22, vol. II[229]

1. [In the event of a conviction, the Trial Chamber shall hold a further hearing [pre-sentencing hearing] to hear any evidence relevant to sentence, to allow the Prosecutor and the defence to make submissions and to consider the appropriate to be imposed.] ~~[The Trial Chamber should take into account such factors as the gravity of the crime and the individual circumstances of the convicted person.]~~ [These submissions may go to aggravation, extenuation or mitigation evidence, or the issue of rehabilitation.]

1 bis. [At such hearing the Parties shall ordinarily present submissions in the following manner:

   (a) presentation by the Prosecutor;
   (b) presentation by the defence;
   (c) prosecution rebuttal;
   (d) defence surrebuttal;
   (e) argument by the Prosecutor on sentence;
   (f) argument by the defence on sentence.]

2. [The Trial Chamber may impose the penalties provided for in the Statute.]

3. ~~[The Trial Chamber shall indicate whether multiple sentences shall be served consecutively or concurrently.]~~

4. [The sentence shall be pronounced in public and in the presence of the convicted person.]

N.B. The deleted texts seem to be redundant in view of similar provisions included in article 70[BCE] (Determination of the sentence) where they may be more appropriately placed.

[*126] PART 7. PENALTIES

N.B. In the Working Group on penalties there were no discussions on the structure of the articles. The following structure is proposed for consideration.

Article 68[A][230]

~~The penalties~~

Applicable penalties

N.B. This title is suggested for consideration.

The Court may impose on a person convicted under this Statute [one or more of the following penalties] [the following penalty]:

---

[229] P. 226.
[230] A/AC.249/1997/L.9/Rev.1, p.67.

(a)[231] [a term of life imprisonment or imprisonment for a specified number of years;]

[a maximum term of imprisonment of [30] years;]

[a definite term of imprisonment between [20] and [40] years [, unless this is reduced according to the provisions of this Statute][232];]

[The Court may attach to the sentence of imprisonment a minimum period during which the convicted person may not be granted any [release under relevant provisions of Part 10 [8] of the Statute].]

[In the case of a convicted person under the age of 18 years at the time of the commission of the crime, a specified term of imprisonment of no more than 20 years];

[*127] [When imposing a penalty on a person under the age of 18 years [at the time of the commission of the crime], the Court shall determine the appropriate measures to ensure the rehabilitation of the offender][233]

N.B. The two preceding paragraphs should be harmonized with article 20[E] (Age of responsibility).

[(b) A fine [in addition to a sentence of imprisonment on conviction of a crime under article 5[20]]];[234]

[(c)

(i) [[disqualification from seeking public office for the person's term of imprisonment and any further period of time that may be imposed] [in the modality and to the extent that the penalty could be imposed in accordance with the laws of the State in which such a penalty is to be enforced];][235]

(ii)[236] a forfeiture of [instrumentalities of crime and] proceeds, property and assets obtained by criminal conduct, without prejudice to the rights of bona fide third parties. [When the whole or part of the [instrumentalities of crime or] proceeds, [*128] property, assets mentioned in ... cannot be forfeited, a sum of money equivalent thereto may be collected.];[237]]

[(d) Appropriate forms of reparation]

---

[231] To meet concerns of several delegations regarding the severity of a life sentence or a long sentence of imprisonment, it was suggested that Part 10[8], article 89[60], should provide a mandatory mechanism by which the prisoner's sentence would be reexamined by the Court after a certain period of time, in order to determine whether he or she should be released. In this way, the Court could also ensure the uniform treatment of prisoners regardless of the State where they served their sentence.

[232] The view was expressed that if such a provision providing for minimum sentencing is included, there should be a reference to factors that may reduce the minimum sentence. In such a case, the list of relevant factors should be exhaustive. It was suggested that among those factors could be the following: (i) diminished mental capacity that falls short of exclusion of criminal responsibility; (ii) the age of the convicted person; (iii) as appropriate, duress; and (iv) the subsequent conduct of the convicted person.

[233] The following proposals were made which should be treated either under age of responsibility or the jurisdiction of the Court:

"[The Court shall have no jurisdiction over those who were under the age of 18 years at the time they are alleged to have committed a crime which would otherwise come within the jurisdiction of the Court] [; however, under exceptional circumstances, the Court may exercise jurisdiction and impose a penalty on a person aged 16 to 18 years, provided it has determined that the person was capable of understanding the unlawfulness of his or her conduct at the time the crime was committed]."

[234] ~~A number of delegations suggested that penalties for procedural crimes be included in relevant provisions of the Statute, along the following lines: "on conviction of perjury or contempt of the Court, as an ordinary penalty or as a supplementary penalty in addition to a sentence of imprisonment".~~

N.B. See article 63[44 bis] (Offences against the integrity of the Court).

[235] Some delegations held the view that such a provision would give rise to difficult issues of enforcement.

[236] Some delegations held the view that such a provision would give rise to difficult issues of enforcement.

[237] It was suggested that forfeiture not be included as a penalty, but instead be included as a mechanism which the Court would request States to use with regard to execution of an order for reparations. According to this view, a provision on forfeiture could be considered as a separate paragraph of this article or elsewhere in the Statute

[[without prejudice to the obligation on every State to provide reparation in respect of conduct engaging the responsibility of the State][238] [or reparation through any other international arrangement], appropriate forms of reparation [,[including] [such as] restitution, compensation and rehabilitation]][239]

N.B. If retained, subparagraph (d) should be examined in the context of the discussions on article 66[45 bis](Compensation to victims).

[(e) (Death penalty)]

Option 1

[death penalty, as an option, in case of aggravating circumstances and when the Trial Chamber finds it necessary in the light of the gravity of the crime, the number of victims and the severity of the damage.]

Option 2

No provision on death penalty.

[*129] [Article 69[47 bis][240] [241] [242]

~~Legal persons~~

Penalties applicable to legal persons

N.B. This title is suggested for consideration if the article is retained.

A legal person shall incur one or more of the following penalties:

    (i)   fines;

    [(ii) dissolution;]

    [(iii) prohibition, for such period as determined by the Court, of the exercise of activities of any kind;]

    [(iv) closure, for such a period as determined by the Court, of the premises used in the commission of the crime;]

    [(v) forfeiture of [instrumentalities of crime and] proceeds, property and assets obtained by criminal conduct;[243]] [and]

    [(vi) appropriate forms of reparation].[244]]

N.B. Subparagraph (vi) should be examined in the context of compensation to victims.

[*130] Article 70[BCE] [245]

Determination of the sentence

N.B. This title is suggested for consideration.

~~Aggravating and mitigating circumstances~~

---

[238]   It was suggested that there was no need for such a clause relating to State responsibility, since it was already dealt with in the context of rules on individual criminal responsibility (see A/AC.249/1997/L.5, article 17[B a.to d.], para. 4).

[239]   A number of delegations suggested that the Statute should address the issue of reparations to victims and their families. Opinions were divided as to whether this issue should be dealt with in the context of penalties. It was suggested that it could usefully be dealt with within the framework of the Working Group on Procedural Matters. It was also noted that the issue of reparations had a bearing on rules of enforcement in Part 10[8]. A number of delegations expressed the view that there might be merit in dealing with these issues in a unified way focusing on all the issues related to compensation.

[240]   A/AC.249/1997/L.9/Rev.1, F on page 71.

[241]   Inclusion of a provision on such penalties would depend on the outcome of considerations in the context of individual criminal responsibility for legal persons.

[242]   It was suggested that such provisions may give rise to issues of enforcement in the context of Part 10[8].

[243]   See footnote 8 concerning forfeiture for natural persons. There may be merit in adopting a unified approach in both provisions, including all relevant qualifications.

[244]   See footnote 8 concerning reparation in the context of natural persons. There may be merit in adopting a unified approach in both provisions, including all relevant qualifications.

[245]   A/AC.249/1997/L.9/Rev.1, B and C on page 70 and E. on page 71.

1. In determining the sentence, the Court shall, in accordance with the Rules of the Court, take into account such factors as the gravity of the crime and the individual circumstances of the convicted person.[246]

~~Prior detention~~

2. In imposing a sentence of imprisonment, the Court shall deduct the time, if any, previously spent in detention in accordance with an order of the Court. The Court may deduct any time otherwise spent in detention in connection with conduct underlying the crime.

N.B. See also article 13[42] (3) (Non bis in idem).

~~Sentences of imprisonment for multiple crimes~~

3. When a person had been convicted of more than one crime, the Court shall:

Option 1

[pronounce a single sentence of imprisonment [not exceeding the maximum sentence prescribed for the gravest crime] [, increased by half]]

[*131] Option 2

[indicate whether multiple sentences of imprisonment shall be served consecutively or concurrently.]

[Article 71[D][247 248]
Applicable national legal standards

Option 1

In determining the length of a term of imprisonment or the amount of a fine to be imposed, [or property to be forfeited,] the Court [may have regard to the penalties provided for by law of] [shall impose the highest penalty provided for by the law of either]:

(a) [the State of which the convicted person is a national];

(b) [the State where the crime was committed;] [or]

(c) [the State which had custody of and jurisdiction over the accused.]

[In cases where national law does not regulate a specific crime, the Court will apply penalties ascribed to analogous crimes in the same national law.]

Option 2

No provision on national legal standards.][249]

[*132] [Article 72[47 ter][250 251]
Fines [and assets] collected by the Court

Fines [and assets] collected by the Court may be transferred, by order of the Court, to one or more of the following:

---

[246] It may be impossible to foresee all of the relevant aggravating and mitigating circumstances at this stage. Many delegations felt that factors should be elaborated and developed in the rules of the Court, while several other delegations expressed the view that a final decision on this approach would depend upon the mechanism agreed for adopting the Rules. Among the factors suggested by various delegations as having relevance were: the impact of the crime on the victims and their families; the extent of damage caused or the danger posed by the convicted person's conduct; the degree of participation of the convicted person in the commission of the crime; the circumstances falling short of exclusion of criminal responsibility such as substantially diminished mental capacity or, as appropriate, duress; the age of the convicted person; the social and economic condition of the convicted person; the motive for the commission of the crime; the subsequent conduct of the person who committed the crime; superior orders; the use of minors in the commission of the crime.

[247] A/AC.249/1997/L.9/Rev.1, D on page 70.

[248] It was suggested that this issue should be dealt with only in the context of article 14[33] on applicable national laws. Another suggestion was to move this issue to section B above. Moreover, the view was held that this kind of provision should be avoided altogether.

[249] Consideration could be given to inserting an express provision to this effect.

[250] A/AC.249/1997/L.9/Rev.1, G on page 72.

[251] It was suggested that there may be options other than (a) and (b) as to the manner in which fines or assets collected by the Court could be distributed to victims.

[(a) [as a matter of priority,] a trust fund [established by the Secretary-General of the United Nations] or [administered by the Court] for the benefit of victims of the crime [and their families];]

　　[(b) a State the nationals of which were the victims of the crime;]

　　[(c) the registrar, to defray the costs of the trial.]]

N.B. This article should be examined in the context of compensation to victims.

[Article H²⁵²,²⁵³

Effect of the judgement.Compliance.Implementation

[(a) The judgement of the Court shall be binding on the national jurisdictions of every State Party as regards the criminal liability of the person convicted and the principles relating to compensation for damage caused to victims and the restitution of property acquired by the person convicted [and other forms of reparation ordered by the Court].

N.B. Paragraph (a) should be deleted as it is already reflected in the second paragraph of article 85[58] (General obligations regarding recognition and enforcement of judgments) and may be more appropriately placed there.

(b) For the purpose of enforcement of fines [or reparation] imposed by the Court, the Presidency may order the forced sale of any property of the person sentenced which is on the territory of a State Party.

For the same purpose, the Presidency may order the confiscation of any sum of money or securities belonging to the person sentenced.

[*133] **N.B. The above text of paragraph (b) should be deleted as it is already reflected in article 88[59 ter](1) (Enforcement of fines and forfeiture measures) and may be more appropriately placed there.**

Decisions by the Presidency are implemented by States Parties in conformity with their domestic laws.

[The provisions of this article shall apply to legal persons.]]

　N. B. The preceding two paragraphs have been moved to article 88[59 ter] (1) (Enforcement of fines and forfeiture measures).

[*134] PART 8. APPEAL AND REVIEW

N.B. The articles in this Part will be considered by the Prep Com at the March/April session.

Article 73[48]²⁵⁴

Appeal against judgement or sentence²⁵⁵

1.　A [decision] [conviction] under article 65[45] may be appealed [to the Appeals Chamber], in accordance with the Rules, as provided for below:

　　(a)　The Prosecutor may make such an appeal [without any specified grounds;] [on the following grounds:

　　　　(i)　procedural error,

　　　　(ii)　error of fact, or

　　　　(iii)　error of law;]

　　(b)　The convicted person may make such an appeal [without any specified grounds.] [on the following grounds:

　　　　(i)　procedural error,

　　　　(ii)　error of fact, or

　　　　(iii)　error of law.]

---

²⁵²　A/AC.249/1997/L.9/L.9/Rev., H on page 72.

²⁵³　It was suggested that all the issues contained here, which include, inter alia, recognition of judgement, should be dealt with in the context of part 8 on enforcement of sentences.

²⁵⁴　A/AC.249/1997/L.9/Rev.1, pp. 35-37.

²⁵⁵　The present text was put forward by individual delegations in order to simplify the existing text and to show more clearly which are the various options. The proposal does not as such constitute a new substantive proposal.

1 bis. A [decision] [sentence] under Part 7[article 47] may be appealed [to the Appeals Chamber], in accordance with the Rules, by the Prosecutor or the convicted person on the ground of disproportion between the crime and the sentence. [In the case of an appeal of sentence, the Appeals Chamber may also render a decision on conviction.]

1 ter.
Option 1
The Prosecutor or the convicted person may, in accordance with the Rules, appeal [to the Appeals Chamber] against a decision rendered in absentia under article 56[37].

[*135] Option 2
The Prosecutor or the convicted person may not appeal against a decision rendered in absentia under article 56[37] except that an appeal against judgement given on the merits in the absence of the accused shall be allowed if the accused accepts the judgement or was represented during the trial before the Trial Chamber by defence counsel appointed by the accused.

2.   Unless the Trial Chamber otherwise orders, a convicted person shall remain in custody pending an appeal.

[2 bis.
Option 1
In case of an acquittal, the accused shall be released immediately.

If, at the time the judgement is pronounced, the Prosecutor advises the Trial Chamber in open court of his or her intention to file notice of appeal, the Trial Chamber may, at the request of the Prosecutor, issue a warrant for the arrest of the acquitted person to take effect immediately.

The Trial Chamber shall not issue an arrest warrant unless it is satisfied that the acquitted person may not be readily returned to custody if judgement is reversed.

Option 2
(a)   If the accused is acquitted, sentenced to payment of a fine or sentenced to a term of imprisonment already covered by the period in detention, the accused shall be released immediately unless he is retained for another case by the organs of the Court or by the judicial authorities of a State Party.

(b)   In all other cases, the Trial Chamber may, if the circumstances justify prolongation of a measure of security, by a special reasoned decision, maintain the detention of the accused. In this case, so long as the judgement is not final and during appeal proceedings, if any, the convicted person shall remain in detention until such time as the period of detention equals the sentence handed down. However, the convicted person has the right to challenge custody by appealing at any time.]

[3.   The sentence shall begin to run from the day it is pronounced. However, as soon as notice of appeal is given, the enforcement of the judgement shall thereupon be stayed until the decision on appeal has been delivered, the convicted person meanwhile remaining in detention.

If, by a previous decision of the Trial Chamber, the convicted person has been released, or is for any other reason at liberty, and he or she is not present when the judgement is pronounced, the Trial Chamber shall issue a warrant for his or her arrest.

[*136] Execution of the judgement shall be suspended during the period allowed for appeal and for the duration of the appeal proceedings.][256]

[4.   The Appeals Chamber may hear interlocutory appeals on the grounds provided for in article 57[38].]

Article 74[49][257]
Proceedings on appeal
1.   The Appeals Chamber has all the powers of the Trial Chamber.

---

[256]   These matters could instead be addressed in Part 7[article 47].

[257]   A/AC.249/1997/L.9/Rev.1, pp. 37-38. The text of article 74[49] was not the subject of a draft revised abbreviated compilation even though it was introduced in the Working Group. Its text comes from the abbreviated compilation of August 1997.

[The Rules of Procedure and Evidence that govern proceedings in the Trial Chambers shall apply <u>mutatis mutandis</u> to proceedings in the Appeals Chamber.] [The Rules of Procedure and Evidence that govern proceedings in the Trial Chambers shall apply <u>mutatis mutandis</u> to proceedings provided by the preceding two paragraphs. Further rules that govern those proceedings shall be provided for in the Rules of Court.] [On the motion of a party, the Appeals Chamber may authorise the presentation of new evidence, which was not available at the time of trial, if it considers that the interests of justice so require.][258]

2.   If the Appeals Chamber finds that the proceedings appealed from were unfair or that the decision is vitiated by error of fact or law, it may:

(a)   if the appeal is brought by the convicted person, reverse or amend the decision, or, if necessary, order a new trial;

(b)   if the appeal is brought by the Prosecutor against an acquittal, order a new trial.

[Those defenses shall only be admissible if already raised in the Trial Chamber or if resulting from the proceedings in that Chamber]

3.   If in an appeal against sentence the Chamber finds that the sentence is manifestly disproportionate to the crime, it may vary the sentence in accordance with Part 7 [article 47].

4.   The decision of the Chamber shall be taken by a majority of the judges, and shall be delivered in open court [on a date of which notice has been given to [*137] the parties and counsel and at which they shall be entitled to be present]. Six judges constitute a quorum.

[The Appeals Chamber shall pronounce judgement on the basis of the record on appeal together with such additional evidence as it has authorized.

[The judgement shall be accompanied or followed as soon as possible by a reasoned opinion in writing, to which separate or dissenting opinions may be appended.]

[The Appeals Chamber may rule only on objections formulated by the parties in their appeals. When the decision has been appealed only by the accused, it cannot be amended to his or her detriment.]

5.   Subject to article 75[50], the decision of the Chamber shall be final.

[6.   A sentence pronounced by the Appeals Chamber shall be enforced immediately.]

[7.   Where the accused is not present when the judgement is due to be delivered, either as having been acquitted on all charges or for any other reason, the Appeals Chamber may deliver its judgement in the absence of the accused and shall, unless it pronounces his or her acquittal, order his or her arrest or surrender to the Court.]

Article 75[50][259]

Revision[260]

1.   The convicted person [and, after his or her death, his spouse, her husband, his or her children, relatives or any persons having express instructions] or the Prosecutor may, in accordance with the Rules, apply to the [Presidency] [Court which rendered the original judgement] for revision of a [conviction] [final judgement in a criminal case][261] on the following grounds:

(a)   that evidence has been discovered which was not available to the applicant at the time the [conviction] [final judgement] was pronounced or affirmed and which could have been a decisive factor in the conviction;

[*138] [(b) it is proved that decisive evidence which was taken into account when passing the conviction does not possess the value which had been assigned to it because it is false, invalid, or has been forged or falsified;

---

[258]   A/51/22, vol. II, p. 242, reformulation of section N.

[259]   A/AC.249/1997/L.9/Rev.1, pp. 38-39.

[260]   The present text was put forward by individual delegations in order to simplify the existing text and to show more clearly which are the various options. The proposal does not constitute as such a new substantive proposal.

[261]   Apparently, the suggested modification implies that an acquittal would also allow an application for revision from the Prosecutor; this would represent a drastic change from the concept of revision adopted by the ILC draft.

(c) it is proved that one or more of the judges who participated in a conviction or in its confirmation has committed in that case a serious breach of his or her duties;

(d) a previous judgement on which the conviction was based has been annulled;

(e) a more benign penal law than the one applied in the sentence becomes retroactively applicable].

2. [[The Presidency] shall reject the application if it considers it unfounded.] [If the [Presidency] [Court which rendered the original judgement] [is of the view that the new evidence could lead to the revision of the conviction] [considers there are valid grounds for the application],

Option 1

it may:

(a) reconvene the Trial Chamber;

(b) constitute a new Trial Chamber; or

(c) refer the matter to the Appeals Chamber,

with a view to the Chamber determining, after hearing the parties, whether the new evidence should lead to a revision of the conviction.

Option 2

it shall annul the conviction and refer the accused to a Chamber at the same level as, but having a composition different from, that of the Chamber which handed down the annulled decision.

[Article 76[50 bis]

Compensation to a suspect/accused]

N.B. This title is suggested in case this article is retained.

N.B.

- **Article 53[29] (8) (Pre-trial detention or release) is also related to this issue.**
- **Consideration should be given to the placement of this article, if retained.**

[*139] Proposals contained in A/51/22, vol. II and DPs (1997)

Proposal 1[262]

Compensation

1. The Court shall make compensation to those who were:

(a) pronounced innocent by an irrevocable adjudication;

(b) arrested or detained for the purpose of prosecution, although the prosecution against him did not eventually take place;

(c) arrested or detained but the lawfulness of that arrest or detention was denied in accordance with this Statute; or

(d) illegally inflicted losses upon by an officer of the Court intentionally or negligently in the course of performing his duties.

2. Procedures and criteria for compensation shall be provided in the Rules, including the expenses to be borne by a complainant State if that State lodged a complaint without sufficient reason.

Proposal 2[263]

The Appeals Chamber may grant compensation to a person who was held in pre-trial detention during proceedings against him that have concluded with a final decision of acquittal. The compensations shall be based on the prejudice caused to him by such detention.

If the Preliminary Investigations Chamber decides to release the person concerned because his arrest or detention was unlawful, it may awards him compensation.

Proposal 3[264]

Compensation in respect of arrest or detention

1. If a person was arrested and no indictment was filed against him or her, and the Trial Chamber finds that there was no basis for the arrest or the detention, or that there are other considerations to justify the

[262] A/51/22, vol II, p. 206, reproduced in A/AC.249/1998/WG.7/CRP.1, p. 24.

[263] A/51/22, vol II, p.206.

[264] Non-Paper/WG.4/No. 1.

compensation of that person, the Trial Chamber may make an order for the payment of compensation in respect of the arrest or detention and reimburse him or her for the costs of his or her defence in an amount to be fixed by the Trial Chamber;

[*140] 2. If a person was arrested or detained and the Trial Chamber finds that the arrest or detention were caused by a frivolous complaint not submitted in good faith, the Trial Chamber may order the complainant State after allowing it to present its arguments in the matter, to make compensation and to pay the costs of defence of the person so arrested or detained, in an amount to be fixed by the Trial Chamber.

Proposal 4[265]

Compensation for irregular or unjustified detention

The Court may award compensation to a person who has held in detention, based on the prejudice caused to him by such detention, when the proceedings against him have concluded with a decision:

-       To release him because of the irregularity of the arrest or detention, or insufficient charges against him;
-       Of acquittal, which has become final;
-       Recognizing his innocence, following an application for revision,

unless it is demonstrated that he was responsible for a failure to produce new evidence or to reveal an unknown factor in good time.

[*141] PART 9. INTERNATIONAL COOPERATION AND JUDICIAL ASSISTANCE[266]
Article 77[51][267]
General obligation to cooperate

States Parties shall, in accordance with the provisions of this [Part] [Statute], fully cooperate with the Court[268] in its investigation and prosecution of crimes under this Statute. States Parties shall so cooperate without [undue] delay.

Article 78[52][269] [270]
[Requests for cooperation: general provisions]

1.   Authorities competent to make and receive requests/Channels for communication of requests

(a)   The Court shall have the authority to make requests to States Parties for cooperation. The requests shall be transmitted through the diplomatic [*142] channel or any other appropriate channel as may be designated by each State Party upon ratification, accession or approval. Such designation and subsequent changes shall be done in accordance with the Rules of Procedure.

(b)   When appropriate, without prejudice to the provisions of paragraph 1 (a), requests may also be transmitted through the International Criminal Police Organization or any appropriate regional organization.

---

[265]   A/AC.249/1997/WG.4/DP.9.

[266]   Articles 78[52], 80[53 bis], 81[54] and 82[55] contain virtually identical provisions, some of which should be harmonized.

[267]   A/AC.249/1997/L.9/Rev.1, p.41.

[268]   "Court" throughout this Part is understood to include its constituent organs, including the Prosecutor, as defined in article 29[5]. Such a provision could be inserted elsewhere in the Statute.

N.B. See N.B. on article 29[5] (Organs of the Court).

[269]   A/AC.249/1997/L.9/Rev.1, pp.41-43.

[270]   It was suggested that the provisions of article 80[53 bis], paragraph 3, and article 82[55], paragraph 7, concerning the protection of witnesses and victims should be combined in a single paragraph in article 78[52], which would read:

"The Court may withhold, in accordance with article 61[43], from the requested State [or a State making a request to the Court under article 82[55] (6)], specific information about any victims, potential witnesses and their families if it considers that this is necessary to ensure their safety or physical and psychological well-being. Any information that is made available to a State under this part shall be provided and handled in a manner that protects the safety or physical or psychological well-being of any victims, potential witnesses or their families."

It was also suggested that the content of such a provision should be considered further.

2.   Language of requests[271]
Requests for cooperation [and supporting documents] shall be [either] in [an official language of the requested State [unless otherwise agreed]] [or in] [one of the working languages reflected in article 42[18], in accordance with the choice made by that State upon ratification, accession or approval].

[The legal effect of such request shall not be diminished if any supporting document is not in such working language provided that a brief summary of any such document in that working language is also submitted.]

3.   Confidentiality of requests from the Court
The requested State shall keep confidential a request and any supporting documents, except to the extent that the disclosure is necessary for execution of the request.

4.   Cooperation by non-States Parties[272]
[(a) The Court may [call on] [invite] any State not party to this Statute to provide assistance under this part on the basis of [comity,] an ad hoc arrangement, an agreement with such State [or any other appropriate basis].]

[(b) Where a State not party to this Statute [which has entered into an ad hoc arrangement or an agreement with the Court][273], fails to cooperate with requests under paragraph (a), thereby preventing the Court from performing its duties under this Statute, the Court may make a finding to that effect and refer the matter to [the Council of States Parties][274] [or] [the United Nations General Assembly] [or, where the Security Council referred the matter to the [*143] Court,] [to the Security Council] [so that necessary measures may be taken to enable the Court to exercise its jurisdiction][275].]

5.   Cooperation of intergovernmental organizations
The Court may ask any intergovernmental organizations to provide information or documents. The Court may also ask for other forms of cooperation and assistance as may be agreed upon with such organizations and in accordance with their respective competencies and/or mandates.

6.[276]   States Parties' failure to cooperate [comply]
Where a State Party fails to comply with a request by the Court contrary to the provisions of the Statute, thereby preventing the Court from performing its duties under this Statute, the Court may make a finding to that effect and refer the matter to [the Council of States Parties][277] [or] [the United Nations General Assembly] [or, where the Security Council referred the matter to the Court] [to the Security Council] [so that necessary measures may be taken to enable the Court to exercise its jurisdiction][278].

N.B. In view of the length of the article, the headings of the paragraphs are retained pending a decision on the text of the article. Consideration may be given to dividing the article into three as follows:

-   **paragraphs 1 to 3;**
-   **paragraphs 4 and 5;**
-   **paragraph 6.**

---

[271]   The language to be used by States in their replies to the Court is dealt with under article 83[56].

[272]   It was suggested that the issue of non-States Parties should be addressed in a separate article 77[51] bis.

[273]   It was suggested that a reference to paragraph (a) would cover this concern.

[274]   It was suggested that the referral be made to a standing committee of the Council of States Parties. This issue needs to be further addressed in Part 4.

[275]   The question of "necessary measures" has to be further examined.

[276]   It was suggested that this paragraph should be inserted in article 77[51].

[277]   It was suggested that the referral be made to a standing committee of the Council of States Parties. This issue needs to be further addressed in the organization of the Court.

[278]   The question of "necessary measures" has to be further examined.

[*144] Article 79[53][279]

[Surrender] [Transfer] [Extradition] of persons[280] to the court

1.   The Court may transmit a request for the arrest and [surrender] [transfer] [extradition] of a person, along with the supporting material outlined in article 80[53 bis], to any State on the territory of which that person may be found, and shall request the cooperation of that State in the arrest and [surrender] [transfer] [extradition] of such person. States Parties shall, in accordance with the provisions of this Part [and the procedure under their national law], comply with requests for arrest and [surrender] [transfer] [extradition] without [undue] delay.

[1 bis. The national law of a requested State shall govern the [conditions] [procedure] for granting or denying a request for [surrender] [transfer] [extradition] [except as otherwise provided in this Part].]

2.

[Option 1: No grounds for refusal.]

[Option 2: A State Party may deny a request for [surrender] [transfer] [extradition] only if:[281]

    (a)   with respect to a crime under [article 5[20] (b) through (e)] [article 5[20] (e)], it has not accepted the jurisdiction of the Court;

    [(b) the person is a national of the requested State;][282]

    (c)   the person has been investigated or has been proceeded against, convicted or acquitted in the requested State or another State for the offence for which his [surrender] [transfer] [extradition] is sought [, except that a request may not be denied if the Court has determined that the case is admissible under article 11[35]];

[*145] [(d) the information submitted in support of the request does not meet the minimum evidentiary requirements of the requested State, as set forth in article 80[53 bis], paragraph 1 (c);]

    (e)   compliance with the request would put it in breach of an existing obligation that arises from [a peremptory norm of] general international law [treaty] obligation undertaken to another State.][283]

N.B. The options in this subparagraph are not clear.

[2 bis. If a request for [surrender] [transfer] [extradition] is denied, the requested State Party shall promptly inform the Court of the reasons for such denial.]

3.   Application to the Court to set aside [surrender] [transfer] [extradition]

    A State Party [having received a request under paragraph 1 may, in accordance with the Rules[284]] [may, in [...] days of receiving a request under paragraph 1], file a written application with the Court to [set aside] [withdraw] the request on specified grounds [including those mentioned in articles 11[35] and 13[42]]. Pending a decision of the Court on the application, the State concerned may delay complying with the request but shall take appropriate measures [as may be available] to ensure the compliance with the request after a decision of the Court to reject the application.

4.   Parallel requests from the Court and State(s)

Option 1

    (a)   A State Party [which has accepted the jurisdiction of the Court] [, if it is a party to the treaty covered by [article 5[20] (e)] with respect to the crime,] shall [, as far as possible,] give priority to a request from the Court under paragraph 1 over requests for extradition from other States [Parties].

---

[279]   A/AC.249/1997/L.9/Rev.1, pp.43-48.

[280]   The term "persons" is understood to include "suspects", "accused" and "convicted persons". [The term "suspect" means a person who is the subject of a pre-indictment arrest warrant.]

[281]   There is no agreement on the list of grounds contained in this option.

[282]   It was suggested that even if a person is a national of the requested State, this does not prevent that State from [transferring] [surrendering] [extraditing] the person to the Court if the latter guarantees that the national in question shall be returned to the requested State to serve the sentence pronounced by the Court (cf. article 86[59] (1)).

[283]   It was suggested that the following ground for refusal should be included: when the imposition or the execution of punishment for the offence for which surrender is requested would be barred by reasons prescribed under the law of the requested State if the requested State were to have jurisdiction over the offence.

[284]   Questions dealing with the consequences of lapse of time will be addressed in the Rules.

(b)   If the requested State also receives a request from a non-State Party to which it is bound by an extradition agreement for the extradition of the same person, either for the same offence or for a different offence for which the Court is seeking the person's [surrender] [transfer] [extradition], the requested State shall determine whether to [surrender] [transfer] [extradite] the person to the Court or to extradite the person to the State. In making its decision the requested State shall consider all relevant factors, including but not limited to:

[*146]   (i)   the respective dates of the requests;

(ii)   if the offences are different, the nature and gravity of the offences;

(iii)   the interests of the State requesting extradition, including, where relevant, whether the offence was committed in its territory and the nationality of the victims of the offence; and

(iv)   the possibility of subsequent [surrender] [transfer] [extradition] or extradition between the Court and the State requesting extradition.

Option 2

(a)   If the requested State also receives a request from a [State] [State Party] [to which it is bound by an extradition agreement] for the extradition of the same person, either for the same offence or for a different offence for which the Court is seeking the person's [surrender] [transfer] [extradition], the appropriate authority of the requested State shall determine whether to [surrender] [transfer] [extradite] the person to the Court or to extradite the person to the State. In making its decision the requested State shall consider all relevant factors, including but not limited to:

(i)   whether the extradition request was made pursuant to a treaty;

(ii)   the respective dates of the requests;

(iii)   if the offences are different, the nature and gravity of the offences;

(iv)   the interests of the State requesting extradition, including, where relevant, whether the offence was committed in its territory and the nationality of the victims of the offence; and

(v)   the possibility of subsequent [surrender] [transfer] or extradition between the Court and the State requesting extradition.

(b)   The requested State may not, however, deny a request for the [surrender] [transfer] [extradition] made under this article in deference to another State's request for extradition of the same person for the same offence if the State requesting extradition is a State Party and the Court has ruled the case before it is admissible, and its decision took into consideration the proceedings in that State which gave rise to its extradition request.

Option 3

(a)   Subject to paragraph (b), a State Party [shall] [may] accord priority to a request by a State over a request by the Court for the extradition, transfer or surrender of a person to the requesting State under the provisions of any existing bilateral or multilateral agreement.

(b)   A State Party shall however accord priority to requests from the Court over a request by a State where the Court has [positively] determined pursuant to article 11[35] that the requesting State is unwilling or unable genuinely to [*147] carry out the investigation or prosecution of the case for which extradition, transfer or surrender is sought.

[5.   Proceeding in requested State

Where the law of the requested State so requires, the person whose [surrender] [transfer] [extradition] is sought shall be entitled to challenge the request for arrest and [surrender] [transfer] [extradition] in the court of the requested State on [only] the following grounds:

[(a)   lack of jurisdiction of the Court;]

[(b)   non bis in idem; or]

[(c)   the evidence submitted in support of the request does not meet the evidentiary requirements of the requested State as set forth in article 80[53 bis], paragraph 1 (b) (v) and (c) (ii).]]

6.   Delayed or temporary [surrender] [transfer] [extradition]

If the person sought is being proceeded against or is serving a sentence in the requested State for an offence different from that for which [surrender] [transfer] [extradition] to the Court is sought, the requested State, after making its decision to grant the request, may:

(a)   temporarily [surrender] [transfer] [extradite] the person to the Court and in that case, the Court shall return the person to that State after the completion of the trial or as otherwise agreed; or

(b)   [with the consent of the Court [Pre-Trial Chamber] which shall rule after having heard the Prosecutor] postpone the [surrender] [transfer] [extradition] of the person until the completion or abandonment of the prosecution [or completion of service of the sentence].[285]

[7.   Extradite or prosecute obligation[286]

(a)   In the case of a crime to which article 5[20] (e) applies, the requested State [, if it is a party to the treaty in question but has not accepted the Court's jurisdiction with respect to that crime,] shall, where it decides not to [surrender] [transfer] [extradite] the accused to the Court, promptly take all necessary steps to extradite the accused to a State having requested extradition or [at the request of the Court] refer the case [through proceedings in accordance with national laws] to its competent authorities for the purpose of prosecution.

[*148] [(b)   In any other case, the requested State Party shall [consider whether it can], in accordance with its legal procedures, take steps to arrest and [surrender] [transfer] [extradite] the accused to the Court, or [whether it should take steps to extradite the accused to a State having requested extradition or [at the request of the Court] refer the case to its competent authorities for the purpose of prosecution.]

[(c)   The [surrender] [transfer] [extradition] of an accused to the Court will constitute, as between States Parties which accept the jurisdiction of the Court with respect to the crime in question, compliance with a provision of any treaty requiring that a suspect be extradited or that the case be referred to the competent authorities of the requested State for the purpose of prosecution.]]

[8.   Provision of evidence irrespective of [surrender] [transfer] [extradition]

[To the extent permitted under the law of the requested State and] without prejudice to the rights of third parties, all items found in the requested State [that have been acquired as a result of the alleged crime or] that may be required as evidence shall, upon request, be transmitted to the Court [if the [surrender] [transfer] [extradition] is granted on conditions to be determined by the Court] [even if the [surrender] [transfer] [extradition] of the person cannot be carried out]. [Any rights which third parties may have acquired in the said items shall be preserved where these rights exist. The property shall be returned without charge to the requested State as soon as possible after the trial.]]

N.B.

-   **It would be more appropriate to deal with the issues raised in this paragraph in the context of article 82[55] (Other forms of cooperation [and judicial and legal [mutual] assistance]).**

-   **Consideration may be given to dealing with some of the details in this paragraph in the Rules.**

9.   Transit of [surrendered] [transferred] [extradited] person[287]

(a)   A State Party shall authorize transportation under its national procedural law through its territory of a person being [surrendered] [transferred] [extradited] to the Court by another State. A request by the Court for transit shall be transmitted in accordance with article 78[52]. The request for transit shall contain a description of the person being transported, a brief statement of the facts of the case and the legal characterization and the warrant for arrest and [transfer] [surrender] [extradition]. A person in transit shall be detained in custody during the period of transit.

[*149] [(b) No authorization is required where air transportation is used and no landing is scheduled on the territory of the State of transit.]

(c)   If an unscheduled landing occurs on the territory of the State of transit, it may require a request for transit as provided for in subparagraph (a). The State of transit shall detain the person to be transported

---

[285]   If it is agreed that consent of the Court will be required for postponement, then the last set of brackets can be removed.

[286]   The text of paragraph 7 (a) and (b) applies if there is a consent regime. If the Court has jurisdiction over core crimes and there is no consent regime, these provisions could be deleted.

[287]   It has been suggested that this or other provisions could form the basis for a separate article. In addition, some felt that a number of details set forth in this text would be more appropriately regulated in the Rules.

until the request for transit is received and the transit is effected, so long as the request is received within 96 hours of the unscheduled landing.

10. Costs

The costs associated with the [surrender] [transfer] [extradition] of a person shall be borne by the [Court] [requested State]] [Court or the requested State depending upon where the cost concerned arises].
N.B. In view of the length of the article, the headings of the paragraphs are retained. Consideration may be given to dividing the article into shorter articles, without prejudice to their retention, as follows:

- **paragraphs 1 and 1 bis;**
- **paragraph 2 and 2 bis;**
- **paragraph 3;**
- **paragraph 4;**
- **paragraph 5;**
- **paragraph 6;**
- **paragraph 7;**
- **paragraph 8;**
- **paragraph 9;**
- **paragraph 10.**

[*150] Article 80[53 bis][288]
Contents of request for [surrender] [transfer] [extradition][289]

1. A request for arrest and [surrender] [transfer] [extradition] shall be made in writing. In urgent cases a request may be made by any medium capable of delivering a written record,[290] provided that a request shall be confirmed [if necessary] through the channel provided for in article 78[52]. The request shall contain or be supported by:

(a) information describing the person sought, sufficient to identify the person and information as to that person's probable location;

(b) in the case of a request for pre-indictment arrest and [surrender] [transfer] [extradition]:

(i) a copy of warrant for arrest;[291]

(ii) a statement of the reasons to believe the suspect may have committed a crime within the jurisdiction of the Court and that the Prosecutor expects to seek an indictment within [90] days;

(iii) a brief summary of the [essential] facts of the case;

(iv) a statement as to why pre-indictment arrest is urgent and necessary;[292]

(v) [such documents, statements, or other types of information regarding the commission of the offence and the person's role therein, which may be required by the laws of the requested State;] [however, in no event may the requested State's requirements be more burdensome than those applicable to requests for extradition pursuant to treaties with other States;]

[*151] (c) in the case of a request for post-indictment arrest and [surrender] [transfer] [extradition]:

(i) a copy of the warrant of arrest and indictment;

(ii) such documents, statements, or other types of information regarding the commission of the offence and the accused's role therein which may be required by the laws of the requested State; [however, in no event may the requested State's requirements be more burdensome than those applicable to requests for extradition pursuant to treaties or other arrangements with other States];]

---

[288] A/AC.249/1997/L.9/Rev.1, pp.48-50.
[289] Portions of this article might also be provided for in the Rules rather than in the Statute.
[290] Issues relating to the security of this type of transmission will have to be discussed.
[291] The question of authentication of a warrant of arrest will be dealt with in the Rules.
[292] Article 52[28] covers pre-indictment arrest, while this paragraph also addresses the form of a request for pre-indictment arrest. The text of these two provisions must be examined together to ensure that there are no inconsistencies or duplications.

(d)   in the case of a request for the arrest and [surrender] [transfer] [extradition] of a person already convicted:[293]

(i)   a copy of any warrant of arrest for that person;

(ii)   a copy of the judgement of conviction;

(iii)   information to demonstrate that the person sought is the one referred to in the judgement of conviction;

(iv)   [if the person sought has been sentenced,] a copy of the sentence imposed and a statement of any time already served and that remaining.

1 bis. A State Party shall notify the Court at the time of ratification, accession or approval whether it can [surrender] [transfer] [extradite] on the basis of a pre-indictment warrant and the information specified in paragraph 1 (b) or it can only [surrender] [transfer] [extradite] following [confirmation of indictment] [issuance of a post-indictment warrant] on the basis of the information in paragraph 1 (c).

[2.   Where the requested State Party considers the information provided insufficient to allow it to comply with the request, it shall seek, without delay, additional information and may fix a reasonable time limit for the receipt thereof. [Any proceedings in the requested State may be continued, and the person sought may be detained, for such period as may be necessary to enable the Court to provide the additional information requested.] If the additional information is not provided within the reasonable time limit fixed by the requested State, the person may be released.]

[3.   The Court may in accordance with article 61[43] withhold from the requested State specific information about any victims, potential witnesses and their families if it considers that it is necessary to ensure their safety or physical or psychological well-being. Any information that is made available under this article shall be provided and handled in a manner that protects the safety or [*152] physical or psychological well-being of any victims, potential witnesses and their families.][294]

N.B. This provision is similar to the text in articles 81[54] (2 bis) (Provisional arrest) and 82[55] (7) (b)(Other forms of cooperation [and judicial and legal [mutual] assistance]). Consideration may be given to combining them in a single article.

Article 81[54][295]
Provisional arrest[296]

1.   In case of urgency, the Court may request the provisional arrest of the person sought pending presentation of the request for [surrender] [transfer] [extradition] and supporting documents under article 80[53 bis].

2.   The request for provisional arrest shall [be made by any medium capable of delivering a written record and shall] contain:

(i)   a description of the person sought and information regarding the probable location of such person;

(ii)   a brief statement of the essential facts of the case, including, if possible, the time and location of the offence;

---

[293]   It was suggested that this paragraph is an enforcement-of-sentence issue to be treated in Part 10.

[294]   This paragraph could also be included under article 78[52].

[295]   A/AC.249/1997/L.9/Rev.1, pp.51-52.

[296]   ILC article 52 (1) (a) addresses provisional arrest, as well as search and seizure and other measures pertaining to mutual assistance. In order to present all proposals in a clear fashion, the present document treats provisional arrest in this article and the other matters in article 82[55]. ~~Article 28 provides for pre-indictment arrest under certain limited circumstances. To avoid confusion with the term of provisional arrest provided for in this article, it is for consideration whether the form of arrest in article 28 should be termed "provisional arrest". This article may have other implications for article 28~~.

N.B. The above text has been deleted because the form of arrest in article 52[28] (Arrest) is now called "pre-indictment arrest".

(iii) a statement of the existence of a warrant of arrest or a judgement of conviction against the person sought, and, if applicable, a description of the specific offence or offences with which the person has been charged or for which he has been convicted; and

(iv) a statement that a request for [surrender] [transfer] [extradition] of the person sought will follow.

[*153] 2 <u>bis</u>. The Court may withhold from the requested State specific information about any victims, potential witnesses and their families or close associates if it considers that it is necessary to ensure their safety or well-being. Any information that is provided under this article to the requested State shall be provided in a manner that protects the safety or well-being of any victims, potential witnesses and their families or close associates.

N.B. See the N.B. in article 80[53 <u>bis</u>](3) (Contents of request for [surrender] [transfer] [extradition]).

3.   A person who is provisionally arrested may be discharged from custody upon the expiration of [ ][297] days from the date of provisional arrest if the requested State has not received the request for [surrender] [transfer] [extradition] and the supporting documents specified under article 80[53 <u>bis</u>]. However, the person may consent to [surrender] [transfer] [extradition] before the expiration of this period if the legislation of the requested State allows, in which case that State shall proceed to [surrender] [transfer] [extradite] the person to the Court as soon as possible.[298]

4.   The fact that the person sought has been discharged from custody pursuant to paragraph 3 shall not prejudice the subsequent rearrest and [surrender] [transfer] [extradition] of that person if the request for [surrender] [transfer] [extradition] and supporting documents are delivered at a later date.

Article 82[55][299]

Other forms of cooperation [and judicial and

legal [mutual] assistance][300]

1.   States Parties shall, in accordance with the provisions of this Part [and their national [procedural] law], comply with requests for assistance by the Court for:

(a)   the identification and whereabouts of persons or the location of items;

[*154] (b)   the taking of evidence, including testimony under oath, and the production of evidence, including expert opinions or reports necessary to the Court;

(c)   the questioning of any suspect or accused;

(d)   the service of documents, including judicial documents;

(e)   facilitating the appearance of persons before the Court;

[(f)   the temporary transfer of persons in custody, with their consent [which cannot be withdrawn], in order to provide testimony [or other assistance] to the Court;]

[(g)   the conduct of on-site investigations and inspections[301] [with the consent of the requested State];]

[(h)   the conduct of proceedings of the Court in its territory with the consent of the requested State;][302]

(i)   the execution of searches and seizures;

(j)   the provision of records and documents, including official records and documents;

(k)   the protection of victims and witnesses and the integrity of evidence;

---

[297]   Some delegations have proposed a 30-day period, some a 40-day period and some a 60-day time period.

[298]   It was suggested that the simplified surrender procedure should be the object of a separate paragraph, since it applies to both the provisional arrest stage and after a full surrender request has been submitted. This paragraph could also be included in article 78[52].

[299]   A/AC.249/1997/L.9/Rev.1, pp. 52-56.

[300]   This issue has to be revisited after the title of Part 9[7] is confirmed.

[301]   This issue is also addressed in article 47[26] (2)(c).

[302]   The relationship between subparagraphs (g) and (h) and article 83[56] (4) needs to be examined.

(l)   the identification, tracing and freezing or seizure of proceeds, property and assets and instrumentalities of crimes for the purpose of eventual ~~confiscation~~ forfeiture without prejudice to the rights of bona fide third parties;[303] and

(m) any other types of assistance [not prohibited by the law of the requested State].

[2.   Grounds for refusal

Option 1

A State Party shall not deny a request for assistance from the Court.

[*155] Option 2

A State Party may deny a request for assistance, in whole or in part, only if:[304]

(a)   with respect to a crime [under [article 5[20] (b) through (e)] [article 5[20] (e)], it has not accepted the jurisdiction of the Court;

(b)   the authorities of the requested State would be prohibited by its national laws from carrying out the action requested with regard to the investigation or prosecution of a similar offence in that State;

(c)   execution of the request would seriously prejudice its national security, <u>ordre public</u> or other essential interests;

(c) <u>bis</u> the request concerns the production of any documents or disclosure of evidence which relates to its national [security] [defence];

(d)   execution of the request would interfere with an ongoing investigation or prosecution in the requested State or in another State [or with a completed investigation or prosecution that might have led to an acquittal or conviction, except that a request may not be denied if the investigation or prosecution relates to the same matter which is the subject of the request and the Court has determined that the case is admissible under article 11[35]];

(e)   compliance with the request would put it in breach of an existing [international law] [treaty] obligation undertaken to another [State] [non-State Party].]

[3.   Before denying a request for assistance, the requested State shall consider whether the requested assistance can be provided subject to specified conditions, or whether the assistance can be provided at a later time or in an alternative manner, provided that if the Court or the Prosecutor accepts the assistance subject to conditions, it shall abide by them.]

4.   If a request for assistance is denied, the requested State Party shall promptly inform the Court or the Prosecutor of the reasons for such denial.

[4 <u>bis</u>. If a requested State does not produce a document or disclose evidence under paragraph 2 (c) <u>bis</u> on the ground that it relates to its national defence, the Trial Chamber shall only make such inferences that relate to the guilt or innocence of the accused.][305]

[*156] 5. Confidentiality[306]

(a)   The Court shall ensure the confidentiality of documents and information except as required for the investigation and proceedings described in the request.

(b)   The requested State may, when necessary, transmit documents or information to the Prosecutor on a confidential basis. The Prosecutor may then use them solely for the purpose of generating new evidence.

(c)   The requested State may, on its own motion or at the request of the Prosecutor, subsequently consent to the disclosure of such documents or information. They may then be used as evidence pursuant to the provisions of Parts 5 [4] and 6 [5] of the Statute and related Rules.

---

[303]   The issue of whether the Court is to be vested with such powers is linked with article 68[A] in Part 7 on Penalties.

[304]   The list of possible grounds for refusal is not an agreed list.

[305]   Views have been expressed that consideration should be given to establishing a mechanism for dealing with such sensitive information.

[306]   Views have also been expressed that subparagraphs (b) and (c) should be addressed in the Rules.

6. Assistance by the Court

(a) The Court [may] [shall], upon request, cooperate with and provide assistance [within its competence] to a State Party conducting an investigation into or trial in respect of acts which constitute a crime under this Statute [or which constitute a serious crime under the national law of the requesting State].

(b)[307] (i) The assistance provided under subparagraph (a) shall include, among others:

(1) the transmission of statements, documents or other types of evidence obtained in the course of an investigation or a trial conducted by the Court; and

(2) the questioning of any person detained by the Court;

(ii) In the case of assistance under subparagraph (b) (i) (1):

(1) If the documents or other types of evidence have been obtained with the assistance of a State, such transmission shall require the consent of that State;[308]

(2) If the statements, documents or other types of evidence have been provided by a witness or expert, such transmission shall be [*157] subject to the provisions of article 61[43][309] [and shall require the consent of that witness or expert];

(c) The Court may, under the conditions set out in this paragraph, grant a request for assistance under this paragraph from a non-State party.

7. Form and contents of the request

(a) Requests for [judicial and legal] [mutual] assistance shall:

(i) be made in writing. In urgent cases, a request may be made by any medium capable of delivering a written record, provided that it shall be confirmed [, if necessary,] through the channel provided for in article 78[52]; and

(ii) contain the following, as applicable:

(1) a brief statement of the purpose of the request and the assistance sought, including the legal basis and grounds for the request;

(2) as much detailed information as possible about the location or identification of any person or place that must be found or identified in order for the assistance sought to be provided;

(3) a brief description of the essential facts underlying the request;

(4) the reasons for and details of any procedure or requirement to be followed;

[(5) such information as may be required under the law of the requested State in order to execute the request;]

(6) any other information relevant to the assistance being sought.

(b) The Court may withhold, in accordance with article 61[43], from the requested State [or a State making a request under paragraph 6] specific information about any victims, potential witnesses and their families if it considers that this is necessary to ensure their safety or physical and psychological well-being. Any information that is made available under this article to the requested State shall be provided and handled in a manner that protects the safety or physical or psychological well-being of any victims, potential witnesses and their families.

N.B. See the N.B. in article 80[53 bis](3) (Contents of request for [surrender] [transfer][extradition]).

[*158] N.B. Consideration may be given to dividing this article into shorter articles, without prejudice to their retention, as follows:

- **paragraph 1;**
- **paragraphs 2 to 4 bis;**
- **paragraph 5;**
- **paragraph 6;**
- **paragraph 7.**

---

[307] Views have also been expressed that subparagraphs (b) and (c) should be addressed in the Rules.
[308] The relationship with article 84[57] needs to be considered.
[309] This relates to the provisions on the protection of victims and witnesses.

Article 83[56][310]

Execution of requests under article 82[55]

1.   Requests for assistance shall be executed in accordance with the law of the requested State [and, unless prohibited by such law, in the manner specified in the request, including following any procedures outlined therein or permitting persons specified in the request to be present at and assist in the execution process[311] [by its competent authorities]].

2.   In the case of an urgent request, the documents or evidence produced in response shall, at the request of the Court, be sent urgently.[312]

3.   Replies from States Parties, including any accompanying documents, [may be in the language of the requested State] [shall be in accordance with paragraph 2 of article 78[52]. The Court may also request the transmission of documents in their original language].

[4.   The [Prosecutor] [Court] may [, if requested,] assist the authorities of the requested State with the execution of the request for judicial assistance [and may, with the consent of the requested State, carry out certain inquiries on its territory].][313]

[*159] [4 bis. [For the purposes of paragraph 4,] the requested State shall, upon request, inform the Court of the time and place of execution of the request for assistance.][314]

5.   (a)   The ordinary costs for execution of requests in the territory of the requested State shall be borne by the requested State except for the following which should be borne by the Court:

(i)   Costs associated with the travel and security of witnesses and experts or the transfer of persons in custody;

(ii)   Costs of translation, interpretation and transcription;

(iii)   The travel and subsistence costs of the Prosecutor, members of his office or any other member of the Court; and

(iv)   The costs of any expert opinion or report requested by the Court.

(b)   Where the execution of a request will result in extraordinary costs, [there shall be consultations to determine how those costs will be met] [those costs shall be met by the Court].

(c)   The provisions in this paragraph shall apply with appropriate modifications to requests made to the Court for assistance.[315]

N.B.

-    **Consideration may be given to whether this provision should constitute a separate article where all the provisions dealing with costs would be combined. See also article 79[53] (10) ([Surrender][Transfer][Extradition] of persons to the Court]).**

-    **Consideration may also be given to dealing with some of the details relating to the costs in the Rules.**

[6.   (a)   Witnesses or experts may not be compelled to testify at the seat of the Court.

[(b)   If they do not wish to travel to the seat of the Court, their evidence shall be taken in the country in which they reside or in such other place as they may agree upon with the Court [in accordance with national requirements [and in compliance with international law standards][316]].

[*160] (c) In order to guarantee the safety of witnesses and experts, any means of communication may be used to take their evidence while preserving their anonymity.[317]][318]

---

[310]   A/AC.249/1997/L.9/Rev.1, pp.55-58.

[311]   There is a link between this provision and the empowerment provisions of paragraph 4.

[312]   Views have been expressed that this should be addressed in the Rules.

[313]   Views have been expressed that paragraph 1 is an alternative to this paragraph.

[314]   Views have been expressed that this should be addressed in the Rules.

[315]   Similar provisions may have to be inserted elsewhere to address the situation where the Court renders assistance to States or States Parties.

[316]   The exact formulation will depend on the formulation adopted for article 62[44].

[317]   The protection of witnesses is also addressed in articles 47[26] and 61[43].

[318]   Views have been expressed on the relationship between subparagraphs (b) and (c) and article 56[37] on trial in the presence of the accused.

[(d) No witness or expert who appears before the Court may be prosecuted, detained or submitted to any restriction of personal freedom by the Court in respect of any acts [or omissions] that preceded the departure of that person from the requested State.]

7.   Provisions allowing a person heard or examined by the Court under article [...] to invoke restrictions designed to prevent disclosure of confidential information connected with national defence or security also apply to the execution of requests for assistance under this article.

[Article 84[57]](319)
Rule of speciality

1.   Limit on other proceedings against [surrendered] [transferred] [extradited] person

A person [surrendered] [transferred] [extradited] to the Court under this Statute shall not be:

(a)   proceeded against, punished or detained for any criminal act other than that for which the person has been [surrendered] [transferred] [extradited];

(b)   [surrendered] [transferred] [extradited] to another State in respect of any criminal act[320]

[except when he or she commits the criminal act after [extradition] [surrender] [transfer]].

2.   Limit on other uses of evidence

Evidence provided by a State Party under this Statute shall [, if that State Party so requests,] not be used as evidence for any purpose other than [*161] that for which it was provided [unless this is necessary to preserve a right of the accused under article 60[41] (2)].

3.   Waiver of rule by the requested State

The Court may request the State concerned to waive the requirements of paragraphs 1 or 2, for the reasons and purposes to be specified in the request. In the case of paragraph 1, this request shall be accompanied by an additional warrant of arrest and by a legal record of any statement made by the accused with respect to the offence.][321]

N.B. The headings of the paragraphs are retained pending a decision on the text of the article.

[*162] PART 10. ENFORCEMENT[322]
Article 85[58][323]
General obligation regarding recognition
[and enforcement] of judgements

States Parties [shall] [undertake to recognize] [[and to] enforce directly on their territory] [give effect to] the judgements of the Court [, in accordance with the provisions of this Part].

[The judgements of the Court shall be binding on the national jurisdictions of every State Party as regards the criminal liability of the person convicted and the principles relating to compensation for damage caused to victims and the restitution of property acquired by the person convicted and other forms of reparation ordered by the Court, such as restitution, compensation and rehabilitation.][324]

N.B. This article should also be considered in the context of the discussions on article 66[45 bis] (Compensation to victims).

---

[319]   A/AC.249/1997/L.9/Rev.1, pp.58-59.

[320]   The issue of transfer, etc., from the State of enforcement of a sentence of imprisonment to a third State is addressed in article 86[59] (4).

[321]   These square brackets reflect the view that there should be no rule of speciality in the Statute.

[322]   One delegation was of the view this Part deals with issues also relevant to judicial assistance and that there might be grounds for non-recognition or non-enforcement of judgements.

[323]   A/AC.249/1997/L.9/Rev.1, p.59.

[324]   There was a question whether this sort of provision should be in article 65[45], Part 7[article 47] or in Part 10.

Article 86[59]³²⁵
Role of States in enforcement [and supervision]
of sentences of imprisonment

1.   Obligation versus consent of States Parties³²⁶
Option 1
A sentence of imprisonment shall be served in a State designated by the [Court] [Presidency].
[*163] Option 2
(a)   A sentence of imprisonment shall be served in a State designated by the [Court] [Presidency] from a list of States which have indicated to the Court their willingness to accept sentenced persons. [The State so designated shall promptly inform the [Court] [Presidency] whether it accepts the request.]

[(b)³²⁷ A State may make its consent conditional [on the applicability of its domestic laws relating to pardon, conditional release and commutation of sentence, and on its administration of the sentence. In this case, the consent of the Court is not required to subsequent actions by that State in conformity with those laws, but the Court shall be given at least 45 days' notice of any decision which might materially affect the terms or extent of the imprisonment].]

1 bis.
(a)   The [Court's] [Presidency's] designation of a State under paragraph 1 shall be governed by principles [of equitable [geographic distribution] [burden sharing]] to be elaborated by [the Permanent Committee of States Parties.]³²⁸ [However, no such designation shall be made with respect to the State where or against which the crime was committed or the State of which the convicted person or the victim is a national [, unless the [Court] [Presidency] explicitly decides otherwise for reasons of social rehabilitation].]

(b)   In making a designation under paragraph 1, the [Court] [Presidency] shall allow the person sentenced to provide views on any concerns as to personal security or rehabilitation. However, the consent of the person is not required for the [Court] [Presidency] to designate a particular State for enforcement of the sentence.

1 ter.
If no State is designated under paragraph 1, the sentence of imprisonment shall be served in the prison facility made available by the host State, in conformity with and under the conditions as set out in the Host State Agreement, as referred to in article 3, paragraph 2.

2.   Enforcement of the sentence³²⁹
(a)   The sentence of imprisonment shall be binding on the States Parties, which may in no case modify it.
[*164] (b)   The Court alone shall have the right to decide any application for review of the [judgement] [sentence]. The State of enforcement shall not impede the sentenced person from making any such application.

3.   Supervision and administration of sentence
(a)   The enforcement of a sentence of imprisonment shall be subject to the supervision of the [Court] [Presidency] [, and the Court shall ensure that internationally recognized standards of treatment of prisoners are fully guaranteed].

(b)
Option 1
[The conditions of detention shall be governed by the law of the State of enforcement. [However, the [Court] [Presidency] may, on its own motion or at the request of the sentenced person, modify the

---

³²⁵   A/AC.249/1997/L.9/Rev.1, pp. 60-62.
³²⁶   The issue arises as to whether provision should be made concerning whether non-States Parties should accept sentenced persons for imprisonment.
³²⁷   If retained, this provision will need to conform with provisions of article 89[60].
³²⁸   This reflects a current proposal for the establishment of a Permanent Committee of States Parties.
³²⁹   It was suggested that this paragraph should be moved to the beginning of the article.

conditions of detention of the sentenced person. The State of enforcement shall enforce the modified conditions of detention. The [Court] [Presidency] may also on its own motion, or at the request of the sentenced person or the State of enforcement, decide that the sentenced person be transferred to another State for the continued serving of the sentence [provided that State agrees].

[Internationally recognized standards of treatment of prisoners shall be fully guaranteed by the State of enforcement.]

Option 2

[The conditions of detention shall be governed by the law of the State of enforcement, in accordance with internationally recognized minimum standards, but in any case not more or less favourable than those available to prisoners convicted of similar offences in the State of enforcement.]

N.B. The placement of the square brackets is unclear in subparagraph (b).

(c) Communications between persons sentenced and the Court shall be unimpeded [and confidential].

4. Transfer of the person upon completion of sentence

(a) Unless the State of enforcement agrees to permit the prisoner to remain in its territory following completion of sentence, the prisoner shall be released into the custody of the State of the person's nationality or another State that has agreed to receive the person.

(b) The costs involved in transporting the prisoner to another State under paragraph 1 shall be borne by the Court, unless the State of enforcement or the receiving State agree otherwise.

[*165] (c) [Unless prohibited by the provisions of article 84[57]] [with the consent of the Court as provided in article 87[59 bis]],[330] the State of enforcement may also, in accordance with its national law, extradite or otherwise surrender the prisoner to the State which has requested the extradition or surrender of the prisoner for purposes of trial or enforcement of a sentence.

N.B. Consideration may be given to dividing this article into shorter articles as follows:

- **paragraph 1 to 1 ter;**
- **paragraph 2;**
- **paragraph 3;**
- **paragraph 4.**

[Article 87[59 bis][331]
Limitation of prosecution/punishment for other offences[332]

1. A sentenced person in the custody of the State of enforcement shall not be subjected to prosecution or punishment [or extradition to a third State] for any conduct committed prior to delivery to the State of detention, unless such prosecution or punishment [or extradition] has been approved by the [Court] [Presidency] [at the request of the State of detention].

2. The [Court] [Presidency] shall rule on the matter after having heard the prisoner.

3. Paragraph 1 of this article shall cease to apply if the sentenced person remains more than 30 days on the territory of the State of enforcement after having served the full sentence imposed by the Court.]

---

[330]   There is a question as to whether the permissibility of re-extradition of the prisoner should be addressed in article 84[57] (Rule of Speciality) or in article 87[59 bis].

[331]   A/AC.249/1997/L.9/Rev.1, p. 62.

[332]   Consideration should be given to the relationship of this article to the rule of speciality, as found in article 84[57]. This article is also related to article 79[53], paragraph 6, regarding temporary or delayed surrender.

[*166] [Article 88[59 ter][333]
Enforcement of fines and forfeiture measures

1. States Parties shall [, in accordance with their national law,] enforce fines and forfeiture measures [and measures relating to compensation or [restitution] [reparation]][334] as fines and forfeiture measures [and measures relating to compensation or [restitution][reparation]] rendered by their national authorities.

[For the purpose of enforcement of fines, the [Court] [Presidency] may order the forced sale of any property of the person sentenced which is on the territory of a State Party. For the same purposes, the [Court] [Presidency] may order the forfeiture of proceeds, property and assets and instrumentalities of crimes belonging to the person sentenced.][335] [336]

[Decisions by the Presidency are implemented by States Parties in conformity with their domestic laws.

[The provisions of this article shall apply to legal persons.]]

N.B. The last two portions of paragraph 1 have been moved from the deleted article H (b) (Effect of the judgement. Compliance. Implementation), p...

2. Property, including the proceeds of the sale thereof, which is obtained by a State Party as a result of its enforcement of a judgement of the Court shall be handed over to the [Court] [Presidency] [which will dispose of that property in accordance with the provisions of article 72[paragraph 3 of article 47].]

[*167] Article 89[60][337] [338]
Pardon,[339] parole and commutation of sentences [early release]

Option 1[340]

1. The prisoner may apply to the [Court] [Presidency] for a [decision on] [ruling regarding the appropriateness of] [pardon,] parole or commutation of sentence, if under a generally applicable law of the State of enforcement, a person in the same circumstances who had been convicted for the same conduct by a court of that State would be eligible for [pardon,] parole or commutation of sentence.

Option 2

1. (a) The State of enforcement shall not release the prisoner before the expiry of the sentence as pronounced by the Court.

(b) The [Court] [Presidency] alone shall have the right to decide any application for [commutation of the sentence] [commutation of the sentence or parole] [commutation of the sentence, parole or [pardon]]. [If appropriate in the circumstances, parole may be granted after the prisoner has served:

---

333   A/AC.249/1997/L.9/Rev.1, p. 63.

334   References to fines, forfeiture, restitution or compensation, or similar terms, will depend on the range of sanctions and compensatory measures ultimately provided for in Part 7[article 47].

N.B. This footnote should be reviewed in the context of the discussions on article 66[45 bis] (Compensation to victims)

335   There is a question whether this provision concerns enforcement of sentences, or rather the powers of the Court to order particular measures relating to enforcement of fines or confiscation. If it is meant to refer to States enforcing specific orders relating to fines or confiscation, then paragraph 1 might be amended to make clear that that enforcement by States Parties would include "giving effect to orders of the Court relating to enforcement of fines or forfeitures, such as the seizure of particular property or the forced sale of property of the convicted person to satisfy a fine".

336   There was a suggestion that this paragraph should be placed first.

337   In the discussion of the Working Group on Penalties, it was suggested that, to meet concerns of several delegations regarding the severity of a life sentence or a long sentence of imprisonment, article 89[60] should provide a mandatory mechanism by which the prisoner's sentence would be re-examined by the Court after a certain period of time, in order to determine whether he or she should be released. In this way, the Court could also ensure the uniform treatment of prisoners regardless of the State where they served their sentence.

338   A/AC.249/1997/L.9/Rev.1, p. 64.

339   A concern was expressed that pardon might involve political considerations which would not be appropriate for determination by the Court, so that the authority to decide on an application for pardon might better be vested in the Permanent Committee of States Parties.

340   This is an abbreviation of article 60 of the ILC text.

     (i) not less than 20 years in case of life imprisonment;

     (ii) not less than two thirds of the term in case of imprisonment for a definite term.

Parole may be revoked when the parolee is convicted of having committed an offence while on parole, or has violated any condition of his parole.]

2.   Procedures regarding an application for commutation of sentence [or parole [or pardon]] and the [Court's][Presidency's] decision on such an application shall be governed by the Rules of Procedure.

[*168] [Article 90[60 bis][341]
Escape

    In the event of an escape, the sentenced person shall, as soon as he has been arrested pursuant to a request of the Court under article 80[53 bis] (1) (d), be delivered to the State in which he was serving his sentence or to another place determined by the Court.]

[*169] PART 11. FINAL CLAUSES
N.B. The articles in this Part were not considered by the Prep Com in 1997.
Article 91[A][342]
Settlement of disputes

1.   Any dispute between two or more States Parties concerning the interpretation or application of this Statute which cannot be settled through negotiation within a reasonable time shall, at the request of any one of them, be submitted to arbitration. If, within six months from the date of the request for arbitration, the parties to the dispute are unable to agree on the organization of the arbitration, any one of those parties may refer the dispute to the International Court of Justice, by application, in conformity with the Statute of that Court. If one or more States Parties to the dispute has made a declaration in accordance with paragraph 2, the present paragraph shall apply to the other parties to the dispute as far as possible.

2.   Each State may at the time of signature, ratification, acceptance or approval of this Statute or accession thereto declare that it does not consider itself bound by paragraph 1 of this article. The other States Parties shall not be bound by paragraph 1 of this article with respect to any State Party which has made such a declaration.

3.   Any State which has made a declaration in accordance with paragraph 2 of this article may at any time withdraw that declaration by notification to the Secretary-General of the United Nations.

Article 92[B][343]
Reservations

No reservations may be made to this Statute.

Article 93[C][344]
Amendments

1.   At any time after the entry into force of this Statute, any State Party may propose amendments thereto. The text of any proposed amendment shall be [*170] submitted to the Registrar, who shall promptly circulate it to all States Parties.

2.   A proposed amendment to this Statute shall be considered at the next Meeting of States Parties, provided that no consideration shall take place until [3] months after its circulation pursuant to paragraph 1.

3.   The adoption of an amendment at a Meeting of States Parties shall require a [2/3] [3/4] majority of [all the States Parties] [those present and voting].

---

[341]   A/AC.249/1997/L.9/Rev.1, p. 65.

[342]   A/AC.249/1998/L.11, p. 1.

[343]   A/AC.249/1998/L.11, p. 2.

[344]   A/AC.249/1998/L.11, p. 2.

4.   The Registrar shall transmit any amendment adopted at a Meeting of States Parties to the Secretary-General of the United Nations, who shall circulate it to all States Parties.
5.   An amendment adopted at a Meeting of States Parties shall enter into force for all States Parties [60] days after instruments of acceptance have been deposited with the Secretary-General of the United Nations by [2/3] [3/4] of [all the States Parties] [those present and voting].

Article 94[D][345] [346]
Simplified amendment procedure

Modification of [articles ... or Part ...] shall be made subject to the following procedure:
   (a)   Any State Party may submit proposals for modifying [articles ... or Part ...], which shall be transmitted to the Registrar who shall promptly circulate such proposals to all States Parties for consideration;
   (b)   On behalf of the Court, the President may propose any modification of [articles ... or Part ...], which shall be transmitted to the Registrar who shall promptly circulate such proposals to all States Parties for consideration;
   (c)   [Five] [Ten] months after the circulation of proposals, they shall be deemed to have been adopted and the provisions amended accordingly unless within that period one third of the States Parties have objected thereto. The proposals shall then come into effect 30 days after their adoption.
   OR
   (c)   Any proposals made under paragraphs (a) and (b) shall be referred to a Standing Committee of the States Parties, which shall be composed of [five] States Parties elected by the Meeting of States Parties. The Standing Committee shall make a recommendation after having considered the proposals. The [*171] recommendation shall be circulated by the Registrar of the United Nations to all States Parties to the Statute. [Five] [Ten] months after the circulation of proposals, they shall be deemed to have been adopted and the provisions amended accordingly, unless within that period one third of the States Parties have objected thereto. The proposals shall then come into effect 30 days after their adoption.

Article 95[E][347]
Review of the Statute

1.   At any time after the entry into force of this Statute, the Meeting of States Parties may decide, by a two-thirds majority [of those present and voting], to convene a special Meeting of States Parties to review the Statute.
2.   Any amendment to the Statute proposed at such a Meeting of States Parties shall be subject to paragraphs 3 to 5 of article 93[C].

Article 96[F][348]
Signature, ratification, acceptance, approval or accession

1.   This Statute shall be open for signature by all States in Rome, at the headquarters of the Food and Agriculture Organization of the United Nations, on 20 July 1998. Thereafter, it will remain open for signature in Rome at the Ministry of Foreign Affairs of Italy until 20 October 1998. After that date, the Statute shall remain open for signature in New York, at United Nations Headquarters, until 31 December 2000.
2.   This Statute is subject to ratification, acceptance or approval. Instruments of ratification, acceptance or approval shall be deposited with the Secretary-General of the United Nations.

---

[345]   This article is intended to provide a simplified procedure for amending those provisions which might require adjustments to meet practical needs.
[346]   A/AC.249/1998/L.11, pp. 2-3.
[347]   A/AC.249/1998/L.11, p. 3.
[348]   A/AC.249/1998/L.11, p. 3.

3.   This Statute shall be open to accession by any State. Instruments of accession shall be deposited with the Secretary-General of the United Nations.

[*172] Article 97[G][349]
Entry into force

1.   This Statute shall enter into force on the [60th] day following the date of the deposit of the [...] instrument of ratification, acceptance, approval or accession with the Secretary-General of the United Nations.

2.   For each State ratifying, accepting, approving or acceding to the Statute after the deposit of the [...] instrument of ratification, acceptance, approval or accession, the Statute shall enter into force on the [60th] day after the deposit by such State of its instrument of ratification, acceptance, approval or accession.

Article 98[H][350]
Withdrawal

1.   Any State Party may withdraw from this Statute by written notification to the Secretary-General of the United Nations.

2.   Withdrawal shall take effect one year following the date on which notification is received by the Secretary-General of the United Nations. The withdrawal shall not affect any obligations of the withdrawing State under the Statute.

Article 99[I][351]
Authentic texts

The original of this Statute, of which the Arabic, Chinese, English, French, Russian and Spanish texts are equally authentic, shall be deposited with the Secretary-General of the United Nations, who shall send certified copies thereof to all States.

IN WITNESS WHEREOF, the undersigned, being duly authorized thereto by their respective Governments, have signed this Statute.

DONE, this 17th day of July 1998, at Rome.

---

[349]   A/AC.249/1998/L.11, p. 4.
[350]   A/AC.249/1998/L.11, p. 4.
[351]   A/AC.249/1998/L.11, p. 4.

DECISIONS TAKEN BY THE PREPARATORY COMMITTEE AT ITS SESSION HELD FROM 1 TO 12 DECEMBER 1997

[Editorial Note - The U.N. page numbers of this document are indicated in bolded brackets [*] in the text].

[*1]. At its 54th meeting, on 1 December 1997, the Preparatory Committee decided to conduct its work through the following working groups: Working Group on Definitions and Elements of Crimes (chaired by Mr. Adriaan Bos); Working Group on General Principles of Criminal Law (chaired by Mr. Per Saland); Working Group on Procedural Matters (chaired by Ms. Silvia Fernandez de Gurmendi); Working Group on International Cooperation and Judicial Assistance (chaired by Mr. Pieter Kruger); and Working Group on Penalties (chaired by Mr. Rolf Einar Fife).

2. At its 55th meeting, on 12 December 1997, the Preparatory Committee took note of the reports of the Working Groups mentioned above, which are annexed to the present document (annexes I to V).

3. The Preparatory Committee also took note that, pursuant to paragraph 7 of General Assembly resolution 51/207 of 17 December 1996, the Secretary-General had established a trust fund for the participation of the least developed countries in the work of the Preparatory Committee and in the diplomatic conference of plenipotentiaries. Guidelines have been established for the administration of the Fund. The following Governments have made contributions to the Fund: Belgium, Canada, Denmark, Finland, Netherlands, Norway and Sweden. Ten States have utilized the Trust Fund to facilitate their participation in the December session. The General Assembly in resolution 51/207 calls upon States to contribute voluntarily to the Trust Fund.

[*3] Annex I
REPORT OF THE WORKING GROUP ON DEFINITIONS AND ELEMENTS OF CRIMES*

The Working Group recommends to the Preparatory Committee the text of the article concerning the definition of war crimes contained in document A/AC.249/1997/WG.1/CRP.9 for inclusion in the draft consolidated text of the convention for an international criminal court. This text supersedes the text contained in document A/AC.249/1997/L.5 on the same subject.

[*4] WAR CRIMES*
Article 20 C**

For the purpose of this Statute, war crimes means the crimes listed in this article.

A. Grave breaches of the Geneva Conventions of 12 August 1949, namely, any of the following acts against persons or property protected under the provisions of the relevant Geneva Convention:

    (a)   wilful killing;

    (b)   torture or inhuman treatment, including biological experiments;

    (c)   wilfully causing great suffering, or serious injury to body or health;

    (d)   extensive destruction and appropriation of property, not justified by military necessity and carried out unlawfully and wantonly;

    (e)   compelling a prisoner of war or other protected person to serve in the forces of a hostile Power;

    (f)   wilfully depriving a prisoner of war or other protected person of the rights of fair and regular trial;

    (g)   unlawful deportation or transfer or unlawful confinement;

    (h)   taking of hostages.

B. Other serious violations of the laws and customs applicable in international armed conflict within the established framework of international law, namely, any of the following acts:

---

   *   Incorporating the documents listed in the opening paragraph.

   *   Views were expressed that certain provisions should be placed within square brackets.

   **   The relative placement of the various options does not indicate in any way the measure of support for such options. Some options commanded very limited support.

(a) [*5] **Option I**
   (a) intentionally directing attacks against the civilian population as such, as well as individual civilians not taking direct part in hostilities;
Option II
   No paragraph (a).
   (a *bis*)
Option I
   (a *bis*) intentionally directing attacks against civilian objects which are not military objectives;
Option II
   No paragraph (a *bis*).
   (b)
Option I
   (b) intentionally launching an attack in the knowledge that such attack will cause incidental loss of life or injury to civilians or damage to civilian objects or widespread, long-term and severe damage to the natural environment which is not justified by military necessity;[1]
Option II
   [*6] (b) intentionally launching an attack in the knowledge that such attack will cause incidental loss of life or injury to civilians or damage to civilian objects or widespread, long-term and severe damage to the natural environment which would be excessive in relation to the concrete and direct overall military advantage anticipated;[1]
Option III
   (b) intentionally launching an attack in the knowledge that such attack will cause incidental loss of life or injury to civilians or damage to civilian objects or widespread, long-term and severe damage to the natural environment;[1]
Option IV   No paragraph (b).
   (b *bis*)
Option I
   (b *bis*) intentionally launching an attack against works or installations containing dangerous forces in the knowledge that such attack will cause excessive loss of life, injury to civilians or damage to civilian objects which would be excessive in relation to the concrete and direct military advantage anticipated;
Option II
   No paragraph (b *bis*).
   (c)
Option I
   (c) attacking or bombarding, by whatever means, towns, villages, dwellings or buildings which are undefended;
Option II
   (c) making non-defended localities and demilitarized zones the objects of attack;
   [*7] (d) killing or wounding a combatant who, having laid down his arms or having no longer means of defence, has surrendered at discretion;
   (e) making improper use of flag of truce, of the flag or of the military insignia and uniform of the enemy or of the United Nations, as well as of the distinctive emblems of the Geneva Conventions, resulting in death or serious personal injury;

---

[1] It has been accepted that it will be necessary to insert a provision, probably in the general principles section, which sets out the elements of knowledge and intent which must be found to have existed for an accused to be convicted of a war crime. For example: "in order to conclude that an accused had the knowledge and criminal intention required to be convicted of a crime, the Court must first determine that, taking account of the relevant circumstances of, and information available to, the accused at the time, the accused had the requisite knowledge and intent to commit the crime."

(f)

Option I

(f)   the transfer by the Occupying Power of parts of its own civilian population into the territory it occupies;

Option II

(f)   the transfer by the Occupying Power of parts of its own civilian population into the territory it occupies, or the deportation or transfer of all or parts of the population of the occupied territory within or outside this territory;

Option III

(f)   (i)   the establishment of settlers in an occupied territory and changes to the demographic composition of an occupied territory;

(ii)   the transfer by the Occupying Power of parts of its own civilian population into the territory it occupies, or the deportation or transfer of all or parts of the population of the occupied territory within or outside this territory;

Option IV

No paragraph (f).

(g)

Option I

[*8] (g)   intentionally directing attacks against buildings dedicated to religion, art, science or charitable purposes, historic monuments, hospitals and places where the sick and wounded are collected, provided they are not being used at the time for military purposes;

Option II

(g)   intentionally directing attacks against buildings dedicated to religion, education, art, science or charitable purposes, historic monuments, hospitals and places where the sick and wounded are collected, provided they are not being used at the time for military purposes;

(h)   subjecting persons who are in the power of an adverse Party to physical mutilation or to medical or scientific experiments of any kind which are neither justified by the medical, dental or hospital treatment of the person concerned nor carried out in his interest, and which cause death to or seriously endanger the health of such person or person;

(i)   killing or wounding treacherously individuals belonging to the hostile nation or army;

(j)   declaring that no quarter will be given;

(k)   destroying or seizing the enemy's property unless such destruction or seizure be imperatively demanded by the necessities of war;

(l)   declaring abolished, suspended or inadmissible in a court of law the rights and actions of the nationals of the hostile party;

(m)   compelling the nationals of the hostile party to take part in the operations of war directed against their own country, even if they were in the belligerent's service before the commencement of the war;

(n)   pillaging a town or place, even when taken by assault;

(o)

Option I

[*9] (o)   employing the following weapons, projectiles and material and methods of warfare which are calculated to cause superfluous injury or unnecessary suffering:

(i)   poison or poisoned weapons,

(ii)   asphyxiating, poisonous or other gases, and all analogous liquids, materials or devices.

(iii)   bullets which expand or flatten easily in the human body, such as bullets with a hard envelope which does not entirely cover the core or is pierced with incisions,

(iv)   bacteriological (biological) agents or toxins for hostile purposes or in armed conflict,

(v)   chemical weapons as defined in and prohibited by the 1993 Convention on the Prohibition of the Development, Production, Stockpiling and Use of Chemical Weapons and On Their Destruction;

Option II

(o)   employing the following weapons, projectiles and material and methods of warfare which are of a nature to cause superfluous injury or unnecessary suffering:

    (i)   poison or poisoned weapons,

    (ii)   asphyxiating, poisonous or other gases, and all analogous liquids, materials or devices,

    (iii) bullets which expand or flatten easily in the human body, such as bullets with a hard envelope which does not entirely cover the core or is pierced with incisions,

    (iv) bacteriological (biological) agents or toxins for hostile purposes or in armed conflict,

    (v)   chemical weapons as defined in and prohibited by the 1993 Convention on the Prohibition of the Development, [*10] Production, Stockpiling and Use of Chemical Weapons and On Their Destruction,

    (vi) such other weapons or weapons systems as become the subject of a comprehensive prohibition pursuant to customary or conventional international law;

Option III

    (o) employing weapons, projectiles and material and methods of warfare which are of a nature to cause superfluous injury or unnecessary suffering or which are inherently indiscriminate;

Option IV

    (o) employing the following weapons, projectiles and material and methods of warfare which are of a nature to cause superfluous injury or unnecessary suffering or which are inherently indiscriminate:

or

employing weapons, projectiles and material and methods of warfare which are of a nature to cause superfluous injury or unnecessary suffering or which are inherently indiscriminate, such as but not limited to:

    (i)   poison or poisoned weapons,

    (ii)   asphyxiating, poisonous or other gases, and all analogous liquids, materials or devices,

    (iii) bullets which expand or flatten easily in the human body, such as bullets with a hard envelope which does not entirely cover the core or is pierced with incisions,

    (iv) bacteriological (biological) agents or toxins for hostile purposes or in armed conflict,

[*11]   (v)   chemical weapons as defined in and prohibited by the 1993 Convention on the Prohibition of the Development, Production, Stockpiling and Use of Chemical Weapons and On Their Destruction,

    (vi) nuclear weapons,

    (vii) anti-personnel mines,

    (viii) blinding laser weapons,

    (ix) such other weapons or weapons systems as become the subject of a comprehensive prohibition pursuant to customary or conventional international law;

    (p)

Option I

    (p) committing outrages upon personal dignity, in particular humiliating and degrading treatment;

Option II

    (p) committing outrages upon personal dignity, in particular humiliating and degrading treatment as well as practices of apartheid and other inhuman and degrading practices involving outrages upon personal dignity based on racial discrimination;

    (p bis) committing rape, sexual slavery, enforced prostitution, enforced pregnancy, enforced sterilization, and any other form of sexual violence also constituting a grave breach of the Geneva Conventions;

    (q) utilizing the presence of a civilian or other protected person to render certain points, areas or military forces immune from military operations;

    (r)   intentionally directing attacks against buildings, material, medical units and transport, and personnel using, in conformity with international law, the distinctive emblems of the Geneva Conventions;

[*12] (s) intentionally using starvation of civilians as a method of warfare by depriving them of objects indispensable to their survival, including wilfully impeding relief supplies as provided for under the Geneva Conventions;

    (t)

Option I

    (t)   forcing children under the age of fifteen years to take direct part in hostilities.

Option II
  (t) recruiting children under the age of fifteen years into armed forces.
Option III
  (t) allowing children under the age of fifteen years to take direct part in hostilities.
Option IV
  (t)
    (i) recruiting children under the age of fifteen years into armed forces or groups; or
    (ii) allowing them to take part in hostilities;
Option V
  No paragraph (t).

* * *

OPTION I
Sections C and D of this article apply to armed conflicts not of an international character and thus do not apply to situations of internal disturbances and tensions, such as riots, isolated and sporadic acts of violence or other acts of a similar nature.
[*13] **C.** In the case of an armed conflict not of an international character, serious violations of article 3 common to the four Geneva Conventions of 12 August 1949, namely, any of the following acts committed against persons taking no active part in the hostilities, including members of armed forces who have laid down their arms and those placed *hors de combat* by sickness, wounds, detention or any other cause:
  (a) violence to life and person, in particular murder of all kinds, mutilation, cruel treatment and torture;
  (b) committing outrages upon personal dignity, in particular humiliating and degrading treatment;
  (c) taking of hostages;
  (d) the passing of sentences and the carrying out of executions without previous judgement pronounced by a regularly constituted court, affording all judicial guarantees which are generally recognized as indispensable.
D. Other serious violations of the laws and customs applicable in armed conflicts not of an international character, within the established framework of international law, namely, any of the following acts:
  (a)
Option I
  (a) intentionally directing attacks against the civilian population as such, as well as individual civilians not taking direct part in hostilities;
Option II   No paragraph (a).
  (b) intentionally directing attacks against buildings, material, medical units and transport, and personnel using, in conformity with international law, the distinctive emblems of the Geneva Conventions;
  (c)
Option I
[*14] (c) intentionally directing attacks against buildings dedicated to religion, art, science or charitable purposes, historic monuments, hospitals and places where the sick and wounded are collected, provided they are not being used at the time for military purposes;
Option II
  (c) intentionally directing attacks against buildings dedicated to religion, education, art, science or charitable purposes, historic monuments, hospitals and places where the sick and wounded are collected, provided they are not being used at the time for military purposes;
  (d) pillaging a town or place, even when taken by assault;
  (e) committing outrages upon personal dignity, in particular humiliating and degrading treatment;
  (e bis) committing rape, sexual slavery, enforced prostitution, enforced pregnancy, enforced sterilization, and any other form of sexual violence also constituting a serious violation of article 3 common to the four Geneva Conventions;

(f)
Option I
 (f) forcing children under the age of fifteen years to take direct part in hostilities;
Option II
 (f) recruiting children under the age of fifteen years into armed forces or groups;
Option III
 (f)
   (i) recruiting children under the age of fifteen years into armed forces or groups; or
[*15] (ii) allowing them to take part in hostilities;
Option IV
 No paragraph (f).
 (g) ordering the displacement of the civilian population for reasons related to the conflict, unless the security of the civilians involved or imperative military reasons so demand;
 (h) killing or wounding treacherously a combatant adversary;
 (i) declaring that no quarter will be given;
 (j) subjecting persons who are in the power of another Party to the conflict to physical mutilation or to medical or scientific experiments of any kind which are neither justified by the medical, dental or hospital treatment of the person concerned nor carried out in his interest, and which cause death to or seriously endanger the health of such person or persons;
 (k) destroying or seizing the property of an adversary unless such destruction or seizure be imperatively demanded by the necessities of the conflict;
 (l)
Option I
 No provision on prohibited weapons.
Option II
 A reference to arms, in the light of the discussions on paragraph B(o).
OPTION II Insert the following provisions in section D:
 - intentionally using starvation of civilians as a method of warfare by depriving them of objects indispensable to their survival, including [*16] wilfully impeding relief supplies as provided for under the Geneva Conventions;
 - intentionally launching an attack in the knowledge that such attack will cause incidental loss of life or injury to civilians or damage to civilian objects or widespread, long-term and severe damage to the natural environment;
 - intentionally launching an attack against works or installations containing dangerous forces in the knowledge that such attack will cause excessive loss of life, injury to civilians or damage to civilian objects which would be excessive in relation to the concrete and direct military advantage anticipated;
 - slavery and the slave trade in all their forms;
OPTION III
 Delete the chapeau of sections C and D.
OPTION IV
 Delete section D.
OPTION V
 Delete sections C and D.

* * *

Elsewhere in the Statute:
Option I
 The jurisdiction of the Court shall extend to the most serious crimes of concern to the international community as a whole. The Court shall have jurisdiction in respect of the crimes listed in article X (war crimes) only when committed as part of a plan or policy or as part of a large-scale commission of such crimes.[2]

---

[2] The view was expressed that the substance and placement of this proposal should be considered.

[*17] **Option II**

The jurisdiction of the Court shall be limited to the most serious crimes of concern to the international community as a whole. The Court shall have jurisdiction in respect of the crimes listed in article X (war crimes) in particular when committed as a part of a plan or policy or as part of a large-scale commission of such crimes.[2]

Option III

No provision on threshold.

* * *

Article Y

(relating to the part of the Statute dealing with the definition of crimes)

Without prejudice to the application of the provisions of this Statute, nothing in this part of the Statute shall be interpreted as limiting or prejudicing in any way existing or developing rules of international law.

[*18] Annex II

REPORT OF THE WORKING GROUP ON GENERAL PRINCIPLES OF CRIMINAL LAW[*]

The Working Group recommends to the Preparatory Committee the text of the following articles concerning general principles of criminal law as a first draft for inclusion in the draft consolidated text of a convention for an international criminal court:

Article L.   Grounds for excluding criminal responsibility (A/AC.249/1997/WG.2/CRP.7);
Article M.   Superior orders and prescription of law (A/AC.249/1997/WG.2/CRP.8);
Article N.   [Possible grounds for excluding criminal responsibility specifically referring to war crimes] (ibid.);
Article O.   Other grounds for excluding criminal responsibility (ibid.);
Article P.   Presumption of innocence (ibid.).

[*19] GENERAL PRINCIPLES OF CRIMINAL LAW

Article L

Grounds for excluding criminal responsibility

1.   In addition to other grounds for excluding criminal responsibility permitted by this Statute,[1] a person is not criminally responsible if at the time of that person's conduct:[2]

(a) the person suffers from a mental disease or defect that destroys that person's capacity to appreciate the unlawfulness or nature of his or her conduct, or capacity to control his or her conduct to conform to the requirements of law;

[(b) the person is in a state of [involuntary] intoxication [by alcohol, drugs or other means] that destroys that person's capacity to appreciate the unlawfulness or nature of his or her conduct, or capacity to control his or her conduct to conform to the requirements of law; [provided, however, that if the person has voluntarily become intoxicated [[with the pre-existing intent to commit the crime] [or knowing that the circumstances would arise that led him or [*20] her to commit the crime and that those circumstances could have that effect]],[3] the person shall remain criminally responsible;]

---

[*]   Incorporating the documents listed in the opening paragraph. The name of the Working Group has been changed from "Working Group on General Principles of Criminal Law and Penalties" as a result of the establishment of a separate Working Group on Penalties (see annex V).

[1]   This formulation presumes that the grounds for excluding criminal responsibility in 1 (a) through (e) are not the exclusive defences available and that, for example, articles N and O would be retained in some form.

[2]   The link between the chapeau of paragraph 1 and paragraph 2 may need to be further considered.

[3]   There are two approaches to the question of voluntary intoxication: If it is decided that voluntary intoxication should in no case be an acceptable defence, the text within brackets "[with the pre-existing intent to commit the crime] [or knowing that the circumstances would arise that led him or her to commit the crime and that those circumstances could have that effect]" would have to be deleted. In that case, however, provision should be made for mitigation of punishment with regard to persons who were not able to form a specific intent, where required, towards the crime committed due to their intoxication. If this text were to be retained, the defence would apply in all cases of voluntary intoxication except for those in which the person became intoxicated in order to commit the crime in an intoxicated condition (actio libera in causa). This would probably lead to a great number of war crimes and crimes against humanity

(c)   the person [, provided that he or she did not put himself or herself voluntarily into a position causing the situation to which that ground for excluding criminal responsibility would apply,] acts [swiftly and] reasonably [, or in the reasonable belief that force is necessary,] to defend himself or herself or another person [or property] against an [imminent ...[4] use of force] [immediate ...[4] threat of force] [impending ...[4] use of force] and [[unlawful] [and] [unjustified]] use of force in a [not excessive] manner[.] [[not disproportionate] [reasonably proportionate] to the degree of danger to the person [or liberty] [or property] protected];

(d)   [the person reasonably believes that][5] there is a threat of [imminent] death or serious bodily harm against that person or another person [or against his or her liberty] [or property or property interests] and the person acts reasonably to avoid this threat, provided that the person's action[6] [causes] [was not intended to cause] [n]either death [n]or a greater harm than the one [*21] sought to be avoided;[7] [however, if the person has [knowingly] [recklessly] exposed him or herself to a situation which was likely to lead to the threat, the person shall remain responsible];

(e)   [the person reasonably believes that there are][8] [there are] [the person necessarily acts in response to] circumstances beyond that person's control which constitute a [threat of [imminent] death or serious bodily harm] [danger] to that person or another person [or property or property rights][9] and the person acts reasonably to avoid the [threat] [danger], [provided that the person intended to prevent a greater harm [and did not intend to cause] [and did not cause] death][10] and provided that there exists no other way to avoid such threat];

[*22] 2.   The Court may[11] determine the applicability of the grounds for exclusion of criminal responsibility[12] [listed in paragraph 1] [permitted by this Statute] [to the case before it].[13]

Article M
Superior orders and prescription of law

1.   The fact that a person's conduct was pursuant to an order of a government or of a superior [whether military or civilian] shall [not] relieve the person of criminal responsibility [[if] [unless] the order [was known to be unlawful or] appeared to be manifestly unlawful].[14]

[The perpetrator of or an accomplice in a crime of genocide [or a crime against humanity] [or a ...] shall not be exempted from criminal responsibility on the sole ground that the person's conduct was

---

going unpunished.

[4]   Dots inserted so as not to repeat "[[unlawful] [and] [unjustified]]" in all three alternatives.

[5]   This should be considered together with article K.

[6]   A proposal was made to replace the rest of the first sentence by "is under the circumstances not reasonably more excessive than the threat or perceived threat".

[7]   A proposal was made to replace "provided that the person's action [causes] [was not intended to cause] [n]either death [n]or a greater harm than the one sought to be avoided" with "employing means which are not disproportionate to the risk faced".

[8]   This should be considered together with article K.

[9]   It was suggested that a mere reference to the law of necessity would suffice in place of the first part of the sentence.

[10]   This applies more to a military situation.

[11]   There was support, in principle, for two proposals regarding application of international law and non-discrimination in the interpretation of general principles of criminal law. The first proposal is to insert, after the word "may" the phrase ", in accordance with international law,". The second proposal is to add the following provision: "The application and interpretation of the general sources of law must be consistent with international human rights standards and the progressive development thereof, which encompasses the prohibition on adverse discrimination of any kind, including discrimination based on gender." These proposals relate to both article 33 of the ILC draft and section 2 of Part 3 bis of the compilation on General Principles of Criminal Law. In order to avoid duplication, discussion could take place in the context of those provisions.

[12]   The issue of the extent to which the facts underlying these grounds, for excluding criminal responsibility, if not sufficient to exclude criminal responsibility, should instead be considered in mitigation of punishment will be dealt with in article [47].

[13]   The link between the chapeau of paragraph 1 and paragraph 2 may need to be reconsidered.

[14]   An unlawful or manifestly unlawful order must be understood as an order in conflict with the rules of international law applicable in armed conflict.

pursuant to an order of a [*23] government or a superior, or pursuant to national legislation or regulations.][15][16]

[2.   Persons who have carried out acts ordered by the Security Council or in accordance with a mandate issued by it shall not be criminally responsible before the Court.][17]

[Article N[18]
Possible grounds for excluding criminal responsibility specifically referring to war crimes]

Article O
Other grounds for excluding criminal responsibility

1.   At trial the Court may consider a ground for excluding criminal responsibility not specifically enumerated in this chapter if the ground:

(a)   is recognized [in general principles of criminal law common to civilized nations] [in the State with the most significant contacts to the crime] with respect to the type of conduct charged; and

(b)   deals with a principle clearly beyond the scope of the grounds for excluding criminal responsibility enumerated in this chapter and is not otherwise inconsistent with those or any other provisions of the Statute.

[*24] 2.   The procedure for asserting such a ground for excluding criminal responsibility shall be set forth in the Rules of the Court.[19]

Article P[20]
Presumption of innocence

Everyone shall be presumed innocent until proved guilty in accordance with law. The onus is on the Prosecutor to establish the guilt of the accused beyond a reasonable doubt.[21]

[*25] Annex III
REPORT OF THE WORKING GROUP ON PROCEDURAL MATTERS[*]

1.[**]   The Working Group recommends to the Preparatory Committee the text of the following articles concerning procedural matters as a first draft for inclusion in the draft consolidated text of the convention for an international criminal court:

Article 26.   (A/AC.249/1997/WG.4/CRP.11/Add.1);

Article 26 bis.) Deferral of an investigation by the Prosecutor)
(A/AC.249/1997/WG.4/CRP.11/Add.1);

Article 26 ter.)

Article 28.   Arrest (A/AC.249/1997/WG.4/CRP.11 and Corr.1);

Article 29.   Pre-trial detention or release (ibid.);

Article 36.   Challenges to the jurisdiction of the Court on the admissibility of a case (A/AC.249/1997/WG.4/CRP.11);

Article 44.   Evidence (A/AC.249/1997/WG.4/CRP.11/Add.2).

---

[15]   This subparagraph should be considered together with article L, paragraph 2.

[16]   For the question of mitigation of punishment, see annex V, sect. B.

[17]   There were widespread doubts about the contents and the placement of this paragraph.

[18]   It was questioned whether such grounds as military necessity could be dealt with in connection with the definition of war crimes.

[19]   This article needs to be further considered together with article L, paragraph 2, and article 33.

[20]   Article P is also dealt with in the report of the Working Group on Procedural Matters (see A/AC.249/1997/L.8/Rev.1, annex II, article 40).

[21]   Reservations were expressed regarding the phrases "in accordance with law" and "beyond a reasonable doubt" contained in the ILC text.

[*]   Incorporating the documents listed in paragraphs 1, 2 and 3.

[**]   Paragraphs 2 and 3 are on the page following the proposed text for [article 44 ter] below.

[*26] [Article 26 bis

1.   States Parties shall promptly inform the Prosecutor about national investigations or proceedings undertaken with respect to the alleged commission of a crime within the jurisdiction of the Court. Such information shall be confidential to the extent necessary and shall include a concise statement of the circumstances of the alleged crime, the identity and whereabouts of any suspect (or accused), and the progress of the investigation or proceeding concerned.
2.   The Prosecutor shall examine the information received from the State(s) Party(ies) concerned and if he/she believes, having regard to the matters referred to in article 35, that the conditions exist for having the Court entertain the case, shall seek a ruling from the Pre-Trial Chamber and inform of his/her decision the State(s) Party(ies) concerned and the suspect (or accused). The Prosecutor may also request the State(s) Party(ies) concerned to provide additional information about the national investigation or proceeding within a given time, and defer a decision until he/she has examined such additional information.
3.   The States Parties to the present Statute undertake to submit periodical reports to the Prosecutor on the measures they have adopted which give effect to the prosecution of crimes falling within the jurisdiction of the Court.]

[*27] [Article 26 ter
Deferral of an investigation by the Prosecutor
1.   In the event that the Prosecutor, having regard to the matters in article 35, defers an investigation, then the Prosecutor [may request that] [may seek an order of the Court that] the relevant State make available to the [Prosecutor] [Court] information on the proceedings.[1]
2.   Any information so provided will, to the extent necessary, be kept confidential.
3.   If the Prosecutor thereafter decides to proceed with an investigation, he or she shall notify the State in respect of whose proceedings deferral has taken place.]

[*28] Article 28
Arrest
1.   At any time after an investigation has been initiated, the [Presidency] [Pre-Trial Chamber] may at the request of the Prosecutor issue a warrant for the pre-indictment arrest of a suspect if there are reasonable grounds[2] [3] to believe that:
    (a)   the suspect has committed a crime within the jurisdiction of the Court; and
    (b)   taking the suspect into custody is necessary to ensure that the suspect does not:
        (i)   fail to appear for trial;
        [(ii)   [interfere with or destroy evidence;][4]
        [(iii) [intimidate] [influence] witnesses or victims;]
        [(iv) engage in collusion with accomplices;] or
        [(v)   [continue to commit a crime within the jurisdiction of the Court.][5]
[The Pre-Trial Chamber may also issue a warrant of judicial supervision in order to place a person under restrictions of liberty other than arrest.][6]
[*29] [No person shall be subjected to arbitrary arrest or detention. Nor shall any person be deprived of his liberty except on such grounds and in accordance with such procedures as are established by the rules of the Court.][7]

---

   [1]   The term "proceedings" covers both investigations and prosecutions (see A/AC.249/1997/L.8/Rev.1, annex I, article 35, note 24).
   [2]   The term "reasonable grounds" was understood to embody objective criteria.
   [3]   Some delegations preferred other terms such as "serious reasons".
   [4]   Some delegations suggested that subparagraphs (ii), (iii) and (iv) could be merged under a more general formulation such as "obstructing or endangering the investigation or the court proceedings".
   [5]   Some delegations favoured addressing situations in which the accused may be harmed or at risk. Other delegations stated that the accused could be adequately protected under article 43.
   [6]   It was suggested that this provision could be deleted because it is addressed in article 29, paragraph 5.
   [7]   It was suggested that this provision could be moved to article 26, paragraph 6.

2.   [a]   The warrant for the pre-indictment arrest shall be deemed to have lapsed and the request for the pre-indictment arrest of a suspect shall be deemed to have been withdrawn if [the indictment has not been confirmed] [a post-indictment warrant has not been served] within [30] [60] [90] days of the arrest, or in exceptional circumstances such longer time up to a total of [60] [90] days as the [Presidency] [Pre-Trial Chamber] may allow.

[b]   In the case of a State Party which has notified the court under article 53 bis (1 bis) that it can surrender pre-indictment, the warrant for the pre-indictment arrest of a suspect shall be deemed to have been withdrawn if [the indictment has not been confirmed] [a post-indictment warrant has not been confirmed] [a post-indictment warrant has not been served] within [30] [60] [90] days of the surrender, or in exceptional circumstances such longer time up to a total of [60] [90] days as the [Presidency] [Pre-Trial Chamber] may allow.

If the Prosecutor decides not to indict the suspect or the [Presidency] [Pre-Trial Chamber] decides not to [confirm the indictment] [not to issue a post-indictment warrant], the Prosecutor shall immediately advise the custodial State of that fact.[8]

3.   [In the case where no pre-indictment warrant has been obtained,] [Prior to the confirmation hearing,] [As soon as practicable] [after the confirmation of the indictment], the Prosecutor shall seek from the Presidency [Pre-Trial Chamber] a [post-indictment] warrant for the arrest and transfer of the accused. The Presidency [Pre-Trial Chamber] shall issue such a warrant unless it is satisfied that:

[Optional chapeau to paragraph 3]
[Upon confirmation of the indictment, a warrant for the arrest of the accused shall be issued by the Pre-Trial Chamber, unless, having heard the views of the Prosecutor, it is satisfied that:]
[*30] (a) the accused will voluntarily appear for trial and none of the other factors in paragraph 1 (b) are present]; or

(b)   there are special circumstances making it unnecessary for the time being to issue the warrant.

4.   The Court[9] shall transmit the warrant to any State where the person may be located, along with a request for the provisional arrest, or arrest and [surrender, transfer, extradition] of the person under part 7.

5.   [Pre-indictment and post-indictment warrants may also be issued when the accused is a fugitive. In this case, the post-indictment warrant issued by the Pre-Trial Chamber shall have the effect of an international warrant and shall be disseminated by all appropriate means. When the accused is apprehended, the authorities shall proceed as provided for in part 7.]

6.   [A post-indictment warrant shall remain in effect until the date of the judgement. The effects of the warrant delivered by the Pre-Trial Chamber shall not be interrupted by the actions challenging the submission of cases to the Court.]

[*31] Article 29
Pre-trial detention or release

1.   [The States [Parties] [in which the person is located] [and in which the crime was committed] shall be notified of a warrant issued by the Pre-Trial Chamber.] The State that has received a pre- or post-indictment warrant and a request for the arrest of a person under article 28 (5) shall immediately [in accordance with its laws][10] [[and] in accordance with the provisions of part 7 of this Statute] take steps to arrest the suspect [on the basis of the warrant issued by the Court or by obtaining a domestic warrant for arrest based on the Court's warrant and request].[11]

---

[8]   It was suggested that the questions of release and re-arrest could be addressed in another provision of this Statute.

[9]   The term "Court" is understood to include its constituent organs, including the Prosecutor, as defined in article 5.

[10]   Under article 28 (5), a warrant for pre-indictment arrest is forwarded to the State in which the individual sought may be located, along with a request for provisional arrest or transfer/surrender under part 7. If part 7 specifies the extent to which national laws apply to requests for provisional arrest or transfer/surrender, it will be unnecessary to treat this issue here as well.

[11]   The issue of whether a State can decline to arrest and detain a person, pending resolution of a challenge under article 36, could be dealt with in that article.

[1 bis. The Prosecutor may, with the consent of the Pre-Trial Chamber, execute a warrant for arrest by him or herself only in cases where the competent authority of the State Party concerned may not be available or may be ineffective.][12]

2.   A person arrested shall be brought promptly before a competent judicial authority in the custodial State who shall determine, in accordance with the law of that State, that the warrant applies to that person and the person has been arrested in accordance with the proper process and that the person's rights have been respected.

3.   The person shall have the right to apply to [the competent judicial authority in the custodial State] [the Pre-Trial Chamber] for interim release pending [surrender] [transfer] [extradition] [in accordance with its national [*32] law]. [The custodial State shall take into account the views of the Prosecutor [and Court] on interim release.]

4.   After the [decision to] [surrender] [transfer] [extradite] to the Court, the person may apply to the [Presidency] [Pretrial Chamber] for interim release pending trial.

5.   The person shall be detained unless the [Presidency] [Pre-Trial Chamber] is satisfied that the person will voluntarily appear for trial and none of the other factors in article 28 (1) (b) are present. If it decides to release the person, it may do so with or without conditions [or may issue a warrant of judicial supervision restricting the person's liberty other than by arrest]. [The [Presidency] [Pre-Trial Chamber] shall also, on its own initiative, review its ruling periodically. If satisfied that changed circumstances require that the ruling be modified, it may order any measure provided for in paragraph 4.]

6.   (a)   The [Presidency] [Pre-Trial Chamber] may, either of its own initiative or at the request of the person concerned or the Prosecutor, modify its ruling as to detention[, judicial supervision] or conditional release in effect at that time.

[(b)   The person may be detained prior to trial for a maximum of one year; however, this period may be extended up to an additional year by the [Presidency] [Pre-Trial Chamber] if the Prosecutor can demonstrate that he or she will be ready for trial within that period and can show good cause for the delay.]

(c)   The person and the Prosecutor may appeal the [Presidency's] [Pretrial Chamber's] determination regarding release or detention to the Appeals Chamber.

7.   If necessary, the [Presidency] [Pre-Trial Chamber] may issue a warrant of arrest to secure the presence of an accused who has been released.

8.   A person arrested may apply to the [Presidency] [Pre-Trial Chamber] for a determination of the lawfulness under this Statute of any arrest warrant or order of detention issued by the Court. If the Presidency [Pre-Trial Chamber] decides that the arrest or detention was unlawful under the Statute, it shall [*33] order the release of the person, [and may award compensation] [in accordance with article ...].[13]

9.   [A person arrested shall be held, pending trial or release on bail, in an appropriate place of detention in the arresting State, in the State in which the trial is to be held, or if necessary in the host State.] [Once ordered [surrendered] [transferred] [extradited] by the custodial State, the person shall be delivered to the Court as soon as possible, and shall be held in an appropriate place of detention in the host State or other State in which the trial is to be held.]

---

[12]   This provision raises a host of issues, including under what conditions the Prosecutor should be able to exercise such authority, whether the Prosecutor would have adequate resources to do so, and whether such issues should be addressed elsewhere in the Statute.

[13]   A number of issues were raised regarding compensation, including whether it should be mandatory or discretionary, whether it should be granted even when the Prosecutor acted in good faith, whether such determination is not appropriate until the judgement becomes final and whether granting compensation may prevent the Prosecutor from diligently carrying out his or her duties.

[*34] Article 36
Challenges to the jurisdiction of the Court
or the admissibility of a case

1. At all stages of the proceedings, the Court (a) shall satisfy itself as to its jurisdiction over a case pursuant to article 24 and (b) may, on its own motion, determine the admissibility of the case pursuant to article 35.[14]

2. Challenges to the admissibility of the case, pursuant to article 35, or challenges to the jurisdiction of the Court may be made by:

(a) an accused [or a suspect];[15]

(b) [A State] [[An interested] State Party] which has jurisdiction over the crime on the ground that it is investigating or prosecuting the case or has investigated or prosecuted[16]

[a State [State Party] of nationality of a person referred to in paragraph 2 (a) [on the ground that it is investigating or prosecuting the case or has investigated or prosecuted]]

[and a State [State Party] which has received a request for cooperation];

The Prosecutor may seek a ruling from the Court regarding a question of jurisdiction or admissibility.

[*35] In proceedings with respect to jurisdiction or admissibility, those having submitted the case pursuant to article 21,[17] [those non-State parties which have jurisdiction over the crimes][18] as well as victims, may also submit observations to the Court.

3.[19] The admissibility of a case or the jurisdiction of the Court may be challenged only once by any person or State referred to in paragraph 2. The challenge must take place prior to or at the commencement of the trial. In exceptional circumstances, the Court may grant leave for a challenge to be brought more than once or at a time later than the commencement of the trial. Challenges to the admissibility of a case, at the commencement of a trial, or subsequently with the leave of the Court as provided in the preceding subparagraph, may only be based on article 35, paragraph 2 (c).[20]

3 bis. A State referred to in paragraph 2 (b) of the present article shall make a challenge at the earliest opportunity.[21]

4. Prior to the confirmation of the indictment, challenges to the admissibility of a case or challenges to the jurisdiction of the Court, shall be referred to the Pre-Trial Chamber. After confirmation of the indictment, they shall be referred to the Trial Chamber.

[*36] Decisions with respect to jurisdiction or admissibility may be appealed to the Appeals Chamber.[22]

[5. If the Court has decided that a case is inadmissible pursuant to article 35, the Prosecutor, may, at any time, submit a request for a review of the decision, on the grounds that conditions required under article 35 to render the case inadmissible no longer exist or that new facts arose.]

---

[14] In the light of the wording to be adopted for article 36, several draft provisions of the statute may have to be reexamined including article 26, paragraph 4, and article 27, paragraph 2 (b).

[15] The term "suspect" includes a person who is the subject to an investigation. Another option is to limit the right to challenge to a suspect arrested on the basis of a pre-indictment arrest warrant.

[16] The final wording of this subparagraph will depend on the content of article 35.

[17] The final wording will depend on the content of article 21 (States, Security Council, Prosecutor).

[18] This provision would apply to the option where only States parties can challenge the jurisdiction of the Court or the admissibility of a case.

[19] It was suggested that if several States have jurisdiction over a case and one of those States has already challenged the jurisdiction of the Court, the remaining States should not bring additional challenges except on different grounds.

[20] The final wording of this subparagraph will depend on the content of article 35.

[21] The question arises as to what consequences, if any, should flow from the failure of a State to make a timely challenge.

[22] Subject to the final decision or the organization of the Court.

[23] The question concerning the suspension of the trial proceeding in case of appeal should be addressed in the Rules of Procedure.

[*37] Article 44
Evidence

1.   Before testifying, each witness shall, in accordance with [or as excepted by] the Rules, give an undertaking as to the truthfulness of the evidence to be given by that witness.[24]

1. bis The testimony of witness at trial shall be given in person, except to the extent provided by the measures set forth in article 43 or in the rules of evidence. These measures shall not be [prejudicial to] [inconsistent with] the rights of the accused.[25] [26]

Note: There was no time to discuss in the Working Group the remaining paragraphs of draft article 44 which follow:

3.   **[The Court has the authority and duty to call all evidence that it considers necessary for the determination of the truth.]**[27] **[It]** The Court may [also] require to be informed of the nature of any evidence before it is offered so that it may rule on its relevance or admissibility **[after hearing the parties to the case].** **[The Court may base its decision only on evidence submitted and discussed before it at the trial.]**[28]

[*38] 4.   The Court shall not require proof of facts of common knowledge but may take judicial notice of them.[29]

5.   Evidence obtained by means of a serious violation of this Statute or of other rules of international law **[or by means which cast substantial doubt on its reliability] [or whose admission is antithetical to, and would seriously damage, the integrity of the proceedings] [or by means which constitute a serious violation of internationally protected human rights] [or which have been collected in violation of the rights of the defence]** shall not be admissible.[30]

[With regard to defences open to the accused under the general principles of criminal law in this Statute, the onus of proof shall be on the accused, subject to a preponderance of probability as applicable in civil cases.][31]

[6.   The Court has, in case of evidence obtained by national authorities, to presume irrebuttably that the national authorities acted in accordance with the domestic provisions. The Rules of Court shall address the admissible motions against this presumption.]

[*39] Article 44 bis[32]
Offences against the integrity of the Court

1.   The Court shall have jurisdiction over the following offences against the integrity of the Court:

    (a)   perjury committed during the course of its proceedings;

---

[24]   Many delegations were of the view that the subject matter of this paragraph was more appropriate to be dealt with in the Rules of Procedure.

[25]   It was suggested that article 43 could be drafted in a more detailed or descriptive manner.

[26]   Some delegations expressed their concern about the possibility of allowing witnesses to testify without revealing personal data.

[27]   This provision is meant to indicate that the relevant evidence cannot be determined by the parties alone, but has also to be determined by the Court's evaluation of the necessary depth of investigation and determination of the facts. This is, of course, basically a civil law concept, but delegations should bear in mind the additional historical dimension and truth-finding mission of the Court.

[28]   These provisions might be better placed in article 45.

[29]   It was questioned whether this provision was strictly necessary.

[30]   This is an attempt to merge the additional proposals (paragraph 5, subparagraphs 2 to 5) concerning the admissibility of evidence with the ILC draft. It was felt that it would be better to refer to "rules of international law" than to single out the International Covenant on Civil and Political Rights, although this will of course be the main focus of this rule. The formula "internationally protected human rights" is intended to cover non-treaty standards as well and would therefore be broader than "international law".

[31]   Such a provision might be better placed either under article 40 or in the context of "Defences" in the part dealing with general principles of criminal law.

[32]   Delegations favoured the options that the Court shall have jurisdiction over offences against its integrity but the precise formulation of this article must be further reflected upon. There was a view that these offences required further definition in the Statute. Some previous proposals in this respect may be found on pages 44 to 46 of the abbreviated compilation of August 1997.

(b)   influencing, impeding or retaliating against officials of the Court;

(c)   obstructing the functions of the Court; and

(d)   contempt committed during the course of its proceedings.

2.   The Court may impose a term of imprisonment not exceeding [X months/years] [or a fine, or both].

3.   The offences referred to in this article shall be tried before a Chamber other than the Chamber in which the alleged offences were committed. The rules shall determine the applicable procedure for these offences.

Note: There was no time to discuss in the Working Group the following formulation:

[Article 44 ter[33]

1.   Any person heard or examined by the Trial Chamber may invoke restrictions provided for in his national law and designed to prevent the disclosure of confidential information connected with national defence or national security.

[*40] 2.   The Trial Chamber may ask the State of which the persons being heard or examined are nationals whether it confirms their claim to be bound to secrecy.

If the State confirms to the Trial Chamber that an obligation of secrecy exists, the Chamber shall note this fact.

3.   The provisions of the preceding paragraphs shall also apply to execution of a request for judicial assistance made under Part 7 of this Statute.]

[*41] 2.   The Working Group also recommends that its deliberations at the 16 March-3 April 1998 session of the Preparatory Committee be centred around the following provisions:

Articles 26 bis and 26 ter (additional discussions) (see above);

Article 44 (remaining paragraphs); 44 bis (additional discussions) and 44 ter (see above);

Article 45)

Article 48)   (see below)

Article 49)

Article 50)

3.   In order to facilitate the Working Group's deliberations at its next session, individual delegations presented draft revised abbreviated compilations on articles 45, 48 and 50, reproduced below. Also reproduced below is the text of article 49, which was not the subject of a draft revised abbreviated compilation even though it was introduced in the Working Group. Its text comes from the abbreviated compilation of August 1996.

[*42] Article 45
Quorum and judgement[35] [36]

1.   A quorum consists of [at least four] (all) members of the Trial Chamber. [The judgement shall be given only by judges who have been present at each stage of the trial before the Trial Chamber and throughout its deliberations.]

[1 bis [The Trial Chamber's judgement shall be based on its evaluation of the evidence and the entire proceedings.] [The judgement shall not exceed the facts and circumstances described in the indictment or its amendment, if any.]][37]

---

[33]   The issues addressed here have also been addressed by a number of proposals on different articles in the procedural part of the Statute.

[35]   The present text was put forward by individual delegations in order to simplify the existing text and to show more clearly which are the various options. The proposal does not constitute as such a new substantive proposal.

[36]   Throughout this article, "Court" has been replaced with "Trial Chamber". Decisions by the Pre-Trial Chamber (as well as its composition) and by the Appeals Chamber are dealt with elsewhere. Furthermore, it is questionable whether this article should only address judgements or whether it should also cover other (procedural) decisions. As currently drafted, it only deals with judgements.

[37]   This is a new paragraph addressing two proposals which are moved here from article 45(5) in the abbreviated compilation and from the revised article 44(3).

2.

Option 1

 The decision [judgement] shall be taken by a majority [at least three] of the judges.

Option 2

 All judges must concur in a decision as to conviction [or acquittal] and at least three judges must concur as to the sentence to be imposed.

Option 3

 All judges must concur in a decision as to conviction [or acquittal] as well as to the sentence to be imposed.

[*43] 3.[38]

Option 1

 If after a sufficient time for deliberation a Chamber which has been reduced to four judges is unable to agree on a decision, it may order a new trial.

Option 2

 If the required majority for a decision as to conviction or the sentence to be imposed cannot be reached, the opinion which is more favourable to the accused shall prevail.

[3 bis. The Trial Chamber shall pronounce its findings separately for each charge in the indictment. If several accused are tried together, the Chamber shall rule separately on the case of each of them.]

4.   The deliberations of the Trial Chamber shall remain secret [confidential].

5.   The judgement shall be in writing and shall contain a full and reasoned statement of the findings [on the evidence] and conclusions. It shall be the sole judgement issued [It may contain dissenting opinions], and shall be delivered in open court.

Article 48
Appeal against judgement or sentence[39]

1.   A decision [conviction] under article 45 may be appealed [to the Appeals Chamber], in accordance with the Rules, as provided for below:

 (a)   The Prosecutor may make such an appeal [without any specified grounds] on the following grounds:

[*44]   (i)   procedural error,

      (ii) error of fact, or

      (iii) error of law;

 (b)   The convicted person may make such an appeal [without any specified grounds] on the following grounds:

      (i)   procedural error,

      (ii) error of fact, or

      (iii) error of law.

1 bis. A decision [sentence] under article 47 may be appealed [to the Appeals Chamber], in accordance with the Rules, by the Prosecutor or the convicted person on the ground of disproportion between the crime and the sentence. [In the case of an appeal of sentence, the Appeals Chamber may also render a decision on conviction.]

1 ter.

Option 1

 The Prosecutor or the convicted person may, in accordance with the Rules, appeal [to the Appeals Chamber] against a decision rendered in absentia under article 37.

Option 2

 The Prosecutor or the convicted person may not appeal against a decision rendered in absentia under article 37 except that an appeal against judgement given on the merits in the absence of the accused shall

---

[38]   This paragraph would only be necessary if majority decisions are allowed and a quorum could consist of an even number of judges.

[39]   The present text was put forward by individual delegations in order to simplify the existing text and to show more clearly which are the various options. The proposal does not as such constitute a new substantive proposal.

be allowed if the accused accepts the judgment or was represented during the trial before the Trial Chamber by defence counsel appointed by the accused.

2.   Unless the Trial Chamber otherwise orders, a convicted person shall remain in custody pending an appeal.

[2 bis. In case of an acquittal, the accused shall be released immediately.

If, at the time the judgement is pronounced, the Prosecutor advises the Trial Chamber in open court of his or her intention to file notice of appeal, the Trial Chamber may, at the request of the Prosecutor, issue a warrant for the arrest of the acquitted person to take effect immediately.

[*45] The Trial Chamber shall not issue an arrest warrant unless it is satisfied that the acquitted person may not be readily returned to custody if judgement is reversed.]

[Option to 2 bis:

      (a)   If the accused is acquitted, sentenced to payment of a fine or sentenced to a term of imprisonment already covered by the period in detention, the accused shall be released immediately unless he is retained for another case by the organs of the Court or by the judicial authorities of a State Party.

      (b)   In all other cases, the Trial Chamber may, if the circumstances justify prolongation of a measure of security, by a special reasoned decision, maintain the detention of the accused. In this case, so long as the judgement is not final and during appeal proceedings, if any, the convicted person shall remain in detention until such time as the period of detention equals the sentence handed down. However, the convicted person has the right to challenge custody by appealing at any time.[40]

[3.   The sentence shall begin to run from the day it is pronounced. However, as soon as notice of appeal is given, the enforcement of the judgement shall thereupon be stayed until the decision on appeal has been delivered, the convicted person meanwhile remaining in detention.

If, by a previous decision of the Trial Chamber, the convicted person has been released, or is for any other reason at liberty, and he or she is not present when the Judgement is pronounced, the Trial Chamber shall issue a warrant for his or her arrest.

Execution of the judgement shall be suspended during the period allowed for appeal and for the duration of the appeal proceedings.][41]

[4.   The Appeals Chamber may hear interlocutory appeals on the grounds provided for in article 38.]

[*46] Article 49
Proceedings on appeal[42]

1.   The Appeals Chamber has all the powers of the Trial Chamber.

[The Rules of Procedure and Evidence that govern proceedings in the Trial Chambers shall apply mutatis mutandis to proceedings in the Appeals Chamber.] [The Rules of Procedure and Evidence that govern proceedings in the Trial Chambers shall apply mutatis mutandis to proceedings provided by the preceding two paragraphs. Further rules that govern those proceedings shall be provided for in the Rules of Court.]

[On the motion of a party, the Appeals Chamber may authorise the presentation of new evidence, which was not available at the time of trial, if it considers that the interests of justice so require.][43]

2.   If the Appeals Chamber finds that the proceedings appealed from were unfair or that the decision is vitiated by error of fact or law, it may:

      (a)   if the appeal is brought by the convicted person, reverse or amend the decision, or, if necessary, order a new trial;

      (b)   if the appeal is brought by the Prosecutor against an acquittal, order a new trial.

[Those defenses shall only be admissible if already raised in the Trial Chamber or if resulting from the proceedings in that Chamber]

---

[40]   This provision appears on page 224 under H of the Report, vol. II.

[41]   Report, vol. II, p. 236. These matters could instead be addressed in article 47.

[42]   The text of article 49 was not the subject of a draft revised abbreviated compilation even though it was introduced in the Working Group. Its text comes from the abbreviated compilation of August 1996.

[43]   Report, vol. II, reformulation of article N, p. 242.

3.   If in an appeal against sentence the Chamber finds that the sentence is manifestly disproportionate to the crime, it may vary the sentence in accordance with article 47.

4.   The decision of the Chamber shall be taken by a majority of the judges, and shall be delivered in open court [**on a date of which notice has been given to [*47] the parties and counsel and at which they shall be entitled to be present**]. Six judges constitute a quorum.

[**The Appeals Chamber shall pronounce judgement on the basis of the record on appeal together with such additional evidence as it has authorized.**

[The judgement shall be accompanied or followed as soon as possible by a reasoned opinion in writing, to which separate or dissenting opinions may be appended.]

[The Appeals Chamber may rule only on objections formulated by the parties in their appeals. When the decision has been appealed only by the accused, it cannot be amended to his or her detriment.]

5:    Subject to article 50, the decision of the Chamber shall be final.

[**6.   A sentence pronounced by the Appeals Chamber shall be enforced immediately.**]

[**7.   Where the accused is not present when the judgement is due to be delivered, either as having been acquitted on all charges or for any other reason, the Appeals Chamber may deliver its Judgement in the absence of the accused and shall, unless it pronounces his or her acquittal, order his or her arrest or surrender to the Tribunal.**]

Note: Paragraph 5 of page 238 of the Report, vol. II, is reproduced in the August 1997 abbreviated compilation under article 43 (other proposals).

Note: Proposals A to M and O on pages 238 to 242 of the Report, vol. II, deal with matters which could be better addressed in the Rules of Court.

Note: The issue of interlocutory appeals is addressed in a proposal made under article 38 (see paras. (e) and (f)). (August 1997 abbreviated compilation).

Article 50
Revision[44]

[*48] 1.   **The convicted person [and, after his or her death, his spouse, her husband, his or her children, relatives or any persons having express instructions] or the Prosecutor may, in accordance with the Rules, apply to the Presidency [Court which rendered the original judgement] for revision of a conviction [final judgement in a criminal case[5]** on the following grounds:

(a)   **that evidence has been discovered which was not available to the applicant at the time the conviction [final judgement] was pronounced or affirmed and which could have been a decisive factor in the conviction;**

[**(b) it is proved that decisive evidence which was taken into account when passing the conviction does not possess the value which had been assigned to it because it is false, invalid, or has been forged or falsified;**

(c)   **it is proved that one or more of the judges who participated in a conviction or in its confirmation has committed in that case a serious breach of his or her duties;**

(d)   **a previous judgement on which the conviction was based has been annulled;**

(e)   **a more benign penal law than the one applied in the sentence becomes retroactively applicable**].

2.   **[[The Presidency] shall reject the application if it considers it unfounded] if the Presidency [Court which rendered the original judgement] is of the view that the new evidence could lead to the revision of the conviction [considers there are valid grounds for the application], it may:**

(a)   **reconvene the Trial Chamber;**

(b)   **constitute a new Trial Chamber; or**

---

[44]   The present text was put forward by individual delegations in order to simplify the existing text and to show more clearly which are the various options. The proposal does not constitute as such a new substantive proposal.

[45]   Apparently, the suggested modification implies that an acquittal would also allow an application for revision from the Prosecutor; this would represent a drastic change from the concept of revision adopted by the ILC draft.

(c)   refer the matter to the Appeals Chamber, with a view to the Chamber determining, after hearing the parties, whether the new evidence should lead to a revision of the conviction.
[*49] [Option to (a)-(c): It shall annul the conviction and refer the accused to a Chamber at the same level as, but having a composition different from, that of the Chamber which handed down the annulled decision.]

[*50] Annex IV
REPORT OF THE WORKING GROUP ON INTERNATIONAL COOPERATION AND JUDICIAL ASSISTANCE*
The Working Group recommends to the Preparatory Committee the text of the following articles concerning international cooperation and judicial assistance as a first draft for inclusion in the draft consolidated text of the convention for an international criminal court:

Article 51.   [General obligation to cooperate] (A/AC.249/1997/WG.5/CRP.2 and Corr.1);
Article 52.   [Requests for cooperation: General provisions] (ibid.);
Article 53.   [Surrender] [Transfer] [Extradition] of persons to the Court (A/AC.249/1997/WG.5/CRP.2/Add.1);
Article 53 bis. [Contents of request for [surrender] [transfer] [extradition] (ibid.);
Article 54.   Provisional arrest (ibid.);
Article 55.   Other forms of cooperation [and judicial and legal [mutual] assistance] (A/AC.249/1997/WG.5/CRP.2/Add.2);
Article 56.   Execution of requests under article 55 (ibid.);
Article 57.   Rule of speciality (ibid.);
Article 58.   General obligation regarding recognition [and enforcement] of judgements (A/AC.249/1997/WG.5/CRP.2/Add.3);
Article 59.   Role of States in enforcement of sentences [and supervision] of sentences of imprisonment (ibid.);
Article 59 bis. Limitation of prosecution/punishment for other offences (ibid.);
[*51] Article 59 ter. Enforcement of fines and forfeiture measures (ibid.);
Article 60.   [Pardon,] parole and commutation of sentences [early release] (ibid.);
Article 60 bis. Escape (ibid.).

[*52] PART 7. [INTERNATIONAL COOPERATION AND JUDICIAL ASSISTANCE]
Article 51
[General obligation to cooperate][2]
States Parties shall, in accordance with the provisions of this [Part] [Statute], fully cooperate with the Court[3] in its investigation and prosecution of crimes under this Statute. States Parties shall so cooperate without [undue] delay.

Article 52[4]
[Requests for cooperation: general provisions]
1.   Authorities competent to make and receive requests/Channels for communication of requests

---

*   Incorporating the documents listed in the opening paragraph.
[2]   It was suggested that there was no need for titles.
[3]   "Court" is understood to include its constituent organs, including the Prosecutor, as defined in article 5. Such a provision could be inserted elsewhere in the Statute.
[4]   It was suggested that the provisions of article 53 bis, paragraph 3, and article 55, paragraph 7, concerning the protection of witnesses and victims should be combined in a single paragraph in article 52, which would read:
"The Court may withhold, in accordance with article 43, from the requested State [or a State making a request to the Court under article 55 (6)], specific information about any victims, potential witnesses and their families if it considers that this is necessary to ensure their safety or physical and psychological well-being. Any information that is made available to a State under this part shall be provided and handled in a manner that protects the safety or physical or psychological well-being of any victims, potential witnesses or their families."
It was also suggested that the content of such a provision should be considered further.

[*53] (a) The Court shall have the authority to make requests to States Parties for cooperation. The requests shall be transmitted through the diplomatic channel or any other appropriate channel as may be designated by each State Party upon ratification, accession or approval.

Such designation and subsequent changes shall be done in accordance with the Rules of Procedure.

(b)   When appropriate, without prejudice to the provisions of paragraph 1 (a), requests may also be transmitted through the International Criminal Police Organization or any appropriate regional organization.

2.   Language of requests[5]

Requests for cooperation [and supporting documents] shall be [either] in [an official language of the requested State [unless otherwise agreed]] [or in] [one of the working languages reflected in article 18, in accordance with the choice made by that State upon ratification, accession or approval].

[The legal effect of such request shall not be diminished if any supporting document is not in such working language provided that a brief summary of any such document in that working language is also submitted.]

3.   Confidentiality of requests from the Court

The requested State shall keep confidential a request and any supporting documents, except to the extent that the disclosure is necessary for execution of the request.

4.   Cooperation by non-States Parties[6]

[(a)   The Court may [call on] [invite] any State not party to this Statute to provide assistance under this part on the basis of [comity], an ad hoc arrangement, an agreement with such State [or any other appropriate basis].]

[*54] [(b)   Where a State not party to this Statute [which has entered into an ad hoc arrangement or an agreement with the Court[7]], fails to cooperate with requests under paragraph (a), thereby preventing the Court from performing its duties under this Statute, the Court may make a finding to that effect and refer the matter to [the Council of States Parties[8]] [or] [the United Nations General Assembly] [or, where the Security Council referred the matter to the Court,] [to the Security Council] [so that necessary measures may be taken to enable the Court to exercise its jurisdiction].[9]]

5.   Cooperation of intergovernmental organizations

The Court may ask any intergovernmental organizations to provide information or documents. The Court may also ask for other forms of cooperation and assistance as may be agreed upon with such organizations and in accordance with their respective competencies and/or mandates.

6.   States Parties' failure to cooperate [comply][10]

Where a State Party fails to comply with a request by the Court contrary to the provisions of the Statute, thereby preventing the Court from performing its duties under this Statute, the Court may make a finding to that effect and refer the matter to [the Council of States Parties[11]] [or] [the United Nations General Assembly] [or, where the Security Council referred the matter to the Court] [to the Security Council] [so that necessary measures may be taken to enable the Court to exercise its jurisdiction].[12]

---

[5]   The language to be used by States in their replies to the Court is dealt with under article 56.

[6]   It was suggested that the issue of non-States Parties should be addressed in a separate article 51 _bis_.

[7]   It was suggested that a reference to paragraph (a) would cover this concern.

[8]   It was suggested that the referral be made to a standing committee of the Council of States Parties. This issue needs to be further addressed in the organization of the Court.

[9]   The question of "necessary measures" has to be further examined.

[10]   It was suggested that this paragraph should be inserted in article 51.

[11]   It was suggested that the referral be made to a standing committee of the Council of States Parties. This issue needs to be further addressed in the organization of the Court.

[12]   The question of "necessary measures" has to be further examined.

[*55] Article 53
[Surrender] [Transfer] [Extradition] of persons[13] to the court

1.   The Court[14] may transmit a request for the arrest and [surrender] [transfer] [extradition] of a person, along with the supporting material outlined in article 53 bis, to any State on the territory of which that person may be found, and shall request the cooperation of that State in the arrest and [surrender] [transfer] [extradition] of such person. States Parties shall, in accordance with the provisions of this Part [and the procedure under their national law], comply with requests for arrest and [surrender] [transfer] [extradition] without [undue] delay.

[1 bis. The national law of a requested State shall govern the conditions [procedure] for granting or denying a request for [surrender] [transfer] [extradition] [except as otherwise provided in this Part].]

2.

[Option 1:   No grounds for refusal.]

[Option 2:   A State Party may deny a request for [surrender] [transfer] [extradition] only if:[15]

    (a)   with respect to a crime under [article 20 (b) through (e)] [article 20 (e)], it has not accepted the jurisdiction of the Court;

[*56] [(b) the person is a national of the requested State;][16]

    (c)   the person has been investigated or has been proceeded against, convicted or acquitted in the requested State or another State for the offence for which his [surrender] [transfer] [extradition] is sought [, except that a request may not be denied if the Court has determined that the case is admissible under article 35];

    [(d) the information submitted in support of the request does not meet the minimum evidentiary requirements of the requested State, as set forth in article 53 bis, paragraph 1 (c);]

    (e)   compliance with the request would put it in breach of an existing obligation that arises from [a peremptory norm of] general international law [treaty] obligation undertaken to another State.][17]

[2 bis. If a request for [surrender] [transfer] [extradition] is denied, the requested State Party shall promptly inform the Court of the reasons for such denial.]

3.   Application to the Court to set aside [surrender] [transfer] [extradition]

    A State Party [having received a request under paragraph 1 may, in accordance with the Rules[18]] [may, in [...] days of receiving a request under paragraph 1], file a written application with the Court to [set aside] [withdraw] the request on specified grounds [including those mentioned in articles 35 and 42]. Pending a decision of the Court on the application, the [*57] State concerned may delay complying with the request but shall take appropriate measures [as may be available] to ensure the compliance with the request after a decision of the Court to reject the application.

4.   Parallel requests from the Court and State(s)

Option 1

    (a)   A State Party [which has accepted the jurisdiction of the Court] [, if it is a party to the treaty covered by [article 20 (e)] with respect to the crime,] shall [, as far as possible,] give priority to a request from the Court under paragraph 1 over requests for extradition from other States [Parties].

    (b)   If the requested State also receives a request from a non-State Party to which it is bound by an extradition agreement for the extradition of the same person, either for the same offence or for a different offence for which the Court is seeking the person's [surrender] [transfer] [extradition], the requested State

---

[13]   The term "persons" is understood to include "suspects", "accused" and "convicted persons". [The term "suspect" means a person who is the subject of a pre-indictment arrest warrant.]

[14]   The term "Court" is understood to include its constituent organs, including the Prosecutor, as defined in article 5. Such a provision could be inserted elsewhere in the Statute.

[15]   There is no agreement on the list of grounds contained in this option.

[16]   It was suggested that even if a person is a national of the requested State, this does not prevent that State from [transferring] [surrendering] the person to the Court if the latter guarantees that the national in question shall be returned to the requested State to serve the sentence pronounced by the Court (cf. article 59 (1)).

[17]   It was suggested that the following ground for refusal should be included: when the imposition or the execution of punishment for the offence for which surrender is requested would be barred by reasons prescribed under the law of the requested State if the requested State were to have jurisdiction over the offence.

[18]   Questions dealing with the consequences of lapse of time will be addressed in the Rules.

shall determine whether to [surrender] [transfer] [extradite] the person to the Court or to extradite the person to the State. In making its decision the requested State shall consider all relevant factors, including but not limited to:

  (i)   the respective dates of the requests;

  (ii) if the offences are different, the nature and gravity of the offences;

  (iii) the interests of the State requesting extradition, including, where relevant, whether the offence was committed in its territory and the nationality of the victims of the offence; and

  (iv) the possibility of subsequent [surrender] [transfer] [extradition] or extradition between the Court and the State requesting extradition.

Option 2

  (a)   If the requested State also receives a request from a [State] [State Party] [to which it is bound by an extradition agreement] for the extradition of the same person, either for the same offence or for a different offence for which the Court is seeking the person's [surrender] [transfer] [extradition], the appropriate authority of the requested State shall determine whether to [surrender] [transfer] [extradite] the person to the Court or to extradite the [*58] person to the State. In making its decision the requested State shall consider all relevant factors, including but not limited to:

  (i)   whether the extradition request was made pursuant to a treaty;

  (ii) the respective dates of the requests;

  (iii) if the offences are different, the nature and gravity of the offences;

  (iv) the interests of the State requesting extradition, including, where relevant, whether the offence was committed in its territory and the nationality of the victims of the offence; and

  (v)   the possibility of subsequent [surrender] [transfer] or extradition between the Court and the State requesting extradition.

  (b)   The requested State may not, however, deny a request for the [surrender] [transfer] [extradition] made under this article in deference to another State's request for extradition of the same person for the same offence if the State requesting extradition is a State Party and the Court has ruled the case before it is admissible, and its decision took into consideration the proceedings in that State which gave rise to its extradition request.

Option 3

  (a)   Subject to paragraph (b), a State Party [shall] [may] accord priority to a request by a State over a request by the Court for the extradition, transfer or surrender of a person to the requesting State under the provisions of any existing bilateral or multilateral agreement.

  (b)   A State Party shall however accord priority to requests from the Court over a request by a State where the Court has [positively] determined pursuant to article ___ that the requesting State is unwilling or unable genuinely to carry out the investigation or prosecution of the case for which extradition, transfer or surrender is sought.

[5.   Proceeding in requested State

  Where the law of the requested State so requires, the person whose [surrender] [transfer] [extradition] is sought shall be entitled to challenge the request for arrest and [surrender] [transfer] [extradition] in the court of the requested State on [only] the following grounds:

[*59] [(a) lack of jurisdiction of the Court;]

  [(b) non bis in idem;[19] or]

  [(c) the evidence submitted in support of the request does not meet the evidentiary requirements of the requested State as set forth in article 53 bis, paragraph 1 (b) (v) and (c) (ii).]]

6.   Delayed or temporary [surrender] [transfer] [extradition]

  If the person sought is being proceeded against or is serving a sentence in the requested State for an offence different from that for which [surrender] [transfer] [extradition] to the Court is sought, the requested State, after making its decision to grant the request, may:

  (a)   temporarily [surrender] [transfer] [extradite] the person to the Court and in that case, the Court shall return the person to that State after the completion of the trial or as otherwise agreed; or

---

[19]   Non bis in idem is treated in article 42.

(b) [with the consent of the Court [Pre-Trial Chamber] which shall rule after having heard the Prosecutor] postpone the [surrender] [transfer] [extradition] of the person until the completion or abandonment of the prosecution [or completion of service of the sentence].[20]

[7. Extradite or prosecute obligation[21]

(a) In the case of a crime to which article 20 (e) applies, the requested State [, if it is a party to the treaty in question but has not accepted the Court's jurisdiction with respect to that crime,] shall, where it decides not to [surrender] [transfer] [extradite] the accused to the Court, promptly take all necessary steps to extradite the accused to a State having requested extradition or [at the request of the Court] refer the case [through proceedings in [*60] accordance with national laws] to its competent authorities for the purpose of prosecution.

[(b) In any other case, the requested State Party shall [consider whether it can], in accordance with its legal procedures, take steps to arrest and [surrender] [transfer] [extradite] the accused to the Court, or [whether it should take steps to extradite the accused to a State having requested extradition or [at the request of the Court] refer the case to its competent authorities for the purpose of prosecution.]

[(c) The [surrender] [transfer] [extradition] of an accused to the Court will constitute, as between States Parties which accept the jurisdiction of the Court with respect to the crime in question, compliance with a provision of any treaty requiring that a suspect be extradited or that the case be referred to the competent authorities of the requested State for the purpose of prosecution.]]

[8. Provisions of evidence irrespective of [surrender] [transfer] [extradition]

[To the extent permitted under the law of the requested State] and without prejudice to the rights of third parties, all items found in the requested State [that have been acquired as a result of the alleged crime or] that may be required as evidence shall, upon request, be transmitted to the Court [if the [surrender] [transfer] [extradition] [is granted on conditions to be determined by the Court] even if the [surrender] [transfer] [extradition] of the person cannot be carried out.] [Any rights which third parties may have acquired in the said items shall be preserved where these rights exist. The property shall be returned without charge to the requested State as soon as possible after the trial.]]

9. Transit of [surrendered] [transferred] [extradited] person[22]

(a) A State Party shall authorize transportation under its national procedural law through its territory of a person being [surrendered] [transferred] [extradited] to the Court by another State. A request by the Court for transit shall be transmitted in accordance with article 52. The request for transit shall contain a description of the person being transported, a brief statement of the facts of the case and the legal characterization and [*61] the warrant for arrest and [transfer] [surrender] [extradition]. A person in transit shall be detained in custody during the period of transit.

(b) [No authorization is required where air transportation is used and no landing is scheduled on the territory of the State of transit.]

(c) If an unscheduled landing occurs on the territory of the State of transit, it may require a request for transit as provided for in subparagraph (a). The State of transit shall detain the person to be transported until the request for transit is received and the transit is effected, so long as the request is received within 96 hours of the unscheduled landing.

10. Costs

The costs associated with the [surrender] [transfer] [extradition] of a person shall be borne by [the [Court] [requested State]] [the Court or the requested State depending upon where the cost concerned arises].

---

[20] If it is agreed that consent of the Court will be required for postponement, then the last set of brackets can be removed.

[21] The text of paragraph 7 (a) and (b) applies if there is a consent regime. If the Court has jurisdiction over core crimes and there is no consent regime, these provisions could be deleted.

[22] It has been suggested that this or other provisions could form the basis for a separate article. In addition, some felt that a number of details set forth in this text would be more appropriately regulated in the Rules.

Article 53 bis
Contents of request for [surrender] [transfer] [extradition][23]

1.   A request for arrest and [surrender] [transfer] [extradition] shall be made in writing. In urgent cases a request may be made by any medium capable of delivering a written record,[24] provided that a request shall be confirmed [if necessary] through the channel provided for in article 52.[25] The request shall contain or be supported by:

(a)   information describing the person sought, sufficient to identify the person and information as to that person's probable location;

[*62] (b)   in the case of a request for pre-indictment arrest and [surrender] [transfer] [extradition]:

(i)   a copy of warrant for arrest;[26]

(ii)   a statement of the reasons to believe the suspect may have committed a crime within the jurisdiction of the Court and that the Prosecutor expects to seek an indictment within [90] days;

(iii)   a brief summary of the [essential] facts of the case;

(iv)   a statement as to why pre-indictment arrest is urgent and necessary;[27]

(v)   [such documents, statements, or other types of information regarding the commission of the offence and the person's role therein, which may be required by the laws of the requested State;] [however, in no event may the requested State's requirements be more burdensome than those applicable to requests for extradition pursuant to treaties with other States;]

(c)   in the case of a request for post-indictment arrest and [surrender] [transfer] [extradition]:

(i)   a copy of the warrant of arrest and indictment;

(ii)   [such documents, statements, or other types of information regarding the commission of the offence and the accused's role therein which may be required by the laws of the requested State; [however, in no event may the requested State's requirements be more burdensome than those applicable to requests for extradition pursuant to treaties or other arrangements with other States;]]

[*63] (d)   in the case of a request for the arrest and [surrender] [transfer] [extradition] of a person already convicted:[28]

(i)   a copy of any warrant of arrest for that person;

(ii)   a copy of the judgement of conviction;

(iii)   information to demonstrate that the person sought is the one referred to in the judgement of conviction;

(iv)   (if the person sought has been sentenced,) a copy of the sentence imposed and a statement of any time already served and that remaining.

1 bis. A State Party shall notify the Court at the time of ratification, accession or approval whether it can [surrender] [transfer] [extradite] on the basis of a pre-indictment warrant and the information specified in paragraph 1 (b) or it can only [surrender] [transfer] [extradite] following [confirmation of indictment] [issuance of a post-indictment warrant] on the basis of the information in paragraph 1 (c).

[2.   Where the requested State Party considers the information provided insufficient to allow it to comply with the request, it shall seek, without delay, additional information and may fix a reasonable time limit for the receipt thereof. [Any proceedings in the requested State may be continued, and the person sought may be detained, for such period as may be necessary to enable the Court to provide the additional information requested.] If the additional information is not provided within the reasonable time limit fixed by the requested State, the person may be released.]

[3.   The Court may in accordance with article 43 withhold from the requested State specific information about any victims, potential witnesses and their families if it considers that it is necessary to ensure their

---

[23]   Portions of this article might also be provided for in the Rules rather than in the Statute.

[24]   Issues relating to the security of this type of transmission will have to be discussed.

[25]   Articles 52, 53 bis, 54 and 55 contain virtually identical provisions, some of which should be harmonized.

[26]   The question of authentication of a warrant of arrest will be dealt with in the Rules.

[27]   Article 28 covers pre-indictment arrest, while this paragraph also addresses the form of a request for pre-indictment arrest. The text of these two provisions must be examined together to ensure that there are no inconsistencies or duplications.

[28]   It was suggested that this paragraph is an enforcement-of-sentence issue to be treated in part 8.

safety or physical or psychological well-being. Any information that is made available under this article shall be provided and handled in a manner that protects the safety or physical or psychological well-being of any victims, potential witnesses and their families.][29]

[*64] Article 54
Provisional arrest

1. In case of urgency, the Court may request the provisional arrest of the person sought pending presentation of the request for [surrender] [transfer] [extradition] and supporting documents under article 53 bis.

2. The request for provisional arrest shall [be made by any medium capable of delivering a written record and shall] contain:

(i) a description of the person sought and information regarding the probable location of such person;

(ii) a brief statement of the essential facts of the case, including, if possible, the time and location of the offence;

(iii) a statement of the existence of a warrant of arrest or a judgement of conviction against the person sought, and, if applicable, a description of the specific offence or offences with which the person has been charged or for which he has been convicted; and

(iv) a statement that a request for [surrender] [transfer] [extradition] of the person sought will follow.

2 bis. The Court may withhold from the requested State specific information about any victims, potential witnesses and their families or close associates if it considers that it is necessary to ensure their safety or well-being. Any information that is provided under this article to the requested State shall be provided in a manner that protects the safety or well-being of any victims, potential witnesses and their families or close associates.

[*65] 3. A person who is provisionally arrested may be discharged from custody upon the expiration of [ ][30] days from the date of provisional arrest if the requested State has not received the request for [surrender] [transfer] [extradition] and the supporting documents specified under article 53 bis. However, the person may consent to [surrender] [transfer] [extradition] before the expiration of this period if the legislation of the requested State allows, in which case that State shall proceed to [surrender] [transfer] [extradite] the person to the Court as soon as possible.[31]

4. The fact that the person sought has been discharged from custody pursuant to subparagraph (c) shall not prejudice the subsequent rearrest and [surrender] [transfer] [extradition] of that person if the request for [surrender] [transfer] [extradition] and supporting documents are delivered at a later date.

Article 55
Other forms of cooperation [and judicial and legal [mutual] assistance][32]

1. States Parties shall, in accordance with the provisions of this Part [and their national [procedural] law], comply with requests for assistance by the Court for:

(a) the identification and whereabouts of persons or the location of items;

---

[29] This paragraph could also be included under article 52.

[30] ILC article 52 (1) (a) addresses provisional arrest, as well as search and seizure and other measures pertaining to mutual assistance. In order to present all proposals in a clear fashion, the present document treats provisional arrest in this article and the other matters in article 55. Article 28 provides for pre-indictment arrest under certain limited circumstances. To avoid confusion with the term of provisional arrest provided for in this article, it is for consideration whether the form of arrest in article 28 should be termed "provisional arrest". This article may have other implications for article 28.

[31] It was suggested that the simplified surrender procedure should be the object of a separate paragraph, since it applies to both the provisional arrest stage and after a full surrender request has been submitted.
This paragraph could also be included in article 52.

[32] This issue has to be revisited after the title of part 7 is confirmed.

(b)   the taking of evidence, including testimony under oath, and the production of evidence, including expert opinions or reports necessary to the Court;

[*66] (c)   the questioning of any suspect or accused;

(d)   the service of documents, including judicial documents;

(e)   facilitating the appearance of persons before the Court;

[(f)   the temporary transfer of persons in custody, with their consent [which cannot be withdrawn], in order to provide testimony [or other assistance] to the Court;]

[(g)   the conduct of on-site investigations and inspections[33] [with the consent of the requested State];]

[(h)   the conduct of proceedings of the Court in its territory with the consent of the requested State;][34]

(i)   the execution of searches and seizures;

(j)   the provision of records and documents, including official records and documents;

(k)   the protection of victims and witnesses and the integrity of evidence;

(l)   the identification, tracing and freezing or seizure of proceeds, property and assets and instrumentalities of crimes for the purpose of eventual confiscation without prejudice to the rights of bona fide third parties;[35] and   (m) any other types of assistance [not prohibited by the law of the requested State].

[*67] [2. Grounds for refusal

Option 1

A State Party shall not deny a request for assistance from the Court.

Option 2

A State Party may deny a request for assistance, in whole or in part, only if:[36]

(a)   with respect to a crime [under [article 20 (b) through (e)] [article 20 (e)], it has not accepted the jurisdiction of the Court;

(b)   the authorities of the requested State would be prohibited by its national laws from carrying out the action requested with regard to the investigation or prosecution of a similar offence in that State;

(c)   execution of the request would seriously prejudice its national security, *ordre public* or other essential interests;

(c) bis the request concerns the production of any documents or disclosure of evidence which relates to its national [security] [defence];

(d)   execution of the request would interfere with an ongoing investigation or prosecution in the requested State or in another State [or with a completed investigation or prosecution that might have led to an acquittal or conviction, except that a request may not be denied if the investigation or prosecution relates to the same matter which is the subject of the request and the Court has determined that the case is admissible under article 35];

(e)   compliance with the request would put it in breach of an existing [international law] [treaty] obligation undertaken to another [State] [non-State Party].]

[3.   Before denying a request for assistance, the requested State shall consider whether the requested assistance can be provided subject to specified conditions, or whether the assistance can be provided at a later time or in an alternative manner, provided that if the Court or the Prosecutor accepts the assistance subject to conditions, it shall abide by them.]

[*68] 4.   If a request for assistance is denied, the requested State Party shall promptly inform the Court or the Prosecutor of the reasons for such denial.

---

[33]   This issue is also addressed in article 26 (2) bis which is being considered by the Working Group on Procedural Matters.

[34]   The relationship between subparagraphs (g) and (h) and article 56 (4) needs to be examined.

[35]   The issue of whether the Court is to be vested with such powers is being considered by the Working Group on Penalties.

[36]   The list of possible grounds for refusal is not an agreed list.

[4 bis. If a requested State does not produce a document or disclose evidence under paragraph 2 (c) bis on the ground that it relates to its national defence, the Trial Chamber shall only make such inferences that relate to the guilt or innocence of the accused.][37]

5.   Confidentiality[38]

(a)   The Court shall ensure the confidentiality of documents and information except as required for the investigation and proceedings described in the request.

(b)   The requested State may, when necessary, transmit documents or information to the Prosecutor on a confidential basis. The Prosecutor may then use them solely for the purpose of generating new evidence.

(c)   The requested State may, on its own motion or at the request of the Prosecutor, subsequently consent to the disclosure of such documents or information. They may then be used as evidence pursuant to the provisions of Parts IV and V of the Statute and related Rules.

6.   Assistance by the Court[39]

(a)   The Court [may] [shall], upon request, cooperate with and provide assistance [within its competence] to a State Party conducting an investigation into or trial in respect of acts which constitute a crime under this Statute [or which constitute a serious crime under the national law of the requesting State].

[*69] (b) (i)   The assistance provided under subparagraph (a) shall include, among others:

(1)   the transmission of statements, documents or other types of evidence obtained in the course of an investigation or a trial conducted by the Court; and

(2)   the questioning of any person detained by the Court;

(ii)   In the case of assistance under subparagraph (b) (i) (1):

(1)   If the documents or other types of evidence have been obtained with the assistance of a State such transmission shall require the consent of that State;[40]

(2)   If the statements, documents or other types of evidence have been provided by a witness or expert, such transmission shall be subject to the provisions of article 43[41] [and shall require the consent of that witness or expert];

(c)   The Court may, under the conditions set out in this paragraph, grant a request for assistance under this paragraph from a non-State party.

7.   Form and contents of the request

(a)   Requests for judicial and legal [mutual] assistance shall:

(i)   be made in writing. In urgent cases, a request may be made by any medium capable of delivering a written record, provided that it shall be confirmed [, if necessary,] through the channel provided for in article 52; and

(ii)   contain the following, as applicable:

(1)   a brief statement of the purpose of the request and the assistance sought, including the legal basis and grounds for the request;

[*70]   (2)   as much detailed information as possible about the location or identification of any person or place that must be found or identified in order for the assistance sought to be provided;

(3)   a brief description of the essential facts underlying the request;

(4)   the reasons for and details of any procedure or requirement to be followed;

[(5)   such information as may be required under the law of the requested State in order to execute the request;]

(6)   any other information relevant to the assistance being sought.

---

[37]   Views have been expressed that consideration should be given to establishing a mechanism for dealing with such sensitive information.

[38]   The work of the Working Group on Procedural Matters on the protection of sensitive information and the protection of victims and witnesses may have an impact on this provision. Views have also been expressed that subparagraphs (b) and (c) should be addressed in the Rules.

[39]   Views have been expressed that subparagraphs (b) (i) and (ii) should be addressed in the Rules.

[40]   The relationship with article 57 needs to be considered.

[41]   This relates to the provisions on the protection of victims and witnesses.

(b)   The Court may withhold, in accordance with article 43, from the requested State [or a State making a request under paragraph 6] specific information about any victims, potential witnesses and their families if it considers that this is necessary to ensure their safety or physical and psychological well-being. Any information that is made available under this article to the requested State shall be provided and handled in a manner that protects the safety or physical or psychological well-being of any victims, potential witnesses and their families.[42]

Article 56
Execution of requests under article 55

1.   Requests for assistance shall be executed in accordance with the law of the requested State [and, unless prohibited by such law, in the manner specified in the request, including following any procedures outlined therein or permitting persons specified in the request to be present at and assist in the execution process[43] [by its competent authorities]].

[*71] 2.   In the case of an urgent request, the documents or evidence produced in response shall, at the request of the Court, be sent urgently.[44]

3.   Replies from States Parties, including any accompanying documents, [may be in the language of the requested State] [shall be in accordance with paragraph 2 of article 52. The Court may also request the transmission of documents in their original language].

[4.   The [Prosecutor] [Court] may [, if requested,] assist the authorities of the requested State with the execution of the request for judicial assistance [and may, with the consent of the requested State, carry out certain inquiries on its territory].][45]

[4 bis. [For the purposes of paragraph 4,] the requested State shall, upon request, inform the Court of the time and place of execution of the request for assistance.][46]

5.   (a)   The ordinary costs for execution of requests in the territory of the requested State shall be borne by the requested State except for the following which should be borne by the Court:

(i)   Costs associated with the travel and security of witnesses and experts or the transfer of persons in custody;

(ii)   Costs of translation, interpretation and transcription;

(iii)   The travel and subsistence costs of the Prosecutor, members of his office or any other member of the Court; and

(iv)   The costs of any expert opinion or report requested by the Court.

(b)   Where the execution of a request will result in extraordinary costs, [there shall be consultations to determine how those costs will be met] [those costs shall be met by the Court].

[*72] (c)   The provisions in this paragraph shall apply with appropriate modifications to requests made to the Court for assistance.[47]

[6.   (a)   Witnesses or experts may not be compelled to testify at the seat of the Court.

[(b)   If they do not wish to travel to the seat of the Court, their evidence shall be taken in the country in which they reside or in such other place as they may agree upon with the Court [in accordance with national requirements [and in compliance with international law standards][48]].

(c)   In order to guarantee the safety of witnesses and experts, any means of communication may be used to take their evidence while preserving their anonymity.[49]][50]

---

[42]   Consideration needs to be given to whether this provision can be relocated to article 52 or article 56.

[43]   There is a link between this provision and the empowerment provisions of paragraph 4.

[44]   Views have been expressed that this should be addressed in the Rules.

[45]   Views have been expressed that paragraph 1 is an alternative to this paragraph.

[46]   Views have been expressed that this should be addressed in the Rules.

[47]   Similar provisions may have to be inserted elsewhere to address the situation where the Court renders assistance to States or States Parties.

[48]   The exact formulation will depend on the formulation adopted for article 44.

[49]   The protection of witnesses is also addressed in articles 26 and 43.

[50]   Views have been expressed on the relationship between subparagraphs (b) and (c) and article 37 on trial in the presence of the accused.

[(d) No witness or expert who appears before the Court may be prosecuted, detained or submitted to any restriction of personal freedom by the Court in respect of any acts [or omissions] that preceded the departure of that person from the requested State.]

7.   Provisions allowing a person heard or examined by the Court under article [...] to invoke restrictions designed to prevent disclosure of confidential information connected with national defence or security also apply to the execution of requests for assistance under this article.

[*73] [Article 57
Rule of speciality
1.   Limit on other proceedings against [surrendered] [transferred] [extradited] person

A person [surrendered] [transferred] [extradited] to the Court under this Statute shall not be:

(a)   proceeded against, punished or detained for any criminal act other than that for which the person has been [surrendered] [transferred] [extradited];

(b)   [surrendered] [transferred] [extradited] to another State in respect of any criminal act[51] [except when he or she commits the criminal act after [extradition] [surrender] [transfer]].

2.   Limit on other uses of evidence

Evidence provided by a State Party under this Statute shall [, if that State Party so requests,] not be used as evidence for any purpose other than that for which it was provided [unless this is necessary to preserve a right of the accused under article 41 (2)].

3.   Waiver of rule by the requested State

The Court may request the State concerned to waive the requirements of paragraphs 1 or 2, for the reasons and purposes to be specified in the request. In the case of paragraph 1, this request shall be accompanied by an additional warrant of arrest and by a legal record of any statement made by the accused with respect to the offence.][52]

[*74] PART 8. ENFORCEMENT[53]
Article 58
General obligation regarding recognition [and enforcement] of judgements

States Parties [shall] [undertake to recognize] [[and to] enforce directly on their territory] [give effect to] the judgements of the Court [, in accordance with the provisions of this Part].

[The judgements of the Court shall be binding on the national jurisdictions of every State Party as regards the criminal liability of the person convicted and the principles relating to compensation for damage caused to victims and the restitution of property acquired by the person convicted and other forms of reparation ordered by the Court, such as restitution, compensation and rehabilitation.][54]

Article 59
Role of States in enforcement [and supervision] of sentences of imprisonment
1.   Obligation versus consent of States Parties[55]
Option 1

A sentence of imprisonment shall be served in a State designated by the Court [Presidency].
Option 2

[*75] (a) A sentence of imprisonment shall be served in a State designated by the Court [Presidency] from a list of States which have indicated to the Court their willingness to accept sentenced persons. [The State so designated shall promptly inform the Court [Presidency] whether it accepts the request.]

---

[51]   The issue of transfer, etc., from the State of enforcement of a sentence of imprisonment to a third State is addressed in article 59 (4).

[52]   These square brackets reflect the view that there should be no rule of speciality in the Statute.

[53]   One delegation was of the view that part 8 deals with issues also relevant to judicial assistance and that there might be grounds for non-recognition or non-enforcement of judgements.

[54]   There was a question whether this sort of provision should be in article 45, article 47 or in part 8.

[55]   The issue arises as to whether provision should be made concerning whether non-States Parties should accept sentenced persons for imprisonment.

[(b)[56] A State may make its consent conditional [on the applicability of its domestic laws relating to pardon, conditional release and commutation of sentence, and on its administration of the sentence. In this case, the consent of the Court is not required to subsequent actions by that State in conformity with those laws, but the Court shall be given at least 45 days' notice of any decision which might materially affect the terms or extent of the imprisonment].]

1 bis.
(a) The Court's [Presidency's] designation of a State under paragraph 1 shall be governed by principles [of equitable [geographic distribution] [burden sharing]] to be elaborated by [the Permanent Committee of States Parties.][57] [However, no such designation shall be made with respect to the State where or against which the crime was committed or the State of which the convicted person or the victim is a national [, unless the Court [Presidency] explicitly decides otherwise for reasons of social rehabilitation].]
(b) In making a designation under paragraph 1, the Court [Presidency] shall allow the person sentenced to provide views on any concerns as to personal security or rehabilitation. However, the consent of the person is not required for the Court [Presidency] to designate a particular State for enforcement of the sentence.

1 ter.
If no State is designated under paragraph 1, the sentence of imprisonment shall be served in the prison facility made available by the host State, in conformity with and under the conditions as set out in the Host State Agreement, as referred to in article 3, paragraph 2.

[*76] 2. Enforcement of the sentence[58]
(a) The sentence of imprisonment shall be binding on the States Parties, which may in no case modify it.
(b) The Court alone shall have the right to decide any application for review of the [judgement] [sentence]. The State of enforcement shall not impede the sentenced person from making any such application.

3. Supervision and administration of sentence
(a) The enforcement of a sentence of imprisonment shall be subject to the supervision of the Court [Presidency] [, and the Court shall ensure that internationally recognized standards of treatment of prisoners are fully guaranteed].

Option 1 for (b)
[(b) The conditions of detention shall be governed by the law of the State of enforcement. [However, the Court [Presidency] may, on its own motion or at the request of the sentenced person, modify the conditions of detention of the sentenced person. The State of enforcement shall enforce the modified conditions of detention. The Court [Presidency] may also on its own motion, or at the request of the sentenced person or the State of enforcement, decide that the sentenced person be transferred to another State for the continued serving of the sentence [provided that State agrees].
[(b) bis Internationally recognized standards of treatment of prisoners shall be fully guaranteed by the State of enforcement.]

Option 2 for (b)
[(b) The conditions of detention shall be governed by the law of the State of enforcement, in accordance with internationally recognized minimum standards, but in any case not more or less favourable than those available to prisoners convicted of similar offences in the State of enforcement.]
(c) Communications between persons sentenced and the Court shall be unimpeded [and confidential].

---

[56] If retained, this provision will need to conform with provisions of article 60 below.
[57] This reflects a current proposal for the establishment of a Permanent Committee of States Parties.
[58] It was suggested that this paragraph should be moved to the beginning of the article.

[*77] 4.   <u>Transfer of the person upon completion of sentence</u>

(a)   Unless the State of enforcement agrees to permit the prisoner to remain in its territory following completion of sentence, the prisoner shall be released into the custody of the State of the person's nationality or another State that has agreed to receive the person.

(b)   The costs involved in transporting the prisoner to another State under paragraph 1 shall be borne by the Court, unless the State of enforcement or the receiving State agree otherwise.

(c)   [Unless prohibited by the provisions of article 57] [with the consent of the Court as provided in article 59 <u>bis</u>],[59] the State of enforcement may also, in accordance with its national law, extradite or otherwise surrender the prisoner to the State which has requested the extradition or surrender of the prisoner for purposes of trial or enforcement of a sentence.

[Article 59 bis

Limitation of prosecution/punishment for other offences[60]

1.   A sentenced person in the custody of the State of enforcement shall not be subjected to prosecution or punishment [or extradition to a third State] for any conduct committed prior to delivery to the State of detention, unless such prosecution or punishment [or extradition] has been approved by the Court [Presidency] [at the request of the State of detention].

2.   The Court [Presidency] shall rule on the matter after having heard the prisoner.

3.   Paragraph 1 of this article shall cease to apply if the sentenced person remains more than 30 days on the territory of the State of enforcement after having served the full sentence imposed by the Court.]

[*78] [Article 59 ter

Enforcement of fines and forfeiture measures[61]

1.   States Parties shall [, in accordance with their national law,] enforce fines and forfeiture measures [and measures relating to compensation or restitution [reparation]][62] as fines and forfeiture measures [and measures relating to compensation or restitution [reparation]] rendered by their national authorities.

[For the purpose of enforcement of fines, the Court [Presidency] may order the forced sale of any property of the person sentenced which is on the territory of a State Party. For the same purposes, the Court [Presidency] may order the forfeiture of proceeds, property and assets and instrumentalities of crimes belonging to the person sentenced.][63] [64]

2.   Property, including the proceeds of the sale thereof, which is obtained by a State Party as a result of its enforcement of a judgement of the Court shall be handed over to the Court [Presidency] [which will dispose of that property in accordance with the provisions to paragraph 3 of article 47].]

[*79] Article 60[65]

---

[59]   There is a question as to whether the permissibility of re-extradition of the prisoner should be addressed in article 57 (Rule of Speciality) or in article 59 <u>bis</u>.

[60]   Consideration should be given to the relationship of this article to the rule of speciality, as found in article 57. This article is also related to article 53, paragraph 6, regarding temporary or delayed surrender.

[61]   The use of the term "forfeiture" rather than "confiscation" reflects the current discussions on this issue in the Working Group on Penalties. This issue is related to the discussion of penalties.

[62]   References to fines, forfeiture, restitution or compensation, or similar terms, will depend on the range of sanctions and compensatory measures ultimately provided for in article 47.

[63]   There is a question whether this provision concerns enforcement of sentences, or rather the powers of the Court to order particular measures relating to enforcement of fines or confiscation. If it is meant to refer to States enforcing specific orders relating to fines or confiscation, then paragraph 1 might be amended to make clear that that enforcement by States Parties would include "giving effect to orders of the Court relating to enforcement of fines or forfeitures, such as the seizure of particular property or the forced sale of property of the convicted person to satisfy a fine".

[64]   There was a suggestion that this paragraph should be placed first.

[65]   In the discussion of the Working Group on Penalties, it was suggested that, to meet concerns of several delegations regarding the severity of a life sentence or a long sentence of imprisonment, article 60 should provide a mandatory mechanism by which the prisoner's sentence would be re-examined by the Court after a certain period of time, in order to determine whether he or she should be released. In this way, the Court could also ensure the uniform treatment of prisoners regardless of the State where they served their sentence.

Pardon,[66] parole and commutation of sentences [early release]
Option 1 (abbreviation of ILC text)
1.   The prisoner may apply to the Court [Presidency] for a [decision on] [ruling regarding the appropriateness of] [pardon,] parole or commutation of sentence, if under a generally applicable law of the State of enforcement, a person in the sa e circumstances who had been convicted for the same conduct by a court of that State would be eligible for [pardon,] parole or commutation of sentence.
Option 2
1.   (a)   The State of enforcement shall not release the prisoner before the expiry of the sentence as pronounced by the Court.
      (b)   The Court [Presidency] alone shall have the right to decide any application for [commutation of the sentence] [commutation of the sentence or parole] [commutation of the sentence, parole or [pardon]]. [If appropriate in the circumstances, parole may be granted after the prisoner has served:
            (i)   not less than 20 years in case of life imprisonment;
            (ii)   not less than two thirds of the term in case of imprisonment for a definite term.
[*80] Parole may be revoked when the parolee is convicte of having committed an offence while on parole, or has violated any condition of his parole.]
2.   Procedures regarding an application for commutation of sentence [or parole [or pardon]] and the Court's decision on such an application shall be governed by the Rules of Procedure.

[Article 60 bis
Escape
      In the event of an escape, the sentenced person shall, as soon as he has been arrested pursuant to a request of the Court under article 53 bis (1) (d), be delivered to the State in which he was serving his sentence or to another place determined by the Court.]

[*81] Annex V
REPORT OF THE WORKING GROUP ON PENALTIES[*]

1.   The Working Group recommends to the Preparatory Committee the text of the provisions concerning penalties contained in documents A/AC.249/1997/WG.6/CRP.2/Rev.1; A/AC.249/1997/WG.6/CRP.3/Rev.1; and A/AC.249/1997/WG.6/CRP.4-13, as a first draft for inclusion in the draft consolidated text of a convention for an international criminal court.
2.   The issue of the death penalty was not discussed by the Working Group, which recommends that the text concerning the death penalty, as contained in A/AC.249/1997/WG.6/CRP.1, under the heading A (e), should be included in the draft consolidated text.
3.   The issue of effect of the judgement, compliance and implementation, as contained in A/AC.249/1997/WG.6/CRP.1, under the heading G, was not discussed by the Working Group, which suggested that it should be dealt with in the context of enforcement of sentences. The text referred to above should accordingly be reflected in the draft consolidated text.

[*82] PENALTIES
A. The penalties
      The Court may impose on a person convicted under this Statute [one or more of the following penalties] [the following penalty]:

---

[66]   A concern was expressed that pardon might involve political considerations which would not be appropriate for determination by the Court, so that the authority to decide on an application for pardon might better be vested in the Permanent Committee of States Parties.
[*]   Incorporating the documents enumerated in paragraph 1 and the texts referred to in paragraphs 2 and 3.

(a)[2] [a term of life imprisonment or imprisonment for a specified number of years;]

[a maximum term of imprisonment of [30] years;]

[a definite term of imprisonment between [20] and [40] years [, unless this is reduced according to the provisions of this Statute][3];]

[The Court may attach to the sentence of imprisonment a minimum period during which the convicted person may not be granted any [release under relevant provisions of Part VIII of the Statute].]

[In the case of a convicted person under the age of 18 years at the time of the commission of the crime, a specified term of imprisonment of no more than 20 years];

[*83] [When imposing a penalty on a person under the age of 18 years [at the time of the commission of the crime], the Court shall determine the appropriate measures to ensure the rehabilitation of the offender][4]

[(b) A fine [in addition to a sentence of imprisonment on conviction of a crime under article 20]];[5]

[(c)

(i) [[disqualification from seeking public office for the person's term of imprisonment and any further period of time that may be imposed] [in the modality and to the extent that the penalty could be imposed in accordance with the laws of the State in which such a penalty is to be enforced];][6]

(ii)[7] a forfeiture of [instrumentalities of crime and] proceeds, property and assets obtained by criminal conduct, without prejudice to the rights of bona fide third parties. [When the whole or part of the [instrumentalities of crime or] proceeds, property, assets mentioned in ... cannot be [*84] forfeited, a sum of money equivalent thereto may be collected.];[8]]

[(d) Appropriate forms of reparation]

[[without prejudice to the obligation on every State to provide reparation in respect of conduct engaging the responsibility of the State][9] [or reparation through any other international arrangement], appropriate forms of reparation [,[including] [such as] restitution, compensation and rehabilitation]][10]

---

[2]   To meet concerns of several delegations regarding the severity of a life sentence or a long sentence of imprisonment, it was suggested that part 8, article 60, should provide a mandatory mechanism by which the prisoner's sentence would be reexamined by the Court after a certain period of time, in order to determine whether he or she should be released. In this way, the Court could also ensure the uniform treatment of prisoners regardless of the State where they served their sentence.

[3]   The view was expressed that if such a provision providing for minimum sentencing is included, there should be a reference to factors that may reduce the minimum sentence. In such a case, the list of relevant factors should be exhaustive. It was suggested that among those factors could be the following: (i) diminished mental capacity that falls short of exclusion of criminal responsibility; (ii) the age of the convicted person; (iii) as appropriate, duress; and (iv) the subsequent conduct of the convicted person.

[4]   The following proposals were made which should be treated either under age of responsibility or the jurisdiction of the Court:

"[The Court shall have no jurisdiction over those who were under the age of 18 years at the time they are alleged to have committed a crime which would otherwise come within the jurisdiction of the Court] [; however, under exceptional circumstances, the Court may exercise jurisdiction and impose a penalty on a person aged 16 to 18 years, provided it has determined that the person was capable of understanding the unlawfulness of his or her conduct at the time the crime was committed]."

[5]   A number of delegations suggested that penalties for procedural crimes be included in relevant provisions of the Statute, along the following lines: "on conviction of perjury or contempt of the Court, as an ordinary penalty or as a supplementary penalty in addition to a sentence of imprisonment".

[6]   Some delegations held the view that such a provision would give rise to difficult issues of enforcement.

[7]   The terms in this provision should be brought into line with similar terms used elsewhere in this Statute once those provisions are finalized.

[8]   It was suggested that forfeiture not be included as a penalty, but instead be included as a mechanism which the Court would request States to use with regard to execution of an order for reparations. According to this view, a provision on forfeiture could be considered as a separate paragraph of this article or elsewhere in the Statute.

[9]   It was suggested that there was no need for such a clause relating to State responsibility, since it was already dealt with in the context of rules on individual criminal responsibility (see A/AC.249/1997/L.5, article B a, para. 4).

[10]   A number of delegations suggested that the Statute should address the issue of reparations to victims and their families. Opinions were divided as to whether this issue should be dealt with in the context of penalties. It was suggested that it could usefully be dealt with within the framework of the Working Group on Procedural Matters. It was also noted that the issue of reparations had a bearing on rules of enforcement in the ILC Statute, part 8. A number of delegations expressed the view that there might be merit in dealing with these issues in a unified way focusing on all the issues related to compensation.

[(e)　(Death penalty)][11]

Option 1

[death penalty, as an option, in case of aggravating circumstances and when the Trial Chamber finds it necessary in the light of the gravity of the crime, the number of victims and the severity of the damage.]

Option 2

[*85] No provision on death penalty.

[*86] B. Aggravating and mitigating circumstances

In determining the sentence, the Court shall, in accordance with the Rules of the Court, take into account such factors as the gravity of the crime and the individual circumstances of the convicted person.[12]

C. Prior detention

In imposing a sentence of imprisonment, the Court shall deduct the time, if any, previously spent in detention in accordance with an order of the Court. The Court may deduct any time otherwise spent in detention in connection with conduct underlying the crime.

D. Applicable national legal standards[13]

Option 1

[In determining the length of a term of imprisonment or the amount of a fine to be imposed, [or property to be forfeited,] the Court [may have regard to [*87] the penalties provided for by law of] [shall impose the highest penalty provided for by the law of either]:

　(a)　[the State of which the convicted person is a national];
　(b)　[the State where the crime was committed;] [or]
　(c)　[the State which had custody of and jurisdiction over the accused.]

[In cases where national law does not regulate a specific crime, the Court will apply penalties ascribed to analogous crimes in the same national law.]]

Option 2

No provision on national legal standards.[14]

E. Sentences of imprisonment for multiple crimes

When a person had been convicted of more than one crime, the Court shall:

Option 1

[pronounce a single sentence of imprisonment [not exceeding the maximum sentence prescribed for the gravest crime] [, increased by half]]

Option 2

[indicate whether multiple sentences of imprisonment shall be served consecutively or concurrently.]

---

[11]　See paragraph 2 of the report of this Working Group, above.

[12]　It may be impossible to foresee all of the relevant aggravating and mitigating circumstances at this stage. Many delegations felt that factors should be elaborated and developed in the rules of the Court, while several other delegations expressed the view that a final decision on this approach would depend upon the mechanism agreed for adopting the Rules. Among the factors suggested by various delegations as having relevance were: the impact of the crime on the victims and their families; the extent of damage caused or the danger posed by the convicted person's conduct; the degree of participation of the convicted person in the commission of the crime; the circumstances falling short of exclusion of criminal responsibility such as substantially diminished mental capacity or, as appropriate, duress; the age of the convicted person; the social and economic condition of the convicted person; the motive for the commission of the crime; the subsequent conduct of the person who committed the crime; superior orders; the use of minors in the commission of the crime.

[13]　It was suggested that this issue should be dealt with only in the context of ILC article 33 on applicable national laws. Another suggestion was to move this issue to section B above. Moreover, the view was held that this kind of provision should be avoided altogether.

[14]　Consideration could be given to inserting an express provision to this effect.

[*88] [F. <u>New article 47 bis. Legal persons</u>][15] [16]
[A legal person shall incur one or more of the following penalties:

(i)   fines;

[(ii) dissolution;]

[(iii) prohibition, for such period as determined by the Court, of the exercise of activities of any kind;]

[(iv) closure, for such a period as determined by the Court, of the premises used in the commission of the crime;]

[(v) forfeiture of [instrumentalities of crime and] proceeds, property and assets obtained by criminal conduct;[17]] [and]

[(vi) appropriate forms of reparation][18]]

[*89] G. <u>New article 47 ter. Fines [and assets] collected by the Court</u>][19]
[Fines [and assets] collected by the Court may be transferred, by order of the Court, to one or more of the following:

[(a) [as a matter of priority,] a trust fund [established by the Secretary-General of the United Nations] or [administered by the Court] for the benefit of victims of the crime [and their families];]

[(b) a State the nationals of which were the victims of the crime;]

[(c) the registrar, to defray the costs of the trial.]]

[H. <u>Effect of the judgement. Compliance. Implementation</u>][20] [21]
[(a) The judgement of the Court shall be binding on the national jurisdictions of every State Party as regards the criminal liability of the person convicted and the principles relating to compensation for damage caused to victims and the restitution of property acquired by the person convicted [and other forms of reparation ordered by the Court].

(b)   For the purpose of enforcement of fines [or reparation] imposed by the Court, the Presidency may order the forced sale of any property of the person sentenced which is on the territory of a State Party.

For the same purpose, the Presidency may order the confiscation of any sum of money or securities belonging to the person sentenced.

[*90] Decisions by the Presidency are implemented by States Parties in conformity with their domestic laws.

[The provisions of this article shall apply to legal persons.]]

---

[15]   Inclusion of a provision on such penalties would depend on the outcome of considerations in the context of individual criminal responsibility for legal persons.

[16]   It was suggested that such provisions may give rise to issues of enforcement in the context of part 8 of the ILC draft.

[17]   See footnote 7 concerning forfeiture for physical persons. There may be merit in adopting a unified approach in both provisions, including all relevant qualifications.

[18]   See footnote 9 concerning reparation in the context of physical persons. There may be merit in adopting a unified approach in both provisions, including all relevant qualifications.

[19]   It was suggested that this issue may be linked to the provisions on fines under section A above and enforcement in Part 8. It was also suggested that there may be options other than (a) and (b) as to the manner in which fines or assets collected by the Court could be distributed to victims. All these issues may be dealt with in the context of a further discussion on matters related to compensation.

[20]   See paragraph 3 of the report of this Working Group, above.

[21]   It was suggested that all the issues contained in this item, which include, <u>inter alia</u>, recognition of judgement, should be dealt with in the context of part 8 on enforcement of sentences.

DECISIONS TAKEN BY THE PREPARATORY COMMITTEE AT ITS SESSION HELD FROM 4 TO 15 AUGUST 1997

[Editorial Note - The U.N. page numbers of this document are indicated in bolded brackets [*] in the text].

[*1]1. At its 52nd meeting, on 4 August 1997, the Preparatory Committee decided to conduct its work through two working groups: the Working Group on Complementarity and Trigger Mechanism (chaired by Mr. Adriaan Bos); and the Working Group on Procedural Matters (chaired by Ms. Silvia Fernández de Gurmendi).

2. At its 53rd meeting, on 15 August 1997, the Preparatory Committee took note of the reports of the Working Group on Complementarity and Trigger Mechanism (annex I) and of the Working Group on Procedural Matters (annex II). The Preparatory Committee also noted that the issues relating to the procedural aspects of article 35 and to the role of the Prosecutor will have to be discussed at a future session.

3. The Preparatory Committee took note that pursuant to paragraph 7 of General Assembly resolution 51/207 of 17 December 1996, the Secretary-General had established a trust fund for the participation of the least developed countries in the work of the Preparatory Committee and in the diplomatic conference of plenipotentiaries. Guidelines have been established for the administration of the Fund. The following Governments have made contributions to the Fund: Belgium, Canada, Denmark, Finland, the Netherlands, Norway and Sweden. Twelve States have utilized the Trust Fund to facilitate their participation in the August session. As at 14 August 1997, a total amount of $300,000 has been received in the Fund. General Assembly resolution 51/207 calls upon States to contribute voluntarily to the Trust Fund.

4. The Preparatory Committee also noted that at the invitation and request of the Government of Italy, Secretariat units responsible for providing services to the proposed diplomatic conference organized a planning mission in June, which made a survey of the facilities intended for the use of the diplomatic conference at the headquarters of the Food and Agriculture Organization of the United Nations in Rome.

[*2]Annex I
REPORT OF THE WORKING GROUP ON COMPLEMENTARITY AND TRIGGER MECHANISM*

The Working Group recommends to the Preparatory Committee the texts of the articles shown on the following pages for inclusion in the draft consolidated text of a convention for an international criminal court: articles 21, 21 bis, 21 ter, 22, 23, 24, 25, 25 bis (A/AC.249/1997/WG.3/CRP.1/Rev.1) and article 35 (A/AC.249/1997/WG.3/CRP.2).

[*3]

Square brackets include also the proposal for total deletion of the text within the square brackets.

If the original International Law Commission text is to be revised, the revision may be as follows:

Article 21
[Exercise of jurisdiction] [Preconditions to the exercise of jurisdiction]

1. The Court [may exercise its] [shall have] jurisdiction [over a person] with respect to a crime referred to in article 20 [(a) to (e) or any combination thereof] [and in accordance with the provisions of this Statute] if:

    [(a) the [matter] [situation] is referred to the Court by the Security Council, [in accordance with article 23] [acting under Chapter VII of the Charter];

    (b) a complaint is lodged by a State Party [two State Parties] [or a non-State Party] in accordance with article 25;

    [(c) the matter is brought by the Prosecutor, in accordance with article 25 bis.]

---

    * Incorporating the documents listed in the opening paragraph.

[2.   [In the case of subparagraphs 1 (b) [and (c)],] the Court [may exercise its] [shall have] jurisdiction [only if the States which have jurisdiction over the case in question have accepted the jurisdiction of the Court in accordance with article 22 and] [if national jurisdiction is either not available or ineffective] [in accordance with article 35] or if [an interested State] [interested States] [those States] have deferred the matter to the Court.]

[¹Article 21 bis
Preconditions to the exercise of jurisdiction

Chapeau of paragraph 1
Option 1²
   [In the case of article 21, subparagraphs 1 (b) [and (c)],] The Court [may exercise its] [shall have] jurisdiction [over a person] if the following [*4] State(s) has/have accepted [the exercise of] the jurisdiction of the Court over the crimes referred to in [article 20 (a) to (e) or any combination thereof] in accordance with article 22:
Option 2
   [In the case of article 21, subparagraphs 1 (b) [and (c)],] the Court [may exercise its] [shall have] jurisdiction [over a person] if the following State(s) has/have accepted the exercise of the jurisdiction of the Court with respect to a case in question which is the subject of a complaint lodged by a State:
   [(a)   the State that has custody of the suspect with respect to the crime ("custodial State")] [by the State on whose territory the person is resident at the time the complaint is lodged] [in accordance with international law];]
   [(b)   the State on the territory of which the act [or omission] in question occurred [or if the crime was committed on board a vessel or aircraft, the State of registration of that vessel or aircraft;]
   [(c)   if applicable, the State that has requested, under an international agreement, the custodial State to surrender a suspect for the purposes of prosecution, [unless the request is rejected];]
   [(d)   the State of which the victim is a national;]
   [(e)   the State of which the [accused] [suspect] of the crime is a national;]
[2.   If a State whose acceptance is required for the exercise of the jurisdiction by the Court rejects such acceptance, that State shall so inform the Court [giving reasons thereof].]³
[3.   Notwithstanding paragraph 1, if a State whose acceptance is required has not indicated whether it gives such acceptance or not within a period of (...), then the Court [may] [may not] exercise its jurisdiction accordingly.]⁴
[4.   When a State that is not a Party to the Statute has an interest in the acts mentioned in the complaint, this State may, by an express declaration deposited with the Registrar of the Court, agree that the Court shall exercise jurisdiction in respect of the acts specified in the declaration.]]

[*5][⁵Article 21 ter⁶

1.   The Court has jurisdiction only in respect of crimes committed after the date of entry into force of this Statute.
   [When a State becomes a Party to this Statute after its entry into force, the Court cannot be seized in respect of crimes committed by its nationals or on its territory or against its nationals, unless those crimes have been committed after the deposit by that State of its instrument of ratification or accession.]
[2.   The Court has no jurisdiction in respect of crimes for which, even if they have been committed after the entry into force of this Statute, the Security Council, acting under Chapter VII of the Charter of the

---

¹   This square bracket ends at the end of article 21 bis.
²   Options are not put in square brackets because they are alternatives supported by only some delegations. Some other delegations suggested the deletion of one or more of the options or have suggested other changes within the options.
³   This paragraph is relevant only to option 2 of the chapeau to paragraph 1.
⁴   Ibid.
⁵   This square bracket ends at the end of article 21 ter.
⁶   The issues raised in this article deserve further reflection as to its place in the Statute.

United Nations, has decided before the entry into force of this Statute to establish an ad hoc international criminal tribunal. The Security Council may, however, decide otherwise.]]

[⁷Article 22
Acceptance of the jurisdiction of the Court

Option 1⁸
1.   A State that becomes a Party to this Statute thereby accepts the [inherent] jurisdiction of the Court with respect to the crimes referred to in article 20, paragraphs [(a) to (d) or any combination thereof].
2.   With regard to the crimes referred to in article 20 other than those mentioned in paragraph 1, a State Party to this Statute may declare:
     (a)   at the time it expresses its consent to be bound by the Statute; or
     (b)   at a later time that it accepts the jurisdiction of the Court with respect to such of the crimes as it specifies in the declaration.
3.   If under article 21 bis the acceptance of a State that is not a Party to this Statute is required, that State may, by declaration lodged with the Registrar, consent to the exercise of jurisdiction by the Court with respect to [*6] the crime. [The accepting State will cooperate with the Court without any delay or exception, in accordance with Part 7 of the Statute.]
Option 2
1.   A State Party to this Statute may:
     (a) at the time it expresses its consent to be bound by the Statute, by declaration lodged with the depositary; or
     (b)   at a later time, by declaration lodged with the Registrar; accept the jurisdiction of the Court with respect to [such of] the crimes referred to in [article 20 (a) to (e) or any combination thereof] as it specifies in the declaration.
2.   A declaration may be of general application, or may be limited to [particular conduct or to conduct] [one or more of the crimes referred to in article 20 (a) to (e)] committed during a particular period of time.⁹
3.   A declaration may be made for a specified period, in which case it may not be withdrawn before the end of that period, or for an unspecified period, in which case it may be withdrawn only upon giving a six month's notice of withdrawal to the Registrar. Withdrawal does not affect proceedings already commenced under this Statute.¹⁰
4.   If under article 21 bis the acceptance of a State that is not a Party to this Statute is required, that State may, by declaration lodged with the Registrar, consent to the exercise of jurisdiction by the Court with respect to the crime. [The accepting State will cooperate with the Court without any delay or exception, in accordance with Part 7 of the Statute.]
[5.   A declaration referred to in paragraphs 1 to 3 may not contain other limitations than those mentioned in paragraphs 1 to 3.]]

[¹¹Article 23
[[Action by] [Role of] The Security Council]] [Relationship between
the Security Council and the International Criminal Court]

Paragraph 1
     [Notwithstanding article 21, [21 bis] [and 22], the Court has jurisdiction in accordance with this Statute with respect to crimes [referred to] [specified] [*7]in article 20 [as a consequence of the referral of] [on the basis of a [formal] decision to refer] a [matter] [situation] in which one or more crimes appear to have been committed to [the Prosecutor of] the Court by the Security Council [acting under Chapter VII of the Charter of the United Nations] [in accordance with the terms of such referral].

---

⁷   The square bracket ends at the end of paragraph 5 of this article.
⁸   Options 1 and 2 are not mutually exclusive and could be combined in such a way that option 1 may be used in respect of some crimes and option 2 in respect of other crimes.
⁹   This paragraph may also apply to option 1.
¹⁰   Ibid.
¹¹   This square bracket ends at the end of option 2 of paragraph 3.

[Paragraph 1 bis
    [Notification of] [A letter from the President of the Security Council conveying] the Security Council decision to the Prosecutor of the Court shall be accompanied by all supporting material available to the Council.]

[Paragraph 1 ter
    The Security Council, on the basis of a formal decision under Chapter VI of the Charter of the United Nations, may lodge a complaint with the Prosecutor specifying that crimes referred to in article 20 appear to have been committed.]

Paragraph 2
Option 1
    [A complaint of or directly related to [an act] [a crime] of aggression [referred to in article 20] may [not] be brought [under this Statute] unless the Security Council has [first] [determined] [formally decided] that the act of a State that is the subject of the complaint, [is] [is not] an act of aggression [in accordance with Chapter VII of the Charter of the United Nations].

Option 2
    [The determination [under Article 39 of the Charter] of the Security Council that a State has committed an act of aggression shall be binding on the deliberation of the Court in respect of a complaint, the subject matter of which is the act of aggression.]

Paragraph 2 bis
    [A referral of a matter to the Court or] [A determination] [A formal decision] by the Security Council [under paragraph 2 above] shall not be interpreted as in any way affecting the independence of the Court in its determination of the criminal responsibility of the person concerned.

Paragraph 2 ter
    [A complaint of or directly related to an act of aggression brought under this Statute and the findings of the Court in such cases is without prejudice to the powers of the Security Council under Chapter VII of the Charter.]

[*8][[12]Paragraph 3
Option 1
    No prosecution may be commenced under this Statute arising from a [dispute or] situation [[pertaining to international peace and security or an act of aggression] which [is being dealt with] [actively] by the Security Council] [as a threat to or breach of the peace or an act of aggression] [under Chapter VII of the Charter], [where the Security Council has decided that there is a threat to or breach of the peace and for which it is exercising its functions under Chapter VII of the Charter of the United Nations], [unless the Security Council otherwise decides] [without the prior consent of the Security Council].

Option 2
1.   [Subject to paragraph 2 of this article], no prosecution may be commenced [or proceeded with] under this Statute [for a period of twelve months] where the Security Council has [decided that there is a threat to or breach of the peace or an act of aggression and], acting under Chapter VII of the Charter of the United Nations, [given a direction] [taken a [formal and specific] decision] to that effect.

2.   [Notification] [A formal decision of the Security Council to the effect] that the Security Council is continuing to act may be renewed at intervals of twelve months [by a subsequent decision].]

3.   [Should no action be taken by the Security Council in accordance with Chapter VII of the Charter of the United Nations within a reasonable time, the Court may exercise its jurisdiction in respect of the situation referred to in paragraph 1 of this article.]]]

Article 24
Duty of the Court as to jurisdiction

The Court shall satisfy itself that it has jurisdiction in any case brought before it.

---

[12]   This square bracket ends at the end of paragraph 3 of option 2.

Article 25
Complaint by State

Paragraph 1
Option 1

[[A State Party which is also a Contracting Party to the Convention on the Prevention and Punishment of the Crime of Genocide of 9 December 1948] [A State [*9] Party [which accepts the jurisdiction of the Court under article 22 with respect to a crime]] may lodge a complaint [referring a [matter] [situation] in which one or more crimes within the jurisdiction of the Court appear to have been committed to] [with] the Prosecutor [alleging that [a crime of genocide] [such a crime] [a crime under article 20, subparagraphs [(a) to (d) or any combination thereof]] appears to have been committed] [and requesting that the Prosecutor investigate the situation for the purpose of determining whether one or more specific persons should be charged with the commission of such crimes.]]

Option 2

[A State Party [which accepts the jurisdiction of the Court under article 22 with respect to a crime] [that has a direct interest] listed under (a) to (d) below may lodge a complaint with the Prosecutor alleging that [such a crime] [a crime under article 20 [(a) to (d) or any combination thereof]] appears to have been committed:

    (a)   a State on the territory of which the act [or omission] in question occurred;
    (b)   a State of the custody;
    (c)   a State of the nationality of a suspect;
    (d)   a State of the nationality of victims.]

[2.   A State Party, which, for a crime under article 20, subparagraph (e), has accepted the jurisdiction of the Court pursuant to article 22 and is a party to the treaty concerned may lodge a complaint with the Prosecutor alleging that such a crime appears to have been committed.][13]

[3.   As far as possible, a complaint shall specify the relevant circumstances and be accompanied by such supporting documentation as is available to the complainant State.][14]

[4.   The Prosecutor shall notify the Security Council of all complaints lodged under article 25.]

[Article 25 bis
Prosecutor

The Prosecutor [may] [shall] initiate investigations [ex officio] [proprio motu] [or] on the basis of information [obtained] [he may seek] from [*10] any source, in particular from Governments, United Nations organs [and intergovernmental and non-governmental organizations]. The Prosecutor shall assess the information received or obtained and decide whether there is sufficient basis to proceed. [The Prosecutor may, for the purpose of initiating an investigation, receive information on alleged crimes under article 20 (a) to (d) from Governments, intergovernmental and non-governmental organizations, victims and associations representing them, or other reliable sources.]][15]

* * *

Article 35
Issues of admissibility

The following draft text represents the results of informal consultations on article 35 and is intended to facilitate the work towards the elaboration of the Statute of the Court. The content of the text represents a possible way to address the issue of complementarity and is without prejudice to the views of any delegation. The text does not represent agreement on the eventual content or approach to be included in this article.

---

[13]   This provision is without any prejudice to the position of delegations with regard to "treaty crimes".
[14]   Further discussion may be necessary in the discussions on procedures. Due regard may be paid to option B on page 110.
[15]   The procedure to be followed by the Prosecutor in relation to this article may be discussed in the context of procedural questions.

1.   [On application of the accused or at the request of [an interested State] [a State which has jurisdiction over the crime] at any time prior to [or at] the commencement of the trial, or of its own motion],[16] the Court shall determine whether a case before it is inadmissible.[17]

2.   Having regard to paragraph 3 of the preamble,[18] the Court shall determine that a case is inadmissible where:

   (a)   the case is being investigated or prosecuted by a State which has jurisdiction over it, unless the State is unwilling or unable genuinely to carry out the investigation or prosecution;*[19]

[*11](b)   the case has been investigated by a State which has jurisdiction over it and the State has decided not to prosecute the person concerned, unless the decision resulted from the unwillingness or inability of the State genuinely to prosecute;

   (c)   the person concerned has already been tried for conduct which is the subject of the complaint,[20] and a trial by the Court is not permitted under paragraph 2 of article 42;[21]
**[22]

   (d)   the case is not of sufficient gravity to justify further action by the Court.[23]

3.   In order to determine unwillingness in a particular case, the Court shall consider whether one or more of the following exist, as applicable:

   (a)   the proceedings[24] were or are being undertaken or the national decision was made for the purpose of shielding the person concerned from criminal responsibility for crimes within the jurisdiction of the Court as set out in article 20;

   (b)   there has been an undue delay in the proceedings which in the circumstances is inconsistent with an intent to bring the person concerned to justice;

   (c)   the proceedings were not or are not being conducted independently or impartially and they were or are being conducted in a manner which, in the [*12] circumstances, is inconsistent with an intent to bring the person concerned to justice.

4.   In order to determine inability in a particular case, the Court shall consider whether, due to a total or partial collapse or unavailability of its national judicial system, the State is unable to obtain the accused or the necessary evidence and testimony or otherwise unable to carry out its proceedings.

*   *   *

An alternative approach, which needs further discussion, is that the Court shall not have the power to intervene when a national decision has been taken in a particular case. That approach could be reflected as follows:

"The Court has no jurisdiction where the case in question is being investigated or prosecuted, or has been prosecuted, by a State which has jurisdiction over it."

---

[16]   The procedural aspects of the provision have not been fully discussed and have yet to be determined. There are other proposals relating to procedure.

[17]   The present text of article 35 is without prejudice to the question whether complementarity-related admissibility requirements of this article may be waived by the State or States concerned.

[18]   Suggestions were made that the principle of complementarity should be further clarified either in this article or elsewhere in the Statute.

[19]   The proposal on extradition or international cooperation is not included in the text, subject to the determination of whether the relevant State would be able to present arguments in the procedure on admissibility.

[20]   If the Security Council can refer situations to the Court or the Prosecutor can initiate investigations, then the appropriate wording may be considered.

[21]   It was noted that article 35 should also address, directly or indirectly, cases in which there was a prosecution resulting in conviction or acquittal, as well as discontinuance of prosecutions and possibly also pardons and amnesties. A number of delegations expressed the view that article 42, as currently worded, did not adequately address these situations for of complementarity. It was agreed that these questions should be revisited in light of further revisions to article 42 to determine whether the reference to article 42 was sufficient or whether additional language was needed in article 35 to address these situations.

[22]   Some delegations preferred the inclusion of the following subparagraph: "the accused is not liable under article 55 to be prosecuted before or punished by the Court".

[23]   Some delegations believed that this subparagraph should be included elsewhere in the Statute or deleted.

[24]   The term "proceedings" covers both investigations and prosecutions.

[*13] Annex II
REPORT OF THE WORKING GROUP ON PROCEDURAL MATTERS[*]
The Working Group recommends to the Preparatory Committee the text of the following articles concerning procedural matters as a first draft for inclusion in the draft consolidated text of the convention for an international criminal court:

Article 26.   Investigation of alleged crimes and article 26 bis (A/AC.249/1997/WG.4/CRP.4)

Article 26.   Paragraph 6: (A/AC.249/1997/WG.4/CRP.4/Add.1)

Article 26 ter.   Functions of the Pre-Trial Chamber in relation with investigation (A/AC.249/1997/WG.4/CRP.4/Add.2)

Article 27.   Commencement of prosecution (A/AC.249/1997/WG.4/CRP.6)

Article 30.   Notification of the indictment (A/AC.249/1997/WG.4/CRP.1*)

Article 37.   Trial in presence of the accused (A/AC.249/1997/WG.4/CRP.2*)

Article 38.   Functions and powers of the Trial Chamber (A/AC.249/1997/WG.4/CRP.5)

Article 38 bis. Proceedings on an admission of guilt (A/AC.249/1997/WG.4/CRP.3 and Corr.1)

Article 40.   Presumption of innocence (A/AC.249/1997/WG.4/CRP.7)

Article 41.   Rights of the accused (A/AC.249/1997/WG.4/CRP.8)

Article 43.   Protection of the [accused], victims and witnesses [and their participation in the proceedings] (A/AC.249/1997/WG.4/CRP.9)

[*14] REVISED ABBREVIATED COMPILATION[1]
Article 26
Investigation of alleged crimes
1.   On receiving a complaint or upon notification of a decision of the Security Council referred to in article 23, paragraph 1 [**or ex officio upon any other substantiated information**], the Prosecutor shall [**subject to paragraph 1 bis and ter**] initiate an investigation unless the Prosecutor concludes that there is no **reasonable basis** for a prosecution under this Statute and decides not to initiate an investigation, in which case the Prosecutor shall so inform the Presidency [**Pre-Trial Chamber**].[2]

[**1 bis. Prior to initiating investigation the Prosecutor shall:**

    (a) [notify the States Parties of any complaint [or any decision of the Security Council referred to in article 23, paragraph 1], and those States Parties shall so inform the persons within their jurisdiction who are referred to by name in the submission; and]

    (b)   determine whether:

        (i)   the complaint provides or is likely to provide a reasonable basis [in law or on the facts] for proceeding with a prosecution under this Statute; and

        (ii)   the case is or would be admissible under article 35; and

        [(ii) bis a prosecution under this Statute would be in the interests of justice [taking into account the gravity of the offences and the] [interests of victims];

        (iii)   [an investigation would be consistent with the terms of any relevant Security Council decision]; and

        (iv)   to seek a preliminary ruling from the Court regarding the Court's jurisdiction if the case could later be challenged under article 34.][3]

[*15][1 ter. The Prosecutor shall not initiate an investigation where the submission of the case to the Court is challenged within one month of notification under article 26, paragraph 1 bis (b) (ii), by a**

---

[*]   Incorporating the documents listed in the opening paragraph.

[1]   In general, the proposed additions or amendments to the ILC text appear in bold and between square brackets in order to distinguish the new text from the ILC text. The fact that the ILC text does not appear within square brackets does not necessarily mean that it was generally acceptable to all delegations.

[2]   Proposed additions originate from the Report of the Preparatory Committee on the Establishment of an International Criminal Court, vol. II (Compilation of Proposals) (Official Records of the General Assembly, Fifty-first Session, Supplement No. 22A (A/51/22)), (hereinafter Report), vol. II, p. 112 (item A.1).

[3]   Report, vol. II, p. 112.

State Party that wishes to proceed or has proceeded with the case or by a person named in the submission and awaits the final ruling of the Court.]⁴

2.   The Prosecutor may:⁵
   (a)   request the presence of and question suspects, victims and witnesses;
   (b)   collect documentary and other evidence [**documents, records and articles of evidence**];
   (c)   option 1: conduct on-site investigations;
   (c)   option 2:

      [(i)   Except as provided for in this paragraph, when evidence is in the territory of a State, the Prosecutor shall, as necessary, seek the cooperation of that State in order to obtain that evidence. The Prosecutor may conduct investigations on the territory of a State only:

      a.   [with the consent of its competent authorities] [upon notification of and where necessary with the consent of its competent authorities] [in accordance with Part 7] [subject to the waiver by the competent authorities of the requirement of consent];

      [b.   When the Pre-Trial Chamber is satisfied that competent authorities to whom a request for assistance under Part 7 can be transmitted are not available [or not functioning].]

      [(ii)   In the case of paragraph (i) (b) above, [such investigations] [investigations of a non-compulsory nature⁶] shall be conducted with the [concurrence] [approval] of the Pre-Trial Chamber [which shall [*16] have regard to the views of [interested States]]. [Notification shall be given to the State in question, in particular for the purpose of the State obtaining an extension of the period for execution of a relevant request for judicial assistance.]

      [(iii)]   In the case of paragraph (i) (b) above, the Prosecutor may use compulsory measures for collecting evidence (such as search and seizure and compelling the attendance of witnesses) based upon a valid warrant issued by the Pre-Trial Chamber.]]

   (d)   take necessary measures to ensure the confidentiality of information or the protection of any person [, **including victims**];

   [(d) bis The Prosecutor shall take appropriate measures to ensure the effective investigation and prosecution of crimes within the jurisdiction of the Court, and in so doing, respect the interests and personal circumstances of victims and witnesses, including age, gender and health, and take into account the nature of the crime, in particular, but not limited to, where it involves sexual or gender violence or violence against children;]

   (e) as appropriate, seek the cooperation of any State or of the United Nations, [**or of any peacekeeping force that may be present in the territory where an investigation is to be undertaken**];

   [(f)   where documents or information have been obtained by the Prosecutor upon a condition as to their confidentiality, which are, or are intended to be, used solely for the purposes of generating new evidence, agree that such documents or information will not be disclosed at any stage of the proceedings unless the provider of the information consents.]

   [(g)   enter into such arrangements or agreements, not otherwise inconsistent with this Statute, as may be necessary to secure the cooperation or assistance of a State or person in the investigation.]

3.   The Presidency [**Pre-Trial Chamber**] may, at the request of the Prosecutor, issue such subpoenas [, **orders**] and warrants as may be required for the purposes of an investigation, including a warrant under article 28, paragraph 1, for the pre-indictment arrest of a suspect.

4.   If, upon investigation and having regard, inter alia, to the matters referred to in article 35, the Prosecutor concludes that [a case is inadmissible under article 35 or] there is [**not a sufficient basis for a prosecution**] [**no prima facie case**] under this Statute [or **a prosecution would not be in the interests of justice**] [**taking into account the interests of victims**] and decides not to file an indictment], the

---

⁴   Report, vol. II, p. 112 (item A.2 (a)). Items A.2 (b) and (c) on p. 112 are addressed in paragraph 1 bis.
⁵   It was proposed that the following text be included as the first line of article 26, paragraph 2:
"When evidence is in the territory of a State Party whose competent authority is functioning properly, the Prosecutor shall request, as necessary, the Pre-Trial Chamber to seek the cooperation of a State Party pursuant to Part 7 of this Statute."
⁶   This set of square brackets will apply if paragraph (iii) is accepted.
⁷   Report, vol. II, p. 115 (item 8).

Prosecutor shall so inform the Presidency [**Pre-Trial Chamber**], as well as the complainant State [or the Security Council, in a case to which article 23, paragraph 1,] applies, giving details of the nature and basis of the complaint and of the reasons for not filing an indictment.

[*17][**4 bis. A decision referred to in paragraph 4 based on considerations of the interests of justice shall only become effective upon its having been confirmed by the Presidency [Pre-Trial Chamber] under paragraph 5 of this article.**]

5.   At the request of a complainant State or, in a case to which article 23, paragraph 1, applies, at the request of the Security Council, the Presidency [**Pre-Trial Chamber**] shall [**may**] review a decision of the Prosecutor not to initiate an investigation or not to file an indictment, and may request the Prosecutor to reconsider the decision [**but it may do so only once**] [: **provided that the Prosecutor, any suspect and the complainant State [or the Security Council (as the case may be)] shall be informed of such review proceedings or confirmation proceedings within the contemplation of paragraph 4 of this article which involves a decision based on considerations of the interests of justice and shall be entitled to submit his/her/their/its viewpoints with regard thereto, which viewpoints shall be considered by the Presidency, [Pre-Trial Chamber] in coming to its decision**].[8]

[When new information is brought to his/her attention regarding the facts in respect of which he or she decided not to initiate an investigation or not to institute proceedings, the Prosecutor may reconsider his/her decision.]

[**5 bis.**[9] **After a determination to initiate an investigation in accordance with article 26, paragraph 2, and prior to the commencement of a trial, a State requested by the Prosecutor to carry out investigations or a State on the territory of which the Prosecutor intends to conduct investigations may challenge the decision of the Prosecutor to initiate an investigation before the Pre-Trial Chamber on the grounds of lack of sufficient basis for a prosecution under this Statute.**][10]

6.   A person suspected of a crime under this Statute shall have the right:

(a)   prior to being questioned, to be informed that the person is a suspect [**, of the conduct that the person is alleged to have committed which may constitute a crime under this Statute**] and of the rights under (b) to (d) hereafter;

(b)   to remain silent, without such silence being a consideration in the determination of guilt or innocence;

(c)   to have [**at all times**] [**in connection with questioning**] the [**prompt**] [**competent**] legal assistance of the person's choosing; [or, if the person does not have legal assistance, to have legal assistance assigned by the Court in any case where the interests of justice so require, including where the person is unable to secure counsel, and without payment if the person lacks sufficient means to pay for such assistance];

[*18][(d) to be questioned in the presence of counsel unless the suspect has voluntarily waived his or her right to counsel;]

(e)   not to be compelled to testify or to confess guilt nor to be subjected to any form of coercion, duress or threat;

(f)   if questioned in a language other than [a language the person understands and speaks] [**his or her own language**], to have, free of any cost, the assistance of a competent interpreter and a translation of any document on which the person is to be questioned;

(g)   not to be subjected to torture, or to cruel, inhuman or degrading treatment or punishment.

[**6 bis.**[11] **Evidence obtained during questioning in violation of these rights shall under no circumstances be used in the trial unless they are favourable to the suspect.**][12]

[**7.**[13] **(a)   The Prosecutor shall fully respect the rights of suspects under the Statute and the Rules.**

---

[8]   Ibid., p. 116 (item C.9).
[9]   This paragraph will be discussed in connection with article 34.
[10]   Report, vol. II, p. 113 (item 4).
[11]   This paragraph will be discussed in connection with article 44.
[12]   Report, vol. II. P. 118 (item 10 (h).
[13]   This paragraph will be discussed in connection with article 12.

(b) [To establish the truth the Prosecutor shall [ex officio] extend the investigation to cover all facts and evidence that are relevant to an assessment of the charge and to the legal consequences that may follow. The Prosecutor shall investigate equally incriminating and exonerating circumstances.]

(c) [If the Prosecutor concludes that there is a basis for prosecution under this Statute, he shall, in accordance with the Rules of the Court, investigate the case by seeking the cooperation of the States concerned or by himself, and such investigation shall be conducted in conformity with international law and fully respecting the sovereignty of the States concerned.][14]

[8.[15] (a) A person suspected of committing a crime within the meaning of this Statute:

(i)   shall, as soon as he is involved in an investigation or prosecuted under this Statute, be entitled to collect all of the evidence that he deems necessary for his defence;

[*19]   (ii)   may either collect this evidence himself or request the Pre-Trial Chamber of the Court to accomplish certain acts, seeking, where necessary, cooperation from any State Party.

The Pre-Trial Chamber may reject the request.

(b) If the suspect elects to collect the evidence himself in accordance with article 26, paragraph 3 (a), he may apply to the Presidency for the following orders and subpoenas: [list to be inserted]][16]

[Article 26 bis][17]

[(a) In the event that the Prosecutor defers investigation on the ground that a State is proceeding with a national investigation, then the Prosecutor may request that the relevant State make available to the Prosecutor, either periodically or on reasonable request, a report on the progress of its investigation, which shall be confidential to the extent necessary. The Prosecutor shall notify the complainant State of the decision to defer to a State and shall notify the complainant State of any known outcome of such national investigation or prosecution.]

(b) [The Prosecutor shall not initiate an investigation into a case that has been investigated and prosecuted by a State following a deferral by the Prosecutor unless:

(i)   the complainant State has lodged a further complaint with the Court on the grounds that the State investigation (or prosecution) has been inadequate, and the Prosecutor agrees;

(ii)   following the Prosecutor's notice to the State where the case was prosecuted of the new complaint and of its opportunity to challenge the initiation of an investigation by the Prosecutor, the State where the case was prosecuted has challenged such an investigation by the Prosecutor and either has failed under the Statute to prevent the new investigation or has failed after a reasonable period of time to challenge the initiation of the new investigation; and

(iii)   the Prosecutor, upon renewed consideration, has not reached any affirmative determination under article 26, paragraph 1 (b) (i), (ii) or (iii).]

Note: Item A, paragraph 4, on page 113, could be addressed in the context of article 34, which could be expanded to address all challenges, or addressed in article 26.

[*20][Article 26 ter][18]

---

[14]   Report, vol. II, pp. 113 and 114 (item B).

[15]   The Working Group decided to defer the consideration of article 26, paragraph 8, until such time as article 41 is considered.

[16]   Report, vol. II, p. 115 (item C.7).

[17]   Ibid., p. 113 (item A.3 (b) and (c)). This article will be discussed in connection with the issues of complementarity and trigger mechanism.

[18]   Article 26 ter was tabled by some 15 interested delegations at the August 1997 meeting of the Preparatory Committee. It was written de novo and did not derive from any particular delegation's proposal.

The proposal contemplates that, in exceptional circumstances in which a unique opportunity appears to exist for the taking or collection of evidence, the Pre-Trial Chamber may be involved in order to assure a fair trial/protect the interests of the defence.

Some delegations believed that the authority of the Pre-Trial Chamber set out in the proposal should be exercised only to collect and preserve evidence for the defence. In relation to the Prosecutor's investigation, the Pre-Trial Chamber should only intervene for the purpose of checking on the lawfulness of the Prosecutor's conduct.

The alternative options reflect differing views as to the balance to be struck between the need to ensure the Prosecutor's independence and the desirability of conferring a limited role on the Pre-Trial Chamber.

Functions of the Pre-Trial Chamber in relation with investigation[19]
1.   [Where the Prosecutor intends to take an investigative action which may] [When the Prosecutor considers an investigation to] present a unique opportunity, which may not be available subsequently for the purposes of a trial, to take testimony or a statement from a witness, or to examine, collect or test evidence, [the Prosecutor shall] [, if the suspect/accused has not been identified or is not available] inform the Pre-Trial Chamber; and] the Pre-Trial Chamber, on the request of the Prosecutor, [or a suspect,] [or on its own initiative,] may take such measures as may be necessary to assure the efficiency and integrity of the proceedings, and in particular to protect the rights of the defence.
2.   These measures may include the power:
       (a)   to make [orders] [recommendations] [orders and recommendations] regarding procedures to be followed;
       (b)   to direct that a record be made of the proceedings;
[*21](c)   to appoint an expert to assist;
       (d)   to authorize counsel for a suspect to assist, or where suspects have not been identified or have not designated counsel, appoint a lawyer to attend and represent the interest of the defence;
       (e)   to name one of its members [or an available judge of the Court]:
             (i)   to observe and make [orders] [recommendations] [orders and recommendations] regarding the collection and preservation of evidence or the questioning of persons;
             (ii)   to decide on questions of law; or
             (iii) to take such other actions as may be necessary to collect or preserve evidence [favourable to the defence] [relevant to the case].
Option: [When in the course of a proceeding a unique opportunity presents itself to collect evidence, the Pre-Trial Chamber may, at the request of the Prosecutor or of the suspect, name one of its members or an available judge of the Court to take necessary measures to collect or preserve evidence, while respecting the rights of the defence.]
3.   [If any [order] [recommendation] [order and recommendation] of the Pre-Trial Chamber is breached or is not complied with, the Pre-Trial Chamber may:
       (a)   reject the admissibility of any evidence obtained as a result or consequence of such a breach or non-compliance; or
       (b)   consider such breach or non-compliance in respect of whether any weight should be attached to any evidence obtained as a result or consequence of such breach or non-compliance.]

* * *

Article 27
Commencement of prosecution
1.   If upon investigation [in the course of an investigation] the Prosecutor, having regard to the matters referred to in article 35, concludes that **[the case is admissible, and]** **[a case does exist against one or more persons named,]** **[there is a prima facie case]** [there is sufficient evidence that could justify a conviction of a suspect, if the evidence were not contradicted at trial,] **[which the accused could be called on to answer and that is desirable in the interests of justice that the case should proceed]**, the Prosecutor shall file with the Registrar an indictment containing a concise statement of the allegations of fact and of the crime or crimes with which the suspect is charged in respect of each of the persons referred to, their name and particulars, a statement of the allegations of fact against them, and the characterization of these facts within the jurisdiction of the Court and shall be accompanied by [relevant] [*22][sufficient] evidence collected by the Prosecutor for the purposes of confirmation [of the indictment] by the Presidency [Pre-Trial Chamber].[20]

If this proposal is adopted, it seems likely that other proposals in relation to article 26 could be deleted or may need revision. Consideration would need to be given to article 26, paragraph 1, article 26, paragraph 2 (a), article 26, paragraph 4 bis, article 26, paragraph 5, article 26, paragraph 5 bis and article 26, paragraph 8.
   [19]   The powers contemplated by this draft provision include the power for the Pre-Trial Chamber to seek judicial assistance from a State.
   [20]   Report, vol. II, pp. 120-121 (item 1.A and B).

[2. The Presidency [**Pre-Trial Chamber**] shall examine the indictment, any amendment[21] and any supporting material and determine:

(a) whether a prima facie case exists [there is sufficient evidence that could justify a conviction of a suspect, if the evidence were not contradicted at trial] [there is strong evidence against the accused] with respect to a crime within the jurisdiction of the Court; and

(b) whether, having regard, <u>inter alia</u>, to the matters referred to in article 35, the case should on the information available be heard by the Court [**if the Court has not yet ruled on this issue**].[22]

[(c) **whether it is desirable in the interest of justice that the case should proceed;**][23]

If so, it shall [**by majority/consensus**] confirm the indictment and establish a trial chamber in accordance with article 9 [**, and inform the Presidency**].[24]]

[2 <u>bis</u>.[25] **Any State concerned may challenge the decision of the Prosecutor to file an indictment before the Pre-Trial Chamber on grounds of inconsistency with this Statute.**][26]

[2 <u>ter</u>. **After the filing of an indictment, the Pre-Trial Chamber shall [in any case] [if the accused is in custody or has been judicially released by the Court pending trial] notify the indictment to the accused, [set a deadline prior to the confirmation hearing, until which the Prosecutor and the defence may add new evidence[27] [for purposes of such confirmation hearing]], and set a date for the review of the indictment. The hearing shall be held in the presence of the Prosecutor and the accused, as well as his/her counsel, subject to the provisions of paragraph 4 <u>bis</u>. In the hearing, the accused shall be allowed to object to the indictment and criticize the material on which it is based.**

[*23] **Following the hearing, the Pre-Trial Chamber may:**

(a) **confirm the indictment in its entirety;**

(b) **confirm only part of the indictment [and amend it], by giving a different qualification to the facts;**

[(c) **order further investigation**];

(d) **refuse to confirm the indictment.**

When it confirms the indictment in its entirety or in part, the Pre-Trial Chamber shall commit the accused to the Trial Chamber for trial on the indictment as confirmed. Confirmation of indictment shall uphold the warrants issued earlier, except if the Court decides otherwise.]

3. If, after any adjournment that may be necessary to allow additional material to be produced, the Presidency [**Pre-Trial Chamber**] decides not to confirm the indictment, it shall so inform the complainant State or, in a case to which article 23 (1) applies, the Security Council.

[If it does not confirm the indictment, all the warrants issued prior to the decision of non-confirmation shall cease immediately to have effect.]

[3 <u>bis</u>. The dismissal of a count in an indictment shall not preclude the Prosecutor from subsequently bringing a new indictment based on the acts underlying that count if supported by additional evidence.[28]]

[4. The Presidency [**Pre-Trial Chamber**] may [, **on its own or**] at the request of the Prosecutor amend the indictment [, **in which case it shall make any necessary orders to ensure that the accused is notified of the amendment and has adequate time to prepare a defence**] [after hearing the accused, provided that the Trial Chamber is satisfied that the accused is not prejudiced in his rights to defend himself].]

[**Alternate paragraph 4. Prior to the confirmation of the indictment by the Pre-Trial Chamber, the Prosecutor may amend or withdraw the indictment. [The accused shall be informed of the withdrawal as well as of any amendment. In the event of withdrawal, the Pre-Trial Chamber may, under the provisions provided for in article 26, ask the Prosecutor to reconsider his/her decision.]**]

---

21 Ibid., p. 122 (item B.1).
22 Ibid., p. 121 (item 2 (c)).
23 Ibid.
24 Ibid., p. 121 (item 2 and 2 (a)).
25 China will submit changes to improve the language of this paragraph.
26 Report, vol. II, p. 121 (item 2).
27 See article 27, paragraph 1 <u>bis</u>, in the abbreviated compilation (p. 9).
28 Report, vol. II, p. 122 (item A (iv)).

After the confirmation of the indictment, the Prosecutor may amend the indictment only with the permission of the Pre-Trial Chamber, and after notice to the accused. If the Prosecutor is seeking to add additional charges or to substitute more serious charges for those in the confirmed indictment, the new or amended charges must be confirmed by the Pre-Trial Chamber in accordance with the procedures for confirmation of the indictment set out in paragraph [...].

[*24] After the commencement of the trial, the Prosecutor may withdraw the indictment or certain charges within the indictment only with the permission of the Trial Chamber].

[In case of withdrawal of the indictment after the confirmation thereof, new prosecution may be instituted for the same offence only based upon a newly discovered material evidence which was not available to the Prosecutor at the time of the withdrawal in the interest of the defence.]

[4 bis.[29] When one or more of the accused has fled or cannot be found, and when all reasonable steps have been taken to inform the accused, the Pre-Trial Chamber may still hold a hearing in order to examine whether it shall confirm the indictment. In that case, the accused cannot be represented by counsel.

When it confirms the indictment, in its entirety or in part, against an accused who has fled or cannot be found, the Pre-Trial Chamber shall issue a warrant to search for, arrest and transfer the accused, which is tantamount to committing him to the Trial Chamber for trial.]

[4 ter. Anyone who has [personally] suffered [direct] injury caused by a crime submitted to the Court, [the legal representatives of victims, victims' relatives, successors and assigns,] may inform the [Prosecutor] [and the] [Pre-Trial Chamber] in writing of the acts having caused injury to him/her/them and the nature and amount of the losses which he/she/they has/have sustained.

When it confirms the indictment, in its entirety or in part, the Pre-Trial Chamber may order provisional measures which may be necessary [in order to enable a Trial Chamber, upon a subsequent conviction,] to compensate the victim designated in the above paragraph. For that purpose, the Pre-Trial Chamber shall seek the cooperation of the interested States.

Such provisions shall also apply when the accused has fled or cannot be found.]

5.   The Presidency [**Pre-Trial Chamber**] [**Trial Chamber**] may make any further orders required for the conduct of the trial, including an order:

(a)   determining the language or languages to be used during the trial;

(b)   requiring the disclosure to the defence [**of the relevant evidence that the defence requests**] within a sufficient time before the trial to enable the preparation of the defence, of [**relevant**] documentary or other evidence available to the Prosecutor [**, whether or not the Prosecutor intends to rely on that evidence**] [**which the Prosecutor intends to rely upon**]; [**if the Prosecutor fails to comply with an order under this subparagraph, the evidence in question will be inadmissible at the trial;**]

[*25][alternative (b) save in respect of documents or information referred to in article 26, paragraph 2 (f), and subject to subparagraph (f) below, requiring the disclosure to the defence of documents or information which are either considered [material] [relevant] to the preparation of the defence, or are intended for use by the Prosecutor at trial or were obtained from the accused [Quaere: definition of "relevant" for the Rules?]]

(c)   providing for the exchange of information between the Prosecutor and the defence, so that both parties are sufficiently aware of the issues to be decided at the trial;

(d)   providing [**, at the request of either party or a State, or at the instance of the Court on its own volition,**] for the protection of the accused, victims and witnesses and of confidential information;

(e)   providing [**, at the request of either party or a State, or at the instance of the Court on its own volition,**] for the protection and privacy of victims and witnesses;

[(f)   providing, at the request of either party or a State, or at the instance of the Court of its own volition, for the non-disclosure or protection of documents or information provided by a State the disclosure of which would [endanger] [prejudice] the national security or national defence interests of a State in accordance with criteria to be specified in rules made pursuant to this Statute.]

---

[29]   The Working Group decided to defer the consideration of paragraph 4 bis of article 27 for such time as article 37 is considered.

* * *

Article 30[30]
Notification of the indictment

1.   The Prosecutor [the Registrar] shall ensure, where necessary with the cooperation of national authorities, that a person who has been arrested is personally served, as soon as possible after being taken into custody, with certified copies of the following documents, in a language understood by that person [a language that the accused understands] [in his own language]:

(a)[31] in the case of the pre-indictment arrest of a suspect, a statement of the grounds for the arrest [[the warrant of arrest or restriction of liberty];[32]

(b)   in any other case, the confirmed indictment;

[*26](c)   a statement of the accused's [arrested person's] rights under [articles 26 or 41 of] this Statute and the Rules [, as applicable].

[1 bis. An indictment shall be made public, except in the following situations:

(a)   The Presidency [Pre-Trial Chamber] may, at the request of the Prosecutor, order that there be no public disclosure of the indictment until it is served on the accused, or in the case of joint accused, on all the accused. In exercising its discretion, the Presidency [Pre-Trial Chamber] shall take account of all relevant factors, including the potential for pre-arrest flight of an accused, destruction of evidence and harm to victims or witnesses if the indictment is made public;

(b)[33] The Presidency [Pre-Trial Chamber] may, at the request of the Prosecutor, also order that there be no disclosure of an indictment, or part thereof, or of all or any part of any particular document or information, if satisfied that the making of such an order is required to give effect to a provision of the Rules, to protect confidential information obtained by the Prosecutor, or is otherwise in the interests of justice.][34]

2.   In any case to which paragraph 1 (a) applies, the indictment shall be served on the accused as soon as possible after it has been confirmed.

3.   If, 60[35] days after the indictment has been confirmed, the accused is not in custody pursuant to a warrant issued under article 28 (3), or for some reason the requirements of paragraph 1 cannot be complied with, the Presidency [Pre-Trial Chamber] [the Registrar] may [shall] on the application of the Prosecutor prescribe some other manner of bringing the indictment to the attention of the accused.

[4.][36]

[5.   [The accused is] [Anyone suspected of committing a crime within the meaning of this Statute shall be] entitled:

(a)   to be informed promptly of the nature and cause of the charge against him or her [and be questioned in a language which he understands, and, to this end, to have the free assistance of a competent interpreter, and to be provided [*27]free of charge with a translation of the documents on the basis of which he is being questioned or that show why a measure infringing upon his liberty or property has been proposed];

(b)   [to have adequate time and facilities for the preparation of his or her defence and to communicate with counsel; [to be assisted promptly by a lawyer of his own choosing, or, if he does not have sufficient means to pay for one, by a lawyer appointed by the [Pre-Trial Chamber] of the Court;]

---

[30]   The wording of this article might be modified in the light of the decisions to be taken as regards the question of hearing of the confirmation of an indictment.

[31]   Subparagraph 1 (a) will be examined in the context of article 28.

[32]   Report, vol. II, p. 146 (item A.1 (a)). Other matters in item A.1 (a) are addressed in article 29, paragraph 2.

[33]   The contents of this subparagraph could become the subject matter of the provision being negotiated on questions of confidentiality, disclosure and protection of information.

[34]   Report, vol. II, p. 127.

[35]   The matter concerning a specific deadline may be more appropriate for the rules of procedure.

[36]   Former paragraph 4 of the abbreviated compilation of proposals on procedural matters (4 August 1997) (hereinafter abbreviated compilation) could become a subject matter for the rules of procedure.

(c)　[before being questioned, or when a measure infringing upon his liberty or property has been proposed and brought to his attention, to be fully informed of the charges against him and the rights to which he is entitled under paragraph 1 of this article.]]

* * *

Article 37
Trial in presence of the accused

Comment: There appear, in essence, to be three options regarding trials in absentia which have emerged to date, in addition to the ILC draft, that appear in the Report, volume II. The ILC text and the proposed options are set out below:

ILC DRAFT

1.　As a general rule, the accused should be present during the trial.

2.　The Trial Chamber may order that the trial proceed in the absence of the accused if:

(a)　the accused is in custody, or has been released pending trial, and for reasons of security or the ill-health of the accused it is undesirable for the accused to be present;

(b)　the accused is continuing to disrupt the trial; or

(c)　the accused has escaped from lawful custody under this Statute or has broken bail.

3.　The Chamber shall, if it makes an order under paragraph 2, ensure that the rights of the accused under this Statute are respected, and in particular:

(a)　that all reasonable steps have been taken to inform the accused of the charge; and

(b)　that the accused is legally represented, if necessary by a lawyer appointed by the Court.

[*28]4.[37] In cases where a trial cannot be held because of the deliberate absence of an accused, the Court may establish, in accordance with the Rules, an Indictment Chamber for the purpose of:

(a)　recording the evidence;

(b)　considering whether the evidence establishes a prima facie case of a crime within the jurisdiction of the Court; and

(c)　issuing and publishing a warrant of arrest in respect of an accused against whom a prima facie case is established.

5.　If the accused is subsequently tried under this Statute:

(a)　the record of evidence before the Indictment Chamber shall be admissible;

(b)　any judge who was a member of the Indictment Chamber may not be a member of the Trial Chamber.

Option 1

[Explanatory note: Option 1 prohibits trial in absentia without any exception; like option 2, it would deal with procedures needed to preserve evidence for trial as a matter separate from trial in absentia. Under this option, article 37 would read in its entirety as follows:]

The trial shall not be held if the accused is not present.

Option 2
General rule

1.　As a general rule, the accused shall be present during the trial.

Exceptions

2.　In exceptional circumstances, the Trial Chamber may order that the trial proceed in the absence of the accused, if the accused, having been present at the commencement of the trial thereafter:

(a)　has escaped from lawful custody or has broken bail; or

[*29][(b) is continuing to disrupt the trial.][38]

Rights of the accused

---

[17]　The questions addressed in paragraphs 4 and 5 may be better dealt with in the context of the pre-trial proceedings.

[18]　Some proponents of option 2 do not agree that this should necessarily be a basis for a trial in absentia.

3.   The Trial Chamber shall, if it makes an order under paragraph 2, ensure that the rights of the accused under this Statute are respected, and in particular that the accused is legally represented, if necessary by a lawyer appointed by the Court.[39]

Proceedings to preserve evidence

[Explanatory note: There is no separate proposal to preserve evidence for trial. This could be dealt with as part of pre-trial proceedings, and would not necessarily be confined to situations where the accused is absent.]

Subsequent trial

[Explanatory note: Under this option, there would be no second trial following a trial in absentia.]

Option 3

1.   *Identical to paragraph 1 of the draft of the International Law Commission.*

2.   In exceptional circumstances, the Trial Chamber may, in the interests of justice [at the request of the Prosecutor] [proprio motu or at the request of one of the parties] order that the trial proceed in the absence of the accused, if the latter, having been duly informed of the opening of the trial:

    (a)   Requests to be excused from appearing for reasons of serious ill-health;

    (b)   Disrupts the trial;

    (c)   Does not appear on the day of the hearing;

    (d)   under detention has, when summoned for the date of the trial, refused to appear without good reason, and made it particularly difficult to bring him to the Court; or

[*30] In the event that the accused is convicted following a trial held in his absence, the Trial Chamber may issue a warrant for the arrest and transfer of the accused for the purposes of executing the judgement. The decision taken under the provisions of this paragraph shall be communicated to the accused and may be appealed.

3.   *Identical to paragraph 3 of the draft of the International Law Commission.*

4.   When the accused has not been duly informed of the opening of the trial and when all reasonable steps have been taken to inform the accused of the charges, the Trial Chamber may also, in very exceptional circumstances, [at the request of the Prosecutor] [proprio motu or at the request of one of the parties], order that the trial proceed in the absence of the accused when required in the interests of justice or the interests of the victims. The accused may not then be represented by a lawyer of the accused's choosing, but the judge presiding over the Trial Chamber may appoint a lawyer on his own motion.

When the accused, having been judged in accordance with the above provisions, is taken prisoner or is arrested, the decisions taken in his absence by the Trial Chamber shall be null and void in all their provisions. The evidence submitted during the trial held in the absence of the accused may not be used, during the second trial, to establish the charges levelled against the accused, except where it is impossible for the depositions to be made a second time or where the evidence cannot again be produced. Nevertheless, the accused may agree to the decision if the sentence pronounced in his absence is less than or equal to 10 years of imprisonment.

Option 4

1.   The accused shall have the right to be present at the trial, unless the Trial Chamber, having heard such submissions and evidence as it deems necessary, concludes that the absence of the accused is deliberate.

2.   [Paragraph 3 of the ILC draft would remain with consequential amendments.]

* * *

Article 38

Functions and powers of the Trial Chamber

1.   At the commencement of the trial, the Trial Chamber shall:

---

[39]   This provision follows paragraph 3 of the ILC draft, except that it omits subparagraph (a), regarding steps to inform the accused of the charges. This is unnecessary under this option since a trial in absentia is permitted only if the accused was present at the commencement of the trial, a stage at which the indictment is to be read out.

(a) have the indictment read;

(b) ensure that articles 27 (5) (b) and 30 have been complied with sufficiently in advance of the trial to enable adequate preparation of the defence;

[*31](c) satisfy itself that the other rights of the accused under this Statute and the Rules have been respected;

(d) allow the accused to enter a plea of not guilty or to make an admission of guilt before the Trial Chamber **[and should the accused fail to do so, enter a plea of not guilty on his or her behalf]**.

2.   The Chamber shall ensure that a trial is fair and expeditious and is conducted in accordance with this Statute and the Rules, with full respect for the rights of the accused and due regard for the protection of victims and witnesses.

[2 bis. The President of the Trial Chamber shall control and direct the hearing, and decide upon the manner by which evidence shall be produced by the parties. In all circumstances, the President shall have the duty to remain impartial.]

3.   The Trial Chamber may, subject to the Rules, hear charges against more than one accused arising out of the same factual situation.

4.   The trial shall be held in public, unless the Trial Chamber determines that certain proceedings be in closed session in accordance with article 43, or for the purpose of protecting confidential or sensitive information which is to be given in evidence. The deliberations of the Court shall remain confidential.

5.   The Trial Chamber shall, subject to this Statute and the Rules, have, <u>inter alia</u>, the power on the application of a party or of its own motion to:

(a) issue a warrant for the arrest and transfer of an accused who is not already in the custody of the Court;

(a) <u>bis</u> exercise the same powers as the Pre-Trial Chamber regarding measures that restrict the liberty of a person;

(a) <u>ter</u> terminate or modify any warrants issued by the Pre-Trial Chamber;

(a) <u>quater</u> rule on any preliminary motions, and such ruling shall not be subject to interlocutory appeal except as provided for in the Rules;

(b) require the attendance and testimony of witnesses, and the production of documents and other evidentiary materials by obtaining, if necessary, the assistance of States as provided in this Statute;

[(b) <u>bis</u> order the production of further evidence to that already collected prior to the trial or presented during the trial by the parties;]

(c) rule on the admissibility or relevance of evidence;

(d) protect confidential information; and

(e) maintain order in the course of a hearing.

[*32]The provisions of article 27, paragraph 5 (f), will apply <u>mutatis mutandis</u> for the purposes of orders sought under subparagraph (d) above.

5 <u>bis</u>. [The Trial Chamber may refer pre-trial issues under this article to the Pre-Trial Chamber for resolution.]

6.   The Trial Chamber shall ensure that a complete record of the trial, which accurately reflects the proceedings, is maintained and preserved by the Registrar.

* * *

Article 38 bis
Proceedings on an admission of guilt

1.   Where the accused makes an admission of guilt under article 38, paragraph 1 (d), the Trial Chamber shall determine whether:

(a) the accused understands the nature and consequences of the admission of guilt and whether the admission is voluntarily made after sufficient consultation with defence counsel; and

(b) the admission of guilt is [firmly] supported by the facts of the case that are contained in:

(i)   the indictment and in any supplementary materials presented by the Prosecutor, and which the accused admits; and

(ii)   any other evidence, including the testimony of witnesses, presented by the Prosecutor or the accused.

2.   Where the Trial Chamber is satisfied that the matters referred to in paragraph 1 are established, the Trial Chamber shall consider the admission of guilt, together with any additional evidence presented and admitted, as an admission of all the essential facts that are required to prove the crime to which the admission of guilt relates, and [may] [shall] convict the accused of that crime.

3.   Where the Trial Chamber is not satisfied that the matters referred to in paragraph 1 are established, the Trial Chamber shall order that the trial be continued under the ordinary trial procedures provided by this Statute, and shall consider the admission of guilt not to have been made [and shall [may] remit the case to another Trial Chamber].

4.   Where the Trial Chamber is of the opinion that a more complete presentation of the facts of the case is otherwise required in the interests of justice, in particular the interests of the victims, the Trial Chamber may request that the Prosecutor present additional evidence, including the testimony of witnesses, or may order that the trial be continued under the ordinary trial procedures provided by this Statute and, in the latter situation, shall consider the [*33]admission of guilt not to have been made[40] [and shall [may] remit the case to another Trial Chamber].

5.   Discussions between the Prosecutor and the defence regarding modification of the charges in the indictment, acceptance of the admission of guilt by the accused, or the penalty to be imposed shall not be legally binding on the Chamber.[41]

* * *

Article 40[*]
Presumption of innocence[42]

Everyone shall be presumed innocent until proved guilty in accordance with law. The onus is on the Prosecutor to establish the guilt of the accused beyond a reasonable doubt.[43]

* * *

[*34] Article 41[44]
Rights of the accused

1.   In the determination of any charge under this Statute, the accused is entitled [, in addition to any rights afforded to a suspect under this Statute,] to a public hearing, having regard to [article 38 and] article 43,[45] and to a fair hearing by an independent and impartial tribunal, and to the following minimum guarantees in full equality:

   (a)[46] to be informed promptly and in detail, in a language that the accused understands [in his own language], of the nature, cause and content of the charge;[47]

   (b)   to have adequate time and facilities for the preparation of the defence, and to communicate freely with counsel of the accused's choosing, in confidence;[48]

   (c)   to be tried without undue [unreasonable] delay and to enjoy a speedy trial;[49]

---

[40]   Report, vol. II, p. 178.

[41]   Concerns were expressed about this paragraph and it was suggested that its formulation should continue to be examined.

[*]   Article 40 is also dealt with in the report of the informal working group on general principles of criminal law.

[42]   The final provision of the Report, vol. II, p. 194, requiring a finding of guilt by a majority of the Trial Chamber, could be addressed in article 45.

[43]   Reservations were expressed regarding the phrases "in accordance with law" and "beyond a reasonable doubt" contained in the ILC text.

[44]   Various rights to be afforded to persons investigated or indicted by the Court are contained in article 26, 28, 29, 30 and 41. One issue that arises is whether or not all of these rights should be set forth in one article. Another issue that should be considered is how to categorize which of those rights apply only to suspects, which apply only to the accused and which aply to any suspect or accused appearing in proceedings before a chamber of the Court.

[45]   The matters relating to the exceptions concerning a public hearing could be addressed in article 38. The matters in section A on pp. 195 and 196 of the Report, vol. II, could be considered under article 38.

[46]   A proposal was made that, as to subparagraphs (a)-(g) of paragraph (1) of article 41 in the abbreviated compilation the wording of subparagraphs (a)-(g) of paragraph (3) of article 14 of the International Covenant on Civil and Political Rights should be used as such.

[47]   The matters referred to in section B of p. 196 of the Report, vol. II, are addressed in article 26.

[48]   The question of privileged communications could be addressed in the context of article 44.

[49]   This addition originates from p. 197 of the Report, vol. II.

(d)[50] subject to article 37 (2), to be present at the trial, to conduct the defence in person or through legal assistance of the accused's choosing, to be informed, if the accused does not have legal assistance, of this right and to [*35] have legal assistance assigned by the Court in any case where the interests of justice so require, including where the person is unable to secure counsel, and without payment if the accused lacks sufficient means to pay for such assistance;[51]

(e) to examine, or have examined, the prosecution witnesses and to obtain the attendance and examination of witnesses for the defence under the same conditions as witnesses for the prosecution; **[In addition the accused shall also be entitled to present any other evidence;]**[52]

(f) if any of the proceedings of or documents presented to the Court are not in a language the accused understands and speaks, to have, free of any cost, the assistance of a competent interpreter and such translations as are necessary to meet the requirements of fairness;

(g) not to be compelled to testify or to confess guilt and to remain silent, without such silence being a consideration in the determination of guilt or innocence;

[[(h) to make an unsworn statement in his or her defence, if desired] [to declare in his or her defence, but need [shall] not take an oath to speak the truth]];[53]

[(i) to request the Pre-Trial Chamber or, after the commencement of the trial, the Trial Chamber to seek the cooperation of a State Party pursuant to Part 7 of this Statute to collect evidence for him/her;]

[(j) no reverse onus or duty of rebuttal shall be imposed on the accused.]

2. Exculpatory evidence **[Evidence which shows or tends to show the innocence]** [or mitigate the guilt] of the accused or may affect the credibility of prosecution evidence that becomes available to the Procuracy prior to the conclusion of the trial shall be made available **[disclosed]** to the defence. In case of doubt as to the application of this paragraph or as to the admissibility of the evidence, the Trial Chamber shall decide. **[The provisions of article 27, paragraph 5 (f), will apply** <u>mutatis mutandis</u> **for the purposes of a decision made under this subparagraph.]**

[*36][3.[54] **The right of all persons to be secure in their homes and to secure their papers and effects against entries, searches and seizures shall not be impaired by the Court except upon warrant issued by the Court [Pre-Trial Chamber], on the request of the Prosecutor, in accordance with Part 7 or the Rules of the Court, for adequate cause and particularly describing the place to be searched and things to be seized, or except on such grounds and in accordance with such procedures as are established by the Rules of the Court.]**

[4. No person shall be deprived of life or liberty, nor shall any other criminal penalty be imposed, without due process of law.]

* * *

Article 43
Protection of the [accused], victims and witnesses
[and their participation in the proceedings]

1. The Court shall take the necessary measures available to it to protect the accused, victims and witnesses and may to that end conduct closed proceedings or allow the presentation of evidence by electronic or other special means.

Notwithstanding the principle of public hearings, the Court may order that the proceedings be closed, in the interest of the accused, the victims or the witnesses. [In camera hearings are mandatory when they are requested by an accused who was a minor at the time of the commission of the acts or at the request of a victim of sexual violence.]

---

[50]   Subparagraphs (d)-(g) will have to be re-examined in the light of article 26, paragraph 6.

[51]   These additions originate from pp. 197 and 116 (paragraph d), respectively, of the Report, vol. II. The matters contained in paragraphs 2 and 3 on pp. 197-199 of the compilation could be considered in the development of the Rules.

[52]   These additions originate from p. 199 of the Report, vol. II.

[53]   These additions originate from pp. 200 and 117 of the Report, vol. II.

[54]   The rights addressed in paragraphs 3 and 4, which are of a general nature, should perhaps be located in another part of the Statute. In addition, paragraph 4 could be reformulated.

2.   [The Prosecutor shall, in ensuring the effective investigation and prosecution of crimes, respect and take appropriate measures to protect the privacy, physical and psychological well-being, dignity and security of victims and witnesses, having regard to all relevant factors, including age, gender and health, and the nature of the crime, in particular, whether the crime involves sexual or gender violence. These measures will be consistent with the rights of the accused.]

3.   The Court shall take such measures as are necessary to ensure the safety, physical and psychological well-being, dignity and privacy of victims and witnesses, at all stages of the process, including, but not limited to, victims and witnesses of sexual and gender violence. However, these measures [may not] [shall not] be [inconsistent with] [prejudicial to] the rights of the accused.

4.   [The Court [shall] [may] permit the views and concerns of the victim to be presented and considered at appropriate stages of the proceedings where their [*37]personal interests are affected in a manner which is consistent with the rights of the accused and a fair and impartial trial.][55]

[5.   The Victims and Witnesses Unit, established under article 13 of this Statute, shall provide counselling and other assistance to victims and witnesses and advise the Prosecutor and the Court on appropriate measures of protection and other matters affecting their rights. These measures may extend to family members and others at risk on account of testimony given by such witnesses.][56]

[6.   Notwithstanding paragraph 1 of article 27, if disclosure of any evidence and/or any of the particulars referred to in that paragraph will probably lead to the security of any witness or his/her family being gravely endangered, the Prosecutor may, for purposes of these proceedings, withhold such particulars and submit a summary of such evidence. Such a summary shall, for purposes of any later trial proceedings before the Court, be deemed to form part of the particulars of the indictment.]

[7.   The rules of procedure shall include provisions giving effect to the United Nations Declaration of Basic Principles of Justice for Victims of Crime and Abuse of Power.][57]

[8.   Legal representatives of victims of crimes have the right to participate in the proceedings with a view to presenting additional evidence needed to establish the basis of criminal responsibility as a foundation for their right to pursue civil compensation.][58]

9.   A State may make an application for necessary measures to be taken in respect of the protection of its servants or agents and the protection of sensitive information.

---

[55] Some delegations thought that there should be further reflection on the paragraph.
[56] This issue will be addressed in the context of the organization of the Court.
[57] Report, vol. II, p. 204, item A (d).
[58] Report, vol. II, p. 204, item A (b).

DECISIONS TAKEN BY THE PREPARATORY COMMITTEE AT ITS SESSION HELD FROM 11 TO 21 FEBRUARY 1997

[Editorial Note - The U.N. page numbers of this document are indicated in bolded brackets [*] in the text].

[*1] 1.   At its 51st meeting, on 21 February 1997, the Preparatory Committee took note of the reports of the Working Group on the Definition of Crimes (see annex I) and of the Working Group on General Principles of Criminal Law and Penalties (see annex II).

2.   At the same meeting, the Preparatory Committee adopted a decision in connection with the invitation by the Government of Italy to host the diplomatic conference (see annex III).

[*2] Annex I
REPORT OF THE WORKING GROUP ON THE DEFINITION OF CRIMES[*]

1.   The Working Group recommends to the Preparatory Committee the text of the definition of the following crimes as a first draft for inclusion in the draft consolidated text of a convention for an international criminal court:

Crime of genocide (A/AC.249/1997/WG.1/CRP.1 and Corr.1);
Crimes against humanity (A/AC.249/1997/WG.1/CRP.5 and Corr.1).

2.   The Working Group recommends to the Preparatory Committee the text of the definition of the following crimes for further consideration at a future time:

War crimes (A/AC.249/1997/WG.1/CRP.2 and Corr.1);
Crime of aggression (A/AC.249/1997/WG.1/CRP.6 and Corr.1);
[Crimes of terrorism, crimes against United Nations and associated personnel and crimes involving the illicit traffic in narcotic drugs and psychotropic substances] (A/AC.249/1997/WG.1/CRP.4 and Corr.1).

[*3] Crime of genocide

For the purpose of the present Statute, the crime of genocide means any of the following acts committed with intent[1] to destroy, in whole or in part, a national, ethnical, racial or religious group,[2] as such:[3]

(a)   Killing members of the group;
(b)   Causing serious bodily or mental harm[4] to members of the group;
(c)   Deliberately inflicting on the group conditions of life calculated to bring about its physical destruction in whole or in part;

---

[*]   Incorporating the documents listed in paras. 1 and 2 of the report.

[1]   The reference to "intent to destroy, in whole or in part ... a group, as such" was understood to refer to the specific intention to destroy more than a small number of individuals who are members of a group.

[2]   The Working Group took note of the suggestion to examine the possibility of addressing "social and political" groups in the context of crimes against humanity.

[3]   The Working Group noted that with respect to the interpretation and application of the provisions concerning the crimes within the jurisdiction of the Court, the Court shall apply relevant international conventions and other sources of international law.

In this regard, the Working Group noted that for purposes of interpreting the present article it may be necessary to consider other relevant provisions contained in the Convention on the Prevention and Punishment of the Crime of Genocide, as well as other sources of international law. For example, article I would determine the question of whether the crime of genocide set forth in the present article could be committed in time of peace or in time of war.

Furthermore, article IV would determine the question of whether persons committing genocide or other acts enumerated in the present article [article III of the Genocide Convention] shall be punished irrespective of their status as constitutionally responsible rulers, public officials or private individuals.

The interrelationship between the various articles of the present Statute would need to be examined in the next phase of the work. For example, the matters dealt with in the first to third paragraphs of the present note would need to be considered in relation to article 33 (Applicable law) of the Statute and the provisions dealing with principles of criminal law.

[4]   The reference to "mental harm" is understood to mean more than the minor or temporary impairment of mental faculties.

(d) Imposing measures intended to prevent births within the group;

(e) Forcibly transferring children of the group to another group;

[*4] [The following acts shall be punishable:

(a) Genocide;

(b) Conspiracy to commit genocide;

(c) Direct and public incitement to commit genocide;

(d) Attempt to commit genocide;

(e) Complicity in genocide.][5]

Crimes against humanity

1.   For the purpose of the present Statute, any of the following acts constitutes a crime against humanity when committed

[as part of a widespread [and] [or] systematic commission of such acts against any population]:

[as part of a widespread [and] [or] systematic attack against any [civilian] population] [committed on a massive scale] [in armed conflict] [on political, philosophical, racial, ethnic or religious grounds or any other arbitrarily defined grounds]:

(a) murder;

(b) extermination;

(c) enslavement;

(d) deportation or forcible transfer of population;

(e) [detention or] [imprisonment] [deprivation of liberty] [in flagrant violation of international law] [in violation of fundamental legal norms];[6]

(f) torture;

(g) rape or other sexual abuse [of comparable gravity,] or enforced prostitution;

(h) persecution against any identifiable group or collectivity on political, racial, national, ethnic, cultural or religious [or gender] [or other [*5] similar] grounds[7] [and in connection with other crimes within the jurisdiction of the Court];

(i) enforced disappearance of persons;[8]

(j) other inhumane acts [of a similar character] [intentionally] causing [great suffering,] or serious injury to body or to mental or physical health.[9]

[2. For the purpose of paragraph 1:

(a) extermination includes the [wilful, intentional] infliction of conditions of life calculated to bring about the destruction of part of a population;

(b) "deportation or forcible transfer of population" means the movement of [persons] [populations] from the area in which the [persons] [populations] are [lawfully present] [present] [resident] [under national or international law] [for a purpose contrary to international law] [without legitimate and compelling reasons] [without lawful justification];

(c) ["torture" means the intentional infliction of severe pain or suffering, whether physical or mental, upon a person [in the custody or physical control of the accused] [deprived of liberty]; except that torture shall not include pain or suffering arising only from, inherent in or incidental to, lawful sanctions [in conformity with international law]]

["torture" as defined in the Convention against Torture and Other Cruel, Inhuman or Degrading Treatment or Punishment of 10 December 1984];

---

[5]   The Working Group will return to the question of the placement of article III of the Genocide Convention once the Working Group on general principles of criminal law has considered this issue in the context of its work.

[6]   It was suggested that this subparagraph does not include freedom of speech and that it includes the unilateral blockade of populations.

[7]   This also includes, for example, social, economic and mental or physical disability grounds.

[8]   It was suggested that some more time was needed to reflect upon the inclusion of this subparagraph.

[9]   It was suggested that the inclusion of this paragraph should be subject to further clarification. It was also suggested that the list of acts should include institutionalized discrimination.

(d) persecution means the wilful and severe deprivation of fundamental rights contrary to international law [carried out with the intent to persecute on specified grounds];

(e) ["enforced disappearance of persons" means when persons are arrested, detained or abducted against their will by or with the authorization, support or acquiescence of the State or a political organization, followed by a refusal to acknowledge that deprivation of freedom or to give information on the fate or whereabouts of those persons, thereby placing them outside the protection of the law] ["enforced disappearance of persons" as defined in the Inter-American Convention on the Forced Disappearance of Persons of 9 June 1994, as referred to [*6] in the Declaration on the Protection of All Persons from Enforced Disappearance (General Assembly resolution 47/133 of 18 December 1992)].

War crimes

[For the purpose of the present Statute, "war crimes" means:]

[For the purpose of the present Statute, any of the following war crimes constitutes a crime within the jurisdiction of the court when committed as part of a systematic plan or policy or as part of a large-scale commission of such crimes:]

A. grave breaches of the Geneva Conventions of 12 August 1949, namely, the following acts against persons or property protected under the provisions of the relevant Geneva Convention:

(a) wilful killing;

(b) torture or inhuman treatment, including biological experiments;

(c) [wilfully causing great suffering, or serious injury to body or health] [wilfully causing great suffering, serious injury to body or health, including rape, enforced prostitution and other sexual violence of comparable gravity];

(d) extensive destruction and appropriation of property, not justified by military necessity and carried out unlawfully and wantonly;

(e) compelling a prisoner of war or other protected person to serve in the forces of a hostile Power;

(f) wilfully depriving a prisoner of war or other protected person of the rights of fair and regular trial;

(g) unlawful deportation or transfer or unlawful confinement;

(h) taking of hostages.

B. [Other war crimes in violation of the laws and customs applicable in international armed conflict within the established framework of international law, namely:]

[Other war crimes in international armed conflict][10]

[other grave breaches]

[*7][[11] 1. [Any of the following acts, when committed wilfully, in violation of international humanitarian law, and causing death or serious injury to body or health:[12]]

[Grave breaches of article 85(3) of Protocol I of 10 June 1977 Additional to the Geneva Conventions of 12 August 1949, namely the following acts, when committed wilfully, in violation of the relevant provisions of the Protocol and causing death or serious injury to body or health:]

(a) making the civilian population or individual civilians the object of attack;

(b) launching an indiscriminate attack affecting the civilian population or civilian objects in the knowledge that such attack will cause excessive loss of life, injury to civilians or damage to civilian objects[;[13]] [, which is excessive in relation to the concrete and direct military advantage anticipated;]

---

[10] Other delegations feel that grave breaches of Protocol Additional I to the 1949 Geneva Conventions should be reflected in the Statute under the heading of grave breaches which would reflect more appropriately the status of those crimes in international humanitarian law.

[11] This square bracket closes after paragraph 3 (c).

[12] The provisions of paragraph 1 are drawn from article 85(3) of Protocol Additional I to the 1949 Geneva Conventions.

It was suggested that crimes listed under section B (1)-(3) could be covered as treaty crimes.

[13] This provision should be read together with article 57(2)(a)(iii) of Protocol Additional I to the 1949 Geneva Conventions. This footnote is an alternative to the words in square brackets following it.

(c)   launching an attack against works or installations containing dangerous forces in the knowledge that such attack will cause excessive loss of life, injury to civilians or damage to civilian objects[;[14]] [, which is excessive in relation to the concrete and direct military advantage anticipated]

(d)   [making non-defended localities and demilitarized zones the object of attack;] [attacking or bombarding, by whatever means, towns, villages, dwellings or buildings which are undefended[15];]

(e)   [making a person the object of attack in the knowledge that he is *hors de combat;*] [*8][killing or wounding an enemy who, having laid down his arms, or having no longer means of defence, has surrendered at discretion[16];]

(f)   the perfidious use of the distinctive emblem of the red cross or red crescent or of other protective signs and signals recognized by international humanitarian law.[17]

2:    [Any of the following acts, when committed wilfully and in violation of international humanitarian law:[18]]

[Grave breaches of article 85(4) of Protocol I of 10 June 1977 Additional to the Geneva Conventions of 12 August 1949, namely the following acts when committed wilfully, in violation of the relevant provisions of the Protocol and causing death or serious injury to body or health:]

(a)   the transfer by the Occupying Power of parts of its own civilian population into the territory it occupies, or the deportation or transfer of all or parts of the population of the occupied territory within or outside this territory;[19]

(b)   unjustifiable delay in the repatriation of prisoners of war or civilians;

(c)   practices of apartheid and other inhuman and degrading practices involving outrages upon personal dignity, based on racial discrimination;

(d)   [making the clearly recognized historic monuments, works of art or places of worship which constitute the cultural or spiritual heritage of peoples and to which special protection has been given by special arrangement, for example, within the framework of a competent international organization, the object of attack, causing as a result, extensive destruction thereof, where there is no evidence of the use by adverse party of such objects in support of a military effort, and when such historic monuments, works of art and places of worship are not located in the immediate proximity of military objectives] [intentionally directing attacks against buildings dedicated to religion, art, science or charitable purposes, historic monuments, hospitals and places [*9] where the sick and wounded are collected, unless such property is used in support of the military effort[20]];

3.   [Wilful acts or omissions, in violation of international humanitarian law, which seriously endangers the physical or mental health or integrity:[21]]

[Grave breaches of article 11 of Protocol I of 10 June 1977 Additional to the Geneva Conventions of 12 August 1949, namely the following acts, when committed wilfully, in violation of the relevant provisions of the Protocol and causing death or serious injury to body or health:]

---

[14]   This provision should be read together with article 57(2)(a)(iii) of Protocol Additional I to the 1949 Geneva Conventions. This footnote is an alternative to the words in square brackets following it.

[15]   This alternative is drawn from article 25 of the Annex to the IV Hague Convention respecting the laws and customs of war on land.

[16]   This alternative is drawn from article 23.1(c) of the Annex to the IV Hague Convention respecting the laws and customs of war on land.

[17]   This provision should be read together with article 37 of Protocol Additional I to the 1949 Geneva Conventions. It is partly overlapping with a proposal in 4(d) below.

[18]   The provisions of paragraph 2 are drawn from article 85(4) of Protocol Additional I to the 1949 Geneva Conventions.

[19]   This provision should be read together with article 49 of the Fourth Geneva Convention.

[20]   This alternative is based on article 27 of the Annex to the IV Hague Convention respecting the laws and customs of war on land.

[21]   The provisions of paragraph 3 are based on article 11 of Protocol Additional I to the 1949 Geneva Conventions.

subjecting persons who are in the power of the adverse Party or who are interned, detained or otherwise deprived of liberty, to any medical procedure which is not indicated by the state of health of the person concerned and which is not consistent with generally accepted medical standards which would be applied under similar medical circumstances to persons who are nationals of the Party conducting the procedure and who are in no way deprived of liberty, in particular to carry out on such persons, even with their consent:

(a)   physical mutilations;

(b)   medical or scientific experiments;

(c)   removal of tissue or organs for transplantation.]

4.[22]   [Other serious violations of international humanitarian law.]

(a)   killing or wounding treacherously individuals belonging to the hostile nation or army [perfidy[23]];

(b)   killing or wounding an enemy who, having laid down his arms, or having no longer means of defence, has surrendered at discretion;[24]

(c)   [declaring that no quarter will be given [thereby inflicting death or serious personal injury upon the enemy]]

[to declare that there shall be no survivors];

[*10](d)   [making improper use of flag of truce of the national flag or of the military insignia and uniform of the enemy, as well as the distinctive emblems of the Geneva Conventions, [thereby inflicting death or serious personal injury upon the enemy]]

[perfidy];

(e)   destroying or seizing the enemy's property [, within one's custody or control,] unless such destruction or seizure be imperatively demanded by the necessities of war;[25]

(f)   [declaring] abolished, suspended or inadmissible in a court of law the rights and actions of the nationals of the hostile party;

(g)   compelling the nationals of the hostile party to take part in the operations of war directed against their own country, even if they were in the belligerent's service before the commencement of the war;

(h)   attacking or bombarding, by whatever means, towns, villages, dwellings or buildings which are undefended;[26]

(i)   [pillaging a town or place, even when taken by assault]

[pillage] [plunder];

(j)   employing poison or poisoned weapons;[27]

[(k)   [employing weapons, projectiles and material and methods of warfare of such a nature as to cause superfluous injury or unnecessary suffering [or inherently indiscriminate] [:][including:]]

[employing arms, projectiles, or material calculated to cause unnecessary suffering [:][including:]]

(i)   using asphyxiating, poisonous or other gases, and all analogous liquids, materials or devices;

(ii)   using bullets which expand or flatten easily in the human body, such as bullets with a hard envelope which does not entirely cover the core or is pierced with incisions;

[*11]   (iii)   using bacteriological (biological) agents or toxins for hostile purposes or in armed conflict;

---

[22]   The numbering of this paragraph depends on the inclusion of paragraphs 1-3 above.

[23]   This alternative provision should be read together with article 37 of Protocol Additional I to the 1949 Geneva Conventions.

[24]   This has also been covered in paragraph B.1(e).

[25]   This subparagraph is drawn from article 23.1(g) of the Annex to the IV Hague Convention respecting the laws and customs of war on land.

[26]   This has also been covered in paragraph B.1(d).

[27]   It was suggested that this subparagraph could be moved to subparagraph (k).

(iv)   using chemical weapons [as defined in and prohibited by the 1993 Convention on the Prohibition of the Development, Production, Stockpiling and Use of Chemical Weapons and On Their Destruction;] in violation of international law;[28]

(v)   [using or the threat of use of nuclear weapons]]

(l)   intentionally directing attacks against buildings dedicated to religion, art, science or charitable purposes, historic monuments, hospitals and places where the sick and wounded are collected, unless such property is used in support of the military effort;[29]

(m)   intentionally directing attacks against the civilian population as such, as well as individual civilians;

(n)   outrages upon personal dignity, in particular rape, enforced prostitution and other sexual violence of comparable gravity;

(o)   utilizing the presence of a civilian or other protected person to render certain points, areas, or military forces, which otherwise would be legitimate military objectives, immune from military operations;

[(p)   to cause wilfully, widespread, long-term and severe damage to the natural environment;

(q)   attacks against buildings, material medical units and transport and personnel entitled to use in conformity with international humanitarian law, the distinctive emblem of the red cross or the red crescent;

(r)   starvation of civilians;

(s)   to recruit children under the age of fifteen years in the armed forces, or to allow them to take part in hostilities;

(t)   violation of armistice, suspensions of fire or local arrangements concluded for the removal, exchange and transport of the wounded and the dead left on the battlefield.]

[*12][[30] C. [...]

1.   Serious violations of Article 3 common to the four Geneva Conventions of 12 August 1949 in the case of an armed conflict not of an international character namely the following acts against persons taking no active part in the hostilities, including members of armed forces who have laid down their arms and those placed *hors de combat* by sickness, wounds, detention or any other cause:

(a)   [violence to the life, health and physical or mental well-being of persons, in particular murder as well as cruel treatment, such as torture, mutilation or any form of corporal punishment]
[violence to life and person, in particular murder of all kinds, mutilation, cruel treatment and torture];

(b)   taking of hostages;

(c)   [outrages upon personal dignity, in particular humiliating and degrading treatment [rape and enforced prostitution];]
[outrages upon personal dignity, in particular rape, enforced prostitution and other sexual violence of comparable gravity;]
[wilfully causing great suffering, serious injury to body or health, including rape, enforced prostitution and other sexual violence of comparable gravity];

(d)   the passing of sentences and the carrying out of executions without previous judgement pronounced by regularly constituted court affording all judicial guarantees which are generally recognized as indispensable;

2.[31]   [Other war crimes in non-international armed conflicts

(e)   collective punishments;

(f)   acts of terrorism;

(g)   slavery and the slave trade in all their forms;

(h)   [pillaging a town or place, even when taken by assault;]
[pillage;] [plunder;]

---

[28]   This provision should be read together with the 1993 Convention on the Prohibition of the Development, Production, Stockpiling and Use of Chemical Weapons and On Their Destruction.

[29]   This has also been covered in paragraph B.2(d).

[30]   This square bracket closes at the end of section C.

[31]   This square bracket closes after the last paragraph of the section.

[*13](i) attacks directed against the civilian population as such, or individual civilians;

(j) employing poison or poisoned weapons;

[(k) [employing weapons, projectiles and material and methods of warfare of such a nature as to cause superfluous injury or unnecessary suffering [:][including:]]
[employing arms, projectiles, or material calculated to cause unnecessary suffering [or inherently indiscriminate] [:][including:]]

[(i) using asphyxiating, poisonous or other gases, and all analogous liquids, materials or devices;

(ii) using bullets which expand or flatten easily in the human body, such as bullets with a hard envelope which does not entirely cover the core or is pierced with incisions;

(iii) using bacteriological (biological) agents or toxins for hostile purposes or in armed conflict;

(iv) using chemical weapons [as defined in and prohibited by the 1993 Convention on the Prohibition of the Development, Production, Stockpiling and Use of Chemical Weapons and On Their Destruction;] [in violation of international law;[32]]]

(l) to cause wilfully widespread, long-term and severe damage to the natural environment;

(m) attacks against buildings, material, medical units and transports, and personnel entitled to use in conformity with international humanitarian law, the distinctive emblem of the red cross or red crescent;

(n) attacks directed against historic monuments, works of art or places of worship which constitute the cultural or spiritual heritage of peoples, and to use them in support of the military effort;

(o) starvation of civilians;

(p) to recruit children under the age of fifteen years in the armed forces, or to allow them to take part in hostilities;

(q) ordering the displacement of the civilian population for reasons related to the conflict, unless the security of the civilians involved or military reasons so demand;

[*14](r) perfidy;

(s) [declaring that no quarter will be given [thereby inflicting death or serious personal injury upon the enemy]]
[declaring that there shall be no survivors];

(t) violation of armistice, suspensions of fire or local arrangements concluded for the removal, exchange and transport of the wounded and the dead left on the battlefield.]]

[[33] Crime of aggression[34]

Note: This draft is without prejudice to the discussion of the issue of the relationship of the Security Council with the International Criminal Court with respect to aggression as dealt with in article 23 of the ILC draft statute.

1. [For the purpose of the present Statute, the crime [of aggression] [against peace] means any of the following acts committed by an individual [who is in a position of exercising control or capable of directing political/military action in a State]:

(a) planning,

(b) preparing,

(c) ordering,

(d) initiating, or

(e) carrying out

[an armed attack] [the use of armed force] [a war of aggression,] [a war of aggression, or a war in violation of international treaties, agreements or assurances, or participation in a common plan or conspiracy for the

---

[12] This provision should be read together with the 1993 Convention on the Prohibition of the Development, Production, Stockpiling and Use of Chemical Weapons and On Their Destruction.

[13] This square bracket closes at the end of paragraph 2.

[14] The proposal reflects the view held by a large number of delegations that the crime of aggression should be included in the statute.
The Working Group considered this crime without prejudice to a final decision on its inclusion in the statute.

accomplishment of any of the foregoing] by a State against the [sovereignty,] territorial integrity [or political independence] of another State [when this] [armed attack] [use of force] [is] [in contravention of the Charter of the United Nations] [[in contravention of the Charter of the United Nations as determined by the Security Council].]

[For the purposes of this Statute, the crime of aggression is committed by a person who is in a position of exercising control or capable of directing political/military actions in his State, against another State, in contravention to the Charter of the United Nations, by resorting to armed [*15] force, to threaten or violate the sovereignty, territorial integrity or political independence of that State.]

[2. [Acts constituting [aggression] [armed attack] include the following:][35]

[Provided that the acts concerned or their consequences are of sufficient gravity, acts constituting aggression [are] [include] the following:]

(a) the invasion or attack by the armed forces of a State of the territory of another State, or any military occupation, however temporary, resulting from such invasion or attack, or any annexation by the use of force of the territory of another State or part thereof;

(b) bombardment by the armed forces of a State against the territory of another State [, or the use of any weapons by a State against the territory of another State];

(c) the blockade of the ports or coasts of a State by the armed forces of another State;

(d) an attack by the armed forces of a State on the land, sea or air forces, or marine and air fleets of another State;

(e) the use of armed forces of one State which are within the territory of another State with the agreement of the receiving State in contravention of the conditions provided for in the agreement, or any extension of their presence in such territory beyond their termination of the agreement;

(f) the action of a State in allowing its territory, which it has placed at the disposal of another State, to be used by that other State for perpetrating an act of aggression against a third State;

(g) the sending by or on behalf of a State of armed bands, groups, irregulars or mercenaries, which carry out acts of armed force against another State of such gravity as to amount to the acts listed above, or its substantial involvement therein.]]

[*16][Crimes of terrorism[36]

The Court has jurisdiction with respect to the following terrorist crimes:

(1) Undertaking, organizing, sponsoring, ordering, facilitating, financing, encouraging or tolerating acts of violence against another State directed at persons or property and of such a nature as to create terror, fear or insecurity in the minds of public figures, groups of persons, the general public or populations, for whatever considerations and purposes of a political, philosophical, ideological, racial, ethnic, religious or such other nature that may be invoked to justify them;

(2) An offence under the following Conventions:

(a) Convention for the Suppression of Unlawful Acts against the Safety of Civil Aviation;

(b) Convention for the Suppression of Unlawful Seizure of Aircraft;

(c) Convention on the Prevention and Punishment of Crimes against Internationally Protected Persons, including Diplomatic Agents;

(d) International Convention against the Taking of Hostages;

(e) Convention for the Suppression of Unlawful Acts against the Safety of Maritime Navigation;

(f) Protocol for the Suppression of Unlawful Acts against the Safety of Fixed Platforms located on the Continental Shelf;

---

[35] Paragraph 2 of the text reflects the view held by some delegations that the definition should include an enumeration of the acts constituting aggression.

[36] The Working Group considered the following three crimes (crimes of terrorism, crimes against United Nations and associated personnel and crimes involving the illicit traffic in narcotic drugs and psychotropic substances) without prejudice to a final decision on their inclusion in the statute. The Working Group also discussed these three crimes only in a general manner and did not have time to examine them as thoroughly as the other crimes.

(3)   An offence involving use of firearms, weapons, explosives and dangerous substances when used as a means to perpetrate indiscriminate violence involving death or serious bodily injury to persons or groups of persons or populations or serious damage to property.]

<u>[Crimes against United Nations and associated personnel</u>[37]

1.   For the purpose of the present Statute, "crimes against United Nations and associated personnel" means any of the following acts [when committed intentionally and in a systematic manner or on a large scale against United Nations and associated personnel involved in a United Nations operation with a view to preventing or impeding that operation from fulfilling its mandate]:

[*17](a)   murder, kidnapping or other attack upon the person or liberty of any such personnel;

(b)   violent attack upon the official premises, the private accommodation or the means of transportation of any such personnel likely to endanger his or her person or liberty.

2.   This article shall not apply to a United Nations operation authorized by the Security Council as an enforcement action under Chapter VII of the Charter of the United Nations in which any of the personnel are engaged as combatants against organized armed forces and to which the law of international armed conflict applies.]

<u>[Crimes involving the illicit traffic in narcotic</u>
<u>drugs and psychotropic substances]</u>[38]

[*18]Annex II
REPORT OF THE WORKING GROUP ON GENERAL PRINCIPLES
OF CRIMINAL LAW AND PENALTIES[*]

1.   The Working Group recommends to the Preparatory Committee the text of the following articles concerning general principles of criminal law as a first draft for inclusion in the draft consolidated text of a convention for an international criminal court.

<u>Nullum crimen sine lege</u> (A/AC.249/1997/WG.2/CRP.1);
Non-retroactivity (A/AC.249/1997/WG.2/CRP.1);
Individual criminal responsibility (Personal jurisdiction) (A/AC.249/1997/WG.2/CRP.2);
Irrelevance of official position (A/AC.249/1997/WG.2/CRP.2/Add.1);
Individual criminal responsibility (A/AC.249/1997/WG.2/CRP.2/Add.2);
Command responsibility (A/AC.249/1997/WG.2/CRP.3);
<u>Mens rea</u> (Mental elements of crime) (A/AC.249/1997/WG.2/CRP.4);
<u>Actus reus</u> (act and/or omission) (A/AC.249/1997/WG.2/CRP.5);
Mistake of fact or of law (A/AC.249/1997/WG.2/CRP.6);
Age of responsibility (report of the Preparatory Committee,[1] part 3 <u>bis</u>, article E);
Statute of limitations (report of the Preparatory Committee,[2] part 3 <u>bis</u>, article F).

2.   The Working Group did not have time to consider articles L to T, contained in part 3 <u>bis</u> of the report of the Preparatory Committee,[3] nor section 2 thereof, nor the question of penalties.[4]

---

[37]   Ibid.
[38]   Ibid.
[*]   Incorporating the documents listed in paragraph 1 of the report.
[1]   <u>Official Records of the General Assembly, Fifty-first Session, Supplement No. 22A</u> (A/51/22), vol. II.
[2]   Ibid.
[3]   Ibid.
[4]   Ibid., part 5.

[*19] Article A[5]
Nullum crimen sine lege

1.   Provided that this Statute is applicable in accordance with article [21, 22 or 23] a person shall not be criminally responsible under this Statute:

(a)   in the case of a prosecution with respect to a crime referred to in articles [20 (a) to (d)], unless the conduct in question constitutes a crime that is defined in this Statute;

(b)   in the case of a prosecution with respect to a crime referred to in article [20 (e)], unless the treaty in question was applicable to the conduct of the person at the time that the conduct occurred.

[2.   Conduct shall not be construed as criminal and sanctions shall not be applied under this Statute by a process of analogy.]

3.   Paragraph 1 shall not affect the character of such conduct as being crimes under international law, apart from this Statute.

Article A bis
Non-retroactivity

1.   Provided that this Statute is applicable in accordance with article A, a person shall not be criminally responsible under this Statute for conduct committed prior to its entry into force.

[2.   If the law as it appeared at the commission of the crime is amended prior to the final judgement in the case, the most lenient law shall be applied.][6]

Other proposals that may also relate to, inter alia, issues concerning trigger mechanism and other jurisdictional questions respectively, and which will be debated by the Preparatory Committee at a later session

[When a State becomes a party to this Statute after its entry into force, the Court has jurisdiction only in respect of acts committed by its nationals or on its territory or against its nationals after the deposit by that State of its instrument of ratification or accession. A non-party State may, however, by an express declaration deposited with the Registrar of the Court, agree that the [*20] Court has jurisdiction in respect of the acts that it specifies in the declaration.

The Court has no jurisdiction in respect of crimes for which, even if they have been committed after the entry into force of this Statute, the Security Council, acting under Chapter VII of the Charter of the United Nations, has decided before the entry into force of this Statute to establish an ad hoc international criminal tribunal. The Security Council may, however, decide otherwise.]

[The present Statute shall apply only to acts committed in the territory of a State party to the present Statute or by the nationals of a State party to the present Statute or against the nationals of a State party to the present Statute.]

Article B a.
Individual criminal responsibility
a. Personal jurisdiction

1.   The Court shall have jurisdiction over natural persons pursuant to the present Statute.

2.   A person who commits a crime under this Statute is individually responsible and liable for punishment.

[3.   Criminal responsibility is individual and cannot go beyond the person and the person's possessions.][7]

4.   The fact that the present Statute provides criminal responsibility for individuals does not affect the responsibility of States under international law.

---

[5]   The letter designation of the articles contained in the present annex correspond to those found in part 3 bis (General principles of criminal law) of volume II of the report of the Preparatory Committee.

[6]   This provision raises issues relating to non-retroactivity, amendment of the statute and penalties. Accordingly, further consideration of this issue is required.

[7]   This proposal deals mainly with the limits of civil liability and should be further discussed in connection with penalties, forfeiture and compensation to victims of crimes.

[5. The Court shall also have jurisdiction over juridical persons, with the exception of States, when the crimes committed were committed on behalf of such juridical persons or by their agencies or representatives.

[*21]6. The criminal responsibility of juridical persons shall not exclude the criminal responsibility of natural persons who are perpetrators or accomplices in the same crimes.][x]

Article B b., c. and d.
Individual criminal responsibility

[Subject to the provisions of articles C, G and H,] a person is criminally responsible and liable for punishment for a crime defined [in article 20] [in this Statute] if that person:

(a)   commits such a crime, whether as an individual, jointly with another, or through another person regardless of whether that person is criminally responsible;

(b)   orders, solicits or induces the commission of such a crime which in fact occurs or is attempted;

[(c)   fails to prevent or repress the commission of such a crime in the circumstances set out in article __ [referring to command/superior responsibility];]

(d)   [with [intent] [knowledge] to facilitate the commission of such a crime,] aids, abets or otherwise assists in the commission [or attempted commission] of that crime, including providing the means for its commission;[9]

(e)   either:

(i)   [intentionally] [participates in planning] [plans] to commit such a crime which in fact occurs or is attempted; or

[*22]   [(ii)   agrees with another person or persons that such a crime be committed and an overt act in furtherance of the agreement is committed by any of these persons that manifests their intent [and such a crime in fact occurs or is attempted];[10]][11]

(f)   [directly and publicly] incites the commission of [such a crime] [genocide] [which in fact occurs], [with the intent that such crime be committed];

(g)[12] [with the intent to commit such a crime,] attempts to commit that crime by taking action that commences its execution by means of a substantial step, but that crime does not occur because of circumstances independent of the person's intentions.[13]

---

[x]   There is a deep divergence of views as to the advisability of including criminal responsibility of juridical persons in the Statute. Many delegations are strongly opposed, whereas some strongly favour its inclusion. Others have an open mind. Some delegations hold the view that providing for only the civil or administrative responsibility/liability of juridical persons could provide a middle ground. This avenue, however, has not been thoroughly discussed. Some delegations, who favour the inclusion of juridical persons, hold the view that this expression should be extended to organizations lacking legal status. Some prefer the term "legal entities".

[9]   It was pointed out that the commentary to the ILC draft Code of Crimes (Official Records of the General Assembly, Fifty-first Session, Supplement No. 10, A/51/10, p. 24, para. (12)) implicitly also includes aiding, abetting or assisting ex post facto. This presumption was questioned in the context of the ICC. If aiding, etc., ex post facto were deemed necessary to be criminalized, an explicit provision would be needed.

[10]   In addition to the two types of conduct described in para. (e), there is a third type of criminal association that may be considered. One formulation of this third category would be to refer to the conduct of a person who "participates in an organization which aims at the realization of such a crime by engaging in an activity that furthers or promotes that realization".

[11]   The inclusion of this subparagraph gave rise to divergent views.

[12]   Questions pertaining to voluntary abandonment or repentance should be further discussed in connection with defences or penalties.

[13]   A view was expressed that it would be preferable that issues connected with attempt be taken up in a separate article rather than in the framework of individual responsibility. In that view, the article on individual responsibility should only refer to the way in which the person takes part in the commission of a crime, regardless of whether it deals with a completed crime or an attempted crime.

Article B e.
Irrelevance of official position

1.   This Statute shall be applied to all persons without any discrimination whatsoever: official capacity, either as Head of State or Government, or as a member of a Government or parliament, or as an elected representative, or as a government official, shall in no case exempt a person from his criminal responsibility under this Statute, nor shall it [per se] constitute a ground for reduction of the sentence.

2.   Any immunities or special procedural rules attached to the official capacity of a person, whether under national or international law, may not be relied upon to prevent the Court from exercising its jurisdiction in relation to that person.[14]

[*23] Article C
Command responsibility[15]Responsibility of [commanders] [superiors][16] for acts of [forces under their command] [subordinates]

[In addition to other forms of responsibility for crimes under this Statute, a [commander] [superior] is criminally responsible] [A [commander] [superior] is not relieved of responsibility][17] for crimes under this Statute committed by [forces] [subordinates] under his or her command [or authority] and effective control as a result of the [commander's] [superior's] failure to exercise properly this control where:

    (a)   the [commander] [superior] either knew, or [owing to the widespread commission of the offences] [owing to the circumstances at the time] should have known, that the [forces] [subordinates] were committing or intending to commit such crimes; and

    (b)   the [commander] [superior] failed to take all necessary and reasonable measures within his or her power to prevent or repress their commission [or punish the perpetrators thereof].

Article E
Age of responsibility

Proposal 1

1.   A person under the age of [twelve, thirteen, fourteen, sixteen, eighteen] at the time of the commission of a crime [shall be deemed not to know the wrongfulness of his or her conduct and] shall not be criminally responsible under this Statute, [unless the Prosecutor proves that the person knew the wrongfulness of his or her conduct at that time.]

2.   [A person who is between the age of [sixteen] and [twenty-one] at the time of the (alleged) commission of a crime shall be evaluated (by the Court) as to his or her maturity to determine whether the person is responsible under this Statute.]

[*24] Proposal 2

Age of persons liable to punishment

[Persons aged 13 to 18 years at the time of the facts shall be criminally responsible but their prosecution, trial and sentence and the regime under which they serve their sentence may give rise to the application of special modalities specified in the Statute.]

[Note. Different views exist among States as to a specific age of responsibility.

    It was observed that many international conventions (such as the International Covenant on Civil and Political Rights, the European Convention on Human Rights, the Inter-American Convention on Human Rights) prohibit the punishment of minors.

---

[14]   Further discussion of paragraph 2 would be required in connection with procedure as well as international judicial cooperation.

[15]   One delegation held the view that this principle should be dealt with in connection with the definitions of the crimes.

[16]   Most delegations were in favour of extending the principle of command responsibility to any superior.

[17]   The alternatives highlight the question whether command responsibility is a form of criminal responsibility in addition to others or whether it is a principle that commanders are not immune for the acts of their subordinates.

The question arising from the draft proposals was whether an absolute age of responsibility should be mandated or whether a presumptive age should be included with a means to rebut the presumption.

It was observed that a consistent approach (in terms of either an evaluation by the Court or proof by the Prosecutor) should be taken in paragraphs 1 and 2 of proposal 1 in respect of both of the age groups mentioned.

A question was raised as to what would be the criteria of the evaluation process, and should this be left for the Court to develop in supplementary rules or by jurisprudence?

It was questioned whether the Statute should specify that mitigation of sentence should or could be appropriate for those minors who were found to be mature enough to be criminally responsible.

It was observed that, in its article 1, the Convention on the Rights of the Child defines as a child every human being younger than eighteen years of age and that, in its article 37, it lays down a series of limitations as regards the applicable penalties, ruling out the death penalty and life imprisonment without parole.]

Article F
Statute of limitations

Proposal 1
[1.   The period of limitations shall be completed upon the lapse of xx years for the offence of ..., and yy years for the offence of ...
2.   The period of limitations shall commence to run at the time when criminal conduct has ceased.
|*25|3. The period of limitations shall cease to run on the institution of the prosecution against the case concerned to this Court or to a national court of any State that has jurisdiction on such case. The period of limitations begins to run when the decision of the national court becomes final, where this Court has jurisdiction over the case concerned.]
Proposal 2
[There is no statute of limitations for those crimes within the [inherent] jurisdiction of the [Tribunal].]
Proposal 3
[There is no statute of limitations for those crimes within the [inherent] jurisdiction of the Court; but [for those crimes not within the Court's inherent jurisdiction] the Court may decline to exercise jurisdiction if, owing to the lapse of time, a person would be denied a fair trial.]
Proposal 4
[Crimes not subject to limitation
The crimes referred to in article 27 (a), (b) and (c)[18] shall not be subject to limitation.
Crimes subject to limitation
1.   Proceedings before the Court in respect of the crimes referred to in article 27 (d) and (e)[19] shall be subject to a period of limitation of 10 full years from the date on which the crime was committed, provided that during this period no prosecution has been brought.
2.   If a prosecution has been initiated during this period, either before the Court or in a State competent to bring a prosecution under its internal law, the proceedings before the Court shall not be subject to limitation until 10 full years have elapsed from the date of the most recent prosecution.
Proposal 5
[1.   The statute of limitations as established hereunder shall extinguish the criminal prosecution and the punishment.
|*26|2. The statute of limitations will be [ ] years and shall commence to run as follows:
  (a)   in case of instantaneous crime, from the moment of its perpetration;

---

[18]   Paragraphs (a), (b) and (c) of article 27 deal, respectively, with the crime of genocide, crimes against humanity and the crime of aggression.

[19]   Paragraphs (d) and (e) of article 27 deal, respectively, with serious violations of the laws and customs applicable in armed conflicts and with grave breaches of the four 1949 Geneva Conventions and of article 3 common to the four 1949 Geneva Conventions.

(b)   in case of attempt, from the moment the last act of execution was performed or the due conduct was omitted;

(c)   in case of permanent crime, from the moment of the cessation of the criminal conduct.

3.   The statute of limitations may be interrupted by the actions taken in the investigation of the crime and its perpetrators. If those actions were stopped, the statute of limitations will run again as of the day the last act of investigation was carried out.

4.   The statute of limitations for definitive sanctions will run as of the moment the condemned person escaped and will be interrupted with its detention.]

Article G

Actus reus (act and/or omission)

1.   Conduct for which a person may be criminally responsible and liable for punishment as a crime can constitute either an act or an omission, or a combination thereof.

2.   Unless otherwise provided and for the purposes of paragraph 1, a person may be criminally responsible and liable for punishment for an omission where the person [could] [has the ability], [without unreasonable risk of danger to him/herself or others,] but intentionally [with the intention to facilitate a crime] or knowingly fails to avoid the result of an offence where:

(a)   the omission is specified in the definition of the crime under this Statute; or

(b)   in the circumstances, [the result of the omission corresponds to the result of a crime committed by means of an act] [the degree of unlawfulness realized by such omission corresponds to the degree of unlawfulness to be realized by the commission of such act], and the person is [either] under a pre-existing [legal] obligation under this Statute[20] to avoid the result of such [*27] crime [or creates a particular risk or danger that subsequently leads to the commission of such crime].[21]

[3.   A person is only criminally responsible under this Statute for committing a crime if the harm required for the commission of the crime is caused by and [accountable] [attributable] to his or her act or omission.][22]

Article H

Mens rea

Mental elements of crime

1.   Unless otherwise provided, a person is only criminally responsible and liable for punishment for a crime under this Statute if the physical elements are committed with intent and knowledge.

2.   For the purposes of this Statute and unless otherwise provided, a person has intent where:

(a)   in relation to conduct, that person means to engage in the act or omission;

(b)   in relation to a consequence, that person means to cause that consequence or is aware that it will occur in the ordinary course of events.

3.   For the purposes of this Statute and unless otherwise provided, "know", "knowingly" or "knowledge" means to be aware that a circumstance exists or a consequence will occur.

[4.[23] [24] [25] For the purposes of this Statute and unless otherwise provided, where this Statute provides that a crime may be committed recklessly, a person is reckless with respect to a circumstance or a consequence if:

[*28](a)   the person is aware of a risk that the circumstance exists or that the consequence will occur;

---

[20]   Some delegations questioned whether the source of this obligation is wider than the statute.

[21]   Some delegations had concerns about including this clause which referred to the creation of a risk. Other delegations thought that, in the context of the offences of the statute, breach of an obligation under the Statute to avoid the result of a crime was sufficient.

[22]   Some delegations thought that a provision on causation was not necessary.

[23]   Further discussion is needed on this paragraph.

[24]   The need for this paragraph will be re-examined once a decision has been taken on the definition of crimes.

[25]   A view was expressed to the effect that there was no reason for rejecting the concept of commission of an offence also through negligence, in which case the offender shall be liable only when so prescribed by the statute.

(b) the person is aware that the risk is highly unreasonable to take;
[and]

[(c) the person is indifferent to the possibility that the circumstance exists or that the consequence will occur.]]

Article K
Mistake of fact or of law[26] [27]

Alternative text A

Unavoidable mistake of fact or of law shall be a defence provided that the mistake is not inconsistent with the nature of the alleged crime. Avoidable mistake of fact or of law may be considered in mitigation of punishment.

Alternative text B

1. A mistake of fact shall be a defence only if it negates the mental element required by the crime [charged provided that said mistake is not inconsistent with the nature of the crime or its elements] [, and provided that the circumstances he reasonably believed to be true would have been lawful].
2. Mistake of law may not be cited as a ground for exemption from criminal responsibility [, except where specifically provided for in this Statute].[28]

[*29] Annex III
DECISION ADOPTED BY THE PREPARATORY COMMITTEE IN CONNECTION WITH THE INVITATION BY THE GOVERNMENT OF ITALY TO HOST THE DIPLOMATIC CONFERENCE

At its 51st meeting, on 21 February 1997, the Preparatory Committee adopted the following decision:

"The Preparatory Committee on the Establishment of an International Criminal Court,

"Welcomes the proposal by the Government of Italy to hold the diplomatic conference in Rome; and

"Recommends to the General Assembly that, pursuant to General Assembly resolution 51/207 of 17 December 1996, after consideration by the Committee on Conferences, a decision in accordance with such proposal be made when dealing with the necessary arrangements for the conference, on the understanding that the organization of the conference in Rome will proceed on the basis of the usual practice concerning the funding of events of this kind taking place outside United Nations Headquarters or other United Nations seats."

---

[26] There were widely divergent views on this matter.

[27] Some delegations were of the view that mistake of fact was not necessary because it was covered by mens rea.

[28] Some delegations felt that paragraph 2 of alternative text B still left some ambiguity, and an alternative approach could read as follows:

"Mistake of law as to whether a particular type of conduct is a crime under this Statute, or whether a crime is within the jurisdiction of the Court, is not a defence. However, a [reasonable] mistake of law may be a defence if it negates the mental element required by such crime."

REPORT OF THE PREPARATORY COMMITTEE ON THE ESTABLISHMENT OF AN INTERNATIONAL CRIMINAL COURT

VOLUME I

(Proceedings of the Preparatory Committee during March-April and August 1996)

[Editorial Note - the U.N. page numbers of this document are indicated in bolded brackets [*] in the text].

[*1] I.   INTRODUCTION

1.   The Preparatory Committee on the Establishment of an International Criminal Court met at United Nations Headquarters from 25 March to 12 April 1996 and from 12 to 30 August 1996, in accordance with General Assembly resolution 50/46 of 11 December 1995.

2.   Under paragraph 2 of that resolution, the Preparatory Committee was open to all States Members of the United Nations or members of the specialized agencies or of the International Atomic Energy Agency. 1/

3.   Mr. Hans Corell, Under-Secretary-General, the Legal Counsel, opened the session, represented the Secretary-General and made an introductory statement.

4.   Mr. Roy S. Lee, Director of the Codification Division of the Office of Legal Affairs, acted as Secretary of the Preparatory Committee; Mr. Manuel Rama-Montaldo, Deputy Director for Research and Studies, acted as Deputy Secretary; Ms. Mahnoush Arsanjani and Ms. Sachiko Kuwabara-Yamamoto, Senior Legal Officers; Ms. Christiane Bourloyannis-Vrailas, Mr. George Korontzis, Mr. Mpazi Sinjela and Ms. Virginia Morris, Legal Officers; and Ms. Darlene Prescott and Mr. Renan Villacis, Associate Legal Officers, acted as assistant secretaries.

5.   At the 1st meeting, on 25 March 1996, the Preparatory Committee elected its Bureau, as follows:

Chairman:	Mr. Adriaan Bos (Netherlands)
Vice-Chairmen:	Mr. Cherif Bassiouni (Egypt)
	Mrs. Silvia A. Fernçndez de Gurmendi (Argentina)
	Mr. Marek Madej (Poland)
Rapporteur:	Mr. Jun Yoshida (Japan)

6.   Also at the 1st meeting, the Preparatory Committee adopted the following agenda (A/AC.249/L.1):

1.   Opening of the session.
2.   Election of officers.
3.   Adoption of the agenda.
4.   Organization of work.
5.   Further consideration of the major substantive and administrative issues arising out of the draft statute for an international criminal court prepared by the International Law Commission and, taking into account the different views expressed during the meetings, drafting of texts, with a view to preparing a widely acceptable consolidated text of a convention for an international criminal court as a next step towards consideration by a conference of plenipotentiaries.
6.   Adoption of the report.

7.   The Preparatory Committee had before it, in addition to the draft statute for an international criminal court adopted by the International Law Commission [*2] (ILC) at its forty-sixth session, 2/ the report of the Ad Hoc Committee on the Establishment of an International Criminal Court, 3/ the comments received pursuant to paragraph 4 of General Assembly resolution 49/53 of 9 December 1994 on the establishment of an international criminal court (A/AC.244/1 and Add.1-4) and a preliminary report submitted by the Secretary-General pursuant to paragraph 5 of that resolution, on provisional estimates of the staffing, structure and costs of the establishment and operation of an international criminal court (A/AC.244/L.2). Also before it was the Draft Code of Crimes against the Peace and Security of Mankind adopted by the International Law Commission at its forty-eighth session; 4/ the Declaration of Basic

Principles of Justice for Victims of Crime and Abuse of Power; 5/ and Principles Guaranteeing the Rights and Interests of Victims in the Proceedings of the Proposed International Criminal Court. 6/

[*3] II.   ORGANIZATION AND METHODS OF WORK

8.   The work of the Preparatory Committee during its March-April session followed the programme suggested by the Bureau and focused on the following questions: scope of jurisdiction and definition of crimes, at its 1st to 6th meetings, on 25, 26 and 27 March; general principles of criminal law, at its 7th to 10th meetings, on 28 and 29 March; complementarity, at its 11th to 14th meetings, on 1 and 2 April; trigger mechanism, at its 15th to 18th meetings, on 3 and 4 April; and cooperation between the court and national jurisdictions, at its 19th to 23rd meetings, on 8, 9 and 10 April.

9.   During the Committee's consideration of the above questions, delegations put forward various suggestions and proposals, some of which were in written form. For the purpose of illustrating some of the major issues involved, they were brought together and compiled under the following headings: general principles of criminal law (A/AC.249/CRP.9); complementarity (A/AC.249/CRP.9/Add.1); trigger mechanism (A/AC.249/CRP.9/Add.2 and 3); and cooperation between the Court and national jurisdictions (A/AC.249/CRP.9/Add.5). These compilations were by no means exhaustive in their inclusion of all suggestions and proposals put forward by the delegations; delegations were encouraged to submit additions to the Secretariat for inclusion. The Committee did not discuss these papers and does not wish to prejudge the future positions of delegations.

10.   With respect to the definition of crimes, a series of Chairman's informal texts was issued in a document (A/AC.249/CRP.9/Add.4) under the following headings: genocide, aggression, war crimes and crimes against humanity. The document also included a compilation of proposals and suggestions submitted by delegations. These are also illustrative texts which are not exhaustive and do not necessarily reflect any general views on the debate. The Committee did not discuss the document.

11.   The work of the Preparatory Committee during its August session followed the programme suggested by the Bureau. To guide the discussion, the Chairman prepared lists of questions which were formulated in connection with specific articles of the draft statute prepared by the International Law Commission. The main topics considered were: procedural questions, fair trial and rights of the accused, at its 33rd to 36th meetings, on 15, 16 and 19 August 1996; organizational questions (composition and administration of the Court), at its 37th to 39th meetings, on 20 and 21 August 1996; and the establishment of the Court and its relationship with the United Nations at its 42nd and 43rd meetings, on 26 August 1996.

12.   At the invitation of the Preparatory Committee, the Office of the Prosecutor of the International Tribunal for the former Yugoslavia presented, in an informal meeting, a statement on its work and an explanation, which were followed by an exchange of views with the representatives of the Tribunal.

13.   During its August session, the following written proposals were submitted:

A/AC.249/L.2	Draft set of rules of procedure and evidence for the Court: working paper submitted by Australia and the Netherlands
A/AC.249/L.3	Draft statute: working paper submitted by France
[*4] A/AC.249/L.4	Applicable law and general principles of law:working paper submitted by Canada
A/AC.249/L.5	International cooperation and judicial [mutual] assistance: working paper submitted by South Africa and Lesotho
A/AC.249/L.6	Rules of procedure: working paper submitted by Argentina
A/AC.249/L.7	Tentative draft on procedure: working paper submitted by Japan
A/AC.249/L.8	Proposals on the organization of the Court: working paper submitted by Japan
A/AC.249/WP.1	Proposal submitted by Germany for article 26
A/AC.249/WP.2	Proposal submitted by Singapore for articles 26, 27, 29 and 33
A/AC.249/WP.3	Proposal submitted by Switzerland for articles 34 and 36
A/AC.249/WP.4	Proposal submitted by Switzerland for articles 9 and 26 to 29
A/AC.249/WP.5	Proposal submitted by the United States of America on general principles of criminal law
A/AC.249/WP.6	Proposal submitted by the Netherlands for articles 5, 27, 37, 38, 44 and 48
A/AC.249/WP.7	Proposal submitted by Singapore for article 38

	A/AC.249/WP.8	Proposal submitted by New Zealand for article 41
	A/AC.249/WP.9	Proposal submitted by Switzerland for article 37
	A/AC.249/WP.10	Proposal submitted by Austria for articles 26 to 29, 34, 36 and 51
	A/AC.249/WP.11	Proposal submitted by Egypt for article 43
	A/AC.249/WP.12	Proposal submitted by Denmark, Finland, Malawi, New Zealand, Nigeria, Norway and Sweden for articles 6 (5) and 12
	A/AC.249/WP.13	Proposal submitted by Singapore for articles 45 and 48
	A/AC.249/WP.14	Proposal submitted by Japan on international cooperation and judicial assistance
	A/AC.249/WP.15	Proposal submitted by the United States of America for part 7
	A/AC.249/WP.16	Proposal submitted by Argentina and Canada for articles 38, 38 bis, 41 and 43
	A/AC.249/WP.17	Proposal submitted by the United Kingdom of Great Britain and Northern Ireland for articles 5, 6, 9 and 12
	A/AC.249/WP.18	Proposal submitted by Austria for articles 9 and 11
	A/AC.249/WP.19	Proposal submitted by Denmark for article 6
[*5]	A/AC.249/WP.20	Proposal submitted by Portugal for article 6
	A/AC.249/WP.21	Proposal submitted by Canada for article 45
	A/AC.249/WP.22	Proposal submitted by the United States for article 6
	A/AC.249/WP.23	Proposal submitted by the United Kingdom for article 6
	A/AC.249/WP.24	Proposal submitted by Singapore for article 6
	A/AC.249/WP.25	Proposal submitted by China for article 6 (3), (5) and (6)
	A/AC.249/WP.26	Proposal submitted by Japan for articles 6 and 13
	A/AC.249/WP.27	Proposal submitted by Switzerland for articles 6, 8 and 9
	A/AC.249/WP.28	Proposal submitted by Austria for article 9
	A/AC.249/WP.29	Proposal submitted by Singapore and Trinidad and Tobago for article 6
	A/AC.249/WP.30	Proposal submitted by Finland for articles 6, 12 and 19
	A/AC.249/WP.31	Proposal submitted by Italy for article 37
	A/AC.249/WP.32	Proposal submitted by Singapore for articles 8 to 10, 12, and 13
	A/AC.249/WP.33	Proposal submitted by Japan for article 59
	A/AC.249/WP.34	Proposal submitted by the United States for articles 8 to 10 and 13
	A/AC.249/WP.35	Proposal submitted by Singapore for article 47
	A/AC.249/WP.36	Proposal submitted by Israel for article 53 (2)
	A/AC.249/WP.37	Proposal submitted by Germany for article 44 (a)
	A/AC.249/WP.38	Proposal submitted by the United Kingdom for article 6
	A/AC.249/WP.39	Proposal submitted by the United States for articles 2 and 4
	A/AC.249/WP.40	Proposal submitted by Singapore on additions to the compilation of proposals on judicial cooperation and enforcement
	A/AC.249/WP.41	Proposal submitted by the United States on offences against the integrity of the Court
	A/AC.249/WP.42	Proposal submitted by Israel for articles 10 (2), 11 (2) and (3) and 16 (1)
	A/AC.249/WP.43	Proposal submitted by Algeria, Egypt, Jordan, Kuwait, the Libyan Arab Jamahiriya and Qatar on the organization of the Court
[*6]	A/AC.249/WP.44	Proposal submitted by Algeria, Egypt, Jordan, Kuwait, the Libyan Arab Jamahiriya and Qatar for article 47
	A/AC.249/WP.45	Proposal submitted by Finland for articles 28 and 29
	A/AC.249/WP.46	Proposal submitted by the Netherlands for article 47
	A/AC.249/WP.47	Proposal submitted by Trinidad and Tobago for article 6
	A/AC.249/WP.48	Proposal submitted by Japan on the definition of war crimes
	A/AC.249/WP.49	Proposal submitted by New Zealand for article 2
	A/AC.249/WP.50	Proposal submitted by Denmark for article 20
	A/AC.249/WP.51	Proposal submitted by Singapore for article 23
	A/AC.249/WP.52	Proposal submitted by Belize for article 20
	A/AC.249/WP.53	Proposal submitted by Israel for articles 44, 45 and 47.

14. For the purpose of organizing the proposals in a coherent and manageable manner, interested States were encouraged to conduct consultations. For those purposes informal groups were formed on the following subjects: procedural questions (chaired by Ms. Silvia A. Fernçndez de Gurmendi, Argentina); international cooperation and judicial assistance (chaired by Mr. Pieter Kruger, South Africa); organizational questions (chaired by Ms. Zaitun Zawiyah Bt. Puteh and Mr. Kian Kheong Wong, Malaysia); and penalties (chaired by Mr. Rolf Einar Fife, Norway). The informal group on the general principles of criminal law continued its work (chaired by Mr. Per Saland, Sweden).

15. At the 45th meeting, on 27 August 1996, the chairmen of the respective informal groups reported on the outcome of their work.

16. At the same meeting, the Committee decided to incorporate into its report (see vol. II), together with the draft articles prepared by the International Law Commission, the compilations of proposals prepared by the informal groups, namely, procedural questions, fair trial and rights of the accused (A/AC.249/CRP.14); international cooperation and judicial assistance (A/AC.249/CRP.17); organization, composition and administration of the Court (A/AC.249/CRP.11); general principles of criminal law (A/AC.249/CRP.13); and penalties(A/AC.249/CRP.13/Add.1). The incorporation into the report of the above-mentioned compilations was done on the understanding that they did not represent texts agreed upon among delegations; they did not affect the status of national proposals nor did they necessarily represent the final position of the delegations which had submitted such proposals. The compilations were not exhaustive and the proposals contained therein had not necessarily been discussed in the informal groups.

17. A view was expressed that only the informal groups on general principles and on international cooperation had had the desirable degree of wide participation. Concern was expressed that in topics such as procedural questions, the compilation of texts on an article-by-article basis might lead to a loss of coherence in the national proposals involved.

18. Some delegations acknowledged the contribution of relevant organizations to the work of the Preparatory Committee as provided for in General Assembly [*7] resolution 50/46, and in particular the representatives of civil organizations in the meetings of the Committee.

19. Appreciation was also expressed by a number of delegations for the renewed generous offer of the Government of Italy to host a conference on the establishment of an international criminal court.

[*8] III. DISCUSSION ON SUBSTANTIVE ISSUES

A.   Establishment of the Court and relationship between the Court and the United Nations

20. The issues on which the debate focused were the following: status and nature of the Court and method of its establishment; relationship between the Court and the United Nations; and financing of the Court.

    1.   Status and nature of the Court and method of its establishment

21. There was general support for the view that the Court should be an independent judicial institution. While some favoured an autonomous international body, others preferred that the Court form part of the United Nations as, for example, a principal or subsidiary organ. It was noted in this regard that the status would be determined or affected by the method of creation selected (for instance, the International Tribunal for the former Yugoslavia was established as a subsidiary organ under Security Council resolutions 808 (1993) and 827 (1993)).

22. It was suggested that the Court should be a full-time, permanent institution, which would sit on a continuous basis for the purpose of prosecuting individuals accused of committing serious crimes. In the view of some delegations, this would promote stability and uniformity in jurisprudence and continuous development of the law. Others, however, favoured a permanent court which would meet only when a complaint was actually submitted to it, as proposed in article 4 of the draft statute of the International Law Commission.

23. It was suggested that the Court should possess international legal personality with treaty-making capacity. There was also a suggestion that the Court should be given competence to request advisory opinions from the International Court of Justice. Others pointed out that this would entail legal implications requiring further consideration.

24. It was suggested that the Court could function at least initially as provided for in articles 4 and 5 of the draft statute. The Presidency, the Prosecutor's office and the Registry (and perhaps one judge for the

conduct of the investigation and indictment phase) could be of a standing nature, while the Trial or Appeals Chambers would be convened as required. This system was regarded as sufficiently balanced, at least for the initial functioning of the Court, and would not result in needless costs.

25. As concerns the method for establishing the Court, various suggestions were made: an amendment to the Charter of the United Nations making the Court a principal organ of the Organization similar to the International Court of Justice; a resolution adopted by the General Assembly and/or the Security Council; or the conclusion of a multilateral treaty. Some delegations expressed reservations on the establishment of the Court by a Security Council resolution. The first approach was considered ideal by some delegations, in that it would make the Statute an integral part of the Charter with binding effect on all Member States. It was, however, noted that this process would be complex and time-consuming, although another suggestion was to retain the option of reviewing the status of the treaty any time proposals for amendment to the Charter were otherwise being considered. To set up the Court by a resolution of [*9] the General Assembly or of the Security Council as a principal or subsidiary organ thereof was considered by some to be efficient, time-saving and feasible pursuant to the advisory opinion of the International Court of Justice of 1954. It was, however, questioned whether a resolution of a recommendatory nature would provide the necessary legal force for the operation of the Court. There was also support for the establishment of the Court under a Security Council resolution. It was, however, pointed out that the Council's competence under the Charter to create ad hoc tribunals in response to a particular situation endangering international peace and security should be distinguished from the current endeavour of creating an international criminal court with general powers and competence.

26. To establish the Court by a multilateral treaty, as recommended by the International Law Commission, seemed to enjoy general support, as the treaty could provide the necessary independence and authority for the Court. States would have the choice whether to become a party to the treaty. The treaty could contain the Court's Statute and other instruments relevant to its creation and work (e.g., rules of the Court, instruments relating to privileges and immunities of the Court). In order to promote wider acceptance of the instrument, the General Assembly could adopt a resolution urging States to become parties to the treaty; the treaty itself could also provide for a review or an amendment mechanism and provisions for the settlement of disputes, which could, according to some, serve as an additional means to attract favourable consideration of the Court by States.

27. In order to maintain the treaty as an integral whole, a suggestion was made that the instrument should not permit reservations; others thought that this question might have to be reviewed at a later stage.

28. Different views were expressed on the number of ratifications required to bring the treaty into force, ranging from 25 to 90 ratifications. According to some, a relatively high number of ratifications would promote the representation of the principal legal systems of the world, all geographical regions and the idea of universality of the Court. On the other hand, the advantage of a lower number was that it could permit a relatively early entry into force of the treaty and would give early effect to the international community's desire to see the Court actually established. Still others suggested that a balance should be achieved to avoid too high a number, which could possibly delay the entry into force of the treaty, or too low a number, which would not provide an effective basis for the Court. It was suggested that the five members of the Security Council should be included among the number of ratifications required for the entry into force of the treaty. Some stressed, however, that early establishment of the Court be given more weight than the other considerations, and that a low number of ratifications would not necessarily preclude the requirement of geographical representation and representation of the major legal systems.

2. Relationship between the Court and the United Nations

29. A close relationship between the Court and the United Nations was considered essential and a necessary link to the universality and standing of the Court, though such a relationship should in no way jeopardize the independence of the Court. A special agreement, either elaborated simultaneously with the Statute (as an annex thereto) or at a later stage, to be concluded between the two institutions would be appropriate for the establishment of such a relationship. The agreement should, however, be [*10] approved by the States parties to the Statute. In this regard, references were made to the agreements between the United Nations and the International Tribunal for the Law of the Sea and the International Atomic Energy Agency respectively.

30.   It was further suggested that the general principles and substantive questions should be dealt in the Statute itself. The relationship agreement should deal only with such technical questions of an administrative nature as issues of representation, exchange of information and documentation, or provisions on cooperation between the two organizations. The agreement should be guided by and not be inconsistent with the provisions of the Statute.

31.   A view was expressed that the Court could have a status analogous to that of a specialized agency. Articles 57 and 63 of the Charter of the United Nations concerning the status of specialized agencies and their cooperation with the United Nations would be relevant in such a case. Others questioned whether such a relationship would be appropriate for the envisaged status of the Court; further careful consideration would be required. Still others were of the opinion that such provisions were not relevant to the nature and functions of the Court and might subject it to the coordination and recommendations of the Economic and Social Council.

       3.   Financing of the Court

32.   As regards the financing of the Court, the views were expressed that it should be effected from the regular budget of the United Nations as is the case with human rights monitoring bodies, since the Court would be dealing with international concerns, and that its financing should be certain and continuing. Moreover, if States parties were required to finance the Court, some States might be deterred from bringing cases before the Court owing to their financial situation, or the State in question might not be a party to the treaty. However, another view considered that the independence of the Court required States parties to finance it through their own contributions on the basis of the scale of assessments of the United Nations or another scale yet to be agreed. It was also noted that States initiating cases, interested States or even the Security Council (if it had referred a matter to the Court) could contribute to the financing. The examples of the Universal Postal Union and the Permanent Court of Arbitration were mentioned in this respect. In addition, the Court should also be open to voluntary contributions by States, organizations or even individuals and corporations. Reference was also made to a proposal for the establishment of a fund to be financed by voluntary contributions, as well as collected fines and confiscated assets. As concerns the institutional aspects of financing, it was suggested that a general assembly of the States parties could be held annually to consider administrative and financial issues and approve the budget. There was also a view that the consideration of the question of financing was premature at the current stage and should be considered later, after the structure and jurisdiction of the Court had been further clarified. It was suggested that a feasibility study be done so that all possible financing options could be considered. It was pointed out that the Secretary-General had prepared in 1995 certain preliminary estimates concerning the establishment of the Court (A/AC.244/L.2).

[*11] B.   Organizational questions (composition and administration of the Court)

Article 5. Organs of the Court

33.   With regard to article 5 dealing with organs of the Court, the view was expressed that an indictment or an investigations chamber for pre-trial procedures should be added and that it should be composed of three judges with the necessary authority to monitor preliminary investigative matters. A view was also expressed that a pre-trial chamber should be established to carry out such pre-trial procedures as issuing warrants and deciding upon indictment and admissibility. Others questioned the need for this, preferring the structure established in the draft by the International Law Commission. Another suggestion was made that there should be no rotation of judges between the various chambers so as to avoid the possibility of having any judge sit on the same case more than once.

34.   A proposal was made to create special chambers to deal with certain cases, for example, genocide.

Article 6. Qualification and election of judges

35.   It was stressed that the qualification of judges for the international criminal court was an issue that needed to be given careful consideration, taking into account the prominence and importance of the future Court. In addition to the qualifications already mentioned in the draft article of the International Law Commission, it was pointed out that the persons to be elected should also possess experience in humanitarian law and the law of human rights. The view was expressed that all judges should have criminal trial experience. In that context, it was further expressed that it was essential that judges to be appointed to the Trial Chamber should have criminal law experience, which does not necessarily imply criminal trial

experience but may include the experience of a lawyer or a prosecutor. Other attributes should include high moral character, impartiality, personal integrity and independence. The view was expressed that the reference to "criminal trial experience" should be clearly defined. Some delegations expressed reservations about the requirement, in the draft prepared by the International Law Commission, of appointment to the highest judicial body, since several legal orders have a judiciary based on a career system. Doubts were expressed as to the advisability of establishing for the Court's composition a strict separation between judges with criminal trial experience and those with recognized competence in international law, as this might unduly complicate the election process. Persons competent in both areas were considered ideally suited for such positions.

36.   It was pointed out that since the Court to be established should be universal in character, representing all systems of the world, there was the need for balance and diversity in its composition. It was therefore considered important that judges be elected on the basis of equitable geographical representation. In this connection, the formulation of the relevant rule of the Statute of the International Tribunal for the Law of the Sea was recalled. It was also emphasized that the Court's composition should ensure gender balance, particularly in the light of the fact that some of the crimes to be considered by the Court related to sexual assault of women and crimes against children. However, the view was also expressed that there should be no quota system for female judges, nor quotas of any kind, since the sole criteria should be the [*12] high qualification and experience of the candidate. It was suggested that rules on qualification and election of judges should be more closely modeled on those governing the International Tribunal for the former Yugoslavia.

37.   In order to attract the most qualified persons, the view was expressed that nomination of candidates for election to the Court should not be confined only to nationals of States parties; nationals of non-States parties should also be permitted. Another view expressed in this connection was that restricting nominations to nationals of States parties would act as an incentive for States to consider becoming parties to the convention. In order to ensure that merit would be a paramount consideration in the election of judges, suggestions were made to the effect that candidates should be nominated either by a nominating committee or by national groups, as in the nomination of candidates for the International Court of Justice.

38.   Support was expressed for the idea that the election of judges should be carried out by the States parties to the Statute of the Court. It was however suggested that elections should be conducted either by the General Assembly, or by the Assembly together with the Security Council, as in the case of the International Court of Justice. According to another point of view, this matter was dependent on the kind of relationship the Court would have with the United Nations.

39.   While there was broad support for the idea that the Court should be composed of 18 judges, the view was also expressed that a higher number, for example 21 or 24, should be considered, depending on the number of Trial Chambers to be created. The view was also expressed that a smaller number should be considered, for example 15 or even 12, particularly at the beginning, in order to cut costs. As a cost-saving measure, it was further suggested that consideration should also be given to the possibility of electing part-time judges who could be called upon on short notice whenever the need arose. The view was also stressed in this connection that consideration of cost savings should not be a major determining factor in the size or nature of the Court to be created.

40.   As for the term of office, while there was widespread support for the proposal of the International Law Commission for a non-renewable nine-year term in order to promote the impartiality and independence of the judges, the view was also expressed that a shorter renewable term (e.g., five or six years) should be given serious consideration, in order to ensure geographic rotation and to attract the best qualified persons. A view was also expressed that while a judge should be allowed to continue in office in order to complete any case the hearing of which has commenced, there should be a limit placed on this extension. It was therefore suggested that the matter should be concluded within five years.

41.   A proposal was made that judges should be subject to a retirement age (e.g., at 70 or 75 years). It was also observed that, in such a case, it would be desirable to set an age ceiling for persons being nominated to stand as candidates to the Court.

Article 8. The Presidency

42. It was suggested that the President's duties should be limited to ceremonial and administrative functions and that States parties should retain an oversight function over the administrative matters of the Court. It was stated [*13] that the line of authority between the President and the Vice-Presidents should be clarified, as well as how decisions are taken within the Presidency (e.g., by consensus, by majority vote). The suggestion was made that the responsibility of the Presidency for the due administration of the Court should include supervision and direction of the Registrar and staff of the Registry, and security arrangements for the defendants, witnesses and the Court. It was also suggested that the functions of the Presidency could be extended to issues such as reviewing decisions of the Prosecutor not to pursue a case. Doubts were expressed as to the appropriateness of the Presidency exercising pre-trial and other procedural functions. In this regard, the establishment of an indictment or investigations chamber was suggested. The Presidency could preserve functions as regards execution of penalties.

Article 9. Chambers

43. It was proposed that paragraph 1 of article 9 should be clarified, particularly regarding the criteria on the basis of which the Appeals Chamber would be established. A body of opinion favoured a completely separate and independent appellate function and was against the rotation of judges between the Trial Chambers and the Appeals Chamber. It was further proposed that the Appeals Chamber, as well as the Trial Chambers, should be elected by the Court rather than appointed by the Presidency, as it was felt that this would enhance the objectivity of the Chambers. The views were also expressed that appointments to the Trial Chambers should be by rotation or by drawing lots. Chambers should invariably be composed of an uneven number of judges to constitute the quorum; judges should always be present at the proceedings of the Court. The need was also stressed for a mechanism to ensure that there would be a sufficient number of judges with criminal law experience in the Appeals Chamber. The suggestion was further made that pre-trial or indictment chambers should be constituted. It was noted in this connection that they could be permanent or established for a particular case or for a specific time period. It was suggested that a remand chamber should be created.

Article 10. Independence of the judges

44. It was pointed out that there were a number of ways to enhance the independence of the judges, such as the election procedure, length of terms, security of tenure and appropriate remuneration. The view was expressed that judges should not engage in any activities that would prejudice their judicial functions. In this connection, activities such as part-time teaching and writing for publication were considered compatible with such functions. It was suggested that any question arising in connection with the outside activities of the judges should be decided not by the Presidency but by an absolute majority of the Court, a solution that was in line with Article 16 of the Statute of the International Court of Justice.

Article 11. Excusing and disqualification of judges

45. The importance of the question concerning the excusing and disqualification of judges was stressed. It was suggested that the relevant article of the draft statute of the International Law Commission needed further elaboration in this respect. A suggestion was made to the effect that the terms of disqualification of a judge contemplated in paragraph 2 of article 11 should not extend to members of an indictment chamber having acted in this capacity. It was also [*14] suggested to include in the Statute such specific grounds for the excusing and disqualification of judges as: that the judge is the injured party or a relative of the accused or of the injured party, or a national of a complainant State or of a State of which the accused is a national, or that the judge has acted as a witness, representative, counsel, public prosecutor or judge at the national level in the case involving the accused. Some of the above suggestions for inclusion gave rise, however, to reservations. The proposal was made that States parties should be able to raise questions concerning the disqualification of a judge. It was also suggested that more detailed rules should be developed to govern conflict of interest problems.

Article 12. The Procuracy

46. The view was expressed that the Statute should provide for an independent Prosecutor with experience in criminal investigations in order to ensure the credibility and integrity of the Court, and that it might be useful to look at the experience of the tribunals for the former Yugoslavia and Rwanda. It was further stated that the Prosecutor's office should be established to seek the truth rather than merely seek a conviction in

a partisan manner. It was suggested that the Prosecutor and the Deputy Prosecutor should have experience in investigation as well as prosecution of criminal cases. It was also proposed that the age limit for the Prosecutor and the Deputy Prosecutor should be 70 years old. Their term of office should be fairly long, such as nine years, and non-renewable. As to the provision concerning the election of the Prosecutor and the Deputy Prosecutor, the view was expressed that further elaboration was required. The view was also expressed that the Prosecutor, like judges, should not be allowed to seek re-election, in order to avoid any political overtones associated with a re-election process. It was observed that the rules for disqualification of the Prosecutor needed further elaboration. It was suggested in that connection that he or she should not engage in any activity likely to interfere with his or her prosecutorial functions or to affect confidence in his or her independence (e.g., being a member of the legislative or executive branches of the Government of a State). It was also suggested that the Prosecutor should not act in relation to a complaint initiated by his or her State of nationality or involving a person of his or her own nationality or in any case in which he or she had previously been involved in any capacity. There were differing views on the need for disqualification based on nationality issues. It was also suggested that the grounds for disqualification of the Prosecutor should be similar to those for a judge. It was suggested that the term "Procuracy" was inappropriate and should be replaced by such designation as "the Office of the Prosecution". The view was also expressed that article 12 should be amended in order to reflect the opinion that the Prosecutor should also be authorized to initiate investigations ex officio, even in the absence of a complaint brought by a State party to the Statute. However, according to another view, such power should not be granted to the Prosecutor.

Article 13. The Registry

47. It was suggested that there should be included in the Statute guidance on the qualifications for the Registrar and the Deputy Registrar, in order to ensure that such offices would be vested in highly qualified persons. It was also suggested that the Registry should be under the direction of the Presidency or of the Court. The view was expressed that the functions of the Registrar needed elaboration and reference was made in this regard to the wording in [*15] article 17, paragraph 1, of the Statute of the International Tribunal for the former Yugoslavia.

Article 15. Loss of office

48. The view was expressed that grounds for the removal of judges, the Prosecutor and the Deputy Prosecutor should be clearly stated in article 15. It was suggested that further to the grounds contemplated in the draft statute of the International Law Commission, reference should also be made to the engagement in delinquency, whether officially or privately, which could erode public confidence in the Court. The view was also expressed that a distinction should be made between conduct triggering loss of office and other kinds of conduct deserving less serious disciplinary measures.

Article 16. Privileges and immunities

49. The view was expressed that the privileges and immunities as expressed in the article were too broad and should be limited to official functions. Moreover, the privileges and immunities of the Court's staff should be waivable. A view was expressed that on-site functions of the Prosecutor and the counsels in the territory of a State were different functions than those performed by a diplomatic agent and that, therefore, the Prosecutor and the counsels did not need full diplomatic privileges and immunities. The point was also made that the scope of the privileges and immunities should be reformulated later, after the functions of each body of the Court had been well defined.

Article 19. Rules of the Court

50. It was suggested that the rules of the Court should be formulated on the basis of the principles set out in the Statute and could initially be reviewed by the States parties. Subsequently, the judges could adopt supplementary rules in accordance with the rules of the Court. According to other delegations, the judges should not be allowed to adopt rules of procedure, but could suggest the adoption of new rules to State parties. The view was expressed that, in the light of the experience of the International Tribunal for the former Yugoslavia, which had amended its rules nine times, a flexible procedure for amendment of the rules of the Court should be established.

C.   Scope of the jurisdiction of the Court and definition of crimes
Article 20. Crimes within the jurisdiction of the Court
   1.   General comments
      (a)   Scope of jurisdiction
51   There was general agreement concerning the importance of limiting the jurisdiction of the Court to the most serious crimes of concern to the international community as a whole, as indicated in the second paragraph of the preamble, to avoid trivializing the role and functions of the Court and interfering with the jurisdiction of national courts. Several delegations emphasized the importance of consistently applying the jurisdictional standard referred to in the second paragraph of the preamble to the various categories of crimes.

[*16]   (b)   Definition of crimes
52.   There was general agreement that the crimes within the jurisdiction of the Court should be defined with the clarity, precision and specificity required for criminal law in accordance with the principle of legality (nullum crimen sine lege). A number of delegations expressed the view that the crimes should be clearly defined in the Statute. However, some delegations envisaged the Statute as a procedural instrument and expressed concern about possible duplication of or interference with the work of the International Law Commission on the draft Code of Crimes against the Peace and Security of Mankind.
53.   Attention was drawn to the definitions of crimes contained in articles 17 to 20 of the draft Code of Crimes against the Peace and Security of Mankind, adopted by the International Law Commission in 1996, with a view to considering the inclusion of such definitions in the Statute. Article 20 of the Statute should be reformulated along the lines of the draft Code, with each crime being defined in a separate article identifying the essential elements of the offences and the minimum qualitative and quantitative requirements. The definition of war crimes should clearly indicate in what circumstances, by which perpetrators and against which victims certain acts would constitute such crimes.

      (c)   Method of definition
54.   Several delegations expressed the view that the crimes referred to in subparagraphs (a) to (d) should be defined by enumeration of the specific offences rather than by reference to the relevant legal instruments, to provide greater clarity and transparency, to underscore the customary law status of the definitions, to avoid a lengthy debate on the customary law status of various instruments, to avoid possible challenges by States that were not parties to the relevant agreements, to avoid the difficulties that might arise if the agreements were subsequently amended and to provide a uniform approach to the definitions of the crimes irrespective of whether they were the subject of a convention. Some delegations suggested that the two approaches could be combined for crimes covered by widely accepted conventions. There were also proposals to define the crimes by reference to the relevant conventions, such as the Genocide Convention and the Geneva Conventions. There was a further proposal to amend article 20 to indicate that the Court should apply the relevant international conventions and other sources of international law in interpreting and applying the definitions of crimes. Several delegations held the view that the Statute should codify customary international law and not extend to the progressive development of international law.

      (d)   Exhaustive or illustrative definition
55.   Several delegations expressed a preference for an exhaustive rather than an illustrative definition of the crimes so as to ensure respect for the principle of legality, to provide greater certainty and predictability regarding the crimes that would be subject to international prosecution and adjudication and to ensure respect for the rights of the accused. However, some delegations expressed the view that it might not be possible to envisage all of the various offences, that exhaustive definitions might excessively restrict the jurisdiction of the Court and that in some instances it might be useful to retain an element of flexibility to permit the continuing development of the law.

[*17]   (e)   Elements of the crimes
56.   Some delegations expressed the view that the constituent elements of the crimes should be set forth in the Statute or in an annex to provide the clarity and precision required for criminal law, to provide additional guidance to the Prosecution and the Court, to ensure respect for the rights of the accused and to avoid any political manipulation of the definitions. It was further stated by some delegations that States,

and not judges, should be responsible for legislating the elements of the crimes. It was also suggested that the Statute could provide a mechanism under which the Court would elaborate the elements similar to the International Tribunal for the former Yugoslavia. However, other delegations expressed the view that it was not necessary to provide the detailed elements of the crimes, that the general definitions contained in the relevant instruments had been sufficiently precise for their practical application and that an elaboration of the elements of the crimes would be a complex and time-consuming task.

(f) Categories of responsible individuals

57. Several delegations expressed the view that it was important to consider the categories of individuals who could incur responsibility for the various crimes in the definitions thereof or in a general provision. Attention was drawn to the draft prepared by a committee of experts at Siracusa concerning the former approach.

2. Genocide

(a) Inclusion

58. There was general agreement that genocide met the jurisdictional standard referred to in the second paragraph of the preamble.

(b) Definition

59. Several delegations expressed the view that the Convention on the Prevention and Punishment of the Crime of Genocide provided an adequate basis for the definition of that crime; that the definition was authoritative, widely accepted and had attained the status of customary law, with reference being made to the advisory opinion of the International Court of Justice in this respect; and that the use of that definition would promote uniform jurisprudence in the field of international law. Several delegations also expressed the view that article II of the Convention should be reproduced without change. It was emphasized that the Preparatory Committee was not the appropriate forum for considering amendments to the Convention or for undertaking the codification or progressive development of law rather than defining the jurisdiction of the Court with respect to existing law.

60. Some delegations suggested that various aspects of the definition contained in article II required further clarification to provide the necessary guidance to the Court in its interpretation and application. With regard to the chapeau of article II, some delegations suggested that it might be necessary to clarify the intent required for various categories of individuals. However, other delegations suggested that the question of intent should be addressed under the applicable law or the general provisions of criminal law. Some delegations also suggested that the term "in part" required further clarification. Some delegations further suggested that consideration should be given to extending the definition to include social and political groups, while recognizing that [*18] that question could also be addressed in connection with crimes against humanity.

61. As regards article II, subparagraph (b), the view was expressed that the term "mental harm" required further clarification.

62. Regarding article II, subparagraph (d), the view was expressed that the phrase "imposing measures intended to prevent births within the group" required further clarification and could be replaced by the phrase "preventing births within the group".

63. With regard to article II, subparagraph (e), the view was expressed that the provision concerning forcible transfers of children should be expanded to include persons who were members of a particular group.

(c) Ancillary crimes

64. Several delegations drew attention to the ancillary crimes addressed in article III of the Genocide Convention, with some delegations suggesting the inclusion of that provision in the definition of genocide and other delegations suggesting that those crimes should be addressed in a general provision in relation to the various crimes.

3. Aggression

(a) Inclusion

65. There were different views concerning the inclusion of aggression.

66. Some delegations were of the view that aggression should be included to avoid a significant gap in the jurisdiction of the Court, as aggression was one of the most serious crimes of concern to the entire

international community, and that it should be regarded as a core crime under general international law; to create a deterrent and to avoid the impunity of the responsible individuals by providing a forum for their prosecution; to enhance the role and stature of the Court; to avoid any negative inference concerning individual criminal responsibility under customary law contrary to the Nurnberg Tribunal precedent affirmed by the General Assembly; and to avoid adopting a retrogressive statute 50 years after the Nurnberg and Tokyo tribunals and the adoption of the Charter of the United Nations.

67.   Some delegations supported the inclusion of this crime if general agreement could be reached on its definition and on the appropriate balance of the respective roles and functions of the Court and the Security Council, without delaying the establishment of the Court.

68.   Still other delegations were of the view that it should not be included because there was no generally accepted definition of aggression for the purpose of determining individual criminal responsibility; there was no precedent for individual criminal responsibility for acts of aggression in contrast to wars of aggression; it would be difficult and inappropriate to attempt to elaborate a sufficiently clear, precise and comprehensive definition of aggression; any attempt to elaborate a generally acceptable definition would substantially delay the establishment of the Court; the crime of aggression necessarily involved political and factual issues (such as territorial claims) that were inappropriate for adjudication by a criminal court; its inclusion could subject the Court to the struggle for political influence among States; the Court would still have jurisdiction over other crimes that often accompanied acts of [*19] aggression; it would be difficult to achieve an appropriate relationship between the judicial functions of the Court and the political functions entrusted to the Security Council under the Charter of the United Nations (for a discussion of this issue and art. 23, see paras. 137-139 below); and its inclusion could jeopardize the general acceptance or universality of the Court.

69.   Some delegations expressed support for providing a review mechanism under which aggression might be added at a later stage to avoid delaying the establishment of the Court pending the completion of a generally accepted definition. Other delegations were opposed to that view. The view was also expressed that appropriate language could be added to the preamble or an operative provision to avoid any negative inferences regarding individual criminal responsibility for such crimes under customary law. (See also the discussion of treaty-based crimes in paras. 103-115 below.)

      (b)   Definition

70.   Several delegations noted the absence of a generally agreed definition of aggression for the purpose of determining individual criminal responsibility under treaty law. Reference was made to various relevant instruments, including Article 2, paragraph 4, of the Charter of the United Nations, the Nurnberg Tribunal Charter, the Tokyo Tribunal Charter, General Assembly resolution 3314 (XXIX) of 14 December 1974, the draft Code and the new definition therefor, and the Siracusa draft.

71.   Some delegations were of the view that the Nurnberg Charter provided a precise definition of particularly serious offences resulting in individual criminal responsibility under customary law, while others described the definition contained therein as too imprecise for these purposes, or too restrictive or outdated.

72.   Some delegations expressed the view that the General Assembly resolution provided a generally accepted definition of aggression and contained elements that could be included in the definition of this crime. Other delegations expressed the view that the resolution did not contain a definition for the purpose of individual criminal responsibility; or indicate the acts that were of sufficient gravity for this purpose; or address a number of fundamental issues that could arise in criminal proceedings, including questions relating to exceptional situations involving the lawful use of force; or deal with possible defences, including self-defence.

73.   Some delegations suggested that it might be easier to reach agreement on a general definition of aggression similar to the new draft Code provision proposed by the ILC. Other delegations expressed a preference for a general definition accompanied by an enumeration of acts to ensure respect for the principle of legality and made reference to the General Assembly resolution and the Siracusa draft. Still other delegations believed it was not necessary to define aggression even if the Court had jurisdiction. Some delegations which had recommended that no definition of aggression should be included in the Statute proposed that a provision should be inserted which specified that, in accordance with the provisions

of the Charter, the Security Council would determine whether or not a situation could be considered aggression. The role of the Court would then be to establish whether or not that situation had given rise to the commission of crimes involving individual responsibility. On the role of the Security Council in relation to the crime of aggression, some delegations pointed out the need to avoid a situation in which the use of the veto in the Council might preclude the prosecution of a person by the Court for the commission of such a crime.

[*20] 4. Serious violations of the laws and customs applicable in armed conflict

(a) Inclusion

74. There was general agreement that serious violations of the laws and customs applicable in armed conflict could qualify for inclusion under the jurisdictional standard referred to in the second paragraph of the preamble.

75. Some delegations expressed the view that this category of crimes should be limited to exceptionally serious violations of international concern; to violations of fundamental protections or particularly serious acts which shocked the conscience of humanity; to situations in which national jurisdiction was unavailable or ineffective to ensure respect for the principle of complementarity and to avoid undermining the existing obligations of States to prosecute or extradite offenders; and to extremely serious situations in which the national courts refused, failed or were unable to exercise jurisdiction given the primary responsibility and interest of a State in maintaining military discipline.

76. Other delegations expressed the view that it was sufficient to refer to serious violations, that the reference to exceptionally serious violations could give rise to confusion regarding a third category of crimes especially regarding grave breaches, that grave breaches were by definition serious offences, that any attempt to distinguish between grave breaches would be inconsistent with the obligation to prosecute or extradite, that the seriousness criterion was more appropriate for distinguishing between violations of the laws and customs applicable in armed conflict which varied in gravity and that issues relating to national court jurisdiction should be addressed elsewhere.

77. There were proposals to include a seriousness criterion in the definition, to apply the criterion in listing the offences to obviate the need for a judicial determination or to include a general provision that would apply to all crimes.

(b) Character of the armed conflict

78. There were different views as to whether this category of crimes should include violations committed in international or non-international armed conflicts. Some delegations expressed the view that it was important to include violations committed in internal armed conflicts given their increasing frequency in recent years, that national criminal justice systems were less likely to be able to adequately address such violations and that individuals could be held criminally responsible for such violations as a matter of international law, with references being made to the Statute of the Rwanda Tribunal and the decision of the Yugoslavia Tribunal Appeals Chamber in the Tadic case. Other delegations expressed the view that violations committed in internal armed conflicts should not be included, that the inclusion of such violations was unrealistic and could undermine the universal or widespread acceptance of the Court, that individual criminal responsibility for such violations was not clearly established as a matter of existing law, with attention being drawn to the absence of criminal offence or enforcement provisions in Additional Protocol II, and that customary law had not changed in this respect since the Rwanda Tribunal Statute. Different views were also expressed concerning the direct applicability of the law of armed conflict to individuals in contrast to States.

[*21] (c) Definition

79. Reference was made to various relevant instruments, including the Nurnberg Tribunal Charter, the Yugoslavia Tribunal Statute, the Rwanda Tribunal Statute, the draft Code of Crimes and the new definition proposed by the ILC Special Rapporteur on the draft Code.

80. Several delegations expressed the view that grave breaches of the Geneva Conventions had attained the status of customary law and should be combined with other serious violations of the laws and customs applicable in armed conflict under subparagraph (c), with attention being drawn to the new definition proposed for the draft Code in contrast to the Yugoslavia Tribunal Statute and a proposal being made to amend the title of this category of crimes accordingly.

81. Several delegations expressed the view that the list of offences should include sufficiently serious violations of the Hague law, with references being made to the 1907 Hague Convention IV respecting the Laws and Customs of War on Land and its annexed regulations and the 1954 Hague Convention for the Protection of Cultural Property in the Event of Armed Conflict; grave breaches of the Geneva Conventions, with references also being made to common article 3 thereof and grave breaches of Additional Protocol I; and comparably serious violations of other relevant conventions that had attained the status of customary law. Different views were expressed concerning the customary law status of Additional Protocols I and II. There were proposals to incorporate provisions of the protocols without referring thereto and to add Additional Protocol II under article 20, subparagraph (e). The view was also expressed that Additional Protocol I had not so far secured the most widespread acceptance by the international community, which would be essential for the Protocol to qualify for inclusion in the statute.

     5.   Crimes against humanity

       (a) Inclusion

82. There was general agreement that crimes against humanity met the jurisdictional standard referred to in the second paragraph of the preamble.

       (b) Definition

83. Several delegations noted the absence of a generally accepted definition of crimes against humanity under treaty law. Reference was however made to such relevant instruments as the Nurnberg Tribunal Charter, Control Council Law Number 10, the Tokyo Tribunal Charter, the Yugoslavia Tribunal Statute, the Rwanda Tribunal Statute, the draft Code of Crimes against the Peace and Security of Mankind and the Siracusa draft. The view was also expressed that the definition of crimes against humanity should only be dealt with upon completion of the International Law Commission's work on the draft Code.

       (c) General criteria

84. A number of delegations attributed particular importance to the general criteria for crimes against humanity to distinguish such crimes from ordinary crimes under national law and to avoid interference with national court jurisdiction with respect to the latter, with the discussion focusing primarily on the criteria contained in article 3 of the Rwanda Tribunal Statute.

[*22]   (d) Widespread or systematic criteria

85. There was general support for the widespread or systematic criteria to indicate the scale and magnitude of the offences. The following were also mentioned as elements to be taken into account: an element of planning, policy, conspiracy or organization; a multiplicity of victims; acts of a certain duration rather than a temporary, exceptional or limited phenomenon; and acts committed as part of a policy, plan, conspiracy or a campaign rather than random, individual or isolated acts in contrast to war crimes. Some delegations expressed the view that this criterion could be further clarified by referring to widespread and systematic acts of international concern to indicate acts that were appropriate for international adjudication; acts committed on a massive scale to indicate a multiplicity of victims in contrast to ordinary crimes under national law; acts committed systematically or as part of a public policy against a segment of the civilian population; acts committed in application of a concerted plan to indicate the necessary degree of intent, concert or planning; acts committed with the consent of a Government or of a party in control of territory; and exceptionally serious crimes of international concern to exclude minor offences, as in article 20, paragraph (e). Some delegations expressed the view that the criteria should be cumulative rather than alternative.

       (e) Attack against any civilian population

86. A number of delegations emphasized that crimes against humanity could be committed against any civilian population, in contrast to the traditional notion of war crimes. However, some delegations expressed the view that the phrase "attack against any civilian population" which appeared in the Rwanda Tribunal Statute was vague, unnecessary and confusing since the reference to attack could be interpreted as referring to situations involving an armed conflict and the term "civilian" was often used in international humanitarian law and was unnecessary in the current context. There were proposals to delete this phrase or to replace the word "attack" by the word "acts". However, the view was also expressed that the word "attack" was intended to indicate some use of force rather than an armed attack and a number of delegations

believed that the phrase should be retained to avoid significantly changing the existing definition of these crimes.

(f) Motivation or grounds

87. There were different views concerning the general motivational requirement or grounds criterion contained in the Rwanda Tribunal Statute. The view was expressed that it would be useful to include these grounds to demonstrate the types of situations in which crimes against humanity were committed, as indicated by the recent events in the former Yugoslavia and in Rwanda which had led to the establishment of the ad hoc tribunals. However, other delegations expressed the view that the inclusion of such a criterion would complicate the task of the Prosecution by significantly increasing its burden of proof in requiring evidence of this subjective element; that crimes against humanity could be committed against other groups, including intellectuals and social, cultural or political groups; that it was important to include crimes against such groups since the definition of genocide might not be expanded to cover them; and that the criterion was not required under customary law, with attention being drawn to the Yugoslavia Tribunal Statute and the draft Code. There was a proposal to include a general reference to the commission of the crimes on discriminatory grounds.

[*23] (g) Nexus to armed conflict

88. There were different views as to whether it was necessary to include a nexus to an armed conflict which was not included in the Rwanda Tribunal Statute. Some delegations expressed the view that crimes against humanity were invariably committed in situations involving some type of armed conflict, as indicated by the ad hoc tribunals; that existing law required some type of connection to an armed conflict in a broad sense, with references being made to the Nurnberg Charter, the Yugoslavia Tribunal Statute, the memorandum of its President and the Nikolic case pending before it; and that customary law had not changed owing to the adoption of human rights instruments which provided specific procedures for addressing violations or the Rwanda Tribunal Statute.

89. However, several delegations expressed the view that crimes against humanity could occur in time of armed conflict or in time of peace and that the armed conflict nexus that appeared in the Nurnberg Tribunal Charter was no longer required under existing law, with attention being drawn to article I of the Genocide Convention, Control Council Law Number 10, the Convention on the Non-Applicability of Statutory Limitations to War Crimes and Crimes against Humanity, the Rwanda Tribunal Statute, the Yugoslavia Tribunal Appeals Chamber decision in the Tadic case and the draft Code. The view was also expressed that although crimes against humanity often occurred in situations involving armed conflict, these crimes could also occur in time of peace or in situations that were ambiguous.

90. The view was expressed that peacetime offences might require an additional international dimension or criterion to indicate the crimes that would be appropriate for adjudication by the Court, possibly by limiting the individuals who could commit such crimes. Some delegations questioned the need for an additional criterion assuming that sufficiently serious, grave or inhumane acts were committed on a widespread and systematic basis, with attention being drawn to proposals for clarifying this general criterion to indicate more clearly the offences that would be appropriate for international adjudication.

(h) List of acts

91. Several delegations expressed the view that the definition should include a list of exceptionally serious, grave or inhumane acts which shocked the conscience of humanity. Some delegations expressed the view that these acts could be drawn from the identical list contained in the Yugoslavia and Rwanda Tribunal statutes, with some delegations indicating provisions that might require further consideration or clarification.

(i) Murder

92. Some delegations expressed the view that murder required further clarification given the divergences in national criminal laws. There were proposals to refer to wilful killing or to murder, including killings done by knowingly creating conditions likely to cause death.

(ii) Extermination

93. The view was expressed that extermination should be deleted as a duplication of murder or clarified to distinguish between the two, with a proposal being made to refer to alternative offences.

[*24]   (iii) Enslavement

94. Some delegations expressed the view that enslavement required further clarification based on the relevant legal instruments. There were proposals to refer to enslavement, including slavery-related practices and forced labour; or the establishment or maintenance over persons of a status of slavery, servitude or forced labour. The view was expressed that forced labour, if included, should be limited to clearly unacceptable acts.

(iv) Deportation

95. Some delegations expressed the view that deportation required further clarification to exclude lawful deportation under national and international law. There were proposals to refer to discriminatory and arbitrary deportation in violation of international legal norms; deportation targeting individuals as members of a particular ethnic group; deportation without due process of law; deportation or unlawful confinement of civilian population; or deportation resulting in death or serious bodily injury.

(v) Imprisonment

96. Some delegations expressed the view that this offence required further clarification to exclude lawful imprisonment in the exercise of State authority. There were proposals to refer to imprisonment in violation of due process or judicial guarantees; imprisonment in violation of international norms prohibiting arbitrary arrest and detention; and imprisonment resulting in death or serious bodily injury.

(vi) Torture

97. Some delegations expressed the view that this offence required further clarification. There was a proposal to incorporate relevant provisions of the Convention against Torture and Other Cruel, Inhuman or Degrading Treatment or Punishment without requiring that the acts be committed by a public official if the other general criteria were met. There was also a proposal to define this offence in terms of cruel treatment, including torture, and to add mutilation as a separate offence.

(vii) Rape

98. There were proposals to refer to rape committed on national or religious grounds; rape, other serious assaults of a sexual nature, such as forced impregnation; or outrages upon person dignity, in particular humiliating and degrading treatment, rape or enforced prostitution, with attention being drawn to recent acts committed as part of a campaign of ethnic cleansing.

(viii) Persecution on political, racial or religious grounds

99. Some delegations expressed the view that persecution should be further clarified and limited to the most egregious cases, while other delegations questioned whether it met the jurisdictional standard and whether it constituted a general policy criterion or a separate offence. These other delegations did not consider it appropriate to include persecution within the jurisdiction of the Court. There was a proposal to include persecution on political, racial, religious or cultural grounds. Reference was also made to the Siracusa draft.

[*25]   (ix) Other inhumane acts

100. Some delegations favoured the inclusion of this category to cover similar acts that were not envisaged and might not be foreseeable; to enable the prosecution of individuals for similar inhumane acts that were not explicitly listed, as in the case of the Yugoslavia Tribunal; and to facilitate the expansion of the Court's jurisdiction in response to the continuing development of international law, with attention being drawn to similar language contained in various definitions of crimes against humanity and national criminal laws

101. Other delegations expressed the view that this category should not be included as it would not provide the clarity and precision required by the principle of legality, would not provide the necessary certainty concerning the crimes that would be subject to international prosecution and adjudication, would not sufficiently guarantee the rights of the accused and would place an onerous burden on the Court to develop the law.

102. There were proposals to limit this category by interpreting it in the context of the definition as a whole, or by referring to other inhumane acts of a similar nature; or by referring to other similar inhumane acts accompanied by a description of their general characteristics and specific examples. There were also proposals to prepare an exhaustive list by adding similar acts that constituted serious violations of the laws and customs applicable in armed conflict or grave breaches of the Geneva Conventions, such as taking civilians as hostages, wilfully depriving a civilian of the right to a fair and regular trial, wilfully causing

great suffering or serious injury to body or health and extensive destruction and appropriation of property carried out unlawfully and wantonly. The view was expressed that the double criminality of such acts would not be inconsistent with the principle of legality since the Court would decide the preponderant elements of an act in determining individual criminal responsibility. The view was also expressed that the Statute could provide an amendment or review procedure that would enable the States parties to the Statute to add other offences at a later stage.

  6.   Treaty-based crimes
      (a)   Inclusion

103. Several delegations expressed the view that the jurisdiction of the Court should be limited to the core crimes under general international law to avoid any question of individual criminal responsibility resulting from a State not being a party to the relevant legal instrument, to facilitate the acceptance of the jurisdiction of the Court by States that were not parties to particular treaties, to facilitate the functioning of the Court by obviating the need for complex State consent requirements or jurisdictional mechanisms for different categories of crimes, to avoid overburdening the limited financial and personnel resources of the Court or trivializing its role and functions, and to avoid jeopardizing the general acceptance of the Court or delaying its establishment.

104. Some delegations expressed support for including various treaty-based crimes which, having regard to the conduct alleged, constituted exceptionally serious crimes of international concern as envisaged in article 20, paragraph (e). The importance of the principle of complementarity was emphasized with respect to these crimes.

105. Some delegations favoured including a separate mechanism for referring exceptional cases where all the interested States concerned agreed. Such a [*26] mechanism would involve a separate State consent regime from that applicable to crimes in respect of which universal jurisdiction already existed.

      (b)   International terrorism

106. A number of delegations were of the view that international terrorism qualified for inclusion under the jurisdictional standard referred to in the second paragraph of the preamble given the serious nature of such acts which shocked the conscience of humanity and the magnitude of the consequences thereof in terms of human suffering and property damage, the increasing frequency of international terrorist acts committed on an unprecedented scale, the resulting threat to international peace and security indicated by recent Security Council practice and the concern of the international community indicated by the condemnation of those crimes in numerous resolutions and declarations. The view was expressed that including those crimes in the Court's jurisdiction would strengthen the ability of the international community to combat those crimes, give States the option of referring cases to the Court in exceptional situations and avoid jurisdictional disputes between States. The view was also expressed that the Court might consider cases of international terrorism in exceptionally serious cases when the Security Council referred the question to the Court for its consideration. Some delegations also emphasized the importance of distinguishing between international terrorism and the right to self-determination, freedom and independence of peoples forcibly deprived of that right, particularly peoples under colonial and racist regimes or other forms of alien domination. References were made to the relevant treaties listed in the annex to the draft statute, the Declaration on Measures to Eliminate International Terrorism adopted by the General Assembly at its forty-ninth session 7/ and the draft Code. The view was expressed that it was precisely these crimes of international terrorism in respect of which national jurisdiction would in many cases not be available.

107. A number of other delegations were of the view that international terrorism should not be included because there was no general definition of the crime and elaborating such a definition would substantially delay the establishment of the Court; these crimes were often similar to common crimes under national law in contrast to the crimes listed in other subparagraphs of article 20; the inclusion of these crimes would impose a substantial burden on the Court and significantly increase its costs while detracting from the other core crimes; these crimes could be more effectively investigated and prosecuted by national authorities under existing international cooperation arrangements for reasons similar to those relating to illicit drug trafficking; and the inclusion of the crimes could lessen the resolve of States to conduct national investigations and prosecutions and politicize the functions of the Court.

(c)   Apartheid

108. Some delegations favoured including apartheid and other forms of racial discrimination as defined in the relevant conventions.

(d)   Torture

109. Some delegations expressed support for the inclusion of torture and referred to the definition contained in the relevant international legal instruments. The view was also expressed that torture was a crime under the domestic law of States and should not be included.

[*27]   (e)   Hostages

110. The view was expressed that the inclusion of the Hostages Convention must be considered.

(f)   Illicit drug trafficking

111. Some delegations expressed the view that particularly serious drug trafficking offences which involved an international dimension should be included, that these offences had serious consequences on the world population and that there was no unified system for addressing these crimes because of divergences in national laws. Reference was made to the convention listed in the annex to the ILC draft statute as well as the new definition proposed by the ILC Special Rapporteur.

112. The view was expressed that drug trafficking should not be included because these crimes were not of the same nature as those listed in other paragraphs of article 20 and were of such a quantity as to flood the Court; the Court would not have the necessary resources to conduct the lengthy and complex investigations required to prosecute the crimes; the investigation of the crimes often involved highly sensitive information and confidential strategies; and the crimes could be more effectively investigated and prosecuted by national authorities under existing international cooperation arrangements.

(g)   Attacks against United Nations and associated personnel

113. Some delegations expressed the view that special consideration should be given to including violations referred to in the Convention on the Safety of United Nations and Associated Personnel since they were undoubtedly exceptionally serious crimes of international concern; the attacks were committed against persons who represented the international community and protected its interests; the attacks were in effect directed or committed against the international community; United Nations and associated personnel were usually involved in situations in which the national law-enforcement or criminal justice system was not fully functional or capable of addressing these crimes; and the international community had a special responsibility to ensure the prosecution and punishment of these crimes. There were different views as to whether and to what extent these violations constituted crimes under general international law which could be included in the jurisdiction of the Court prior to the entry into force of the Convention.

(h)   Serious threats to the environment

114. The view was expressed that the inclusion of serious threats to the environment must be considered.

(i)   Review procedure

115. Some delegations favoured limiting the initial jurisdiction of the Court and including a review procedure for considering the addition of other crimes at a later stage to avoid delaying the establishment of the Court and to take account of the adoption or entry into force of relevant treaties in the future. A number of delegations presented a proposal to this effect. Others were not in favour of the inclusion of such a procedure since there was no point in delaying decision-making. There were different views concerning the effectiveness of review procedure clauses. The consideration of this question was described as premature. The view was expressed that treaties adopted after the establishment of the Court could include appropriate jurisdictional clauses similar to those relating to the International Court of Justice.

[*28] D.   Trigger mechanism

116. The trigger mechanism touches upon two main clusters of issues: acceptance of the Court's jurisdiction, State consent requirements and the conditions for the exercise of jurisdiction (arts. 21 and 22); and who can trigger the system and the role of the Prosecutor (arts. 23 and 25).

1.   Acceptance of the Court's jurisdiction, State consent requirements and the conditions for the exercise of jurisdiction: articles 21 and 22

117. Some delegations felt that the treatment of jurisdiction in articles 21 and 22 of the Statute was insufficient. In their view, the inherent jurisdiction of the Court should not be limited to genocide, but

should extend to all the core crimes. Acceptance of inherent jurisdiction for the core crimes would require significant revision of articles 21 and 22. From this perspective, the Court would not need specific State consent to establish its jurisdiction. States, by virtue of becoming party to the Statute, would be consenting to its jurisdiction. This meaning of inherent jurisdiction, some delegations felt, was fully compatible with respect for State sovereignty, since States would have expressed their consent at the time of ratification of the Statute as opposed to having to express it in respect of every single crime listed in the Statute at different stages. Hence, there would be no need for a selective "opt in" or "opt out" approach. In accord with this view, the opening clause of article 21 should be changed to state that the Court should have jurisdiction over the crimes listed in article 20. Article 22 would become superfluous and should be deleted. It was, however, noted that if the Statute were to include crimes other than core crimes, the "opt in" regime could be maintained for them. In this regard, a remark was made that a distinction should be made between the jurisdiction of the Court per se and the exercise of that jurisdiction or the terms and conditions for the exercise of jurisdiction; these issues all linked to the question of admissibility under article 35. In this context, a comment was made that article 21 dealt with the conditions of the exercise of jurisdiction by the Court, by establishing the Court's jurisdiction ratione personae.

118. Some delegations found inherent jurisdiction to be a contradiction in terms, for the jurisdiction of the Court would arise exclusively out of the contractual stipulations in the instrument by which the Court would be created. They also found inherent jurisdiction incompatible with complementarity. Other delegations saw it differently. For them, the concept of inherent jurisdiction meant that the Court was invested with jurisdiction by virtue of its constituent instrument, with no need for additional consent to exercise its jurisdiction. Inherent jurisdiction also did not, in their view, imply that the Court, in all circumstances, had a better claim than national Courts to exercise jurisdiction. It was therefore possible that a case could arise in relation to a crime which was within the Court's inherent jurisdiction but which would none the less be tried by a national jurisdiction, because it was determined that the exercise of national jurisdiction would be more appropriate in that particular case.

119. Some other delegations expressed reservations about the inherent jurisdiction of the Court over any crime, including the core crimes. They believed that the regime of "opt in" provided for in article 22 was more likely to maximize universal participation. In their view, this approach was also consistent with the principle of sovereignty and the regimes set out by the treaties on the core crimes themselves. A comment was made that the "opt in" approach was compatible with the practice of adherence to the jurisdiction of the International Court of Justice. Similarly, in the current context, by [*29] becoming party to the Statute of the Court, States did not automatically accept the jurisdiction of the Court in a particular case. This would be done by means of a declaration, in accordance with article 22 of the Statute.

120. Some delegations saw merit in having genocide come under the inherent jurisdiction of the Court. Reference was made to article VI of the Genocide Convention, which provides that persons accused of genocide should be tried by a competent tribunal or by such international penal tribunal as may have jurisdiction with respect to those contracting parties which shall have accepted its jurisdiction. However, a view was expressed that taking into account that the Genocide Convention contained provisions on national jurisdiction and that the number of States parties to it was less than 120, the inclusion of genocide as a crime within the so-called inherent jurisdiction of the Court would not only undermine the relevant provisions of the Genocide Convention on national jurisdiction, but would also run the risk of discouraging the non-States parties to that Convention from signing the Statute.

121. It was noted that the question of acceptance of the Court's jurisdiction was inextricably linked to the question of preconditions for the exercise of that jurisdiction, or consent, as well as to the question of who might bring complaints. In this connection, a comment was made that the jurisdiction of the Court, even under the core crimes approach, embraced different categories of crimes of different degrees of seriousness required for bringing charges. For example, the threshold for establishing genocide was rather high, compared to many war crimes which were not as high. However, not every single war crime was of sufficient serious international concern to warrant its submission to the Court.

122. Some delegations supported the requirement, set out in article 21 (1) (b), calling for the consent of the custodial State and the State where the crime was committed. In their view, such a consent requirement was essential, since the Court could not function without the cooperation of these States. A comment was

made that custody over a suspect, however, should be in accordance with international law; the maxim *male captus, bene detentus* should have no application to the jurisdiction of the Court. It was further stated that, as a general rule, the number of States whose consent was required should be kept to the minimum. Otherwise, the likelihood of one of these States not being party to the Statute would increase, precluding the Court from initiating proceedings.

123. The remark was made that the word "custody" in article 21 (1) (b) (i) was misleading, for it appeared to include mere presence, even a transitory presence. This was inconsistent with current State practice, according to which an accused is normally located in or extradited to the State in which he or she committed the crime. Furthermore, in current State practice, the potential for political abuse was controlled in a number of ways, including comity and diplomatic immunity. In contrast, the current draft, according to this view, left open significant possibilities for efforts by States to embroil the Court in legal controversies and political disputes, which could undermine its effectiveness.

124. In addition, it was noted that the actual location of the accused was not important at the initial stage of the proceedings, but only at the stage of arrest. Hence, the role of the custodial State should be addressed in connection with the obligation to cooperate with the Court, and not in connection with jurisdiction. Even in that context, it sufficed, according to this view, for the custodial State to be party to the Statute; it was not necessary for it to have accepted a particular type of jurisdiction.

[*30] 125. A view was expressed that the precondition to the exercise of the Court's jurisdiction imposed by article 21 (1) (b) (i) was not consistent with subsequent provisions in the Statute, namely those that allowed the Court to confirm an indictment against a person who was not detained, and with article 53 (2) (b) and (c).

126. As regards the requirement of consent of the State where the crime was committed, a comment was made suggesting modifying the language of article 21 (1) (b) (ii) by means of the addition of the words "if applicable" in order to cover situations where the crime might have been committed outside the territory of any State, such as on the high seas.

127. It was also stated that in certain types of conflict, in order to determine the States whose consent were necessary for the proceedings of the Court, one should look at the whole situation and not just the State where the crime was committed. The example given was war crimes, where at least two States would have interests in the case and the State where the war crime had been committed could be the one that started the war in violation of international law. Going beyond the core crimes, to terrorism, for example, it was noted that there would be other States, such as the one which was the target of the crime, with a real interest in the proceedings, yet whose interests were not taken into account by the current draft. It was further stated that a large number of States were precluded by their domestic law from extraditing their nationals for criminal prosecution abroad. The view was also expressed that the consent of the State of nationality of the accused to the jurisdiction of the Court should also be a precondition to the exercise of that jurisdiction. The reasons for that suggestion are set out in paragraph 105 of the report of the Ad Hoc Committee on the establishment of an International Criminal Court. 8/ Alternatively, the State of nationality of the suspect would have to extradite only if it refused to commence prosecution, in good faith, within a reasonable period of time. This approach, according to this view, was compatible with the principle of universal jurisdiction and should be taken into account in the Statute.

128. It was also noted that the Court could not exercise jurisdiction in relation to States not party to the Statute. This, it was agreed, could become a particularly difficult issue when the State not party was the custodial State or its cooperation was indispensable to the prosecution. For this reason, some delegations were of the view that it would be proper for the Security Council to have a role which was respectful of the independence of the Court in humanitarian situations.

    2.   Who can trigger the system and the role of the Prosecutor: articles 23 and 25
      (a) The Security Council: article 23

129. Delegates in their comments appeared to agree that the Statute would not affect the role of the Security Council as prescribed in the Charter of the United Nations. The Council would, therefore, continue to exercise primary authority to determine and respond to threats to and breaches of the peace and to acts of aggression; the obligation of Member States to accept and carry out the decisions of the Council under Article 25 of the Charter would remain unchanged. However, some delegations voiced three

concerns: first, that it was important, in the design of the Statute, to ensure that the international system of dispute resolution - and in particular the role of the Security Council - would not be undermined; secondly, that the Statute should not confer any more authority on the Security Council than that already assigned to it by the Charter; and thirdly, that the relationship between the Court and the Council [*31] should not undermine the judicial independence and integrity of the Court or the sovereign equality of States.

130. In the light of the above concerns, some delegations found that article 23 was completely unacceptable and should be deleted. Others felt it was in need of substantial revision precisely because it conferred more authority on the Security Council than did the Charter or than was necessary in contemporary international relations; it also diminished the requisite judicial independence of the Court. In their view, the Security Council was a political organ whose primary concern was the maintenance of peace and security, resolving disputes between States and having sufficient effective power to implement its decisions. The Council made its decisions, according to these delegations, taking into account political considerations. The Court, in contrast, was a judicial body, concerned only with the criminal responsibility of individuals who committed serious crimes deeply offensive to any moral sense.

131. Some other delegations, however, favoured the proposed article 23 of the Statute. In their view, the article corresponded with the role for the Security Council carved out in the Charter and properly took account of the current situation of international relations. They did not agree with the view that decisions of the Security Council were exclusively political in nature. They were convinced that, while it was a political organ, the Security Council made decisions in accordance with the Charter of the United Nations and international law and that these decisions, in particular those adopted under Chapter VII of the Charter, had legal or political-legal character. On the contrary, according to this view, it was more likely for a State to lodge a complaint with the Court inspired purely by political motives.

      (i)   Article 23 (1)

132. Some delegations requested the deletion of article 23 (1), empowering the Security Council to refer a "matter" to the Court. Others favoured its retention. For the former delegations, a referral by the Security Council would affect the independence of the Court in the administration of justice. Delegations holding this view believed that a political body should not determine whether a judicial body should act. In addition, referral by the Security Council would dispense with the requirements of article 21 as well as complementarity and the sovereign equality of States. It was further noted that article 23 (1) assigned the right of referral of a matter to the Court only to the Security Council. Taking into account current efforts to define the new world order, in which the relationship between the Security Council and the General Assembly had come under scrutiny, these delegations wondered if such right should also be conferred upon the General Assembly.

133. Those delegations favouring the retention of article 23 (1) based their views on the following: the Security Council had already demonstrated a capacity to address the core humanitarian law crimes through the creation of two ad hoc tribunals, for the former Yugoslavia and for Rwanda, and had created the International Commission of Inquiry in Burundi to report on violations of international humanitarian law; one of the purposes of the Court was to obviate the creation of ad hoc tribunals. In this context, the Council's referral should activate a mandatory jurisdiction, similar to the powers of the ad hoc tribunals. The Council's referral would not, according to these delegations, impair the independence of the Court because the Prosecutor would be free to decide whether there was sufficient evidence to indict a particular individual for a crime.

[*32] 134. It was also noted that article 23 (1) limited the Security Council's referral authority to Chapter VII situations. Some delegations proposed that the Council's referral authority should be extended to matters under Chapter VI as well. They mentioned Articles 33 and 36 of the Charter, which encourage Council action of a peaceful character with respect to any dispute, the continuance of which was likely to endanger the maintenance of international peace and security. One of the "appropriate procedures" described, it was noted, was "judicial settlement". Those pressing this point suggested deleting "Chapter VII of" from article 23 (1) so that Chapter VI actions would also be covered. Some other delegations did not favour the extension of the Council's right of referral to Chapter VI, while some other delegations reserved their position on this issue.

135. It was suggested that the effective functioning of the Court could be enhanced without interfering with the primary responsibility of the Security Council for the maintenance of international peace and security by allowing the Court to investigate or prosecute a case unless the Security Council directed otherwise.

136. As regards the use of the word "matter" in article 23 (1), a suggestion was made to replace it with "case". The suggestion was also made to provide that any referral should be accompanied by such supporting documentation as was available to the Security Council. This modification of article 23, according to the latter suggestion, would impose on the Council the same burdens and responsibilities imposed on a complainant State. A number of delegations, while not disagreeing with the latter, did not agree with the proposal to change the word "matter" to "case". They held the view that the Council, while having the power to refer a situation to the Court, should not be able to refer an individual to the Court. The word "situation" was however considered too broad by some delegations.

(ii) Article 23 (2)

137. With respect to the requirement of article 23 (2) that the Security Council should have determined that an act of aggression had already been committed before the Court could process complaints on individual responsibility for an act of aggression, two different views were expressed. According to one view, the paragraph should be retained if aggression was going to be included in the list of crimes in the Statute. According to another view, paragraph 2 should be deleted even if aggression was included in the list of crimes in the Statute. Some delegations reserved their position pending a final decision on the inclusion of aggression in the list of crimes.

138. A number of delegations recalled their opposition to the inclusion of the crime of aggression in the list of crimes in the Statute (for their views, see para. 68 above) and observed that if aggression were excluded from the list of crimes, there would be no need to maintain article 23 (2). But article 23 (2) would be indispensable if aggression were included in the list. They referred to Article 39 of the Charter, according to which the Security Council has the exclusive power to determine whether an act of aggression has been committed. In their view, it was difficult to see how an individual could be charged with an act of aggression - assuming a definition for individual culpability were agreed upon - without the threshold requirement of an act of aggression first being determined by the Security Council.

139. Delegations that favoured the deletion of article 23 (2), while supporting the retention of aggression as a crime under the Statute, based their view on the following grounds. First, in practice, the Security Council often responded to situations under Chapter VII of the Charter without explicitly determining [*33] the existence of an act of aggression; requiring such a determination for the exercise of jurisdiction by the Court could impede the effective functioning of the Court. Secondly, because of the veto power, the Council might be unable to characterize an act as aggression. Thirdly, the Council's determination of an act of aggression was based on political considerations, while the Court would have to establish criminal culpability on legal grounds. In this connection and to protect the prerogatives of the Council, it was suggested that a provision should be included to the effect that the Statute was without prejudice to the functions of the Security Council under Chapter VII. However, a view was expressed that the determination by the Security Council on the existence of an act of aggression should be binding on the deliberations of the Court. Yet another view was expressed that article 23 (2) could remain in place if supplemented by a provision clarifying that the decisions by the Security Council on the commission of an act of aggression by a State was not binding on the Court as regards the question of individual responsibility.

(iii) Article 23 (3)

140. As regards article 23 (3), providing that no prosecution may be commenced arising from a situation being dealt with by the Security Council in accordance with Chapter VII unless the Council otherwise decides, a number of different views were expressed.

141. According to one view, the necessity for the retention of the paragraph arose from the fact that the Security Council had the primary responsibility for the maintenance of international peace and security. Delegations expressing this view thought it would be unacceptable if the Court were empowered to act in defiance of the Charter of the United Nations and to interfere in delicate matters under consideration by the Security Council. According to this view, paragraph 3 should be revised to include, not only Chapter VII situations, but all situations which were being dealt with by the Council.

142. According to another view, because paragraph 3 was designed to function as the political equivalent of the sub judice rule, its ambit was so wide as to infringe on the judicial independence of the Court. Reference was made to the large number of situations currently under consideration by the Security Council and the fact that in many cases the Security Council had been "seized" of these same situations continuously for more than 30 years without taking effective action. It was noted that, under paragraph 3, the Council would have the authority to preclude the Court from examining any complaint in respect of them. It was further noted that the Statute of the International Court of Justice did not prevent the Court from hearing cases relating to international peace and security which were being dealt with concurrently by the Security Council. According to this view, paragraph 3 should therefore be deleted.

143. Yet another view, while concerned about the implication of paragraph 3 for the judicial independence of the Court, found some ground for a safeguard clause, but not as currently formulated. According to this view, the words "being dealt with" should be narrowly defined to limit their scope. A narrow interpretation of these words was found compatible with the intention of the Commission as explained in its commentary to the paragraph, which interpreted it to mean "a situation in respect of which Chapter VII action is actually being taken" by the Security Council. Even this interpretation, according to this view, left many questions unresolved; for example, the words "threat to or breach of the peace" were open to broad interpretation and could conceivably cover all cases likely to fall within the Court's jurisdiction. Considering that national Courts could prosecute a case relating to a situation under consideration by the Security Council, the reasonableness of denying the Court the same power as national Courts was questioned. It was proposed to include a [*34] provision stating that "should no action be taken in relation to a situation which has been referred to the Security Council as a threat to or breach of the peace or an act of aggression under Chapter VII of the Charter within a reasonable time, the Court shall exercise its jurisdiction in respect of that situation". The purpose of this proposal was to allow the Court to take action in situations where the Security Council, though seized of a matter, would not or could not act upon it. A suggestion was also made to change the emphasis in the paragraph, by allowing the Court to proceed with a complaint unless the Security Council took a formal decision in accordance with Article 27 of the Charter to ask the Court not to proceed on the basis that the Council was taking effective action in relation to that situation or a matter referred to the Council as a threat to or breach of the peace. This would avoid the veto being available in respect of the Court's jurisdiction.

144. Concern was voiced about the possibility of conflict between decisions by the Court and the Security Council on the same issue. There was a feeling that those concerns were not adequately dealt with in the current wording of article 23.

    (b)   States: article 25

145. It was observed that the complaint mechanism set out in article 25 was premised on the right of any State party, under certain conditions, to lodge a complaint with the Prosecutor alleging that a crime "appears to have been committed". Some delegations found this arrangement satisfactory. Others, for different reasons, felt that it needed substantial modification.

146. Some delegations were uneasy with a regime that allowed any State party to select individual suspects and lodge complaints with the Prosecutor with respect to them, for this could encourage politicization of the complaint procedure. Instead, according to these delegations, States parties should be empowered to refer "situations" to the Prosecutor in a manner similar to the way provided for the Security Council in article 23 (1). Once a situation was referred to the Prosecutor, it was noted, he or she could initiate a case against an individual. It was suggested, however, that in certain circumstances a referral of a situation to the Prosecutor might point to particular individuals as likely targets for investigation.

147. Some delegations felt that only those States parties to the Statute with an interest in the case should be able to lodge a complaint. Interested States were identified as the custodial State, the State where the crime was committed, the State of nationality of the suspect, the State whose nationals were victims and the State which was the target of the crime. Some other delegations opined that the crimes under the Statute were, by their nature, of concern to the international community as a whole. They also noted that the jurisdiction of the Court would only be engaged if some Government failed to fulfil its obligations to prosecute an international crime; then, in their view, all States parties would become interested parties. Some delegations felt that articles 34, 35 and 36 of the Statute provided adequate safeguards against abuse.

In addition to preventing political abuse of the process, they suggested that the Prosecutor should notify all other States parties to the Statute, allowing them the opportunity to express their views on whether to proceed with the case before the Court decided. Some delegations proposed that one could require more than one State to lodge a complaint in order to signify that a serious crime of interest to the international community was at issue.

148. Some other delegations were of the view that the States which could lodge a complaint not only should be party to the Statute, but should also have accepted the Court's jurisdiction in respect of the specific crime for which the State [*35] had made a complaint. In this respect, it was noted that for the crime of genocide a complaint could be made to the Court by a State party to the Genocide Convention but not party to the Statute. In other words, the acceptance requirements of articles 21 (1) and 25 (2) would be circumvented.

    (c) The Prosecutor

149. Some delegations found the role of the Prosecutor, under article 25, too restricted. In their view, States or the Security Council, for a variety of political reasons, would be unlikely to lodge a complaint. The Prosecutor should therefore be empowered to initiate investigations ex officio or on the basis of information obtained from any source. It was noted that the Prosecutors of the two existing ad hoc tribunals were granted such rights; there was no reason to deny the same power to the Prosecutor of this Court. Hence the suggestion to add a new paragraph to article 25 along the lines of article 18 (1) of the Statute of the Tribunal for the former Yugoslavia and article 17 (1) of the Statute of the Tribunal for Rwanda. Under this system, therefore, individuals would also be able to lodge complaints.

150. In order to prevent any abuse of the process by any of the triggering parties, a procedure was proposed requiring that in case a complaint was lodged by a State or an individual or initiated by the Prosecutor, the Prosecutor would first have to satisfy himself or herself that a prima facie case against an individual obtained and the requirements of admissibility had been satisfied. The Prosecutor would then have to present the matter to a chamber of the Court (which would not ultimately try the case) and inform all interested States so that they would have the opportunity to participate in the proceedings. In this respect the indictment chamber was considered as the appropriate chamber. The chamber, upon a hearing, would decide whether the matter should be pursued by the Prosecutor or the case should be dropped. Up to this point, the procedure would be in camera and confidential, thus preventing any publicity about the case and protecting the interest of the States.

151. Some other delegations could not agree with the notion of an independent power for the Prosecutor to institute a proceedings before the Court. In their view, such an independent power would lead to politicization of the Court and allegations that the Prosecutor had acted for political motives. This would undermine the credibility of the Court. This power could also lead to overwhelming the limited resources of the Prosecutor with frivolous complaints. A view was expressed that the complaint lodged by the Prosecutor on his or her own initiative lacking the support of the complainant State would be ineffective. A view was further expressed that developments in international law had yet to reach a stage where the international community as a whole was prepared to empower the Prosecutor to initiate investigations. It was unrealistic to seek to expand the Prosecutor's role, according to this view, if widespread acceptance of the Court was to be achieved.

    (d) Other comments

152. Two other comments were made in respect of article 25. First, preconditions to the exercise of jurisdiction should be looked at and satisfied at the very beginning and before the stage of investigation, lest the Court invest substantial resources only to discover that it could not exercise jurisdiction. Secondly, some delegations felt that article 25 on complaint was too complicated and would make the exercise of the jurisdiction of the Court unpredictable.

[*36] E. Complementarity

    1. General comments

153. It was observed that complementarity, as referred to in the third paragraph of the preamble to the draft statute, was to reflect the jurisdictional relationship between the International Criminal Court and national authorities, including national courts. It was generally agreed that a proper balance between the two was crucial in drafting a statute that would be acceptable to a large number of States. Different views were

expressed on how, where, to what extent and with what emphasis complementarity should be reflected in the statute.

154. Some delegations felt that complementarity should more explicitly reflect the intention of the Commission, in respect of the role of an international criminal court, in order to provide clear guidance for interpretation. That intention was for such a court to operate in cases where there was no prospect of persons who had been accused of the crimes listed in the statute being duly tried in national courts; but such a court was not intended to exclude the existing jurisdiction of national courts or to affect the right of States to seek extradition and other forms of international judicial assistance under existing arrangements. The Commission's intention, it was further noted, applied not only to national decisions as to whether or not to prosecute, but also to decisions by national authorities to seek assistance, including extradition, from another State and decisions by such other State to cooperate accordingly, particularly where that State was under an international obligation to do so. In this regard, therefore, complementarity becomes a constant in the arrangements for the Court and needs to be taken into account at each point at which the respective roles of the Court and national authorities can or do coincide. From this perspective, it is not a question of the Court having primary or even concurrent jurisdiction. Rather, its jurisdiction should be understood as having an exceptional character. There may be instances where the Court could obtain jurisdiction quickly over a case because no good-faith effort was under way at the national level to investigate or prosecute the case, or no credible national justice system even existed to consider the case. But as long as the relevant national system was investigating or prosecuting a case in good faith, according to this view, the Court's jurisdiction should not come into operation. A view was also expressed that a possible safeguard against sham trials could also be for the Statute to set out certain basic conditions relating to investigations, trials and the handling of requests for extradition and legal assistance.

155. It was also observed that the limited resources of the Court should not be exhausted by taking up the prosecution of cases which could easily and effectively be dealt with by national courts. In addition, taking into account that under international law, exercise of police power and penal law is a prerogative of States, the jurisdiction of the Court should be viewed only as an exception to such State prerogative.

156. Some delegations expressed the view that the establishment of the Court did not by any means diminish the responsibility of States to investigate vigorously and prosecute criminal cases. Therefore, they wanted the preamble of the Statute to reiterate the obligation of States in this respect. Caution, however, was voiced against placing such a paragraph in the preamble because it might tilt the bias in favour of national jurisdiction in interpreting complementarity. According to this view, the establishment of such a court was itself a manifestation of States exercising their obligations to prosecute vigorously perpetrators of serious crimes.

[*37] 157. Some other delegations expressed concern that without specifying clear exceptions to the concept, complementarity would render the Court meaningless by undermining its authority. In their view, a suggestion that in each and every case the Prosecutor had to prove that circumstances required the Court's intervention would reduce it to a mere residual institution, short of necessary status and independence. In this context it was noted that while national authorities and courts had the primary responsibility for prosecuting the perpetrators of the crimes listed in the Statute, the Court was an indispensable asset in enhancing the prevention of impunity, which too often had been the reward for violators of human rights and humanitarian law. While attempts should be made to minimize the risk of the Court dealing with a matter that could eventually be dealt with adequately on the national level, it was, according to this view, still preferable to the risk of perpetrators of serious crimes being protected by sympathetic national judiciaries or authorities. In addition, a concern was raised that complementarity should not be used to uphold the sanctity of national courts. Such an approach would shift the emphasis from what the Court could do to what the Court should not do. Some delegations proposed the inclusion of a reference to complementarity in article 1; the proposal received some support.

158. The remark was also made that complementarity was closer to the concept of concurrent jurisdiction. The jurisdiction of the Court, it was stated, should be looked at in different contexts. While for certain crimes the Court would have inherent jurisdiction, the primary jurisdiction of national courts would be more appropriate for other crimes. The remark was further made that in respect of core crimes, there would always be a "perception" problem: it would be difficult to believe that national courts could be fair and

impartial. For other types of crimes, such as terrorism, drug trafficking, etc., this would not be a problem. In addition, it was noted that, in cases of inherent jurisdiction, complementarity should not be construed so as to make the Court's jurisdiction dependent on factors beyond the Court's control. However, it was noted, even in respect of core crimes, the important role of national courts should not be undermined. Reference was made to the recent practice with respect to the establishment of ad hoc tribunals whereby the tribunals exercised inherent and primary jurisdiction over certain individual cases, with some deference to national justice systems as they currently existed.

159. It was suggested that the principle of complementarity should be defined as an element of the competence of the Court; the conditions, timing and procedures for invoking this principle should be clearly indicated; the person named in the submission to the Court or the State party invoking this principle should provide supporting information; the Court could hold a hearing before reaching a decision; the Prosecutor should be able to obtain protective measures to preserve evidence or to detain suspects pending the Court's decision; and the person named in the request for transfer or the State requested to transfer an accused should be able to invoke the principle for the first time before the trial.

160. It was further suggested that consideration should be given to how the complementarity regime would take account of national reconciliation initiatives entailing legitimate offers of amnesty or internationally structured peace processes.

2. Third preambular paragraph

161. A number of delegations agreed that while the preambular reference to complementarity should remain, a more explicit definition of the concept, enumerating its constituent elements, should also be embodied in an article of [*38] the Statute. In this context it was noted that the words "unavailable" or "ineffective" should be further defined; it was also suggested that the words should be omitted altogether. Suggestions were also made to replace the words "trial procedures" with "systems" for further clarity. It was noted that while the determination of "availability" of national criminal systems was more factual, the determination of whether such a system was "ineffective" was too subjective. Such a determination would place the Court in the position of passing judgement on the penal system of a State. That would impinge on the sovereignty of national legal systems and might be embarrassing to that State to the extent that it might impede its eventual cooperation with the Court.

162. As regards who is to decide on whether the Court should exercise jurisdiction, three views emerged. According to one view, taking into account that the exercise of penal jurisdiction was the prerogative of States, the Court's jurisdiction was an exception to be exercised only by State consent. An optional clause regime, according to this view, was consistent with this approach. According to another view, the Court itself should make the final determination of jurisdiction, but in accordance with precise criteria set out in the Statute. According to yet a third view, while agreeing that the Court should decide on its own jurisdiction in accordance with the Statute, the Statute should leave some discretion to the Court.

163. It was recommended that the consequences of a State's refusal to consent to the Court's jurisdiction, if required by the Statute, should also be examined. The question would be whether, in such cases, the State would entail such responsibility as existed in the classical international law of State responsibility, or whether different consequences would ensue which should be specified in the Statute itself.

3. Article 35

164. It was noted that the principle of complementarity involved, besides the third preambular paragraph, a number of articles of the Statute, central among which was article 35 on admissibility. Several delegations felt that the three grounds indicated in that article, on the basis of which the Court may decide that a case before it is inadmissible, seemed too narrow. Paragraph (a) refers, for example, only to decisions of a State not to proceed to a prosecution, ignoring other national decisions to discontinue the proceedings, acquit, convict of a lesser offence, sentence or pardon or even requests for mutual assistance or extradition. Moreover, it was observed that other grounds of inadmissibility contained in other articles of the Statute (for example articles 42 and 55) could be included in article 35, which would then constitute the main article on complementarity in the operative part of the Statute. The view was expressed that the article should be expanded to include cases which are being or have been prosecuted before national jurisdictions, subject to qualifications in respect of impartiality, diligent prosecution, etc. It was further noted that the

Court should abstain from exercising jurisdiction unless no domestic court was properly fulfilling this responsibility.

165. It was observed that paragraph (b) of article 35 indicated a crime under investigation as a ground for inadmissibility without taking into account the circumstances under which a crime was investigated and the possibilities of ineffective or unavailable procedures or even sham trials. A view was expressed that allowance should be made for parallel investigations to be conducted by national authorities and the Court under certain circumstances, as for example when an interested State did not object for the Court to investigate other aspects of the same conflict. It was generally agreed that "parallel" procedures between national courts and the Court should be avoided to the extent [*39] possible. The necessity of additional procedural checks and review was also stressed, particularly in cases where the procedure of article 36 was applicable.

166. Other delegations recalled once again the difficulties in assessing when procedures were ineffective and pointed out the essentially subjective character of the proposed criteria. It was felt that more stringent and objective criteria, possibly included in the text of the Statute itself, would be needed for the purposes of greater clarity and security. The efficiency of national proceedings (as juxtaposed to the intention to "shield" the accused) was one such criterion: several delegations noted that notions such as "absence of good faith" and "unconscionable delay" in the conduct of the proceeding on the part of national authorities would be useful tools for the clarification of this issue. However, other delegations felt that these terms were also vague and might be confusing.

167. On the subject of who might raise the issue of inadmissibility, the question was raised as to whether the accused should be permitted to file an application or this right should rest only with "interested States". It was noted, however, that the notion "interested States" should be further defined. In this context several suggestions were made, notably mentioning the State of which the accused is a national, the State(s) of which the victim or victims are nationals, the State which has custody of the accused, the State on the territory of which the alleged crime was committed (State of locus delicti) or any other State which could exercise jurisdiction in respect of the crime. It was also pointed out that in such a case, article 36 would have to be modified to include any "interested State" in this sense. Other delegations noted that any State could have the right to file such a request. A view was also expressed that the accused could bring a challenge only after indictment and only on specific grounds.

168. As for the time of raising the issue of admissibility, it was generally agreed that it should be prior to, or at the beginning of the trial and not later. The view was expressed that the Court should be able to declare, at any time and of its own motion, or upon the request of the accused, a case inadmissible. In this respect, it was also noted that the Court should retain the right to recommence proceedings after a fundamental change of circumstances, or to review its own decision on the admissibility of a case.

169. Concerning the non-gravity of the crime as a ground for inadmissibility, it was pointed out that the inclusion of a more detailed definition of crimes in article 20 would suffice to indicate that the crime did not pertain to the jurisdiction of the Court as defined in that article.

    4.   Article 42

170. As regards article 42, the remark was made that the principle of non bis in idem was closely linked with the issue of complementarity. This paragraph, it was noted, should apply only to res judicata and not to proceedings discontinued for technical reasons. In addition, non bis in idem should not be construed in such a way as to permit criminals to escape any procedure.

171. Some delegations felt that the term "ordinary crime" in paragraph 2 (a) of article 42 needed further clarification. Some others thought that the term was sufficiently clear and should be retained. Yet some other delegations considered that it could be left out altogether since it might create a certain confusion. In this connection, it was mentioned that the principle [*40] non bis in idem could apply when a person had already been tried for only a part of a crime. The view was also expressed that it was the nature of the crimes that was significant and this should be taken into consideration for the distinction between "ordinary crimes" and "other crimes" falling under the jurisdiction of the Court. It was suggested that a formulation to the effect that the national proceedings did not take account of the international character and the grave nature of the act might be useful.

172. With regard to the other precondition for the Court to try a person already tried in another court, indicated in paragraph 2 (b) of article 42, many delegations voiced their concern about the vagueness and the subjectivity of the criteria. It was pointed out that several core crimes could not effectively be tried in national courts because of their very nature and the circumstances of their commission. Several delegations felt that this wording would grant the Court an excessive right of control over national jurisdictions and would even undermine the principle of complementarity. According to this view, the Court should not be considered as an appellate court. However, several other delegations considered the article as drafted by the Commission sufficiently clear and comprehensive.

173. A view was also expressed that article 42 should include cases where the sentence imposed by the national jurisdiction was manifestly inadequate for the offence as an exception to non bis in idem. It was noted, however, that a possible solution would provide for the Court to try a person already tried in another court, only if the proceedings in the other court manifestly intended to shield the accused from his/her international criminal responsibility.

174. The view was also expressed that the "exception" to the principle non bis in idem as set out in article 42 (b) should extend beyond the trial proceedings to embrace parole, pardon, amnesty, etc. Others pointed out that the conditions and modalities laid down in article 35 should also apply to article 42. It was also noted that both articles 35 and 42 could be consolidated in order to constitute a unique central article on complementarity in the operative part of the Statute. A question was raised as to the possibility of a preliminary hearing on the question of admissibility between any interested State and the Court. The view was further expressed that article 42 (b) should not include any wording which could be conducive to subjective interpretation.

    5.   Article 27

175. It was noted that the decision of the Prosecutor not to prosecute should be subject to subsequent revision if, for example, new evidence appeared or a new complaint was lodged by a State. The view was also expressed that the Prosecutor should examine ex officio, on receiving a complaint, the question of the inadmissibility of the case.

176. Moreover, in a case where the Prosecutor defers investigation since a State is proceeding with a national investigation, a mechanism of mutual information between the Prosecutor, the investigating and the complainant States should be established. This mechanism would allow for the complainant State to lodge further complaints with the Court, should the third State's investigation be inadequate. The view was also expressed that in such a case a new complaint would not be required. In the same context, other delegations expressed their concern with regard to the powers of the Prosecutor to conduct investigations under article 26 and the possibility that they might be in conflict with domestic judicial procedures. 9/ According to a number of delegations, however, [*41] the provisions of articles 26 and 27 adequately reflected the issue of complementarity and avoided the risk of "double jeopardy".

    6.   Article 51

177. As concerns article 51, which imposes an obligation on States to cooperate with the Court in connection with its investigations and proceedings, it was observed that this obligation should be confined to cases which are not inadmissible. Other delegations felt that the obligation should not be limited but should embrace all aspects of cooperation, even for the determination of grounds of inadmissibility.

    7.   Article 53

178. A view was expressed that paragraph 4 of article 53, which gives priority to court requests among possibly completing extradition obligations, should be deleted in the context of a strict application of complementarity. However, under another view it was pointed out that the provision was satisfactory and did not really affect complementarity insofar as a case had not been declared inadmissible.

F.   General principles of criminal law

179. The discussion of the Preparatory Committee followed the guidelines set out in annex II to the report of the Ad Hoc Committee on the Establishment of an International Criminal Court 10/ on the question of the general principles of criminal law.

1. Process issues

   (a) Methods of elaboration

180. There was broad agreement that the fundamental principles of criminal law to be applied to the crimes punishable under the Statute should be clearly laid down in the Statute in accordance with the principle of legality, nullum crimen sine lege, nulla poena sine lege. It was noted that conventions defining international crimes provided only one aspect of the substantive criminal law; they usually did not contain principles of liability and defence and other general rules of criminal law to be used to apply the definitions of crimes. It was considered important, therefore, that all general elements of crimes and the basic principles of liability and defence should be elaborated by States and laid down in the Statute itself, or in an annex thereto which would have the same legal value as the Statute. Suggestions were also made that punishment to be imposed on each offence, including the enforcement of penalties, should be elaborated in the Statute. The view was widely shared that the elaboration of those essential elements and principles, if left to the Court to deal with on a case-by-case basis, would not ensure predictability or equality before and in the law. Some delegations, however, suggested that technical and detailed rules should be developed by judges of the Court and incorporated in the rules of the Court, subject to the approval of the States parties to the Statute.

181. The articulation of the fundamental principles of criminal law in the Statute was considered consistent with the prerogative of legislative powers of sovereign States. It would give potential States parties a clear understanding [*42] of the obligations entailed. It would also provide clear guidance to the Court and promote consistent jurisprudence. Furthermore, it would ensure predictability and certainty in the application of law, which would be essential for the protection of the rights of the accused.

182. Several delegations, however, cautioned against the risk of compounding the Statute with extensive and detailed rules. The goal, it was said, should not be to replicate an exhaustive criminal code in the Statute. It was recognized that the Statute could not specify all rules, nor could it predict all types of issues which might come before the Court. It was suggested, therefore, that a proper balance must be struck between the Statute laying down basic rules of applicable law and the rules of the Court supplementing and further elaborating those basic rules for the effective functioning of the Court. In this connection, it was also suggested that account be taken of the fact that the jurisdiction of the Court might be limited only to certain core crimes, and that the role of the Court would be complementary to that of national courts when addressing the issues of the Statute or the rules, or the application by the Court of general principles of criminal law.

183. It was emphasized by some delegations that the concept of an international criminal court with universal jurisdiction would be sustainable only on the basis of a flexible and concise statute. The more detailed the Statute, it was said, the more difficult would be the problem of reconciling the existing different legal systems. The statement of law in the "general part" of the Statute, therefore, should reflect a common and balanced approach drawing upon all the major legal systems of the world.

184. It was proposed that, in order to achieve a concise and flexible document, the Statute should provide for a mechanism or include a general mandating clause whereby the judges of the Court would elaborate the elements of the crimes set out in article 20 as well as the principles of liability and defence that were not otherwise set out in the Statute. Any rules to be elaborated by the judges would be of a subsidiary nature, conforming to the elements and principles laid down in the Statute. It was also proposed that the Court should be allowed to draw upon the major legal systems of the world to establish general principles of criminal law, the application of which would be subject to the approval of the States parties to the Statute. Some delegations were of the view, however, that conferring the substantive legislative power upon the judges of the Court would not be consistent with the principle of legality.

185. Furthermore, a number of delegations suggested that, in order to satisfy the requirements of fairness, transparency, consistency and equality in criminal proceedings, not only the fundamental principles of criminal law, but also the general and most important rules of procedure and evidence should be articulated in the Statute. It was also suggested that the principle of procedural legality and its legal consequences should be firmly established in the Statute itself. It was further stressed that the procedural rules of the Court should be determined not on the basis of which system of law was to be applied but rather by reference to the rules of law that would be more appropriate to ensure justice.

186. The view was generally expressed that the method used for the statutes of the International Tribunal for the former Yugoslavia and of the International Tribunal for Rwanda, which left it to the judges to elaborate and adopt substantive rules of procedure and evidence, was not an appropriate model for the elaboration of such rules for a permanent court to be established on a consensual basis by States parties to its Statute. At the same time, the relevance of certain specific provisions contained in their statutes, [*43] particularly those relating to individual criminal responsibility, was noted by a number of delegations. Some delegations also drew attention in this regard to the relevant provisions contained in the Draft Code of Crimes against the Peace and Security of Mankind.

    (b) Relevance of national law

187. The direct application of national law provided in article 33 (c) of the draft statute was viewed with concern by a number of delegations. It was remarked that in view of the divergences in national criminal laws and in the absence of precise rules in the provisions of article 33 as to which national law should be applied, a direct reference to national law would lead to inequality of treatment of the suspect and the accused in criminal proceedings and inconsistent jurisprudence. Some delegations considered that a certain residual role of national law should be recognized, bearing in mind that international law did not yet contain a complete system of substantive criminal law. Recourse to national law should be made only as a last resort, failing the application of the Statute, the relevant treaties and the principles and rules of general international law, and only to the extent that the rules of national law in question were consistent with the Statute. It was also suggested that the Court should apply national law concerning general rules of criminal law which were not addressed in the Statute and that the Statute should clearly determine which national law should be applied in each specific case. The view was also expressed that the proper applicable law would be the law of the State where the crime was committed but that other national laws might also be applied if considered fit by the Court under the circumstances of the case. It was also stated that the Court should take into account general principles of criminal law that were common to the major legal systems, rather than relying on the national law of a particular State to resolve issues in particular cases, which were not addressed in the Statute or the rules of the Court. The suggestion was also made that the reference to national law should be allowed for general rules of criminal law only and, as far as procedural rules were concerned, the Statute and the rules of the Court should be the exclusive sources of applicable law.

188. As regards the specific provisions contained in the draft statute relevant to the general rules of criminal law, the provisions of article 33 concerning applicable law were considered vague and should be revised by: (a) substantiating in more detail the sources of the substantive law which the Court would apply; and (b) elaborating the essential elements of the general principles of criminal law, including the principles of liability and defence. Several specific proposals to this effect were submitted by delegations. It was also suggested that the primacy of the Statute and the order of relevance and applicability of other sources of applicable law should be made explicit in the revision of the article.

    2. Substantive issues

    (a) Non-retroactivity

189. The principle of non-retroactivity was considered fundamental to any criminal legal system. A number of delegations recognized the substantive link between this concept and article 39 of the Statute (nullum crimen sine lege) and suggested that the principle should be clearly and concisely set out in the Statute, even though some of the crimes referred to in the Statute were recognized as crimes under customary international law. It was further noted that the principle nulla poena sine lege also required that the principle of non-retroactivity be clearly spelled out in the Statute and that the temporal [*44] jurisdiction of the Court should be limited to those crimes committed after the entry into force of the Statute.

    (b) Punishment under customary international criminal law

190. The view was expressed that the principle of legality required not only clear definitions of the crimes under the jurisdiction of the Court which should be set out in the Statute, or in an annex thereto, but also a clear and full statement of the related punishment so as to avoid problems often associated with the issue of punishment under the different legal systems. However, doubts were expressed by some delegations as to whether customary international law covered the issue of punishment in relation to individuals held responsible for their acts or omissions.

(c) Individual criminal responsibility

191. It was generally accepted that the concept of individual criminal responsibility for the crimes, including those acts of planning, instigating and assisting the person who actually committed the crime, was essential and should be stipulated in the Statute. Some delegations suggested, therefore, that a provision laying down the basic elements of the responsibility should be included in the Statute itself. Reference was made to articles 7 and 6, respectively, of the Yugoslavia and Rwanda tribunal statutes. Other delegations were of the opinion that such an explicit and elaborate provision was not needed, as it could lead to complex negotiations, a lengthy statute and a difficult task of defining such elements as participation, conspiracy and complicity.

192. The view was also expressed that an essential question which should be addressed in the Statute was whether some kind of safeguard provision was needed to ensure that individual criminal responsibility did not absolve the State of any of its responsibility in a given case.

(d) Irrelevance of official position

193. Taking into account the precedents of the Nürnberg, Tokyo, Yugoslavia and Rwanda tribunals, there was support for the Statute to disallow any plea of official position as Head of State or Government or as a responsible government official; such official position should not relieve an accused of criminal responsibility. Some delegations thought that this issue could be included in relation to "defences". The opinion was also expressed that further consideration would be useful on the question of diplomatic or other immunity from arrest and other procedural measures taken by or on behalf of the Court.

(e) Criminal liability of corporations

194. Some delegations held the view that it would be more useful to focus attention on individual responsibility, noting at the same time that corporations were in fact controlled by individuals. Several delegations stated that such liability ran counter to their domestic law. The point was made, however, that the liability of a corporation could be important in the context of restitution. It was recalled that the principle had been applied in the Nurnberg Judgement.

[*45]   (f) Appropriateness of the statute of limitations

195. Some delegations were of the view that, owing to the serious nature of the crimes to be dealt with by the Court, there should be no statute of limitations for such crimes. On the other hand, some delegations felt that such a provision was mandatory and should be included in the Statute so as to ensure fairness for the accused. The view was expressed that statutory limitation might apply to crimes that were relatively less serious than that of genocide or crimes against humanity.

196. In the view of some delegations, this question should be considered in connection with the issue of the availability of sufficient evidence for a fair trial. Some delegations suggested that, instead of establishing a rigid rule, the Prosecutor or the President should be given flexible power to make a determination on a case-by-case basis, taking into account the right of the accused to due process. In this connection, it was noted that article 27 of the Statute was relevant to this issue. It was suggested that an accused should be allowed to apply to the Court to terminate the proceedings on the basis of fairness, if there was lack of evidence owing to the passage of many years.

(g) Actus reus

197. The general view was that a provision on the objective elements of omissions should be established to set out clearly and carefully in the Statute all conditions under which a crime could be committed, and that this should not be left to the discretion of the Court, especially when considering that it would be placed in the difficult position of choosing between the different rules in the various national legal systems. Some delegations were of the view that it would not be necessary to include such a provision, and that it would be sufficient to have the definition of the crimes in the Statute.

198. Regarding the element of causation, several delegations were of the view that it was not necessary to include causation in the Statute, as it was largely a factual matter which the Court itself could consider and decide upon. Still other delegations felt it was preferable to include rules on causation and accountability.

(h) Mens rea

199. A general view was that since there could be no criminal responsibility unless mens rea was proved, an explicit provision setting out all the elements involved should be included in the Statute. There was no

need, however, to distinguish between general and specific intention, because any specific intent should be included as one of the elements of the definition of the crime.

200. Regarding recklessness and gross negligence, there were differing views as to whether these elements should be included. Motives were seen as being relevant at the penalty stage of the proceedings. There were also doubts expressed concerning the appropriateness of including these elements in the Statute.

201. The need for including a provision setting an age limit at which an individual could be regarded as not having the requisite mens rea was widely supported. The question of what that age should be, however, would require common agreement. There was support for various proposals to this effect, including one that would give the Court discretion to evaluate an offender - within a certain age range - as to his or her maturity at the time of the commission of the crime. Attention was also drawn to a number of international [*46] instruments relevant to this issue, including the Convention on the Rights of the Child.

    (i)   Other types of responsibility

202. The view was expressed that such types of responsibility as solicitation, attempt, conspiracy, aiding and abetting, accessory after the fact, complicity and responsibility of superiors for acts of subordinates were also important and relevant to the task of the Preparatory Committee and, according to some delegations, they should be defined in the Statute. Several delegations stressed the need to resolve these issues in the Statute having regard to the different meanings and definitions used in national laws.

203. As to the definitions themselves, the opinion was expressed that the terms of incitement would have to be carefully worded so as to avoid any violations of the right of free speech. Regarding the crime of attempt, it was stated that something more than mere preparation was needed to qualify as an attempt; another suggested definition was one where the perpetrator had commenced the crime but failed to complete it. Concerning aiding and abetting and conspiracy, some delegations stressed that a formula acceptable to all would have to be found before it could be included in the Statute. The issue of the responsibility of superiors for acts of subordinates was viewed as critical and should be defined for inclusion in the Statute. It was further suggested that responsibility of superiors, in this regard, also might be relevant to the question of a defence. Reference was made to provisions of the statutes of the tribunals for the former Yugoslavia and Rwanda.

    (j)   Defences

204. Some delegations stated that they were still formulating their position with regard to this issue. It was generally felt, however, that it was necessary to set out the fundamental elements of defences, and, some delegations stated that the definitions contained in the Siracusa draft provided a good starting-point. Concern was expressed over adopting an overly generalized approach, particularly involving war crimes where specific defences already had been developed. The view was expressed that the list of defences should not be exhaustive given the difficulty of trying to cover every conceivable defence, while others believed that leaving to the Court the power to add other defences would be tantamount to giving legislative power to the Court. It was also generally felt that only defences relevant to the type of crimes under the Statute should be included. Accordingly, it was suggested, for example, that it was not necessary to include intoxication and insanity in the Statute. A proposal was made to add renunciation to the list of defences.

205. The view was expressed that it was not necessary to refer to mistake of law or fact as this was, to a large extent, a question of common sense. In other words, if a particular negation existed, then of course mens rea did not exist. Some delegations found it necessary that such provisions should be made.

206. The opinion was expressed that self-defence should also include defence of others, as well as the concept of pre-emptive self-defence. The latter was particularly important to military situations where it would be justifiable to act pre-emptively in response to an imminent threat of force. It was also suggested that the concept of proportionality should be inserted in the definition of self-defence.

207. Several delegations were of the view that defence of property was not needed because of the type of crimes over which the Court would have [*47] jurisdiction, but the point was made that it would be relevant in cases of certain war crimes.

208. Attention was drawn to the need to avoid an overlap between superior orders, and necessity and duress in the Statute; specific language would, therefore, be required in defining these terms, especially

considering the subtle distinction between necessity and duress. Doubt was expressed with regard to the need to include the law-enforcement defence.

209. Some delegations stated that they were still in the process of defining their positions on defences under public international law. Doubt was expressed over grouping together military necessity, reprisals and Article 51 of the Charter of the United Nations, and concern was also expressed over the inclusion of reprisals under defences.

210. The view was expressed that because many legal systems included the elements of aggravating and mitigating circumstances, these issues would need to be addressed in the Statute. The remark was made that perhaps they should be dealt with in connection with penalties.

   (k)   Penalties 11/

211. It was generally stated that if the Court was to have jurisdiction over crimes, then it would have to impose penalties on individuals found guilty of those crimes. Whether specific penalties should be written in the Statute and, if not, what law applied in this regard would have to be discussed; article 47 of the draft statute offered a solution. The remark was also made that under paragraph 2 of article 47, preference was given to the law of the State where the crime had been committed. It was suggested that the issues relating to penalties, as well as to aggravating and mitigating circumstances, should be discussed fully at the resumed session of the Preparatory Committee under procedural questions.

G.   Procedural questions, fair trial and rights of the accused

212. The Preparatory Committee considered this topic at its session in August 1996.

213. To facilitate and guide the discussion, the Chairman put forward a list of questions formulated in the context of certain specific articles of the draft statute prepared by the International Law Commission.

214. There was general agreement on the importance of the topic and the need to elaborate further the relevant provisions. Different views were expressed as to how best to meet this need. One view was that all the necessary principles and rules should be formulated in an integral manner, contained in the Statute or annexes thereto, and adopted by the States parties. Another view was that the Statute itself should contain only the general principles, leaving the implementation and subsidiary rules to be embodied in a second or third instrument; while these instruments could all be adopted initially by the States parties, the second and third instruments could be amended as needed by a simpler procedure (e.g., by the Court itself) without resorting to treating amendment provisions. Still another view was to assemble at the current stage those principles and rules deemed relevant and to leave the question of their placement for a later stage. The view was also expressed that it would not be practical to prepare all necessary rules down to every last detail and that the Court must be given the flexibility to add detailed rules, provided that they were consistent with the principles and rules laid down by the States parties.

[*48] 215. A view was expressed that the procedural rules should maintain a balance between different penal systems of States and draw from their positive elements. Reference was made in this context to the penal law approach adopted by civil law States in matters dealing with hearings and investigations, steps which were taken to ensure equality between the prosecution and the defence, with regard to the means available to them, and in which the judge also played a more active role in conducting hearings. It was stressed that an international criminal jurisdiction should draw upon the practice of any system that could assist it in the performance of its functions. It should not be used as a standard to test the credibility of penal systems of individual States.

Article 25. Complaint

216. It was noted that the complaint should contain information sufficient to indicate that investigation by the Court was warranted and should meet a certain threshold in indicating that a crime had been committed that was within the jurisdiction of the Court and as to which the Court's exercise of jurisdiction was appropriate. The complaint should, also, address the issue of consent by a certain number of States, admissibility or complementarity, so as to assist the Court in determining whether it should take action in a particular case. It was further stressed that the purpose of the complaint should be to describe criminal acts which appeared to warrant investigation by the Court.

217. It was noted in this context, that, as a minimum, a complaint should contain information on: (a) the jurisdiction relied upon in making the complaint; (b) the circumstances of the alleged crime (e.g., specific criminal conduct occurring in a specific place and during a specific time); (c) the identity and whereabouts

of any suspects, if known; (d) the identity and whereabouts of any witnesses, if known; (e) the location of evidence; and (f) details of any investigation carried out by the complaining State party or, to its knowledge, any other State.

218. Concerns were expressed however, about stipulating a mandatory list of requirements for a complaint, because such a list might make it more difficult for States with fewer resources to lodge a bona fide complaint. For that reason, some support was expressed for the words "as far as possible" in paragraph 3 of article 25, as they allowed a degree of flexibility.

219. As regards the wording of paragraph 3 of article 25, it was according to one view sufficient for the Statute; more detailed rules specified in the preceding paragraphs could be placed in a second-tier instrument. According to another view, the paragraph required detailed elaboration of the rules of procedure.

220. As regards the role of the Prosecutor, the following points were made: (a) he or she should be able to ask for clarifications of a complaint; (b) he or she should not be bound by allegations in the complaint about who is or should be a suspect or accused; (c) he or she should be able to pursue criminal acts that are closely related to those in the complaint or which form a continuing pattern of criminal activity; but (d) if the complaint is to serve as a trigger, the investigation should not stray into unrelated or clearly collateral matters. Views differed as to whether the Prosecutor was bound by the content of complaint or whether the Prosecutor's investigation might extend beyond the content of a complaint. One view supported the former, while another expressed preference for the latter. There were uncertainties as to whether a complaint by a State should be too specific or should only refer, as in the case of a referral by the Security Council, a situation to the Court.

[*49] 221. With respect to who can make a complaint, different views were expressed. According to one view, only States parties should be empowered to lodge a complaint. Some delegations holding this view felt that the Security Council or the Prosecutor should not initiate proceedings before the Court. According to another view, States parties and the Security Council should be able to lodge a complaint. Some other delegations expressed the view that the Prosecutor should be allowed to initiate investigation based on any credible information provided to him or her from any source, whether as a result of inherent jurisdiction or referral of a situation by a State, the Security Council or another source, a model similar to that provided in the Statute of the International Tribunal for the former Yugoslavia.

222. The dual complaint system under article 25, one for genocide and the other for other crimes, was considered by some as undesirable. Preference was expressed for a single unified system, applicable to all crimes.

223. It was suggested that the question of the trigger mechanism be addressed in two separate articles, one dealing with complaints by States and the other complaints by the Security Council. This would allow any necessary special requirements to be prescribed for referral of situations to the Court by the Security Council under Chapter VII of the Charter.

Article 26. Investigation of alleged crimes

224. As regards the initiation of investigations, various suggestions were made for providing a minimum threshold, a screening mechanism or a judicial filter to distinguish between well-founded complaints of sufficiently serious crimes and frivolous or vexatious complaints. It was suggested that a State party, or a person referred to by name in a complaint, should be allowed to challenge before a trial chamber the submission of a complaint prior to the initiation of an investigation, on various grounds (e.g., the sufficiency of the complaint, the basis for jurisdiction and the admissibility of the case in terms of the principle of complementarity and the gravity of the alleged crime). A State party which was conducting a related investigation should also be allowed to send its objections to the Prosecutor.

225. Different views were expressed as to whether the Prosecutor should be authorized to initiate investigations ex officio. It was suggested that he or she should be authorized to do so based on sufficient, verifiable information received from any reliable source, with a view to strengthening the independence of the Prosecutor and the effectiveness of the Court.

226. With respect to the role of the Prosecutor, a spectrum of views were expressed: the Prosecutor should conduct an independent and impartial investigation on behalf of the international community and should collect incriminating and exonerating information to determine the truth of the charges and to protect the

interests of justice; he or she should seek the cooperation of States in conducting investigations rather than carrying out such activities directly for reasons of efficiency and effectiveness, and the investigations would be conducted in accordance with the Statute and the rules of the Court as well as the national law of the State in whose territory the investigation was conducted; the Prosecutor should be able to seek cooperation directly from States or could be authorized to conduct direct investigations in exceptional situations in which there were concerns regarding the objectivity of the national authorities.

227. With regard to on-site investigations, different ways to conduct such activities were mentioned: the investigations should only be conducted with the [*50] consent of the State concerned so as to ensure respect for its sovereignty, with the possible exception of situations in which the national criminal justice system was not fully functioning; the Presidency could empower the Prosecutor to conduct such investigations if there were no civil authorities to whom a request for assistance could be transmitted; the Presidency should appoint a judge or a chamber to supervise on-site investigations and thereby protect the rights of the suspect or the accused, whose counsel could also be present.

228. There was some question as to whether the Presidency was the appropriate body to issue investigative orders, with questions being raised as to the legal effect of such orders. It was stated that the reference to orders concerning "provisional arrest" in this context could create confusion with the use of this term in relation to extradition. It was suggested that an investigations chamber should monitor the investigative activities of the Prosecutor to give judicial authority to his or her actions to decide on requests for State cooperation, to ensure equality between the prosecution and the defence and to enable the suspect to request that certain investigations be carried out. Some delegations observed, however, that undue judicial control over the investigation would interfere with the separation of the judicial and prosecutorial functions. Such a chamber could also decide on objections of States to decisions on investigative measures prior to an indictment. However, the view was also expressed that such tasks could be entrusted to a single judge or magistrate rather than creating an additional chamber.

229. Attention was drawn to the need to consider further and clarify the standard to be applied by the Prosecutor in deciding whether to initiate an investigation or to file an indictment. It was suggested that the Prosecutor should, for example, have broad discretion to decide not to initiate or to discontinue an investigation or prosecution in the interests of justice owing to the age or illness of an individual or a national investigation or prosecution, or to have the authority to decline to investigate or to prosecute certain cases which were not of sufficient gravity and to select the most important cases when crimes were committed on a massive scale.

230. The view was expressed that the complainant State or the Security Council, as appropriate, should be informed of the Prosecutor's decision not to initiate an investigation or to seek an indictment. Any State whose cooperation had been requested during an investigation should also be informed of the latter decision. There were various suggestions to provide for the judicial review of these decisions by the Presidency, a trial chamber, an investigations chamber, an indictment chamber or a judge at the request of the complainant State, the Security Council or the victims. There was some question as to whether the complainant State or an appropriate judicial body should be entitled to initiate a review of such a decision and the manner in which the complainant State should submit its views. It was suggested, for example, that the judicial review should be based on a specific legal standard, such as that of manifestly inappropriate, which would defer to the appropriate exercise of prosecutorial discretion; that the authority of the judicial body should be limited to requesting the Prosecutor to reconsider a decision to preserve prosecutorial discretion and independence; and that the Prosecutor should be able to reconsider such decisions based on new information.

231. As regards the rights of the suspect, the view was expressed that they should be further elaborated in accordance with international standards and contained in a separate article. Emphasis was placed, inter alia, on the right of the suspect to receive a sufficient warning before being questioned, to remain silent during questioning, to not be compelled to testify or to confess guilt, to receive the assistance of competent counsel irrespective of the ability to pay for such assistance, to communicate in confidence with the [*51] counsel, to equal protection before the law and in the case of a minor to be dealt with in a manner that takes account of the child's age. It was stated that, if the accused decides to testify, his or her testimony may be

used as evidence in the trial. The view was expressed that the enumeration of the rights of the suspect should, however, be non-exhaustive.

Article 27. Commencement of prosecution

232. It was suggested that the indictment filed by the Prosecutor in a particular case should contain more detailed information than that stipulated in paragraph 1 of the article. However, if the evidence collected in the case was excessive, a summary could be provided to the reviewing body, which would have the right to request further information as needed.

233. As regards the reviewing body, concerns were expressed over the concentration of authority vested with the Presidency as envisaged in the draft statute, and it was suggested that it would be more appropriate to give certain pre-trial responsibilities to another body, independent of the Prosecutor and the trial, and appeals chambers. In this connection, it was proposed that a pre-trial, indictment or investigations chamber be established to examine the indictment and to hold confirmation hearings, which would provide the accused with further necessary guarantees considering the very public nature of an indictment for serious crimes. The point was made that a permanent reviewing chamber would have the advantages of consistency of approach and avoidance of difficulties associated with a rotation of judges.

234. It was also suggested that either a single judge or a panel of three judges, serving on a rotational basis, should have the function of ruling on pre-trial matters. The same judge performing pre-trial functions should not, however, be involved with the case at later stages. In addition, the judges of the reviewing body should not be of the same nationality as the accused.

235. Regarding the standard on which the indictment would be based, the statement was made that whatever standard was ultimately employed should be sufficiently high to justify trial proceedings. It was suggested that the timing of the exercises contained in paragraph 2 (a) and (b), i.e., determination of a prima facie case and the admissibility of a case before the Court, should be clearly delineated.

236. The view was expressed that the Statute should address the Court's ability to issue arrest warrants prior to any confirmation of an indictment, as well as the need to maintain the confidentiality of an indictment until the arrest is made, in order to ensure the custody of the suspect and to prevent the destruction of evidence. It was further proposed, as also provided for in rule 61 of the Rules of Procedure of the International Tribunal for the former Yugoslavia, that provision should be made in the Statute allowing for seizure of the accused's assets under certain circumstances.

237. With respect to paragraph 3, it was proposed that in those cases where the reviewing body refused to confirm the indictment it should indicate the reasons for its refusal.

238. As regards the requirements under paragraph 4, it was pointed out that the grounds for amendment of the indictment should be clarified. One view was that any amendments to the indictment should not result in the charging of new crimes against the accused. Before deciding upon an amendment of the indictment, the Court should hear the accused. Moreover, the requirement of notifying the accused of any amendments should be fulfilled promptly and in the language of [*52] the accused, in accordance with the International Covenant on Civil and Political Rights (art. 14, para. 3 (a)).

Article 28. Arrest

Article 29. Pre-trial detention or release

Article 30. Notification of the indictment

239. It was stressed that certain matters were within the purview of the State and others were within the purview of the Court and only those functions performed by the Court should be regulated by the Statute. It was recognized that the cooperation of States with the Court was essential for the carrying out of effective and efficient arrest and detention procedures. Attention was also drawn to proposals, submitted at the first session of the Preparatory Committee, for the reformulation of articles 28 and 29 so as to provide for greater clarification and more concise wording regarding arrest and detention.

240. As regards the arrest of the suspect, the view was expressed that the proceedings under article 28 should be conducted under the control of the relevant national authority. Moreover, since many countries would not accept the direct execution of an arrest warrant on their territory, the Statute should provide that States should execute the warrant on behalf of the Court.

241. It was suggested that the term "provisional arrest" used in article 28 should be replaced by another term to avoid improper analogizing to the extradition model.

242. It was deemed reasonable to hold the suspect for a period of 90 days to allow time for confirmation of the indictment considering the serious nature of the crimes in question and the complicated investigation that would ensue. On the other hand, the view was also expressed that the 90-day period was too long and should be reduced. It was also suggested that once the Presidency was satisfied that there was no prospect that the required arrest criteria would be met, the suspect should be immediately released. Concern was also expressed over the provision contained in paragraph 2 of article 28 allowing the Presidency to extend the 90-day period to a seemingly indefinite period of time, and in this regard the suggestion was made to have a fixed period. Provision could also be made for an extension based on compelling reasons.

243. It was felt that article 29 on pre-trial detention or release needed further clarification in respect, inter alia, of the determination by the judicial officer of the warrant duly served and the purpose of such determination. It was suggested that the determination of the lawfulness of the arrest or detention, as well as bail, should be made by the relevant national authorities. A view was expressed that what the Court could determine was the lawfulness of its arrest warrants and its requests for the detention of the suspect. However, the Statute should provide guidelines for the grounds for detention and release for those occasions when the Court had custody of the suspect.

244. It was proposed that, in accordance with the International Covenant on Civil and Political Rights, detention of a suspect before trial should be limited to exceptional cases, such as danger of flight of the suspect, threat to others or the likelihood of destruction of evidence. It was also suggested that provision should be made for other options, such as allowing the custodial State to guarantee the availability of the suspect before the Court without actually [*53] detaining the suspect, or by placing the suspect under judicial remand, for example by confining him to his home.

245. It was considered useful to make clear in the provision on notification of the indictment, as contained in article 30, that State authorities should normally perform service of documents. It would not be cost-effective nor would it be necessary for reasons of fairness for the Registrar of the Court to travel to each country where the suspect was detained to serve the indictment.

Article 34. Challenges to jurisdiction

Article 35. Issues of admissibility

Article 36. Procedure under articles 34 and 35

246. As a general comment, it was noted that the provisions dealing with the organization of the trial should be more detailed than those provided for in the draft articles formulated by the International Law Commission. Such provisions should, in addition to providing for a speedy and fair trial, also provide for the following: protection of witnesses; right of the victim to reparation; possibility of trial in places other than the site of the Court; the possibility of trial in absentia, if the accused is a fugitive; confidentiality of information and evidence; and suppression of false evidence.

247. The discussion on articles 34, 35 and 36 was focused on three main questions and it showed that further elaboration and clarification were requested.

248. As regards the question of who may challenge the jurisdiction of the Court or object to the admissibility of the case (article 34), it was noted that the term "interested State" was too vague and should be defined as those States entitled to exercise jurisdiction, including the State of nationality of the accused, the State where the crime had been committed, the State of nationality of the victims and the custodial State. According to one view, such interested States should also be parties to the Statute. According to another view, there was no logical reason to deprive a non-State party that had a direct and material interest in the case of the right to challenge the Court's jurisdiction. Thus, according to this view, any State that had a right to consent to the Court's jurisdiction under the Statute should be able to challenge that jurisdiction. It was also pointed out that the accused should have the right to challenge the jurisdiction of the Court. The question was raised however as to whether the accused should be permitted to challenge the Court's jurisdiction on grounds of lack of consent where the State whose consent was required had not done so. The competence of the Court could be contested by the interested State or by individuals in question upon receipt of a notification of complaint by the Court, when a request for transfer had been made or at the beginning of the trial.

249. As regards the question of when such a challenge might be made (article 35), a preference was expressed for as early a time as possible. It was suggested that the right to challenge jurisdiction or

admissibility should be limited to pre-trial hearings or to the commencement of the trial. To avoid any misuse of the Court or unnecessary expenditure, it was suggested that any challenge to jurisdiction or admissibility should be raised and decided upon before any step in the trial was taken. In addition, challenges to jurisdiction should be permitted only once and not at multiple stages of the process. Preference was expressed for limiting the time within which challenges to jurisdiction or admissibility might be made. It was noted in this regard that [*54] States with an interest in a case should be given notice of indictment. This could be facilitated by notification of an indictment from the Court to all States parties. One delegation expressed the view that the case provided for in article 35 (c), inasmuch as it involved a question inseparable from the merits, could not constitute a preliminary objection and accordingly could not be treated as one.

250. It was stated that only in exceptional cases should challenges to jurisdiction be permitted during the trial. Such exceptional cases would include the discovery of new facts which could affect the question of jurisdiction. It was also noted that a fugitive at large should not be permitted to challenge jurisdiction, thereby taking advantage of the processes of the Court, while maintaining the option of refusing to submit to it if it ruled against him or her. The question was also raised as to whether an accused should be permitted to wait until the later stages of a trial to raise a jurisdictional challenge that could have been brought much earlier. A view was also expressed that there should be no distinction between the right of the State and that of the accused with regard to when either could challenge the jurisdiction of the Court. Hence paragraph (b) of article 34 should be deleted. It was further stated that an accused should not be able to challenge admissibility on the grounds of a parallel investigation by national authorities where those national authorities had in fact declined to challenge the Court's jurisdiction. These issues involved how best to allocate prosecutorial power between the Court and those States where the accused did not have a proper role.

251. As regards the procedure by which challenges could be made (article 36), different views were expressed. One view was that objections to jurisdiction should be raised before a chamber other than the trial chamber; such a chamber might be the indictment chamber or the investigative chamber. This procedure, it was suggested, was compatible with maintaining the independence of the trial chamber. According to another view, the question of objections to jurisdiction should be dealt with by the trial chamber itself. It was noted that there should be a decision as to whether decisions on challenges to jurisdiction or admissibility could be appealable. If so, the Statute should clearly provide the procedure for such appeals. It was also noted that article 36, paragraph 2, on the referral of a matter to the appeals chamber, required further guidance with respect to the prerequisites for such a referral.

252. It was stated that when an individual has been investigated and/or prosecuted by national authorities, the decision to override that national process should be by a two-thirds majority of the Court, in deference to national processes.

Article 37. Trial in the presence of the accused

253. Different views were expressed on this question. According to one view, trial in the presence of the accused constituted a fundamental right of the accused and this right must be observed. Consequently there could be no trial in absentia.

254. Another view was that the current context was different; it involved exceptional circumstances (e.g. crimes affecting the international community) and pertained to a special international judiciary organ which would not have an enforcement mechanism to ensure the presence of the accused. There was therefore room to consider trial in absentia at least in certain specific cases, such as the one in which the accused deliberately flees justice and every effort to bring him or her to trial has proved fruitless. It was stressed however that the rights of the accused must be fully guaranteed and the circumstances and [*55] conditions clearly stipulated. In particular, the sentence would not be mandatory and if the accused were subsequently to reappear before the Court there should be a retrial.

255. Specific comments were made on the text of article 37.

256. Concerns were expressed over article 37, paragraph 2, which provided for exceptions to the general rule. It was pointed out that even the limited exceptions provided for in that paragraph were not in conformity with the rights of the accused as contained in various international human rights instruments and national constitutions, and should therefore be deleted. It was further observed that the reference to

"ill-health" in paragraph 2 (a) constituted only a reason for the adjournment or the suspension of a trial and not for a trial in absentia; continuing disruption of the trial caused by the behaviour of the accused was not a legitimate excuse and it should be remedied by such practical measures as the use of video conferencing or creating a security area for the accused, treating such behaviour as contempt of court. As far as trial in absentia for reasons of security was concerned, it was noted that practical alternatives should be sought (e.g. temporary relocation of the Court or the use of video conferencing).

257. It was also observed that in the case of escape from bail or from lawful custody, the focus for the international community should be on cooperation in locating and re-apprehending the accused. The accused should be warned in advance that in case of escape he or she could be tried in absentia. It was suggested that the term "lawful custody" needed further clarification. It was also pointed out that the distinction between "deliberate absence" referred to in article 37, paragraph 4, and escape "from lawful custody" referred to in paragraph 2 (c) of the same article was not clear and should be clarified.

258. It was stressed that in cases of trial in absentia, the rights of the accused should be set out in detail to include, for example: the possibility for the Court to review the order to exclude the accused, the right of the accused to be informed (through the Registrar) of the proceedings, in case of sickness to be questioned whenever he or she is in the presence of his or her counsel and of the Prosecutor or to be always legally represented by a counsel of his or her choice (or appointed ex officio).

259. Specific comments were also made with regard to paragraph 4, which permitted the establishment of an indictment chamber for certain specific purposes in cases of the deliberate absence of the accused. Concerns were expressed that the effectiveness of the Court might be undermined in those cases. Support was expressed, however, for such an indictment chamber for the purpose of recording the evidence or issuing and publishing an international warrant of arrest for the accused. This should not, in some members' view, lead to either partial or full trial in absentia. The view was also expressed that trial in absentia might take place when the accused was deliberately absent, or when the accused implicitly or explicitly waived his or her rights, provided that rigorous safeguards were taken to preserve the rights of the accused. It was further suggested that a verdict should not be reached nor imprisonment imposed in a trial in absentia. In any case, the trial should be reopened if it had already taken place in absentia. The accused should be able to challenge the admissibility of the evidence recorded in his or her absence. Also, the right of appeal against any decision granted in absentia should be allowed so as to strike a balance between the necessities of justice and the rights of the accused.

[*56] Article 38. Functions and powers of the Trial Chamber

260. A number of general remarks were made in this regard: consideration should be given to when the trial chamber was constituted and whether pre-trial motions should be dealt with by another entity; the accused should be informed of the composition of the chamber to facilitate challenges under article 11; some matters addressed in paragraph 1 should be dealt with during the first appearance of the accused before a chamber rather than at the commencement of the trial; and pre-trial motions should be addressed, possibly along the lines of rule 73 of the International Tribunal for the former Yugoslavia.

261. As regards paragraph 1 (d), there were different views as to whether the accused should be allowed to enter a plea of guilty or not guilty and the consequences of a guilty plea. The view was expressed that the accused should be allowed to enter a plea of guilty, which would have the procedural effect of obviating the need for a lengthy and costly trial: the accused would be allowed to admit his wrongdoing and accept his sentence; the victims and witnesses would be spared any additional suffering; and the Court would be allowed to take the guilty plea into account in sentencing the convicted person. The accused would also be allowed to enter a plea of not guilty, so as to benefit from the presumption of innocence and to offer a defence without affecting the duty of the prosecution to prove the charges. A court was not bound to accept a plea or a recommendation for leniency.

262. In contrast, the view was also expressed that the accused should be able to acknowledge the deeds attributed to him or her and the Court should be able to consider this admission as evidence; the admission should not be the only evidence considered by the Court; the admission should not have any consequences for the trial procedures; the Chamber had a duty to determine the guilt or innocence of the accused notwithstanding an admission; and a full trial was necessary given the seriousness of the crimes and the interests of the victims as well as the international community. It was suggested that the Court should not

have the power to convict the accused based solely on his or her confession or a single testimony; the Court should be subject to a minimum evidentiary rule concerning admissions or confessions made in Court; and the Court should be subject to a rule of legal reasoning for its decisions concerning guilt and the elements of the indictment, and therefore paragraph 1 (d) should be deleted. It was noted that this paragraph was contrary to the constitutions of some States and could prevent their acceptance of the Statute.

263. Attention was drawn to the need to bridge the gap between different legal systems, some of which did not provide for a plea by the accused with respect to the charges, with emphasis being placed on finding the common denominators in different legal systems. It was suggested that if the accused admitted the facts contained in the indictment, the trial chamber could decide to conduct an abbreviated proceeding to hear a summary of the evidence presented by the prosecution or to continue with the trial if the accused failed to reaffirm the admission or to accept the proceeding. It was further suggested that the trial chamber should determine whether the accused fully understood the nature and consequences of admission of guilt, whether the admission was made voluntarily without coercion or undue influence and whether the admission was supported by the facts contained in the indictment and a summary of the evidence presented by the prosecution before deciding whether to request additional evidence, to conduct an expedited proceeding or to proceed with the trial. It was stated that the Court must have the power to satisfy itself before taking a decision.

264. Paragraph 1 (d) was described as relating to the question of plea bargaining, which should be excluded given the fact that it is in contradiction with the structure of the Court and also given the serious nature of the crimes [*57] which affected the interests of the international community as a whole. However, it was also stated that guilty pleas were not inseparable from plea bargaining.

265. Regarding paragraph 2, the view was expressed that the President of the chamber should play an active role in guiding the trial proceedings by conducting the debate and monitoring the manner in which evidence for or against the accused was reported. It was also stated that procedural matters relating to the order of presentation of evidence should be dealt with in the rules of procedure, while protective measures for victims and witnesses should be elaborated in the Statute.

266. As regards paragraph 3, it was suggested that joinder of accused and joinder of crimes should be addressed in the rules of procedure.

267. With regard to paragraph 4, the view was expressed that the principle of public trials should be clearly stated as the strong preference in the Statute and that any exceptions should be very limited. Suggested exceptions to this principle related to public order; the dignity of the proceedings; the security or safety of the accused, victims or witnesses; crimes allegedly committed by minors; and victim or witness testimony concerning sexual violence. Various concerns were expressed regarding the reference to "confidential or sensitive information". The power of the chamber to maintain order might obviate the need for conducting trials in the absence of a disruptive accused under article 37. The chamber should also have the power to impose sanctions for failure to respect its orders to provide deterrence, as in rule 77 of the International Tribunal for the former Yugoslavia. Decisions concerning in camera proceedings and the verdict should be announced in a public session.

268. A number of remarks were made concerning paragraph 5: subparagraphs (b) and (c) should be amended to refer to witnesses who appear before the Court; a new paragraph 5 (c) bis should be added to enable the chamber to request the assistance of States in taking witness testimony and producing documents or other evidence outside of Court; a chamber should rule at an early stage on the admissibility of evidence under paragraph 5 (d); the chamber should rule on evidentiary questions only after hearing the parties; and such matters could be addressed in article 44.

269. Regarding paragraph 6, it was suggested that the Registrar should be required to prepare a complete written record of the proceedings and possibly a video or audiovisual recording as well.

<u>Article 41. Rights of the accused</u>

270. It was recognized that respect for the rights of the accused were fundamental and reflected the credibility of the Court and that there was already a large body of international law on the subject, as contained in such instruments as the Universal Declaration of Human Rights, the International Covenant on Civil and Political Rights, standard minimum rules for the treatment of prisoners and the statutes of the Yugoslavia and Rwanda tribunals, which should be elaborated in the Statute. An issue which needed to

be explored was the interaction of the Court and the national jurisdiction prior to the transfer of an accused to the Court. It was also noted that the fundamental rights of an accused to be treated equally by the Court, and the right of minors to be dealt with in a manner taking account of the child's age, needed to be explicitly addressed.

[*58] 271. It was stated that the important right of the accused to be promptly informed of the charge needed further elaboration in the Statute, as well as a broader guarantee than was currently in the draft statute of speedy conduct of all proceedings. The point was also made that an expeditious trial process would prevent a guilty person from delaying the proceedings and would secure the early release of an innocent person. What was needed in this regard was a proactive court which would properly manage the case so as to achieve an early resolution of the case.

272. It was suggested that the Statute should provide for the appointment of counsel if the accused could not afford one. In this connection, a list of defence counsel should be developed to allow the accused a choice of counsel. It was pointed out that the qualification for defence counsel should be based on the capacity to practise before the highest criminal court in the country; in the case of court-appointed counsel, a panel could be established to review counsel according to such criteria as high moral character, competency and relevant experience. It was recommended that there be a presumption in the Statute in favour of the accused being represented by counsel. However, in the event the accused chose to conduct his or her own defence, given the grave crimes the accused would be charged with, consideration could be given to the Court's providing counsel to give legal advice to the accused if so requested. Moreover, provision should be made specifically for the right of confidential communication between the accused and the defence counsel.

273. Given the fact that the Prosecutor would have earlier access to evidence and other information, it was recommended that a mechanism be found that would neutralize any potential advantage of the Prosecutor over the defence.

274. It was stated that it was also fundamental to a fair trial that provision be made for the full disclosure of evidence by the Prosecutor to the defence, as well as a reciprocal duty of disclosure on the part of the defence, including notice to the Prosecutor of any alibi evidence the defence might bring before the Court during trial. It was also stated that the provision, contained in paragraph 2 of the article, requesting the Prosecutor to make available to the defence exculpatory evidence should also include the requirement to make available inculpatory evidence prior to the conclusion of the trial; others stated however that these provisions need further elaboration. It was further observed that the need to protect sensitive information supplied by a State would have to be balanced with the general duty to disclose.

275. It was also pointed out that the right to confront and cross-examine all witnesses was a fundamental right, and concern was expressed in this regard over the possible use of anonymous witnesses, since the defence's ability to probe the credibility of the witness to show a motive to lie or to show that a mistake had been made depended to a large extent on who the witness was. The view was further expressed that there was a need to take into account special measures for a child witness.

276. The right of the accused not to be compelled to give testimony was supported, as was the right of witnesses to enjoy some degree of protection from giving self-incriminating testimony.

277. Concerning the need for the translation of documents, a suggestion was made that the Statute should not allow for the translation of all relevant documents if the accused's counsel had command of either of the working languages of the Court. The question of the costs involved in the translation of documents was also raised.

[*59] 278. It was recommended that provision be made in the Statute for the right of the accused to compensation in the event of reversal of or pardon on the ground of newly discovered evidence.

279. With respect to specific drafting points, it was suggested, for example, that the words "subject to article 43" contained in paragraph 1 be replaced with "having due regard to article 43" so as not to place the rights contained in article 43 in a superior position over the rights of the accused. It was further suggested that the words "subject to article 37 (2)" contained in paragraph 1 (d) should be deleted.

Article 43. Protection of the accused, victims and witnesses

280. It was pointed out that the article was of a very general nature and should be further elaborated and more precisely formulated. Attention was drawn in this regard to the principles of justice for victims of

crimes contained in the 1985 United Nations Declaration on the topic, as well as principles, recently elaborated by an expert group, guaranteeing the rights and interests of victims in the proceedings of the Court. The view was also expressed that the protection of the accused, victims and witnesses should be the obligation of the State concerned. Given the importance of protecting victims and witnesses, it was further recommended that their protection should be addressed in a separate provision from that concerning protection of the accused. At the same time, the point was made that the Statute must contain a balance of rights between the two groups and that any protections bestowed on victims and witnesses should not undermine the right of the accused to receive a fair trial.

281. It was stated that measures of protection employed should be non-exhaustive. Reference was made to the witness protection programmes found in many national jurisdictions. It was suggested that provision be made to protect the identity of victims and witnesses in particular cases which, at the same time, would not unduly prejudice the defence. It was further suggested that the Court should obtain the cooperation of the victim or witness before offering any type of protection. The view was also expressed that victims and witnesses should be encouraged to come forward, and in this connection a Court should be created that treated these individuals with concern and respect. Particular concern should be given to children and the mentally impaired and victims of sexual assault. Proposals were also put forward regarding the need to keep victims and witnesses informed of the progress of the case. Attention was drawn to proposals, as well as the precedent of the Yugoslavia Tribunal, for a witness and victim unit to be established to provide services and support to victims and witnesses, under the supervision of the office of either the Registrar or the Prosecutor.

282. It was recommended that provision be made in the Statute for payment of compensation to victims who have suffered damages. Several proposals were made concerning this issue, including the possibility of the Court being empowered to make decisions on these matters, among them the administration of a compensation fund, as well as to decide on other types of reparation. It was further proposed that both the victim and the accused should be allowed to take part in such a proceeding. Concern was expressed however over the Court's ability to follow through adequately and to ensure that restitution was made. The view was also put forward that since the question of compensation was essentially a civil matter, the Court could decide the scope of the victimization and determine the principles relating to compensation for damage caused to the victim; relying on this judgement, the victim could pursue the matter of remedies through the [*60] appropriate national jurisdiction, which would be bound by the decision of the Court.

283. With respect to specific drafting points, it was suggested that the words "subject to article 41" should be added to article 43.

<u>Article 44. Evidence</u>

284. Among the questions raised by this article was that of whether the rules of evidence should appear in the Statute or in the rules of procedure of the Court or in some other form.

285. It was noted that the rules of evidence constituted an integral part of the due process of law and of the rights of the accused.

286. A commonly shared view seemed to be that fundamental or substantive principles of evidence should figure in the Statute itself while secondary and subsidiary rules could appear in the rules of the Court or other instruments. This approach would be more flexible since the latter could be more easily amended than the Statute and would also allow the Court the flexibility to adopt rules according to its practice and requirements. Certain examples of such principles were given: the judicial notice, the presumption of innocence of the accused, the capacity of witnesses to testify, the right to refuse to answer incriminating questions or the evaluation of documentary evidence. Written proposals were submitted for that purpose. It was recognized however that the task would be difficult since it would first involve a selection of the fundamental principles from the main legal systems of the world and would then entail a differentiation between the principles, the rules and the subsidiary rules.

287. The issue of perjury was also at the centre of the debate on the article. One view was that States parties should extend their national laws on perjury to cover evidence given by their nationals before the Court. The Court should only be concerned with whether perjury had taken place; the consequences of perjury should be left to the States concerned. In effect the jurisdiction of the Court would only cover crimes defined by the Statute.

288. Another view was that the Court should be able to control its proceedings, address the reliability of evidence presented and impose penalties in case of perjury; to leave such issues to States would entail many legal and practical difficulties, lengthy proceedings and jurisdictional conflicts. Rules concerning perjury should therefore be included in the Statute. The view was also expressed that the term "perjury" should be replaced by the words "false testimony", that false testimony should be made an offence under the Statute and that the Court should be empowered to order the arrest of a suspect for this offence and his trial by a specially constituted chamber.

289. Another issue related to the means of obtaining evidence and the exclusion of evidence (of article 44, para. 5). This raised, inter alia, the important question of judicial cooperation between the Court and national jurisdictions since very often evidence presented to the Court would have been obtained in the States concerned, in accordance with their national rules. Consideration was given to the possibility for the Court to inquire whether such evidence had been obtained in accordance with national rules. It was suggested that a mechanism should be created whereby the Court, in cases of allegations of evidence obtained by national authorities by illegal means, could decide on the credibility of the allegations and the seriousness of "violations". According to another view, the Court should not get involved in intricate inquiries about [*61] domestic laws and procedures and it should rather rely on ordinary principles of judicial cooperation. It should apply international law and should exclude, for example, evidence obtained in violation of fundamental human rights, or minimum internationally acceptable standards (such as the Guidelines of the United Nations Congress on Prevention of Crime and Treatment of Offenders), or by methods casting substantive doubts on its reliability.

Article 45. Quorum and judgement

290. With respect to the question of quorum and presence in the trial chamber, a general view seemed to be that the number of the members should preferably be odd (e.g., five) and that all members as well as the Prosecutor should be present at all stages of the trial in the interests of due process and fair trial (the same judges should be present at all hearings when relevant evidence was given, for example). A temporary absence of a judge should result either in the continuation of the trial with the remaining judges or the suspension of the trial. In case of prolonged absence of a judge, replacement should take place.

291. As for the method of decision-taking in the trial chamber, some delegations expressed the view that it should be by a majority of judges, although some supported a unanimity rule (at least in case of a conviction). The judgement should be in writing and as complete as possible, including the questions of the competence and admissibility, as well as reasons for the judgement. The view was also expressed that the Court should have power to convict the accused on the strength of evidence put forward of a crime different from that included in the indictment provided that the accused had an opportunity to defend himself or herself and that the punishment to be imposed would not be more severe than the punishment which may have been imposed under the original indictment.

292. A view was expressed that there was no need to hold two separate hearings - one for the conviction or acquittal of the accused, and one for the sentence, since no jury trial was envisaged and both issues would be decided by judges. It was also suggested that in case of conviction, compensation for the victims or restitution of goods should be considered when appropriate. The view was also expressed that the accused, when sentenced, should be notified of his right of appeal and the time limit within which that right must be exercised.

293. Another issue was how to deal with dissenting or separate opinions. A view was expressed that such opinions should be made known together with the majority decision, as this would be consistent with the established practice in national and international courts; they might also become particularly relevant in cases of appeals or retrials. Another view was that the criminal proceedings were completely different from proceedings involving civil cases and that dissenting or separate opinions would undermine the credibility and authority of the Court.

H. Appeal and review

294. Three substantive issues were raised regarding appeal: (a) the grounds of appeal, (b) the persons who have the right to appeal, and (c) the proceedings on appeal.

295. Some support was expressed for the grounds enumerated in paragraph 1 of article 48: procedural error, error of fact or of law, or disproportion between the crime and the sentence. Whether an appeal on

the grounds of jurisdiction and admissibility would be possible and at which point it should be made were issues also raised and it was suggested that they should be considered further. A suggestion was that appeals of the Prosecutor should only be allowed on the [*62] ground of error of law. Another view was that the grounds of appeal for the Prosecutor and the accused should be the same. It was also suggested that the ground of disproportion between the crime and the sentence as well as the notion of procedural error needed to be further clarified and elaborated. One view was that the convicted person should be able to appeal on any substantive grounds. If the appeal by the convicted person was general (i.e., not only against the sentence), the appeals chamber should re-examine the case in its entirety. The idea was expressed that the right of appeal should be made available as broad as possible without the appellant having to justify why this recourse was sought.

296. As for the question of the proceedings, it was pointed out that a provision on the time period in which an appeal ought to be made should appear in the Statute (for example 30 days or longer should the Presidency allow it). Stress was placed upon the necessity to include more detailed and specific provisions concerning the manner in which the appeals chamber would apply rules of procedure and evidence.

297. It was also suggested that the judges of the appeals chamber should have the right to make public their dissenting opinions. The opposite opinion was also put forward: it was suggested that the number of judges should be odd (for example, seven).

298. In case of new evidence, a suggestion was that the appeals chamber should be able to transmit the case for review to the trial chamber with different composition. It was stressed that a complete separation of membership between the trial and appeals chambers was necessary. Terms such as "unfair [proceedings]" or "error of fact or law" in article 49 were considered unclear and in need of further clarification. It was also considered necessary to define clearly the criteria according to which a new trial should be ordered as distinguished from those for a reversal or an amendment of a decision.

299. With regard to the effect of an appeal, it was suggested that unless the trial chamber decided otherwise, a convicted person should remain in custody pending an appeal, though the appeal should have an effect of suspending the execution. The idea was also expressed that during the appeal the execution of sentence should be suspended and the accused should be detained as long as the trial chamber is determining its decision.

300. As concerns the question of the revision of a conviction, it was felt that the grounds should go beyond those indicated in article 50 and should possibly include cases where evidence proved to be false or invalid, a grave violation of duties of judges had occurred, or when new facts had come to light which were unknown at the time of the trial. But the grounds for revision should be more limited than those for appeal. It seemed to be a general view that revision should not be subject to a time limit and could take place at any time (even after the death of the convicted person, if requested by his or her relatives or any other person concerned).

301. It was considered necessary to elaborate the rules for the determination of when to constitute a new trial chamber or reconvene the trial chamber or to refer the matter to the appeals chamber.

302. In case of a revision of a conviction or of acquittal of a convicted person, it was suggested that provision for compensation should be included in the Statute.

[*63] I.   Penalties
Article 46. Sentencing
Article 47. Applicable penalties

303. Two main issues emerged from the discussion: the type of penalties and the relevant laws for determining penalties.

304. It was noted that the principle of legality (nulla poena sine lege) required that penalties be defined in the draft statute of the Court as precisely as possible. The link was stressed between sentencing and penalties which should reflect the different degrees of culpability. A view was expressed that maximum and minimum penalties for each crime should be carefully set out in the draft statute. There was also a suggestion to include detailed regulations concerning, for example, minors, aggravating or attenuating circumstances (severity of damage or injury, prior conduct of the accused, means of commission of the crime, etc.), cumulative penalties for multiple crimes, an exhaustive list of aggravating circumstances and a non-exhaustive list of attenuating circumstances. Other delegations expressed support for the more

flexible approach of the draft proposed by the International Law Commission, owing to the difficulties of reaching agreement as to specific rules in this matter.

305. It was considered that deprivation of freedom would form the basis of penalties under the Statute. Some delegations expressed some difficulties with the concept of life imprisonment. Some others considered that life imprisonment and imprisonment for a specified period of time (years and/or months) should be the basic penalties under the draft statute. Fines as a separate penalty were considered inadequate in view of the seriousness of the crimes and, moreover, the Court might have difficulty collecting the fines owing to the lack of an enforcement mechanism under the draft statute. It was recognized however that fines might be appropriate for such "procedural" crimes as perjury or contempt of court or as supplementary to a penalty of imprisonment or as penalties to be applied to juridical persons. Other penalties suggested for imposition included disenfranchisement, denial or suspension of political rights or public office for the convicted person and forfeiture of property.

306. Some delegations expressed their strong support for the exclusion of the death penalty from the penalties that the Court would be authorized to impose in accordance with article 47 of the draft statute. While the death penalty was ruled out by those delegations, others suggested that the death penalty should not be excluded a priori since it was provided for in many legal systems, especially in connection with serious crimes.

307. It was also noted that provisions concerning compensation of victims, restitution of property acquired through crime and the confiscation of property of the convicted person, as well as provisions concerning penalties for juridical persons (political organizations, trade organizations and other organizations) such as dissolution, confiscation and the like, should also be considered for inclusion in the draft statute. Many problems were raised in connection with the complex issue of compensation for the victims, including compensating a large number of victims of civil war, locating the source of funding and establishing criteria for distributing funds. Reference was made to the ongoing work on reparation for victims of crime under the auspices of both the Commission on Human Rights and the Commission on Crime Prevention and Criminal Justice.

308. Regarding the relevant laws for determining penalties, various comments were made with respect to the States whose national laws the Court might take [*64] into account: (a) the State of nationality of the convicted person; (b) the State where the crime had been committed; and (c) the State which had custody of and jurisdiction over the accused. A view was expressed that taking into account the various national laws had the drawback of vagueness and imprecision, which could be contrary to the principle of legality. Moreover, this could result in manifest inequality and inconsistency, since domestic laws were not always identical in the penalties prescribed even for the same crimes. The idea was expressed that recourse to internal law should be used on a subsidiary basis and could only be applied if it did not run counter to international criminal law. One suggestion was that the draft statute should include an international standard for the various crimes; the jurisprudence and the experience of the Court could gradually expand this area. Another view, however, considered that the "renvoi" (referral) to national legislation could constitute a compromise among differing concepts and a solution to the difficult problem of determining the gravity of penalties. In the event that the national legislation did not provide for a specific crime, its provisions for an analogous crime could be taken into account.

309. It was suggested that the Court should have competence to impose appropriate punishment in cases where the convicted person was sentenced for a lesser crime than that for which he or she had originally been indicted. It was further suggested that the period of incarceration already served by the convicted person prior to trial should be taken into account in his or her serving of the term of imprisonment.

J.   Cooperation between States and the International Criminal Court
    1.   General issues relating to States' cooperation with the Court

310. The view was widely shared that since the proposed International Criminal Court would not have its own investigative or enforcement agencies, the effectiveness of the Court would depend largely upon the cooperation of national jurisdiction in obtaining evidence and securing the presence of accused persons before it. It was considered essential, therefore, that the Statute provide the Court with a sound, workable and predictable framework to secure the cooperation of States. There was the position that the legal framework governing cooperation between States and the Court should be broadly similar to that existing

between States on the basis of extradition and legal assistance agreements. This approach would ensure that the framework of cooperation would be set forth explicitly and the procedure in which each State would meet its obligations would be controlled by its national law, although there would be instances in which a State must amend its national law in order to be able to meet those obligations. There was also the position, however, that the Statute should provide for an entirely new regime which would not draw upon existing extradition and legal assistance conventions, since the system of cooperation between the Court and States was fundamentally different from that between States, and extradition existed only between sovereign States. The obligation to cooperate imposed by the Statute on States parties would not prevent the application of national laws in implementing such cooperation.

311. The principle of complementarity was considered particularly important in defining the relationship and cooperation between the Court and States. It was suggested that the principle called for the establishment of a flexible system of cooperation which would allow for special constitutional requirements of States, as well as their obligations under existing treaties.

[*65] 312. It was noted that the nature and scope of cooperation was closely linked with the basic issue of the jurisdiction of the Court under article 20 of the Statute, and with such other issues as admissibility, consent mechanisms and the choice between "opt in" and "opt out" systems.

313. There was general support for the view that all basic elements of the required cooperation between the Court and States should be laid down explicitly in the Statute itself, while the list of such elements need not be exhaustive. It was suggested that a State would need to have a clear understanding of the types of assistance required to qualify their obligations in accordance with its domestic law, or to make provisions in their law for specific forms of assistance to be available.

314. As regards the question of the extent to which national law should be a source for determining the obligations of States under the Statute, the view was expressed that since the Statute was to provide all basic requirements of cooperation between States parties and the Court, national law should not be regarded as a source for determining such requirements, although the importance of its role in implementing the cooperation required by the Statute should be emphasized. It was noted further that, in order for the system of cooperation to be workable, there must be some deference to national law, but it could not be so dependent on national law that there would be real doubts about the extent to which States would provide meaningful cooperation of the Court in appropriate circumstances. The view was expressed by some delegations that matters of substance should be governed by the Statute and matters of procedure by national law.

315. Concerning the issue of the extent to which States parties to the Statute would be bound to grant assistance and cooperation to the Court, it was suggested that the obligations of States should be clearly and exhaustively defined in the Statute, together with the exceptions to that obligation. The suggestion was also made that the Statute itself should stipulate that in general a request of the Court was mandatory. The view was expressed, however, that the obligation could not be absolute, as inferred from the principle of complementarity. It was furthermore suggested that, if the jurisdiction of the Court was to be limited to the core crimes, there should be no need for acceptance of its jurisdiction by the State to cooperate, and some kind of safeguard should be provided to enable the Court to take further action should the State fail to comply with the Court's request. Some delegations also stated, however, that if jurisdiction was not limited to core crimes those States that had not accepted jurisdiction over a crime might not be obligated to cooperate. The view was expressed that precise mechanisms should be provided for situations where a State party refused to honour the Court's requests, and for cooperation with non-parties. Recourse to the Security Council in some cases was mentioned.

316. It was generally felt that the grounds for refusing compliance with requests from the Court should be limited to a minimum, taking into account the special character of the jurisdiction of the Court and the seriousness of the crimes to be covered under the Statute. Some exceptions referred to by delegations included deference to the principle of complementarity, urgency to exercise national jurisdiction, non-acceptance of the jurisdiction of the Court by the requested State, competing requests received by the requested State from the Court and from another State under existing treaty arrangements and constitutionally protected rights. The view was expressed by some delegations that essential security interests of the requested State should also qualify for refusal. As regards traditional exceptions to

extradition, many of them, such as lack of dual criminality, political offence and nationality, were considered inappropriate in the light of the type of crimes to be dealt with by the Court. [*66] The view was expressed that such traditional exceptions to extradition had their merits in this context.

317. It was noted that the relation between the obligations under parts 7 and 8 of the draft statute and existing conventions between States in the same area raised a particularly difficult problem. The point was made that the principle of complementarity would suggest that the requested State had the discretionary power to make a determination as to which request should have priority in the interest, for example, of effective prosecution. On the other hand, some delegations insisted on the primacy of requests from the Court, which would be established by an international convention and whose jurisdiction would be limited to core crimes, in the case where a State party had received competing requests from the Court and from another State party. The situations involving a competing request by a State which was not a party to the Statute was considered particularly complex and it was suggested that the matter should be examined further.

318. It was noted that additional discussions would be required to consider situations where the national authority of a State party did not exist for the Court to establish contact to seek cooperation.

319. The question was raised as to what would be the effect of the Court's exercise of inherent jurisdiction where the State requested to grant cooperation denied such cooperation without a justifiable reason. It was further stated that under the existing norms of international law, the State that did not comply with the obligations of the Statute would be held in violation of international law, which would impose State responsibility upon that State.

2. Apprehension and surrender

320. It was noted that the system of apprehension and surrender under article 53 of the draft statute, which embodied a strict transfer scheme without contemplating any significant role of the national courts and other authorities on the matter, was a departure from the traditional regime of cooperation between States established under the existing extradition treaties. In this regard, some delegations indicated that they were in favour of a system based exclusively on the traditional extradition regime, modified as necessary. Some other delegations supported the transfer regime as envisaged in the Statute. Some further delegations expressed their view in support of reconciling the two regimes so as to ensure the consistent application of the Statute. The suggestion was made also that, in order to facilitate its acceptance by States, the Statute should provide for a choice between a modified extradition regime and a strict transfer regime, subject to different national laws and practices. It was emphasized however that whatever might be its character, it was a unique system of cooperation which must be tailored to the special needs of the Court, taking into account national constitutional requirements, particularly those for guaranteeing the protection of the fundamental rights of individuals, and States' obligations under existing extradition treaties. It was further stated that the relationship between surrender and traditional extradition required further examination. The suggestion was made that the system of surrender should be extended to cover the convicted as well as the accused persons.

321. It was generally agreed that the basis for a request by the Court for arrest of an accused as a preliminary measure for surrender should be a warrant of arrest issued by the International Criminal Court in accordance with the provisions of article 26 (3) of the draft statute. It was considered that such a request to a State party should contain a full description of the identity of the person sought, together with a full summary of the facts of the case in [*67] question, including details of the offence or offences of which the person was accused and a copy of a warrant for his or her arrest. Such information, it was said, should be provided at the time when the request was made, and not later as contemplated in article 57. In this regard, it was suggested that the Statute should formulate a procedure for what is the traditional form of provisional arrest whereby a request could be made in an abbreviated form in cases of urgency, to be followed by the transmission of a formal request for surrender accompanied by supporting documentation. As for the transmission of a formal request, it was suggested that, although some States might need to follow a modified extradition approach, rather than a pure transfer regime, documentary and evidentiary requirements under a modified extradition approach should be the least burdensome possible. In this connection, support was expressed for the proposal that States specify those requirements in advance at the time of their ratification or accession to the Statute. On the question of the means of transmission, it

was stated that the Court should have the freedom of using in each case the channel and the method it deemed appropriate, including the use of new technology such as telefax.

322. The point was made that there should be a clear distinction between the Court's request for pre-indictment arrest of a suspect and the Court's provisional request for post-indictment arrest of an accused, pending the transmission of a formal arrest warrant. It was stated that, in either case, a warrant of arrest should be the basis for a request for arrest. Some delegations suggested that, if the warrant of arrest was issued in the pre-indictment stage, there should be a determination by national courts of some sufficiency of underlying evidentiary basis for the warrant and of the existence of a specific charge. A number of delegations felt, however, that there was no need to require the transmission of any evidence in support of the arrest warrant. Concern was nevertheless expressed that pre-indictment arrest was not permissible under certain constitutions, nor was the unusually long period of 90 days of the pre-indictment detention provided for in article 28 (2). As for a need for a provision in the Statute concerning arrest of persons other than the accused, doubts were expressed as regards the possibility of the Court's ordering the arrest and transfer of a reluctant witness. In this regard, it was considered preferable to ensure that the Court itself had flexibility to receive testimony taken outside of its seat with the assistance of States or through, for example, electronic means.

323. On the question of the role of national authorities, in particular the judiciary, in the execution of the Court's requests for provisional arrest, pre-surrender detention or surrender of the accused to the Court, there was general support for the view that the Statute should permit involvement of national courts in the application of national law where those requirements were considered fundamental, especially to protect the rights of individuals, as well as to verify procedural legality. Mention was made in this connection, of the difficulties that many States would have with a direct enforcement of an arrest warrant issued by the Court, as opposed to an indirect enforcement through available national mechanisms. It was suggested that, as a minimum, it should be possible to challenge in a national court of the requested State a document purporting to be a warrant - without the examination of the warrant in relation to substantive law - and that there should be a national forum in which to adjudicate upon any admissibility dispute, at least as regards double jeopardy. It was further suggested that issues of detention prior to surrender, including bail or provisional release, should be determined by national authorities and not by the International Criminal Court, as envisaged in the draft statute. It was considered necessary, however, that the requested State should ensure that the views of the Prosecutor in regard to any release of the suspect or the accused should be brought to the attention of the judicial officer. In this regard, it was emphasized that there must be a very close working relationship [*68] between the Prosecutor and States parties in implementing the Court's request for assistance and surrender, and that the Statute should be sufficiently flexible so as to take this into account, while at the same time giving due attention to the rights of the individuals and the State's international obligations. The view was also expressed that the transfer of the accused to the Court or to the detaining State could be an appropriate point for shifting the primary responsibility over the accused from the national authorities to the International Criminal Court. With regard to the question of who should execute surrender, it was suggested that, for practical reasons, the Statute should provide for an option for execution by the custodial State, although there was also the view in favour of execution, in principle, by officials of the Court only.

324. With regard to the question of exceptions to the obligation to surrender, the view was reiterated that they should be kept to a minimum and that they should be specifically laid down in the Statute. In this connection, some delegations questioned the appropriateness of such traditional limitations or exceptions as the nationality of the accused, political or military offences, essential interests/ordre public or sufficiency of evidence. They also considered as inappropriate the principle of dual criminality, in view of the seriousness of crimes within the jurisdiction of the Court. Other delegations felt that some of these elements should be taken into account in laying down exceptions. Suggestions for possible exceptions included the principle of non bis in idem, non-acceptance of the Court's jurisdiction over a particular crime other than the crime of genocide, manifest errors of facts or law by the Court, the lack of a prima facie case, the statute of limitations, pendency of national proceedings relating to the same crime and competing requests from the Court and another State where the requested State might favour cooperation with that

other State for effective prosecution of the crime, or might be obliged to render such cooperation to that other State.

325. On the rule of speciality, the view was expressed that, while some provision concerning speciality was required in order to safeguard the rights of the accused, the Statute should provide for application only to offences committed before surrender and also for the possibility of waiver by the States concerned. It was further noted that the question of competing international obligations would arise in respect of apprehension or surrender where a person whom the requested State had secured from another State for offences unconnected with the Court was transferred to the Court without the consent of that State. The view was also expressed that the Court should not, without the consent of the requested State, re-surrender to another State party or to a third State a person surrendered to it by the requested State in respect of offences committed before his surrender.

K.   International cooperation and judicial assistance
    1.   Nature of assistance

326. While the term "judicial assistance" was described as sufficiently broad to cover the types of assistance envisaged, a preference was expressed for the term "mutual assistance" as a term of art used in recent legal instruments and as a more accurate description of the various types of assistance that might be required. A doubt was also expressed, however, concerning the appropriateness of the use of the term "mutual" considering the unique character of the Court.

[*69] 2.   Obligation of States parties to provide assistance (article 51, paragraph 1)

327. Several delegations expressed the view that the Statute should provide the legal basis for the obligation of States parties to provide the widest assistance to the Court and the general framework that would govern such matters. It was suggested that States parties should be required to use their best efforts in responding without delay to requests for assistance.

328. Some delegations expressed the view that the obligation to provide assistance should apply to all States parties, while others suggested that it should apply only to States parties which have accepted the jurisdiction of the Court with respect to the crime concerned. It was also suggested that requests for assistance should be made only after the Court had determined the question of jurisdiction, including State consent requirements, and the question of admissibility under the principle of complementarity.

329. While noting differences between the assistance to be provided by States to the Court and the traditional assistance provided between States in criminal matters, it was suggested that the Statute should be guided by the relevant existing conventions and the United Nations Model Treaty on Mutual Assistance in Criminal Matters. The view was also expressed that the Court could utilize existing arrangements for cooperation and mutual legal assistance in criminal matters.

    3.   Exceptions or limitations

330. The view was expressed that traditional exceptions to requests for assistance between States in criminal matters should not apply to the assistance to be provided to the Court given the serious nature of the crimes and the interest of the international community in the effective investigation and prosecution of those crimes. It was emphasized that any exceptions should be expressly provided in the Statute to provide predictability and uniformity with respect to the obligations of States parties, should be sufficiently narrow in scope to avoid abuse and should be kept to a minimum to avoid hampering the effective functioning of the Court. The view was also expressed that States could indicate the applicable exceptions under national law when becoming a party to the Statute. A question was raised as to whether the Statute would provide a self-contained regime of obligations and exceptions. A question was also raised as to whether the exceptions provided under international public law, such as reprisals or self-defence of States, would be applicable.

        (a)   National laws and constitutions

331. The view was expressed that national laws and constitutions should provide the procedures for implementing the requests for assistance but should not affect the obligation to provide such assistance under the Statute. It was suggested that national law could also provide the basis for the compulsory nature of investigative actions taken by the national authorities, such as search and seizure orders.

(b) Public or national security interests

332. While the view was expressed that national security interests should constitute a valid exception, as in existing conventions, concerns were expressed about recognizing a broad exception based on public or national security interests. It was suggested that consideration should be given to addressing the legitimate concerns of States regarding requests for information [*70] or evidence relating to national security interests or other sensitive information while limiting the possibility of abuse which could impede the effective functioning of the Court.

(c) National investigation or prosecution

333. Some delegations expressed the view that the traditional exception to requests for assistance based on pending national investigations or prosecutions should not be applicable since the Court would consider this matter in determining the admissibility of a case under the principle of complementarity as a preliminary matter. Other delegations expressed the view that consideration should be given to providing a limited exception in situations in which complying with a request for assistance would interfere with an effective national investigation or prosecution.

(d) Political or military offences

334. Many delegations expressed the view that the traditional exception concerning political or military offences should not apply to requests for assistance.

(e) Dual criminality

335. It was suggested that the dual criminality requirement should not be applied to requests for assistance by the Court.

(f) Manifestly unfounded request

336. Some delegations expressed the view that a State party should be able to refuse to comply with a request for assistance which was
manifestly unfounded.

4. General provision or enumeration (article 51, paragraph 2)

337. A number of delegations expressed the view that the Statute should contain a list of the types of assistance that might be requested of States parties so as to indicate clearly their obligations and to facilitate the adoption of implementing legislation. While several delegations favoured a non-exhaustive list to provide a measure of flexibility and to enable the Court to request appropriate kinds of assistance in particular cases not specifically envisaged in the Statute, other delegations favoured a comprehensive list to provide greater clarity concerning the obligation of States parties and thereby facilitate the enactment of implementing legislation. It was suggested that the list contained in article 51, paragraph 2, should be further elaborated based on existing instruments.

5. On-site investigations (article 26, paragraph 2 (c))

338. Several delegations expressed the view that the Prosecutor should not be authorized unilaterally to initiate and conduct on-site investigations in the territory of a State party without its consent since that authority would be contrary to the principle of State sovereignty; it would be difficult for the Prosecutor to conduct on-site investigations and to ensure compliance with divergent national and constitutional law guarantees of individual rights without the assistance of national authorities; and such authorization would go beyond existing international law and would not be generally acceptable to States.

[*71] 339. The view was expressed that the on-site investigations envisaged under article 26, paragraph 2 (c), should be considered as a kind of assistance to be provided by States in response to an appropriate request from the Court. It was emphasized that on-site investigations should be carried out only with the consent of the State concerned and by its competent national authorities in accordance with the national and constitutional law guarantees of individual rights. The view was expressed that there might be a limited exception to the State consent requirement in extraordinary situations involving the referral of a matter to the Court by the Security Council under Chapter VII of the Charter of the United Nations. Other delegations felt that the Prosecutor should be authorized to carry out on-site investigations with the consent of the State concerned, and without its consent if the national authorities were unable to conduct an investigation that would meet the Court's needs. In the view of those delegations, it would be up to the Court to decide if that condition had been met.

6. Requests for assistance (article 57)
(a) Form and content of requests

340. Several delegations expressed the view that requests for assistance should include sufficiently detailed, relevant information concerning the crime, the alleged offender, the type of assistance requested, the reasons for requesting assistance and its objective as well as other relevant information depending on the type of assistance requested, such as the identity and location of the alleged offender, the identity and location of witnesses, the location of documents or other evidence. There was an indication of general satisfaction with article 57, paragraphs 3 and 4, while noting the possibility of further refinement based on the relevant instruments. It was suggested that it might be necessary to retain a degree of flexibility in view of divergent national law requirements.

(b) Competent authority for making such requests

341. The view was expressed that the Prosecutor should be competent to request assistance given his or her responsibility for the investigation and prosecution of alleged offenders. There were different views as to the extent to which the Prosecutor should be required to request the assistance of States in obtaining exculpatory information and evidence or the defence should be permitted to request the assistance of States in this regard. The view was further expressed that the Presidency, the Court or the trial chamber should also be competent to request assistance from a State party depending on the stage of the investigation or the judicial proceeding. It was suggested that the Court should be competent to request assistance either ex officio, upon the request of the Prosecutor or of the defence. It was also suggested that the Registry should be responsible for transmitting requests for assistance, as indicated in article 51, paragraph 2.

(c) Means of communication

342. Several delegations expressed the view that States parties should designate the competent national authority to receive requests for assistance to provide an expeditious and direct line of communication, as envisaged in article 57, paragraph 1. A preference was expressed for using diplomatic channels to communicate requests for assistance, while there was also an indication that this was not the current practice. It was suggested that there should be some flexibility to enable States parties to select different channels of communication.

[*72] 343. In the view of some delegations modern means of communication should be used to facilitate expeditious communications, such as by fax or other electronic means. It was emphasized that it might be necessary to provide subsequently an original written request without delay to enable the national authorities to take appropriate action. However, concerns were expressed regarding the reliability and the confidentiality of such means.

7. Role of national authorities

344. It was emphasized that requests for assistance should be carried out by the competent national authorities in accordance with national law and constitutional guarantees of individual rights. It was also emphasized that it would be necessary for the national authorities to comply with relevant international standards in implementing the requests for assistance. It was suggested that the national authorities could carry out investigations pursuant to instructions provided by the Court and that the Prosecutor or staff members could be present during the investigation and possibly participate therein.

8. Non-compliance

345. The view was expressed that consideration should be given to situations in which a State refused to assist in an investigation in an attempt to shield an individual from criminal responsibility or was unable to provide such assistance owing to the lack of an effective, functioning judicial or legal system. It was suggested that it might be possible to envisage a role for the Security Council in certain situations. It was also suggested that the Statute should envisage a special chamber that would consider refusals or failures to comply with requests for assistance and render appropriate decisions.

9. Rule of speciality (article 55)

346. The view was expressed that the rule of speciality should apply to information or evidence transmitted to the Court by a State. There was an indication of general satisfaction with the limited rule contained in article 55, paragraph 2. Emphasis was also placed on envisaging an exception to the rule based on the express consent or waiver given by the State that had provided the information or evidence, with reference being made to article 55, paragraph 3. It was suggested that such an exception should be based on the

consent or waiver of the accused. It was also suggested that the rule of speciality could be limited to situations in which the State concerned raised an objection.

10. Reciprocity

347. Some delegations were of the view that the rule of reciprocity should apply to the relation between the Court and States, to the effect that the Court should be under an obligation to comply with requests by States exercising jurisdiction in conformity with the notion of complementarity. The view was also expressed that the Statute should merely envisage the possibility of the Court providing information or evidence to a State to assist with a national investigation or prosecution of a similar or related case without overburdening the Court. Although some delegations raised this issue under the rubric of reciprocity, other delegations pointed out that since the Court would not be a State and could not be obligated to reciprocate assistance rendered by a State in a strict sense, it would be more appropriate to consider the issue as [*73] possible cooperation provided by the Court to a State. It was further stated that a provision stipulating such cooperation by the Court could be included in the Statute. The view was expressed that the Court could not provide information obtained from one State to another State without the consent of the former State.

11. Assistance of non-States parties (article 56)

348. The view was expressed that non-States parties should be encouraged to provide assistance to the Court as envisaged in article 56. It was suggested that the Court should be authorized to enter into special agreements or ad hoc arrangements with non-States parties to encourage and enable such States to provide assistance to the Court in general or in particular cases. It was also suggested that reciprocity or mutual cooperation might be an important factor in obtaining the assistance of non-States parties.

12. Recognition of judgements and enforcement of sentences

349. It was generally recognized that because this subject involved novel features and therefore only preliminary comments could be made at the current stage, these issues would require further consideration and elaboration.

350. Concerning the issue of penalties, it was felt that penalties other than imprisonment, e.g., fines, restitution, compensation, might have to be considered under part 8.

(a) Recognition of judgements (article 58)

351. The view was expressed that by accepting the jurisdiction of the Court States parties would, by definition, recognize the Court's judgements. Therefore, it was not necessary to provide for a particular recognition procedure in the Statute. Article 58, therefore, should be modified to provide that a State not only should recognize a judgement of the Court but also should enforce the Court's sentences in its territory. The view was also expressed that States parties were bound to recognize the Court's judgements upon the entry into force of the Statute, and it was proposed that article 58 be amended by adding the sentence: "States parties have to recognize the judgements of the Court as judgements rendered by their national judiciaries." It was further proposed that, as a consequence of the rule of reciprocity, a provision in article 58 should stipulate that the Court also should recognize the judgements of the States parties.

352. Some delegations felt that automatic recognition of judgements and enforcement of sentences of the Court should be subject to the provision that recognition should not be inconsistent with fundamental provisions of the domestic law of States parties.

353. A contrasting view envisaged the Court as being on equal footing with national legal systems and that the Court's judgements, therefore, should not be automatically recognized, but rather examined by the national Court concerned.

354. There was support for both a method of continued enforcement and a national exequatur procedure. Regarding a national exequatur procedure, the point was made that the Statute should ensure that the reasons for a State's refusal to execute the Court's judgement were kept to an absolute minimum.

[*74] 355. The need for article 58 was also questioned on the ground that if the Court was to impose only imprisonment, vis-ê-vis fines or restitution, then article 59 alone would appear to specify adequately a State's obligation to the Court.

(b) Enforcement of sentences (article 59)

356. There was support among the delegations for the Court to designate a State where the sentence of imprisonment would be served from a list of States which had indicated their "willingness" to accept convicted persons. The view was further expressed that in designating a State the Court should take into

account the interests of the Court itself and of the State concerned as well as the fundamental rights of the prisoner. The remark was made, however, that article 59 should be redrafted so as to exclude any element of "willingness" on the part of States parties in executing the Court's sentences, as this would run counter to the idea of the Court being an extension of the judiciary of the States parties. In other words, article 59 should make it clear that States parties would be obligated to execute sentences of the Court if they were so designated by the Court.

357. Concerning the issue of the supervision of a sentence of imprisonment, it was generally agreed that the Court should exercise control in critical areas, in order to ensure consistency and compliance with international norms regarding conditions of incarceration (e.g., the 1955 United Nations Standard Minimum Rules for the Treatment of Prisoners), and leaving to the custodial State the day-to-day supervision of the prisoner. The remark was also made that control by the Court was necessary to prevent national law being used, for example, to reduce a sentence imposed on a prisoner by the Court.

358. The point was also made that the issues of enforcement of sentences in article 59 and the issues of pardon, parole and commutation of sentences in article 60 merged to a certain extent, and that the temporary or permanent release of a convicted person should be decided upon by the Court. It was recognized that that might require the establishment of an additional arm of the Court to monitor when prisoners should be released.

(c) Pardon, parole and commutation of sentences (article 60)

359. The view was expressed that the issues of pardon, parole and commutation of sentences should be left to the Court. Another view supported the retention of paragraph 4 of article 60 as an essential provision in the Statute for a State's acceptance of prisoners.

360. There was also the view that since the Court was a judicial body and should not be put in a position to consider extra-legal matters associated with pardons and parole, perhaps a separate entity should be created to deal with these issues.

361. Remarks were made however questioning the role of the power of pardon since the Court's powers of revision, parole and commutation of sentences seemed sufficient to address the interests of the convicted person.

L. Other issues

362. It was suggested that the final clauses should provide a transitional arrangement for the transfer of cases from the ad hoc tribunals to the Court to avoid concurrent or parallel jurisdiction. However, attention was drawn to the differences in the temporal jurisdiction of the ad hoc tribunals and the Court, which obviated the need for such an arrangement.

[*75] 363. Some delegations expressed their concern that there had been no negotiation of texts during the deliberations of the Preparatory Committee which would allow the fixing of a specific date for the holding of the conference. For those delegations, the date of the conference was closely linked to the progress in the preparatory work and its results.

364. The view was also expressed that the process of negotiation should be democratic and transparent, that the question of the scheduling of the conference was a political one and did not fall within the mandate of the Preparatory Committee and that it should be considered in a political body such as the Sixth Committee. According to the same view, taking a decision on the date of the conference before the trend of future developments became clearer might compromise the quality of negotiations in the future.

365. Other delegations, however, were of the view that in order to ensure an effective negotiating process it would be necessary to establish a deadline for the preparatory work and to that effect fix a date for the conference of plenipotentiaries in 1997.

M. Conclusions of the Preparatory Committee 12/

366. The General Assembly, by its resolution 50/46 of 11 December 1995, established the Preparatory Committee on the Establishment of an International Criminal Court and directed it "to discuss further the major substantive and administrative issues arising out of the draft Statute prepared by the International Law Commission and, taking into account the different views expressed during the meetings, to draft texts, with a view to preparing a widely acceptable consolidated text of a convention for an international criminal Court as a next step towards consideration by a conference of plenipotentiaries", and decided "to include in the provisional agenda of its fifty-first session an item entitled 'Establishment of an international criminal

Court', in order to study the report of the Preparatory Committee and, in light of that report, to decide on the convening of an international conference of plenipotentiaries to finalize and adopt a convention on the establishment of an international criminal Court, including on the timing and duration of the conference."

367. In accordance with its mandate, the Preparatory Committee discussed the major substantive and administrative issues arising out of the draft Statute and proceeded to consider draft texts, with a view to preparing a widely acceptable consolidated text of a convention for an international criminal Court. The Preparatory Committee undertook its mandate on the basis of the draft Statute prepared by the International Law Commission, taking into account the report of the Ad Hoc Committee on the Establishment of an International Criminal Court, the written comments submitted by States to the Secretary-General pursuant to General Assembly resolution 49/53 of 9 December 1994 and proposals for amendments submitted by delegations and taking into account also the contributions of relevant organizations. Written proposals for amendments to the draft Statute of the International Law Commission already submitted by delegations or prepared by the Chairman are included in the present report in the form of a compilation (see vol. II). They contain consolidated texts prepared by informal groups without prejudice to the national positions of delegations.

368. The Preparatory Committee wishes to emphasize the usefulness of its discussions and the cooperative spirit in which the debates took place. In light of the progress made and with an awareness of the commitment of the international community to the establishment of an international criminal Court, [*76] the Preparatory Committee recommends that the General Assembly reaffirm the mandate of the Preparatory Committee and give the following directions to it:

(a)   To meet three or four times up to a total of nine weeks before the diplomatic conference. To organize its work so that it will be finalized in April 1998 and so as to allow the widest possible participation of States. The work should be done in the form of open-ended working groups, concentrating on the negotiation of proposals with a view to producing a draft consolidated text of a convention to be submitted to the diplomatic conference. No simultaneous meetings of the working groups shall be held. The working methods should be fully transparent and should be by general agreement in order to secure the universality of the convention. Submission of reports on its debates will not be required. Interpretation and translation services will be available to the working groups;

(b)   To deal with by the following:

(i)   Definition and elements of crimes;
(ii) Principles of criminal law and penalties;
(iii) Organization of the Court;
(iv) Procedures;
(v)   Complementarity and trigger mechanism;
(vi) Cooperation with States;
(vii) Establishment of the International Criminal Court and its relationship with the United Nations;
(viii) Final clauses and financial matters;
(ix) Other matters.

369. The Preparatory Committee recalls that the General Assembly resolved in its resolution 50/46 to decide at its fifty-first session, in the light of the report of the Preparatory Committee, on the convening of an international conference of plenipotentiaries to finalize and adopt a convention on the establishment of an international criminal court, including on the timing and the duration of the conference.

370. Recognizing that this is a matter for the General Assembly, the Preparatory Committee, on the basis of its scheme of work, considers that it is realistic to regard the holding of a diplomatic conference of plenipotentiaries in 1998 as feasible.

Notes

<u>1</u>/   The list of delegations to the Preparatory Committee is contained in documents A/AC.249/INF/1 and A/AC.249/INF/2.

<u>2</u>/   Official Records of the General Assembly, Forty-ninth Session, Supplement No. 10 (A/49/10), chap. II.B.I.5; and A/49/355, chap. II.

<u>3</u>/   Ibid., Fiftieth Session, Supplement No. 22 (A/50/22).

[*77] <u>4</u>/   A/CN.4/L.532 and Corr.1 and 3. This document will appear in Official Records of the General Assembly, Fifty-first Session, Supplement No. 10 (A/51/10).

<u>5</u>/   General Assembly resolution 40/34, annex.

<u>6</u>/   E/CN.15/1996/16/Add.5, recommendation 2, annex.

<u>7</u>/   General Assembly resolution 49/60, annex.

<u>8</u>/   Official Records of the General Assembly, Fiftieth Session, Supplement No. 22 (A/50/22).

<u>9</u>/   For further discussion on the role of the Prosecutor, see paras. 149 to 151 above.

<u>10</u>/   Official Records of the General Assembly, Fiftieth Session, Supplement No. 22 (A/50/22).

<u>11</u>/   See also paras. 303-309 below.

<u>12</u>/   Some delegations expressed reservations on the conclusions of the Preparatory Committee and felt that these conclusions do not prejudge the position of the States in the General Assembly.

REPORT OF THE PREPARATORY COMMITTEE ON THE ESTABLISHMENT OF AN INTERNATIONAL CRIMINAL COURT

VOLUME II

(Compilation of Proposals)

[Editorial Note - The U.N. page numbers of this document are indicated in bolded brackets [*] in the text].

[*1] Preamble*
I. ILC DRAFT

The States parties to this Statute,

Desiring to further international cooperation to enhance the effective prosecution and suppression of crimes of international concern, and for that purpose to establish an international criminal court;

Emphasizing that such a court is intended to exercise jurisdiction only over the most serious crimes of concern to the international community as a whole;

Emphasizing further that such a court is intended to be complementary to national criminal justice systems in cases where such trial procedures may not be available or may be ineffective;

Have agreed as follows:

II. PROPOSALS

Desiring to further international cooperation ...;

Emphasizing that such a court is intended ...;

[**Recognizing** that it is the primary duty of States to bring to justice persons responsible for such serious crimes;]

Emphasizing further that such a court is intended to be complementary to national criminal justice systems **[in cases where such systems may be ineffective AND/OR in cases where national jurisdiction is unavailable]** (in cases where such trial procedures may not be available or may be ineffective);

[*2] OR

Emphasizing further that **the international criminal court shall complement national criminal justice systems when they are unable or unwilling to fulfil their obligations to bring to trial such persons;**

[*3] PART 1. ESTABLISHMENT OF THE COURT
Article 1
The Court
I. ILC DRAFT

There is established an International Criminal Court ("the Court"), whose jurisdiction and functioning shall be governed by the provisions of this Statute.

II. PROPOSALS

There is established an International Criminal Court ("the Court") **[which shall be complementary to national criminal justice systems. Its jurisdiction and functions]** (whose jurisdiction and functioning) shall be governed by the provisions of this Statute.

---

*   Note concerning the preamble and articles 1 to 4 and 20 to 24

Unless otherwise indicated, where the text of proposals is based on the original text of the ILC draft statute, the latter is reproduced in ordinary type and delegations' proposals for amendment appear in bold type.

Where a deletion of text has been proposed, the original text is surrounded by parentheses which are in bold type. Where an addition to the text has been proposed, the original text is interrupted by square brackets, which contain the proposed addition in bold type.

This compilation is not exhaustive. The texts included do not reflect any generally held views. The Committee did not discuss these texts and does not wish to prejudice the future positions of delegations.

This compilation has been prepared on the basis of the proposals made in the March-April meeting of the Preparatory Committee (A/AC.249/1, annexes I-VI) and the written proposals submitted at the August meeting of the Preparatory Committee (A/AC.249/L.3).

* * *

A Permanent International Criminal Court ("the Court"), whose jurisdiction and functioning shall be governed by the provisions of this Statute, is hereby established.

[*4] Article 2
Relationship of the Court to the United Nations
I. ILC DRAFT

The President, with the approval of the States parties to this Statute ("States parties"), may conclude an agreement establishing an appropriate relationship between the Court and the United Nations.

II. PROPOSALS

The Court shall, as soon as possible, be brought into relationship with the United Nations. It shall constitute one of the specialized agencies provided for in Article 57 of the Charter of the United Nations. The relationship shall form the subject of an agreement with the United Nations pursuant to Article 63 of the Charter.

The agreement, proposed by the Presidency of the Court, shall be submitted to the General Assembly of the States parties for approval. It shall provide the means for establishing effective cooperation between the Court and the United Nations in the pursuit of their common aims. It shall, at the same time, set forth the autonomy of the Court in its particular field of competence, as defined in this Statute.

[*5] Article 3
Seat of the Court
I. ILC DRAFT

1.   The seat of the Court shall be established at ... in ... ("the host State").
2.   The President, with the approval of the States parties, may conclude an agreement with the host State establishing the relationship between that State and the Court.
3.   The Court may exercise its powers and functions on the territory of any State party and, by special agreement, on the territory of any other State.

II. PROPOSALS

1.   The seat of the Court shall be established at ... in ... ("the host State").

The Presidency of the Court shall submit for the approval of the General Assembly of the States parties an agreement establishing relations between the host State and the Court.

2.   The Court may also, for a particular case and when travel by the members of the Court is likely to make the proceedings simpler and less costly, sit in a State party other than the host State.

The Presidency of the Court shall make inquiries with the State party that appears likely to receive the Court.

After the State party likely to receive the Court has agreed, the decision under the preceding paragraph to hold a session away from the Court's seat shall be taken by the General Assembly of the States parties, which shall be informed either by one of its members, the Presidency, the Prosecutor or the General Assembly of Judges of the Court.

With the express agreement of the State party receiving the Court, the privileges, immunities and facilities provided for in article x shall continue to be effective when the Court holds a session pursuant to the three preceding subparagraphs.

3.   The provisions of paragraph 2 of this article shall also apply to non-party States which, after inquiries by the Presidency, state that they agree to receive the Court and to grant the privileges, immunities and facilities provided for in article x.

[*6] Article 4
Status and legal capacity
I. ILC DRAFT

1.   The Court is a permanent institution open to States parties in accordance with this Statute. It shall act when required to consider a case submitted to it.

2.   The Court shall enjoy in the territory of each State party such legal capacity as may be necessary for the exercise of its functions and the fulfilment of its purposes.

II. PROPOSALS

1.   The Court is a permanent institution open to States parties under the conditions set out in this Statute. It shall act when required to consider a case submitted to it.

2.   Without prejudice to the provisions of paragraph 1 of this article, the Presidency, the Preliminary Investigations Chambers, the Procuracy and the Registry shall perform their functions at the Court on a permanent basis.

3.   When the Presidency considers that the Court's case-load requires the permanent presence of all the judges of the Court, it shall so inform the General Assembly of the States parties, which may decide that all judges shall perform their duties full-time, for a period determined by the General Assembly or until further notice.

[*7] PART 2. COMPOSITION AND ADMINISTRATION OF THE COURT
Article 5
Organs of the Court*
I. ILC DRAFT

The Court consists of the following organs:

(a)   a Presidency, as provided in article 8;

(b)   an Appeals Chamber, Trial Chambers and other chambers, as provided in article 9;

(c)   a Procuracy, as provided in article 12; and

(d)   a Registry, as provided in article 13.

II. PROPOSALS
UNITED STATES OF AMERICA

Throughout the text

(a)   Replace the term "Presidency" by the term "Administrative Council";

(b)   Replace the term "President" by the term "Chief Judge";

(c)   Replace the term "Vice-President" by the term "Deputy Chief Judge".

UNITED KINGDOM OF GREAT BRITAIN AND NORTHERN IRELAND

Replace the term "Procuracy" by the term "Prosecutor's Office".

[*8] FRANCE

The Court shall consist of the following organs:

(a)   a Presidency, as provided for in article ...;

(b)   Preliminary Investigations Chambers, as provided for in article ...;

(c)   Trial Chambers, an Appeals Chamber and a Remand Chamber, as provided for in article ...;

(d)   a procuracy, as provided for in article ...;

(e)   a Registry, as provided for in article ...; and

(f)   a General Assembly of Judges, consisting of all the judges of the Court.

NETHERLANDS

Insert after subparagraph (b) the following subparagraph (b.1):

"(b.1) an Investigative Judge, as provided in article 26 (2) (c);"

---

*   Note concerning articles 5 to 19

The following is a compilation which was prepared by an informal group and contains written proposals submitted by various delegations to the Preparatory Committee in the course of discussion on issues pertaining to the composition and administration of the International Criminal Court. Nothing in this compilation necessarily represents the final position of the delegations which submitted the proposals.

The compilation is not exhaustive and does not necessarily reflect any generally held views. The informal group did not discuss the proposals and does not wish to prejudge the future position of the delegations. The informal group compiled notes submitted by certain delegations. Such compilation of notes is not intended to be comprehensive.

[*9] Article 6
Qualification and election of judges
I. ILC DRAFT

1.   The judges of the Court shall be persons of high moral character, impartiality and integrity who possess the qualifications required in their respective countries for appointment to the highest judicial offices, and have, in addition:

(a)   criminal trial experience;

(b)   recognized competence in international law.

2.   Each State party may nominate for election not more than two persons, of different nationality, who possess the qualification referred to in paragraph (1) (a) or that referred to in paragraph 1 (b), and who are willing to serve as may be required on the Court.

3.   Eighteen judges shall be elected by an absolute majority vote of the States parties by secret ballot. Ten judges shall first be elected, from among the persons nominated as having the qualification referred to in paragraph 1 (a). Eight judges shall then be elected, from among the persons nominated as having the qualification referred to in paragraph 1 (b).

4.   No two judges may be nationals of the same State.

5.   States parties should bear in mind in the election of the judges that the representation of the principal legal systems of the world should be assured.

6.   Judges hold office for a term of nine years and, subject to paragraph 7 and article 7 (2), are not eligible for re-election. A judge shall, however, continue in office in order to complete any case the hearing of which has commenced.

7.   At the first election, six judges chosen by lot shall serve for a term of three years and are eligible for re-election; six judges chosen by lot shall serve for a term of six years; and the remainder shall serve for a term of nine years.

8.   Judges nominated as having the qualification referred to in paragraph 1 (a) or 1 (b), as the case may be, shall be replaced by persons nominated as having the same qualification.

II. PROPOSALS
FRANCE

1.   The judges of the Court shall be persons of high moral character and possess all the qualifications required for appointment to the highest judicial offices. They shall, in addition, have great practical criminal trial experience or recognized competence in international criminal law. They shall [*10] also possess an excellent knowledge of and be fluent in at least one of the working languages referred to in article 25.

2.   Each State Party may nominate for election not more than three persons who are willing to serve as may be required on the Court.

3.   The judges shall be 24 in number. They shall be elected by the General Assembly of the States Parties. No two judges may be of the same nationality. States Parties shall endeavour in the election of the judges to ensure that the principal legal systems of the world are represented.

4.   A judge's term of office shall be nine years. It shall end in all cases when the judge reaches 75 years of age. Judges shall not be eligible for re-election, subject to the provisions of paragraphs 5 and 6 of this article. In addition, a judge who has started to hear a case shall continue to deal with it, even beyond the limit fixed by this article.

5.   Following the first election of the judges, eight judges chosen by lot shall serve for a term of three years, eight more for a term of six years, and the remaining eight for a term of nine years. The judges chosen for a term of three years shall be eligible for re-election.

UNITED STATES OF AMERICA

1.   The judges of the Court shall be persons of high moral character, impartiality and integrity who are qualified for the practice of law and have, in addition:

(a)   [at least five years] experience in the conduct of criminal proceedings [as judge, Prosecutor, or defending attorney], and/or

(b)   recognized competence in [relevant] international law.

2.   (a)   When an election is required, the Nominating Committee shall develop a list of candidates, equal in number to the number of positions to be filled, taking into account such views as may be submitted to it by the Presidency, the Procuracy and States Parties and such other sources as the Committee may consult. [In addition to the mandatory requirements set forth in this article, the Committee shall consider as desirable criteria the degree of excellence in meeting the mandatory requirements, technical ability in professional skills and expertise in criminal law.]

       (b)   The Nominating Committee shall be composed by the [Secretary-General of the United Nations] [Assembly of States Parties] [the Chairmen of the Regional Groups] and shall consist of two members from each Regional Group, selected from among nominations by States party.

       (c)   Once the Nominating Committee is established, the Registrar shall provide the Committee, upon request, with any necessary facilities and administrative and staff support.

3.   [12-24?] judges shall be elected by an [absolute majority] [two-thirds majority] vote of the States Parties by secret ballot. In the event that a sufficient number of judges is not elected, the Nominating Committee shall provide a further list of candidates and there shall be another election.

[*11] [Election may be by diplomatic note, with the results to be compiled and announced by the Depositary or, once the Court is established, the Registrar.]

4.   No two judges may be nationals of the same State, nor may any judge be over the age of [?] at the time of nomination.

5.   In compiling the nominations, the Nominating Committee should bear in mind that the representation of the principal legal systems of the world should be assured and should aim for overall balanced representation of geographic regions [and cultures] and representation of women as well as men [gender balance] [gender diversity]. [At least two thirds of the candidates should have experience in criminal proceedings.]

6.   Judges hold office for a term of [nine years and, subject to paragraph 7 and article 7 (2), are not eligible for re-election] [six years and may be re-elected]. A judge shall continue in office in order to complete any case the hearing of which has commenced.

7.   At the first election, [six] [?] judges chosen by lot shall serve for a term of [three] [two] years and are eligible for re-election; [six] [?] judges chosen by lot shall serve for a term of [six] [four] years; and the remainder shall serve for a term of [nine] [six] years. [In the event that the number of judges is increased at any stage, the terms of the additional judges shall be similarly staggered.]

       [Note: This allows for a decision to increase the number of judges, but the means by which this decision is made depends on overall administrative arrangements and will be addressed elsewhere.]

Article 6, paragraph 1
SINGAPORE AND TRINIDAD AND TOBAGO

Insert at the end of subparagraph 1 (a) the words "as an advocate or as a member of the judiciary."

PORTUGAL

Paragraph 1 of article 6 should read:

"The judges of the Court shall be persons of high moral character, <u>independence</u>, impartiality and integrity who <u>are highly competent jurists</u> and have, in addition:

"(a) criminal trial experience [insert the proposal of Trinidad and Tobago]; and/or

"(b) recognized competence in international law."

SWITZERLAND

Replace paragraph 1 of article 6 by the following:

[*12] "The judges of the Court shall be persons of the highest moral character, impartiality and integrity who, in their respective countries, fulfil the requirements for the exercise of the highest judicial offices. In the composition of the Court and its Chamber, due account shall be taken of the experience of the judges in criminal law and international law, including international humanitarian law and human rights law."

UNITED KINGDOM

In paragraph 1, delete subparagraphs (a) and (b) and insert after the words "in addition" the words "criminal trial experience and, where possible, recognized competence in international law".

JAPAN

Replace subparagraph 1 (b) by the following: "recognized competence in international law or criminal law".

FINLAND

Insert in subparagraph 1 (b) after the words "international law" the following: ", including international humanitarian law and human rights law."

ALGERIA, EGYPT, JORDAN, KUWAIT, LIBYAN ARAB JAMAHIRIYA AND QATAR

The qualification of judges should be the same as those formulated in the ICTFY statute. The principle of equitable geographic distribution and other factors are needed to achieve diversity and balance. Experience in criminal matters (judicial prosecutorial or defence advocacy) is, in part, necessary, but not to the exclusion of other expertise. The words of article 6 "... for appointment to the highest judicial offices ..." are too limiting since most legal systems do not have judicial appointments but career judges. This present formulation means that only career judges are eligible, and therefore, this formulation should be changed. We share the views of other delegations that gender representation is necessary, but voice our opposition to a quota system. It would be useful to have a nomination and screening process by the Committee of States Parties.

Article 6, paragraph 2
FINLAND

Insert at the end of the paragraph:
"Persons over [65] years of age at the time of election shall not be nominated for election."

[*13] SINGAPORE

Amend paragraph 2 as follows:
"Each State Party may nominate for election not more than two persons of different nationality, who possess the qualification referred to in paragraph 1 (a) or that referred to in paragraph 1 (b), who are not above the age of [61/66] years at the time of election, and who are willing to serve as may be required on the Court."

SWITZERLAND AND UNITED KINGDOM OF GREAT BRITAIN AND NORTHERN IRELAND

Replace the words "the qualification referred to in paragraph 1 (a) or that referred to in paragraph 1 (b)" by the words "the qualifications referred to in paragraph 1".

UNITED KINGDOM

Replace the words "each State Party" by "each national group".

ALGERIA, EGYPT, JORDAN, KUWAIT, LIBYAN ARAB JAMAHIRIYA AND QATAR

As stated by other delegations, a judge nominated by a State Party can be a national of any other State. This would broaden the universality of a Court and allow for a broader choice of qualified candidates.

Article 6, paragraph 3
CHINA

Replace paragraph 3 by the following: "The judges shall be elected by the General Assembly of the United Nations."

UNITED KINGDOM

Replace paragraph 3 by the following: "The judges of the Court shall be elected by the General Assembly and the Security Council from a list of persons nominated by national groups appointed for the purpose by their Governments."

SWITZERLAND

Replace paragraph 3 by the following: "Twelve judges shall be elected, by secret ballot, by an absolute majority of the Assembly of States Parties."

ALGERIA, EGYPT, JORDAN, KUWAIT, LIBYAN ARAB JAMAHIRIYA AND QATAR

The overall number of judges should be determined at a later stage. The proposals of 18 and up to 24 by several delegations are reasonable, but [*14] consideration should be given to the subsequent appointment of judges if the volume of work of the Court requires it. Such a mechanism should be established without the need to amend the statute.

Article 6, paragraph 5
CHINA
Replace paragraph 5 by the following:
"In the election of the judges, the representation of the main forms of civilization and of the principal legal systems of the world and the equitable geographical distribution should be assured in the Court as a whole."

DENMARK, FINLAND, MALAWI, NEW ZEALAND, NORWAY AND SWEDEN
Replace paragraph 5 by the following:
"In the election of the judges, States Parties should bear in mind that in the Court as a whole the representation of the principal legal systems of the world, equitable geographical distribution and gender balance should be assured."

Article 6, paragraph 6
CHINA
Replace paragraph 6 by the following: "The judges may hold office for a term of nine years and be eligible for re-election."

DENMARK
Insert the following as a second sentence: "Judges shall retire at the age of [70/75]."

TRINIDAD AND TOBAGO
Add the following words at the end of the paragraph: "on the understanding that the matter be concluded within five years."

ALGERIA, EGYPT, JORDAN, KUWAIT, LIBYAN ARAB JAMAHIRIYA AND QATAR
The term of office should be limited in number of years, for example, five years with only one potential renewal. Also an age limit of 70 years should be established.

[*15] Article 6, paragraph 7
UNITED KINGDOM OF GREAT BRITAIN AND NORTHERN IRELAND
Replace the words "six judges" wherever they appear by the words "five judges".

Article 6, paragraph 8
SWITZERLAND AND UNITED KINGDOM
Delete paragraph 8.

[*16] Article 7
Judicial vacancies
I. ILC DRAFT
1.   In the event of a vacancy, a replacement judge shall be elected in accordance with article 6.
2.   A judge elected to fill a vacancy shall serve for the remainder of the predecessor's term, and if that period is less than five years is eligible for re-election for a further term.
II. PROPOSALS
FRANCE
In the event of a vacancy, a new election shall be held in accordance with this article. A judge elected to fill a vacancy shall serve for the remainder of the predecessor's term. If the remainder of the term is less than three years, he shall be eligible for re-election for a further term.

[*17] Article 8
The Presidency
I. ILC DRAFT
1.   The President, the first and second Vice-Presidents and two alternate Vice-Presidents shall be elected by an absolute majority of the judges. They shall serve for a term of three years or until the end of their term of office as judges, whichever is earlier.
2.   The first or second Vice-President, as the case may be, may act in place of the President in the event that the President is unavailable or disqualified. An alternate Vice-President may act in place of either Vice-President as required.
3.   The President and the Vice-Presidents shall constitute the Presidency which shall be responsible for:

(a)   the due administration of the Court; and

(b)   the other functions conferred on it by this Statute.

4.   Unless otherwise indicated, pre-trial and other procedural functions conferred under this Statute on the Court may be exercised by the Presidency in any case where a chamber of the Court is not seized of the matter.

5.   The Presidency may, in accordance with the Rules, delegate to one or more judges the exercise of a power vested in it under articles 26 (3), 27 (5), 28, 29 and 30 (3) in relation to a case, during the period before a Trial Chamber is established for that case.

II. PROPOSALS
FRANCE
Internal organization

1.   The college of judges of the Court shall consist of:

(a)   a president;

(b)   six Vice-Presidents, including a First Vice-President and a Second Vice-President;

(c)   seventeen judge counsellors.

2.   The President, First Vice-President, Second Vice-President and four other Vice-Presidents shall be elected by an absolute majority at a General Assembly of Judges following their first election. They shall be elected for three years or until expiry of their term as a judge if the term ends before expiry of those three years. They shall be eligible for re-election once.

[*18] The General Assembly of Judges of the Court shall be convened when one of the posts referred to in paragraph 1 (a) and (b) of this article falls vacant.

Presidency of the Court

The Presidency of the Court shall be responsible for due administration of the Court. It shall consist of the President, the First Vice-President and the Second Vice-President.

UNITED STATES

1.   Add the following to paragraph 1: "The Vice-Presidents and Alternates shall be chosen so as to represent both the appellate and trial judges."

2.   Replace paragraph 3 by the following:

"The President and the Vice-Presidents [Chief and Deputy Chief Judges] shall constitute the Presidency [Administrative Council] which shall be responsible for the due administration of the Court, including the supervision and direction of the Registrar and staff of the Registry and Court. The Presidency [Administrative Council] shall consult with the Prosecutor and include the Prosecutor or Deputy in their meetings on all matters of mutual concern including, for example, functioning of the Registry and security arrangements for defendants, witnesses and the Court."

3.   Delete paragraphs 4 and 5.

SINGAPORE

1.   Paragraph 2 should be amended as follows:

"The first Vice-President <u>shall</u> act in place of the President in the event that the President is unavailable or disqualified. <u>The second Vice-President shall act in place of the President in the event that both the President and the first Vice-President are unavailable or disqualified. The President may appoint an</u> alternate Vice-President <u>to</u> act in place of either Vice-President as required."

2.   Add the following new paragraph after paragraph 4:

"4 (<u>bis</u>). Decisions of the Presidency shall be taken [by consensus] [majority vote] of the members. [The President shall have a casting vote in the event of a tie.]"

AUSTRALIA AND NETHERLANDS
Election of the President

As provided for in article X (A 8 ILC), the President shall be elected by an absolute majority of the votes of the judges composing the Court. The procedure for conducting the election shall be laid down in the supplementary rules.

[*19] Death, loss of office or resignation of the President

If the President dies, ceases to hold office pursuant to article X (A 15 ILC) or resigns before the expiration of his or her term, the judges shall by absolute majority elect from among their number a successor for the remainder of the term. The election shall be governed by the procedure determined by the judges for the election of the President.

Election of Vice-Presidents and alternate Vice-Presidents

As provided for in article X (A 8 ILC), the Vice-Presidents and alternate Vice-Presidents shall be elected by an absolute majority of the votes and the judges composing the Court. The procedure for conducting these elections shall be laid down in the supplementary rules.

Death, loss of office or resignation of a Vice-President or an alternate Vice-President

If a Vice-President or alternate Vice-President dies, ceases to hold office pursuant to article X (A 15 ILC) or resigns before the expiration of his or her term, the judges shall by absolute majority elect from among their number a successor for the remainder of the term. The election shall be governed by the procedure determined by the judges for the election of Vice-Presidents and alternate Vice-Presidents.

Functions of the Presidency

(a)   The Presidency shall exercise the powers and functions conferred upon it by the Statute and these rules.

(b)   The procedures to govern the delegation of the powers of the Presidency provided for in article X (A 8(5) ILC) of the Statute shall be laid down in the supplementary rules.

(c)   The Presidency shall exercise any powers and functions conferred upon it by the supplementary rules.

The President

(a)   The President shall exercise the powers and functions conferred upon him or her by the Statute and these rules.

(b)   The President shall exercise any powers and functions conferred upon him or her by the supplementary rules.

The Vice-Presidents

(a)   The Vice-Presidents shall exercise the powers and functions conferred upon them by the Statute and these rules.

(b)   The Vice-Presidents shall exercise any powers and functions conferred upon them by the supplementary rules.

Replacements

If neither the President nor the Vice-Presidents (or alternate Vice-Presidents when acting as Vice-Presidents) can carry out the functions of the [*20] President, these functions shall be assumed by the senior judge, determined in accordance with the precedence of judges provided for in the supplementary rules.

SWITZERLAND

Delete paragraph 4.

ALGERIA, EGYPT, JORDAN, KUWAIT, LIBYAN ARAB JAMAHIRIYA AND QATAR

As several delegations stated, the "Presidency" should be limited in number and power. In addition to the President, two Vice-Presidents would suffice.

[*21] Article 9
Chambers
I. ILC DRAFT

1.   As soon as possible after each election of judges to the Court, the Presidency shall in accordance with the Rules constitute an Appeals Chamber consisting of the President and six other judges, of whom at least three shall be judges elected from among the persons nominated as having the qualification referred to in article 6 (1) (b). The President shall preside over the Appeals Chamber.

2.   The Appeals Chamber shall be constituted for a term of three years. Members of the Appeals Chamber shall, however, continue to sit on the Chamber in order to complete any case the hearing of which has commenced.

3.   Judges may be renewed as members of the Appeals Chamber for a second or subsequent term.

4.	Judges not members of the Appeals Chamber shall be available to serve on Trial Chambers and other chambers required by this Statute, and to act as substitute members of the Appeals Chamber in the event that a member of that Chamber is unavailable or disqualified.

5.	The Presidency shall nominate in accordance with the Rules five such judges to be members of the Trial Chamber for a given case. A Trial Chamber shall include at least three judges elected from among the persons nominated as having the qualification referred to in article 6 (1) (a).

6.	The Rules may provide for alternate judges to be nominated to attend a trial and to act as members of the Trial Chamber in the event that a judge dies or becomes unavailable during the course of the trial.

7.	No judge who is a national of a complainant State or of a State of which the accused is a national shall be a member of a chamber dealing with the case.

II. PROPOSALS
FRANCE
Preliminary Investigations Chambers

1.	The Preliminary Investigations Chambers perform pre-trial functions, in accordance with Part 4 of this Statute.

2.	A Preliminary Investigations Chambers shall be established for each case by the President of the Court. It shall consist of two Vice-Presidents and either the First Vice-President or Second Vice-President, who shall preside over it.

[*22] Chambers of the Court

1.	The Trial Chamber shall consist of four judge counsellors and a Vice-President, who shall preside over it. The Appeals Chamber shall consist of six judge counsellors and either the First Vice-President or Second Vice-President, who shall preside over it. The Remand Chamber shall consist of four judge counsellors and either the First Vice-President or Second Vice-President, who shall preside over it.

2.	All members of the chambers referred to in paragraph 1 of this article shall be chosen by lot. Judges drawn by lot may be excluded as a result of incompatibilities under article ... When the membership of a chamber drawn by lot encounters difficulties owing to incompatibilities under article ..., the First and the Second Vice-President may be replaced by a Vice-President, and a Vice-President by the most senior judge counsellor in the Court or, failing such a judge, the oldest.

3.	The President of the Court may, if he so wishes, preside over one of the chambers referred to in paragraph 1 of this article, subject to the provisions of article 13.

Alternate judge counsellors

1.	For the membership of each of the chambers referred to in article ..., the President of the Court may arrange for as many alternate judge counsellors as he deems necessary to be chosen by lot. They attend hearings of the chamber for which they have been designated, but do not participate in the deliberations. They are not, in that event, subject to the incompatibilities referred to in article ....

2.	In the course of a hearing, an alternate judge counsellor may be required to replace a member of the chamber to which he has been designated, when that member is temporarily unable to perform his duties, either for medical reasons or for one of the reasons set out in articles ... and .... The judge shall be chosen by lot from among the alternate judge counsellors designated for that chamber. Incompatibilities under article ... shall apply to alternate judge counsellors required to sit under the conditions referred to in the preceding paragraph.

Plurality of offices and incompatibilities

For the purposes of ruling on a case, the following functions may not be combined:

...

(b)	Serving as a member of the Trial Chamber and as a member of the Appeals Chamber.

JAPAN

1.	Replace paragraph 1 by the following:

"As soon as possible after each election of judges to the Court, the Presidency shall in accordance with the Rules constitute an Appeals Chamber consisting of seven judges, of whom at least three shall be judges elected [*23] from among the persons nominated as having the qualification referred to in article 6(1)(b)."

2.	Replace paragraph 4 by the following:

"Judges not members of the Appeals Chamber shall be available to serve on Trial Chambers and Pre-trial Chambers required by this Statute, and to act as substitute members of the Appeals Chamber in the event that a member of that Chamber is unavailable or disqualified."

3.   Replace paragraph 5 by the following:

"The Presidency shall nominate in accordance with the rules three such judges to be members of the Pre-trial Chamber for a given case. A Pre-trial Chamber shall include at least two judges elected from among the persons nominated as having the qualification referred to in article 6(1)(a). A Pre-trial Chamber shall be responsible in the given case for such functions as prescribed in [articles 26(3) and (5), 27(2) to (4), 27(5)(b), 28(1) to (3), 30(3), and any other functions concerning pre-trial process]."

4.   Replace paragraph 6 by the following:

"The Presidency shall nominate in accordance with the rules five such judges who are not members of the Pre-trial Chamber for a given case to be members of the Trial Chamber for the same case. A Trial Chamber shall include at least three judges elected from among the persons nominated as having the qualification referred to in article 6(1)(a)."

5.   Add new paragraph 6 bis:

"The rules may provide for alternate judges to be nominated to attend a trial and to act as members of the Pre-trial Chamber and Trial Chamber in the event that a judge dies or becomes unavailable during the course of the trial."

AUSTRALIA AND THE NETHERLANDS
Deliberations
The deliberations of the Chambers shall take place in private and remain secret.
Presiding Judges
(a)   If the President is unable to exercise his or her functions as Presiding Judge of the Appeals Chamber under article X (A 9(1) ILC), that Chamber shall elect a Presiding Judge from among its number. The procedure for conducting the election shall be laid down in the supplementary rules.

(b)   Where a Vice-President is a member of a Trial Chamber, he or she shall serve as its Presiding Judge. If the Vice-President is unable to exercise his or her functions as Presiding Judge of a Trial Chamber, that Chamber shall elect a Presiding Judge from among its number. The procedure for conducting the election shall be laid down in the supplementary rules.

[*24] Plenary sessions of the Court
The Judges shall meet in plenary to:

(i)   elect the President, the Vice-Presidents and alternate Vice-Presidents;

(ii)   elect the Registrar and Deputy Registrar;

(iii) adopt and amend the supplementary rules;

(iv)   decide upon matters relating to the internal functioning of the Chambers and the Court;

(v)   adopt the annual report provided for in article X of the Statute; and

(vi)   exercise any other functions provided for in the Statute, the rules or the supplementary rules or as necessitated by the operation of the Court.

Timing and conduct of plenary sessions
The timing and the conduct of plenary sessions shall be governed by the supplementary rules.

[Note. The provisions under the previous two hearings may be more appropriately included as a separate article headed "plenary sessions".]

Article 9, paragraph 1
UNITED KINGDOM
Replace the word "six" by the word "four" and delete the words "of whom at least three shall be judges elected from among the persons nominated as having the qualification referred to in article 6(1)(b)" in the first sentence.

SWITZERLAND
Replace the first sentence in paragraph 1 by the following:

"As soon as possible after each election of judges to the Court, the Presidency shall, in accordance with the rules, constitute an Appeals Chamber consisting of the President and two other judges."

AUSTRIA

The first sentence in paragraph 1 is amended as follows: "As soon as possible ... the Presidency shall in accordance with the rules constitute <u>an Indictment Chamber consisting of three judges and</u> an Appeals Chamber ..."

[*25] SINGAPORE

Replace paragraph 1 by the following:

"As soon as possible after each election of judges to the Court, an Appeals Chamber shall be constituted consisting of the President and six other judges to be elected by an absolute majority of the judges of the Court. Of these six other judges, [at least three] shall be judges elected from among the persons nominated as having the qualification referred to in article 6(1)(a) and [at least three] shall be judges elected from among the persons nominated as having the qualification referred to in article 6(1)(b). The President shall preside over the Appeals Chamber."

Article 9, paragraph 2
AUSTRIA

Paragraph 2 is amended as follows:

"The <u>Indictment Chamber and the</u> Appeals Chamber shall ... Members of the <u>Indictment Chamber and the</u> Appeals Chamber ..."

UNITED KINGDOM

Paragraph 2 is replaced by the following:

"Judges who have served in the Appeals Chamber shall not serve in any other Chamber and judges who have served in a Trial Chamber shall not serve in the Appeals Chamber."

Article 9, paragraph 3
UNITED KINGDOM

Delete paragraph 3.

Article 9, paragraph 4
AUSTRIA

Add the following second sentence in paragraph 4: "Judges of the Indictment Chamber shall not serve in the Trial Chambers or in the Appeals Chamber at the same time."

ALGERIA, EGYPT, JORDAN, KUWAIT, LIBYAN ARAB JAMAHIRIYA AND QATAR

The proposed practice of rotation of judges between the appellate and Trial Chambers is incompatible with basic principles of judicial independence, impartiality and fairness. Reviewing judges must therefore, remain in that position and not rotate to trial functions.

It is also useful to consider a general practice of limited rotation and specialization. This would apply, for example, to the Chamber on Indictments and preliminary matters. This proposed Chamber, which would consist of three [*26] judges and one alternate judge, would be assigned for a period of a number of years. This would provide for specialization, and also for consistency and predictability of outcomes.

Article 9, paragraph 5
SWITZERLAND

Replace paragraph 5 by the following:

"The Presidency shall nominate, in accordance with the rules and for a period of three years, two Trial Chambers consisting of three judges each. The members of the Trial Chambers shall continue to sit in order to complete any case the hearing of which has commenced."

SINGAPORE

Paragraph 5 is amended as follows:

"The Presidency shall nominate <u>on a rotational basis as far as possible and</u> in accordance with the Rules ..."

UNITED KINGDOM

Replace the word "five" by the word "three" and delete the second sentence in paragraph 5.

ALGERIA, EGYPT, JORDAN, KUWAIT, LIBYAN ARAB JAMAHIRIYA AND QATAR

In order to provide for greater stability in the Chambers and to avoid frequent rotations resulting in conflicts that would reduce the number of available judges who would be conflicted out of carrying out judicial functions in certain cases, assignment of judges to specific trial chambers should be for a certain number of years. Every chamber should consist of three judges, and should have one alternate judge to sit if one of the judges becomes unavailable to continue in his or her function.

Article 9, paragraph 6
SWITZERLAND

Replace paragraph 6 by the following:

"Rules may provide for alternate judges to be nominated to act as members of the Trial or Indictment Chambers and the Appeals Chamber in the event of death or unavailability of a judge."

ARGENTINA

For the cases of illness or other incapacity, death, loss of office or resignation of a member of the Trial Chamber, the following formula is proposed:

[*27] "If a judge sitting as a member of the Trial Chamber is unable to continue sitting in a part-heard trial owing to illness or other incapacity, the Presiding Judge may adjourn the proceedings, if the cause of that inability seems likely to be of short duration. Otherwise, or if the cause of the inability is still present 10 days after the adjournment, the Presiding Judge shall report to the Presidency, which shall order a retrial. If the Trial Chamber has comprised more than the required number of judges from the start of the trial, the judge in question shall be replaced immediately by an alternate judge. This rule shall also apply to cases of death, loss of office or resignation of a judge from the Trial Chamber."

[Note. Only a judge who has been present without interruption throughout the trial is in a position to pass judgement in a case. Alternative measures, such as audio and video recordings, cannot substitute for the judge's direct sensory perception of what takes place in the courtroom, and therefore do not constitute justifiable exceptions to the principle in question. In appellate proceedings, on the other hand, the principle of immediacy is much more limited in scope, since, as a rule, the Appeals Chamber bases its decision on the trial record. The rules applicable in the case of death, incapacity or other impediment of a member of the Appeals Chamber have not therefore been amended.]

Article 9, paragraph 7
UNITED STATES

Delete paragraph 7.

[*28] Article 10
Independence of the judges
I. ILC DRAFT

1.   In performing their functions, the judges shall be independent.
2.   Judges shall not engage in any activity which is likely to interfere with their judicial functions or to affect confidence in their independence. In particular they shall not while holding the office of judge be a member of the legislative or executive branches of the Government of a State, or of a body responsible for the investigation or prosecution of crimes.
3.   Any question as to the application of paragraph 2 shall be decided by the Presidency.
4.   On the recommendation of the Presidency, the States parties may by a two-thirds majority decide that the workload of the Court requires that the judges should serve on a full-time basis. In that case:
      (a)   existing judges who elect to serve on a full-time basis shall not hold any other office or employment; and
      (b)   judges subsequently elected shall not hold any other office or employment.

II. PROPOSALS
FRANCE

1.   The judges of the Court shall be independent. They may not engage in any activity which is likely to be incompatible with their judicial functions or to affect confidence in their independence. They may not, moreover, be a member of the legislative or executive branches of the Government of a State or a body responsible for the investigation or prosecution of crimes.
2.   Judges who are required to serve permanently on the Court, pursuant to article 5(2) or (3), may not engage in any other employment or hold any other office.
3.   When the Presidency considers that the Court's case load requires the permanent presence of all the judges of the Court, it shall so inform the General Assembly of the States Parties, which may decide that

all judges shall perform their duties full-time, for a period determined by the General Assembly or until further notice.

[*29] SINGAPORE

Paragraph 3 is amended as follows:

"Any question as to the application of paragraph 2 shall be decided by an absolute majority of the judges of the Court."

UNITED STATES

In subparagraphs 4(a) and (b) insert the words "full time" before the words "office or employment".

ISRAEL

Replace paragraph 2 by the following:

"Judges should be prohibited from exercising any political or administrative function or engaging in any other occupation of a professional nature".

[*30] Article 11
Excusing and disqualification of judges
I. ILC DRAFT

1.   The Presidency at the request of a judge may excuse that judge from the exercise of a function under this Statute.

2.   Judges shall not participate in any case in which they have previously been involved in any capacity or in which their impartiality might reasonably be doubted on any ground, including an actual, apparent or potential conflict of interest.

3.   The Prosecutor or the accused may request the disqualification of a judge under paragraph 2.

4.   Any question as to the disqualification of a judge shall be decided by an absolute majority of the members of the Chamber concerned. The challenged judge shall not take part in the decision.

II. PROPOSALS
FRANCE

1.   A judge of the Court shall not participate in a case:

(a)   in the event of one of the incompatibilities under article ...;

(b)   when his impartiality may be doubted on any ground, including an actual, apparent or potential conflict of interest.

2.   In situations provided for in paragraph 1 of this article, a judge may:

(a)   be excused from a case by the Presidency, with his agreement;

(b)   be disqualified, at the request of the Presidency, the Prosecutor or the accused, in which case the decision shall be taken by the Appeals Chamber, and the judge concerned shall not be present if he forms part of that Chamber; he shall then be replaced by another judge chosen by lot.

3.   For the purposes of ruling on a case, the following functions may not be combined:

(a)   serving as a member of the Preliminary Investigations Chamber appointed for a case under article 10 and as a member of one of the chambers hearing the same case;

(b)   serving as a member of the Trial Chamber and as a member of the Appeals Chamber.

[*31] JAPAN

1.   Replace paragraph 2 by the following:

"In the following cases a judge shall be excluded from the exercise of his functions under this Statute:

(a)   if he himself is the injured party;

(b)   if he is or was a relative of the accused or the injured party;

(c)   if he is a national of a complainant State or of a State of which the accused is a national;

(d)   if he is the legal representative, supervisor of the guardian or curator of the accused or the injured party;

(e)   if he has acted as a witness or an expert witness in the case involving the accused or the injured party;

(f)   if he has acted as the representative, counsel or assistant of the accused in the case involving that accused;

(g)   if he has exercised the functions of a public prosecutor or a judicial officer in the case involving the accused;

(h)   if he has previously exercised the functions of a judge in the case involving the accused at the national level; or

(i)   if he has participated in the decision mentioned in article 8 or 37 (4), in the decision by the Court below, in the original judgment of the case which has been sent back in accordance with the provisions of article 50 or in the investigations which form the basis of such decisions."

2.   Add new paragraph 5 as follows:

"Procedures of the trial subsequent to the change of the judges in accordance with this article shall be prescribed by the rules."

ARGENTINA

1.   No member of the Presidency who has participated in a decision by the Presidency under articles 26(3), 27(5), 28, 29 or 30(3) of the Statute concerning the case being tried or under appeal may sit as a member of the Trial or Appeals Chamber in that case. No judge who has made a decision under articles 26(3), 27(5), 28, 29 or 30(3) of the Statute concerning the case being tried or under appeal pursuant to a delegation from the Presidency under article 8(5) of the Statute may sit as a member of the Trial or Appeals Chamber in that case.

2.   A member of the Presidency who participated in the confirmation of the indictment against a suspect under article 27(2) of the Statute may not subsequently sit as a member of the Trial Chamber for the trial of that accused or as a member of the Appeals Chamber hearing an appeal in relation to that trial.

[*32] 3.   If a judge is disqualified from continuing to sit in a part-heard trial and thereby deprives the Trial Chamber of its required quorum under article 45(1) of the Statute, he or she shall be replaced immediately by an alternate judge if the Trial Chamber has from the start of the trial comprised more than the required number of judges. Otherwise, the Presidency shall order a retrial.

[Note. This proposal is based on a strict interpretation of the principle of impartiality; it is felt that a judge who has sat previously in the same case, even if he or she has not played a decisive role, runs the risk of being subjected to influences which may prevent him or her from making an impartial decision. It is therefore preferable to establish an explicit rule, in line with part of the jurisprudence of the European Court of Human Rights in the cases of Piersack v. Belgium (1982) and De Cubber v. Belgium (1984) which prohibits the subsequent participation of the judge in the decision of the case and thereby avoiding an interminable discussion of the potential effect of the specific action taken by the judge in question.]

AUSTRIA

In paragraph 2, after the word "Judges" add the words "except the members of the Indictment Chamber having acted in this capacity,".

ISRAEL

Add new paragraph 3(bis) as follows:

"3 (bis). Any request for the disqualification of a judge should include detailed reasons for the request."

AUSTRALIA AND NETHERLANDS
Disqualification

(a)   A member of the Presidency shall not be subject to disqualification from a trial or appeal because he or she participated in a decision by the Presidency under articles **X** (A 26(3), 27(5), 28, 29, 30(3) ILC) of the Statute concerning the case being tried or under appeal. A judge shall not be subject to disqualification from a trial or appeal who has made a decision under articles **X** (A 26(3), 27(5), 28, 29, 30(3) ILC) of the Statute concerning the case being tried or under appeal pursuant to a delegation from the Presidency under article X (A 8(5) ILC) of the Statute.

(b)   A member of the Presidency, who participated in the confirmation of the indictment against an accused under article **X** (A 27(2) ILC) of the Statute may sit as a member of the Trial Chamber for the trial of that accused or as a member of the Appeals Chamber hearing an appeal in relation to that trial.

(c)   No member of the Appeals Chamber shall sit on any appeal in a case in which he or she sat as a member of the Trial Chamber.

(d)   As provided for in article **X** (A 37(5) ILC) of the Statute, any judge who was a member of an Indictment Chamber may not subsequently sit as a member of a Trial Chamber hearing the case against the accused who was the subject of the proceedings before the Indictment Chamber.

[*33] (e) If a judge is disqualified from continuing to sit in a part-heard trial and thereby deprives the Trial Chamber of its required quorum under article **X** (A 45(1) ILC) of the Statute, the Presidency may assign another judge to the Chamber and order either a rehearing or continuation of the proceedings from that point. However, after the beginning of the presentation of evidence, the continuation of the proceedings may only be ordered with the consent of the accused.

(f)   If a judge is disqualified from continuing to sit in a part-heard appeal and thereby deprives the Appeals Chamber of its required quorum under article **X** (A 49(4) ILC) of the Statute, the Presidency may assign another judge to the Chamber drawn, subject to sub-rule (C) of this rule, from those available for duty in a Trial Chamber.

Assignment of judges

The Assignment of judges shall be governed by the procedure laid down in the supplementary rules.

Conflict of interest

(a)   In order to assist the application of article X (A 11(2) ILC) of the Statute, the supplementary rules shall contain detailed conflict of interest rules.

(b)   States Parties shall be able to make submissions to the President about the content of these rules.

[*34] Article 12
The Procuracy
I. ILC DRAFT

1.   The Procuracy is an independent organ of the Court responsible for the investigation of complaints brought in accordance with this Statute and for the conduct of prosecutions. A member of the Procuracy shall not seek or act on instructions from any external source.

2.   The Procuracy shall be headed by the Prosecutor, assisted by one or more Deputy Prosecutors, who may act in place of the Prosecutor in the event that the Prosecutor is unavailable. The Prosecutor and the Deputy Prosecutors shall be of different nationalities. The Prosecutor may appoint such other qualified staff as may be required.

3.   The Prosecutor and Deputy Prosecutors shall be persons of high moral character and have high competence and experience in the prosecution of criminal cases. They shall be elected by secret ballot by an absolute majority of the States parties, from among candidates nominated by States parties. Unless a shorter term is otherwise decided on at the time of their election, they shall hold office for a term of five years and are eligible for re-election.

4.   The States parties may elect the Prosecutor and Deputy Prosecutors on the basis that they are willing to serve as required.

5.   The Prosecutor and Deputy Prosecutors shall not act in relation to a complaint involving a person of their own nationality.

6.   The Presidency may excuse the Prosecutor or a Deputy Prosecutor at their request from acting in a particular case, and shall decide any question raised in a particular case as to the disqualification of the Prosecutor or a Deputy Prosecutor.

7.   The staff of the Procuracy shall be subject to Staff Regulations drawn up by the Prosecutor.

II. PROPOSALS
FRANCE
Procuracy of the Court

1.   The Procuracy shall be an independent organ of the Court responsible under this Statute for receiving complaints addressed to the Court, for examining them and for conducting investigations and prosecutions before the Court.

2.   The Procuracy shall be headed by the Prosecutor, assisted by two Deputy Prosecutors. The Procuracy is an indivisible body; the Deputy Prosecutors are entitled to carry out any of the acts required of the Prosecutor under this Statute.

[*35] 3. The Prosecutor and the Deputy Prosecutors shall be persons of high moral character, possess great competence and have practical experience in the prosecution of criminal cases. They shall, furthermore, have an excellent knowledge of and be fluent in at least one of the working languages referred to in article 25.

4. Each State Party may nominate two persons who are willing to serve as may be required in the Procuracy of the Court.

5. The Prosecutor and Deputy Prosecutors shall be elected by the General Assembly of the States Parties. The election of the Prosecutor shall be held first, followed by that of the two Deputy Prosecutors. No two members of the Procuracy of the Court may be of the same nationality.

6. The Prosecutor and Deputy Prosecutors shall hold office for nine years. The term shall end in all cases when the person reaches 70 years of age. They shall not be eligible for re-election.

7. The Prosecutor or a Deputy Prosecutor may not participate in a case in which his impartiality might be doubted on any ground, including an actual, apparent or potential conflict of interest. The Presidency of the Court may on its own motion or at the request of the Prosecutor or of a suspect or accused person, excuse a member of the Procuracy from following a case for one of the reasons set out in the preceding paragraph.

Investigators

The Prosecutor may choose investigators who shall assist him in his duties and shall be placed under his sole authority. They may carry out any acts for which they have been delegated by the Prosecutor or a Deputy Prosecutor, with the exception of requests for cooperation referred to in Part 4 of this Statute. They shall be staff members of the Court within the meaning of this Statute.

Article 31 of the ILC draft Statute should be placed in Part 2 of the Statute with the following amendments:

(a) The Prosecutor may request a State Party to make persons available to him to assist him in a particular case;

(b) Such persons shall be under the authority of the Prosecutor for the duration of the case for which they have been made available. They may carry out acts under the conditions established for investigators in article ...

JAPAN

1. Replace paragraph 5 by the following:

"The Prosecutor and Deputy Prosecutors shall not act in relation to a complaint falling in the following cases:

(a) if they themselves are the injured party;

(b) if they are or were a relative of the accused or the injured party;

[*36] (c) if they are a national of a complainant State or of a State of which the accused is a national;

(d) if they are the legal representative, supervisor of the guardian or curator of the accused or the injured party;

(e) if they have acted as a witness or an expert witness in the case involving the accused or the injured party; or

(f) if they have acted as the representative, counsel or assistant of the accused in the case involving that accused."

2. Replace paragraph 6 by the following:

"In case the Prosecutor or a Deputy Prosecutor falls in the cases prescribed in the preceding paragraph, he may be challenged by the accused. The Presidency shall decide on challenges against the Prosecutor or a Deputy Prosecutor made before the first day of the public trial. Challenges made afterwards shall be decided by the Trial Chamber concerned."

UNITED KINGDOM

1. In the first sentence of paragraph 3 after the words "moral character" add the words ", impartiality and integrity in" and replace the words "high competence and experience" by the words "the highest level of competence and experience in the investigation and".

2. Replace the second sentence of paragraph 3 by the following:

"They should be elected by secret ballot by an absolute majority of the [States Parties, from among candidates nominated by the members of the Court] [members of the Court, from among candidates nominated by the States Parties]."

SINGAPORE

1.   The third sentence of paragraph 3 is amended as follows: "Unless a shorter term ... they shall hold office for a term of [seven/nine] years and are not eligible for re-election."

2.   After paragraph 4 add the following paragraph:

"4 bis. The Prosecutor and Deputy Prosecutors shall not engage in any activity which is likely to interfere with their prosecutorial functions or to affect confidence in their independence. In particular they shall not, while holding office, be a member of the legislative or executive branches of the Government of a State [, or of a body responsible for the investigation or prosecution of crimes]."

3.   Paragraph 5 is amended as follows:

"The Prosecutor and Deputy Prosecutors shall not act in relation to a complaint initiated by their State of nationality or involving a person of [*37] their own nationality or in any case in which they have previously been involved in any capacity."

FINLAND

Add the following sentence at the end of paragraph 5:

"They shall not participate in any case in which they are or have previously been involved in any capacity or in which their impartiality might reasonably be doubted on any ground, including an actual, apparent or potential conflict of interest."

DENMARK, FINLAND, MALAWI, NEW ZEALAND, NIGERIA, NORWAY AND SWEDEN

Add a new paragraph 8 as follows:

"The paramount consideration in the employment of the staff of the Procuracy and in the drawing up of the staff regulations shall be the necessity of securing the highest standards of efficiency, competence and integrity. In the employment of the staff the Prosecutor should bear in mind the criteria set forth in article [6(5)] (as amended)."

AUSTRALIA AND NETHERLANDS

Powers and functions of the Prosecutor

(a)   The Prosecutor shall exercise the powers and functions conferred upon him or her by the Statute and these rules.

(b)   The Prosecutor shall be responsible for the organization and administration of the Procuracy.

(c)   The Prosecutor may put in place such internal procedures as he or she considers necessary to govern the operation of the Procuracy.

(d)   The Prosecutor's powers under the rules may be exercised by staff members of the Procuracy authorized by him or her, or by any person acting under his or her direction.

Role of a Deputy Prosecutor

(a)   A Deputy Prosecutor shall assist the Prosecutor, act as Prosecutor in the latter's absence and, in the event of the office becoming vacant, exercise the functions of Prosecutor until the office has been filled.

(b)   If States parties elect more than one Deputy Prosecutor under article **X** (A 12(3) ILC), the Prosecutor shall establish a mechanism for determining which Deputy Prosecutor is to act as Prosecutor in his or her absence and, in the event of the office becoming vacant, exercise the functions of Prosecutor until the office has been filled by election under article **X** (A 12(3) ILC) of the Statute.

[*38] Acting Prosecutor

(a)   If both the Prosecutor and Deputy Prosecutor(s) are unable to carry out the duties of the Prosecutor on a temporary basis, an acting Prosecutor shall discharge those duties for such time as may be necessary. The acting Prosecutor shall be appointed from a list of other lawyers serving as prosecutors on the staff of the Procuracy, which shall be compiled by the Prosecutor. The list shall prescribe the order in which the persons identified therein are to be called upon to serve as acting Prosecutor.

(b)   If the offices of Prosecutor and Deputy Prosecutor(s) are vacant at the same time, an acting Prosecutor shall discharge the duties of Prosecutor pending an election to that office under article **X** (A 12(3) ILC) of the Statute. The acting Prosecutor shall be appointed from the list referred to in sub-rule (a). He or she shall be subject to the provisions of the Statute governing the loss of office by the Prosecutor.

Solemn undertaking

(a)   Upon commencing employment, every staff member of the Procuracy shall make the same undertaking as required of judges and other officers of the Court.

(b)   The undertaking, signed by the staff member and witnessed by the Prosecutor or a Deputy Prosecutor, shall be kept in the records of the Court.

Retention of information and evidence

The Prosecutor shall be responsible for the retention, storage and security of information and physical evidence obtained in the course of the Procuracy's investigations.

Agreements with States

The Prosecutor may enter into agreements with States governing the provision of resources by States to assist in investigations and prosecutions, including the use of national scientific analysis or forensic facilities and the secondment of persons to the staff of the Prosecutor, as provided for in article **X** (A 31 ILC) of the Statute.

Conflict of interest

(a)   In order to assist the application of article **X** (A 12(6) ILC) of the Statute, the Prosecutor shall put in place a set of detailed conflict of interest rules for the staff of the Procuracy.

(b)   States Parties shall be able to make submissions to the Prosecutor about the content of these rules.

[*39] Article 13
The Registry
I. ILC DRAFT

1.   On the proposal of the Presidency, the judges by an absolute majority by secret ballot shall elect a Registrar, who shall be the principal administrative officer of the Court. They may in the same manner elect a Deputy Registrar.

2.   The Registrar shall hold office for a term of five years, is eligible for re-election and shall be available on a full-time basis. The Deputy Registrar shall hold office for a term of five years or such shorter term as may be decided on, and may be elected on the basis that the Deputy Registrar is willing to serve as required.

3.   The Presidency may appoint or authorize the Registrar to appoint such other staff of the Registry as may be necessary.

4.   The staff of the Registry shall be subject to Staff Regulations drawn up by the Registrar.

II. PROPOSALS
FRANCE

1.   The General Assembly of judges shall elect the Registrar and the Deputy Registrar of the Court by an absolute majority by secret ballot. The Registrar and the Deputy Registrar shall hold office for five years. Their term shall end in all cases when they reach 65 years of age. They shall be eligible for re-election once.

2.   The Registrar shall be the principal administrative officer of the Court. He shall be under the authority of the President of the Court.

JAPAN

Add the following new paragraph before paragraph 1 of the ILC draft statute:

"1 (bis). The Registry shall be responsible for the administration and serving of the Court."

SINGAPORE

The second sentence in paragraph 2 is amended as follows:

"The Deputy Registrar shall hold for a term of five years or such shorter term as may be decided on [by the judges by consensus/by an absolute majority of the judges], and may be elected on the basis that the Deputy Registrar is willing to serve as required."

[*40] UNITED STATES

1.   Add a second sentence in paragraph 4 as follows:

"Such regulations shall be circulated to the States parties for comment, whenever possible before they take effect."

2.   Add a new paragraph 5 as follows:
"The Registry may be removed by a majority vote of the judges for inadequate performance, malfeasance or other good cause."

AUSTRALIA AND NETHERLANDS
Composition of the Registry
The Registry shall comprise the Registrar, the Deputy Registrar (if one has been elected) and such other staff appointed by the Registrar pursuant to article **X** (A 13 (3) ILC) of the Statute.

Qualifications of the Registrar
The Presidency shall satisfy itself that the candidates it puts forward for the consideration of judges in the ballot for the position of Registrar are of the highest calibre.

Election of the Registrar
As provided for in article **X** (A 13 (1) ILC) of the Statute, the judges shall elect the Registrar by an absolute majority by secret ballot. The necessary procedure for conducting the election shall be laid down in the supplementary rules.

[*41] Death, loss of office or resignation of the Registrar
If the Registrar dies, ceases to hold office pursuant to article **X** (A 15 ILC) of the Statute or resigns before the expiration of his or her term, the judges shall by an absolute majority by secret ballot elect a replacement. The election shall be governed by the procedure determined by the judges.

Qualifications of the Deputy Registrar
The Presidency shall satisfy itself that the candidates it puts forward for the consideration of judges in the ballot for the position of Deputy Registrar are of the highest calibre.

Election of the Deputy Registrar
As provided for in article **X** (A 13 (1) ILC) of the Statute, the judges shall elect the Deputy Registrar by an absolute majority by secret ballot. The election shall be governed by the procedure determined by the judges for the election of the Registrar.

Death, loss of office or resignation of the Deputy Registrar
If the Deputy Registrar dies, ceases to hold office pursuant to article **X** (A 15 ILC) of the Statute or resigns before the expiration of his or her term, the judges shall by an absolute majority by secret ballot elect a replacement. The election shall be governed by the procedure determined by the judges.

Solemn undertaking
(a)   Upon commencing employment, every staff member of the Registry shall make the same undertaking as required of judges and other officers of the Court.

(b)   The undertaking, signed by the staff member and witnessed by the Registrar or Deputy Registrar, shall be kept in the records of the Court.

Functions of the Registrar
(a)   The Registrar is charged with being the principal administrative officer of the Court by article **X** (A 13 (1) ILC) of the Statute. Accordingly, under the authority of the Presidency, he or she shall be responsible for organizing the Registry and for the administration and servicing of the Court and shall serve as its channel of communication, in accordance with the Statute, rules and supplementary rules of the Court. The Registrar shall assist the Chambers, the plenary meetings of the Court, the judges and the Prosecutor in the performance of their functions.

(b)   The Registrar shall also be responsible for the security of the Court in consultation with other organs of the Court and the host State.

(c)   The duties of the Registrar shall be elaborated in the supplementary rules.

Role of the Deputy Registrar
(a)   The Deputy Registrar shall assist the Registrar, act as Registrar in the latter's absence and, in the event of the office becoming vacant, exercise the functions of Registrar until the office has been filled by election.

(b)   The duties of the Deputy Registrar shall be elaborated in the supplementary rules.

Official of the Registry to serve as Registrar

(a)   If both the Registrar and the Deputy Registrar are unable to carry out the duties of the Registrar on a temporary basis, the Presidency shall appoint an official of the Registry to discharge those duties for such time as may be necessary.

(b)   If both offices are vacant at the same time, the Presidency, after consulting the other judges, shall appoint an official of the Registry to discharge the duties of the Registrar pending an election to that office. The official shall be subject to the provisions of the Statute, rules and supplementary rules governing the loss of office by the Registrar.

[*42] Records

(a)   The Registrar shall maintain records which shall list all the particulars of each case brought before the Court. The records shall be open to the public.

(b)   The Registrar shall also maintain the other records of the Court.

[Note. The issue of whether some records may need to be sealed should be addressed.]

Minutes

Except where a full record is made, the Registrar, or Registry staff designated by him or her, shall take minutes of the plenary meetings of the Court and of the sittings of the Chambers, other than private deliberations.

Victims and Witnesses Unit

(a)   There shall be set up under the authority of the Registrar a Victims and Witnesses Unit consisting of qualified staff to:

(i)   recommend protective measures for victims and witnesses in accordance with article **X** (A 43 ILC) of the Statute; and

(ii)   provide counselling and support for them, in particular in cases of rape and sexual assault.

(b)   Due consideration shall be given, in the appointment of staff, to the employment of qualified women.

[*43] Article 14
Solemn undertaking
I. ILC DRAFT

Before first exercising their functions under this Statute, judges and other officers of the Court shall make a public and solemn undertaking to do so impartially and conscientiously.

II. PROPOSALS
FRANCE

1.   Before taking office pursuant to this Statute, all officers of the Court shall make a public and solemn undertaking to perform their duties impartially and conscientiously.

2.   In performing their duties, the officers of the Court and the staff of the Court shall not seek or accept instructions from any Government or any authority outside the Court. They shall refrain from any act incompatible with their status and shall be accountable only to the Court.

3.   The States Parties undertake to respect the exclusive international character of the duties of the officers of the Court and the staff of the Court and not to seek to influence them in the performance of their duties.

AUSTRALIA AND NETHERLANDS
Solemn undertaking

(a)   As required by article **X** (A 14 ILC) of the Statute, before first exercising their functions under the Statute, judges and other officers of the Court shall make the following solemn undertaking:

"I solemnly undertake that I will perform my duties and exercise my powers as **X** of the International Criminal Court honourably, faithfully, impartially and conscientiously and that I will respect the provisions of the Statute, rules and supplementary rules of the Court."

(b)   The undertaking, signed by the judge or other officer of the Court and witnessed by **X** or his or her representative, shall be kept in the records of the Court.

[Note. Specific proposals for the solemn undertaking to be made by staff members of the Prosecutor's Office and the Registry are contained in the proposals under articles 12 and 13 respectively.]

[*44] Article 15
Loss of office
I. ILC DRAFT

1. A judge, the Prosecutor or other officer of the Court who is found to have committed misconduct or a serious breach of this Statute, or to be unable to exercise the functions required by this Statute because of long-term illness or disability, shall cease to hold office.
2. A decision as to the loss of office under paragraph 1 shall be made by secret ballot:
(a) in the case of the Prosecutor or a Deputy Prosecutor, by an absolute majority of the States Parties;
(b) in any other case, by a two-thirds majority of the judges.
3. The judge, the Prosecutor or any other officer whose conduct or fitness for office is impugned shall have full opportunity to present evidence and to make submissions but shall not otherwise participate in the discussion of the question.

II. PROPOSALS
FRANCE

1. An officer of the Court who has seriously breached the rules laid down in this Statute or has committed misconduct such as to jeopardize his independence or his impartiality, or is unable to continue to perform his duties for medical reasons duly established by at least two experts, shall be dismissed under the conditions laid down in paragraph 2 of this article.
2. The decision to dismiss an officer of the Court under the preceding paragraph shall be taken, further to an assenting opinion of the General Assembly of Judges of the Court, by the General Assembly of States Parties.
3. An officer of the Court whose activity is challenged under this article may in defence produce any arguments and evidence that he deems necessary. All evidence against him shall be communicated to him.

JAPAN
Discipline and loss of office

1. A judge, the Prosecutor or a Deputy Prosecutor shall not be removed against his will except by procedures in this article unless judicially declared mentally or physically incompetent to perform his official duties.
2. A judge can be removed by a two-thirds majority of the States Parties upon request by either more than three judges or more than one tenth of the States Parties, if that judge falls in either of the following cases:
[*45] (a) if he/she has committed grave misconduct in performing his/her functions, or a serious breach of his/her official duties; or
(b) if he/she has been engaged in delinquency, whether officially or privately, which raises serious doubts in public confidence in his/her capacity as a judge.
3. A judge who has committed misconduct other than those mentioned in the preceding paragraph shall be subject to disciplinary measures as decided by a two-thirds majority of the judges excluding himself/herself.
4. The Prosecutor or a Deputy Prosecutor can be removed by a majority of the States Parties upon request by either the Presidency or more than one tenth of the States Parties, if he/she falls in either of the following cases:
(a) if he/she has committed grave misconduct in performing his/her functions, or a serious breach of his/her official duties; or
(b) if he/she has been engaged in delinquency, whether officially or privately, which raises serious doubts in public confidence in his/her official capacity.
5. The Prosecutor or a Deputy Prosecutor who has committed misconduct other than those mentioned in the preceding paragraph shall be subject to such disciplinary measures as decided by ...
6. Discipline including loss of office against other staff of the Court shall be governed by the rules and the staff regulations.
7. The third paragraph of article 15 of the ILC draft statute should be retained and renumbered as paragraph 7 in this proposal.

AUSTRALIA AND NETHERLANDS

Illness or other incapacity

(a) If a judge is, for reason of illness or other incapacity, unable to continue sitting in a part-heard trial, and thereby deprives a Trial Chamber of its required quorum under article **X** (A 45 (1) ILC) of the Statute, the Presiding Judge may, if that inability seems likely to be of short duration, adjourn the proceedings. Otherwise he or she shall report to the Presidency which may assign another judge to the Chamber and order either a rehearing or continuation of the proceedings from that point. However, after the beginning of the presentation of evidence, the continuation of the proceedings may only be ordered with the consent of the accused.

(b) If a judge is, for reason of illness or other incapacity, unable to continue sitting in a part-heard appeal, and thereby deprives the Appeals Chamber of its required quorum under article **X** (A 49 (4) ILC) of the Statute, the Presiding Judge may, if that inability seems likely to be of short duration, adjourn the proceedings. Otherwise, he or she shall report to the Presidency which may assign a Judge to the Chamber, drawn from those available for duty in a Trial Chamber.

[*46] Death

(a) If the death of a judge deprives a Trial Chamber of its required quorum under article **X** (A 45 (1) ILC) of the Statute, the Presidency may assign another Judge to the Chamber and order either a rehearing or continuation of the proceedings from that point. However, after the beginning of the presentation of evidence, the continuation of the proceedings may only be ordered with the consent of the accused.

(b) If the death of the judge deprives the Appeals Chamber of its required quorum under article **X** (A 49 (4) ILC) of the Statute, the Presidency may assign another Judge to the Chamber, drawn from those available for duty in a Trial Chamber.

Loss of office

(a) If a judge ceases to hold office pursuant to the application of article **X** (A 15 ILC) of the Statute during a part-heard trial and thereby deprives a Trial Chamber of its required quorum under article **X** (A 45 (1) ILC) of the Statute, the Presidency may assign another judge to the Chamber and order either a rehearing or continuation of the proceedings from that point. However, after the beginning of the presentation of evidence, the continuation of the proceedings may only be ordered with the consent of the accused.

(b) If a judge ceases to hold office pursuant to the application of article **X** (A 15 ILC) of the Statute, and thereby deprives the Appeals Chamber of its required quorum under article **X** (A 49 (4) ILC) of the Statute, the Presidency may assign another judge to the Chamber, drawn from those available for duty in a Trial Chamber.

Resignation

(a) A judge who wishes to resign shall communicate that decision in writing to the President who shall transmit it to **X**. The judge shall endeavour to discharge his or her responsibilities in relation to uncompleted trials or appeals before the resignation takes effect.

(b) Where the resignation of a judge takes effect during a part-heard trial and thereby deprives the Chamber of its required quorum under article **X** (A 45 (1) ILC) of the Statute, the Presidency may assign another judge to the Chamber and order either a rehearing or continuation of the proceedings from that point. However, after the beginning of the presentation of the evidence, the continuation of the proceedings may only be ordered with the consent of the accused.

(c) Where the resignation of a judge takes effect during a part-heard appeal and thereby deprives the Chamber of its required quorum under article **X** (A 49 (4) ILC) of the Statute, the Presidency may assign another judge to the Chamber drawn from those available for duty in a Trial Chamber.

The judges

(a) In any case in which the application of article **X** (A 15 ILC) to a judge is under consideration, the judge concerned shall be so informed by the President in a written statement which shall include the grounds therefor and any relevant evidence. He or she shall subsequently, in a close plenary session of the Court specially convened for the purpose, be afforded full opportunity, [*47] in accordance with article **X**

(A 15 (4) ILC) of the Statute, to present evidence and make submissions. He or she shall also have full opportunity to supply answers, orally or in writing, to any questions put to him or her.

(b)   At a further closed plenary session of the Court specially convened for the purpose, the question of whether the judge concerned should continue to hold office shall be put to a vote in accordance with article **X** (A 15 (2) ILC) of the Statute. The procedure for conducting the vote shall be laid down in the supplementary rules.

The Registrar and Deputy Registrar

(a)   In any case in which the application of article **X** (A 15 ILC) of the Statute to the Registrar or Deputy Registrar is under consideration, the Registrar or Deputy Registrar shall be so informed by the President in a written statement which shall include the grounds therefor and any relevant evidence. He or she shall subsequently, in a closed plenary session of the Court specially convened for the purpose, be afforded full opportunity, in accordance with article **X** (A 14 (4) ILC) of the Statute, to present evidence and make submissions. He or she shall also have full opportunity to supply answers, orally or in writing, to any question put to him or her.

(b)   At a further closed plenary session of the Court specially convened for the purpose, the question of whether the Registrar or Deputy Registrar should continue to hold office shall be put to a vote in accordance with article **X** (A 15 (2) ILC) of the Statute. The procedure for conducting the vote shall be laid down in the supplementary rules.

[*48] Article 16
Privileges and immunities
I. ILC DRAFT

1.   The judges, the Prosecutor, the Deputy Prosecutors and the staff of the Procuracy, the Registrar and the Deputy Registrar shall enjoy the privileges, immunities and facilities of a diplomatic agent within the meaning of the Vienna Convention on Diplomatic Relations of 16 April 1961.

2.   The staff of the Registry shall enjoy the privileges, immunities and facilities necessary to the performance of their functions.

3.   Counsel, experts and witnesses before the Court shall enjoy the privileges and immunities necessary to the independent exercise of their duties.

4.   The judges may by an absolute majority decide to revoke a privilege or waive an immunity conferred by this article, other than an immunity of a judge, the Prosecutor or Registrar as such. In the case of other officers and staff of the Procuracy or Registry, they may do so only on the recommendation of the Prosecutor or Registrar, as the case may be.

II. PROPOSALS
FRANCE

1.   The judges, the Prosecutor, the Deputy Prosecutors, the Registrar and the Deputy Registrar shall enjoy the privileges, immunities and facilities of a diplomatic agent within the meaning of the Vienna Convention on Diplomatic Relations of 16 April 1961.

2.   The staff of the Registry and other staff members of the Court shall enjoy the privileges, immunities and facilities necessary for the independent performance of their functions.

3.   Counsel, experts and witnesses before the Court shall enjoy the privileges and immunities necessary for the independent exercise of their duties.

4.   With the exception of those referred to in paragraph 1 of this article, the privileges, immunities and facilities granted may be revoked or waived by a decision taken by an absolute majority, by secret ballot, of the General Assembly of Judges of the Court.

ISRAEL

Replace paragraph 1 by the following:

"Members of the Court shall enjoy diplomatic privileges and immunities when engaged in the business of the Court".

[*49] Article 17
Allowances and expenses
I. ILC DRAFT

1. The President shall receive an annual allowance.
2. The Vice-Presidents shall receive a special allowance for each day they exercise the functions of the President.
3. Subject to paragraph 4, the judges shall receive a daily allowance during the period in which they exercise their functions. They may continue to receive a salary payable in respect of another position occupied by them consistently with article 10.
4. If it is decided under article 10 (4) that judges shall thereafter serve on a full-time basis, existing judges who elect to serve on a full-time basis, and all judges subsequently elected, shall be paid a salary.

II. PROPOSALS
FRANCE
Remuneration

All permanent members of the Court, as defined in article 5 (2) and (3) shall receive remuneration. Judges who sit only on a temporary basis shall receive a daily allowance during the period in which they perform their functions. They may continue to receive a salary payable in respect of another position occupied by them.

ALGERIA, EGYPT, JORDAN, KUWAIT AND LIBYAN ARAB JAMAHIRIYA

Several delegations have argued that judges should be paid on a per diem basis. This is, in principle, offensive to judicial dignity and judicial independence. It would also limit the pool of candidates who would be willing to serve under those conditions. All judges should receive a base salary of no less than half of the salary received by ICJ judges. Those who are in function should receive additional compensation on a pro-rata basis up to the maximum of the equivalent compensation received by ICJ judges.

[*50] Article 18
Working languages
I. ILC DRAFT

The working languages of the Court shall be English and French.

II. PROPOSALS
AUSTRALIA AND NETHERLANDS

(a)   As provided for in article **X** (A 18 ILC) of the Statute, the working languages of the Court shall be English and French.

(b)   An accused shall have the right to use his or her own language and to have the benefit of interpretation and translation provided for in article **X** (A 41.1 (f) ILC) of the Statute.

(c)   Any other person appearing before the Tribunal, other than as counsel, who does not have sufficient knowledge of either of the two working languages, may use his or her own language and have the benefit of interpretation and translation on the basis of the same criteria applied to an accused under article **X** (A 41.1 (f) ILC) of the Statue.

(d)   Counsel for an accused may apply to the Presiding Judge of a chamber for leave to use a language other than the two working languages or the language of the accused. If such leave is granted, the expenses of interpretation and translation shall be borne by the Court to the extent, if any, determined by the President, taking into account the rights of the defence and the interests of justice.

(e)   Documents filed with the Court shall be in one of the working languages or accompanied by a translation into one of those languages.

(f)   The Registrar shall make any necessary arrangements for interpretation and translation into and from the working languages.

[*51] Article 19
Rules of the Court
I. ILC DRAFT

1.   Subject to paragraphs 2 and 3, the judges may by an absolute majority make rules for the functioning of the Court in accordance with this Statute, including rules regulating:

(a)   the conduct of investigations;

(b)   the procedure to be followed and the rules of evidence to be applied;

(c)   any other matter which is necessary for the implementation of this Statute.

2.   The initial Rules of the Court shall be drafted by the judges within six months of the first elections for the Court, and submitted to a conference of States parties for approval. The judges may decide that a rule subsequently made under paragraph 1 should also be submitted to a conference of States parties for approval.

3.   In any case to which paragraph 2 does not apply, rules made under paragraph 1 shall be transmitted to States parties and may be confirmed by the Presidency unless, within six months after transmission, a majority of States parties have communicated in writing their objections.

4.   A rule may provide for its provisional application in the period prior to its approval or confirmation. A rule not approved or confirmed shall lapse.

II. PROPOSALS
FRANCE

The rules of organization, functioning and procedure of the Court not set out in this Statute shall appear in the regulations and the rules of procedure of the Court.

Draft regulations and rules of procedure of the Court shall be prepared by the General Assembly of judges. They shall be adopted by the General Assembly of the States parties, which may amend them.

The rules and regulations adopted in accordance with the preceding paragraph may be amended under the same conditions.

FINLAND

1.   The States Parties [may] [shall] by an absolute majority adopt rules for the functioning of the Court in accordance with this Statute, including rules regulating:

[*52] (a)   the conduct of investigations;

(b)   the procedure to be followed and the rules of evidence to be applied;

(c)   any other matter which is necessary for the implementation of this Statute.

2.   [Any State Party] [Five States Parties] may propose an amendment to the rules of the Court and file it with the [Registrar] [Secretary-General of the United Nations]. The judges may decide by an absolute majority to propose an amendment to the rules of the Court. The [Registrar] [Secretary-General] shall communicate to States parties the amendment proposed by any State Party or by the judges. The amendment shall be considered adopted unless within [three] months from the date of such communication [a majority] of States Parties have communicated in writing their objection.

3.   The judges may by an absolute majority adopt supplementary rules in accordance with the rules of the Court.

AUSTRALIA AND NETHERLANDS
Interpretation of the rules

(a)   To the extent that the plain language of the rules does not require otherwise, they should be interpreted to ensure simplicity in procedure, fairness to the parties and the elimination of unjustified delay.

(b)   In the rules, the singular shall include the plural, and vice versa.

Authentic texts

The English and French texts of the rules shall be equally authentic. In case of discrepancy, the version which is more consonant with the spirit of the Statute and the rules shall prevail.

Non-compliance with the rules

(a)   Any objection by a party to an act of another party on the ground of non-compliance with the rules shall be raised with the Presidency, Trial Chamber or Appeals Chamber, as appropriate, at the earliest opportunity.

(b)   The Presidency, Trial Chamber or Appeals Chamber shall rule without delay on whether there has been non-compliance with the rules.

(c)   When non-compliance is ruled to have occurred, the Presidency, Trial Chamber or Appeals Chamber shall have the discretion not to make an order if the non-compliance with a rule is not of a serious nature. The party at fault, however, must subsequently comply with the rule in question.

(d)   When the Presidency, the Trial Chamber or the Appeals Chamber rules that the non-compliance is of a serious nature, they may make an appropriate order, including the exclusion of evidence. In cases where the non-compliance is contrary to the fundamental principles of fairness and has occasioned a miscarriage of justice, an order may be made for the indictment against the accused to be dismissed.

[*53] (e) A party may appeal a ruling or order made by the Presidency or a Trial Chamber under this rule to the Appeals Chamber.

[Note. Some delegations proposed that article 19 might suitably be discussed in connection with the Rules of Procedure, Fair Trial and Rights of the Accused.]

[*54] Article A 1/
Compensation
PROPOSAL
JAPAN

1.   The Court shall make compensation to those who were:

(a)   pronounced innocent by an irrevocable adjudication;

(b)   arrested or detained for the purpose of prosecution, although the prosecution against him did not eventually take place;

(c)   arrested or detained but the lawfulness of that arrest or detention was denied in accordance with this Statute; or

(d)   illegally inflicted losses upon by an officer of the Court intentionally or negligently in the course of performing his duties.

2.   Procedures and criteria for compensation shall be provided in the rules, including the expenses to be borne by a complainant State if that State lodged a complaint without sufficient reason.

[Note. The question of compensation is also addressed in the document compiled by the informal group on the Rules of Procedure, Fair Trial and Rights of the Accused.]

[*55] PART 3. JURISDICTION OF THE COURT
Article 20*
Crimes within the jurisdiction of the Court
I. ILC DRAFT

The Court has jurisdiction in accordance with this Statute with respect to the following crimes:

(a)   the crime of genocide;

(b)   the crime of aggression;

(c)   serious violations of the laws and customs applicable in armed conflict;

(d)   crimes against humanity;

(e)   crimes, established under or pursuant to the treaty provisions listed in the Annex, 2/ which, having regard to the conduct alleged, constitute exceptionally serious crimes of international concern.

II. PROPOSALS

The Court has jurisdiction in accordance with this Statute with respect to the following crimes:

(a)   the crime of genocide;

(b)   crimes against humanity;

(c)   the crime of aggression;

(d)   serious violations of the laws and customs applicable in armed conflicts;

---

1   There is no equivalent article in the draft proposal by the International Law Commission.

*   Note. See the footnote to the proposals on the preamble, at the beginning of the present volume.

2/   See appendix II of the annex to the ILC draft.

(e)
- grave breaches of the four Geneva Conventions of 12 August 1949;
- grave breaches of article 3 common to the four Geneva Conventions of 12 August 1949.

[*56] A. Genocide
Alternative 1. Definition by reference

The Court has jurisdiction in accordance with this Statute with respect to the following crimes:

(a) the crime of genocide **[as defined in the Convention on the Prevention and Punishment of the Crime of Genocide of 1948;]**

[With respect to the interpretation and application of the crimes within the jurisdiction of the Court, the Court shall apply relevant international conventions and other sources of international law.]

Alternative 2. Definition modelled on Genocide Convention with or without modification

Genocide means any of the following acts committed with intent to destroy, in whole or in part, a national, ethnic, racial or religious group, as such:

(a) killing members of the group;

(b) causing serious bodily or mental harm to members of the group;

(c) deliberately inflicting on the group conditions of life calculated to bring about its physical destruction in whole or in part;

(d) imposing measures intended to prevent births within the group;

(e) forcibly transferring children of the group to another group.

[The following acts shall also be punishable:

(a) conspiracy to commit genocide;

(b) direct and public incitement to commit genocide;

(c) attempt to commit genocide;

(d) complicity in genocide.] 3/

* * *

1. Genocide means any of the following acts committed **[, whether in time of peace or in time of armed conflict]** with intent to destroy, in whole or in [*57]**[substantial]** part, a national, ethnic, racial or religious group, **[social or political]** as such: 4/

(a) killing members of the group;

(b) causing serious bodily or mental harm to members of the group;

(c) deliberately inflicting on the group conditions of life calculated to bring about its physical destruction in whole or in part;

(d) imposing measures intended to prevent **[preventing]** births within the group;

(e) forcibly transferring children **[persons]** of the group to another group.

2. The following acts shall be punishable: 5/

(a) genocide;

(b) conspiracy to commit genocide;

(c) direct and public incitement to commit genocide;

(d) attempt to commit genocide;

(e) complicity in genocide.

3/   Chairman's informal text (see A/AC.249/1, p. 58); see also A/AC.249/L.3, article 28. The acts enumerated here are identical to those of articles II and III of the 1948 Convention on the Prevention and Punishment of Genocide.
The paragraph in square brackets above may become unnecessary if there is a separate article covering those elements.

4/   Text reproduced from article II of the 1948 Convention on the Prevention and Punishment of the Crime of Genocide. Additions are indicated in bold type.

5/   Another suggestion is to delete this paragraph and to include, in the General Part of the Statute, provisions regarding conspiracy, incitement, attempt and complicity in the commission of the core crimes under the court's jurisdiction.

[3. Persons committing genocide or any of the other acts enumerated above shall be punished, whether they are constitutionally responsible rulers, public officials or private individuals.] 6/

[4. "Intent to destroy, in whole or in part, a national ethnical, racial or religious group" means the specific intent to destroy, in whole or in substantial part, a national, ethnical, racial or religious group as such by the acts specified in the definition.

5. "Mental harm" means permanent impairment of mental faculties through drugs, torture or similar techniques.]

[*58] B. Aggression 7/

Paragraph 1

[1. Aggression means an act committed by an individual who, as leader or organizer, is involved in the use of armed force by a State against the territorial integrity or political independence of another State, or in any other manner inconsistent with the Charter of the United Nations.]

* * *

[1. The crime of aggression is committed by a person who is in a position of exercising control or capable of directing political/military actions in his State, against another State, in contravention to the Charter of the United Nations, by resorting to armed force, to threaten or violate that State's sovereignty, territorial integrity or political independence.]

Paragraph 2

2. Acts constituting aggression include the following:

* * *

[(a) the invasion or attack by the armed forces of a State of the territory of another State, or any military occupation, however, temporary, resulting from such invasion or attack, or any annexation by the use of force of the territory of another State or part thereof;

(b) bombardment by the armed forces of a State against the territory of another State, [or the use of any weapons by a State against the territory of another State.]

(c) the blockade of the ports or coasts of a State by the armed forces of another State;

(d) an attack by the armed forces of a State on the land, sea or air forces, or marine and air fleets of another State;

(e) the use of armed forces of one State which are within the territory of another State with the agreement of the receiving State in contravention of the conditions provided for in the agreement, or any extension of their presence in such territory beyond the termination of the agreement;

(f) the action of a State in allowing its territory, which it has placed at the disposal of another State, to be used by that other State for perpetrating an act of aggression against a third State;

(g) the sending by or on behalf of a State of armed bands, groups, irregulars or mercenaries, which carry out acts of armed force against another State of such gravity as to amount to the acts listed above, or its substantial involvement therein.]

* * *

[*59] [Crimes against peace, namely, planning, preparation, initiation or waging of a war of aggression, or a war in violation of international treaties, agreements or assurances, or participation in a common plan or conspiracy for the accomplishment of any of the foregoing.]

* * *

[1. Aggression means the use of force or the threat of use of force [by a State] against the sovereignty, territorial integrity or political independence of [another] [a] State, or the use of force or threat of use of force in any other manner inconsistent with the Charter of the United Nations and customary international law.]

6/   Text reproduced from article IV of the Genocide Convention.

7/   The following proposals represent a number of alternatives for illustrative purposes. Some delegations believe that they are all inadequate.

Some delegations are for and some are against the inclusion of "aggression" in the crimes covered by the International Criminal Court.

[2.   The crime of aggression is committed by an individual who as leader or organizer plans, commits or orders the commission of an act of aggression.]

* * *

The crime of aggression means planning, preparation, initiation or waging of a war of aggression, or a war in violation of international treaties, agreements or assurances, or participation in a common plan or conspiracy for the accomplishment of any of the foregoing acts.

C. War Crimes

[War crimes] means: 8/

1.Grave breaches referred to in the Geneva Conventions of 12 August 1949 [and of Additional Protocol I thereto of 8 June 1977] [such as] [namely]:

[(a)   wilful killing;

(b)   torture or inhuman treatment, including biological experiments;

(c)   wilfully causing great suffering or serious injury to body or health;

(d)   extensive destruction and appropriation of property, not justified by military necessity and carried out unlawfully and wantonly;

(e)   compelling a prisoner of war or a civilian to serve in the forces of a hostile Power;

(f)   wilfully depriving a prisoner of war or a civilian of the rights of fair and regular trial;

(g)   unlawful deportation or transfer or unlawful confinement of a civilian;

(h)   taking civilians as hostages.]

[*60] [(i) making the civilian population or individual civilians the object of attack;

(j)   the perfidious use of the distinctive emblem of the red cross, red crescent or red lion and sun or of other recognized protective signs recognized under international law;

(k)   launching an attack against works or installations containing dangerous forces in the knowledge that such attacks will cause excessive loss of life, injury to civilians or damage to civilian objects;

(l)   practices of apartheid and other inhuman and degrading practices involving outrages upon personal dignity, based on racial discrimination;

(m)   making clearly recognized historic monuments, works of art or places of worship which constitute the cultural or spiritual heritage of peoples and to which special protection has been given by special arrangement, for example, within the framework of a competent international organization, the object of attack, causing, as a result, intensive destruction thereof, where there is no evidence of the violation by the adverse party of using such objects in support of a military effort, and when such historic monuments, works of art and places of worship are not located in the immediate proximity of military objectives;

(n)   the transfer by the occupying Power of parts of its own civilian population into the territory it occupies, or the deportation or transfer of all or parts of the population of the occupied territory within or outside this territory in violation of article 49 of the Fourth Convention;

(o)   making non-defended localities and demilitarized zones the object of attack;

(p)   unjustifiable delay in the repatriation of prisoners of war or civilians.]

[2.   Other serious violations of the laws and customs [of war] [applicable in armed conflict], [whether of an international or of a non-international character] [which include, but are not limited to,] [namely] the violations referred to in the 1907 Hague Convention No. IV, [and the serious violations of article 3 common to the Geneva Conventions of 12 August 1949] [and of Additional Protocol II thereto of 8 June 1977] [include but are not limited to] [are]:

[(a)   employment of poisonous weapons or other weapons calculated to cause unnecessary suffering;

(b)   wanton destruction of cities, towns or villages, or devastation not justified by military necessity;

(c)   attack, or bombardment, by whatever means, of undefended towns, villages, dwellings or buildings;

8/   The present text (Chairman's revised informal text) represent a compilation of different possibilities for illustrative purposes. Adaptations of this text may be required after completion of the definitions of crimes and discussion of jurisdiction and other related issues.

[*61] (d) seizure of, destruction of or wilful damage done to institutions dedicated to religion, charity and education, the arts and sciences, historic monuments and works of art and science;

(e) plunder of public or private property;

(f) violence to the life, health and physical or mental well-being of persons, in particular murder, manslaughter, [rape] [and sexual violence] as well as cruel treatment such as torture, mutilation or any form of corporal punishment, [and human experimentation];

(g) collective punishments;

(h) taking of hostages;

(i) acts of terrorism;

(j) outrages upon personal dignity, in particular humiliating and degrading treatment, rape, enforced prostitution and any form of indecent assault;

(k) slavery, [and the slave trade,] [slave-related practices, and forced labour] in all their forms;

(l) pillage;

(m) usage of human shields;

(n) acts of violence designed to inspire or instil terror into that population in whole or in part;

(o) the passing of sentences and the carrying out of executions without previous judgement pronounced by a regularly constituted court, affording fundamental judicial guarantees which are recognized [under general principles of international law];

(p) forcibly using members of the civilian population, including children, to take part in hostilities or to perform forced labour or labour related to military purposes];

(q) failure to remove or protect civilians, particularly children, from areas in which hostilities are taking place to safer areas within the State of nationality of the civilian population, and with respect to children, to ensure that they are accompanied by persons responsible for their safety and well-being];

(r) starving of the civilian population and prevention of humanitarian assistance from reaching them;

(s) intentionally separating children from parents or persons responsible for their safety and well-being;

(t) failure to medically treat the wounded, the sick, the shipwrecked and persons deprived of their liberty for reasons related to the armed conflict;

[*62] (u) mistreatment of persons detained or interned].

* * *

[Unless they constitute crimes mentioned in the subparagraph (above) 9/ (below),] An individual who commits or orders the commission of an exceptionally serious war crime shall, on conviction thereof, be sentenced to [...].

For the purposes of this Code [of the present Statute] [of the present Convention], a war crime means:

1. Grave breaches of the Geneva Conventions of [12 August] 1949, namely: [, the following acts against persons or property protected under the provisions of the relevant Geneva Conventions:]

(a) wilful killing;

(b) torture or inhuman treatment, including biological experiments;

(c) wilfully causing great suffering or serious injury to body or health;

(d) extensive destruction and appropriation of property, not justified by military necessity and carried out unlawfully and wantonly;

(e) compelling a prisoner of war or a civilian to serve in the forces of a hostile Power;

(f) wilfully depriving a prisoner of war or a civilian of the rights of fair and regular trial;

(g) unlawful deportation or transfer or unlawful confinement of a civilian;

(h) taking civilians as hostages.

2. [The following] [Other serious] Violations of the laws [applicable in armed conflicts] or [and] customs of war, [whether international or internal in character,] which include, but are not limited to:

9/ Unless indicated in bold type, the present text is based on the revised article on war crimes proposed by the Special Rapporteur of the International Law Commission for consideration in second reading of the draft Code of Crimes against the Peace and Security of Mankind (A/CN.4/466, p. 26). In the text of one proposal, the order of paragraphs 1 and 2 of the draft article should be inverted.

|, including serious violations of article 3 common to the Geneva Conventions of 12 August 1949 for the Protection of War Victims, and of Additional Protocol thereto of 8 June 1977. These violations shall include, but shall not be limited to:|

   |(a) **making the civilian population or individual civilians the object of attack|**
   (a)   employment of poisonous weapons or other weapons calculated to cause unnecessary suffering;
   (b)   wanton destruction of cities, towns or villages, or devastation not justified by military necessity;
|*63| (c) attack, or bombardment, by whatever means, of undefended towns, villages, dwellings or buildings;
   (d)   seizure of, destruction of or wilful damage done to institutions dedicated to religion, charity and education, the arts and sciences, historic monuments and works of art and science;
   (e)   plunder of public or private property.

   |3.   **In the case of armed conflict not of an international character occurring in the territory of a State Party:|**
   |(a) **violence to life, health and physical or mental well-being of persons, in particular murder as well as cruel treatment such as torture, mutilation or any form of corporal punishment;**
   (b)   **collective punishment;**
   (c)   **taking of hostages;**
   (d)   **acts of terrorism;**
   (e)   **outrages upon personal dignity, in particular humiliating and degrading treatment, rape, enforced prostitution and other forms of indecent assault;**
   (f)   **pillage;**
   (g)   **the passing of sentences and the carrying out of executions without previous judgement pronounced by a regularly constituted court, affording all the judicial guarantees which are recognized as indispensable by civilized peoples.|**
   |(h) **threats to commit any of the acts listed under paragraph 3 above.|**
                                   * * *

Serious violations of the laws and customs of war

The following acts are considered serious violations of the laws and customs of war:
   (a)   killing or wounding treacherously individuals belonging to the hostile nation or army;
   (b)   killing or wounding an enemy who, having laid down arms, or having no longer means of defence, has surrendered at discretion;
   (c)   declaring that no quarter will be given;
   (d)   making improper use of a flag of truce, of the national flag or of the military insignia and uniform of the enemy, of the uniform of multinational forces in the context of a peace-making or peace-keeping operation, as well as the distinctive badges of the Geneva Convention;
   (e)   destroying or seizing the enemy's property, unless such destruction or seizure be imperatively demanded the necessities of war;
|*64| (f) declaring abolished, suspended or inadmissible in a court of law the rights and actions of the nationals of the hostile party;
   (g)   compelling the nationals of the hostile party to take part in the operations of war directed against their own country, even if they were in the belligerent's service before the commencement of the war;
   (h)   attacking or bombarding by whatever means towns, villages, dwellings or buildings which are undefended;
   (i)   pillaging a town or place, even when taken by assault;
   (j)   using certain categories of projectiles which are explosive or charged with fulminating or inflammable substances, such as those referred to in the St. Petersburg Declaration of 1868;
   (k)   using bullets which expand or flatten easily inside the human body, as defined in the Hague Declaration of 29 July 1899;
   (l)   using asphyxiating, poisonous or other gases and bacteriological methods as defined in the Geneva Protocol of 1925, as well as microbial agents or toxins, as defined in the 1972 Biological Weapons Convention;

(m) using chemical weapons as defined in article 2 of the 1993 Convention on the Prohibition of the Development, Production, Stockpiling and Use of Chemical Weapons and on Their Destruction;

(n) directing attacks against historical monuments, works of art or clearly recognized places of worship constituting the cultural heritage, unless such attacks be imperatively demanded by the necessities of war.

Grave breaches of the Geneva Conventions

1. Grave breaches of the Geneva Conventions of 12 August 1949 are:

(a) With regard to the wounded and sick in armed forces in the field and wounded, sick and shipwrecked members of armed forces at sea: wilful killing, torture or inhuman treatment, including biological experiments, wilfully causing great suffering or serious injury to body or health, and extensive destruction and appropriation of property, not justified by military necessity and carried out unlawfully and wantonly;

(b) With regard to prisoners of war: wilful killing, torture or inhuman treatment, including biological experiments, wilfully causing great suffering or serious injury to body or health, compelling a prisoner of war to serve in the forces of the hostile Power, or wilfully depriving a prisoner of war of the rights of fair and regular trial prescribed in the Conventions referred to in this article;

(c) With regard to the protection of civilian persons in time of war: wilful killing, torture or inhuman treatment, including biological experiments, wilfully causing great suffering or serious injury to body or health, unlawful deportation or transfer or unlawful confinement of a protected person, compelling a protected person to serve in the forces of a hostile Power, or wilfully depriving a protected person of the rights of fair and regular trial prescribed in the Conventions referred to in this article, taking of hostages, [*65] and extensive destruction and appropriation of property, not justified by military necessity and carried out unlawfully and wantonly.

2. Grave breaches of article 3 common to the four Geneva Conventions of 12 August 1949 are, at all times and in any place, in the case of an armed conflict not of an international character occurring on the territory of one of the States parties, the following acts against persons taking no active part in the hostilities, including members of armed forces who have laid down their arms and those placed <u>hors de combat</u> by sickness, wounds, detention or any other cause:

(a) violence to life and person, in particular murder of all kinds, mutilation, cruel treatment and torture;

(b) taking of hostages;

(c) outrages upon personal dignity, in particular humiliating and degrading treatment;

(d) the passing of sentences and the carrying out of executions without previous judgement pronounced by a regularly constituted court affording all the judicial guarantees which are recognized as indispensable by civilized peoples.

* * *

Violations of article 3 common to the Geneva Conventions and of Additional Protocol II

The International Criminal Court shall have the power to prosecute persons committing or ordering to be committed serious violations of article 3 common to the Geneva Conventions of 12 August 1949 for the Protection of War Victims and of Additional Protocol II thereto of 8 June 1977 where, having regard to the conduct alleged, these acts constitute serious causes of international concern, including but not limited to:

[subparagraphs (a) to (g) as in para. 3 of the preceding formulation]

D. Crimes against humanity

"Crimes against humanity" means the following [crimes] [acts], when committed as part of a widespread [and] [or] systematic attack [on a massive scale] against any civilian population:

(a) [murder] [wilful killing];

(b) extermination;

(c) enslavement;

(d) deportation [or forcible transfer of population];

(e) imprisonment [, including taking of civilian hostages];

(f)   torture [or other forms of cruel treatment];

(g)   rape [or other serious assaults of a sexual nature];

[*66] (h) persecutions on political, [national, ethnic,] racial and religious grounds [in connection with any [other] crime within the jurisdiction of the Court];

(i)   [other inhumane acts of a similar character [, such as] wilfully causing great suffering or serious injury to body and health];

[other inhumane acts which cause serious injury to body or health]. 10/

* * *

[1. A person commits crimes against humanity, whether in time of peace or in time of war, when:

(a) he is in a position of authority and orders, commands, or fails to prevent the systematic commission of the acts described below, against a given segment of the civilian population;

(b) he is in a position of authority and participates in the making of a policy or programme designed to systematically carry out the acts described below against a given segment of the civilian population;

(c) he is in a senior military or political position and knowingly carries out or orders others to carry out systematically the acts described below against a segment of the civilian population;

(d) he knowingly commits the acts described below with intent to further a policy of systematic persecution against a segment of the civilian population without having a moral choice to do otherwise.]

* * *

[The International Criminal Court] shall have the power to prosecute persons responsible for the following crimes when committed as part of a widespread or systematic attack against any civilian population on [discriminatory] [national, political, ethnic, racial or religious] grounds: [and which, having regard to the conduct alleged, constitute serious crimes of international concern];

* * *

[For the purposes of the present Convention "crimes against humanity" means the following acts when committed as part of a widespread and systematic attack against any civilian population unless they constitute crimes defined in the preceding provision:]

* * *

[*67] [The acts constituting "crimes against humanity" when committed systematically or as part of a public policy against a segment of the civilian population are:]

* * *

[A crime against humanity means the widespread or systematic commission, raising international concern, of any or more of the following acts:]

* * *

[The following acts when committed as part of a widespread and systematic attack against any civilian population shall be punishable:]

* * *

[Crimes against humanity means the following: crimes when committed in armed conflicts, whether international or internal in character, as part of a widespread or systematic attack on a massive scale against any civilian population.]

* * *

1.   A person commits a crime against humanity when:

(a) he commits one of the acts described in paragraph 2; and

[(b) that act is part of a widespread and systematic attack against a civilian population]

* * *

[(c) he commits that act [knowing it is part of] [with the intent to further] a widespread and systematic attack against a civilian population]

10/   Chairman's informal text. Adaptations of this text may be required after completion of the definitions of crimes and discussion of jurisdiction and other related issues.

2. Acts constituting a crime against humanity when committed as part of a widespread and systematic attack against a civilian population are the following:

* * *

[(a) A person commits crimes against humanity, whether in time of peace or in time of war, when he knowingly commits the acts described below against a segment of the civilian population, and when these acts are part of a systematic policy or when they are committed on a widespread basis. 11/

   (b) The acts constituting "crimes against humanity" are:]

   (a) [wilful] murder [killing or extermination] [, including killings by knowingly creating conditions likely to cause death];

   [(b) mutilation];

   (b) extermination;

   [*68] (c) enslavement [, including slavery-related practices and forced labour]; [establishing or maintaining over persons a status of slavery, servitude or forced labour];

   (d) [discriminatory and arbitrary] deportation [or unlawful confinement of civilian population] [in violation of international legal norms] [which inflicts death or serious bodily injury];

   (e) imprisonment [, in violation of international norms on the prohibition of arbitrary arrest and detention] [which inflicts death or serious bodily injury];

   (f) [cruel treatment including] torture [, rape and other serious assaults of a sexual nature];

   (g) [outrages upon personal dignity, in particular humiliation and degrading treatment,] rape [, enforced prostitution];

   (h) persecutions on political, racial and religious [or cultural] grounds [, whether based on laws or practices targeting selected groups or their members in ways that seriously and adversely affect their ethnic, cultural or religious life, their collective well-being and welfare, or their ability to maintain group identity];

   [(h bis) taking civilians as hostages];

   [(h ter) wilfully depriving a civilian of the rights of fair and regular trial];

   (i) other inhumane acts [of a similar nature] [, including but not limited to attacks upon physical integrity, personal safety and individual dignity, such as physical mutilation, forced impregnation or forced carrying to term of fetuses that are the product of forced impregnation, and unlawful human experimentation].

   [Annex

   (a) Wilful killing means intentionally or knowingly causing the death of another person, or [causing the death of another person under circumstances manifesting extreme indifference to human life.]

   (b) Extermination means:

      (i) mass murder; or

      (ii) intentionally inflicting conditions of life [calculated to] [which the accused knew or had reason to know would] bring about the physical destruction of a defined segment of the population.

   (c) Enslavement means intentionally placing or maintaining a person in a condition in which any or all of the powers attaching to the right of ownership are exercised over him.

   (d) Deportation means mass deportation or forced transfer of persons from the territory of a State [or from an area within a State] of which such persons are nationals or lawful permanent residents, except where the acts constituting [*69] deportation or transfer are for purposes of an evacuation for safety or other legitimate and compelling reasons.

   (e) Imprisonment means the forcible confinement of a person for a prolonged or indefinite period of time in manifest and gross violation of governing legal norms regarding arrest and detention.

   11/ Unless indicated in bold type, this text is based on article 3 on crimes against humanity of the Statute of the International Criminal Tribunal for Rwanda.

(f)   **Torture means the intentional infliction of severe pain or suffering, whether physical or mental, upon a person in the accused's custody or physical control; except that torture shall not include pain and suffering arising only from, inherent in or incidental to, lawful sanctions.**

(g)   **Rape means causing a person to engage in or submit to a sexual act by force or threat of force.**

(h)   **Enforced prostitution means intentionally placing or maintaining a person in circumstances in which the person is expected or directed to engage repeatedly over time in sexual acts, and the person's capacity or freedom to refuse has been substantially negated because of the force or threat of force, the circumstances, loss of physical liberty, mental impairment or prolonged periods of serious mental or physical abuse.**

(i)   **Persecution means the intentional and severe deprivation of fundamental rights, without lawful justification.**

(j)   **The term "widespread" means the attack is massive in nature and directed against large numbers of individuals.**

(k)   **The term "systematic" means the attack constitutes, or is part of, consistent with or in furtherance of, a policy or concerted plan, or repeated practice over a period of time.]**

* * *

Crimes against humanity mean any of the following acts committed on a massive and systematic scale against a group of the civilian population on political, philosophical, racial, ethnic or religious grounds:

(a)   wilful killing;
(b)   enslavement;
(c)   kidnapping followed by the disappearance of the person;
(d)   deportation;
(e)   arbitrary detention;
(f)   rape;
(g)   any form of persecution on these grounds;
(h)   torture or any other inhumane act causing great suffering or serious injury to physical or mental integrity or health.

[*70] Article 21
Preconditions to the exercise of jurisdiction
I. ILC DRAFT

1.   The Court may exercise its jurisdiction over a person with respect to a crime referred to in article 20 if:

(a)   in a case of genocide, a complaint is brought under article 25 (1);
(b)   in any other case, a complaint is brought under article 25 (2) and the jurisdiction of the Court with respect to the crime is accepted under article 22:

(i)   by the State which has custody of the suspect with respect to the crime ("the custodial State"); and
(ii)   by the State on the territory of which the act or omission in question occurred.

2.   If, with respect to a crime to which paragraph 1 (b) applies, the custodial State has received, under an international agreement, a request from another State to surrender a suspect for the purposes of prosecution, then, unless the request is rejected, the acceptance by the requesting State of the Court's jurisdiction with respect to the crime is also required.

II. PROPOSALS

1.   The Court (may exercise its) [shall have] jurisdiction (over a person with respect to a crime) referred to in article 20 (f):

(a)   in a case of genocide, a complaint is brought under article 25 (1);
(b)   in any other case, a complaint is brought under article 25 (2) and the jurisdiction of the Court with respect to the crime is accepted under article 22:

(i)   by the State which has custody of the suspect with respect to the crime ("the custodial State") [in accordance with international law]; (and)

(ii)   by the State on the territory of which the act or omission in question occurred [**if applicable**].

2.   If, with respect to a crime to which paragraph 1 (b) applies, the custodial State has received, under an international agreement, a request from another State to surrender a suspect for the purposes of prosecution, then, unless the request is rejected, the acceptance by the requesting State of the Court's jurisdiction with respect to the crime is also required.

[*71] Proposals for replacing article 21

[1.   **The Court may exercise its jurisdiction over a person with respect to a crime referred to in article 20 in accordance with the provisions of this Statute if:**

(a)   **the matter is referred to the Court by the Security Council acting under Chapter VII of the Charter of the United Nations;**

(b)   **a complaint is lodged by an interested State in accordance with article 25;**

(c)   **the matter was notified to the Prosecutor and he/she concludes that there is sufficient basis for a prosecution in accordance with articles 26 and 27.**

2.   **In the case of subparagraphs 1 (b) and (c) the Court may exercise its jurisdiction only if the States which have jurisdiction over the case in question have accepted the jurisdiction of the Court in accordance with article 22 and if national jurisdiction is either not available or ineffective or if those States have deferred the matter to the Court.]**

* * *

[1.   **The Court may exercise its jurisdiction over a person with respect to a crime referred to in article 20 if a complaint is brought under article 25 and the jurisdiction of the Court with respect to the crime is accepted under article 22:**

(a)   **by the State which has custody of the suspect with respect to the crime ("custodial State"); and**

(b)   **by the State on the territory of which the act or omission in question occurred.**

2.**If, with respect to a crime to which paragraph 1 applies, the custodial State has received, under an international agreement, a request from another State to surrender a suspect for the purposes of prosecution, then, unless the request is rejected, the acceptance by the requesting State of the Court's jurisdiction with respect to the crime is also required.]**

* * *

[1.   **The Court may exercise its jurisdiction over a person with respect to a crime referred to in Article 20 and in accordance with the provisions of this Statute if:**

(a)   **the matter is referred to the Court by the Security Council acting under Chapter VII of the Charter of the United Nations; or**

(b)   **a complaint is brought by a State Party.**

2.**The Court shall not exercise its jurisdiction with respect to the crime referred to in article 20 (d) unless the Security Council has first determined that a State has committed an act of aggression.]**

* * *

[*72] Consent of States

The jurisdiction of the Court extends to all crimes referred to in articles __ to __ when the following have expressed their agreement:

(a)   the State(s) on whose territory the acts were committed;

(b)   the State(s) of the nationality of the victim(s) of those acts; and

(c)   the State(s) of the nationality of the person(s) suspected to having committed the acts.

[*73] Article 22
Acceptance of the jurisdiction of the Court for the purposes of article 21
I. ILC DRAFT

1.   A State party to this Statute may:

(a)   at the time it expresses its consent to be bound by the Statute, by declaration lodged with the depositary; or

(b)   at a later time, by declaration lodged with the Registrar;

accept the jurisdiction of the Court with respect to such of the crimes referred to in article 20 as it specifies in the declaration.

2.   A declaration may be of general application, or may be limited to particular conduct or to conduct committed during a particular period of time.

3.   A declaration may be made for a specified period, in which case it may not be withdrawn before the end of that period, or for an unspecified period, in which case it may be withdrawn only upon giving six months' notice of withdrawal to the Registrar. Withdrawal does not affect proceedings already commenced under this Statute.

4.   If under article 21 the acceptance of a State which is not a party to this Statute is required, that State may, by declaration lodged with the Registrar, consent to the Court exercising jurisdiction with respect to the crime.

II. PROPOSALS
Proposal 1

[1.   **A State which becomes a party to this Statute thereby accepts the inherent jurisdiction of the Court with respect to crimes referred to in article 2, paragraphs (a) to (d).**

2.   With regard to the crimes referred to in article 20 (e) a State party to this Statute may declare:

      (a)   at the time it expresses its consent to be bound by the Statute, or

      (b)   at a later time that it accepts the jurisdiction of the Court with respect to such of the crimes as it specifies in the declaration. (Para. 2 shall be maintained only if "treaty crimes" are included in the statute)]

Proposal 2

[The Court shall satisfy itself that it has jurisdiction in any case brought before it.]

[Part 3 has optional jurisdiction of the Court.]

[*74] (If the so-called "treaty crimes" were to be comprised in the jurisdiction of the Court, this part would organize the regime thereof along the lines contained in article 21 (i) (b), (2) and article 22 of the present ILC draft statute.)

[*75] Article 23
Action by the Security Council
I. ILC DRAFT

1.   Notwithstanding article 21, the Court has jurisdiction in accordance with this Statute with respect to crimes referred to in article 20 as a consequence of the referral of a matter to the Court by the Security Council acting under Chapter VII of the Charter of the United Nations.

2.   A complaint of or directly related to an act of aggression may not be brought under this Statute unless the Security Council has first determined that a State has committed the act of aggression which is the subject of the complaint.

3.   No prosecution may be commenced under this Statute arising from a situation which is being dealt with by the Security Council as a threat to or breach of the peace or an act of aggression under Chapter VII of the Charter, unless the Security Council otherwise decides.

II. PROPOSALS

[1. A State Party may lodge a complaint with the Prosecutor alleging that a crime referred to in article 20 appears to have been committed.

2.   As far as possible a complaint shall specify the circumstances of the alleged crime and the identity and whereabouts of any suspect, and be accompanied by such supporting documentation as is available to the complainant State.

3.   In a case to which article 21 (a) applies, a complaint is not required for the initiation of an investigation.]

* * *

1.   Notwithstanding article 21, the Court has jurisdiction in accordance with this Statute with respect to crimes (referred to) [**specified**] in article 20 as a consequence of the referral of a (matter) [**situation**] to the Court by the Security Council (acting under Chapter VII of the Charter of the United Nations.) [**in accordance with the terms of such referral.**]

Delete original paragraph 2 of the ILC draft.

2.　No prosecution may be commenced under this Statute arising from a [**dispute or**] situation (which is being dealt with by the Security Council as a threat to or breach of the peace or an act of aggression under Chapter VII of the Charter, unless the Security Council otherwise decides.) [**pertaining to international peace and security or an act of aggression which is being dealt with by the Security Council without the prior consent of the Security Council.**]

[**If "aggression" were to be included in article 20, then, according to the above proposal, the retention of the original paragraph 23 (2) of the ILC draft statute would be necessary, with the renumbering of the above-stated subparagraph 2 as article 23 (3).**]

* * *

[*76] Role of the Security Council

1.　Notwithstanding article 34, the Security Council acting under Chapter VII of the Charter of the United Nations, can decide to refer a situation or acts constituting crimes to the Prosecutor of the Court when one or more of the crimes referred to in article 27 **appear** to **have been committed**.

Notification of the Security Council decision to the Prosecutor of the Court shall be accompanied by all evidence available to the Council.

2.　A complaint of or directly related to a crime of aggression referred to in articles 27 (c) and 30 may not be brought unless the Security Council has first determined that a State has committed the act of aggression which is the subject of the complaint, in accordance with Chapter VII of the Charter of the United Nations.

3.　No prosecution may be commenced under this Statute arising from a situation which is being dealt with by the Security Council as a threat to or breach of the peace or an act of aggression under Chapter VII of the Charter, unless the Security Council otherwise decides.

* * *

Other proposals
Paragraph 1

Notwithstanding article 21, the Court has jurisdiction in accordance with this Statute with respect to crimes referred to in article 20 as a consequence of the referral of a (matter) [**case**] to the Court by the Security Council (acting under Chapter VII of the Charter of the United Nations) or [**acting under Chapters VI and VII of the Charter of the United Nations**]. [**As far as possible a referral shall specify the circumstances of the alleged crime and be accompanied by such supporting documentation as is available to the Security Council.**]

Paragraph 2

The determination of the Security Council that a State has committed an act of aggression shall be binding on the deliberation of the Court in respect of a complaint, the subject matter of which is the act of aggression.

Paragraph 3

(a)　No prosecution may be commenced under this Statute arising from (a situation which is being dealt with by the Security Council) [**a situation where the Security Council has decided that there is a threat to or breach of the peace and for which it is exercising its functions under Chapter VII of the Charter of the United Nations**] as a threat to or breach of the peace or an act of aggression under Chapter VII of the Charter, unless the Security Council otherwise decides.

[*77] (b) [**The determination by the Security Council under paragraph 2 above shall not be interpreted as in any way affecting the independence of the Court in deciding on the commission of the crime of aggression by a given person.**]

(c)　[**Should no action be taken in relation to a situation which has been referred to the Security Council as a threat to or breach of the peace or an act of aggression under Chapter VII of the Charter within a reasonable time, the Court shall exercise its jurisdiction in respect of that situation.**]

(d)　[**Prosecution may be commenced under this Statute except where the Security Council decides in accordance with Article 27 of the Charter that it arises from a situation in respect of which**

effective action is being taken by the Security Council (as a threat to or breach of the peace or an act of aggression under Chapter VII of the Charter).]
Proposals were also made to retain paragraph 1 of article 23 and to delete paragraphs 2 and 3.
Proposals were also made for the deletion of article 23.

[*78] Article 24
Duty of the Court as to jurisdiction
I. ILC DRAFT
The Court shall satisfy itself that it has jurisdiction in any case brought before it.
II. PROPOSALS
Concurrent jurisdiction
The Court has no jurisdiction under this Statute when:
(a)   the acts mentioned in the submission to the Court are still being investigated by a State and the investigation is not manifestly intended to relieve the person concerned of criminal responsibility;
(b)   the acts mentioned in the submission to the Court have already been duly investigated by a State and the decision not to institute proceedings was taken by that State when it had knowledge of all the acts mentioned in the submission and the decision was not motivated by a manifest willingness to relieve the persons concerned of any criminal responsibility;
(c)   any person(s) mentioned in the submission to the Court have already been acquitted or convicted by a final ruling in a State for the acts involved unless the decision failed to take account of all facts contained in the submission or the proceedings were conducted in the State concerned by evading the rule of international law for the manifest purpose of relieving the persons concerned of criminal responsibility.
Verification of jurisdiction
The Court shall satisfy itself that it has jurisdiction in any case brought before it. Any State party competent to institute proceedings in connection with all or part of the acts brought before the Court, and any person named in the document of submission to the Court, may challenge the jurisdiction of the Court. The forms and periods set out in article 39, paragraphs 2 and 3, shall apply.

[*79] PART 3 bis. GENERAL PRINCIPLES OF CRIMINAL LAW* 12/
SECTION 1. SUBSTANTIVE ISSUES
Article A
Nullum crimen sine lege/Non-retroactivity
Proposal 1
1.   [Provided that this Statute is applicable in accordance with articles 21, 22 or 23] a person shall not be criminally responsible under this Statute:
(a)   In the case of a prosecution with respect to a crime referred to in articles 20 (a) to (d), unless the conduct in question constituted a crime [under international law] [under the definition of the crimes of this Statute] [or by national law which is in accordance with international law] at the time that the conduct occurred and such conduct occurred after the entry into force of this Statute;
(b)   In the case of a prosecution with respect to a crime referred to in article 20 (e), unless the treaty in question was applicable to the conduct of the person at the time that the conduct occurred.
2.   Paragraph 1 [1 (a)], above, shall not affect the character of such conduct as being crimes under international law, apart from this Statute.
3.   If the law as it appeared at the commission of the crime is amended prior to the final judgement in the case, the most lenient law shall be applied.

Note. The following is a compilation prepared by an informal group dealing with general principles of criminal law neither represents a text agreed upon among delegations nor suggests that every item should be included in the Statute. It identifies possible elements to be included and examples of some possible texts. The order of the articles as well as the headings are only of an indicative character and have not been finally agreed upon.
Delegations should bear in mind, wherever appropriate, the need to check the consistency of the texts in this compilation with those of existing international instruments.
12/   There is no equivalent of this part in the draft proposed by the International Law Commission.

[Note. A question was raised as to whether the term "international law" in paragraph 1 (a) needed to be clarified. Is it clear that the Statute's definition of a crime would be sufficient and exclusive for the purpose of establishing "a crime under international law" within the meaning of paragraph 1 (a), and that for the purposes of determining whether conduct constitutes a crime for this article, no reference need or should be made to other sources of international law, such as other conventions or customary international law? If it is not clear, should the paragraph refer to crimes as defined by the Statute?

Is a reference in paragraph 1 (a) to national law necessary if all crimes within the jurisdiction of the Court are defined by the Statute?

[*80] Should paragraph 1 (b) also be qualified by the addition of the words "and such conduct occurred after the entry into force of this Statute", as in paragraph 1 (a)?]

Proposal 2

This Statute applies only to a conduct that is done after the entry into force of this Statute, and no conduct shall be punished by this Court unless it is an offence under the definition of the crimes of this Statute.

[2. The Statute shall describe precisely and unequivocally the punishable conducts under its competence and shall not leave doubts about their prohibition.

3.   Punishable conducts shall not be construed and sanctions shall not be applied by analogy.]

Proposal 3
Jurisdiction ratione temporis

1.   The Court has jurisdiction only in respect of acts committed after the date of entry into force of this Statute.

When a State becomes party to this Statute after its entry into force, the Court has jurisdiction only in respect of acts committed by its nationals or on its territory or against its nationals after the deposit by that State of its instrument of ratification or accession.

A non-party State may, however, by an express declaration deposited with the Registrar of the Court, agree that the Court has jurisdiction in respect of the acts that it specifies in the declaration.

2.   The Court has no jurisdiction in respect of crimes for which, even if they have been committed after the entry into force of this Statute, the Security Council, acting under Chapter VII of the Charter of the United Nations, has decided before the entry into force of this Statute to establish an ad hoc international criminal tribunal.

The Security Council may, however, decide otherwise.

Article B
Individual criminal responsibility
a. Personal jurisdiction
Proposal 1

1.   The International Tribunal shall have jurisdiction over [natural] persons pursuant to the provisions of the present statute.

2.   A person who commits a crime under this statute is individually responsible and liable for punishment.

[*81] [2 bis. Criminal responsibility is individual and cannot go beyond the person and his/her possessions.]

3.   The fact that the present Statute provides criminal responsibility for individuals does not [prejudice] [affect] the responsibility of States under international law.

Proposal 2
Physical persons and juridical persons

1.   The Court shall be competent to take cognizance of the criminal responsibility of:

(a)   Physical persons;

(b)   Juridical persons, with the exception of States, when the crimes committed were committed on behalf of such juridical persons or by their agencies or representatives.

2.   The criminal responsibility of juridical persons shall not exclude the criminal responsibility of physical persons who are perpetrators of or accomplices in the same crimes.

3.   These provisions shall be without prejudice to the responsibility of States with respect to international law.

Note

Some delegations indicated that the expression "juridical persons" should extend to organizations lacking a legal status.

Some delegations expressed doubts about including the criminal responsibility of juridical persons into the Statute.

It was proposed as an alternative the possibility of referring to the "responsibility" of the juridical persons without including the word "criminal".

b. Principle of criminal responsibility

Criminal responsibility of principals

1.   A person is criminally responsible as a principal and is liable for punishment for a crime under this Statute if the person, with the mental element required for the crime:

    (a)   Commits the conduct specified in the description (definition) of the crime;

    (b)   Causes the consequences, if any, specified in that description (definition); and

    (c)   Does so in the circumstances, if any, specified in that description (definition).

[*82] 2.   Where two or more persons jointly commit a crime under this Statute with a common intent to commit such crime, each person shall be criminally responsible and liable to be punished as a principal.

[3.   A person shall be deemed to be a principal where that person commits the crime through an innocent agent who is not aware of the criminal nature of the act committed, such as a minor, a person of defective mental capacity or a person acting under mistake of fact or otherwise acting without mens rea.]

[Note. This article establishes the general principle regarding the liability of principal perpetrators of a crime. Further elaboration of the elements of this general principle, such as "mental element", "conduct" and causation, are elaborated in articles G and H.

Other persons who participate in the commission of a crime under this Statute would be criminally responsible and liable for punishment in the manner provided in articles B (c), I and J [and C] of this draft general part.

A question was raised whether this article is required, and whether it would be sufficient merely to state that a person who commits a crime under the Statute is criminally responsible and liable for punishment? On the other hand, it was noted that specificity of the essential elements of the principle of criminal responsibility was important; it serves as a foundation for many of the other subsequent principles and avoids the need to elaborate defences within the Statute that merely constitute negations of the existence of essential mental or physical elements.

It was noted that the choice of using the word "description" or "definition" was dependent upon answering the question whether the definition of crimes would be solely within the Statute (in which case the term "definition" would be appropriate) or whether further elaboration of the elements of the definition of a crime in the Statute might be contained in an annex (in which case the term "description" might be appropriate given that this term could encompass both the statutory definition and the annexed elaboration of elements)].

c. Participation/Complicity

Proposal 1

Responsibility of other persons in the completed

crimes of principals

[1.   A person who [plans,] aids, abets or solicits the commission of a crime under this Statute is criminally responsible and liable for punishment in accordance with that person's own individual responsibility apart from the responsibility of other participants.]

[2.   A person who plans the commission of a crime under this Statute, which is committed by that person or another person, is criminally responsible and liable for punishment [shall be liable to the same punishment as provided in this Statute for a person who commits such crime as a principal].]

[3.   A person may only be criminally responsible for planning the commission of a crime where so provided in this Statute.]

[*83] 4.   A person solicits the commission of a crime if, with the purpose of encouraging another person [making another person decide] to commit [or participate in the commission of] a specific crime, the person commands, [orders], requests, counsels or incites the <u>other</u> person to engage [or participate] in the commission of such crime, and the other person commits a crime [or is otherwise criminally responsible for such crime] as a result of such solicitation.

5.   A person who solicits the commission of a crime is criminally responsible and liable for punishment [shall be liable to the same punishment as provided in this Statute for a <u>person</u> who commits such crime as a principal].

6.   A person aids or abets the commission of a crime if the person does anything for the purpose of facilitating the commission of such crime by another person.

7.   A person who aids or abets the commission of a crime is criminally responsible and liable for punishment {shall be liable to [a reduced punishment] [to the same punishment as provided in this Statute for a person who commits such crime as a principal]}.

[Note. The importance of being able to punish the planners was recognized. Under this article, planners are punishable only if a principal actually committed a crime as a result of such planning or soliciting. An alternative way of addressing the situation of planners is through the concept of "conspiracy"; see article J and notes relating to "conspiracy", below.

It was questioned whether paragraph 1 was redundant and should be deleted in light of the specific paragraphs that followed, which describe in greater detail the forms of participation, responsibility and liability for punishment.

A question was raised whether a person who solicits another person to commit a crime should be responsible and liable not only if the other person commits the crime that was solicited but also for any other crime that the other person committed which the solicitor foresaw (or reasonably could foresee) would be committed as a result of the solicitation.

A question raised by the draft proposals is whether a person should be liable as a solicitor only if the person solicits another to be a principal perpetrator or whether the person should also be liable for soliciting another person to participate in its commission as an aider and abettor (i.e. "otherwise criminally responsible").

It was questioned whether the Statute (in a new and separate article?) should also criminalize and punish a person in the situation where that person solicits another person to commit or criminally participate in a crime, but the other person does not commit the crime.

It was also questioned whether the Statute (in a new and separate article?) should also criminalize and punish persons who aid and abet another person after the commission of a crime; (e.g. aiding a person to escape detection or arrest, or destroying or concealing evidence).

It was suggested that provisions concerning the quantum of sentence should not be included in the General Part, but be located elsewhere in the Statute.]

[*84] Proposal 2
Criminal solicitation

1.   A person is guilty of criminal solicitation, if, with the purpose of making another person decide to commit an offence, he/she commands, encourages or requests another person to engage in specific criminal conduct, when such person did criminal conduct according to such solicitation.

2.   The punishment of criminal solicitation shall be the same as that of principals which is provided for in this Statute.

Accessories

1.   A person is guilty of accessories if he/she did a conduct that facilitates the commission of an offence.

2.   The punishment of accessories shall be reduced.

Proposal 3
Perpetrator and accomplice

1.   An accomplice in a crime shall be punished as the perpetrator.

2.   An accomplice is a person who knowingly, through aid or assistance, facilitates the preparation or commission of a crime.

3.   An accomplice is also a person who knowingly, by whatever means, plans, incites the commission, orders or assists and encourages the planning, preparation or commission of a crime.

d. Combined proposal covering both: (b) principle of criminal responsibility and (c)
participation/complicity

1.   The following shall be considered perpetrators or participants of the crimes defined in the present Statute:

(a)   Those who agree or prepare its perpetration;

(b)   Those who commit such crimes;

(c)   Those who jointly commit such crimes;

(d)   Those who commit such crimes by means of a third person;

(e)   Those who order intentionally a third person to perpetrate such crimes;

(f)   Those who assist intentionally others in the perpetration of such crimes;

(g)   Those who intervene without prior agreement with other persons in the perpetration of such crimes, when it is not possible to determine the result that each one produced.

[*85] 2.   The persons mentioned above will be liable in proportion to their responsibility.

e. Irrelevance of official position
Proposal 1

[1.   This Statute shall be applied to all persons without any discrimination whatsoever.] The official position of a person who commits a crime under this Statute, in particular whether the person acts as Head of State or of Government or as a responsible government official, shall not relieve that person of criminal responsibility nor mitigate punishment.

2.   Immunity

In the course of investigations or procedures performed by, or at the request of the court, no person may make a plea of immunity from jurisdiction irrespective of whether on the basis of international or national law.

Proposal 2
Official capacity of the accused

1.   The official capacity of the accused, either as Head of State or Government, or as a member of a Government or parliament, or as an elected representative, or as an agent of the State shall in no case exempt him from his criminal responsibility under this Statute, nor shall it constitute a ground for reduction of the sentence.

2.   The special procedural rules, the immunities and the protection attached to the official capacity of the accused and established by internal law or by international conventions or treaties may not be used as a defence before the Court.

Article C
Command responsibility
Responsibility of [commanders] [superiors] 13/ for acts
of [forces under their command] [subordinates]

[In addition to other forms of responsibility for crimes under this Statute, a [commander] [superior] is criminally responsible] [A [commander] [*86] [superior] is not relieved of responsibility] [A [commander] [superior] shall be regarded as the perpetrator] 14/ for crimes under this Statute committed by [forces] [subordinate[s]] under his or her command [and effective control] 15/ as a result of the [commander's] [superior's] failure to exercise proper control where:

13/   A significant question is whether the principle of command responsibility should be restricted to military commanders or be extended to any superior regarding the actions of subordinates.

14/   The alternatives highlight the major question under this article of whether command responsibility is a form of criminal responsibility in addition to other modes of participation and complicity, or whether it is a principle that commanders are not immune for the acts of their subordinates. Option 1 takes the former approach, while option 2 takes the latter approach. Option 3 treats the commander as a principal.

15/   A question arises as to whether the commander must have a certain level of de facto control over subordinates at the time of the crime before a duty to act arises.

(a) The [commander] [superior] either knew, or [owing to the widespread commission of the offences should have known] [should have known] 16/ that the [forces] [subordinate[s]] were committing or intending to commit such crimes; 17/ and

(b) The [commander] [superior] failed to take all necessary [and reasonable] measures within his or her power to prevent or repress their commission [or punish the perpetrators thereof]. 18/

Article D
Non bis in idem
Proposal 1

No person shall be tried before any other court for acts constituting a crime of the kind referred to in article 20 for which that person has already been tried by the Court.

Proposal 2

1. Once convicted or acquitted by a final judgement of the Court, a person may no longer be accused on the basis of the same evidence, even for a [*87] different offence, either by the organs of the Court or by the judicial authorities of the States parties.

2. However, if new evidence is made known to the prosecutor following acquittal, he may institute new proceedings.

[Note. The insertion of the above text does not intend to cover all the matters encompassed by article 42 of the Statute of the International Law Commission, but only those pertaining to the principle of non bis in idem stricto sensu, as it does not address the possible application of this principle by the international criminal court in relation to decisions of national courts. It was noted that this aspect was linked to questions of complementarity and procedure, although some delegations had the view that it belonged in the chapter on general principles.]

Article E
Age of responsibility
Proposal 1

1. A person under the age of [twelve, thirteen, fourteen, sixteen, eighteen] at the time of the commission of a crime [shall be deemed not to know the wrongfulness of his or her conduct and] shall not be criminally responsible under this Statute, [unless the Prosecutor proves that the person knew the wrongfulness of his or her conduct at that time].

2. [A person who is between the age of [sixteen] and [twenty-one] at the time of the (alleged) commission of a crime shall be evaluated (by the Court) as to his or her maturity to determine whether the person is responsible under this Statute.]

Proposal 2
Age of persons liable to punishment

[Persons aged 13 to 18 years at the time of the facts shall be criminally responsible but their prosecution, trial and sentence and the regime under which they serve their sentence may give rise to the application of special modalities specified in this Statute.]

[Note. Different views exist among States as to a specific age of responsibility.

It was observed that many international conventions (such as the International Covenant on Civil and Political Rights, the European Convention on Human Rights, the Inter-American Convention on Human Rights) prohibit the punishment of minors.

The question arising from the draft proposals was whether an absolute age of responsibility should be mandated or whether a presumptive age should be included with a means to rebut the presumption.

16/ Alternatively, "had reason to know" could be substituted for "should have known".

17/ The major questions raised by the alternatives are (a) what level of knowledge or foresight is required with respect to actions of subordinates; and (b) what should be the subject of this knowledge.

18/ Questions arise as to what type of action, the failure of which leads to liability, should be required of the commander (e.g. necessary or reasonable measures to prevent, repress or punish)? In addition, should the imposition of punishment by the commander alone be sufficient to relieve a commander of responsibility for crimes committed by a subordinate, which the commander could have but failed to prevent?

It was observed that a consistent approach (in terms of either an evaluation by the Court or proof by the Prosecutor) should be taken in paragraphs 1 and 2 of proposal 1 in respect of both of the age groups mentioned.

[*88] A question was raised as to what would be the criteria of the evaluation process, and should this be left for the Court to develop in supplementary rules or by jurisprudence?

It was questioned whether the Statute should specify that mitigation of sentence should or could be appropriate for those minors who were found to be mature enough to be criminally responsible.

It was observed that, in its article 1, the Convention on the Rights of the Child, defines as a child every human being younger than eighteen years of age and that, in its article 37, it lays down a series of limitations as regards the applicable penalties, ruling out the death penalty and life imprisonment without parole.]

Article F
Statute of limitations
Proposal 1

[1.   The period of limitations shall be completed upon the lapse of xx years for the offence of .... and yy years for the offence of ...

2.   The period of limitations shall commence to run at the time when criminal conduct has ceased.

3.   The period of limitations shall cease to run on the institution of the prosecution against the case concerned to this Court or to a national court of any State that has jurisdiction on such case. The period of limitations begins to run when the decision of the national court becomes final, where this Court has jurisdiction over the case concerned.]

Proposal 2

[There is no statute of limitations for those crimes within the [inherent] jurisdiction of the [Tribunal].]

Proposal 3

[There is no statute of limitations for those crimes within the [inherent] jurisdiction of the Court; but [for those crimes not within the Court's inherent jurisdiction] the Court may decline to exercise jurisdiction if, owing to the lapse of time, a person would be denied a fair trial.]

Proposal 4
[Crimes not subject to limitation

The crimes referred to in articles 27 19/ (a), (b) and (c) shall not be subject to limitation.

[*89] Crimes subject to limitation

1.   Proceedings before the Court in respect of the crimes referred to in articles 27 20/ (d) and (e) shall be subject to a period of limitation of 10 full years from the date on which the crime was committed, provided that during this period no prosecution has been brought.

2.   If a prosecution has been initiated during this period, either before the Court or in a State competent to bring a prosecution under its internal law, the proceedings before the Court shall not be subject to limitation until 10 full years have elapsed from the date of the most recent prosecution.

Proposal 5

[1.   The statute of limitations as established hereunder shall extinguish the criminal prosecution and the punishment.

2.   The statute of limitations will be [ ] years and shall commence to run as follows:

   (a)   In case of instantaneous crime, from the moment of its perpetration;

   (b)   In case of attempt, from the moment the last act of execution was performed or the due conduct was omitted;

   (c)   In case of permanent crime from the moment of the cessation of the criminal conduct.

19/ Paragraphs (a), (b) and (c) of article 27 deal, respectively, with the crime of genocide, crimes against humanity and the crime of aggression.

20/ Paragraphs (d) and (e) of article 27 deal, respectively, with serious violations of the laws and customs applicable in armed conflicts and with grave breaches of the four 1949 Geneva Conventions and of article 3 common to the four 1949 Geneva Conventions.]

3.   The statute of limitations may be interrupted by the actions taken in the investigation of the crime and its perpetrators. If those actions were stopped, the statute of limitations will run again as of the day the last act of investigation was carried out.

4.   The statute of limitations for definitive sanctions will run as of the moment the condemned person escaped and will be interrupted with its detention.]

[*90] Article G
Actus reus (act and/or omission)
Proposal 1
Physical elements of crime

1.   Conduct for which a person may be criminally responsible and liable for punishment as a crime under this Statute can constitute either an act or an omission, or combination thereof. 21/

2.   For the purposes of paragraph 1, a person may be criminally responsible and liable for punishment for an omission if:

(a)   The omission is specified in the description of the crime, and the person could have, but [intentionally or knowingly] failed to avoid the omission; or

(b)   In the circumstances

(i)   a.   the person is under a [pre-existing] legal obligation (duty) to avoid the consequences specified as an [constituent; material] element in the description of a crime;

[Alternative: (I) a. the person is under a [pre-existing] legal obligation (duty) to avoid the result of a crime;]

b.   [or The person is responsible for having created a particular risk or danger that subsequently led to the crime]

(ii)   The consequence caused [result realized] by the omission corresponds to the consequence [result] that would be caused [realized] by a commission of such crime by means of an act; and

(iii)   The person could have, but [intentionally or knowingly] failed to avoid the consequences [results] of such crime.

[3.   A person is only criminally responsible under this Statute if the harm required for the commission of a crime is caused by and accountable to the principal's (perpetrator's) act or omission (conduct).]

[Note. The concept of "omission" presents particular problems to various legal systems.

The extent to which the concept of omission could raise the question of liability may be considered.

Delegations may wish to omit these two elements [i.e., omissions and causation] from the statute.

[*91] Regarding paragraphs 2 (a) and (b) (iii), it was questioned whether references to "intentionally or knowingly" were necessary in view of the subsequent article concerning mental elements, which requires proof of intent or knowledge as the general rule. On the other hand, it was noted that it should be made clear that a failure to avoid an omission due to negligence is insufficient for criminal liability, thereby, possibly justifying the retention of these words.

Regarding paragraph 2 (b) (ii), a question was raised as to the origin of the legal obligation or duty to avoid the consequences or result of a crime. Does this obligation arise only by way of the Statute, or might the obligation arise by virtue of other sources of international or national law? Should it be clarified that any legal obligation must be an obligation pursuant to the Statute?

Also regarding paragraph 2 (b), the draft proposals raise the question whether the obligation is to avoid the "consequences" specified in the definition of the crime or to avoid the "result" of a crime (which may be a broader concept and may include crimes of conduct that have no separate consequences)?

Regarding paragraph 3, it was questioned whether the draft should specify that the "act or omission" be voluntary. Others thought that this was not necessary, as voluntariness was addressed by the principles concerning mental elements in article H.

A question was raised as to whether liability in respect of omissions should be limited only to specific crimes as defined by the Statute [see proposals concerning command responsibility].]

21/   New proposal. This paragraph would link the concepts of act and omission with the concept of "conduct" to which reference is made in article 33-4, and would provide a conceptual link for paragraph 2 of article 33-5.

Proposal 2
Omission

A person who fails to avoid the result of an offence is responsible for such offence if:

(a)   He/she is under a legal obligation to avoid such result;

(b)   The degree of the unlawfulness realized by such omission corresponds to that of the unlawfulness to be realized by the commission of such offence; and

(c)   He/she could have avoided such result.

[Note. It was suggested that the Committee might wish to include in the Statute the classification of instantaneous and permanent crimes.]

[*92] Article H
Mens rea
Mental elements of crime
Proposal 1

1.   Unless otherwise provided, a person is only criminally responsible and liable for punishment for a crime under this Statute if the physical elements are committed with intent [or] [and] knowledge [, whether general or specific or as the substantive crime in question may specify].

2.   For the purposes of this Statute and unless otherwise provided, a person has intent where:

(a)   In relation to conduct, that person means to engage in the act or omission;

(b)   In relation to a consequence, that person means to cause that consequence or is aware that it will occur in the ordinary course of events.

3.   For the purposes of this Statute and unless otherwise provided, "know", "knowingly" or "knowledge" means:

(a)   To be aware that a circumstance exists or a consequence will occur; or

(b)   [To be aware that there is a substantial likelihood that a circumstance exists and deliberately to avoid taking steps to confirm whether that circumstance exists] [to be wilfully blind to the fact that a circumstance exists or that a consequence will occur.]

[4.   For the purposes of this Statute and unless otherwise provided, where this Statute provides that a crime may be committed recklessly, a person is reckless with respect to a circumstance or a consequence if:

(a)   The person is aware of a risk that the circumstance exists or that the consequence will occur;

(b)   The person is aware that the risk is highly unreasonable to take; [and]

[(c) The person is indifferent to the possibility that the circumstance exists or that the consequence will occur.]

[Note. The concepts of recklessness and dolus eventualis should be further considered in view of the seriousness of the crimes considered.

Therefore, paragraph 4 would provide a definition of "recklessness", to be used only where the Statute explicitly provides that a specific crime or element may be committed recklessly. In all situations, the general rule, as stated in paragraph 1, is that crimes must be committed intentionally and knowingly.

[*93] It was questioned whether further clarification might be required to the above definitions of the various types and levels of mental elements. It was noted that this could occur either in the General Part, in the provisions defining crimes or in an annex.

It was questioned whether it was necessary in paragraph 1 to make reference to general and specific intent, as in either case the general rule would be that intent or knowledge is required.

Likewise, it was noted that any reference to "motive" should not be included; if relevant, motive or purpose would be an integral element of the definition of a crime.]

Proposal 2

At the time of a conduct, if a person is not aware of the facts constituting an offence, such conduct is not punishable.

Proposal 3
Moral element

There cannot be a crime without the intention to commit it.

Article I
Attempt
Proposal 1

1.   A person is criminally responsible and is liable for punishment for attempting to commit a crime if, with the intent to commit that crime, the person

[engages in conduct for the purpose of carrying out that intent which is more than mere preparation to commit the crime]

[engages in conduct constituting a substantial step towards the accomplishment of such crime]

[or concludes all necessary steps within the person's control and according to his or her plan towards execution of the crime]

[commences execution of the crime]

, but fails to complete the commission of the crime due to [circumstances independent of that person's will] [or a fortuitous event], [or the object of the attempt is impossible to achieve].

[2.   A person shall only be criminally responsible for attempting to commit a crime where so provided in this Statute.]

3.   A person who is criminally responsible for attempting to commit a crime may be liable to [a reduced punishment] [a reduced period of imprisonment].

[4.   If the person abandons his or her efforts to commit the crime or otherwise prevents the accomplishment of the crime, the person is not punishable if the person completely and voluntarily has given up his or her criminal purpose before the crime was committed.] [without prejudice to applying the penalties to acts committed or omitted that constitute by themselves crimes.]

[*94] [Note. With regard to paragraph 4 above, it was noted that some jurisdictions do not recognize "abandonment" as a defence. Questions were raised whether the concept of "abandonment" should be included in the definition of "attempt", or should be dealt with separately in the statute.

It was observed that an intervening event might break the chain of causation.

It was observed that the three alternatives in paragraph 1 were not mutually exclusive and could be combined as: "commences execution of the crime by engaging in conduct for the purpose of carrying out that intent, which is more than mere preparation and constitutes a substantial step towards the accomplishment of such crime".

It was questioned whether the three proposed reasons in paragraph 1 for the failure to complete the commission of a crime were mutually exclusive, or could be combined.

It was observed that the offence of attempt could apply generally to all crimes.

A question was raised as to when mitigation of punishment for an attempt was appropriate and whether such mitigation should only be for certain crimes.]

Proposal 2
Commission and attempted commission

[1.   The perpetrator of a crime is the person who commits or attempts to commit it.

2.   A crime is attempted when its commission has been commenced and has been interrupted or ceased to have effect only owing to circumstances beyond the control of the perpetrator. The commencement of the commission of a crime is characterized by one or more acts which must have the direct consequence of commission of the crime when the crime has entered its period of commission.]

[Article J
Conspiracy

1.   A person is criminally responsible and is liable for punishment for conspiracy if that person, [with the intent to commit a specific crime] agrees with one or more persons to perpetrate that crime [or that a common intention to commit a crime will be carried out] and an overt act is committed by that person [or by another party to the agreement] [for the purpose of furthering the agreement] [that manifests the intent].

2.   A person is guilty of conspiracy even if the object of the conspiracy is impossible or is prevented by a fortuitous event.

3.   A person shall only be criminally responsible for conspiracy in respect of a crime where so provided in this Statute.

[*95] 4. A person who is criminally responsible for conspiracy is liable for the same punishment as the person who committed or would have committed the crime as a principal.]

[Note. See also article 6.1 of the Rwanda Statute.

It was noted that there were conceptual differences concerning conspiracy among the different legal systems.

The question was raised whether a "planner" should be punished when the crime was not completed, yet action had been taken to implement the plan.

Some delegations questioned whether this concept should be included in the General Part of the Statute, although it might be necessary to punish such conduct in cases of exceptionally serious crimes. (Delegations are invited to look at the explanatory note contained in pages 76 and 77 of document A/AC.249/1.)

Others thought that it would be retrogressive not to include it since it was a form of liability at the Nuremberg trials.

It was questioned whether, in the situation where the crime agreed upon is actually committed, would the crime of conspiracy merge with the completed crime or remain a distinct and separate crime? If the conspiracy were merged with the completed crime, should a conspirator also be responsible for other foreseeable crimes that may have been committed in carrying out the conspiracy? (If the conspiracy remained a distinct crime, the conspirator would only be responsible (absent any other mode of participation) for a conspiracy to commit the crime that was agreed to be committed, as this is the subject-matter of the unlawful agreement.)

Questions arising from the proposed drafts include:

(a) whether the accused conspirator must have an intent to commit the crime or whether it is sufficient that there is an intention that a crime be carried out and that others might be the actual committers;

(b) whether the accused conspirator must commit the overt act or whether it is sufficient if one of the other co-conspirators commits the overt act;

(c) what must be the nature of the overt act (e.g. the act is undertaken for the purpose of furthering the agreement or must it actually manifest the agreement);

(d) whether a conspiracy exists even if the object of the conspiracy is factually impossible to achieve;

(e) whether conspiracy should be limited in respect of an agreement to commit certain listed crimes;

and

(f) the appropriate punishment for the crime.]

Article K

Mistake of fact [or law]

Proposal 1

Mental element

1. At the time of a conduct, if a person is not aware of the facts constituting an offence, such conduct is not punishable.

[*96] 2. Even if a person, at the time of a conduct, does not realize its unlawfulness, he/she is criminally responsible in the case unless such error is unavoidable; provided that the sentence may be reduced.

Proposal 2

Mistake of fact [or of law]

Invincible [Unavoidable] mistake of fact [or of law] shall be a defence provided that the mistake is not inconsistent with the nature of the alleged crime. Avoidable mistake of fact [or of law] may be considered in mitigation of punishment.

Proposal 3

1. [A mistake of law or] a mistake of fact shall be a defence if it negates the mental element required by the crime charged provided that said mistake is not inconsistent with the nature of the crime or its elements, and provided that the circumstances he reasonably believed to be true would have been lawful.

[2. The person who commits a crime in the mistaken belief that he is acting lawfully is not punishable, provided that he has done everything under the circumstances which could reasonably be demanded of him to inform himself about the applicable law. If he could have avoided his mistake of law, the punishment may be reduced.]

Proposal 4
Mistake of law

Mistake of law may not be cited as a ground for exemption from criminal responsibility.
[Note. Some delegations expressed doubts over including these concepts in the Statute.

Doubts were also expressed as to whether these concepts are negations of responsibility or a defence.

In view of the proposed statutory requirements for the existence of particular mental elements in order to establish criminal responsibility (see articles B (b) and H), it was questioned whether this defence need be explicitly mentioned as it is merely one example of the various factors that could negate the existence of the required mental element.

Some delegations held the view that mistake of law should not be permitted as a defence.]

[*97] Article L
Insanity/Diminished mental capacity
Proposal 1

1.   A person is not criminally responsible [is legally insane] if at the time of that person's conduct that (would otherwise) constitutes a crime, the person suffers from a mental disease or mental defect that results in the person lacking substantial capacity either to appreciate the criminality [unlawfulness] of his or her conduct or to confirm his or her conduct to the requirements of the law [, and such mental disease or mental defect caused the conduct constituting a crime.]"
2.   Where a person does not lack substantial capacity of the nature and degree mentioned in paragraph 1, but such capacity is nevertheless substantially diminished at the time of the person's conduct, the sentence shall [may] be reduced."
[Note. The question was raised whether this defence should be included.

The question was also raised whether a provision was required to deal with the issue of whether the accused is fit to stand for trial. That provision might be included in the chapter on trial/procedural rules.

The question was raised as to what should happen to a person who is found insane. Should the person be released or be detained in a mental institution? If the latter, where? Should provision for this be made in the articles concerning enforcement of sentences by the Court and States Parties?

It was observed that this defence might be more relevant for some crimes (e.g. a war crime, such as killing of a prisoner of war) than for others (e.g. crimes involving the formulation of policy, such as genocide). If the defence is included, possibly it should be available only for some types of crimes?]

Proposal 2
Mental disorders

1.   A person who, at the time of the facts, was suffering from a mental or neuropsychic disorder that destroyed his judgement or his control over his actions shall not be criminally responsible.
2.   When the mental or neuropsychic disorder from which the person was suffering at the time of the facts merely altered his judgement or impeded his control over his actions without destroying such judgement or control, he shall remain criminally responsible. However, the Court shall take such circumstances into account in determining the sentence and the regime under which it shall be served.

[*98] Article M
Intoxication
Proposal 1

A person is intoxicated or in a drugged condition when under the effect of alcohol or drugs at the time of the conduct that would otherwise constitute a crime he is unable to formulate the mental element required by said crime. Such a defence shall not apply to a person who engages in voluntary intoxication with the pre-existing intent to commit a crime. With respect to crimes requiring the mental element of recklessness, voluntary intoxication shall not constitute a defence.
[Note. The point was made that there were essentially two questions:

(a)   Whether intoxication should be available as a defence or as a negation of <u>mens rea</u>; and

(b)   If available as a defence, should it be spelled out in the Statute or elaborated in another way (see section B below).

It was observed that this defence might be relevant for some individual crimes (e.g. a war crime, such as killing a prisoner of war). On the other hand, it was observed that it might be better to leave this defence to be resolved by the Court through its jurisprudence rather than to include such a defence in the Statute.

It was also observed that intoxication is merely a factor relevant to the existence of, or which may negate, a required mental element. In light of the proposed statutory requirements for the existence of particular mental elements in order to establish criminal responsibility (see articles B (b) and H), it was questioned whether such a defence need be explicitly mentioned as it is merely an example of one factor that could negate the existence of the required mental element.

Differences exist among national legal systems as to how intoxication is addressed, and other formulations of a defence could equally be suggested.

If the defence is available (either expressly by the Statute or by the Court's jurisprudence), should it be limited to only certain crimes?]

Proposal 2
Voluntary drunkenness and narcotic intoxication

A state of drunkenness caused by the voluntary consumption of alcohol or a state of intoxication caused by voluntarily taking a narcotic product may in no case be regarded as grounds for exemption from criminal responsibility.

[*99] Article N
Self-defence/defence of others/defence of property
Proposal 1
Self-defence and defence of others

1.   A person [is not criminally responsible and] is not liable for punishment if that person acts in self-defence or in defence of others.

2.   A person acts in self-defence, or in defence of others, if the person acts [reasonably] [and as necessary] [with the reasonable belief that force is necessary] to defend himself or herself, or another person, against a[n] [reasonable apprehension of] [imminent] [present] unlawful force or threatened unlawful force, [in a manner which is reasonably proportionate to the threat or use of force].

[3.   Self-defence, in particular defence of property, shall not exclude punishment if it causes damage disproportionate to the degree of danger involved or the interest to be protected by the defensive act].

[4.   If a person exceeds the limits of the justifiable defence as described in paragraph 2, the sentence may be reduced.]

[Note. Several questions were raised:

(a)   whether a provision relating to defence of property should be included in the Statute;

(b)   whether self-defence should be used as a defence in response to a threat of unlawful force;

(c)   whether pre-emptive self-defence is valid;

(d)   whether self-defence should be limited to certain types of crimes under article 20; and

(e)   whether or not self-defence should be allowed in specific cases, at the discretion of judges.

Other questions raised by the draft include the extent to which the availability of the defence should be limited by requirements of reasonableness, necessity and/or proportionality.

The question also arises as to whether the defence should be available only if the defensive action is actually necessary or whether it is sufficient if the accused, although honestly mistaken, reasonably believes that the defensive action is necessary.

The degree of responsibility and punishment for excessive use of force in self-defence also arises as an issue.]

Proposal 2
Legitimate defence

1.   A person who, in the face of an unjustified attack on himself or another person, carries out at that same time an act dictated by the necessity of legitimate self-defence or defence of another person shall not

be criminally responsible except when the means of defence use is incommensurate with the seriousness of the attack.

2.   The argument of legitimate defence cannot be accepted when the unjustified attack which the person cites in accordance with the preceding paragraph constitutes only an attack on property.

[*100] Article O
Necessity
Proposal 1

1.   A person [is not criminally responsible and] is not liable for punishment if that person acts due to necessity.

2.   A person acts due to necessity if:

   (a)   [The person reasonably believes that] there is a threat of [imminent] [present] [or otherwise unavoidable] death or serious bodily harm to [or a threat to the freedom of] that person or another person; [alternative: (a)   Circumstances beyond a person's control are likely to create an unavoidable private or public harm];

   (b)   [The person acts reasonably to avoid the threat] [there exists no other way to avoid the threat]; (and)

   (c)   [The person acts only to avoid greater imminent harm] [the interests protected by such conduct exceed the interest infringed by such conduct].

[3.   This defence does not include the use of deadly force.]

[4.   A person does not act due to necessity if [the circumstances are (within) not beyond a person's control] [(or if) that person knowingly and without reasonable excuse has exposed himself or herself to the circumstances creating the necessity].]

[5.   If a person exceeds the limitation of the justifiable defence as described in paragraph 2 [this article], the sentence may be reduced.]

[Note. The question was raised as to the crimes to which the defence of necessity might apply.

The question was also raised whether the defence of necessity should include the use of deadly force.

   It was questioned whether the defence of necessity should apply to the crimes of genocide and crimes against humanity.

   Other questions arising from the proposed drafts include:

   (a)   the degree of immediacy of the threat (e.g. present, imminent or otherwise unavoidable);

   (b)   the nature of the threatened harm to be avoided (e.g. serious bodily harm, death, freedom, or private or public harm);

   (c)   whether the defence should be available only if the threat actually exists or whether it is sufficient if the accused, although honestly mistaken, reasonably believes that the threat exists;

   (d)   whether the accused need only act reasonably to avoid the threat if there is more than one equally harmful means of avoidance or must there be no other way to avoid the threatened harm other than by the accused's acts;

   (e)   the necessity for proportionality between the harm to be avoided and the harm caused by the accused; and

   (f)   what factors (such as voluntary exposure to the risk or control of circumstances) should deny the availability of the defence, and whether these are mutually exclusive or could be conjunctive.]

[*101] Proposal 2

1.   A conduct done, in the present danger for life, body or freedom to avoid such danger of himself/herself or any other person, is not punishable, if (a) there exists no other way to avoid such danger, and (b) the interest protected by such conduct exceeds the interest infringed by such conduct.

2.   If a person exceeds the limitation of justifiable defence of paragraph 1, the sentence may be reduced.

Article P
Duress/Coercion

1.   A person [is not criminally responsible and] is not liable for punishment if the person acts under duress or coercion.

2.   A person acts under duress or coercion if:

[(a) [[the person reasonably believes that] there is a threat of [imminent] [present] [or otherwise unavoidable] [unlawful] force or use of such force against that person or another person];

[(a) [the person reasonably believes that] there is a threat of [imminent] [present] [or otherwise unavoidable] death or serious bodily harm to that person or another person];

(b)   [the person acts reasonably in response to that threat] [the threat could not reasonably have been resisted by [an ordinary] [the] person]; and

[(c)   the coerced conduct does not produce a greater harm than the one likely to be suffered (sought to be avoided) and is not likely to produce death].

[3.   A person does not act under duress or coercion if that person knowingly and without reasonable excuse has exposed himself or herself to that duress or coercion].

[Note. Questions arising from the proposed drafts include:

(a)   the degree of immediacy of the threat (e.g. present, imminent or otherwise unavoidable);

(b)   the nature of the threatened harm to be avoided (e.g. force serious bodily harm, death), and whether it need be unlawful;

(c)   whether the defence should be available only if the threat actually exists or whether it is sufficient if the accused, although honestly mistaken, reasonably believes that the threat exists;

(d)   whether the accused need only act reasonably to avoid the threat or whether no reasonable person could have resisted the threat;

(e)   the necessity for proportionality between the harm to be avoided and the harm caused by the accused;

(f)   whether causing death is a permitted response to a threat; and

(g)   what factors (such as voluntary exposure to the risk) should deny the availability of the defence.]

[*102] Article Q
Superior orders
Proposal 1

1.   The fact that a person acted pursuant to an order of a Government or of a superior, [whether military or political] shall not relieve the person of criminal responsibility [if the order appears to be manifestly unlawful] [and the person has a greater risk to himself or herself no alternative but to obey, or has no other moral choice].

2.   Where the person has acted pursuant to an order of a government or of a superior in the circumstances as described in paragraph 1, the sentence may be reduced having regard to the circumstances [this fact may be considered in mitigation of punishment if the court determines that justice so requires].

[Note. Three questions were raised:

(a)   Should those troops who obey what appears to them at the time to be a manifestly lawful order, be criminally responsible if it transpires that their commander was acting illegally in giving the order?

(b)   Should those troops who receive an order which is not manifestly lawful but simply lawful, be criminally responsible if it transpires that their commander was acting illegally in giving the order, and if they should have made further inquiries before obeying the order?

(c)   What rules of law govern the legality or otherwise of an order? It was also suggested that the defence not apply to the crimes of genocide and crimes against humanity. Should the defence be limited to only some types of crimes?]

Proposal 2
Prescription by law, and orders of the legitimate authority

1.   With regard to genocide, crimes against humanity and the crime of aggression, the perpetrator of or accomplice in one of these crimes may not be exempted from his criminal responsibility by the sole fact that he carried out an act prescribed or authorized by legislation or regulations or an act ordered by the legitimate authority. However, the Court shall take this circumstance into account when determining the sentence and its severity.

2.   With regard to the crimes referred to in articles 31 and 32, 22/ a person who carries out an act ordered by the legitimate authority shall not be criminally responsible except when such an act is manifestly illegal or in conflict with the rules of international law applicable in armed conflicts or with duly ratified or approved international conventions.

3.   However, persons who have carried out acts ordered by the Security Council or who have acted on its behalf and in accordance with a mandate issued by it shall not be criminally responsible and may not be prosecuted before the Court.

[*103] [Article R
Possible defences specifically referring to war crimes and grave breaches of the Geneva Conventions of 1949

Such defences might include:

-    Military necessity;
-    Reprisals.]

[Note. It was questioned whether defences under public international law should be included in the General Part of the Statute, since they to a large extent relate to inter-state relations. It was also questioned which set of rules governing reprisals should apply.

As regards the question of Article 51 of the Charter of the United Nations, it was suggested that a savings clause could be included in reference to the rights and duties of States under the Charter and the functions and powers of the principal organs of the United Nations under the Charter. Such a clause should not necessarily be in a chapter on General Principles.

It was questioned whether such defences could be dealt with in connecting with the definition of war crimes and grave breaches of the Geneva Conventions of 1949.]

Article S
Exhaustive or enumerative list of defences
Proposal 1
Other defences

1.   At trial the Court may consider a defence not specifically enumerated in this chapter if the defence:

  (a)   Is recognized [in general principles of criminal law common to civilized nations] 23/ [in the State with the most significant contacts to the crime] 24/ with respect to the type of conduct charged; and

  (b)   Deals with a principle clearly beyond the scope of the defences enumerated in this chapter and is not otherwise inconsistent with those or any other provisions of the Statute.

2.   If an accused wishes to raise such a defence, he must notify the Court and the Prosecutor a reasonable time prior to trial. The Court shall give the Prosecutor the opportunity to be heard and shall issue an order deciding the matter. An accused who has failed to provide adequate notice shall be precluded [*104] from asserting the defence at trial; except that, where compelling circumstances exist, the Court may instead grant the Prosecutor a reasonable postponement to prepare for the issue at trial. 25/

3. Denial of a request under this article shall not preclude an accused from seeking consideration of the basis of the asserted defence as a grounds for mitigation of punishment to the extent otherwise permitted by this Statute.

Proposal 2

The Court shall determine the admissibility of reasons excluding punishment in view of the character of each crime.

22/   Articles 31 and 32 deal, respectively, with "serious violations of the laws and customs of wars" and with "grave breaches of the Geneva Conventions".

23/   This text represents the approach of Article 38 (c) of the Statute of the International Court of Justice.

24/   This approach draws upon principles applied in international private law matters and would presumably require the Court to craft a test for determining which State's contacts are most significant.

25/   The Rules of Procedure could provide further clarification regarding the conduct of any hearings required by the Court prior to ruling. The Statute or Rules might also permit interlocutory appeal by the Prosecutor of an adverse ruling.

[Note 1. Different views were held as to whether the finally agreed upon list of defences in the Statute should be exhaustive or enumerative. This leads to the question under section B below.]

[Note 2. It was noted that if the nature of a defence was really the negation of a mental element, there was no need to specify that defence in the Statute. Further, it could be applicable by means of the savings clause as proposed in this article.]

Article T
Presumption of innocence

An accused shall be presumed innocent [until] [unless] [proved guilty] [convicted] in accordance with [this Statute] [law]. [The onus is on the prosecutor to establish the guilt of the accused [beyond reasonable doubt].]

[Note 1. The presumption of innocence is also a procedural matter.]

[Note 2. Presumption of innocence [also] constitutes a substantive right of the accused.]

SECTION 2. FURTHER ELABORATION BY THE COURT OF GENERAL PRINCIPLES OF CRIMINAL LAW, INCLUDING THE QUESTION OF APPLICABLE LAW

[Note. The question was raised as to whether the Court should be empowered to elaborate/legislate further the general principles of criminal law that are not written in the Statute. (Please note that the draft ILC Statute contains a provision on this question in article 19.):

(a) If so, one of the possible solutions may be found in the proposal by one delegation concerning article 20 (bis), which reads as follows:

"1. Subject to paragraphs 2 and 3, the judges may by absolute majority elaborate the elements of the crimes set out in article 20 and elaborate principles of liability and defence that are not otherwise set out in, and [*105] that are not inconsistent with, the elements and principles in the Statute or in annex B. In elaborating elements and principles, the Court shall not create any new offences or crimes.

"2. The initial elements and principles elaborated by the Court shall be drafted by the judges within six months of the first elections for the Court, and submitted to a conference of States parties for approval. The judges may decide that an element or principle subsequently elaborated under paragraph 1 should also be submitted to a conference of States parties for approval.

"3. In any case to which paragraph 2 does not apply, elements or principles elaborated under paragraph 1 shall be transmitted to States parties and may be confirmed by the Presidency unless, within six months after transmission, a majority of States parties have communicated in writing their objections.

"4. An element or principle may provide for its provisional application in the period prior to its approval or confirmation. An element or principle not approved or confirmed shall lapse."]

[Note should be taken of the link to the choice of sources of law in connection with possible further elaboration of general principles of criminal law by the Court.

(b) It was stated by some delegations, however, that the Court should not be empowered to legislate general principles of criminal law. In this case, a possible solution is found in the proposal by another delegation on article 33, which reads:

"1. The Court shall apply this Statute.

"2. When the Court cannot find the necessary provision to be applied, the Court may apply:

(a) The national law of the State where the crime was committed;

(b) If the crime was committed in the territories of more than one State, the national law of the State where the substantial part of the crime was committed;

(c) If the laws of the States mentioned in (a) and (b) do not exist, the national law of the State of nationality of the accused, or if the accused does not have any nationality, the national law of the State of permanent residence of the accused; or

(d) If the laws of the States mentioned in (a), (b) and (c) do not exist, the national law of the State which had custody of the accused, as far as these laws are consistent with the objectives and purposes of this Statute."]

[Note should be taken of other proposals submitted on article 33, which are:

(a)<u>Proposal submitted by one delegation</u>

"1.   The Court shall apply:

[*106] (a) The Statute, including annexes A and B, rules adopted pursuant to article 19, and elements of crimes and principles of liability and defence elaborated pursuant to article 20 <u>bis</u>;

(b)   Applicable treaties and the principles and rules of general international law; and

(c)   Principles of law developed by the Court from national law.

"2.   In developing principles of law as referred to in paragraph 1 (c), the Court shall [conduct and] take into account [a survey of] the national laws of States representing the major legal systems of the world, where those laws are not inconsistent with international law and internationally recognized norms and standards.

"The Court shall only apply paragraph 1 (c) to the extent that a matter is not covered by paragraphs 1 (a) or (b)."

(b)<u>Proposal submitted by another delegation</u>

"The Court shall apply:

(a)   Its Statute, including the annexes thereto;

(b)   The other relevant rules of international law;

(c)   General principles of criminal law identified by it and approved by States parties to the statute;

(d)   Rules of national law, to the extent authorized by the Statute, and

(e)   Its Rules of Procedure and Evidence."

(c)<u>Proposal submitted by another delegation</u>

"1.   This Statute (and the rules promulgated thereunder) shall be the primary source of law for the Court.

"2.   To the extent not inconsistent with the above, the Court may apply principles and rules of law that are generally recognized in national legal systems as a subsidiary source of law.

"3.   To the extent not inconsistent with the above, the Court may apply specific rules of applicable national law, or applicable treaty provisions, where necessary to the determination of a specific question that is governed by such law or treaty, or where the application or interpretation of such specific law or treaty is in fact at issue in the case."]

[*107] <u>Proposal submitted by another delegation</u>

<u>Applicable law</u>

The Court shall apply:

(a)   In the first place, this Statute and the treaties to which it makes reference;

(b)   If necessary, the principles and rules of general international law;

(c)   Failing that, and provided that such action does not conflict with the provisions mentioned above, the internal law of the State in whose territory the crime has been committed and, on a subsidiary basis, the internal law of the State of which the accused is a national.

<u>Proposal submitted by still another delegation</u>

The Court may apply principles and rules of law enunciated in its previous decisions.

[Note. Article 33 obviously has a bearing on many parts of the Statute. The fact that it is taken up here does not imply that it should be placed in the part dealing with the general principles of criminal law.

Delegations are invited to look at page 26 of document A/AC.249/L.4.

The question of penalties is not included in this document.]

[*108] PART 4. INVESTIGATION AND PROSECUTION*

Note. The following is a compilation prepared by an informal group dealing with procedural questions, fair trial and rights of the accused covering parts4, 5 and 6. It neither represents a text agreed upon among delegations nor suggests that every provision should be included in the Statute. It contains only written proposals. Proposals for some of the articles have been consolidated to various degrees by some of their authors and may not necessarily represent the views of all the delegations who submitted proposals. The order of the articles as well as the proposed content and headings are only of an indicative character and have not been finally agreed upon. The compilation does not prejudice discussion on other topics related to the establishment of an international criminal court.

Articles 25, 26, 27, 30, 32, 37, 40 to 43, 45, 46 and 48 to 50 have been consolidated to various degrees. Articles 28, 29, 34 to 36, 38 and 44 are only compilations of written proposals. Articles 31, 33, 39 and 47 are related to other issues and are not dealt with here.

Article 25
Complaint
I. ILC DRAFT

1.   A State party which is also a Contracting Party to the Convention on the Prevention and Punishment of the Crime of Genocide of 9 December 1948 may lodge a complaint with the Prosecutor alleging that a crime of genocide appears to have been committed.

2.   A State party which accepts the jurisdiction of the Court under article 22 with respect to a crime may lodge a complaint with the Prosecutor alleging that such a crime appears to have been committed.

3.   As far as possible a complaint shall specify the circumstances of the alleged crime and the identity and whereabouts of any suspect, and be accompanied by such supporting documentation as is available to the complainant State.

4.   In a case to which article 23 (1) applies, a complaint is not required for the initiation of an investigation.

II. PROPOSALS
A. Who can make a complaint

[1.   A State Party which is also a Contracting Party to the Convention on the Prevention and Punishment of the Crime of Genocide of 9 December 1948, and any State Party may lodge a complaint [in writing] with the Prosecutor

-     [alleging that a crime appears to have been committed.]

[*109] -   [specifying that acts constituting crimes referred to in article 20 appear to have been committed.]

-     [that refers a situation to the Prosecutor as to which such crime appears to have been committed and requesting that the Prosecutor investigate the situation for the purpose of determining whether one or more specific persons should be charged with commission of such crime.] 26/

2.   A State Party [which accepts the jurisdiction of the Court under article 22 with respect to a crime] 27/ [which has jurisdiction over the crime, or of which a victim of the alleged crime is or was its national,] may lodge a complaint [in writing] with the Prosecutor

-     [alleging that a crime appears to have been committed]

-     [specifying that acts constituting crimes referred to in article 20 appear to have been committed]

-     [that refers a situation to the Prosecutor as to which such crime appears to have been committed and requesting that the Prosecutor investigate the situation for the purpose of determining whether one or more specific persons should be charged with commission of such crime].

[2 bis.   In a case to which article 23 (1) applies, a complaint is not required for the initiation of an investigation.] 28/

[2 bis. Notwithstanding article 21, the Security Council, acting under Chapter VII of the Charter of the United Nations, can decide to refer a [matter] [situation or acts constituting crimes] to the Prosecutor when one or more of the crimes referred to in article 20 appear to have been committed.]

[2 ter. Notification of the Security Council decision to the Prosecutor shall be accompanied by all evidence available to the Council.]

[2 quat. The Prosecutor shall initiate investigations ex officio or on the basis of information obtained from any source, particularly from Governments, United Nations organs, intergovernmental and non-governmental organizations. The Prosecutor shall assess the information received or obtained and decide whether there is sufficient basis to proceed.]

A chart of written proposals on the articles dealing with procedural questions, fair trial and rights of the accused is contained in annexII to the present volume.

26/   Depending upon which crimes will be within the inherent jurisdiction of the Court or whether all crimes will be treated in the same manner in terms of preconditions to the exercise of jurisdiction (see article 21), paragraph 1 could be expanded to include other crimes or be deleted.

27/   An alternative would be to require at least one other State party which accepts the jurisdiction of the Court under article 22 with respect to the same crime to join in the complaint and affirm that in their joint opinion the crime is a most serious one of interest to the international community as a whole.

28/   This paragraph is former paragraph 4 of article 25 of the ILC draft.

[*110] B. <u>Contents of a complaint</u>

3.   As far as possible a complaint shall [specify] [provide as much information as possible to assist the Prosecutor in deciding whether an investigation should be initiated, including]:

(a)   [the facts which indicate] the basis of jurisdiction relied upon in making the complaint;

(b)   the specific crime or crimes within the jurisdiction of the Court, which the complainant State believes has been committed;

(c)   the circumstances of the alleged crime;

(d)   the identity and location of any persons suspected of committing such crime, [if known];

(e)   the identity and location of any witnesses, if known;

(f)   a description of evidence or believed sources of evidence pertinent to the investigation; and

(g)   whether the complaint State, or other States to its knowledge, may be investigating or prosecuting the matter, and the details of such investigation or prosecution; and be accompanied by such supporting documentation as is available to the complaint State. The complainant State may request or the Prosecutor may require that the complaint or any part thereof remain confidential pending the Prosecutor's review.

3 <u>bis</u>. The Prosecutor may seek clarification of any matter contained in the complaint or further information from the complainant State Party.

C. <u>Miscellaneous</u>

4. <u>29/</u> The Prosecutor shall inform the Security Council of all complaints lodged under this article.

[*111] <u>Article 26</u>
<u>Investigation of alleged crimes</u>
I. ILC DRAFT

1.   On receiving a complaint or upon notification of a decision of the Security Council referred to in article 23(1), the Prosecutor shall initiate an investigation unless the Prosecutor concludes that there is no possible basis for a prosecution under this Statute and decides not to initiate an investigation, in which case the Prosecutor shall so inform the Presidency.

2.   The Prosecutor may:

(a)   request the presence of and question suspects, victims and witnesses;

(b)   collect documentary and other evidence;

(c)   conduct on-site investigations;

(d)   take necessary measures to ensure the confidentiality of information or the protection of any person;

(e)   as appropriate, seek the cooperation of any State or of the United Nations.

3.   The Presidency may, at the request of the Prosecutor, issue such subpoenas and warrants as may be required for the purposes of an investigation, including a warrant under article 28 (1) for the provisional arrest of a suspect.

4.   If, upon investigation and having regard, <u>inter alia</u>, to the matters referred to in article 35, the Prosecutor concludes that there is no sufficient basis for a prosecution under this Statute and decides not to file an indictment, the Prosecutor shall so inform the Presidency giving details of the nature and basis of the complaint and of the reasons for not filing an indictment.

5.   At the request of a complainant State or, in a case to which article 23 (1) applies, at the request of the Security Council, the Presidency shall review a decision of the Prosecutor not to initiate an investigation or not to file an indictment, and may request the Prosecutor to reconsider the decision.

6.   A person suspected of a crime under this Statute shall:

(a)   prior to being questioned, be informed that the person is a suspect and of the rights:

(i)   to remain silent, without such silence being a consideration in the determination of guilt or innocence; and

[*112]   (ii)   to have the assistance of counsel of the suspect's choice or, if the suspect lacks the means to retain counsel, to have legal assistance assigned by the Court;

(b)   not be compelled to testify or to confess guilt; and

29/   Former ILC paragraph 4 has been moved to paragraph 2 <u>bis</u>.

(c) if questioned in a language other than a language the suspect understands and speaks, be provided with competent interpretation services and with a translation of any document on which the suspect is to be questioned.

II. PROPOSALS

A. Conditions for the Prosecutor to initiate an investigation [and review of Prosecutor's decision]

1.   On receiving a complaint [under article 25] or upon notification of a decision of the Security Council referred to in article23(1) [or upon any other substantiated information] the Prosecutor shall:

[(a) notify the States Parties of any matter submitted to the Court in accordance with [French articles 37 and 38] and those States Parties shall so inform the persons referred to by name in the submission; and]

[(b) determine prior to initiating an investigation

(i)   whether the complaint provides or is likely to provide a [possible] [reasonable] basis [in law or on the facts] for proceeding with a prosecution under this Statute; and

(ii)   whether the case is or would be admissible under article 35; and

(iii) whether an investigation would be consistent with the terms of any relevant Security Council decision; and

(iv) whether to seek a preliminary ruling from the Court regarding the Court's jurisdiction if the case could later be challenged under article 34.]

2.The Prosecutor shall [may] initiate an investigation unless:

(a) the submission of the case to the Court under [French articles 37 and 38] is challenged within one month of notification under article 26(1)(a) by a State Party which wishes to proceed or has proceeded with the case or by a person named in the submission; or

(b) the Prosecutor considers any determination within article 26 (1) (b) (i) to (iii) prevents further action; or

(c) the Prosecutor determines to seek a preliminary ruling in accordance with article 26 (1) (b) (iv); in which case the Prosecutor shall so inform the Presidency [Indictment Chamber] [Preliminary Investigations Chamber of the Court] [and await its final ruling.]

[*113] As soon as an investigation is initiated, the Presidency shall designate one of the Trial Chambers constituted in accordance with article 9 (5) as an Indictment Chamber, the other then automatically becoming the Trial Chamber for the case.

3.   (a) At the request of a complainant State or, in a case to which article 23 (1) applies, at the request of the Security Council, the Presidency [Preliminary Investigations Chamber] [Indictment Chamber] shall review a decision of the Prosecutor not to initiate an investigation and may request the Prosecutor to reconsider his decision.

(b) [In the event that the Prosecutor defers investigation on the ground that a State is proceeding with a national investigation, then the Prosecutor may request that the relevant State make available to the Prosecutor, either periodically or on reasonable request, a report on the progress of its investigation, which shall be confidential to the extent necessary. The Prosecutor shall notify the complainant State of the decision to defer to a State and shall notify the complainant State of any known outcome of such national investigation or prosecution.]

(c) [The Prosecutor shall not initiate an investigation into a case that has been investigated and prosecuted by a State following a deferral by the Prosecutor unless:

(i)   the complainant State has lodged a further complaint with the Court on the grounds that the State investigation (or prosecution) has been inadequate, and the Prosecutor agrees;

(ii)   following the Prosecutor's notice to the State where the case was prosecuted of the new complaint and of its opportunity to challenge the initiation of an investigation by the Prosecutor, the State where the case was prosecuted has challenged such an investigation by the Prosecutor and either has failed under the Statute to prevent the new investigation or has failed after a reasonable period of time to challenge the initiation of the new investigation; and

(iii) the Prosecutor, upon renewed consideration, has not reached any affirmative determination under article 26 (1) (i), (ii) or (iii).]

4.   After a determination to initiate an investigation in accordance with article 26 (2), and prior to the commencement of a trial, a State requested by the Prosecutor to carry out investigations or a State on the

territory of which the Prosecutor intends to conduct investigations may challenge the decision of the Prosecutor to initiate investigation before the Indictment Chamber on the grounds of lack of sufficient basis for a prosecution under this Statute.]

B. Duty of the Prosecutor

5. (a)   The Prosecutor shall fully respect the rights of suspects under the Statute and the rules.

(b)   [To establish the truth the Prosecutor shall [ex officio] extend the investigation to cover all facts and evidence that are relevant to an assessment of the charge and to the legal consequences that may follow. He shall investigate equally incriminating and exonerating circumstances.]

[*114] (c) [If the Prosecutor concludes that there is a basis for prosecution under this Statute, he shall, in accordance with the rules of the Court, investigate the case, by seeking the cooperation of the States concerned or by himself, and such investigation shall be conducted in conformity with international law and fully respecting the sovereignty of the States concerned.]

C. Powers of the Prosecutor to gather evidence

6.   The Prosecutor may:

(a)   request the presence of and question suspects, victims and witnesses;

(b)   collect documentary and other evidence;

(c)   [under the supervision of an investigative judge appointed by the Presidency] [on application of the Presidency] conduct on-site investigations [if the Presidency, having regard to the views of interested States, is satisfied that there are no civil authorities to whom a request for assistance under Part 7 of the Statute can be transmitted;]

(d)   take necessary measures to ensure the confidentiality of information or the prosecution of any person;

(e)   as appropriate, seek the cooperation of any State or of the United Nations, and

(f)   (i)   whenever it is necessary to carry out a reconnaissance, inspection, reconstruction or a scientific or technical test that, because of its nature and characteristics cannot be reproduced in full at a later stage during the trial, or whenever it is assumed that a witness will not be able to testify during trial because of some unsurmountable obstacle, the Prosecutor shall request the Presidency to appoint a judge to carry out or supervise the act;

(ii)   the judge shall carry out or supervise the act in question notifying the Prosecutor, the accused and his or her counsel, who shall be authorized to be present and shall have the same right to intervene as during the rest of the trial. If the accused is detained, his or her counsel shall act in the accused's behalf, unless the accused expressly asks to be present in person, provided his place of detention is in the territory where the act is to be carried out;

(iii)   when the accused is yet unknown or any of the acts described under (i) is extremely urgent, the Prosecutor may request the Presidency orally to appoint a judge, who shall carry out or supervise the act. The notifications provided in (ii) shall not be necessary but a counsel for the defence shall be appointed ex officio to control the act or to take part in it.

(g)   apply to the Presidency [the Indictment Chamber] for the following orders, subpoenas and warrants in the course of his or her investigation:
[list to be inserted]

[*115] 7. (Rights of suspect to gather evidence):

(a)   (i)   A person suspected of committing a crime within the meaning of this Statute shall, as soon as he is involved in an investigation or prosecuted under this Statute, be entitled to collect all of the evidence which he deems necessary for his defence;

(ii)   He may either collect this evidence himself or request the Preliminary Investigations Chamber of the Court to enjoin the Prosecutor to accomplish certain acts, seeking, where necessary, cooperation from any State party. In that event, the Preliminary Investigations Chamber shall have a period of two months in which to respond to the accused's request;

(b)   (i)   The Prosecutor shall be required to accomplish any act which the Preliminary Investigations Chamber enjoins him to carry out pursuant to paragraph 3 of this article;

(ii)   If the Preliminary Investigations Chamber rejects a request made pursuant to paragraph 3 of this article, its decision must be based on the futility of the act requested in the light of the patently dilatory nature of the request;

(iii)   Notice of the decision by the Preliminary Investigations Chamber rejecting the request, which is not subject to appeal, must, in accordance with paragraph 3 of this article, be served on the person involved within two months following the date of his request. No other request may be made by the accused until the Preliminary Investigations Chamber has taken its decision or the two-month period expires;

(c)   If the suspect elects to collect the evidence himself in accordance with article 26 (3) (a), he may apply to the Presidency for the following orders and subpoenas:
[list to be inserted]
8.   If upon investigation the Prosecutor concludes that:

(a)   a case is inadmissible under article 35; or

(b)   there is no sufficient basis for a prosecution; or

(c)   a prosecution would not be in the interests of justice and decides not to file an indictment, the Prosecutor shall so inform the Presidency [Preliminary Investigations Chamber], the State which lodged the complaint under [French article 37] or the Security Council if the matter was submitted to the Court under [French article 38], giving details of the nature [, origin] and basis of complaint and the reasons why he is not instituting proceedings.

9.   When the Prosecutor has decided not to file an indictment following an investigation, the Presidency [Preliminary Investigations Chamber] [Indictment Chamber] shall [may, either at the request of the State which lodged the complaint under or at the request of the Security Council, if the matter was [*116] submitted to the Court under article 23 (1)] request the Prosecutor to reconsider his decision [but it may do so only once.]

D. Additional rights of suspects [and questioning of suspects]

10.   (a)   A person suspected of a crime under this Statute shall, prior to being questioned, be informed that the person is a suspect [and of the details, circumstances and evidence of the case and the laws applicable] and of entitlement to the rights:

[(i)   to be presumed innocent in accordance with article 40; and]

(ii)   to remain silent without such silence being a consideration in the determination of guilt or innocence; and

(iii)   not to be compelled to testify [against himself] or to confess guilt; and

(iv)   to have [at all times] the [prompt] assistance of [competent] counsel of, if the suspect lacks the means [efforts] to retain counsel, to have legal assistance provided by the [Preliminary Investigations Chamber of the] Court [and assignment of counsel shall be in accordance with the following rules:

a.   A list of counsel who speak one or both of the working languages of the Court, meet the requirements of subrule 51 (b) and have indicated their willingness to be assigned by the Court to indigent suspects or accused, shall be kept by the Registrar;

b.   The criteria for determination of indigency shall be established by the Registrar and approved by the judges;

c.   In assigning counsel to an indigent suspect or accused, the following procedure shall be observed:

i.   A request for assignment of counsel shall be made to the Registrar;

ii.   The Registrar shall inquire into the means of the suspect or accused and determine whether the criteria of indigency are met;

iii.   If he or she decides that the criteria are met, he or she shall assist counsel from the list; if he or she decides to the contrary, he or she shall inform the suspect or accused that the request is refused;

d.   The suspect or accused may seek from the Presidency a review of a decision to refuse a request. The decision of the Presidency shall be final. The procedure governing review by the Presidency shall be laid down in the supplementary rules;

e.   If a request is refused, a further request may be made by a suspect or an accused to the Registrar upon showing a change in circumstances;

[*117]   f.   The Registrar shall, in consultation with the judges, establish the criteria for the payment of fees to assigned counsel;

g.   If a suspect or an accused elects to conduct his own defence, he or she shall so notify the Registrar in writing at the first opportunity;

h.   Where an alleged indigent person is subsequently found not to be indigent, the Trial or Appeals Chamber may make an order of contribution to recover the cost of providing counsel for proceedings before that Chamber;]

[(v) not to be subject to torture or to cruel, inhuman or degrading treatment or punishment; and]

(vi) to be informed of the charges against him and questioned in a language which he understands and speaks, or if otherwise, to the [free] assistance of a competent interpreter, and to be provided [free of charge] with the translation of any document on which the suspect is to be questioned [or that show why a measure infringing his liberty or property has been proposed];

(b) Any person suspected of committing a crime within the meaning of this Statute must, before being questioned, or when a measure infringing his liberty or property has been proposed and brought to his attention, be fully informed of the charges against him and to the rights to which he is entitled under article 26 (1) (a) above;

(c) Questioning of a suspect shall not proceed without the presence of counsel unless the suspect has voluntarily waived his or her right to counsel. In case of waiver, if the suspect subsequently expresses the desire to have counsel, questioning shall thereupon cease, and shall only resume when the suspect has obtained or been assigned counsel;

(d) Before being questioned the suspect shall be invited to declare whatever he or she may deem advisable concerning the crime that is being investigated and to point out the evidence the suspect considers should be obtained [in accordance with article 26 (7)];

(e) Under no circumstances shall the suspect be asked to take an oath to speak the truth, nor shall he or she be subjected to any kind of coercion, duress, threat or promise, except those expressly authorized by [this Statute or the rules], nor shall any means to force or induce the suspect to speak the truth be used against him or her;

(f) No means in detriment to the freedom of decision of the suspect shall be used during questioning. The questions asked shall be clear and precise. When due to the length of questioning, it is, or should be, noticed that the suspect is too tired to continue or is no longer calm, questioning shall be adjourned until the suspect is fit to continue;

(g) Whenever the Prosecutor questions a suspect, the questioning shall be audio-recorded or video-recorded in accordance with the following procedure:

(i) The suspect shall be informed in a language he or she speaks and understands that the questioning is being audio-recorded or video-recorded;

[*118]   (ii) In the event of a break in the course of the questioning, the fact and the time of the break shall be recorded before audio-recording or video-recording ends and the time of resumption of the questioning shall also be recorded;

(iii) At the conclusion of the questioning the suspect shall be offered the opportunity to clarify anything he or she has said, and to add anything he or she may wish, and the time of conclusion shall be recorded;

(iv) The tape shall then be transcribed as soon as practicable after the conclusion of questioning and a copy of the transcript supplied to the suspect, together with a copy of the recorded tape or, if multiple recording apparatus was used, one of the original recorded tapes;

(v) After a copy has been made, if necessary, of the recorded tape for purposes of transcription, the original recorded tape or one of the original tapes shall be sealed in the presence of the suspect under the signature of the Prosecutor and the suspect;

[(h) Evidence obtained during questioning in violation of these rules shall under no circumstances be used in the trial unless they are favourable to the suspect.]

[*119] Article 27
Commencement of prosecution
I. ILC DRAFT

1.   If upon investigation the Prosecutor concludes that there is a prima facie case, the Prosecutor shall file with the Registrar an indictment containing a concise statement of the allegations of fact and of the crime or crimes with which the suspect is charged.

2.   The Presidency shall examine the indictment and any supporting material and determine:

      (a)   whether a prima facie case exists with respect to a crime within the jurisdiction of the Court; and

      (b)   whether, having regard, <u>inter alia</u>, to the matters referred to in article 35, the case should on the information available be heard by the Court.

If so, it shall confirm the indictment and establish a trial chamber in accordance with article 9.

3.   If, after any adjournment that may be necessary to allow additional material to be produced, the Presidency decides not to confirm the indictment, it shall so inform the complainant State or in a case to which article 23 (1) applies, the Security Council.

4.   The Presidency may at the request of the Prosecutor amend the indictment, in which case it shall make any necessary orders to ensure that the accused is notified of the amendment and has adequate time to prepare a defence.

5.   The Presidency may make any further orders required for the conduct of the trial, including an order:

      (a)   determining the language or languages to be used during the trial;

      (b)   requiring the disclosure to the defence, within a sufficient time before the trial to enable the preparation of the defence, of documentary or other evidence available to the Prosecutor, whether or not the Prosecutor intends to rely on that evidence;

      (c)   providing for the exchange of information between the Prosecutor and the defence, so that both parties are sufficiently aware of the issues to be decided at the trial;

      (d)   providing for the protection of the accused, victims and witnesses and of confidential information.

[*120] II. PROPOSALS

1.   If [upon investigation] [following the investigation] [in [during] the course of an investigation] the Prosecutor [concludes] [is satisfied] that

[the case is admissible, that]

[there is a prima facie case [which the accused could be called on to answer and that is desirable in the interests of justice that the case should proceed]]

[a suspect has committed a crime within the jurisdiction of the Court]

[a case does exist against one or more persons named],

the Prosecutor shall

[file with the Registrar [of the Court]]

[prepare in writing and forward to the Registrar]

an indictment containing

[a concise statement of the allegations of fact and of the crime or crimes with which the suspect is charged]

[in respect of each of the persons referred to, their name, a statement of the allegations of fact against them, and the characterization of these facts in accordance with articles ... to ...] 30/

[for confirmation by the Presidency [the Indictment Chamber] [the Pre-Trial Chamber] together with supporting material]

A.   [(i) The indictment shall be accompanied by all evidence collected by the Prosecutor. Other evidence may be freely added by the Prosecutor up until the time when the indictment is considered by the Preliminary Investigations Chamber. However, without prejudice to the provisions of paragraph (iii) of this article, no evidence submitted to the Registrar for purposes of accompanying the indictment may be withdrawn by the Prosecutor];

      [(ii) The Prosecutor may amend the indictment up until the time it is considered by the Preliminary Investigations Chamber];

30/   Articles of the Statute dealing with crimes within the jurisdiction of the Court.

[(iii) The Prosecutor may also withdraw an indictment together with all the accompanying evidence until the time when the indictment is considered by the Preliminary Investigations Chamber];

[In that event the Preliminary Investigations Chamber may, under the conditions provided for in article ...., 31/ ask the Prosecutor to reconsider his decision.]

[*121]B. [(i) The indictment shall set forth the name and particulars of the suspect, a concise statement of the allegations of fact and of the crime or crimes with which the suspect is charged];

[(ii) The indictment shall also contain a statement regarding the basis for the Court to exercise jurisdiction];

[(iii) The supporting material referred to in subrule A shall include the evidence gathered by the Prosecutor];

[(iv) The Registrar shall forward the indictment and supporting material to the Presidency [the Indictment Chamber], which will inform the Prosecutor of the date fixed for review of the indictment]

2. [The Presidency] [the Indictment Chamber] [the Pre-trial Chamber] shall [constitute an Indictment Chamber comprising (a single judge/three judges) who are not members of the Trial Chamber to] examine the indictment and any supporting material and determine:

(a) whether a prima facie case exists with respect of a crime within the jurisdiction of the Court; [and]

(b) whether, having regard, inter alia, to the matters referred to in article 35, the case should on the information available be heard by the Court; [and]

[(c) whether it is desirable in the interests of justice that the case should proceed].

If so, it shall confirm the indictment [and establish a Trial Chamber in accordance with article 9 [and inform so the Presidency].

[Any State concerned may challenge the decision of the Prosecutor to file an indictment before the Indictment Chamber on grounds of inconsistency with this Statute]

[2a.Decisions of the Indictment Chamber shall be taken by a majority of the judges of the Chamber/by consensus]

A. [(i) On reviewing the indictment, the Presidency [the Indictment Chamber] shall hear the Prosecutor, who may present additional material in support of any count. The Presidency [Indictment Chamber] may also require the Prosecutor to present additional material in support of any count. The proceedings may be adjourned to allow additional material to be produced]

[(ii) if the accused is detained at the disposal of the Court, or, being free, he or she voluntarily submits himself or herself to its jurisdiction, the Indictment Chamber shall notify the accused of the date set for the review of the indictment, and shall provide him or her with a copy of the indictment by the Prosecutor. On the day of the hearing, the Indictment Chamber shall listen to the accused, who shall be allowed to raise objections to the indictment, to point out any flaws it may contain, to criticize the material on which the indictment is based and to point out the evidence that he or she deems relevant to decide about the existence of a criminal case and which has been omitted by the Prosecutor. If this is the first time the accused presents himself or [*122] herself, he or she shall be allowed to bring any motions contained in rule 79 (A), or wait until the term of 60 days established in rule 74 (B) has elapsed]

[(iii) The Presidency [Indictment Chamber] shall determine in relation to each count whether a prima facie case exists with respect to a crime within the Court's jurisdiction and shall dismiss those counts where such a case does not exist]

[(iv) The dismissal of a count in an indictment shall not preclude the Prosecutor from subsequently bringing a new indictment based on the acts underlying that count if supported by additional evidence]

[(v) If a prima facie case is found to exist in relation to one or more counts in the indictment, the Presidency [Indictment Chamber] shall determine whether, having regard, inter alia, to the matters referred to in article X (A 35 ILC) of the Statute, the case should on the information available be heard by the Court]

31/ Article of the Statute dealing with the closing of the case.

[(vi) If the Presidency [Indictment Chamber] determines that the case should be heard by the Court, it shall confirm the indictment and establish [shall ask the Presidency to establish] a Trial Chamber]
B.[1.   The Preliminary Investigations Chamber shall proceed to consider indictment and any amendment thereto together with all the accompanying evidence.
2.   It shall take a decision:
      (a)   on the admissibility of the case on the basis of the reasons in article 35, if the Court has not yet ruled on this issue;
      (b)   on the serious nature of the charges against the person or persons named in the indictment with respect to an offence within the Court's jurisdiction.]
1.   If after considering the indictment, or after the further investigation requested in accordance with article 46, the Preliminary Investigations Chamber proposes to confirm the indictment it shall so inform the Prosecutor and the persons named in the indictment and shall indicate to them that it sill hold a hearing to consider the charges contained in the indictment.
The hearing shall be held at a date determined by the Preliminary Investigations Chamber, one month, at the earliest, from the day on which the persons named in the indictment were notified that the Preliminary Investigations Chamber proposed to confirm the indictment, and no later than three months from that same date.
2.   The Registrar of the Court shall serve the Prosecutor and the persons named in the indictment with a summons to appear, containing the indictment, the place, date and time of the hearing and mentioning the rights which the suspects are recognized as having in accordance with article 51.
3.   The persons named in the indictment are entitled to receive from the Registrar of the Court certified copies of all the evidence accompanying the indictment.
[*123] 4. During the hearing organized before it, the Preliminary Investigations Chamber shall consider the indictment and the accompanying evidence. It shall hear the arguments of the Prosecutor, followed by those of the persons named in the indictment, the latter always being heard last.
5.   Following the hearing and after deliberations, the Preliminary Investigations Chamber may:
      (a)   confirm the indictment in its entirety;
      (b)   confirm only part of the indictment and amend it, either by declaring the case inadmissible in part, for the reasons listed in article 35, if the Court has not already ruled on this issue or by withdrawing certain charges deemed not sufficiently serious or by giving some facts another characterization, in accordance with articles 27 and 32;
Refuse to confirm the indictment.
It must give the reasons for its decision based on the provisions of article 45 (2).
6.   When it confirms the indictment in its entirety or in part, the Preliminary Investigations Chamber must commit the accuse to the Trial Chamber for trial on the facts referred to in the confirmation decision and with the characterization accepted in that decision. It shall uphold the warrants for the arrest and transfer of the accused or the warrants for judicial supervision issued earlier. It may, by taking a special decision, decide not to uphold these warrants or decide to amend the warrants for judicial supervision.
If it does not confirm the indictment, all the warrants issued prior to the decision of non-confirmation shall cease immediately to have effect.

                                    * * *

[1.   When the Preliminary Investigations Chamber proposes to confirm an indictment, but one or more of the persons named in the indictment has fled or cannot be found, it may still hold a hearing under the conditions provided for in article 48.
2.   When it confirms the indictment, in its entirety or in part, against a person who has fled or cannot be found, the Preliminary Investigations Chamber shall issue a warrant to search for, arrest and transfer the accused, which is tantamount to committing him to the Trial Chamber for trial. This warrant must contain, in addition to the particulars listed in article 55, the statement of facts referred to in the confirmation decision, with the characterization accepted in that decision.
The warrant shall be disseminated by the Registrar of the Court using all appropriate means. When the person is found, the warrant shall be executed as a warrant of arrest and transfer, in accordance with the provisions of title II of this part.]

* * *

[1.   Anyone who has personally suffered direct injury caused by a crime submitted to the Court may inform the Registrar of the Court in writing of the [*124] acts having caused injury to him and the nature and amount of the losses which he has sustained.

2.   When a hearing is held under article 48, the Registrar of the Court shall transmit to the Preliminary Investigations Chamber the correspondence received from victims pursuant to paragraph 1 of this article.

3.   When it confirms the indictment in its entirety or in part, the Preliminary Investigations Chamber may order the provisional seizure of all or part of the property of the person committed for trial, if it believes that such a measure is necessary to compensate the victims who have come forward in accordance with paragraph 1 of this article.

In that event, the Preliminary Investigations Chamber shall ask the Prosecutor to secure the cooperation of the States in whose territory the provisionally seized property is situated requesting them, inter alia, to freeze assets and to appoint official receivers.

The provisions of the preceding subparagraph shall also apply in the situations described in article 49.]

C.   [The Presidency shall nominate in accordance with the rules three such judges to be members of the Pre-trial Chamber for a given case. A Pre-trial Chamber shall include at least two judges elected from among the persons nominated as having the qualification referred to in article 6 (1) (a). A Pre-trial Chamber shall be responsible in the given case for such functions as prescribed in [articles 26 (3) and (5), 27 (2) to (4), 27 (5) (b), 28 (1) to (3), 30 (3), and any other functions concerning pre-trial process].

6.   The Presidency shall nominate in accordance with the rules five such judges who are not members of the Pre-trial Chamber for a given case to be members of the Trial Chamber for the same case. A Trial Chamber shall include at least three judges elected from among the persons nominated as having the qualification referred to in article 6 (1) (a).]

3.   If after any adjournment that may be necessary to allow additional material to be produced, the presidency [the Indictment Chamber [the Pre-trial Chamber] decides not to confirm the indictment, it shall so inform the complainant State or, in a case to which article 23 (1) applies, the Security Council.

A.[1. After having considered the indictment in accordance with article4, the Preliminary Investigations Chamber may defer ruling and may ask the Prosecutor to conduct a further investigation.

2.   The Preliminary Investigations Chamber may indicate to the Prosecutor which issues it feels need to be investigated further.]

* * *

[1.   After considering the indictment, or after the further investigation requested in accordance with article 46, the Preliminary Investigations Chamber may decide not to confirm the indictment. This decision must be based on the provisions of article 45 (2).

All warrants issued prior to this decision of non-confirmation shall cease immediately to have effect.

[*125] 2. The Registrar of the Court shall immediately notify the persons named in the indictment, the Prosecutor, the States which, in accordance with titles II and II of this part, have been charged with executing a warrant or asked to cooperate and either the State which lodged the complaint under article 37, or the Security Council, if the matter was submitted to the Court under article 38 (1), of the non-confirmation of the indictment.

3.   Non-confirmation of an indictment under this article shall not prevent the Prosecutor from preparing, in accordance with article 44, a new indictment on the basis of facts which were the grounds for the initial indictment which was not confirmed, in so far as additional supporting evidence is provided.]

4.   [The Presidency [Indictment Chamber] [the Pre-trial Chamber] may at the request of the Prosecutor amend the indictment, in which case it] [In case of an amendment of the indictment by the Prosecutor or the Indictment Chamber, the Presidency] shall make any necessary orders to ensure that the accused is notified of the amendment and has adequate time to prepare a defence.

A.   [The Prosecutor may amend an indictment, without leave, at any time before it is confirmed in the review proceedings under article X (A 27 ILC) of the Statute, but thereafter only with the leave of the Presidency [Indictment Chamber] or, if at trial, with leave of the Trial Chamber. If leave to amend is granted, the amended indictment shall be transmitted to the accused and to his or her counsel and where necessary, the date for trial shall be postponed to ensure adequate time for the preparation of the defence]

[The amendment of the indictment shall be possible only when the Prosecutor wishes to introduce a new fact or circumstance which modifies the legal characterization or the punishment for a crime or crimes contained in the indictment, or when it has been found out that a new crime has been committed in connection with the fact or facts contained in the indictment]

B.   [5. Following the hearing and after deliberations, the Preliminary Investigations Chamber may:

(a)   confirm the indictment in its entirety;

(b)   confirm only part of the indictment and amend it, either by declaring the case inadmissible in part, for the reasons listed in article 35, if the Court has not already ruled on this issue, or by withdrawing certain charges deemed not sufficiently serious, or by giving some facts another characterization, in accordance with articles 27 to 32;

(c)   refuse to confirm the indictment.

It must give the reasons for its decision based on the provisions of article 45 (2).]

[7.   The Registrar of the Court shall promptly inform the accused, the Prosecutor, the States which, in accordance with titles II and III of this part have been charged with executing a warrant or asked to cooperate and either the State which lodged the complaint under article37 or the Security Council, if the matter was submitted to the Court under article 38 (1), of the Preliminary Investigations Chamber's decision.]

* * *

[*126] [5.   When an indictment is drawn up pursuant to article 44, the evidence collected in accordance with this article shall be attached to the indictment, shall be subject to the same conditions.

* * *

The accused shall enjoy the rights afforded to suspects under article 51, paragraph 1. He shall also be entitled:

-     to a fair hearing by an independent and impartial tribunal. Subject to the provisions of article 104, the hearing shall be public;

-     to have adequate time and facilities for the preparation of his defence;

-     to be tried without undue delay;

-     to examine or have examined the witnesses against him and to obtain the attendance and examination of witnesses on his behalf under the same conditions as witnesses against him;

-     to have communicated to him all evidence submitted to the Court.]

5.   The Presidency may make any further orders required for the conduct of the trial, including an order:

(a)   determining the language or languages to be used during the trial;

(b)   requiring the disclosure to the defence, within a sufficient time before the trial to enable the preparation of the defence, of documentary or other evidence available to the Prosecutor, whether or not the Prosecutor intends to rely on that evidence;

(c)   providing for the exchange of information between the Prosecutor and the defence, so that both parties are sufficiently aware of the issues to be decided at the trial;

(d)   providing for the protection of the accused, victims and witnesses and of confidential information. 32/

A.   [The working languages of the Court shall be English and French.]

* * *

[At the opening of the trial, the President of the Chamber shall ensure that the accused understands and speaks the language employed at the hearing. Should this not be the case, the accused shall be entitled to be assisted free of charge by an interpreter appointed by the President of the Trial Chamber;]

* * *

[1.   Anyone suspected of committing a crime within the meaning of the present Statute shall be entitled to be informed of the charges against him and [*127] questioned in a language which he understands, and, to this end, to have the free assistance of a competent interpreter, and to be provided free of charge with

---

32/   Subparagraph (d) relates to the measures for protection of the accused, victims and witnesses available to the Court. See the different proposals on this issue under article 43.

a translation of the documents on the basis of which he is being questioned or that show why a measure infringing upon his liberty or property has been proposed.]

B.[1.   The Prosecutor may withdraw an indictment or one or more counts thereof, without leave, at any time before it is confirmed in the review proceedings under article X (A 27 ILC) of the Statute, but thereafter only with leave of the Presidency or, if at trial, only with leave of the Trial Chamber.

2.   The withdrawal of the indictment or one or more counts thereof shall be promptly notified to the accused and to his or her counsel.]

* * *

[Subject to rule 68, upon the decision of the Presidency to confirm an indictment and establish a Trial Chamber under article X (A 27 ILC) of the Statute, the indictment shall be made public.

(a)   The Presidency may, at the request of the Prosecutor, order that there be no public disclosure of the indictment until it is served on the accused, or in the case of joint accused, on all the accused. In exercising its discretion, the Presidency shall take account of all relevant factors, including the potential or pre-arrest flight of an accused, destruction of evidence and harm to victims or witnesses if the indictment is made public.

(b)   The Presidency may, at the request of the Prosecutor, also order that there be no disclosure of an indictment, or part thereof, or of all or any part of any particular document or information, if satisfied that, the making of such an order is required to give effect to a provision of the rules, to protect confidential information obtained by the Prosecutor, or is otherwise in the interests of justice.]

[*128] Article 28
Arrest
I. ILC DRAFT

1.   At any time after an investigation has been initiated, the Presidency may at the request of the Prosecutor issue a warrant for the provisional arrest of a suspect if:

(a)   there is probable cause to believe that the suspect may have committed a crime within the jurisdiction of the Court; and

(b)   the suspect may not be available to stand trial unless provisionally arrested.

2.   A suspect who has been provisionally arrested is entitled to release from arrest if the indictment has not been confirmed within 90 days of the arrest, or such longer time as the Presidency may allow.

3.   As soon as practicable after the confirmation of the indictment, the Prosecutor shall seek from the Presidency a warrant for the arrest and transfer of the accused. The Presidency shall issue such a warrant unless it is satisfied that:

(a)   the accused will voluntarily appear for trial; or

(b)   there are special circumstances making it unnecessary for the time being to issue the warrant.

4.   A person arrested shall be informed at the time of arrest of the reasons for the arrest and shall be promptly informed of any charges.

II. PROPOSALS

A. Is it possible - and on which grounds - to order measures restricting or suppressing the liberty of an accused before the indictment?

At any time after an investigation has been initiated, the Presidency may at the request of the Prosecutor issue a warrant for the provisional arrest of a suspect if:

(a)   there is probable cause to believe that the suspect may have committed a crime within the jurisdiction of the Court; and

(b)   the suspect may not be available to stand trial unless provisionally arrested.

* * *

Any person implicated under this Statute shall remain free during the proceedings, unless he is placed under judicial supervision or taken into [*129] custody prior to the judgement, in accordance with the rules and conditions set forth below.

Persons aged 13 to 18 at the time of the proceedings may be taken into custody prior to the judgement only under exceptional circumstances.

The decision to place a person under judicial supervision prior to the judgement shall be taken by the Preliminary Investigations Chamber of the Court at the request of the Prosecutor.

The Preliminary Investigations Chamber may also place a person under judicial supervision when it declines to grant the Prosecutor's request that he be taken into custody, but wishes to impose certain restrictions on his freedom, or when it releases a person and wishes to impose certain restrictions on his release.

When it issues a warrant for judicial supervision, the Preliminary Investigations Chamber subjects a person to one or more obligations, in particular:

(a)   not to go outside the territorial limits established by the Preliminary Investigations Chamber without its explicit agreement;

(b)   not to leave his place of abode or a residence established by the Preliminary Investigations Chamber except under the conditions and for the reasons determined by it;

(c)   not to frequent certain places and to refrain from contact with certain persons designated by the Preliminary Investigations Chamber;

(d)   to respond to attendance notices issued by any authority or qualified person designated by the Preliminary Investigations Chamber;

(e)   not to engage in certain professional activities;

(f)   to pay a security deposit, the amount, time limits and payment terms of which shall be determined by the Preliminary Investigations Chamber;

(g)   to hand-over to the Registrar of the Court all documents establishing his identity, including his passport;

(h)   to furnish securities in rem or in personam designed to guarantee the rights of the victims.

Persons aged 13 to 18 at the time of the proceedings may also be placed in appropriate educational institutions.

Warrants for judicial supervision may be issued at any time before trial.

Prior to the confirmation of the indictment, the Preliminary Investigations Chamber may issue warrants of provisional arrest and detention after the investigation has been initiated.

While it is considering the confirmation of the indictment, the Preliminary Investigations Chamber may issue warrants of arrest and transfer.

* * *

[*130] Replace "Presidency" by "Indictment Chamber".

* * *

No person shall be subjected to arbitrary arrest or detention. Nor shall any person be deprived of his liberty except on such grounds and in accordance with such procedure as are established by the rules of the Court.

* * *

When the Trial Chamber deems that the danger of the accused escaping or hindering the proceedings may reasonably be avoided by methods other than detention, it may order any of the following measures:

(a)   home arrest, in his own home or under somebody else's custody, and watched or guarded in the way the Trial Chamber shall determine;

(b)   the obligation of submitting himself to the care or guard of a certain person or institution, who shall periodically report to the tribunal;

(c)   the prohibition to absent himself without leave from the territory of the State where he is or to absent himself from the territory determined by the Trial Chamber.

The Trial Chamber may impose one of these measures or combine some of them, depending on the case, and shall order the steps to be taken and the notifications necessary to guarantee their enforcement.

* * *

In cases of urgency, when the Court makes a request for provisional detention, notifying the requested Party that a warrant of arrest has been issued or a sentence had been imposed for an offence specified in article [ ], the requested State party may provisionally detain the person sought in accordance with its national laws.

* * *

At any time after an investigation has been initiated, the Presidency may at the request of the Prosecutor issue a warrant for the arrest of a suspect before indictment if:

    (a) there is probable cause to believe that the suspect may have committed a crime within the jurisdiction of the Court; and

    (b) the suspect may not be available to stand trial unless arrested before indictment.

B. <u>Maximum duration of detention before indictment</u>

A suspect who has been provisionally arrested is entitled to release from arrest if the indictment has not been confirmed within 90 days of the arrest, or such longer time as the Presidency may allow.

* * *

[*131] Any person for whom a warrant of arrest and detention is issued shall be released if the indictment concerning him, accompanied by a warrant of arrest and transfer replacing the initial warrant, are not served on him within 60days from the date of his arrest.

Notwithstanding the provisions of paragraph 2 of this article and article 66 (5), the effects of a warrant of arrest and detention shall not be interrupted by the actions challenging the submission of cases to the Court provided for in article 69.

* * *

"... within <u>60</u> days of the arrest _____. <u>Upon request of the Prosecutor, the Indictment Chamber may under exceptional circumstances extend this period to a maximum extent of 90 days.</u>"

* * *

1.   A warrant of arrest issued pursuant to article X (A 28(3) ILC) of the Statute shall be signed by the Presidency or the Judge (or Trial Chamber) who has dealt with the matter pursuant to a delegation under article X (A 8 (5) ILC) of the Statute and shall bear the seal of the Court. It shall be accompanied by a copy of the indictment and a statement of the rights of the accused under the Statute and rules.

2.   A warrant for the arrest of the accused and an order for his surrender to the Court shall be transmitted by the Registrar to the national authorities of the State in whose territory or under whose jurisdiction or control the accused resides, or was last known to be, together with instructions that at the time of arrest the indictment and the statement of the rights of the accused be read to him or her in a language he or she understands and that he or she be cautioned in that language.

3.   When an arrest warrant issued by the Court is executed, a member of the Prosecutor's Office may be present as from the time of arrest with the agreement of the State concerned.

[<u>Note</u>. If provisional arrest as contemplated in A 28 (1) of the ILC Statute is retained, a similar rule to this one will need to be elaborated in part VI, Investigation and rights of suspects.]

* * *

A suspect who has been provisionally arrested is entitled to release from arrest if the indictment has not been confirmed within <u>30</u> days of the arrest, or such longer time as the Presidency may allow <u>if the special circumstances so require</u>.

* * *

If the Court fails to present the request for extradition within [30] days from the date of provisional detention, the person detained shall be set at liberty; provided that this stipulation shall not prevent the requested State from instituting a proceeding with a view to extraditing the person sought if a request for extradition is subsequently received.

* * *

[*132] (a) The Prosecutor shall transmit the warrant to the State where the suspect is located, along with a request for the arrest of the suspect and a statement of the reasons to believe that the suspect may have committed a crime within the jurisdiction of the Court and that the Prosecutor expects to file an indictment and make a request for indictment within [90] days. The arrest request should be accompanied by a description of the person sought, together with all available information that will help to identify and locate the person. Where necessary under the law of the State where the suspect is located, the Prosecutor should also provide a brief summary of the facts of the case and the reasons why pre-indictment arrest is believed to be urgent and necessary.

    (b) Where a suspect is arrested before the indictment and an indictment is subsequently filed against the suspect, the Prosecutor shall transmit a copy of the indictment to the State with custody of the accused, along with a request that the accused be surrendered to the Court for trial. The request should be followed by such other additional material as may be required by the law of the State with custody of the accused.

(c)   In the case where a suspect has been arrested before indictment, if before the expiry of [90] days, a decision is taken by the Prosecutor not to indict the suspect or the Presidency decides not to confirm the indictment, the Prosecutor shall immediately advise the custodial State of that fact and the custodial State shall take steps to have the suspect immediately released from custody or any conditions of bail. 33/

C. Measures that can be taken at the time of or after the indictment

As soon as practicable after the confirmation of the indictment, the Prosecutor shall seek from the Presidency a warrant for the arrest and transfer of the accused. The Presidency shall issue such a warrant unless it is satisfied that:

(a)   the accused will voluntarily appear for trial; or

(b)   there are special circumstances making it unnecessary for the time being to issue the warrant.

* * *

Under a warrant of arrest and detention, the person shall be arrested by the competent national authorities and brought before the appropriate national judicial authority pursuant to article 55 (3).

If the accused is already in custody under a warrant of arrest and detention, pursuant to article 58, the warrant of arrest and transfer shall replace the initial warrant.

[*133] The warrant of arrest and transfer and the confirmed indictment shall be served on the accused in his place of detention. He shall be brought before the appropriate national judicial authority pursuant to article 55 (3).

The accused shall be kept in custody and transferred to the Court in the conditions provided for in Part 4, Title III, of this Statute.

If the accused is not in custody and his place of residence is known, he shall be arrested by the competent national authorities and brought before the appropriate national judicial authority pursuant to article 55 (3). The accused shall be taken into custody pursuant to the warrant of the Preliminary Investigations Chamber, in an appropriate place of detention in the State responsible for executing the warrant and shall be transferred to the Court in the conditions provided for in Part 4, Title III, of this Statute.

If the accused is a fugitive, the warrant of arrest and transfer issued by the Preliminary Investigations Chamber shall have the effect of a warrant to search for the wanted person and shall be disseminated by all appropriate means. Once the accused is apprehended, the authorities shall proceed in accordance with paragraph 2 of this article.

A warrant of arrest and transfer shall remain in effect until the date of the judgement. Its effects shall not be interrupted by the actions challenging the submission of cases to the Court provided for in article 69.

* * *

In the case where no pre-indictment warrant has been obtained, as soon as practicable after the confirmation of the indictment, the Prosecutor shall seek from the Presidency a warrant for the arrest of the accused. The Presidency shall issue such a warrant unless it is satisfied that:

(a)   the accused will voluntarily appear for trial;

(b)   there are special circumstances making it unnecessary for the time being to issue the warrant.

The Prosecutor shall transmit the warrant to the State where the accused is located along with a request that the accused be arrested and surrendered to the Court for trial. The request should be accompanied by a description of the person sought, together with all available information that will help identify and locate the person. The request should be followed by such other additional material as may be required by the law of the State where the accused is located.

D. Who can request - and following which formal requirements and procedure - such measures to be taken, whether before or after the indictment

A request for arrest or surrender [duly signed by the Prosecutor] shall:

33/   A concern is that this provision may create constitutional problems for certain States for which it would be unacceptable for a person to be in custody for a period and then not be indicted. A possible solution is to insert a provision that some form of assurance should be given that an indictment will follow the request for arrest.

(a)   be made by letter, fax, e-mail or any medium capable of delivering a written record (provided that a request shall be confirmed through the diplomatic channel);

[*134] (b) contain or be supported by:

(i)   information describing the person sought, sufficient to identify the person and information as to that person's probable location;

(ii)   in the case of a request for pre-indictment arrest:

    a.   a copy of the warrant for arrest;

    b.   a statement of the reasons to believe the suspect may have committed a crime within the jurisdiction of the Court and that the Prosecutor expects to seek an indictment within [90] days;

    c.   a brief summary of the facts of the case;

    d.   a statement as to why pre-indictment arrest is urgent and necessary;

(iii)   in the case of a request for post-indictment arrest and surrender of a person not yet convicted:

    a.   a copy of the warrant of arrest and indictment;

    b.   such information, documents or statements outlining the facts of the case as may be required by the law of the requested State;

(iv)   in the case of a request for the arrest and surrender of a person already convicted:

    a.   a copy of any warrant of arrest for that person;

    b.   a copy of the judgement of conviction;

    c.   information to demonstrate that the person sought is the person referred to in the judgement of conviction;

    d.   (if the person sought has been sentenced) a copy of the sentence imposed and a statement of any time already served and that remaining.

Where the requested State Party considers the information provided insufficient to allow it to comply with the request it may seek, without delay, additional information.

* * *

The decision to detain a person prior to the judgement shall be taken by the Preliminary Investigations Chamber of the Court at the request of the Prosecutor. The Preliminary Investigations Chamber must give a reason for its decision based on paragraphs 2 and 3 of this article.

Under this Statute, a person may be detained prior to the judgement when, notwithstanding his assertions to the contrary, there are serious reasons for believing that he has participated in a crime, either as perpetrator or as accomplice, and that taking him into custody is the only way to:

(a)   preserve the evidence or material clues;

[*135] (b) avoid pressure on witnesses and victims;

(c)   prevent fraudulent consultation with other possible perpetrators and accomplices;

(d)   protect him;

(e)   put a stop to the crime or prevent its recurrence;

(f)   ensure that he remains at the disposal of the Court if the risks of flight appear to be high.

Detention prior to the judgement may also be decided on if the person wilfully evades the obligations of judicial supervision to which he has been subjected under article 53.

The Prosecutor's written request for the issuance of a warrant of arrest or restriction of liberty prior to the judgement must contain the name of the person concerned, a statement of the charges against him and the reasons for which the warrant is necessary, along with a list of States Parties capable of executing the warrant. The Preliminary Investigations Chamber shall request the Prosecutor to provide it with all available evidence.

The warrant issued by the Preliminary Investigations Chamber must contain:

(a)   the name of the person concerned;

(b)   a statement of the charges against him;

(c)   the reasons for the issuance of the warrant;

(d)   a statement of the suspect's rights under article 51 (1);

(e)   a statement of the suspect's right to request, at any time, either his release or the suspension or amendment of judicial supervision, pursuant to article 56.

The States Parties listed in the Prosecutor's request shall be notified of a warrant issued by the Preliminary Investigations Chamber. The warrant shall take effect as soon as it is brought to the attention of the person concerned by the national authorities charged with executing it.

Any person for whom the Preliminary Investigations Chamber issues a warrant of arrest or restriction of liberty must receive a certified copy of the warrant and must be promptly brought before the appropriate judicial authority of the State in which the warrant is executed. The national judicial authority shall ensure that the warrant does, in fact, apply to that person and that it meets the formal requirements laid down in this Statute.

* * *

[*136] 1. A warrant of arrest issued pursuant to article X (A 28 (3) ILC) of the Statute shall be signed by the Presidency or the Judge (or Trial Chamber) who has dealt with the matter pursuant to a delegation under article X (A 8 (5) ILC) of the Statute and shall bear the seal of the Court. It shall be accompanied by a copy of the indictment, and a statement of the rights of the accused under the Statute and Rules.

2.   A warrant for the arrest of the accused and an order for his surrender to the Court shall be transmitted by the Registrar to the national authorities of the State in whose territory or under whose jurisdiction or control the accused resides, or was last known to be, together with instructions that at the time of arrest the indictment and the statement of the rights of the accused be read to him or her in a language he or she understands and that he or she be cautioned in that language.

3.   When an arrest warrant issued by the Court is executed, a member of the Prosecutor's Office may be present as from the time of arrest with the agreement of the State concerned.

[Note. If provisional arrest as contemplated in A 28 (1) of the ILC Statute is retained, a similar rule will need to be elaborated in Part VI, Investigation and rights of suspects.]

* * *

The request for provisional detention shall describe the identity of the person to be sought and the facts of the case, and shall contain such further information as may be required by the laws of the requested State.

If the Court fails to present the request for extradition within [30] days from the date of provisional detention, the person detained shall be set at liberty; provided that this stipulation shall not prevent the requested State from instituting a proceeding with a view to extraditing the person sought if a request for extradition is subsequently received.

When ratifying this Statute, States Parties shall notify the Secretary-General of the United Nations of the conditions under which they would refuse provisional detention and shall specify elements which must be included in a written request for provisional detention. States Parties shall not refuse a request for detention for reasons other than those indicated.

E. Information which should be given to the arrested person

[Note. The question of the rights of the arrested is dealt with in detail in paragraph 26 (6); the question of the information to be provided to the suspected/accused is dealt with in paragraph 30.]

A person arrested shall be informed at the time of arrest of the reasons for the arrest and shall be promptly informed of any charges.

* * *

If the accused is already in custody under a warrant of arrest and detention, pursuant to article 58, the warrant of arrest and transfer shall replace the initial warrant.

The warrant of arrest and transfer and the confirmed indictment shall be served on the accused in his place of detention. He shall be brought before the appropriate national judicial authority pursuant to article 55 (3).

[*137] The accused shall be kept in custody and transferred to the Court under the conditions provided for in Part 4, Title III, of this Statute.

* * *

Any person who is arrested or provisionally arrested shall be informed, at the time of arrest or provisional arrest, of the reasons for his arrest or provisional arrest and shall be promptly informed of any charges against him/her in accordance with the rules of the Court.

Any person arrested, provisionally arrested or detained on a criminal charge shall, in accordance with the rules of the Court, be brought promptly before a judge or other officer authorized to exercise judicial power and shall be entitled to trial within a reasonable time or to release.

* * *

[Note. The question of challenge against such measures is dealt with under paragraph 29. The questions of the content of a warrant of arrest and transfer and of provisional arrest are also dealt with in articles 53, 53 bis and 53 ter of the report of the working group on cooperation. See in particular pages 117, 121, 122, 123 and 124 of the report of the first session of the Preparatory Committee (A/AC.249/1).]

* * *

The following proposal for article 28 was also made by the informal group on judicial cooperation and enforcement:

1.   At any time after an investigation has been initiated, the Presidency may at the request of the Prosecutor issue a warrant for the arrest of a suspect before indictment if:

(a)   there is probable cause to believe that the suspect may have committed a crime within the jurisdiction of the Court; and

(b)   the suspect may not be available to stand trial unless arrested before indictment.

2.   (a)   The Prosecutor shall transmit the warrant to the State where the suspect is located, along with a request for the arrest of the suspect and a statement of the reasons to believe that the suspect may have committed a crime within the jurisdiction of the Court and that the Prosecutor expects to file an indictment and make a request for indictment within [90 days]. The arrest request should be accompanied by a description of the person sought, together with all available information that will help to identify and locate the person. Where necessary under the law of the State where the suspect is located, the Prosecutor should also provide a brief summary of the facts of the case and the reasons why pre-indictment arrest is believed to be urgent and necessary.

(b)   Where a suspect is arrested before the indictment and an indictment is subsequently filed against the suspect, the Prosecutor shall transmit a copy of the indictment to the State with custody of the accused, along with a request that the accused be surrendered to the Court for trial. The request should be followed by such other additional material as may be required by the law of the State with custody of the accused.

[*138] (c) In the case where a suspect has been arrested before indictment, if before the expiry of [90 days], a decision is taken by the Prosecutor not to indict the suspect or the Presidency decides not to confirm the indictment, the Prosecutor shall immediately advise the custodial State of that fact and the custodial State shall take steps to have the suspect immediately released from custody or any conditions of bail. 34/

3.   In the case where no pre-indictment warrant has been obtained, as soon as practicable after the confirmation of the indictment, the Prosecutor shall seek from the Presidency a warrant for the arrest of the accused. The Presidency shall issue such a warrant unless it is satisfied that:

(a)   the accused will voluntarily appear for trial; or

(b)   there are special circumstances making it unnecessary for the time being to issue the warrant.

3 bis.   The Prosecutor shall transmit the warrant to the State where the accused is located along with a request that the accused be arrested and surrendered to the Court for trial. The request should be accompanied by a description of the person sought, together with all available information that will help identify and locate the person. The request should be followed by such other additional material 35/ as may be required by the law of the State where the accused is located.

34/   A concern is that this provision may create constitutional problems for certain States, for which it would be unacceptable for a person to be in custody for a period and then not be indicted. A possible solution is to insert a provision that some form of assurance should be given that an indictment will follow the request for arrest.

35/   Only information pertaining to elements of fact, and not of law, is envisaged under this provision.

[*139] <u>Article 29</u>
<u>Pre-trial detention or release</u>
I. ILC DRAFT

1.   A person arrested shall be brought promptly before a judicial officer of the State where the arrest occurred. The judicial officer shall determine, in accordance with the procedures applicable in that State, that the warrant has been duly served and that the rights of the accused have been respected.

2.   A person arrested may apply to the Presidency for release pending trial. The Presidency may release the person unconditionally or on bail if it is satisfied that the accused will appear at the trial.

3.   A person arrested may apply to the Presidency for a determination of the lawfulness under this Statute of the arrest or detention. If the Presidency decides that the arrest or detention was unlawful, it shall order the release of the accused, and may award compensation.

4.   A person arrested shall be held, pending trial or release on bail, in an appropriate place of detention in the arresting State, in the State in which the trial is to be held or if necessary, in the host State.

II. PROPOSALS

A. <u>Is the control over the legality of the detention (or other measures) within the competence of the national judicial authorities, the Court or both?</u>

A person arrested shall be brought promptly before a judicial officer of the State where the arrest occurred. The judicial officer shall determine, in accordance with the procedures applicable in that State, that the warrant has been duly served and that the rights of the accused have been respected.

* * *

1.   Once detained, an accused may not be released except upon an order of the Trial Chamber.

2.   When the Trial Chamber deems that the danger of the accused escaping or hindering the proceedings may reasonably be avoided by methods other than detention, it may order any of these measures:

    (a)   home arrest, in his own home or under somebody else's custody, and watched or guarded in the way the Trial Chamber shall determine;

    (b)   the obligation of submitting himself to the care or guard of a certain person or institution, who shall periodically report to the tribunal;

    (c)   the prohibition to absent himself without leave from the territory of the State where he is or to absent himself from the territory determined by the Trial Chamber.

[*140] The Trial Chamber may impose one of these measures or combine some of them depending on the case, and shall order the steps to be taken and the notifications necessary to guarantee their enforcement. An accused who has been detained may request the Trial Chamber to order his or her release with no restrictions or the substitution of his or her detention for any of the measures provided in the <u>chapeau</u> of paragraph 2 above. The accused shall also have the right to appeal any resolution against his request before the Appeals Chamber pursuant to rule 128.

* * *

Once detained, an accused may not be released except upon an order of the Presidency.

* * *

A person against whom a warrant of arrest has been issued may challenge the warrant before the Indictment Chamber on the grounds of inconsistency with this Statute.

* * *

The States Parties listed in the Prosecutor's request shall be notified of a warrant issued by the Preliminary Investigations Chamber. The warrant shall take effect as soon as it is brought to the attention of the person concerned by the national authorities charged with executing it.

Any person from whom the Preliminary Investigations Chamber issues a warrant of arrest or restriction of liberty must receive a certified copy of the warrant and must be promptly brought before the appropriate judicial authority of the State in which the warrant is executed. The national judicial authority shall ensure that the warrant does, in fact, apply to that person and that it meets the formal requirements laid down in this Statute.

Under a warrant of arrest and detention, the person shall be arrested by the competent national authorities and brought before the appropriate national judicial authority pursuant to article 55 (3).

If the accused is already in custody under a warrant of arrest and detention, pursuant to article 58, the warrant of arrest and transfer shall replace the initial warrant.

The warrant of arrest and transfer and the confirmed indictment shall be served on the accused in his place of detention. He shall be brought before the appropriate national judicial authority pursuant to article 55 (3).

The accused shall be kept in custody and transferred to the Court in the conditions provided for in Part 4, Title III, of this Statute.

If the accused is not in custody and his place of residence is known, he shall be arrested by the competent national authorities and brought before the appropriate national judicial authority pursuant to article 55 (3). The accused shall be taken into custody, pursuant to the warrant of the Preliminary Investigations Chamber, in an appropriate place of detention in the [*141] State responsible for executing the warrant and shall be transferred to the Court in the conditions provided for in Part 4, Title III, of this Statute.

* * *

A person arrested may apply to the Presidency for a determination of the lawfulness under this Statute of any arrest warrant or order of detention issued by the Court.

* * *

Replace "the Presidency" by "the indictment Chamber".

* * *

The State that has received a pre- or post-indictment warrant and a request for the arrest of a suspect shall immediately, in accordance with its law, take steps to arrest the suspect on the basis of the warrant of the Court or by obtaining a domestic warrant for arrest based on the Court's warrant and request.

A person arrested shall be brought promptly before a judicial officer in the custodial State who shall determine, in accordance with the law of that State, that the person has been arrested in accordance with the proper process and that the person's rights have been respected.

       B. <u>What are the conditions and procedures for conditional release (probational bail)</u>
<u>and how is detention re-examined by the Court</u>?

A person arrested may apply to the Presidency for release pending trial. The Presidency may release the person unconditionally or on bail if it is satisfied that the accused will appear at the trial.

* * *

Release may only be ordered by the Trial Chamber once the host State has been heard, and only if it is satisfied that the accused will appear for trial and that, if released, will neither pose a danger to any victim, witness or any other person nor hinder the investigation or the trial by destroying or concealing evidence or by threatening or intimidating witnesses.

The Trial Chamber may impose such conditions upon the release of the accused as it may determine appropriate, including the execution of a bail bond and the observance of such conditions as are necessary to ensure his or her presence for trial and the protection of others.

Every three months the Trial Chamber shall re-examine the reasons why it ordered the detention of the accused and, depending on the case, shall order that it shall be continued or substituted for some other measure or that the accused shall be released. The provisional detention of the accused shall not continue for a longer period than a year since the detention was ordered. At the request substantiated by the Prosecutor, the Presidency may order that the detention be extended for an additional year under the condition that the Prosecutor explains that there are sufficient reasons for the need of the [*142] extension and can reasonably estimate the time necessary to bring the accused to trial.

* * *

Release may be ordered by the Presidency only in exceptional circumstances, after hearing the host country and only if it is satisfied that the accused will appear for trial and, if released, will not pose a danger to any victim, witness or other person.

The Presidency may impose such conditions upon the release of the accused as it may determine appropriate, including the execution of a bail bond and the observance of such conditions as are necessary to ensure his or her presence for trial and the protection of others.

* * *

At any time during the proceedings, the Preliminary Investigations Chamber may, either of its own initiative or at the request of the person concerned or the Prosecutor, release the person concerned or suspend or amend the terms of judicial supervision.

Even in the absence of any request made under the preceding paragraph, the warrant issued by the Preliminary Investigations Chamber must be reviewed every four months, failing which it shall cease to have effect.

When the Preliminary Investigations Chamber receives a request for release under paragraph 1 of this article, it shall have 15 days in which to respond, failing which the person concerned shall be released immediately. The Registrar of the Court shall promptly notify the Prosecutor, the person in custody and the State in which he is held of the decision of the Preliminary Investigations Chamber.

* * *

An accused surrendered to the Court may apply to the Presidency for interim release pending trial. The Presidency may release the accused with or without conditions if satisfied the person will appear for trial.

* * *

In the case of a person arrested before indictment, if no indictment is received within [90 days] of that person's arrest or the Prosecutor advises the custodial State that no indictment will be filed, the person shall be released from custody or any terms of interim release. The release of the person shall not preclude that person's re-arrest should an indictment and a warrant be submitted at a later date.

An accused surrendered to the Court may apply to the Presidency for interim release pending trial. The Presidency may release the accused with or without conditions if satisfied the person will appear for trial.

[*143] C. If the Court (or the appropriate national authorities) decides that the arrest or detention was illegal, what are the consequences of that decision?

A person arrested may apply to the Presidency for a determination of the lawfulness under this Statute of the arrest or detention. If the Presidency decides that the arrest or detention was unlawful, it shall order the release of the accused, and may award compensation.

* * *

If the Preliminary Investigations Chamber decides to release the person concerned because his arrest or detention was unlawful, it may award him compensation.

The decisions of the Preliminary Investigations Chamber to release a person or to suspend or amend his judicial supervision shall be executed by the State Party in which the person concerned is being held or which is responsible for such judicial supervision, as soon as it has received notification through the Registrar of the Court.

* * *

The Court shall make compensation to those who were:

(a) pronounced innocent by an irrevocable adjudication;

(b) arrested or detained for the purpose of prosecution, although the prosecution against him did not eventually take place;

(c) arrested or detained but the lawfulness of that arrest or detention was denied in accordance with this Statute; or

(d) illegally inflicted losses upon by an officer of the Court, intentionally or negligently in the course of performing its duties.

Procedures and criteria for compensation shall be provided in the rules, including the expenses to be borne by a complaint State if that State lodged a complaint without enough reason.

* * *

If the Presidency decides that the arrest warrant or order of detention was unlawful, it shall order the withdrawal of all requests for surrender and for provisional arrest made pursuant to the warrant or order, and may award compensation.

* * *

[*144] A person arrested may apply to the Presidency for a determination of the lawfulness under this Statute of the arrest or detention. The Presidency shall in any case review ex officio every 30 days the lawfulness under this Statute of the arrest or detention. If the Presidency decides ...

* * *

A person arrested may apply to the Presidency for a determination of the lawfulness under this Statute of any arrest warrant or order of determination issued by the Court. If the Presidency decides that the arrest or detention was unlawful under the Statute, it shall order the release of the accused, and may award compensation.

A person arrested shall have the right to apply to a judicial officer in the custodial State for interim release pending the indictment or surrender of the person. The custodial State shall ensure that the views of the Prosecutor on interim release are brought to the attention of the judicial officer.

D. Appropriate place for detention

A person arrested shall be held, pending trial or release on bail, in an appropriate place of detention in the arresting State, in the State in which the trial is to be held or, if necessary, in the host State.

* * *

Upon his or her transfer to the seat of the Court, the accused shall be detained in facilities provided by the host country, or by another country. The Presidency may under article X (A 29 ILC) of the Statute, on the application of a party, modify the conditions of detention of an accused.

Note: There is a question as to whether the Trial Chamber should carry out this function instead. There is also the issue of whether the host State should have standing in relation to detention decisions.

* * *

A person arrested shall be held, pending trial or release on bail, in an appropriate place of detention in the arresting State, in the State in which the trial is to be held or, if necessary, in the host State.

E. Case of an accused absent or fugitive

If necessary, the Presidency may issue a warrant of arrest to secure the presence of an accused who has been released or is for any other reason at liberty.

* * *

If the accused is a fugitive, the warrant of arrest and transfer issued by the Preliminary Investigations Chamber shall have the effect of a warrant to search for the wanted person and shall be disseminated by all appropriate means. Once the accused is apprehended, the authorities shall proceed in accordance with paragraph 2 of this article.

* * *

Note. The question of implementation of the warrants of detention, arrest, transfer, is dealt with in the part on assistance and cooperation.

* * *

[*145] The following proposal for article 29 was also made by the informal group on judicial cooperation and enforcement:

1. The State that has received a pre- or post-indictment warrant and a request for the arrest of a suspect shall immediately, in accordance with its law, take steps to arrest the suspect on the basis of the warrant of the Court or by obtaining a domestic warrant for arrest based on the Court's warrant and request.

2. A person arrested shall be brought promptly before a judicial officer in the custodial State who shall determine, in accordance with the law of that State, that the person has been arrested in accordance with the proper process and that the person's rights have been respected.

3. A person arrested may apply to the Presidency for a determination of the lawfulness under this Statute of any arrest warrant or order of determination issued by the Court. If the Presidency decides that the arrest or detention was unlawful under the Statute, it shall order the release of the accused, and may award compensation.

3 bis.   A person arrested shall have the right to apply to a judicial officer in the custodial State for interim release pending the indictment or surrender of the person. The custodial State shall ensure that the views of the Prosecutor on interim release are brought to the attention of the judicial officer.

4. A person arrested shall be held, pending trial or release on bail, in an appropriate place of detention in the arresting State, in the State in which the trial is to be held or, if necessary, in the host State.

4 bis. In the case of a person arrested before indictment, if no indictment is received within [90 days] of that person's arrest or the Prosecutor advises the custodial State that no indictment will be filed, the person shall be released from custody or any terms of interim release. The release of the person shall not preclude that person's re-arrest should an indictment and a warrant be submitted at a later date.

5 bis.   An accused surrendered to the Court may apply to the Presidency for interim release pending trial. The Presidency may release the accused with or without conditions if satisfied the person will appear for trial.

[*146] Article 30
Notification of the indictment
I. ILC DRAFT

1.   The Prosecutor shall ensure that a person who has been arrested is personally served, as soon as possible after being taken into custody, with certified copies of the following documents, in a language understood by that person:(a)in the case of a suspect provisionally arrested, a statement of the grounds for the arrest;(b)in any other case, the confirmed indictment;(c)a statement of the accused's rights under this Statute.

2.   In any case to which paragraph (1) (a) applies, the indictment shall be served on the accused as soon as possible after it has been confirmed.

3.   If, 60 days after the indictment has been confirmed, the accused is not in custody pursuant to a warrant issued under article 28 (3), or for some reason the requirements of paragraph 1 cannot be complied with, the Presidency may on the application of the Prosecutor prescribe some other manner of bringing the indictment to the attention of the accused.

II. PROPOSALS
A. Information to be provided relating to the indictment or warrant 36/

1.   The [Prosecutor] [Registrar] shall ensure that a person who has been arrested is personally served, as soon as possible after being taken into custody, with certified copies of the following documents, in a language understood by that person:

    (a)   in the case of a suspect provisionally arrested, [a statement of the grounds for arrest] [the warrant of arrest or restriction of liberty] [and must be promptly brought before the appropriate judicial authority of the State in which the warrant is executed. The national judicial authority shall ensure that the warrant does, in fact, apply to that person and that it meets the formal requirements laid down in this Statute];

    (b)   in any other case, the confirmed indictment;

    (c)   a statement of the [accused's] [arrested person's] rights under [articles 26 or 41 of] this Statute [, as applicable].

[*147] [2. The States Parties listed in the Prosecutor's request shall be notified of a warrant issued by the Preliminary Investigations Chamber. The warrant shall take effect as soon as it is brought to the attention of the person concerned by the national authorities charged with executing it.]

3.Option 1:

In any case to which paragraph (1) (a) applies, the indictment shall be served on the accused as soon as possible after it has been confirmed.

Option 2:

The Registrar shall promptly inform the accused, the Prosecutor and the States which in accordance with titles _____ and_____ of this part 37/ have been charged with executing a warrant or asked to cooperate and either the State which lodged the complaint under article_____ 38/ or the Security Council, if the matter was submitted to the Court under article_____, 39/ of the Preliminary Investigations Chamber's decision. If the accused is already in custody under a warrant of arrest and detention, pursuant to article_____, 40/ the warrant of arrest and transfer shall replace the initial warrant. The warrant of arrest and transfer and the

---

36/   Questions under this topic include: (a) what should be provided to the accused and his counsel; (b) who informs the accused of the charges against him before and after the indictment; (c) who should be notified; (d) when should notification be provided?

37/   Relating to "warrants of arrest or restrictions of liberty prior to the judgement" and "cooperation and judicial assistance", respectively.

38/   Relating to complaints submitted by States.

39/   Relating to referrals by the Security Council.

40/   Relating to pre-indictment arrest.

confirmed indictment shall be served on the accused in his place of detention. He shall be brought before the appropriate national judicial authority pursuant to article____. 41/

If the accused is not in custody and his place of residence is known, he shall be arrested by the competent national authorities and brought before the appropriate national judicial authorities pursuant to article_____.] 42/

B. Rights of the suspect or accused related to notification 43/

1.   [The accused is] [Anyone suspected of committing a crime within the meaning of this Statute shall be] entitled:

(a) to be informed promptly of the nature and cause of the charge against him or her [and be questioned in a language which he understands, and, to this end, to have the free assistance of a competent interpreter, and to be provided [*148] free of charge with a translation of the documents on the basis of which he is being questioned or that show why a measure infringing upon his liberty or property has been proposed]; 44/

(b) [to have adequate time and facilities for the preparation of his or her defence and to communicate with counsel; [to be assisted promptly by a lawyer of his own choosing, or, if he does not have sufficient means to pay for one, by a lawyer appointed by the Preliminary Investigations Chamber of the Court;] 45/

(c) [before being questioned, or when a measure infringing upon his liberty or property has been proposed and brought to his attention, to be fully informed of the charges against him and the rights to which he is entitled under paragraph 1 of this article.]

C. Alternative means to personal service or notification

Option 1:

[If 60 days after the indictment has been confirmed, the accused is not in custody pursuant to a warrant issued under article _____, 46/ or for some reason the requirements of paragraph_1 cannot be complied with,] the [Presidency may] [Registrar shall], on application of the Prosecutor, [prescribe some other manner of bringing the indictment to the attention of the accused] [transmit to the national authorities of any State or States in whose territory the Prosecutor has reason to believe the accused may be found, for publication in newspapers having wide circulation in that territory, intimating to the accused that service of an indictment against him or her is sought].

Option 2:

If the accused is a fugitive, the warrant of arrest and transfer issued by the Preliminary Investigations Chamber shall have the effect of a warrant to search for the wanted person and shall be disseminated by all appropriate means. Once the accused is apprehended, the authorities shall proceed in accordance with [paragraph 3 of topic A above, option 2, last sentence].

[Note. In the case of a hearing by an indictment chamber, notification of the indictment takes a specific form which is reflected in the consolidation attempt of article 27.]

[*149] Article 31
Persons made available to assist in a prosecution 47/
ILC DRAFT

1.   The Prosecutor may request a State party to make persons available to assist in a prosecution in accordance with paragraph 2.

41/   See footnote 13.

42/   Ibid.

43/   Rights of suspects are generally dealt with under article 27 (6) while rights of the accused are generally treated under article 41. Accordingly, there is a question of whether instead of appearing under article30, these provisions should be consolidated under articles 27 or 41, as appropriate.

44/   As to the accused, compare with ILC article 41 (1) (a), (e); as to suspects, compare with ILC article 26 (6) (c).

45/   As to the accused, compare with ILC article 41 (1) (b); as to suspects, compare with ILC article 26 (6) (a) (ii).

46/   See footnote 13.

47/   This article was not considered by the informal working group on procedural questions, fair trial and rights of the accused, as it deals with other matters.

2.   Such persons should be available for the duration of the prosecution, unless otherwise agreed. They shall serve at the direction of the Prosecutor, and shall not seek or receive instructions from any Government or source other than the Prosecutor in relation to their exercise of functions under this article.

3.   The terms and conditions on which persons may be made available under this article shall be approved by the Presidency on the recommendation of the Prosecutor.

[*150] PART 5. THE TRIAL 48/
Article 32
Place of trial
I. ILC DRAFT

Unless otherwise decided by the Presidency, the place of the trial will be the seat of the Court.

II. PROPOSALS
Competent organ and criteria to decide the place of the trial

1.   Unless otherwise decided in accordance with paragraph 2, the place of the trial will be the seat of the Court.

2.   The [Presidency] [General Assembly of the States parties] may authorize the [Trial Chamber] [Court] to [exercise its functions at a place other than the seat of the Court] [sit in a State Party other than the host State] [for a particular case] [where it will ensure the efficient conduct of the trial and is in the interests of justice] [or] [when travel by the members of the Court is likely to make the proceedings simpler and less costly]. 49/

3.   [(a)] The Presidency of the Court shall make inquiries with the State Party that appears likely to receive the Court.

    [(b)] After the State Party likely to receive the Court has agreed, the decision [under the preceding paragraph] to hold a session away from the Court's seat shall be taken by the General Assembly of the States Parties, which shall be informed either by one of its members, the Presidency, the Prosecutor or the General Assembly of the Judges of the Court.]

4.   With the express agreement of the State Party receiving the Court, the privileges, immunities and facilities provided for in article [23?] shall continue to be effective when the Court holds a session pursuant to [this article] [the three preceding paragraphs].

5.   The provisions of this article shall also apply to non-party States which, after inquiries by the Presidency, state that they agree to receive the Court and to grant the privileges, immunities and facilities provided for in article [23?].

[*151] Article 33 50/
Applicable law
ILC DRAFT

The Court shall apply:

(a)   this Statute;

(b)   applicable treaties and the principles and rules of general international law; and

(c)   to the extent applicable, any rule of national law.

[*152] Article 34
Challenges to jurisdiction
I. ILC DRAFT

Challenges to the jurisdiction of the Court may be made, in accordance with the Rules:

(a)   prior to or at the commencement of the hearing, by an accused or any interested State; and

---

48/   See the note to Part 4.

49/   This raises a number of issues, including the need for agreement of States Parties or the host State for a trial chamber to exercise its functions away from the seat of the Court and whether authority to initiate such a step should rest with the President or the trial chamber.

50/   This article was not considered by the informal working group on procedural questions, fair trial and rights of the accused, as it deals with other matters.

(b)   at any later stage of the trial, by an accused.

II. PROPOSALS
AUSTRALIA AND NETHERLANDS
Rule 78
General provisions

(A)   After the initial appearance of the accused, either party may move before the Trial Chamber for appropriate relief or ruling. Such motions may be written or oral, at the discretion of the Trial Chamber.

(B)   The Trial Chamber shall dispose of preliminary motions *in limine litis* and without interlocutory appeal, save in the following cases wherein the Chamber:

(i)   dismisses an objection by the accused based on lack of jurisdiction;

(ii)   dismisses all or part of an indictment which prohibits the Prosecutor from bringing new charges based on the acts underlying the dismissed indictment, or portion thereof;

(iii)   excludes evidence and the Prosecutor represents to the Trial Chamber that the appeal is not taken for the purpose of delay and that the evidence is a substantial proof of a fact material in the proceeding.

(C)   The supplementary rules shall provide for matters such as the length, format and manner of service of preliminary motions where those motions are in written form.

Rule 79
Preliminary motions by accused

(A)   Preliminary motions open to the accused shall include:

(i)   objections based on lack of jurisdiction;

(ii)   objections based on defects in the form of the indictment;

[*153] (iii) applications for the exclusion of evidence obtained from the accused or having belonged to him or her;

(iv)   applications for severance under rule 64;

(v)   objections based on the denial of request for assignment of counsel.

(B)   Any of the motions by the accused referred to in subrule (A) shall be brought within sixty days after his or her initial appearance, and in any case before the hearing on the merits.

(C)   Failure to apply within the time-limit prescribed shall constitute a waiver of the right. Upon a showing of good cause, the Trial Chamber may grant relief from the waiver.

[Note. Subrules (B) and (C) conflict with article 34 of the ILC draft Statute.]

Rule 80
Opportunity to respond

Upon the submission of a motion, the other party shall be afforded a reasonable opportunity to respond to it. The supplementary rules may set time-limits for responses.

Rule 81
Ruling on motions

Motions shall be decided as expeditiously as possible. A motion may be summarily denied on the grounds that insufficient allegations of fact or law have been set forth to justify further inquiry by the Trial Chamber.

ARGENTINA
Rule 61

(B)   If the accused is detained at the disposal of the Court, or, being free, he or she voluntarily submits himself or herself to its jurisdiction, the Indictment Chamber shall notify the accused of the date set for the review of the indictment, and shall provide him or her with a copy of the indictment by the Prosecutor. On the day of the hearing, the Indictment Chamber shall listen to the accused, who shall be allowed to raise objections to the indictment, to point out any flaws it may contain, to criticize the material on which the indictment is based and to point out the evidence that he or she deems relevant to decide about the existence of a criminal case and which has been omitted by the Prosecutor. If this is the first time the accused presents himself or herself, he or she shall be allowed to bring any motions contained in rule 79 (A), or wait until the term of 60 days established in rule 79 (B) has elapsed.

[*154] FRANCE
Article 36
Verification of jurisdiction

The Court shall satisfy itself that it has jurisdiction in any case brought before it. Any State Party competent to institute proceedings in connection with all or part of the acts brought before the Court, and any person named in the document of submission to the Court, may challenge the jurisdiction of the Court. The forms and periods set out in article 39, paragraphs 2 and 3, shall apply.

Article 39
Challenge of a submission to the Court

1.   The Prosecutor of the Court, before initiating an investigation, shall notify the States Parties of any matter submitted to the Court in accordance with articles 37 and 38. The States Parties shall so inform the persons referred to by name in the submission.

2.   A State Party which wishes to continue to proceed with a prosecution or which has already proceeded with one in the case brought before the Court may then challenge the submission of the case within a period of one month after notification of the submission has been sent under paragraph 1 of this article. The person referred to by name in the submission may also dispute it under the same conditions. As soon as the Court has received notice that the submission is being challenged under the preceding subparagraph, article 40, paragraph 2, shall apply.

3.   The State Party or person challenging the submission to the Court may present his arguments either in writing or at a hearing held at his request. The Court may also decide of its own motion or at the request of the Prosecutor of the Court to hold such a hearing.

The decision shall be handed down by the Trial Chamber after it has heard the State or person disputing the submission and the Prosecutor. The State or person in question or the Prosecutor can appeal the decision handed down by the Trial Chamber before the Appeals Chamber.

The rules set forth in the preceding subparagraphs of this paragraph shall apply to any dispute brought before the Court under this article, during both the initial review of the dispute provided for in paragraph 6 of this article and the subsequent reviews provided for in paragraph 7 hereof.

4.   The Court may decide, having regard to the principle of complementarity referred to in the preamble of this Statute, that a case brought before it is inadmissible for the reasons stated in article 35 (a), (b) and (c).

5.   In every case, the State or person challenging a submission to the Court under paragraph 2 of this article shall provide all information concerning the conduct of the investigations and the judicial procedures which may support a finding of inadmissibility in the case submitted to the Court.

[*155] 6. If the Court recognizes the plea of inadmissibility by the State or person challenging the submission on the grounds of article 35 (a), it shall declare the case before it provisionally inadmissible. In that event, the Prosecutor may question the State proceeding with the prosecution as to the status of the investigation and the action that will be taken on it.

If the Court recognizes the plea of inadmissibility by the State or person challenging the submission on the grounds of article 35 (b) or (c), it shall declare the case inadmissible.

7.   In the case of the situation described in the first paragraph of paragraph 6 hereof, the Prosecutor may at any time refer back to the Court the same acts if it appears to him that the conditions required in article 35 (a) no longer exist. The Chamber which has made the initial finding that the Court lacks jurisdiction in the matter shall rule on the Prosecutor's request. After it has heard the arguments of the Prosecutor and the State or person concerned, it may either find that the conditions of article 35 (a) have been fulfilled or authorize the Prosecutor to initiate a prosecution in accordance with this Statute.

In the case of the situation envisaged in the second paragraph of paragraph 6 hereof, the Prosecutor of the Court may, if new facts arise, submit a request to the Court for a review of the decision of inadmissibility. The chamber which has handed down the initial decision of inadmissibility shall decide on the Prosecutor's request. After it has heard the arguments of the Prosecutor and the State or person concerned, it can either confirm its decision of inadmissibility or authorize the Prosecutor to initiate a prosecution before it in accordance with this Statute.

Article 69
Concurrent requests for transfer or extradition

1.   The States Parties shall undertake to give priority to requests for transfer submitted by the Court over requests for extradition submitted by other States Parties.

2.   If the State Party to which the request for transfer is addressed has also received a request for extradition from a State Party to which it is bound by an extradition agreement, it shall rule on that request for extradition, unless the Court, pursuant to article 39, has already rejected the challenge to submission to the Court made by the State requesting the extradition.

3.   The State requesting the extradition may, if it has not already contested submission to the Court pursuant to article 39, request the Court to withdraw its request for transfer, on the basis of the principle of complementarity stated in the preamble to this Statute. The person named in the request for transfer may, under the same conditions, challenge submission to the Court and seek the withdrawal of the request for transfer.

Taking into account the facts and the identity of the persons named in the request for transfer, the Court shall rule in accordance with article 35, paragraphs (a) and (c), and article 39, paragraphs 3, 5, 6 and 7. The warrants issued earlier by the Court shall remain in force and the States parties shall be bound to cooperate.

[*156] 4. If the State detaining the person concerned rejects the request for extradition, it shall so inform the Court without delay. The request referred to in paragraph 3 of this article shall then cease to have effect, and the Court shall note this fact in a decision.

5.   If the Court decides not to grant the request submitted under paragraph 3 of this article, the Registrar shall immediately so inform the requested State, and the demand for extradition submitted by the requesting State shall cease to have effect. The person concerned shall then be transferred to the Court as soon as possible.

6.   If the State detaining the person concerned decides to grant the request for extradition before the Court has finally ruled on the request submitted under paragraph 3 of this article, it may either keep the person concerned at its disposal or transfer him to the Court, in which case it shall notify its decision in favour of extradition to the requesting State and to the Court.

If the Court subsequently accepts the request submitted by the requesting State in accordance with paragraph 3 of this article and if the person concerned has been transferred to it pursuant to the preceding paragraph, it shall order the return of the person concerned to that State.

For the purposes of prosecution the requesting State shall be bound by the decision on extradition taken by the requested State and by all other provisions of the extradition treaty between the two States. The duration of the person's detention in the requested State and at the seat of the Court or in the place which it specifies shall be deducted in full from any sentence imposed in that requesting State.

7.   If the State party requested to make a transfer to the Court has also received a request for extradition from a State non-party but one to which it is bound by an extradition agreement, it shall rule as in the case of concurrent requests for extradition, taking into account the following circumstances:

-    The respective dates of the requests;
-    The respective seriousness of the offences in question, with priority given to the request based on the most serious offences;
-    The possibility that an agreement may be concluded between the State non-party requesting the extradition and the Court providing either that, following his trial by that State or after he has served his sentence, the person concerned may be transferred to the Court, or that the Court agrees to return him temporarily to the State requesting his extradition after having tried him, in order that that State may try him in turn or have him serve his sentence.

[*157] Article 107
Notification of the indictment to the States Parties for the purpose of
challenging the submission of the case to the Court

1.   At least three months before the date of opening of the trial, the Registrar shall notify the States Parties of the confirmed indictments and shall inform them that they are allowed a period of one month from the date of such notification in which to advise him if they challenge the submission of the case to the Court.

2.   If a State has declared its intention to challenge the submission of the case to the Court, under articles 115 and 116, and within the time-limit laid down in the preceding paragraph, the prosecutor shall notify to the State the date on which the trial is to be held, such notification to be given at least two months before that date.

Article 115
Challenging of submission of the case to the Trial Chamber

Upon the opening of the trial, and in accordance with the procedure laid down in article 116, the right to challenge submission of the case to the Court lies with the accused and with the State which has already exercised its jurisdiction, provided the accused and the State in question have not previously challenged the submission to the Court.

Article 116
Challenge procedure

1.   At the opening of the trial, following completion of the formalities provided for in article 113, the accused and the States that have indicated their wish to challenge submission of the case to the Court, in accordance with article 107, paragraph 2, may submit a memorandum raising the question of inadmissibility of a case of which the Court is seized, having regard to the principle of complementarity enunciated in the preamble to this Statute.

Submission of the case to the Court may not subsequently be challenged.

2.   If an accused or a State challenges submission of the case to the Court, the Trial Chamber shall adjourn the trial until a final decision has been taken on the matter.

The Trial Chamber shall rule on the defence of inadmissibility. The hearing may take place immediately or at a later date set by the Chamber, either of its own motion or at the request of the prosecutor, the accused or the State challenging the submission to the Court.

3.   During the hearing on the question of submission to the Court, the President of the Trial Chamber shall invite the accused or the State challenging submission to the Court to present their arguments, following which he shall request the prosecutor to present his observations.

[*158] 4. The Prosecutor, the accused and the State that has challenged submission to the court may appeal the decision of the Trial Chamber to the Appeals Chamber.

5.   At this stage of the proceedings, the Court may decide, having regard to the principle of complementarity enunciated in the preamble to this Statute, that the case brought before it is inadmissible on the ground that the accused has already been acquitted or convicted in final judgement within a State, in respect of the acts specified in the confirmed indictment, unless the proceedings took place in the State concerned in violation of the rules of international law with the aim of protecting the accused from criminal liability.

6.   If the Court allows the defence of inadmissibility, it shall declare the case inadmissible and the trial initiated in accordance with this title may not proceed. The case may be declared partly inadmissible, in which case the trial may proceed in respect of the acts and of the accused that do not fall under the provisions of paragraph 5 of the present article.

AUSTRIA
Article 34

"...

(a)   ...

(b)   ..., by an accused or any State concerned only upon production of new relevant facts."

SWITZERLAND

Challenges to the jurisdiction of the Court may be made, under the conditions laid down in the rules, prior to or at the commencement of the hearing, by an accused or interested State.

Preparatory Committee (spring session)

(2)   (An application by the accused or) a request by a State (OR an interested State) to the Court to declare a case inadmissible under paragraph 1 may be made at any time before (or at the commencement of) the trial (and must give reasons). (The accused may bring a challenge only after indictment and only on the grounds specified in article 35 (1)(c).)

[*159] Article 35 51/
Issues of admissibility
I. ILC DRAFT

The Court may, on application by the accused or at the request of an interested State at any time prior to the commencement of the trial, or of its own motion, decide, having regard to the purposes of this Statute set out in the preamble, that a case before it is inadmissible on the ground that the crime in question:

(a) has been duly investigated by a State with jurisdiction over it, and the decision of that State not to proceed to a prosecution is apparently well-founded;

(b) is under investigation by a State which has or may have jurisdiction over it, and there is no reason for the Court to take any further action for the time being with respect to the crime; or

(c) is not of such gravity to justify further action by the Court.

II. PROPOSALS
FRANCE
Article 36
Verification of jurisdiction

The Court shall satisfy itself that it has jurisdiction in any case brought before it. Any State Party competent to institute proceedings in connection with all or part of the acts brought before the Court, and any person named in the document of submission to the Court, may challenge the jurisdiction of the Court. The forms and periods set out in article 39, paragraphs 2 and 3, shall apply.

[*160] Article 36
Procedure under articles 34 and 35
I. ILC DRAFT

1. In proceedings under articles 34 and 35, the accused and the complainant State have the right to be heard.

2. Proceedings under articles 34 and 35 shall be decided by the Trial Chamber, unless it considers, having regard to the importance of the issues involved, that the matter should be referred to the Appeals Chamber.

II. PROPOSALS
AUSTRALIA AND NETHERLANDS
Rule 78

(B) The Trial Chamber shall dispose of preliminary motions in limine litis and without interlocutory appeal, save in the following cases wherein the Chamber:

(i) dismisses an objection by the accused based on lack of jurisdiction;

(ii) dismisses all or part of an indictment which prohibits the Prosecutor from bringing new charges based on the acts underlying the dismissed indictment, or portion thereof;

(iii) excludes evidence and the Prosecutor represents to the Trial Chamber that the appeal is not taken for the purpose of delay and that the evidence is a substantial proof of a fact material in the proceeding.

Rule 128
Interlocutory appeals

(A) Subject to subrule (B), a party seeking to make an interlocutory appeal as permitted by subrule 78 (B) shall not more than ten days from the date on which the Trial Chamber ruled on the preliminary motion, file with the Registrar and serve upon the other party a written notice of interlocutory appeal, setting forth the grounds. The supplementary rules shall provide for the form and any related requirements of an interlocutory notice of appeal.

(B) The Appeals Chamber may extend the period up to an additional five days for good cause.

[Note. This rule needs further elaboration. The matter might also need to be addressed in the Statute.]

51/ Only procedural issues are discussed by the informal group. Issues of complementarity in the context of this article are not considered here.

[*161] FRANCE

Article 39

Challenge of a submission to the Court

1.   The Prosecutor of the Court, before initiating an investigation, shall notify the States Parties of any matter submitted to the Court in accordance with articles 37 and 38. The States Parties shall so inform the persons referred to by name in the submission.

2.   A State Party which wishes to continue to proceed with a prosecution or which has already proceeded with one in the case brought before the Court may then challenge the submission of the case within a period of one month after notification of the submission has been sent under paragraph 1 of this article. The person referred to by name in the submission may also dispute it under the same conditions. As soon as the Court has received notice that the submission is being challenged under the preceding subparagraph, article 40, paragraph 2, shall apply.

3.   The State Party or person challenging the submission to the Court may present his arguments either in writing or at a hearing held at his request. The Court may also decide of its own motion or at the request of the Prosecutor of the Court to hold such a hearing.

The decision shall be handed down by the Trial Chamber after it has heard the State or person disputing the submission and the Prosecutor. The State or person in question or the Prosecutor can appeal the decision handed down by the Trial Chamber before the Appeals Chamber.

The rules set forth in the preceding subparagraphs of this paragraph shall apply to any dispute brought before the Court under this article, during both the initial review of the dispute provided for in paragraph 6 of this article and the subsequent reviews provided for in paragraph 7 hereof.

4.   The Court may decide, having regard to the principle of complementarity referred to in the preamble of this Statute, that a case brought before it is inadmissible for the reasons stated in article 35 (a), (b) and (c).

5.   In every case, the State or person challenging a submission to the Court under paragraph 2 of this article shall provide all information concerning the conduct of the investigations and the judicial procedures which may support a finding of inadmissibility in the case submitted to the Court.

6.   If the Court recognizes the plea of inadmissibility by the State or person challenging the submission on the grounds of article 35 (a), it shall declare the case before it provisionally inadmissible. In that event, the Prosecutor may question the State proceeding with the prosecution as to the status of the investigation and the action that will be taken on it.

If the Court recognizes the plea of inadmissibility by the State or person challenging the submission on the grounds of article 35 (b) or (c), it shall declare the case inadmissible.

[*162] 7. In the case of the situation described in the first paragraph of paragraph 6 hereof, the Prosecutor may at any time refer back to the Court the same acts if it appears to him that the conditions required in article 35 (a) no longer exist. The Chamber which has made the initial finding that the Court lacks jurisdiction in the matter shall rule on the Prosecutor's request. After it has heard the arguments of the Prosecutor and the State or person concerned, it may either find that the conditions of article 35 (a) have been fulfilled or authorize the Prosecutor to initiate a prosecution in accordance with this Statute.

In the case of the situation envisaged in the second paragraph of paragraph 6 hereof, the Prosecutor of the Court may, if new facts arise, submit a request to the Court for a review of the decision of inadmissibility. The chamber which has handed down the initial decision of inadmissibility shall decide on the Prosecutor's request. After it has heard the arguments of the Prosecutor and the State or person concerned, it can either confirm its decision of inadmissibility or authorize the Prosecutor to initiate a prosecution before it in accordance with this Statute.

Article 69

3.   The State requesting the extradition may, if it has not already contested submission to the Court pursuant to article 39, request the Court to withdraw its request for transfer, on the basis of the principle of complementarity stated in the preamble to this Statute. The person named in the request for transfer may, under the same conditions, challenge submission to the Court and seek the withdrawal of the request for transfer.

Taking into account the facts and the identity of the persons named in the request for transfer, the Court shall rule in accordance with article 35, paragraph (a) and (c), and article 39, paragraphs 3, 5, 6 and 7. The warrants issued earlier by the Court shall remain in force and the States Parties shall be bound to cooperate.

Article 70
Request for transfer addressed to a State which invokes the principle of complementarity

1. A State Party which brings a prosecution in respect of the facts referred to in the request for transfer addressed to it by the Court, or which had already tried the person named in that request and which has not challenged submission to the Court under article 39, may request the Court to withdraw its request for transfer, on the basis of the principle of complementarity stated in the preamble to this Statute. The person named in the request for transfer may, under the same conditions, challenge submission to the Court and seek the withdrawal of the request for transfer.

The State shall notify the Court which, taking into consideration the facts and the identity of the persons named in the request for transfer, shall rule in accordance with the provisions of article 35, paragraphs (a) and (c), and article 39, paragraphs 3, 5, 6 and 7. Warrants issued subsequently by the Court shall remain in force, and the State Parties shall be bound to cooperate.

[*163] 2. The persons named in a request for transfer addressed to a State which challenges submission to the Court under paragraph 1 of this article shall in no circumstances be placed in detention at the request of the Court before it has finally ruled on submission.

At the request of the Prosecutor of the Court, the Preliminary Investigations Chamber may nevertheless issue against such persons a warrant for judicial supervision, in order, <u>inter alia</u>, to prevent them leaving the territory of the requested State before the Court has finally ruled on submission.

Article 116
Challenge procedure

1. At the opening of the trial, following completion of the formalities provided for in article 113, the accused and the States that have indicated their wish to challenge submission of the case to the Court, in accordance with article 107, paragraph 2, may submit a memorandum raising the question of inadmissibility of a case of which the Court is seized, having regard to the principle of complementarity enunciated in the preamble to this Statute.

Submission of the case to the Court may not subsequently be challenged.

2. If an accused or a State challenges submission of the case to the Court, the Trial Chamber shall adjourn the trial until a final decision has been taken on the matter.

The Trial Chamber shall rule on the defence of inadmissibility. The hearing may take place immediately or at a later date set by the Chamber, either of its own motion or at the request of the Prosecutor, the accused or the State challenging the submission to the Court.

3. During the hearing on the question of submission to the Court, the President of the Trial Chamber shall invite the accused or the State challenging submission to the Court to present their arguments, following which he shall request the prosecutor to present his observations.

4. The Prosecutor, the accused and the State that has challenged submission to the court may appeal the decision of the Trial Chamber to the Appeals Chamber.

5. At this stage of the proceedings, the Court may decide, having regard to the principle of complementarity enunciated in the preamble to this Statute, that the case brought before it is inadmissible on the ground that the accused has already been acquitted or convicted in final judgement within a State, in respect of the acts specified in the confirmed indictment, unless the proceedings took place in the State concerned in violation of the rules of international law with the aim of protecting the accused from criminal liability.

6. If the Court allows the defence of inadmissibility, it shall declare the case inadmissible and the trial initiated in accordance with this title may not proceed. The case may be declared partly inadmissible, in which case the trial may proceed in respect of the acts and of the accused that do not fall under the provisions of paragraph 5 of the present article.

[*164] AUSTRIA
Article 36
(2) "Proceedings under articles 34 <u>(a) and 35</u> shall be decided by the <u>Indictment</u> Chamber, <u>under article 34 (b) by the Trial Chamber,</u> unless ..."

SWITZERLAND
Article 36, paragraph 2
1. Proceedings under articles 34 and 35 shall be decided by the Trial Chamber to which the matter has been submitted prior to its examination of the issues involved.
2. The accused, the Prosecutor and the interested States may appeal against this decision in accordance with the procedure provided for in article 48 and the following articles.

Preparatory Committee (spring session)
Article 36
(3) In cases where the jurisdiction of the Court is called into question, the proceedings shall be interrupted until the competent chamber has reached its decision on this point.

Requirement of super-majority
Preparatory Committee (spring session)
Article 35
((4) A vote of two thirds of the members of the Court shall be required before the Prosecutor can investigate and prosecute a case under article 35 (1) (c).)

[*165] Article 37
Trial in the presence of the accused
I. ILC DRAFT
1. As a general rule, the accused should be present during the trial.
2. The Trial Chamber may order that the trial proceed in the absence of the accused if:
    (a) the accused is in custody, or has been released pending trial, and for reasons of security or the ill-health of the accused it is undesirable for the accused to be present;
    (b) the accused is continuing to disrupt the trial; or
    (c) the accused has escaped from lawful custody under this Statute or has broken bail.
3. The Chamber shall, if it makes an order under paragraph 2, ensure that the rights of the accused under this Statute are respected, and in particular:
    (a) that all reasonable steps have been taken to inform the accused of the charge; and
    (b) that the accused is legally represented, if necessary by a lawyer appointed by the Court.
4. In cases where a trial cannot be held because of the deliberate absence of an accused, the Court may establish, in accordance with the Rules, an Indictment Chamber for the purpose of:
    (a) recording the evidence;
    (b) considering whether the evidence establishes a <u>prima facie</u> case of a crime within the jurisdiction of the Court; and
    (c) issuing and publishing a warrant of arrest in respect of an accused against whom a <u>prima facie</u> case is established.
5. If the accused is subsequently tried under this Statute:
    (a) the record of evidence before the Indictment Chamber shall be admissible;
    (b) any judge who was a member of the Indictment Chamber may not be a member of the Trial Chamber.

[*166] II. PROPOSALS
A. Scope of general rule and exceptions
1. [As a general rule, the accused should be present during the trial.] [The accused shall be present during the trial] [The trial shall not be held if the accused is not present].
[2. The Trial Chamber may [exceptionally and by a specially reasoned decision] [in the interests of justice] [having heard such submissions and evidence as it deems necessary] [<u>proprio motu</u> or at the request of either party] order that the trial proceed in the absence of the accused, if the accused:

(a) [is in custody, or has been released pending trial, and for reasons of security or the ill-health of the accused it is undesirable for the accused to be present] [because of his state of health, requests that he be excused from appearing and the Chamber considers that his presence is not essential to the holding of the trial. In this case, the Chamber may appoint one of its members to hear the accused at his place of residence or in the local prison where he is held after his defense counsel has been duly notified. The judge so appointed, assisted by the Registrar, shall examine the accused. The Prosecutor and the counsel of the parties may also put questions to him by requesting authorization to do so from the appointed judge. The Registrar shall prepare a record of the examination of the accused and shall transmit it as soon as possible to the Trial Chamber];

(b) [is continuing to disrupt the trial] [disrupts the trial or refuses to appear. In this case, the accused shall, until the end of the trial, be held at the disposal of the Chamber by the police. After each hearing, the Registrar shall read the record of the deliberations to the accused and deliver to him a copy of the submissions by the prosecutor and of the judgements given by the Trial Chamber];

(c) [has escaped from lawful custody under this Statute or has broken bail]; or

(d) [under detention has, when summoned for the date of trial, refused to appear without good reason, and made it particularly difficult to bring him to the Court];

(e) [has failed to appear for trial and all reasonable steps have been taken to inform the accused of the charge.]

Another alternative

If the accused is at liberty, he must give himself up no later than the day before the trial; he may, however, apply to the President of the Trial Chamber for exemption from this requirement. He shall be informed of the decision of the President by any available means. The accused shall be warned that, in the event of his failure to present himself for the opening of the trial, he will be tried in absentia in accordance with the provisions of paragraph 4 of this article. There shall be no appeal against denial of such exemption by the President.

If the accused has been placed under judicial supervision by the Trial Chamber, this supervision shall continue in force until such time as the accused gives himself up or, if he is exempted from the requirement to give himself up, [*167] until such time as the Trial Court takes the decision referred to in article 100. If the accused does not give himself up in accordance with the provisions of paragraph 1, or, if he has been exempted from the requirement to give himself up, does not present himself at the opening of the trial, or if he escapes during the course of the trial before the Chamber has withdrawn to deliberate, the Trial Chamber may issue a warrant requiring that he be sought, arrested and transferred. This warrant must contain a statement of the acts referred to in the decision confirming the indictment for the offence specified in the decision.

This warrant shall be circulated by the Registrar of the Court by any appropriate means; if the accused is found, he shall be served with the warrant and shall be informed of the confirmed indictment if this has not already been done. He shall be brought before the competent national authority, which shall proceed in accordance with article 55, paragraph 3. The accused shall be placed in detention and transferred as soon as possible to the local prison closest to the seat of the Court, or to any other place specified by the Court, in the manner provided for in Part 4, Title III, of this Statute, with a view to being brought before the Trial Chamber.

If the accused has not given himself up on the day before the trial in accordance with the provisions of paragraph 1, or if he was exempted from the requirement to give himself up but did not present himself at the opening of the trial, or if he escapes during the trial before the Chamber retires for deliberation, and he still cannot be found, he may be tried in absentia upon the express application of the prosecutor. The Trial Chamber shall issue a warrant for the arrest and transfer of the accused for the purpose of enforcement of its judgement. This warrant, which shall replace any previous warrant, shall be executed in accordance with the provisions of Part 4, Title II, of this Statute.]

B. Rights of the accused

3. The Chamber shall, if it makes an order under paragraph 2, ensure that the rights of the accused under this Statute [and the rules] are respected [, and in particular:

(a) that all reasonable steps have been taken to inform the accused of the charge; and

(b)   that the accused is legally represented, if necessary by a lawyer appointed by the Court.]

[*168] C. <u>Proceedings to preserve evidence and to issue</u>
<u>international warrants</u> <u>52/</u>

4. <u>Option 1</u>
An exception shall be made in the case of measures for recording the evidence.

<u>Option 2</u>
In cases where a trial cannot be held because of the deliberate absence of an accused, the court may establish, in accordance with the rules, an Indictment Chamber for the purpose of:

(a)   recording the evidence;

(b)   considering whether the evidence establishes a <u>prima facie</u> case of a crime within the jurisdiction of the Court; and

(c)   issuing and publishing a warrant of arrest in respect of an accused against whom a <u>prima facie</u> case is established.

<u>Option 3</u>
When the Preliminary Investigations Chamber proposes to confirm an indictment, but one or more of the persons named in the indictment has fled or cannot be found, it may still hold a hearing under the conditions provided for in article ___. <u>53/</u>

When it confirms the indictment, in whole or in part, against a person who has fled or cannot be found, the Preliminary Investigations Chamber shall issue a warrant to search for, arrest and transfer the accused, which is tantamount to committing him to the Trial Chamber for trial. This warrant must contain, in addition to the particulars listed in article ___, <u>54/</u> the statement of facts referred to in the confirmation decision, with the characterization accepted in that decision.

The warrant shall be disseminated by the Registrar using all appropriate means. When the person is found, the warrant shall be executed as a warrant of arrest and transfer, in accordance with the provisions of title ___ of this part. <u>55/</u>

D. <u>Subsequent trial</u>

5. <u>Option 1</u>
If the accused is subsequently tried under this Statute:

[*169] (a) the record of evidence before the Indictment Chamber shall be admissible;

(b)   any judge who was a member of the Indictment Chamber may not be a member of the Trial Chamber.

<u>Option 2</u>
If an accused person tried <u>in absentia</u> under the provisions of this article gives himself up or is arrested, the decision taken <u>in absentia</u> by the Trial Chamber shall be void in all its provisions and the accused shall be retried, except in the case provided for in paragraph 7.

However, the accused may accept the decision if the sentence pronounced is one of imprisonment for not more than 10 years. Such acceptance must be recorded, in the presence of defense counsel, appointed by the accused or by the court at his request, by the President of the Trial Chamber or by any judge appointed by him.

The Trial Chamber may allow the accused to be represented by counsel whom he has appointed. In this case, the accused shall be tried <u>in absentia</u>, but the Trial Chamber shall inform the defense counsel of the accused that the latter may not be retried.

<u>Option 3</u>
In case an accused has been tried <u>in absentia</u> in accordance with this article, the Trial Chamber may, according to circumstances, admit an authorized representative to appear on trial to plea for the accused. In case the accused still appears pending procedures, the Trial Chamber shall recommence the trial entirely.

<u>52/</u>   An important question here is how to control the recording of evidence in order to prevent prejudice to the accused at the time of trial.

<u>53/</u>   Relating to confirmation of the indictment.

<u>54/</u>   Relating to formal requirements for the issuance of an arrest warrant.

<u>55/</u>   Relating to arrest or restrictions of liberty prior to judgement.

[*170] Article 38
Functions and powers of the Trial Chamber
A. Procedures related to the commencement of the trial
I. ILC DRAFT

1.   At the commencement of the trial, the Trial Chamber shall:
   (a)   have the indictment read;
   (b)   ensure that articles 27 (5) (b) and 30 have been complied with sufficiently in advance of the trial to enable adequate preparation of the defence;
   (c)   satisfy itself that the other rights of the accused under this Statute have been respected.

II. PROPOSALS
AUSTRALIA AND NETHERLANDS
Rule 74
Initial appearance of accused

Upon his or her transfer to the seat of the Court or where the trial is to be held, the accused shall be brought before the Trial Chamber established by the Presidency under article X (A 27 ILC) of the Statute without delay, and shall be formally charged. The Trial Chamber shall:
   (i)   satisfy itself that the right of the accused to counsel is respected;
   (ii)   read or have the indictment read to the accused in a language he or she speaks and understands, and satisfy itself that the accused understands the indictment;
   (iii)   call upon the accused to enter a plea of guilty or not guilty on each count; and should the accused fail to do so, enter a plea of guilty on his or her behalf;
   (iv)   in the case of a plea of not guilty, instruct the Registrar to set a date for trial;
   (v)   in the case of a plea of guilty, instruct the Registrar to set a date for the pre-sentencing hearing under rule 118;
   (vi)   instruct the Registrar to set such other dates as appropriate.
[Note. A number of issues are raised by this rule which flow from the different approaches taken under the common law and civil law systems. For example, civil law systems do not make provision for guilty pleas. The proposal that a guilty plea would lead directly to a pre-sentencing hearing would also raise concerns from the perspective of a civil law system.]

[*171] Rule 78
General provisions

(A)   After the initial appearance of the accused, either party may move before the Trial Chamber for appropriate relief or ruling. Such motions may be written or oral, at the discretion of the Trial Chamber.
(B)   The Trial Chamber shall dispose of preliminary motions in limine litis and without interlocutory appeal, save in the following cases wherein the Chamber:
   (i)   dismisses an objection by the accused based on lack of jurisdiction;
   (ii)   dismisses all or part of an indictment which prohibits the Prosecutor from bringing new charges based on the acts underlying the dismissed indictment, or portion thereof;
   (iii)   excludes evidence and the Prosecutor represents to the Trial Chamber that the appeal is not taken for the purpose of delay and that the evidence is a substantial proof of a fact material in the proceeding.
(C)   The supplementary rules shall provide for matters such as the length, format and manner of service of preliminary motions where those motions are in written form.

FRANCE
Article 98
Submission to the Trial Chamber

The Trial Chamber shall have jurisdiction over accused persons brought before it by a decision of the Preliminary Investigations Chamber taken under the provisions of article 48, paragraph 6, and article 49, paragraph 2.

Article 113
Opening of trial

At the opening of the trial, the President of the Chamber shall:
   (a)   examine the accused in order to verify his identity;

(b)   ensure that the accused has actually been notified of the confirmed indictment and has since then been allowed adequate time and facilities for the preparation of his defence;

(c)   ensure that a defence counsel for the accused is present. If the accused has no counsel, the President of the Chamber shall appoint one of his own motion;

(d)   ensure that the accused understands and speaks the language employed at the hearing. Should this not be the case, the accused shall be entitled to [*172] be assisted free of charge by an interpreter appointed by the President of the Trial Chamber;

(e)   have the confirmed indictment read out.

TITLE II. FORMALITIES PRIOR TO THE OPENING OF THE TRIAL
Article 106
Summons for the accused to appear

The Registrar of the Court shall inform the accused of the date of opening of the trial at least two months before that date.

Article 107
Notification of the indictment to the States Parties
for the purpose of challenging the submission of the case to the Court

1.   At least three months before the date of opening of the trial, the Registrar shall notify the States Parties of the confirmed indictments and shall inform them that they are allowed a period of one month from the date of such notification in which to advise him if they challenge the submission of the case to the Court.

2.   If a State has declared its intention to challenge the submission of the case to the Court, under articles 115 and 116, and within the time limit laid down in the preceding paragraph, the Prosecutor shall notify to the State the date on which the trial is to be held, such notification to be given at least two months before that date.

Article 108
Summoning of witnesses and experts

1.   The Prosecutor shall communicate to the accused and the accused shall communicate to the Prosecutor, as soon as possible and in any event within 15 days of the opening of the trial, the list of persons they wish to have heard as witnesses or experts in support of the evidence obtained during the investigation.

The communication shall indicate the name, forename, occupation and place of residence of such witnesses or experts.

2.   Upon application by the accused, the Prosecutor shall, at least one month before the beginning of the trial, summon to appear the witnesses and experts the list of whom has been communicated to him by the accused. This list may not include more than 10 names.

Further witnesses or experts or witnesses or experts whose names were communicated to the prosecutor after the time limit shall, at the request of the accused and at his expense, be summoned to appear. However, if the accused does not have sufficient resources to bear the cost of their [*173] appearance, he may request the Trial Chamber to summon, upon his petition, further witnesses or experts. The Trial Chamber shall determine by a non-appealable decision whether the appearance of the persons concerned will be useful in ascertaining the true facts.

TITLE III. CONDUCT OF THE TRIAL
Article 109
Assistance by a Registrar

During the trial, the Trial Chamber shall have the assistance of a Registrar.

Article 110
Means of constraint

Means of constraint, such as handcuffs, shall not be used except to avoid a risk of escape during transfer or for reasons of security; they shall be removed when the accused appears before the Trial Chamber.

1 (a). Guilty plea

ARGENTINA
Rule 74

...

(iii) [The Trial Chamber] shall request the accused, once all counts have been read, to say whatever he or she deems convenient about the indictment and the counts he or she is being indicted for;

(iv) If the accused admits the facts he or she is being indicted for, [the Trial Chamber] shall order the trial to be carried out pursuant to the abbreviated proceedings established in rule 145 and instruct the Registrar to set a date for the hearing;

(v) In any other case, once the accused has been heard, [the Trial Chamber] shall instruct the Registrar to set a date for the trial;

(vi) [The Trial Chamber] shall instruct the Registrar to set such other dates as appropriate.

ARGENTINA AND CANADA

1.Amend article 38, paragraph 1 (d), to read:

"(d)allow the accused to enter a plea of not guilty or to make an admission of guilt before the Trial Chamber."

[*174] 2.Add a new article 38 bis:

"Article 38 bis

"Abbreviated proceedings on an admission of guilt

"1. Where the accused makes an admission of guilt under article 38, paragraph 1 (d), the Trial Chamber shall determine whether:

(a) the accused appreciates the nature and consequences of the admission of guilt and whether the admission is voluntarily made; and

(b) the admission of guilt is firmly supported by the facts of the case that are contained in:

(i) the indictment and in any supplementary materials presented by the Prosecutor, and which the accused admits; and

(ii) any other evidence, including the testimony of witnesses, presented by the Prosecutor or the accused.

"2. Where the Trial Chamber is satisfied that the natters referred to in paragraph 1 are established, the Trial Chamber shall consider the admission of guilt as an admission of all the essential facts that are required to prove the crime to which the admission of guilt relates, and may convict the accused of that crime.

"3. Where the Trial Chamber is not satisfied that the matters referred to in paragraph 1 are established, the Trial Chamber shall order that the trial be continued under the ordinary trial procedures provided by this Statute, and shall consider the admission of guilt not to have been made.

"4. Where the Trial Chamber is of the opinion that a more complete presentation of the facts of the case is otherwise required in the interests of justice, the Trial Chamber may request that the Prosecutor present additional evidence, including the testimony of witnesses, or may order that the trial be continued under the ordinary trial procedures provided by this Statute and, in the latter situation, shall consider the admission of guilt not to have been made."

[*175] B. Rights of the accused/witnesses/victims
I. ILC DRAFT

2. The Chamber shall ensure that a trial is fair and expeditious and is conducted in accordance with this Statute and the rules, with full respect for the rights of the accused and due regard for the protection of victims and witnesses.

II. PROPOSALS
AUSTRALIA AND NETHERLANDS
Rule 75
Questioning of accused

After the initial appearance of the accused the Prosecutor shall not question him or her unless his or her counsel is present and the questioning is tape-recorded or video-recorded in accordance with the procedure provided for in rules 58 and 59. The Prosecutor shall at the beginning of the questioning caution the accused that he or she is not obliged to say anything unless he or she wishes to do so but that whatever he or she says may be given in evidence.

ARGENTINA
Rule 100
(C) The accused shall be able to declare in his or her defence, should he or she wish to do so. If this were the case, the provisions of rules 57 bis and 75 shall be applicable.

FRANCE
Article 101 Rights of the accused
The accused shall enjoy the rights afforded to suspects under article 51, paragraph 1. He shall also be entitled:-to a fair hearing by an independent and impartial tribunal. Subject to the provisions of article 104, the hearing shall be public;-to have adequate time and facilities for the preparation of his defence;-to be tried without undue delay;-to examine or have examined the witnesses against him and to obtain the attendance and examination of witnesses on his behalf under the same conditions as witnesses against him; [*176]-to have communicated to him all evidence submitted to the Court.

Article 127 Consideration of decisions
Following the submission by the Prosecutor and the pleadings of the accused, the President shall declare the deliberations concluded and the Chamber shall withdraw to deliberate in camera. The accused shall be found guilty only if the majority of the Trial Chamber considers that his guilt has been proved beyond reasonable doubt. The Trial Chamber shall pronounce its finding separately for each charge in the indictment. If several accused are tried together, the Chamber shall rule separately on the case of each one of them. If the Trial Chamber finds the accused guilty, it shall decide on the sentence by majority vote. Where necessary, it shall also establish principles relating to compensation for damage caused to the victims and to restitution of property unlawfully acquired by the persons convicted. The manner in which the decisions of the Trial Chamber are taken shall be covered by the confidentiality of deliberations.

[*177] C. Disclosure of evidence
PROPOSALS
AUSTRALIA AND NETHERLANDS SECTION
4. DISCLOSURE OF EVIDENCE
Rule 82 Disclosure by the Prosecutor
(A) The Prosecutor shall make available to the defence, as soon as practicable after the initial appearance of the accused, copies of the supporting material which accompanied the indictment when confirmation was sought as well as all prior statements obtained by the Prosecutor from the accused or from prosecution witnesses.

(B) The Prosecutor shall on request, subject to subrule (C), permit the defence to inspect any books, documents, photographs and tangible objects in his or her custody or control, which are material to the preparation of the defence, or are intended for use by the Prosecutor as evidence at trial or were obtained from or belonged to the accused.

(C) Where information is in the possession of the Prosecutor, the disclosure of which may prejudice further or ongoing investigations, or for any other reasons may be contrary to the public interest or affect the security interests of any State, the Prosecutor may apply to the Trial Chamber sitting in camera to be relieved from the obligation to disclose pursuant to subrule (B). When making such application the Prosecutor shall provide the Trial Chamber (but only the Trial Chamber) with the information that is sought to be kept confidential.

(D) Information subject to an order of the Trial Chamber pursuant to subrule (C) must be subsequently disclosed if it is intended to be used as evidence at trial.

[Note. The requirement of disclosure throws up a number of important issues. One relates to the need to ensure that the rights of the accused are not prejudiced through limiting the duty on the Prosecutor to disclose information. There is also the matter of protecting sensitive information supplied by States to the Prosecutor. In this regard, should the relevant State have standing to argue for the non-disclosure of information it has supplied to the Prosecutor? It should be noted that the approach taken in this rule conflicts with aspects of article 27 (5) of the ILC draft Statute.]

Rule 83
Reciprocal disclosure

(A) As early as reasonably practicable and in any event prior to the commencement of the trial:

(i)   The Prosecutor shall notify the defence of the names of the witnesses that he or she intends to call in proof of the guilt of the accused [*178] and in rebuttal of any defence plea of which the Prosecutor has received notice in accordance with (ii) below;

(ii)   The defence shall notify the Prosecutor of its intent to offer:

(a)   the defence of alibi; in which case the notification shall specify the place or places at which the accused claims to have been present at the time of the alleged crime and the names and addresses of witnesses and any other evidence upon which the accused intends to rely to establish the alibi;

(b)   any special defence, including those of (defences to be identified); in which case the notification shall specify the names and addresses of witnesses and any other evidence upon which the accused intends to rely to establish the special defence.

(B) Failure of the defence to provide notice under this rule shall not limit the right of the accused to testify on the above defences.

(C) If the defence makes a request pursuant to subrule (B) of rule 82, the Prosecutor shall be entitled to inspect any books, documents, photographs and tangible objects, which are within the custody or control of the defence and which it intends to use as evidence at the trial.

Rule 84
Disclosure of exculpatory evidence

(A) The Prosecutor shall, as soon as practicable, disclose to the defence the existence of evidence known to the Prosecutor which in any way tends to suggest the innocence or mitigate the guilt of the accused or may affect the credibility of prosecution evidence.

(B) The Prosecutor may request an ex parte hearing in camera before the Trial Chamber for the purpose of obtaining a ruling on whether or not particular evidence falls within the category of exculpatory evidence.

Rule 85
Continuing duty to disclose

(A) The duty to disclose is ongoing for both parties.

(B) If either party discovers additional evidence or material which should have been produced earlier pursuant to the rules, that party shall promptly notify the other party and the Trial Chamber of the existence of the additional evidence or material.

[Note. The issue of sanctions for non-disclosure needs to be addressed.]

[*179] Rule 86
Protection of victims and witnesses

(A) In exceptional circumstances, the Prosecutor may apply to a Trial Chamber to order the non-disclosure of the identity of a victim or witness who may be in danger or at risk until such person is brought under the protection of the Tribunal.

(B) In the determination of protective measures for victims and witnesses, the Trial Chamber may consult the Victims and Witnesses Unit.

(C) Subject to rule 95, the identity of the victim or witness shall be disclosed in sufficient time prior to the trial to allow adequate time for preparation of the defence.

[Note. The protection of victims and witnesses will be an important responsibility of the Court. The non-disclosure of the identity of victims and witnesses needs to be balanced against the right of an accused to prepare his or her defence.]

Rule 87
Matters not subject to disclosure

(A) Notwithstanding the provisions of rules 82 and 83 reports, memoranda, or other internal documents prepared by a party, its assistants or representatives in connection with the investigation or preparation of the case, are not subject to disclosure or notification under those rules.

(B) If the Prosecutor is in possession of information which has been provided to him or her on a confidential basis and which has been used solely for the purpose of generating new evidence, that initial information and its origin shall not be disclosed by the Prosecutor without the consent of the person or entity providing the initial information and shall in any event not be given in evidence without prior disclosure to the accused.

(C) If, after obtaining the consent of the person or entity providing information under this rule, the Prosecutor elects to present as evidence any testimony, document or other material so provided, the Trial Chamber, notwithstanding rule 116, may not order either party to produce additional evidence received from the person or entity providing the initial information, nor may the Trial Chamber for the purpose of obtaining such additional evidence itself summon that person or a representative of that entity as a witness or order their attendance.

(D) If the Prosecutor calls as a witness the person providing, or a representative of the entity providing, information under this rule, the Trial Chamber may not compel the witness to answer any question the witness declines to answer on grounds of confidentiality.

(E) The right of the accused to challenge the evidence presented by the Prosecution shall remain unaffected subject only to limitations contained in subrules (C) and (D).

[*180] (F) Nothing in subrule (C) or (D) above shall effect a Trial Chamber's power under subrule 105 (D) to exclude evidence if its probative value is substantially outweighed by the need to ensure a fair trial.

Rule 95
Measures for the protection of victims and witnesses

(A) As provided for in article X (A 38 (4), 43 ILC) of the Statute, a Trial Chamber may, proprio motu or at the request of either party, or of the victim or witness concerned, or of the Victims and Witnesses Unit, order appropriate measures for the privacy and protection of victims and witnesses, provided that the measures are consistent with the rights of the accused as provided for in the Statute and the rules, in particular the right to examine, or have examined, prosecution witnesses.

(B) A Trial Chamber may hold an in camera proceeding to determine whether to order:

(i) Measures to prevent disclosure to the public or the media of the identity or whereabouts of a victim or a witness, or of persons related to or associated with him or her by such means as:

    (a) expunging names and identifying information from the Chamber's public records;
    (b) non-disclosure to the public of any records identifying the victim;
    (c) giving of testimony through image or voice altering devices or closed circuit television;
    (d) assignment of a pseudonym;

(ii) Closed sessions, in accordance with rule 91;

(iii) Appropriate measures to facilitate the testimony of vulnerable victims and witnesses, such as one-way closed circuit television.

(C) A Trial Chamber shall, whenever necessary, control the manner of questioning to avoid any harassment or intimidation.

[Note. The power of the Trial Chamber to issue a protective order to ensure the safety and security of a particular victim or witness needs to be considered.]

[*181] D. Multiple accused and joinder of crimes
I. ILC DRAFT

3.   The Chamber may, subject to the rules, hear charges against more than one accused arising out of the same factual situation.

II. PROPOSALS
AUSTRALIA AND NETHERLANDS
Rule 62
Joinder of accused

Persons accused of the same or different crimes committed in the course of the same transaction may be jointly charged and tried.

Rule 63
Joinder of crimes

Two or more crimes may be joined in one indictment if the series of acts committed together form the same transaction, and the said crimes were committed by the same accused.

Rule 92
Joint trials

In joint trials, each accused shall be accorded the same rights as if he or she were being tried separately.

[*182] E. Public v. closed proceedings
I. ILC DRAFT

4.   The trial shall be held in public, unless the Chamber determines that certain proceedings be in closed session in accordance with article 43, or for the purpose of protecting confidential or sensitive information which is to be given in evidence.

II. PROPOSALS
AUSTRALIA AND NETHERLANDS
Rule 90
Open sessions

(A)   All proceedings before a Trial Chamber, other than deliberations of the Chamber, shall be held in public, unless otherwise provided.

(B)   Photography, video recording or audio recording of the trial, other than by the Registry under rule 98 is within the discretion of the Trial Chamber.

(C)   In order to protect the accused's right to a fair trial or maintain the dignity and decorum of proceedings, the Trial Chamber may limit the number of spectators in, exclude specific persons from, or restrict access to the courtroom.

[Note. Questions arising under this rule include whether the Trial Chamber should have the power to order a closed hearing and whether photography, video recording or audio recording of the trial, other than by the Registry under rule 98, should be permitted.]

Rule 91
Closed sessions

(A)   As provided for in article X (A 38 (4) ILC) of the Statute, the Trial Chamber may order that the press and the public be excluded from all or part of the proceedings for reasons of:

(i)   public order or morality;

(ii)   safety, security or non-disclosure of the identity of a victim or witness as provided in rule 95;

(iii)   the protection of the interests of justice.

(B)   The Trial Chamber shall make public the reasons for its order.

[Note. This rule is wider in some respects than article 38 (4) of the ILC draft statute.]

[*183] ARGENTINA
Rule 91

(C)   The trial shall be carried out in open sessions as soon as the reasons why the proceedings were being carried out in closed sessions have ceased to exist.

FRANCE
Article 104
Public nature of trial

1.   The trial, with the exception of the consideration of findings, shall be public.

2.   Nevertheless, the Trial Chamber may, of its own motion or at the request of the Prosecutor, the accused, a victim or a witness, order, by a decision given in public, that the entire trial or a part thereof be held in camera:

(a)   for reasons connected with protection of public order or of human dignity;

(b)   to ensure the safety and protection of the accused, of the victims or of witnesses.

3.   Proceedings shall be held in camera as of right:

(a)   at the request of the accused if he was a minor at the time of commission of the acts;

(b)   at the request of a witness or a victim who suffered sexual violence.

When in camera proceedings have been ordered, the judgement on the merits shall always be pronounced in public hearing.

JAPAN

1. The accused shall enjoy the right to a speedy and public trial by an impartial tribunal.
2. Trials shall be conducted and judgement declared publicly. Where the Court unanimously determines publicity to be dangerous to public order, a trial may be conducted privately.

[*184] F. Powers of the Trial Chamber/Preliminary motions
I. ILC DRAFT

5. The Chamber shall, subject to this Statute and the rules, have, _inter alia_, the power on the application of a party or of its own motion to:

(a) issue a warrant for the arrest and transfer of an accused who is not already in the custody of the Court;
(b) require the attendance and testimony of witnesses;
(c) require the production of documentary and other evidentiary materials;
(d) rule on the admissibility or relevance of evidence;
(e) protect confidential information; and
(f) maintain order in the course of a hearing.

II. PROPOSALS
AUSTRALIA AND NETHERLANDS
Rule 79 Preliminary motions by accused

(A) Preliminary motions open to the accused shall include:
(i) objections based on lack of jurisdiction;
(ii) objections based on defects in the form of the indictment;
(iii) applications for the exclusion of evidence obtained from the accused or having belonged to him or her;
(iv) applications for severance under rule 64;
(v) objections based on the denial of request for assignment of counsel.

(B) Any of the motions by the accused referred to in subrule (A) shall be brought within sixty days after his or her initial appearance, and in any case before the hearing on the merits.

(C) Failure to apply within the time limit prescribed shall constitute a waiver of the right. Upon a showing of good cause, the Trial Chamber may grant relief from the waiver.

[Note. Subrules (B) and (C) conflict with article 34 of the ILC draft statute.]

[*185] Rule 80
Opportunity to respond

Upon the submission of a motion, the other party shall be afforded a reasonable opportunity to respond to it. The supplementary rules may set time limits for responses.

Rule 81
Ruling on motions

Motions shall be decided as expeditiously as possible. A motion may be summarily denied on the grounds that insufficient allegations of fact or law have been set forth to justify further inquiry by the Trial Chamber.

Rule 94
Instruments of restraint

Instruments of restraint, such as handcuffs, shall not be used except as a precaution against escape during transfer or for security reasons, and shall be removed when the accused appears before a Trial Chamber.

Rule 116
Power of Trial Chambers to order production of additional evidence

A Trial Chamber may order either party to produce additional evidence. It may itself summon witnesses and order their attendance.

FRANCE
Article 99
Pre-trial detention and judicial supervision

The Trial Chamber, upon being seized of a case, must decide whether the accused is to be placed under judicial supervision or in pre-trial detention, in accordance with the rules and modalities laid down in articles 52 to 56.Appeals against decisions of the Trial Chamber concerning court supervision or pre-trial detention shall be submitted to the Appeals Chamber.

Article 100
Warrants issued by the Trial Chamber

Warrants issued by the Trial Chamber shall remain effective during the trial unless the Trial Chamber decides to terminate or modify them, of its own [*186] motion, on application by the prosecutor or the accused, or upon expiry of the four-month period referred to in article 56, paragraph 1.

Article 105
Determination of proof

The commission of a crime may be established by any method of proof and the Trial Chamber shall decide in accordance with its innermost conviction.

It may base its decision only on evidence submitted to it during the deliberations and discussed before it on an adversary basis.

The accused must have the benefit of the doubt.

Article 118
Request for judicial assistance

The provisions of Part 4, Title III, subtitle 2, of this Statute shall apply before the Trial Chamber.

The request for judicial assistance shall be made by the President of the Chamber. The President of the Chamber or a judge appointed by him may assist in the execution of the request for judicial assistance on the territory of the State to which the request is made.

Article 117
Decision to postpone

The Trial Chamber may, either of its own motion or at the request of the prosecutor or the accused, order postponement of the case to a later date in the interest of proper administration of justice and respect for the rights of the defence.

The parties shall be called upon to submit their observations. The decision shall be taken without prejudice to implementation of the provisions of article 99. It shall not be subject to appeal.

Article 120
Powers of the President

The President shall control the hearing and direct the deliberations. He shall reject anything which might compromise their dignity or prolong them without giving reason to hope for greater certainty in their results.

He shall have a duty to remain impartial in all circumstances.

He shall determine the order of the examination of the accused, the hearing of experts and the depositions of witnesses.

[*187] The accused, the witnesses, the experts and any person called to the bar shall be examined first of all by the President. Following this, the Prosecutor and the defence counsel of the accused may also examine them with the authorization of the President.

Article 121
Powers of the Chamber

1.   The Trial Chamber may of its own motion call witnesses or experts to appear or have placed before it any new evidence which it deems useful for ascertainment of the truth.

2.   The Prosecutor or the accused may request the appearance of a witness or of an expert who was not summoned to appear in accordance with article 118. The Chamber may deny such an appearance only if it can show that, for stated reasons, the appearance is not possible or if it will not contribute to ascertainment of the truth. The decision of the Chamber shall not be subject to appeal.

SINGAPORE

1. Subparagraph (b) to be amended to read:
     "(b)require the attendance and testimony of witnesses who appear before the Court;"
2. Subparagraph (c) to be amended to read:
     "(c)require the production of documentary and other evidential materials from witnesses who appear before the Court;"
3. Insert a new subparagraph (c) bis as follows:
     "(ca) request the assistance of States in the taking of testimony from witnesses and the production of documentary and other evidence;"

[*188] G. Amicus curiae
AUSTRALIA AND NETHERLANDS
Rule 96
Amicus curiae

A Trial Chamber may, if it considers it desirable for the proper determination of the case, invite or grant leave to a State, organization or person to appear before it and make submissions on any issue specified by the Chamber.

[*189] H. Records of proceedings
I. ILC DRAFT

6. The Chamber shall ensure that a complete record of the trial, which accurately reflects the proceedings, is maintained and preserved by the Registrar.

II. PROPOSALS
AUSTRALIA AND NETHERLANDS
Rule 97
Solemn undertaking by interpreters and translators

Before performing any duties, an interpreter or a translator shall solemnly undertake to do so faithfully, independently, impartially and with respect for the duty of confidentiality.

Rule 98
Records of proceedings and evidence

(A) The Registrar shall cause to be made and preserve a full and accurate record of all proceedings, including audio recordings, transcripts and, when deemed necessary by the Trial Chamber, video recordings.

FRANCE
Article 119
Recording of deliberations and preservation of evidence

1. The Registrar shall prepare and keep a complete record of all the deliberations, including a sound recording, the transcription thereof and, where deemed necessary by the Trial Chamber, an audiovisual record. The latter shall be made from fixed points.
2. The Trial Chamber may, with the consent of a person who had requested that the case be heard in camera, order the disclosure of all or part of the record of the deliberations in camera, if the reasons justifying proceedings in camera no longer exist.
3. The Registrar shall ensure the preservation and custody of all material evidence produced in the course of the proceedings.
4. The Trial Chamber shall determine whether photographs, video recordings or sound recordings may be taken during the hearing other than by the Registrar.
5. All sound or audiovisual recordings made during the deliberations may be used in the event of appeal or revision.
[*190] 6. Once the trial has concluded with a judgement that has become final, reproduction or full or partial broadcasting of these recordings, in such manner as is laid down in the rules of procedure, may be authorized by the President of the Court.

[*191] I. Trial procedures
AUSTRALIA AND NETHERLANDS
Rule 99
Opening statements
Before presentation of evidence by the Prosecutor, each party may make an opening statement. The defence may however elect to make its statement after the Prosecutor has concluded his presentation of evidence and before the presentation of evidence for the defence.

Rule 100
Presentation of evidence
(A) Each party is entitled to call witnesses and present evidence. Unless otherwise directed by the Trial Chamber in the interests of justice, evidence at the trial shall be presented in the following sequence:

(i)   evidence for the prosecution;

(ii) evidence for the defence;

(iii) prosecution evidence in rebuttal;

(iv) defence evidence in rejoinder;

(v) evidence ordered by the Trial Chamber pursuant to rule 116.

(B) Examination-in-chief, cross-examination and re-examination shall be allowed in each case. It shall be for the party calling a witness to examine him or her in chief, but a judge may at any stage put any question to the witness.

(C) The accused may, if he or she so desires, appear as a witness in his or her own defence.

Rule 101
Postponements
The Trial Chamber shall have the power to order a postponement of proceedings, proprio motu or on the application of either party, on the following grounds:[Grounds to be listed]

[*192] Rule 102
Closing arguments
After the presentation of all the evidence, the Prosecutor may present an initial argument, to which the defence may reply. The Prosecutor may, if he or she wishes, present a rebuttal argument, to which the defence may present a rejoinder.

[*193] Article 39
Principle of legality (nullum crimen sine lege) 56/
ILC DRAFT
An accused shall not be held guilty:

(a)   in the case of a prosecution with respect to a crime referred to in article 20 (a) to (d), unless the act or omission in question constituted a crime under international law;

(b)   in the case of a prosecution with respect to a crime referred to in article 20 (e), unless the treaty in question was applicable to the conduct of the accused;at the time the act or omission occurred.

[*194] Article 40*
Presumption of innocence
I. ILC DRAFT
An accused shall be presumed innocent until proved guilty in accordance with law. The onus is on the Prosecutor to establish the guilt of the accused beyond reasonable doubt.
II. PROPOSALS
Anyone [accused][charged with a criminal offence][suspected of committing a crime within the meaning of this statute] shall be presumed innocent until proved guilty [in accordance with law].[The onus is on the Prosecutor to establish the guilt of the accused][The accused is declared guilty only when the

---

56/   This article was not considered by the informal working group on procedural questions, fair trial and regrets of the accused, as it deals with other matters.

*   Article 40 is also dealt with in the report of the informal group on general principles of criminal law (see Part 3 bis above).

majority of the Trial Chamber considers that the guilt of the accused has been proved] beyond a reasonable doubt.

[*195] Article 41
Rights of the accused
I. ILC DRAFT

1.   In the determination of any charge under this Statute, the accused is entitled to a fair and public hearing, subject to article 43, and to the following minimum guarantees:

(a)   to be informed promptly and in detail, in a language which the accused understands, of the nature and cause of the charge;

(b)   to have adequate time and facilities for the preparation of the defence, and to communicate with counsel of the accused's choosing;

(c)   to be tried without undue delay;

(d)   subject to article 37 (2), to be present at the trial, to conduct the defence in person or through legal assistance of the accused's choosing, to be informed, if the accused does not have legal assistance, of this right and to have legal assistance assigned by the Court, without payment if the accused lacks sufficient means to pay for such assistance;

(e)   to examine, or have examined, the prosecution witnesses and to obtain the attendance and examination of witnesses for the defence under the same conditions as witnesses for the prosecution;

(f)   if any of the proceedings of or documents presented to the Court are not in a language the accused understands and speaks, to have, free of any cost, the assistance of a competent interpreter and such translations as are necessary to meet the requirements of fairness;

(g)   not to be compelled to testify or to confess guilt.

2.   Exculpatory evidence that becomes available to the Procuracy prior to the conclusion of the trial shall be made available to the defence. In case of doubt as to the application of this paragraph or as to the admissibility of the evidence, the Trial Chamber shall decide.

II. PROPOSALS

The accused shall be entitled to the following minimum guarantees:

A. Public hearing

1.   In the determination of any charge under this Statute, the accused, [in addition to the rights afforded to suspects under article [?]] is entitled to a fair and public hearing [by an independent and impartial tribunal]. The right to a public hearing is subject to the following exceptions:

[*196] (a) the deliberations of the Court shall be private;

(b)   the Trial Chamber may, of its own motion or at the request of the prosecutor, the accused, a victim or a witness, order, by a decision given in public, that the entire trial or a part thereof be held in camera:

(i)   for reasons connected with protection of public order or of human dignity;

(ii) to ensure the safety and protection of the accused, of the victims or of witnesses;

(c)   proceedings shall be held in camera as of right:

(i)   at the request of the accused if he was a minor at the time of the commission of the acts;

(ii) at the request of a witness or a victim who suffered sexual violence;

(d)   when in camera proceedings have been ordered, the judgement on the merits shall always be pronounced in a public hearing.

B. Notification of charge 57/

1.   The accused [Any one suspected of committing a crime within the meaning of this Statute] is entitled to be informed promptly [and in detail], in a language which the accused understands, of the [nature and cause of the] charge against him/her [and, to this end, to have the free assistance of a competent interpreter, and to be provided free of charge with a translation of the documents on the basis of which the

---

57/   Articles 26 and 30 of this compilation also currently contain provisions related to the right of suspects or accused to be notified of the charges. Delegations should consider where in the Statute or rules such rights would be most appropriately located.

[accused/suspect] is being questioned or that show why a measure infringing upon the [accused/suspect]'s liberty or property has been proposed].

[2. Anyone suspected of committing a crime within the meaning of this Statute must before being questioned, or when a measure infringing upon his liberty or property has been proposed and brought to his attention, be fully informed of the charges against him and the rights to which he is entitled as a suspect under paragraph [?] of article [?]].

C. Preparation of defence

1. The accused is entitled to have adequate time and facilities for the preparation of the defence, and to communicate with counsel of the accused's choosing.

2. All communications between lawyer and client shall be regarded as privileged, and consequently not subject to disclosure at trial, unless:

[*197] (i) the client consents to such disclosure; or

(ii) the client has voluntarily disclosed the content of the communication to a third party, and that third party then gives evidence of that disclosure.

D. Speedy trial

1. The accused shall enjoy the right to [be tried without undue delay] [a speedy and public trial by an impartial tribunal].

E. Right to counsel

1. Subject to article 37 (2), the accused is entitled to be present at the trial and

[to conduct the defence in person or through legal assistance of the accused's choosing]

[at all times, shall have the [prompt] assistance of competent counsel] [of the accused's choosing] and to be informed, if the accused does not have legal assistance, of this right and to have legal assistance assigned by the [Court] [Preliminary Investigations Chamber of the Court], without payment if the accused [lacks sufficient means to pay for such assistance] [is unable to secure the same by his/her own efforts].

2. Matters concerning the qualification of counsel, including counsel assigned by the Court shall be [provided in the rules of the Court] [determined as follows:

(a) counsel engaged by a suspect or an accused shall file his or her power of attorney with the Registrar at the earliest opportunity;

(b) a counsel shall be considered qualified to represent a suspect or accused if he or she satisfies the Registrar that he or she is admitted to the practice of law in a State;

(c) a person who has witnessed the crime for which the accused has been indicted may not act as counsel for the defence. A person may not act as counsel for the defence or shall be immediately dismissed from such office if it is proved or deemed very probable according to objective facts that:

(i) he or she has participated or is participating in any of the crimes being investigated in the proceedings;

(ii) he or she is a participant in the crime of aiding in the commission of those crimes, or of harbouring a suspect, or destroying or concealing evidence in connection with such crimes;

[*198] (iii) he or she is participating together with the accused in an illicit association or any other kind of illegal organization related to the crime that is being investigated in the proceedings;

(iv) he or she has participated or is participating in an attempt to escape by the accused.]

3. Matters concerning the assignment of counsel shall be [provided in the rules] [determined as follows:

(a) a list of counsel who speak one or both of the working languages of the Court, meet the requirements of paragraph [2] and have indicated their willingness to be assigned by the Court to indigent suspects or accused, shall be kept by the Registrar;

(b) the criteria for determination of indigency shall be established by the Registrar and approved by the judges;

(c) in assigning counsel to an indigent suspect or accused, the following procedure shall be observed:

(i) a request for assignment of counsel shall be made to the Registrar;

(ii) the Registrar shall inquire into the means of the suspect or accused and determine whether the criteria of indigency are met;

(iii) if he or she decides that the criteria are met, he or she shall assign counsel from the list; if he or she decides to the contrary, he or she shall inform the suspect or accused that the request is refused;

(d) the suspect or accused may seek from the Presidency a review of a decision to refuse a request; the decision of the Presidency shall be final; the procedure governing review by the Presidency shall be laid down in the supplementary rules;

(e) if a request is refused, a further request may be made by a suspect or an accused to the Registrar upon showing a change in circumstances;

(f) the Registrar shall, in consultation with the judges, establish the criteria for the payment of fees to assigned counsel;

(g) [if the suspect or an accused is not indigent, but does not wish to retain defence counsel, the Court shall nevertheless assign defence counsel from the list kept by the Registrar, and shall then seek to recover the cost of providing defence counsel according to the procedure laid down in subrule (h)];

[If a suspect or an accused person elects to conduct his or her own defence, he or she shall so notify the Registrar in writing at the first opportunity. However, if the Trial or Appeals Chamber considers that the technical defence is thereby impaired, it shall automatically order the assignment of defence counsel from the list kept by the Registrar];

(h) where an alleged indigent person is subsequently found not to be indigent, the Trial or Appeals Chamber may make an order of contribution to recover the cost of providing counsel for proceedings before that Chamber;

[*199] (i) no defence counsel may represent more than one indicted person or accused in the same trial;

(j) if the defence counsel of a suspect or accused resigns the defence or abandons it during the proceedings, the Trial or Appeals Chamber shall give the suspect or the accused a specific time period in which to retain other defence counsel. If, at the end of that time, the suspect or the accused has not retained counsel or stated his or her intention to defend him or herself in person, defence counsel shall be assigned automatically from the list kept by the Registrar. Subrules (g) and (h) will still apply.]

F. Examination of witnesses

1. The accused shall be entitled to examine or have examined [the prosecution witnesses] [witnesses against him/her] and to obtain the attendance and examination of witnesses [for the defence] [on his behalf] under the same conditions as witnesses [for the prosecution] [against him/her]. [In addition the accused shall also be entitled to present any other evidence.]

2. The accused may, if he or she so desires, [make an unsworn statement in his or her defence] appear as a witness in his or her own defence.

G. Interpretation and translation

1. Anyone suspected of committing a crime within the meaning of this Statute shall be entitled to be informed of the charges against him and questioned in a language which he understands and to this end, to have, free of any cost, the assistance of a competent interpreter and to be provided free of charge with a translation of the documents on the basis of which he is being questioned or that show why a measure infringing upon his liberty or property has been proposed.

2. If any of the proceedings of or documents presented to the Court are not in a language the accused understands and speaks, the accused is entitled to have, free of any cost, the assistance of a competent interpreter and such translations as are necessary to meet the requirements of fairness.

[3. The working languages of the Court shall be English and French.]

[4. Any other person appearing before the Court, other than as counsel, who does not have sufficient knowledge of either of the two working languages may use his or her own language and have the benefit of interpretation and translation on the basis of the same criteria applied to an accused under this article.] 58/

[5. Counsel for an accused may apply to the Presiding Judge of a Chamber for leave to use a language other than the two working ones or the language of the accused. If such leave is granted, the expenses of

---

58/ Paragraphs 3 to 7 could more appropriately to be added to article 18, concerning working languages, rather than be addressed in article 41, concerning the rights of the accused.

interpretation and translation shall be borne by the Court to the extent, if any, determined by the President, taking into account the rights of the defence and interests of justice.]

[*200] [6. Documents filed with the Court shall be in one of the working languages or accompanied by a translation into one of those languages.]

[7. The Registrar shall make any necessary arrangements for interpretation and translation into and from the working languages.]

H. Self-incrimination

1. The accused [anyone suspected of committing a crime within the meaning of this Statute] shall be entitled not to be compelled to testify [against himself/herself] or to confess guilt.

2. Anyone suspected of committing a crime within the meaning of this Statute shall be entitled to remain silent without such silence being taken into consideration by the Court at a later stage in the determination of his guilt or innocence.

3. No person shall be subject to torture or to cruel, inhuman or degrading treatment.

I. Disclosure of evidence

1. [Inculpatory evidence and] exculpatory evidence [evidence which in any way tends to suggest the innocence or mitigate the guilt of the accused or may affect the credibility of prosecution evidence][that becomes available][the existence of which is known] to the [Procuracy] [Prosecutor] prior to the conclusion of the trial shall be made available [disclosed] to the defence [as soon as practicable].

2. The duty to disclose is ongoing and if the Prosecutor discovers additional evidence or material which should have been produced earlier [pursuant to the rules] he shall promptly notify the other party and the Trial Chamber of the existence of the additional evidence or material.

3. The Prosecutor may request an ex parte hearing in camera before the Trial Chamber for the purpose of obtaining a ruling on whether or not particular evidence falls within the category of exculpatory evidence. In case of doubt as to the application of this [paragraph] or as to the admissibility of the evidence, the Trial Chamber shall decide.

4. The accused shall be entitled to have communicated to him or her all evidence submitted to the Court.

J. Search and seizure

The right of all persons to be secure in their homes, papers and effects against entries, searches and seizures shall not be impaired except upon warrant issued, in accordance with the rules of the Court, for adequate cause and particularly describing the place to be searched and things to be seized, or [*201] except on such grounds and in accordance with such procedures as are established by the rules of the Court.

K. Due process

1. No person shall be deprived of life or liberty, nor shall any other criminal penalty be imposed, without due process of law.

2. No person shall be found guilty unless the [Prosecutor proves beyond a reasonable doubt] [Court is convinced] that the accused has committed every element of the offence with which he/she is charged. 59/

[*202] Article 42
Non bis in idem
I. ILC DRAFT

1. No person shall be tried before any other court for acts constituting a crime of the kind referred to in article 20 for which that person has already been tried by the Court.

2. A person who has been tried by another court for acts constituting a crime of the kind referred to in article 20 may be tried under this Statute only if:

(a) the acts in question were characterized by that court as an ordinary crime and not as a crime which is within the jurisdiction of the Court; or

(b) the proceedings in the other court were not impartial or independent or were designed to shield the accused from international criminal responsibility or the case was not diligently prosecuted.

59/ This issue is also addressed above in Part 3 bis on general principles of criminal law.

3.   In considering the penalty to be imposed on a person convicted under this Statute, the Court shall take into account the extent to which a penalty imposed by another court on the same person for the same act has already been served.

II. PROPOSALS

1.   [No person shall be tried before any other court for acts constituting a crime referred to in article 20 for which that person already has been tried by the Court.] [Once convicted or acquitted by a final judgement of the Court] for acts constituting a crime of the kind referred to in article 20 a person may no longer be accused on the basis of the same evidence, even for a different offence, either by the organs of the Court or by the judicial authorities of the States Parties, unless new evidence is made known [in which case the Prosecutor of the Court may institute new proceedings].

2.   [No person shall be tried before any other court for acts constituting a crime referred to in article 20 for which that person already has been tried by the Court.] A person who has been tried by another court for acts constituting a crime of the kind referred to in article 20 may be tried under this Statute only if:

(a)   the acts in question were characterized by that court as an ordinary crime and not as a crime which is within the jurisdiction of the Court; or

(b)   the proceedings in the other court were not impartial or independent or were designed to shield the accused from international criminal responsibility or the case was not diligently prosecuted.

[*203] [2 bis. The court has no jurisdiction under this Statute when:

(a)   The acts mentioned in the submission to the Court are still being investigated by a State and the investigation is not manifestly intended to relieve the person concerned of criminal responsibility;

(b)   The acts mentioned in the submission to the Court have already been duly investigated by a State and the decision not to institute proceedings was taken by that State when it had knowledge of all the facts mentioned in the submission and the decision was not motivated by a manifest willingness to relieve the persons concerned of any criminal responsibility;

(c)   Any person(s) mentioned in the submission to the Court have already been acquitted or convicted by a final ruling in a State for the acts involved unless the decision failed to take account of all facts contained in the submission or the proceedings were conducted in the State concerned by evading the rule of international law for the manifest purpose of relieving the persons concerned of criminal responsibility.

3.   In considering the penalty to be imposed on a person convicted under this Statute, the Court shall take into account the extent to which a penalty imposed by another court on the same person for the same act has already been served.

[*204] Article 43
Protection of the accused, victims and witnesses
I. ILC DRAFT

The Court shall take necessary measures available to it to protect the accused, victims and witnesses and may to that end conduct closed proceedings or allow the presentation of evidence by electronic or other special means.

II. PROPOSALS
A. Victims and Witnesses Services Unit (Rights of the victims)

[(a) The Court shall ensure the safety of the accused, victims and witnesses, as well as that of their families, from intimidation and retaliation before, during and after the trial. To this end a special service shall be established to achieve that purpose and States Parties should cooperate with this service in their respective territories. In particular this service, as well as States Parties, shall take additional measures to protect the integrity, privacy and physical and psychological well-being of victims of sexual assault and of children who are victims or witnesses.";

(b)   Legal representatives of victims of crimes have the right to participate in the proceedings with a view to presenting additional evidence needed to establish the basis of criminal responsibility as a foundation for their right to pursue civil compensation;

(c)   The judgement of the Court shall also include a determination of the scope and extent of the victimization in order to allow victims to rely on that judgement for the pursuit of civil remedies, including compensation, either in national courts or through their Governments, in accordance with international law;

(d)   The rules of procedure shall include provisions giving effect to the United Nations Declaration of Basic Principles of Justice for Victims of Crime and Abuse of Power adopted by the General Assembly in its resolution 40/34 of 29 November 1985, which was recalled by the Economic and Social Council in its resolution 1996/14 of 23 July 1996 in paragraph 6 of which the Council "requests the Secretary-General to bring to the attention of the Preparatory Committee for the Establishment of an International Criminal Court the potential applicability of the basic principles, contained in the Declaration", and the Principles Guaranteeing the Rights and Interests of Victims in the Proceeding of the Proposed International Criminal Court adopted by the Commission on Crime Prevention and Criminal Justice.]

* * *

Victims and Witnesses Unit

[(A) There shall be set up under the authority of the Registrar a Victims and Witnesses Unit consisting of qualified staff to:

[*205]   (i)   recommend protective measures for victims and witnesses in accordance with article X (A 43 ILC) of the Statute;

(ii)   provide counselling and support for them, in particular in cases of rape and sexual assault.

(B)   Due consideration shall be given, in the appointment of staff, to the employment of qualified women.]

B. Measures for protection

[As provided for in article X (A 38 (4), 43 ILC) of the Statute a] [the] Trial Chamber may [proprio motu or] at the request of [either party] [the Prosecutor, the accused [or of] the victim or the witness concerned [or of the Victims and Witnesses Unit] order appropriate measures to protect the privacy and security protection of victims and witnesses, provided the said measures are [consistent with] [not prejudicial to] the rights of the accused [as provided for in the Statute and the rules, in particular the right to examine, or have examined, prosecution witnesses]. [The States Parties are required, where necessary, to execute these measures, subject to observance of their internal law].

The [a] Trial Chamber may hold a hearing [proceeding] in camera [to determine] [for the purpose of determining, without prejudice to the rights of the accused] [whether to order] [the necessity of ordering]:

(a)   measures to prevent disclosure to the public or the [information] media of the identity [or whereabouts] of a victim or a witness, of persons related to them or associated with them, [or of their locality], by such means as:

(i)   [deletion from the court records of the name of the person concerned and of particulars by means of which he might be identified] [expunging names and identifying information from the Chamber's public records];

(ii)   [prohibition of access by the public to any evidence in the file by means of which the victim might be identified] [non-disclosure to the public of any records identifying the victim];

(iii) [the use during testimony of [image or voice altering devices] [of technical methods for altering appearances or voices] or [the use of] closed circuit television];

(iv) [assignment of a pseudonym]; 60/

(b)   [closed sessions, in accordance with rule 91] [the holding of hearings in camera, in accordance with article 38];

(c)   appropriate measures to facilitate testimony [of vulnerable victims and] [by a victim or by a vulnerable] witness[es], [such as] [by means of] [one-way] closed circuit television.

[*206] [A Trial Chamber shall, whenever necessary, control the manner of questioning to avoid any harassment or intimidation.]

* * *

60/   Concerns were raised regarding the restriction of the right of the accused to cross-examine and contradict witnesses that the measures provided for in sections (iii) and (iv) may lead to.

Rule 86
Protection of victims and witnesses

[(A) In exceptional circumstances, the Prosecutor may apply to a Trial Chamber to order the non-disclosure of the identity of a victim or witness who may be in danger or at risk until such person is brought under the protection of the Tribunal.

(B) In the determination of protective measures for victims and witnesses, the Trial Chamber may consult the Victims and Witnesses Unit.

(C) Subject to rule 95, the identity of the victim or witness shall be disclosed in sufficient time prior to the trial to allow adequate time for preparation of the defence.]

[Note. The protection of victims and witnesses will be an important responsibility of the Court. The non-disclosure of the identity of victims and witnesses needs to be balanced against the right of an accused to prepare his or her defence.]

C. Compensation to the accused

1.   The Court shall make compensation to those who were:

(a) Pronounced innocent by an irrevocable adjudication;

(b) Arrested or detained for the purpose of prosecution, although the prosecution against him did not eventually take place;

(c) Arrested or detained but the lawfulness of that arrest or detention was denied in accordance with this Statute; or

(d) Illegally inflicted losses upon by an officer of the Court intentionally or negligently in the course of performing its duties.

2.   Procedures and criteria for compensation shall be provided in the rules including the expenses to be borne by a complainant State if that State lodged a complaint without sufficient reason.

* * *

The Appeals Chamber may grant compensation to a person who was held in pre-trial detention during proceedings against him that have concluded with a final decision of acquittal. The compensation shall be based on the prejudice caused to him by such detention.

If the Preliminary Investigations Chamber decides to release the person concerned because his arrest or detention was unlawful, it may award him compensation.

[*207] Article 44
Evidence
I. ILC DRAFT

1.   Before testifying, each witness shall, in accordance with the Rules, give an undertaking as to the truthfulness of the evidence to be given by that witness.

2.   States parties shall extend their laws of perjury to cover evidence given under this Statute by their nationals, and shall cooperate with the Court in investigating and where appropriate prosecuting any case of suspected perjury.

3.   The Court may require to be informed of the nature of any evidence before it is offered so that it may rule on its relevance or admissibility.

4.   The Court shall not require proof of facts of common knowledge but may take judicial notice of them.

5.   Evidence obtained by means of a serious violation of this Statute or of other rules of international law shall not be admissible.

II. PROPOSALS
A. Determination of proof
GERMANY

In order to determine the truth, the court shall, ex officio, extend the taking of evidence to all facts and evidence that are important for the decision. The court will decide on the taking of evidence according to its [free] conviction obtained from the entire trial.

FRANCE
Article 105
Determination of proof
The commission of a crime may be established by any method of proof and the Trial Chamber shall decide in accordance with its innermost conviction.

It may base its decision only on evidence submitted to it during the deliberations and discussed before it on an adversary basis.

The accused must have the benefit of the doubt.

[*208] NETHERLANDS
Article 44a
Evidentiary sources. Rule of legal reasoning and exclusionary rule
1.   The Trial Chamber shall rely [for the determination of guilt] only on the following means of evidence, presented or realized on trial in open court:

(a)   the confession or admission of the accused;

(b)   the testimony of witnesses and experts;

(c)   documents drafted in their legal form in accordance with the legal procedures either of the administering State or of the Court;

(d)   the judicial observations.

2.   No judgement containing a determination of guilt shall be based only on the confession of the accused nor can any judgement be based on one testimony alone.

3.   Decisions of evidentiary nature shall be based on reasons explicitly stated in the judgement.

Article 44b
Evidence obtained by national authorities
1.   The Court has, in case of evidence obtained by national authorities, to presume irrebuttably that the national authorities acted in accordance with the domestic provisions.

2.   In case of a plea on behalf of the accused to the contrary of this presumption, the Court may refer the accused in that respect to the national procedures of the administering State to decide on that plea. The Court may decide to a discontinuation of procedure during that referral until an irrevocable decision of the administering State has been received [by the Registrar].

3.   In case the Court rejected a motion on behalf of the accused for application for referral in accordance with paragraph 2 or for discontinuation of procedure, the accused shall have the right of appeal on the ground of non-compliance with the rules of evidence.

4.   In case the Court decided to a referral or discontinuation of procedure in accordance with paragraph 2, the Prosecutor shall have the right of appeal on the ground mentioned in paragraph 3.

[*209] B. Undertaking as to truthfulness
[See paragraph 1 of the ILC draft.]
AUSTRALIA AND NETHERLANDS
Rule 106
Testimony of witnesses
(A)   Witnesses shall, in principle, be heard directly by the Chambers unless a Chamber has ordered that the witness be heard by means of a deposition [see note on section 5 of Part IX].

(B)   Every witness shall, before giving evidence, make the following solemn declaration: "I solemnly declare that I will speak the truth, the whole truth and nothing but the truth."

(C)   A child who, in the opinion of the Chamber, does not understand the nature of a solemn declaration, may be permitted to testify without that formality, if the Chamber is of the opinion that he or she is sufficiently mature to be able to report the facts of which he or she had knowledge and that he or she understands the duty to tell the truth. A judgement, however, cannot be based on such testimony alone.

(D)   A witness, other than an expert, who has not yet testified shall not be present when the testimony of another witness is given. However, a witness who has heard the testimony of another witness shall not for that reason alone be disqualified from testifying.

(E)   A witness may object to making any statement which might tend to incriminate him or her. The Chamber may, however, compel the witness to answer the question. Testimony compelled in this way shall not be used as evidence in a subsequent prosecution against the witness for any offence other than perjury. 61/

FRANCE
Article 122
Testimony

...

3.   Each witness shall, at the request of the President, state his name, forenames, age, occupation and domicile or place of residence. The President may dispense a witness from the requirement to reveal his identity, his occupation or his domicile or place of residence. Before commencing their testimony, the witnesses shall declare on oath that they will speak without hatred and without fear and that they will speak the truth and only the truth.

[*210] C. Perjury: punishable by national courts v. the Court
[See paragraph 2 of the ILC draft.]
AUSTRALIA AND THE NETHERLANDS
SECTION 3. CONTEMPT OF COURT, MISCONDUCT AND PERJURY

[As is the case with national courts, the Court must have the power to deal with contempt and perjury. The Statute should address the point with necessary elaboration to be undertaken in the rules. Following for information is rule 77 of the Rules of the Tribunal for the former Yugoslavia dealing with contempt:

Rule 77
Contempt of the Tribunal

(A)   Subject to the provisions of subrule 90(E), a witness who refuses or fails contumaciously to answer a question relevant to the issue before a Chamber may be found in contempt of the Tribunal. The Chamber may impose a fine not exceeding US$ 10,000 or a term of imprisonment not exceeding six months.

(B)   The Chamber may, however, relieve the witness of the duty to answer, for reasons which it deems appropriate.

(C)   Any person who attempts to interfere with or intimidate a witness may be found guilty of contempt and sentenced in accordance with subrule (A).

(D)   Any judgement rendered under this rule shall be subject to appeal.

(E)   Payment of a fine shall be made to the Registrar to be held in a separate account.][The Court will also need the power to deal with the misconduct of counsel. Following for information is rule 46 of the Rules of the Tribunal for the former Yugoslavia dealing with this matter:

Rule 46
Misconduct of Counsel

(A) A Chamber may, after a warning, refuse audience to counsel if, in its opinion, his conduct is offensive, abusive or otherwise obstructs the proper conduct of the proceedings.

(B)   A judge or a Chamber may also, with the approval of the President, communicate any misconduct of counsel to the professional body regulating the conduct of counsel in his State of admission or, if a professor and not otherwise admitted to the profession, to the governing body of his University.][The Court must also be able to deal with perjury. Article 44(2) of the ILC draft Statute currently provides for the States parties to extend their laws of perjury to cover evidence given by their nationals. This provision has been criticized and it has been proposed that the Statute deal with the issue of [*211] perjury. One of the shortcomings of article 44(2) is that it would not cover the situation where the national of a non-State party was giving evidence. Following for information is rule 91 of the Rules of the Tribunal for the former Yugoslavia:

61/   There is a need to list fully the grounds on which a witness could refuse to give evidence, for example, where a witness is the spouse of an accused.

<u>Rule 91</u>
False testimony under Solemn Declaration

(A)   A Chamber, on its own initiative or at the request of a party, may warn a witness of the duty to tell the truth and the consequences that may result from a failure to do so.

(B)   If a Chamber has strong grounds for believing that a witness has knowingly and wilfully given false testimony, it may direct the Prosecutor to investigate the matter with a view to the preparation and submission of an indictment for false testimony.

(C)   The rules of procedure and evidence in Parts Four to Eight shall apply <u>mutatis mutandis</u> to proceedings under this Rule.

(D)   No judge who sat as a member of the Trial Chamber before which the witness appeared shall sit for the trial of the witness for false testimony.

(E)   The maximum penalty for false testimony under solemn declaration shall be a fine of US$ 10,000 or a term of imprisonment of twelve months, or both. The payment of any fine imposed shall be made to the Registrar to be held in the account referred to in subrule 77(E).]

[<u>Note</u>. An alternative view on dealing with contempt and perjury is that States should punish their nationals for committing contempt and perjury when appearing as witnesses before the Court.]

FRANCE
Article 124
Perjury

If, following the deliberations, the testimony of a witness appears to be false, the Trial Chamber shall request the Registrar to prepare a record of this testimony, which shall be transmitted promptly to the judicial authorities of the State that may undertake prosecution of the witness. The States parties shall extend the provisions of their legislation that are applicable to perjury to testimony given by their nationals under this Statute.

JAPAN

The detailed regulations of procedure concerning trial and judgement including perjury shall be provided in the rules of the Court.

[*212] D. <u>Offences against the integrity of the Court</u>
Article Perjury

A person who:

(a)   has given to an organ of the International Criminal Court <u>62/</u> an undertaking as to truthfulness <u>63/</u> regarding testimony, or any written statement made by him or her; and

(b)   intentionally and contrary to such undertaking communicates any material matter in that testimony or statement that he or she does not believe to be true;

shall be punished by a maximum of [five] years' imprisonment.

<u>Article Influencing, impeding or retaliating against officials of the Court 64/</u>

A person who:

(a)   directly or indirectly offers anything of value to an official of the International Criminal Court with intent to corruptly influence any official act; or

(b)   uses physical force, intimidation, or threats against [an official of the International Criminal Court] [any person] with intent to impede, intimidate, or interfere with an official of the International Criminal Court while performing official duties, or with intent to retaliate against such official on account of the performance of official duties;

shall be punished by a maximum of [ten] years' imprisonment.

<u>Article Obstructing the functions of the Court</u>

1.   A person who:

<u>62/</u>   There will be a need to define "organ of the International Criminal Court".
<u>63/</u>   ILC article 44 (1) provides for an "undertaking" as to the truthfulness of matters asserted before the Court.
<u>64/</u>   There will be a need to define the term "official of the Court".

(a)   intentionally uses physical force, intimidation, or threats against another with intent to prevent the attendance or testimony of [any] [such] person or the production of evidence in a proceeding of the International [*213] Criminal Court, or prevent the communication of material information regarding a crime under this statute, an investigation or proceeding before the Court;

(b)   intentionally uses physical force, intimidation, or threats against another with intent to retaliate against [any] [such] person for attendance, testimony, or the production of evidence in a proceeding of the International Criminal Court, or the communication of material information regarding a crime under this Statute or an investigation or proceeding before the Court; or

(c)   directly or indirectly offers anything of value to another with intent to prevent the attendance or testimony of [any] [such] person, the production of evidence in a proceeding of the International Criminal Court, or the communication of material information regarding a crime under this statute. an investigation or proceeding before the Court;

shall be punished by a maximum of [10] years' imprisonment.

2.   A person who:

destroys, alters or conceals a record or other object with intent to withhold it or impair its integrity in an investigation or proceeding before the International Criminal Court;

shall be punished by a maximum of [ten] years' imprisonment.

Article Contempt

The Court shall have the power to punish by fine or [ ] months' imprisonment, at its discretion, such contempt of its authority as:

(a)   misbehaviour of any person in its presence or so near thereto as to obstruct the administration of justice; or

(b)   misbehaviour of any of its officials in their official transactions.

[Note. The question arises as to whether attempt and other inchoate crimes should be punishable. This issue is related to general principles of criminal law.

There is also an issue of whether actions to influence those involved in official Court matters by trick, harassment, or other methods should also be punishable.

There is also the question of whether the regime for cooperation or enforcement regarding these crimes would be the same as for the core crimes.]

E. Determination of relevance and admissibility
[See paragraph 3 of the ILC draft.]
[*214] AUSTRALIA AND NETHERLANDS
Rule 105
General provisions

(A)   The rules of evidence set forth in this section together with article X (A 44 ILC) of the Statute shall govern the proceedings before the Trial Chambers. The Chambers shall not be bound by national rules of evidence.

(B)   In cases not otherwise provided for in this section, a Trial Chamber shall apply rules of evidence which will best favour a fair determination of the matter before it and are consonant with the spirit of the Statute and the general principles of law.

(C)   A Trial Chamber may admit any relevant evidence which it deems to have probative value. Irrelevant evidence shall not be admitted.

(D)   A Trial Chamber may exclude evidence if its probative value is substantially outweighed by the need to ensure a fair trial.

(E)   A Trial Chamber may request verification of the authenticity of evidence obtained out of court.

(F)   The Trial Chamber shall place on the record its reasons for excluding relevant evidence.

Rule 106
Testimony of witnesses

(A)   Witnesses shall, in principle, be heard directly by the Chambers unless a Chamber has ordered that the witness be heard by means of a deposition [see note on section 5 of Part IX].

Rule 108
Confessions

(A) A confession or admission by the accused given during questioning by the Prosecutor shall, provided the relevant requirements of the Statute and rules were strictly complied with, be presumed to have been free and voluntary unless the contrary is proved.

(B) A confession or admission by a suspect given during questioning by the Prosecutor shall, provided the relevant requirements of the Statute and rules were strictly complied with, be presumed to have been free and voluntary unless the contrary is proved.

(C) A confession or admission by a suspect given during questioning by national authorities shall, provided the relevant requirements of the Statute and the rules were strictly complied with, be presumed to have been free and voluntary unless the contrary is proved.

[*215] (D) A confession is an out-of-court acknowledgement of guilt of any element of an offence of any out-of-court self-incriminating statement made by an individual. An admission is any other statement made by an individual with respect to his or her participation or participation in an offence.

Rule 109
Evidence of consistent pattern of conduct

(A) Evidence of a consistent pattern of conduct relevant to serious violations of international humanitarian law under the Statute may be admissible in the interests of justice.

(B) Acts tending to show such a pattern of conduct shall be disclosed by the Prosecutor to the defence pursuant to rule 82.

Rule 111
Agreements by the parties regarding facts in issue

(A) The parties may make oral or written agreements that a fact in issue should be considered proven without the need for evidence to be produced.

(B) The Trial Chamber may, in the interest of justice, decline to accept an agreement under subrule

Rule 113
Evidence in cases of sexual assault

In cases of sexual assault:

(i)   No corroboration of the victim's testimony shall be required;

(ii) Consent shall not be allowed as a defence if the victim

(a)   Has been subjected to or threatened with or has had reason to fear violence, duress, detention or psychological oppression, or

(b)   Reasonably believed that if the victim did not submit, another might be so subjected, threatened or put in fear;

(iii) Before evidence of the victim's consent is admitted, the accused shall satisfy the Trial Chamber in camera that the evidence is relevant and credible;

(iv) Prior sexual conduct of the victim shall not be admitted in evidence.

[Note. Should there be an absolute prohibition on prior sexual conduct of a victim being admitted in evidence?]

[*216] Rule 114
Joint trials

In joint trials, evidence which is admissible against only some of the joint or several accused may be considered only against the accused concerned.

ARGENTINA
Rule 89 bis

(A) Whenever it is necessary to carry out a reconnaissance, inspection, reconstruction or a scientific or technical test that, because of its nature and characteristics cannot be reproduced in full at a later stage during the trial, or whenever it is assumed that a witness will not be able to testify during trial because of some unsurmountable obstacle, the Prosecutor shall request the Presidency to appoint a judge to carry out or supervise the act.

(B) The judge shall carry out or supervise the act in question notifying the Prosecutor, the accused and his or her counsel, who shall be authorized to be present and shall have the same right to intervene as during the rest of the trial. If the accused is detained, his or her counsel shall act in the accused's behalf, unless the accused expressly asks to be present in person, provided his place of detention is in the territory where the act is to be carried out.

(C)   When the accused is yet unknown or any of the acts described under (A) is extremely urgent, the Prosecutor may request the Presidency orally to appoint a judge, who shall carry out or supervise the act. The notifications provided in (B) shall not be necessary but a counsel for the defence shall be appointed ex officio to control the act or to take part in it.

Rule 113
(It is suggested that paragraph (b) (iv) be omitted.)
FRANCE
Article 114
Defence of nullity and plea of inadmissibility of evidence
The Trial Chamber shall have competence to rule on defences based on nullity of the proceedings prior to the opening of the trial. It shall also have competence to rule on defences based on the inadmissibility of evidence recorded during the investigation of the accused, particularly with respect to its compatibility with the rights of the defence.

These defences, to be admissible, must be raised by the parties at the opening of the trial, prior to the reading of the confirmed indictment.

The Trial Chamber may rule on these defences by a decision separate from the judgement on the merits and such decision may be appealed to the Appeals Chamber in the manner provided for in article 7 of this Statute.

[*217] JAPAN
Evidence
1.   The accused shall be permitted full opportunity to examine all witnesses, and he/she shall have the right of compulsory process for obtaining witnesses on his/her behalf at public expense.

2.   A document, audio recording, or video recording containing a statement of a person other than the accused, which was given before a judge of the court of a State Party, is admissible in evidence when that person is not able to testify before the Court because of death, illness, injury, old age or other good cause.

4.   Confession made under compulsion, torture or threat, or after prolonged arrest, provisional arrest or detention, or which is suspected not to have been made voluntarily shall not be admitted in evidence.

5.   No person shall be convicted or punished in all cases where the only proof against him/her is his/her own conviction.

6.   The right of all persons to be secure in their homes, papers and effects against entries, searches and seizures shall not be impaired except upon warrant issued, in accordance with the rules of the Court, for adequate cause and particularly describing the place to be searched and things to be seized, or except on such grounds and in accordance with such procedure as are established by the rules of the Court.

7.   No person shall be found guilty unless the Prosecutor proves beyond a reasonable doubt that the defendant has committed every element of the offence with which he/she is charged.

F. Facts of common knowledge
[See paragraph 4 of the ILC draft.]
[*218] AUSTRALIA AND NETHERLANDS
Rule 110
Judicial notice
A Trial Chamber shall not require proof of facts of common knowledge but shall take judicial notice thereof.

G. Exclusion of evidence
[See paragraph 5 of the ILC draft.]
AUSTRALIA AND NETHERLANDS
Rule 112
Evidence obtained by means contrary to internationally protected human rights

No evidence shall be admissible if obtained by methods which cast substantial doubt on its reliability or if its admission is antithetical to, and would seriously damage, the integrity of the proceedings.

ARGENTINA
Rule 112

No evidence shall be admissible if obtained by methods which cast substantial doubt on its reliability. The tribunal shall not admit evidence obtained in violation to this Statute or the rules subsequently made by the Court or by means which constitute a violation to internationally protected human rights.

NETHERLANDS
Article 44a
Evidentiary sources. Rule of legal reasoningand exclusionary rule

4.   No evidence shall be admissible if obtained by methods which cast substantial doubts on its reliability or if its admission is antithetical to, and would seriously damage, the integrity of the proceedings [international standards of due process].

JAPAN

Evidence obtained by means of a serious violation of this Statute or International Covenant on Civil and Political Rights shall not be admitted in evidence.

H. Privileges
AUSTRALIA AND NETHERLANDS
Rule 115
Lawyer-client privilege

All communications between lawyer and client shall be regarded as privileged, and consequently not subject to disclosure at trial, unless:

(i)   the client consents to such disclosure; or

[*219] (ii)   the client has voluntarily disclosed the content of the communication to a third party, and that third party then gives evidence of that disclosure.

ARGENTINA
Rule 106

...

(F)   The spouse of the accused, his or her ascendants, descendants, close relatives by consanguinity or adoption, whoever lives with the accused or is bound to him or her by ties of affection shall be exempted from testifying. They shall be informed of their right to refrain from testifying before giving testimony. They shall have the right to refrain from testifying even when giving testimony or with respect to some questions only.

(G)   A person who, with respect to the object of his or her testimony is under the obligation to keep a professional, official or private secret may not be admitted as a witness. Should such witness be summoned before the Court, he or she shall present himself or herself and explain the reason why he or she is under the obligation to keep a secret and to refrain from testifying.

(H)   If the Trial Chamber considers that the witness is wrong about invoking his or her right to refrain from testifying or to keep a secret, it shall order him or her to give testimony.

FRANCE
Article 125
Confidentiality of communications between the accused and his defence counsel

1.   The accused and his defence counsel may converse to the extent necessary for the organization of the defence, without their conversation being supervised.

2.   All communications between an accused and his defence counsel shall be covered by professional secrecy and their disclosure may not be ordered unless:

(a)   the accused consents to their disclosure;

(b)   the accused has voluntarily disclosed their contents to a third party and this third party refers to them during the trial.

[*220] I. Procedure for depositions
FRANCE
Article 122
Testimony

1. In principle, the Trial Chamber shall hear witnesses in person.
However, in exceptional circumstances and in the interest of justice, the Trial Chamber may, of its own motion or at the request of the prosecutor or the accused, order that a deposition be taken for the purposes of the trial in the manner provided in article 118.

2. The witnesses shall testify separately from each other, in the order determined by the President.

4. A minor or a person whose judgement has been impaired and who, in the opinion of the Chamber, does not understand the nature of an oath, may be allowed to testify without this formality if the Chamber considers that they are able to describe acts which came to their knowledge and that they understand the meaning of the duty to speak the truth. However, a judgement may not be based on such testimony alone.

5. A witness, other than an expert, who has not yet given evidence, may not be present during the testimony of another witness. However, if he has heard that other testimony this does not mean that his own testimony is inadmissible.

J. National defence secrets
FRANCE
Article 123
Secrecy on defence grounds

1. Any person heard or examined by the Trial Chamber may invoke restrictions provided for in his national law and designed to prevent the divulgation of confidential information connected with national defence.

2. The Trial Chamber may ask the State of which the persons being heard or examined are nationals whether it confirms their claim to be bound to secrecy.
If the State confirms to the Trial Chamber that an obligation of secrecy exists, the Chamber shall note this fact.

3. The provisions of the preceding paragraphs shall also apply to execution of a request for judicial assistance made under article 72.

[*221] ISRAEL
Article 44

In paragraph 2, replace the word "perjury" with the words "false testimony".In paragraph 3, after the words "relevance or admissibility", add the words "after hearing the parties to the case".Add a new paragraph 5 bis reading:"With regard to defences open to the accused under the general principles of criminal law in this statute, the onus of proof shall be on the accused, subject to a preponderance of probability as applicable in civil cases."

[*222] Article 45
Quorum and judgement
I. ILC DRAFT

1. At least four members of the Trial Chamber must be present at each stage of the trial.

2. The decisions of the Trial Chamber shall be taken by a majority of the judges. At least three judges must concur in a decision as to conviction or acquittal and as to the sentence to be imposed.

3. If after sufficient time for deliberation a Chamber which has been reduced to four judges is unable to agree on a decision, it may order a new trial.

4. The deliberations of the Court shall be and remain secret.

5. The judgement shall be in writing and shall contain a full and reasoned statement of the findings and conclusions. It shall be the sole judgement issued, and shall be delivered in open court.

II. PROPOSALS
A. Preliminary procedural questions
1.   The Preliminary Investigations Chamber shall proceed to consider the indictment and any amendment thereto together with all accompanying evidence.
2.   It shall take a decision:
   (a)   on the admissibility of the case on the basis of the reasons listed in article 35, 65/ if the Court has not yet ruled on this issue;
   (b)   on the serious nature of the charges against the person or persons named in the indictment with respect to an offence within the Court's jurisdiction.

B. Quorum and presence of judges
1.   [At least four] [All] members of the Trial Chamber must be present at each stage of the trial. [The decision shall be taken by the judges who attended throughout the deliberations.]

C. Deliberations/Secrecy of deliberations
1.   [When both parties have completed their presentation of the case] [Following submission by the Prosecutor and the pleadings of the accused], the [*223] Presiding Judge shall declare the [hearing closed] [deliberations concluded], and the Trial Chamber shall [withdraw to] deliberate in [private] [camera].
2.   The deliberations of the Court shall be and remain [secret] [confidential].
3.   The Trial Chamber shall vote separately on each charge contained in the indictment. If two or more accused are tried together under rule ___, 66/ separate findings shall be made as to each accused.

D. Pronouncement of judgement/Majority decision
1.   [The decisions of the Trial Chamber shall be taken by a majority of the judges.] [At least three] [All] judges must concur in a decision as to conviction [or acquittal] and [at least three judges must concur] as to the sentence to be imposed.
2.   The accused shall be found guilty only if [a majority of] the Trial Chamber considers that his guilt has been proved beyond reasonable doubt.
3.   The Trial Chamber shall pronounce its finding separately for each charge in the indictment. If several accused are tried together, the Chamber shall rule separately on the case of each one of them.
4.   Where necessary, it shall also establish principles relating to compensation for damage caused to the victims and to restitution of property unlawfully acquired by the persons convicted.
5.   The judgement shall be [pronounced] [delivered] [at a public hearing] [in open court] on a date to be notified to the parties and to the counsel and at which [they] [the latter] shall be entitled to be present.
6.   If the Trial Chamber finds the accused guilty it shall decide on the sentence by a majority vote.
7.   The detailed regulations of procedure concerning judgement shall be provided in the rules of the Court.

E. Mistrial/Failure to reach a verdict
1.   [If after sufficient time for deliberation a Chamber which has been reduced to four judges is unable to agree on a decision, it may order a new trial.]
[Note. Some delegations were of the view that in such circumstances, the accused would be entitled to an acquittal.]

F. Judgements/Dissenting opinions
1.   The [judgement] [grounds for the judgement] shall be given in writing [as soon as possible] and shall contain:
   [a full and reasoned statement of the findings and conclusions]
[*224] [(a) the name of the tribunal and the date it is delivered, the first names and surname of the accused and any other personal data that may help to determine his identity;
   (b)   the description of the facts and circumstances set forth in the indictment or its amendment;
   (c)   the vote of the judges and a brief exposition of their grounds on fact and law;
   (d)   the precise determination of the fact that the Trial Chamber deems proved;

65/   The provision in the current ILC text dealing with admissibility of a case.
66/   The provision on joint trials, currently contained in rule 62 of the Australia/Netherlands paper (A/AC.249/L.2).

(e)   the verdict, mentioning the legal dispositions applicable;

(f)   the signatures of the judges, but if one of the members of the Trial Chamber were unable to sign the judgement because of an impediment [posterior] [subsequent] to the deliberation and voting, the fact shall be recorded and the judgement shall be valid without his or her signature][The judgement shall not exceed the facts and circumstances described in the indictment or in its amendment, if any].It [shall be the sole judgement issued] [may contain dissenting opinions].

G. Compensation for the victims

1.   The Registrar shall transmit to the competent authorities of the States concerned the judgement by which the accused was found guilty of an offence which caused damage to the victim.

2.   The victims or his successors and assigns may, in accordance with the applicable national law, institute proceedings in a national jurisdiction or any other competent institution in order to obtain compensation for the prejudice caused to them.

3.   The judgement of the Court shall be binding on the national jurisdictions of every State party as regards the criminal liability of the person convicted and the principles relating to compensation for damage caused to victims and the restitution of property unlawfully acquired by the person convicted.

[Note. The fifth paragraph of article 127 of the French paper (A/AC.249/L.3) dealing with the power of the Court to establish principles relating to compensation and restitution is found in section D (Pronouncement of judgement/majority decision) above.]

H. Consequences of a judgement on the individual

1.   If the accused is acquitted, if he is sentenced to payment of a fine or if he is sentenced to a term of imprisonment already covered by his period in detention, he shall be released immediately unless he is retained for another case by the organs of the Court or by the judicial authorities of a State Party.

2.   In all other cases, the Trial Chamber may, if the circumstances justify prolongation of a measure of security, by a special reasoned decision, maintain [*225] the detention of the accused. In this case, so long as the judgement is not final and during appeal proceedings, if any, the convicted person shall remain in detention until such time as the period of detention equals the sentence handed down, without prejudice to application of the provisions of article____. 67/

[*226] Article 46
Sentencing
I. ILC DRAFT

1.   In the event of a conviction, the Trial Chamber shall hold a further hearing to hear any evidence relevant to sentence, to allow the Prosecutor and the defence to make submissions and to consider the appropriate sentence to be imposed.

2.   In imposing sentence, the Trial Chamber should take into account such factors as the gravity of the crime and the individual circumstances of the convicted person.

II. PROPOSALS

1.   [In the event of a conviction, the Trial Chamber shall hold a further hearing [pre-sentencing hearing] to hear any evidence relevant to sentence, to allow the Prosecutor and the defence to make submissions and to consider the appropriate sentence to be imposed.] [The Trial Chamber should take into account such factors as the gravity of the crime and the individual circumstances of the convicted person.] [These submissions may go to aggravation, extenuation or mitigation evidence, or the issue of rehabilitation.]

1 bis.   [At such hearing the parties shall ordinarily present submissions in the following manner:

(a)   presentation by the Prosecutor;

(b)   presentation by the defence;

(c)   prosecution rebuttal;

(d)   defence surrebuttal;

(e)   argument by the Prosecutor on sentence;

(f)   argument by the defence on sentence.]

67/   Provision on pre-trial detention [and judicial supervision]; see article 29 of the ILC draft and article 99 of the French paper (A/AC.249/L.3).

2. [The Trial Chamber may impose the penalties provided for in the Statute.]
3. [The Trial Chamber shall indicate whether multiple sentences shall be served consecutively or concurrently.]
4. [The sentence shall be pronounced in public and in the presence of the convicted person.]

[*227] Article 47*
Applicable penalties
I. ILC DRAFT

1. The Court may impose on a person convicted of a crime under this Statute one or more of the following penalties:
    (a) a term of life imprisonment, or of imprisonment for a specified number of years;
    (b) a fine.
2. In determining the length of a term of imprisonment or the amount of a fine to be imposed, the Court may have regard to the penalties provided for by the law of:
    (a) the State of which the convicted person is a national;
    (b) the State where the crime was committed; and
    (c) the State which had custody of and jurisdiction over the accused.
3. Fines paid may be transferred, by order of the Court, to one or more of the following:
    (a) the Registrar, to defray the costs of the trial;
    (b) a State the nationals of which were the victims of the crime;
    (c) a trust fund established by the Secretary-General of the United Nations for the benefit of victims of crime.

[*228 II. PROPOSALS
Paragraph 1 68/

"(The Court may impose on a person convicted of a crime under this Statute one or more of the following penalties:
    (a) a term of life imprisonment, or of imprisonment for a specified number of years;
    (b) a fine. 69/
    [(c) a disenfranchisement in the modality and to the extent such penalty could be imposed in accordance with the laws mentioned in paragraph 2.] or [(c) a forfeiture]). 70/
OR
[1.In the case of a physical person who is found guilty, the penalty of imprisonment incurred shall be life imprisonment.
2. The Court may, however, impose a sentence of imprisonment for a specified number of years if there are grounds for mitigation of criminal responsibility or if it recognizes the existence of

---

*   Note The compilation on article 47 was prepared by an informal group. It is designed to reflect the proposals of delegations made during the course of discussions on the issue of penalties. It follows the original text of the ILC draft Statute; amendments are represented in bold type. Where a deletion of text has been proposed, the original text is surrounded by parentheses which are in bold type. Where an addition of text has been proposed, the original text is interrupted by square brackets, which contain the proposed additional text in bold type. This compilation is not exhaustive. The texts included do not reflect any generally held views and do not prejudge the future positions of delegations.

68/   Some delegations expressed the view that there should be more precise maximum penalties of imprisonment set forth as part of the definitions of specific crimes within the jurisdiction of the International Criminal Court. For example, as to certain violations of the laws and customs of war, delegations may wish to consider whether it would be appropriate to specify a maximum penalty of a fixed number of years' imprisonment.

69/   The question has been raised as to whether the International Criminal Court should concern itself with the collection of pecuniary sanctions, other than for the purpose of compensating victims.

70/   One delegation observed that the inclusion of the penalty of forfeiture in article 47 will provide effective enforcement mechanism for the economic crime resulting in international social problems such as crimes of drug trafficking which may fall under the definition of the serious crimes of international concern under article 20 (e) of the ILC draft. Should in the future these crimes be listed in the Annex of article 20 (e), there will be no need to amend the Statute to incorporate such penalty to govern the said crimes.

mitigating circumstances, bearing in mind in particular the special circumstances of the case, the personality of the guilty party and his degree of involvement in the crime in question.

In the case referred to in the preceding paragraph, the sentence of imprisonment imposed may not be more than 30 years.

3.   In the case of a person aged 13 to 18 years at the time of the facts who is found guilty, the Court may not impose a sentence of more than 20 years imprisonment. However, by way of exception and taking into account the circumstances of the case and the personality of the person concerned, the Court may decide that there are no grounds for mitigation and impose a sentence under the same conditions as those referred to in paragraphs 1 and 2 of this article. The Court shall give its specific reasons for such a decision.

[*229]4. In the case of a physical person who is found guilty, the Court may also impose a fine, the amount of which shall be freely set by it.

5.In the case of physical persons who are found guilty, fines may be imposed in addition to sentences of imprisonment.]

OR

[The Court may impose on a person convicted of a crime under this Statute a life imprisonment, or of imprisonment for a specified number of years and months.

The Court may impose on a person convicted of a perjury or contempt of the Court a fine.[71/

OR

[The Court may impose terms of imprisonment on persons convicted of crimes under this Statute. Terms of imprisonment may be combined with fines.]

OR

[The punishment which this Court may impose is:

(a)   imprisonment for life; or

(b)   imprisonment for a definite term between twenty and forty years, unless it is reduced according to the provisions of this Statute.]

OR

[The Court may impose on a person convicted of a crime under this Statute one or more of the following penalties:

(a)   death penalty, as an option, in case of aggravating circumstances and when the Trial Chamber finds it necessary in light of the gravity of the crime, the number of victims and the severity of the damage;

(b)   a term of life imprisonment, or of imprisonment for a specified number of years;

(c)   a fine.]

OR

[*230] [The Court may apply the following penalties and security measures: 72/

(a)   imprisonment;

(b)   pecuniary sanctions; 73/

(c)   seizure of instruments and objects of the crime;

(d)   suspension or loss of rights;

(e)   disqualification, dismissal or suspension from office or employment.]"

A. Aggravating and mitigating circumstances

[Note. Delegates may wish to deal in this context with the issues treated in article 46 (2) of the ILC draft. Thus, a possibility would be to delete article 46 (2) and insert it as a new paragraph of article 47, as is done here:

71/   One delegation pointed out that article 44 of the report by the informal group on procedure, which contains proposals for definitions of crimes, including perjury and contempt, should also be reviewed. Some of those proposals contain provisions for penalties of imprisonment.

72/   The type of sanction applicable to each one of the crimes which come under the jurisdiction of the Court should be specified in the chapter on definitions, so as to include both the provision as well as the penalty in the same article.

73/   Pecuniary sanctions may include both a fine and a compensation.

In imposing sentence, the Trial Chamber (should) [shall] take into account such factors as the gravity of the crime[, **the extent and severity of the damage or injury caused**] and the individual circumstances of the convicted person[, **including any previous convictions of the convicted person**].
> OR

[When the Court finds extenuating circumstances concerning criminal conduct of the defendant, it may reduce the sentence of imprisonment.]
> OR

[In determining the sentence, the Trial Chamber shall take into account the factors mentioned in article ... of the Statute, as well as any factors such as

(a) any aggravating circumstances, including:
  (i) the impact of the crime on the victims;
  (ii) the extent of damage caused by the convicted person's conduct;
(b) any mitigating circumstances, including: the substantial cooperation with the Prosecutor by the convicted person before or after conviction;
(c) the time which the convicted person has already been detained for on the charges;
(d) the extent to which any penalty imposed by a court of any State on the convicted person for the same act has already been served, as referred to in article ... (A 42 (3) (ILC) of the Statute.] [*231]
> OR

[The Court may, within the limits permitted by this Statute, apply the penalties established for each crime, individualizing them on the basis of the severity of the crime and the agent's degree of responsibility, bearing in mind:

(a) the extent of the damage caused or the danger posed;
(b) the nature of the illicit behaviour and the means employed to execute it;
(c) the circumstances of time, mode and place of the act executed;
(d) the form and degree of intervention of the agent in the commission of the crime, as well as his or her capacity and that of the victim;
(e) the age, education, culture, customs, social and economic condition of the agent, as well as the motives which induced him to commit the crime.]

B. Minimum periods of imprisonment

[1. When the Court imposes a sentence of imprisonment of more than five years, it may attach to the sentence a minimum period during which the guilty party may not be granted any reduction or amendment of his sentence as provided for in Part [...] of this Statute.
2. The duration of the minimum period shall be freely set by the Court, but it may not exceed either two thirds of the sentence in the case of imprisonment for a specified number of years or 22 years in the case of life imprisonment.]

C. Concurrence of offences

[When a person has committed more than one offence, the Court shall:

(a) when imprisonment for life is to be imposed for one of these offences, pronounce a single sentence of imprisonment for life; or
(b) otherwise, pronounce a single sentence for a definite term, the maximum of which shall be the maximum sentence prescribed for the gravest crimes increased by one half.]
> OR

[1. Concurrence of offences occurs when an offence is committed by a person before he has finally been sentenced by the Court for another offence.
2. When, in the course of the same proceedings, a physical person is convicted by the Court of several concurrent offences within the meaning of paragraph 1 of this article, only one sentence of imprisonment may be imposed on him, under the conditions provided for in [...]. This sentence shall be deemed common to the concurrent offences.
3. When, in the course of separate proceedings, a physical person is convicted by the Court of several concurrent offences within the meaning of paragraph 1 of [*232] this article, several sentences of imprisonment may be imposed on him, under the conditions provided for in [...]. Such sentences shall run consecutively.

In such cases the Court may order that all or part of the sentences of imprisonment shall be served concurrently. Concurrency shall be automatic when one of the sentences is life imprisonment.
4.   Fines imposed on physical persons may be cumulative with each other and with fines imposed for concurrent crimes within the meaning of paragraph 1 of this article.]

D. Prior detention

[If a sentence of imprisonment is imposed, the actual period of imprisonment to be served by the convicted person shall be reduced by the time which he or she has already been detained prior to sentencing.]

OR

[If the accused is acquitted, if he is sentenced to payment of a fine or if he is sentenced to a term of imprisonment already covered by his period in detention, he shall be released immediately unless he is retained for another case by the organs of the Court or by the judicial authorities of a State Party.]

Paragraph 2

(In determining the length of a term of imprisonment or the amount of a fine to be imposed, the Court may have regard to the penalties provided for by the law of) or [In determining the length of a term of imprisonment, the amount of a fine to be imposed, or the property to be forfeited, the Court shall impose the highest penalty provided for by the law of either]: 74/

    (a)   the State of which the convicted person is a national;
    (b)   the State where the crime was committed; [or]
    (c)   the State which had custody of and jurisdiction over the accused.)

OR

[In determining the penalty imposed, the Court will have regard to the penalties provided for by the law of the State of the nationality of the offender. In cases where national law does not regulate a specific crime, the Court will apply penalties ascribed to analogous crimes in the same national law.] 75/

[*233] E. Confiscation

[1.   The following may be confiscated:
    (a)   an object which has been used or was intended to be used in the commission of the criminal conduct;
    (b)   an object or profit obtained by criminal conduct.
2.   When the whole or a part of an object or profit mentioned in paragraph 1 cannot be confiscated, a sum of money equivalent thereto may be collected.]

OR

[The Court may confiscate any object which has served to commit a crime and order the return to their rightful owners of any property and proceeds acquired by criminal conduct.]

AND/OR

[1.   The judgement of the Court shall be binding on the national jurisdictions of every State Party as regards the criminal liability of the person convicted and the principles relating to compensation for damage caused to victims and the restitution of property acquired by the person convicted.
2.   For the purpose of enforcement of fines imposed by the Court, the Presidency may order the forced sale of any property of the person sentenced which is on the territory of a State Party.

For the same purpose, the Presidency may order the confiscation of any sum of money or securities belonging to the person sentenced.

74/   One delegation expressed the view that the language of the present article 47, paragraph 2, will result in an uncertainty arising from problems of concurrent jurisdictions. The Court will be accorded too broad discretion as to the degree of penalty it will impose on the defendant. The amendment to the second paragraph, therefore, is necessary to provide more certainty and transparency to such a provision.

75/   This proposal intends to solve the question of legality and at the same time accommodate differences of legal systems concerning penalties.

Decisions by the Presidency are implemented by States Parties in conformity with their domestic laws.

The provisions of this article shall apply to juridical persons.]

Paragraph 3

"(Fines paid may be transferred, by order of the Court, to one or more of the following:

(a)   the Registrar, to defray the costs of the trial;

(b)   a State the nationals of which were the victims of the crime;

(c)   a trust fund established by the Secretary-General of the United Nations for the benefit of victims of crime.)

OR

[Fines paid will be transferred to the Registrar to defray the costs of the trial.]"

OR

[*234] [Fines may be transferred, by order of the Court, to one or the other of the following, or be distributed between:

(a)   the Registrar, to defray the costs of the trial;

(b)   a trust fund administered by the Court for the benefit of victims of crime.]

F. Juridical persons (article 47 bis)

[1.   In respect of all the crimes referred to in [...], juridical persons who are held to be criminally responsible by the Court shall incur the following penalties:

(a)   fines, the amount of which shall be freely set by the Court;

(b)   dissolution;

(c)   prohibition, in perpetuity or for a period freely determined by the Court, of the direct or indirect exercise of one or more professional or social activities;

(d)   closure, in perpetuity or for a period freely determined by the Court, of the establishments used in the commission of the crimes;

(e)   confiscation of any item used in the commission of the crimes or which is a product of the crimes.

2.   The penalties provided for in paragraph 1 of this article may be cumulative with each other or with penalties imposed for concurrent crimes within the meaning of [...] of this Statute.]

[*235] PART 6. APPEAL AND REVIEW 76/

Article 48

Appeal against judgement or sentence

I. ILC DRAFT

1.   The Prosecutor and the convicted person may, in accordance with the Rules, appeal against a decision under articles 45 or 47 on grounds of procedural error, error of fact or of law, or disproportion between the crime and the sentence.

2.   Unless the Trial Chamber otherwise orders, a convicted person shall remain in custody pending an appeal.

II. PROPOSALS

1.   The Prosecutor and the convicted person [accused], may in accordance with the rules (of the Court), appeal [before the Appeals chamber] against (his) (his/her) (a)

[decision under articles 45 or 47 (ILC) on the grounds of procedural error, error of fact or of law, or disproportion between the crime and the sentence [or against a decision rendered in absentia under article 37, paragraph 2]]

[conviction and sentence on grounds of procedural error, error of fact or law, or disproportion between the crime and the sentence].

[Judgements given on the merits of the case by the Trial Chamber, with the exception of those given in the absence of the accused, as provided for in article 112, paragraph 4.

76/   See the footnote to the proposals on the preamble, at the beginning of the present volume.

An appeal against judgements given on the merits in the absence of the accused shall be allowed if the latter accepts the judgement or was represented during the trial before the Trial Chamber by defence counsel appointed by him.
The appeal may be general or may relate exclusively to the magnitude of the penalty.]
2.   [The Appeals Chamber may hear interlocutory appeals on the grounds provided for in article X.]
3.   [An appeal shall be lodged within [30] days of the decision being challenged, or such longer time as the Presidency may allow.]
4.   [Unless the Trial Chamber otherwise orders, a convicted person shall remain in custody pending an appeal.]
[In case of an acquittal, the accused shall be released immediately.
[*236] If, at the time the judgement is pronounced, the Prosecutor advises the Trial Chamber in open court of his or her intention to file notice of appeal, the Trial Chamber may, at the request of the Prosecutor, issue a warrant for the arrest of the acquitted person to take effect immediately.
The Trial Chamber shall not issue an arrest warrant unless it is satisfied that the acquitted person may not be readily returned to custody if judgement is reversed.]
[The sentence shall begin to run from the day it is pronounced. However, as soon as notice of appeal is given, the enforcement of the judgement shall thereupon be stayed until the decision on appeal has been delivered, the convicted person meanwhile remaining in detention.
If, by a previous decision of the Trial Chamber, the convicted person has been released, or is for any other reason at liberty, and he or she is not present when the Judgement is pronounced, the Trial Chamber shall issue a warrant for his or her arrest.]
[Execution of the judgement shall be suspended during the period allowed for appeal and for the duration of the appeal proceedings.]

[*237] Article 49
Proceedings on appeal
I. ILC DRAFT
1.   The Appeals Chamber has all the powers of the Trial Chamber.
2.   If the Appeals Chamber finds that the proceedings appealed from were unfair or that the decision is vitiated by error of fact or law, it may:
        (a)   if the appeal is brought by the convicted person, reverse or amend the decision, or, if necessary, order a new trial;
        (b)   if the appeal is brought by the Prosecutor against an acquittal, order a new trial.
3.   If in an appeal against sentence the Chamber finds that the sentence is manifestly disproportionate to the crime, it may vary the sentence in accordance with article 47.
4.   The decision of the Chamber shall be taken by a majority of the judges, and shall be delivered in open court. Six judges constitute a quorum.
5.   Subject to article 50, the decision of the Chamber shall be final.
II. PROPOSALS
1.   [The Appeals Chamber has all the powers of the Trial Chamber.]
[The rules of procedure laid down for the Trial Chamber shall apply in the Appeals Chamber, subject to articles 107, 115, 116 and 130 and the following provisions.]
[The rules of procedure and evidence that govern proceedings in the Trial Chambers shall apply mutatis mutandis to proceedings in the Appeals Chamber.]
[The rules of procedure and evidence that govern proceedings in the Trial Chambers shall apply mutatis mutandis to proceedings provided by the preceding two paragraphs. Further rules that govern those proceedings shall be provided for in the rules of Court.]
2.   [If the Appeals Chamber finds that the proceedings appealed from were unfair or that the decision is vitiated by error of fact or law, it may:
        (a)   if the appeal is brought by the convicted person, reverse or amend the decision, or, if necessary, order a new trial;
        (b)   if the appeal is brought by the Prosecutor against an acquittal, order a new trial.]

[*238] [The Court shall admit a plea of nullity based on nullity of the procedure followed in the Trial Chamber with regard to evidence produced in that Chamber, if the nullity is referred to by the President, the prosecutor or the accused in the course of proceedings in the Appeals Chamber and has already been raised in the Trial Chamber.

Other defences based on nullity of the procedure followed in the Trial Chamber shall not be admissible. Defences based on nullity of the summons to appear before the Appeals Chamber must, to be admissible, be raised by the parties at the opening of proceedings, before the reading of the judgement of the Trial Chamber and of the notice of appeal.]

3.   [If in an appeal against sentence the Chamber finds that the sentence is manifestly disproportionate to the crime, it may vary the sentence in accordance with article 47.]

4.   [The decision of the Chamber shall be taken by a majority of the judges, and shall be delivered in open court [on a date of which notice has been given to the parties and counsel and at which they shall be entitled to be present]. Six judges constitute a quorum.]

[The Appeals Chamber shall pronounce judgement on the basis of the record on appeal together with such additional evidence as it has authorized.

The judgement shall be accompanied or followed as soon as possible by a reasoned opinion in writing, to which separate or dissenting opinions may be appended.]

[The Appeals Chamber may rule only on objections formulated by the parties in their appeals. When the decision has been appealed only by the accused, it cannot be amended to his or her detriment.]

5.   [The Appeals Chamber may grant compensation to a person who was held in pre-trial detention during proceedings against him that have concluded with a final decision of acquittal. The compensation shall be based on the prejudice caused to him by such detention.]

6.   [Subject to article 50, the decision of the Chamber shall be final.]

7.   [A sentence pronounced by the Appeals Chamber shall be enforced immediately.

Where the accused is not present when the judgement is due to be delivered, either as having been acquitted on all charges or for any other reason, the Appeals Chamber may deliver its Judgement in the absence of the accused and shall, unless it pronounces his or her acquittal, order his or her arrest or surrender to the Tribunal.]

A. Notice of appeal

1.   [Subject to (B), a party seeking to appeal under article X (A 48 ILC) of the Statute a judgement or sentence shall, not more than thirty days from the date on which the judgement or sentence was pronounced, file with the Registrar and serve upon the other party a written notice of appeal, setting forth the grounds. [The supplementary rules shall provide for the form and any related [*239] requirements of a notice of appeal.] [It shall be signed by the Registrar and by the appellant or by his defence counsel.]

[If the appellant is in detention, the appeal may be effected by means of a declaration to the head of the prison facility. The declaration shall be noted, dated and signed by the head of the prison facility and the appellant. It shall be transmitted promptly to the Registrar of the Court who shall notify the other parties of the appeal.]

[(B) The Appeals Chamber may extend the period up to an additional thirty days for good cause.]

[The Appeals Chamber shall be seized of the case by the notice of the appeal.]

[An appeal shall be lodged within [30] days of the decision being challenged, or such longer time as the Presidency may allow.]

[An appeal shall be lodged within 30 days if it relates to the judgement on merits or to a judgement terminating the proceedings.

The time limit shall be eight days where the Court rules on an application for release or on an application for the lifting of a restriction or a modification of judicial supervision.

This period shall run from the date of the pronouncement of the judgement.

However, it shall run only from the date of notification of the judgement:

(a)   for an accused who was not present or represented at the hearing where the judgement was pronounced, but only in those cases where he himself or his defence counsel was not informed of the date on which the judgement would be pronounced;

(b) for an accused who requested that he be tried <u>in absentia</u> in accordance with the provisions of article 111, paragraph 1 (b).]

[If notice of appeal is not filed within the required time limit, or if a properly filed appeal is discontinued in all respects, the judgement or sentence shall be deemed to be final and subject only to revision pursuant to article X (A 50 ILC) of the Statute.]

B. Interlocutory appeals

[Subject to (B), a party seeking to make an interlocutory appeal shall not more than ten days from the date on which the Trial Chamber ruled on the preliminary motion, file with the Registrar and serve upon the other party a written notice of interlocutory appeal, setting forth the grounds. The supplementary rules shall provide for the form and any related requirements of an interlocutory appeal notice of appeal.

(B) The Appeals Chamber may extend the period up to an additional five days for good cause.]

[Judgements of the Trial Chamber other than those given on the merits may be appealed against if: |*240| (a) they terminate the proceedings;

(b) they provide for committal in custody or judicial supervision.

Judgements of the Trial Chamber other than those given on the merits and which are not referred to in the present article may not be the subject of appeal.

Appeals lodged against the judgements referred to in the present article shall not have suspensive effect. They shall be brought before the Appeals Chamber.] <u>77/</u>

C. Appeals by both parties

[When both parties file a notice of appeal, the party lodging the earliest notice shall be deemed to be the appellant and, accordingly, the other party shall be deemed to be the respondent.]

D. Discontinuance of appeal

[An appellant, including the party deemed to be the respondent, may at any time file with the Registrar a written notice of discontinuance of appeal. The Registrar shall inform the other party that the notice has been filed. Upon filing of the notice, the appeal shall be abandoned.]

E. Record on appeal

[The record on appeal shall consist of the trial record, as certified by the Trial Chamber.]

[<u>Note</u>. There may be grounds for limiting the record on appeal to that part of the trial record going to the matters in dispute.]

F. Copies of record

[The Registrar shall make a sufficient number of copies of the record on appeal for the use of the Judges of the Appeals Chamber and of the parties.]

[Persons who have been convicted shall be entitled to delivery to them by the Registrar of the Court of certified true copies of the judgement of the Trial Chamber and of the complete record of the deliberations.]

G. Appellant's brief

[An appellant's brief of argument and authorities shall be served on the other party and filed with the Registrar within thirty days of the date of the filing of the notice of appeal. The Appeals Chamber may for good cause extend the period up to additional ten days.

|*241| The appellant's brief shall satisfy the requirements as to the form, content and length of briefs laid down in the supplementary rules.]

H. Respondent's brief

[A respondent's brief of argument and authorities shall be served on the other party and filed with the Registrar within thirty days of the filing of the appellant's brief. The Appeals Chamber may extend the period up to an additional ten days for good cause.

The respondent's brief shall satisfy the requirements as to the form, content and length of briefs laid down in the supplementary rules.]

I. Brief in reply

[An appellant may file a brief in reply within ten days after the filing of the respondent's brief. The Appeals Chamber may extend the period up to an additional five days for good cause.]

77/ See also rule 78 proposed by Australia and the Netherlands (A/AC.249/L.2).

J. <u>Requirement for brief where appellant or respondent is not represented by counsel</u>
[Where the appellant or respondent is not represented by counsel, the Appeals Chamber may order that he or she need not file a brief, or may file a brief in a modified form.]

K. <u>Briefs submitted on behalf of interested persons or organizations</u>
[A brief submitted on behalf of an interested person may be filed only by invitation of the Appeals Chamber or by motion for leave to file granted by the Appeals Chamber.

A brief submitted shall be filed with the Registrar who shall provide copies to the appellant and respondent.

The Appeals Chamber shall determine what time limits should govern the filing of such briefs.

The supplementary rules shall specify the requirements as to the form, content and length of such briefs.]

L. <u>Date of hearing</u>
[After the expiry of the time-limits for filing the briefs, the Appeals Chamber shall set the date for the hearing and the Registrar shall notify the parties.]

M. <u>Conduct of hearing</u>
[The supplementary rules shall govern the conduct of the hearing.]

[*242] N. <u>Additional evidence</u>
[A party may apply by motion to present before the Appeals Chamber additional evidence which was not available to it at the trial. Such motion must be served on the other party and filed with the Registrar not less than fifteen days before the date of the hearing.

The Appeals Chamber shall authorize the presentation of such evidence if it considers that the interests of justice so require.]

O. <u>Expedited appeals procedure</u>
[An interlocutory appeal shall be heard expeditiously on the basis of the original record of the Trial Chamber and without the necessity of any written brief.

All delays and other procedural requirements shall be fixed by an order of the President issued on an application by one of the parties or <u>proprio motu</u> should no such application have been made within fifteen days after the filing of the notice of interlocutory appeal.]

[*243] Article 50
Revision
I. ILC DRAFT

1.   The convicted person or the Prosecutor may, in accordance with the Rules, apply to the Presidency for revision of a conviction on the ground that evidence has been discovered which was not available to the applicant at the time the conviction was pronounced or affirmed and which could have been a decisive factor in the conviction.

2.   The Presidency shall request the prosecutor or the convicted person, as the case may be, to present written observations on whether the application should be accepted.

3.   If the Presidency is of the view that the new evidence could lead to the revision of the conviction, it may:

(a)   reconvene the Trial Chamber;

(b)   constitute a new Trial Chamber; or

(c)   refer the matter to the Appeals Chamber;

with a view to the Chamber determining, after hearing the parties, whether the new evidence should lead to a revision of the conviction.

II. PROPOSALS

1.   An application for the revision of a conviction [final judgement in a criminal case] may be made to the [Presidency] [court which rendered the original judgement], in accordance with the rules (of the Court), by:

(a)   the Prosecutor (of the Court); or

(b)   the person convicted [and, after the death of the latter, by his spouse, his children, his relatives or any persons having express instructions to apply for revision].

2.   An application may be made on the following grounds:

[evidence has been discovered which was not available to the applicant at the time the conviction was pronounced or affirmed and which could have been a decisive factor in the conviction]

[a new circumstance or evidence of which the Court was unaware at the time of the trial occurs or becomes known and is such as to create doubt as to the guilt of the person convicted]

[new evidence is found which was not available at the time of the passing or confirmation of the sentence and which could have had a decisive influence on the sentence]

[it is proved that a decisive piece of evidence which was taken into account when passing the sentence does not possess the value which had been assigned to it because it is false, invalid, or it has been forged or falsified]

[*244] [it is proved that one of the judges who participated in the sentence or in its confirmation has committed in that case a serious breach of his duties]

[a previous judicial judgement on which the sentence was based has been annulled]

[a more benign penal law than the one applied in the sentence becomes retroactively applicable]

3.   [The applicant shall file with the Registrar and serve upon the other party a written application for revision, setting forth the grounds.] [The supplementary rules shall provide for the form and any related requirements of an application for revision.]

4.   [[The Presidency] shall request the Prosecutor or the convicted person, as the case may be, to present written observations on whether the application should be accepted.]

[[The Presidency] shall, either directly or within the framework of an application for judicial assistance, undertake such investigation and verification as may be required. It may, at any time, order the suspension of execution of the sentence.]

[[The Presidency] shall rule on the application following a public hearing at which the oral or written observations of the appellant or his defence counsel and of the Prosecutor shall be recorded. [The Presidency] shall announce the grounds for the decision, which shall not be subject to appeal.]

5.   [The rules of procedure and evidence that govern proceedings in the Trial Chambers shall apply <u>mutatis mutandis</u> to proceedings provided by the previous paragraphs. Further rules that govern those proceedings shall be provided in the rules of the Court.]

6.   [If the [Presidency] is of the view that the new evidence could lead to the revision of the conviction, it may:

   (a)   reconvene the Trial Chamber;
   (b)   constitute a new Trial Chamber; or
   (c)   refer the matter to the Appeals Chamber,

with a view to the Chamber determining, after hearing the parties, whether the new evidence should lead to the revision of the conviction.]

[[The Presidency] shall reject the application if it considers the latter unfounded. If it considers there are valid grounds for the application, it shall annul the conviction and refer the accused to a jurisdiction at the same level as but having a composition different from that of the jurisdiction which handed down the annulled decision.]

[The Court may award compensation to a convicted person who is found innocent under the present title, the compensation to be in the amount of the prejudice caused by the conviction, unless it is demonstrated that he was responsible for a failure to produce new evidence or to reveal an unknown factor in good time.]

[*245] PART 7. INTERNATIONAL COOPERATION AND JUDICIAL ASSISTANCE* 78/

Note. These proposals and compilations were prepared by an informal group dealing with Part 7. They neither represent a text agreed upon among delegations nor suggest that every item should be included in the Statute. They identify possible elements to be included and examples of some possible texts. The order of the articles as well as the headings are only of an indicative character and have not been finally agreed upon.

78/   Not all assistance is provided by judicial authorities. "Mutual assistance", which is developing into a term of art, may be a better option and has throughout the text been inserted in square brackets after "judicial".

[Article X 79/
[Reciprocity] Obligation to cooperate and general provisions 80/
A. General obligation to cooperate

1.   States Parties shall, in accordance with the provisions of this Part, cooperate with the Court in its investigation and prosecution of crimes under this Statute. A State shall not deny a request for cooperation except as specifically provided in this Part.

* * *

[[States Parties shall afford to the Court the widest possible measure of mutual assistance] or [States Parties and the Court shall afford each other reciprocal cooperation and mutual assistance] in connection with [the] criminal investigations and proceedings under this Statute.]

* * *

States Non-Parties may offer their assistance to the Court under conditions determined by them or pursuant to a specific agreement.

* * *

States Parties shall respond without undue delay to the request.

* * *

States Parties shall respond without delay to any request for cooperation submitted by the Court under this Statute. They may request the Court to provide any additional information which they consider necessary to enable them to respond to the request.

[*246] The obligation to cooperate provided for in paragraph 1 of this article shall be discharged in accordance with the conditions set out in this Statute.

* * *

States Parties shall respond without delay to any request for cooperation submitted by the Court under this Statute. They may request the Court to provide any additional information which they consider necessary to enable them to respond to the request.

* * *

The Court may request the extradition of a fugitive to States Parties as regards an offence specified in article [ ] when the Court has issued a warrant of arrest.

* * *

[Note. Another option is to couch this provision in reciprocal terms.]

B. Channels for communication of requests/Authorities competent to make and receive requests

2.   [Requests for cooperation may be made by the Court, [or Prosecutor] and shall be transmitted through diplomatic channels, unless the Court and the requested State agree on another mode for transmitting the requests.] 81/

* * *

The request under paragraph 1 shall be made in written form through diplomatic channels. If a requested State considers the information and evidence provided by the Court insufficient as a basis for decisions whether to offer assistance, it may seek further information and evidence from the Court as it deems necessary.

All the documents to be provided by the Court to State Party shall be accompanied by a duly certified translation in the language of the party.

* * *

79/   Some delegations are of the view that the obligation to cooperate should be subject to certain preconditions. Therefore, there is no need as such in the Statute for an article X, which may cause some confusion on the understanding of obligation and limitations on it.

80/   This provision reflects the need for a general statement of the obligation of States to cooperate with the Court and related matters.

81/   An alternative would be to provide that "Communications relating to a request under this Part shall be between the Registrar, or Prosecutor acting under article 26, and the national authority designated by each State party for this purpose [unless otherwise permitted by the laws of that State party]. See also article 53 (1) and 57 (2).The ILC draft Statute commingles provisions of mutual assistance on the one hand, and arrest and surrender on the other. In this text these two aspects have been separated into two distinct provisions, respectively articles 51 and 53. Each provision contains its own provisions relating to the obligation to cooperate and the grounds for denial of the request.

The requested State shall through diplomatic channels promptly notify the court of its decision as regards the request for extradition.

* * *

[*247] Each State Party shall designate, at the time of deposition of its instruments of ratification, the national authority competent to receive requests for cooperation transmitted by the Court and the various authorities to which requests for cooperation may be submitted, as determined by the urgency of the request and the means of its transmission.

However, a State Party may amend the list of competent national authorities subsequent to ratification, but such amendment shall not be opposable until six months have elapsed from the date of its deposition.

* * *

Requests for cooperation shall be transmitted to States by the Registrar. The replies of States shall be addressed to him, as shall any accompanying documents or papers.

* * *

[Note. Alternatively reliance could be had on cooperation between States (see A/AC.249/1, para. 179) or a combination of the two systems.]

C. States Parties' failure to cooperate 82/

3.   Where non-cooperation by States with requests by the Court [or Prosecutor] prevents the Court from performing its duties in terms of this Statute, the Court may request the Security Council to take the measures necessary to enable the Court to exercise its jurisdiction, in relation to both States Parties to this Statute, or States not parties.

* * *

The Preliminary Investigations Chamber of the Court may bring to the attention of the Security Council any failure to discharge the obligation to cooperate provided for in paragraph 1 of this article which obstructs the performance of the Chamber's functions. 83/

[*248] D. Cooperation by non-States Parties

4.   The Court may call on any State not party to this Statute to provide assistance 84/ provided for in this Part on the basis of comity, an ad hoc arrangement or through entry into agreement with such State. 85/

* * *

The Court may also make a request under paragraph 1 to any non-State Party. Non-State Parties may honour the request and provide necessary assistance in accordance with their national laws.

* * *

States non-parties may offer their assistance to the Court under conditions determined by them or pursuant to a specific agreement with the Court.

E. Language of requests and answers 86/

5.   [Requests for cooperation shall be in an official language of the requested State unless otherwise agreed.]

* * *

82/   Reservations were expressed regarding the role of the Security Council in the Court. Some delegations consider that it should not be involved in any way in the work of the Court while others underscored that all provisions in the Statute pertaining to its role should confirm to the agreement to be reached on principles of relationship between the Court and the United Nations among the States Members of the United Nations. The legal basis of the role of the Security Council will also have to be viewed in the context of the powers of the Security Council in the Charter of the United Nations.

83/   Paragraph 1 deals with the general obligation to cooperate with the Court.

84/   See Siracusa draft, article 56. This is preferable to article 56 of the ILC draft, which formulates the same principle in the form of an entitlement to States which are not party to the Statute. It appears more correct to formulate the principle as empowering the Court to request cooperation, leaving open the reaction of the requested State.

85/   This could form the substance of a separate article. It should also be considered whether a provision should be added providing that the Court shall have the power to respond to any counter-request by such a State that has been requested to cooperate.

86/   The issue of the working languages of the Court has not yet been addressed by the Preparatory Committee. Some delegations expressed doubts about the current drafting of article 25 of the Statute.

The request under paragraph 1 shall be made in written form through diplomatic channels. If a requested State considers the information and evidence provided by the Court insufficient as a basis for decisions whether to offer assistance, it may seek further information and evidence from the Court as it deems necessary.

All the documents to be provided by the Court to State Party shall be accompanied by a duly certified translation in the language of the Party.

* * *

Requests for cooperation addressed to States Parties by the Court shall be drafted in one of the two working languages referred to in article 25, in accordance with the choice made by that State at the time of deposition of its instruments of ratification.

[*249] The same shall apply to papers and documents transmitted to the Court by States Parties in response to the requests referred to in paragraph 1 of this article. The Court may also request the transmission of documents in their original language.

* * *

[Note. It was mentioned that in the field of international cooperation there exists no obligation to translate documents transmitted in the execution of a request.]

F. Extent to which national law controls procedures for execution of requests

6.   States Party to this Statute shall inform the Registrar of any conditions under their laws that requests for cooperation and judicial [mutual] assistance are required to comply with, and of any amendments to such laws.

* * *

The obligation to cooperate provided for in paragraph 1 of this article shall be discharged in accordance with the conditions set out in this Statute.

Subject to the provisions of paragraph 2 of this article, the procedure by which a State Party discharges its obligation to cooperate shall be governed by its internal law. 87/

* * *

The Court may also make a request under paragraph 1 to any Non-State Party. Non-State Parties may honour the request and provide necessary assistance in accordance with their national laws.

* * *

States Parties shall undertake to extradite to the Court any fugitive requested for extradition and found in their territories in accordance with this Statute and their national laws.

When a State Party honours the request for extradition, it shall promptly detain the fugitive under its national laws.

The request for extradition shall include a description of the identity of the fugitive and the facts of the case, and shall contain such further information as may be required by the laws of the requested State.

* * *

In cases of urgency, when the Court makes a request for provisional detention, notifying the requested Party that a warrant of arrest has been issued or a sentence has been imposed for an offence specified in article [ ], the requested State Party may provisionally detain the person sought in accordance with its national laws.

[*250] The request for provisional detention shall describe the identity of the person to be sought and the facts of the case, and shall contain such further information as may be required by the laws of the requested State.

* * *

States Parties shall honour and comply with the request for assistance through proceedings according to their national laws.

States Parties shall give approval for the transportation of the persons to the Court through their territories in accordance with their national laws.]

87/   Paragraph 2 deals with the obligation to cooperate.

[*251] Article 51
Cooperation and judicial assistance

I. ILC DRAFT

1.   States parties shall cooperate with the Court in connection with criminal investigations and proceedings under this Statute.

2.   The Registrar may transmit to any State a request for cooperation and judicial assistance with respect to a crime, including, but not limited to:

     (a)   the identification and location of persons;

     (b)   the taking of testimony and the production of evidence;

     (c)   the service of documents;

     (d)   the arrest or detention of persons; and

     (e)   any other request which may facilitate the administration of justice, including provisional measures as required.

3.   Upon receipt of a request under paragraph 2:

     (a)   in a case covered by article 21 (1) (a), all States parties;

     (b)   in any other case, States parties which have accepted the jurisdiction of the Court with respect to the crime in question;

shall respond without undue delay to the request.

II. PROPOSALS

The title of the article should read: "Cooperation and judicial [mutual] assistance".

A. Obligation to provide judicial [mutual] assistance

1.   [States Parties shall] [in a case which is not inadmissible under article 35] [afford to the Court the widest possible measures of judicial [mutual] assistance] OR [States have the obligation to provide assistance to the Court] 88/ in connection with any investigations and proceedings under this Statute.

* * *

[*252] States Parties shall [in a case which is (decided by the Court as) not inadmissible under article 35] cooperate with the Court in connection with criminal investigations and proceedings under this Statute.

* * *

States Parties shall honour and comply with the request for assistance through proceedings according to their national laws.

* * *

The obligation to cooperate provided for in article 60 89/ shall take precedence over all the legal obstacles which the State to which the request for judicial assistance is made invokes against the Court pursuant to its internal law or the treaties to which it is a party.

B. Types/categories of assistance (exhaustive or non-exhaustive) 90/

2.   The Registrar, or the Prosecutor [in the performance of his functions under article 26], 91/ may with respect to a crime under article 20 transmit a request in accordance with article 57 92/ to any State Party for cooperation and judicial [mutual] assistance, pertaining to: 93/

88/   The success of the Court depends on the effectiveness of the provisions pertaining to cooperation by States with requests for assistance. In this regard the imposition of a definite obligation on States to cooperate, as opposed to a more vague provision allowing a discretion on whether to cooperate, should be considered. The argument for the former option is that a rigid and absolute obligation, allowing for no discretion to States party which accept the jurisdiction of the Court, would be crucial to, and strengthen, the principle of complementarity. Consideration could be given to making the same rigid principles applicable to requests by States with preferent jurisdiction over a crime.

89/   Article 60 deals with the general obligation to cooperate with the Court.

90/   Depending on the Court's remedies, is there a need to include assistance relating to compensation or restitution to victims?

91/   See article 26 (2) (e), which empowers the Prosecutor to seek the assistance of States, or article 26 of the ILC draft, which refers to pre-indictment requests. Requests by the Prosecutor after the indictment could also be provided for.

92/   See the note under article 52 in the present compilation. If elements of article 57 of the ILC draft are slotted in as article 52, bringing them into close proximity of these assistance provisions, this reference would change to "article 52".

93/   Paragraph (j) is already a catch-all, obviating the need for "including, but not limited to".

* * *

The Court's requests for judicial assistance may concern, without being limited thereto:

(a) The seizure and transmission to the Court of all papers, files or documents, including judicial decisions, extracts from criminal records, and documents of governmental bodies;

(b) The service of procedural documents;

(c) The hearing of witnesses;

[*253] (d) The questioning of any suspect or accused, including those named in a request for transfer;

(e) The production and transmission of any expert opinion or report necessary to the Court.

* * *

Scope of assistance. States Parties shall, in accordance with the provisions of this article, comply with requests for legal assistance by the Court [or Prosecutor] with respect to the investigation or prosecution of a crime under the Court's jurisdiction, which assistance shall include:

(a) the identification and whereabouts of persons or the location of items;

(b) the taking of testimony and the production of evidence;

* * *

the taking and production of [testimony or other] evidence and statements of persons; 94/

(c) the service of documents;

(d) the temporary transfer of persons in custody, with their consent, in order to provide testimony or other assistance to the Court;

(d bis) assisting in the [making available/transfer] of other persons not in custody, in order to provide testimony or other assistance to the Court; 95/

(e) the conduct of on-site investigations and inspections; 96/

(f) permitting the Court to sit on its territory for the purpose of taking of evidence or of conducting a proceeding before the Court;

[*254] (g) executing searches and seizures; 97/

(h) provision of originals and certified copies of relevant records and documents;

(i) taking action as permitted by law to prevent injury to, or the intimidation of, a witness or the destruction of evidence; 98/ or

(j) identifying, tracing, freezing, seizing and forfeiting proceeds and instrumentalities of crime;

(k) any other assistance [not prohibited by the law of the requested State 99/] which the Court may require. 100/

* * *

The Court may request the cooperation and assistance of any State party on matters including, but not limited to:

(a) the extradition of fugitives;

(b) the provisional detention of fugitives;

94/ Other aspects that could be included in this provision are "including records of government" in regard to the production of evidence, and "whether or not under oath" with regard to statements.

95/ The problem of the arrest and forcible transfer of recalcitrant witnesses to the Court creates problems for many States. Provision could be made in the rules of the Court for the Court to accept testimony recorded by the requested State in alternative ways, for instance by way of video recordings (see footnote 106 below). Another alternative would be to allow the Prosecutor/ Court to take a deposition from such a witness within the territory of the requested State, provided of course that the defence would also be allowed to cross-examine the witness if the Prosecutor takes the deposition.

96/ See ILC draft Statute article 26 (2) (c). It has been observed that this is also a form of cooperation. This provision as drafted is conceivably wide enough to allow not only the Prosecutor to utilize it, but the Court as well.

97/ This provision appeared as a provisional measure in article52(1)(b) of the ILC draft Statute.

98/ These measures also appeared in the ILC draft Statute as provisional measures.

99/ If inserted here, this qualification may only apply to subparagraph (k), and not all the forms of assistance provided for in this article. The aim is, however, to allay concerns States may have regarding the open-endedness of the provision.

100/ Despite the open-endedness created by this subparagraph, it should be considered whether there are any other forms of assistance that need to be specifically provided for.

(c)　the taking of statements of suspects, witnesses or any other persons, including testimony upon oath;

(d)　search and seizure;

(e)　inspections and expert examinations;

(f)　the identification and location of suspects, witnesses or any other persons;

(g)　the forwarding of evidentiary documents and seizable evidentiary materials;

(h)　the approval of transportation of persons surrendered through its territory.

The Court may make a request to States Parties for assistance as provided for in subparagraphs 1 (c) to (g) inclusive of article 1 (hereinafter referred [*255] to as request for assistance) as regards offences specified in article [ ], either <u>ex officio</u> or upon request of the prosecution or a defence counsel.

C. <u>Limitations on obligation; bases for denial of requests; assistance</u>
<u>pursuant to conditions (paragraph 5 (c))</u>

3.　With regard to a request pertaining to a crime under: 101/

(a)　article 20 (a) to (d), all States Parties;

(b)　article 20 (e), States Parties which have accepted the jurisdiction of the Court with respect to the crime in question, shall respond without undue delay to the request.

* * *

3.... request, <u>without prejudice to the rights under article 26</u>.

* * *

Secrecy of defence

The obligation to cooperate provided for in article 60 shall take precedence over all the legal obstacles which the State to which the request for judicial assistance is made invokes against the Court pursuant to its internal law or the treaties to which it is a party.

1.　Any person heard or examined by the Trial Chamber may invoke restrictions provided for in his national law and designed to prevent the divulgation of confidential information connected with national defence.

2.　The Trial Chamber may ask the State of which the persons being heard or examined are nationals whether it confirms their claim to be bound to secrecy.

If the State confirms to the Trial Chamber that an obligation of secrecy exists, the Chamber shall note this fact.

3.　The provisions of the preceding paragraphs shall also apply to execution of a request for judicial assistance made under article 72.

* * *

When ratifying this Statute, States Parties shall notify the Secretary-General of the United Nations of the conditions under which they would refuse assistance and shall specify elements which must be included in a written [*256] request. States Parties shall not refuse assistance for reasons other than those indicated.

The following conditions do not constitute conditions under which a requested State may refuse to provide assistance, irrespective of paragraph 3: 102/

(a)　when the act constituting the offence for which extradition is requested does not constitute an offence under the laws, regulations or ordinances of the requested State;

(b)　when the requested State does not deem it appropriate to honour the request.All the offences specified in article [ ] shall not be deemed to be offences of a political nature as regards a request for assistance under this Statute.

* * *

101/ The final wording of this provision, as well as that of the whole article, depends on which crimes are ultimately included under the jurisdiction of the Court. This drafting reflects a situation where the core crimes are under the inherent jurisdiction of the Court. If treaty crimes are excluded initially and a provision is inserted for the revision of the list of crimes, then a proviso could be considered along with such revision provision, providing for the cooperation by a requested State that has accepted the expanded jurisdiction of the Court with regard to the crime in question.

102/ It was emphasized that other traditional grounds for refusal, such as the public order clause, should also not be allowed to be invoked with respect to requests of the Court for assistance.

5.   (a)   A requested State Party may deny a request for assistance, in whole or in part, if: 103/
(i)   except for [the crime of genocide under article 20 (a)] [the crimes under article 20 (a) to (d)], it has not accepted the jurisdiction of the Court with respect to the offence which is the subject of the investigation or prosecution; or
(ii)   [the action requested is prohibited by the law of the requested State] 104/
OR
[the authorities of requested State would be prohibited by its domestic laws from carrying out the action requested with regard to the investigation or prosecution of a similar offence in that State];
[*257]   (iii)   execution of the request would seriously prejudice its security [, ordre public] or other of its essential interests; 105/
(iv)   [if the request would be manifestly ungrounded]; or
(v)   [if the request is not made in conformity with the provisions of this article.]
(b)   [Except where the Court has determined that a case is admissible under section 35, the requested State may postpone or refuse assistance where, in its opinion, execution of the request would interfere with an ongoing investigation or prosecution of the same matter in the requested State or in another State [or with a completed investigation or prosecution of that matter that might have led to an acquittal]]
OR
[A State may deny a request for assistance, in whole or in part, if:
(i)   execution would interfere with an ongoing criminal investigation or proceeding in that State; or
(ii)   execution would conflict with an obligation to provide assistance to another State in its investigation or prosecution.
(b bis)   Assistance may not be denied on the basis of subparagraph (b) (i) or (b) (ii) if the Court has already declared the case giving rise to the request for assistance to be admissible, and
(i)   in a case under subparagraph (b) (i), its decision took into consideration the investigation or proceedings pending in the requested State; or
(ii)   in a case under subparagraph (b) (ii), the other State is a State Party, and the Court's decision took into consideration the investigation or proceedings in the other State.]
(c)   Before denying a request for assistance, the requested State shall consider whether the requested assistance can be provided subject to specified conditions, or whether the assistance can be provided at a later time or in an alternative manner: 106/ Provided that if the Court or the Prosecutor accepts the assistance subject to conditions, it shall abide by them;
[*258] (d) If a request for assistance is denied, the requested State Party shall promptly inform the Court or the Prosecutor of the reasons for the denial.

* * *

103/ The Preparatory Committee generally felt that the grounds on which the request may be refused should be limited in nature and should be specifically spelt out in the Statute. In this regard non bis in idem could also be considered for inclusion, as well as manifest errors of fact or law by the Court, and a statute of limitations if such a provision is included.

104/ This provision should not allow proliferation of grounds for refusal of a request on the basis of national law. The grounds for denial should remain limited to only those contained in this Statute. This provision is intended to cover the situation where, for instance, telephone tapping is requested and the law of the requested State does not allow such action. Consideration could also be given to formulating the provision in positive terms, for instance that "compliance with a request for assistance shall be in accordance with the national law of the requested State".

105/ The inherent danger of this provision is that it is possible to interpret it so broadly as to be ultimately counterproductive to the obligation to provide assistance. In this regard a proposal has been made to, where a witness refuses to give evidence on the basis of not wishing to disclose government secrets, provide for the Court to approach the State concerned to confirm the status of the information. The Court would then have to abide by the classification of that State.

106/ In this regard it is conceivable that testimony could, for instance, be recorded electronically and made available to the Court in that format. It should be considered whether it is necessary to include a specific provision to the effect that the Court will be allowed to receive and consider such testimony. See footnote 95 above.

[A requested State Party may deny a request for assistance, in whole or in part, if compliance with the request would put it in breach of an existing [international law] [treaty] obligation undertaken to another [State] [non-State Party].] 107/

D. Application to the Court to set aside assistance request

4.   [A State Party] may, within 28 days of receiving a request under paragraph 2, file a written application with the Registrar [, or with the Prosecutor where the request is made by the Prosecutor during the investigation phase,] requesting that the Court set aside the request on specified grounds. Pending a decision of the Court on the application, the State concerned may delay complying with paragraph 3, but shall take any provisional measure necessary to ensure that assistance can be given at a later moment. 108/

[*259] E. Priority of the Court's requests

5.   [States Parties and the Court shall give absolute priority to the request under paragraph 1 of this article even over concurring requests from other States [Parties] not having primary jurisdiction according to this Statute. 109/

F. Confidentiality

6.   The Court shall ensure the confidentiality of evidence and information except as required for the investigation and proceedings described in the request.

The requested State shall keep confidential a request and any supporting documents, except to the extent that the disclosure is necessary for execution of the request.

* * *

The requested State may, when it deems it to be in its interest, transmit documents, papers, files or information to the Prosecutor on a confidential basis. The Prosecutor may then use them only for the purpose of collecting new evidence.

The State may automatically or at the request of the Prosecutor subsequently authorize the publication of such documents, papers, files or information. They may then be used as evidence, provided that they are previously communicated to the accused.

G. Reciprocal cooperation of the Court with States Parties

7.   If requested, the Court shall reciprocally cooperate with and 110/ provide assistance to a State Party conducting an investigation into actions which constitute a crime under this Statute.

* * *

1.   The States parties may, for the purposes of a current investigation or legal proceeding, request the Court to transmit papers or documents obtained in the course of an investigation or a legal proceeding conducted by the Court.

2.   If such papers or documents have been obtained with the assistance of a State, this State must give its prior consent to any communication addressed to the requesting State. It shall be invited, at the request of the Preliminary Investigations Chamber and through the Registrar, to make its decision known.

107/ If a breach of another international law obligation is a ground for denying assistance, what is its precise scope?(a)Is it confined to obligations owed to non-States Parties only? As between States Parties to the International Criminal Court, participation in the Statute could override earlier inconsistent treaty obligations (see article 30 of the 1969 Vienna Convention on the Law of Treaties) but would it be desirable to have an express provision in the Statute stating so?(b)Is it confined to obligations arising out of treaties only?(c)Does it cover requests for arrest and transfer (e.g., requests for the surrender of a foreign diplomat accredited to the requested State Party) or only requests for other forms of assistance (e.g., search and seizure of diplomatic premises)?Consideration should be given to the relationship between the obligations of States Parties to cooperate with the Court and their other existing but inconsistent international law obligations, e.g., arising from bilateral extradition treaties, the Vienna Convention on Diplomatic Relations.

108/ An expressed concern is that this provision could allow States, in bad faith, to block or delay compliance with requests for assistance. It has been pointed out that it is not in accordance with State practice for a State to challenge the decision of another State to request assistance. Does the provision therefore serve a useful purpose in the context of the Court? Two views are that: (a) the provision opens up other grounds for denial of a request, in direct opposition to the intention that the grounds for refusal should be exhaustively enumerated in the Statute; and (b) that the provision is necessary. It allows for a useful interplay between the Court and national jurisdictions in order to allow the latter to better (in view of the principle of complementarity) take an informed decision.

109/ If the option, expressed in paragraph3, is found to be undesirable in view of arguments related to the principle of complementarity, this alternative, reflecting a reciprocal and rigid obligation approach, could be considered.

110/ Some support exists for providing a reciprocal obligation on the Court also to provide assistance to States.

3.   In the case of the testimony of a witness or expert, such witness or expert must also give his prior consent to any communication addressed to the [*260] requesting State. He shall be invited to do so at the request of the Preliminary Investigations Chamber and through the Registrar.

4.   The Preliminary Investigations Chamber shall grant the request after having obtained the necessary consents.

The Preliminary Investigations Chamber may, under the same conditions, grant such a request from a State non-party. In taking its decision it shall bear in mind the behaviour of that State in connection with earlier requests for cooperation addressed to it by the Court and the interests of justice.

[*261] Article 52
Provisional measures
I. ILC DRAFT

1.   In case of need, the Court may request a State to take necessary provisional measures, including the following:

   (a)   to provisionally arrest a suspect;
   (b)   to seize documents or other evidence; or
   (c)   to prevent injury to or the intimidation of a witness or the destruction of evidence.

2.   The Court shall follow up a request under paragraph 1 by providing, as soon as possible and in any case within 28 days, a formal request for assistance complying with article 57.

II. PROPOSALS
The title of the article should read:
[Provisional measures] [Request for assistance in case of urgency]

[Note. In view of the proposal at the first session of the Preparatory Committee that provisional arrest be included under the provisions of articles 28 and 29 (as pre-indictment arrest and post-indictment arrest) this provision as contained in the ILC draft Statute could be deleted. 111/ The provisional measures pertaining to protection of evidence and witnesses can be seen as assistance measures and have been inserted under article 51 (2).

If this is done, the current ILC draft Statute's article 57 pertaining to the form and contents of the request could be inserted here as article 52, bringing it in closer proximity to article 51 to which it applies.The question of provisional detention is dealt with in article 53 bis.

The question of provisional arrest in case of urgency is dealt with in article 53 ter.]

In cases of urgency, when the Court makes a request for provisional detention, notifying the requested Party that a warrant of arrest has been issued or a sentence has been imposed for an offence specified in article [ ], the requested State Party may provisionally detain the person sought in accordance with its national laws.

[*262] The request for provisional detention shall describe the identity of the person to be sought and the facts of the case, and shall contain such further information as may be required by the laws of the requested State.

If the Court fails to present the request for extradition within [30] days from the date of provisional detention, the person detained shall be set at liberty; provided that this stipulation shall not prevent the requested State from instituting a proceeding with a view to extraditing the person sought if a request for extradition is subsequently received.

When ratifying this Statute, States Parties shall notify the Secretary-General of the United Nations of the conditions under which they would refuse provisional detention and shall specify elements which must be included in a written request for provisional detention. States Parties shall not refuse a request for detention for reasons other than those indicated.

* * *

111/ It should be noted, however, that other provisional measures, such as for instance deprivation of freedom through the seizure of passports, may indeed exist that may warrant the retention of this provision if these measures cannot be read in under the catch all provision of article 51 (2) (i).

In an emergency the request for transfer referred to in paragraph 1 of this article may be transmitted to a State by any means producing a written communication. It shall be accompanied by a statement of the facts and shall indicate the existence of one of the warrants referred to in paragraph 4 of this article.

The person named in a request for transfer transmitted in this way may be arrested and placed in detention in the manner prescribed for the execution of the warrant mentioned in the said request. This person shall be released automatically if the request for transfer accompanied by the documents referred to in paragraphs 3 and 4 of this article does not reach the State which is detaining him within 30 days from the date of his arrest. However, the person may consent to his transfer to the Court before the expiry of this period if the legislation of the requested State so allows, in which case that State shall proceed to transfer him to the Court as soon as possible.

The release of this person pursuant to the preceding paragraph shall not prevent his re-arrest and transfer to the Court if a request for transfer satisfying the requirements of paragraphs 3 and 4 of this article arrives subsequently.

* * *

In an emergency, the request referred to in paragraph 1 of this article may be transmitted to a State by any means producing a written communication.

At the request of the Court, the documents produced in response to the request shall also be sent urgently by any means. The procedure described in paragraphs 2 and 3 of this article shall subsequently be followed.

[*263] Article 53
Transfer of an accused to the Court
I. ILC DRAFT

1.   The Registrar shall transmit to any State on the territory of which the accused may be found a warrant for the arrest and transfer of an accused issued under article 28, and shall request the cooperation of that State in the arrest and transfer of the accused.

2.   Upon receipt of a request under paragraph 1:

    (a)   all States Parties:

        (i)   in a case covered by article 21 (1)(a), or

        (ii)   which have accepted the jurisdiction of the Court with respect to the crime in question;

shall, subject to paragraphs 5 and 6, take immediate steps to arrest and transfer the accused to the Court;

    (b)   in the case of a crime to which article 20 (e) applies, a State Party which is a Party to the treaty in question but which has not accepted the Court's jurisdiction with respect to that crime shall, if it decides not to transfer the accused to the Court, forthwith take all necessary steps to extradite the accused to a requesting State or refer the case to its competent authorities for the purpose of prosecution;

    (c)   in any other case, a State Party shall consider whether it can, in accordance with its legal procedures, take steps to arrest and transfer the accused to the Court, or whether it should take steps to extradite the accused to a requesting State or refer the case to its competent authorities for the purpose of prosecution.

3.   The transfer of an accused to the Court constitutes, as between States Parties which accept the jurisdiction of the Court with respect to the crime, sufficient compliance with a provision of any treaty requiring that a suspect be extradited or the case referred to the competent authorities of the requested State for the purpose of prosecution.

4.   A State party which accepts the jurisdiction of the Court with respect to the crime shall, as far as possible, give priority to a request under paragraph 1 over requests for extradition from other States.

5.   A State Party may delay complying with paragraph 2 if the accused is in its custody or control and is being proceeded against for a serious crime, or serving a sentence imposed by a court for a crime. It shall within 45 days of receiving the request inform the Registrar of the reasons for the delay. In such cases, the requested State:

[*264] (a) may agree to the temporary transfer of the accused for the purpose of standing trial under this Statute; or

(c)   shall comply with paragraph 2 after the prosecution has been completed or abandoned or the sentence has been served, as the case may be.

6.   A State party may, within 45 days of receiving a request under paragraph 1, file a written application with the Registrar requesting the Court to set aside the request on specified grounds. Pending a decision of the Court on the application, the State concerned may delay complying with paragraph 2 but shall take any provisional measures necessary to ensure that the accused remains in its custody or control.

II. PROPOSALS

The title of the article should read:

Surrender of accused or convicted persons to the Court 112/

The Court may request the extradition of a fugitive to States Parties as regards offences specified in article [ ] when the Court has issued a warrant of arrest.

* * *

A. Transmittal and purposes of request

1.   The Registrar shall transmit to any State on the territory of which the accused or convicted person may be found the warrant for the arrest and [a request for the] transfer [surrender] of such person issued under article 28, or in order to enforce the sentence of the convicted person, [along with the supporting material outlined in article 53 bis] and shall request the cooperation of that State in the arrest and surrender of such person. 113/

* * *

The request for transfer, in written form and signed by the Prosecutor, shall be addressed by the Registrar to the competent authority of the requested State designated in accordance with article 62. 114/

[*265] States parties shall respond without delay to any request for cooperation submitted by the Court under this Statute. They may request the Court to provide any additional information which they consider necessary to enable them to respond to the request.

The competent authority of the requested State and the Registrar of the Court shall agree on the date and modalities of the transfer of the person concerned to the seat of the Court or to the place which it specifies.

* * *

The request under paragraph 1 shall be made in written form through diplomatic channels. If a requested State considers the information and evidence provided by the Court insufficient as a basis for decisions whether to offer assistance, it may seek further information and evidence from the Court as it deems necessary.

All the documents to be provided by the Court to the State Party shall be accompanied by a duly certified translation in the language of the party.

B. Limitations on obligation/Basis for denial 115/

2.   A requested State Party on whose territory the accused or convicted person is found 116/ shall, subject to paragraphs 8 and 9, take immediate steps to arrest and surrender a convicted person to the authorities

---

112/ This article will require especial consideration of the principle of complementarity, and specific drafting to reinforce the principle may be necessary. It is conceivable that convicted persons may be at large for some reason. It may therefor be necessary to provide for the arrest of such convicted persons. Although this aspect is dealt with under this article, it has been pointed out that it may be more appropriate to deal with this aspect under article 59 on enforcement of sentences.

113/ See article 53 (4) of both the ILC and the Siracusa drafts.

114/ Article 62 deals with the designation of a competent national authority.

115/ The refusal to transfer on the grounds that a State exercises its jurisdiction is neither a denial nor a limitation on the obligation to transfer but a question of complementarity to be addressed in the appropriate section of the draft Statute.

116/ Apart from stating the obvious fact that, since the request will in all probability be transmitted to more than one State, the State on whose territory the person is found should arrest and surrender that person, the text basically accords with article 53 (2) of the Siracusa draft. See, however, article 53 (2) of the ILC draft.

identified in the warrant of arrest in the case of a convicted person, 117/ or arrest and surrender an accused to the Court if the case is covered by:

(a)   articles 20 (a) to (d) [(a) or Article 23 (1)]; 118/ or

(b)   if the requested State has accepted the jurisdiction of the Court with respect to the crime in question.

* * *

[*266] The extradition legislation of a requested State shall be opposable by that State to any request for transfer of the accused or the suspect to the Court.

* * *

When ratifying this Statute, States parties shall inform the Secretary-General of the United Nations of the conditions under which they would refuse extradition and shall specify elements which must be included in a written request for extradition. States Parties shall not refuse extradition for reasons other than those indicated.

The following do not constitute conditions under which a requested State may refuse extradition, irrespective of paragraph 4:

(a)   The act constituting the offence for which extradition is requested does not constitute an offence under the laws, regulations or ordinances of the requested State;

(b)   The requested State does not deem it appropriate to honour the request;

[(c) The requested State has substantial grounds for believing that the request for extradition has been made for the purpose of prosecuting or punishing the person concerned on account of that person's race, religion, nationality, ethnic origin, political opinions, sex or status, or that that person's position may be prejudiced for any of those reasons;]

[(d) The requested State has grounds for believing that the person whose extradition is requested has been or would be subjected in the Court to torture or cruel, inhuman or degrading treatment or punishment or if that person has not received or would not receive the minimum guarantees in a criminal proceeding, as contained in the International Covenant on Civil and Political Rights, article 14.]

All the offences specified in article [ ] shall not be deemed to be offences of a political nature as regards extradition under this Statute.

States Parties shall not be bound to extradite their own nationals, but may extradite them at their discretion.

* * *

Where the law of the requested State Party so requires, the accused person shall be entitled to challenge the request for arrest and surrender in the court of the requested State Party on the ground that the evidence submitted in support of the request would not be sufficient to commit him to trial for such an offence in a court of the requested State.

* * *

[A requested State Party may deny a request for arrest or surrender if compliance with the request would put it in breach of an existing [international [*267] law] [treaty] obligation undertaken to another [State] [non-State party].] 119/

C. Competing [parallel] requests from the Court and State(s)

3.   The requested State Party, if it is a party to the treaty covered by article 20 (e) and has accepted the jurisdiction of the Court, shall give priority to surrender the accused to the Court over requests for extradition from other States.

* * *

[3.   If the requested State also receives a request from a State for the extradition of the same person, either for the same offence or for a different offence for which the Court is seeking the person's surrender, the

---

117/ It is conceivable that a convicted fugitive should be surrendered to the authorities of the State which has been designated as the administering State, and that warrant would provide for this.

118/ The first option would apply if the Court was given inherent jurisdiction over the core crimes.

119/ Consideration should be given to the relationship between the obligations of States Parties to cooperate with the Court and their other existing but inconsistent international law obligations, e.g. arising from bilateral extradition treaties, the 1961 Vienna Convention on Diplomatic Relations, etc. See footnote 107 above.

appropriate authority of the requested State shall determine whether to surrender the person to the Court or to extradite the person to the State. In making its decision the requested State shall consider all relevant factors, including but not limited to

  (a) whether the extradition request was made pursuant to a treaty;

  (b) if the offences are different, the nature and gravity of the offences;

  (c) the interests of the State requesting extradition, including, where relevant, whether the offence was committed in its territory and the nationality of the victims of the offence;

  (d) the possibility of subsequent surrender or extradition between the Court and the State requesting extradition; and

  (e) the chronological order in which the requests were received.

3 bis. The requested State may not, however, deny a request for the surrender made under this article in deference to another State's request for extradition of the same person for the same offence, if the State requesting extradition is a State party, and the Court has ruled the case before it admissible, and its decision took into consideration the proceedings in that State which gave rise to its extradition request.] 120/

* * *

1. The States Parties shall undertake to give priority to requests for transfer submitted by the Court over requests for extradition submitted by other States Parties.

[*268] 2. If the State Party to which the request for transfer is addressed has also received a request for extradition from a State Party to which it is bound by an extradition agreement, it shall rule on that request for extradition, unless the Court, pursuant to article 39, has already rejected the challenge to submission to the Court made by the State requesting the extradition.

3. The State requesting the extradition may, if it has not already contested submission to the Court pursuant to article 39, request the Court to withdraw its request for transfer, on the basis of the principle of complementarity stated in the preamble to this Statute. The person named in the request for transfer may, under the same conditions, challenge submission to the Court and seek the withdrawal of the request for transfer.

Taking into account the facts and the identity of the persons named in the request for transfer, the Court shall rule in accordance with article 35, paragraphs (a) and (c), and article 39, paragraphs 3, 5, 6 and 7. The warrants issued earlier by the Court shall remain in force and the States parties shall be bound to cooperate.

4. If the State detaining the person concerned rejects the request for extradition, it shall so inform the Court without delay. The request referred to in paragraph 3 of this article shall then cease to have effect, and the Court shall note this fact in a decision.

5. If the Court decides not to grant the request submitted under paragraph 3 of this article, the Registrar shall immediately so inform the requested State, and the demand for extradition submitted by the requesting State shall cease to have effect. The person concerned shall then be transferred to the Court as soon as possible.

6. If the State detaining the person concerned decides to grant the request for extradition before the Court has finally ruled on the request submitted under paragraph 3 of this article, it may either keep the person concerned at its disposal or transfer him to the Court, in which case it shall notify its decision in favour of extradition to the requesting State and to the Court.

If the Court subsequently accepts the request submitted by the requesting State in accordance with paragraph 3 of this article and if the person concerned has been transferred to it pursuant to the preceding paragraph, it shall order the return of the person concerned to that State.

For the purposes of prosecution the requesting State shall be bound by the decision on extradition taken by the requested State and by all other provisions of the extradition treaty between the two States. The duration of the person's detention in the requested State and at the seat of the Court or in the place which it specifies shall be deducted in full from any sentence imposed in that requesting State.

120/ This issue may be considered as part of the wider question of whether a State Party can rely on an existing but inconsistent international law obligation to deny such a request. See footnote 107.

7. If the State Party requested to make a transfer to the Court has also received a request for extradition from a State non-party but one to which it is bound by an extradition agreement, it shall rule as in the case of concurrent requests for extradition, taking into account the following circumstances:

- The respective dates of the requests;
- The respective seriousness of the offences in question, with priority given to the request based on the most serious offences;

[*269] - The possibility that an agreement may be concluded between the State non-party requesting the extradition and the Court providing either that, following his trial by that State or after he has served his sentence, the person concerned may be transferred to the Court, or that the Court agrees to return him temporarily to the State requesting his extradition after having tried him, in order that that State may try him in turn or have him serve his sentence.

D. Extradite or prosecute obligation

4. In the case of a crime to which article 20 (e) applies, the requested State Party, if it is a party to the treaty in question but has not accepted the Court's jurisdiction with respect to that crime shall, where it decides not to surrender the accused to the Court, promptly take all necessary steps to extradite the accused to a State having requested extradition or refer the case to its competent authorities for the purpose of prosecution. 121/

* * *

If the requested State refuses to carry out a transfer, it shall, at the request of the Court, submit the case to the competent authorities in order that judicial proceedings may be instituted if grounds exist.

* * *

If a State Party decides not to extradite a fugitive who is present in its territory, it shall submit, without undue delay, the case to its competent authority for the purpose of prosecution, through proceedings in accordance with its national laws. This provision shall not apply in the following cases:

    (a) if it is deemed that under the laws, regulations or ordinances of the requested State it would be impossible to impose or to execute punishment upon the fugitive; if the act constituting the offence for which extradition is requested was committed in the territory of the requested State; or if the trial therefore would be held in a court of requested State;

    (b) if there is no probable cause to suspect that the fugitive has committed an act which constitutes an offence for which extradition is requested.

5. In any other case, the requested State Party shall [consider whether it can], 122/ in accordance with its legal procedures, take steps to arrest and surrender the accused to the Court, or [whether it should] take steps to extradite the accused to a State having requested extradition or refer the case to its competent authorities for the purpose of prosecution. 123/

[*270] 5 bis. A requested State Party may not deny a request for surrender on the grounds that

    (a) the person sought is a national of the requested State;

    (b) the offence for which the person is being sought is a political or military offence [or an offence connected to such offences]; 124/ or

* * *

5 ter. A requested State may deny a request for surrender if the person is being proceeded against or has been proceeded against, convicted or acquitted in the requested State or another State for the offence for which his surrender is sought, unless the Court has declared the case before it to be admissible under article 35 or 42, notwithstanding such proceedings or such prior conviction or acquittal.

121/ It is conceivable that a convicted fugitive should be surrendered to the authorities of the State which has been designated as the administering State, and that the warrant would provide for this.

122/ Should there be a discretion in this regard? If not, then both the phrases in square brackets in this provision could be deleted.

123/ See ILC draft article53(2)(c) and Siracusa draft article53(5).

124/ The separation of provisions dealing with mutual assistance and with arrest and transfer necessitates the insertion in this article of a provision dealing with the grounds on which the request for arrest and surrender may be refused. Further grounds such as double criminality and public order should also be inserted.

6.   The surrender of an accused to the Court constitutes, as between States Parties which accept the jurisdiction of the Court with respect to the crime in question, compliance with a provision of any treaty requiring that a suspect be extradited or the case be referred to the competent authorities of the requested State for the purpose of prosecution. 125/

7.   A State Party which has accepted the jurisdiction of the Court with respect to the crime in question shall, as far as possible, give priority to a request under paragraph 1 over requests for extradition from other States. 126/

E. Delayed or temporary surrender of persons in custody for different offence

8.   The requested 127/ State Party may delay complying with a request under paragraphs 2 to 4 if the accused or convicted person is in its custody or control and is being proceeded against for a serious crime, or serving a [*271] sentence imposed by [a/the] 128/ Court for a crime. It shall within [28 days] of receiving the request inform the Registrar of the reasons for the delay. In such case it:

(a)   may agree to the temporary surrender of the accused for the purpose of standing trial under this Statute; or

(b)   shall comply with the request under paragraphs 2 to 4 after the prosecution has been completed or abandoned or the sentence has been served, as the case may be. 129/

* * *

The requested State may, with the consent of the Preliminary Investigations Chamber, which shall rule after having heard the Prosecutor, defer the transfer of the person in question if he is being prosecuted or serving a sentence in respect of facts different from those for which he is being sought.

If the requested State does not request deferment of the transfer or if such deferment is denied by the Preliminary Investigations Chamber, that State may request the Preliminary Investigations Chamber to return the person concerned after completion of his trial by the Court, in order that he may be prosecuted or serve his sentence in respect of facts different from those for which he has finally been sentenced by the Court.

* * *

F. Application to the Court to set aside surrender request

9.   A [requested] State Party may, within [28 days] of receiving a request under paragraph 1, file a written request with the Registrar requesting the Court to set aside the request on specified grounds including those mentioned in articles 35 and 42. Pending a decision of the Court on the application, the State concerned may delay complying with paragraphs 2 to 4 but shall take any provisional measures necessary to ensure that the accused or convicted person remains in its custody or control. 130/

G. Provisions of evidence irrespective of surrender

10.   To the extent permitted under the law of the requested State and subject to the rights of third parties, all [property] found in the requested State that has been acquired as a result of the alleged offence or that may be required as evidence shall, upon request, be transmitted to the Court if surrender is granted, even if the surrender cannot be carried out, on conditions to be determined by the Court. 131/

125/ This specific language of such a provision would need to reflect whether, in the final analysis, such situations are governed as matters of admissibility, under a separate non bis in idem provision, or a combination of the two. The notion here is to preserve the traditional non bis in idem concept, save where the Court, in accordance with the Statute, has specifically ruled that the exercise of its jurisdiction over the case is proper notwithstanding the prior proceedings in a State.

126/ See Siracusa draft article 53 (7) and ILC draft article 53 (4).

127/ Siracusa draft article 53 (8). If "requested" is retained here, it should also be inserted at the beginning of the next paragraph for the sake of uniformity. It would, however, appear to be redundant owing to the specific reference to "request" in both provisions and could therefore be deleted.

128/ Article 53 (8) of the Siracusa draft contains an error here: either "a" or "the" depending on whether any court, or specifically the International Criminal Court is being referred to.

129/ See Siracusa draft article 53 (8).

130/ See ILC draft article 53 (6) and Siracusa draft article53(9).

131/ Siracusa draft article 53 (10). Some delegations questioned the utility of this paragraph.

[*272] H. <u>Transit of surrendered person</u>

11. <u>132/</u> (a)   A State Party shall authorize transportation through its territory of a person being surrendered to the Court by another State. A request by the Court for transit shall be transmitted through diplomatic channels, unless otherwise agreed. The request for transit shall contain a description of the person being transported and a brief statement of the facts of the case. A person in transit shall be detained in custody during the period of transit.

   (b)   No authorization is required where air transportation is used and no landing is scheduled on the territory of the State of transit. If an unscheduled landing occurs on the territory of the State of transit, it may require a request for transit as provided for in subparagraph (a). The State of transit shall detain the person to be transported until the request for transit is received and the transit is effected, so long as the request is received within 96 hours of the unscheduled landing.

* * *

1.   Transit through the territory of one of the States Parties shall be granted on application to the competent authority designated in accordance with article 62.

2.   The transit of a national of the transit State may be refused.

3.   Subject to the provisions of paragraph 4 of this article, the documents referred to in article 66, paragraphs 3 (a) and 4 (a) and (b), shall be produced.

4.   If air transport is used, the following provisions shall apply:

   (a)   when no intermediate landing is envisaged, the Court shall notify the State over whose territory the aircraft will fly and certify the existence of one of the documents referred to in article 66, paragraph 4;

   (b)   in the event of an unscheduled landing or when a landing is envisaged, the Court shall submit a regular transit request as provided for in paragraph 3 of this article.

5.   The transit of the person concerned shall not be effected through a territory where there are grounds for believing that his life or liberty may be threatened by reason of his race, religion, nationality or political opinions.

* * *

States Parties shall give approval for the transportation of the persons to the Court through their territories in accordance with their national laws.

[*273] Article 53 bis <u>133/</u>
<u>Form and content of requests for arrest or surrender</u>

1.   A request for arrest or surrender [duly signed by the Prosecutor] shall:

   (a)   be made by letter, fax, e-mail or any medium capable of delivering a written record (provided that a request shall be confirmed through the diplomatic channel):

   (b)   contain or be supported by:

      (i)   information describing the person sought, sufficient to identify the person and information as to that person's probable location;

      (ii)   in the case of a request for pre-indictment arrest:

         a.   a copy of the warrant for arrest;

         b.   a statement of the reasons to believe the suspect may have committed a crime within the jurisdiction of the Court and that the Prosecutor expects to seek an indictment within (90) days;

         c.   a brief summary of the facts of the case;

         d.   a statement as to why pre-indictment arrest is urgent and necessary.

      (iii)   in the case of a request for post-indictment arrest and surrender of a person not yet convicted:

         a.   a copy of the warrant of arrest and indictment;

132/ The need for a transit provision has been identified. It is suggested that this provision should form a separate article.

133/ This article has no equivalent in the draft proposed by the International Law Commission.

     b.   such information, documents or statements outlining the facts of the case as may be required by the law of the Requested State.

    (iv) in the case of a request for the arrest and surrender of a person already convicted:

     a.   a copy of any warrant of arrest for that person;

     b.   a copy of the judgement of conviction;

     c.   information to demonstrate that the person sought is the person referred to in the judgement of conviction;

     d.   (if the person sought has been sentenced) a copy of the sentence imposed and a statement of any time already served and that remaining.

2.   Where the requested State Party considers the information provided insufficient to allow it to comply with the request it may seek, without delay, additional information.

* * *

[*274] Article 53 ter 134/
Provisional arrest

1.   In case of urgency, the Court may request the provisional arrest of the person sought pending presentation of the request for surrender and supporting documents under paragraph 53 <u>bis</u>.

2.   The request for provisional arrest shall contain:

    (a) a description of the person sought and information regarding the probable location of such person;

    (b) a brief statement of the essential facts of the case, including, if possible, the time and location of the offence;

    (c) a statement of the existence of a warrant of arrest or a judgement of conviction against the person sought, and a description of the specific offence or offences with which the person has been charged or for which he has been convicted; and

    (d) a statement that a request for surrender of the person sought will follow.

3.   A person who is provisionally arrested may be discharged from custody upon the expiration of [60] days from the date of provisional arrest if the Requested State has not received the formal request for surrender and the supporting documents specified under paragraph [ ].

4.   The fact that the person sought has been discharged from custody pursuant to paragraph 3 shall not prejudice the subsequent rearrest and surrender of that person if the request for surrender and supporting documents are delivered at a later date.

[*275] Article 54
Obligation to extradite or prosecute
I. ILC DRAFT

In a case of a crime referred to in article 20 (e), a custodial State party to this Statute which is a party to the treaty in question but which has not accepted the Court's jurisdiction with respect to the crime for the purposes of article 21 (1) (b) (i) shall either take all necessary steps to extradite the suspect to a requesting State for the purpose of prosecution or refer the case to its competent authorities for that purpose.

II. PROPOSALS

[Note. Owing to the insertion of article 53 (4), (5) and (6), the need for article 54 of the ILC draft falls away. The provisions of the proposed article 54 (Judicial assistance) of the Siracusa draft have been absorbed into article 51 and therefore do not require incorporation as a separate article. 135/]

134/ This article has no equivalent in the draft prepared by the International Law Commission.

135/ This provision has a tight connection with the item under article 59 dealing with the recognition of the Court's sentences.

[*276] Article 55
Rule of speciality
I. ILC DRAFT

1.   A person transferred to the Court under article 53 shall not be subject to prosecution or punishment for any crime other than that for which the person was transferred.

2.   Evidence provided under this Part shall not, if the State when providing it so requests, be used as evidence for any purpose other than that for which it was provided, unless this is necessary to preserve the right of an accused under article 41 (2).

3.   The Court may request the State concerned to waive the requirements of paragraphs 1 or 2, for the reasons and purposes specified in the request.

II. PROPOSALS
A. Limit on other proceedings against surrendered person

1.   A person surrendered to the Court under Article 53 shall not be proceeded against, sentenced or detained for any crime other than that for which the person has been surrendered. 136/

* * *

1.   A person extradited under this Statute shall not, except under any one of the following circumstances, be detained, prosecuted, tried or punished for an offence other than that for which extradition was effected:

   (a)   when a person extradited commits an offence after extradition;
   (b)   when a requested State has consented to his detention, prosecution, trial or punishment for an offence other than that for which the extradition has been effected.

B. Limit on other uses of evidence

2.   A State providing evidence under this Part may require that the evidence not be used for any purpose other than that for which it was provided unless [*277] this is necessary to preserve a right of the accused under article 41 (2). 137/

* * *

2.   Evidence provided by States Parties under this Statute shall not be used in connection with any offence other than that which is mentioned in the request for assistance as being a subject of investigation unless the requested State offers its consent.

C. Waiver of rule by requested State

3.   The Court may request the State concerned to waive the requirements of paragraphs 1 or 2, for the reasons and purposes to be specified in the request. In a case of paragraph 1, the request shall be accompanied by an additional warrant of arrest and by a legal record of any statement made by the accused with respect to the offence.

[*278] Article 56
Cooperation with States not parties to this Statute
I. ILC DRAFT

States not parties to this Statute may assist in relation to the matters referred to in this Part on the basis of comity, a unilateral declaration, an ad hoc arrangement or other agreement with the Court.

II. PROPOSALS

[Note. This provision has been inserted as subparagraph 4 of the proposed article X of this Part, obviating the need for its inclusion as a separate article.]Certain delegations suggested that there should be a separate provision for cooperation with non-State Parties.

136/ See article 55 (1) of both the ILC draft and the Siracusa draft. This wording is based on the more comprehensive formulation of the Siracusa draft.

137/ The Preparatory Committee expressed general satisfaction with the limited rule contained in article 55 (2) of the ILC draft. The proposed wording reflects the wording of article 55 (2) of the Siracusa draft.

[*279] Article 57
Communications and documentation
I. ILC DRAFT

1. Requests under this Part shall be in writing, or be forthwith reduced to writing, and shall be between the competent national authority and the Registrar. States parties shall inform the Registrar of the name and address of their national authority for this purpose.

2. When appropriate, communications may also be made through the International Criminal Police Organization.

3. A request under this Part shall include the following, as applicable:

(a) a brief statement of the purpose of the request and of the assistance sought, including the legal basis and grounds for the request;

(b) information concerning the person who is the subject of the request on the evidence sought, in sufficient detail to enable identification;

(c) a brief description of the essential facts underlying the request; and

(d) information concerning the complaint or charge to which the request relates and of the basis for the Court's jurisdiction.

4. A requested State which considers the information provided insufficient to enable the request to be complied with may seek further particulars.

[*280] II. PROPOSALS

The title of the article should be changed to read:
Form and contents of the request 138/[for assistance] 139/

1. Requests for judicial (mutual) assistance shall: 140/

A. Assistance

The request for judicial assistance, in written form and signed by the Prosecutor, shall be addressed by the Registrar to the competent authority of the requested State designated in accordance with article 62.

The request referred to in paragraph 1 of this article shall be accompanied by the following information:

(a) A statement of the facts in respect of which the request for judicial assistance is made, the date and place of their commission and their legal characterization in accordance with articles 27 to 32;

(b) The identity, and if possible, the address of any person named in the request;

(c) The fullest possible details of the requested assistance.

The documents produced in response to the request for judicial assistance shall be addressed by States to the Registrar of the Court.

The Court may request the transmission of the original copies of these documents or of any other documents. In such cases the requested State may, with the consent of the Preliminary Investigations Chamber, defer the dispatch of these documents for as long as is necessary for the conduct of an investigation or legal proceeding in its territory. If the original copies of the documents are transmitted to the Court, they shall be returned as soon as possible to the State which transmitted them, if that State so requests.

[* 281] If the Court does not make any request under the preceding paragraph, the requested State may transmit merely certified copies or photocopies of the documents.

138/ The deletion of article 52 has been proposed so that the matters previously dealt with as "provisional measures" may be dealt with in articles 28 and 29 as pre-indictment and post indictment arrest. The present article could then be inserted as article 52. If this is done it may be necessary to let the provisions inserted as article 52 deal with the form and content for requests for mutual assistance. A separate provision would then need to be inserted after article 53 to deal with the form and content of a request for arrest and surrender of persons.

139/ In this report article 57 embodies only those proposals that bear on the form that requests for judicial assistance should take and not requests for transfer.

140/ Siracusa draft article 57 (1), elaborates on ILC draft article 57 (1) and (2). The Preparatory Committee was generally satisfied with the ILC draft but indicated that article 57 (3) and (4) could be further refined.

B. Transfer

The request for transfer, accompanied by the documents specified in paragraphs 3 and 4 of this article, may also be addressed to all the States Parties in whose territory the suspect or accused may be found, as well as to all the States non-parties willing to comply with the request.

In all cases the request for transfer shall be accompanied by:

(a)   A statement of the facts in respect of which the transfer is requested, the date and place of their commission and their legal characterization in accordance with articles 27 to 32;

(b)   The fullest possible description of the suspect or accused and any other information which may help to determine his identity;

(c)   If possible, the place where the suspect or accused may be found.

The request for transfer shall also be accompanied by:

(a)   Either the warrant for arrest and transfer, together with the indictment, in an original copy or a copy certified by the Registrar, if the request for transfer is made after the filing of the indictment;

(b)   Either the warrant for arrest and detention, in the original copy or a copy certified by the Registrar, if the request for transfer is made before the filing of the indictment, article 58, paragraph 2, being then applicable.

* * *

(a)   be made by letter, fax, e-mail or any medium capable of delivering a written record[, provided that a request shall be confirmed through the diplomatic channel];

(b)   contain the following, as applicable:

(i)   a brief statement of the purpose of the request and the assistance sought including the legal basis [and grounds] for the request;

(ii)   as much detailed information as possible about the location or identification of any person or place that must be found or identified in order for the assistance sought to be provided; 141/

(iii)   a brief description of the [essential] facts underlying the request including a statement explaining the nexus between the assistance sought and the matter under investigation or subject to prosecution;

[*282]   (iv)   information 142/ concerning the complaint or charge to which the request relates and of the basis of the Court's jurisdiction;

(v)   such information as may be required under the law of the requested State in order to execute the request;

(vi)   any other information relevant to the assistance being sought; 143/ and

The request for extradition shall include a description of the identity of the fugitive and the facts of the case, and shall contain such further information as may be required by the laws of the requested State.

* * *

The request for provisional detention shall describe the identity of the person to be sought and the facts of the case, and shall contain such further information as may be required by the laws of the requested State.

(c)   where applicable and unless otherwise agreed, as soon as practicable be provided to a requested State in the form of a duly certified translation in the official language of that State. 144/

141/ At the Preparatory Committee it was proposed that the "identity and location of witnesses" should also be included in this list. This provision appears to be wide enough to encompass witnesses as well.

142/ "Information" includes the charge and any relevant evidence.

143/ This catch-all provision derives from a proposal during the discussions of the Preparatory Committee.

144/ To provide for such translations would conceivably facilitate the procedures to be followed in the requested State. The provision as drafted provides for later transmission of the translation. This could avoid delays in urgent situations where the immediate preparation in a specific language could take time.

2.   Communications relating to a request under this Part shall be between the Registrar, or Prosecutor acting under article 26, and the national authority designated by each State Party for this purpose, 145/ and where appropriate may be made through the International Criminal Police Organization. 146/

Transmittal of Requests. Requests for cooperation may be made by the Court [or Prosecutor], and shall be transmitted through diplomatic channels, unless the Court and the requested State agree on another mode for transmitting requests.

* * *

[*283] The request under paragraph 1 shall be made in written form through diplomatic channels. If a requested State considers the information and evidence provided by the Court insufficient as a basis for decisions whether to offer assistance, it may seek further information and evidence from the Court as it deems necessary.

All the documents to be provided by the Court to a State Party shall be accompanied by a duly certified translation in the language of the Party.

* * *

3.   Where the requested State Party considers the information provided insufficient to allow it to comply with the request it may seek, without delay, additional information. 147/

4.   Provided that the request contains sufficient information to meet the requirements of the relevant law of the administering party, the latter shall execute the request as expeditiously as possible and transmit the results to the requesting party. 148/

* * *

(a)   The requested State shall promptly execute the request and transmit the result to the Court [or Prosecutor];

(b)   The requested State shall, to the extent permitted by its law, execute the request in accordance with any procedures specified in the request and permit persons specified in the request to be present at or assist in execution of the request.

Article 57 bis
Execution of requests 149/

1.   Requests for assistance shall be executed as expeditiously as possible and the results transmitted to the requesting party.

2.   Requests for assistance shall be executed in accordance with the law of the requested State except that the requested State shall execute the request in the manner specified in the request, including following any procedures outlined therein or permitting persons specified in the request to be present at and assist in the execution process; unless prohibited by the law of that State.

3.   The ordinary costs for execution of requests shall be borne by the requested State except for the following which should be borne by the requesting party:

[*284] (a) Costs associated to the travel of witnesses or the surrender of an accused or convicted person;

(b)   Costs of translation, interpretation and transcription.

Where the execution of a request will result in extraordinary costs, there should be consultations to determine how those costs will be met.

* * *

145/ Siracusa draft article 57 (1), with the added provision for requests by the prosecutor during the investigative phase. ILC draft article 57 (1) refers only to "between the competent national authority and the Registrar". The Preparatory Committee had some divergence of views on this aspect. The proposed wording is intended to be a compromise that could accommodate all views.

146/ ILC draft article 57 (2), Siracusa draft article57(1)(2). This provision has, in this draft, been linked to the provision contained in paragraph 1 of both the ILC and the Siracusa drafts.

147/ Siracusa draft article 57 (2), which elaborates on ILC draft article 57 (4).

148/ This provision is drafted in reciprocal terms to allow for the Court to be subject to the same obligation if requested to assist a State.

149/ This article will require some alteration if the decision is taken to make the obligation to assist reciprocal.

A. Assistance

Subject to the provisions of paragraph 2 of this article, the procedure by which a State Party discharges its obligation to cooperate shall be governed by its internal law.

The Prosecutor or members of the procuracy may assist with the execution of the request for judicial assistance by the authorities of the requested State. The requested State may authorize them to carry out certain inquiries in its territory.

If the competent authorities of the requested State are no longer able, owing to their lack of organization, to respond to requests for judicial assistance submitted by the Prosecutor, he may request from the Preliminary Investigations Chamber authorization to conduct the necessary inquiries directly in the territory of the requested State. The requested State shall be given prior notification and may submit comments to the Preliminary Investigations Chamber, in particular for the purpose of obtaining an extension of the period for execution of the request for judicial assistance.

Witnesses or experts may not be compelled to testify at the seat of the Court. If they do not wish to travel to the seat of the Court, their testimony shall be taken in the country in which they reside or in some other place which they may determine by common accord with the Court.

In order to guarantee the safety of witnesses and experts, any means of communication may be used in order to take their testimony while preserving their anonymity.

No witness or expert who appears before the Court may be prosecuted, detained or submitted to any other restriction of personal freedom by the Court.

Notwithstanding the provisions of the second and third sentences of paragraph 1 of this article, any detainee whose appearance as a witness or for the purposes of confrontation is requested by the Court shall, if necessary, be transferred temporarily to the seat of the Court or to the place which it specifies.

If this person must pass in transit through the territory of another State party, the Registrar of the Court shall proceed in accordance with article 68.

A person transferred in this manner shall remain in detention for as long as is necessary for his testimony or confrontation, unless the State in whose territory he was detained requests his release. In such circumstances the Court [*285] shall grant the request as soon as possible, and the person may not be prosecuted, detained or subjected to any other restriction of his personal freedom by the Court.

If the State which has transferred the person concerned to the seat of the Court or to the place which it specifies does not request his release, he shall be transferred back to that State as soon as possible after his testimony or confrontation.

B. Transfer

The competent authority of the requested State and the Registrar of the Court shall agree on the date and modalities of the transfer of the person concerned to the seat of the Court or to the place which it specifies.

The duration of the person's detention in the territory of the requested State shall be communicated to the Court and deducted in full from any sentence imposed by the Court.

The requested State may, with the consent of the Preliminary Investigations Chamber, which shall rule after having heard the Prosecutor, defer the transfer of the person in question if he is being prosecuted or serving a sentence in respect of facts different from those for which he is being sought.

If the requested State does not request deferment of the transfer or if such deferment is denied by the Preliminary Investigations Chamber, that State may request the Preliminary Investigations Chamber to return the person concerned after completion of his trial by the Court, in order that he may be prosecuted or serve his sentence in respect of facts different from those for which he has finally been sentenced by the Court.

On the completion of the proceedings or after the person has served his sentence, he may be transferred back to the Court or to the place which it specifies, in order to serve the sentence handed down by the Court. 150/

Articles found in the possession of the suspect or accused shall be handed over to the Court, at its request, at the time of his transfer. This may be done even if the transfer cannot take place owing to the

---

150/ The view was expressed that this provision required further clarification.

death or escape of the individual sought. The Court shall return such articles free of charge as soon as possible after the trial, if they are the property of a third party or the requested State.

C. <u>Costs</u>

The costs of the transfer of a suspect to the seat of the Court or to the place which it specifies shall be borne by the requested State.

The costs of executing requests for judicial assistance in the territory of States parties shall be borne by them, except with respect to the travel and subsistence costs of the Prosecutor, members of his office or any other member of the Court.

[*286] The costs of transmitting documents or papers, including urgent transmission, to the seat of the Court or to the place which it specifies shall be borne by the States parties.

The costs of transferring to the seat of the Court, or to the place which it specifies, detainees whose appearance is requested by the Court as witnesses or for the purposes of confrontation shall be borne by the States parties.

The costs of the travel of witnesses or experts to the seat of the Court or to the place which it specifies and the costs of their subsistence shall be borne by the budget of the Court.

The costs of any expert opinion or report requested by the Court shall be borne by the budget of the Court.

[*287] PART 8. ENFORCEMENT
Article 58
Recognition of judgements
I. ILC DRAFT

States parties undertake to recognize the judgements of the Court.

II. PROPOSALS

The title of the article should be changed to read:

General Rule 151/

General obligation to recognize judgements [and enforce sentences]
States parties undertake to recognize the judgements of the Court.

* * *

States Parties undertake to abide by the judgements of the Court 152/ and shall enforce the sentences of the Court in their territory. 153/

* * *

States Parties have to recognize the judgements of the Court as judgements rendered by their national authorities.

* * *

1. The States Parties undertake to enforce directly on their territory the decisions handed down by the Court, in accordance with the provisions of this Part.

2. A sentence pronounced by the Court shall be binding on the States Parties, which may in no case modify it, whether by reducing it, or increasing it or by altering its nature.

[*288] However, if the sentence pronounced by the Court exceeds the maximum sentence for the same offence provided for in the internal law of a State designated by the Presidency under article 149, it may, with the prior and express consent of the Presidency, be reduced by that State to the maximum incurred under its internal law.

151/ Under this article four different options are reflected based on different concepts concerning the mode of recognition.

152/ In article 58 of the Siracusa draft, "abide by" appears preferable to "recognize", which appears in ILC draft article 58. The latter conjures up images of special recognition procedures.

153/ At the Preparatory Committee a view was expressed that article 58 should provide not only for "recognition" of judgements, but also for enforcement of sentences. It should be noted that this is merely a statement of a general rule. A further proposal at the Preparatory Committee was to provide reciprocally that the Court shall recognize the judgements of courts of the States Parties. Some delegations felt that this obligation should be subject to certain conditions.

[*289] Article 59
Enforcement of sentences 154/
I. ILC DRAFT

1.   A sentence of imprisonment shall be served in a State designated by the Court from a list of States which have indicated to the Court their willingness to accept convicted persons.

2.   If no State is designated under paragraph 1, the sentence of imprisonment shall be served in a prison facility made available by the host State.

3.   A sentence of imprisonment shall be subject to the supervision of the Court in accordance with the Rules.

II. PROPOSALS
A. Obligation v. agreement of States Parties to enforce sentences of imprisonment

1.   [All States Parties shall assist the Court in enforcing prison sentences by accepting 155/ convicted persons and thus becoming the administering State. A sentence of imprisonment shall be served in a State designated by the Court from the list of available administering States. To that end, the Court shall provide the State so designated with a certified copy of the Court's judgement to be enforced. The State so designated shall promptly inform the Court whether it accepts the request.]

* * *

A sentence of imprisonment shall be served in a State designated by the Court from a list of States which have indicated to the Court their willingness to accept convicted persons. [The Court cannot designate an interested State of a given case as the place of imprisonment.]

* * *

[*290] 1. A sentence of imprisonment shall be served in a State designated by the Court from a list of States which have indicated to the Court their willingness to accept convicted persons.

* * *

1.   A sentence of imprisonment imposed by the Court shall be served in a State designated by the Presidency from a list of States which have indicated to the Presidency their willingness to accept sentenced persons. Before taking its decision, the Presidency shall request the person sentenced to comment on the matter.

3.   Although not included in the list referred to in paragraph 1 of this article, a State may, on a case-by-case basis, either of its own motion or at the request of the Presidency, give its consent to a person sentenced by the court serving his sentence on its territory. It may make its consent subject to the condition referred to in paragraph 2 of this article.

* * *

2.   If no State is designated under paragraph 1, the sentence of imprisonment shall be served in a prison facility made available by the host State.

* * *

3.   A sentence of imprisonment shall be subject to the supervision of the Court in accordance with the rules [including the rules concerning treatment of prisoners.]

* * *

B. Conditions for accepting convicted persons

4.   When imposing a sentence of imprisonment, a Chamber may stipulate that the sentence is to be served in accordance with specified laws as to pardon, parole or commutation of sentence of the State of imprisonment. The consent of the Court is not required to subsequent action by that State in conformity with those laws, but the Court shall be given at least 45 days' notice of any decision which might materially affect the terms or extent of the imprisonment.

154/ It has been stipulated that there is a strong connection between the items under articles 47 and 55. A view was expressed at the Preparatory Committee that article 58 should not only provide for "recognition" of judgements, but also for enforcement of sentences. It should be noted that this is merely a statement of a general rule. A further proposal at the Preparatory Committee was to provide reciprocally that the Court shall recognize the judgements of courts of the State Parties. Some delegations felt that the obligation should be subject to certain conditions.

155/ "Accepting" creates the possibility that this provision does not create a binding obligation. Should an alternative word be considered?

* * *

2. A State may make its consent conditional on the applicability of its internal law relating to pardons, conditional release and commutation of sentences to persons sentenced by the Court. Notwithstanding the provisions of article 152, paragraph 1, only the State of detention shall then have competence to apply these measures.

* * *

C. Designation of State by Court

Appropriateness of territorial or national State Designation of host State

[*291] 2. If no State is designated under paragraph 1, the sentence of imprisonment shall be served in a prison facility made available by the host State where the Court has its official seat.]

* * *

1. [States parties shall enforce the judgement of the Court on designation by the Registrar on [geographical] criteria formulated by Rules of the Court in accordance with the rule of burden sharing.

2. No designation to enforce shall be notified to the territorial State, or the State of active or passive nationality.]

* * *

4. If no State is designated by the Presidency under paragraphs 1 or 3 of this article, the sentence imposed by the Court shall be served in a prison facility made available by the host State.

D. Consent of convicted person

3. The consent of the sentenced person is not required for the enforcement of a sentence.

* * *

The Court shall admit a plea of nullity based on nullity of the procedure followed in the Trial Chamber with regard to evidence produced in that Chamber, if the nullity is referred to by the President, the Prosecutor or the accused in the course of the proceedings in the Appeals Chamber and has already been raised in the Trial Chamber.

Other defences based on nullity of the procedure followed in the Trial Chamber shall not be admissible.

Defences based on nullity of the summons to appear before the Appeals Chamber must, to be admissible, be raised by the parties at the opening of the proceedings, before the reading of the judgement of the Trial Chamber and of the notice of appeal.

E. Application of national law in enforcement of sentence

4. A sentence of imprisonment shall be subject to the supervision of the Court and be enforced:
   (a) as pronounced by the Court; and
   (b) in accordance with the applicable law of the administering State.

* * *

1. The conditions of detention shall be governed by the law of the State of detention.

2. A sentence shall be enforced under the supervision of the Presidency.

[*292] 3. Communications between persons sentenced and the Court shall be free and confidential.

Any sentenced person may address a petition to the Presidency in order to complain about his conditions of detention.

4. The Presidency, having requested any necessary information of the State on whose territory the sentenced person is incarcerated, may, if it believes there are grounds for the petition, take such measures as it deems appropriate in order to modify the conditions of detention of the sentenced person.

The State of detention shall be obliged to enforce these measures.

The Presidency may also, of its own motion or at the request of the sentenced person or the State of detention, decide that the sentenced person be transferred to another State party for the continued serving of his sentence.

F. Enforcement of fines and confiscatory measures 156/

156/ With the exception of paragraph 5, and perhaps paragraph 6, all other provisions of article 59 appear to deal solely with enforcement of sentences of imprisonment. If the remedies of the Court include fines, restitution, compensation and/or confiscation, there may need to be separate articles dealing with enforcement of those remedies (unless a simple "undertake to recognize" approach of ILC article 58 is adopted).

5.   The same applies <u>mutatis mutandis</u> to the enforcement of fines and confiscatory measures. The proceeds therefrom shall be handed over to the Court which will dispose thereof in accordance with the provisions of paragraph 4 of article 47.

* * *

1.   For the purpose of enforcement of fines imposed by the Court, the Presidency may order the forced sale of any property of the person sentenced which is on the territory of a State party.

For the same purpose, the Presidency may order the confiscation of any sum of money or securities belonging to the person sentenced.

2.   The sums thus collected shall be disposed of by the Presidency of the Court.

3.   The provisions of this article shall apply to legal persons.

G. <u>Competence to review the Court's judgements</u>

6.   The Court alone shall have the right to decide on any application for review of the judgement. The administering State shall not impede the sentenced person from making any such application.

[*293] H. <u>Limitation on punishment for other offences</u>

7.   A sentenced person in the custody of the administering State shall not be subjected to prosecution or punishment for any conduct committed prior to transfer unless such prosecution or punishment has been agreed to by the Court.

* * *

1.   Subject to the provisions of article 67, paragraphs 3 and 4, the State on whose territory a convicted person is serving the sentence imposed by the Court may not prosecute or try him, cause him to serve a sentence imposed by its courts or subject him to any other restriction of his personal freedom for any act committed prior to his incarceration on its territory.

2.   However, the Presidency may, at the request of the State of detention, authorize prosecution or the execution of a penalty imposed by the courts of that State. The Presidency shall rule on the matter after having requested the comments of the prisoner.

3.   The rule established by paragraph 1 of this article shall cease to have effect if the sentenced person remains more than 30 days on the territory of the State of detention after having served the full sentence imposed by the Court.

* * *

1.   Upon designation by the Court, States shall enforce sentences of imprisonment, imposed by the Court. Internationally recognized standards of treatment of prisoners shall thereby be fully guaranteed.

2.   In making a designation as referred to in paragraph 1, the Court shall, <u>inter alia</u>, take into consideration reasons of burden sharing, the modalities of which shall be elaborated by the States parties.

3.   No designation as referred to in paragraph 1 shall be made with respect to the State where the crime was committed or the State of which the convicted person or the victim is a national, unless the Court explicitly decides otherwise for reasons of social rehabilitation.4. A sentence of imprisonment shall be subject to the supervision of the Court in accordance with the rules.

* * *

1.   A sentence of imprisonment shall be served in a State not involved in the case designated by the Court from a list of States which have indicated to the Court their willingness to accept convicted persons.

2.   If no State is designated under paragraph 1, the sentence of imprisonment shall be served in a prison facility made available by the host State.

3.   A sentence of imprisonment shall be subject to the supervision of the Court in accordance with the rules concerning the treatment of the prisoners.

[*294] Article 60
Pardon, parole and commutation of sentences
I. ILC DRAFT

1.   If, under a generally applicable law of the State of imprisonment, a person in the same circumstances who had been convicted for the same conduct by a court of that State would be eligible for pardon, parole or commutation of sentence, the State shall so notify the Court.

2.   If a notification has been given under paragraph 1, the prisoner may apply to the Court in accordance with the Rules, seeking an order for pardon, parole or commutation of the sentence.

3.   If the Presidency decides that an application under paragraph 2 is apparently well founded, it shall convene a Chamber of five judges to consider and decide whether in the interests of justice the person convicted should be pardoned or paroled or the sentence commuted, and on what basis.

4.   When imposing a sentence of imprisonment, a Chamber may stipulate that the sentence is to be served in accordance with specified laws as to pardon, parole or commutation of sentence of the State of imprisonment. The consent of the Court is not required to subsequent action by that State in conformity with those laws, but the Court shall be given at least 45 days' notice of any decision which might materially affect the terms or extent of the imprisonment.

5.   Except as provided in paragraphs 3 and 4, a person serving a sentence imposed by the Court is not to be released before the expiry of the sentence.

II. PROPOSALS

The title of the article should be changed to read:

Early release 157/

1.   The administering State shall not release the prisoner before the expiry of the sentence as pronounced by the Court.

2.   The Court alone shall have the right to decide on the release of a prisoner before the expiry of the sentence and determine the conditions and effects of the release. That decision shall be taken by a Chamber of five judges, who may [*295] in arriving at their decision take representations by the administering State or any other interested party into account. 158/

3.   The prisoner may apply to the Court for a decision according to paragraph 2.

4.   When imposing a sentence of imprisonment, a Chamber may stipulate that the sentence is to be served in accordance with specified laws as to early release of the administering State. The consent of the Court is not required to subsequent action by that State in conformity with those laws, but the Court shall be given at least 45 days' notice of any decision which might materially affect the terms or extent of the imprisonment. 159/

* * *

The Court, according to the circumstances, may parole a convict who served his/her sentence:

(a)   more than 20 years in case of life imprisonment.

(b)   more than two thirds of its term in case of imprisonment for a definite term.

A parole shall be revoked when the parolee commits a further offence during its period and is convicted by this Court.

* * *

1.   If, under a generally applicable law of the State of imprisonment, a person in the same circumstances who had been convicted for the same conduct by a court of that State would be eligible for pardon, parole or commutation of sentence, the State shall so notify the Court.

2.   If a notification has been given under paragraph 1, the prisoner may apply to the Court in accordance with the rules, seeking an order for pardon, parole or commutation of the sentence.

3.   If the Presidency decides that an application under paragraph 2 is apparently well founded, it shall convene a Chamber of five judges to consider and decide whether in the interests of justice the person convicted should be pardoned or paroled or the sentence commuted, and on what basis.

* * *

157/ This wording is based on article 60 of the Siracusa draft, which appears to be simpler than the system envisaged under article 60 of the ILC draft. It appears appropriate that the Court should be the authority to decide on matters of pardon, parole and commutation of sentences.

158/ The insertion of the last phrase would make clear that representations may be made to the Court concerning the release of the prisoner. In ILC draft article 60 (1) and (2) it was made especially clear that the early release conditions pertaining in the administering State could be taken into account in determining early release.

159/ ILC draft article 60 (4).

1.   Subject to the provisions of article 149, paragraph 2, if a person sentenced by the Court may benefit from a pardon, parole or commutation of his sentence under the internal law of the State of detention, the latter shall notify the Registrar of the Court and the prisoner of this fact.

[*296] The prisoner may also petition the Presidency for a pardon, parole or commutation of his sentence.

The Presidency shall decide whether the prisoner shall be granted a pardon, parole or commutation of his sentence and shall specify the modalities thereof.

The State of detention shall promptly implement the decision of the Presidency, which shall be notified to it and to the prisoner by the Registrar.

2.   If the provisions of article 149, paragraph 2, apply, the State of detention shall notify the Registrar of the Court, who shall inform the Presidency, at least 45 days in advance, of any decision that may appreciably alter the duration of the detention.

* * *

5.   Except as provided in paragraphs 3 and 4, a person serving a sentence imposed by the Court is not to be released before the expiry of the sentence.

* * *

1.   Subject to the provisions of article 149, paragraph 2, if a person sentenced by the Court may benefit from a pardon, parole or commutation of his sentence under the internal law of the State of detention, the latter shall notify the Registrar of the Court and the prisoner of this fact.

The prisoner may also petition the Presidency for a pardon, parole or commutation of his sentence.

The Presidency shall decide whether the prisoner shall be granted a pardon, parole or commutation of his sentence and shall specify the modalities thereof.

The State of detention shall promptly implement the decision of the Presidency, which shall be notified to it and to the prisoner by the Registrar.

2.   If the provisions of article 149, paragraph 2, apply, the State of detention shall notify the Registrar of the Court, who shall inform the Presidency, at least 45 days in advance, of any decision that may appreciably alter the duration of the detention.

[*297] Article Y 160/
Escape
PROPOSAL
Escape (article 154)

1.   In the event of an escape, the Presidency shall request from any State Party the transfer of the convicted person who has escaped.

The provisions of article 66 shall apply to this request for a transfer for the purposes of enforcement of the sentence still to be served, with the exception of the documents accompanying the request, which shall be limited to the decision pronounced by the Court - either the original or a copy certified by the Registrar as a true copy - and as detailed a description as possible of the convicted person.

2.   The convicted person shall be transferred as soon as possible after his arrest to the territory of the State in which he was serving his sentence or to another place determined by the Presidency.

The period of detention in the territory of the State where the convicted person was arrested after his escape shall be deducted in full from the sentence still to be served.

3.   If the State Party in whose territory the escaped person is arrested agrees, the convicted person may serve the rest of his sentence in that State provided that the Presidency gives its consent.

The application of the provisions of article 149, paragraph 2, shall in that case also be subject to the agreement of the Presidency.

[*298] ANNEX I
Crimes pursuant to Treaties (see article 20 (e))
ILC DRAFT

1.   Grave breaches of:

160/ There is no equivalent of this article in the draft prepared by the International Law Commission.

(i)   the Geneva Convention for the Amelioration of the Condition of the Wounded and Sick in Armed Forces in the Field of 12 August 1949, as defined by Article 50 of that Convention;

(ii) the Geneva Convention for the Amelioration of the Condition of Wounded, Sick and Shipwrecked Members of Armed Forces at Sea of 12 August 1949, as defined by Article 51 of that Convention;

(iii) the Geneva Convention relative to the Treatment of Prisoners of War of 12 August 1949, as defined by Article 130 of that Convention;

(iv) the Geneva Convention relative to the Protection of Civilian Persons in Time of War of 12 August 1949, as defined by Article 147 of that Convention;

(v)   Protocol I Additional to the Geneva Conventions of 12 August 1949 and relating to the Protection of Victims of International Armed Conflicts of 8 June 1977, as defined by Article 85 of that Protocol.

2.   The unlawful seizure of aircraft as defined by Article 1 of the Hague Convention for the Suppression of Unlawful Seizure of Aircraft of 16 December 1970.

3.   The crimes defined by Article 1 of the Montreal Convention for the Suppression of Unlawful Acts against the Safety of Civil Aviation of 23 September 1971.

4.   Apartheid and related crimes as defined by Article II of the International Convention on the Suppression and Punishment of the Crime of Apartheid of 30 November 1973.

5.   The crimes defined by Article 2 of the Convention on the Prevention and Punishment of Crimes against Internationally Protected Persons, including Diplomatic Agents of 14 December 1973.

6.   Hostage-taking and related crimes as defined by Article 1 of the International Convention against the Taking of Hostages of 17 December 1979.

7.   The crime of torture made punishable pursuant to Article 4 of the Convention against Torture and Other Cruel, Inhuman or Degrading Treatment or Punishment of 10 December 1984.

8.   The crimes defined by Article 3 of the Convention for the Suppression of Unlawful Acts against the Safety of Maritime Navigation of 10 March 1988 and by Article 2 of the Protocol for the Suppression of Unlawful Acts against the Safety of Fixed Platforms Located on the Continental Shelf of 10 March 1988.

[*299] 9. Crimes involving illicit traffic in narcotic drugs and psychotropic substances as envisaged by Article 3 (1) of the United Nations Convention against Illicit Traffic in Narcotic Drugs and Psychotropic Substances of 20 December 1988 which, having regard to Article 2 of the Convention, are crimes with an international dimension.

Procedural questions, fair trial and rights of the accused
Table of ILC draft articles and various proposed articles a/

PART 4. INVESTIGATION AND PROSECUTION

ILC A/49/355	Australia/ Netherlands A/AC.249/L.2	France A/AC.249/L.3	Argentina A/AC.249/L.6	Japan A/AC.249/L.7	Japan A/AC.249/L.8	Germany A/AC.249/WP.1	Singapore A/AC.249/WP.2
Art. 25 Complaint	Rule 53, 54	Art. 37, 38(1)					
Art. 26 Investigation of alleged crimes	Rule 52, 55-59	Art. 40, 42, 43, 51, 57(2)	Rule 57 bis, 89 bis	I(4); II(1)		Art. 26	Art. 26
Art. 27 Commencement of prosecution	Rule 60, 61, 65-68	Art. 25; 44-50; 51(1e); 101; 102; 113(d)	Rule 60, 61, 65	II(7)	Art. 9		Art. 27
Art. 28 Arrest	Rule 69	Art. 51(1), (2); 52; 55; 57(1), (2); 58(2); 59(1), (2)		II(2), (3)			
Art. 29 Pre-trial detention or release	Rule 70, 71, 76, 77	Art. 55(1); 56(1), (2), (3); 58	Rule 77	II(4), (5)	Art. X		
Art. 30 Notification of the indictment	Rule 72	Art. 48(7); 51(1), (2); 55(3); 59(1), (2), (3)		III(3)			

a/ Prepared by the informal group dealing with procedural questions, fair trial and rights of the accused.

ILC A/49/355	Switzerland A/AC.249/WP.4	Netherlands A/AC.249/WP.6	Austria A/AC.249/WP.10	Prep Com A/AC.249/1
Art. 25 Complaint				Page 107-109
Art. 26 Investigation of alleged crimes	Art. 26		Art. 26	Page 96-97
Art. 27 Commencement of prosecution	Art. 27	Art. 27	Art. 27	Page 97-98
Art. 28 Arrest	Art. 28		Art. 28	Page 110-111
Art. 29 Pre-trial detention or release	Art. 29		Art. 29	Page 111-112, 120
Art. 30 Notification of the indictment				

PART 5. THE TRIAL

ILC A/49/355	Australia /Netherlands A/AC.249/L.2	France A/AC.249/L.3	Argentina A/AC.249/L.6	Japan A/AC.249/L.7	Japan A/AC.249/L.8	Switzerland A/AC.249/WP.3	Netherlands A/AC.249/WP.6
Art. 32 Place of trial	Rule 8	Art. 4(2), (3); 103					
		Art. 98-100,106-110					
Art. 34 Challenges to jurisdiction	Rule 78-81, 128	Art. 36, 39, 69, 70(1), 107, 115, 116	Rule 61(B)			Art. 34, 36	
Art. 35 Issues of admissibility							
Art. 36 Procedure under articles 34 and 35							
Art. 37 Trial in the presence of the accused	Rule 93	Art. 49, 111, 112		III(4)			Art. 37
Art. 38 Functions and powers of the Trial Chamber	Rule 62, 63, 74, 75, 78-87, 90-92, 94-102, 116	Art. 98-101, 104-110, 113, 117-121, 127	Rule 38 bis, 74, 91, 100	III(1), (2)			Art. 38
Art. 39 Principle of legality (nullum crimen sine lege)		Art. 101, 125		I(5)			
Art. 40 Presumption of innocence		Art. 51, 101		I(2)			
Art. 41 Rights of the accused	Rule 4, 51, 52, 84, 85, 100, 115	Art. 51(1), (2); 101, 104	Rule 51, 52, 100	I(1), (3), (4); II(6); III(1), (3), (5), (7)			
Art. 42 Non bis in idem		Art. 35, 131					

ILC A/49/355	Australia /Netherlands A/AC.249/L.2	France A/AC.249/L.3	Argentina A/AC.249/L.6	Japan A/AC.249/L.7	Japan A/AC.249/L.8	Switzerland A/AC.249/WP.3	Netherlands A/AC.249/WP.6
Art. 43 Protection of the accused victims and witnesses	Rule 40, 86, 91, 95	Art. 102	Rule 95		Art. X		
Art. 44 Evidence	Part III, Sect. 3:Rule 105, 106, 108-115	Art. 105, 114, 122, 125	Rule 89 bis, 106, 112. 113	II(6); III(6), (7); IV(1)-(5)			Art. 44
Art. 45 Quorum and judgement	Rule 103, 104	Art. 45, 127-130	Rule 104	III(6)			
Art. 46 Sentencing	Rule 118-119	Art. 94(2)		III(8)			

ILC A/49/355	Singapore A/AC.249/WP.7	New Zealand A/AC.249/WP.8	Switzerland A/AC.249/WP.9	Austria A/AC.249/WP.10	Egypt A/AC.249/WP.11	Singapore A/AC.249/WP.13	Argentina A/AC.249/WP.16
Art. 32 Place of trial							
Art. 34 Challenges to jurisdiction				Art. 34, 36			
Art. 35 Issues of admissibility							
Art. 36 Procedure under articles 34 and 35							
Art. 37 Trial in the presence of the accused			Art. 37				
Art. 38 Functions and powers of the Trial Chamber	Art. 38						Art. 38
Art. 39 Principle of legality (nullum crimen sine lege)							
Art. 40 Presumption of innocence							
Art. 41 Rights of the accused		Art. 41					Art. 41
Art. 42 Non bis in idem							
Art. 43 Protection of the accused, victims and witnesses					Art. 43		Art. 43
Art. 44 Evidence							
Art. 45 Quorum and judgement						Art. 45	
Art. 46 Sentencing							

ILC A/49/355	Canada A/AC.249/WP. 21	Italy A/AC.249/WP. 31	Germany A/AC.249/W P.37	United States A/AC.249/W P.41	A/AC.249/W P.__	A/AC.249/W P.__	Prep Com A/AC.249/1
Art. 32 Place of trial							
Art. 34 Challenges to jurisdiction							Page 98 (Sect. VI, VII) [Art. 34(b), 35]
Art. 35 Issues of admissibility							Page 100 [alternate Art. 35(2)]
Art. 36 Procedure under articles 34 and 35							Page 101 (Sect. VII-VIII) [Art._35(4), 36(3)]
Art. 37 Trial in the presence of the accused		Art. 37					Page 131 [Art._37]
Art. 38 Functions and powers of the Trial Chamber							
Art. 39 Principle of legality (nullum crimen sine lege)							
Art. 40 Presumption of innocence							
Art. 41 Rights of the accused				Art. 41			
Art. 42 Non bis in idem							
Art. 43 Protection of the accused, victims and witnesses			Art. 44(a)				
Art. 44 Evidence							
Art. 45 Quorum and judgement	Art. 45						
Art. 46 Sentencing							

PART 6 APPEAL AND REVIEW

ILC A/49/355	Australia/Netherlands A/AC.249/L.2	France A/AC.249/L.3	Argentina A/AC.249/L.6	Japan A/AC.249/L.7	Netherlands A/AC.249/W P.6	Singapore A/AC.249/W P.13	A/AC.249/W P.__
Art. 48 Appeal against judgement or sentence	Rule 78(b), 117. 120	Art. 132-135		V(1)	Art. 48	Art. 48	
Art. 49 Proceedings on appeal	Rule 126-143	Art. 136-143	Rule 142	V(3)			
Art. 50 Revision	Rule 144	Art. 144-147	Rule 74, 144	V(2), (3)			

[*307] ANNEX III
Working paper prepared by interested delegations regarding Part 7*
PART 7. INTERNATIONAL COOPERATION AND JUDICIAL [LEGAL] [MUTUAL] a/
ASSISTANCE
[Article X
Obligation to cooperate and general provisions b/
General obligation to cooperate

1.   States parties shall, in accordance with the provisions of this Part, cooperate with the Court in its investigation and prosecution of crimes under this Statute. A State shall not deny a request for cooperation except as specifically provided in this Part.

* * *

States Parties and the Court shall afford each other reciprocal cooperation and mutual assistance in connection with criminal investigations and proceedings under this Statute.

[*308] Channels for communication of requests/Authorities competent to make and receive requests c/

2.   Requests for cooperation may be made by the Court [or Prosecutor] and shall be transmitted [by the Registrar] through diplomatic channels, unless the Court and the requested State agree on another mode for transmitting the requests.

* * *

Each State Party shall designate at the time of deposition of its instruments of ratification, the national authority competent to receive requests for cooperation transmitted by the Court [, and such authorities to which requests for cooperation may be submitted in cases of urgency,] and the means of transmission of requests.

States Parties' failure to cooperate d/

3.   Where non-cooperation by States with requests by the Court [or Prosecutor] prevents the Court from performing its duties in terms of this Statute, [the Preliminary Investigations Chamber of] the Court may request the Security Council to take the measures necessary to enable the Court to exercise its jurisdiction, in relation to both States Parties to this Statute, or States not parties.

Cooperation by non-States Parties e/

4.   The Court may call on any State not party to this Statute to provide assistance provided for in this Part on the basis of comity, an ad hoc arrangement, or through entry into agreement with such State.]

---

*   Note. This annex contains a working paper prepared by interested delegations. It neither represents a text agreed upon among delegations nor suggests that every item should be included in the Statute. It identifies possible elements to be considered for inclusion, with alternative views of some of those elements, and examples of some possible texts. The order of the articles as well as the headings are only of an indicative character and have not been finally agreed upon. Because of time constraints, it was not possible to reflect all formulations or the results of substantive discussions of proposals. The working paper aims at helping the reading and further discussion of the compilation of proposals on judicial cooperation, and is not intended in any way to prejudice the future positions of delegations.

a/   Not all assistance is necessarily provided by judicial authorities; also there is a question whether use of term "judicial" assistance would limit the ability of the Prosecutor to request assistance directly.   "Mutual assistance", which is developing into a term of art, may be a better option but is more commonly used with respect to truly reciprocal cooperation between States (the issue of reciprocal cooperation by the Court being itself a topic of discussion). "Legal" assistance is a third option.

b/   This provision reflects the need for a general statement of the obligation of States to cooperate with the Court, and related matters.

c/   The two alternatives are not necessarily mutually exclusive of each other in all respects.

d/   The Working Group notes that there has been little discussion of the failure of States Parties to cooperate with the Court. The possibility of referral to the Security Council, reflected above, has been the only approach subject of a written proposal to date.

e/   Some proposals treat cooperation with non-States Parties as a separate article. The ILC draft and certain other proposals referred to the possibility of cooperation of non-States Parties. This text takes the approach of providing explicit authority for the Court to request cooperation, leaving the reaction of the requested State open. It also provides clear authority for the Court to enter into agreements or ad hoc arrangements with non-States Parties.

Article 51
Cooperation and judicial [legal] [mutual] assistance

1.   States Parties shall, in accordance with the provisions of this article [and their national law], comply with requests for judicial [legal] [mutual] [*309] assistance by the Court, which assistance shall include [but is not limited to] f/

(a)   the identification and whereabouts of persons or the location of items;

(b)   the taking of testimony, including testimony under oath, and the production of evidence, including expert opinions or reports necessary to the Court;

(c)   the service of [procedural] documents;

(d)   facilitating the appearance of persons before the Court;

(e)   the temporary transfer of persons in custody, with their consent, in order to provide testimony or other assistance to the Court;

(f)   the conduct of on-site investigations, inspections and expert examination;

(g)   the conduct of proceedings of the Court in its territory;

(h)   executing searches and seizures;

(i)   provision of records and documents;

(j)   taking action to protect victims and witnesses and the integrity of evidence;

(k)   identifying, freezing and forfeiture of proceeds and instrumentalities of crimes; and

(l)   any other assistance not prohibited by the law of the Requested State.

2.   Grounds for refusal.[A State Party may deny a request for assistance, in whole or in part, if - g/ [*310] (a) with respect to a crime under [article 20 (b) through (e)] [Article20(e)], it has not accepted the jurisdiction of the Court; h/

(b)   the authorities of the requested State would be prohibited by its domestic laws from carrying out the action request with regard to the investigation or prosecution of a similar offence in that State;

(c)   execution of the request would seriously prejudice its security [, ordre public] or other of its essential interests;

(d)   the request is manifestly ungrounded;

(e)   execution of the request would interfere with an ongoing investigation or prosecution requested State or in another State [or with a completed investigation or prosecution that might have led to an acquittal], except that a request may not be denied if the investigation or prosecution relates to the same matter which is the subject of the request and the Court has determined that the case is admissible under article 35;

[(f)] Compliance with the request would put it in breach of an existing [international law] [treaty] obligation undertaken to another [State] [non-State party]] i/

---

f/   [The enumeration of types of assistance above is not intended in any way to limit or otherwise prejudice the rights of the Prosecutor or Court to exercise their powers and duties as described in Article 26 or other provisions of this Statute, or to seek the cooperation of States Parties in doing so.] If the list of forms of assistance contains a final "catch-all" clause, the phrase "but not limited to" may not be necessary. The purpose of the list was to include in substance the various types of assistance set out in written proposals, rather than to select among them.

g/   This list is not an exhaustive one, but attempts to reflect some of the more frequently raised possible grounds for denial of requests for assistance. Other bases for denial that could be considered would include, but are not limited, to ne bis in idem, dual criminality, expiry of statute of limitations.

h/   The final wording of such a paragraph, if it is retained, may depend on which crimes are ultimately included under the jurisdiction of the Court, the extent to which an "opting" (or consent regime) as to jurisdiction is included, and the extent to which the Court might be deemed to have inherent jurisdiction. The brackets suggest two possible approaches, if such a provision is deemed appropriate: one where acceptance of jurisdiction could be a consideration with respect to all crimes but genocide, the other where it would be a consideration only with respect to treaty crimes.

i/   Consideration should be given to the relationship between the obligations of States Parties to cooperate with the Court and their other existing but inconsistent international law obligations, e.g. arising from bilateral extradition treaties, the Vienna Convention on Diplomatic Relations, etc.If a breach of another international law obligation is a ground for denying assistance, what is its precise scope?(a)Is it confined to obligations owed to non-States Parties only? As between States Parties to the Court, participation in the Statute could override earlier inconsistent treaty obligations (see article 30 of the 1969 Vienna Convention on the Law of Treaties) but would it be desirable to have an express provision in the Statute stating so?;(b)Is it confined to obligations arising out of treaties only?; and(c)Does it cover requests for arrest and transfer (e.g., requests for the surrender of a foreign diplomat accredited to the requested State

* * *

[*311] [When ratifying this Statute, States Parties shall notify the Secretary-General of the United Nations of the conditions under which they would refuse assistance and shall specify elements which must be included in a written request. States Parties shall not refuse assistance for reasons other than those indicated.] j/

* * *

[3.   A State may not deny a request for assistance, in whole or in part, on the grounds that:

(a)   the act constituting the offence to which the request relates does not constitute an offence under the laws, regulations or ordinances of the requested State;

(b)   the offence is a political or military offence, or an offence connected to such an offence; or

(c)   the requested State does not deem it appropriate to honour the request.]

4.   Before denying a request for assistance, the requested State shall consider whether the requested assistance can be provided subject to specified conditions, or whether the assistance can be provided at a later time or in an alternative manner; k/ provided that if the Court or the Prosecutor accepts the assistance subject to conditions, it shall abide by them.

5.   Confidentiality.

The Court shall ensure the confidentiality of evidence and information except as required for the investigation and proceedings described in the request.

[(a)   The requested State may, when it deems it to be in its interest, transmit documents, files or information to the Prosecutor on a confidential basis. The Prosecutor may then use them only for the purpose of collecting new evidence.

[(b)   The requested State may automatically or at the request of the Prosecutor subsequently authorize the publication of such documents, papers, files or information.]

[*312] [6. Reciprocity. l/

[If requested, the Court shall reciprocally cooperate with and provide assistance to a State Party conducting an investigation into actions which constitute a crime under this Statute.]

* * *

[(a) The States Parties may, for the purposes of a current investigation or a legal proceeding, request the Court to transmit papers or documents obtained in the course of an investigation or a legal proceeding conducted by the Court.

(b)   If such papers or documents have been obtained with the assistance of a State, that State must give its prior consent to any communication addressed to the requesting State. It shall be invited, at the request of the Preliminary Investigations Chamber and through the Registrar, to make its decision known.

(c)   In the case of the testimony of a witness or expert, such witness or expert must also give his prior consent to any communication addressed to the requesting State. He shall be invited to do so at the request of the Preliminary Investigations Chamber and through the Registrar.

(d)   The Preliminary Investigations Chamber shall grant the request after having obtained the necessary consents.

(e)   The Preliminary Investigations Chamber may, under the same conditions, grant such a request from a State non-party. In taking its decision it shall bear in mind the behaviour of that State in connection with earlier requests for cooperation addressed to it by the Court and the interests of justice.]

---

party) or only requests for other forms of assistance (e.g., search and seizure on diplomatic premises)?

j/   This proposal contemplates, however, that certain grounds would be excluded as bases for denying request, such as those set out in paragraph 3 below.

k/   In this regard it is conceivable that testimony could, for instance, be recorded electronically and made available to the Court in this format. It should be considered whether it is necessary to include a specific provision to the effect that the Court will be allowed to receive and consider such testimony.

l/   In view of the issue of reciprocity having been inserted in the general provision (article X), this whole provision has been inserted in square brackets to highlight the necessity to reconsider whether a separate provision should be retained.

Article 53
[Surrender] [Extradition] [Transfer] m/ of accused or convictedpersons n/ to the court

1.   Transmittal of requests; obligation of States.

[*313] The [Court] [Prosecutor] [Registrar] shall transmit to any State on the territory of which the accused or convicted person may be found, a request for the surrender of that person, along with the supporting material outlined in article 53 bis, and shall request the cooperation of that State in the arrest and surrender of such person. States Parties shall, in accordance with the provisions of this article [and their national law], comply with requests for surrender without delay.

2.   Grounds for refusal.

[A State Party may deny a request for surrender, if o/

(a)   with respect to a crime under [article 20 (b) through (e)] [article 20 (e)], it has not accepted the jurisdiction of the Court; p/

(b)   the person is a national of the requested State;

(c)   the person is being proceeded against or has been proceeded against, convicted or acquitted in the requested State or another State for the offence for which his surrender is sought, except that a request may not be denied if the Court has determined that the case is admissible under article 35.

(d)   the request is manifestly unfounded;

(e)   compliance with the request would put it in breach of an existing [international law] [treaty] obligation undertaken to another [State] [non-State party] q/

[When ratifying this Statute, States Parties shall notify the Secretary-General of the United Nations of the conditions under which they would refuse [provisional arrest or] surrender and shall specify elements which must be included in a written request. States Parties shall not refuse surrender for reasons other than those indicated.] r/

[*314] [OR]

[The extradition legislation of a requested State may be relied upon by that State as a basis for denying a request for surrender.]

* * *

[3.   Impermissible grounds for refusal.

A State may not deny a request for assistance, in whole or in part, on the grounds that:

(a)   the act constituting the offence to which the request relates does not constitute an offence under the laws, regulations or ordinances of the requested State;

(b)   the offence is a political or military offence, or an offence connected to such an offence; or

(d)   the person is a national of the requested State;

[(e) [the requested State has substantial grounds for believing that the request for surrender has been made for the purpose of prosecuting or punishing the person on account of that person's race, religion,

---

m/   There is an issue of what is the appropriate term for the process of delivering accused or convicted persons to court, and whether that process is sui generis, or more in the vein of traditional extradition. The use of the term "surrender" here does not denote any choice of approach, but is used as a matter of convenience and is to be broad enough to encompass either approach.

n/   It is conceivable that convicted persons may be at large for some reason. It may therefore be necessary to provide for the arrest of such convicted persons. Although this aspect is dealt with under this article, it has been pointed out that it may be more appropriate to deal with this aspect under article 59 (Enforcement of sentences).

o/   This list is not an exhaustive one, but attempts to reflect some of the more frequently raised possible grounds for denial of requests for surrender. Other bases for denial that could be considered would include, but are not limited, to non bis in idem, dual criminality, expiry of statute of limitations.

p/   The final wording of such a paragraph, if it is retained, may depend on which crimes are ultimately included under the jurisdiction of the Court, the extent to which an "opting" (or consent regime) as to jurisdiction is included, and the extent to which the Court might be deemed to have inherent jurisdiction. The brackets suggest two possible approaches, if such a provision is deemed appropriate: one where acceptance of jurisdiction could be a consideration with respect to all crimes but genocide, the other where it would be a consideration only with respect to treaty crimes.

q/   See footnote j/ above.

r/   This proposal contemplates, however, that certain grounds would be excluded as bases for denying request, such as those set out in paragraph3 below.

nationality, ethnic origin, political opinions, sex or status, or that person's position may be prejudiced for any of those reasons;]

* * *

[the requested State has grounds for believing that the person whose extradition is requested has been or would be subjected in the Court to torture or cruel, inhuman or degrading treatment or punishment or if that person has not received or would not receive minimum guarantees in a criminal proceeding, as is contained in the International Covenant on Civil and Political Rights, article 4;]

    (f)   the requested State does not deem it appropriate to honour the request.]

4.   Parallel requests from the Court and State(s).

[A State Party [, if it is a Party to the treaty covered by article 20 (e) and has accepted the jurisdiction of the Court,] shall [undertake to] give priority to surrender the accused to the Court over requests for extradition from other States [Parties].

* * *

[If the requested State also receives a request from a State [State Party] [to which it is bound by an extradition agreement] for the extradition of the same person, either for the same offence or for a different offence for which the Court is seeking the person's surrender, the appropriate authority of the requested State shall determine whether to surrender the person to the Court or to extradite the person to the State. In making its decision the requested State shall consider all relevant factors, including but not limited to: [*315] [(a) whether the extradition request was made pursuant to a treaty;]

    (b)   the respective dates of the requests;

    (c)   if the offences are different, the nature and gravity of the offences;

    (d)   the interests of the State requesting extradition, including, where relevant, whether the offence was committed in its territory and the nationality of the victims of the offence; and

    (e)   the possibility of subsequent surrender or extradition between the Court and the State requesting extradition.

The requested State may not, however, deny a request for the surrender made under this article in deference to another State's request for extradition of the same person for the same offence, if the State requesting extradition is a State Party, and the Court has ruled the case before it admissible, and its decision took into consideration the proceedings in that State which gave rise to its extradition request.]

5.   Proceeding in requested State.

Where the law of the requested State so requires, the person whose surrender is sought shall be entitled to challenge the request for arrest and surrender in the court of the requested State on the following grounds:

    (a)   lack of jurisdiction of the International Criminal Court;

    (b)   non bis in idem; or

    (c)   the evidence submitted in support of the request would not be sufficient to commit him for trial for such an offence in a court of the requested State.

6.   Delayed or temporary surrender.

    (a)   If the person sought is being proceeded against or is serving a sentence in the requested State for an offence different from that for which his surrender to the Court is sought, the requested State may [with the consent of the Preliminary Investigations Chamber, which shall rule after having heard the Prosecutor,]

      (i)   delay the surrender of person until the prosecution has been completed or abandoned or the sentence has been served, at which time the person shall be surrendered to the Court; or

      (ii)   temporarily surrender the person to the Court;

    (b)   if the surrender of the person is not delayed, the requested State may request the [Court] [preliminary Investigations Chamber] to return the person after the completion of his trial by the Court, in order that he may be prosecuted or serve his sentence in the requested State.

7.   Extradite or prosecute obligation.

    (a)   [In the case of a crime to which article 20 (e) applies,] the requested State [, if it is a party to the treaty in question but has not [*316] accepted the Court's jurisdiction with respect to that crime] shall, where it decides not to surrender the accused to the Court, promptly take all necessary steps to extradite the accused to a State having requested extradition or [at the request of the Court] refer the case [through proceedings in accordance with national laws] to its competent authorities for the purpose of prosecution.

[This provision shall not apply in the following cases:

[(i) if it is deemed that under the laws, regulations or ordinances of the requested State it would be impossible to impose or to execute punishment upon the person; if the act constituting the offence for which surrender is requested was committed in the territory of the requested State; or if the trial therefore would be held in a court of the requested State;

[(ii) if there is no probable cause to suspect that the person has committed an act which constitutes an offence for which surrender is requested;]

(b) The surrender of an accused to the Court constitutes, as between States Parties which accept the jurisdiction of the Court with respect to the crime in question, compliance with a provision of any treaty requiring that a suspect be extradited or the case be referred to the competent authorities of the requested State for the purpose of prosecution.

8.   Provision of evidence irrespective of surrender.

To the extent permitted under the law of the requested State and subject to the rights of third parties, all [property] found in the requested State that has been acquired as a result of the alleged offence or that may be required as evidence shall, upon request, be transmitted to the Court if surrender is granted, even if the surrender cannot be carried out, on conditions to be determined by the Court.

9.   Transit of surrendered person.

(a) A State Party shall [, in accordance with its national laws,] authorize transportation through its territory of a person being surrendered to the Court by another State. A request by the Court for transit shall be transmitted through diplomatic channels, unless otherwise agreed. The request for transit shall contain a description of the person being transported and a brief statement of the facts of the case [and their legal characterization, and the warrant for arrest and transfer]. A person in transit shall be detained in custody during the period of transit.

(b) [No authorization is required where air transportation is used and no landing is scheduled on the territory of the State of transit.]

                              * * *

[If air transport is used an no intermediate landing is envisioned, the Court shall notify the State over whose territory the aircraft will fly and certify the existence of the documents referred to in paragraph (a)]

If an unscheduled landing occurs on the territory of the State of transit, it [may require] [the Court shall submit] a request for transit as provided for in subparagraph (a). The State of transit shall detain the person to be transported until the request for transit is received and the transit is [*317] effected, so long as the request is received within 96 hours of the unscheduled landing.

(c) The transit of the person shall not be effected through a territory where there are grounds for believing that his life or liberty may be threatened by reason of his race, religion, nationality or political asylum.

(d) The transit of a national may be refused.

10.   Arrangements for surrender.

The competent authority of the requested State and the [Court] [Prosecutor] [Registrar] shall agree on the date and arrangements for the surrender of the person concerned to the seat of the Court or to the place which it specifies.

[*318] Article 53 bis

1.   A request for arrest or surrender [duly signed by the Prosecutor] shall:

(a) be made by letter, fax, e-mail or any medium capable of delivering a written record (provided that a request shall be confirmed through the diplomatic channel):

(b) contain or be supported by:

(i) information describing the person sought, sufficient to identify the person and information as to that person's probable location;

(ii) in the case of a request for pre-indictment arrest:

a. a copy of the warrant for arrest;

b.   a statement of the reasons to believe the suspect may have committed a crime within the jurisdiction of the Court and that the Prosecutor expects to seek an indictment within [90] days;

c.   a brief summary of the facts of the case;

d.   a statement as to why pre-indictment arrest is urgent and necessary.

(iii)   in the case of a request for post-indictment arrest and surrender of a person not yet convicted:

a.   a copy of the warrant of arrest and indictment;

b.   such information, documents or statements outlining the facts of the case as may be required by the law of the requested State.

(iv)   in the case of a request for the arrest and surrender of a person already convicted:

a.   a copy of any warrant of arrest for that person;

b.   a copy of the judgment of conviction;

c.   information to demonstrate that the person sought is the person referred to in the judgment of conviction;

d.   (if the person sought has been sentenced) a copy of the sentence imposed and a statement of any time already served and that remaining.

2.   Where the requested State Party considers the information provided insufficient to allow it to comply with the request it may seek, without delay, additional information.

[*319] Article 53 ter

(a)   In case of urgency, the Court may request the provisional arrest of the person sought pending presentation of the request for surrender and supporting documents under paragraph 53 <u>bis</u>.

(b)   The request for provisional arrest shall contain:

(i)   a description of the person sought and information regarding the probable location of such person;

(ii)   a brief statement of the essential facts of the case, including, if possible, the time and location of the offence;

(iii)   a statement of the existence of a warrant of arrest or a judgement of conviction against the person sought, and a description of the specific offence or offences with which the person has been charged or for which he has been convicted; and

(iv)   a statement that a request for surrender of the person sought will follow.

(c)   A person who is provisionally arrested may be discharged from custody upon the expiration of [ ] <u>s/</u> days from the date of provisional arrest if the requested State has not received the formal request for surrender and the supporting documents specified under paragraph [ ]. However, the person may consent to surrender before the expiration of this period if the legislation of the requested State so allows, in which case that State shall proceed to surrender the person to the Court as soon as possible.

(d)   The fact that the person sought has been discharged from custody pursuant to paragraph (c) shall not prejudice the subsequent rearrest and surrender of that person if the request for surrender and supporting documents are delivered at a later date.

Article 55
Rule of speciality Limit on other proceedings against surrendered person

1.   A person [surrendered to the Court under article 53] [extradited under this Statute] shall not [except under any one of the following circumstances] be proceeded against/prosecuted [tried], sentenced/punished or detained for [any crime] [an offence] other than that for which [the person has been surrendered] [extradition was effected]:

[(a)   when a person extradited commits an offence after extradition;

(b)   when a requested State has consented to his detention, prosecution, trial or punishment for an offence other than that for which extradition has been effected.]

<u>s/</u>   Some delegations have proposed a 30-day time period and some a 60-day time period.

[*320] <u>Limit on other uses of evidence</u>

2.   [A State providing evidence under this Part] [Evidence provided by States Parties under this Statute] [may require that the evidence not be used] [shall not be used] [for any purpose] [in connection with any offence] other than that [for which it was provided] [which is mentioned in the request for assistance as being a subject of investigation] unless [this is necessary to preserve a right of the accused under article 41 (2)] [the requested State offers its consent]. t/

<u>Waiver of rule by requested State</u>

3.   The Court may request the State concerned to waive the requirements of paragraphs 1 or 2, for the reasons and purposes to be specified in the request. In a case of paragraph 1, the request shall be accompanied by an additional warrant of arrest and by a legal record of any statement made by the accused with respect to the offence. u/

Article 57
Form and contents of the request

1.   Requests for judicial [mutual] [legal] assistance shall:

(a)   be made by letter, fax, e-mail or any medium capable of delivering a written record [, provided that a request shall be confirmed through the diplomatic channel];

(b)   be in [accompanied by a duly certified translation] an official language of the requested State.

(b (<u>bis</u>)) be in one of the two languages referred to in article 25 in accordance with the choice made by that State.

(c)   contain the following, as applicable:

(i)   a [brief] statement of the purpose of the request and the assistance sought including the legal basis [and grounds] for the request;

(ii)   as much detailed information as possible about the location or identification of any person or place that must be found or identified in order for the assistance sought to be provided;

(iii) a [brief] description of the [essential] facts underlying the request including a statement explaining the nexus between the assistance sought and the matter under investigation or subject to prosecution;

[*321]   (iv) information concerning the complaint or charge to which the request relates and of the basis of the Court's jurisdiction;

(v)   such information as may be required under the law of the requested State in order to execute the request;

(vi) any other information relevant to the assistance being sought.

Article 57 bis
Execution of requests v/

1.   Requests for assistance shall be executed as expeditiously as possible and the results transmitted to the requesting Party.

2.   Requests for assistance shall be executed in accordance with the law of the requested State except that the requested State shall execute the request in the manner specified in the request, including following any procedures outlined therein or permitting persons specified in the request to be present at and assist in the execution process; unless prohibited by the law of that State.

3.   The ordinary costs for execution of requests shall be borne by the requested State except for the following which should be borne by the requesting Party:

(a)   Costs associated to the travel of witnesses or the surrender of an accused or convicted person;

(b)   Costs of translation, interpretation and transcription.

---

t/   The Preparatory Committee expressed general satisfaction with the limited rule contained in article 55 (2) of the ILC draft. The first alternative reflects the wording of article 55 (2) of the Siracusa draft.

u/   Siracusa draft article 55 (3). The Preparatory Committee emphasized that the exception to the rule should be based on the express consent or waiver given by the State involved.

v/   This article will require some alteration if the decision is taken to make the obligation to assist reciprocal.

Where the execution of a request will result in extraordinary costs, there should be consultations to determine how those costs will be met.

Article 59
Enforcement of sentences
1.Obligation versus agreement of States Parties to enforce sentencesof imprisonment
[On designation by the Court] [a State not involved in the case, taken from a list of States] [all States Parties] [which have indicated to the Court their willingness thereto] shall assist the Court in enforcing prison sentences [by accepting convicted persons and thus becoming the administering State. To that end, the Court shall provide the State so designated with a certified copy of the Court's judgement to be enforced. The State so designated shall promptly inform the Court whether it accepts the request.]
2. Criteria for designation
In making a designation [as referred to in paragraph 1] the Court [the Registrar] shall take into consideration [[geographical] criteria formulated by [*322] Rules of the Court] in accordance with the rule of burden sharing [the modalities of which shall be elaborated by the States Parties].

No designation [as referred to in paragraph 1] shall be made with respect to the State where the crime was committed or the State of which the convicted person or the victim is a national, [unless the Court explicitly decides otherwise for reasons of social rehabilitation].
3. Provision in case no detention facilities are made available
[If no State is designated [under paragraph 1] the sentence of imprisonment shall be served in a prison facility made available by the host State [where the Court has its official seat].]
4. No consent of convicted person
The consent of the convicted person is not required for enforcement of a sentence.
5. Role of the Court, national law and international standards in enforcement of sentences
1.A sentence of imprisonment [shall be subject to the supervision of the Court [the Presidency]] [in accordance with the rules [concerning the treatment of prisoners]] and be enforced:
  (a) as pronounced by the Court;
  (b) in accordance with the applicable law of the administering State.
  [The conditions of detention shall be governed by the law of the State of detention.]
  [Internationally recognized standards of treatment of prisoners shall thereby be fully guaranteed.]
2.   Communications between persons sentenced and the Court shall be free and confidential. Any sentenced person may address a petition to the Presidency in order to complain about his condition of detention.
3.   The Presidency [The Court], having requested any necessary information of the State on whose territory the sentenced person is incarcerated, may, if it believes there are grounds for the petition, take such measures as it deems appropriate in order to modify the conditions of detention of the sentenced person. The State of detention shall be obliged to enforce these measures. The Presidency [The Court] may also, of its own motion or at the request of the sentenced person or the State of detention, decide that the sentenced person be transferred to another State Party for the continued serving of his sentence.
6 .Enforcement of fines and confiscatory measures
[The same applies mutatis mutandis to the enforcement of fines and confiscatory measures. The proceeds therefrom shall be handed over to the Court which will dispose thereof in accordance with the provisions of paragraph 4 of article 47.]
[*323] [For the purpose of enforcement of fines imposed by the Court, the Presidency may order the forced sale of any property of the person sentenced which is on the territory of a State Party. For the same purpose, the Presidency may order the confiscation of any sum of money or securities belonging to the person sentenced.]
7.Review
The Court alone shall have the right to decide on any application for review of the judgement. The administering State shall not impede the sentenced person from making any such application.

8. Limitation on prosecution/Punishment for other offences

A sentenced person in the custody of the administering State shall not be subjected to prosecution or punishment for any conduct committed prior to transfer unless such prosecution or punishment has been agreed to by the Court.

REPORT OF THE *AD HOC* COMMITTEE ON THE
ESTABLISHMENT OF AN INTERNATIONAL CRIMINAL COURT

[Editorial Note - the U.N. page numbers of this document are indicated in bolded brackets [*] in the text].

I.   INTRODUCTION

[*1] 1.   The Ad Hoc Committee on the Establishment of an International Criminal Court met at United Nations Headquarters from 3 to 13 April and from 14 to 25 August 1995, in accordance with General Assembly resolution 49/53 of 9 December 1994.

2.   Under paragraph 2 of that resolution, the Ad Hoc Committee was open to all States Members of the United Nations or members of the specialized agencies. 1/

3.   The session was opened by Mr. Hans Corell, Under-Secretary-General, the Legal Counsel, who represented the Secretary-General and made an introductory statement.

4.   Ms. Jacqueline Dauchy, Director of the Codification Division of the Office of Legal Affairs, acted as Secretary of the Ad Hoc Committee; Mr. Andronico O. Adede, Deputy Director (Codification Division, Office of Legal Affairs), acted as Deputy Secretary; Ms. Mahnoush Arsanjani and Ms. Sachiko Kuwabara-Yamamoto, Senior Legal Officers, and Ms. Virginia Morris and Ms. Darlene Prescott, Associate Legal Officers (Codification Division, Office of Legal Affairs), acted as assistant secretaries.

5.   At its 1st meeting, on 3 April 1995, the Ad Hoc Committee elected its Bureau, as follows:

Chairman: Mr. Adriaan Bos (Netherlands)
Vice-Chairmen: Mr. Cherif Bassiouni (Egypt)
                  Mrs. Silvia A. Fernandez de Gurmendi (Argentina)
                  Mr. Marek Madej (Poland)
Rapporteur: Ms. Kuniko Saeki (Japan)

6.   Also at its 1st meeting, the Ad Hoc Committee adopted the following agenda (A/AC.244/L.1):

1.   Opening of the session.
2.   Election of officers.
3.   Adoption of the agenda.
4.   Organization of work.
5.   Review of the major substantive and administrative issues arising out of the draft statute for an international criminal court prepared by the International Law Commission and consideration, in the light of that review, of arrangements for the convening of an international conference of plenipotentiaries.
6.   Adoption of the report.

7.   The Ad Hoc Committee had before it, in addition to the draft statute adopted by the International Law Commission at its forty-sixth session, 2/ the relevant chapter of the topical summary of the discussion held in the Sixth Committee of the General Assembly during its forty-ninth session[*2] (A/CN.4/464/Add.1), the comments received pursuant to paragraph 4 of General Assembly resolution 49/53 on the establishment of an international criminal court (A/AC.244/1 and Add.1-4) 3/ and a report submitted by the Secretary-General pursuant to paragraph 5 of that resolution, on provisional estimates of the staffing, structure and costs of the establishment and operation of an international criminal court (A/AC.244/L.2). It also had before it a number of valuable informal papers prepared by some of its members, and received documents prepared by experts and by non-governmental organizations.

8.   In accordance with its mandate, the Ad Hoc Committee conducted its work in two   phases.

9.   In a first phase (3-13 April and 14-23 August 1995), the Ad Hoc Committee conducted a review of the major substantive and administrative issues arising out of the draft statute for an international criminal court prepared by the International Law Commission. During that phase, the Committee established an open-ended Working Group chaired by Mr. Gerhard Hafner (Austria) and entrusted it with the preparation of an informal paper on methods of proceedings (due process). The Committee agreed to include the paper it received from the Working Group in its report (see paras. 128-194 below), as an extremely useful basis for further discussion. It subsequently instructed the Working Group to prepare guidelines for the consideration of: (a) the question of the relationship between States parties, non-States

parties and the international criminal court; and (b) the question of general rules of criminal law. Both questions were considered by the Committee on the basis of the schedule prepared by the Working Group. The guidelines are annexed to the present report. The outcome of the first phase of the proceedings is reflected in section II below.

10.   In the second phase of its proceedings, the Ad Hoc Committee considered, in the light of its review of the major substantive and administrative issues arising out of the draft prepared by the International Law Commission, arrangements for the convening of an international conference of plenipotentiaries. The outcome of this phase of the proceedings is reflected in section III of the present report.

11.   Section IV of the report contains the conclusions of the Ad Hoc Committee.

[*3] II.   REVIEW OF THE MAJOR SUBSTANTIVE AND ADMINISTRATIVE ISSUES ARISING OUT OF THE DRAFT STATUTE FOR AN INTERNATIONAL CRIMINAL COURT PREPARED BY THE INTERNATIONAL LAW COMMISSION

A.   Establishment and composition of the Court

12.   There was broad recognition that the establishment of an effective and widely accepted international criminal court could ensure that the perpetrators of serious international crimes were brought to justice and deter future occurrences of such crimes. The remark was made that the establishment of a single, permanent court would obviate the need for setting up ad hoc tribunals for particular crimes, thereby ensuring stability and consistency in international criminal jurisdiction. The hope was expressed that an independent court free from political pressure, established on a legal basis to deal with well-defined crimes and offering maximum guarantees to the defendants, would prevent crises which had adverse effects on entire peoples. A note of caution was however struck in this respect by some representatives, who drew attention to the far-reaching legal and financial implications of the project. A remark was also made that the result of the discussion in the Committee would inform the decision of those States which were not committed to the establishment of an international criminal court on this matter.

13.   It was emphasized that the proposed court should be established as a body whose jurisdiction would complement that of national courts and existing procedures for international judicial cooperation in criminal matters and that its jurisdiction should be limited to the most serious crimes of concern to the international community as a whole.

14.   It was also emphasized that without universal participation the court would not serve the interests of the international community.

1.   Method of establishment

15.   The view was widely shared that the proposed court should be established as an independent judicial organ by means of a multilateral treaty, as recommended by the Commission. Such an approach based on the express consent of States was considered consistent with the principle of State sovereignty and with the goal of ensuring the legal authority of the court. That approach was also recognized by many delegations as the most practical in the light of the difficulties that would be involved in establishing the court as an organ of the United Nations through an amendment to the Charter of the United Nations. It was suggested that a relatively high number of ratifications and accessions, for instance 60, should be required for the entry into force of the treaty, as a way of ensuring general acceptance of the regime. Concern was however expressed about the delays which such an approach might entail, and it was suggested that no more than 20 or 25 ratifications should be required. Emphasis was placed on the need to promote the general acceptability of the statute of the court by giving due reflection therein to the various legal systems.

16.   Some delegations, on the other hand, advocated the establishment of the proposed court as a principal organ of the United Nations, in order to ensure its universality, moral authority and financial viability. The view was expressed that the difficulties involved in the required amendment to the Charter should not be overemphasized, bearing in mind the ongoing discussions[*3] concerning the restructuring of the Security Council, and that resort could be had to the amendment procedure provided for in Article 109 of the Charter.

2. Relationship with the United Nations

17. A close relationship between the proposed court and the United Nations was viewed as an essential condition of the universality and moral authority of the new institution, as well as of its financial and administrative viability. The conclusion of a special agreement between the court and the United Nations as envisaged in article 2 of the draft statute was considered by a number of delegations to be an appropriate way of establishing the required links of functional cooperation between the two institutions, while at the same time preserving the court's independence as a judicial organ. Some delegations however warned that complex issues were involved, and it was suggested that the content of the agreement and the method of its adoption should be provided for in the statute itself, or that the agreement should be elaborated simultaneously with the statute.

3. Nature of the proposed court as a permanent institution

18. The approach reflected in article 4, paragraph 1, of the draft statute, whereby the court would be established as a permanent institution which would act when required to consider a case submitted to it, was described as an acceptable compromise which sought to strike a balance between, on the one hand, the requirements of flexibility and cost-effectiveness in the operation of the court and, on the other hand, the need to promote, as an alternative to ad hoc tribunals, a permanent judicial organ, able to ensure uniformity and consistency in the application and further development of international criminal law. Other delegations agreed with this proposal as long as it would not undermine the permanence, the stability and the independence of the court.

19. It was suggested that the permanence and independence of the court would be enhanced if some officials, such as the judges, the Presidency, the Registrar and/or the prosecutor, were appointed on a full-time basis.

4. Appointment of the judges and of the prosecutor

20. As regards the appointment of judges, paragraphs 1 and 2 of article 6 pertaining to the qualifications and election of judges gave rise to objections. Concern was voiced by some delegations that too rigid a distinction between judges with criminal trial experience and those with competence in international law might result in an unjustifiable quota system and complicate the selection of candidates. The singling out of those two areas of the law was furthermore considered by some delegations as unduly restricting the sources of expertise on which the court should be able to rely. A more flexible formulation, drawing inspiration from article 13, paragraph 1, of the statute of the Tribunal for the former Yugoslavia, was found preferable by some delegations. Other delegations emphasized the importance of expertise in criminal law, consistent with the character of the court, some of them suggesting that every judge should have criminal law qualifications and experience. The remark was also made that the procedures for the nomination and election of judges applicable in the context of the International Court of Justice and the International Tribunal for the former Yugoslavia afforded better guarantees of independence and universality.

[*5]21. It was accordingly suggested by some delegations that the pool from which candidates would be selected should go beyond the circle of States parties and that there should be an initial screening, for example through nomination by national groups. It was also suggested that the elections should be conducted by the General Assembly and the Security Council rather than by the States parties, in order to enhance the acceptability of the institution, that a filtering role might be envisaged for the Security Council and that a two-thirds majority should be required for election. It was observed that other delegations were not in favour of extending the role of the Security Council in this regard given that it could create limitations in the ultimate selection of judges for the court.

22. It was further suggested that paragraph 5 of article 6 should be amended to provide for equitable geographical representation as well as the representation of the principal legal systems of the world. The view was expressed that the principal legal systems of the world should be identified for the purposes of representation. Some delegations emphasized that small States should be adequately represented in the court. Other delegations questioned the relevance of those criteria.

23. Concerning the appointment of the prosecutor, expertise in the investigation and prosecution of criminal cases was considered to be an important requirement. It was suggested that impartiality would be better guaranteed if the prosecutor and deputy prosecutors were of different nationality and that a

system of appointment by the court on the recommendation of States parties, or vice versa, would reinforce the authority and independence of the officials concerned.

24. The powers of the Presidency were considered by many delegations to be excessive and in need of further examination. The rotation system between the Trial Chambers and the Appeals Chamber was also criticized.

    5.   Role of the prosecutor

25. Suggestions were made to give the prosecutor the power to initiate investigations and prosecutions. The view was expressed that the prosecutor should have the consent of interested States before initiating investigations and prosecutions. Another suggestion was to include in the statute rules on disqualification.

    6.   Adoption of the rules of the court

26. The substantive link between the statute and the rules of the court was widely recognized, as was also the special importance of the rules of evidence and of particular elements of substantive criminal law. Many delegations suggested that the rules of the court should be elaborated and adopted simultaneously with the statute, or incorporated in the statute itself. Some delegations however considered that internal rules could be elaborated and adopted by the judges themselves.

[*6] 7.   Other issues

27. Several delegations noted that the draft statute allowed rotation of the judges between the Trial and Appeals Chambers and expressed concern about the compatibility of such arrangements with the requirements of due process.

28. Some delegations favoured the inclusion of a provision on the non-retroactivity of the statute, bearing in mind article 28 of the 1969 Vienna Convention on the Law of Treaties.

B.   The principle of complementarity

    1.   Significance of the principle of complementarity

29. The third preambular paragraph of the draft statute provides that the establishment of an international criminal court "is intended to be complementary to national criminal justice systems in cases where such trial procedures may not be available or may be ineffective". The principle of complementarity 4/ thus deals with the relationship between the proposed international criminal court and national criminal and investigative procedures. Many delegations referred to the commentary to the preamble as clearly indicating that the International Law Commission did not intend the proposed court to replace national courts. The principle of complementarity was described as an essential element in the establishment of an international criminal court. It was, however, also viewed as calling for further elaboration so that its implications for the substantive provisions of the draft statute could be fully understood.

30. Several delegations felt that an abstract definition of the principle would serve no useful purpose and found it preferable to have a common understanding of the practical implications of the principle for the operation of the international criminal court. Some saw merit in regrouping certain provisions of the draft statute on which the principle of complementarity had a direct bearing such as those relating to admissibility and judicial assistance.

31. A number of delegations stressed that the principle of complementarity should create a strong presumption in favour of national jurisdiction. Such a presumption, they said, was justified by the advantages of national judicial systems, which could be summarized as follows: (a) all those involved would be working within the context of an established legal system, including existing bilateral and multilateral arrangements; (b) the applicable law would be more certain and more developed; (c) the prosecution would be less complicated, because it would be based on familiar precedents and rules; (d) both prosecution and defence were likely to be less expensive; (e) evidence and witnesses would normally be more readily available; (f) language problems would be minimized; (g) local courts would apply established means for obtaining evidence and testimony, including application of rules relating to perjury; and (h) penalties would be clearly defined and readily enforceable. It was also noted that States had a vital interest in remaining responsible and accountable for prosecuting violations of their laws - which also served the interest of the international community, inasmuch as national systems would be expected to maintain and enforce adherence to international standards of behaviour within their own jurisdiction.

32. Other delegations pointed out that the concept of complementarity should not create a presumption in favour of national courts. Indeed while such courts[*7] should retain concurrent jurisdiction with the court, the latter should always have primacy of jurisdiction.

33. The view was also expressed that in dealing with the principle of complementarity a balanced approach was necessary. According to such view, it was important not only to safeguard the primacy of national jurisdictions, but also to avoid the jurisdiction of the court becoming merely residual to national jurisdiction.

34. The comment was made that the issue of complementarity and the relationship between the international criminal court and national courts would have to be examined in a number of other areas, e.g., international judicial cooperation and various issues involving surrender, extradition, detention, incarceration, recognition of decisions and applicable law.

35. On the question whether the principle of complementarity should be reflected in the preamble or embodied in an article of the draft statute, two views were expressed.

36. According to one view, a mere reference in the preamble was insufficient, considering the importance of the matter, and a definition or at least a mention of the principle should appear in an article of the statute, preferably in its opening part. Such a provision would, it was stated, remove any doubt as to the importance of the principle of complementarity in the application and interpretation of subsequent articles.

37. According to another view, the principle of complementarity could be elaborated in the preamble. Reference was made in this context to article 31 of the Vienna Convention on the Law of Treaties, according to which the preamble to a treaty was considered part of the context within which a treaty should be interpreted, and the remark was made that a statement on complementarity in the preamble to the statute would form part of the context in which the statute as a whole was to be interpreted and applied.

    2.   Implications of the principle of complementarity as regards the list of crimes which would fall under the jurisdiction of an international criminal court

38. According to a number of delegations, the principle of complementarity required that the draft statute provide for a single legal system for all crimes within the jurisdiction of the court. Such a legal system should be transparent and efficient and aimed at enhancing the credibility and, therefore, the acceptability of the court. It was argued that such a single legal system was conceivable only if the jurisdiction of the court was limited to a few "hard-core" crimes. Otherwise, a multiplicity of jurisdictional mechanisms would have to be established and there would be an increased risk of endless challenges to the jurisdiction of the court. It was also noted that limiting the jurisdiction of the court to a few crimes would simplify the problem of consent to the exercise of jurisdiction, whereas expanding the list of crimes would have the opposite effect.

[*8] 3.   Role of national jurisdiction

39. A number of delegations observed that the meaning of the expression "national jurisdiction" needed to be clarified. "National jurisdiction", it was stated, was not limited to territorial jurisdiction but also included the exercise of jurisdiction by the States competent to exercise jurisdiction in accordance with established principles and arrangements: thus, with respect to the application of military justice, it was not so much the territorial State that was important, but the State whose military was involved. The status-of-forces agreements and extradition agreements also had to be taken into consideration in determining which State had a strong interest in the issue and should consequently exercise jurisdiction.

40. As regards exceptions to the exercise of national jurisdiction, the following issues were raised: (a) nature of the exceptions to the exercise of national jurisdiction; (b) authority competent to decide on such exceptions; and (c) timing requirements.

    (a) Nature of the exceptions to the exercise of national jurisdiction

41. As regards the nature of the exceptions, and with reference to the phrase, in the third preambular paragraph of the draft statute, "where such trial procedures [in national criminal justice systems] may not be available or may be ineffective", there was a wide measure of agreement that the words "available" and "ineffective" were unclear. Questions were raised as to the standards for determining whether a particular national judicial system was "ineffective". The principle of complementarity as reflected in the above-

quoted phrase was furthermore viewed by some delegations as barring inherent jurisdiction as provided for in paragraph 1 (a) of article 21 of the draft statute, as well as "exclusive" jurisdiction.

42.   In this context, the observation was made that the commentary to the preamble clearly envisaged a very high threshold for exceptions to national jurisdiction and that the International Law Commission only expected the international criminal court to operate in cases in which there was no prospect that alleged perpetrators of serious crimes would be duly tried in national courts. It was further stressed that the exercise of national jurisdiction encompassed decisions not to prosecute. In this context, it was suggested that the presumption in article 35 of the draft statute should be reversed so that decisions of acquittal or conviction by national courts or decisions by national prosecution authorities not to prosecute were respected except where they were not well-founded. Some delegations put forward the view that it would be preferable if the principles set out in article 35 in regard to admissibility and conferring a discretion upon the court to decide that a case before the court was inadmissible on the grounds set out in subparagraphs (a) to (c) were laid down as a condition rather than by way of conferring a discretionary power. Another remark was that article 25 of the draft should allow the international criminal court to pursue a complaint only when no State was investigating, or had already investigated, the case. A comparable provision could, it was suggested, be included in articles 26 and 27, as well as in articles 51 and 52, where it would set a limit on the obligation of States to assist the international criminal court. While such a provision was viewed by some delegations as giving adequate expression to the concept of complementarity, others felt that the duty of the international criminal court to respect the decisions of national courts extended only to manifestly well-founded decisions.

[*9]43.   It was stressed that the standards set by the Commission were not intended to establish a hierarchy between the international criminal court and national courts, or to allow the international criminal court to pass judgement on the operation of national courts in general. In this context, concern was expressed by some delegations that article 42 on non bis in idem conferred upon the international criminal court a kind of supervisory role vis-à-vis national courts, notwithstanding the fact that the jurisdiction of the international criminal court was concurrent with that of national courts. Also in relation to article 42, it was suggested to delete the distinction between ordinary crimes and crimes of international concern, since such a distinction was not common to all legal systems and could cause substantial legal problems.

44.   A provision that was viewed by some delegations as departing from the concept of complementarity was paragraph 4 of article 53, which required a State party to give priority, as far as possible, to requests for arrest and transfer emanating from the court over extradition requests from other States.

45.   According to several delegations, the decision on whether national jurisdiction should be set aside should be made on a case-by-case basis, taking into account, among other factors, the probability that national jurisdiction would be exercised in a particular instance. It was noted that, while the jurisdiction of an international criminal court was compelling where there was no functioning judicial system, the intervention of the court in situations where an operating national judicial system was being used as a shield required very careful consideration. The remark was also made that if national authorities failed, without a well-founded reason, to take action in respect of the commission of a crime under the draft statute, the international criminal court should exercise its jurisdiction.

46.   Some delegations felt that the statute should address the issue of national amnesties and provide guidelines on the matter, indicating the circumstances in which the international criminal court might ignore, or intervene ahead of, a national amnesty.

47.   It was also suggested that the draft statute should provide for the possibility that a State might voluntarily decide to relinquish its jurisdiction in favour of the international criminal court in respect of crimes expressly provided for under its statute. This suggestion gave rise to reservations on the ground that it was not consistent with some delegations' view of the principle of complementarity. In this respect, the remark was made that the international criminal court should in no way undermine the effectiveness of national justice systems and should only be resorted to in exceptional cases.

(b) Authority competent to decide on exceptions to the exercise of national jurisdiction

48. Some delegations felt that the power to decide on the exceptions to national jurisdiction should be vested in the international criminal court. The latter court should, it was stated, have primacy over national courts, and article 9 of the statute of the International Tribunal for the former Yugoslavia was viewed as a good model to follow in this respect. Reference was also made to article 24 of the draft statute, which spelled out the duty of the international criminal court to satisfy itself that it had jurisdiction. Practical reasons were furthermore invoked in favour of leaving it to the international criminal court to decide whether it should exercise jurisdiction or yield to national jurisdiction.

[*10]49. Other delegations found the above arguments unconvincing. They did not view article 9 of the statute of the International Tribunal for the former Yugoslavia as an appropriate precedent inasmuch as the international community was aware, at the time of the establishment of the said Tribunal, of the special circumstances of the situation and had consequently made certain assumptions in creating the Tribunal; in the present instance, it was necessary to define criteria and establish standards to be applied in many diverse situations in the future. Similarly, the view was expressed that caution should be exercised in referring to past war crimes tribunals and the ad hoc Tribunal on Rwanda as relevant precedents for discussing the future international criminal court. The view was also expressed that the burden of proof as to the appropriateness of an exception to the exercise of national jurisdiction should be on the international criminal court.

50. According to some delegations, one could envisage an international criminal court with inherent jurisdiction over a few "hard-core" crimes which would be presumed to have a superior claim to exercise jurisdiction, on the understanding, however, that the presumption would be rebuttable on the basis of criteria to be defined in the statute. If, on the other hand, the jurisdiction of the international criminal court encompassed treaty-based crimes, then the regimes set out in those treaties should have primacy, and only if they proved ineffective should the international criminal court intervene.

(c) Timing requirements

51. The remark was made that exceptions to national jurisdiction should be considered at the very first stage, before the prosecutor of the international criminal court initiated an investigation, because even the initiation of an investigation might interfere with the exercise of national jurisdiction. It was also said that if a case was being investigated or was pending before a national court, the international criminal court should suspend the exercise of its jurisdiction, even though it might subsequently resume consideration of the case in accordance with article 42 of the draft statute.

C. Other issues pertaining to jurisdiction

1. Applicable law and jurisdiction of the court

52. As regards article 33 of the draft statute, the view was expressed that, to satisfy the requirements of precision and certainty in criminal proceedings, the law to be applied by the court should be clearly determined by the statute rather than through reliance on national conflict-of-law rules. Applicable law, it was suggested, should be understood to cover not only the offences and penalties but also principles of individual criminal responsibility, defences and the procedural and evidentiary law to be addressed in the rules of the court under article 19. While some delegations felt that the statute itself should provide the applicable law by elaborating or incorporating the relevant conventional and customary law, other delegations emphasized the importance of accelerating the work on the draft Code of Crimes against the Peace and Security of Mankind to address such matters. Some delegations advocated a link between the draft Code and the statute.

53. Subparagraph (a) of article 33 was described as self-evident. The suggestion was made to include in subparagraph (b) a reference to the treaties listed in the annex and to bring the wording in line with Article 38 of the Statute of the International Court of Justice to avoid uncertainty or confusion,[*11] although some delegations questioned the appropriateness of applying the principles and rules of international law. Subparagraph (c), it was stated, should be amended to make it clear that national law was a subsidiary means for determining general principles of law common to the major legal systems or, alternatively, should clearly indicate the relevant national law, the State whose law would apply and the circumstances in which such law would apply, particularly as national law was far from uniform. It was also suggested

that a new provision should be added concerning customary law, bearing in mind Article 38 of the Statute of the International Court of Justice.

    (a)   <u>Question of the crimes to be covered by the statute and the specification of the crimes</u>
        (i)   <u>General observations</u>

54. As to the scope of the subject-matter jurisdiction of the court, several delegations emphasized the importance of limiting it to the most serious crimes of concern to the international community as a whole, as indicated in the second preambular paragraph, for the following reasons: to promote broad acceptance of the court by States and thereby enhance its effectiveness; to enhance the credibility and moral authority of the court; to avoid overloading the court with cases that could be dealt with adequately by national courts; and to limit the financial burden imposed on the international community. It was suggested that the principle of limited jurisdiction should be reflected not only in the preamble but also in an operative provision, possibly in a new article 1 or in article 20, and should be further clarified through the identification of precise criteria.

55. With regard to the selection of crimes, a number of delegations suggested that the jurisdiction of the court should be limited to three or four of the crimes under general international law listed in subparagraphs (a) to (d) of article 20 because of the magnitude, the occurrence and the inevitable international consequences of these crimes, with different views being expressed concerning subparagraph (b). The view was expressed that the inclusion of the three crimes covered by subparagraphs (a), (c) and (d) would be sufficient to obviate the need for the creation of additional ad hoc tribunals given the scope of jurisdiction of the two existing tribunals. Further, some delegations were of the view that various treaty-based crimes referred to in subparagraph (e), among which individual delegations singled out terrorist and drug-related offences, torture and apartheid, were also serious crimes of international concern and should be included. In the view of some delegations, the list of crimes mentioned under this subparagraph was not exhaustive. There were also suggestions to add to the list of treaty-based crimes violations of the Convention on the Safety of United Nations and Associated Personnel as well as environmentally related offences. Various delegations suggested an approach to the selection of crimes consisting in initially limiting the court's jurisdiction to the first three or four crimes, while providing for some type of mechanism to enable the States parties to the statute to consider the addition of other crimes at a later stage. A suggestion was also made for an approach in which States could agree to refer to the court extraordinary cases which were not otherwise covered.

56. The remark was made that the selection of crimes would define the role to be played by the future court. Attention was also drawn to the implications that the selection of crimes would have on other issues relating to the court, including the principle of complementarity, the State consent requirements and the trigger mechanism for the exercise of jurisdiction, as well as the[*12] obligations of States parties with respect to the cooperation and judicial assistance to be provided to the court. In particular, some delegations felt that limiting the jurisdiction of the court to a few "core crimes" under general international law would facilitate the consideration of other issues relating to the court and the adoption of a coherent, unified approach to the various requirements for the exercise of jurisdiction. However, it was also stated that broadening the court's jurisdiction might make it possible to use this institution as a further means for the peaceful settlement of disputes.

57. As regards the specification of crimes, the view was expressed that a procedural instrument enumerating rather than defining the crimes would not meet the requirements of the principle of legality (<u>nullum crimen sine lege</u> and <u>nulla poena sine lege</u>) and that the constituent elements of each crime should be specified to avoid any ambiguity and to ensure full respect for the rights of the accused. The following methods were suggested for defining the crimes listed in article 20: referring to, or incorporating, the provisions of relevant treaties; elaborating definitions by using the Nürnberg Charter and the statutes of the International Tribunals for the former Yugoslavia and for Rwanda as a starting-point; or finalizing the draft Code of Crimes against the Peace and Security of Mankind as a matter of priority to avoid delays in the establishment of the court. Some delegations expressed reservations about using the draft statutes for the ad hoc Tribunals or the draft Code of Crimes as a basis for defining the crimes.

58. Several delegations were of the view that it would be important to include in the statute the principle of the non-retroactivity of its provisions. The view was also expressed that the statute should include a provision that would prevent the court from imposing punishment on the basis of customary law without a clear definition of the crime being included in the statute.

(ii) Genocide

59. As regards subparagraph (a) of article 20, many delegations agreed that the crime of genocide met the criteria for inclusion in the jurisdiction of the court set forth in the preamble.

60. A number of delegations were of the view that the authoritative definition of the crime of genocide was to be found in the 1948 Convention on the Prevention and Punishment of the Crime of Genocide, 5/ which was widely accepted by States and had been characterized as reflecting customary law by the International Court of Justice. 6/ Some delegations favoured reproducing the relevant provisions in the statute of the court, as had been done in the statutes of the ad hoc Tribunals for the former Yugoslavia and for Rwanda.

61. There was a suggestion to expand the definition of the crime of genocide contained in the Convention to encompass social and political groups. This suggestion was supported by some delegations who felt that any gap in the definition should be filled. However, other delegations expressed opposition to amending the definition contained in the Convention, which was binding on all States as a matter of customary law and which had been incorporated in the implementing legislation of the numerous States parties to the Convention. The view was expressed that the amendment of existing conventions was beyond the scope of the present exercise. Concern was also expressed that providing for different definitions of the crime of genocide in the Convention and in the statute could result in the International Court of Justice and the international criminal court rendering conflicting decisions with respect to the same situation under the two respective instruments. It was suggested that acts such[*13] as murder that could qualify as genocide when committed against one of the groups referred to in the Convention could also constitute crimes against humanity when committed against members of other groups, including social or political groups.

62. There was a further suggestion to clarify the intent requirement for the crime of genocide by distinguishing between a specific intent requirement for the responsible decision makers or planners and a general-intent or knowledge requirement for the actual perpetrators of genocidal acts. Some delegations felt that it might be useful to elaborate on various aspects of the intent requirement without amending the Convention, including the intent required for the various categories of responsible individuals, and to clarify the meaning of the phrase "intent to destroy", as well as the threshold to be set in terms of the scale of the offence or the number of victims. The view was expressed that the International Court of Justice might shed some light on these aspects of the definition of genocide in relation to the case that was currently before it. 7/ It was also suggested that the question of intent could be addressed in greater detail with respect to the various crimes within the jurisdiction of the court in connection with the applicable law.

(iii) Aggression

63. Some delegations supported the inclusion of aggression or the planning, preparation, initiation or waging of a war of aggression among the crimes falling within the jurisdiction of the court. In this respect, it was noted that the question of the inclusion of this crime in the draft statute and the issue of the powers of the Security Council under article 23 of the draft statute were closely related. While recognizing that defining aggression for the purpose of the statute would not be an easy task, those delegations drew attention to article 6 (a) of the Nürnberg Charter, which, it was stated, reflected the position of the 20 States participating in the London Agreement as regards the principle of individual criminal responsibility for aggression and was part of existing applicable law, as well as to the Definition of Aggression contained in General Assembly resolution 3314 (XXIX) of 14 December 1974, to the definition proposed in the context of the ongoing work of the International Law Commission on the draft Code of Crimes against the Peace and Security of Mankind and to the definition worked out by the Committee of Experts which had met in June 1995 under the auspices of the International Association of Penal Law, the International Institute of Higher Studies in Criminal Sciences and the Max Planck Institute for Foreign and International Criminal Law. In their opinion, the United Nations, whose Charter enshrined the principle of the non-use of force and which had been created to save future generations from the scourge of war, could not, 50 years

after the Nürnberg trial, exclude aggression from the jurisdiction of the international criminal court, thereby taking a retrogressive step and ignoring the contrary line taken by the International Law Commission in the context of its work on the draft Code of Crimes against the Peace and Security of Mankind.

64.　Other delegations opposed the inclusion of aggression. Many questioned the possibility of arriving at a definition of aggression for the purpose of the statute within a reasonable time-frame and expressed concern that such a time-consuming exercise would unduly delay the finalization of the statute. They pointed out that the ultimate goal - namely, to create an effective organ for the administration of justice - should not be sacrificed to political considerations. In their opinion, the Nürnberg Charter was unhelpful in the present context because it referred to a war of aggression that had already been waged and characterized as such; in contrast, a prospective definition would[*14] have to tackle the difficult issue of possible justifications such as self-defence or humanitarian intervention. As for the 1974 Definition of Aggression, it was not intended for the establishment of individual criminal responsibility. The question was also raised whether the reference in both instruments to wars of aggression - as opposed to acts of aggression - still provided an acceptable test, and attention was drawn in this context to common article 2 of the Geneva Conventions of 1949. The Definition of Aggression was furthermore viewed as unhelpful for criminal law purposes inasmuch as (a) the list of acts of aggression contained in its article 3 was not exhaustive; and (b) it differentiated between wars of aggression, which were described as criminal, and acts of aggression, which amounted to international torts entailing State responsibility. The remark was made in this connection that for the International Law Commission to attach individual criminal responsibility to acts of aggression involved a substantive amount of progressive development of international law.

65.　Some among the latter delegations also pointed out that aggression was not punishable under national penal codes. In response to this argument, the remark was made that the penal code currently under consideration in the Parliament of a Member State did provide for the punishment of aggression. Furthermore, the fact that most national legislations were silent on the matter was a mere consequence of the lack of a definition at the international level and of the corresponding implementation mechanism; it provided an additional reason to include aggression in the statute, bearing in mind the principle of complementarity and the concept of unavailability of criminal procedures reflected in the preamble to the draft prepared by the International Law Commission.

66.　With reference to the practical difficulty of bringing political leaders to trial for aggression, some delegations observed that the problem also arose in relation to other crimes, such as genocide. Other delegations considered it ill-advised to extend the jurisdiction of the court to acts that could not, in fact, form the basis of actual prosecution, and thereby run the risk of discrediting the court and undermining its moral authority.

67.　In the view of some delegations, the goal of those who favoured the inclusion of aggression among the crimes falling within the jurisdiction of the court could be achieved without getting embroiled in the considerable difficulties referred to above, bearing in mind that aggression often entailed violations of humanitarian law. This argument was found unconvincing inasmuch as a violation of jus ad bellum was quite conceivable without a violation of jus in bello.

68.　As regards the justiciability of the conduct under consideration, some members pointed out that aggression was an act of State and that the qualification of a particular act as aggression was a political decision. Others observed that aggression was not a mere political act entailing no legal consequences but a breach of a fundamental norm of international law and that a finding of aggression, although part of a political process, was a legal decision taken in accordance with the Charter. It was also said that, while aggression undoubtedly involved political aspects, the same was true of other acts generally recognized as qualifying for inclusion within the jurisdiction of the court.

69.　A number of delegations commented on the problem of reconciling, on the one hand, the primary responsibility of the Security Council in the maintenance of international peace and security and its role in making determinations of acts[*15] of aggression and, on the other hand, the responsibility that would devolve on the court to establish individual criminal responsibility for the same act - difficulties that article 23 of the Commission's draft vividly brought to light.

70. Some delegations objected to the idea of leaving it to the Security Council to determine the existence of an act of aggression and relying on the future court to ascribe criminal responsibility to specific individuals. Such a solution, it was stated, gave rise to problems of due process and would deprive the court of its independence: could the court find that a Head of State was not guilty of aggression notwithstanding a prior determination by the Security Council that the State concerned had committed an act of aggression? On the other hand, could the court be allowed to act independently in determining the existence of a situation of aggression notwithstanding the prerogatives of the Security Council? Caution was also urged on the ground that the question of the existence and/or consequences of an act of aggression might come up not only before the Security Council and the future court but also before the International Court of Justice and that legal coherence required that the three forums should not arrive at inconsistent or conflicting conclusions.

71. Other delegations considered it necessary and possible to find a proper balance between the requirement of the independence of the court and the need to respect the primary role of the Security Council in the maintenance of international peace and security. Concern was, however, expressed that such a balance was not achieved in article 23 of the Commission's draft. Most delegations commented on article 23 in the context of the discussion of the role of the Security Council in relation to the exercise of jurisdiction (see paras. 120-126 below). In the present context, however, the remark was made that the limitation contemplated in paragraph 2 had no counterpart in the Statute of the International Court of Justice and that the paragraph should be redrafted so as to provide that the court could consider a complaint of aggression if no decision had been taken by the Council on the matter. In the opinion of the delegations concerned, the responsibility of the Council in qualifying a particular conduct as aggression did not result in the court being deprived of a role in determining the criminal responsibility of individuals as regards the planning, preparation or launching of aggression.

(iv) Serious violations of the laws and customs applicable in armed conflict

72. Regarding subparagraph (c) of article 20, many delegations agreed that serious violations of the laws and customs applicable in armed conflict met the criteria for inclusion in the jurisdiction of the court set forth in the preamble. The view was expressed that the concept of seriousness might require further clarification or possibly be accompanied by additional criteria to distinguish between violations of greater or lesser gravity, magnitude, scale or duration and to ensure that only the former would be included in the jurisdiction of the court. In this regard, the view was also expressed that not all violations of the relevant laws and customs amounted to crimes of such seriousness that they should be dealt with by an international court.

73. A number of delegations felt that, under general international law, this category of crimes should encompass not only serious violations of the laws and customs applicable in armed conflict in terms of the Hague Conventions and Regulations but also grave breaches of the 1949 Geneva Conventions that were currently covered by subparagraph (e), as well as comparably serious violations of other relevant conventions that had attained the status of customary law. While some delegations felt that subparagraph (c) should also include violations[*16] of Additional Protocol I to the 1949 Geneva Conventions, a question was raised as to whether that instrument as a whole reflected customary law. A preference was also expressed for a more limited approach to this category of crimes based on the 1949 Geneva Conventions, which were widely accepted by States.

74. There were different views as to whether the laws and customs applicable in armed conflict, including treaty crimes, should include those governing non-international armed conflicts, notably common article 3 of the 1949 Geneva Conventions and Additional Protocol II thereto. Those who favoured the inclusion of such provisions drew attention to the current reality of armed conflicts, the statute of the ad hoc Tribunal for Rwanda and the recent decision of the ad hoc Tribunal for the former Yugoslavia recognizing the customary-law status of common article 3. However, other delegations expressed serious reservations concerning the possibility of covering non-international armed conflicts and questioned the consistency of such an approach with the principle of complementarity. As regards Additional Protocol II, the view

was expressed that that instrument as a whole had not achieved the status of customary law and therefore was binding only on States parties thereto. The view was also expressed that non-international armed conflicts should not fall within the jurisdiction of the court either with respect to common article 3 or Additional Protocol II.

75. In considering the related offences committed in armed conflict that could be regrouped within a single category, attention was drawn to the inconsistency and possible confusion resulting from the use of the term "serious violations" in subparagraph (c), the term "exceptionally serious violations" in subparagraph (e) and the term "grave breaches" in the Geneva Conventions. It was suggested that this terminological problem could be solved by using the term "war crimes" to cover all of the relevant offences.

76. With regard to the specification of the crimes, some delegations felt that the reference to serious violations of the laws and customs applicable in armed conflict was not sufficiently precise for the purposes of the principle of legality. In this regard, particular emphasis was placed on the need to define the specific content or constituent elements of the violations in question with a view to indicating the onus on the prosecution, ensuring due process and respect for the rights of the accused and providing guidance to the court in its determination of the merits of the charges. Some delegations drew attention to the relevant provisions of the Nürnberg Charter and of the statutes of the ad hoc Tribunals for the former Yugoslavia and for Rwanda as possible starting-points for the elaboration of the definitions of the crimes concerned, with a preference being expressed, however, for an exhaustive list of offences to ensure respect for the <u>nullum crimen sine lege</u> principle. In terms of the list of offences, the remark was made that rape and similar offences should be included. The view was furthermore expressed that the specification of the violations provided for in common article 3 of the 1949 Geneva Conventions - assuming they were to be included - would need to take into account the absence of any explicit provision for international criminal responsibility in that article.

(v)   Crimes against humanity

77. As regards subparagraph (d) of article 20, many delegations expressed the view that crimes against humanity met the criteria for inclusion in the jurisdiction of the court set forth in the preamble. It was suggested that the jurisdiction of the court with respect to this category of crimes should be subject to further qualification to ensure a balanced approach in comparison to[*17] the one reflected in subparagraph (c), which made room for the seriousness criterion. In this regard, attention was drawn to the reference to armed conflict in the statute of the ad hoc Tribunal for the former Yugoslavia and to the requirement in the statute of the ad hoc Tribunal for Rwanda that the offences provided for therein should be of a systematic or widespread nature.

78. With regard to the specification of the crimes, it was pointed out that there was no convention containing a generally recognized and sufficiently precise juridical definition of crimes against humanity. Several delegations were of the view that the definitions contained in the Nürnberg Charter, the Tokyo Tribunal Charter, Control Council Law Number 10 and the statutes of the ad hoc Tribunals for the former Yugoslavia and for Rwanda could provide guidance in the elaboration of such a definition; at the same time, they recognized the need to reconcile differences in those definitions and to further elaborate the specific content of such offences as extermination, deportation and enslavement. More specific remarks with respect to the elements that should be reflected in the definition of crimes against humanity included the following: the crimes could be committed against any civilian population in contrast to war crimes; the crimes usually involved a widespread or systematic attack against the civilian population rather than isolated offences; the additional persecution grounds contained in the statute of the ad hoc Tribunal for Rwanda were questionable and unnecessary in the present context; and the list of offences should include rape but not persecution, which was described as too vague a concept. While some delegations favoured an exhaustive list of offences, other delegations felt that it might be useful to retain a residual category of offences; it was, however, recognized that the term "other inhumane acts" required further clarification.

79. There were different views as to whether crimes against humanity could be committed in peacetime in the light of the Nürnberg precedent, as well as the statute of the ad hoc Tribunal for the former Yugoslavia. Some delegations singled out, among the developments since the Nürnberg precedent which

militated in favour of the exclusion of any requirement of an armed conflict, the precedent of the statute of the ad hoc Tribunal, for Rwanda and the recent decision of the ad hoc Tribunal for the former Yugoslavia in the Tadič case. However, the view was also expressed that the crimes in question were usually committed during an armed conflict and only exceptionally in peacetime, that the existence of customary law on this issue was questionable in view of the conflicting definitions contained in the various instruments and that the matter called for further consideration.

80. With regard to the relationship between crimes against humanity and genocide, the view was expressed that any overlap between the two categories of crimes should be avoided and that the same standard of proof should be required for both, notwithstanding any differences in the intent requirements.

(vi) Treaty-based crimes

81. With regard to subparagraph (e) of article 20, (see para. 55 above), the view was expressed that the offences established in the treaties listed in the annex might be of lesser magnitude than the other offences provided for in article 20 and that their inclusion within the jurisdiction of the international criminal court entailed a risk of trivializing the role of the court, which should focus on the most serious crimes of concern to the international community as a whole. Also in favour of the exclusion of the crimes in question from the jurisdiction of the court, it was argued that the said crimes were more effectively dealt with by national courts or through international cooperation.[*18] With specific reference to terrorism and illegal drug trafficking, concern was expressed that extending the jurisdiction of the court to the corresponding crimes would result in an overburdening of the court.

82. Merit was, however, also found in retaining all or some of the crimes dealt with in the treaties listed in the annex. It was pointed out in this connection that the international criminal court was not meant to replace existing mechanisms for the prosecution of such treaty crimes as terrorism and drug-related offences. Rather, it was intended to be an option available to States parties to the statute, which would determine whether a particular crime was better dealt with at the domestic or the international level. The fact that many countries did not have the resources to engage in large-scale intelligence gathering, which was often required for the prosecution of terrorist and drug-related crimes, was also mentioned as militating in favour of the inclusion of treaty-based crimes within the jurisdiction of the court.

83. The view was expressed that it was necessary to include the conventions dealing with acts of terrorism in the list contained in the annex so as to bring the acts in question within the court's jurisdiction without prejudice to the principle of complementarity and national jurisdiction. Other delegations, however, expressed grave doubts as to the wisdom and feasibility of proceeding along those lines.

84. On the question whether other instruments should be added to the list contained in the annex, some delegations proposed the inclusion of the Convention on the Safety of United Nations and Associated Personnel inasmuch as it was likely to operate in situations where there would be no adequate domestic courts and where the international criminal court would therefore fill a gap. However, the view was expressed that that Convention, which was not yet in force, dealt with offences that did not have the same degree of seriousness as those categories of crimes provided for in the draft. Some delegations doubted the usefulness of the inclusion of the Convention within the court's jurisdiction.

85. It was suggested that a provision should be included in the statute to allow for periodic reviews of the list of crimes as a way of keeping it attuned to the requirements of the international community. A number of delegations expressed support for this suggestion.

(b) General rules of criminal law

86. The Committee considered various items listed in the guidelines for consideration of the question of general principles of criminal law, prepared by the Working Group (see para. 9 above), as set out in annex II to the present report.

87. As regards process issues, several delegations expressed support for a combined approach to the method of elaboration of the general rules of criminal law under which (a) the fundamental principles would be included in the statute or in an annex thereto; (b) other important issues would be addressed in the rules; and (c) questions of lesser importance could be determined by the court in a particular case, possibly by drawing upon the national law of a particular State or principles that were common to the major legal systems. This approach would enable the States parties to the statute to participate in the

elaboration of the essential rules that would form part of the statute, as well as the elaboration of other important provisions to be included in the rules of the court. It would also give potential States parties a clear understanding of the[*19] general legal framework in which the court would operate. Furthermore, it would provide clear guidance to the court, secure the degree of predictability and certainty required for the rights of the accused and the ability of defence counsel to respond to the charges to be fully respected, and promote consistent jurisprudence on fundamental questions of general criminal law, such as mens rea, principles of individual criminal responsibility and possible defences. The view was expressed that the nature of the crimes within the jurisdiction of the court should be taken into account when addressing the issues of the statute or the rules or the application by the court of general principles of criminal law. The statute of the International Tribunal for the former Yugoslavia did not, it was stated, provide an appropriate model for the elaboration or determination of general rules of criminal law in relation to a permanent court to be established on a consensual basis by the States parties to its statute. Some delegations, on the other hand, drew attention to the principles of general criminal law addressed in article 7 of that statute. Other delegations indicated that they had not yet taken a final position on the question.

88.   With respect to the relevance of national law, some delegations expressed concern regarding the direct applicability of national law envisaged in article 33, subparagraph (c), of the draft statute in view of the uncertainty as to which national law should be applied and bearing in mind the divergences in national criminal laws. The view was expressed that it might be preferable for the court to take into account general principles of criminal law that were common to the major legal systems rather than relying on the national law of a particular State to resolve issues in particular cases which were not addressed in the statute or the rules of the court. Attention was also drawn to the differences in the criminal law and procedures of common-law and civil-law countries. While a preference was expressed by some delegations for the investigation approach of the latter, the remark was also made that an attempt should be made to find a generally acceptable and balanced approach, taking into account both types of legal systems.

89.   Regarding substantive issues, a number of delegations expressed the view that the various questions identified by the Working Group deserved further examination and that consideration should be given to the possibility of including relevant provisions in the statute or in an annex thereto, in particular on general principles such as the principle of non-retroactivity and principles of individual criminal responsibility; the necessary intent or mens rea; the question of mental capacity; the various types of criminal responsibility; possible defences to the crimes within the jurisdiction of the court; the aggravating or mitigating circumstances that might affect the determination of an appropriate sentence; the penalties that might be imposed by the court; the discrepancy in the maximum penalty that might be imposed by the court and by national courts; and the inclusion of fines and other financial sanctions as possible penalties. A question was also raised as to the applicability of State defences to individual liability.

2.   Exercise of jurisdiction

90.   Commenting in general on the issue of the exercise of jurisdiction, a number of delegations drew attention to the close links between the various elements relevant to the issue (complementarity, jurisdiction, consent, triggering mechanism, role of the Security Council, etc.). The remark was also made that the question of how the court exercised its jurisdiction was central to how Governments would react to the statute: the extent of participation in[*20] the statute, the credibility and independence of the court, its day-to-day functioning and the importance of its work would in large measure be determined by the way in which cases came before it for adjudication.

(a)   Inherent jurisdiction

91.   A number of delegations elaborated on their understanding of the concept of inherent jurisdiction. It was pointed out in this connection that, if the court was given inherent jurisdiction over a crime, then any State that became party to the statute would ipso facto accept that the court had the power to try an accused for that crime without additional consent being required from any State party. The remark was also made that inherent jurisdiction did not mean exclusive jurisdiction and would not strip States parties of the power to exercise jurisdiction at the national level and that the question of priority of jurisdiction would have to be resolved by the international criminal court on the basis of the principle of complementarity.

92. Some delegations objected to the inclusion of the concept of inherent jurisdiction in the statute on a number of grounds. In their view, the concept was incompatible with the principle of State sovereignty as embodied in Article 2, paragraph 1, of the Charter of the United Nations. The phrase "inherent jurisdiction" was furthermore viewed as involving a contradiction in terms inasmuch as the court's authority to exercise jurisdiction could only stem - at a time when the international criminal court was not yet in existence and where jurisdiction for the prosecution of the crimes concerned was vested in national courts - from the States parties' consent, expressed through the treaty or on a case-by-case basis. The concept of inherent jurisdiction was also considered as inconsistent with the principle of complementarity, under which the court was only intended to have jurisdiction where trial procedures at the national level were unavailable or would not be effective. The point was made in this connection that instead of assuming a priori that certain categories of crimes were better suited for trial by an international criminal court, it would be preferable to determine the circumstances when trial by such a court was appropriate. The remark was made in this context that the principle of complementarity needed to be much more fully developed than it was in the draft prepared by the International Law Commission and that the concepts of admissibility under article 35 and non bis in idem under article 42, which were paramount and must be applied in every case by the court, should be further elaborated in order to implement the principle of complementarity. With reference to the risk of conflicts of jurisdiction, the point was made that it would not be fair to give the international criminal court the power to settle such conflicts, nor would it be wise to place before it dilemmas from which it might come out with its dignity impaired.

93. Other delegations emphasized that inherent jurisdiction could not be viewed as incompatible with State sovereignty since it would stem from an act of sovereignty, namely, acceptance of the statute. The remark was also made that the crimes under consideration were crimes of international concern, the prosecution of which would be of interest to a number of States, if not to the international community as a whole, and that, in case the custodial State was unable to prosecute, insistence on sovereignty would affect the legitimate interests of other States. It was furthermore pointed out that the alternative solution - subordinating the exercise of jurisdiction by the court to a declaration of acceptance - would leave the future fate of the court in the hands of States on whose discretion the ability of the court to operate would depend. Concern was expressed that such an approach, apart from enabling States to manipulate the functioning of the court, would set aside the interests of the[*21] international community - which could not be reduced to the sum total of the States forming part of it - and would prevent the court from playing its role as the guardian of international public order. With reference to the argument that inherent jurisdiction interfered with the principle of complementarity, the delegations in question stressed that inherent jurisdiction was not exclusive jurisdiction and that the court would have concurrent jurisdiction, i.e., would only intervene when it appeared to the court, on the basis of criteria to be clearly established in the statute, that national courts could not function adequately. The remark was made in this context that the effect of the principle of complementarity could only be, at most, to defer the intervention of the court, whereas rejection of the inherent jurisdiction concept would result in the court's complete inability ab initio to be seized of a case. As regards possible conflicts of jurisdiction, the remark was made that appropriate provisions could be included in the statute.

94. The approach of the International Law Commission to the issue of inherent jurisdiction, as reflected in article 21, 8/ was supported by several delegations. It was, however, viewed by some as inconsistent with the 1948 Convention on Genocide and by others as too restrictive.

95. Under the first set of criticisms, it was said that the 1948 Convention, to which most States were parties, did not envisage inherent jurisdiction and that the question arose whether the Committee had competence to engage in progressive development of the relevant substantive law. The Convention, it was further observed, envisaged the possible jurisdiction of an international criminal court over genocide only in the hypothesis of failure of national authorities to prosecute; a complaint from any State party to the Convention could not by itself trigger the jurisdiction of an international criminal court. It was accordingly suggested that the court should only be entitled to exercise jurisdiction over genocide if, within a given period from the commission of the crime, no State had initiated an investigatory process. The assumption

underlying the approach of the International Law Commission that national courts would be less able or in a less favourable position to prosecute a crime of genocide was furthermore viewed as questionable.

96. In response to these views, the remark was made that the relevant Convention had not only confirmed, almost 50 years ago, the already accepted notion that genocide was a crime under general international law but had envisaged in its article 6 the creation of an international criminal tribunal competent to try that crime. The view was expressed in this context that the implementation of the letter and spirit of existing treaties that had come to embody general international law ought to have at least as much of a priority as the formulation of new norms and that it was difficult to see how the objectives of the 1948 Convention could be achieved if inherent jurisdiction was not conferred on the court.

97. Under the second set of criticisms, the Commission's approach was too restrictive and the sphere of inherent jurisdiction should encompass, in addition to genocide, other crimes under general international law. Such a broadening of the sphere of inherent jurisdiction would, it was observed, have less far-reaching consequences than might appear inasmuch as, for the court to have jurisdiction over the crimes concerned, the complainant State, the territorial State and the custodial State would all have to be parties to the statute. In favour of the suggested new approach, a number of delegations invoked the gravity of the so-called "core crimes" and the desirability of including them in the sphere of inherent jurisdiction if the new institution was to provide an adequate judicial answer to the concerns to which its creation was[*22] intended to respond. It was pointed out in this connection that the Commission's approach lagged behind present-day requirements and led to legally untenable results since it made it possible to exclude from the jurisdiction of the court crimes that constituted violations of legal norms of the highest order, namely, rules of a jus cogens character, and, by way of consequence, to formulate a reservation to a jus cogens rule. It was also argued that extending the scope of inherent jurisdiction to crimes other than genocide would make it possible to simplify the rules on the exercise of jurisdiction and, for the crimes concerned, to do away with the requirements of a declaration of acceptance. The remark was made in this context that the requirement of State consent, as a building-stone for international jurisdiction, traditionally gave rise to a number of separate proceedings on the issue of jurisdiction alone and that inherent jurisdiction would limit the possibility of recurrent objections on the competence of the court - in particular with regard to the interpretation in each particular case of the provisions of article 22 - and thereby contribute to eliminating substantial delays in trial proceedings. Emphasis was also placed on the fact that more than 185 countries already had jurisdiction over serious crimes of international concern addressed by the 1948 Convention: universal jurisdiction had thus already been given away to every State in the world and the question was whether it should also be given to a just, fair and effective international court which States could agree to set up or not by signing its statute.

98. The delegations favouring the suggested new approach generally agreed that the sphere of inherent jurisdiction should extend to crimes against humanity and to war crimes, the latter category being intended to encompass, according to a number of delegations, not only serious violations of the laws and customs of war, but also crimes under the 1949 Geneva Conventions. Some delegations strongly argued in favour of adding aggression to the two above-mentioned categories of crimes. Others were of a different opinion. The views on this issue are reflected in more detail in paragraphs 63-71 above.

99. A number of delegations, while reserving their position on the matter, expressed readiness to envisage inherent jurisdiction for the "core crimes" subject to the inclusion in the statute of satisfactory provisions on complementarity.

100. Other delegations objected to extending the sphere of inherent jurisdiction to crimes other than genocide. It was noted in particular that, although the draft prepared by the International Law Commission was the basic proposal before the Committee, the discussion had brought to light an alternative model which ignored the contemporary realities at the international level. The presumption that States would agree by signing a treaty to defer to the court mandatory jurisdiction over the "core crimes" was viewed as highly questionable and concern was expressed that, when the matter of ratifying the statute was before national parliaments, very few Governments would agree to such mandatory jurisdiction. Reference was made in this context to the lessons to be drawn from the record of acceptance of the compulsory jurisdiction of the International Court of Justice. It was also said that the issues of sovereignty raised

during the course of the debate could not be disposed of by providing for a single expression of consent at the time of acceptance of the statute and that, for the membership of the court to have the required broad geographical basis, the concerns of all regions should be duly taken into account.

101. The proponents of the extension of the sphere of inherent jurisdiction to the "core crimes" indicated that such extension could have as a corollary the exclusion from the subject-matter jurisdiction of the court of treaty-based [*23] crimes - an approach that would make it easier to achieve the goal of complementarity. They did not, however, exclude the possibility of retaining the latter crimes and bringing them under the jurisdiction of the court by way of a declaration of acceptance, on the basis of the opting-in or opting-out system.

(b) Mechanism by which States accept the jurisdiction of the court

102. As regards the distinction made in article 22 between acceptance of the statute and acceptance of the jurisdiction of the court, reservations were expressed on the opt-in approach, which, it was stated, leaned too much on the side of conservatism to the detriment of the interests of the international community and might leave the court with a very narrow field of competence and thus run counter to the general aim of the statute. Some delegations, however, expressed preference for the opt-in approach, which would promote broader acceptance of the statute and make it easier to present national legislation organs with convincing arguments on a case-by-case basis. Several delegations favoured adopting an opt-out approach for the "core crimes" while retaining the opt-in approach for lesser crimes and crimes to be brought within the jurisdiction of the court at a later stage. Such a combination, it was argued, would give the court a jurisdiction of reasonable scope and make it more responsive to the current needs of the international community. It was also suggested that article 22 should make it clear whether ratification of the relevant treaty was a prerequisite to the acceptance of the corresponding jurisdiction of the court.

(c) State consent requirements and conditions for the exercise of jurisdiction

103. Paragraph 1 (b) of article 21 was viewed by some delegations as well balanced and consistent with the consensual basis of the court's jurisdiction. Other delegations felt that, to avoid subjecting the operation of the court to undue restrictions, the consent requirement should be limited to the territorial State, which had a particular interest in the prosecution of the case, or to the custodial State, whose consent was necessary for the court to obtain custody of the accused. Still other delegations took the view that the consent requirements should be extended to additional States which could have a significant interest in a case, including the State of nationality of the victim, the State of nationality of the accused and the target State of the crime. It was also suggested that consideration should be given to the interests of States in specific categories of cases and to the need to obtain the consent of the custodial State at the time of arrest. The view was expressed that the provision would need to be further examined in conjunction with article 20 and paragraph 1 (a) of article 21.

104. A number of delegations emphasized that, for practical reasons, only the consent of the State in whose territory the crime was committed or of the custodial State, as provided in article 21, was necessary. They were in favour of keeping to the minimum the number of States whose consent would be needed for the international criminal court to exercise jurisdiction. They pointed out that the international criminal court could not conduct an effective prosecution without the cooperation of the territorial State, nor could a prosecution be conducted unless the alleged offender was surrendered to the court by the custodial State. The point was further made that, under general international law, the custodial State was in a key position to determine who should prosecute a crime. It would be necessary to determine how much of this power the custodial State should cede to the international criminal court.

[*24] 105. The requirement for the consent of the State of nationality of the accused was considered by some delegations necessary not only because some States might be constitutionally barred from extraditing their own nationals, but also because of an anomaly that would result if a complaint could be brought before the court against a person based solely on the acceptance of the jurisdiction of the court by the custodial State and by the territorial State while the acceptance of the jurisdiction by the State of nationality to which the accused owed allegiance and which had jurisdiction over the accused would not be required. Other delegations felt that the requirement of consent of the State of nationality would complicate the exercise of jurisdiction by the international criminal court in cases of multiple offenders.

106. The view was also expressed that in cases of international conflict it was not acceptable to give all control to the territorial State, which might be only one party to the conflict. In the case of terrorism, moreover, the State against which the act was politically directed was concerned as well.

107. The comment was further made that the question of State consent should be examined from the perspective of a basic goal of the planned court: to allow and to encourage States to exercise jurisdiction over the perpetrators of a particular crime. Only when such States were unable to exercise jurisdiction should the international criminal court be called upon to intervene. This approach was found by some delegations to be consistent with the concept of complementarity.

108. As regards paragraph 2 of article 21, the view was expressed that a requesting State or a sending State entitled to assert jurisdiction under an extradition treaty or a status-of-forces agreement, respectively, should be able to prevent the court from exercising jurisdiction even if the custodial State denied the request to surrender a suspect. However, the view was also expressed that the legal basis for requiring such consent was questionable; that attention should be paid to situations in which an extradition request was denied without legal justification or was a pretext for requiring the requesting State's consent; and that the complexities of status-of-forces agreements called for further consideration. Care should be taken not to create irreconcilable obligations for States.

109. The view was expressed that the provisions of article 35 should be viewed as preconditions for the exercise of jurisdiction by the court in all cases, rather than in terms of a discretionary power to be exercised by the court in certain situations. It was suggested that the principle of complementarity should be reflected more clearly in the form of a precondition to ensure that the court would not interfere with the legitimate investigative activities of national authorities or exercise jurisdiction when a State was willing and able to do so, including under bilateral extradition treaties or status-of-forces agreements. Also in relation to the complementary role of the court, it was suggested that national courts should have priority as regards violations of international humanitarian law and alleged crimes of their armed forces involved in United Nations operations. Other comments included: (a) that subparagraph (a) should be redrafted to provide that a case would be inadmissible if it had been duly investigated by a State and there was no reason to believe that the decision of that State not to prosecute was not well founded; (b) that subparagraph (c) of article 35 should be revised to be consonant with the second paragraph of the preamble; (c) that grounds deriving from the principle <u>non bis in idem</u> (art. 42, para. 2) and from the rule of speciality (art. 55) should also be included among grounds for inadmissibility; and (d) that a vexatious complaint constituting an abuse of legal process, or[*25] unjust prosecution, taking into account the circumstances of the accused such as age or ill-health, should also be considered inadmissible.

110. It was pointed out that the draft statute provided for two forms of consent: a State could consent to the jurisdiction of the international criminal court by a declaration of general consent as provided for in article 22, paragraph 1, or by an ad hoc declaration, as stipulated in article 22, paragraph 2. It was noted that the draft statute did not treat a third form of consent: consent with respect to particular crimes. A related issue, not yet considered, it was observed, was whether State consent was a precondition for prosecution by the international criminal court of a particular crime, and whether such consent was among the factors and elements to be considered by the court in determining whether it should exercise jurisdiction or yield to national jurisdiction. In this context, the comment was made that the draft statute should distinguish between consent to prosecution and consent to jurisdiction, inasmuch as consent to jurisdiction might not always be consent to prosecution in a particular case.

111. It was further noted that, in so far as consent implied cooperation, various situations had to be envisaged. The consent of the territorial State might not be crucial in certain circumstances, e.g., peacekeeping operations or belligerent occupation. There were also situations, e.g., belligerency between two States where the same State was at once the custodial State, the territorial State and the State of nationality.

(d) <u>Trigger mechanism</u>

112. As regards the complaint envisaged as a trigger mechanism under articles 21 and 25, some delegations expressed the view that any State party to the statute should be entitled to lodge a complaint with the prosecutor with respect to the serious crimes under general international law that were of concern to the international community as a whole, referred to in article 20, subparagraphs (a) to (d). It was further

suggested that complaints with respect to the crime of genocide as a crime under general international law should not be limited to States parties to the relevant convention. However, the view was also expressed that only the States concerned that had a direct interest in the case, such as the territorial State, the custodial State or the State of nationality of the victim or suspect, and were able to provide relevant documents or other evidence should be entitled to lodge complaints to avoid the substantial costs involved in a lengthy investigation in response to frivolous, politically motivated or unsubstantiated complaints. It was also suggested that the consent of a group of States whose size would be proportional to the number of States having accepted the jurisdiction of the court should be obtained before the prosecutor initiated an investigation, or as soon as the relevant States were identified, to avoid wasting efforts on the investigation of cases over which the court would not be able to exercise jurisdiction. There were further suggestions that the complainant should be a State party to the relevant convention and should pay some portion of the costs of the proceedings. A number of delegations opposed the latter suggestion. It was further suggested that the complaint should not automatically trigger the jurisdiction of the court without notice being given to the States concerned and a determination having been made as to whether any State was willing and able to effectively investigate and prosecute the case.

113. Some delegations felt that the role of the prosecutor should be more fully elaborated and expanded to include the initiation of investigation or prosecution in the case of serious crimes under general international law that[*26] were of concern to the international community as a whole in the absence of a complaint. These delegations were of the view that this expanded role would enhance the independence and autonomy of the prosecutor, who would be in a position to work on behalf of the international community rather than a particular complainant State or the Security Council. In this regard, attention was drawn to the limited role played by state complaints in the context of certain human rights conventions. Reference was also made to the more prominent role assigned to the prosecutor of the ad hoc Tribunals, who was authorized to initiate an investigation ex officio or on the basis of information obtained from any source, including States, international organizations and non-governmental organizations.

114. There were different views as to whether the proposed expanded role of the prosecutor would be consistent with the functions of the procuracy as envisaged in article 12 of the draft statute, which was similar to the corresponding provisions of the statutes of the ad hoc tribunals. It was suggested that consideration be given to the implications of such a role on other provisions of the draft statute, including those relating to the question of determining the admissibility of a case under article 35. Opinions also differed as to whether, in the absence of a State complaint, it would be appropriate for the prosecutor to initiate an investigation: according to one view, the absence of such a complaint was an indication that the crime was not of sufficient gravity or concern to the international community; according to another view, it might mean that the States concerned were unable or unwilling to pursue the matter.

115. Regarding paragraph 3, the view was expressed that the threshold for initiating an investigation was too low since a State could file a complaint without conducting any investigation or providing any proof and that the prosecutor was not given sufficient discretion to determine whether a complaint warranted initiating an investigation by the court without exonerating the suspect for purposes of national prosecution. With regard to article 26, the view was also expressed that a higher threshold should be required for the initiation of an investigation following a complaint or, alternatively, that the prosecutor should be given broader discretion to determine whether to initiate an investigation.

116. As regards article 27, the remark was made that the authority of the prosecutor to file indictments under the article required further consideration with respect to the principle of complementarity.

117. There was a further suggestion that the victims of crimes or their relatives be authorized to trigger the jurisdiction of the court if three criteria were met, namely, (a) the crimes were within the jurisdiction of the court; (b) the territorial State was a party to the statute and had accepted the jurisdiction of the court with respect to the crime; and (c) the court was entitled to initiate an investigation or prosecution in conformity with the principle of complementarity. In this regard, it was also suggested that a special commission should be established within the court to review complaints filed by individuals and to determine before the initiation of any further action whether the necessary criteria were met so as to avoid overloading the court.

118. The view was expressed that it might be appropriate to consider different trigger mechanisms for different categories of crimes. The view was also expressed that the paragraph should be further considered in the light of the appropriateness of the so-called "inherent jurisdiction" concept.

[*27] 119. Several delegations emphasized the relationship between the question of the trigger mechanism for the exercise of jurisdiction and other issues such as the position of State consent requirements and that of the mechanism by which States would indicate their consent.

(e)   Role of the Security Council

120. As regards article 23, paragraph 1, of the draft statute, several delegations were of the view that the Security Council should be authorized to refer matters to the court to obviate the need for the creation of additional ad hoc tribunals and to enhance the effectiveness of the court as a consequence of referrals made under Chapter VII of the Charter of the United Nations. The role envisaged for the Security Council was described as consistent with its primary responsibility for the maintenance of international peace and security and its existing powers under the Charter as reflected in recent practice. The Council, it was observed, would merely refer a general matter or situation to the court, as opposed to bringing a case against a specific individual - which would preserve the independence and autonomy of the court in the exercise of its investigative, prosecutorial and judicial functions. In this regard, reference was made to the modus operandi of the two ad hoc Tribunals established by the Security Council. The view was expressed that the intervention of the Security Council in triggering the jurisdiction of the court under the paragraph under consideration would be particularly relevant if the jurisdiction of the court were limited to the most serious crimes that might threaten international peace and security. It was observed that the provisions of this paragraph might help to solve the issue of extending the jurisdiction of the court to several treaty-based crimes, in particular, terrorist acts. It was also suggested that the elimination of the Council's role as envisaged in that paragraph would necessitate a more complex State consent regime, which would have the further drawback of resting on the political agenda of individual States rather than on the collective decision of the Security Council. There were different views as to whether a Security Council referral should obviate the need for State consent, as envisaged by the phrase "notwithstanding article 21" as well as the commentary to the article. A question was also raised concerning the effects of a Security Council referral in terms of the possible primacy of the court's jurisdiction and the concurrent jurisdiction of national courts under the principle of complementarity, with attention being drawn to the statutes of the ad hoc tribunals in this respect.

121. Several other delegations expressed serious reservations or opposition to the role envisaged for the Security Council, which, in their view, would reduce the credibility and moral authority of the court; excessively limit its role; undermine its independence, impartiality and autonomy; introduce an inappropriate political influence over the functioning of the institution; confer additional powers on the Security Council that were not provided for in the Charter; and enable the permanent members of the Security Council to exercise a veto with respect to the work of the court. The necessity of envisaging a role for the Security Council in relation to a permanent court was also questioned on the ground that States parties to the statute could trigger the jurisdiction of the court by means of filing a complaint, with the prosecutor acting as a filter or screening mechanism with respect to frivolous complaints. The remark was also made that a distinction should be drawn between the ad hoc Tribunals instituted by the Security Council under Chapter VII and the future permanent court to be established on a consensual basis by the States parties to its statute.

[*28] 122. With reference to paragraph 2 of article 23, some delegations were of the view that the role envisaged for the Security Council was appropriate and necessary in view of Article 39 of the Charter. Emphasis was placed on the need to draw a clear distinction between a finding of aggression by the Council with respect to a State and a determination of individual criminal responsibility by the court and to keep in mind the differences between the mandates to be performed independently by the two bodies. In this regard, it was suggested that the court should not be able to question or contradict a finding of the Security Council. There were different views on the extent to which the court should be permitted to consider a plea of self-defence raised by the accused since a Security Council finding under Article 39 would have clear implications with respect to Article 51 of the Charter.

123. Other delegations expressed serious concern regarding paragraph 2. It was argued in particular that the judicial functions of the court would be unduly curtailed with respect to the determination of the existence of the crime of aggression as well as the defences that could be considered in relation to the question of individual criminal responsibility; the independence and impartiality of the court would be undermined by its dependence on the finding of a political body; the court could be precluded from performing its functions with respect to the crime of aggression as a result of the exercise of the veto by a permanent member of the Security Council; the work of the court in terms of the investigation and prosecution of the crime of aggression could also be impeded or delayed as a result of the failure of the Security Council to make an express finding of aggression. It was also mentioned that paragraph 2 of article 23 would be superfluous in any case if the crime of aggression were not covered under article 20. The point was further made that no provision similar to paragraph 2 was to be found, in relation to the International Court of Justice, in the Charter of the United Nations or the Statute of the Court. Some delegations felt that paragraph 2 should be deleted, possibly together with article 20, paragraph (b). 9/

124. Paragraph 3 was viewed by some delegations as necessary to prevent the risk of interference in the Security Council's fulfilment of its primary responsibility for the maintenance of international peace and security under Article 24 of the Charter, with attention being drawn to the priority given to the Council in this regard under Article 12 of the Charter. The remark was made that the role of the Security Council with respect to the maintenance of international peace and security could eclipse the judicial functions of the International Court of Justice in some situations.

125. Other delegations expressed serious reservations concerning paragraph 3 in relation to the prerogative conferred on the Security Council by article 23 of the draft statute as regards the activation of the court, bearing in mind the political character of the organ in question. It was observed in particular that the judicial functions of the court should not be subordinated to the action of a political body. Concern was also voiced that the court could be prevented from performing its functions through the mere placing of an item on the Council's agenda and could remain paralysed for lengthy periods while the Security Council was actively dealing with a particular situation or retained the item on its agenda for possible future consideration. The necessity of the provision was also questioned on the ground that no similar priority was given to the Security Council under Article 12 of the Charter with respect to judicial decisions on legal questions to be rendered by the International Court of Justice.

[*29]126. Still other delegations expressed the view that the current text was too vague and should be reformulated so as to expressly limit the application of the paragraph to situations in which the Council was taking action with respect to a particular situation, as indicated in the commentary to the article. Other issues that were viewed as calling for further consideration included: the criteria or method for determining when the Security Council should be considered as actively seized of, or performing its responsibilities with respect to, a particular situation for the purposes of paragraph 3; the question of whether the paragraph should apply to situations in which the Security Council was performing its responsibilities under so-called "Chapter VI and a half" as well as Chapter VII; the relationship between the said paragraph and paragraph 1; and the implications of the Security Council assuming its responsibilities with respect to a particular situation after the court had commenced investigations or judicial proceedings relating to the same situation.

> (f) Statute of limitations

127. Some delegations felt that the question of the statute of limitations for the crimes within the jurisdiction of the court should be addressed in the statute in the light of divergences between national laws and bearing in mind the importance of the legal principle involved, which reflected the decreasing social importance of bringing criminals to justice and the increasing difficulties in ensuring a fair trial as time elapsed. However, other delegations questioned the applicability of the statute of limitations to the types of serious crimes under consideration and drew attention to the 1968 Convention on the Non-applicability of Statutory Limitations to War Crimes and Crimes against Humanity.

D. Methods of proceedings: due process

128. The present summary endeavours to list the main issues raised with regard to Parts 4 (Investigation and prosecution), 5 (The trial) and 6 (Appeal and review) of the draft statute during the Ad Hoc

Committee's debate on 6 April 1995. It reflects only the views expressed and the proposals made in that debate, and is presented without prejudice to the written comments on the draft statute as contained in document A/AC.244/1 and Add.1-4 as well as to the comments reflected in document A/CN.4/464/Add.1, or to any other views or proposals that delegations may wish to put forward.

    1.   General observations

129. The question of the methods of proceedings was viewed as going beyond technical concerns and touching upon fundamental aspects of the proposed institution. It was felt essential to bear in mind, first, that the court, in view of the considerable powers it would enjoy in relation to individuals, should be bound to apply the highest standards of justice, integrity and due process; secondly, that the demand for due process was of special cogency in relation to defendants involved in proceedings conducted away from their home country and away from where the evidence and witnesses were readily available; and thirdly, that precedents would be scarce or unavailable. Emphasis was placed on the need to have the rules of the court prepared by States rather than by the judges and to have them eventually adopted by States parties to the statute.

[*30]130. The remark was made that in drafting the statute the International Law Commission had drawn inspiration from common-law practice. Bearing in mind that both the civil-law and common-law systems would be represented on the court, it was felt necessary to give appropriate reflection to both systems in the statute as well as in the rules of the court.

131. There seemed to be a general agreement that the articles on due process as formulated by the ILC served as a useful point of departure for the further deliberations. However, as was evidenced by the debate, there was a need for further elaboration of those articles as well as further work on the rules of evidence and procedure, and for determining whether such rules should be elaborated in conjunction with the statute itself. Referring to the intention expressed in the third paragraph of the preamble to the statute that the court was to "be complementary to national criminal justice systems", several delegations highlighted the difficulties involved in establishing an adequate relationship between the court and national authorities for the purpose of implementing the provisions of the statute on due process.

132. It was generally recognized that Part 4 (Investigation and prosecution) should be carefully reviewed to ensure, inter alia, a proper balance between two concerns, namely effectiveness of the prosecution and respect for the rights of the suspect or the accused. Emphasis was placed on the need to formulate the provisions on due process in such a way as to allow for the application of standards contained in relevant human rights instruments. Some concern was voiced, particularly in relation to articles 28, 30 and 46, that the statute drew extensively on the common-law system, even though the civil-law system might afford greater protection to the suspect or the accused at the early stage of investigation or prosecution.

133. It was pointed out that some issues, such as that of the powers of the Presidency, were not confined to one article and needed to be examined comprehensively. The remark was also made that the role of the Security Council under Part 4, for example in relation to article 25, paragraph 4, and article 26, paragraph 5, would depend upon the nature and extent of the court's jurisdiction, to be defined in Part 3 of the draft statute. Attention was also drawn to the complex interplay between, and division of, responsibilities of the court and those of the national authorities which required a further analysis in the context of several articles, including articles 28, 29, 35, 38 and 42.

    2.   Specific issues

Article 25

134. The general point was made that the precise formulation of this article would have to be determined in the light of the outcome of the discussion on the jurisdiction of the court under Part 3.

135. A proposal was made that there should be a certain minimum number of States before a complaint could be lodged under the article, as opposed to individual States.

136. Paragraph 3 was viewed by several delegations as calling for further scrutiny to prevent the submission of frivolous cases or cases for purely political reasons. In this connection, it was suggested that the phrase "as far as possible" should be deleted.

[*31] Article 26

137. The remark was made that the relationship between investigations conducted under national procedures and those carried out in relation to the same conduct under the present article called for a careful review. Attention was drawn to the relevance, in this context, of issues addressed in article 35.

138. The view was expressed that the prosecutor, in investigating alleged crimes under paragraph 2, should act in conformity with established practice in matters of international judicial assistance. The provision enabling the prosecutor to conduct on-site investigations gave rise to special concern; it was argued that the provisions should be brought in line with the established practice of cooperation and judicial assistance, as well as with constitutional requirements of certain States.

139. Paragraphs 3 and 5 were considered by some delegations as further examples of overly broad powers of the Presidency and as requiring further examination to ensure that they were fully consistent with the principle of "complementarity". The question was asked whether safeguards for the rights of witnesses should not be provided.

140. As regards paragraph 4, it was suggested that the limits of the prosecutor's discretion to decide not to prosecute should be clarified, taking into account, in particular, issues on inadmissibility addressed in connection with article 35. It was generally felt that similar concerns arose in relation to the provisions of article 27, paragraphs 1 and 4, relating to the filing, confirmation or amendment of an indictment.

141. With respect to paragraph 5, the point was made by some delegations that States parties to the statute having accepted the jurisdiction of the court should have the possibility to participate in the review of the prosecutor's decision.

142. Doubts were expressed about paragraph 6. It was asked, in particular, whether subparagraph (a) (i) was not going beyond what was strictly necessary, whether the suspect should not be entitled to be informed of the charge against him or her, and whether subparagraph (b) was appropriate. The remark was made that these issues were also relevant to article 43.

Article 27

143. A substantial number of delegations expressed concern over the broad powers of the Presidency with respect to indictments. There was a view that these powers undermined the independence of the prosecutor.

144. Emphasis was placed on the need to clarify the prosecutor's discretion to file and possibly amend the indictment. It was suggested that the suspect should be entitled to be heard, in order to ensure that the amendment of indictment did not infringe upon his or her rights.

145. With respect to paragraph 5, the remark was made that attention should be paid to the disclosure of sensitive information because of possible adverse consequences. It was pointed out that the same issue arose in the context of article 38, paragraph 4, and article 41, paragraph 2.

[*32] Article 28

146. There was extensive discussion on the issue of provisional arrest which brought forward the difficult problem of the division of responsibilities between the court and national judicial systems. It was noted that the problem arose in the context of article 30 as well. Concern was expressed over the permissible length of detention and the consequences of its expiry, the powers of the Presidency, the adequacy of criteria for arrest and the consequences of release from arrest. The legal basis for the provisional arrest of a suspect was also queried.

Article 29

147. With respect to the pre-trial stage, the nature of the proceedings before the national judicial officer and the extent of the rights of the suspect were viewed as calling for clarification. The question was asked whether the article should lay down specific standards for the protection of the rights of the suspect. In this connection the question was asked whether the article should not reflect or represent a more balanced division of responsibilities between the international criminal court and national authorities. Attention was also drawn to the constitutional problems which some States would face, and to the practical difficulties which many States would encounter with the article as currently drafted, in achieving such a balanced division.

148. Practical and constitutional concerns were expressed, in particular with respect to paragraph 2.

149. Concern was expressed about the need to clarify the meaning of provisional arrest and its relationship to other forms of arrest throughout the statute. Attention was drawn to the need to keep to a minimum the duration of detention following arrest, as well as to provide procedures for dealing with applications for release.

150. As regards paragraph 3, the point was made that the issue of compensation also arose in relation to provisional arrest (art. 28) and in case of exoneration (arts. 45 and 50).

151. Questions were furthermore raised as to the eligibility for, and mechanics of, compensation as well as the need to identify the authorities which would be liable for payment.

152. The article was also viewed as insufficiently detailed with respect to procedures at the pre-trial stage and it was stated that more detailed provisions were required, including those on arrest, detention and appearance before, and so also the role of, the judicial authorities.

Article 30

153. The duty imposed on the prosecutor in paragraph 1 raised once again the difficulties involved in reconciling the respective responsibilities of the international criminal court and those of national authorities. Particular difficulty arose over the uncertainty as to which jurisdiction, the national one or that of the court, should govern provisional arrest. Furthermore, it was reiterated that the suspect should be served with the indictment prior to its confirmation.

[*33] Article 31

154. A question was raised as to the extent to which persons made available to the prosecutor to assist in a prosecution would have the power to act; this was seen as connected with the problem of the overall powers of the prosecutor, as already referred to in paragraph 138 above in connection with article 26.

Article 33

155. This provision was mostly discussed in connection with issues pertaining to jurisdiction and has therefore been left out of the purview of the present summary.

Article 34

156. The reference to "interested State" was viewed as calling for clarification. The timing of challenges, in particular after the commencement of the hearing, and the locus standi to make challenges in that phase of the trial gave rise to divergent opinions.

Article 35

157. This provision was considered as one which should give clear expression to the principle of "complementarity".

158. It was suggested that the various grounds of inadmissibility, including those covered by articles 42 and 55, should be grouped in a separate part of the statute.

159. With reference to the word "may" in the introductory phrase of this article, the view was widely held that there should be no discretion for the court to declare a case admissible if the grounds for inadmissibility had been duly made out.

160. The previous calls for a clarification of the term "interested State" were reiterated in the present context.

161. It was also remarked that the wording of the article needed to be reviewed in the light of article 27.

162. Whereas subparagraph 9 (a) was viewed by some delegations as redundant in the light of article 26, paragraph 1, others proposed the insertion of additional grounds of inadmissibility such as acquittal after a properly brought case. Subparagraph (b) was considered as problematic in so far as its wording gave rise to divergent interpretations. As for subparagraph (c), the question of the entitlement of the accused to invoke insufficient gravity was raised. There was also a view that the subparagraph should be deleted.

Article 36

163. Some delegations raised the question whether further parties should have the right to be heard, in particular in the exercise of the right of diplomatic protection by the State of which the accused was a national.

[*34] Article 37

164. The rule that the accused should be present during the trial was widely endorsed. Some delegations, which invoked, inter alia, constitutional reasons, argued that the rule should not be accompanied by any exceptions. For others, exceptions should only be permitted in clearly specified circumstances.

165. Paragraph 2 as a whole was viewed by some delegations as too broad or imprecise, but was considered by others as striking an adequate balance between the rule and the exceptions.

166. With reference to subparagraph (a), reservations were expressed on the appropriateness of the ground of "ill-health" and it was queried whether, at least in some cases, this ground would not already amount to incapacity to stand trial. 10/ Whether reasons of security had a place in this context was also questioned.

167. With reference to paragraph 4, the need for an Indictment Chamber was queried and it was suggested either to delete the paragraph or to establish a permanent indictment chamber which would take over the powers of the Presidency such as those under article 27.

168. It was furthermore proposed to limit the function of an Indictment Chamber in in absentia proceedings to the preservation of evidence. In this context, concern was expressed about the subsequent use of evidence and attention was drawn to the desirability of providing safeguards to protect the rights of the accused. To some delegations, this article also raised the question of the entitlement of the accused to legal representation before the Indictment Chamber.

Article 38

169. A number of delegations reiterated in the context of this provision their view that the draft was not explicit enough on procedures and that more details should be provided, possibly through the rules of the court.

170. With reference to paragraph 1 (d), the notion of "plea of guilty or not guilty" gave rise to criticisms. The view was expressed by some delegations that the effect of a guilty plea would need to be spelled out in view of the differences between civil-law and common-law systems. The remark was made that, in view of the gravity of the crimes within the jurisdiction of the court, it would be inappropriate to permit plea bargaining.

Article 39

171. Attention was drawn to the need to define more precisely the concept of treaty applicability so as not to infringe upon the principle of nullum crimen sine lege. It was generally asked, in relation to the treaty crimes referred to in article 20 (e), whether ratification or accession by a certain State was necessary for a treaty to be applicable for the purpose of the statute. The question was also raised whether, once a person had been handed over to the court, the relevant treaty remained applicable in the sense of subparagraph (b), despite the fact that the court was not a party to the relevant treaty.

172. Subparagraph (a) raised the problem of the non-retroactive applicability of penal provisions and was viewed as calling for further examination once the final shape of article 20 had been determined and for certain redrafting. A[*35] view was expressed that the qualification of a crime under international law seemed redundant in view of the reference to article 20 (a) to (d).

Article 41

173. A substantial number of delegations stressed the need to guarantee minimum rights for the accused in conformity with article 14 of the International Covenant on Civil and Political Rights.

174. Consequently, it was argued that a special regime should be provided for juveniles in accordance with that article.

175. The issue of mandatory legal assistance was viewed as particularly important in view of the seriousness of the crimes within the jurisdiction of the court. Emphasis was placed in this context on the need to establish rules on the qualifications, powers and remuneration of defence attorneys and on the procedure governing the appointment of court-assigned attorneys.

176. The views expressed in the context of article 27 on the limits to be placed on the disclosure of sensitive information were reiterated in the context of paragraph 2.

Article 42

177. The crucial importance of the non bis in idem principle in the interplay between national jurisdiction and the jurisdiction of the court was widely recognized. In this context one view was however expressed

that article 42 in its current form came close to undermining the principle of "complementarity". The appropriateness of empowering the court to pass judgement on the impartiality or independence of national courts was seriously questioned.

178. Certain countries raised constitutional difficulties with regard to this provision.

179. With reference to subparagraph (a) of paragraph 2, some delegations expressed serious reservations about a criterion based on the concept of "ordinary crime". It was proposed to delete the subparagraph.

180. Subparagraph (b) was considered by some delegations as too vaguely formulated and as involving subjective assessments.

Article 43

181. This provision was viewed by a few delegations as calling for further elaboration, particularly with regard to the protection of victims and witnesses. Also noted was the need to consider the rights of the accused in this context.

Article 44

182. There was a general feeling that this article required further scrutiny in the framework of the statute and/or in the context of the rules of the court.

183. As regards paragraph 2, it was widely held that cases of perjury should be prosecuted by the international criminal court rather than by national courts.

[*36]184. Several delegations supported the principle set forth in paragraph 5. The view was however expressed that careful attention should be paid to the way in which the provision would operate in practice and it was suggested that the grounds for inadmissibility of evidence should be more narrowly circumscribed.

Article 45

185. As regards paragraph 1, several delegations felt that the presence of all members of the Trial Chamber should be required throughout the proceedings. With reference to paragraphs 2 and 5, the question was raised whether judges should be entitled to deliver separate or dissenting opinions. Divergent views were expressed in this connection. It was noted that the issues of the quorum and dissenting opinions would also arise in connection with article 49.

186. As to paragraph 3, questions were raised concerning the meaning of the expression "sufficient time" and as to what should be the consequence of the failure of the Trial Chamber to agree on a decision.

Article 47

187. In the view of many delegations, this article gave rise to a serious problem with regard to its conformity with the principle nulla poena sine lege. It was generally held that there was a need for maximum penalties applicable to various types of crimes to be spelled out. The view was also expressed that minimum penalties should also be made explicit in view of the seriousness of the crimes. It was also proposed to introduce criteria as to the choice of appropriate penalty.

188. With regard to paragraph 1, the exclusion of the death penalty was supported by many delegations. Some delegations suggested provision for such exclusion, while one delegation proposed that the death penalty be included in the list of possible penalties. It was suggested that suspension of penalties should be addressed. A number of delegations wondered whether a fine would be commensurate with the seriousness of the crimes under the jurisdiction of the court. Some delegations further questioned the enforceability of fines and asked whether failure to pay could lead to the imposition of a term of imprisonment. Proposals were also made that the statute should provide for confiscation, restitution of property and compensation for victims.

189. Paragraph 2 gave rise to serious concern on the part of many delegations owing to the lack of certainty regarding the law to be applied. There was a proposal to apply only the law of the State where the crime had been committed; another proposal was to apply exclusively the law of the State of the nationality of the accused.

190. Several delegations suggested the need for further consideration of paragraph 3. Concern was expressed, in particular, as to the appropriateness of subparagraphs (a) and (b).

Article 48

191. A number of delegations questioned the adequacy of, or necessity for, the grounds for appeal as laid down in this article.

[*37] Article 49

192. A number of delegations thought it necessary to introduce a time-limit for the lodging of an appeal.

Article 50

193. The question was raised whether the grounds for revision listed in article 50 were broad enough to accommodate developments in relevant national law. Concern was also expressed that the article did not contain any provisions regarding compensation for the wrongly convicted person, bearing in mind the provisions of article 14, paragraph 6, of the International Covenant on Civil and Political Rights.

   3.   Additional remarks

194. Some delegations thought it necessary to provide for sanctions and other consequences, including compensation, in case of misconduct of the prosecutors, judges or other officers of the court.

E.   Relationship between States parties, non-States parties and the international criminal court 195. Discussion of topics under this subheading was based on the guidelines prepared by the Working Group (see para. 9 above), as set out in annex I to the present report.

   1.   General issues

196. It was widely recognized that the question of cooperation between States and the court was intrinsically linked with that of the relationship between the provisions of the statute and their implementation under national law, and the nature and extent of obligations of States to guarantee such cooperation. Given the importance and complexity of that relationship, it was suggested that the basic elements of the required cooperation be laid down explicitly in the statute itself.

197. It was emphasized that the effectiveness of the international criminal court would depend largely on the cooperation of national jurisdiction through the organs of which requests of the court for assistance would primarily have to be put into effect. It was suggested that only in limited circumstances, where national jurisdiction failed to provide such assistance, would the question of the court's direct exercise of its investigative powers in the territory of the State, either on its own or through agents of the State acting on its behalf, arise.

198. Strict adherence to the principle of complementarity was considered particularly important in defining the relationship and cooperation between the court and national authorities. It was further stated that the role to be played by the principle of complementarity in this connection was ultimately connected with other issues such as the overall scope and nature of the jurisdiction of the court, the regime of States' consent, or the trigger mechanism, to be provided under the statute.

[*38]199. The view was expressed that the choice of cooperation to be afforded to the international criminal court and the nature and extent of obligations of States to assist would have a significant bearing not only on issues of sovereignty and constitutional laws of many States, but also on the effective functioning of the court itself. It was noted that neither complete reliance on national laws and practices nor direct implementation and enforcement of the statute by the court itself would be a reasonable option. The appropriate option, it was suggested, was to establish a mechanism for effective cooperation, built on existing regimes of cooperation and judicial assistance, with full regard to the requirements of national laws and procedure, adjusting them, as required, to the special character of cooperation between the court and States. Mention was also made of the possibility of providing for an entirely new regime which would not draw upon existing extradition and judicial assistance conventions.

200. It was further recognized that the divergence of national laws and procedures would call for a flexible scheme, providing viable options and sub-schemes to allow for variations in national requirements, as opposed to a rigid and monolithic scheme. The question was however raised as to the need for guaranteeing a homogeneous system for all or some forms of cooperation between the court and national authorities in the relationship between the national law and the law of the statute. The view was also expressed that any impediments arising from the application of existing regimes of cooperation or considerations of national constitutional requirements should be clearly identified for the purpose of devising appropriate schemes for cooperation.

201. As regards the extent of obligations of States parties to assist, the view was widely shared that such obligations could not be absolute since, under the principle of complementarity, States would have the discretionary power of deciding whether or not to comply with the court's request for assistance. In this connection, concern was expressed regarding the presumption made in the draft statute of the primacy of the requests of the international criminal court in full for the apprehension and surrender of persons over requests from another State. The view was also expressed, however, that the primacy of the jurisdiction of the court should prevail in all cases of most serious crimes, as defined in article 20, subparagraphs (a) to (d).

202. It was noted, however, that the grounds for refusing compliance with such requests from the court should be limited to a minimum, taking into account the special character of the jurisdiction of the court and the seriousness of the crimes to be covered under the statute, and that the results should be explicitly laid down in the statute itself. Many traditional exceptions to extradition were considered inappropriate in the light of the type of crimes to be dealt with by the court.

203. The issue of competing treaty obligations was recognized as a particularly difficult one. It was pointed out that the issue would not only relate to States' obligations under existing extradition treaties but also to the obligations under the status-of-forces agreements. The point was also made that different regimes of cooperation would have to apply to situations where both or only one of the States parties to the statute were parties to the treaty in question. It was further suggested that the issue would have to be dealt with in the context of the question of applicable law and the respective roles of the court and the custodial State. In this connection, note was taken of the fact that article 21, paragraph 2, of the draft statute adopted one approach to addressing this issue.

[*39]204. The importance of the role of national laws and courts in guaranteeing the fundamental rights of individuals was emphasized. It was pointed out that, in many States, such safeguards were part of constitutional requirements. It was also noted that, in some cases, national safeguards for the protection of the rights of accused persons might be greater than those existing in international law and the appropriateness of the direct application of standards established by the court, as envisaged in article 29, paragraphs 2 and 3, of the draft statute with regard to release, bail and a determination of the lawfulness of arrest, was questioned. It was emphasized, however, that care should be taken that adherence to national safeguards did not become an unjustifiable impediment to cooperation with the court.

2.   Apprehension and surrender

205. The view was expressed that the system of apprehension and surrender under article 53 of the draft statute was a departure from the traditional regime of cooperation between States established under the existing extradition treaties. It was noted, in particular, that the article embodied a strict transfer scheme which did not seem to contemplate any significant role of the national courts and other authorities on this matter, and that it established a presumption of preference of the requests for transfer of accused persons to the court over requests by States. It was suggested that, while a case could be made for creating a new scheme of cooperation tailored to the special needs of the court, national constitutional requirements, particularly those for guaranteeing the protection of the fundamental rights of individuals, as well as the principles and established practices of the existing extradition treaties, should be fully taken into account if a truly effective system of cooperation was to be developed.

206. But there was also the view that, as long as the competence of the court was restricted to all or some of the most serious crimes as defined in article 20, subparagraphs (a) to (d), the primacy of the jurisdiction of the court in all cases of requests for transfer should indeed prevail. Otherwise, it was further noted, a homogeneous system of cooperation between the court and national authorities could not be guaranteed in relation to the application of national law and procedures and the provisions of the statute. According to this view, for those crimes referred to above, the jurisdiction of the court would be in respect of all persons arrested in a State that had accepted the jurisdiction of the court.

207. The point was made that these two different approaches to the question of surrender of the accused to the court militated in favour of the creation of two different schemes of cooperation within the statute: one being a transfer scheme similar to that proposed in the draft statute for those States that were able and

willing to provide expedited transfers, and another based on the traditional notion of extradition for those States that were not able constitutionally to provide expedited transfers of the accused.

208. It was further remarked that the choice of concepts such as extradition, surrender and transfer was a matter that could have very different and far-reaching consequences in various States. It was therefore considered important that, whatever concept might be chosen or the number of schemes adopted, a list should be established, preferably in article 53, specifically indicating certain traditional limitations or exceptions that could not be invoked in connection with the court's requests for transfer of the accused. [*40]209. With regard to the issues relating to apprehension, it was emphasized that domestic constitutional requirements should be taken into account when considering the roles of the court and national authorities in the arrest of an accused person. As to the question of the arrest warrant issued by the court, it was noted that the use of the term "provisional arrest" in two very distinct contexts - the pre-indictment arrest warrant, which was provisional for the court's own purposes, and the provisional arrest request, pending a formal request for surrender of the accused to the court - was confusing and needed to be clarified. With respect to provisional measures under article 52, it was suggested that inclusion of the notion of "emergency" might be appropriate.

210. As to the form and content of the court's requests for the arrest of the accused, some greater specificity about the content of those requests was suggested. The point was made that this issue could be particularly important for the court and for the requested States, where there might be the need for a review of the matters pertaining to the underlying case, as a matter of judicial confirmation of a request for surrender by national authorities.

211. The unusually long period of the pre-indictment detention provided for in article 28, paragraph 2, was noted with special concern as not being consistent with the national laws of many States. In this connection, the question was raised as to whether there was really a need in most instances for the Presidency to determine those issues as a matter of protecting the rights of the accused when, for most States, those same rights must be respected in national courts as well. Attention was drawn to the fact that the national court in which the accused was actually present with counsel and with the familiarity of the laws might afford a greater degree of protection and understanding of the rights of the accused.

212. With respect to the issues relating to surrender, it was noted that the question of the applicability of national judicial procedures to the surrender decision raised the difficult issue of the national inquiry into substantive matters pertaining to the accusation by the court. In this regard, the view was expressed that national authorities should not have the right to examine the warrant in relation to substantive law, while certain formal requirements might be made. The issue of different national requirements regarding sufficiency of evidence was also noted as a particularly difficult problem. It was suggested that this should be an issue only where it was an absolute requirement and care should be taken not to burden those national proceedings with issues that were not truly necessary under national law. As to the question of the relevance of dual criminality and statutes of limitations, doubts were expressed as to the appropriateness of such rules in relation to cases of surrender of the accused to the court, in view of the most serious character of the crimes under its jurisdiction.

213. The suggestion was also made that the system of apprehension and surrender under the statute should be extended to cover convicted persons, since there was the possibility that the arrest and surrender of a convicted person who had escaped custody might be sought.

214. As regards exceptions to the obligation to surrender, the view was reiterated that they should be kept to the absolute minimum and that they should be specifically articulated in the statute. In this connection, the appropriateness of such traditional limitations or exceptions as the nationality of the accused, the level of social integration and excuses and justifications under national law, or the political exception, was questioned. It was also[*41] suggested that the lapse of time as well as the age and health of the suspected person should not be grounds for refusing surrender.

215. On the question of the applicability of some of the traditional delays, it was noted that domestic proceedings could involve a more serious offence than those before the court and therefore the notion of deferral of surrender or a scheme of temporary surrender should be considered, ensuring that both the domestic and the court prosecution could proceed on the basis of a temporary surrender of the accused to

the court. It was also suggested that the State concerned could enforce both the domestic and the court sentences. Pendency of national proceedings relating to the same crime was also considered relevant, being consistent with the principle of complementarity.

216. With regard to the issue of the transfer of the accused to the court or to the detaining State, the view was expressed that such a transfer could be an appropriate cut-off point for shifting the primary responsibility over the accused from the national authorities to the international criminal court. It was suggested that the same consideration could equally apply to the pre-trial detention of the accused. It was further noted that this might be an appropriate solution for those States in which the initial proceedings regarding surrender would require some degree of national court involvement.

217. With regard to the issue of transit through third States in the course of transfer of the accused to the court or to the detaining State, there was recognition of the need to include in the statute a special provision concerning the duties of those transit States and the differences that should be made in this regard depending on whether the State concerned was a party to the statute or not. The possibility of ad hoc arrangements between the court and States not parties to the statute was mentioned.

218. Concerning other surrender issues, the importance of the question of competing treaty obligations was again emphasized. It was suggested that the requested State make its decision taking into account the overall purposes of the court, the principle of complementarity and the objective of producing the most appropriate jurisdiction for trying the accused. The suggestion was also made that the statute stipulate that, in cases of conflicting transfer/ extradition obligations, a State party to the statute should recognize the obligation to transfer an accused person to the court unless another State that had an extradition relation with the requested State could make, immediately, a prima facie case that it had sufficient jurisdiction and that the circumstances supported the claim that national prosecution would be effective. However, the view was expressed with respect to the provision of article 53, paragraph 4, that the presumption of the primacy of jurisdiction should be in favour of States rather than the court.

219. On the rule of specialty, the view was expressed that, while some provision concerning specialty was required in order to safeguard the rights of the accused, the statute should also provide for waiver by the requested State, the custodial State, as well as by the accused, in a manner similar to that envisaged under traditional forms of extradition treaty arrangements. It was further suggested that the rule of specialty might need to be expanded to encompass the question of the ability of the court to surrender to a third State according to its own proceedings as well as possibly, the need to distinguish between crimes committed after surrender, to which the rule of specialty generally did not apply. The view was also expressed, however, that the rule of specialty should not be applied with respect to the court.

[*42]220. The entire issue of re-extradition, namely, the transfer of the accused by the court to a third State, was considered important and worthy to be addressed specifically in the statute. In particular, the point was made that the question of whether there was a continuing right on the part of the custodial State to refuse to allow the court to hand over an accused needed to be explored.

221. The suggestion was also made that the question of international liability of national authorities when undertaking actions at the request of the court and the issue of the legal status of the court when involved in national proceedings should be examined.

3.   Judicial assistance

222. The remark was made that, in common-law systems, "judicial assistance" did not encompass certain types of assistance, such as those requiring the use of the police force. It was accordingly suggested to use the term "mutual assistance", as did the United Nations Model Treaty on Mutual Assistance in Criminal Matters (General Assembly resolution 45/117). While concern was expressed that the term "mutual" might imply reciprocity, which was not appropriate in the present context, the remark was made that mutual assistance implied equal access to evidence and information and not necessarily reciprocity.

223. Emphasis was placed by several delegations on the need for full cooperation between the international criminal court and national authorities, each taking account of the other's concerns and needs.

224. As regards judicial assistance during the investigation phase (prior to indictment), support was expressed for the establishment of a list itemizing the forms of assistance that States parties to the statute

would be expected to provide to the international criminal court; that list would not necessarily be exhaustive but should identify the types of assistance that were compulsory.

225. As to whether the prosecutor should be entitled to carry out activities related to the preparation and prosecution of a case in the territory of a State, many delegations took the view that the consent of the State was a prerequisite and that the activities in question should be conducted in conformity with domestic constitutional and other requirements. For others, a differentiation should be made between the types of activities involved. The prosecutor might, for instance, be permitted, under the statute, to interview witnesses in the territory of a State party in accordance with domestic law, subject to, for comity reasons, informing the national judicial or police authorities concerned. Activities requiring coercive measures such as search and seizure or surrender should, however, be the exclusive prerogative of national police authorities, particularly as liability issues might arise. Multilateral treaties on mutual assistance and the United Nations Model Treaty on Mutual Assistance in Criminal Matters were mentioned as possible bases for the drafting of the relevant provisions of the statute.

226. It was pointed out that the limits to the prosecutor's authority to conduct activities relating to the preparation of a case in the territory of a State largely depended on whether or not that State had a functioning judicial system.

227. The remark was made that the statute should provide for exceptions to the obligation of a State to comply with a request for assistance from the[*43] prosecutor. In this context, reference was made to constitutional barriers to compellability of witnesses, as well as to privileges exempting individuals from the obligation to testify.

228. Attention was drawn to the need to make it clear whether the obligation concerning the rights of the accused prior to questioning, which was provided for under article 26, paragraph 6, applied only to the prosecutor or also to national authorities when questioning a suspect for purposes of prosecution by the international criminal court.

229. The view was expressed that the statute should address the question of the gathering and confidentiality of information and evidence. It was recalled in this context that, in criminal proceedings, an accused should have full access to, and the opportunity to examine, the evidence against him or her.

230. Considering that one of the goals of the planned court was to encourage national prosecution of alleged offenders, and bearing in mind that not all States were bound by mutual judicial assistance agreements, it was suggested to include in the statute appropriate provisions on which States could rely in requesting assistance from each other.

231. Attention was also drawn to the guidelines elaborated by the International Tribunal for the former Yugoslavia for national implementing legislation aimed at facilitating cooperation with States under article 21 of its statute. Those guidelines dealt with the following issues: duty to cooperate; national authority responsible for cooperation with the Tribunal; concurrent jurisdiction; arrest, detention and surrender of the accused; provisional arrest; witnesses and experts; data from police files; immunity and free transit; seizure; return of property and proceeds of crime; and enforcement of sentences. Similar guidelines could be elaborated for the international criminal court on the major aspects of cooperation with States, other aspects being left to ad hoc arrangements between the court and the States concerned.

232. The remark was further made that, while a State party to the statute having consented to the jurisdiction of the court for a particular crime would obviously be obliged to comply with a request for assistance connected with that crime, it was not clear whether, in the absence of such consent, the State party would be under an obligation to comply with a request for assistance connected with the crime concerned. It was also noted that the draft statute did not address the question of the obligation of States to provide assistance to the defence or the role, if any, of the court or the prosecutor in processing such requests.

233. The delegations that commented on the issue of witnesses noted that, in relation to an international criminal court, the problem arose whether attendance of witnesses could be compelled directly or through State authorities. It was noted that, in many countries, it was not constitutionally possible to force a citizen to leave the country to attend judicial proceedings in another country. One solution to the problem was to obtain the testimony by way of a request for assistance to the State of residence of the witness; the

requested State would use the means of compulsion allowed under its internal law and provide the international criminal court with a transcript of the examination and cross-examination. It was suggested that the relevant rules should be drafted flexibly to allow a judge or prosecutor of the international criminal court to be present and to play an active role. One delegation took the view that, in highly exceptional cases, some measures of indirect compulsion in the form of a fine or imprisonment could be taken by the requested State to[*44] compel attendance of a witness. Other solutions that were mentioned included testimony by way of a live video link hooked up with the court or, subject to the agreement of the State concerned, the hearing of evidence, by the court, on the territory of the said State.

234. Attention was drawn to the need to address, preferably, in the view of one delegation, in the rules of evidence to be drawn up by the chambers, the question of the privileges of witnesses to refuse to testify (solicitor-client privilege, marital privilege, etc.). Other issues that were mentioned in this context related to safe conduct and to costs and expenses, including advance payments.

235. The issues connected with cooperation relating to indictment, judicial assistance during the post-indictment phase, provisional measures, specialty and communications and documents, as itemized in the guidelines reproduced in annex II to the present report, were viewed by the delegations that commented on them as important and worthy of further consideration.

236. The remark was made that, in discussing the question of judicial assistance, due account should be taken of the fact that the investigation process and the gathering of evidence might well start before an alleged criminal was identified and that provision should be made for cooperation between the States parties to the statute and the international criminal court prior to the stage in question. It was furthermore pointed out that the discussion had so far proceeded on the assumption that national judicial systems were able to cooperate. The question arose as to how the international criminal court would discharge its duties if it could not rely on functioning national judicial systems.

   4.   Recognition of the judgements of the court, enforcement of sentences and mutual recognition of judgements

237. As regards articles 58 and 59 of the draft statute, there were different views as to whether the statute should provide for the direct recognition and enforcement of the orders, decisions and judgements of the court under the continued enforcement approach or envisage some type of further action by the national authorities under the conversion approach. A suggestion was made that the statute should accommodate both approaches rather than choose one. A view was expressed that the extent to which States generally should be bound by decisions of the court was related to the questions of jurisdiction, consent and complementarity.

238. Attention was drawn to the question of the rights of third parties, particularly in those cases involving confiscation of property, forfeiture of profits and restitution issues. The question was raised whether third parties should have their rights determined by the international criminal court or be able to turn to domestic courts if their concerns were not addressed by the court.

239. With reference to article 59 of the draft statute, support was expressed for reliance, for the enforcement of sentences, on the States that had expressed willingness to accept prisoners for incarceration either in general terms or on an ad hoc basis. There was however also a view that article 59 should be amended to provide for an obligation of all States parties to enforce sentences of the court, except the State of the nationality of the accused and the State where the crime was committed.

[*45]240. The question whether the consent of the accused regarding the place of incarceration should be required elicited a negative reply, although it was suggested that the views of the accused could be taken into account.

241. Regarding which law should govern the enforcement of sentences, the view was expressed that the terms and conditions of imprisonment should be in accordance with international standards. It was also said that, while custodial and administrative authority over the convicted person should be delegated to the State that accepted responsibility for enforcing the sentence, the international criminal court should play some role in the supervision of the prisoner, perhaps through an appropriate international organization. The issue was also raised whether provision should be made for some form of communication channel between the court and the prisoner.

242. The question of fines and other financial sanctions was viewed by several delegations as requiring further consideration. The view was expressed that in light of article 47 of the draft statute, which provided for the imposition of fines, it was necessary to include a provision addressing the enforcement of this kind of penalty. However, it was also suggested that the difficulty of establishing such an enforcement mechanism should be considered in determining the appropriateness of including the provision concerning fines.

243. As regards article 60, the remark was made that, while the court should have control over the pardon, parole, commutation of sentence or release of the convicted person, care should be taken to ensure a relatively uniform administration at the national level. It was suggested that national authorities be allowed to make recommendations to the court based, for example, on the behaviour of the prisoner, or that national authorities and the court make a joint decision.

F.   Budget and administration

244. As regards budgetary aspects, three main trends emerged: according to one trend, the costs of the court should be financed from the regular budget of the United Nations; according to another trend, they should be borne by States parties to the statute; and under a third trend, it was premature to discuss budgetary matters in detail until the nature of the court and the degree of its general acceptability had been clarified.

245. The proponents of the first approach emphasized the need to ensure the universal character of the court by making it part of the United Nations system. They felt it was necessary, given the nature of the crimes over which the court would exercise jurisdiction, to make it possible for all States to initiate proceedings without financial burdens - an objective which could not be achieved if only the States parties to the statute were to contribute to the financing of the institution. It was also observed that on a practical level it had been difficult to finance other institutions in this area by any voluntary or opting-in method alone.

246. Those favouring the second approach pointed out that a wide interest in the court on the part of States would translate itself into wide participation in its statute and, therefore, in a large number of contributing parties. Mention was made of the possibility of resorting to a formula similar to that applicable in the framework of the Permanent Court of Arbitration.

[*46]247. It was suggested that consideration should be given to making a State which initiated a procedure before the court share in the costs involved, with due regard to the special position of developing countries. A view was also expressed that costs of judicial assistance at the request of the court could be considered costs of the court itself. In response to the argument that a State might be precluded from seeking justice for lack of means, the opinion was expressed that very few States were so lacking in resources that they could not make some contribution, bearing in mind, in particular, that in the absence of an international criminal court, they themselves would have to bear the relevant costs. The remark was also made that the United Nations should bear financial responsibility in relation to cases referred by the Security Council.

248. In order to reduce costs, however funded, it was suggested that, whenever possible, the court should move to the location where a particular crime had been committed. It was also suggested that a State which had lodged a frivolous complaint should be made to pay some of the costs. Mention was further made of the possibility of establishing an auditing mechanism to monitor the expenditures of the court, as well as a supervisory mechanism to oversee the administration of the court.

249. It was pointed out that the court would need to have a legal personality. It was also suggested that the statute should include provisions regarding the privileges and immunities of the court and its officials.

[*47] III. CONSIDERATION, IN THE LIGHT OF THE AD HOC COMMITTEE'S REVIEW OF THE MAJOR SUBSTANTIVE AND ADMINISTRATIVE ISSUES ARISING OUT OF THE DRAFT STATUTE PREPARED BY THE INTERNATIONAL LAW COMMISSION, OF ARRANGEMENTS FOR THE CONVENING OF AN INTERNATIONAL CONFERENCE OF PLENIPOTENTIARIES

250. In the second phase of its work, the Ad Hoc Committee considered the above issue on the basis of proposals prepared by the Chairman (see paras. 255-259 below).

251. All the delegations that spoke placed emphasis on the quality of the work accomplished by the Ad Hoc Committee, which reflected a general awareness of the importance of the exercise and augured well for the future, as well as on the need to enlist the participation of all countries in what was termed an important and historic venture.

252. A large number of delegations observed that the Committee had fulfilled the mandate entrusted to it by the General Assembly and that the time had now come to enter into a new phase of negotiations to prepare the text of a convention to be adopted by a conference of plenipotentiaries. They therefore welcomed the proposal that the mandate for future work be changed to that effect. Appreciation was at the same time expressed to the International Law Commission for its valuable draft. While the delegations in question were prepared to accept the text proposed by the Chairman as a compromise text, they nevertheless regretted that that text did not provide for a precise timetable for the completion of what they considered as an urgent task. Most of them felt that it was not unrealistic, provided the necessary ingredients (political will, resources and broadly based expertise) were available, to envisage concrete scenarios involving the consideration of specific issues by working groups meeting simultaneously over a given period of time in the course of 1996, which would make it possible to complete the preparatory work in time for a conference to be convened in 1997. Some delegations expressed the view that such a conference could be envisaged in 1996. While regret was expressed that the proposals of the Chairman did not touch on the timing aspect, it was noted that all options, among which several delegations singled out the convening of a preparatory committee in 1996, remained open and that it would be for the Sixth Committee and the General Assembly to determine the future course of action.

253. Some delegations agreed that the Ad Hoc Committee had achieved useful results and welcomed the constructive approach taken thus far; they stressed that much more work was needed. They pointed out that the ultimate goal was not an international conference but the establishment of an effective international criminal court endowed with moral authority and independence and enjoying universal support and participation. Emphasis was placed in this connection on the complexity of the current exercise, which had to solve many difficult and novel problems and to take account of the diversity of constitutional and legal systems if it was to result in a truly international court. The delegations in question stressed that a fruitful continuation of the work required in-depth exploration of a number of issues as well as the active involvement of the widest possible number of countries. Some delegations expressed concern that these tasks could not be accomplished over a period of one year. While some among them took the view that some issues were ripe for drafting, others were not and felt that it was inadvisable, at the current stage, to change the character of the work as conducted so far. Some were of the view that there was still a long way to go before negotiations could meaningfully be initiated. The[*48] delegations in question warned that if the goal was to establish an international criminal court rather than sending political signals of progress, it was unwise to set unrealistic timetables and refer to the convening of a conference, thereby pre-empting the authority of the General Assembly and prematurely interfering with the normal course of things. The view was expressed by a delegation that the third sentence of the third paragraph of the Chairman's proposal could read: "In the light of the progress made, the Committee is of the opinion that issues can be addressed most effectively by further discussions with a view to the drafting of the text of a convention by a conference of plenipotentiaries to be convened."

254. Appreciation was expressed by a number of delegations for the renewed generous offer of the Italian Government to host a conference on the establishment of an international criminal court.

[*49] IV. CONCLUSIONS OF THE AD HOC COMMITTEE

255. By its resolution 49/53 of 9 December 1994, the General Assembly established the Ad Hoc Committee on the Establishment of an International Criminal Court and directed it "to review the major substantive and administrative issues arising out of the draft statute prepared by the International Law Commission and, in the light of that review, to consider arrangements for the convening of an international conference of plenipotentiaries", and decided "to include in the provisional agenda of its fiftieth session an item entitled 'Establishment of an international criminal court', in order to study the report of the Ad Hoc Committee and the written comments submitted by States and to decide on the convening of an

international conference of plenipotentiaries to conclude a convention on the establishment of an international criminal court, including on the timing and duration of the conference."

256. The Ad Hoc Committee for the Establishment of an International Criminal Court wishes to emphasize the usefulness of its discussions, during which it conducted a review of the major substantive and administrative issues arising out of the draft statute for the establishment of an international criminal court. The Committee has made considerable progress during both its sessions on key issues such as complementarity, jurisdiction and judicial cooperation between States and the international criminal court.

257. Further work on the establishment of an international criminal court has to be done. Work should be based on the draft statute of the International Law Commission and should take into account the reports of the Ad Hoc Committee and the comments submitted by States and, as appropriate, contributions of relevant organizations. In the light of the progress made, the Committee is of the opinion that issues can be addressed most effectively by combining further discussions with the drafting of texts, with a view to preparing a consolidated text of a convention for an international criminal court as a next step towards consideration by a conference of plenipotentiaries. The Committee proposes therefore that the mandate for future work be changed to that effect.

258. Aware of the interest of the international community in the establishment of an international criminal court which would be widely accepted, the Committee recommends that the General Assembly take up the organization of future work with a view to its early completion. 11/

259. In order to promote universality, which is an important element for a successful international criminal court, the Committee encourages participation by the largest number of States in future work.

Notes

1/   For the membership of the Ad Hoc Committee at its first session, see A/AC.244/INF/1 and Add.1 and A/AC.244/INF/2 and Add.1.

2/   Official Records of the General Assembly, Forty-ninth Session, Supplement No. 10 (A/49/10), chap. II.B.I; and A/49/355, chap. II.

3/   Comments were received from: Azerbaijan, Barbados, Belarus, China, Cyprus, Czech Republic, France, Libyan Arab Jamahiriya, Singapore, Sudan, Sweden, Switzerland, Trinidad and Tobago, United States of America and[*50] Venezuela, as well as from the Crime Prevention and Criminal Justice Branch and the United Nations International Drug Control Programme and from the International Tribunal for the Prosecution of Persons Responsible for Serious Violations of International Humanitarian Law Committed in the Territory of the Former Yugoslavia since 1991.

4/   It was pointed out that complementarity might be regarded not as a principle but rather as an objective to be achieved.

5/   United Nations, Treaty Series, vol. 78, No. 1021, p. 277.

6/   Reservations to the Convention on Genocide, Advisory Opinion, I.C.J. Reports 1951, p. 23.

7/   Application of the Convention on the Prevention and Punishment of the Crime of Genocide (Bosnia and Herzegovina v. Yugoslavia (Serbia and Montenegro); see Official Records of the General Assembly, Fiftieth Session, Supplement No. 4 (A/50/4), paras. 98-119.

8/   One representative felt that paragraph 1 (b) (i) of article 21 did not fit well with paragraph 1 of article 53 and that in any event the requirement established in the said subparagraph (b) (i) should be removed. To make his thinking more readily understandable, he stated that his concerns would be met if the text of subparagraph (b) was replaced with the following:

"(b)   in any other case where:

       (i)   a complaint is brought under article 25 (a);

       (ii)   the jurisdiction of the Court is accepted under article 22 by the State on the territory of which the act or omission in question occurred; and

       (iii) the suspect has been surrendered to the Court, voluntarily or not, by a State to which the Registrar of the Court has submitted a warrant for arrest in accordance with article 53 (1)."

9/   See paras. 63-71 above for the different views expressed on the question of whether the crime of aggression should be included in the jurisdiction of the court.

10/ It was noted in this connection that the draft contained no provision on the competence of the accused to stand trial.

11/ Some delegations saw merit in setting a date for the completion of the work. 1996 was mentioned. Others considered that it was not yet possible to fix a realistic date at this stage.

[*51] ANNEX I
Guidelines for the consideration of the question of the relationship between States parties, non-States parties and the International Criminal Court

I. GENERAL ISSUES RELATING TO STATES' COOPERATION WITH THE INTERNATIONAL CRIMINAL COURT

1. The question of cooperation is intrinsically linked with the overall problem of the applicability of national law to the national part of the cooperation: in this context the question arises as to whether the State, when acting within the framework of cooperation, acts within the ambit of the court's authority as its organ or whether the cooperation is performed by the State on its own authority and subject to national law.

2. Choice of mutually non-exclusive approaches for dealing with assistance (both surrender and judicial assistance) in the Statute:

(a) A general facilitating provision, relying on existing judicial assistance and extradition regimes; for example, for judicial assistance, a general provision supplemented by a non-exclusive list of the type of assistance that could be sought;

(b) A detailed regime in, or annexed to, the statute; for example, for surrender of accused persons, a new mechanism of "transfer" as proposed by the ILC.

3. Extent of obligations of States Parties to assist:

(a) Absolute, or subject to exceptions; if exceptions, what should be the exceptions and what are the justifications for those exceptions?

(b) Factors which may influence the extent of obligations: State's consent to jurisdiction of the international criminal court for the type of crime, or for the specific crime at issue;

(c) Principle of complementarity;

(d) Traditional considerations of essential interests (ordre public);

(e) Compliance with other conventions.

4. Role of national laws/courts in guaranteeing fundamental rights: can or should national authorities defer to the international criminal court on these matters?

II. CLUSTERS OF ISSUES RELATING TO SPECIFIC ASPECTS OF COOPERATION
First cluster: apprehension and surrender

1. Triggering act by the international criminal court: arrest warrant issued by the court.

[*52] Confusion created by concept of "provisional arrest" in article 28 (as compared to article 52). The difference between pre-indictment arrest and post-indictment arrest. Are a court arrest warrant and some form of accusation prerequisites to the apprehension of the accused by a State?

2. Request by the international criminal court for arrest of accused - form and content of the request and its communication to national authorities:

(a) For provisional arrest (art. 52); for formal request for arrest and surrender (art. 57);

(b) Extent to which detailed guidance is needed in the statute (or in an annex thereto).

3. Arrest of accused by national authorities for purposes of surrender to the international criminal court (based either on a request for provisional arrest (art. 52) or a formal request for arrest and surrender (art. 57)).

Roles of national authorities and of the international criminal court at the phase of initial arrest:

(a) Executing warrant of the court versus executing request to arrest, pursuant to national authority and laws?

(b) Applicability of national judicial proceedings [constitutional requirements/fundamental rights];

(c)   Protection of the rights of the accused in connection with arrest - application of the standards of the court versus national standards;

(d)   Arrest of persons other than the accused.

4.   Pre-surrender detention:

(a)   Determined by the court (application of art. 29 to be considered) or determined by national authorities?

(b)   Governed by national law, relevant international standards, or standard provided in the statute of the international criminal court?

5.   The surrender decision:

(a)   Role, if any of national courts or other authorities;

(b)   Applicability of national judicial proceedings; in the affirmative, what legal issues may be addressed (e.g., identity of accused, whether valid court accusation and arrest warrant; crime charged is a crime within the jurisdiction of the court, legal rights of the accused concerning the request for surrender):

- Different national requirements regarding sufficiency of evidence;

- Relevance of dual criminality and statutes of limitation.

[*53] (c) Application of national law, particularly issues/rights of fundamental or constitutional dimension.

6.   Absolute obligation to surrender versus general obligation subject to exceptions. If exceptions, to what extent are traditional limitations on extradition appropriate in the context of the international criminal court? Some examples of traditional limitations or exceptions include:

- <u>Non bis in idem</u>;

- Political offence;

- Nationality of the accused;

Some examples of traditional delays include:

- Pendency of national proceedings relating to same crime;

- Deferral of surrender versus temporary surrender where accused subject to proceedings for other offence.

7.   Transfer of accused to the court or to a "detaining" State acting as custodian for court pre-trial detainees:

(a)   Does transfer of the accused (or the decision to surrender) occasion a shift in primary responsibility for the accused from the national authorities to the international criminal court?

(b)   Which authorities are responsible for transfer?

8.   Problems of transit through third States in the course of transfer of accused to the international criminal court or to a "detaining" State:

- Scope of the duties of the transit State.

9.   Pre-trial detention of the accused:

(a)   (The text of the draft statute does not clearly distinguish between (a) detention by national authorities pending national decision to surrender and (b) detention (pre- or post-trial) by national authorities agreeing to act as custodial agent for the court -referred to here as a "detaining" State);

(b)   Determined by the court (art. 29) or by "detaining" State authorities?

(c)   Whether the statute of the court, other relevant international standards or national law should control;

(d)   Accused's challenges to the lawfulness of detention:

- Decided by the court (art. 29(3)) or by national authorities?

- Does recourse to the court under article 29(3) exclude accused's fundamental rights under national law to challenge in national courts the lawfulness of detention? If not, what is <u>locus standi</u> of the international criminal court in proceedings before a national court?

[*54]10. Other surrender issues:

(a)   Obligations to the international criminal court versus obligations/rights under existing extradition treaties, other bilateral or multilateral arrangements, or status-of-forces agreements:

- Should the international criminal court's request be given priority (art. 53(4))?
- Should the answer to this question depend on whether a State party to the statute has consented to the jurisdiction of the court over the crime at issue?

    (b)   Rule of speciality (art. 55).

Second cluster: judicial assistance

1.   Judicial assistance during investigation phase (prior to the indictment)

- Different kinds of judicial assistance (should an enumerative list be included; should a distinction be drawn between compulsory and non-compulsory measures?);
- Should the prosecutor be entitled to carry out activities on the territory of a State other than the host State
- On its own (such as to collect documentary and other evidence, to conduct on-site investigations);
- On its own but subject to the consent to the State concerned; or should the State concerned carry out those activities (in conformity with traditional practice in matters of international judicial assistance)?
- Possibility of different approaches under different circumstances;
- Examination of lawfulness of on-site activities undertaken by the prosecutor or carried out on behalf of the prosecutor by a State; sanction and compensation for unlawful acts;
- Need to clarify the relation between articles 26 and 51;
- Requirement and conditions of consent of the State concerned;
- Extent of the legal obligation to comply with a request by the international criminal court to carry out such activities:
- Exceptions and limitations to such obligation;
- Which States are obliged? Is the criterion consent to the jurisdiction of the court over the crime, participation in the statute or any other factor?
- Applicability of constitutional requirements or of standards of fundamental human rights to the activities of the prosecutor;

[*55] - Applicability of national law and procedures;

- Possibility of ad hoc arrangements of the prosecutor with a State concerning modalities for transfer of information.

2.   Cooperation relating to indictment (arts. 30 and 38)

- Notification of the indictment to the suspect through national authorities;
- Forms of assistance of States to the court to bring the indictment to the attention of the accused.

3.   Judicial assistance during post-indictment phase and during trial (art. 38) (many of the issues described under point 1 arise in this context as well)

- Legal effect of a request by the court under paragraph 5 (b) and (c); legal obligation incumbent on (which) State?
- Legal consequences of a refusal to comply with such a request for the refusing State (impact on process?);
- Request for cooperation made on behalf of the accused;
- Capacity to compel attendance of witnesses (are there other alternatives?).

4.   Provisional measures (art. 52)

- Form and content of a request for provisional measures;
- Legal consequences of the provisional seizure of documents and other evidence (compensation for costs incurred);
- Which procedures are applicable to a State's measures to prevent injury to or intimidation of a witness or the destruction of evidence?
- Legal implications of the absence of a subsequent formal request.

5.   Speciality (art. 55)

- Power of the international criminal court to deviate from the rule of speciality in respect of evidentiary documents and materials
- condition of the consent of State?
- Power of the court to request waiver of the condition of speciality - duty to comply?

6.   Communications and documents (art. 57)
- Form and content of communications and documents required in the context of cooperation;
- Modern methods of communication and conditions of their use.

[*56] 7.   Obligations
- Obligations to the court versus obligations/rights under existing extradition treaties and arrangements on judicial assistance.

Third cluster: recognition of judgements of the international criminal court
- Different types of judgements of the court and their impact on their recognition and implementation;
- Character of a judgement of the court - qualified as a national judgement?
- Is it subject to examination through national procedures? If so, to what extent?
- Applicability of national law on recognition procedures (continued enforcement or conversion);
- Protection of the rights of third parties.

Fourth cluster: enforcement of sentences
- Requirement of consent of State (case-by-case or general acceptance?) (see subtopics (a) and (b) below);
- Necessary documentation (see subtopics (a) and (b) below):
(a)   Enforcement of sentences involving imprisonment:
- Imprisonment according to national law or international standards;
- Applicability of national procedure (to, for example, temporary absences);
- Status of the international criminal court in the supervision of the imprisonment;
- State's duties concerning communications between the prisoner and the international criminal court;
- National court versus international criminal court responsibility for decisions on pardon, parole and commutation of sentences;
(b)   Enforcement of sentences involving penalties other than imprisonment:
- Procedure for the enforcement of judgements (national versus internationally regulated);
- Protection of the rights of third parties;
- Asset sharing.

[*57] Fifth cluster: mutual recognition of judgements
- Non bis in idem:
- As a bar to judicial assistance;
- As a bar to trial proceedings;
- Recognition by the international criminal court of other national judgements.

[*58] ANNEX II
Guidelines for consideration of the question of general principles of criminal law
The following items could be discussed under this topic
A.   Process issues
1.   Method of elaboration:
- By States in the statute (or in an annex thereto);
- By the international criminal court on a case-by-case basis;
- By the international criminal court as part of the rules (to be confirmed by State parties?);
- Combination (e.g., major issues determined in the statute or in an annex thereto and others left for the court to determine).
2.   Relevance of internal law:
- Application of the law of a particular State;
- Which State?
- Reference to national law as interpretative aid;
- Particular State (which State?);
- Common principles represented within the world's legal systems.
B.   Substantive issues
1.   General principles:

- Non-retroactivity;
- Punishment by customary international criminal law;
- Individual responsibility;
- Irrelevance of official position;
- Criminal liability of corporations?
- Appropriateness of statutes of limitations.
2.   Actus reus:
- Act or omission;
- Causation and accountability.
[*59]3.   Mens rea:
- Intention (culpa, dolus/intentionally, knowingly, recklessly/dolus eventualis, gross negligence);
- General intention - specific intention? (motives);
- Age of responsibility.
4.   Other types of responsibility:
- Solicitation/incitement;
- Attempts;
- Conspiracy/complot;
- Aiding and abetting;
- Accessory;
- Complicity;
- Command responsibility/responsibility of superiors for acts of subordinate.
5.   Defences:
      (a)   Negation of liability:
      - Error of law?
      - Error of fact?
      - Diminished mental capacity:
            To stand trial
            Regarding liability;
      (b)   Excuses and justification:
      - Self-defence;
      - Defence of others;
      - Defence of property?
      - Necessity;
      - Lesser of evils;
      - Duress/coercion/force majeure;
      - Superior orders;
      - Law enforcement/other authority to maintain order;
[*60]   (c)   (Defences under public international law/depending on jurisdiction):
      - Military necessity
      - Reprisals
      - Article 51 of the Charter of the United Nations (cf. justifications in the International Law
Commission draft on State responsibility)
6.   Aggravating and mitigating circumstances:
- Effect on liability and/or penalty?
7.   Penalties:
      (a)   Discharge of penalties;
      (b)   Types of penalties (imprisonment, fines, restitution/forfeiture/confiscation);
      (c)   Maximum and minimum amount of punishment.

REPORT OF THE INTERNATIONAL LAW COMMISSION
ON THE WORK OF ITS FORTY-SIXTH SESSION

DRAFT STATUTE FOR AN INTERNATIONAL CRIMINAL COURT

[Editorial Note - The U.N. page numbers of this document are indicated in bolded brackets [*] in the text].

[*43] DRAFT STATUTE OF THE INTERNATIONAL CRIMINAL COURT

The States parties to this Statute,
Desiring to further international cooperation to enhance the effective suppression and prosecution of crimes of international concern, and for that purpose to establish an international criminal court;
[*44] Emphasizing that such a court is intended to exercise jurisdiction only over the most serious crimes of concern to the international community as a whole;
Emphasizing further that such a court is intended to be complementary to national criminal justice systems in cases where such trial procedures may not be available or may be ineffective;
Have agreed as follows:

PART 1. ESTABLISHMENT OF THE COURT
Article 1
The Court
There is established an International Criminal Court ("the Court"), whose jurisdiction and functioning shall be governed by the provisions of this Statute.

[*45] Article 2
Relationship of the Court to the United Nations
The President, with the approval of the States parties to this Statute ("States parties"), may conclude an agreement establishing an appropriate relationship between the Court and the United Nations.

[*48] Article 3
Seat of the Court
1.   The seat of the Court shall be established at ... in ... ("the host State").
2.   The President, with the approval of the States parties, may conclude an agreement with the host State establishing the relationship between that State and the Court.
3.   The Court may exercise its powers and functions on the territory of any State party and, by special agreement, on the territory of any other State.

Article 4
Status and legal capacity
1.   The Court is a permanent institution open to States parties in accordance with this Statute. It shall act when required to consider a case submitted to it.
2.   The Court shall enjoy in the territory of each State party such legal capacity as may be necessary for the exercise of its functions and the fulfillment of its purposes.

[*49] PART 2. COMPOSITION AND ADMINISTRATION OF THE COURT
Article 5
Organs of the Court
The Court consists of the following organs:
(a)   a Presidency, as provided in article 8;
(b)   an Appeals Chamber, Trial Chambers and other chambers, as provided in article 9;
(c)   a Procuracy, as provided in article 12; and
(d)   a Registry, as provided in article 13.

[*50] Article 6
Qualification and election of judges

1.   The judges of the Court shall be persons of high moral character, impartiality and integrity who possess the qualifications required in their respective countries for appointment to the highest judicial offices, and have, in addition:
   (a)   criminal trial experience;
   (b)   recognized competence in international law.
2.   Each State party may nominate for election not more than two persons, of different nationality, who possess the qualification referred to in paragraph 1 (a) or that referred to in paragraph 1 (b), and who are willing to serve as may be required on the Court.
3.   Eighteen judges shall be elected, by an absolute majority vote of the States parties by secret ballot. Ten judges shall first be elected, from among the persons nominated as having the qualification referred to in paragraph 1 (a). Eight judges shall then be elected, from among the persons nominated as having the qualification referred to in paragraph 1 (b).
4.   No two judges may be nationals of the same State.
5.   States parties should bear in mind in the election of the judges that the representation of the principal legal systems of the world should be assured.
6.   Judges hold office for a term of nine years and, subject to paragraph 7 and article 7 (2), are not eligible for reelection. A judge shall, however, continue in office in order to complete any case the hearing of which has commenced.
7.   At the first election, six judges chosen by lot shall serve for a term of three years and are eligible for reelection; six judges chosen by lot shall serve for a term of six years; and the remainder shall serve for a term of nine years.
8.   Judges nominated as having the qualification referred to in paragraph 1 (a) or 1 (b), as the case may be, shall be replaced by persons nominated as having the same qualification.

[*52] Article 7
Judicial vacancies

1.   In the event of a vacancy, a replacement judge shall be elected in accordance with article 6.
2.   A judge elected to fill a vacancy shall serve for the remainder of the predecessor's term, and if that period is less than five years is eligible for reelection for a further term.

Article 8
The Presidency

1.   The President, the first and second Vice-presidents and two alternate Vice-presidents shall be elected by an absolute majority of the judges. They shall serve for a term of three years or until the end of their term of office as judges, whichever is earlier.
2.   The first or second Vice-president, as the case may be, may act in place of the President in the event that the President is unavailable or disqualified. An alternate Vice-president may act in place of either Vice-president as required.
[*53]3.   The President and the Vice-presidents shall constitute the Presidency which shall be responsible for:
   (a)   the due administration of the Court; and
   (b)   the other functions conferred on it by this Statute.
4.   Unless otherwise indicated, pre-trial and other procedural functions conferred under this Statute on the Court may be exercised by the Presidency in any case where a chamber of the Court is not seized of the matter.
5.   The Presidency may, in accordance with the Rules, delegate to one or more judges the exercise of a power vested in it under articles 26 (3), 27 (5), 28, 29 or 30 (3) in relation to a case, during the period before a Trial Chamber is established for that case.

[*55] Article 9
Chambers

1. As soon as possible after each election of judges to the Court, the Presidency shall in accordance with the Rules constitute an Appeals Chamber consisting of the President and six other judges, of whom at least three shall be judges elected from among the persons nominated as having the qualification referred to in article 6 (1) (b). The President shall preside over the Appeals Chamber.

2. The Appeals Chamber shall be constituted for a term of three years. Members of the Appeals Chamber shall, however, continue to sit on the Chamber in order to complete any case the hearing of which has commenced.

3. Judges may be renewed as members of the Appeals Chamber for a second or subsequent term.

4. Judges not members of the Appeals Chamber shall be available to serve on Trial Chambers and other chambers required by this Statute, and to act as substitute members of the Appeals Chamber, in the event that a member of that Chamber is unavailable or disqualified.

5. The Presidency shall nominate in accordance with the Rules five such judges to be members of the Trial Chamber for a given case. A Trial Chamber shall include at least three judges elected from among the persons nominated as having the qualification referred to in article 6 (1) (a).

6. The Rules may provide for alternate judges to be nominated to attend a trial and to act as members of the Trial Chamber in the event that a judge dies or becomes unavailable during the course of the trial.

7. No judge who is a national of a complainant State or of a State of which the accused is a national shall be a member of a chamber dealing with the case.

[*56] Article 10
Independence of the judges

1. In performing their functions, the judges shall be independent.

2. Judges shall not engage in any activity which is likely to interfere with their judicial functions or to affect confidence in their independence. In particular, they shall not while holding the office of judge be a member of the legislative or executive branches of the Government of a State, or of a body responsible for the investigation or prosecution of crimes.

3. Any question as to the application of paragraph 2 shall be decided by the Presidency.

[*57]4. On the recommendation of the Presidency, the States parties may by a two-thirds majority decide that the work-load of the Court requires that the judges should serve on a full-time basis. In that case:

    (a) existing judges who elect to serve on a full-time basis shall not hold any other office or employment; and

    (b) judges subsequently elected shall not hold any other office or employment.

[*58] Article 11
Excusing and disqualification of judges

1. The Presidency at the request of a judge may excuse that judge from the exercise of a function under this Statute.

2. Judges shall not participate in any case in which they have previously been involved in any capacity or in which their impartiality might reasonably be doubted on any ground, including an actual, apparent or potential conflict of interest.

3. The Prosecutor or the accused may request the disqualification of a judge under paragraph 2.

4. Any question as to the disqualification of a judge shall be decided by an absolute majority of the members of the Chamber concerned. The challenged judge shall not take part in the decision.

Article 12
The Procuracy

1. The Procuracy is an independent organ of the Court responsible for the investigation of complaints brought in accordance with this Statute and for the conduct of prosecutions. A member of the Procuracy shall not seek or act on instructions from any external source.

2.   The Procuracy shall be headed by the Prosecutor, assisted by one or more Deputy Prosecutors, who may act in place of the Prosecutor in [*59] the event that the Prosecutor is unavailable. The Prosecutor and the Deputy Prosecutors shall be of different nationalities. The Prosecutor may appoint such other qualified staff as may be required.

3.   The Prosecutor and Deputy Prosecutors shall be persons of high moral character and have high competence and experience in the prosecution of criminal cases. They shall be elected by secret ballot by an absolute majority of the States parties, from among candidates nominated by States parties. Unless a shorter term is otherwise decided on at the time of their election, they shall hold office for a term of five years and are eligible for reelection.

4.   The States parties may elect the Prosecutor and a Deputy Prosecutor on the basis that they will be available to serve as required.

5.   The Prosecutor and Deputy Prosecutors shall not act in relation to a complaint involving a person of their own nationality.

6.   The Presidency may excuse the Prosecutor or a Deputy Prosecutor at their request from acting in a particular case, and shall decide any question raised in a particular case as to the disqualification of the Prosecutor or a Deputy Prosecutor.

7.   The staff of the Procuracy shall be subject to Staff Regulations drawn up by the Prosecutor so far as possible in conformity with the United Nations Staff Regulations and Staff Rules and approved by the Presidency.

[*60] Article 13
The Registry

1.   On the proposal of the Presidency, the judges by an absolute majority by secret ballot shall elect a Registrar, who shall be the principal administrative officer of the Court. They may in the same manner elect a Deputy Registrar.

2.   The Registrar shall hold office for a term of five years, is eligible for reelection and shall be available on a full-time basis. The Deputy Registrar shall hold office for a term of five years or such shorter term as may be decided on, and may be elected on the basis that the Deputy Registrar will be available to serve as required.

3.   The Presidency may appoint or authorize the Registrar to appoint such other staff of the Registry as may be necessary.

4.   The staff of the Registry shall be subject to Staff Regulations drawn up by the Registrar so far as possible in conformity with the United Nations Staff Regulations and Staff Rules, and approved by the Presidency.

[*61] Article 14
Solemn undertaking

Before first exercising their functions under this Statute, judges and other officers of the Court shall make a public and solemn undertaking to do so impartially and conscientiously.

Article 15
Loss of office

1.   A judge, the Prosecutor or other officer of the Court who is found to have committed misconduct or a serious breach of this Statue, or to be unable to exercise the functions required by this Statute because of long-term illness or disability, shall cease to hold office.

2.   A decision as to the loss of office under paragraph 1 shall be made by secret ballot:

    (a)   in the case of the Prosecutor or a Deputy Prosecutor, by an absolute majority of the States parties;

    (b)   in any other case, by a two-thirds majority of the judges.

3.   The judge, the Prosecutor or other officer whose conduct or fitness for office is impugned shall have full opportunity to present evidence and to make submissions but shall not otherwise participate in the discussion of the question.

[*62] Article 16
Privileges and immunities

1.   The judges, the Prosecutor, the Deputy Prosecutors and the staff of the Procuracy, the Registrar and the Deputy Registrar shall enjoy the privileges, immunities and facilities of a diplomatic agent within the meaning of the Vienna Convention on Diplomatic Relations of 16 April 1961.

2.   The staff of the Registry shall enjoy the privileges, immunities and facilities necessary to the performance of their functions.

3.   Counsel, experts and witnesses before the Court shall enjoy the privileges and immunities necessary to the independent exercise of their duties.

4.   The judges may by an absolute majority decide to revoke a privilege or waive an immunity conferred by this article, other than an immunity of a judge, the Prosecutor or Registrar as such. In the case of other officers and staff of the Procuracy or Registry, they may do so only on the recommendation of the Prosecutor or Registrar, as the case may be.

[*63] Article 17
Allowances and expenses

1.   The President shall receive an annual allowance.

2.   The Vice-presidents shall receive a special allowance for each day they exercise the functions of the President.

3.   Subject to paragraph 4, the judges shall receive a daily allowance during the period in which they exercise their functions. They may continue to receive a salary payable in respect of another position occupied by them consistently with article 10.

4.   If it is decided under article 10 (4) that judges shall thereafter serve on a full-time basis, existing judges who elect to serve on a full-time basis, and all judges subsequently elected, shall be paid a salary.

[*64] Article 18
Working languages

The working languages of the Court shall be English and French.

Article 19
Rules of the Court

1. Subject to paragraphs 2 and 3, the judges may by an absolute majority make rules for the functioning of the Court in accordance with this Statute, including rules regulating:

    (a)   the conduct of investigations;

    (b)   the procedure to be followed and the rules of evidence to be applied;

    (c)   any other matter which is necessary for the implementation of this Statute.

2.   The initial Rules of the Court shall be drafted by the judges within six months of the first elections for the Court, and submitted to a conference of States parties for approval. The judges may decide that a rule subsequently made under paragraph 1 should also be submitted to a conference of States parties for approval.

3.   In any case to which paragraph 2 does not apply, rules made under paragraph 1 shall be transmitted to States parties and may be confirmed by the Presidency unless, within six months after transmission, a majority of States parties have communicated in writing their objections.

4.   A rule may provide for its provisional application in the period prior to its approval or confirmation. A rule not approved or confirmed shall lapse.

[*66] PART 3. JURISDICTION OF THE COURT
[*70] Article 20
Crimes within the jurisdiction of the Court

The Court has jurisdiction in accordance with this Statute with respect to the following crimes:

    (a)   the crime of genocide;

    (b)   the crime of aggression;

(c)   serious violations of the laws and customs applicable in armed conflict;

(d)   crimes against humanity;

(e)   crimes, established under or pursuant to the treaty provisions listed in the Annex, which, having regard to the conduct alleged, constitute exceptionally serious crimes of international concern.

[*79] Article 21
Preconditions to the exercise of jurisdiction

1.   The Court may exercise its jurisdiction over a person with respect to a crime referred to in article 20 if:

(a)   in a case of genocide, a complaint is brought under article 25(1);

(b)   in any other case, a complaint is brought under article 25 (2) and the jurisdiction of the Court with respect to the crime is accepted under article 22:

(i)   by the State which has custody of the suspect with respect to the crime ("the custodial State"); and

(ii)   by the State on the territory of which the act or omission in question occurred.

2.   If, with respect to a crime to which paragraph 1 (b) applies, the custodial State has received, under an international agreement, a request from another State to surrender a suspect for the purposes of [*80] prosecution, then, unless the request is rejected, the acceptance by the requesting State of the Court's jurisdiction with respect to the crime is also required.

[*82] Article 22
Acceptance of the jurisdiction of the Court for the purposes of article 21

1.   A State party to this Statute may:

(a)   at the time it expresses its consent to be bound by the Statute, by declaration lodged with the depository; or

(b)   at a later time, by declaration lodged with the Registrar;

accept the jurisdiction of the Court with respect to such of the crimes referred to in article 20 as it specifies in the declaration.

2.   A declaration may be of general application, or may be limited to particular conduct or to conduct committed during a particular period of time.

3.   A declaration may be made for a specified period, in which case it may not be withdrawn before the end of that period, or for an unspecified period, in which case it may be withdrawn only upon giving six months' notice of withdrawal to the Registrar. Withdrawal does not affect proceedings already commenced under this Statute.

4.   If under article 21 the acceptance of a State which is not a party to this Statute is required, that State may, by declaration lodged with the Registrar, consent to the Court exercising jurisdiction with respect to the crime.

[*84] Article 23
Action by the Security Council

1.   Notwithstanding article 21, the Court has jurisdiction in accordance with this Statute with respect to crimes referred to in article 20 as a consequence of the referral of a matter to the Court by the Security Council acting under Chapter VII of the Charter of the United Nations.

2.   A complaint of or directly related to an act of aggression may not be brought under this Statute unless the Security Council has first determined that a State has committed the act of aggression which is the subject of the complaint.

[*85] 3.   No prosecution may be commenced under this Statute arising from a situation which is being dealt with by the Security Council as a threat to or breach of the peace or an act of aggression under Chapter VII of the Charter, unless the Security Council otherwise decides.

[*88] Article 24
Duty of the Court as to jurisdiction
The Court shall satisfy itself that it has jurisdiction in any case brought before it.

[*89] PART 4. INVESTIGATION AND PROSECUTION
Article 25
Complaint
1. A State party which is also a Contracting Party to the Convention on the Prevention and Punishment of the Crime of Genocide of 9 December 1948 may lodge a complaint with the Prosecutor alleging that a crime of genocide appears to have been committed.
2. A State party which accepts the jurisdiction of the Court under article 22 with respect to a crime may lodge a complaint with the Prosecutor alleging that such a crime appears to have been committed.
3. As far as possible a complaint shall specify the circumstances of the alleged crime and the identity and whereabouts of any suspect, and be accompanied by such supporting documentation as is available to the complainant State.
4. In a case to which article 23 (1) applies, a complaint is not required for the initiation of an investigation.

[*90] Article 26
Investigation of alleged crimes
1. On receiving a complaint or upon notification of a decision of the Security Council referred to in article 23 (1), the Prosecutor shall initiate an investigation unless the Prosecutor concludes that there is no possible basis for a prosecution under this Statute and decides not to initiate an investigation, in which case the Prosecutor shall so inform the Presidency.
[*91] 2. The Prosecutor may:
    (a) request the presence of and question suspects, victims and witnesses;
    (b) collect documentary and other evidence;
    (c) conduct on site investigations;
    (d) take necessary measures to ensure the confidentiality of information or the protection of any person;
    (e) as appropriate, seek the cooperation of any State or of the United Nations.
3. The Presidency may, at the request of the Prosecutor, issue such subpoenas and warrants as may be required for the purposes of an investigation, including a warrant under article 28 (1) for the provisional arrest of a suspect.
4. If, upon investigation and having regard, inter alia, to the matters referred to in article 35, the Prosecutor concludes that there is no sufficient basis for a prosecution under this Statute and decides not to file an indictment, the Prosecutor shall so inform the Presidency giving details of the nature and basis of the complaint and of the reasons for not filing an indictment.
5. At the request of a complainant State or, in a case to which article 23 (1) applies, at the request of the Security Council, the Presidency shall review a decision of the Prosecutor not to initiate an investigation or not to file an indictment, and may request the Prosecutor to reconsider the decision.
6. A person suspected of a crime under this Statute shall:
    (a) prior to being questioned, be informed that the person is a suspect and of the rights:
        (i) to remain silent, without such silence being a consideration in the determination of guilt or innocence; and
        (ii) to have the assistance of counsel of the suspect's choice or, if the suspect lacks the means to retain counsel, to have legal assistance assigned by the Court;
    (b) not be compelled to testify or to confess guilt; and
    (c) if questioned in a language other than a language the suspect understands and speaks, be provided with competent interpretation services and with a translation of any document on which the suspect is to be questioned.

[*94] Article 27

Commencement of prosecution

1.   If upon investigation the Prosecutor concludes that there is a prima facie case, the Prosecutor shall file with the Registrar an indictment containing a concise statement of the allegations of fact and of the crime or crimes with which the suspect is charged.

2.   The Presidency shall examine the indictment and any supporting material and determine:

(a)   whether a prima facie case exists with respect to a crime within the jurisdiction of the Court; and

(b)   whether, having regard, inter alia, to the matters referred to in article 35, the case could on the information available be heard by the Court. If so, it shall confirm the indictment and establish a trial chamber in accordance with article 9.

3.   If, after any adjournment that may be necessary to allow additional material to be produced, the Presidency decides not to confirm the indictment, it shall so inform the complainant State or, in a case to which article 23 (1) applies, the Security Council.

4.   The Presidency may at the request of the Prosecutor amend the indictment, in which case it shall make any necessary orders to ensure that the accused is notified of the amendment and has adequate time to prepare a defence.

5.   The Presidency may make any further orders required for the conduct of the trial, including an order:

(a)   determining the language or languages to be used during the trial;

[*95] (b) requiring the disclosure to the defence, within a sufficient time before the trial to enable the preparation of the defence, of documentary or other evidence available to the Prosecutor, whether or not the Prosecutor intends to rely on that evidence;

(c)   providing for the exchange of information between the Prosecutor and the defence, so that both parties are sufficiently aware of the issues to be decided at the trial;

(d)   providing for the protection of the accused, victims and witnesses and of confidential information.

[*97] Article 28

Arrest

1.   At any time after an investigation has been initiated, the Presidency may at the request of the Prosecutor issue a warrant for the provisional arrest of a suspect if:

(a)   there is probable cause to believe that the suspect may have committed a crime within the jurisdiction of the Court; and

(b)   the suspect may not be available to stand trial unless provisionally arrested.

2.   A suspect who has been provisionally arrested is entitled to release from arrest if the indictment has not been confirmed within 90 days of the arrest, or such longer time as the Presidency may allow.

3.   As soon as practicable after the confirmation of the indictment, the Prosecutor shall seek from the Presidency a warrant for the arrest and transfer of the accused. The Presidency shall issue such a warrant unless it is satisfied that:

(a)   the accused will voluntarily appear for trial; or

(b)   there are special circumstances making it unnecessary for the time being to issue the warrant.

4.   A person arrested shall be informed at the time of arrest of the reasons for the arrest and shall be promptly informed of any charges.

[*98] Article 29

Pretrial detention or release

1.   A person arrested shall be brought promptly before a judicial officer of the State where the arrest occurred. The judicial officer shall determine, in accordance with the procedures applicable in that State, that the warrant has been duly served and that the rights of the accused have been respected.

2.   A person arrested may apply to the Presidency for release pending trial. The Presidency may release the person unconditionally or on bail if it is satisfied that the accused will appear at the trial.

3.   A person arrested may apply to the Presidency for a determination of the lawfulness under this Statute of the arrest or detention. If the Presidency decides that the arrest or detention was unlawful, it shall order the release of the accused, and may award compensation.

4.   A person arrested shall be held, pending trial or release on bail, in an appropriate place of detention in the arresting State, in the State in which the trial is to be held or if necessary, in the host State.

[*100] Article 30
Notification of the indictment

1.   The Prosecutor shall ensure that a person who has been arrested is personally served, as soon as possible after being taken into custody, with certified copies of the following documents, in a language understood by that person:

(a)   in the case of a suspect provisionally arrested, a statement of the grounds for the arrest;

(b)   in any other case, the confirmed indictment;

(c)   a statement of the accused's rights under this Statute.

2.   In any case to which paragraph (1) (a) applies, the indictment shall be served on the accused as soon as possible after it has been confirmed.

3.   If, 60 days after the indictment has been confirmed, the accused is not in custody pursuant to a warrant issued under article 28 (3), or for some reason the requirements of paragraph 1 cannot be complied with, the Presidency may on the application of the Prosecutor prescribe some other manner of bringing the indictment to the attention of the accused.

[*101] Article 31
Designation of persons to assist in a prosecution

1.   A State party may, at the request of the Prosecutor, designate persons to assist in a prosecution.

2.   Such persons should be available for the duration of the prosecution, unless otherwise agreed. They shall serve at the direction of the Prosecutor, and shall not seek or receive instructions from any Government or source other than the Prosecutor in relation to their exercise of functions under this article.

3.   The terms and conditions on which persons may be designated under this article shall be approved by the Presidency on the recommendation of the Prosecutor.

[*102] PART 5. THE TRIAL
Article 32
Place of trial

1.   Unless otherwise decided by the Presidency, the place of the trial will be the seat of the Court.

[*103] Article 33
Applicable law

The Court shall apply:

(a)   this Statute;

(b)   applicable treaties and the principles and rules of general international law; and

(c)   to the extent applicable, any rule of national law.

[*104] Article 34
Challenges to jurisdiction

Challenges to the jurisdiction of the Court may be made, in accordance with the Rules:

(a)   prior to or at the commencement of the hearing, by an accused or any interested State; and

(b)   at any later stage of the trial, by an accused.

[*105] Article 35
Issues of admissibility

The Court may, on application by the accused or at the request of an interested State at any time prior to the commencement of the trial, or of its own motion, decide, having regard to the purposes of this

Statute set out in the preamble, that a case before it is inadmissible on the ground that the crime in question:

(a)   has been duly investigated by a State with jurisdiction over it, and the decision of that State not to proceed to a prosecution is apparently well-founded;

(b)   is under investigation by a State which has or may have jurisdiction over it, and there is no reason for the Court to take any further action for the time being with respect to the crime; or

(c)   is not of such gravity to justify further action by the Court.

[*106] Article 36
Procedure under articles 34 and 35

1.   In proceedings under articles 34 and 35, the accused and the complainant State have the right to be heard.

2.   Proceedings under articles 34 and 35 shall be decided by the Trial Chamber, unless it considers, having regard to the importance of the issues involved, that the matter should be referred to the Appeals Chamber.

[*107] Article 37
Trial in the presence of the accused

1.   As a general rule, the accused should be present during the trial.

2.   The Trial Chamber may order that the trial proceed in the absence of the accused if:

(a)   the accused is in custody, or has been released pending trial, and for reasons of security or the ill health of the accused it is undesirable for the accused to be present;

(b)   the accused is continuing to disrupt the trial; or

(c)   the accused has escaped from lawful custody under this Statute or has broken bail.

3.   The Chamber shall, if it makes an order under paragraph 2, ensure that the rights of the accused under this Statute are respected, and in particular:

(a)   that all reasonable steps have been taken to inform the accused of the charge; and

(b)   that the accused is legally represented, if necessary by a lawyer appointed by the Court.

4.   In cases where a trial cannot be held because of the deliberate absence of an accused, the Court may establish, in accordance with the Rules, an Indictment Chamber for the purpose of:

(a)   recording the evidence;

(b)   considering whether the evidence establishes a prima facie case of a crime within the jurisdiction of the Court; and

(c)   issuing and publishing a warrant of arrest in respect of an accused against whom a prima facie case is established.

5.   If the accused is subsequently tried under this Statute:

(a)   the record of evidence before the Indictment Chamber shall be admissible;

(b)   any judge who was a member of the Indictment Chamber may not be a member of the Trial Chamber.

[*110] Article 38
Functions and powers of the Trial Chamber

1.   At the commencement of the trial, the Trial Chamber shall:

(a)   have the indictment read;

(b)   ensure that articles 27 (5) (b) and 30 have been complied with sufficiently in advance of the trial to enable adequate preparation of the defence;

(c)   satisfy itself that the other rights of the accused under this Statute have been respected; and

(d)   allow the accused to enter a plea of guilty or not guilty.

2.   The Chamber shall ensure that a trial is fair and expeditious, and is conducted in accordance with this Statute and the Rules, with full respect for the rights of the accused and due regard for the protection of victims and witnesses.

3.   The Chamber may, subject to the Rules, hear charges against more than one accused arising out of the same factual situation.

4.   The trial shall be held in public, unless the Chamber determines that certain proceedings be in closed session in accordance with article 43, or for the purpose of protecting confidential or sensitive information which is to be given in evidence.

5.   The Chamber shall, subject to this Statute and the Rules have, inter alia, the power on the application of a party or of its own motion, to:

   (a)   issue a warrant for the arrest and transfer of an accused who is not already in the custody of the Court;

   (b)   require the attendance and testimony of witnesses;

   (c)   require the production of documentary and other evidentiary materials;

   (d)   rule on the admissibility or relevance of evidence;

   (e)   protect confidential information; and

   (f)   maintain order in the course of a hearing.

6.   The Chamber shall ensure that a complete record of the trial, which accurately reflects the proceedings, is maintained and preserved by the Registrar.

[*112] Article 39
Principle of legality (nullum crimen sine lege)

An accused shall not be held guilty:

   (a)   in the case of a prosecution with respect to a crime referred to in article 20 (a) to (d), unless the act or omission in question constituted a crime under international law;

   (b)   in the case of a prosecution with respect to a crime referred to in article 20 (e), unless the treaty in question was applicable to the conduct of the accused;

at the time the act or omission occurred.

[*114] Article 40
Presumption of innocence

An accused shall be presumed innocent until proved guilty in accordance with law. The onus is on the Prosecutor to establish the guilt of the accused beyond reasonable doubt.

Article 41
Rights of the accused

1.   In the determination of any charge under this Statute, the accused is entitled to a fair and public hearing, subject to article 43, and to the following minimum guarantees:

   (a)   to be informed promptly and in detail, in a language which the accused understands, of the nature and cause of the charge;

   (b)   to have adequate time and facilities for the preparation of the defence, and to communicate with counsel of the accused's choosing;

   (c)   to be tried without undue delay;

   (d)   subject to article 37 (2), to be present at the trial, to conduct the defence in person or through legal assistance of the [*115] accused's choosing, to be informed, if the accused does not have legal assistance, of this right and to have legal assistance assigned by the Court, without payment if the accused lacks sufficient means to pay for such assistance;

   (e)   to examine or have examined, the prosecution witnesses and to obtain the attendance and examination of witnesses for the defence under the same conditions as witnesses for the prosecution;

   (f)   if any of the proceedings of or documents presented to the Court are not in a language the accused understands and speaks, to have, free of any cost, the assistance of: a competent interpreter and such translations as are necessary to meet the requirements of fairness;

   (g)   not to be compelled to testify or to confess guilt.

2.   Exculpatory evidence that becomes available to the Procuracy prior to the conclusion of the trial shall be made available to the defence. In case of doubt as to the application of this paragraph or as to the admissibility of the evidence, the Trial Chamber shall decide.

[*117] Article 42
Non bis in idem

1.   No person shall be tried before any other court for acts constituting a crime of the kind referred to in article 20 for which that person has already been tried by the Court.

2.   A person who has been tried by another court for acts constituting a crime of the kind referred to in article 20 may be tried under this Statute only if:

    (a)   the acts in question were characterized by that court as an ordinary crime and not as a crime which is within the jurisdiction of the Court; or

    (b)   the proceedings in the other court were not impartial or independent or were designed to shield the accused from international criminal responsibility or the case was not diligently prosecuted.

3.   In considering the penalty to be imposed on a person convicted under this Statute, the Court shall take into account the extent to which a penalty imposed by another court on the same person for the same act has already been served.

[*119] Article 43
Protection of the accused, victims and witnesses

The Court shall take necessary measures available to it to protect the accused, victims and witnesses and may to that end conduct closed proceedings or allow the presentation of evidence by electronic or other special means.

[*120] Article 44
Evidence

1.   Before testifying, each witness shall, in accordance with the Rules, give an undertaking as to the truthfulness of the evidence to be given by that witness.

2.   States parties shall extend their laws of perjury to cover evidence given under this Statute by their nationals, and shall cooperate with the Court in investigating and where appropriate prosecuting any case of suspected perjury.

3.   The Court may require to be informed of the nature of any evidence before it is offered so that it may rule on its relevance or admissibility.

4.   The Court shall not require proof of facts of common knowledge but may take judicial notice of them.

5.   Evidence obtained by means of a serious violation of this Statute or of other rules of international law shall not be admissible.

[*121] Article 45
Quorum and judgment

1.   At least four members of the Trial Chamber must be present at each stage of the trial.

2.   The decisions of the Trial Chamber shall be taken by a majority of the judges. At least three judges must concur in a decision as to conviction or acquittal and as to the sentence to be imposed.

3.   If after sufficient time for deliberation a Chamber which has been reduced to four judges is unable to agree on a decision, it may order a new trial.

[*122] 4. The deliberations of the Court shall be and remain secret.

5.   The judgment shall be in writing and shall contain a full and reasoned statement of the findings and conclusions. It shall be the sole judgment issued, and shall be delivered in open court.

[*123] Article 46
Sentencing
1.   In the event of a conviction, the Trial Chamber shall hold a further hearing to hear any evidence relevant to sentence, to allow the Prosecutor and the defence to make submissions and to consider the appropriate sentence to be imposed.
2.   In imposing sentence, the Trial Chamber should take into account such factors as the gravity of the crime and the individual circumstances of the convicted person.

Article 47
Applicable Penalties
1.   The Court may impose on a person convicted of a crime under this Statute one or more of the following penalties:
(a)   a term of life imprisonment, or of imprisonment for a specified number of years;
(b)   a fine.
[*124] 2. In determining the length of a term of imprisonment or the amount of a fine to be imposed, the Court may have regard to the penalties provided for by the law of:
(a)   the State of which the convicted person is a national;
(b)   the State where the crime was committed; and
(c)   the State which had custody of and jurisdiction over the accused.
3.   Fines paid may be transferred, by order of the Court, to one or more of the following:
(a)   the Registrar, to defray the costs of the trial;
(b)   a State the nationals of which were the victims of the crime;
(c)   a trust fund established by the secretary-general of the United Nations for the benefit of victims of crime.

[*125] PART 6. APPEAL AND REVIEW
Article 48
Appeal against judgement or sentence
1.   The Prosecutor and the convicted person may, in accordance with the Rules, appeal against a decision under articles 45 or 47 on grounds of procedural unfairness, error of fact or of law, or disproportion between the crime and the sentence.
2.   Unless the Trial Chamber otherwise orders, a convicted person shall remain in custody pending an appeal.

[*126] Article 49
Proceedings on appeal
1.   The Appeals Chamber has all the powers of the Trial Chamber.
2.   If the Appeals Chamber finds that the proceedings appealed from were unfair or that the decision is vitiated by error of fact or law, it may:
(a)   if the appeal is brought by the convicted person, reverse or amend the decision, or, if necessary, order a new trial;
(b)   if the appeal is brought by the Prosecutor against an acquittal, order a new trial.
3.   If in an appeal against sentence the Chamber finds that the sentence is manifestly disproportionate to the crime, it may vary the sentence in accordance with article 47.
4.   The decision of the Chamber shall be taken by a majority of the judges, and shall be delivered in open court. Six judges constitute a quorum.
5.   Subject to article 50, the decision of the Chamber shall be final.

[*127] Article 50
Revision
1.   The convicted person or the Prosecutor may, in accordance with the Rules, apply to the Presidency for revision of a conviction on the ground that evidence has been discovered which was not available to

the applicant at the time the conviction was pronounced or affirmed and which could have been a decisive factor in the conviction.

2.   The Presidency shall request the Prosecutor or the convicted person, as the case may be, to present written observations on whether the application should be accepted.

[*128] 3. If the Presidency is of the view that the new evidence could lead to the revision of the conviction, it may:

(a)   reconvene the Trial Chamber;

(b)   constitute a new Trial Chamber; or

(c)   refer the matter to the Appeals Chamber; with a view to the Chamber determining, after hearing the parties, whether the new evidence should lead to a revision of the conviction.

[*129] PART 7. INTERNATIONAL COOPERATION AND JUDICIAL ASSISTANCE
Article 51
Cooperation and judicial assistance

1.   States parties shall cooperate with the Court in connection with criminal investigations and proceedings under this Statute.

2.   The Registrar may transmit to any State a request for cooperation and judicial assistance with respect to a crime, including, but not limited to:

(a)   the identification and location of persons;

(b)   the taking of testimony and the production of evidence;

(c)   the service of documents;

(d)   the arrest or detention of persons; and

(e)   any other request which may facilitate the administration of justice, including provisional measures as required.

3.   Upon receipt of a request under paragraph 2:

(a)   in a case covered by article 21 (1) (a), all States parties;

(b)   in any other case, States parties which have accepted the jurisdiction of the Court with respect to the crime in question; shall respond without undue delay to the request.

[*130] Article 52
Provisional measures

1.   In case of need, the Court may request a State to take necessary provisional measures, including the following:

(a)   to provisionally arrest a suspect;

(b)   to seize documents or other evidence; or

(c)   to prevent injury to or the intimidation of a witness or the destruction of evidence.

2.   The Court shall follow up a request under paragraph 1 by providing, as soon as possible and in any case within 28 days, a formal request for assistance complying with article 57.

[*131] Article 53
Transfer of an accused to the Court

1.   The Registrar shall transmit to any State on the territory of which the accused may be found a warrant for the arrest and transfer of an accused issued under article 28, and shall request the cooperation of that State in the arrest and transfer of the accused.

2.   Upon receipt of a request under paragraph 1:

(a)   all States parties:

(i)   in a case covered by article 21 (1) (a), or

(ii)   which have accepted the jurisdiction of the Court with respect to the crime in question; shall, subject to paragraphs 5 and 6, take immediate steps to arrest and transfer the accused to the Court;

(b)   in the case of a crime to which article 20 (e) applies, a State party which is a party to the treaty in question but which has not accepted the Court's jurisdiction with respect to that crime shall, if it decides not to transfer the accused to the Court, forthwith take all necessary steps to extradite the accused to a requesting State or refer the case to its competent authorities for the purpose of prosecution;

(c) in any other case, a State party shall consider whether it can, in accordance with its legal procedures, take steps to arrest and [*132] transfer the accused to the Court, or whether it should take steps to extradite the accused to a requesting State or refer the case to its competent authorities for the purpose of prosecution.

3.   The transfer of an accused to the Court constitutes, as between States parties which accept the jurisdiction of the Court with respect to the crime, sufficient compliance with a provision of any treaty requiring that a suspect be extradited or the case referred to the competent authorities of the requested State for the purpose of prosecution.

4.   A State party which accepts the jurisdiction of the Court with respect to the crime shall, as far as possible, give priority to a request under paragraph 1 over requests for extradition from other States.

5.   A State party may delay complying with paragraph 2 if the accused is in its custody or control and is being proceeded against for a serious crime, or serving a sentence imposed by a court for a crime. It shall within 45 days of receiving the request inform the Registrar of the reasons for the delay. In such cases, the requested State:

(a) may agree to the temporary transfer of the accused for the purpose of standing trial under this Statute; or

(c) shall comply with paragraph 2 after the prosecution has been completed or abandoned or the sentence has been served, as the case may be.

6.   A State party may, within 45 days of receiving a request under paragraph 1, file a written application with the Registrar requesting the Court to set aside the request on specified grounds. Pending a decision of the Court on the application, the State concerned may delay complying with paragraph 2, but shall take any provisional measures requested by the Court.

[*135] Article 54
Obligation to extradite or prosecute

In a case of a crime referred to in article 20 (e), a custodial State party to this Statute which is a party to the treaty in question but which has not accepted the Court's jurisdiction with respect to the crime for the purposes of article 21 (1) (b) (i) shall either take all necessary steps to extradite the suspect to a requesting State for the purpose of prosecution or refer the case to its competent authorities for that purpose.

[*136] Article 55
Rule of sociality

1.   A person transferred to the Court under article 53 shall not be subject to prosecution or punishment for any crime other than that for which the person was transferred.

2.   Evidence provided under this Part shall not, if the State when providing it 80 requests, be used as evidence for any purpose other than that for which it was provided, unless this is necessary to preserve the right of an accused under article 41(2).

3.   The Court may request the State concerned to waive the requirements of i paragraphs 1 or 2, for the reasons and purposes specified in the request.

[*137] Article 56
Cooperation with States not parties to this Statute

States not parties to this Statute may assist in relation to the matters, referred to in this Part on the basis of comity, a unilateral declaration, an ad hoc arrangement or other agreement with the Court.

Article 57
Communications and documentation

1.   Requests under this Part shall be in writing, or be forthwith reduced to writing, and shall be between the competent national authority and the Registrar. States parties shall inform the Registrar of the name and address of their national authority for this purpose.

2.   When appropriate, communications may also be made through the International Criminal Police Organization.

3.   A request under this Part shall include the following, as applicable:

    (a)   a brief statement of the purpose of the request and of the assistance sought, including the legal basis and grounds for the request;

    (b)   information concerning the person who is the subject of the request on the evidence sought, in sufficient detail to enable identification;

    (c)   a brief description of the essential facts underlying the request; and

    (d)   information concerning the complaint or charge to which the request relates and of the basis for the Court's jurisdiction.

4.   A requested State which considers the information provided insufficient to enable the request to be complied with may seek further particulars.

[*138] PART 8. ENFORCEMENT
Article 58
Recognition of judgments

States parties undertake to recognize the judgments of the Court.

[*139] Article 59
Enforcement of sentences

1.   A sentence of imprisonment shall be served in a State designated by the Court from a list of States which have indicated to the Court their willingness to accept convicted persons.

2.   If no State is designated under paragraph 1, the sentence of imprisonment shall be served in a prison facility made available by the host State.

3.   A sentence of imprisonment shall be subject to the supervision of the Court in accordance with the Rules.

[*140] Article 60
Pardon, parole and commutation of sentences

1.   If, under a generally applicable law of the State of imprisonment, a person in the same circumstances who had been convicted for the same conduct by a court of that State would be eligible for pardon, parole or commutation of sentence, the State shall so notify the Court.

2.   If a notification has been given under paragraph 1, the prisoner may apply to the Court in accordance with the Rules, seeking an order for pardon, parole or commutation of the sentence.

3.   If the Presidency decides that an application under paragraph 2 is apparently well-founded, it shall convene a Chamber of five judges to consider and decide whether in the interests of justice the person convicted should be pardoned or paroled or the sentence commuted, and on what basis.

4.   When imposing a sentence of imprisonment, a Chamber may stipulate that the sentence is to be served in accordance with specified laws as to pardon, parole or commutation of sentence of the State of imprisonment. The consent of the Court is not required to subsequent action by that State in conformity with those laws, but the Court shall be given at least 45 days' notice of any decision which might materially affect the terms or extent of the imprisonment.

5.   Except as provided in paragraphs 3 and 4, a person serving a sentence imposed by the Court is not to be released before the expiry of the sentence.

[*141] Annex
Crimes pursuant to Treaties (see art. 20 (e))

1.   Grave breaches of:

(i)   the Geneva Convention for the Amelioration of the Condition of the Wounded and Sick in Armed Forces in the Field of 12 August 1949, as defined by Article 50 of that Convention;

(ii)   the Geneva Convention for the Amelioration of the Condition of Wounded, Sick and Shipwrecked Members of Armed Forces at Sea of 12 August 1949, as defined by Article 51 of that Convention;

(iii)   the Geneva Convention relative to the Treatment of Prisoners of War of 12 August 1949, as defined by Article 130 of that Convention;

(iv)   the Geneva Convention relative to the Protection of Civilian Persons in Time of War of 12 August 1949, as defined by Article 147 of that Convention;

(v)   Protocol I Additional to the Geneva Conventions of 12 August 1949 and relating to the Protection of Victims of International Armed Conflicts of June 1977, as defined by Article 85 of that Protocol.

2.   The unlawful seizure of aircraft as defined by Article 1 of the Hague Convention for the Suppression of Unlawful Seizure of Aircraft of 16 December 1970.

3.   The crimes defined by Article 1 of the Montreal Convention for the Suppression of Unlawful Acts against the Safety of Civil Aviation of 23 September 1971.

[*142] 4. Apartheid and related crimes as defined by Article II of the International Convention on the Suppression and Punishment of the Crime of Apartheid of 30 November 1973.

5.   The crimes defined by Article 2 of the Convention on the Prevention Punishment of Crimes against Internationally Protected Persons, including Diplomatic Agents of 14 December 1973.

6.   Hostage-taking and related crimes as defined by Article 1 of the International Convention against the Taking of Hostages of 17 December 1979.

7.   The crime of torture made punishable pursuant to Article 4 of the Convention against Torture and Other Cruel, Inhuman or Degrading Treatment or Punishment of 10 December 1984.

8.   The crimes defined by Article 3 of the Convention for the Suppression of Unlawful Acts against the Safety of Maritime Navigation of 10 March 1988 and by Article 2 of the Protocol for the Suppression of Unlawful Acts against the Safety of Fixed Platforms Located on the Continental Shelf of 10 March 1988.

9.   Crimes involving illicit traffic in narcotic drugs and psychotropic substances as envisaged by Article 3 (1) of the United Nations Convention against Illicit Traffic in Narcotic Drugs and Psychotropic Substances of 20 December 1988 which, having regard to Article 2 of the Convention, are crimes with an international dimension.

IMPLEMENTATION OF THE INTERNATIONAL CONVENTION ON THE SUPPRESSION AND PUNISHMENT OF THE CRIME OF <u>APARTHEID</u>

STUDY ON WAYS AND MEANS OF INSURING THE IMPLEMENTATION OF INTERNATIONAL INSTRUMENTS SUCH AS THE INTERNATIONAL CONVENTION ON THE SUPPRESSION AND PUNISHMENT OF THE CRIME OF APARTHEID, INCLUDING THE ESTABLISHMENT OF THE INTERNATIONAL JURISDICTION ENVISAGED BY THE CONVENTION*

[Editorial Note - The U.N. page numbers of this document are indicated in bolded brackets [*] in the text].

1.   At its thirty-sixth session, on 26 February 1980, the Commission on Human Rights adopted resolution 12 (XXXVI) entitled "Implementation of the International Convention on the Suppression and Punishment of the Crime of <u>Apartheid</u>". By paragraph 7 of that resolution, the Commission requested the <u>Ad Hoc</u> Working Group of Experts, in co-operation with the Special Committee against <u>Apartheid</u> and in accordance with paragraph 20 of the annex to General Assembly resolution 34/24 of 15 November 1979, to undertake a study on ways and means of insuring the implementation of international instruments such as the International Convention on the Suppression and Punishment of the Crime of <u>Apartheid</u>, including the establishment of the international jurisdiction envisaged by the Convention.
2.   At the request of the <u>Ad Hoc</u> Working Group of Experts a Consultant was commissioned to prepare a study and a draft Statute of the proposed International Criminal Court.
3.   The Working Group considered the study and the draft Statute at its meetings in Geneva in August 1980 and January 1981.
4.   The attached interim Report is referred to the Commission on Human Rights with a recommendation that the Commission invites States Parties to the Convention on the Suppression and Punishment of the Crime of <u>Apartheid</u> to submit their comments and/or views to the study to enable the Working Group to give further consideration to it.

[*1] INTRODUCTION
1.   This study is submitted in response to the request made by the Commission on Human Rights in its resolution 12 (XXXVI) that the <u>Ad Hoc</u> Working Group of Experts, in co-operation with the Special Committee against <u>Apartheid</u> and in accordance with paragraph 20 of the annex to General Assembly resolution 34/24 of 15 November 1979, should undertake a study on ways and means of ensuring the implementation of international instruments such as the International Convention on the Suppression and Punishment of the Crime of <u>Apartheid</u>, including the establishment of the international jurisdiction envisaged by the Convention. The study was prepared with implementation as its central consideration, and begins with an inquiry into the significance of the term "implementation" in view of the nature of the <u>Apartheid</u> Convention.
2.   The report concludes that, in the present context, "implementation" signifies creation of an international criminal court. From this it proceeds to consider the state of international criminal law in terms of theory and practicality of operations of such a court, and with special attention to the particular nature of the crime of <u>apartheid</u>.
3.   It is upon this foundation of relevant concerns that adoption of any instrument creating such a court, must be considered.
4.   An assessment is included of the possible usefulness of such a court in combating the crime of <u>apartheid</u>.
5.   Finally, a summary of issues requiring attention and means of addressing such issues is provided.

---

*   This draft statute was prepared by M. Cherif Bassiouni as special consultant to the Commission on Human Rights Working Group on Southern Africa. The author subsequently updated the text and prepared a commentary which appears as an appendix in this volume as M. Cherif Bassiouni, *Draft Statute: International Criminal Court*, 9 Nouvelles Études Pénales (1993).

6.   Throughout, an effort has been made to present a range of options and to describe modalities for achieving the widest possible acceptance of implementation steps. In keeping with this goal of flexibility, particular approaches are not strongly advocated for outright adoption. Rather, it is left to the Working Group and other concerned organs to identify especially promising alternatives based on their competence. In particular, the possibility of formalizing the quest for consensus in formulating an appropriate implementation scheme is outlined in the concluding portion of the report.

7.   Although southern Africa is the chief concern of the Convention and of the Working Group, the discussion of implementation is general. This is not out of a spirit of neutrality; on the contrary, it is out of concern that <u>apartheid</u> be recognized and dealt with for what it is, regardless of where it occurs. Accordingly, general discussion ensures that implementation measures would be suitable for application in every context. That the official government policy labelled "<u>apartheid</u>" is not the sole concern of those combating the crime of the same name is readily apparent from such works as the progress report of the Ad Hoc Working Group of Experts (E/CN.4/136) prepared in accordance with Commission on Human Rights resolution 12 (XXXV) and Economic and Social Council decision 1979/34.

8.   Two major reports preceding the present report have been prepared by distinguished members of the Ad Hoc Working Group, one by Professor Felix Ermacora entitled "Study concerning the question of <u>apartheid</u>, from the point of view of international penal law" (E/CN.4/1075), and the other by Professor Brarimir Jankovic entitled "<u>Aide-Memoire</u>" (E/CN.4/AC.22/1980/WP.2).

[*2]9. The study contains two models. The first is the Draft Convention on the Establishment of an International Penal Tribunal for the Suppression and Punishment of the Crime of <u>Apartheid</u> and Other International Crimes, which is based on article V of the International Convention on the Suppression and Punishment of the Crime of <u>Apartheid</u>, and permits States parties to add, by Supplemental Agreement, other convention international crimes which are the subject of multilateral conventions. The draft convention contemplates the creation of a new international legal entity, an International Penal Tribunal, through a multilateral convention open to States parties to the <u>Apartheid</u> Convention and to other States. The second model is the Draft Additional Protocol for the Penal Enforcement of the International Convention on the Suppression and Punishment of the Crime of <u>Apartheid</u>, which is based on article V of the International Convention on the Suppression and Punishment of the Crime of <u>Apartheid</u>. It does not contemplate the potential addition of other international crimes than those listed in article II of the Convention. This model does not contemplate the creation of a new international legal entity but the use of existing United Nations structures, with the addition of one new structure, namely an international panel of judges to adjudicate violations of article II ov the Convention. It requires an Additional Protocol to the Convention and is open to States parties to the said Convention.

10.   The idea of establishing an international criminal court is not new, as is shown by the reference to foot-note 14. Particular care and attention has been given to the reports of Professors Ermacora and Jankovic referred to in paragraph 8, to the texts of a draft Statute for an international Criminal court prepared by the Committee on International Criminal Jurisdiction in 1953 and to the texts of a draft statute for an international criminal inquiry and a draft statute for the establishment of an international criminal court prepared by the International Law Association in 1979. Other studies relevant to this subject have also been considered.

11.   Parts A and D establish the basis for the two alternative models, proposed in parts C and D, for an international penal enforcement system. Parts A and B describe the relationship between international criminal law and internationally protected human rights and lay the foundation for resort to international criminal law as a means to enforce internationally protected human rights. Furthermore, they establish the legal basis and arguments for an international penal enforcement mechanism under the Convention on the Suppression and Punishment of the Crime of <u>Apartheid</u>. The proposal in part C is for a multilateral convention, with the creation of new institutions pertaining thereto, which would deal not only with the crime of <u>apartheid</u> but with other international crimes. The proposal in part D is for an additional protocol to the <u>Apartheid</u> Convention limiting the jurisdiction of the enforcement organs to the crime of <u>apartheid</u> and maximizing the use of existing institutions and instruments to implement the draft protocol.

[*3] I. THE MANDATE FOR IMPLEMENTATION: ITS MEANING INTERPRETED
IN VIEW OF THE NATURE OF THE CONVENTION ON THE SUPPRESSION AND
PUNISHMENT OF THE CRIME OF APARTHEID

12.   The conduct prescribed under the Convention on the Suppression and Punishment of the Crime of Apartheid (hereinafter referred to as the Apartheid Convention) is also prescribed under other, more basic instruments, some of which embody their own measures and mechanisms of implementation. For this reason, implementation of the Apartheid Convention requires consideration of the relationship of it to these other instruments in order to appreciate its distinctive motivations and objectives.

13.   This consideration may begin with the duplicativeness of the Apartheid Convention as to the substantive norm enunciated. Apartheid is defined in article II of the apartheid Convention as acts for the purpose of dominating a racial group including murder, infliction of harm, infringement of freedom or dignity, torture, imposing harmful living conditions, segregation, preventing development, depriving of freedoms, creating reserves and ghettoes, exploitation and persecutions of those who would resist such acts. In this respect the Apartheid Convention merely describes a norm narrower than but contained within the norms previously enunciated in more basic instruments.

14.   For example, the Universal Declaration of Human Rights provides in article 2 that "Everyone is entitled to all the rights and freedoms set forth in this Declaration without distinction of any kind, such as race, colour...national or social origin..." and among the rights set forth are: freedom from servitude (article 4); freedom from discrimination and a guarantee of equal protection of the laws (article 7); freedom of movement and residence (article 15); freedom of interracial marriage (article 16(1)); equal access to public service (article 21(2); choice of employment, equal pay and the right to form and join unions (article 23); and the right to an opportunity for higher education based on merit (article 26). Likewise, the International Covenant on Civil and Political Rights forbids discrimination on the basis of race, colour or origin (article 2), and provides rights to: means of subsistence for peoples (article 1); freedom of citizens to vote and be elected (article 25); equal protection of the laws (article 26); and for minority groups, cultural and developmental opportunities (article 27). In addition, the International Convention on the Elimination of All Forms of Racial Discrimination defines and condemns racial discrimination in terms that are comprehensive (article 1), condemns apartheid without defining it (article 3) and particularly condemns discrimination regarding listed civil, political, economic and social rights (article 5).

15.   The obvious duplicativeness of the Apartheid Convention as to its proscription must find explanation in terms of other aspects of the instrument. Obligations of States parties with respect to the norms enunciated may be considered first, and may be divided for that purpose into obligations of a domestic orientation and those of an international orientation.

16.   The Universal Declaration contains no express provision for domestic measures to be taken, but both the International Covenant and the Convention on the Elimination of All Forms of Racial Discrimination do so. The former obligates States parties to ensure that all rights under it are protected within their territory (article 2). The latter imposes general duties to see that its norms are respected as to discrimination (article 2) and apartheid (article 3), and a more emphatic duty to [*4] eliminate discrimination regarding listed rights (article 5), plus more specific duties to oppose racist propaganda (article 4), assure remedies for deprivations of rights under it (article 6) and to promote racial tolerance (article 3). In contrast, the duties under the Apartheid Convention are highly specific: States Parties are to declare apartheid and those engaging in it as criminal (article I), and to take steps to prevent, prosecute, try and punish in accordance with their jurisdiction crimes of apartheid (article IV).

17.   As to internationally-oriented obligations, a similar pattern may be observed. The Universal Declaration lacks specific provisions. The International Covenant requires submission of reports on compliance (article 40), and for States parties to inform other States parties should they derogate from that instrument's provisions (article 4(3)), and to respond to complaints by other States parties regarding compliance (article 41). In addition, the Optional Protocol to the Covenant provides for responses to certain complaints by individuals (article 4(2)). The Discrimination Convention also calls for reports (article 9(1)), responses to complaints (article 11(1)) and article 14(6) (b)), plus informing other States parties whether an acceptable solution to a dispute regarding compliance has been found (article 13(2)). Under the Apartheid Convention, the obligations are rather dissimilar. Parties undertake to accept and carry

out anti-<u>apartheid</u> decisions of certain international organs (article VI), but this appears to be redundant in that such duties are already imposed in more general terms by the instruments relating to those organs. A reporting requirement is imposed (article VII(1)), and States parties are to settle their disputes regarding the Convention by means of the International Court of Justice or as they may otherwise agree (article XI). Also, in matters of extradition the States parties are not to regard crimes of <u>apartheid</u> as political offenses (article XI).

18.   Related to these internationally-oriented obligations and provisions for implementation machinery, which merit consideration before assessing the patterns of obligations of the various instruments. No such machinery is created under the Universal Declaration, but the International Covenant establishes a Human Rights Committee (article 28), and assigns it the tasks of receiving, studying and transmitting reports of States parties (article 49), considering and reporting on disputes (article 41), and, when appropriate, referring such disputes to a conciliation commission (article 42(1)). The Optional Protocol to the Covenant confers similar competence upon the Human Rights Committee with respect to individuals' complaints (article 4), and provides for possible reporting of the views of the Committee (article 5). Comparable functions are assigned to a Committee on Elimination of Racial Discrimination under the Racial Discrimination Convention (articles 8, 9, 11, 12(1) and 14). Under the <u>Apartheid</u> Convention, however, the function of considering its chairman (article IX), and, as already mentioned, dispute settlement is otherwise provided for. A monitoring function is provided for the Commission on Human Rights (article X). Finally, it is provided that an accused may be tried by an international penal tribunal (article V).

19.   The above patter of obligations and implementation mechanisms does not present a clear spectrum in terms of effectiveness. Reporting is the chief vehicle for implementation under all of the instruments having express provisions for duties of States parties. Obviously the Optional Protocol, which has relevance not only to the Covenant but also to the Racial Discrimination Convention, represents an enhancement of potential effectiveness in that individual complaints are capable of bringing to light problems unlikely to be dealt with by complaints of States. Notable, no [*5]provision is included in the <u>Apartheid</u> Convention for individuals' complaints. Dispute resolution is treated differently under the <u>Apartheid</u> Convention than under the other instruments, yet all of them make it possible for disputes to be settled without compulsory process if the complainant so agrees.

20.   Instead of constituting a pattern of increasing or decreasing effectiveness, the above patter may be understood as a function of the perceived purpose of each instrument. The Universal Declaration, as an embodiment of the widest possible consensus on human rights deserving international attention, contains no express provisions regarding duties of States or creating implementation machinery. As discussed elsewhere, it amplifies terms of the Charter, which has its own effectiveness, and certain of its principles are given heightened effectiveness through more narrow instruments, such as the International Covenant on Civil and Political Rights. The Covenant is itself an instrument of wide consensus and its provisions reflect this by shaping implementation-related measures to deal only with States parties, it being apparently contemplated that te Covenant should act as a vehicle for enhancing implementation of the rights provided under it within States that have already manifested acceptance of the validity of such rights. No express provision attempts to deal with States that have not manifested such acceptance, and the Optional Protocol is also limited to States manifesting acceptance. A similar treatment is provided under the Racial Discrimination Convention, although the duties under it are more detailed.

21.   It is against this background that the distinctiveness of the <u>Apartheid</u> Convention may be appreciated. Its name is derived from the term given by South Africa to its racial policies [for reviews of such policies, see United Nations, Dag Hammarskjhold Library, <u>apartheid: A Selective Bibliography on the Racial Policies of the Government of the Republic of South Africa, 1970-1978</u> (1979)], and its purpose is to oppose such policies. Accordingly, although it may be viewed as aiming in part at preventing the spread of such practices to States parties, its primary thrust is against the practices of a non-State party. Moreover, to the extent that the term <u>apartheid</u> is given a generic definition applicable to practices of States other than South Africa, it must be presumed that no State indulging in such practices would also be a State party to the <u>Apartheid</u> Convention. Accordingly, the distinctive essence of the Apartheid Convention is that it addresses the consequences for States generally of conduct occurring within another State.

22.   This distinctiveness is of central importance to the question of implementation, for unlike other related instruments the Apartheid Convention cannot and does not rely on co-operation of the States wherein the reported human rights violation has occurred. On the contrary, it concerns itself with co-operation of States within which no such violations have occurred. Such an orientation requires explanation in view of the general concept of non-intervention by States in the domestic affairs of other States.

23.   Such an explanation may be found in the use by the Apartheid Convention of the terms "crime against humanity" (article I), and "international criminal responsibility" (article III), together with the general concept of international human rights. As described within a general obligation to respect human rights attaches to all members of the United Nations by virtue of the Charter and the Universal Declaration. The precise dimensions of such an obligation, however, are not explicitly stated in these instruments and the specificity with which the rights that must be respected are defined varies. The International Covenant and its Optional Protocol provide further elaboration of these rights and, for States parties, of the obligations regarding them. To the extent that such elaboration amounts to a statement of a general principle of [*6] international law, it is binding upon non-States parties as well, and clearly this is more likely to be true with respect to elaboration of a norm than of institutional duties as reporting and dispute resolution. With respect tor acial discrimination, even more detailed elaboration is contained in the Racial Discrimination Convention, with comparable effect.

24.   As a result, the human rights instruments leading up to the Racial Discrimination Convention may be viewed on the one hand as progressively elaborating upon general principles of international law respecting treatment of races, and on the other as providing appropriate means for States parties to assure and enhance their compliance with these principles. The former is not dependent on express consent of particular States whereas the latter is largely dependent on such consent.

25.   The Apartheid Convention has a similar duality in its nature but what must be recognized is that two such dualities are involved. In defining apartheid and indicating that persons ought not be subjected to a general treatment, there is an elaboration of a general principle comparable in purpose to the definitional portions of related human rights instruments, but highly specific. In assigning certain obligations to States respecting such conduct, such as reporting and dispute resolution requirements, there is an elaboration of a consent-dependent regime not greatly different from those of other, related human rights instruments.

26.   However, there is a significant departure from prior instruments of similar vein in the pronouncements of criminality and the provisions dealing with consequences of this criminalization. Not all violations of rights enunciated in other human rights instruments have been described as criminal. Even racial discrimination is not described within the Racial Discrimination Convention as necessarily amounting to a crime. This terminology is applied exclusively to apartheid. Accordingly, the specific conduct elaborated in the Apartheid Convention's proscription is not merely a more detailed treatment of a human rights violation, but also a seminal description of a class of international crime. As to the impact of this on no-States parties, consonance of the conventional language with general principles of international law is crucial, and to the extent such consonance exists, that language is applicable notwithstanding the consent of States.

27.   Moreover, the same is true with respect to the duties of States to criminalize, prosecute and punish such conduct. This is in stark contrast to the consequences of reporting and dispute-resolution measures. The difference lies in the fact that particular consequences attach to international crimes under general principles of international law, including duties of action against such crimes.

28.   Thus, just as the mere describing of certain conduct as violating international law does not make it so, yet it may be so as a general principle of international law, so also describing certain conduct as criminal under international law does not *ipso facto* make it an international crime. Likewise, stating that certain action ought to be taken by States with respect to certain conduct does not *ipso facto* establish a general rule of international law, but if the conduct in question is actually an international crime, then certain obligations of States flow from that.

29.   In sum, if the various human rights instruments teaching upon racial matters are viewed simply as consensual arrangements among States parties, the Apartheid Convention appears duplicative though some of its provisions are not themselves repetitive. However, when these instruments are considered as declarations regarding general rules of international law, the distinctive role of the Apartheid Convention

becomes clearer. [*7] It strives to define the international crime of <u>apartheid</u> and to express the consequences for States of that crime, while at the same time extending particular attention had protective measures to that matter in a manner similar to that done under other human rights instruments.

30. As a human rights instrument, the <u>Apartheid</u> Convention is as well implemented and as well founded and drafted as kindred human rights instruments. It is as a declaration of international criminal law that the <u>Apartheid</u> Convention merits special attention.

31. The particular legal questions relating to mode of implementation are addressed and assessed below. It is useful, however, to first consider very general matters.

32. First, it must be noted that the <u>Apartheid</u> Convention does not by its terms attempt to class <u>apartheid</u> as a mere crime of extraterritorial effect, suitable fo independent action by individual States or concerted action by groups of States. Rather, it treats <u>apartheid</u> as a "crime against humanity," and one entailing "international criminal responsibility." Accordingly, although various states may feel the harmful effects of the crime, it is to be punished in the name of or on behalf of the world community. This suggests in itself that a uniform standard should be applied.

33. Second, although the <u>Apartheid</u> Convention is designed to be declaratory s to the acts constituting the international crime of <u>apartheid</u>, it may in that respect be either over-inclusive or under-inclusive or both, in that the actual crime's existence and character are dependent not on that Convention but on general principles of international law. As a result, the definition given in article II of the <u>Apartheid</u> Convention may be viewed as conventionally binding upon States parties, but as to States that are not parties its binding quality depends on its correspondence to the general rule of international law. Accordingly, actions by States parties under the <u>Apartheid</u> Convention, even when fully in keeping with the terms of that Convention, as justifiable as exercises of general international criminal law only to the extent that the terms of the Convention correspond with such general international criminal law. This is not to say that actions under the Convention would not be otherwise justifiable. Rather, it is to say that in so far as the <u>Apartheid</u> Convention purports to be a declaration of general rules of international law, actions taken pursuant to that convention seek justification in terms of that body of law.

34. Third, the search for appropriate means of implementation for this aspect of the <u>Apartheid</u> Convention is, if not easy, narrowly drawn. By its very nature implementation of criminal law is by criminal process, and although significant variations in such process exist in different legal systems, the general nature of such process may readily be recognized.

35. The distinctive character of criminal process may be appreciated not only by its particular form but also by its distinctive purposes. Criminal law does not merely wpecify proper or improper forms of behaviour, a function of other law generally. Rather, it identifies behaviour in response to which particular measures are to be imposed not in the name of or on behalf of someone disadvantaged by that conduct, but rather in the name of and on behalf of the community and its sense of justice. Such measures are commonly termed "penal" or "punitive" in order to indicate that they are but designed merely to remedy past harm of a remediable type. On the contrary, they are directed at the future in the sense of generally deterring future conduct of that kind, by incapacitating the offender or by affecting the offender's will or inclination [*8] to engage in such conduct. Only in the sense of retribution do such measures have a remedial aspect, and this is aimed at vindicating the community's sense of justice, which was not in a tangible sense harmed and cannot in tangible form be repaired.

36. Because of this ultimate purpose of criminal process, initiation and direction of such process cannot be left merely to interested persons or organizations, but must rather be supervised by someone qualified to act on behalf of the relevant community. The appropriate motivation for initiation and direction of such process is concern for justice.

37. A second consequence of the purposes of criminal process is that an orderly and reliable method for establishing facts must be utilized. The broad outlines of such methods include both general investigation and consideration of allegation by the accused. In some systems the manner of receiving and considering evidence may be highly elaborate, but in every system an effort is made to gather evidence widely with particular care to utilize the most reliable sources. [It should be noted that, although instruments with an affirmative, human rights protection function, have involved some investigative activity, the procedures followed have not been as orderly and reliable as would be required for punitive purposes. See, e.g., Franck

and Fairley "Procedural Due Process in Human Rights Fact-finding by International Agencies," A.J.I.L. 308 (1980)].

38.   A third consequence is that criminal norms are specified in great detail. This is because of the special need to be right when acting in the name of the community's sense of justice. Conduct cannot be fairly punished when the community has not clearly expressed its intention that such conduct be avoided. The matter is given further attention in connection with the principle nulla poena sine lege.

39.   The foregoing demonstrates that a mandate to implement the Apartheid Convention constitutes a mandate to create the mechanisms necessary to set in motion criminal process. Indeed, bringing international criminal law to bear on this wrongful conduct has been an enduring consideration of those involved in anti-apartheid activities. See, for example, the report of the Ad Hoc Working Group of Experts, entitled "Study concerning the question of apartheid from the point of view of the international penal law," (E/CN.4/1075). The central institution in such a process is a court, but related institutions may also be appropriate in order to assist the functioning of the court. The tasks that require treatment in order for such a court to operate merit separate attention.

40.   The ultimate implementation goal of the Apartheid Convention may obviously be served by such an approach in that the goals of criminal process are prevention and suppression of specific conduct. The extent to which criminal process on an international scale can secure in practice such goals also merits separate consideration.

[*9] II. INTERNATIONAL CRIMINAL LAW CONSIDERATIONS

A.   The application of international criminal law principles to internationally protected human rights

41.   The International Convention on the Suppression and Punishment of the Crime of Apartheid is an harmonious part of the global scheme of international protection of human rights. As such it must be considered and interpreted in the light of other conventions in pari materia. To the extent that these other relevant conventions are specifically embodied in the language and spirit of the Apartheid Convention, in particular article II thereof, they are incorporated therein.

42.   These relevant conventions fall into two categories: (1) conventions which are declaratory of certain specific human rights deemed protected by the international law of human rights; and (2) conventions which require signatories to criminalize certain violations of human rights in their national laws, to prosecute the violators or alternatively to extradite persons accused or found guilty thereof to a requesting State. Some of these conventions specifically declare the conduct in question to be a "crime under international law" while others do not state this specifically; the object and outcome remain however the same.

43.   The conventions included in the first category, which contain declaratory principles on the protection of specific human rights, do not however deem their violations to be crimes under international law nor do they contemplate criminalization of the conduct in question under the national laws of the signatory States. However, they are non the less relevant in the historical process in that, as the embodiment of a worldwide consensus of certain minimum standards, these prescriptions may evolve into proscriptions which may become the object of enforcement measures including their criminalization under international law, or the imposition under international law of a duty to prosecute or extradite the violators of these protected rights. This has been the case with respect to many international instruments aimed at the protection of human rights which evolved from declaratory principles to specific international proscriptions having a penal character.

44.   The principal conventions in this category which, because they refer to a prohibition or protection against "racial discrimination", are relevant to the interpretation and implementation of the Apartheid Convention are: the Universal Declaration of Human Rights; the International Covenant on Civil and Political Rights; the Optional Protocol to the International Covenant on Civil and Political Rights; the International Convention on the Elimination of All Forms of Racial Discrimination; the Convention on the

Reduction of Statelessness; and, the Convention on Refugees.[1] Each of these instruments specifically refers to the protection of individuals against racial discrimination and is relevant in whole or in part to the Apartheid Convention, and more particularly to the meaning of Article II, of the said [*10] Convention and other provisions which implement it. (In addition other Conventions of the United Nations and its specialized agencies such as the ILO and UNESCO, which also include provisions against "racial discrimination" and its consequent practices could be deemed included in this category).

45.   The significance of these Conventions lies first in that the Universal Declaration of Human Rights was deemed by the International Court of Justice in its 1970 "Advisory Opinion on the Legal Consequences for States of the Continued Presence of South Africa in Namibia"[2] as incorporated in the meaning of Article 55 of the Charter of the United Nations.[3] Thus, since the Universal Declaration of Human Rights is deemed to be the further expression of the words "Human Rights" of Article 55 of the Charter and since Article 56 of the Charter states that the protection of "human rights" under Article 55 is "self-executing", the protections afforded by the Universal Declaration of Human Rights are applicable to Member States of the United Nations and binding upon them.

46.   To the extent that the conventions deemed relevant and listed in paragraph 4 above interpret the specific rights enunciated in the Universal Declaration of Human Rights they may, by incorporation, be considered binding on all Member States of the United Nations and not only on their signatory States. Such a binding effect would not derive from each convention qua, but from the fact that it gives specific meaning to specific rights embodied in the Universal Declaration of Human Rights which, under the decision of the International Court of Justice referred to in paragraph 45 above, is deemed as incorporated in the meaning of Article 55 of the Charter of the United Nations; and that Article 56 of the Charter requires the Member States to enforce the protection of these human rights.

47.   In so far as the Apartheid Convention prohibits conduct predicated on "racial discrimination" which is specifically defined in the Conventions listed in paragraph 44 it can be said that the Apartheid Convention incorporates in its meaning of the prohibited conduct stated in article II thereof the provisions of these other conventions to the extent they are applicable.

48.   Mutatis mutandi, to the extent that the Apartheid Convention criminalizes certain extreme forms of "racial discrimination" as defined and prohibited by the Convention on the Elimination of All Forms of Racial Discrimination, and that these two conventions give meaning to the protection against "racial discrimination" which is guaranteed by the Universal Declaration of Human Rights which Declaration is applicable to Member States of the United Nations through Articles 55 and 56 of the Charter as discussed in paragraphs 45 and 46 it could be argued that by incorporation of the relevant provisions of these Conventions in the Declaration that Member States of the United Nations are obligated under the Charter not to engage in the practices of apartheid as defined in article II of the Apartheid Convention.

49.   The second category of relevant conventions, namely those which either declare given conduct to be "a crime under international law", or that the conduct in question should be criminalized under the national criminal law of the signatory States and thus embody the maxim aut dedere aut judicare, are:

[*11] (i)   The Nuremberg Principles[4]

---

[1]   For the texts of these and other international instruments on the protection of human rights, see Human Rights: A compilation of international instruments (United Nations publication, Sales No. E.70.XIV.2). See also United Nations Action in the Field of Human Rights (United Nations publication, Sales No. #.74.XIV.2); L. Sohn and T. Buergenthal, International Protection of Human Rights (1973); J. Graven, Problèmes de protection internationale des droits de l'homme (Institut internationale des droits de l'homme, 1969).

[2]   (1971) I.C.J., 16.

[3]   Ibid., p. 57 et seq. See also Schwelb, "The International Court of Justice and the Human Rights Clauses of the Charter", 66 A.J.I.L. 337 (1972).

[4]   In connection with the Nuremberg Principles, see General Assembly resolution 95 (I) of 11 December 1946 and the Report of the International Law Commission covering its second session (Official Records of the General Assembly, Fifth Session, Supplement No. 12 (A/1316), part III, pp. 11-14). See also M.C. Bassiouni and V.P. Nanda, A Treatise on International Criminal Law, vol. I, (1973) p. 587. See also Proceedings in the Trial of the Major War Criminals Before the International Military Tribunal, 42 vols. (1949), known as the "Blue Series". The ensuing trials were published under the title Trials of War Criminals before the Nuremberg Military Tribunal, 14 vols. (1940), known as the "Green Series". For an interesting account of the trial and the accused, see E. Davidson, The Trial of the Germans

(ii)   Crimes Against Humanity[5]

(iii)   The Genocide Convention[6]

(iv)   The four Geneva Conventions of 12 August 1949 and the 1977 Additional Protocols thereto[7]

(v)   The Slavery Conventions[8]

(vi)   The Convention of the Non-applicability of Statutes of Limitation to War Crimes and Crimes Against Humanity[9]

[*12] In addition a Convention which is currently at the drafting stage should be added:

The draft Convention on the Prevention and Suppression of Torture[10]

50.   The relevance of these Conventions is first that article I of the Apartheid Convention declares the conduct defined in article II thereof as "a crime against humanity" and thus incorporates by reference Crimes Against Humanity which derive their meaning from the Nuremberg Principles. In addition the conduct prohibited by article II of the Apartheid Convention includes inter alia conduct deemed a "crime under international law" and conduct regarding which an international duty to prosecute or extradite exists under the provisions of the Convention listed in paragraph 49. Thus article II incorporated to the extent applicable some of the provisions stated in these conventions and is to be interpreted in light of the meaning of these other Conventions which prohibit the same conduct. The difference between the prohibition of article II and the prohibition stated in these other Conventions is that the Apartheid Convention prohibition refers to specific conduct done in furtherance of a policy of "racial discrimination" while the other Conventions with the exception of the Genocide Convention do not limit their prohibitions and violations to that particular purpose.

51.   Article II of the Apartheid Convention includes a number of specific prohibitions and violations thereof deemed criminal under international law which, as discussed above, incorporate the meaning of other specific protections and prohibitions contained in some relevant conventions listed in paragraph 44 whose binding effect on Member States of the United Nations is discussed in paragraphs 45 and 46 and other specific prohibitions and violations contained in some relevant Conventions listed in paragraph 9.

(1966). For a legal appraisal and description of the proceedings, see R. Woetzel, The Nuremberg Trials in International Law (1960); J. Keenan and B. Brown, Crimes against International Law (1950); S. Glueck, War Criminals, Their Prosecution and Punishment (1944), see also, P. Poltorak, The Nuremberg Epilogue (1977), translated from the Russian by D. Skvirsky.

[5]   For "Crimes Against Humanity" see the Nuremberg Principles supra, note 4, principle VI (C). For a historical-legal analysis of "Crimes Against Humanity" see Bassiouni, "International Law and the Holocaust" 9 Calif. West. Int'l L.J. 201 (1979).

[6]   Supra notes 1 and 5; and see also, E. Aronneau Le Crime Contre l'Humanité (1961) and P. Drost, The Crime of State (2 vol.) (1959).

[7]   Geneva Conventions of 12 August 1949:

For the Amelioration of the Condition of the Wounded and Sick in Armed Forces of the Field, 75 United Nations, Treaty Series, 31; For the Amelioration of the Condition of Wounded, Sick and Shipwrecked Members of Armed Forces at Sea, 75 United Nations, Treaty Series, 85; Relative to the Treatment of Prisoners of War, 75 United Nations, Treaty Series, 135; Relative to the Protection of Civilian Persons in Time of War, 75 United Nations, Treaty Series, 287.

Protocols Additional to the Geneva Convention of 12 August 1949, 19 June 1977, KRC, (August-September 1977).

[8]   See supra note 1, but also other conventions on the subject listed in M.C. Bassiouni, International Criminal Law: A Draft International Criminal Code (1980), at "A list of the Principal International Instruments" p. xiii, under "Slavery and Slave-Related Practices" that lists 25 international instruments. Appendix 2; see also B. DeSchutter, A Bibliography on International Criminal Law (1972) and Bibliography on International Criminal Law and International Criminal Courts prepared by the Secretariat of the United Nations (A/CN.4/28).

[9]   Supra note 1; see also 37 Revue International de Droit Penal Vol. 3-4 devoted to that subject.

[10]   See the United Nations "Declaration on the protection of all persons from being subjected to torture and other cruel, inhuman or degrading treatment or punishment" (General Assembly resolution 3453 (XXX) of 9 December 1975), the "Draft Convention on the Prevention and Suppression of Torture" introduced by the Association Internationale de Droit Penal before the Sub-Commission on Prevention of Discrimination and Protection of Minorities, (E/CN.4 NGO/213) and 48 Revue Internationale de Droit Penal No. 3-4 (1977) devoted to that subject. The Draft Articles before the Commission's Working Group are those contained in the official Swedish draft (E/CN.4/1285) which is quite similar to the AIDP Draft and Comments thereon (E/CN.4/1314).

52. In so far as article IV of the Apartheid Convention requires States parties to "prosecute" and "punish" the violators of article II of the Convention, and article V contemplates the enforcement of these violations by means of an "international penal tribunal", and, article IX requires States parties to "extradite" perpetrators of such violations, it is therefore necessary in order to satisfy the principle of legality in criminal law, nullum crimen sine lege, nulla poena sine lege, which is a "general principle of international law recognized by civilized nations", that article II be given more specificity in order to avoid vagueness, ambiguity and incorporation by reference or analogy of other relevant treaty provisions deemed incorporated within the meaning of article II of the Apartheid Convention.

[*13] B. Institutional setting: progress towards creation of an international criminal court

53. Article V of the Apartheid Convention contemplates the creation of an "international penal tribunal" to enforce the violations of Article II of the said Convention. Thus the legislative authority for the creation of an International Criminal Court is clearly established.

54. The only precedents save for an isolated historical instance[11] are the Nuremberg and Tokyo war crimes tribunals which were ad hoc international criminal courts.[12] There are no other examples of such tribunals in contemporary history.

55. In 1951, a draft statute of an international criminal jurisdiction (A/2126) repared by a committee of experts was submitted to the United Nations and in 1953 a second draft (A/2645) was submitted based on the work of another committee of experts. Both drafts were tabled but no further action was taken by the United Nations on them.[13]

[*14] 56. The principal reasons for this action could be summarized as follows:

---

[11]   Professor A. Schwartzenberger reported that in 1474 one Peter Von Hagenbush was prosecuted by an international tribunal of the Holy Roman Empire for war crimes in Breisach, Germany, "The Breisach War Crime Trial of 1474" The Manchester Guardian 17 September 1946, see also de Barrante, Histoire des Ducs de Bourgogne, Vol. IX (1837). Another precedent could be that of the trial in Naples of Couradin Von Hohenstofen for initiating an "unjust war" in 1268, though the composition of the tribunal was not international, see Bierzaneck, "The Prosecution of War Crimes" in Bassiouni and Nanda, supra note 4, p. 559, 560. Another possible precedent is the decision of the "Allies" at the Congress of Aix-La-Chapelle of 1810 to detain Napoleon Bonaparte on the Island of Elba for waging unjust wars. See Bellot, "The Detention of Napoleon Bonaparte" 19 Temple L. Rev. 170 (1923).

[12]   See Wright, History of the United Nations War Crimes Commission (1948); Proceedings in the Trial of the Major War Criminals Before International Military Tribunals (1942) 42 vols; R. Woetzel, The Nuremberg Epilogue (1971); Roling, "The Nuremberg and Tokyo War Crimes Trials", in Bassiouni and Nanda, supra note 4, p. 590.

[13]   See General Assembly resolution 1187 (XII) of 11 November 1957. See also the note by the Secretary-General entitled "International Criminal Jurisdiction" (Official Records of the General Assembly, Twelfth session, document A/3649) and the memorandum submitted by the Secretary-General of the United Nations entitled "Historical Survey of the Question of Criminal Jurisdiction" (United Nations publication, Sales No. 1949.V.8). For a documentary history of the various projects for the creation of an international criminal jurisdiction, see B. Ferencz, aThe International Criminal Court (1980) 2 Vols. See also, J. Stone and R. Woetzel, Toward a Feasible International Criminal Court (1970); 35 Revue Internationale de Droit Penal No. 1-2 (1964) devoted to that subject, and 45 Revue Internatione de Droit Penal No. 3-4 (1974) containing the contributions of the AIDP to V United Nations Congress on Crime Prevention and Criminal Justice, Geneva, September 1975 devoted to the subject of "La Creation d'une Justice Penale Internationale". The Revue International de Droit Penal contained scholarly writings on this subject in its issues of 1928, 1935, 1945 and 1952 as well as others. The AIDP has traditionally supported the creation of an international criminal court as witnessed by the positions it has taken at its various International Congresses, and those of its distinguished members among them: Pella, Donnedieu de Vabres, Saldana, Graven, Jimenez de Asua, Setille, Cornil, Bouzat, Jescheck, Romoshkiin, Herzog, Glaser, Dautricourt, Quaintano-Rippoles, Arroneau, Mueller, de Schutter, Triffterer, Lambois, Plawski, Ferencz, Oehler, Zubkowski. Because of the numerous writings on the subject by the above-mentioned scholars and others it would be impossible to cite them all, but see Bassiouni supra note 8 "Bibliography" p. 175. For three more recent initiatives resulting in the submission of a draft statute, see the International Law Association, "Draft Statute for an International Commission of Criminal Injury" adopted by its International Criminal Law Committee in Paris, May 1979. Proceedings of the International Law Association (Belgrade Conference 1980) p. 4; the "Draft Statute for an International Criminal Court", World Peace through Law, Abidjan World Conference, August 1973 (edited by Robert K. Woetzel); and a "Draft Statute for an International Criminal Court" prepared by the Foundation for the Creation of an International Criminal Courts, see also K. de Haan "The Procedural Problems of a Permanent International Criminal Jurisdiction" in De bestraffing van inbreuken tegen het corlegs - en het humanitair recht (A. Beirlaen, S. Dockx, K. de Haan, C. Van den Wifngaert, eds., 1980) p. 191.

(i) There existed no codification of international crimes. In particular aggression[14] had not been defined and those other customary and conventional crimes were insufficiently defined, with few exceptions;

(ii) The proposed international criminal jurisdiction contemplated the exercise of its jurisdiction over all international crimes, including those as of then deemed insufficiently defined;

(iii) A "General Part" dealing with principles of responsibility and other matters usually included in a "General Part" of the criminal codes or laws of most legal systems had not been elaborated and what was proposed by the two United Nations Committees of Experts who prepared the 1951 and 1953 drafts dis not obtain sufficient consensus;

(iv) The absence of an international criminal code containing both a "General Part" and a "Special Part" (the crimes) violated the generally accepted principle nullum crimen sine lege, nulla neona sine lege; and

(v) The two drafts necessitated an amendment to the Charter of the United Nations which was impractical.

[*15] 57. In 1972, a Special Report was prepared by the Ad Hoc Working Group of Experts of the Commission on Human Rights entitled "Study Concerning the Question of Apartheid from the Point of View of International Penal Law" (E/CN.4/1075) which sets forth the basis for the creation of an international criminal jurisdiction in accordance with article V of the Apartheid Convention. No action was taken on that report and no further implementation of article V of the Apartheid Convention has been proposed until recently.

C.   Apartheid as an international crime: special issues on responsibility
58. Based on article III of the Apartheid Convention and in accordance with resolutions of the Commission on Human Rights and the Ad Hoc Group of Experts on Southern Africa, the basic principle of responsibility adopted is that of direct individual responsibility. However, this basis of responsibility is much too narrow under article III and under international criminal law.[15]
59. In so far as the Apartheid Convention declares that the conduct proscribed in article II constitutes a crime under international law, the principle of responsibility thereunder should conform to established norms which are:[16]

---

[14]   General Assembly resolution 3314 (XXIX) of 14 December 1974. See also B. Ferencz, Defining International Aggression (1975).

[15]   See Bassiouni supra note 8.

[16]   "For direct responsibility of individual conduct", "Command responsibility for acts of subordinates", "Individual responsibility for failure to act" and "Individual responsibility for participating in criminal organizatons", see the "Nuremberg Principles" supra note 4. For some general works see Komarov, "Individual Responsibility Under International Law: The Nuremberg Principles in Domestic Legal Systems:, 29 Int'l & Comp. L.Q. 21 (1980) Diritto (Penale Internazionale (Consiglio Superiore della Nagistratura, 1979); C. Lombois, Droit Penal International 1st ed. 1971, 2d ed. 1979); Green, "An International Criminal Code - Now?" 3 Dalhousie L.J. 560, 561 (1976); Dinstein, "International Criminal Law", 5 Israel Y.B. of Human Rights 55, 72 (1975); La Belgique et le Droit International Penal, B. DeSchutter ed. (1975); D. Oehler, Internationales Strafrecht (1974); Special issue 45 Revue Internationale de Droit Penal 3-4 (1974) on International Criminal Law; Triffterer in Bassiouni and Nanda, A Treatise on International Criminal Law vol. II (1974) pg. 86-96; M.C. Bassiouni and V.P. Nanda, A Treatise on Criminal Law vol. II (1973) two volumes; Munch, in Bassiouni and Nanda, A Treatise on International Criminal Law vol. I (1973) pg. 143-55; B. DeSchutter, A Bibliography on International Criminal Law (1972); S. Plawski, Etude des Principes Fondamentaux du Droit International Penal (1972); S. Glaser, Droit Penal International Conventionnel (1970); O. Triffterer, Dogimatische Untersuchungen zur Entwicklung des Materiellen Völkerstrafrechts seit Nürnberg (1966); G.O.W. Mueller and E.M. Wise, International Criminal Law (1965); V. Pella, La Guerre-Crime et les Criminels de Guerre 1964); S. Glaser, Infraction Internationale (1957); A. Quintano-Rippoles, Tratado de Derecho Penal Internacional y Internacional Penal (1956) two volumes; H.-H. Jescheck, Die Vorantlichkeit der Staatsorgane Nach Völkerstrafrecht (1952); V. Pella, La Codification du Droit Penal International (1952); N. Lavi, Il Diritto Penale Internazionale (1949); Radin, "International Crimes", 32 Iowa L. Rev. 33, 46 (1946); H. Donnedieu de Vabres, Introduction a l'Etude du Droit Penal International (1928); M. Travers, Le Droit Penal Internationale et sa Mise en Oeuvre en Temps de Paix et en Temps de Guerre (1920-22) five volumes; Meili, Lehrbuch des Internationalen Strafrechts und Strafprocessrechts (1910); Hegler, Prinzipin des Internationaled Strafrechts (1906).

(i)   Direct responsibility for individual conduct;
(ii) Command responsibility for acts of subordinates;
(iii) Individual responsibility for failure to act;
[*16](iv) Responsibility of corporate entities;
(v)   The non-applicability of the defense of superior orders (if a moral choice existed).[17]

60. While international criminal law contemplates only the punishment of individuals, the responsibility of corporate entities and that of the State can be deemed to be a quasi-criminal responsibility for which fines and punitive damages are the appropriate remedies.

61. The principle of State responsibility for wrongful conduct should also apply,[18] and the appropriate remedies would be remedial legislative and administrative action, reparations and damages.

D. Some considerations on the potential impact of creating an international penal system to prevent and punish the crime of apartheid

62. The prevention of apartheid can be accomplished through the processes of international criminal law only to the extent that the threat of punishment deters such conduct, the corollary of which is that actual imposition of punishment can be accomplished in order to achieve specific deterrence through retribution, [*17] incapacitation, and finally rehabilitation. Accordingly, he effectiveness of any penal measures depends on the machinery implementing the system and its prompt and certain operation. In that respect, an international penal system.[19]

1. Individuals in States with apartheid as policy
    (a) Present threat of punishment

63. It may be assumed that no State with apartheid as an official policy would adhere to a draft convention and protocol as proposed in the present study (Parts III and IV), and therefore no such State would be bound by its express terms. As a result, the existence of such an instrument would in itself have no effect on the amenability of persons within such a State to an international criminal process. Such States would refuse to comply with requests and orders of an international enforcement system and such refusal would leave matters as they were before the instrument came into existence. However, any individual who had committed crimes of apartheid would find it necessary as a matter of prudence to refrain from going into the territory of any State who is a party to the draft convention (Part III) and the Protocol (Part IV). The

---

[17]   See the "Nuremberg Principles", supra note 4, Y. Dinstein The Defense of Obedience to Superior Orders in International Law (1965) and Vogler "The Defense of Obedience to Superior Orders in International Criminal Law" in Bassiouni and Nanda, supra note 4.

[18]   See Yearbook of the International Law Commission, 1978, vol. II (Part Two) (United Nations publication, Sales No. E.CN.4/246 and Add.1-3) reproduced in ibid., 1971, pp. 199 et seq., citing landmark decisions of the P.C.I.J. and I.C.J. as well as arbitral decisions. See also M. Whiteman, A Digest of International Law, vols. 1 and 8 (1968); A. Verdross, Völkerrecht (5th ed. 1964); G. Balladore-Pallieri, Diritto Internazionale Publico (8th ed. 1962); C. Rousseau, Principles Generaux de Droit International Public (1953); P. Guggenheim, Traite de Droit International Public (1953); H. Kelsen, Principles of International Law (1952); L. Oppenheim, International Law, vol. 1 (Lauterpacht 8th ed. 1955); G. Schwarzenberg, International Law (3rd ed. 1957); J. Personnaz, La Reparation du Prejudice en Droit International Public (1939); C. Eagleton, The Responsibility of States in International Law (1928); C. de Visscher, La Responsabilite des Etats (1924); D. Apzilotti, Teoria Generale della Responsabilite della Stata nel Diritto Internazionale (1902), reprinted in D. Anzilotti, Corso di Diritto Internazionale (1928); K. Strupp, Handbuch des Völkerrechts - Das völkerrechtliche Delikt, vol. 3 (1920); G. Vattel, Le Droit de Gens (1887).

[19]   See A. Pagliaro, Prinipip di Diritto Penale (1980); The Criminal Justice System of the USSR (M.C. Bassiouni and V. Savitski eds.) (1979); E.R. Zaffaroni, Manuel de Derecho Penal (1979); M.C. Bassiouni, Substantive Criminal Law (1978); L. Carranca, Y Trujillo Derecho Penala Mexicano (1977); N. Hungria and H. Fragoso, Comentarios ao Condigo Penal (1977); A. Odah, Islamic Criminal Law Compared to Positive Law (in Arabic) two volumes (1977) 3rd ed.; F. Munoz Conde, Derecho Penal (1976); S. Renneberg, Strafrecht (1976); H.-H. Jescheck, Lehrbuch das Strafrecht (1975); M. Mostafa, Principes de Droit Penal des Pays Arabes (1973); R. Merla and G. Vitu, Droit Criminal (1967); a and M. Ancel and Y. Marx, Les Code Penaux Europeens, three volumes (1958).

same deterrence applies to other States with which States parties to the Draft Convention and Protocol have extradition relations and could secure the surrender to them of such a person.[20]

64. Accordingly, the chief impact of the draft convention and protocol would be to limit offenders' freedom of travel, which is a small but perceptible punishment. The greater the number of States parties to the draft convention and protocol, and the stronger the expectation that that individual's acts were known to the machinery under the draft convention and protocol, the greater the impact of the restrictions and limitations.

[*18] 65. Individuals may also be tried <u>in absentia</u>, as is theoretically possible under the draft convention and protocol and that would have the same if not a greater deterrent effect on the mobility of such persons beyond their State's boundaries. Another consideration which has negative implications on the preservation of world order is the possibility that such persons found guilty may become targets for violence or death by liberation movements or terrorist organizations or even by individuals. Such a result might serve as a deterrent, but no legal system would tolerate, much less advocate, enforcement of its judgements by lawless action, all authorities concurring that such conduct undermines the integrity of the legal system as an instrument of justice and the stability of world order.

66. Expectation of investigation and prosecution and actual commencement of an investigation for prosecution is also a deterrent, but it could also be relied upon by lawless persons or organizations as pretexts for violence.

67. Stigmatization resulting from investigation, prosecution or conviction would also be an effective remedy, particulary where world wide publicity attaches to the fact. But such factors are contrary to all theories of rehabilitation and resocialization.

    (b) <u>Future threat of punishment</u>

68. The greatest threat to individuals residing in States with <u>apartheid</u> as policy would be in the future. Policies of Stats are subject to change, and in the case of <u>apartheid</u> the policy is most kindly described as a doomed anachronism. However, offenders may view their efforts as postponing the inevitable so that they may reap the benefits of the exploitation aspects of <u>apartheid</u> as long as possible before fleeing the State. The absence of a jurisdictional basis for other States to prosecute them may leave such offenders with the impression that they cannot be punished outside their State, and it should be noted that the <u>Apartheid</u> Convention itself merely requires States parties to punish offenders according to their own rules of jurisdiction. Thus, the absence of any mechanism for exercise of international jurisdiction is a serious problem.

69. Extradition limits the possibility of evading punishment, but offenders may be optimistic about finding themselves in a State that will not hold them for extradition. Unfortunately that optimism may not be without basis. Many States would regard <u>apartheid</u> as a political offence and would refuse to extradite an offender to the State wherein the crimes were committed if the government were changed. Moreover, even States parties to the <u>Apartheid</u> Convention, which are obligated not to regard <u>apartheid</u> as a political offence, might lack a legal basis to hold such an offender until a treaty of extradition was arranged with that offender's former State, so that during the period of government change many offenders would be able to pass through even such States.

70. Under the draft convention and protocol, however, the list of places for even the most temporary asylum would shrink in relationship to the number of States parties to that Statute and the multiplier effect of their extradition relations with other non States parties. Thus, the choice of an ultimate place of asylum might be severely limited.

71. States reluctant to enforce the provisions of the <u>Apartheid</u> Convention in their national system, may find it more politically convenient and acceptable to do so by recognizing and international penal jurisdiction.

---

[20]   See B.E.H. Booth, <u>British Extradition La and Procedures</u> (1980); C. Van den Wijngaert, <u>The Political Offence Exception to Extradition</u> (1980); M.C. Bassiouni, <u>International Extradition and World Public Order</u> (1974); I. Shearer, <u>Extradition in International Law</u> (1971); T. Vogler, <u>Auslieferingsrecht und Brundgesetz</u> (1960); Bedi, <u>International Extradition</u> (1968); and A. Billot, <u>Traite de l'Extradition</u> (1874). See also M. Pisani and F. Mosconi, <u>Codice della Convenzioni di Estradizione E Di Assistenza Giudiziaria in Materia Penale</u> (1979).

[*19] 2.   Individuals in other States

72. In States not having an official policy of <u>apartheid</u> but which may be occasionally instituted may consider acts of <u>apartheid</u> either as individual perpetrators, illegal government activities, or so possible future government policy. If that State is a party to the draft convention an protocol, complaints to the Procuracy could result in their conduct's being brought to and attention of government officials, or other government officials, and that would be an effective deterrent to such activities.

73. With respect to non States parties, the draft convention and protocol permits the investigation, prosecution, adjudication and punishment of such acts irrespective of where they are committed. Thus a certain deterrent effect can be expected.

74. The independence and impartiality of the draft convention and protocol machinery, and particularly the court, are an inducement to States, whether parties or non-parties, to assist in the effective functioning of these organs, particularly where States can foresee, as in the case of the draft convention, the possible expansion of the jurisdictions of its organs to other international crimes, which is a prospect frequently hoped for by a number of responsible personalities in many States.

3.   Threat of punishment to States

75. Historically, penalties for a State's wrongful conduct can be imposed only by virtue of military domination or the coerced consent of the affected State. However, the United Nations has angered a new era and such sanctions are now within the exclusive province of the Security Council.

76. At issue here is not the resort to the Security Council for sanctions whether economic or military because that is defined by the law of the Charter of the United Nations. What is at issue is the concept of fines or reparations as a measure of punitive damages against States who engage in internationally established wrongful conduct.[21]

77. The economic impact of such fines could have an impact on the international trade of such a State and be the most effective deterrent against what is basically a crime of State policy, even though it is carried out by individuals.

78. Finally, the effect of condemnation on world public opinion, and the potential diplomatic isolation of such a State would also have serious deterrent implications.

4.   Transnational corporations

79. Surprisingly, perhaps, one of the most promising areas for deterring <u>apartheid</u> may be in connection with transnational corporations (TNCs). Because TNCs may have property in the territory of States parties to the draft convention and protocol, the threat of fines to be levied against such property may be a very real and effective [*20] deterrent. In the face of such a threat, TNCs could be forced to choose between dealing with States with a policy of <u>apartheid</u> and States parties to the draft convention and protocol.

80. One major qualification must be stated, however. Further elaboration is required before any process against TNCs could be attempted to distinguish between corporate policy that in fact aids <u>apartheid</u> and employees who may or may not be part of that decision-making process, and corporate policy that in fact defeats <u>apartheid</u>.

5.   Other considerations

81. The creation of international penal systems as proposed in the draft convention and protocol while largely dependent for their effectiveness on the co-operation and support of States parties, will none the less create a momentum of its own. World public opinion would be affected by the very establishment of any of these two alternative systems, and it would certainly be shaped by its activities. Ultimately it is not international instruments or institutions which significantly alter State or individual conduct, though they contribute to it, but it is the change in individual and social values which produces the desired result. One has only to consider that slavery has now been almost eradicated not by the force of international enforcement machinery but by the cumulative impact of measures including international instruments which brought the change in social values that was the direct cause for its quasi-eradication.[22]

---

[21]   See <u>supra</u> note 18.

[22]   See the memorandum prepared by the Secretary-General of the United Nations on the suppression of slavery (ST/SOA/4). See, too, Nanda and Bassiouni, "Slavery and the slave trade: steps towards its eradication", 12 <u>Santa Clara Law</u>, 424 (1972).

82. It should also be noted that States parties to the Apartheid Convention are bound to use their national legal system to investigate, prosecute and punish the crime of apartheid irrespective of whether there is an international penal enforcement machinery. That duty would still continue to exist even if an international penal system is established.[23]

[*21] III. DRAFT CONVENTION ON THE ESTABLISHMENT OF AN INTERNATIONAL PENAL TRIBUNAL FOR THE SUPPRESSION AND PUNISHMENT OF THE CRIME OF APARTHEID AND OTHER INTERNATIONAL CRIMES
PART I. NATURE OF THE TRIBUNAL AND ITS ORGANS AND POWERS
Article 1
PURPOSES

An International Penal Tribunal is hereby established for the specific purpose of enforcing the penal provisions of the International Convention for the Prevention and Suppression of the Crime of Apartheid, and any other international crime the States Parties may wish to include within the jurisdiction of the Tribunal by Supplemental Agreement.

Article 2
NATURE OF THE TRIBUNAL

The Tribunal shall be a permanent body, occupying facilities and performing its chief functions at the Palace of Justice in the Hague, and using as its official languages, those of the United Nations.

Article 3
ORGANS OF THE TRIBUNAL

1. The Tribunal shall consist of the following organs
   (a) The Court;
   (b) The Procuracy;
   (c) The Secretariat; and
   (d) The Standing Committee of States Parties to the Statute of the International Penal Tribunal.
2. The functions and competence of the above organs shall be as descried in Part III of this Convention.

Article 4
JURISDICTION

1. The Tribunal shall have jurisdiction over "grave breaches" of article II of the International Convention for the Prevention and Punishment of the Crime of apartheid, namely: murder; torture; cruel, inhuman, or degrading treatment or punishment; arbitrary arrest and detention; and,
2. Any other act or conduct deemed an international crime by virtue of a multilateral convention in force which declares that act or conduct to be an international crime or which requires its contracting parties to criminalize it under their national laws and to prosecute or extradite its perpetrators, provided that any party hereto who wishes the Tribunal to exercise such jurisdiction does so by virtue of a Supplemental Agreement to this Convention.
[*22] 3. The Tribunal shall have universal jurisdiction with respect to the investigation, prosecution, adjudication and punishment of persons and legal entities accused or found guilty of these crimes which are within its jurisdiction.

Article 5
COMPETENCE

1. The Tribunal shall be competent to investigate, prosecute, adjudicate and punish any person or legal entity accused or guilty of:

---

[23]   See the Report of the Group of Three established under the International Convention on the Suppression and Punishment of the Crime of Apartheid (E/CN.4/1328).

(a)   A "grave breach" of article II of the International Convention of the Suppression and Punishment of the Crime of <u>Apartheid</u> as defined in article 4, paragraph 1; and,

(b)   Any other international crime as defined in article 4, paragraph 2, of this Convention and subject to any specific provisions of a Supplemental Agreement making a crime subject to the jurisdiction of this Tribunal.

2.   The Tribunal shall, subject to the provisions of the present Convention, exercise its competence in accordance with international law whose sources are stated in article 30 of the Statute of the International Court of Justice.

3.   The Competence of the Organs of the Tribunal shall be interpreted and exercised in light of the purposes of the Tribunal as set forth in this Convention.

Article 6
SUBJECTS UPON WHOM THE TRIBUNAL SHALL EXERCISE ITS JURISDICTION

The Tribunal shall exercise its jurisdiction over natural persons and legal entities as defined in article 20.

Article 7
SANCTIONS

1.   The Court as an organ of the Tribunal shall upon entering a finding of guilty and in accordance with article 24 and standards set forth in this Convention have the power to impose the following sanctions:

(a)   Deprivation of liberty or any lesser measures of control where the person found guilty is a natural person; and,

(b)   Fines to be levied against a natural person or legal entity; and

(c)   Injunctions against natural persons or legal entities restricting them from engaging in certain conduct or activities.

2.   Sanctions shall be established by the rules of the Court and shall be published before their entry into effect. Such sanctions shall be equivalent to those penalties existing in the major criminal systems of the world for the same type of offence.

[*23] PART II. THE PENAL PROCESSES OF THE TRIBUNAL
Article 8
INITIATION OF PROCESS

1.   No criminal process shall be initiated unless a complaint is communicated to the Procuracy or originated within the Procuracy.

2.   The Investigative Division of the Procuracy shall determine whether such complaints are "manifestly unfounded" or not, and that determination shall be reported immediately to the source of the communication, if any,

3.   No complaint by a State Party to the present Convention or an Organ of the United Nations shall be deemed "manifestly unfounded". Other States and intergovernmental organizations whose complaints are determined to be "manifestly unfounded" may appeal such determinations to the Court pursuant to article 12 of this Convention.

4.   Unless otherwise directed by the Court, the Procuracy may either take no further action on "manifestly unfounded" complaints or may continue further investigation.

5.   Communications determined "not manifestly unfounded" shall be transferred together with the record of investigation to the Prosecutorial Division of the Procuracy, which shall immediately inform the accused and assume responsibility for development of the case.

6.   When a case is ready for prosecution, the Procurator shall submit it to an appropriate Chamber of the Court pursuant to article 9 of this Convention, or to the Standing Committee pursuant to Article XVII of this Convention, or to both, but if a case based on a complaint submitted by a State Party to this Convention or by an organ of the United Nations has not been presented to the Court within one year of submission to the Standing Committee the source of the complaint may request the Court to examine the case and act pursuant to article 9 of this Convention.

<u>Article 9</u>
PRE-TRIAL PROCESS

1.   The Prosecutorial Division of the Procuracy may request an appropriate Chamber of the Court pursuant to this Article of the Convention to issue orders in aid of development of a case, in particular, orders in the nature of:

 (a)   Arrest warrants;
 (b)   Subpoenas;
 (c)   Injunctions;
 (d)   Search warrants;
 (e)   Warrants for surrender of an accused so as to enable accused persons to be brought before the Court and to transit States without interference.

[*24] 2.   Requests for such orders may be granted with or without prior notice if opportunity to be heard would jeopardize the effectiveness of the requested order.

3.   All such orders shall be executed pursuant to the relevant laws of the State in which they are to be executed.

4.   The ultimate merits of a case shall not be considered pursuant to article 10 of this Convention until the case has been submitted to an appropriate Chamber of the Court, sitting in a preliminary hearing at which the accused is represented by Counsel and the Chamber, made the following determinations:

 (a)   The case is reasonably founded in fact and law;
 (b)   No prior proceedings before the Tribunal or elsewhere bar the process in accordance with the principle <u>non bis in idem</u> or fundamental notions of fairness; and
 (c)   No conditions exist that would render the adjudication unreliable or unfair.

5.   The schedule of proceedings shall be established by the appropriate Chamber in consultation with the Procuracy and Counsel for the accused with due regard to the principle of fairness to the parties and the principle of "speedy trial".

<u>Article 10</u>
ADJUDICATION

1.   Hearings on the ultimate merits of cases shall be conducted in public before a designated Chamber of the Court but deliberations of the Chamber shall be <u>in camera</u>.

2.   A Chamber may at any time dismiss a case and enter appropriately motivated orders. In case of dismissal for any reason other than on the merits, the principle <u>non bis in idem</u> shall not apply.

3.   In all proceedings a Chamber shall give equal weight to evidence and arguments presented by the Procurator and on behalf of the accused in accordance with the principle of "equality of arms" of the parties.

4.   When all evidence respecting guilt or responsibility for wrongful acts has been presented, and argued by the parties, the Chamber shall close the Hearings and retire for deliberations.

5.   The decisions of the Chambers shall be publicly announced orally, in summary or entirely, accompanied by written findings of fact and conclusions of law, or entered 30 days from the date of pronouncement of the oral decision, and any judge of that Chamber may write a separate dissenting or concurring opinion.

6.   A determination of guilt shall be deemed entered when recorded by the Secretariat, which shall communicate it forthwith to the Procuracy and the accused, but no such determination shall be regarded as effective until 30 days after the date of recording at which time the deciding Chamber may no longer modify its findings.

7.   Each chamber shall consist of three judges selected by lot, and cases shall be assigned to each Chamber by lot.

[*25] Article 11

SANCTIONING

1.   Upon a determination of guilt or responsibility, a separate hearing shall be held regarding sanctions to be imposed at which hearing evidence of mitigation and aggravation shall be introduced and argued by the parties.

2.   Other appeals from actions of Chambers may be taken before a final judgement is entered only if such actions are conclusive as to independent matters.

3.   The Procuracy may appeal questions of law in the same manner as an accused under paragraphs 1 and 2.

4.   Decisions on appeals shall be delivered in the same manner as other decisions of the Court en banc as provided in article 10, paragraphs 5 and 6, of this Convention.

5.   Decisions of the Court en banc and unappealed determinations or orders of Chambers shall be deemed final unless it is shown that:

   (a)   Evidence unknown at the time of the determination or order has been discovered, which would have had a material effect on the outcome of the said determination or order; or,

   (b)   The Court or Chamber was flagrantly misled as to the nature of matters affecting the outcome; or,

   (c)   On the face of the record the facts alleged have not been proved beyond a reasonable doubt; or,

   (d)   The facts proved do not constitute a crime within the jurisdiction of the Tribunal; or,

   (e)   Other grounds for which the Court may provide by its rules.

6.   Appealed determinations may be revised or vacated or remanded for new determination, and when vacating a determination the Court shall specify what if any non bis in idem effect shall be given to the prior proceedings.

[*26]Article 13

SANCTIONS AND SUPERVISION

1.   The Court may call upon any State Party to execute measures imposed in respect of guilt, in accordance with the laws of the said State Party.

2.   With respect to each accused determined to be guilty, a judge of the Court shall be selected by lot as supervisor of the sanction imposed.

3.   All requests to modify sanctions shall be directed in the first instance to the sanction supervising judge who may submit the request to the adjudicating chamber for modification provided such action in no way increases the sanction or conditions imposed upon the person or legal entity found guilty.

4.   Decisions of the sanction supervising judges regarding modification requests may be appealed to the Chamber which imposed the sanction, but such appeals in the Chamber's discretion need not be the subject of full hearings and detailed written decision.

5.   Nothing herein precludes the Court in accordance with its rules to suspend its sanctions or place pre-conditions to their application in accordance with its rules.

PART III. ORGANS OF THE TRIBUNAL

Article 14

THE COURT

1.   The Court shall consist of twelve judges, no more than two of whom shall be of the same nationality, who shall be elected by the Standing Committee of States Parties from nominations submitted thereto.

2.   Nominees for positions as judges shall be of distinguished experts in the fields of international criminal law or human rights and other jurists qualified to serve on the highest courts of their respective States who may be of any nationality or have no nationality.

3.   Judges shall be elected by secret ballot and the Standing Committee of States Parties shall strive to elect persons representing diverse backgrounds and experience with due regard to representation of the major legal and cultural systems of the world.

4.   Elections shall be co-ordinated by the Secretariat under the supervision of the presiding officer of the Standing Committee of States Parties and shall be held whenever one or more vacancies exist on the Court.

5.   Judges shall be elected for the following terms: four judges for four-year terms, four judges for six-year terms, and four judges for eight-year terms. Judges may be re-elected for any term at that time available.

6.   No judge shall perform any public function in any State.

7.   Judges shall have no other occupation or business than that of judge of this Court. However, judges may engage in scholarly activity for remuneration provided such activity in no way interferes with their impartiality and appearance of impartiality.

[*27] 8.   A judge shall perform no function in the Tribunal with respect to any matter in which he may have had any involvement prior to his election to this Court.

9.   A judge may withdraw from any matter at his discretion, or be excused by a two-thirds majority of the judges of the Court for reasons of conflict of interest.

10.   Any judge who is unable or unwilling to continue to perform functions under this statute may resign. A judge may be removed for incapacity to fulfill his functions by a unanimous vote of the other judges of the Court.

11.   Except with respect to judges who have been removed, judges may continue in office beyond their term until their replacement are prepared to assume the office and shall continue in office to complete work on any pending matter in which they were involved even beyond their term.

12.   The judges of the Court shall elect a president, vice-president and such other officers as they deem appropriate. The president shall serve for a term of two years.

13.   Judges of the Court shall perform their judicial functions in three capacities:
    (a)   Sitting with other judges as the Court en banc;
    (b)   Sitting in panels of three on a rotational basis in Chambers; and
    (c)   Sitting individually as Supervisors of sanctions.

14.   The salary of judges shall be equal to that of the judges of the International Court of Justice.

15.   The Court en banc shall subject to the provisions of this Convention, adopt Rules governing procedures before its Chambers and the Court en banc, and provide for establishment and rotation of Chambers.

16.   The Court en banc shall announce its decisions orally in full or in summary, accompanied by written findings of fact and conclusions of law at the time of the oral decision or within thirty days thereafter, and any judge so desiring may issue a concurring or dissenting opinion.

17.   Decisions and orders of the Court en banc are effective upon certification of the written opinion by the Secretariat, which is to communicate such certified opinion to parties forthwith.

18.   The Court en banc may within thirty days of the certification of the judgement take its decisions without notice.

19.   No actions taken by the Tribunal may be contested in any other forum than before the Court en banc, and in the event that any effort to do so is made, the Procurator shall be competent to appear on behalf of the Tribunal and in the name of all States Parties of this Convention to oppose such action.

20.   States Parties agree to enforce the final judgements of the Court in accordance with the provisions of this Convention.

[*28] Article 15
THE PROCURACY

1.   The Procuracy shall have as its chief officer the Procurator and shall consist of an administrative division, an investigative division and a prosecutorial division, each headed by a deputy procurator, and employing appropriate staff.

2.   The Procurator shall be elected by the Standing Committee of States Parties from a list of at least three nominations submitted by members of the Standing Committee, and shall serve for a renewable term of six years, barring resignation or removal by two-thirds vote of the judges of the Court en banc for incompetence, conflict of interest, or manifest disregard for the provisions of this Convention or material Rules of the Tribunal.

3.   The Procurator's salary shall be the same as that of the judges.

4.   The deputy procurators and all other members of the Procurator's staff shall be named and removed by the Procurator at will.

Article 15
THE SECRETARIAT

1.   The Secretariat shall have as its chief officer the Secretary, who shall be elected by a majority of the Court sitting en banc and serve for a renewable term of six years barring resignation or removal by a majority of the Court sitting en banc for incompetence, conflict of interest or manifest disregard of the Provisions of this Convention or material Rules of the Tribunal.

2.   The Secretary's salary shall be equivalent to that of the judges.

3.   The Secretariat shall employ such staff as appropriate to perform its chancery and administrative functions and such other functions as may be assigned to it by the Court that are consistent with the provisions of this Convention and the rules of the Tribunal.

4.   In particular, the Secretary shall twice each year prepare:
(a)   Budget requests for each of the organs of the Tribunal; and
(b)   Make and publish an annual report on the activities of each organ of the Tribunal.

5.   The Secretariat staff shall be appointed and removed by the Secretary at will.

6.   An annual summary of investigations undertaken by the Procuracy shall be presented to the Secretariat for publication, but certain investigations may be omitted where secrecy is necessary, provided that a confidential report of the investigation is made to the Court and to the Standing Committee and filed separately with the Secretariat, but either the Court or the Standing may order by majority vote that the report be made public.

[*29] 7.   Upon request by the Procuracy, or by a party to a case presented for adjudication to a Chamber of the Court, the Standing Committee may be seized with a mediation and conciliation petition. In that case the Standing Committee shall within 60 days decide on granting or denying the petition from which there is no appeal. In the event that the Standing Committee grants the petition, Court proceedings shall be stayed until such time as the Standing Committee concludes its mediation and conciliation efforts, but not for more than one year except by stipulation of the Parties and with the consent of the Court.

Article 18
GENERAL INSTITUTIONAL MATTERS

1.   Each of the organs of the Tribunal shall formulate and publish its own rules in accordance with the standards set forth in Part IV to regulate its functions under this Convention, but the rules of the Procuracy and Secretariat shall be subject to approval by a majority of the Court en banc.

2.   The Procurator shall participate without a vote in formulating the rules of the Court and of the Secretariat. The President of the Court shall participate without a vote in formulating the rules of the Procuracy and of the Secretariat.

[*30] 3.   Except to the extent of the adopted rules, procedures of the Court shall be those of the International Court of Justice and those of the Secretariat shall be as for the Registrar of the International Court of Justice.

4.   Each of the Organs of the Tribunal shall co-operate with the Secretariat in formulating its budget request and such budget requests shall be presented to the Court en banc for modification or approval, subject to adoption or rejection in their entirety by the Standing Committee.

5.   The Judges, the Procurator and Deputy Procurators and their assistants and the Secretary shall be deemed officers of the Court, as well as Counsels appearing in a given case, and they shall enjoy immunity from legal processes of States with respect to the performance of their official duties.

6.   No officer of the Court other than counsel in a given case shall perform any function under this Convention without having first made a public, solemn declaration of impartiality and adherence to this Convention and the rules of the Tribunal.

PART IV. TRIBUNAL STANDARDS
Article 19
STANDARDS FOR RULES AND PROCEDURES

1.   In all proceedings of the Tribunal and in the formulation of any rules by any of its organs, the accused shall be entitled to those fundamental human rights enunciated in the Universal Declaration of Human Rights and the International Covenant on Civil and Political Rights, which for these purposes are:

(a)   The presumption of innocence

The presumption of innocence is a fundamental principle of criminal justice. It includes inter alia:

1.   No one may be convicted or formally declared guilty unless he has been tried according to law in a fair trial;

2.   No criminal punishment or any equivalent sanction may be imposed upon a person unless he has been proved guilty in accordance with the law.

3.   No person shall be required to prove his innocence;

4.   In case of doubt the decision must be in favour of the accused.

[*31] (b)   Procedural rights ("equality of arms")

The accused shall have substantial parity in proceedings and procedures and shall be given effective ways to challenge any and all evidences produced by the prosecution and to present evidence in defence of the accusation.

(c)   Speedy trial

1.   Criminal proceedings should be established for each stage of the proceedings and should not e extended without reason by the appropriate Chamber of the Court.

2.   Complex cases involving multiple defendants or charges may be severed by the appropriate Chamber of the Court when it is deemed in the interest of fairness to the parties and justice to the case.

3.   Administrative or disciplinary measures shall be taken against officials of the Tribunal and deliberately or by negligence violate the provisions of this Convention and the rules of this Tribunal.

(d)   Evidentiary questions

1.   All procedures and methods for securing evidence which interfere with internationally guaranteed human rights shall be in accordance with the standards of justice set forth in this Convention and in the rules of the Tribunal.

2.   The admissibility of evidence of criminal proceedings must take into account the integrity of the judicial system, the rights of the defence, the interests of the victim and the interests of the world community.

3.   Evidence obtained directly or indirectly by illegal means which constitute a serious violation of internationally protected human rights, violate the provisions of this Convention, and Rules of this Tribunal shall hold this inadmissible.

4.   Evidence obtained by means of lesser violations shall be admissible only subject to the judicial discretion of the Court on the basis of the veracity of the evidence presented and the values and interests involved.

(e)   The right to remain silent

Anyone accused of a criminal violation has the right to remain silent and must be informed of this right.

[*32] (f)   Assistance of counsel

1.   Anyone suspected of a criminal violation has the right to defend himself and to competent legal assistance of his own choosing at all stages of the proceedings.

2.   Counsel shall be appointed ex officio whenever the accused by reason of personal conditions is unable to assume his own defence or to provide for such defence, and in those complex or grave cases where in the best interest of justice and in the interest of the defence such counsel is deemed necessary by the Court.

3.   Appointed counsel shall receive reasonable compensation from the Tribunal whenever the accused is financially unable to do so.

4.   Anyone arrested or detained shall be promptly brought before a judge of the Court and shall be informed of the charges against him: after appearance before such judicial authority he may be returned

to the custody of the arresting authority but he shall be subject to the jurisdiction of the Court even when in the custody of a State Party.

[*33]   5.   Preliminary or provisional arrest and detention shall take place only whenever necessary and as much as possible should be reduced to a minimum of cases and to the minimum of time.

6.   Preliminary or provisional detention shall not be compulsory but subject to the determination of the Court and in accordance with its rules.

7.   Alternative measures to detention shall be used whenever possible and include inter alia:
    Bail;
    Limitations of freedom of movement;
    Imposition of other restrictions.

8.   No detainee shall be subject to rehabilitative measures prior to conviction unless he freely consents thereto.

9.   No administrative preventive detention shall be permissible as part of any criminal proceedings.

10.   Any period of detention prior to conviction shall be credited toward the fulfilment of the sanction imposed by the Court.

11.   Anyone who has been the victim of illegal or unjustified detention shall have the right to compensation.

(h)   Rights and interests of the victim
The rights and interests of the victim of a crime shall be protected and in particular:

1.   The opportunity to participate in the criminal proceedings;

2.   The right to protect his civil interests;

3.   Due regard shall be given in formulation of Rules of the Organs of the Tribunal to the principle of non bis in idem, but a seemingly duplicative prosecution shall not be barred provided that the record in the prior proceeding is taken into account along with any prior measures in respect of guilt of the accused;

4.   Arrest and detention shall be in conformity with the Standard Minimum Rules for the Treatment of Prisoners and the principles on freedom from arbitrary arrest and detention of the United Nations;

5.   Maximum flexibility regarding restrictive measures should be encouraged, including use of such mechanisms as house arrest, work release and bail, and credit shall be given for any pre-conviction restrictions to an accused;

[*34]   6.   The Tribunal shall include all of the above in the formulation of its rules of practice and procedures which shall be effective upon promulgation.

7.   No proceedings before the Tribunal shall commence prior to the promulgation of the Rules of practice and procedures of the Court, the Procuracy and the Secretariat.

PART V. PRINCIPLES OF ACCOUNTABILITY (PROVISIONS IN THE NATURE OF A GENERAL PART)
Article 20
DEFINITIONS

1.   An international crime is any offence arising out of the provisions of this Statute and any supplemental agreement thereto as defined in Article 4.

2.   A State is an international legal entity defined under international law.

(a)   This term is used without prejudice to questions of recognition or membership in the United Nations.

(b)   This term also includes a group of States acting collectively.

3.   The words "person" or "individual" for the purposes of this Convention are used interchangeably and each one of them refers to a physical human being alive.

4.   For the purposes of this Convention, the words "group" and "organization" are interchangeable. A group consists of more than one person, acting in concert with respect to the performance of a particular act.

5.   The term "entity" is used herein to include groups, organs of State, States or groups of States.
6.   Participation in group action is a person's conduct which directly contributes to the group's ability to perform a given act or which directly influences the decision of the group to perform a given act.
7.   A person commits solicitation when, with the intent that an offence be committed, he instigates, commands, encourages or requests another to commit that offence.
8.   A person commits conspiracy when, with intent to commit a specific offence, he agrees with another to the commission of that offence and one of the members of the conspiracy commits an overt act in furtherance of the agreement.
9.   A person commits an attempt when, with the intent to commit a specific offence, he engages in unequivocal and direct conduct which constitutes a substantial step toward the commission of that offence and which if not for a fortuitous event or misapprehension of the actor, would result in the completion of the crime.
[*35] 10.   A person in authority is a person who has legal authority under domestic law or a person who by virtue of the power structure of a group is deemed to be in command or has the power to command others, and to whom obedience is generally expected.
11.   Omission by a State, group or organization or failure to act occurs whenever a person in authority having power to act and having knowledge of the facts requiring action fails to take reasonable measures to prevent, or terminate and commission of a crime or to apprehend, or prosecute, or punish any person who has or may have committed a crime. Omission by an individual is conscious failure to act in accordance with a pre-existing legal obligation.
12.   The masculine "he" used throughout this article refers equally to the feminine "she".

Article 21
RESPONSIBILITY

1.   A person is criminally responsible under this article when he reaches the age of 18.
2.   Direct personal responsibility
    (a)   A person who commits or attempts to commit a crime is responsible for it and criminally punishable under article 24.
    (b)   A person who conspires with another or solicits another to commit a crime as defined is criminally responsible for it and criminally punishable.
    (c)   A person who commits a crime is not relieved from responsibility by the sole fact that he was acting in the capacity of Head of State, responsible Government official, acting for or on behalf of a State, or pursuant to "superior orders" except where the provisions of article 24, paragraph 6 are applicable.
3.   Responsibility for the conduct of others
    (a)   A person is responsible for the conduct of another if, before, during or after the commission of a crime, and with the intent to promote or facilitate the commission of a crime, he aids, abets, solicits, conspires or attempts to aid another person in the planning, perpetration or concealment of the crime, or facilitates the concealment or escape of a perpetrator.
    (b)   A person is not responsible for the acts of others if hat individual is a victim of the crime, or when, before the commission of the crime, that person terminates his efforts of participation as described in paragraph 3(a) and such termination wholly deprives others of his efforts and of their effectiveness or if such a person gives timely warning and advice to appropriate government authorities.
    (c)   The vicarious responsibility for the conduct of another under this section is not dependent upon the conviction of a person accused as a principal.
[*36] (d)   The person is responsible for the conduct of another with respect to any crime committed in furtherance of a solicitation, conspiracy and for those crimes which are reasonably foreseeable to be committed by others in furtherance of a common criminal scheme, design or plan.
4.   Collective responsibility
    (a)   A group or organization other than a State or an organ of a State is collectively responsible for its acts, irrespective of the responsibility of its members.
    (b)   A person is responsible for crimes committed by a group or organization, if he knew of or could reasonably foresee the commission of such crime and remained a member thereof.

5.   Responsibility of persons in authority
     (a)   A person in authority in a State, group or organization, if he knew of or could reasonably foresee the commission of such crime and remained a member thereof.
6.   State responsibility
     (a)   Conduct for which States are responsible
          1.   A State is responsible for any crime committed on its behalf, behest or benefit by a person in authority, regardless of whether such acts are deemed lawful under its municipal law.
          2.   Conduct is attributed to a State if i is performed by persons or groups acting in their official capacity, who under the domestic law of that State possess the authority to make decisions for the State or any political subdivision thereof or possess the status of organs, agencies or instrumentalities of that State or a political subdivision thereof.
          3.   Conduct outside the scope of authority of any of the entities listed in this article is attributed to the State.
     (b)   State responsibility for failure to act
          1.   Failure to act by a State in accordance with its obligation under this Code shall constitute an international offence.
          2.   Any revolutionary movement which establishes a State or overthrows a Government is responsible in the new State or new Government to prosecute or extradite any individual within such group or any individual who has been omitted from the group for any international crime. Failure to do so shall constitute a basis for State responsibility.

[*37]Article 22
ELEMENTS OF AN INTERNATIONAL CRIME

7.   Definition
     (a)   An international crime shall contain four elements: a material element; a mental element; a causal element; and, harm, as defined in paragraphs 2 through 5 inclusive, except when in the definition of a given crime those requirements are altered.
8.   Material element
     (a)   Any voluntary act or omission which constitutes part of a crime as defined in article 4 will constitute the material element.
9.   Causal element
     (a)   Conduct is the cause of a result when it is an antecedent but for which the result in question would not have occurred, and that the result was a foreseeable consequence of such conduct.
10.   Harm
     (a)   The element of harm shall depend upon the definition of the crime, except where no harm is needed in the definition of the crime.
11.   Mental element
     (a)   The mental element of an offence at the time of the commission of the material element shall consist of either intent, knowledge, or recklessness, unless the definition of the crime specifies any of these three.
     (b)   A person "intends" to accomplish a result or engage in conduct described by the law defining the offence, when his conscious objective or purpose is to accomplish that result or engage in that conduct.
     (c)   A person "knows" or acts "knowingly" when he is consciously aware of the attendant circumstances of his conduct or of the substantial probability of existing facts and circumstances likely to produce a given result.
     (d)   A person is reckless or acts recklessly when he consciously disregards a substantial and unreasonable risk that a likely result would be a foreseeable consequence of such conduct.

Article 23
IMMUNITIES

1.   For purpose of this article, no person shall enjoy any international immunity except that Head of State, Head of Government, official representative of a State having diplomatic status, employees of international

organizations and the members [*38] of the families and staffs of the above-enumerated persons shall be exempt and immune from the criminal process of all States other than their own and this International Criminal Tribunal, provided that in the event of the commission of a crime as defined herein, the State party whose national is entitled to the immunity and exemption stated herein shall undertake to investigate, prosecute and punish the allegation or crime charged.

2. Any State may waive this immunity on behalf of its nationals without prejudice to its interests in favour of any other State.

3. Any person who falls into any of the categories of paragraph 1 of this article may specifically waive that immunity with the consent of the State of which he is a national or of the international organization by which he is employed without prejudice to that State or organization.

4. A person who no longer has the privileges of the positions covered by immunity in paragraph 1 of this article may no longer benefit from said immunity except with respect to those acts committed or alleged to have been committed while that person held the position that granted immunity.

Article 24
PENALTIES

1. Punishability

(a) All crimes defined in this article are punishable in proportion to the seriousness of the violation, to the harm threatened or caused, and to the degree of the responsibility of the individual actor in accordance with a schedule to be promulgated by rules of the Tribunal before it exercises its jurisdiction in a given case.

2. Penalties for individuals

(a) Penalties for persons who have been convicted of the commission of a crime shall consist of imprisonment or such alternatives to imprisonment or fines as promulgated by the International Criminal Court.

3. Penalties for a group or organization

(a) Penalties for crimes for which groups are collectively responsible under article 21, paragraph 4, shall consist of fines or other sanctions established in accordance with the principle of proportionality set forth in paragraph 1 of this article and as promulgated by the rules of the Court.

(b) Fines shall be collectively levied against the assets of group and individual participants and enforced by the States Parties wherein such assets may be found.

4. Penalties for States

(a) Penalties for States which are responsible for crimes shall consist of fines assessed on the basis of proportionality as set forth in section 1 of this article, without prejudice to the duties or reparations and civil damages.

[*39](b) Such fines shall be due from a State, provided that they do not critically impair the economic viability of the State.

(c) The determination and assessment of fines against a State shall be made by the Court and the enforcement of such fines shall be by and through the United Nations.

(d) The provisions of this article are without prejudice to the rights and duties of the United Nations to impose sanctions against a State as provided for in the Charter of the United Nations.

(e) Special remedies

Nothing in this article shall prevent the International Criminal Court to rely on its inherent judicial power to order a State to cease and desist from a given activity which is an international crime or to order by injunctions the correction of previous violations and prevent their reoccurrence.

5. Multiple crimes and penalties

(a) The Court may with respect to a single criminal transaction involving the commission of more than one crime all of which are related and are based on substantially the same facts impose a single penalty with discretion concerning aggravating and mitigating circumstances as may be found by the Court.

6. Mitigation of punishment

(a) A person acting pursuant to superior orders may present such a claim in mitigation of punishment.

(b)   Subject to the defence of double jeopardy a person who was sentenced in one State for substantially the same criminal conduct and resentenced by the Court shall receive credit for any part of a sentence already executed.

(c)   The Court may take into account any mitigating fact such as imperfect or incomplete defences stated in article 25.

Article 25
EXONERATION

1.   Definition

(a)   A person shall be exonerated from responsibility arising under this Convention if in the commission of an act which constitutes a crime any of the defences stated in paragraphs 2 through 11 inclusive is applicable.

2.   Self-Defence (Individual)

Self-defence consists in the use of force against another person which may otherwise constitute a crime when and to the extent that he reasonably believes that such force is necessary to defend himself or anyone else against such other person's imminent use of unlawful force, and in a manner which is reasonably proportionate to the threat or use of force.

[*40] 3.   Necessity

(a)   A person acts under necessity when by reason of circumstances beyond his control, likely to create a private or public harm, he engages in conduct which may otherwise constitute a crime which he reasonably believes to be necessary to avoid the imminent greater harm likely to be produced by such circumstances, but not likely to produce death.

4.   Coercion

(a)   A person acts under coercion when he is compelled by another under an imminent threat of force or use of force directed against him or another, to engage in conduct which may otherwise constitute a crime which he would not otherwise engage in, provided that such coerced conduct does not produce a greater harm than the one likely to be suffered and is not likely to produce death.

5.   Obedience to superior orders

(a)   A person acting in obedience to superior orders shall be exonerated from responsibility for his conduct which may otherwise constitute a crime or omission unless, under the circumstances, he knew that such act would constitute a crime.

6.   Refusal to obey a superior order which constitutes a crime

(a)   No person shall be punished for refusing to obey an order of his Government or his superior which, if carried out, would constitute a crime.

7.   Mistake of law or fact

(a)   A mistake of law or a mistake of fact shall be a defence if it negates the mental element required by the crime charged provided that said mistake is not inconsistent with the nature of the crime or its elements.

8.   Double jeopardy

(a)   The Court may not retry or resentence the same individual for the same conduct irrespective of what the crime or charge may be.

(b)   In the event a person has been tried by the national courts of a State party he could be retried for the same conduct by the Court but he shall receive credit for a sentence rendered by a national criminal court and executed by that State or any other State.

(c)   No individual who has been tried and convicted or acquitted on the merits by the Court shall be retried or resentenced by the domestic court of any State party.

(d)   Amnesty or pardon by any State shall not constitute a bar to adjudication before the Court and shall not be deemed to fall within the defence of double jeopardy.

[*41] 9.   Insanity

(a)   A person is legally insane when at the time of the conduct which constitutes a crime, he suffers from a mental disease or mental defect, resulting in his lacking substantial capacity either to appreciate the criminality of his conduct or to conform his conduct to the requirements of the law, and such mental disease or mental defect caused the conduct constituting a crime.

10.   Intoxication or drugged condition

(a)   A person is intoxicated or in a drugged condition when under the effect of alcohol or drugs at the time of the conduct which would otherwise constitute a crime he is unable to formulate the mental element required by the said crime.

(b)   Such a defence shall not apply to a person who engages in voluntary intoxication with the pre-existing intent to commit a crime.

(c)   With respect to crimes requiring the mental element of recklessness, voluntary intoxication shall not constitute a defence.

11.   Renunciation

(a)   It shall be a defence to the crimes of attempt, conspiracy and solicitation if a person renounces or voluntarily withdraws from the commission of the said crimes before any harm occurs and if he has engaged in any individual activity by doing any of the following:

(i)   Wholly deprives others from the use or benefit of his participation in the commission of the crime;

(ii)   Notifies law enforcement officials in time in order to prevent the occurrence or the commission of the crime.

Article 26
STATUTE OF LIMITATION

1.   Duration

(a)   No prosecution or punishment by the Court of an international crime shall be barred by a period of limitations of lesser duration than the maximum penalty ascribed to the crime in question in the laws of the State where the crimes was committed.

(b)   The period of limitation shall commence at the time that legal proceedings under the provisions of this Convention may commence but shall not apply to any period during which a person is escaping or evading appearance before the appropriate authorities. It is interrupted by the arrest of the accused but shall recommence ab initio if the accused or convicted person escapes and in no case shall it run for a period which would be longer than twice the original period of limitation.

(c)   In the case of State responsibility, the period of limitation for commencing any action before the Court shall be measured with reference to the acts of those State officials whose conduct has implicated the responsibility of the State in question.

[*42] PART VI. DUTIES OF STATES PARTIES
Article 27
GENERAL PRINCIPLES

1.   States Parties shall surrender upon request of the Court any individual where it appears that there are reasonable grounds to believe that such a person has committed an international crime within the jurisdiction of the Tribunal.

2.   States Parties shall provide the Court with all means of judicial assistance and co-operation, including but not limited to letters rogatory, service of writs, assistance in securing testimony and evidence, transmittal of records and transfer of proceedings.

3.   States Parties shall recognize the judgements of the Court and execute provisions of such judgements in accordance with their national laws.

4.   In the event the Court does not have detentional facilities under its direct control, States Parties will honour requests from the Court to execute its sentences in accordance with their own correctional systems, but subject to continuing jurisdiction of the Court over the transferred offender.

5.   States Parties may receive requests for transfers of offenders.

6.   States Parties to this Convention undertake to provide co-operation to organs of the Tribunal in accordance with the terms of this Convention and the purpose of the Tribunal, and in particular to:

(a) Provide financial support to the Tribunal in the proportion they would be assessed under contemporaneous General Assembly apportionment established in article 17 of the Charter of the United Nations, payments being due within six months of the adoption of a budget by the Standing Committee; and

(b) Budgetary needs of the Tribunal shall be computed after taking into account income from voluntary contributions and fines collected by the Tribunal.

Article 28
SURRENDER OF ACCUSED PERSONS

1. States Parties shall surrender upon a request of the Court any individual sought to appear before the Court for any proceeding arising out of the Court's jurisdiction provided that the Court's request shall be based on reasonable grounds to believe that the person sought has committed a violation of this Code.

2. The following acts shall not be a bar to surrender a person to the International Penal Tribunal for any acts constituting a crime:

(a) That person sought to be surrendered claims or the State wherein he may be located claims that the act falls within the meaning of the "political offence exception";

(b) That the individual is a national of the requested State;

[*43](c) That the requested State otherwise imposes certain conditions or restriction to the practice of extradition to and from other States.

3. Procedures regulating such transfers shall be determined by the rules of the Court subject to the laws of the requested State.

Article 29
JUDICIAL ASSISTANCE AND OTHER FORMS OF CO-OPERATION

1. The States Parties shall provide the International Penal Tribunal with all means of judicial assistance and co-operation including but not limited to letters rogatory, service of writs, assistance in securing testimony and evidence, transmittal of records, transfer of proceedings where applicable.

2. The procedures for such judicial assistance and other forms of co-operation shall be determined by the Court's rules of practice.

Article 30
RECOGNITION OF THE JUDGEMENTS OF THE
INTERNATIONAL PENAL TRIBUNAL

1. The States Parties agree to recognize the judgements of the Court and to execute its provisions. For the purposes of double jeopardy and evidentiary matters the International Penal Tribunal shall recognize the sanctions of other States in accordance with the provisions of article 24.

2. The Court's rules of practice shall govern the recognition of the judgements of the Court by States Parties and those of the other States by the Court.

Article 31
TRANSFER OF OFFENDERS AND EXECUTION OF SENTENCES

1. In the event the International Penal Tribunal does not have detentional facilities under its direct control it may request a State Party to execute the sentence in accordance with that Party's correctional system and in that case the Court shall continue to exercise jurisdiction over the offender including his transfer to another State or facility.

2. In the event the International Penal Tribunal has placed an offender in its own detention facilities, this person may by agreement be transferred for detention to his country of origin subject to the Court's jurisdiction.

3. The Court's rule of practice shall determine the basis and condition of the transfer of offenders and the execution of sentences.

[*44] PART VII. TREATY PROVISIONS
Article 32
ENTRY INTO FORCE
1. This Convention is open for signature to all States, including after its entry into force.
2. This Convention is subject to ratification, instruments of ratification being deposited with the Secretary-General of the United Nations.
3. Accession to this Convention shall be effected by deposit of an instrument of accession with the Secretary-General of the United Nations.
4. This Convention shall enter into force on the thirtieth day after the deposit of the sixth instrument of ratification or accession, and for States thereafter ratifying or acceding to this Convention, on the thirtieth day after deposit of the applicable instrument.
5. The Secretary-General of the United Nations shall inform all signatory States of:
   (a) All signatures, ratifications, accessions and reservations to this Convention; and
   (b) The date of entry into force of this Convention.
6. This Convention, of which the Arabic, Chinese, English, French, Spanish and Russian texts are equally authentic, shall be deposited in the archives of the United Nations and copies thereof shall be transmitted to all signatories.

Article 33
RESERVATIONS
1. States may make any reservations to this Convention but shall not be deemed States Parties for the purposes of representation in the Standing Committee if the reservation is as to a material aspect of the Tribunal's jurisdiction, competence and the effects of its judgements.
2. The Secretary-General shall keep separate count of signatories making reservations not in conformity of paragraph 1 of this article.

Article 34
INITIAL IMPLEMENTAL STEPS
1. Upon entry into force of this Convention, the Secretary-General of the United Nations shall call the first meeting of the Standing Committee, and shall preside over that meeting until a presiding officer is chosen.
[*45]2. The Standing Committee shall undertake as its first order of business measures toward election of judges of the Court.

Article 35
AMENDMENTS
1. The Convention may at any time be amended by a vote of three-fourths of the members of the Standing Committee, subject to ratification of such amendments by the same number of States Parties represented in the Standing Committee.
2. Upon petition by a State Party to the Standing Committee the jurisdiction of the Court may be expanded to include additional crimes or classes of offenders and measures in respect of guilt when this is sought by a State capable of exercising compulsory process upon the accused; and this may be on either an ad hoc or permanent basis and shall be embodied in a supplemental agreement between the requesting State and the presiding officers of the Standing Committee acting for and on behalf of the said Standing Committee.

[*46] COMMENTARY
DRAFT CONVENTION ON THE ESTABLISHMENT OF AN
INTERNATIONAL PENAL TRIBUNAL FOR THE SUPPRESSION AND
PUNISHMENT OF THE CRIME OF <u>APARTHEID</u> AND OTHER
INTERNATIONAL CRIMES

General Observations

The International Convention on the Suppression and Punishment of the Crime of <u>Apartheid</u> (hereinafter referred to as <u>Apartheid</u> Convention) in article V is the only international convention which specifically contemplates an "international penal tribunal." No other international convention, which has as its objective to criminalize a certain conduct, contains a similar requirement. In fact only the Convention on the Protection and Punishment of Genocide incidentally recognizes the eventual jurisdiction of an International Criminal Court. The introductory notes to this study, seek to retrace the history of the creation of an International Criminal Court and cite appropriate authorities. It remains, however, that the only international legislative authority for an International Penal Tribunal is the <u>Apartheid</u> Convention. Consequently, this draft Convention relies on this legislative basis as its authoritative source. Thus, having secured an international legislative basis, nothing precludes the States parties to this draft Convention from enlarging upon its jurisdiction by a device referred to in this draft Convention as "Supplemental Agreement" in order to permit the International Penal Tribunal to investigate, prosecute, adjudicate and punish other conventional international crimes.

The approach, though characterizable as "direct enforcement model" [See M.C. Bassiouni, <u>International Criminal Law: A Draft International Criminal code</u> (1980)] meaning the existence of an international system for the investigation, prosecution, adjudication and punishment of international crimes, is nevertheless dependant upon States parties for substantial aspects of its functioning. Thus there is in this approach still much of the "indirect enforcement model" which characterizes contemporary international criminal law in that States assume certain international duties which they enforce through their national systems. In that respect the enforcement mechanisms of the International Penal Tribunal rely on the "indirect enforcement model." Such an approach by necessity must not only rely on the voluntary compliance of States, but must also accept the inherent differences of national legal systems through which enforcement of the Tribunal's functions and orders are to be channelled.

The Court and the investigative and prosecutorial functions are internationally institutionalized, as is contemplated by the 1979 International Law Association Draft Statute of an International Criminal Court and its 1978 Draft Statute for an International Commission of Criminal Inquiry. Such institutional mechanisms solve some problems, but no others due to the absence of an international legislative apparatus.

To remedy this situation a quasi-legislative body is created in the form of the "Standing Committee of States Parties" which is given policy and administrative functions. Furthermore, a rule-making power is given to the organs of the Tribunal subject to certain "standards" of international fairness embodied in the draft Convention.

[*47] The administrative needs of the Court are met by a Secretariat, which also provides support to the other organs of the Tribunal and serves as a vehicle for assuring that record-keeping and registry functions as well as other requirements essential to fairness and effectiveness are met.

In view of the conceptual framework chosen and outlined above, an appropriate organizational approach was adopted in the formulation of the sequence of the provisions of the draft Convention:

Part I: Nature of the Tribunal and its organs and powers

    Article 1 Purposes
    Article 2 Nature of the Tribunal
    Article 3 Organs of the Tribunal
    Article 4 Jurisdiction
    Article 5 Competence
    Article 6 Subjects upon whom the Tribunal shall Exercise its jurisdiction
    Article 7 Sanctions

PART I: NATURE OF THE TRIBUNAL AND ITS ORGANS AND POWERS

This text relies in part on article I of the Revised draft statute for an international criminal court (A/2645), prepared by the United Nations 1953 Committee on International Criminal Jurisdiction (the Geneva Committee) hereinafter referred to as the 1953 Geneva Committee draft and the draft statute of an international criminal court of the International Law Association (ILA), of May 1979, in proceedings of the International Law Association's Belgrade Conference, 1980, p. 11, hereinafter referred to as 1979 ILA Draft.

Article 1 - Purposes. Establishes an International Penal Tribunal which is to be a new international legal institution consisting of several organs discussed in article 3 below. The legislative authority of the Tribunal and, of course, all of its organs is predicated on Article V of the Apartheid Convention. But this draft Convention provides States parties with the opportunity to include, by Supplemental Agreement, within the jurisdiction of the Court other international crimes which are defined in article 4, paragraph 2.

Article 2 - Nature of the Tribunal. Considers the Tribunal as a newly created institution and in order to minimize logistical problems the suggested location is the Palace of Justice in The Hague since it is already established and equipped as an international judicial body. The official languages are those of the United Nations which represent a recognized world consensus.

Article 3 - Organs of the Tribunal. Establishes four bodies with separate functions and purposes which are described throughout Part II in the allocation of their respective duties in connection with the penal processes but which are more adequately described in Part II though that Part deals more with the institutional and operational aspects of these organs. It is important at this juncture to conceptualize the inter-relationship of these organs which are, with respect to the Court, the Procuracy and the Secretariat, very similar to the traditional organs of the national penal systems of most countries of the world. Clearly an attempt has been made to integrate different institutional concepts which are represented by the major criminal justice systems of the world (see Bassiouni, "A Survey of Major Criminal Justice Systems of the World" in Handbook of Criminology ed. D. Glaser (1974)). In effect, the Court as an organ of the Tribunal and its functions does not differ from their traditional role in any legal system. The distinguishing characteristics pertaining to the role of the judges and the degree of their [*49] discretion in the conduct of the proceedings are left to the formulation of the rules of the Court which are to be promulgated as specified in article 18 and subject to those minimum standards of fairness embodied in international instruments for the protection of human rights which are stated in Part IV.

The Procuracy is a combination of the Soviet Union and Eastern European Socialist systems (see M.C. Bassiouni and V. Savitski, The Criminal Justice System of the USSR (1979); the judge of instruction in the Romanist-Civilist system (M. Ancel and Y. Marx, Les Code Penaux Europeens, three volumes (1958)) and the Common Law system's prosecutor (Archbold Pleading, Evidence and Practice in Criminal Cases (39th ed.) S. Mitchell ed. (1976) and Y. Kamisar, W. LaFave, J. Israel, Modern Criminal Procedure (1980)). In balance, there is more emphasis toward the Romanist-Civilist tradition than to the Common Law tradition since it would be more consonant with the need for effective investigation and prosecution of international crimes subject to the guarantees enunciated in Part V which are adequate to secure individual human rights protection.

The Secretariat fulfills the traditional administrative support functions as well as the functions of court registrar.

The Standing Committee is a novelty in the structural approach to the creation of now international institutions. To a large extent the Standing Committee is to the organs of the Tribunal what the General Assembly is to the United Nations. It represents the States parties, assists in insuring compliance with the provisions of the Convention and oversees the administrative and financial affairs of the Tribunal.

Article 4 - Jurisdiction. The jurisdiction of the Tribunal is limited to what is defined in paragraph 1 as "grave breaches" of the Apartheid Convention. The analogy here is to the conception of grave breaches in the Four Geneva Conventions of 12 August 1949 (For the Amelioration of the Condition of the Wounded and Sick in Armed Forces of the Field, United Nations, Treaty Series, vol. 75, p. 31; For the Amelioration of the Condition of Wounded, Sick and Shipwrecked Members of Armed Forces at Sea, ibid., p. 85; Relative to the Treatment of Prisoners of War, ibid., p. 135; Relative to the Protection of Civilian Persons in Time of War, ibid., p. 287; and in the Protocols Additional to the Geneva Convention on 12 August 1949, 19 June 1977 (ICRC, August-September, 1977)). In addition, paragraph 2 defines these additional international crimes which may be part of the Court's jurisdiction by Supplemental Agreement and binding only upon the States parties entering into such an agreement with the Standing Committee. International Crimes, however, are limited to those so declared in a multilateral convention and which can be so construed by the institution of penal procedures or the obligation to prosecute or extradite. This embodies the maxim aut dedere aut judicare which characterizes international crimes.

Paragraph 3 establishes the Tribunal's jurisdiction over such crimes and, of course, over persons and entities charged with them as universal in terms of its scope and in terms of the power of the Court.

The 1953 Geneva Committee draft does not define the crimes to be dealt with beyond the phrase "crimes generally recognized under international law," whereas the 1979 ILA draft incorporates by reference definitions of crimes in 16 international conventions, but notably omitting the Apartheid Convention.

[*50] Article 5 - Competence. While penal theoreticians may argue the merits of a distinction between jurisdiction and competence, it is suggested that jurisdiction establishes a Tribunal's geographic and subject-matter authority, and in personam authority, while competence determines the specific powers of

the Court with respect to its jurisdiction and provides the legal framework of reference for the Tribunal's exercise of its jurisdictional authority.

Article 6 - Subjects upon whom the Tribunal shall exercise its jurisdiction. Though Article 4 on jurisdiction refers to the Court's authority over natural persons and legal entities, it was deemed of importance to emphasize this authority under a separate article though it may appear duplicative.

Article 7 - Sanctions. Only the Court upon a finding of guilty, subject to the provisions of this Convention, the procedures and rules which would be developed by the different organs and the standards of fairness set forth in Part V, can impose a sanction against a natural person or legal entity. Clearly deprivation of liberty applies to natural persons and not to legal entities but fines and injunctions apply to natural persons and legal entities. It is to be noted that there is no schedule of penalties affixed to any specific crime and to some this may raise a question of nulla poena sine lege. To avoid this problem the Convention proconizes that the Court shall enact appropriate and specific Rules on sanctions to be promulgated prior to the Tribunal's commencement of activities which would satisfy the element of notice. There is, however, the objection that such penalty will apply to persons who have committed "grave breaches" of the Apartheid Convention or violations of other international conventions made subject to the Court's jurisdiction by supplemental agreement (as discussed in the Commentary to articles 1 and 4) before the promulgation of these sanctions. In effect this would be tantamount to applying a penalty which was not promulgated at the time of the commission of a given crime. In some ways this may be deemed a violation of the principle nulla poena sine lege though it could be argued that if the penalty is commensurate with or equivalent to the same penalty provided for in the State in which the crime was committed for equivalent crimes the objection would lose much of its substance. If, however, the sanction is to be the same as that for the equivalent crime in the national legal system of the State in which the international crime had been committed the principle nulla poena sine lege would be complied with.

PART II: THE PENAL PROCESSES OF THE TRIBUNAL

Article 8 - Initiation of process. The desirability of such a process has substantial support. See General Assembly resolution 1107 (XII) of 11 November 1957. See also the note by the Secretary-General entitled "International Criminal Jurisdiction" (Official Records of the General Assembly, Twelfth Session, document A/3649) and the memorandum submitted by the Secretary-General of the United Nations entitled "Historical Survey of the Question of Criminal Jurisdiction" (United Nations publication, Sales No. 1949.V.8).

For a documentary history of the various projects for the creation of an international criminal jurisdiction, see B. Ferencz, The International Criminal Court (1980) 2 Vols. See also J. Stone and R. Woetzel, Toward a Feasible International Criminal Court (1970); 35 Revue Internationale de Droit Penal No. 1-2 (1964) devoted to that subject, and 45 Revue Internationale de Droit Penal No. 3-4 (1974) containing the contributions of the AIDP to V United Nations Congress on Crime Prevention and Criminal Justice, Geneva, September 1975 devoted to the [*51] subject of "Creation d'una Justice Penale Internationale." The Revue Internationale de Droit Penal contained scholarly writings on this subject in its issues of 1928, 1935, 1945 and 1952 as well as others. The AIDP has traditionally supported the creation of an international criminal court as witnessed by the positions it has taken at its various International Congresses, and those of its distinguished members among them: Pella, Donnedieu de Vabres, Saldana, Graven, Jimenez de Asua, Setille, Cornil, Bouzat, Jescheck, Romeahkiin, Herzog, Glaser, Dautricourt, Quaintano-Reppele Arreneau, Mueller, de Schutter, Triffterer, Lombois, Plawski, Ferencz, Oehler, Zubkowski. Because of the numerous writings on the subject by the above-mentioned scholars and others it would be impossible to cite them all. For three more recent initiatives resulting in the submission of a draft statute, and the International Law Association, "Draft Statute for an International Commission of Criminal Injury" adopted by its International Criminal Law Committee in Paris May 1978 Proceedings of the International Law Association (Belgrade Conference 1980) p. 4; and "Draft Statute for an International Criminal Court," World Peace through Law, Abidjan World Conference August 1973 (edited by Robert K. Woetzel); and a "Draft Statute for an International Criminal Court" prepared by the Foundation for the Creation of an International Criminal Court, see also, K. de Haan "The Procedural Problems of a Permanent International Criminal Jurisdiction" in De bestraffing van inbreuken tegen het oorlogs - en het humanitair recht (A. Bierlaen, S. Dockx, K. de Haan, C. Van den Wijngaert, eds., 1980) p. 191.

The 1953 Geneva Committee draft, in article 29, provides that the penal processes could commence only by action of a State party. The 1979 ILA Draft in Article 23 allows only States to approach the Commission which at its turn would present a case to the Court. The procedures presented herein differ from the 1953 Geneva Committee draft and 1979 ILA Draft in that it concentrates the investigation and prosecution of any case with the Procuracy, but a State party, organ of the United Nations, intergovernmental organization, non-governmental organization and individual may file a complaint with the Procuracy which shall accept such communications. The Procuracy then makes an initial determination as to whether the complaint is "not manifestly unfounded" or "manifestly unfounded". That determination is quite similar to the one made by the European Commission on Human Rights as to complaints concerning violations of the European Convention on Human Rights. However, the Procuracy is not without controls as to its discretion in that a State party and an organ of the United Nations are entitled to recognition of their complaints as being "not manifestly unfounded" while other States and intergovernmental organizations are entitled to an appeal to the Court of a determination by the Procuracy that the complaint has been found "manifestly unfounded". Communications and complaints by individuals and non-governmental organizations are not entitled to the same status. The Procuracy's decisions are thus reviewable in the case of certain complaints and communications and a decision holding a complaint "not manifestly unfounded" will then travel two alternate channels: (a) the possibility of mediation and conciliation through the Standing Committee; (b) adjudication before the Court. A period of one year is allowed for the conciliation process which is the same period allowed for the Procuracy's investigation and preparation of the case. Thereafter the case may be presented to the Court at the request of the complaining State party or organ of the United Nations if it is the initiator of the complaint. Otherwise that period of one year is extendable subject to the Court's review.

[*52] Article 9 - Pre-trial process. A non-exhaustive list of orders that may be issued by the Court in aid of the preparation of a case is specified. It is expected that the Rules of the Court will go into the details of the form, content, and other formalities pertaining to these orders. They are among the traditional powers of either a Court, or a judge of instruction respectively in the Common Law and Romanist-Civilist tradition. Similar provisions may be found in the 1953 Geneva Committee draft, articles 40, 41, and 42, and in the 1979 ILA Draft, Articles 36, 37. It must be noted here that the Tribunal in general and the Court in particular will in this and in other respects rely on the co-operation of the States parties to implement its orders. It must also be noted that where a State party has with a State which is not a party, treaties or relations on the subject of extradition and judicial assistance and co-operation, the Court's orders and determinations of any sort would have an impact beyond that State party and thus give this Convention a multiplier effect with respect to its impact. (See e.g., V.E.H. Booth, British Extradition Law and Procedure (1980); C. Van de Wijngaert, The Political Offence Exception in Extradition (1980); M.C. Bassiouni, International Extradition and World Public (1974); I. Shearer, Extradition in International Law (1971); T. Vogler, Auslieferingsrecht und Grundgesetz (1969); Bode, International Extradition (1968); A. Billot, Traite de l'Extradition (1874) and, M. Pisani and F. Mosconi, Codice delle Convenzioni di Estradizione E Di Assistenza Giudiziaria in Materia Penale (1979)). The observations made herein are also relevant to Part VI on the duties of State parties since such duties will not only extend to the carrying out of the obligations of this Convention within their own territories but also whenever possible in their relations with other States. It is clear that the carrying out and execution of all such obligations to assist the Tribunal where required by this Convention, and in particular Part VII, but a State party is only requested to act pursuant to its relevant national laws. It must, however, be noted that a State party cannot enact national laws which will frustrate the carrying out of the obligations arising under this Convention.

Paragraph 4 establishes a procedure analogous to an indictment, such as was proposed in articles 33 to 35 and 31 of the 1953 Geneva Committee and the 1979 ILA drafts respectively, by means of a Committing Chamber in the former and Commission processes in the latter. Under the present draft, however, this process is but a step toward determination as to guilt, it being unnecessary to give it special consequences because prior procedures in the Procuracy have been given appropriate consequences and progress under the present draft after the initial Procuracy action is gradual rather than involving thresholds.

The subparagraph (a) determination is primarily for the sake of efficiency, as a means of detecting any errors by the Procuracy as to the suitability of the matter for further action. Subparagraph (b) provides an opportunity for early consideration of whether misconduct in preparation of the case may have impugned the Tribunal's integrity in such a way to impair credibility or acceptability of its determinations, as well as for early consideration of non bis in indem (double jeopardy) problems. (See M.C. Bassiouni, Substantive Criminal Law (1978), pp. 499-512).

Subparagraph (c) is particularly intended to deal with the need to consider the possibility that non-co-operation of States, particularly non-parties, may render evidence of either incriminatory or exculpatory character unavailable, so that a fair trial of the case may be impossible. Early detection of problems of this type would not only be more efficient but also would tend to avoid unnecessary and difficult non bis in idem questions regarding aborted proceedings.

[53] Article 10 - Adjudication. Paragraph 1 parallels articles 39 of the 1953 Geneva Committee draft and 35 of the 1979 IFA draft, conforming more closely to the latter, which makes no express provision for secret sessions. This treatment appears appropriate in that any confidential evidence may be submitted in public in a form or manner that protects essential matters of confidentiality such as identity of a witness or a particular technique for obtaining evidence, and the details for such presentations may be treated in rules of the Court and Procuracy, which may be elaborated at a time when the actual needs in this regard are clearer.

Paragraph 2 describes the inherent power of courts to dismiss cases, particularly in respect of evidentiary problems. Article 38, paragraph 4, of the 1953 Geneva Committee draft has a similar dismissal provision. No express provision is made for withdrawal of a matter, as was done in articles 43 and 38 of the Geneva Committee and ILA drafts, respectively, it being implicit in the nature of the powers of the Procuracy to determine whether to take such action.

Paragraphs 4 and 5 are self-explanatory.

It is contemplated that rules of the Court will address non bis in idem issues. Paragraph 3, it should be noted, relates to the principle of equality of arms, which has been observed under the European Convention on Human Rights. (Applications No. 596/59 and 789/60, Franz Pataki and Johann Dunshirn vs. Austria, Report of the Commission of 28 March 1963, Yearbook of the European Convention on Human Rights pp. 730, 734 (1963)).

Paragraph 6 is in part motivated by the availability of appeal and also the fact that Chambers, being constituted on a rotational basis, may be unavailable in their prior form for subsequent arguments. Details of the rotational constitution of Chambers are left for elaboration in Court rules.

Article 11 - Sanctioning. These provisions are self-explanatory, but this article is to be read in pari materie with article VII and the Commentary thereto and articles XIII and XXIV.

Article 12 - Appeals. Appeals from Chambers determinations and orders, which may be entered only on behalf of an accused or the Procuracy on questions of law, are permitted including post-conviction orders. This is consonant with the provisions of the International Covenant on Civil and Political Rights concerning the dual level of judgement and review.

No appeal is permitted for the accused under articles 49 and 43 of the Geneva Committee and ILA drafts, respectively. Also interlocutory appeals are permitted as practical necessity may require them.

Paragraph 6 on revision of judgements parallels articles 52 and 45 of the Geneva Committee and ILS drafts respectively, but is broader in scope.

Article 13 - Sanctions and Supervision. Paragraph 1 corresponds to article 46 of the 1979 ILA draft, Article 51 of the 1953 Geneva Committee draft having left such matters to future conventions. The terminology "sanctions" is capable of including not only punishments of imprisonment or fines, but also levies of compensation or injunctive orders, thus maintaining the possibility for such broad ranges of action.

[*54] As noted previously, the supervisory mechanism of paragraph 2 replaces the clemency and parole boards provided for by the Geneva Committee and ILA drafts, and appeal is made possible under paragraph 3.

It should be noted that these provisions govern only the procedures relating to sanctions. Standards relating to sanctions may be elaborated further in Court rules but subject to article 24.

PART III: ORGANS OF THE TRIBUNAL

Article 14 - The Court. Except for mechanical differences, the terms of their article as to selection, tenure and replacement of judges closely parallel those of articles 4 through 12 and 13 through 20 of the 1953 Geneva Committee draft and 3 through 9 and 12 through 15 of the 1979 ILA draft , although the latter makes no provision for removal of judges.

This article represents an innovation, in that the other drafts dealt with a single court organ and created a separate clemency and parole board. As discussed below, the provision for separate functions of Chambers and the Court en banc permits appeals, a right called for in article 14, paragraph 5, of the International Covenant on Civil and Political Rights. Rather than create a separate institution to deal with such matters as clemency and parole it was deemed more efficient to have such functions performed by individual judges, subject to possible appeals from their decisions, as discussed in connection with article 11.

Paragraph 5 contemplates that judges will be elected with reference to specific terms. Accordingly, when a given judge is considered for re-election, any of the terms that are vacant at that time may be regarded as available for that judge.

Paragraph 7 addresses the concern that any conduct by a judge may create an appearance of impropriety, and narrowly circumscribes permitted non-Court activity.

Paragraph 11 is intended to permit judges to remain in their official capacity for the sole purpose of completing work on Court action begun prior to expiration of their terms.

Paragraph 12, it should be noted, does not bar re-election of the Court president.

Article 15 - The Procuracy. The significance of the three-part division of the Procuracy is apparent in connection with budgets and reports and transfer of cases from investigative to prosecutorial divisions, as well as to the rights of the accused.

Paragraph 2, providing for joint action by the Court and Standing Committee for selection of a Procurator, appears appropriate because such an officer should be politically acceptable and States are in a superior position to become aware of suitable candidates, while the Court is in a superior position to judge legal competence and estimate probable devotion to impartiality. Removal power is vested in the Court in the belief that deficiencies of the kind the Court would be likely to note would e the appropriate bases for dismissal.

Deputies are placed under control of the Procurator in paragraph 4 in the interest of effective management.

[*55] Article 16 - The Secretariat. Although most of the functions of the Secretariat are ministerial in character, its duties to oversee communications and prepare reports serve an inspectorate function as well. Accordingly, control over the Secretariat is vested in the Court, as a neutral body.

Article 17 - The Standing Committee. The 1953 Geneva Committee draft assumed that the court created under it would be a part of the United Nations, and therefore any governing-body needs or political issues regarding its operations would be addressed by the political organs and the United Nations, especially the General Assembly. Under the 1979 ILA draft, a similar assumption appears to have been made in that no treaty-type provisions are included and, although references have consented to be subject to operation of the court. Nevertheless, the commission contemplated in the ILA draft would have had a somewhat political character, in that only nationals of States consenting to be subject to operations of the commission could have been members and the commission's own statute is referred to as a "Convention" in its article 3.

The present Statute, in contrast, would be entirely conventional in character, although there are various express provisions for co-ordination of action with the United Nations. Accordingly, the need for an organ to deal with governance of the Tribunal and political issues relating to its activities promoted provision for a Standing Committee. It should be noted that the express functions of the Standing Committee are of a governing-body nature for the most part, and that its functions beyond these are largely unspecified. This would permit the representatives of States parties who constitute that organ to have wide flexibility in pursuing non-juridical matters helpful to international criminal justice. The requirement of meetings twice a year assures that the Standing Committee will be available for consultation on political questions.

One of the most significant functions of the Standing Committee may be in Articles 17, paragraph 6, with respect to proposing action to initiate and propose new norms of international criminal law or standards for its application by the Tribunal. In view of the vagueness of existing instruments purporting to define international crimes, such proposals and adoption may be essential in order that criminal responsibility may be dealt with without violating the principle of nulla peona sine lege.

It should be noted that this article does not contemplate deprivation of the status of State party in response to non-payment of financial support, but mere suspension.

No provision has been made for terms of representatives, it being assumed that their tenure shall be at the pleasure of the appointing State.

Article 18 - General institutional matters. Paragraph 1 rules, it should be noted, are subject to further provisions in Article 19. Recognition that flexibility should be provided for such rules was expressed in article 24 of the 1953 Geneva Committee draft and article 10 of the 1979 ILA draft. Court approval of rules for the Procuracy and Secretariat appears appropriate in view of the need to assure that such rules are fair and conform to legal requirements. Participation by the Procurator in formulation of Court rules recognizes the desirability that such rules interrelate properly with Procuracy procedures and capabilities.

[*56] Paragraph 2 gives the Court, a neutral body, a key role in shaping the budget of the Tribunal, but leaves a veto power with the Standing Committee, which represents the States obliged to meet the budget. Prior draft statutes did not deal in detail with budgetary approval. See 1953 General Committee article 23 and 1979 ILA article 17.

Paragraph 5 parallels article 14 of the 1953 General Committee draft, which has no counterpart in the 1979 ILA draft, as to judges. Expansion to other Tribunal officers is clearly appropriate. Expansion to other parties before the court is necessary in the interest of fairness. (See. e.g., the European Agreement Relating to Persons Participating in Proceedings of the European Commission and Court of Human Rights (Council of Europe, May 1969; E.T.S. No. 69)).

Paragraph 6's requirement of a solemn declaration parallels article 13 of the 1953 Geneva Committee draft and article 11 of the 1979 ILA draft, but is expanded to include officers of the Tribunal.

PART IV: TRIBUNAL STANDARDS

Article 19 - Standards for rules and procedures. The standards of fairness which are to be guaranteed in all proceedings before the organs of the Tribunal and which are to be reflected in the rules to be promulgated by the said Organs emboding rights are contained in the 1948 Universal Declaration of Human Rights, the 1966 International Covenant on Civil and Political Rights, the 1980 Body of Principles on the Protection of Persons from All Forms of Arbitrary Arrest and Detention, the 1950 European Convention for the Protection of Human Rights and Fundamental Freedoms, and the 1969 Inter-American Convention on Human Rights. These standards are also embodied in the resolutions of the XIIth International Congress of Penal Law held in Hambourg 1979 whose draft and explanatory notes are in 49 Revue International de Droit Penal vol. 3, 1978. These provisions are particularly consonant with the European Convention for the Protection of Human Rights and Fundamental Freedoms and Additional Protocols. (See A. Robertson, Human Rights in Europe (1977), and D. Poncet, La Protection de l'Accusé par la Convention Europeènne des Droits de l'Homme (1977). See also, e.g., L. Sohn and T. Buergenthal, International Protection of Human Rights (1973)).

PART V: PRINCIPLES OF ACCOUNTABILITY (PROVISIONS IN THE NATURE OF A GENERAL PART)

The principles of accountability set forth in Part VI are from the General Part of the Draft International Criminal Code in M.C. Bassiouni, International Criminal Law: A Draft International Criminal Code (Sijthoff, 1980).

Article 20 - Definitions. Paragraph 1 defines international crimes with reference to the Convention, thus permitting expansion.

Paragraph 2 incorporates by reference the definition of a State as recognized under international law. This approach was preferred to repetition of one of the generally accepted formulations of a definition of a State because use of such a formulation would call for definition of the terms used in it, such as the Montevideo Convention's provision that a State has the capacity to conduct "international relations". See the Convention on the Rights and Duties of States of 26 December 1933 (United Nations, Treaty Series, vol. 176, p. 19). See also, United Nations debates on statehood in connection with Israel and Liechtenstein (Official Records of the Security Council, Third Year, 383rd meeting, No. 128, pp. 9-12, and ibid., Fourth Year, 433rd meeting, No. 35, pp. 4-5).

For the sake of convenience, the term "State" is deemed to include groups.

[*57] Paragraph 3 exemplifies a correlation between "person" and individual", and confines the meaning of these terms to exclude such entities as corporations or other so-called juridical persons.

Paragraphs 4 and 5. Begin with another correlation for the sake of convenience, with respect to the terms "group" and "organization." the definition is provided because of the use of these terms in provisions dealing with collective responsibility, which is discussed below.

Paragraph 6. On participation in a group action is designed for the same purpose. The model of responsibility arose out of the Nuremberg trials and Tokyo war crimes trials. (See article 9 of the London Charter of 8 August 1945, Control Council Ordinance No. 10 of 20 December 1945; for a discussion of the basis of this responsibility and the cases decided at Nuremberg and Tokyo, see L. Friedman, The Law of War: A Documentary History (1972); see also Wright, History of the United Nations War Crimes Commission (1949)).

Paragraphs 7 and 8. Are basically the provisions of the Model Penal Code relating to solicitation and conspiracy, American Law Institute Model Penal Code (1962). (See generally M.C. Bassiouni, Substantive Criminal Law (1978), and W. LaFave and A. Scott, Criminal Law (1972) see also for a comparison with the German Penal Code, G. Fletcher, Rethinking Criminal Law (1978)).

The definition of "solicitation" was found to be workable under civil law, as well as common law systems. On the other hand, the concept of conspiracy is not generally recognized under the civil law systems, so that inclusion of this term required a common law definition even though the requirement of an "overt act" brings such a definition close to preparatory acts in civilist-Romanist systems. (See R. Merle and A. Vitu, Traite de Droit Criminal (1967). It is to be noted that conspiracy and participation in a group action are separate terms with separate definitions. The concept, however, is found in the Nuremberg and Tokyo War Crimes trials.

In paragraph 9, "Attempt" was given a definition based on the Model Penal Code, but with modifications reflecting the concern of civil law jurists. For example, the term "preparation" has been omitted and "substantial step" has been amplified by the addition of the words "unequivocal and direct." This modification was intended to provide a meaning that would be recognized under civil law as being as limited as the meaning that these provisions would be given under common law systems. See Fletcher, op. cit.

The definitions for the terms "participation in a group action," "solicitation," "conspiracy" and "attempt" are provided in the "General Part." Such conduct in reference to the proscriptions of the "Special Part" is included in the "General Part" as opposed to the "Special Part" as is more consonant with the civil law system. (See generally R. Merle and A. Vitu, Traite de Droit Criminel (1967); P. Bouzat and J. Pinatel, Traite de Droit Penale (mise a jour 1975); H.H. Jescheck, Lehrbuch des Strafrechts (1975)).

Paragraphs 10 and 11. Deal with "person in authority" and "omission" and are included for the purpose of criminalizing failure of persons in authority to fulfill their legal duties arising out of any specific duty referred to in the "Special part."

[*58] It is clear that the definitions provided reflect a certain conceptual choice and the attempt to integrate civilist-Romanist and common law principles and those principles which have emerged from the history and practice of international criminal law. (In that respect see S. Glaser, Infractions Internationale (1957) and S. Plawski, Etude des Principes Fond mentaux du Droit International Penal (1972)).

Article 21 - Responsibility. The basis of responsibility of accountability follows the "Definitions" and precedes "Elements of an International Crime" because of the view that the various levels and types of accountability should be set forth first so as to define to whom and on what basis responsibility can be imputed. This approach neither fits the common law nor the civil law models. It was deemed appropriate subject to the special status of these Tribunals and the historical peculiarities of international criminal law in light of the precedents of the Leipzig War Crimes Trials, though these were subject to German laws, and the Nuremberg and Tokyo War Crimes Trials. There is no analogy to be found in the writings of scholars to that approach. This identification of criminally accountable subjects should be read in pari materiae with the Provision on "Definitions."

Under paragraph 1 through 5, criminal responsibility is assigned not only to committing a crime, but also to attempting, soliciting or conspiring to commit any crime. However, because the element of harm is required unless that requirement is modified by the definition of the specific offence, criminal responsibility for acts not constituting a "commission" are controlled by the definitions of the crime, which may have a different requirement. Other provisions relating to individual responsibility are taken from parallel provisions of national penal codes. It was noted that the provision relating to responsibility for acts of others is not intended to create a new crime, but rather to express the principle of derivative responsibility which exists in one way or another in every penal system. These provisions are more in conformity to the common law approach than to the continental approach.

The provisions regarding group responsibility were framed to serve two purposes: to make groups themselves accountable under the Article dealing with penalties, and to prevent an individual from escaping responsibility where he provided a group with continued intangible support despite its foreseeable criminal conduct as reflected in the principles of the Nuremberg and Tokyo War Crimes Trials. Special provision is made for responsibility of persons in authority in order to incorporate responsibility for failure to act. This provision is based on military law and command responsibility as it is incorporated in the Four Geneva Conventions of 12 August 1949 and in particular in the 1977 Additional Protocol Amending the Geneva Conventions of August 12, 1949 concerning failure of superiors to control acts of subordinates and other sources of international criminal law.

Paragraph 6, on State responsibility, is essentially drawn from the draft principles of State responsibility (A/CN.4/246) adopted by the International Law Commission. P. Guggenheim, Traite de Droit International (1952) and C. Eagleton, The Responsibility of States in International Law (1928); Strupp, Handbuch des Volkerrechts - Das volkerrechtliche Delikt (1920) and more recently, F. Munch, Das volkerrechtliche Delikt (1963) and H.H. Jescheck, Die Verantwartlichkeit der Staatserganen - Nach Volkerstrafrecht (1952)).

These provisions are intended to cover both responsibility for failure to act and non-state entities that subsequently become states by analogy to principles of state succession in international law. (See generally D.P. O'Connell, State Succession in International Law (1967)).

[*59] Article 22 - Elements of an international crime. This provision seeks to synthesize common law and civil law concepts as well as to take into account fundamental principles of international criminal law in providing for and defining the four essential elements of an international crime. There seems to be agreement on the need for all such elements, even though there are divergences with respect to the meaning and content of each one. Probably the most authoritative work on the subject is Stefan Glaser, Infraction Internationale (1957). In it, Glaser starts, as does this Article, with the material element, but then interjects certain legal justifications before dealing with the mental element. He concludes his work with participation and complicity. In this respect, a conceptual difficulty arises and the choice was to separate the required elements of a crime from the "responsibility," and conditions of "exoneration." The approach of dividing "Responsibility," "Element of an International Crime," and "Exoneration" into three different provisions seeks to avoid doctrinal differences between common law and civil law by devising a neutral approach.

The material element satisfies both the common law and civil law systems, as does to a great extent the mental element, though it is couched in more objective terms.

In recognition of the fact that most civil law criminal codes do not specify causation as a separate element, the element of causation could be interpreted as included in the material element of a crime in civil law systems and separate for common law systems.

It was agreed that the mental element should not extend to mere negligence, but it was feared that mere exclusion of negligence would result in responsibility under civil law systems for mental states between mere negligence and recklessness. Accordingly, the decision was made to list the mental states of intent, knowledge, and recklessness with the understanding that recklessness went beyond the dolus eventualis, described under the 1976 German Penal Code as a state of mind such that the person knew that harm would result.

For common law systems, however, a separate provision on causation was added.

The fourth such element, harm, was recognized as requiring interpretation in connection with the offence in question. It was determined that provision should be made for circumstances where an offence did not require an outcome whose character would match the usual meaning of the word "harm." similar concern was voiced regarding the element of causation, so that it was determined to qualify the listing of elements with a clause providing that these elements may be altered by the definition of a given crime.

Article 23 - Immunities. This provision is set forth immediately after principles of responsibility and imputability, the elements of a crime, because of the peculiarity of international law with respect to immunities which derive from the principles of sovereignty. (See Sutton, "Jurisdiction Over Diplomatic Personnel and International Organizations' Personnel for Common Crimes and for Internationally Defined Crimes," in M.C. Bassiouni and V.P. Nanda, A Treatise in International Criminal Law (1973), Vol. II, p. 97. See also Oppenheim, International Law (8th ed., Lauterpacht, 1955), p. 757; Harvard Research on International Law, Diplomatic Privileges and Immunities, 26 A.J.I.L. 15-187 (Supp. 1932); ad Immunite, Extraterritorialite et Droit d'Asile en Droit Penal International, 49 Revue Int'le de Droit Penal, No. 2 (1978)).

[*60] This text is based on the provisions of: 1961 Vienna Convention on Diplomatic Relations; 1963 Convention on Consular Relations; 1968 United Nations Draft Convention on Special Missions; 1946 Convention on the Privileges and Immunities of the United Nations; 1947 Convention on the Privileges and Immunities of the Specialized Agencies; Draft Articles on the Representation of States in their Relations with International Organizations of the International Law Commission, 1972; Draft Articles on the Protection and Inviolability of Diplomatic Agents and Other Persons Entitled to Special Protection Under International Law, of the Organization of American States, 1971; Convention to the Prevent and Punish the Acts of Terrorism Taking the Form of Crimes Against Persons and Related Extortions that are of International Significance, 1971; the 1973 Convention on the Prevention and Punishment of Crimes Against Internationally Protected Persons Including Diplomatic Agents; the General Agreement of 18 March 1950, and the four additional Protocols to the General Agreement on Privileges and Immunities of the Council of Europe (1952, 1961).

The text also takes into account customary principles of international law on the immunity of Heads of State and the practice of states. The nature of the immunity provided herein is, however, more narrowly circumscribed, as it is not absolute. The text obligates the Contracting Parties whose national is the subject of any immunity category contained herein to take appropriate action against such persons, but permits waiver of that jurisdiction in favour of the International Court much as do the NATO and Warsaw Pact countries on Status of Forces Agreement; (see Coker, "The Status of Visiting Military Forces in Europe," in M.C. Bassiouni and V.P. Nanda (eds), A Treatise on International Criminal Law (1973) Vol. II, p. 115.)

Article 24 - Penalties. Separate provisions are made for punishment of different types of offenders, all subject to the requirement in Section 1 that punishment by proportional to seriousness of the violation and the harm threatened or caused as well as to the degree of responsibility of the actor.

The Court is directed to develop appropriate Rules before exercising its jurisdiction. It must be noted that principles of legality are not violated by these provisions because the Court should first promulgate the penalties and the criteria for their application.

Paragraph 3 recognizes the principle of the Nuremberg Tribunals that organizations as such may be punished by means of fines. (See Dinstein, infra). This provision goes beyond continental principles.

Paragraph 4, punishment of states by imposition of fines is provided, it being considered beyond the scope of the court's ability to impose other sanctions. (See Triffterer, "Jurisdiction Over States for Crimes of State," and Baxter, "Jurisdiction Over War Crimes and Crimes Against Humanity: Individual and State Accountability," in M.C. Bassiouni and V.P. Nanda (eds), A Treatise on International Criminal Law (1973) Vol. II, pp. 86-96 and 65-85. See also Munch, "State Responsibility in International Law," in Bassiouni and Nanda, supra, Vol. I, pp. 143 35 seq.; C. Eagleton, The Responsibility of States in International Law (1924), C. de Visscher, La responsabilite des Etats (1924); F. Munch, Das volkerrechtliche Delikt (1963);

J. Castillon, Les Reparations allemandes - Deux experiences (1919-1932, 1945-1952), (1953), and H.H. Jescheck, Die Verantwertlichkeit der Staatsarganen - Nach Volkerestrafrecht (1952)).

[*61] Paragraph 5 confers discretion on the court whether to impose cumulative sentences for crimes arising from a single transaction.

Paragraph 6, dealing with mitigation, provides for the possibility that the fact that an accused was acting under orders could be considered a mitigating factor. This reflects the content of Article 8 of the London Charter of 8 August 1945 establishing the International Military Tribunal at Nuremberg, (See Y. Dinstein, The Defense of "Obedience to Superior Orders" in International Law p. 260 and 283 (1985)).

Article 25 - Exoneration. While the civil law system would view the conditions of exoneration listed in this Article as a questionable combination of principles of responsibility and legal defence, it was felt that a single provision containing all conditions which ultimately result in exoneration from responsibility, irrespective of their doctrinal or dogmatic basis should be placed together, as it gives these aspects a sense of cohesion and practical use by an international tribunal.

The self-defence provision in paragraph 2, is based on that contained in article 2, paragraph 2(a) of European Convention for the Protection of Human Rights and Fundamental Freedoms as well as on the language used in the Model Penal Code. The requirement that the defender reasonably believes that forceful response is necessary is a common law requirement which is superfluous for civil law systems. On the other hand, the introduction of the requirement that the response be to an "imminent" use of unlawful force may be viewed under the common law as surplusage.

The defence of necessity is limited in paragraph 3 to use of force not likely to produce death as a policy decision to restrain individuals.

Coercion, under paragraph 4, was limited as a defence to situations where the threat or use of force is "imminent."

Paragraph 5 makes obedience to superior orders a defence where the person accused was not in a position to know of the criminal nature of his acts. Conversely, paragraph 6 protects persons from prosecutions for refusing to follow orders to commit crimes.

Paragraph 7 adapts the formulation of the Model Penal Code relating to mistake of law or fact, conditioning this defence on negation of criminal intent.

Paragraph 8, on double jeopardy, simply seeks to give effect to the principle non bis in idem. The fourth paragraph recognizes the competence of the International Criminal Court to overlook pardons and amnesties of other jurisdictions in order to avoid that states resort to that practice from negotiating a person's punishability. It applies to the actual conduct involved rather than to any legal characterization of that conduct by any State.

Paragraph 9 is based on the Model Penal Code's provision on the defence of insanity. This differs from civilist systems where such a condition is deemed a pre-condition to criminal responsibility.

Paragraph 10 on the defence of intoxication springs from the same source, and excludes voluntary intoxication as a defence to crimes requiring intent.

The renunciation principles set forth in Section 11 also stem from the Model Penal Code but are in keeping with the continental approach.

[*62] This provision includes principles of justification, conditions negating criminal responsibility, excusability and procedural defences. From a Romanist-Civilist perspective it is doctrinally challengeable on the very grounds that it encompasses too much diversity. However, its justification rests on pragmatic reasons which avoid the dogmatism that has been at the basis of so much debate between European penalists for so long.

Article 26 - Statute of Limitation. The approach adopted measures the limitation period by the maximum potential penalty required for similar offences under the national law of the State where the crime was committed as is the case under penalties. It should be noted that, under this approach, where the maximum penalty is life imprisonment or death, there is no limitation period. Also, it was necessary to add paragraph 1 (c) because offences by States are punishable only by fines under this Code. This approach was preferred notwithstanding the Convention on the Non-Applicability of Statutory Limitations to War Crimes and Crimes Against Humanity, of 9 December 1968 (see also 39 Revue International de Droit Penal (1968) dedicated to this topic, and the European Convention on the Non-Applicability of Statutory

Limitations to Crimes Against Humanity and War Crimes of 1974). In fact, the result of this approach and that of the Conventions referred to above, is for all practical purposes the same except for minor offences and in fact avoids the difficulties which have prevented the ratification of these treaties by a number of states.

PART VI: DUTIES OF STATES PARTIES

Article 27 - General principles. The basis of international enforcement and co-operation derives from the maxim aut dedere aut judicare from Hugo Grotius, De Jure Belli ac Pacis (1924). It is now recognized as a general principle of international law to "prosecute or extradite"; (see Bassiouni, "International Extradition and World Public Order," in Aktuelle Problema des Internationalen Strafrechts (1970) pp. 10, 15 (ed. D. Oehler and P.G. Pötz)) and it is the conceptual basis of the indirect enforcement scheme, that international law has relied upon. It is embodied in international criminal law conventions. The mechanism by which the indirect enforcement scheme operates, is that a state obligates itself under an international convention to include appropriate provisions in its national laws which would make the internationally proscribed conduct a national crime. This approach is found in all international criminal law conventions establishing such a duty upon its Contracting Parties. (See e.g., the Four Geneva Conventions of 12 August 1949 in their respective Articles 49-50/50-51/129-130/146-147). It is also the case with respect to all other international criminal law conventions.

Article 28 - Surrender of accused persons. Surrender of the accused is equivalent to extradition. Because of the importance of extradition in this enforcement scheme, it is covered herein with as much detail as possible in light of existing problems perceived in the practice. The "political offence exception" is excluded from all international crimes herein. (See article VII of the 1948 Genocide Convention; the European Convention on the Suppression of Terrorism of 27 January 1977; the 1973 Draft Additional Protocol Amending the Geneva Conventions of 12 August 1949, Protocol I, Article 78. See also Bassiouni, "Repression of Breaches of the Geneva Conventions under the Draft Additional Protocol to the Geneva Conventions of August 12, 1949," 8 Rutgers-Camden L.J. 185 (1977); D. Poncet and P. Neyreud, L'Extradition et l'Aisle Politique en Suisse (1976); C. Van den Wijngaert, The Political offence exception to extradition: The delicate problem of balancing the rights of the individual and international public order (1980)). The language used in this article is patterned after the [*63] 1970 Hague Convention for the Suppression of Unlawful Seizure of Aircraft. (See e.g., M.C. Bassiouni, International Extradition and World Public Order (1974), and I. Shearer, Extradition in International Law (1971). See also the European Convention on the Suppression of Terrorism of 1979 and the European Convention on Extradition of 13 December 1957. See also, Legal Aspects of Extradition Among European States (Council of Europe, 1970). For different national perspectives, see 38 Revue Int'le de Droit Penal (1968), and T. Vogler, Auslieferungsrecht und Grunigesetz (1969). For a historical perspective, see A. Billot, Traite de l'Extradition, (1974). See also,M. Pisani and P. Mosconi, Codice Belle Convenzioni di Estradizione e di Assistenza Giudiziaria in Materia Penale (1979)). In general the laws of the requested State are applicable as is the case in all multilateral and bilateral extradition treaties.

Article 29 - Judicial Assistance and Other Forms of Co-operation. The requested party shall execute in the manner provided for by its law any letters rogatory relating to a criminal matter and addressed to it by the judicial authorities of the requesting Party for the purpose of procuring evidence or transmitting objects, records or documents to be produced in evidence.

The requested party shall effect service of writs and records of judicial decisions which are transmitted to it for this purpose by the requesting party. Service may be effected by simple transmission of writ or record to the person to be served. Other formalities shall be established by Rules of the Court. See the 1959 European Convention on Mutual Assistance in Criminal Matters, and in part on the 1972 European Convention on Transfer of Proceedings in Criminal Matters. See also, Grutzner, "International Judicial Assistance and Co-operation in Criminal Matters," in M.C. Bassiouni and V.P. Nanda (eds), A Treatise on International Criminal Law, Vol. 2, pp. 189 and 217-218 (1973). See also, Explanatory Report on the European Convention on the Transfer of Proceedings in Criminal Matters (Council of Europe, 1972); Problems Arising from the Practical Application of the European Convention on Mutual Assistance in Criminal Matters (Council of Europe 1971); de Schutter, "International Criminal Law in Evolution: Mutual

Assistance in Criminal Matters between the Benelux Countries," 14 <u>Neth. Int'l L. Rev.</u> 382 (1967); Grützner, <u>International Judicial Assistance and Co-operation in Criminal Matters</u>, and Markees, "The Difference in Concept Between Civil and Common Law Countries as to Judicial Assistance and Co-operation in Criminal Matters," in M.C. Bassiouni and V.P. Nanda (eds), <u>A Treatise in International Criminal Law</u>, Vol. 2, pp. 189 and 171 (1973). See also, H. Grützner, <u>Internationales Rechshilfeverkehr</u> (1967). For the text of these and other treaties see, M. Pisani and F. Mosconi, <u>Codice Delle Convenzione di Estradizione e di Assistenza Giudiziaria in Materia Penale</u> (1979)).

    <u>Article 30 - Recognition of the judgements of the International Penal Tribunal.</u> This article is applicable to: (a) sanctions involving deprivation of liberty; (b) fines or confiscations; (c) disqualifications. A State party shall under the conditions provided for in this Convention enforce a sanction imposed by the Court, and vice versa. (See the 1970 <u>European Convention on the International Validity of Criminal Judgements</u>. See also <u>Aspects of International Validity of Criminal</u> Judgements (Council of Europe, 1968) and <u>Explanatory Report on the European Convention on the International Validity of Criminal Judgements</u> (Council of Europe, 1970). See also Harari, McLean and Silverwood, "Reciprocal Enforcement of Criminal Judgements, 45 <u>Revue Internationale de Droit Penal</u> 585 (1974); D. Oehler, "Recognition of Foreign Penal Judgements and their Enforcement," in M.C. Bassiouni and V.P. Nanda (eds), <u>A Treatise on International Criminal Law</u>, vol. II, p. 261 (1973); Schearer, "Recognition and Enforcement of Foreign Criminal Judgement," 47 <u>Aust. L.J.</u> 585 (1973); D. Oehler, <u>Internationalen Strafrecht</u> (1973). For the Benelux Convention, see <u>Convention Concerning Customs and Excise</u>, 5 September, 1972, [*64] Belgium-Luxembourg-The Netherlands, United Nations, <u>Treaty Series</u>, vol. 247, p. 329. See also K. Kraelle, <u>Le Benelux Commente, Textes Officiels</u> 147, 209, 306 (1961); De Schutter, "International Criminal Cooperation: the Benelux Example," in M.C. Bassiouni and V.P. Nanda (eds), <u>A Treatise in International Criminal Law</u>, Vol. 2, p. 261 (1973). The Scandinavian countries' arrangement for recognition and enforcement of penal judgements is reproduced in H. Grützner, <u>Internationales Rechtshilfeverkehr in Strafsache</u>, pt. IV (1967). The arrangement between France and certain African states is reproduced in 52 <u>Rev. Critique de Droit International Prive</u> 863 (1973)).

    <u>Article 31 - Transfer of offenders and execution of sentences.</u> This article relies on the concepts embodied in the 1970 <u>European Convention on the International Validity of Criminal Judgements</u> and the 1964 <u>European Convention on the Supervision of Conditionally Sentenced or Conditionally Released Offenders</u>. It also relies on the treaties on the execution of penal sentences between the United States and Mexico, 5 November 1976, between the United States and Canada, 2 march 1977, and between the United States and Bolivia, 10 February 1978, all treaties having entered into force. Furthermore, special reliance was placed on United States legislation implementing the above treaties, 18 U.S.C., Sections 4100-4115. (See Bassiouni, "Perspectives on the Transfer of Prisoners Between the United States and Mexico and the United States and Canada," 11 <u>Vanderbilt J. Transnational L.</u> 249 (1978); Bassiouni, "A Practitioner's Perspective on Prisoner Transfer," 4 <u>Nat'l J. Crim. Defense</u> 127 (1978); Abramovsky and Eagle, "A Critical Evaluation of the Newly-Ratified Mexican-American Transfer of Penal Sanctions Treaty" 64 <u>Iowa L. Rev.</u> 325 (1979) and Professor Vagt's response thereto in the same issue).

    A scheme for transfer of offenders can be said to rely in part on the assumption that a given state will recognize the criminal judgement of another and of the Court. The manner in which this article is drafted makes that assumption. (See in particular article 6 of the 1970 <u>European Convention on the International Validity</u> of Criminal Judgements).

PART VII: TREATY PROVISIONS

    The treaty provisions are somewhat standard, except for the reservations clause which though in keeping with the Vienna Convention on treaty interpretation also takes into account the relevant aspects of the "Advisory Opinion By The International Court of Justice on Reservations to the Convention on the Prevention and Punishment <u>of Genocide</u>," 1951 <u>I.C.J.</u> 15.

    One of the conditions for this Convention's implementation in, of course, the need for the Standing Committee to be created and to start functioning and that is why a special provision has been made to that effect.

[*65] IV. DRAFT ADDITIONAL PROTOCOL FOR THE PENAL ENFORCEMENT
OF THE INTERNATIONAL CONVENTION ON THE SUPPRESSION
AND PUNISHMENT OF THE CRIME OF <u>APARTHEID</u>
PART I: NATURE OF THE PROCESS
Article 1
PURPOSE AND INSTITUTIONAL FRAMEWORK

1.   There are hereby established penal measures for the implementation of article V of the Convention on the suppression and Punishment of the Crime of <u>Apartheid</u>, that is to say, adjudication of culpability and imposition of punishment for crimes of <u>apartheid</u> as stated in article II of the <u>Apartheid</u> Convention.

2.   The following enforcement organs shall enforce the provisions of this Protocol according to their powers and duties as described in this Protocol: a Charging Committee; a Prosecutorial Commission; a panel of judges to adjudicate a crime of <u>apartheid</u>, hereinafter referred to as the "Tribunal"; and, a Standing Committee of States Parties.

Article 2
JURISDICTION AND COMPETENCE

1.   The enforcement organs established in article 1 shall have the power to investigate, prosecute and adjudicate violations of the convention on the Suppression and Punishment of the Crime of <u>apartheid</u>, and, in the case of the Tribunal, to impose penal sanctions against those found responsible for the Commission of a crime of <u>apartheid</u> as defined in article II of the said Convention.

2.   The enforcement organs established in article 1 shall have universal jurisdiction in their investigation, prosecution, adjudication, and punishment of the crime of <u>apartheid</u>.

3.   The power and authority to investigate all complaints and claims of violations of the Convention on the Suppression and Punishment of the Crime of <u>Apartheid</u> shall be in the Charging Committee, whose functions are described in article 5.

4.   The power and authority to prosecute cases whose investigation have been completed by the Charging Committee before the Tribunal shall be in the Prosecutorial Commission whose functions are described in article 6.

5.   The power and authority to adjudicate criminal charges of <u>apartheid</u>, determination of guilt and innocence, and the imposition of sanctions on the basis of cases presented by the Prosecutorial commission shall be in the Tribunal whose functions are described in article 7.

Article 3
SANCTIONS

1.   The Tribunal shall have the power to impose the following sanctions with respect to the following types of persons who have been found to be responsible of the following types of conduct:

[*66] (a) Terms of deprivation of liberty and lesser penalties where the accused is a natural person who has been determined to be guilty of a "grave crime" under article II of the Convention on the Suppression and Punishment of the Crime of <u>Apartheid</u>, that is to say:

  (i)   Murder;
  (ii) Torture;
  (iii) Cruel, inhuman or degrading treatment or punishment; or
  (iv) Arbitrary arrest and detention.

  (b) Fines and injunctive orders where the accused is a natural or juridical person and has been determined to be responsible for any conduct prohibited by article II of the Convention on the Suppression and Punishment of the Crime of <u>Apartheid</u>.

  (c) Terms of deprivation of liberty when the accused is a natural person, and fines where the accused is either a natural or a juridical person, and has been determined to e responsible for violations of lawful orders of the Court.

2.   Procedural and other aspects of sanctions are described in article 8.

Article 4
SUBJECTS UPON WHOM THE ORGANS OF ENFORCEMENT
SHALL EXERCISE THEIR JURISDICTION

The organs of enforcement shall exercise their jurisdiction over natural persons and legal entities as defined in Part VI.

PART II: THE PENAL PROCESS
Article 5
INITIATION OF THE PROCESS

1.   A complaint or crime of violation of the Convention on the Suppression and Punishment of the Crime of <u>Apartheid</u> shall be brought by anyone to the Charging Committee who shall receive and investigate any such information.

2.   Upon review of the information and on the basis of a majority vote by the Charging Committee that it believes a violation of the Convention has taken place it may submit it to the Prosecutorial Commission along with its investigation and findings to prosecute the person believed to have committed such a crime.

3.   Nothing herein shall preclude the Charging Committee from undertaking any action other than submission of a case to the Prosecutorial Commission which would be in conformity with the intents and purposes of this Protocol and of the Convention on the Suppression and Punishment of the Crime of <u>Apartheid</u>.

[*67] Article 6
THE PROSECUTION AND PRE-TRIAL PROCESS

1.   The Prosecutorial Commission shall undertake no action with respect to any alleged violation of this Protocol or of the Convention on the Suppression and Punishment of the Crime of <u>Apartheid</u> unless it is so instructed by the Charging Committee.

2.   The Prosecutorial Commission upon being instructed by the Charging Committee to proceed with the prosecution of a given case shall prepare the said case for submission to the Court for adjudication.

3.   In aid of such preparation the Prosecutorial Commission may request the Tribunal to issue orders in the nature of:

    (i)   Arrest warrants;

    (ii)   Subpoenas;

    (iii)   Injunctions;

    (iv)   Search warrants;

    (v)   Warrants for surrender of an accused so as to enable the accused to be transported to attend proceedings and to transit States without interference.

4.   Any pre-trial order in aid of the preparation of a case for adjudication shall be issued by the Tribunal in accordance with the standards set forth in this Convention in Part V.

5.   Prior to commencement of the adjudication on the ultimate merits of a given case, the Tribunal shall conduct a preliminary hearing to determine:

    (a)   Whether the case is founded in fact and law;

    (b)   Whether prior proceedings has the case in accordance with the principle of <u>non bis in idem</u>;

    (c)   Whether there are circumstances that would render the trial unreliable or unfair; and

    (d)   Set a schedule for the adjudication and determine relevant procedural questions pertaining to the adjudication.

6.   After the preliminary hearing described in paragraph 5 above the Tribunal may either dismiss the case or hold it for adjudication.

Article 7
THE ADJUDICATION PROCESS

1.   The Tribunal shall conduct its hearings in accordance with the standards set forth in Part V.

[*68] 2.   After hearing evidence and arguments in a public hearing except as the Tribunal may otherwise decide if it is in the best interest of the accused or in the best interest of justice the Tribunal shall deliberate

in camera and shall thereafter upon reaching a determination announce its decision orally in summary fashion or by a complete reading of a written opinion in open Court.

3.   If an opinion is announced orally in summary fashion the written opinion shall be submitted no less than 30 days from the date of the oral opinion.

4.   The date in which the written opinion shall be deposited with the Secretariat of the Tribunal shall be the effective date of judgement.

5.   Any judge may issue a separate concurring or dissenting opinion.

6.   All decisions of the Tribunal shall take effect 30 days after the effective date of judgement in order to permit post-trial modifications of the Tribunal's determination as described in article 9.

Article 8
THE SANCTIONING PROCESS

1.   Upon a determination by the Tribunal that the person charged is responsible for a crime within the jurisdiction and competence of the Tribunal, a hearing shall be held to determine the appropriate sanction for purposes of hearing evidence and arguments of mitigation and aggravation.

2.   The Tribunal shall then pronounce its determination of the applicable sanction in accordance with article 3 of this Protocol.

3.   Decisions relating to sanctions shall be reached and announced in the same manner as decisions regarding determination of responsibility as stated in article 7.

4.   The sanctioning hearing shall be held anytime after the effective date of entry of the Court's determination of responsibility which is after 30 days of the date of recording of the judgement provided that no post-adjudication review procedures have been initiated pursuant to article 9. In the event that post-trial procedures have been initiated, the sanctioning hearing shall commence after the date of entry of judgement on the said hearing.

Article 9
THE POST-ADJUDICATION REVIEW PROCESS

1.   Within 30 days of the effective date of entry of a determination of responsibility by the Tribunal the Prosecutorial commission or the accused may file a petition for review with the Tribunal for purposes of vacating or modifying any part or all of the Tribunal's determination.

2.   The bases upon which such a petition for review can be presented are:

    (a)   Discovery of evidence unknown at the time of the prior determination which if known at the time would have materially affected the outcome of the determination;

    (b)   The Court was misled as to material affecting the outcome of the determination;

[*69](c)   On the face of the record the facts alleged are not proven beyond a reasonable doubt; or

    (d)   The facts alleged and proved do not constitute responsibility for a crime of apartheid.

3.   The Tribunal shall hold such hearings in accordance with the same standards and procedures set forth for adjudication of responsibility pursuant to article 6 of this Protocol.

4.   Upon a determination on the merits of the petition for review the Tribunal shall announce its decision in the same manner prescribed in article 7 and the determination shall be final upon its recording.

PART III: THE ENFORCEMENT ORGANS
Article 10
THE TRIBUNAL

1.   The Tribunal shall consist of five judges, no two of whom shall be of the same nationality, who shall be elected by representatives of States Parties to this Protocol acting through the Standing Committee of States Parties.

2.   Election of judges shall be by secret ballot at a meeting called for that purpose by the Standing Committee of States Parties from a list of nominees submitted by States Parties, no more than two of which shall be submitted by the same State Party.

3.   Nominees shall be distinguished experts in the fields of international criminal law and human rights or other jurists qualified to sere on the highest courts of their respective States.

4.   In electing judges due consideration shall be given to the diversity of personal backgrounds and experience and to the representation of the major legal and cultural systems of the world.
5.   Judges shall have no occupation or business that would conflict with the performance of their duties on the Tribunal.
6.   Judges shall be compensated for time spent on Tribunal matters and on a basis proportionate to the salaries of judges of the International Court of Justice.
7.   The five judges shall be elected for terms of three years, which can be renewed.
8.   No judge shall perform any judicial function with respect to an accused of the same nationality or with respect to any matter with which the judge was involved in any other capacity.
9.   A judge may withdraw from a case or be excluded for good cause by unanimous vote of the other judges.
10.   A judge may be removed from the Tribunal for good cause by a unanimous vote of the other judges.
[*70]11. Except with respect to judges who have been removed, judges may continue in office beyond their term as acting judges until their replacement assumes the office and shall continue in office to complete work on any pending matter in which they were involved.
12.   The judges of the Tribunal shall elect a President and such other officers as they deem appropriate. The president shall serve for a term of one year which is renewable.

Article 11
THE CHARGING COMMITTEE

1.   The Charging Committee shall be the three members of the Commission on Human Rights designated pursuant to article IX of the Convention on the Suppression and Punishment of the Crime of Apartheid.
2.   Meetings may be held regularly or on an ad hoc basis to perform the functions required by this Protocol.
3.   The Charging Committee shall adopt rules to govern performance of its functions.
4.   The members of the Charging Committee shall elect every year a President who may be re-elected.
5.   Members of the Charging Committee shall be reimbursed for their expenses and compensated for their services on the same basis as for the performance of their functions under article IX of the Convention on the Suppression and Punishment of the Crime of Apartheid and under existing United Nations procedures.
6.   The Charging Committee may designate qualified experts to investigate and research matters considered by the Committee. The compensation of such experts shall be determined by the Committee on an ad hoc basis.

Article 12
THE PROSECUTORIAL COMMISSION

1.   The Prosecutorial Commission shall consist of the members of the Ad Hoc Working Group of Experts established under resolution 2 (XXIII) of the Commission on Human Rights.
2.   Meetings of the Commission may be held regularly or on an ad hoc basis to perform its functions under this Protocol.
3.   The Prosecutorial Commission shall adopt rules to govern performance of its functions.
4.   The members of the Commission shall elect a President every year who can be re-elected.
5.   Members of the Prosecutorial Commission shall be reimbursed for their expenses and compensated for their services on the same basis as for their functions under article IX of the Convention on the Suppression and Punishment of the Crime of Apartheid and under existing United Nations procedures.
[*71] 6. The Prosecutorial Commission may engage the services of a qualified expert to present cases before the Tribunal. The compensation of such experts shall be determined by the Commission on an ad hoc basis.

Article 13
THE STANDING COMMITTEE OF STATES PARTIES

1.   The Standing Committee shall consist of one representative appointed by each State Party to this Protocol.

2.   The Standing Committee shall elect by majority vote a President and such other officers as it deems appropriate for one year who may be re-elected.

3.   The President shall convene meetings in accordance with such rules as may be adopted by the Standing Committee.

4.   The Standing Committee shall have the power to perform the functions expressly assigned to it under this Protocol and may:

      (a)   Determine the operating budget of the organs of enforcement set up under this Protocol and costs relating to the machinery of enforcement and in general all financial and administrative matters arising under this Protocol including assessing States Parties for their <u>pro rata</u> share of the costs incurred.

      (b)   Encourage States to accede to this Protocol;

      (c)   Propose international instruments to enhance the performance of the Tribunal; and

      (d)   Encourage States to assist the enforcement organs of this Protocol and to comply with the Tribunal's determinations.

5.   The Standing Committee may exclude from participation representatives of States Parties that have failed to provide financial support to the Tribunal as required by this Protocol or that have failed to carry out other express obligations under this Protocol.

PART IV: INSTITUTIONAL MATTER
Article 14
THE STANDING COMMITTEE OF STATES PARTIES

1.   The Standing Committee shall consist of one representative appointed by each State party to this Protocol.

2.   The Standing Committee shall elect by majority vote a President and such other officers as it deems appropriate for one year who may be re-elected.

3.   The President shall convene meetings in accordance with such rules as may be adopted by the Standing Committee.

4.   The Standing Committee shall have the power to perform the functions expressly assigned to it under this Protocol and may:

      (a)   Determine the operating budget of the organs of enforcement set up under this Protocol and costs relating to the machinery of enforcement and in general all financial and administrative matters arising under this Protocol including assessing States Parties for their <u>pro rata</u> share of the costs incurred.

      (b)   Encourage States to accede to this Protocol;

      (c)   Propose international instruments to enhance the performance of the Tribunal; and

      (d)   Encourage States to assist the enforcement organs of this Protocol and to comply with the Tribunal's determinations.

5.   The Standing Committee may exclude from participation representatives of States Parties that have failed to provide financial support to the Tribunal as required by this Protocol or that have failed to carry out other express obligations under this Protocol.

PART IV: INSTITUTIONAL MATTER
Article 14
RULE MAKING

1.   Each of the enforcement organs and the Standing Committee shall formulate their own rules of procedures to fulfil the interests and purposes of this Protocol and in accordance with the standards of fairness as stated in Part V of this Protocol.

2.   The rules of the Charging Committee and of the Prosecuting Commission shall first be approved by the Tribunal before they become effective.

[*72] 3.   To insure the independence and impartiality of the Tribunal its rules shall not be reviewable. The Standing Committee may, however, request the Tribunal to consider proposed rules or reconsider established ones. Nothing herein precludes and accused or the Prosecutorial Commission from presenting to the Tribunal a challenge to a rule for failure to comply with the provisions of this Protocol or its standards in Part V.

4. No rule shall take effect until 60 days after publication.

5. All rules and amendments shall be published and made available to the public through the Division of Human Rights of the United Nations.

6. All Administrative and financial matters pertaining to this Protocol shall be undertaken by the Division of Human Rights of the United Nations which shall appoint with the approval of the Standing Committee a chief administrative officer to carry out these functions.

7. All costs and expenses incurred by the administration of this Protocol shall be borne by the States Parties who shall be assessed by the Standing Committee on a pro rata basis.

8. In all matters except judicial matters in which this Protocol or its provisions are called into question, the President of the Standing Committee of States Parties shall be the competent authority.

9. In all judicial matters and matters involving the Organs of Enforcement of this Protocol the President of the Tribunal shall be the competent authority and he may delegate any member of the Charging Committee or Prosecutorial Commission to act on his behalf or appoint a special expert on an ad hoc basis.

PART V: STANDARDS
Article 15
STANDARDS FOR RULES AND PROCEDURES

In all proceedings and in the formulation of any rules by the organs of enforcement, the accused where applicable shall be entitled to those fundamental human rights enunciated in the Universal Declaration of Human Rights and the International Covenant on Civil and Political Rights, which are:

(a) The presumption of innocence

The presumption of innocence is a fundamental principle of criminal justice. It includes inter alia:

    1. No one may be convicted or formally declared guilty unless he has been tried according to law in a fair trial;

    2. No criminal punishment or any equivalent sanction may be imposed upon a person unless he has been proven guilty in accordance with the law;

    3. No person shall be required to prove his innocence;

    4. In case of doubt the decision must be in favour of the accused.

(b) Procedural rights ("equality of arms")

The accused shall have substantial parity in proceedings and procedures and shall be given effective ways to challenge any and all evidence produced by the prosecution and to present evidence in defence of the accusation.

(c) Speedy trial

Criminal proceedings shall be speedily conducted without, however, interfering with the right of the defence to prepare adequately for trial. To this effect:

    1. Time limitations should be established for each stage of the proceedings and should not be extended without reason by the appropriate Chamber of the Court.

    2. Complex cases involving multiple defendants or charges may be severed by the appropriate Chamber of the Court when it is deemed in the interest of fairness to the parties and justice to the case.

    3. Administrative or disciplinary measures shall be taken against officials of the Tribunal who deliberately or by negligence violate the provisions of this Convention and the rules of this Tribunal.

(d) Evidentiary questions

    1. All procedures and methods for securing evidence which interfere with internationally guaranteed human rights shall be in accordance with the standards of justice set forth in this Convention and in the rules of the Tribunal.

    2. The admissibility of evidence in criminal proceedings must take into account the integrity of the judicial system, the rights of the defence, the interests of the victim and the interests of the world community.

    3. Evidence obtained directly or indirectly by illegal means which constitute a serious violation of internationally protected human rights, violate the provisions of this Convention, and rules of this Tribunal shall hold them inadmissable.

4.   Evidence obtained by means of lesser violations shall be admissible only subject to the judicial discretion of the Court on the basis of the veracity of the evidence presented and the values and interests involved.

(e)   The right to remain silent

Anyone accused of a criminal violation has the right to remain silent and must be informed of this right.

(f)   Assistance of counsel

1.   Anyone suspected of a criminal violation has the right to defend himself and to competent legal assistance of his own choosing at all stages of the proceedings.

[*74]   2.   Counsel shall be appointed ex officio whenever the accused by reason of personal conditions is unable to assume his own defence or to provide for such defence, and in those complex or grave cases where in the best interest of justice and in the interest of the defence such counsel is deemed necessary by the Court.

3.   Appointed counsel shall receive reasonable compensation from the Tribunal whenever the accused is financially unable to make such compensation.

4.   Counsel for the accused shall be allowed to be present at all critical stages of the proceedings.

5.   Counsel for the accused or the accused shall be provided with all incriminating evidence available to the prosecution as well as all exculpatory evidence as soon as possible but no later than at the conclusion of the investigation or before adjudication and in reasonable time to prepare the defence.

6.   Anyone detained shall have the right of access to and to communicate in private with his counsel personally and by correspondence, subject only to reasonable security measures decided by a judge of the Court.

(g)   Arrest and detention

1.   No one shall be subjected to arbitrary arrest or detention.

2.   No one shall be deprived of his liberty except on such grounds and in accordance with such procedure as established by this Protocol and rules of the Tribunal and only on the basis of a determination by the Court.

3.   No one shall be arrested or detained without reasonable grounds to believe that he committed a criminal violation within the jurisdiction of the Tribunal.

4.   Anyone arrested or detained shall be promptly brought before a judge of the Court and shall be informed of the charges against him; after appearance before such judicial authority he may be returned to the custody of the arresting authority but he shall be subject to the jurisdiction of the Court even when in the custody of a State party.

5.   Preliminary or provisional arrest and detention shall take place only whenever necessary and as much as possible should be reduced to a minimum of cases and to the minimum of time.

6.   Preliminary or provisional detention shall not be compulsory but subject to the determination of the Court and in accordance with its rules.

7.   Alternative measures to detention shall be used whenever possible and include inter alia:
Bail;
Limitations of freedom of movement;
Imposition of other restrictions.

[*75]   8.   No detainee shall be subject to rehabilitative measures prior to conviction unless he freely consents thereto.

9.   No administrative preventive detention shall be permissible as part of any criminal proceedings.

10.   Any period of detention prior to conviction shall be credited toward the fulfillment of the sanction imposed by the Court.

11.   Anyone who has been the victim of illegal or unjustified detention shall have the right to compensation.

(h)   Rights and interests of the victim

The rights and interests of the victim of a crime shall be protected, in particular:

1.   The opportunity to participate in the criminal proceedings;

2.   The right to protect his civil interests;

3.   Due regard shall be given in formulation of rules of the organs of the Tribunal to the principle of non bis in idem, but a seemingly duplicative prosecution shall not be barred provided that the record in the prior proceeding is taken into account along with any prior measures in respect of guilt of the accused.

4.   Arrest and detention shall be in conformity with the Standard Minimum Rules for Treatment of Prisoners and the Body of Principles on the Protection of Persons from All Forms of Arbitrary Arrest and Detention of the United Nations.

5.   Maximum flexibility regarding restrictive measures should be encouraged, including use of such mechanisms as house arrest, work release and bail, and credit shall be given for any pre-conviction restrictions to an accused.

6.   The Tribunal shall include all of the above in the formulation of its rules of practice and procedures which shall be effective upon promulgation.

7.   No proceedings before the Tribunal shall commence prior to the promulgation of the rules of practice and procedures of the Court, the Procuracy and the Secretariat.

PART VI: PRINCIPLES OF ACCOUNTABILITY
(PROVISIONS IN THE NATURE OF A GENERAL PART)
Article 16
DEFINITIONS

1.   An international crime is any offence arising out of the provisions of this Statute and any supplemental agreement thereto.

[*76]2.   A State is an international legal entity defined under international law.

(a)   This term is used without prejudice to questions of recognition or membership in the United Nations.

(b)   This term also includes a group of States acting collectively.

3.   The words "person" or "individual" for the purposes of this Protocol are used interchangeably and each one of them refers to a physical human being alive.

4.   For the purposes of this Protocol, the words "group" and "organization" are interchangeable. A group consists of more than one person, acting in concert with respect to the performance of a particular act.

5.   The term "entity" is used herein to include groups, organs of state, states or groups of states.

6.   Participation in group action is a person's conduct which directly contributes to the group's ability to perform a given act or which directly influences the decision of the group to perform a given act.

7.   A person commits solicitation when, with the intent that an offence be committed, he instigates, commands, encourages or requests another to commit that offence.

8.   A person commits conspiracy when, with intent to commit a specific offence, he agrees with another to the commission of that offence and one of the members of the conspiracy commits an overt act in furtherance of the agreement.

9.   A person commits an attempt when, with the intent to commit a specific offence, he engages in unequivocal and direct conduct which constitutes a substantial step toward the commission of that offence and which if not for a fortuitous event or misapprehension of the actor, would result in the completion of the crime.

10.   A person in authority is a person who has legal authority under domestic law or a person who by virtue of the power structure of a group is deemed to be in command or has the power to command others, and to whom obedience is generally expected.

11.   Omission by a State, group or organization or failure to act occurs whenever a person in authority having power to act and having knowledge of the facts requiring action fails to take reasonable measures to prevent, or terminate the commission of a crime or to apprehend, or prosecute, or punish any person who has or may have committed a crime. Omission by an individual is conscious failure to act in accordance with a pre-existing legal obligation.

12.   The masculine "he" used throughout this article refers equally to the feminine "she".

Article 17
RESPONSIBILITY

1.   A person is criminally responsible under this article when he reaches the age of eighteen.

[*77] 2.   Direct personal responsibility

(a)   A person who commits or attempts to commit a crime is responsible for it and criminally punishable under article 20 and also articles 3 and 8.

(b)   A person who conspires with another or solicits another to commit a crime as defined is criminally responsible for it and criminally punishable.

(c)   A person who commits a crime is not relieved from responsibility by the sole fact that he was acting in the capacity of Head of State, responsible Government official, acting for or on behalf of a State, or pursuant to "superior orders" except where the provisions of article 21, paragraph 5, are applicable.

3.   Responsibility for the conduct of others

(a)   A person is responsible for the conduct of another if, before, during or after the commission of a crime, and with the intent to promote or facilitate the commission of a crime, he aids, abets, solicits, conspires or attempts to aid another person in the planning, perpetration or concealment of the crime, or facilitates the concealment or escape of a perpetrator.

(b)   A person is not responsible for the acts of others if that individual is a victim of the crime, or when, before the commission of the crime, that person terminates his efforts of participation as described in paragraph 3 (a) and such termination wholly deprives others of his efforts and of their effectiveness or if such a person gives timely warning and advice to appropriate Government authorities.

(c)   The vicarious responsibility for the conduct of another under this section is not dependent upon the conviction of a person accused as a principal.

(d)   A person is responsible for the conduct of another with respect to any crime committed in furtherance of a solicitation, conspiracy and for those crimes which are reasonably foreseeable to be committed by others in furtherance of a common criminal scheme, design or plan.

4.   Collective responsibility

(b)   A group or organization other than a State or an organ of a state is collectively responsible for its acts, irrespective of the responsibility of its members.

(c)   A person is responsible for crimes committed by a group or organization, if he knew of or could reasonably foresee the commission of such crime and remained a member thereof.

5.   Responsibility of persons in authority

(a)   A person in authority in a State, group or organization is personally responsible for the commission of a crime when such crime is committed at his instigation, suggestion, command or request, or if he fails to act.

[*78] 6.   State responsibility

(a)   Conduct for which states are responsible

1.   A State is responsible for any crime committed on its behalf, behest or benefit by a person in authority, regardless of whether such acts are deemed lawful under its municipal law.

2.   Conduct is attributed to a State if it is performed by persons or groups acting in their official capacity, who under the domestic law of that state possess the authority to make decisions for the State or any political subdivision thereof or possess the status of organs, agencies or instrumentalities of that state or a political subdivision thereof.

3.   Conduct outside the scope of authority of any of the entities listed in paragraph 6 (a) 2 of this article is attributed to the State.

(b)   State responsibility for failure to act

1.   Failure to act by a State in accordance with its obligation under this Code shall constitute an international offence.

2.   Any revolutionary movement which establishes a State or overthrows a Government is responsible in the new State or new Government to prosecute or extradite any individual within such group or any individual who has been omitted from the group for any international crime. Failure to do so shall constitute a basis for State responsibility.

Article 18
ELEMENTS OF AN INTERNATIONAL CRIME

1. Definition

(a) An international crime shall contain four elements: a material element, a mental element, a causal element and harm, as defined in sections 2 through 5 inclusive, except when in the definition of a given crime these requirements are altered.

2. Material element

(a) Any voluntary act or omission which constitutes part of a crime as defined in article 21 will constitute the material element.

3. Causal element

(a) Conduct is the cause of a result when it is an antecedent but for which the result in question would not have occurred, and that the result was a foreseeable consequence of such conduct.

4. Harm

(a) The element of harm shall depend upon the definition of the crime, except where no harm is needed in the definition of the crime.

[*79] 5. Mental element

(a) The mental element of an offence at the time of the commission of the material element shall consist of either intent, knowledge, or recklessness, unless the definition of the crime specifies any of these three.

(b) A person "intends" to accomplish a result or engage in conduct described by the law defining the offence, when his conscious objective or purpose is to accomplish that result or engage in that conduct.

(c) A person "knows" or acts "knowingly" when he is consciously aware of the attendant circumstances of his conduct or of the substantial probability of existing facts and circumstances likely to produce a given result.

(d) A person is reckless or act recklessly when he consciously disregards a substantial and unreasonable risk that a likely result would be a foreseeable consequence of such conduct.

Article 19
IMMUNITY

1. For purposes of this article, no person shall enjoy any international immunity except that Head of State, Head of Government, official representative of a State having diplomatic status, employees of international organizations and the members of the families and staffs of the above enumerated persons shall be exempt and immune from the criminal process of all States other than their own and this International Criminal Tribunal, provided that in the event of the commission of a crime as defined herein, the State Party whose national is entitled to the immunity and exemption stated herein shall undertake to investigate, prosecute and punish the allegation or crime charged.

2. Any State may waive this immunity on behalf of its nationals without prejudice to its interests in favour of any other State.

3. Any person who falls into any of the categories of paragraph 1 of this article may specifically waive that immunity with the consent of the State of which he is a national or of the international organization by which he is employed without prejudice to that State or organization.

4. A person who no longer has the privileges of the positions covered by immunity in paragraph 1 of this article may no longer benefit from said immunity except with respect of those acts committed or alleged to have been committed while that person held the position that granted immunity.

Article 20
PENALTIES

1. Punishability

(a) All crimes defined in this article are punishable in proportion to the seriousness of the violation, to the harm threatened or caused, and to the degree of the responsibility of the individual actor in accordance with a schedule to be promulgated by rules of the Tribunal before it exercises its jurisdiction in a given case.

[*80]2.	Penalties for individuals

(a)	Penalties for persons who have been convicted of the commission of a crime shall consist of imprisonment or such alternatives to imprisonment or fines as promulgated by the International Criminal Court.

3.	Penalties for a group or organization

(a)	Penalties for crimes for which groups are collectively responsible under article 21, paragraph 4, shall consist of fines or other sanctions established in accordance with the principle of proportionality set forth in paragraph 1 of this article and as promulgated by the rules of the Court.

(b)	Fines shall be collectively levied against the assets of group and individual participants and enforced by the States Parties wherein such assets may be found.

4.	Penalties for States

(a)	Penalties for States which are responsible for crimes shall consist of fines assessed on the basis of proportionality as set forth in section 1 of this article, without prejudice to the duties or reparations and civil damages.

(b)	Such fines shall be due from a State, provided that they do not critically impair the economic viability of the State.

(c)	The determination and assessment of fines against a State shall be made by the Court and the enforcement of such fines shall be by and through the United Nations.

(d)	The provisions of this article are without prejudice to the rights and duties of the United Nations to impose sanctions against a State as provided for in the United Nations Charter.

(e)	Special remedies

Nothing in this article shall prevent the Criminal Court to rely on its inherent judicial power to order a State to cease and desist from a given activity which is an international crime or to order by injunctions and correction of previous violations and prevent their reoccurrence.

5.	Multiple crimes and penalties

(a)	The Court may with respect to a single criminal transaction involving the commission of more than one crime all of which are related and are based on substantially the same facts impose a single penalty with discretion concerning aggravating and mitigating circumstances as may be found by the Court.

6.	Mitigation of punishment

(a)	A person acting pursuant to superior orders may present such a claim in mitigation of punishment.

(b)	Subject to the defence of double jeopardy a person who was sentenced in one State for substantially the same criminal conduct and resentenced by the Court shall receive credit for any part of a sentence already executed.

[*81](c) The Court may take into account any mitigating fact such as imperfect or incomplete defences stated in article 21.

Article 21
EXONERATION

1.	Definition

(a)	A person shall be exonerated from responsibility arising under this Protocol if in the commission of an act which constitutes a crime any of the defences stated in paragraphs 2 through 11 inclusive is applicable.

2.	Self-Defence (Individual)

(a)	Self-defence consists in the use of force against another person which may otherwise constitute a crime when and to the extent that he reasonably believes that such force is necessary to defend himself or anyone else against such other person's imminent use of unlawful force, and in a manner which is reasonably proportionate to the threat or use of force.

3.	Necessity

(a)	A person acts under necessity when by reason of circumstances beyond his control, likely to create a private or public harm, he engages in conduct which may otherwise constitute a crime which he reasonably believes to be necessary to avoid the imminent greater harm likely to be produced by such circumstances, but not likely to produce death.

4.   Coercion

(a)   A person acts under coercion when he is compelled by another under an imminent threat of force or use of force directed against him or another, to engage in conduct which may otherwise constitute a crime which he would not otherwise engage in, provided that such coerced conduct does not produce a greater harm than the one likely to be suffered and is not likely to produce death.

5.   Obedience to superior orders

(a)   A person acting in obedience to superior orders shall be exonerated from responsibility for his conduct which may otherwise constitute a crime or omission unless, under the circumstances, he knew that such act would constitute a crime.

6.   Refusal to obey a superior order which constitutes a crime.

(a)   No person shall be punished for refusing to obey an order of his Government or his superior which if carried out, would constitute a crime.

7.   Mistake of law or fact

(a)   A mistake of law or a mistake of fact shall be a defence if it negates the mental element required by the crime charged provided that said mistake is not inconsistent with the nature of the crime or its elements.

[*82] 8.   Double Jeopardy

(a)   The Court may not retry or resentence the same individual for the same conduct irrespective of what the crime or charge may be.

(b)   In the event a person has been tried by the national courts of a State Party he could be retried for the same conduct by the Court but he shall receive credit for a sentence rendered by a national criminal court and executed by that state or any other State.

(c)   No individual who has been tried and convicted or acquitted on the merits by the Court shall be retried or resentenced by the domestic court of any State Party.

(d)   Amnesty or pardon by any State shall not constitute a bar to adjudication before the Court and shall not be deemed to fall within the defence of double jeopardy.

9.   Insanity

(a)   A person is legally insane when, at the time of the conduct which constitutes a crime, he suffers from a mental disease or mental defect, resulting in his lacking substantial capacity either to appreciate the criminality of his conduct or to conform his conduct to the requirements of the law, and such mental disease or mental defect caused the conduct constituting a crime.

10.   Intoxication or drugged condition

(a)   A person is intoxicated or in a drugged condition when under the effect of alcohol or drugs at the time of the conduct which would otherwise constitute a crime he is unable to formulate the mental element required by the same crime.

(b)   Such a defence shall not apply to a person who engages in voluntary intoxication with the pre-existing intent to commit a crime.

(c)   With respect to crimes requiring the mental element of recklessness, voluntary intoxication shall not constitute a defence.

11.   Renunciation

(a)   It shall be a defence to the crimes of attempt, conspiracy and solicitation if a person renounces or voluntarily withdraws from the commission of the said crimes before any harm occurs and if he has engaged in any individual activity by doing any of the following:

(i)   Wholly deprives others from the use or benefit of his participation in the commission of the crime;

(ii)   Notifies law enforcement officials in time in order to prevent the occurrence or the commission of the crime.

[83]Article 22
STATUTE OF LIMITATION

1. Duration
    (a) No prosecution or punishment by the Court of an international crime shall be barred by a period of limitations of lesser duration than the maximum penalty ascribed to the crime in question.
    (b) The period of limitation shall commence at the time that legal proceedings under the provisions of this Protocol may commence but shall not apply to any period during which a person is escaping or evading appearance before the appropriate authorities. It is interrupted by the arrest of the accused but shall recommence ab initio if the accused or convicted person escapes and in no case shall it run for a period which would no longer than twice the original period of limitation.
    (c) In the case of State responsibility, the period of limitation for commencing any action before the Court shall be measured with reference to the acts of those State officials whose conduct has implicated the responsibility of the State in question.

PART VII: DUTIES OF STATES PARTIES
Article 23
GENERAL PRINCIPLES

1. States Parties shall surrender upon request of the Tribunal any individual where it appears that there are reasonable grounds to believe that such a person has committed the international crime of apartheid.
2. States Parties shall provide the Tribunal with all means of judicial assistance and co-operation, including but not limited to letters rogatory, service of writs, assistance in securing testimony and evidence, transmittal of records and transfer of proceedings.
3. States Parties shall recognize the judgements of the Tribunal and execute provisions of such judgements in accordance with their national laws.
4. In the event the Tribunal does not have detentional facilities under its direct control, States Parties will honour requests from the Tribunal to execute its sentences in accordance with their own correctional systems, but subject to continuing jurisdiction of the Tribunal over the transferred offender.
5. States Parties may receive requests for transfers of offenders.
6. States Parties to this Protocol undertake to provide co-operation to organs of enforcement in accordance with the terms of this Protocol, and in particular to:
    (a) Organs of enforcement on a pro rata basis as determined by the Standing Standing Committee of States Parties.
    (b) Budgetary needs of the organs of enforcement shall be computed after taking into account income from voluntary contributions and fines collected by the Tribunal.

[*84]Article 24
SURRENDER OF ACCUSED PERSONS

1. States Parties shall surrender upon a request of the Tribunal any individual sought to appear before the Tribunal for any proceeding arising out of the Tribunal's jurisdiction provided that the Tribunal's jurisdiction provided that the Tribunal's request shall be based on reasonable grounds to believe that the person sought has committed a violation of the Convention on the Suppression and Punishment of the Crime of Apartheid.
2. The following acts shall not be a bar to surrender a person to the Tribunal for any acts constituting a crime:
    (a) That the person sought to be surrendered claims or the State wherein he may be located claims that the act falls within the meaning of the "political offence exception";
    (b) That the individual is a national of the requested State;
    (c) That the requested State otherwise imposes certain conditions or restrictions to the practice of extradition to and from other States.
3. Procedures regulating such transfers shall be determined by the rules of the Tribunal subject to the laws of the requested state.

Article 25
JUDICIAL ASSISTANCE AND OTHER FORMS OF CO-OPERATION

1. The States Parties shall provide the Tribunal with all means of judicial assistance and co-operation including but not limited to letters rogatory, service of writs, assistance in securing testimony and evidence, transmittal of records, transfer of proceedings where applicable.

2. The procedures for such judicial assistance and other forms of co-operation shall be determined by the Tribunal's rules of practice.

Article 26
RECOGNITION OF THE JUDGEMENTS OF THE TRIBUNAL

1. The States Parties agree to recognize the judgements of the Tribunal and to execute its provisions. For the purposes of double jeopardy and evidentiary matters the Tribunal shall recognize the penal judgements of the States Parties.

2. The Tribunal's rules of practice shall govern the recognition of the judgements of the Tribunal and those of the States Parties.

[*85]Article 27
TRANSFER OF OFFENDERS AND EXECUTION OF SENTENCES

1. In the event the Tribunal does not have detentional facilities under its direct control it may request a State Party to execute the sentence in accordance to that Party's correctional system and in that case the Tribunal shall continue to exercise jurisdiction over the offender including his transfer to another State.

2. In the event the Tribunal has placed an offender in its own detention facilities, this person may by agreement transfer to his country of origin.

3. The Tribunal's rule of practice shall determine the basis and condition of the transfer of offenders and the execution of sentences.

PART VIII: TREATY PROVISIONS
Article 28
ENTRY INTO FORCE

1. This Protocol is open for signature to all States Parties to the Convention on the Suppression and Punishment of the Crime of <u>Apartheid</u>, including after its entry into force.

2. This Protocol is subject to ratification, instruments of ratification being deposited with the Secretary-General of the United Nations.

3. Accession to this Protocol shall be effected by deposit of an instrument of accession with the Secretary-General of the United Nations.

4. This Protocol shall enter into force on the thirtieth day after the deposit of the sixth instrument of ratification or accession, and for States thereafter ratifying or acceding to this Protocol, on the thirtieth day after deposit of the applicable instrument.

5. The Secretary-General of the United Nations shall inform all signatory States of:
   (a) All signatures, ratifications, accessions and reservations to this Protocol; and
   (b) The date of entry into force of this Protocol.

6. This Convention, of which the Arabic, Chinese, English, French, Spanish and Russian texts are equally authentic, shall be deposited in the archives of the United Nations and copies thereof shall be transmitted to all signatories.

[*86]Article 29
RESERVATIONS

1. States may make any reservations to this Protocol but shall not be deemed States Parties for the purposes of representation in the Standing Committee if the reservation is as to a material aspect of the Tribunal's jurisdiction, competence and the effects of its judgement.

2. The Standing Committee shall undertake as its first order of business measures toward election of judges of the Tribunal.

Article 30
INITIAL IMPLEMENTATION STEPS

1.   Upon entry into force of this Convention, the Secretary-General of the United Nations shall call the first meeting of the Standing Committee, and shall preside over that meeting until a presiding officer is chosen.

2.   The Standing Committee shall undertake as its first order of business measures toward election of judges of the Tribunal.

Article 31
AMENDMENT

1.   This Protocol may at any time be amended by a vote of three-fourths of the members of the Standing Committee, subject to ratification of such amendments by the same number of States Parties represented in the Standing Committee.

[*87]COMMENTARY
DRAFT OPTIONAL PROTOCOL FOR THE PENAL ENFORCEMENT OF THE INTERNATIONAL CONVENTION FOR THE SUPPRESSION AND PUNISHMENT OF THE CRIME OF <u>APARTHEID</u>

The provisions of this Protocol are largely self-explanatory and require little in the form of commentary. This is particularly obvious in view of the commentary to the Draft Convention on the Establishment of an International Penal Tribunal for the Suppression and Punishment of the Crime of Apartheid and Other International Crimes. Consequently, the commentary which follows is a chronological listing of observations which are more descriptive of the system proposed than its specific details. To facilitate linkage between the provisions of the Protocol and this commentary, an outline of the provisions of the Protocol follows:

1.   This document does not require an amendment to the Charter of the United Nations nor a separate multilateral convention but only an Additional Protocol to the International Convention for the Suppression and Punishment of the Crime of Apartheid.

2.   The Additional Protocol is predicated on the authority of article V of the Apartheid Convention and thus has a legislative basis.

3.   It establishes penal procedures and sanctions in accordance with article V of the Apartheid Convention for violations of article II of the said Convention.

4.   The structure, institutions and organs of enforcement rely essentially on existing institutions. This applies to the Charging Committee, the Prosecutorial Commission and the Division of Human Rights of the United Nations. The Tribunal, however, is anew institution but it relies in its functions on the other already existing organs. Institutional matters are dealt with in a way to minimize the creation of new institutional entities and bodies. It emphasizes the utilization of existing United Nations organs with the addition of new functions and of course the addition of the Standing Committee and the Tribunal. However, all administrative and financial matters have been established in away to preserve the above stated policy.

5.   The enforcement organs were designed to facilitate their implementation and would present few practical difficulties.

6.   It is to be noted however that the Tribunal will have no direct enforcement mechanism and that it relies essentially on the States Parties.

7.   The Standing Committee of States Parties though a new institution will present few problems of implementation. It will have certain general policy functions as well as specific administrative and technical functions on which it will rely on existing institutions.

8.   The jurisdiction and competence of the enforcement organs are universal in geography but limited to violations of article II of the Apartheid Convention.

9.   A distinction between a "crime" and "grave crime" is made in article 3 of the Protocol with respect to sanctions and is both self-explanatory and justified in view of the need to have the Tribunal concern itself only with the more serious violations.

[*89] 10. The jurisdiction of the organs of enforcement shall extend not only to natural persons but to legal entities based on the belief that as a policy greater impact could be obtained by subjecting corporations and public entities to criminal responsibility even though sanctions against them would be in the nature of fines and injunctions.

11.   The penal process commences only upon a decision of the Charging Committee which may interact with the Standing Committee for purposes of mediation of any complaint or claims and their possible resolution outside the framework of the penal process. The Charging committee, however, in the exclusive authority competent to decide on whether the penal process shall be set in motion. Because of the composition of the Charging Committee it is clear that such a body would have the necessary sensitivity to make the appropriate decisions as to the prosecutorial or non-prosecutorial and to undertake any other appropriate measure.

12.   The Prosecutorial Commission acts only pursuant to a determination made by the Charging Committee. In fact the Prosecutorial Commission has no autonomous decision-making and acts exclusively in the prosecution of cases. The Prosecutorial Commission, however, has the power to resort to a variety of measures which may be necessary for the effective performance of its prosecutorial functions.

13.   The adjudication process describes the manner in which hearings on the determination of guilt or innocence shall be conducted which are much the same as for the sanctioning process.

14.   The standards and procedures for each of the organs responsible for the investigation, prosecution, adjudication and sanctioning are subject to certain minimum standards of fairness descried in Part V. Each enforcement organ is to promulgate its rules which are to be published so as to inform the public. This approach maximizes efficiency and legislative economy.

15.   To preserve the right of appeal required by the International Covenant on Civil and Political Rights a post-adjudication process is established.

16.   The judicial integrity, impartiality, and independence of the Tribunal is emphasized by the provisions of article 10 of the Protocol.

17.   The costs of operating this system will be borne by the States Parties and the mechanics for it will be through the Standing Committee. The actual administration of the budget will be left to an administrator who will be appointed by the Division of Human Rights with the approval of the Standing Committee. This is designed to reduce the necessity of creating new institutions.

18.   In keeping with the policy prevailing throughout this Protocol all administrative matters and support will be given by the Division of Human Rights which will be charged to the account of the Protocol and paid through the budget as approved by the Standing Committee.

19.   A provision is established for the enforcement organs to rely on experts for ad hoc assignments which is a device designed to eliminate the need for permanent staffing beyond the administrative and support staff which the Division of Human Rights is to provide.

[*90] 20.   The section's function for the organs of enforcement and the court registry function for the Tribunal shall be performed by the Division of Human Rights.

21.   In so far as the organs of enforcement have no direct enforcement capabilities these duties are to be carried out by the States Parties in accordance with their undertakings as stated in Part VII. Among those duties are those of recognition of the Tribunal orders and their enforcement in accordance with the natural laws of the requested States Parties whose co-operation is requested.

22.   A General Part describing the basic principle of accountability is also included so that the Protocol contains in effect a special part as is also found in criminal codes namely the Apartheid Convention and more specifically article II thereof which is incorporated by reference in this Protocol; a General Part which is made part of this Protocol; and, a sanctioning part which is part of the Protocol. These provisions satisfy the requirements of nullum crimen sine lege, nullum poena sine lege with the exception of the lack of specific sentencing parameters namely the leniency of imprisonment for each crime and the amount of fine to be levied. This short-coming however can be cured by the appropriate enactment of the Tribunal rules which could embody those with specificity. The promulgation and publication of these rules containing specific sentencing considerations would satisfy the requirements of the provisions of legality recognized in most legal systems of the world.

23.   The standards of fairness which are to be guaranteed in all proceedings before the enforcement organs and which are to be reflected in the rules to be promulgated by the said enforcement organs emboding those rights which are contained in the Universal Declaration of Human Rights, the International Covenant on Civil and Political Rights, the Body of Principles on the Protection of Persons from All Forms of Arbitrary Arrest and Detention, the European Convention on the Protection of Fundamental Freedoms, and the Inter-American Convention on the Protection of Human Rights. These standards are also embodied in the resolutions of the XIIth International Congress of Penal Law held in Hamburg in 1979, whose draft and explanatory notes are to be found in 49 Revue Internationale de Droit Penal, vol. 3, 1978.

These provisions are consonant with the European Convention for the Protection of Human Rights and Fundamental Freedoms of 4 November 1950, and additional Protocols. See a. Robertson, Human Rights in Europe (1977), and D. Poncet, La Protection de l'Accuse par la Convention Europeenne des Droits de l'Homme (1977). They are also consonant with the Universal Declaration on Human Rights

(1948), the International Covenant on Civil and Political Rights (1966), the Inter-American Convention on Human Rights (1969), and other applicable conventions. See, e.g., L. Sohn and T. Buergenthal, International Protection of Human Rights (1973).

24. The principles of accountability set forth in Part VI are from the General Part of the Draft International Criminal Code in M.C. Bassiouni, International Criminal Law: A Draft International Criminal Code (Sijthoff 1980), pp. 141 et. seq. and excerpts thereof.

[*91] Article 16 - Definitions

Paragraph 1 defines international crimes with reference to the Protocol thus permitting expansion.

Paragraph 2 incorporates by reference the definition of a State as recognized under international law. This approach was preferred to repetition of one of the generally accepted formulations of a definition of a State because use of such a formulation would call for definition of the terms used in it, such as the Montevideo Convention's provision that a State has the capacity to conduct "international relations", Convention on Rights and Duties of States of 26 December 1933, United Nations, Treaty Series, vol. 165, p. 19; see also United Nations debates on Statehood in connection with Israel and Liechtenstein (Official Records of the Security Council, Third Year, 385rd meeting, No. 128, pp. 9-12, and ibid., fourth Year, 433rd meeting, No. 35, pp. 4-5).

For the sake of convenience, the term "State" is deemed to include groups of States acting collectively.

Paragraph 3 exemplifies a correlation between "person" and "individual", and confines the meaning of those terms to exclude such entities as corporations or other so-called juridical persons.

Paragraph 5 begins with another correlation for the sake of convenience, with respect to the terms "group" and "organization". The definition is provided because of the use of these terms in provisions dealing with collective responsibility, which is discussed below.

Paragraph 6 on participation in a group action, is designed for the same purpose. The model of responsibility arose out of the Nuremberg trials and Tokyo war crimes trials. See article 9 of the London Charter of 8 August 1945, Control Council Ordinance No. 10 of 20 December 1945; for a discussion of the basis of the responsibility and the cases decided at Nuremberg and Tokyo, see L. Friedman, The Law of War: A Documentary History (1972); see also Wright, History of the United Nations War Crimes Commission (1949).

Paragraph 7 and 8 are basically the provisions of the Model Penal Code relating to solicitation and conspiracy, American Law Institute Model Penal Code (1962). See generally M.C. Bassiouni, Substantive Criminal Law (1978), and W. LaFave and A. Scott, Criminal Law (1972); see also for a comparison with the German Penal Code, G. Fletcher, Rethinking Criminal Law (1978).

The definition of "solicitation" was found to be workable under civil law, as well as common law systems. On the other hand, the concept of conspiracy is not generally recognized under the civil law systems, so that inclusion of this term required a common law definition even though the requirement of an "overt act" brings such a definition close to preparatory acts in civilist-Romanist systems. See R. Merle and A. Vitu, Traite de Droit Criminel (1967). It is to be noted that conspiracy and participation in a group action are separate terms with separate definitions. The concept, however, is found in the Nuremberg and Tokyo War Crimes trials.

[*92] In paragraph 9 "attempt" was given a definition based on the Model Penal Code but with modifications reflecting the concern of civil law jurists. For example, the term "preparation" has been omitted and "substantial step" has been amplified by the addition of the words "unequivocal and direct". This modification was intended to provide a meaning that would be recognized under civil law as being as limited as the meaning that these provisions would be given under common law systems. See Fletcher, op. cit.

The definitions for the terms "participation in a group action", "solicitation", "conspiracy" and "attempt" are provided in the "General Part". Such conduct, in reference to the proscriptions of the "Special Part", is included in the "General Part" as opposed to the "Special Part" as is more consonant with the civil law system. (See generally R. Merle and A. Vitu, Traite de Droit Criminel (1967); P. Bouzat and J. Pinatel, Traite de Droit Penale (mise a jour 1975); H.-H. Jescheck, Lehrbuch des Strafrechts (1975)).

Paragraphs 10 and 11 deal with "person in authority" and "omission" and are included for the purpose of criminalizing failure of persons in authority to fulfil their legal duties arising out of any specific duty referred to in the "Special Part".

It is clear that the definitions provided reflect a certain conceptual choice and the attempt to integrate civilist-Romanist and common law principles and those principles which have emerged from the history and practice of international criminal law. (In that respect see S. Glaser, Infractions Internationale (1957) and S. Plawski, Etude des Principes Foundamentaux du Droit International Penal (1972)).

Article 17 - Responsibility

The basis of responsibility or accountability follows the "Definitions" and precedes "Elements of an International Crime" because of the view that the various levels and types of accountability should be set forth first so as to define to whom and on what basis responsibility can be imputed. This approach fits neither the common law nor the civil law models. It was deemed appropriate subject to the special status of these Tribunals and the historical peculiarities of international criminal law in light of the precedents of the Leipzig War Crimes Trials, though these were subject to German laws, and the Nuremberg and Tokyo War Crimes Trials. There is no analogy to be found in the writings of scholars to that approach. This identification of criminally accountable subjects should be read in pari materiae with the provision on "Definitions".

Under paragraphs 1 through 5 criminal responsibility is assigned not only to committing a crime, but also to attempting, soliciting or conspiring to commit any crime. However, because the element of harm is required unless that requirement is modified by the definition of the specific offence, criminal responsibility for acts not constituting a "commission" are controlled by the definitions of the crime, which may have a different requirement. Other provisions relating to individual responsibility are taken from parallel provisions of national penal codes. It was noted that the provision relating to responsibility for acts of others is not intended to create a new crime but rather to express the principle of derivative responsibility which exists in one way or another in every penal system. These provisions are more in conformity to the common law approach than to the continental approach.

[*93] The provisions regarding group responsibility were framed to serve two purposes: to make groups themselves accountable under the article dealing with penalties, and to prevent an individual from escaping responsibility where he provided a group with continued intangible support despite its foreseeable criminal conduct as reflected in the principles of the Nuremberg and Tokyo War Crimes Trials. Special provision is made for responsibility of persons in authority in order to incorporate responsibility for failure to act. This provision is based on military law and command responsibility as it is incorporated in the Formal Geneva Convention of 12 August 1949 and in particular in article 76 of the 1977 Additional Protocol Amending the Geneva Conventions of 12 August 1949 concerning failure of superiors to control acts of subordinates and other sources of international criminal law.

Paragraph 6 on State responsibility is essentially drawn from the draft Principles of State Responsibility adopted by the International Law Commission (A/CN.4/246). See also P. Guggenheim, Traite de Droit International (1952) and C. Eagleton, The Responsibility of States in International Law (1923); Strupp, Handbuch des Volkerrechts - Das volkerrechtliche Delikt (1920), and more recently P. Munch, Das volkerrechtlicke Delikt (1963) and H.-H. Jescheck, Die Verantwortlichkeit der Staatsorganen - Nach Volkerstrafrecht (1952).

These provisions are intended to cover both responsibility for failure to act and non-State entities that subsequently become State by analogy to principles of State succession in international law. (See generally D.P. O'Connell, State Succession in International Law (1967)).

Article 18 - Elements of an International Crime

This provision seeks to synthesize common law and civil law concepts as well as to take into account fundamental principles of international criminal law in providing for and defining the four essential elements of an international crime. There seems to be agreement on the need for all such elements, even though there are divergences with respect to the meaning and content of each one. Probably the most authoritative work on the subject in Stefan Glaser, Infraction Internationale (1957). In it, Glaser starts, as does this article, with the material element, but then interjects certain legal justifications before dealing with the mental element. He concludes his work with participation and complicity. In this respect, a conceptual difficulty arises and the choice was to separate the required elements of a crime from the "responsibility", and conditions of "Exoneration". The approach of dividing "Responsibility", "Element of an International Crime", and "Exoneration" into three different provisions seeks to avoid doctrinal differences between common law and civil law by devising a neutral approach.

The material element satisfies both the common law and civil law systems, as does a great extent the mental element, though it is couched in more objective terms.

In recognition of the fact that most civil law criminal codes do not specify causation as a separate element, the element of causation could be interpreted as included in the material element of a crime in civil law systems and separate for common law systems.

[*94] It was agreed that the mental element should not extend to mere negligence, but it was feared that mere exclusion of negligence would result in responsibility under civil law systems for mental states between more negligence and recklessness. Accordingly, the decision was made to list the mental states of intent, knowledge, and recklessness with the understanding that recklessness went beyond the dolus eventualis, described under the 1976 German Penal Code as a state of mind much that the person knew that harm would result.

For common law systems, however, a separate provision on causation was added.

The forth such element, harm, was recognized as requiring interpretation in connection with the offence in question. It was determined that provision should be made for circumstances where an offence did not require an outcome whose character would match the usual meaning of the word "harm". Similar concern was voiced regarding the element of causation, so that it was determined to qualify the listing of elements with a clause providing that these elements may be altered by the definition of a given crime.

Article 19 - Immunities

This provision is set forth immediately after principles of responsibility and imputability, the elements of a crime, because of the peculiarity of international law with respect to immunities which derive from the principles of sovereignty. (See Sutton, "Jurisdiction over Diplomatic Personnel and International Organizations' Personnel for Common Crimes and for Internationally Defined Crimes", in M.C. Bassiouni and V.P. Nanda, A Treatise in International Criminal Law (1973), vol. II, p. 97. See also Oppenheim, International Law (8th ed., Lauterpacht, 1955), p. 757; Harvard Research on International Law, Diplomatic Privileges and Immunities, 226 A.J.I.L. 15-187 (Supp. 1932); and "Immunité, Extraterritorialité et Droit d'Asile en Droit Penal International", 49 Revue Internationale de Droit Penal, No. 2 (1978)).

This text is based on the provisions of: 1961 Vienna Convention on Diplomatic Relations; 1963 Convention on Consular Relations; 1968 United Nations Draft Convention on Special Missions; 1946 Convention on the Privileges and Immunities of the United Nations; 1947 Convention on the Privileges and Immunities of the Specialized Agencies; Draft Articles on the Representation of States in their Relations with International Organizations of the International Law Commission, 1972; Draft Articles on the Protection and Inviolability of Diplomatic Agents and Other Persons Entitled to Special Protection Under International Law of the Organization of American States, 1971; Convention to Prevent and Punish the Acts of Terrorism Taking the Form of Crimes Against Persons and Related Extortions that are of International Significance, 1971; the 1973 Convention on the Prevention and Punishment of Crimes Against Internationally Protected Persons, including Diplomatic Agents; The General Agreement of Privileges and Immunities of the Council of Europe of 1949; the Supplementary Agreement of 18 March 1959; and, the four additional Protocols to the General Agreement on Privileges and Immunities of the Council of Europe (1952, 1961).

The text also takes into account customary principles of international law on the immunity of Heads of State and the practice of States. The nature of the immunity provided herein is, however, more narrowly circumscribed, as it is not absolute. [*95] the text obligates the contracting parties whose national is the subject of any immunity category contained herein to take appropriate action against such persons, but permits waiver of that jurisdiction in favour of the International Court much as do the NATO and Warsaw Pact countries on Status of Forces Agreement; (see Coker, "the Status of Visiting Military Forces in Europe", in M.C. Bassiouni and V.P. Nanda (eds), A Treatise on International Criminal Law (1973) vol. II, p. 115).

Article 20 - Penalties

Separate provisions are made for punishment of different types of offenders, all subject to the requirement in section 1 that punishment be proportional to seriousness of the violation and the harm threatened or caused as well as to the degree of responsibility of the actor.

The International Criminal Court is directed to develop appropriate rules before exercising its jurisdiction. It must be noted that principles of legality are not violated by these provisions because the Court should first promulgate the penalties and the <u>criteria</u> for their application.

Paragraph 3 recognizes the principle of the Nuremberg Tribunals that organizations as such may be punished by means of fines. See Dinstein, <u>infra</u>. This provision goes beyond continental principles.

Under paragraph 4, punishment of States by imposition of fines is provided, it being considered beyond the scope of the court's ability to impose other sanctions. (See Triffterer, "Jurisdiction Over States for Crimes of State", and Baxter, "Jurisdiction Over War Crimes and Crimes Against Humanity: Individual and State Accountability" in M.C. Bassiouni and V.P. Nanda (eds), <u>A Treatise on International Criminal Law</u> (1973) vol. II, pp. 86-96 and 65-85. See also Munch, "State Responsibility in International Law", in Bassiouni and Nanda, <u>supra</u>, Vol. I, pp. 143 <u>et seq.</u>; C. Eagleton, <u>The Responsibility of States in International Law</u> (1924); C. de Visscher, <u>La responsabilite des Etats</u> (1924); F. Munch, <u>Das volkerrechtlicke Delikt</u> (1963); J. Castillon, <u>Les Reparations allemandes - Deux experiences</u> (1919-1932, 1945-1952), (1953), and H.-H. Jescheck, <u>Die Verantwortlichkeit der Staatsorganen - Nach Volkersstrafrecht</u> (1952)).

Paragraph 5 confers discretion on the Court whether to impose cumulative sentences for crimes arising from a single transaction.

Paragraph 6, dealing with mitigation, provides for the possibility that the fact that an accused was acting under orders could be considered a mitigating factor. This reflects the content of article 8 of the London Charter of 8 August 1945 establishing the International Military Tribunal at Nuremberg. (See Y. Dinstein, <u>The Defense of "Obedience to Superior Orders" in International Law</u>, p. 260 at 283 (1965)).

Article 21 - Exoneration

While the civil law system would view the conditions of exoneration listed in this article as a questionable combination of principles of responsibility and legal defence, it was felt that a single provision containing all conditions which ultimately result in exoneration from responsibility, irrespective of their doctrinal or dogmatic basis should be placed together, as it gives these aspects a sense of cohesion and practical use by an international tribunal.

|96| The self-defence provision, paragraph 2, is based on that contained in article 2, paragraph 2 (a). of the European Convention for the Protection of Human Rights and Fundamental Freedoms as well as on the language used in the Model Penal Code. The requirement that the defender reasonably believe that forceful response is necessary is a common law requirement which is superfluous for civil law systems. On the other hand, the introduction of the requirement that the response be to an "imminent" use of unlawful force may be viewed under the common law as surplusage.

The defence of necessity is limited in paragraph 3 to use of force not likely to produce death as a policy decision to restrain individuals.

Coercion, under paragraph 4, was limited as a defence to situations where the threat or use of force as "imminent".

Paragraph 5 makes obedience to superior orders a defence where the person accused was not in a position to know of the criminal nature of his acts. Conversely, paragraph 6 protects persons from prosecutions for refusing to follow orders to commit crimes.

Paragraph 7 adopts the formulation of the Model Penal Code relating to mistake of law or fact, conditioning this defence on negation of criminal intent.

Paragraph 8 on double jeopardy simply seeks to give effect to the principle <u>non bis in idem</u>. Subparagraph (d) recognizes the competence of the International Criminal Court to overlook pardons and amnesties of other jurisdictions in order to avoid that States resort to that practice from negotiating a person's punishability. It applies to the actual conduct involved rather than to any legal characterization of that conduct by any State.

Paragraph 9 is based on the Model Penal Code's provision on the defence of insanity. This differs from civilist systems where such a condition is deemed a pre-condition to criminal responsibility.

Paragraph 10 on the defence of intoxication springs from the same source, and excludes voluntary intoxication as a defense to crimes requiring intent.

The renunciation principles set forth in section 11 also stem from the Model Penal Code but are in keeping with the continental approach.

This provision includes principles of justification, conditions negating criminal responsibility, excusability and procedural defenses. From a Romanist-Civilist perspective it is doctrinally challengeable on the very grounds that it encompasses too much diversity. However, its justification rests on pragmatic reasons which avoid the dogmatism that has been at the basis of so much debate between European penalists for so long.

Article 22 - Statute of Limitation

The approach adopted measures the limitation period by the maximum potential penalty required for similar offences under the national law of the State in which the crime was committed as is the case under Penalties. It should be noted that, [*97] under this approach, where the maximum penalty is life imprisonment or death, there is no limitation period. Also, it was necessary to add paragraph 1 (c) because offences by states are punishable only by fines under this Code. This approach was preferred notwithstanding the Convention on Non-Applicability of Statutes of Limitations to War Crimes and Crimes Against Humanity, of 9 December 1968; (see also 39 Revue Internationale de Droit Penal (1968) dedicated to this topic, and the European Convention on the Non-Applicability of Statutory Limitation to Crimes Against Humanity and War Crimes of 1974). In fact, the result of this approach and that of the Conventions referred to above, is for all practical purposes the same except for minor offences and in fact avoids the difficulties which have prevented the ratification of these treaties by a number of States.

The duties of States Parties are to provide financial support for the enforcement organs and for the effective function and implementation of this Protocol. In addition they must provide such judicial assistance and co-operation as to make this Protocol effective. In particular, the means of surrendering of accused persons to the Tribunal much as an obligation to extradition between States, noting, however, that the crime of apartheid is not to be considered within the meaning of the political offence exception (see M.C. Bassiouni, International Extradition and World Public Order (1974)). Other forms of judicial assistance involves the traditional method of letters rogatory, securing of testimony, transmittal of records, etc. In addition the very important provisions dealing with recognition of the judgements of the Tribunal so that they may be given effect in the States which are States Parties. A provision is also made for the transfer of offenders and execution of sentencing which may be a useful device. To a large extent the model for these provisions may be found in M.C. Bassiouni, International Criminal Law: A Draft International Criminal Code, pages 107 through 130.

The treaty provisions are somewhat standard, except for the reservations clause which though in keeping with the Vienna Convention on treaty interpretation also takes into account the relevant aspects of the Advisory Opinion By the International Court of Justice On Reservations To The Convention On The Prevention And Punishment of Genocide, 1951 I.C.J. 15.

One of the conditions for this Protocol's implementation is, of course, the need for the Standing Committee to be created and to start functioning and that is why a special provision has been made to that effect.

DRAFT STATUTE FOR AN INTERNATIONAL CRIMINAL COURT (ANNEX TO THE REPORT OF THE COMMITTEE ON INTERNATIONAL CRIMINAL JURISDICTION ON ITS SESSION FROM 1 TO 31 AUGUST 1951

ANNEXES
Annex I. Draft statute for an international criminal court[1]

CHAPTER I
General Principles
Article 1
Purpose of the Court

There is established an International Criminal Court to try persons accused of crimes under international law, as may be provided in conventions or special agreements among States parties to the present Statute.

Article 2
Law to be applied by the Court

The Court shall apply international law, including international criminal law, and where appropriate, national law.

Article 3
Permanent Nature of the Court

The Court shall be a permanent body. Sessions shall be called only when matters before it require consideration.

CHAPTER II
Organization of the Court
Article 4
Qualifications of Judges

The Court shall be composed of a body of independent judges, elected regardless of their nationality from among persons of high moral character, who possess the qualifications required in their respective countries for appointment in the highest judicial offices, or are jurisconsults of recognized competence in international criminal law.

Article 5
Number of Judges

The Court shall consist of nine judges.

Article 6
Nationality of Judges

1. Judges may be elected from candidates of any nationality or without nationality.
2. No two judges may be nationals of the same State. A person who, for the purpose of membership in the Court, could be regarded as a national of more than one State, shall be deemed to be a national of the State in which he ordinarily exercises civil and political rights.

Article 7
Nomination of Candidates

1. Judges shall be elected from a list of candidates nominated by the States parties to the present Statute.
2. Each State may submit the names of not more than four candidates.

---

[1]   Titles of articles have been included for purposes of reference and identification only, and shall not be considered as elements of interpretation.

Article 8
Invitation to Nominate

1.   The date of each election shall be fixed by the Secretary-General of the United Nations.
2.   At least three months before this date, he shall address a written request to the States parties to the present Statute, inviting them to undertake, within a time specified, the nomination of qualified persons in a position to accept the duties of a judge.

Article 9
List of Candidates

The Secretary-General of the United Nations shall prepare a list, in alphabetical order, of all candidates. He shall submit the list to the States parties to the present Statute.

Article 10
Representative Character of the Court

The electors shall bear in mind that the judges, as a body, should, as far as possible, represent the main forms of civilization and the principal legal systems of the world.

Article 11
Election of Judges

1.   The judges shall be elected at meetings of representatives of the States parties to the present Statute by an absolute majority of those present and voting. The Secretary-General of the United Nations shall, after due notice to each of such States, convene these meetings.
2.   In the event of more than one national of the same State obtaining a sufficient number of votes for election, the one who obtains the greatest number of votes shall be considered as elected and if the votes are equally divided the elder or eldest candidate shall be considered as elected.

Article 12
Terms of Office

1.   The judges shall be elected for nine years and may be re-elected; provided, however, that of the judges elected at the first election, the terms of three judges shall expire at the end of three years and the terms of three more judges shall expire at the end of six years.
2.   The judges whose terms are to expire at the end of the initial periods of three and six years shall be chosen by lot drawn by the Secretary-General of the United Nations immediately after the first election has been completed.
3.   Each judge shall continue to discharge his duties until his place has been filled. Though replaced, he shall finish any case which he may have begun.
4.   In the case of the resignation of a judge, the resignation shall be addressed to the President of the Court, who shall transmit the resignation to the Secretary-General. This transmission shall make that place vacant.

Article 13
Solemn Declaration

Each judge shall, before taking up his duties, make a solemn declaration in open court that he will perform his functions impartially and conscientiously.

Article 14
Privileges and Immunities

Each judge, when engaged on the business of the Court, shall enjoy diplomatic privileges and immunities.

Article 15
Occupations of Judges

1. No judge shall engage in any occupation which interferes with his judicial function during sessions of the Court. Nor shall he engage in any occupation which is incompatible with his function as a judge.
2. Any doubt on this point shall be settled by the decision of the Court.

Article 16
Disability of Judges

1. No judge may participate in proceedings relating to any case in which he has previously taken part in any capacity whatsoever.
2. Any doubt on this point shall be settled by the decision of the Court.

Article 17
Disqualification of Judges

1. If, for some special reason, a judge considers that he should not participate in a particular proceeding, he shall so inform the President.
2. Any party to a proceeding may submit that a judge should not participate in that proceeding. Such submission shall be addressed to the President.
3. If the President, upon receipt of such submission or of his own motion, considers that a judge should not participate in particular proceeding, the President shall so advise the judge.
4. If the President and the judge disagree on the issue, the Court shall decide.

Article 18
Dismissal of Judges

1. No judge shall be dismissed unless, in the unanimous opinion of the other judges, he has ceased to fulfil the conditions required for his continuance in office.
2. Formal notification of such unanimous opinion shall be made to the Secretary-General of the United Nations by the Registrar.
3. This notification shall make the place vacant.

Article 19
Vacancies

1. Vacancies shall be filled by the same method as that prescribed for the first election, except that the Secretary-General of the United Nations, shall within one month of the occurrence of a vacancy, issue the invitations provided for in article 8.
2. A judge elected to replace a judge whose term of office has not expired shall hold office for the remainder of his predecessor's term.

Article 20
Officers

1. The Court shall elect its President and Vice-President for three years; each may be re-elected.
2. The Court shall appoint its Registrar and shall provide for the appointment of such other officers as may be necessary.

Article 21
Seat of the Court

The permanent seat of the Court shall be established at . . . The Court may, however, sit and exercise its functions elsewhere whenever the Court considers it desirable.

ARTICLE 22
Emoluments

Each participating judge shall be paid travel expenses, and a daily allowance when the Court is in session. Each judge shall be paid an annual remuneration.

Article 23
Finances

The States parties to the present Statute shall create and maintain a fund to be collected and administered in accordance with regulations adopted by the parties. From this fund shall be paid the costs of maintaining and operating the Court, the Committing Authority, the Prosecution and the Board of Clemency, including the fees and expenses of counsel for the defence as provided in article 38, paragraph 2, sub-paragraph (c).

Article 24
Rules of Court

1.   The Court shall adopt rules for carrying out its functions. In particular, it shall prescribe rules of procedure and such general principles governing the admission of evidence as the Court may deem necessary.
2.   These rules and any amendments thereto shall be published without delay and shall not be altered so as to affect pending proceedings.

CHAPTER III
Competence of the Court
Article 25
Jurisdiction as to persons

The Court shall be competent to judge natural persons only, including persons who have acted as Head of State or agent of government.

Article 26
Attribution of Jurisdiction

Jurisdiction may be conferred upon the Court by States parties to the present Statute, by convention or, with respect to a particular case, by special agreement or by unilateral declaration.

Article 27
Recognition of Jurisdiction

No person shall be tried before the Court unless jurisdiction has been conferred upon the Court by the State or States of which he is a national and by the State or States in which the crime is alleged to have been committed.

Article 28
Approval of Jurisdiction by the United Nations

No jurisdiction may be conferred upon the Court without the approval of the General Assembly of the United Nations.

Article 29
Access to the Court

Proceedings before the Court may be instituted only by:
(a)   The General Assembly of the United Nations,
(b)   Any organization of States so authorized by the General Assembly of the United Nations, or
(c)   A State party to the present Statute which has conferred jurisdiction upon the Court over such offence as are involved in those proceedings.

Article 30
Challenge of Jurisdiction

1.   The jurisdiction of the Court may be challenged not only by the parties to any proceeding, but also by any State referred to in article 27, which may intervene for this purpose.
2.   Such challenges made prior to the beginning of trial, shall be considered by the Court before the trial begins.
3.   Such challenges made after the beginning of trial, shall be considered by the Court at such time as the Court thinks fit.

Article 31
Assistance of States

1.   The Court may request national authorities to assist it in the performance of its duties.
2.   A State shall be obliged to render such assistance only in conformity with any convention or other instrument in which the State has accepted such obligation.

Article 32
Penalties

The Court shall impose upon an accused, upon conviction, such penalty as the Court may determine, subject to any limitations prescribed in the instrument conferring jurisdiction upon the Court.

CHAPTER IV
Committing Authority and Prosecuting Attorney
Article 33
Committing authority

1.   There shall be established within the framework of the United Nations a Committing Authority composed of nine members, elected in the same manner, at the same time, on the same terms, and possessing the same qualifications as the judges.
2.   The function of the Authority shall be to examine the evidence offered by the complainant to support the complaint.
3.   The complainant shall designate an agent or agents who shall present the evidence before the Authority.
4.   If the authority is satisfied that the evidence is sufficient to support the complaint, the authority shall so certify to the Court and the complainant.
5.   Before issuing any such certificate, the authority shall give the accused reasonable opportunity to be heard and to adduce such evidence as he may desire.
6.   The authority shall adopt its own rules of procedure.

Article 34
Prosecuting Attorney

1.   The States parties to the present Statute, at the meetings and in the manner provided for in article 11, shall elect a panel of ten persons whose duty it shall be, whenever a certificate for trial is issued by the Committing Authority to elect forthwith a Prosecuting Attorney who shall possess the same qualifications as a member of the Court.
2.   The Prosecuting Attorney shall file with the Court an indictment of the accused based on the findings certified by the Committing Authority and shall be responsible for conducting the prosecution before the Court.

CHAPTER V
Procedure
Article 35
Indictment

1. The indictment shall contain a concise statement of the facts which constitute each alleged offence and a specific reference to the law under which the accused is charged.
2. The Court may authorize amendment of the indictment.

Article 36
Notice of the Indictment

1. The Court shall bring the indictment to the notice of the accused, of the State of which the accused is alleged to be a national and of the State in which the crime is alleged to have been committed.
2. The Court shall not proceed with the trial unless satisfied that the accused has had the indictment or any amendment thereof, as the case may be, served upon him and has sufficient time to prepare his defence.

Article 37
No Jury

Trials shall be without a jury.

Article 38
Rights of the accused

1. The accused shall be presumed innocent until proved guilty.
2. The accused shall have a fair trial and, in particular:
    (a) The right to be present at all stages of the proceedings;
    (b) The right to conduct his own defence or to be defended by counsel of his own choice, and to have his counsel present at all stages of the proceedings;
    (c) The right to have the expenses of his defence charged to the fund referred to in article 23 in case the Court is satisfied that the accused is financially unable to engage the services of counsel;
    (d) The right to have the proceedings of the Court, including documentary evidence, translated into his own language;
    (e) The right to interrogate, in person or by his counsel, any witness and to inspect any document or other evidence introduced during the trial;
    (f) The right to adduce oral and other evidence in his defence;
    (g) The right to the assistance of the Court in obtaining access to material which the Court is satisfied may be relevant to the issues before the Court;
3. The accused shall have the right to be heard by the Court but shall not be compelled to speak. His refusal to speak shall not be relevant to the determination of his guilt. Should he elect to speak, he shall be liable to questioning by the Court and by counsel.

Article 39
Publicity of Hearings

1. The Court shall sit in public unless there are exceptional circumstances in which the Court finds that public sittings might prejudice the interests of justice.
2. The deliberations of the Court shall take place in private and shall not be discussed.

ARTICLE 40
Warrants of Arrest

The Court shall have power to issue warrants of arrest related to crimes over which the Court has jurisdiction.

Article 41
Provisional Liberty of Accused

The Court shall decide whether the accused shall remain in custody during the trial or be provisionally set at liberty, and the conditions under which such provisional liberty shall be granted.

Article 42
Powers of the Court

The Court shall have the powers necessary to the proper conduct of the trial, including the power to require the attendance of witnesses, require production of documents and other evidentiary material, rule out irrelevant issues, evidence and statements, and maintain order at the trial.

Article 43
Dismissal of Case

The Court may dismiss at any stage of the proceedings any case in which the Court is satisfied that no fair trial can then be had. In the event of such dismissal, the Court shall discharge the accused and may also acquit him.

Article 44
Withdrawal of Prosecution

A prosecution may be withdrawn only with the approval of the Court. In the event of such approval, the Court shall discharge the accused and may also acquit him.

Article 45
Quorum

The participation of seven judges shall suffice to constitute the Court.

Article 46
Required Majority

1.   Final judgments and sentences of the Court shall require a majority vote of the judges participating in the trial.
2.   The same requirement shall apply to other decisions of the Court, provided that, in the event of an equality of votes, the vote of the presiding judge shall be decisive.

Article 47
Contents and Signature of Judgment

1.   The judgment shall state, in relation to each accused, the reasons upon which it is based.
2.   The judgment shall contain the names of the judges who have taken part in the decision. It shall be signed by the President and the Registrar.

ARTICLE 48
Separate Opinions

If the judgment of the Court does not represent the unanimous opinion of the judges, any judge shall be entitled to deliver a separate opinion.

ARTICLE 49
Delivery of Judgment

The judgment shall be read in open Court

Article 50
No Appeal

The judgment shall be final and without appear.

Article 51
Subsequent Trial

No person who has been tried and acquitted or convicted before the Court shall be subsequently tried for the same offence in any court, within the jurisdiction of any State which has conferred jurisdiction upon the Court with respect to such offence.

Article 52
Execution of Sentences

Sentences shall be executed in accordance with conventions relating to the matter. In the absence of such conventions, arrangements for the execution may be made, upon motion of the Court, by the Secretary-General of the United Nations with any State.

Article 53
Revision of Judgment

1.　An accused who has been found guilty may apply to the Court for revision of the judgment.
2.　An application for revision shall not be entertained unless the Court is satisfied:
　　(a)　That a fact was discovered of such a nature as to be a decisive factor; and
　　(b)　That that fact was, when the judgment was given, unknown to the Court and the applicant.
3.　Revision proceedings shall be opened by a judgment of the Court expressly recording the existence of the new fact and recognizing that it has such a character as to lay the case open to revision.

CHAPTER VI
Clemency
Article 54
Board of Clemency

1.　A Board of Clemency consisting of five members shall be established by the States parties to the present Statute.
2.　The Board shall have the powers of pardon and parole and of suspension, reduction and other alteration of a sentence of the Court.
The Board shall adopt its own rules of procedure.

CHAPTER VII
Final Provisions
Article 55
Special Tribunals

Nothing in the present Statute shall be taken to prejudice the right of two or more States parties thereto jointly to set up special tribunals to try the perpetrators of crimes over which each of such States has jurisdiction according to the general rules of international law.

Annex . Vœu

The Committee on International Criminal Jurisdiction,

Considering that the crime of genocide—a crime under international law—has been exactly defined in the Convention on the Prevention and Punishment of the Crime of Genocide,

Considering that this Convention has been ratified by twenty-eight States,

Considering that special mention of the crime of genocide was made in the terms of reference of the International Law Commission under General Assembly resolution 260 II (111), and in those of this Committee under General Assembly resolution 489 (V),

Expresses the *Vœu* that along with the instrument establishing the International Criminal court a protocol shall be drawn up conferring jurisdiction on that Court in respect of the crime of genocide.

REVISED DRAFT STATUTE FOR AN INTERNATIONAL CRIMINAL COURT (ANNEX TO THE REPORT OF THE 1953 COMMITTEE ON INTERNATIONAL CRIMINAL JURISDICTION ON ITS SESSION HELD FROM 27 JULY TO 20 AUGUST 1953

ANNEX
Revised draft statute for an international criminal court

CHAPTER I
General Principles
Article 1
Purpose of the Court

There is established an International Criminal Court to try natural persons accused of crimes generally recognized under international law.

Article 2
Law to be applied by the Court

The Court shall apply international law, including international criminal law, and where appropriate, national law.

Article 3
Permanent Nature of the Court

The Court shall be a permanent body. Sessions shall be called only when matters before it require consideration.

CHAPTER II
Organization of the Court
Article 4
Qualifications of Judges

The Court shall be composed of a body of independent judges, elected regardless of their nationality from among persons of high moral character, who possess the qualifications required in their respective countries for appointment to the highest judicial offices, or are jurisconsults of recognized competence in international law, especially in international criminal law.

Article 5
Number of Judges

The Court shall consist of fifteen judges.

Article 6
Nationality of Judges

1. Judges may be elected from candidates of any nationality or without nationality.
2. No two judges may be nationals of the same State. A person who, for the purpose of membership in the Court, could be regarded as a national of more than one State shall be deemed to be a national of the State in which he ordinarily exercises civil and political rights.

Article
Nomination of candidates
Alternative A

1. Judges shall be elected from a list of candidates nominated by the States which have conferred jurisdiction upon the Court.

Alternative B

1 Judges shall be elected from a list of candidates nominated by the Members of the United Nations and by those non-member States which have conferred jurisdiction upon the Court.

2.   Each State may submit the names of not more than four candidates.

Article 8
Invitation to Nominate

1.   The date of each election shall be fixed by the Secretary-General of the United Nations.

Alternative A

2.   At least three months before this date, he shall address a written request to the States which have conferred jurisdiction upon the Court, inviting them to undertake, within a time specified, the nomination of qualified persons in a position to accept the duties of a judge.

Alternative B

2.   At least three months before this date, he shall address a written request to the States referred to in article 7 [alternative B], inviting them to undertake, within a time specified, the nomination of qualified persons in a position to accept the duties of a judge.

Article 9
List of Candidates

Alternative A

The Secretary-General of the United Nations shall prepare a list, in alphabetical order, of all candidates. He shall submit the list to the States which have conferred jurisdiction upon the Court.

Alternative B

The Secretary-General of the United Nations shall prepare a list, in alphabetical order, of all candidates. He shall submit the list to the States referred to in article 7 [alternative B].

Article 10
Representative Character of the Court

The electors shall bear in mind that the judges, as a body, should, as far as possible, represent the main forms of civilization and the principal legal systems of the world.

Article 11
Election of Judges

Alternative A

1.   The Judges shall be elected, at meetings of representatives of the States which have conferred jurisdiction upon the Court, by an absolute majority of those present and voting. The Secretary-General of the United Nations shall, after due notice to each of such States, convene these meetings.

Alternative B

1.   The Judges shall be elected at meetings of the States referred to in article 7 [alternative B], by an absolute majority of those present and voting. The Secretary-General of the United Nations shall, after due notice to each of such States, convene these meetings.

2.   In the event of more than one national of the same State obtaining a sufficient number of votes for election, the one who obtains the greatest number of votes shall be considered as elected and if the votes are equally divided the elder or eldest candidate shall be considered as elected.

Article 12
Terms of Office

1.   The judges shall be elected for nine years and may be re-elected; provided, however, that of the judges elected at the first election, the terms of five judges shall expire at the end of three years and the terms of five more judges shall expire at the end of six years.

2.   The judges whose terms are to expire at the end of the initial periods of three and six years shall be chosen by lot drawn by the Secretary-General of the United Nations immediately after the first election has been completed.

3.   Each judge whose term of office has expired shall continue to discharge his duties until his place has been filled. Though replaced, he shall finish any case which he may have begun.

4.   In the case of the resignation of a judge, the resignation shall be addressed to the President of the Court, who shall transmit the resignation to the Secretary-General. This transmission shall make the place vacant.

Article 13
Solemn Declaration
Each judge shall, before taking up his duties, make a solemn declaration in open court that he will perform his functions impartially and conscientiously.

Article 14
Privileges and immunities
Each judge shall, when engaged on the business of the Court, shall enjoy diplomatic privileges and immunities.

Article 15
Occupations of Judges
1.   No judge shall engage in any occupation which interferes with his judicial function during sessions of the Court. Nor shall he engage in any occupation which is incompatible with his functions as a judge.
2.   Any doubt on this point shall be settled by the decision of the Court.

Article 16
Disability of Judges
1.   No judge may participate in proceedings relating to any case in which he has previously taken part in any capacity whatsoever.
2.   Any doubt on this point shall be settled by the decision of the Court.

Article 17
Disqualification of Judges
1.   If, for some special reason, a judge considers that he should not participate in a particular proceeding, he shall so inform the President.
2.   Any party to a proceeding may submit that a judge should not participate in that proceeding,. Such submission shall be addressed to the President.
3.   If the President, upon receipt of such submission or of his own motion, considers that a judge should not participate in a particular proceeding, the President shall so advise the judge.
4.   If the President and the judge disagree on the issue, the Court shall decide.

Article 18
Dismissal of Judges
1.   No judge shall be dismissed unless, in the unanimous opinion of the other judges, he has ceased to fulfil the conditions required for his continuance in office.
2.   Formal notification of such unanimous opinion shall be made to the Secretary-General of the United Nations by the Registrar.
3.   This notification shall make the place vacant, and thereupon the dismissed judge shall immediately cease to perform all functions as a member of the Court.

Article 19
Vacancies
1.   Vacancies shall be filled by the same method as that prescribed for the first election, except that the Secretary-General of the United Nations shall, within one month of the occurrence of a vacancy, issue the invitations provided for in article 8.
2.   A judge elected to replace a judge whose term of office has not expired shall hold office for the remainder of his predecessor's term.

Article 20
Officers

1.   The Court shall elect its President and Vice-President for three years; each may be re-elected.
2.   The Court shall appoint its Registrar and shall provide for the appointment of such other officers as may be necessary.

Article 21
Seat of the Court

The permanent seat of the Court shall be established at _____. The Court may, however, sit and exercise its functions elsewhere whenever the Court considers it desirable.

Article 22
Emoluments

Each participating judge shall be paid travel expenses, and a daily allowance when the Court is in session. Each judge shall be paid an annual remuneration.

Article 23
Finances

The States which have conferred jurisdiction upon the Court shall create and maintain a fund to be collected and administered in accordance with regulations adopted by the parties. From the fund shall be paid the costs of maintaining and operating the Court and the Board of Clemency and Parole, and the expenses for the defence as provided in article 38, paragraph 2, sub-paragraph (c), and as approved by the Court.

Article 24
Rules of the Court

1.   The Court shall adopt rules for carrying out its functions. In particular, it shall prescribe rules of procedure and such general principles governing the admission of evidence as the Court may deem necessary.
2.   These rules and any amendments thereto shall be published without delay and shall not be altered so as to affect pending proceedings.

CHAPTER III
Competence of the Court
Article 25
Jurisdiction as to persons

The Court shall be competent to judge natural persons, whether they are constitutionally responsible rulers, public officials or private individuals.

Article 26
Attribution of Jurisdiction

1.   Jurisdiction of the Court is not to be presumed.
2.   A State may confer jurisdiction upon the Court by convention, by special agreement or by unilateral declaration.
3.   Conferment of jurisdiction signifies the right to seize the Court, and the duty to accept its jurisdiction subject to such provisions as the State or States have specified.
4.   Unless otherwise provided for in the instrument conferring jurisdiction upon the Court, the laws of a State determining national criminal jurisdiction shall not be affected by that conferment.

Article 27
Recognition of Jurisdiction

No person shall be tried before the Court unless jurisdiction has been conferred upon the Court by the State or States of which he is a national and by the State or States in which the crime is alleged to have been committed.

Article 28
Withdrawal of Jurisdiction

A State may withdraw its conferment of jurisdiction. Such withdrawal shall take effect one year after the delivery of notice to that effect to the Secretary-General of the United Nations.

Article 29
Access to the Court
Alternative A

Proceedings before the Court may be instituted by a State which has conferred jurisdiction upon the Court over such offences as are involved in these proceedings.

Alternative B

1.   Proceedings before the Court may be instituted by a State which has conferred jurisdiction upon the Court over such offences as are involved in those proceedings.

2.   In the interest of the maintenance of peace, a United Nations organ to be designated by the United Nations may stop the presentation or prosecution of a particular case before the Court.

Article 30
Challenge of Jurisdiction

1.   The jurisdiction of the Court may be challenged by the parties to any proceeding or by any State referred to in article 27.

2.   Such challenge made at the beginning of trial shall be decided by the Court at once.

3.   Such challenge made after the beginning of trial shall be decided by the Court at such time as the Court thinks fit.

Article 31
Assistance of States

1.   The Court, including the Committing Chamber, may request national authorities to assist it in the performance of its duties.

2.   A State shall be obliged to render such assistance only in conformity with any convention or other instrument in which the State has accepted such obligation.

Article 32
Penalties

The Court shall impose upon an accused, upon conviction, such penalty as the Court may determine, subject to any limitations prescribed in the instrument conferring jurisdiction upon the Court.

CHAPTER IV
Committing Chamber and Prosecuting Attorney
Article 33
Committing Chamber

1.   The Committing Chamber shall be composed of five judges appointed annually for one year at a sitting of the whole Court by a majority of the members present. Retiring members of the Chamber shall not be eligible for immediate reappointment. No judge who has participated in committing a case may adjudicate on the substance thereof.

2.   The function of the Chamber shall be to examine the evidence offered by the complainant to support the complaint.

3.   The complainant shall designate an agent or agents who shall present the evidence before the Chamber.

4.   If the Chamber is satisfied that the evidence is sufficient to support the complaint, the Chamber shall so certify to the Court and to the complainant.

5.   Before issuing any such certificate, the Chamber shall give the accused reasonable opportunity to be heard. If necessary and, in particular, to ensure that the accused shall have a fair trial, the Chamber may order further inquiry or the investigation of specific matters.

6.   The Court shall determine the rules of procedure of the Committing Chamber.

Article 34
Prosecuting Attorney

1.   A jurisconsult appointed by the complainant or complainants shall assume the functions of Prosecuting Attorney.

2.   The Prosecuting Attorney shall file with the Court an indictment of the accused based on the findings certified by the Committing Chamber and shall be responsible for conducting the prosecution before the Court.

CHAPTER V
Procedure
Article 35
Indictment

1.   The indictment shall contain a concise statement of the facts which constitute each alleged offence and a specific reference to the law under which the accused in charged.

2.   The Court may authorize amendment of the indictment.

Article 36
Notice of the Indictment

1.   The Court shall bring the indictment to the notice of the accused, of the State or States of which the accused is alleged to be a national, of the State in which the crime is alleged to have been committed and, as far as possible, of the States of which the victims are nationals.

2.   The Court shall not proceed with the trial unless satisfied that the accused has had the indictment and any amendment thereof served upon him and has sufficient time to prepare his defence.

Article 37
Jury

Trials shall be without jury, except where otherwise provided in the instrument by which jurisdiction has been conferred upon the Court.

Article 38
Rights of the Accused

1.   The accused shall be presumed innocent until proved guilty.

2.   The accused shall have a fair trial and, in particular:

(a)   The right to be present at all stages of the proceedings;

(b)   The right to conduct his own defence or to be defended by counsel of his own choice, and to have his counsel present at all stages of the proceedings;

(c)   The right to have reasonable expenses of his defence charged to the fund referred to in article 23 in so far as the Court is satisfied that the accused is unable to engage the services of counsel;

(d)   The right to have the proceedings of the Court, including documentary evidence, translated into his own language;

(e)   The right to interrogate, in person or by his counsel, any witness and to inspect any document or other evidence introduced during the trial;

(f)   The right to adduce oral and other evidence in his defence;

(g)   The right to the assistance of the Court in obtaining access to material which the Court is satisfied may be relevant to the issues before the Court.

3.   The accused shall have the right to be heard by the Court but shall not be compelled to speak. His refusal to speak shall not be relevant to the determination of his guilt. Should he elect to speak, he shall be liable to questioning by the Court and by counsel. He shall not be compelled to take an oath.

4.   If the Court considers it impossible to ensure a fair trial, the Court may, by a decision supported by reasons, suspend the proceedings and, if they are not resumed within a time limit determined by the Court, dismiss the case. If the case be dismissed, the accused shall be automatically released.

Article 39
Publicity of Hearings

1.   The Court shall sit in public unless there are exceptional circumstances in which the Court finds that public sittings might prejudice the interests of justice.

2.   The deliberations of the Court shall take place in private and shall not be disclosed.

Article 40
warrants of arrest

The Court shall have power to issue warrants of arrest related to crimes over which the Court has jurisdiction.

Article 41
Provisional Liberty of Accused

The Court shall decide whether the accused shall remain in custody during the trial or be provisionally set at liberty, and the conditions under which such provisional liberty shall be granted.

Article 42
Authority of the Court

The Court shall have the authority necessary to the proper conduct of the trial, including the authority to require the attendance of witnesses and the production of documents and other evidentiary material, to rule out irrelevant issues, evidence and statements, and to maintain order at the trial.

Article 43
Withdrawal of Prosecution

If the complainant State withdraws the complaint, the Court alone shall decide whether the accused shall be discharged; if the complaint is not substantiated, the Court shall acquit the accused.

Article 44
Quorum

The participation of seven judges shall suffice to constitute the Court.

Article 45
Required Majority

1.   All questions shall be decided by a majority of votes of the judges participating in the trial.

2.   With the exception of a decision to impose the death penalty or life imprisonment, in the event of an equality of votes, the presiding judge shall have a casting vote.

Article 46
Contents and Signature of Judgment

1.   The judgment shall state, in relation to each accused, the reasons upon which it is based.

2.   The judgment shall contain the names of the judges who have taken part in the decision. It shall be signed by the President and the Registrar.

Article 47
Separate Opinions

If the judgment of the Court does not represent the unanimous opinion of the judges, any judge shall be entitled to deliver a separate opinion.

Article 48
Delivery of Judgment

The judgment shall be read in open Court.

Article 49
No Appeal

The judgment shall be final and without appeal.

Article 50
Double Jeopardy

No person who has been tried and acquitted or convicted before the Court shall be subsequently tried for the same offence in any court within the jurisdiction of any State which has conferred jurisdiction upon the Court with respect to such offence.

Article 51
Execution of Sentences

Sentences shall be executed in accordance with conventions relating to the matter.

Article 52
Revision of Judgment

1.   An accused who has been found guilty may apply to the Court for revision of the judgment.
2.   An application for revision shall not be entertained unless the Court is satisfied:
    (a)   That a fact was discovered of such a nature as to be a decisive factor; and
    (b)   That that fact was, when the judgment was given, unknown to the Court and the applicant.
3.   Revision proceedings shall be opened by a judgment of the Court expressly recording the existence of the new fact and recognizing that it has such a character as to lay the case open to revision.

CHAPTER VI
Clemency and Parole
Article 53
Board of Clemency and Parole
Alternative A

1.   The States which have conferred jurisdiction upon the Court, shall, at the meetings and in the manner provided in article 11, elect a Board of Clemency and Parole consisting of five persons.
2.   Subject to the provisions of the instruments by which States have conferred jurisdiction upon the Court, the Board shall have the powers of clemency and parole.
3.   Before deciding on a petition for clemency or parole, the Board shall request the advice of the Court.
4.   The Board shall adopt its own rules of procedure.
Alternative B

1.   The States referred to in article 7 [alternative B] shall designate a Board of Clemency and Parole.

CHAPTER VII
Final Provisions
Article 54
Special Tribunals

Nothing in the present Statute shall be taken to prejudice the right of two or more States which have conferred jurisdiction upon the Court jointly to set up special tribunals to try the perpetrators of crimes over which each of such States has jurisdiction according to the general rules of international law.

DRAFT STATUTE: INTERNATIONAL CRIMINAL TRIBUNAL, BY M. CHERIF BASSIOUNI (9 NOUVELLES ÉTUDES PÉNALES 1993)*

This draft relies in part on the following: The Statute and Rules of the International Court of Justice; the 1953 UNITED NATIONS REVISED DRAFT STATUTE FOR AN INTERNATIONAL CRIMINAL COURT (9 GAOR, Supplement XII, U.N. Doc. A/2645, 1954, hereinafter referred to as 1953 Draft); the DRAFT STATUTE OF AN INTERNATIONAL COMMISSION OF CRIMINAL INQUIRY, prepared by the International Law Association (Report of the Sixtieth Conference, Montreal 1982, *in* Proceedings of the International Law Association's Conference, 1983, p. 424, hereinafter referred to as ILA Draft); the UNITED NATIONS DRAFT STATUTE FOR THE CREATION OF AN INTERNATIONAL CRIMINAL JURISDICTION TO IMPLEMENT THE INTERNATIONAL CONVENTION ON THE SUPPRESSION AND PUNISHMENT OF THE CRIME OF *APARTHEID* (19 January 1980, U.N. Doc. E/CN.4/1426 (1980)), (prepared by M. Cherif Bassiouni, reprinted in 9 HOFSTRA L. REV. 533 (1987)); and the DRAFT STATUTE FOR AN INTERNATIONAL CRIMINAL TRIBUNAL (prepared by a Committee of Experts of the International Institute of Higher Studies in Criminal Sciences (ISISC), which presented it to the United Nations Congress on the Prevention of Crime and the Treatment of Offenders (Havana, Cuba, 27 August to 7 September 1990, U.N. Doc. A/CONF.144/NGO.7 ISISC, reprinted in 15 NOVA L. REV. 354 (1991)). For a more detailed study, see M. CHERIF BASSIOUNI, A DRAFT INTERNATIONAL CODE AND DRAFT STATUTE FOR AN INTERNATIONAL CRIMINAL TRIBUNAL (1987) [hereinafter Bassiouni, Draft Code and Statute]. For explanatory studies, see M. Cherif Bassiouni, *The Time Has Come for an International Criminal Court*, 1 INDIANA J. OF INT'L & COMP. L. 1 (1991) [hereinafter Bassiouni, The Time Has Come]; M. Cherif Bassiouni & Christopher L. Blakesley, *The Need for an International Criminal Court in the New World Order*, 25 VAND. J. TRANSNAT'L L. 151 (1992) [hereinafter Bassiouni & Blakesley, The Need for an ICC].

All official and unofficial instruments and texts listed at the end of this document as part of the chronology of efforts to establish an International Criminal Court were also taken into account.

CHAPTER 1. DEFINITIONS

Article 1. The Convention
The instrument by virtue of which the State-Parties establish the Tribunal and promulgate its Statute.

Article II. The Statute
The Statute of the International Criminal Tribunal is the legal basis regulating the Tribunal and its Organs. It is promulgated by the Convention.

Article III. The International Criminal Tribunal
Consists of all the Organs created by the Statute, which include the Court, the Procuracy, the Secretariat, and the Standing-Committee of State-Parties.

Article IV. The Court
The Court is the judicial organ of the Tribunal which, in accordance with its jurisdiction (Article XIX), adjudicates matters constituting violations of international criminal law, as between State-Parties; and determines, with respect to natural persons, guilt or innocence, and metes out penalties in accordance with the provisions of the Statute.

Article V. The Standing-Committee
The body which represents the State-Parties to the Convention.

Article VI. The Procuracy
The Organ of the Tribunal that investigates, prosecutes, and oversees the execution of the decisions of the Court.

Article VII. The Secretariat
The clerical, administrative, and financial organ of the Tribunal.

---

* A French and Spanish translation of this Draft Statute can be found in 10 NOUVELLES ÉTUDES PÉNALES 1993

Article VIII. The Judge or Judges
The person or persons who sit on the Court.
Article IX. The Procurator-General
The person elected by the Standing-Committee to head the Procuracy.
Article X. The Secretary
The person elected by the Standing-Committee to head the Secretariat.
Article XI. Crimes
1.   The term crimes used throughout this Convention shall refer to those crimes listed in Annex 1 with respect to the general subject-matter jurisdiction of the Tribunal, and Annexes 2 and 3 with respect to the Tribunal's jurisdiction as described in Article XIX, paragraphs 2, 3 and 4.
2.   It is understood that State-Parties shall only be obligated under Article XIX with respect to those crimes listed in the respective schedules, which will differ for each State-Party.

Commentary
     The Tribunal is to be a complete, self-contained international institution established pursuant to a multilateral convention developed by the United Nations. The United Nations can have the General Assembly act as a Plenipotentiary Conference for purposes of adopting the Convention, and the General Assembly could also elect a drafting committee. This Plenipotentiary Conference would avoid the costs and time consuming process.
     The Tribunal, like the International Court of Justice (ICJ), would be a specialized organ of the United Nations.
     The Statute of the Tribunal is part of the Convention, like the ICJ's Statute is part of the United Nations Charter.
     The competence and composition of the various organs of the Tribunal are described in Chapter 3.

CHAPTER 2. GENERAL PROVISIONS
Article XII. - Purposes of the International Criminal Tribunal
     The purposes of this International Criminal Tribunal are as follows:
1.   To adjudicate conflicts, disputes or contentions between the State-Parties as to the interpretation of conventional and customary international criminal law with respect to those crimes listed in Annex 1, in accordance with Article XIX, paragraph 1.
2.   To adjudicate the criminal responsibility of individuals charged by the State Parties with the violation of international criminal law and domestic criminal law, embodying international criminal law with respect to those crimes listed in Annexes I and 2, in accordance with Article XIX paragraphs 2, 3, and 4.

Commentary
     This formula is intended to give the State-Parties the flexibility they may need to induce them to ratify the Convention. The purposes of the Tribunal relate to the Court's jurisdiction.
     Annex 1 contains all the recognized international crimes that the State-Parties agree could be the object of the Court's jurisdiction with respect to resolution of conflicts between them as to obligations arising out of conventional and customary international law.
     The crimes listed in Annex 2 are a subset of the crimes listed in Annex 1, which the State-Parties agree to submit to the Court's exclusive jurisdiction.
     The crimes listed in Annex 3 are another subset of the crimes listed in Annex 1, which the State-Parties agree to submit to Court's concurrent or transferred criminal jurisdiction. This formula is intended to give the State-Parties the greatest flexibility they may need to determine the application of the Tribunal's purposes, in accordance with the jurisdictional formula embodied in Article XIX as supplemented by schedules of crimes listed in the annexes.
     Thus, the Tribunal 's purposes reflect its jurisdictional competence, pursuant to Article XIX, which gives the State-Parties the opportunity to agree on the Tribunal's subject-matter. Each given jurisdictional basis shall have its own Applicable Law in accordance with Article XX.

There are 24 categories of international crimes represented hy some 316 international instruments established between 1815 and 1989, *see* M. CHERIF BASSIOUNI, INTERNATIONAL CRIMES: A DIGEST/INDEX OF INTERNATIONAL INSTRUMENTS 1815-1985 (1985) [hereinafter BASSIOUNI, DIGEST] (which lists only 22, the two others are merceranism, INTERNATIONAL CONVENTION AGAINST THE RECRUITMENT, USE, FINANCING AND TRAINING OF MERCENARIES, December 4, 1989, *reprinted in* 29 I.L.M. 91 (1990), and maritime attacks, CONVENTION FROM THE INTERNATIONAL CONFERENCE ON THE SUPPRESSION OF UNLAWFUL ACTS AGAINST THE SAFETY OF MARITIME NAVIGATION, March I0, 1988, *reprinted in* 27 I.L.M. 668 (1988)), but only some of these adequately define the offenses proscribed, *see generally*, BASSIOUNI, DRAFT CODE AND STATUTE. Customary international law which supplements these Conventions in some cases is also inadequate in defining these offenses with specificity. *Id. See also* 1 INTERNATIONAL CRIMINAL LAW: CRIMES (M. Cherif Bassiouni ed. 1986) [hereinafter BASSIOUNI, ICL]. This situation creates difficulties in ascertaining, at the international level, the specifics of a given international crime in order to satisfy the principles of legality recognized in the world's major criminal justice systems. An international criminal code is needed for just this reason. *Id.* However, when the Tribunal's jurisdiction is founded upon a transfer of criminal jurisdiction from a State-Party or concurrent jurisdiction (as provided in Article XIX) *see, e.g.,* EUROPEAN CONVENTION ON THE TRANSFER OF PROCEEDINGS IN CRIMINAL MATTERS, Europ. T.S. No. 73; MULLER-RAPPARD & BASSIOUNI, 2 EUROPEAN INTER-STATE CO-OPERATION IN CRIMINAL MATTERS chapter IV (1987) [hereinafter MULLER-RAPPARD & BASSIOUNI, EUROPEAN INTER-STATE COOPERATION]; this problem would not arise because in such a case the Tribunal would apply the substantive law of the transferring State as described in Article XX.

For a discussion of what constitutes an international crime see generally the following major texts: A. HEGLER, PRINZIPEN DES INTERNATIONALEN STRAFRECHTS (1906); E. MELLI, LEHRBUCH DES INTERNATIONALEN STRAFRECHTS UND STRAFPROCESSRECHTS (1910); H. DONNEDIEU DE VABRES, INTRODUCTION A L'ETUDE DU DROIT PÉNAL INTERNATIONAL (1922); V. V. PELLA, LA CODIFICATION DU DROIT PÉNAL INTERNATIONAL (1922); M. TRAVERS, LE DROIT PENAL INTERNATIONAL ET SA MISE EN EUOVRE EN TEMPS DE PAIX ET EN TEMPS DE GUERRE (5 VOLS. 1920-1922); H. DONNEDIEU DE VABRES, LES PRINCIPLES MODERNES DU DROIT PÉNAL INTERNATIONAL (1928); N. LEVI, DIRITTO PENALE INTERNAZIONALE (1944); H.-H. JESCHECK, DIE VORANTWORTLICHKEIT DER STAATSORGANE NACH VOLKERSTRAFRECHT (1952); S. GLASER, INTRODUCTION A L'ETUDE DU DROIT INTERNATIONAL PENAL (1954); A. QUINTANO-RIPOLES, TRATADO DE DERECHO PENAL INTERNACIONAL Y INTERNACTIONAL PENAL (2 vols. 1955-1957); S. GLASER, LES INFRACTIONS INTERNATIONALES (1957); INTERNATIONAL CRIMINAL LAW (Gerhard O.W. Mueller & Edward M. Wise eds., 1965); O. TRIFFTERER, DOGMATISCHE UNTERSUCHUNGEN ZUR ENTWICKLUNG DES MATERIELLEN VOLKERSTRAFRECHTS SEIT NURNBERG (1966); S. PLAWSKI, ETUDE DES PRINCIPES FONDAMENTEAUX DU DROIT INTERNATIONAL PÉNAL (1972); 1 A TREATISE ON INTERNATIONAL CRIMINAL LAW (M. Cherif Bassiouni & Ved P. Nanda eds., 1973); LA BELGIQUE ET LE DROIT INTERNATIONAL PÉNAL (B DeSchutter ed. 1975); S. GLASER, LE DROIT PÉNAL INTERNATIONAL CONVENTIONEL (2 vols. 1977-1979); G. FIERRO, LA LEY PENAL Y EL DERECHO INTERNACIONAL (1977-1979); C. LOMBOIS, DROIT PÉNAL INTERNATIONAL (2d ed. 1979); H. EBEID, AL-GARIMA AL-DAWLIA (THE INTERNATIONAL CRIME) (1979); D. OEHLER, INTERNATIONALES STRAFRECHT (2d ed. 1983); M. CHERIF BASSIOUNI, INTERNATIONAL CRIMES DIGEST/INDEX OF INTERNATIONAL INSTRUMENTS 1815-1985 (2 vols. 1985); INTERNATIONAL CRIMINAL LAW (M. Cherif Bassiouni ed., 3 vols. 1986); M. CHERIF BASSIOUNI, A DRAFT INTERNATIONAL CODE AND DRAFT STATUTE FOR AN INTERNATIONAL CRIMINAL TRIBUNAL (1987); F. MALEKIAN, INTERNATIONAL CRIMINAL LAW (2 vols. 1991). *See also inter alia* the following major articles: Radin, *International Crimes*, 32 IOWA L. REV. 33 (1946); Edward M. Wise, *Prolegomenon to the Principles of International Criminal Law*, 16 N.Y.L.F. 562 (1970); Schwarzenberger, *The Problem of an International Criminal Law*, 3 CURRENT LEGAL PROB. 263 (1950); Dinstein, *International Criminal Crimes*, 5 ISR. Y.B. H.R. 55 (1975); Wright, *The Scope of International Criminal Law: A Conceptual Framework*, 15 VA. J. INT'L L. 562 (1975); Wise, *War Crimes and Criminal Law, in* STUDIES IN COMPARATIVE LAW 35 (Edward M. Wise & Gehard O.W. Mueller eds., 1975); Green, *An International Criminal Code - Now?*, 3 DALHOUSIE W. 560 (1976); Mueller, *International Criminal Law: Civitas Maxima*, 15 CASE W. RES. J. INT'L L. I (1983); Dinstein, *International Criminal Law*, 20 ISR. L. REV. 206 (1985); Schindler, *Crimes Against the Law of Nations*, 8 ENCYCLOPEDIA OF PUB. INT'L L. 109

(1985); Wise, *Terrorism and the Problems of an International Criminal Law*, 19 CONN. L. REV. 799 (1987); Green, *International Criminal Law and the Protection of Human Rights, in* CONTEMPORARY PROBLEMS OF INTERNATIONAL LAW: ESSAYS IN HONOR OF GEORG SCHWARZENBERGER 116 (B. Cheng & E. Brown eds., 1988); Clark, *Offenses of International Concern: Multilateral State Treaty Practice in the Forty Years Since Nuremberg*, 57 NORDIC J. INT'L L. 49 (1988); Wise, *International Crimes and Domestic Criminal Law*, 38 DEPAUL L. REV. 923 (1989). *See also* 52 RIDP, Nos. 3-4 (1981), symposium issue on a Draft International Criminal Code; Bouzat, *Introduction* 331; Jescheck, *Development Present State and Future Prospects of International Law* 377; Decker, *A Critique of the Draft International Criminal Code* 373; Ottenhof, *Considerations sur la Forme le Style, et la Methode d'Elaboration du Project de Code Penal International* 385; Friedlander, *Some Observations Relating to the Draft International Criminal Code* 407; Nanda, *International Crimes under the Draft Criminal Code* 627. *See also* the Draft Code of Offenses and, since 1987, the Draft Code of Crimes which have been in process of revision since 1977; Symposium Issue on International Criminal Law, 15 NOVA L. REV. 343 *et seq.* (1991); Annual Reports of the ILC on the Work of its Thirty-Second Session, (1984), up to its Forty-Third Session (1991).

Article XIII. Nature and Seat of the Tribunal
1.   The Tribunal shall be a permanent organ of the United Nations, occupying facilities and performing its chief functions at the Palace of Justice in The Hague, and utilizing as its official languages those of the United Nations.
2.   The Court may from time to time sit in the territory of any State-Party, or in the territory of any other State upon approval of the Standing- Committee.

Commentary
This article establishes the Tribunal as a permanent independent organ of the United Nations. The actual physical presence of all the Tribunal's organs would be at The Hague, or until such time as the Tribunal's volume of work requires a separate seat.

For a variety of practical and security reasons, the Court can sit at The Hague, or elsewhere. A State-Party can offer its court facilities to the ICC. A non-State-Party can also offer its facilities to the ICC, but then the Standing-Committee must approve the offered location. This approval emphasizes the role of the Standing-Committee in sharing responsibilities for the good functioning of the Tribunal.

This formula also eliminates the need to provide for new physical facilities and reduces costs. In fact, the Tribunal can easily be established within a few offices for a small secretariat at the Hague, with the judges and prosecutors remaining in their respective countries and carrying out their permissible occupations until they are called to sit on a given case. The various organs of the Tribunal could easily meet at the Peace Palace without inconvenience to the ICJ, which does not utilize its facilities at all times. The ICC could also share the ICJ's library.

This formula meets the cost concerns of many States and also minimizes the creation of a new international bureaucracy. It also provides the opportunity for prompt operational readiness of the Tribunal without logistical problems.

CHAPTER 3. ORGANS OF THE TRIBUNAL
Article XIV. General Provision
The Tribunal shall consist of the following organs whose functions and competence are described below. They are:
    a.   The Court,
    b.   The Procuracy,
    c.   The Secretariat, and
    d.   The Standing-Committee of State-Parties.

Commentary
This article establishes four bodies, each with a separate function and competence, which are further described in this chapter. This detailed structure does not, however, entail the creation of a cumbersome,

costly international bureaucracy as stated in the Commentary to Article XII below in the description of these organs and their functions.

Article XV. The Court

1.   The Court shall consist of fifteen judges, no more than one of whom shall be of the same nationality, and ten alternate judges, no more than one of whom shall be of the same nationality, who shall be elected by the Standing-Committee from nominations submitted thereto by State-Parties. The alternate judges shall have no official function until they are called to fill a vacancy on the Court, either for the remaining part of a term, or for a given case. The selection of individual alternate judges to fill the vacancies or to sit on a given case shall be by the Standing-Committee.

2.   Judicial nominees shall be persons of the highest caliber of integrity and legal competence, with specific expertise in the fields of international criminal law or human rights.

3.   Judges shall be elected by secret ballot and the Standing-Committee of State-Parties shall strive too elect persons representing diverse backgrounds and experience with due regard to representation of the major legal systems of the world.

4.   Judges and alternate judges shall be elected for the following terms: five judges for four-year terms, five judges for six-year terms, and five judges for eight year terms. Judges and alternate judges may not be re-elected for more than two consecutive terms.

5.   Once elected, a judge may not occupy a public function or official position in any State other than that of judge of any court of law.

6.   Judges shall have no other occupation or business other than that of judge in the State from which they have been elected, or a member of the faculty of a university. Judges shall not engage in any activity which interferes with their judicial functions at the ICC and avoid any appearance of lack of impartiality.

7.   A judge shall perform no function in the Tribunal with respect to any matter in which he may have had any involvement prior to his election to this Court, nor with respect to any matter involving actual or apparent conflict of interest.

8.   A judge may withdraw from any matter at his discretion, or be excused by a two-thirds majority of the judges of the Court for reasons of actual, apparent or potential conflict of interest.

9.   A judge may be removed by a unanimous vote of the other judges of the Court for incapacity to fulfill his functions.

10.   A judge may continue in office beyond his term until his replacement has been inducted to the office. A judge shall, however, continue in office in order to complete work on any pending matter in which he was involved until final disposition of that matter.

11.   The judges of the Court shall elect a president, vice-president and such officers as they deem appropriate. The president shall serve for a term of two years, and may be re-elected, although not for more than two consecutive terms.

12.   Judges of the Court shall perform their judicial functions in four capacities:
    a.   sitting with other judges *en banc*;
    b.   sitting in panels of five judges as an Appellate Chamber;
    c.   sitting in panels of three judges on a rotational basis in Chambers; and
    d.   sitting individually as supervisors of sanctions.

13.   The Court *en banc* shall, subject to the provisions of this Statute, be the final reviewing judicial body of the Tribunal, adopt Rules governing procedures and practice before its Chambers, promulgate penalties and sanctions, and provide for establishment of Chambers and selection of judges.

14.   The Court, whether sitting *en banc*, in Appellate Chamber, or in other Chambers, shall announce its decisions orally, in full or in summary, in open or closed Court at their discretion, accompanied by written findings of facts and conclusions of law. Any judge may issue a concurring or dissenting opinion. These decisions shall be presented at the time of the oral decision or within thirty days thereafter.

15.   Decisions and orders of the Court are effective upon certification of the written opinion or order by the Secretariat, which is to communicate such certified opinion to all interested parties forthwith.

16.   No actions taken by the Court may be contested in any other forum than before the Court.

17.   The Court shall sit as follows:
    a.   as Indictment Chambers of three judges;
    b.   as Adjudication Chambers of three judges;
    c.   as Appellate Chambers of five judges; and

 d. *en banc* of all the judges of the Court.
18. Decisions of the Court's Chambers and *en banc* shall be by simple majority.
19. The presiding judge of the Court shall request the Standing-Committee to nominate alternate judges whenever needed, and the nomination by the Standing-Committee shall be within sixty days of the request.
20. Election of the judges to the various Chambers shall be by the Court *en banc*, by lot, and conducted by the Secretary under the supervision of the presiding judge of the Court.
21. The Standing-Committee shall determine the salary of the judges, but may not reduce salaries once established.
22. The judgments of the Court shall be enforced by the State-Parties in accordance with their national laws, provided they are not inconsistent with the provisions of this Statute. The Court *en banc* shall decide whether enforcement by a State-Party is inconsistent with its judgment or this Statute and shall refer its decision to the Standing-Committee.
23. The Court *en banc* with a two-thirds vote can, for cause, disallow or suspend anyone but the Procurator-General from appearing before the Court or one of its Chambers.

Commentary

Except for some slight differences particularly with respect to the alternate judge formula, which provides an additional pool of judges, the formula is similar to that of the ICJ. Since no more than one judge can be a national of a State-Party from the panel of 15 judges and from the panel of the 10 alternates, it is possible to have 2 judges from a given State-Party. But no panel or Chamber of the Court can have more than one nationality represented. In case of dual citizenship, the Court *en banc* shall decide on the appropriateness of the diversity of citizenship composition of the Chamber. The terms of this Article as to selection, tenure and replacement of judges closely parallel those of Articles 4 through 12 and 15 through 20 of the 1953 Draft and 3 through 9 and 12 through 15 of the ILA Draft, although the latter makes no provision for removal of judges. The judges may preside for more than two terms, as long as the terms are not consecutive. Any time spent as an alternate judge does not apply towards this limitation. There are also many other similarities with the provisions of the ICJ. *See generally* SHABTAI ROSENNE, THE WORLD COURT: WHAT IT IS AND HOW IT WORKS (1988).

This Article, however, presents several functional innovations, with respect to the separate functions of Chambers and the Court *en banc*. The Appellate Chamber provides for a right of appeal, a right called for in Article 14, paragraph 5 of the *International Covenant on Civil and Political Rights*.

Rather than create a separate institution to deal with supervision of sanctions, it was deemed more efficient to have such functions performed by individual judges as overseers of sanctions as provided for in Article XXIX.

Judges are elected for specific terms. Accordingly, when a given judge's term ends, he may be re-elected or an Alternate Judge is to be elected to take his place. In this case, another Alternate Judge is elected in accordance with the established procedure.

Paragraphs 7, 8, and 9 address the concern that conduct by a judge may create an appearance of impropriety, and narrowly circumscribes permitted non-judicial activity. Academic and scholarly activities are permitted. But removal by the Court *en banc*, or excuse from a given Case is provided for as a mechanism for the Court to preserve its own judicial integrity.

Paragraph 10 permits judges to remain in their official capacity beyond their term of office for the sole purpose of completing work on Court action begun prior to the expiration of their terms.

Paragraphs 12-17 describe the Chamber system, which is operationally described in Chapter 6.

Paragraph 13 is one of the important functions of the Court *en banc*, namely the adoption of rules of procedure and practice as referred to in Chapter 5 and penalties and sanctions as referred to in Articles XXI and XXVII. Furthermore, the Court *en banc* establishes the Chambers and selects the judges by a random system, as determined by the Court *en banc*.

While Paragraph 22 reaffirms that the enforcement of the Court's judgments depends upon the State-Parties, the Court nonetheless has the power to make findings of non-compliance and to report them to the Standing-Committee for action. This method provides the sanction of embarrassment which may deter non-complying States. Although, only the Standing-Committee can take action against the non-compliant State-Party. This inducement-compliance device may yield beneficial results.

If the Court has its own detention facilities, it may directly enforce its judgments and supervise their execution. Until such a time, the enforcement of execution of sentences will depend on the cooperation of states who will carry out the sentences in their own detention facilities. This formula avoids many practical difficulties during the early stages of the Court's development. It will also be a cost saving method for the Court.

Article XVI. The Procuracy

1.   The Procuracy shall have the Procurator-General as its chief officer and such other prosecutors, investigators, and clerical staff as may be necessary to carry out its responsibilities in accordance with the budget provided by the Standing-Committee.

2.   The Procurator-General shall be elected by the Standing-Committee of State-Parties from a list of at least three nominees submitted by members of the Standing-Committee, and shall serve for a renewable term of six years, barring resignation or removal by two-thirds vote of the judges of the Court *en banc* for incompetence, conflict of interest, or manifest disregard of the provisions of this Statute or material Rules of the Tribunal.

3.   The Procurator-General's salary shall be the same as that of judges.

4.   All other members of the Procurator-General's staff shall be named and removed at will by the Procurator-General and their salaries determined by the Procurator-General within the budgetary parameters established by the Standing-Committee.

5.   State-Parties who transfer criminal proceedings to the Tribunal in accordance with Article XIX Paragraph 3 may elect to have a prosecuting official from their State join the Procurator-General in prosecuting a given case under the said Article XIX Paragraph 3. In such cases, the prosecuting official from the transferring State shall act as Deputy Procurator-General for that case.

Commentary

Paragraph 2 provides for joint action by the Court and Standing-Committee for selection and removal of the Procurator-General. This process is appropriate because such an officer should be acceptable to the State-Parties who are in a better position to evaluate suitable candidates. The Court is, however, in a better position to evaluate legal competence and to determine proper conduct. Thus, removal power is vested in the Court. This vesting of the removal power with the Court *en banc* insulates the Procurator-General from political pressures, which could be exercised by the Standing-Committee if it had such power.

Deputies and staff are placed under control of the Procurator-General in Paragraph 4 in the interest of effective management.

Paragraph 5 provides States the right of direct representation and active involvement. This formula enhances the image of the transferring state in its domestic public arena. It also insures that in these cases, where the applicable law is that of the transferring state (*see* Article XX), this expert knowledge of the applicable law will be directly available to the prosecution and to the Court. But, the Procurator-General remains the lead person responsible for the prosecution and the conduct of the case. Primacy of the Procurator-General will enhance uniform compliance with the Court's procedures and ensure appropriate conduct and decorum in Court proceedings. This formula is intended to satisfy the interests of justice, the Court's processes, and the interests of the transferring State.

Article XVII. The Secretariat

1.   The Secretariat is the administrative, financial, and clerical organ of the Tribunal.

2.   The Secretariat shall have as its chief officer the Secretary of the Tribunal, who shall be elected by a majority of the Court sitting *en banc* and serve for a renewable term of six years barring resignation or removal by a majority of the Court sitting *en banc* for incompetence, conflict of interest, or manifest disregard of the provisions of this Statute or material Rules of the Tribunal.

3.   The Secretary is the Clerk of the Tribunal as a whole and of the Court m particular.

4.   The Secretary of the Tribunal's salary shall be the same as that of the judges.

5.   The Secretariat shall employ such staff as appropriate to perform its chancery and administrative functions and such other functions as may be assigned to it by the Court that are consistent with the provisions of this Statute or Rules of the Tribunal in accordance with the budget provided by the Standing-Committee. The Secretariat staff shall be appointed and removed by the Secretary at will. The salary of the Secretariat staff shall be established by the Secretary within the budgetary parameters established by the Standing-Committee.

6.   The Secretary of the Tribunal shall during the first calendar month of each year:

a.   Prepare budget requests for each of the Organs of the Tribunal on the basis of the information provided thereto by the other organs; and

b.   Publish an annual financial report and a report on the activities of the Tribunal on the basis of information provided by the President of the Court and the Procurator-General.

7.   An annual summary of investigations undertaken by the Procuracy shall be presented to the Secretariat for publication, but certain investigations may be omitted where secrecy is necessary, provided that a confidential report of the investigation is made to the Court and to the Standing-Committee. But, either the Court or the Standing-Committee may order by majority vote that the report be made public.

Commentary

Although most of the functions of the Secretariat are ministerial in character, its duties to oversee communications and prepare reports serve an inspectorate function as well. Accordingly, control over the Secretariat is vested in the Court, since it is the organ most affected by the performance of the Secretary. This reason supports vesting removal power in the Court.

Article XVIII. The Standing-Committee

1.   The Standing-Committee shall have the power to perform the functions expressly assigned to it under the Statute, and any other functions that it determines appropriate in furtherance of the purposes of the Tribunal and are not inconsistent with the Statute. In no way shall these functions impair the independence and integrity of the Court as a judicial body.

2.   The Standing-Committee shall:
   a.   elect the judges and alternate judges;
   b.   elect the Procurator-General;
   c.   determine the annual budget of the Tribunal;
   d.   assist the Tribunal in carrying out its functions;
   e.   insure compliance by the State-Parties of the provisions of the Convention and Statute;
   f.   insure compliance with the judgments of the Court; and
   g.   any other function provided in the Convention and Statute.
   h.   it may also mediate disputes between State- Parties relating to the functions of the Tribunal, encourage States to accede to the Convention, and propose to State-Parties international instruments to enhance the functions of the Tribunal.

3.   The Standing-Committee shall consist of one representative and no more than two alternate representatives appointed by each State-Party for a term of two years except where exigent circumstances require a shortening of the representative's accreditation.

4.   It shall elect by majority vote a presiding officer, an alternate presiding officer, a secretary, and such other officers as it deems appropriate.

5.   The presiding officer shall convene meetings at least twice each year, at the seat of the Tribunal, and call other meetings at the request of one third of the Committee. Meetings of the Standing-Committee can also be held in a location other than the seat of the Tribunal if a majority of State-Parties agree. The Standing-Committee may also meet whenever it deems it appropriate to discharge its responsibilities pursuant to the Convention and the Statute.

6.   The Standing-Committee may exclude from participation at a given session by a majority vote the representative of a State-Party that failed to provide financial support for the Tribunal as per the annual budget as required by the Statute, and, a State-Party that failed to carry out its obligations under the Convention and the Statute, including, but not limited to, the failure to carry out the orders of the Court for the enforcement of its judgments.

7.   Upon request by the Procurator-General, or by a State-Party involved in a given case, the Standing-Committee may be seized with a mediation and conciliation petition. In this case, the Standing-Committee shall decide within 60 days whether to grant or deny the petition, from which decision there is no appeal. In the event that the Standing-Committee grants the petition, Court proceedings shall be stayed until such time as the Standing- Committee concludes its mediation and conciliation efforts, but not for more than one year except by stipulation of the State-Party or State-Parties to the case and with the consent of the Court.

8.   Nothing in this Article prevents the Standing-Committee from forming an executive board or other sub-committees as a it may deem appropriate.

9.   The Standing-Committee shall promulgate its own rules of procedure and conduct.

Commentary

    The 1953 Draft assumes that the Court created under it would be a part of the United Nations and, therefore, any governing-body facing certain issues, particularly political issues, would address them to political organs of the United Nations. Under the ILA Draft, a similar assumption appears to have been made in that no similar provisions are included.

    The present Statute is a creature of the Convention. Accordingly, the need for an organ to deal with governance of the Tribunal and issues relating to its activities prompts the need for a Standing-Committee. It should be noted that the express functions of the Standing-Committee are of a governing-body. This permits in pursuing non juridical matters helpful to international criminal justice. The requirement of meetings twice a year assures that the Standing-Committee will be available for consultation on a variety of questions, and for support of the Tribunal's work.

    The Standing-Committee also acts as a watchdog of the State-Parties' compliance with their treaty obligations and the orders and judgments of the Court, and also over the Tribunal as a whole.

    The power to select the Procurator-General, elect the judges and alternate judges, and establish the annual budget should provide all the assurances that States may require in order to become State-Parties.

    The Standing-Committee also has duties of insuring compliance and financial support by State-Parties. As a governing body, it is given powers to carry out these tasks, including suspension of State-Parties from voting in the Standing-Committee. It should be noted, however, that this Article does not contemplate deprivation of the status of State-Party in response to non-payment of financial support, but mere suspension.

    No provision has been made for terms of office for State-Parties' representatives, it being assumed that their tenure shall be at the pleasure of the appointing State. Thus, individual members serve in their official representative capacity and should, therefore, be appropriately accredited. The termination of their accreditation ends their membership in the Standing-Committee. Paragraph 5 brings two new requirements to the practice of international and inter-governmental organizations. The first is to limit delegations to a maximum of three persons, and that is done to increase efficiency and reduce the temptation for State-Parties to send large delegations of observers. The second is to require State-Parties to nominate their representatives for a minimum of two year terms. This is intended to provide for better continuity of management and enhanced knowledge of the Tribunal and other State-Parties' activities and concerns. Obviously, State-Parties can shorten the term of their representative, but it puts a certain pressure on them to maintain continuity in representation.

    Paragraph 9 gives the Standing-Committee the right to establish an executive board to deal with urgent matters, or sub-committees to deal with specific matters.

    Paragraph 10 gives it the power to develop its own rules and procedures, but these rules and procedures must be promulgated for the benefit of State-Parties, though not necessarily rendered public. They may also be amended at the pleasure of the Standing-Committee. Obviously, these rules and procedures cannot be in contradiction with the spirit or letter of the Convention and Statute.

CHAPTER 4. JURISDICTION AND APPLICABLE LAW
Article XIX. Jurisdictional Bases of the Tribunal

    The Tribunal's jurisdiction shall be limited to the following bases:

1.   *Resolution of disputes between State-Parties* with respect to international criminal law conventions applicable to those crimes listed in Annex 1 of this Statute, including but not limited to:
      a.   the duty to extradite or prosecute;
      b.   conflicts of criminal jurisdiction;
      c.   extradition;
      d.   mutual legal assistance; and
      e.   other modalities of inter-state cooperation in penal matters.

2.   *Original jurisdiction* to prosecute, try and enforce sentences (penalties) against natural persons with respect to those crimes listed in Annex 2 which the State-Parties have agreed to as being subject to the Tribunal's original jurisdiction.

3.   *Concurrent jurisdiction* to try, prosecute and enforce sentences (penalties) against natural persons with respect to those crimes listed in Annex 3 on the basis of explicit or implicit consent by a State-Party, or on the basis of transfer of the criminal proceedings.

4.   *Ad Hoc jurisdiction* to prosecute, try, and enforce sentences (penalties) against natural persons with respect to any crime listed in Annex 1 which a given State-Party may wish to submit to the Tribunal's jurisdiction.

Commentary

In Paragraph 1, the Court may act in a conflict resolution capacity between States concerning issues arising out of the interpretation and application of conventional and customary international law. But it is limited to questions arising out of, or pertaining to, those crimes listed in Annex 1. The Convention could even provide for compulsory jurisdiction in certain matters involving the duty to prosecute or extradite. Compulsory jurisdiction is embodied, for example in the OPTIONAL PROTOCOL TO THE VIENNA CONVENTION ON DIPLOMATIC RELATIONS CONCERNING THE COMPULSORY SETTLEMENT OF DISPUTES, 23 U.S.T. 3374, 3375, 500 U.N.T.S. 241, 241 states, at article I: "Disputes arising out of the interpretation or application of the Convention shall lie within the compulsory jurisdiction of the [ICJ] and may accordingly be brought before the Court by an application made by any party to the dispute being a Party to the present Protocol." *See also Case Concerning United States Diplomatic and Consular Staff in Tehran* (U.S. v. Iran), 1979 I.C.J. 7 (Request for the Indication of Provisional Measures); B. CARTER & P. TRIMBLE, INTERNATIONAL LAW 56-75 (1991); Mark W. Janis, *Somber Reflections on the Compulsory Jurisdiction of the International Court*, 81 AM. J. INT'L. L. 144 (1987).

The benefits of compulsory jurisdiction are quite obvious, especially in the area of conflicting concurrent jurisdiction. One contemporary example deserves mention: the case where the United States and the United Kingdom seek to prosecute two Libyan officials for the sabotage and explosion of Pan American Flight 103 over Lockerbie, Scotland. The position of the Libyan government is that it is willing to prosecute them in Libya in accordance with and as required by its national law, which, like that of virtually all European and Latin American nations, prohibits extradition of its nationals. The position of the United States and the United Kingdom is that it cannot rely on the effectiveness of national prosecution because these individuals were part of a state structure that engaged in such acts of international terror-violence and that they were supported by state action or policy. The United States and the United Kingdom argue that the duty to prosecute in this case is meaningless because the conditions for effective prosecution do not exist. They insist, therefore, that the individuals be surrendered by extradition or other means for prosecution either in the United States or the United Kingdom. The Libyan case indicates the political nature of the current system. The United States and British governments certainly know that Libya legally cannot extradite its nationals. The United States and the British governments, however, actually might not expect extradition, but would prefer the propaganda benefits of condemning Libya for not extraditing. France is also seeking four Libyans in connection with the sabotage and explosion of a French UTA aircraft. *See* Bassiouni & Blakesley, The Need for an ICC 150-51.

For similar cases involving issues of jurisdiction, prosecution and extradition, *see* Gerald P. McGinley, *The Achille Lauro Case: A Case Study in Crisis Law, Policy and Management, in* LEGAL RESPONSES TO INTERNATIONAL TERRORISM: U.S. PROCEDURAL ASPECTS 323 (M. Cherif Bassiouni ed. 1988); David M. Kennedy et al., *The Extradition of Mohammed Hamadei*, 31 HARV. INT'L L.J. 5 (1990). *See also* M. Cherif Bassiouni, *Effective National and International Action Against Organized Crime and Terrorist Criminal Activities*, 4 EMORY INT'L L. REV. 9 (1990); and JOHN MURPHY, PUNISHING INTERNATIONAL TERRORISTS: E LEGAL FRAMEWORK FOR POLICY INITIATIVES 1-5 (1985).

The jurisdictional basis of Paragraph 1 is similar to that of the ICJ, whether optional or compulsory. But to have a specialized Court deal with these questions offers greater expertise. Furthermore, it is complementary to the other jurisdictional bases which, unlike this one, is limited to States, applies to natural persons under Paragraphs 2, 3, and 4.

Under the jurisdictional basis of Paragraph 1, only States can bring the action and if jurisdiction for these issues is optional, the consent of the State against which the action is brought must be obtained. This requirement is similar to the requirements of the ICJ.

Only those crimes listed in Annex 1 are within the Court's subject-matter jurisdiction. The State-Parties can choose among themselves to determine which will be subject to the Court's exclusive jurisdiction (Paragraph 2). The selected crimes are listed in Annex 2. The crimes listed in Annex 3 will be subject to concurrent or transferred jurisdiction (Paragraph 3). Under Paragraph 4, the *Ad Hoc* Jurisdiction of the Court can only be exercised with respect to the crimes listed in Annex 1. The Court must have jurisdiction over the merits of cases involving an international or a transnational crime. For this reason, and with respect to Paragraphs 2, 3 and 4, a schedule list approach is provided.

Paragraph 2 provides for the Court's exclusive jurisdiction. Of all the jurisdictional bases, exclusive jurisdiction is the most politically difficult to achieve. States are reluctant to relinquish jurisdiction to an international criminal court for a variety of xenophobic reasons, as well as legitimate political and practical concerns. That is why a choice is left to those State-Parties willing to confer such exclusive jurisdiction to the Court to do so on the basis of an annexed schedule (Annex 2). However this formula may be confusing, since State-Parties will not always select the same international crimes. The result, if a number of State-Parties accept this formula and choose a wide variety of different crimes, may create confusion and uncertainty in world public opinion, and, reduce the credibility and standing of the Court. Furthermore, it could tend to create unfavorable reactions in the public opinion of some State-Parties who did not accept such a jurisdictional basis. The best approach would be to have all State-Parties agree to the exclusive jurisdiction of the Court with respect to certain crimes to which they can all agree.

The question remains, however, as to whether a state can relinquish jurisdiction over certain offenses. In other words, can a state allow the international criminal court to have exclusive jurisdiction over specific crimes or under certain circumstances? Furthermore, can a sovereign state surrender sovereignty to adjudicate and enforce certain crimes in instances when the Court's jurisdiction would supersede national criminal jurisdiction?

Paragraph 3 is the most feasible jurisdictional basis because it provides for the initial discretion of the State-Party wishing to allow the Court to exercise its jurisdiction. Two alternative formulas are proposed - concurrent jurisdiction and transfer of proceedings. Concurrent jurisdiction implies that a state having jurisdiction under any of the four internationally recognized theories of jurisdiction, namely territoriality, nationality, passive personality, and protected interest, would be able to exercise that jurisdiction, but elects to allow the ICC to exercise it in its stead. It implies that the Court would exercise its jurisdiction with respect to those crimes listed in Annex 3. A problem with concurrent jurisdiction, however, is the potential for jurisdictional conflict between two or more states and the Court.

Concurrent jurisdiction exists primarily to permit State-Parties who cannot, for constitutional reasons, transfer jurisdiction in accordance with a scheme similar to that of the EUROPEAN CONVENTION ON THE TRANSFER OF PROCEEDINGS IN CRIMINAL MATTERS, Europ. T.S. No. 73. *See also* MULLER-RAPPARD & BASSIOUNI, 2 EUROPEAN INTER-STATE CO-OPERATION chapter IV. For a positive view on the formula see Michael P. Scharf, *The Jury Is Still Out on the Need for An International Criminal Court*, 1991 DUKE J. COMP. & INT'L L. REV. 135, 159-64.

Thus, this provision allows States to explicitly "transfer" criminal proceedings and jurisdiction to the ICC, or alternatively by not exercising national jurisdiction, they would allow the ICC to exercise its "concurrent" jurisdiction. In these cases, the State allowing the ICC to exercise jurisdiction in its stead, must still provide the Court with judicial assistance and cooperation as provided in Chapter 8.

Paragraph 4 provides for *Ad Hoc* Jurisdiction which the Convention could leave open to non-State-Parties as a way of enhancing future adhesion. But with respect to State-Parties, this formula also allows a given State-Party to confer *Ad Hoc* jurisdiction for any crime listed in Annex 1 without being permanently committed to the Court's jurisdiction. This approach creates an inducement for State-Parties to experiment with the Court's jurisdiction and eventually to gain the confidence necessary to rely more frequently on the Court.

Article XX. Applicable Law

1.   The Tribunal shall, subject to the provisions of the present Statute, exercise its jurisdiction in accordance with international law whose sources are stated in Article 38 of the Statute of International Court of Justice.

2.   Whenever the Tribunal exercises its jurisdiction pursuant to Article XIX, paragraph 1, the applicable law shall be as stated in paragraph 1 of this Article.

3.   Whenever the Tribunal exercises its jurisdiction Pursuant to Article XIX, paragraph 2, the applicable law shall be as stated in paragraph 1 of this Article, provided that it does not violate the "principles of legality" recognized in the world's major criminal justice systems.

4.   Whenever the Tribunal's jurisdiction is exercised on the basis of Article XIX, paragraph 3, the applicable substantive law (general part, special part and sanctions and penalties) shall be that of the transferring State-Party or the State-Party having jurisdiction on the basis of territoriality, passive personality and active personality which has allowed the Court to exercise jurisdiction in such cases where concurrent jurisdiction exists.

5.   Whenever the Tribunal exercises its jurisdiction on the basis of Article XIX, paragraph 4, it shall apply the substantive law agreed to by the State Party or State-Parties submitting a given case to the Tribunal, providing that such agreed upon applicable substantive law is not contrary to international law.

6.   In all cases before the Court, the Procedures, Rules, and Standards of the Court shall apply irrespective of the procedural laws of any State.

Commentary

With respect to matters of international law, the Tribunal shall apply the provisions of Article 38 of the ICJ Statute. The Tribunal must, however, in its choice of specific applicable law, satisfy the "principles of legality." Until such time as a comprehensive international code is adopted, the Tribunal will have to rely on the applicable sources of international law. *See* BASSIOUNI, DRAFT CODE AND STATUTE. For the problems of legality see M. CHERIF BASSIOUNI, CRIMES AGAINST HUMANITY IN INTERNATIONAL CRIMINAL LAW 87-146 (1992).

Whenever the Tribunal's jurisdiction is predicated on Article XIX, paragraph 3, it shall apply the national law of the transferring State, both State-Party and non-State-Party alike. This mechanism provides the greatest level of certainty and fairness.

Paragraph 4 provides for the basis of the applicable substantive law by the State or States submitting the case on the basis of *Ad Hoc* jurisdiction pursuant to Article XIX, paragraph 4.

Paragraph 5 provides for the uniform application of the Court's Procedures, Rules and Standards as provided in Chapter 5, and supplemented by the Rules and Standards promulgated by the Court.

Whenever the Court exercises its jurisdiction pursuant to Article XIX, paragraph 2, the Sanctions and Penalties shall be in accordance with the provisions of Article XXI. Otherwise, the applicable substantive law shall govern these matters.

Article XXI. Sanctions and Penalties

1.   The Court, as an organ of the Tribunal shall, when exercising its jurisdiction over natural persons pursuant to Article XIX, paragraphs 2, 3 and 4, upon entering a finding of guilty, and in accordance with Article XXIX and the procedures and standards set forth in chapter 5 have the power to impose the following penalties and sanctions.

   a.   The penalties shall be:
       i.   Deprivation of liberty or any lesser measures of control where the person found guilty is a natural person; and
       ii.   Fine to be levied against a natural person; and
       iii. Confiscation of the proceeds of proscribed (or criminal) conduct
   b.   The sanctions shall be:
       i.   Injunctions against natural persons or legal entities restricting them from engaging in certain conduct or activities; and
       ii.   Order restitution and provide for damages.

2.   Sanctions shall be established by the Rules of the Court and approved by the Standing-Committee and shall be established before their entry into effect.

3.   Whenever the Tribunal's jurisdiction is predicated on Article XIX, paragraph 3, the applicable penalties and sanctions shall be those of the State-Party whose substantive law shall apply provided it does not conflict with international law. In such a case, the Court shall modify these penalties and sanctions to comply with international legal norms and standards.

Commentary

Only the Court, upon a finding of guilty, shall apply with respect to jurisdiction under Article XIX, paragraph 2, those penalties promulgated prior to the Tribunal's commencement of activities. Those penalties must, of course, conform to international legal norms and standards.

Whenever the Tribunal's jurisdiction is based on the provisions of Article XIX, paragraph 3, the Court should apply the sanctions and penalties of the transferring State, provided they are in conformity with international legal norms and standards, or modify their application accordingly. The same applies to sanctions arising out of the Court's jurisdiction pursuant to Article XIX, paragraph 4.

In keeping with the principle of legality, it is necessary that precise sanctions and penalties be promulgated prior to trial. This legislative responsibility is delegated by the Statute to the Court.

CHAPTER 5. PROCEDURES AND RULES OF THE FAIRNESS OF THE TRIBUNAL
Article XXII. Standards for Procedures and Rules of the Tribunal

1. In all proceedings of the Tribunal and in the formulation of any of its organs' Rules, the accused shall be entitled to those fundamental human rights established in conventional and customary international law, and recognized in "general principles of law," which shall be promulgated before the commencement of any legal proceedings.
2. Principles of Legality
   In all cases before the Tribunal the "Principles of Legality" shall be applied. They include:
   a. Prohibition of *ex post facto* laws;
   b. non-retroactivity of criminal laws and penal sanctions;
   c. *Nullum crimen sine lege*, and
   d. *Nulla poena sine lege*.
3. Presumption of Innocence
   a. The presumption of innocence is a fundamental principle of criminal justice and all organs of the Tribunal shall act in keeping therewith.
   b. No one may be convicted of a crime unless he has been tried according to law in a fair trial and before an impartial Court, and proven guilty beyond a reasonable doubt.
   c. No criminal punishment or any equivalent sanction may be imposed upon. a person unless he was convicted of a crime in the manner prescribed by law in accordance with the provisions of the Statute.
   d. The burden of proof of guilt rests on the prosecution;
   e. No person shall be required to prove his innocence; and
   f. In case of reasonable doubt, the decision must be in favor of the accused.
4. Speedy Trial
   All proceedings shall be speedily conducted without, however, interfering with the right of the Prosecution and the defense to adequately prepare for trial.
   Administrative or disciplinary measures shall be taken against officials of the Tribunal, including counsels for the defense, who deliberately violate the provisions of the Statute and the Rules of the Tribunal.
5. Evidentiary Questions
   All procedures and methods of securing evidence shall be in accordance with internationally guaranteed human rights, the standards of justice set forth in the Statute. and in the Rules of the Tribunal.
   a. The admissibility of evidence in all proceedings must take into account the lawfulness of the process by which the evidence was obtained, the truth and veracity of the evidence, the integrity of the judicial system, the rights of the defense, the interests of the victim, and the interests of the world community.
   b. Evidence obtained directly or indirectly, by illegal means which constitute a gross violation of internationally protected human rights, or by means which violate the provisions of the Convention, or the Rules of the Tribunal shall be inadmissible in Court proceedings.
   c. An accused person shall be afforded the opportunity to challenge evidence produced by the prosecution and to present evidence in defense of the charges.
   d. An accused person has the right to be present at all judicial proceedings and to confront and examine the witnesses against him/her.
   e. Counsel for the accused shall be provided with all incriminating evidence available to the prosecution as well as all exculpatory evidence as soon as possible but no later than at the conclusion of the investigation or before adjudication and in reasonable time to prepare the defense.
6. The Right to Remain Silent
   Anyone charged or accused of a criminal violation has the right to remain silent and must be informed of this right, and cannot be compelled to be a witness against himself/herself.

7.   Assistance of Counsel
    a.   Anyone suspected, charged or tried of a criminal violation has the right to effectively defend himself/herself and to have competent legal assistance of his own choosing at all stages of the proceedings.
    b.   Counsel shall be appointed by the Court in accordance with the Rules of the Court, whenever a person charged or brought to a trial is financially unable to retain counsel, and whenever the Court deems it in the best interests of justice in accordance with the Rules of the Court enacted pursuant to the Statute. Appointed counsel shall receive reasonable compensation from the Tribunal.
    c.   Counsel for the accused shall be allowed to be present at all stages of the proceedings.
    d.   Anyone detained shall have the right to access and to communicate in private with his counsel, personally and by correspondence, subject only to reasonable security measures decided by the Adjudication Chamber in the case or by the President of the Court if the Adjudication Chamber has not been established.
8:    Arrest and Detention
    a.   Arrest and detention shall be in conformity with the *United Nations Basic Principles on Freedom from Arbitrary Arrest and Detention and the United Nations Standard Minimum Rules for Treatment of Prisoners.*
    b.   No one shall be deprived of his liberty before trial except on such grounds and in accordance with such procedure as established by the Statute and Rules of the Court and only on the basis of a judicial determination by the Indictment Chamber of the Court.
    c.   Anyone arrested or detained shall be promptly brought before an Adjudication Chamber of the Court to be informed of the charges against him. After such an appearance the accused may be returned to the custody of the arresting authority or State but he shall be subject to the jurisdiction of the Court even when in the custody of a State.
    d.   Any period of detention prior to conviction shall be credited toward the fulfillment of the penalty imposed by the Court.
    e.   Anyone who has been the victim of illegal or unjustified detention shall have the right to compensation. An action for damages may be brought and damages awarded for accusations which are found by the Court to be vexatious or brought in bad faith.
9.   Rights and Interests of the Victim
    The rights and interests of the victim of a crime shall be protected in accordance with the *United Nations Declaration on Principles of Justice for Victims of Crime and Abuse of Power.* Particularly, a victim shall have the following:
    a.   the opportunity, through private counsel, to participate in the criminal proceedings in accordance with the provisions of the Statute and the Rules of the Court; and
    b.   the right to protect his civil interests.
10.   *Ne Bis in Idem*
    The principle of *ne bis in idem* shall apply in all cases with respect to individuals charged with a crime under the jurisdiction of the Tribunal.

Commentary
    The standards of fairness which are to be guaranteed in all proceedings before the Organs of the Tribunal and which are to be reflected in the Procedures and Rules to be promulgated by the said Organs embodying those rights are contained *inter alia*: 1948 UNIVERSAL DECLARATION OF HUMAN RIGHTS, the 1966 INTERNATIONAL COVENANT ON CIVIL AND POLITICAL RIGHTS, G.A. Res. 2200A (XXI), 16 December 1966, the 1980 BODY OF PRINCIPLES ON THE PROTECTION OF PERSONS FROM ALL FORMS OF ARBITRARY ARREST AND DETENTION, THE 1950 EUROPEAN CONVENTION FOR THE PROTECTION OF HUMAN RIGHTS AND FUNDAMENTAL FREEDOMS, 213 U.N.T.S. 262, and ADDITIONAL PROTOCOLS Nos. 5-10., and the 1969 AMERICAN CONVENTION ON HUMAN RIGHTS, OAS Off. Rec. Ser. K/XVI 1.1 Doc. 65, Rev. 1, Cor. 1, 22 November 1969. These standards are also embodied in the resolutions of the XIIth International Congress of Penal Law held in Hamburg 1979 whose draft and explanatory notes are in 49 *Revue International de Droit Pénal* vol. 3, 1978. *See, e.g.,* LOUIS B. SOHN & THOMAS BUERGENTHAL, INTERNATIONAL PROTECTION OF HUMAN RIGHTS (1973); A. ROBERTSON, HUMAN RIGHTS IN EUROPE (1977); D. PONCET, LA PROTECTION DE L'ACCUSE PAR LA CONVENTION EUROPEENNE DES DROITS DE L'HOMME (1977); FLAVIA LATTANZI, GARANZIE DEL DIRITTI DELL'UOMO NEL DIRITTO INTERNAZIONALE GENERALE (1983); HERBERT PETZOLD, THE EUROPEAN CONVENTION ON HUMAN RIGHTS (5th ed. 1984);THOMAS BUERGENTHAL, ROBERT

NORRIS & DINAH SHELTON, PROTECTING HUMAN RIGHTS IN THE AMERICAS: SELECTED PROBLEMS 52 (2d ed. 1986); THEODOR MERON, HUMAN RIGHTS IN INTERNATIONAL LAW: LEGAL AND POLICY ISSUES (1989); THE FUTURE OF HUMAN RIGHTS PROTECTION IN A CHANGING WORLD: FIFTY YEARS SINCE THE FOUR FREEDOMS ADDRESS, ESSAYS IN HONOUR OF TORKEL OPSHAL (Asbjorn Eide & Jan Helgesen eds., 1991).

CHAPTER 6. THE PENAL PROCESSES OF THE TRIBUNAL
Article XXIII. General Provision
1. The penal processes of the Tribunal shall consist as follows:
    a. Initiation of the Process,
    b. Pre-trial Processes,
    c. Adjudication,
    d. Sanctioning,
    e. Appeals, and
    f. Supervision of sanctions.
2. No prosecution shall initiate without an Indictment Chamber of the Court issuing an indictment. The composition of the Indictment Chamber shall consist of a panel of three judges randomly selected.
3. Decisions by the Indictment Chamber are reviewable by, and at the discretion of, an Appellate Chamber sitting without the participation of the three judges who were members of the Indictment Chamber.
4. Adjudication shall be by a panel of three judges randomly selected, excluding the three judges of the Indictment Chamber.
5. Appeals shall be before a panel of five judges randomly selected, excluding the judges of the Indictment Chamber and the judges of the Adjudication Panel.

Commentary
Prosecution may commence on the basis of a criminal complaint brought by a State-Party. In addition, a State-Party that does not have either subject matter or *in personam* jurisdiction, or which does not wish to bring a criminal complaint within its own jurisdiction, may petition the Procurator-General of the Tribunal to inquire about the potential direct prosecution by the Court. In such cases, the request by a State-Party will be confidential. Only after the Procurator-General of the Tribunal has deemed the evidence sufficient, will the case for prosecution be presented to the Indictment Chamber of the Court. Once this Chamber issues its order to prosecute, a formal indictment shall be brought against the accused and appropriate procedures and steps taken by the Procurator-General to assure the surrender of the accused to the Court by the State-Party where the accused may be found.

In Chapter 8, the Statute includes provisions on surrendering the accused to the Tribunal and providing the Tribunal with legal assistance (including administrative and judicial assistance) for the procurement of evidence (both tangible and testimonial). *See, e.g.,* THE EUROPEAN CONVENTION ON MUTUAL LEGAL ASSISTANCE Europ. T.S. No. 30, MULLER-RAPPARD & BASSIOUNI, 1 EUROPEAN INTER-STATE CO-OPERATION chapter 1, and the various bilateral Conventions between various states. *See also, e.g.,* Hans-Heinrich Jescheck, *Moglichkeiten und Probleme eines Europaischen Strafrechts,* FESTSCHRIFT FUR JHONG-WON KIM ZUM 60. GEBURTSTAG 947 (1991); A. Ellis and R. Pisani, *The United States Treaties on Mutual Assistance in Criminal Matters, in* BASSIOUNI, ICL 151.

The desirability of such a penal process has substantial support in several studies and prior drafts. *See* G.A. Res. 1187 (XII) 11 November 1957; *Report of the Secretary-General on International Criminal Jurisdiction* U.N. GAOR (XII) (1957), Doc. A/13649; *U.N. Historical Survey on the Question of the International Criminal Jurisdiction* Doc. A/CN.4/7, Rev. 1 (1949). For a documentary history of the various projects for the creation on an international criminal jurisdiction, see BENJAMIN FERENCZ, THE INTERNATIONAL CRIMINAL COURT (1980) 2 vols; Bassiouni & Blakesley, The Need for an ICC; Bassiouni, The Time Has Come; Bassiouni, Draft Code and Statute. *See also* 52 RIDP, Nos. 3-4 (1981), symposium issue on a Draft International Criminal Code; Bouzat, *Introduction* 331; Jescheck, *Development Present State and Future Prospects of International Law* 377; Decker, *A Critique of the Draft International Criminal Code* 365; Shupilov, *General Comments on the Draft International Criminal Code* 373; Ottenhof, *Considerations sur la Forme le Style et la Methode d Elaboration du Project de Code Penal International* 385; Friedlander, *Some Observations Relating to the Draft International Criminal Code* 407; Nanda, *International Crimes under the Draft Criminal Code* 627; 45 RIDP Nos. 3-4 (1974) containing the contributions of the AIDP to V U.N. Congress on Crime Prevention and Criminal Justice, Geneva, September 1975 devoted to the subject of *La Creation d'une Justice Penale Internationale*; 35 RIDP 102 (1964) devoted to this subject. The Revue Internationale de Droit Penal presented scholarly writings on this subject in its issues of 1928, 1935, 1945, 1952, and 1974, as well as other individual scholarly reports between 1928-1992. For other works see K. de Haan, *The Procedural Problems of a Permanent International Criminal Jurisdiction, in* DE BESTRAFFING VAN INBREUKEN TEGEN HET OORLOGS - EN HET HUMANITAIR RECHT (A. Berlaen et al. eds. 1980); Kos-Rabcewicz-Zubkowski, *The Creation of an International Criminal Court, in* INTERNATIONAL TERRORISM AND POLITICAL CRIMES 519 (M. Cherif Bassiouni ed. 1975); J. STONE & ROBERT WOETZEL, TOWARD A FEASIBLE INTERNATIONAL CRIMINAL COURT (1970); Klein & Wilkes, *United Nations Draft Statute for an International Criminal Court: An American Evaluation, in* INTERNATIONAL CRIMINAL LAW 573 (Gerhard O.W. Mueller & Edward M. Wise eds. 1965); P. CAJEU, PROJECT D'UNE JURISDICTION PENALE INTERNATIONALE (1953); A SOTTILE, THE PROBLEM OF THE CREATION OF A PERMANENT INTERNATIONAL CRIMINAL COURT (1951); *Project for the Establishment of a Convention for the Creation of a United Nations Tribunal for War Crimes,* established by the United Nations War Crimes Commission, 1944, *see* WRIGHT, UNITED NATIONS WAR CRIME COMMISSION (1946); L'UNION INTERPARLIAMENTAIRE. COMPTE RENDU DE LA XXVII CONFERENCE TENUE A ROME EN 1948 (1949); *Projet d'une Cour Criminelle Internationale,* adopted by the International Law Association at its 34th Conference in Vienna, August 1926, THE INTERNATIONAL LAW ASSOCIATION, REPORT OF THE 34TH CONFERENCE VIENNA, AUGUST 5-11, 1926 (1927); Project of the International Association of Penal Law, *in* ACTES DU PREMIER CONGRES INTERNATIONAL DE DROIT PENAL, BRUXELLES, JUNE 26-29, 1926 (1927); *Projet de Statut pour la Creation d'une Chambre Criminelle au Sein de la Cour Permanente de Justice Internationale,* presented by the International Association of Penal Law to the League of Nations in 1927, 5 RIDP (1928); *Constitution et Procedure D 'un Tribunal Approprié pour Juger de la Responsabilite des Auteurs des Crime de Guerre, Presente a la Conference Preliminaires de Paix par la Commission des Responsabilites des Auteurs de la Guere et Sanctions,* III, LA PAIX DE VERSAILLES (1930); and *see* V. V. Pella the InterParliamentary Union, XXII Conference, held in Berne and Geneva, 1924, *in* L'UNION INTERPARLIAMENTIARE. COMPTE RENDU DE LA XXII CONFERENCE TENUE A BERNE ET A GENEVE EN 1924, PUBLIE PAR LE BUREAU INTERPARLIAMENTAIRE. COMPTE RENDU DE LA XXIII CONFERENCE TENUE A WASHINGTON ET A OTTOWA EN 1925 (1926).

The 1953 Draft in Article 29 provides that the penal processes could commence only by action of a State-Party. The ILA Draft in Article 23 allows only States to approach the Commission, which at its turn would present a case to the Court. The procedures presented herein differ from the 1953 Draft and the ILA Draft in that they centralize the prosecution of any case with the Procurator-General. The Procurator-General then makes an initial determination as to whether the complaint is "not manifestly unfounded" or "manifestly unfounded." This determination is quite similar to the one made by the European Convention on Human Rights. The Procuracy's decisions are reviewable by the Court *en banc.* Furthermore, the Standing-Committee may provide mediation and conciliation as provided for in Chapter 3.

The procedure set forth herein prevents vexatious or malicious prosecutions. The fact that an Indictment Chamber decides on prosecutability provides such a guarantee, as does the provision for appeal to the Court *en banc.* The Right of Appeal is also ensured before a Chamber consisting of five judges, who were neither on the Indictment nor the Adjudication Chambers.

Article XXIV. Initiation of the Process
1.   No criminal process shall be initiated unless a complaint is communicated to the Procuracy by a State-Party or originated by the Procuracy with respect to cases arising under the Tribunal 's exclusive jurisdiction as established in Article XIX, paragraph 2.
2.   The Procuracy shall determine whether such complaints are "manifestly unfounded" or not, and that determination shall be reported immediately to the State-Party who filed the complaint.
3.   State-Parties whose complaints are determined to be "manifestly unfounded" may appeal such determinations to the Court *en banc* pursuant to Chapters 3 and 6 of this Statute.
4.   When a case is ready for prosecution, the Procurator-General shall submit it to an Indictment Chamber of the Court pursuant to Chapter 3 of this Statute.
5.   The adjudication process shall commence only as often as the Indictment Chamber orders it.

Article XXV. Pre-trial Processes

1. The ultimate merits of a case shall not be considered until the case has been submitted to an Indictment Chamber of the Court, sitting in a preliminary hearing at which the accused has the opportunity of being represented by Counsel, and the Chamber has made the following determinations:

   a. the case is reasonably founded in fact and law;

   b. no prior proceedings before the Tribunal or elsewhere bar the process in accordance with principle *ne bis in idem* or fundamental notions of fairness, and

   c. no conditions exist that would render the adjudication unreliable or unfair.

2. The Procuracy may request the Adjudication Chamber of the Court to issue orders in aid of development of a case, in particular, orders in the nature of:

   a. Arrest warrants;

   b. Subpoenas;

   c. Injunctions;

   d. Search warrants; and

   e. Warrants for surrender of an accused so as to enable accused persons to be brought before the Court and to transit States without interference.

3. Requests for such orders may be granted with or without prior notice to the accused if it would jeopardize the pursuit of justice.

4. All such orders shall be executed pursuant to the relevant laws of the state in which they are to be executed.

5. The schedule of proceedings shall be established by the Adjudication Chamber in consultation with the Procuracy and Counsel for the accused with due regard to the principle of fairness to the parties and the principle of speedy trial.

Commentary

A non-exhaustive list of orders that may be issued by the Court to aid in the preparation of a case is specified. It is expected that the Rules of the Court will go into the details of the form, content, and other formalities pertaining to these orders. They are among the traditional powers of either a Court, or a judge of instruction respectively, in the Common Law and Romanist-Civilist tradition. Similar provisions may be found in the 1953 Draft, Articles 40, 41, and 42 and in the ILA Draft Articles 36 and 37. It must be noted here that this Court will in this and other respects rely on the cooperation of the State-Parties to implement its orders. It m also be noted that where a State-Party has treaties or relations with a non-State-Pa on the subject of extradition and judicial assistance and cooperation, the Court orders and determinations of any sort would have an impact beyond that State-Par and thus give this Convention a multiplier effect with respect to its impact. *See, e.g.*, MULLER-RAPPARD & BASSIOUNI, EUROPEAN INTER-STATE COOPERATION. The duties of the State-Parties extend to the carrying out of the obligations of this Statute within their own territories and also whenever possible in their relations with other States. Th, carrying out and execution of all such obligations to assist the Tribunal where required by this Statute, and in particular under Chapter 8, are pursuant to the relevant national laws of the requested State. It must, however, be noted that a State-Party cannot enact national laws that will frustrate the carrying out of the obligations arising under this Statute.

These provisions establish a procedure analogous to an indictment, such as was proposed in Articles 33 to 35 and 31 of the 1953 Draft and ILA Drafts, respectively, by means of a Committing Chamber in the former and Commission processes in the latter.

Article XXVI. Adjudication

1. Hearings on the ultimate merits of cases shall be conducted before a designated Adjudication Chamber of the Court consisting of three judges randomly selected whose deliberations shall be *in camera*.

2. Hearings shall be open to the public unless, the Court determines that it is in the best interest of justice or security to conduct all or part of the proceedings *in camera*.

3. The Adjudication Chamber may dismiss a case and enter an appropriately motivated order. In case of dismissal on the merits, the principle *ne bis in idem* shall apply, unless the Appellate Chamber reverses the findings of the Adjudication Chamber.

4.   In all proceedings an Adjudication Chamber shall give equal weight to evidence and arguments presented by the Procurator-General and on behalf of the accused in accordance with the principle of "equality of arms" of the parties.

5.   When all evidence respecting guilt and innocence has been presented and argued by the parties, the Adjudication Chamber shall close the Hearings and retire for deliberations.

6.   The decisions of the Adjudication Chambers may be rendered orally, but a written opinion containing findings of fact and conclusions of law must always be made by the Adjudication Chamber. Any judge of that Chamber may write a separate dissenting or concurring opinion.

7.   A Determination of guilt shall be deemed entered when recorded by the Secretariat, which shall communicate it forthwith to the interested State-Party or State-Parties and to the accused.

8.   The Rules of the Tribunal shall establish procedures and rules of evidence in keeping with the standards established in Chapter 5.

Commentary

Paragraphs 1 and 2 parallel Article 39 of the 1953 Draft and 35 of the ILA Draft, conforming more closely to the latter. Paragraph 2 specifically provides for eventual *in camera* hearings whenever security requires it. This treatment appears appropriate to protect essential matters of confidentiality, such as identity of a witness or a particular technique for obtaining evidence in sensitive cases such as terrorism. The details for such presentations should be covered by the Procedures and Rules of the Tribunal and the Procuracy.

Paragraph 3 describes the inherent powers of courts to dismiss cases. Article 38, paragraph 4, of the 1953 Draft has a similar dismissal provision. No express provision is made for withdrawal of a matter, as was done in Articles 43 an~1 38 of the 1953 Draft and ILA Draft, respectively, it being implicit in the nature of the powers of the Procuracy to determine whether to take such action. It also provides for the application of the principle *non bis in idem* when the dismissal is on the merits of the case. But since appeals are provided for, the judgment becomes final after appeal, if one is sought.

Paragraph 4 relates to the principle of "equality of arms," which has been applied under the EUROPEAN CONVENTION ON HUMAN RIGHTS. [Applications No. 596159 and 789/60, Franz Pataki and Johann Dunshim v. Austria, *Report of the Commission*, 28 March 1963, YEARBOOK OF THE EUROPEAN CONVENTION ON HUMAN RIGHTS, 730-34 (1963)].

Article XXVII. Sanctioning

1.   Upon a Determination of guilt, a separate hearing shall be held regarding sanctions to be imposed, at which hearing evidence of mitigation and aggravation shall be introduced and argued by the parties.

2.   At the conclusion of this hearing the Adjudication Chamber shall retire for deliberation and shall issue its Determination in the same manner and subject to the same conditions as for a Determination of guilt, as set forth in Article XIX.

3.   The sanctioning hearing shall be subject to the procedures and standards of the Tribunal as set forth in chapter 5.

Commentary

The Court, upon a finding of guilt in accordance with the provisions of this Convention, the Procedures, and Rules and the Standards of Fairness set forth in Chapter 5, can impose a sanction against natural persons. If the case is brought pursuant to Article XIX, paragraphs 3 and 4, the Court will apply the law of the transferring State, or applicable law agreed to by the State referring the case to the Court. If the case is brought pursuant to Article XIX, paragraph 2, the Court shall apply its own penalties and sanctions pursuant to its promulgated rules. The Court shall enact appropriate and specific sanctions to be promulgated prior to the Tribunal's commencement of activities, in order to satisfy the element of notice required by the "principles of legality."

Upon conviction, the individual may be returned to the surrendering state, which will carry out the sentence on the basis of provisions in the Convention in the nature of transfer of prisoners' agreements, as in the EUROPEAN CONVENTION ON TRANSFER OF SENTENCED PERSONS Europ. T.S. No. 112; MULLER-RAPPARD & BASSIOUNI, EUROPEAN INTER-STATE CO-OPERATION chapter IV. *See* H. Epp, *The European Convention on Transfer of Prisoners, in* 2 BASSIOUNI, ICL 253 (1986); and M. Cherif Bassiouni, *Perspectives on the Transfer of Prisoners between the United States and Mexico and the United States and*

Canada, 11 VAND. J. TRANSNAT'L L. 239 (1978). Alternatively, the convicted person can be transferred to any other State Party on the same legal basis. The Tribunal may also place the convicted persons in its own detention facilities, which could be established by the Convention in accordance with a host-state agreement between the Tribunal and the State wherein the detention facility will be established.

Article XXVIII. Appeals

1.   Appeals from Determinations of the Adjudication Chamber may be commenced by the accused upon written notice filed with the Secretariat and communicated to all interested parties within 30 days of the date of entry of judgment.
2.   Appeals shall be heard by a five judge panel, randomly selected but excluding those judges who sat on the panels of the Indictment and Adjudication Chambers.
3.   Other appeals from actions of the Indictment or Adjudication Chambers may be taken before a final judgment is entered only if such actions are conclusive as to procedural matters.
4.   The Procuracy may appeal questions of law in the same manner as an accused under paragraphs 1 and 2 of this Article.
5.   Decisions on Appeals shall be delivered in the same manner as other decisions as provided in Article XXVI, paragraphs 5 and 6 of this statute.
6.   Appellate decisions and unappealed judgments of the Indictment and Adjudication Chambers shall be deemed final unless the Court en banc intervenes to withhold execution of a judgment. The Court en banc can exercise this prerogative if:
    a.   Evidence has been discovered, which was unknown at the time of the judgment, has a material effect on the outcome of the judgment;
    b.   The Court was flagrantly misled as to the nature of matters affecting the outcome;
    c.   The facts proved do not constitute a crime within the jurisdiction of the Tribunal; or
    d.   Other grounds for which the Court may provide in its Rules.
7.   If the Court *en banc* intervenes to withhold execution of the judgment, it may reopen the case and vacate the judgment or remand the case for a new trial before an Adjudication Chamber.

Commentary

The provisions of the *International Covenant on Civil and Political Rights* concerning the dual level of judgment and review provide for a right of appeal, which is provided herein in the form of an Appellate Chamber. Also, interlocutory appeals are permitted in certain cases. The paragraph on revision of judgments parallels Articles 52 and 45 of the 1953 Draft and ILA Draft, respectively, but is broader in scope.

Appeals by the Procuracy on questions of law are permitted, including post-conviction orders.

The Court *en banc* may, under the circumstances described in Paragraph 6, review the judgments of the Chambers. This provision parallels Articles 52 and 45 of the 1953 Draft and ILA Draft, respectively, but is broader in scope.

Article XXIX. Supervision of Sanctions

1.   The Court may call upon any State-Party to execute measures imposed in respect of guilt and sanctions meted out by the Court in accordance with the laws of the said State-Party.
2.   With respect to each accused found guilty, a judge of the Court shall be selected by the Adjudication Chamber to act as Supervisor of the sanction imposed.
3.   All requests to modify sanctions shall be directed in the first instance to the Sanction Supervising judge who may submit the request to the Adjudication Chamber for modification, provided such action in no way increases the sanction or conditions imposed upon the person or legal entity found guilty.
4.   Decisions of the Sanction Supervising judges regarding modification requests may be reviewed by the Adjudication Chamber which imposed the sanction, but such reviews are in the Chamber's discretion and need not be the subject of full hearings and detailed written decisions.
5.   Nothing herein precludes the Court in accordance with its Rules to suspend its sanctions or place pre-conditions to their application in accordance with its published Rules in accordance with Chapters 3 and 5.

Commentary

Paragraph 1 corresponds to Articles 46 of the ILA Draft, Article 51 of the 1953 Draft having left such matters to future conventions. The terminology "sanctions" is capable of including not only punishments of imprisonment or fines but also levies of compensation or injunctive orders, thus maintaining the possibility for broad ranges of action.

The supervisory mechanism of Paragraph 2 replaces the Clemency and Parole Boards provided by the 1953 Draft and ILA Draft.

It should be noted that these provisions govern only the procedures relating to sanctions. Standards relating to sanctions may be elaborated by the Tribunal Rules.

The supervision of sentences is known to some legal systems, for example in France, *Juge de l'exécution des peines*. This formula is particularly important whenever the sanction is to be carried out by a State-Party.

CHAPTER 7. GENERAL INSTITUTIONAL MATTERS

Article XXX. Rule-Making

1.   The Tribunal shall formulate and publish its Rules in accordance with the norms and standards set forth in the Statute in order to regulate its functions and activities.
2.   Rules of the Tribunal shall be those of the International Court of Justice and those of the Secretariat shall be as for the Registrar of the International Court of Justice, unless any of these sources for rules and procedures are changed by this Statute or by the Rules of the Tribunal as provided for in this Article.

Commentary

This Article deals with the indispensable questions of Rule-Making, since it is impossible for the Statute to anticipate all the questions and problems of the Tribunal. This practical mechanism will eliminate the need to amend the Convention or Statute in the future. Recognition that flexibility should be provided for by such Rules was expressed in Article 24 of the 1953 Draft and Article 10 of the ILA Draft. Court approval of Rules for the Procuracy and Secretariat appear appropriate in view of the need to assure that such rules are both fair and conform to legal requirements. Participation by the Procurator in formulation of Tribunal Rules recognizes the desirability that such Rules interrelate properly with Procuracy procedures and capabilities.

Article XXXI. Immunity

1.   The Judges, the Procurator-General, the Deputy Procurators, and the prosecutorial staff, and the Secretary shall be deemed officers of the Court, as well as other Counsels appearing in a given case, and they shall enjoy immunity from legal processes in the State-Parties with respect to and during the performance of their legal duties.
2.   Immunity shall be indefinite with respect to the performance of duties by those persons covered by this paragraph, and limited in time for the duration of the person's function with respect to any other matter.
3.   The Court *en banc* may revoke any person's immunity with a two-thirds vote, except for Judges and the Procurator-General.
4.   The terms and provisions of the 1969 *Vienna Convention on Diplomatic Relations* shall apply.

Commentary

A certain level of immunity is necessary for the personnel of such an institution and for those who participate in its activities. This immunity requires the application of the VIENNA CONVENTION ON DIPLOMATIC RELATIONS 500 U.N.T.S. 95 (1961), but limits it in a number of ways. One of these is that immunity for Private Counsels and Counsels representing State-Parties is transactional, i.e. for the purposes of the case before the Court, and lasts only for the duration of the case. Another limitation is derived from the Court's ability to revoke it, although only by a two-thirds majority vote.

Article XXXII. Private Counsels

1.   Any person admitted to the practice of law before the highest court of law of a State-Party, and who is in good standing, can be retained by a person who is being investigated by the Procurator-General or charged with a crime, or otherwise subject to the Court's jurisdiction. Said persons may also be appointed by the Court.

2. The victims of a crime which is subject to the Court's jurisdiction can also be represented by private counsel of their choice who can submit written material to the Court and to the Procurator-General. Said counsel can orally address the Court during legal proceedings but only at the Court's discretion.

3. All Private Counsels must be admitted by the Court and take the oath described in Article XXXIII.

4. Any person investigated, charged, or tried by the Tribunal shall be represented by Counsel of his choice. In the event such a person is determined by the Court to be without sufficient means to obtain Private Counsel, he shall be represented at no cost by Court appointed counsel. The Rules of the Tribunal shall establish the criteria and method for Court appointed Counsel.

Commentary

This Article minimally regulates Private Counsels, deferring the regulation of lawyers to the Rules of the Tribunal. But, the Court *en banc* has the power to suspend Private Counsels for cause. The innovation in this Paragraph is that it provides the right of victims to representation. *See International Protection of Victims*, 7 NOUVELLES ÉTUDES PÉNALES (M. Cherif Bassiouni ed. 1988). Private Counsel for victims can submit written material to the Tribunal, but can only address the Court at its discretion. This right of victim's counsel presence in the case is in the capacity of *Partie Civile* as known in the civilist legal systems, it is likely to enhance the quality of justice and to partially vindicate the victim.

Article XXXIII. Oaths

1. No officer or employee of the Tribunal, except for external Counsels in a given case, shall perform any function in and before the Tribunal without having first made a solemn declaration before a judge of the Court of impartiality and adherence to the Statute and the Rules of the Tribunal's Organs.

2. Private Counsel and Counsels representing States shall make a solemn declaration of observance of the Tribunal's Rules before a judge of the Court.

3. The Rules of the Tribunal shall provide for the manner and content of such oaths.

Commentary

This Article parallels Article 14 of the 1953 Draft, which has no counterpart in the ILA Draft. Extension to other Tribunal officers is clearly appropriate in the interest of fairness. *See, e.g.*, the EUROPEAN AGREEMENT RELATING TO PERSONS PARTICIPATING IN PROCEEDINGS OF THE EUROPEAN COMMISSION AND COURT OF HUMAN RIGHTS Europ. T.S. No. 69.

The oath for Private Counsels parallels Article 13 of the 1953 Draft and Article 11 of the ILA Draft.

Article XXXIV. Budget Approval

1. The budget of the Tribunal shall be subject to approval by the Standing Committee and the State-Parties shall equally contribute to the costs of the Tribunal. Payment by State-Parties of their share of the cost shall be made to the Tribunal's Secretariat within 120 days of the budget's approval by the Standing-Committee.

2. In case financial contribution by a State-Party is in arrears, the Standing Committee may seek financing from other sources or authorize the Secretary to do so from public or private sources, but all costs shall be charged to the State-Party or State-Parties in arrears.

3. If a State-Party is in arrears for three consecutive years, it shall be automatically suspended from the Tribunal, and the Tribunal shall have a claim against the delinquent State-Party which it can directly enforce through the Secretary.

Commentary

This Article gives the Court a key role in shaping the budget of the Tribunal, but leaves the decision to the Standing-Committee. The Standing-Committee represents the States who are obliged to meet the costs. Prior draft statutes did not deal in detail with budgetary questions. *See* 1953 Article 23 and ILA Draft Article 17. This provision gives the Standing-Committee an important responsibility in the activities of the institution.

CHAPTER 8. JUDICIAL ASSISTANCE AND OTHER FORMS OF COOPERATION
Article XXXV. Applicability

1. The provisions of this chapter shall apply as between the following:

a.   The State-Parties and the International Criminal Tribunal; and

b.   Any state willing to cooperate with and assist the Tribunal or any other State-Party in connection with matters within the jurisdiction of the Tribunal on the basis of comity or by virtue of a special agreement between a non-State-Party and the Tribunal.

2.   The State-Parties shall provide the Tribunal with all internationally recognized means of legal assistance and cooperation including, but not limited to; extradition, service of notices and writs, assistance in securing testimony and other forms of tangible and intangible evidence, transmittal of records, transfer of proceedings, transfer of prisoners, and recognition of the Court's judgments.

3.   State-Parties shall enact specific legislation necessary to implement the provisions of this Chapter.

Commentary

Legal assistance includes administrative as well as judicial assistance. This provision includes the possibility the Tribunal may cooperate with non-State-Parties, whether by comity or agreement.

Sections 1 and 2 of this Article refer to the modalities and procedures set forth below.

The requested Party executes these duties in the manner provided for by its national laws.

The requested Party shall effect service of notices, writs, and records of judicial decisions that are transmitted to it for this purpose by the Tribunal. Service may be effected by simple transmission of the writ or record to the person to be served. Other formalities shall be established by the Rules of the Tribunal. *See* 1959 EUROPEAN CONVENTION ON MUTUAL ASSISTANCE IN CRIMINAL MATTERS, Europ. T.S. No. 30; MULLER-RAPPARD & BASSIOUNI, 1 EUROPEAN INTER-STATE COOPERATION chapter I (1987); and in part on the 1972 EUROPEAN CONVENTION ON TRANSFER OF PROCEEDINGS IN CRIMINAL MATTERS Europ. T.S. No. 73; MULLER-RAPPARD & BASSIOUNI, 2 EUROPEAN INTER-STATE COOPERATION chapter IV (1987). *See also* GRUTZNER, INTERNATIONALES RECHTSHILFEVERKEHR (1967); de Schutter, *International Criminal Law in Evolution: Mutual Assistance in Criminal Matters between the Benelux Countries*, 14 NETH. INT'L L. REV. 382 (1967); *Problems Arising from the Practical Application of the European Convention on Mutual Assistance in Criminal Matters* (Council of Europe, 1971); Grutzner, *International Judicial Assistance and Cooperation in Criminal Matters*, *in* 2 A TREATISE ON INTERNATIONAL CRIMINAL LAW, vol. 2, 189, 217-18 (M. Cherif Bassiouni and Ved P. Nanda eds. 1973)[hereinafter Bassiouni & Nanda, A TREATISE ON ICL]; Grutzner, *International Judicial Assistance and Cooperation in Criminal Matters*, and Markees, *The Difference in Concept Between Civil and Common Law Countries as to Judicial Assistance and Cooperation in Criminal Matters*, both *in* 2 Bassiouni & Nanda, A TREATISE ON ICL 171, 189 (1973); and M. PISANI & F. MOSCONI, CODICE DELLE CONVENZIONI DI ESTRADIZIONE E DI ASSISTENZA GIUDIZIARIA IN MATERIAL PÉNALE (1979); COOPERACION INTERAMERICANA EN LOS PROCEDIMIENTOS PENALES (L. Kos-Rabcewicz-Zubkowski ed. 1983); PAOLO LASZLOCZKY, LA CONVENZIONE EUROPEA DI ASSISTENZA GIUDIZIARIA IN MATERIA PENALE (1984); and *see also generally* 2 BASSIOUNI, ICL (1986).

With respect to the enforcement of judgments, *see* the 1970 EUROPEAN CONVENTION ON THE INTERNATIONAL VALIDITY OF CRIMINAL JUDGMENTS Europ. T.S. No. 70; *Aspects of International Validity of Criminal Judgments* (Council of Europe, 1968); *Explanatory Report on the European Convention on the International Validity of Criminal Judgments* (Council of Europe, 1970); 2 MULLER-RAPPARD & BASSIOUNI, EUROPEAN INTER-STATE COOPERATION chapter III. *See also* H. GRUZNER, INTERNATIONALES RECHTSHIFEVERKEHR IN STRAFSACHE, pt. IV (1967); 52 REV. CRITIQUE DE DROIT INTERNATIONAL PRIVÉ 863 (1973); D. Oehler, *Recognition of Foreign Penal Judgments and their Enforcement*, *in* 2 Bassiouni & Nanda, A TREATISE ON ICL 261; D. Oehler, INTERNATIONALEN STRAFRECHT (1973); I. A. Schearer, *Recognition and Enforcement of Foreign Criminal Judgments*, 47 AUST. L. J. 585; de Schutter, *International Criminal Cooperation: The Benelux Example*, *in* 2 Bassiouni & Nanda, A TREATISE ON ICL 261; Harari et. al., RECIPROCAL ENFORCEMENT OF CRIMINAL JUDGMENTS, 45 RIDP 585 (1974). *See also, e.g.*, 2 BASSIOUNI, ICL (1986).

With respect to transfer of sentences, *see* EUROPEAN CONVENTION ON THE SUPERVISION OF CONDITIONALLY SENTENCED OR CONDITIONALLY RELEASED OFFENDERS Europ. T.S. No. 51; 2 MULLER-RAPPARD & BASSIOUNI, EUROPEAN INTER-STATE COOPERATION chapter III; M. Cherif Bassiouni, *Perspectives on the Transfer of Prisoners between the United States and Mexico and the United States and Canada*, 11 VAND. J. TRANSNAT'L L. 249 (1978); M. Cherif Bassiouni, *A Practitioner's Perspective on Prisoner Transfer*, 4 NAT'L J. CRIM. DEFENSE 127 (1978); Abramovsky & Eagle, *A Critical Evaluation on the Newly-Ratified Mexican American Transfer of Penal Sanction Treaty*, 64 IOWA L. REV. 325 (1979), and Professor Vagt's response thereto in the same issue.

Article XXXVI. Cooperation with non-State-Parties

1.   Non-State-Parties may provide the Tribunal with assistance on the basis of comity or pursuant to *ad hoc*, or permanent agreements to provide the Tribunal with the assistance and cooperation modalities identified in Article XXXVII
2.   The Standing-Committee shall be empowered to negotiate and enter into such agreements after consultation with the Court. No agreement shall be entered into with any State over the express opposition of a majority of the Court sitting *en banc.*

Commentary

Paragraph 1 offers the opportunity for non-State-Parties to cooperate with the Tribunal. It is a way to enlarge the network of cooperating states in order to enhance the Court's effectiveness. In order to accomplish that, interested States can provide assistance on the basis of comity, *ad hoc* agreements, or permanent agreements. The Rules of the Tribunal should provide for such modalities. Since the Tribunal will have an independent juridical personality, it can, like other international organizations, enter into such agreements.

Paragraph 2 leaves the negotiations of such agreements to the Standing committee but subject to the Court's veto. Thus, the State-Parties have the political task of negotiating and entering into such agreements, but subject to the Court's judicial oversight and veto. This formula provides for an adequate balance between judicial and political considerations. It also leaves the Court outside the negotiating process in order to preserve its high dignity.

Article XXXVII. General Provisions on Judicial Assistance and Cooperation

1.   Applicable Law
    The law of the requested Party shall be applicable with respect to all procedures described in this Chapter, subject, however, to the provisions of the Convention.
2.   Communications
        a.   All communications between the State-Parties shall be in writing and shall be between the Ministries of Justice and the Secretariat of the International Criminal Tribunal.
        b.   Whenever appropriate, communications may also be made through the International Criminal Police Organization (ICPO/Interpol), but these communications shall only be deemed an official communication if accompanied by the certification of the Secretariat with a copy to the interested State or States, unless such a copy could affect security or the best interests of justice.
3.   Contents of Documentation
    Documentation pertaining to judicial assistance and cooperation shall include the following:
        a.   the basis and legal reasons for the request;
        b.   information concerning the individual who is the subject of the request;
        c.   information concerning the evidence sought to be seized, including: a description with sufficient detail to identify it, the reasons why it is sought and the legal basis relied on;
        d.   a description of the basic facts underlying the request; and
        e.   a description of the evidence concerning the charges, accusations, or conviction of the person who is the subject of the request.
4.   Languages
    All requests and communications made pursuant to this Convention shall be in any of the official languages of this Convention.
5.   Multiple Requests
    Requests for judicial assistance and cooperation by the Tribunal shall receive priority over any other request that a State-Party may receive.
6.   Provisional Measures
        a.   In cases of urgency, the Tribunal may ask of the requested State Party any or all of the following: to provisionally arrest the person sought for surrender, to seize evidence needed in connection with any proceedings which shall be the object of a formal request under the provisions of this Chapter, or to undertake protective measures to prevent the escape of the person or destruction of the evidence sought.
        b.   Provisional measures of arrest or seizure of evidence are valid only for a period of thirty days, and if all the necessary documents are not received within such period, the person seized shall be released forthwith and the evidence seized shall be returned to the person or entity from which it was taken. The

requested Party may at its discretion, grant an extension to the Tribunal for the submission of a formal request accompanied by the necessary documents, provided it shall not exceed an additional thirty days.

c.   The person affected by any provisional order, whether for provisional arrest or provisional seizure of evidence, shall have the right to be heard by a court of ordinary criminal jurisdiction in the requested State in connection with those provisional measures, subject to the applicable laws of the requested Party.

7.   Delivery of Persons

a.   The surrender or transfer of individuals, for any reason, from a State to the Tribunal and vice-versa, shall be in accordance with established legal procedures under both the Tribunal's Statute and Rules, and the laws of the requested state.

b.   Surrendered or transferred individuals shall be transported under humane and safe conditions, taking into account their health conditions. They shall also be transported by the shortest available route, and, when possible, without actual transit through any other territory. In the event of transit, permission from the State of transit shall be requested by the State who shall have custody of the individual to insure safe-passage. Transit shall not take place through any territory where there is reason to believe that the individual in question may fear for his life, freedom, or well-being.

8.   Rule of Speciality

a.   A person surrendered to the Tribunal shall not be subject to prosecution or punishment for any offense other than that for which he has been surrendered.

b.   Evidence surrendered shall not be used for any purpose other than the purpose for which it was surrendered.

c.   Waiver of the requirements of subparagraphs (a) and (b) shall be made by the requested State on the basis of a motivated request by the Tribunal and shall be examined by the appropriate authorities of the requested State in accordance with its laws, subject, however, to any other requirements set forth in the provisions of this Chapter.

9.   Re-extradition and Surrender of Evidence to a Third Party

a.   Neither the Tribunal nor a State-Party shall, without the consent of the individual or the originally requested State, surrender to any other third State a person with respect to any offense committed prior to the date of surrender.

b.   The procedure for obtaining consent of the requested State shall be the same as for an original request.

10.   Conditional Surrender

The Tribunal may accept limitations or conditions attached by the requested Party to the surrender of an individual or evidence in connection with any proceedings before the Tribunal.

11.   Property Rights

a.   Property seized by a requested Party at the request of the Tribunal, or by the Tribunal, shall be returned to the person from whom it was seized unless it was the subject of a judicial sanction of confiscation or destroyed.

b.   Issues involving seizure of property in connection with the provisions of this Chapter shall be adjudicated before the Court or, where applicable, before the judicial organs of the State wherein the property was seized. All persons having an interest in the outcome of such a judicial determination shall have the right to be heard. The person or legal entity from which the property was seized and any known owner of record shall receive notice and shall have the opportunity to be heard.

c.   In the event the property seized is surrendered to another State, it shall be subject to the same requirements set forth in subparagraph (b).

d.   No State-Party shall impose any customs or any other taxes upon the transfer and return of property seized, transferred, and returned under the provisions of this Chapter.

e.   The Tribunal and the requested State have the duty to exercise reasonable care in the protection and preservation of property seized, surrendered and returned, for the benefit of the owner, and any other person having an interest therein.

12.   Costs

The costs involved in surrender and transfer of persons and evidence for judicial assistance and cooperation, as well as execution of sentences shall be borne by the Tribunal whenever it exercises its jurisdiction pursuant to Article XIX, paragraph 2. When the Tribunal exercises its jurisdiction pursuant to Article XIX, paragraphs 3 and 4, the transferring State or submitting State shall bear these costs and refund them to the Tribunal.

Commentary

These General Provisions are to a large extent common to the various modalities of enforcement and mechanisms of cooperation contained in a number of bilateral and multilateral conventions on judicial assistance and cooperation in penal matters. They are also found in the European Conventions on Inter-State Cooperation in Penal Matters. *See, e.g.*, MULLER-RAPPARD & BASSIOUNI, EUROPEAN INTER-STATE CO-OPERATION (3 vols.).

Paragraph 1 on applicable law can be found in almost all multilateral and bilateral conventions on extradition and judicial assistance and cooperation in penal matters.

Paragraph 2 also reflects the prevailing practices of communication of many members of the world community, although a number of States use their ministries of Foreign Affairs or diplomatic missions as the appropriate channel communications. Experience has demonstrated that this usually lengthens the process, and that direct communication between the Ministries of Justice speeds it up. As to Interpol communications, it is presently a common practice in course with over one hundred members of that organization.

Paragraph 3 on documentation is also inspired by a number of multilateral and bilateral conventions and the practices of many States. *See, e.g.*, EUROPEAN CONVENTION ON EXTRADITION, Europ. T.S. No. 24, (1957), article 12, MULLER-RAPPARD & BASSIOUNI, L EUROPEAN INTER-STATE COOPERATION chapter II; the EUROPEAN CONVENTION ON MUTUAL ASSISTANCE, Europ. T.S. No. 30 (1959) article 14, MULLER-RAPPARD & BASSIOUNI, 1 EUROPEAN INTER-STATE COOPERATION chapter I; AMERICAN CONVENTION ON EXTRADITION, *signed* at Montevideo, December 26, 1933, 34 O.A.S. T.S. 51 (1967); the EUROPEAN CONVENTION ON TRANSFER OF PROCEEDINGS, Europ. T.S. No. 73 (1972), article 13, MULLER-RAPPARD & BASSIOUNI, 2 EUROPEAN INTER-STATE COOPERATION chapter IV; *Draft International Inter-American Convention on Mutual Assistance in Criminal Matters*, February 28, 1992. For useful commentary upon judicial assistance and cooperation, see Christine Van den Wijngaert, *Stuctures et Methodes de la Cooperation Internationale et Regionale en Matiere Penale*, 517 REVUE DROIT PENAL CRIMINOLOGIE (1984); MARIO PISANI, COOPERAZIONE GUIDIZIARIA INTERNAZIONALE DIZIONARIO DI DIRITTO E PROCEDURA PENALE (1986); D. Krapac, *An Outline of the Recent Development of the Yugoslav Law of International Judicial Assistance and Cooperation in Criminal Matters*, 324 NILR vol. XXXIV (1987); Didier Opertti, *Juridical Mutual Cooperation in Criminal Matters*, 89 NILR vol. XXXIX (1992).

Paragraph 4 is common to multilateral and bilateral treaties.

Paragraph 5 concerns multiple requests. Multiple requests concerning the same person or subject are infrequent. But, since it is a possibility, it is important to establish a basis for resolving conflicts that might arise from such a situation. The Tribunal's requests will always have precedence.

Paragraph 6 reflects the prevailing practice evidenced in multilateral and bilateral extradition treaties. However, paragraph 6 also extends to provisional measures dealing with evidence - which is not found in any existing convention.

Paragraph 7 provides for the means and manner by which an individual, as well as evidence, is to be delivered. The language is self-explanatory. It takes into account certain human rights standards embodied, in language and spirit, in a number of human rights instruments.

Paragraph 8 embodies the well-established rule of speciality that can be found in a variety of bilateral and multilateral extradition conventions and which has now become part of customary international law. It is placed in these general provisions because of its applicability to areas other than extradition. Its language is inspired by the EUROPEAN CONVENTION ON EXTRADITION, Europ. T.S. No. 24 (1957), MULLER-RAPPARD & BASSIOUNI, 2 EUROPEAN INTER-STATE COOPERATION chapter VI. *See also* M. CHERIF BASSIOUNI, INTERNATIONAL EXTRADITION IN UNITED STATES LAW AND PRACTICE (2d rev. ed. 1987).

Paragraph 9 intends to clarify problems relating to re-extradition and surrender of evidence to a Party other than the one to which extradition or surrender of the evidence has been granted. It is seldom found explicitly stated in multilateral and bilateral conventions and is, at times. a source of conflict.

Paragraph 10 recognizes the right of a State-Party to conditionally surrender a person or evidence. A similar provision can be found in the EUROPEAN CONVENTION ON EXTRADITION, Europ. T.S. No. 24 (1957), article 19, Muller-Rappard & Bassiouni, 2 European Inter-State Cooperation chapter VI.

The provisions of Paragraph 11 are fairly self-explanatory. They seek to. protect the rights of owners, persons and parties having an interest in the property, while at the same time ensuring the orderly surrender and transfer of property needed in connection with criminal proceedings. It also establishes the proper judicial forum for the adjudication of property rights and confiscatory measures in order to avoid conflicts between the State-Parties and undue hardship on persons having a right of ownership or other economic rights and interests in the property. While there are practically no multilateral and bilateral conventions that go into such detail, the EUROPEAN CONVENTION ON EXTRADITION, Europ. T. S. No. 24 (1957), article 20, MULLER-RAPPARD & BASSIOUNI, 2 EUROPEAN INTER-STATE COOPERATION chapter VI, deals with the preservation of property and its return, and the EUROPEAN CONVENTION ON INTERNATIONAL VALIDITY OF CRIMINAL JUDGMENTS, Europ. T.S. No. 70 (1970), article 12, MULLER-RAPPARD & BASSIOUNI, 2 EUROPEAN INTER-STATE COOPERATION chapter 3, deals with the non-imposition of duties. Two recent conventions need to be taken into account with respect to seizure and forfeiture of assets they are: UNITED NATIONS CONVENTION AGAINST ILLICIT TRAFFIC IN NARCOTIC DRUGS AND PSYCHOTROPIC SUBSTANCES, Dec. 19, 1988, 28 I.L.M. 493 (1989), and CONVENTION ON LAUNDERING, SEARCH, SEIZURE AND CONFISCATION OF THE PROCEEDS FROM CRIME (opened for signature on 8 November 1990) and *Council of Europe Explanatory Report on the Convention on laundering, Search, Seizure and Confiscation of the Proceeds from Crime* (Strasbourg, 1991).

Paragraph 12 concerns costs. It was deemed advisable to include a provision allocating costs of proceedings under this Convention in order to avoid any conflicts between the State-Parties and the Tribunal. This provision recognizes that the Party requesting assistance ought to bear the cost of such proceedings. This subject has frequently arisen in the European context, where such practices are more frequent. Some observers have argued that the high costs of judicial assistance and cooperation may work as an impediment thereto. Consequently, it was felt desirable to meet this argument head-on and to resolve the question.

Article XXXVIII. *Aut Dedere Aut Judicare*

1.   The State-Parties undertake to surrender, extradite, or transfer to the International Criminal Tribunal, on the basis of this Convention, any person under investigation, charged, sought to be tried, or convicted by the Court pursuant to the Tribunal's jurisdiction under Article XIX, paragraph 2. State-Parties further agree to surrender, extradite or transfer a person to the Tribunal pursuant to Article XIX, paragraph 3, if the given State-Party has not assumed the investigation, prosecution, or punishment of the said person who is believed, accused, or convicted of an offense listed in Annex 3.

2.   A State-Party that decides to prosecute a person does not have the obligation to surrender or extradite that person to the Tribunal, provided the anticipated prosecution is reasonably expected to be effective and fair. Whenever there is doubt as to effectiveness or fairness, another interested State-Party may raise the issue before the Court which in these cases will sit *en banc* pursuant to Article XIX, paragraph 1.

3.   A State-Party may, as an alternative to prosecution and as an alternative to using the Tribunal's jurisdiction pursuant to Article XIX, paragraph 3, extradite a person to another State having jurisdiction and willing to prosecute effectively and fairly. A State-Party may also transfer the proceedings and the accused to another State willing to accept the transfer and to prosecute effectively and fairly.

Commentary

The basis of international enforcement and cooperation derives from the maxim *aut dedere aut judicare* from Hugo Grotius, *De Jure Belli ac Pacis* (1624). It is now recognized as a general principle of international law to "prosecute or extradite." *See* M. Cherif Bassiouni, *International Extradition and World Public Order*, in AKTUELLE PROBLEME DES INTERNATIONALEN STRAFRECHTS 10, 15 (D. Oehler & P.G. Potz eds. 1970); CHRISTINE VAN DEN WIJNGAERT, THE POLITICAL OFFENSE EXCEPTION TO EXTRADITION: THE DELICATE PROBLEM OF BALANCING THE RIGHTS OF THE INDIVIDUAL AND THE INTERNATIONAL PUBLIC ORDER 218-29 (1980); M. CHERIF BASSIOUNI, INTERNATIONAL EXTRADITION IN U.S. LAW & PRACTICE 10-29 (2d. ed. 1987); Edward M. Wise, *International Crimes and Domestic Criminal Law*, 38 DEPAUL L. REV. 923 (1989).

This duty is the conceptual basis of the indirect enforcement scheme, which international law relies upon and is embodied in over 70 international criminal law conventions. The mechanism of the indirect enforcement scheme operates through a State's obligation to include appropriate provisions in its national laws to criminalize and prosecute the internationally proscribed conduct as a national crime. *See, e.g.*, the

Four Geneva Conventions, 12 August 1949, in their respective Articles 49-50/50-51/129-130/146-147. It is also the case with respect to other international criminal law conventions. *See generally* BASSIOUNI, DIGEST.

The formula proposed herein provides a number of alternative options which favor flexibility while enhancing the execution of the duty to prosecute or extradite. Paragraphs 3 and 4 introduce a new approach to the traditional formulation of the duty to prosecute or extradite, namely adding the requirements that prosecution when it is an alternative to extradition, be effective (to avoid sham prosecutions) and fair to the accused.

Article XXXIX. Priorities in Theories of Criminal Jurisdiction

Priority in theories of jurisdiction for the prosecution and punishment of any international offense to which the State-Parties have conferred jurisdiction to the Court pursuant to Article XIX paragraphs 3 and 4, shall be in the following order:

a. the State-Party in whose territory the offense occurred in whole or in part (territorial);
b. the State-Party of which the accused is a national (active personality);
c. the State-Party of which the victim is a national (passive personality);
d. the State-Party whose interests have been affected (protective); and
e. any other State-Party within whose territory the accused may be found (universality).

Commentary

The approach followed is that of ranking the priority of jurisdictional theories based on recognized international law and practice. The primary jurisdictional theory in Paragraph l(a) is that of territorial jurisdiction. *See* The S.S. *Lotus* case (France v. Turkey), 1927 P.C.I.J. Ser. A. No. 9. Sound policy reasons as well as international practice favor this theory. Ranking after territoriality in order of international acceptance are the theories of active personality, passive personality, protective, and universality. *See Harvard Draft Convention on Jurisdiction with Respect to Crime*, 29 A.J.I.L. SUPP. 439 (1935); D. GREIG, INTERNATIONAL LAW 168 (1970); Feller, *Jurisdiction over Offenses wi~h Foreign Element, in* Bassiouni & Nanda, 2 A TREATISE ON ICL 5 *et seq.*; and M. Cherif Bassiouni, *Theories of Jurisdiction and Their Application in Extradition Law and Practice*, 5 CALIF. W. INT'L L. J. 1 (1974); Christopher L. Blakesley, *Extraterritorial Jurisdiction, in* BASSIOUNI, 2 ICL 3. Universal jurisdiction is embodied in Subparagraph (e), and is generally a corollary of the recognition that a given offense constitutes an international crime. *See* Attorney General of Israel v. Eichmann, 36 I.L.R. S (Israel, 1961) and I.L.R.277 (1962); *see also* P. PAPADATOS, THE EICHMANN TRIAL (1964).

Article XL. Basic Principles Applicable to the Surrender of Persons

1. Basis for Surrender

a. State-Parties shall consider this Convention as the legal basis for surrendering persons to the Tribunal.

b. State-Parties undertake to include violations listed respectively in Annexes 2 and 3, and for which they have given jurisdiction to this Court pursuant to Article XIX, paragraphs 2 and 3, as extraditable offenses in their appropriate legislation and in their extradition treaties.

2. Priority in Extradition and Surrender Requests

If a State-Party receives multiple extradition requests for the same person, it shall give precedence to the Tribunal's request.

3. Conditional Surrender

a. Whenever the laws of the requested State-Party prohibit extradition or surrender for a violation susceptible to punishment by the death penalty, the requesting State-Party may, as a precondition to surrender, stipulate that such penalty shall not be imposed and, upon receipt of such assurances, the person requested shall be surrendered to the Tribunal subject to the assurances given.

b. In the event that the national constitution of a State-Party prohibits extradition of its nationals, the person requested may be conditionally delivered to the Tribunal for prosecution on the condition that the accused be returned to the requested Party after the trial and, in this case, the Party shall recognize such a foreign penal judgment and execute its sentencing provisions in accordance with the judgment of the Court. Alternatively, the requested State-Party may consider, by virtue of this Convention, that the Tribunal is part of or an extension of its judiciary.

4.   Bar to Extradition

    a.   A State-Party shall not surrender a person requested by the Tribunal if the prosecution is barred by the principle *ne bis in idem* or the statute of limitation of the requested State.

    b.   A State-Party may deny extradition to the Tribunal if it is in the process of prosecuting a person accused of committing any violation of this Convention, except where the State-Party in question has conferred exclusive jurisdiction to the Court pursuant to Article XIX, paragraph 2.

5.   Judicial Determination

    Surrender shall be granted to the Tribunal on the basis of a judicial determination made by a court of ordinary jurisdiction under the laws of the requested Party.

6.   Rule of Speciality

    A surrendered person shall be tried or judged by the Tribunal only for the offense or offenses for which he was surrendered.

Commentary

    This article is provided for whenever the Court exercises its jurisdiction pursuant to Article XIX, paragraph 2, whereby the Court has exclusive jurisdiction over those offenses listed in Annex 2, and pursuant to Article XIX, paragraph 4, *Ad Hoc* jurisdiction. The grounds and exceptions, as well as the procedures, are those recognized in conventional and customary international law, as well as the prevailing practices of States.

    Because of the importance of extradition, and in light of existing problems perceived in the practice, it is covered herein with detail. *See* THEO VOGLER, AUSLIEFERUNGSRECHT UND GRUNDGESETZ (1970); I. A. SHEARER, EXTRADITION INTERNATIONAL LAW (1971); M. CHERIF BASSIOUNI, INTERNATIONAL EXTRADITION AND WORLD PUBLIC ORDER (1974); V. E. HARTLEY BOOTH, I BRITISH EXTRADITION LAW AND PROCEDURE (1980); CHRISTINE VAN DEN WIJNGAERT, THE POLITICAL OFFENSE EXCEPTION TO EXTRADITION: THE DELICATE PROBLEM OF BALANCING THE RIGHTS OF THE INDIVIDUAL AND INTERNATIONAL PUBLIC ORDER (1980); ROBERT LINKE, GRUNDISS DES AUSLIEFERUNGS-RECHTS (1983); MANUEL ADOLFO VIERIRA, L'EVOLUTION RECENTE DE L'EXTRADITION DANS LE CONTINENT AMERICAIN; BLANCA PASTOR BORGONON, ASPECTOS PROCESALES DE LA EXTRADICION EN DERECHO ESPANOL (1984); HAFID ALAOUI BAOUKHRISS, LA COOPERATION PÉNALE INTERNATIONALE PAR VOIE D'EXTRADITION AU MAROC (1986); M. CHERIF BASSIOUNI, INTERNATIONAL EXTRADITION IN U.S. LAW AND PRACTICE (2 vols. 2d rev. ed. 1987); OTTO LAGODNY, DIE RECHTSSTELLUNG DES AUSZULIEFERNDEN IN DER BUNDESREPUBLIK DEUTSCHLAND (1987); TIZIANA TREVISSON LUPACCHINI, L'ESTRADIZIONE DALL'ESTERO PER L'ITALIA (1989); MARIA RICCARDA MARCHETTI, LA CONVENZIONE EUROPEA DI ESTRADIZIONE (1990)

Article XLI. Basic Principles Applicable to Legal Assistance

1.   General Principles

    The State-Parties undertake to afford the Tribunal, in accordance with the provisions of this Chapter, the widest measure of legal assistance in administrative and judicial proceedings with respect to offenses for which they have conferred jurisdiction to the Tribunal pursuant to Article XIX, and in accordance with the Principles set forth herein and the Rules of the Tribunal. Such legal assistance shall be performed with a view to protecting the rights of all persons affected by such proceedings in accordance with the provisions of Chapter 5.

2.   Information

    a.   The State-Parties undertake to supply each other and the Tribunal with information on their substantive and procedural laws and regulations, judicial organization, and the authority of various administrative, prosecutorial, judicial and law enforcement bodies with respect to criminal matters.

    b.   Whenever a person is investigated or prosecuted by the Tribunal, State Parties shall inform the Tribunal of all criminal convictions and subsequent measures.

3.   Notices, Writs, and Records

    State-Parties shall effect service of notices and writs and give proof of records of judicial decisions and verdicts transmitted to it by the Tribunal in accordance with their national laws.

4.   Witnesses

    a.   A witness or expert requested by the Tribunal for appearance before the Court in connection with a matter relating to any of the offenses within the Court's jurisdiction shall be notified by the Requested State Party in accordance with its national laws.

b.   A person sought by the Tribunal as a witness or expert who is in the requested State-Party shall be transferred for testimonial purposes.

c.   A witness or expert, whatever his nationality, who voluntarily responds to a notice, writ, or summons to testify in whatever capacity in legal proceedings before the Tribunal shall be given safe conduct to and from other State-Parties for the period of his appearance before the Tribunal and during his travel to and from the Tribunal. Such safe conduct shall include immunity from prosecution, detention, and other restrictions of his personal liberty. Seizure of personal property shall be prohibited, excluding, of course, items whose possession may constitute a violation of the criminal laws of that Party. In such a case, their seizure is permitted, but not the arrest, detention or prosecution of the witness.

Commentary

This Article is adapted from provisions of the 1959 EUROPEAN CONVENTION ON MUTUAL ASSISTANCE IN CRIMINAL MATTERS, Europ. T.S. No. 30, MULLER-RAPPARD & BASSIOUNI, 1 EUROPEAN INTER-STATE COOPERATION chapter I; and the ADDITIONAL PROTOCOL TO THE EUROPEAN CONVENTION ON MUTUAL ASSISTANCE IN CRIMINAL MATTERS, Europ. T.S. No. 99 (1978), MULLER-RAPPARD & BASSIOUNI, 1 EUROPEAN INTER-STATE COOPERATION chapter I. *See also* FIRST ADDITIONAL PROTOCOL TO THE EUROPEAN CONVENTION ON INFORMATION ON FOREIGN LAW, Europ. T.S. 98 (1978), MULLER-RAPPARD & BASSIOUNI, 1 EUROPEAN INTER-STATE COOPERATION chapter I.

Paragraph 1 is self-explanatory as it is a general statement of principles. It also relies on article 1 of the EUROPEAN CONVENTION ON MUTUAL ASSISTANCE IN CRIMINAL MATTERS, Europ. T.S. No. 30 (1959), MULLER-RAPPARD & BASSIOUNI, 1 EUROPEAN INTER-STATE COOPERATION chapter I.

Paragraph 2 relies on the provisions of article 1 of the EUROPEAN CONVENTION ON INFORMATION ON FOREIGN LAW, Europ. T.S. No. 97 (1978), and SECOND ADDITIONAL PROTOCOL Europ. T.S. No. 98 (1978) as well as on article 22 of the COOPERATION IN PENAL MATTERS. *See, e.g.,* MULLER-RAPPARD & BASSIOUNI, EUROPEAN INTER-STATE CO-OPERATION chapter I

Paragraph 3 relies on articles 7 an 13 of the EUROPEAN CONVENTION ON MUTUAL LEGAL ASSISTANCE IN CRIMINAL MATTERS, but is more explicit.

Paragraph 4 relies on articles 9 and 10 of the EUROPEAN CONVENTION ON MUTUAL LEGAL ASSISTANCE IN CRIMINAL MATTERS and is to be read as complementary to Paragraphs 3 and 4. It adds certain conditions on safe conduct which are found also in article 12 of the EUROPEAN CONVENTION ON MUTUAL LEGAL ASSISTANCE IN CRIMINAL MATTERS.

There is no compulsory transfer of witnesses: The process is voluntary, and the requested Party may oppose it, even if the witness volunteers. *See, e.g., Explanatory Report on the European Convention on the Transfer of Proceedings in Criminal Matters* (Council of Europe, 1972); *Problems Arising from the Practical Application of the European Convention on Mutual Assistance in Criminal Matters* (Council of Europe, 1971); de Schutter, *International Criminal Law in Evolution: Mutual Assistance in Criminal Matters between the Benelux Countries,* 14 NETH. INT'L L. REV. 382 (1967); H. Grutzner, *International Judicial Assistance and Cooperation in Criminal Matters, in* Bassiouni & Nanda, 2 A TREATISE ON ICL 189; Markees, *The Difference in Concept Between Civil and Common Law Countries as to Judicial Assistance and Cooperation in Criminal Matters, in* Bassiouni & Nanda, 2 A TREATISE ON ICL 171 (1973). *See also* M. PISANI & F. MOSCONI, CODICE DELLE CONVENZIONI DI ESTRADIZIONE E DI ASSISTENZA GIUDIZIARIA IN MATERIA PENAL (1979); A. Ellis & R.L. Pisani, *The United States Treaties on Mutual Assistance in Criminal Matters, in* 2 BASSIOUNI, ICL; L. Gardocki, *The Socialist System, in* 2 BASSIOUNI, ICL 133; Ekkehart Muller-Rappard, *The European System, in* 2 BASSIOUNI, ICL 195.

Article XLII. Basic Principles on the Transfer of Criminal Proceedings

1.   Basis

a.   A State-Party may request the Tribunal to undertake the prosecution of a person when it has the power to exercise criminal jurisdiction in accordance with the Tribunal's jurisdiction in accordance with Article XIX, paragraphs 3 and 4, and with respect to Annex 3.

b.   The Court has the right to accept or refuse such a transfer in accordance with its judicial processes established in this Statute.

2.　　Surrender of the Accused
　　　Whenever the Tribunal has agreed to assume prosecution, the accused shall be surrendered to the Tribunal in accordance with the Basic Principles Applicable to the Surrender of Persons set forth in Article XL and the Rules of the Tribunal.
3.　　Transfer of Records
　　　The State-Party who has requested or consented to the transfer of proceedings to the Tribunal undertakes to transmit, at its expense, all the records and materials pertaining to the transferred matter and shall provide the Tribunal with every reasonable and available form of assistance in connection with the prosecution in accordance with the Basic Principles Applicable to the Legal Assistance set forth in Article XLI and the Rules of the Tribunal.

Commentary
　　　This Article is based on the EUROPEAN CONVENTION ON THE TRANSFER OF PROCEEDINGS IN CRIMINAL MATTERS, Europ. T.S. No. 73 (1972), MULLER-RAPPARD & BASSIOUNI, 2 EUROPEAN INTER-STATE COOPERATION chapter IV . It also relies in part on the EUROPEAN CONVENTION ON THE PUNISHMENT OF ROAD TRAFFIC OFFENSES, Europ. T.S. No. 52 (1964), MULLER-RAPPARD & BASSIOUNI, 3 EUROPEAN INTER-STATE COOPERATION chapter 4; and the EUROPEAN CONVENTION ON MUTUAL ASSISTANCE IN CRIMINAL MATTERS, Europ. T.S. No. 30, MULLER-RAPPARD & BASSIOUNI, 1 EUROPEAN INTER-STATE COOPERATION chapter I.

Article XLIII. Basic Principles Applicable to the Enforcement of Judgments
1.　　The administering State-Party shall assume, for and on behalf of the Tribunal, the duty to enforce a sanction imposed by the Court, with respect to a given sentenced person, in accordance with their national laws, but subject to the continued supervision of the Court.
2.　　A State-Party may refuse to enforce the Court's judgment whenever any of the following may exist:
　　　a.　　the administering State-Party is unable to administer the sanction;
　　　b.　　the sentenced person is neither a national nor a permanent resident of the administering State-Party;
　　　c.　　the age of the sentenced person at the time of the execution or enforcement of the sanction is below the age prescribed for this type of sanction by the laws of the requested State-Party;
　　　d.　　the nature, type, and length of sentence is contrary to the public policy of the requested Party; and
　　　e.　　the sentence of the Court is not final, and all available means of review before the Tribunal have not been exhausted.
3.　　Effects of Acceptance by a State-Party to Enforce a Sanction
　　　a.　　The acceptance by the administering State-Party of the request to enforce a sentence by the Tribunal grants that State-Party subject to the Court's supervision over the sentenced person.
　　　b.　　The administering State-Party may, for good cause, elect to terminate its enforcement of the sanction and thereby offer to return the sentenced person to the custody of the Tribunal.
　　　c.　　The judicial, executive, or administrative organs of the administering State-Party shall not have jurisdiction to review any aspect of the prosecution, judgment, or sentence rendered by the Tribunal.
　　　d.　　The laws of the administering State-Party, as well as its administrative regulations concerning the enforcement and execution of the sentence, shall apply, including conditional release or alternative measures provided under its laws.
　　　e.　　Nothing in this Article shall preclude or limit the right of a sentenced person, even after his surrender to the administering State-Party, to resort to the legal processes of the Tribunal with respr,ct to any available means of review of the conviction and sentence. In such a case, the administering State-Party shall not impede the right of a sentenced person to such available recourse.
　　　f.　　A transferred sentenced person shall be given credit toward service of the sentence by the administering State-Party for any period of time served before conviction or any fine paid to the Tribunal irrespective of whether the period of time served was for pre-trial detention or for administrative reasons.
4.　　Sentence Administration
　　　The administration of sentences shall be subject to the supervision of the Court, acting through the judge supervising the sentence. The administering State-Party shall give the judge of supervision of sentences all the assistance and access necessary to carry out his/her duties.

5.   Prosecution and Punishment of the Sentenced Person by the Administering Party A sentenced person within the custody of the administering State-Party shall not be subjected to prosecution or punishment for any conduct committed prior to the transfer of the sentenced person from the custody of the Tribunal to that of the administering State-Party unless such prosecution or punishment has been agreed to by the Tribunal.

6.   Fines and Confiscations
The enforcement of a fine or a confiscatory measure shall be governed by the same provisions contained in this Article. The proceeds of fines or confiscatory measures shall go to the Tribunal.

Commentary
This article relies on a number of European Conventions. EUROPEAN CONVENTION ON THE SUPERVISION OF CONDITIONALLY SENTENCED OR CONDITIONALLY RELEASED OFFENDERS, Europ. T.S. No. 51 (1970), MULLER-RAPPARD & BASSIOUNI, 1 EUROPEAN INTER-STATE COOPERATION chapter 3; the EUROPEAN CONVENTION ON THE PUNISHMENT OF ROAD TRAFFIC OFFENCES, Europ. T.S. No. 52 (1964), MULLER-RAPPARD & BASSIOUNI, 2 EUROPEAN INTER-STATE COOPERATION chapter 5; The EUROPEAN CONVENTION ON THE INTERNATIONAL VALIDITY OF CRIMINAL JUDGMENTS, Europ. T.S. No. 70 (1970), MULLER-RAPPARD & BASSIOUNI, 1 EUROPEAN INTERSTATE COOPERATION chapter 3; EUROPEAN CONVENTION ON THE TRANSFER OF SENTENCED PERSONS, Europ. T.S. No. 112 (1983), MULLER-RAPPARD & BASSIOUNI, EUROPEAN INTER-STATE COOPERATION chapter 3.

Concerning the validity of foreign criminal judgments, *see* Harari et al., *Reciprocal Enforcement of Criminal Judgments*, 45 REV. INT'L DROIT PENAL 585 (1974); Dietrich Oehler, *Recognition of Foreign Penal Judgments and their Enforcement, in* Bassiouni & Nanda, 2 A TREATISE ON ICL 261; I. A. Schearer, *Recognition and Enforcement of Foreign Criminal Judgment*, 47 AUST. L.J. 585(1973); DIETRICH OEHLER, INTERNATIONALEN STRAFRECHT (1973). For the Benelux Convention, *see* CONVENTION CONCERNING CUSTOMS AND EXCISE, September 5, 1972, Belgium-Luxembourg-The Netherlands, 247 U.N.T.S. 329 (1956). *See also* K. KRAELLE, LE BENELUX COMMENTE, TEXTES OFFICIELS 147, 209, 306 (1961); De Schutter, *International Criminal Cooperation: The Benelux Example, in* Bassiouni & Nanda, 2 A TREATISE ON ICL 261. The Scandinavian countries' arrangement for recognition and enforcement of penal judgments is reproduced in H. GRUTZNER, INTERNATIONALES RECIITSHILFEVERKEHR IN STRAFSACHE, pt. IV (1967). The arrangement between France and certain African states is reproduced in 51 REV. CRITIQUE DROIT INT'L PRIVE 863 (1973).

Concerning transfer of offenders *see* M. Cherif Bassiouni, *Perspectives on the Transfer of Prisoners Between the United States and Mexico and the United States and Canada*, 11 VAND. J. TRANSNAT'L L. 249 (1978); M. Cherif Bassiouni, *A Practitioner's Perspective on Prisoner Transfer*, 4 NAT'L J. CRIM. DEFENSE 127 (1978); Abramowsky & Eagle, *A Critical Evaluation of the Newly-Ratified Mexican-American Transfer of Penal Sanctions Treaty*, 64 IOWA L. REV. 325 (1979) and Professor Vagt's response thereto in the same issue. The provision requires: the existence of double criminality; that the transferee be a citizen or a permanent resident of the country to which he is to be transferred; that the transfer be subject to his consent; that the transfer be only after a conviction or sentence is final; that the receiving state shall give the transferee any legal advantages that the legal system under which the sentence was imposed provides to him, and that all other conditions of detention and custody are subject to the laws of the receiving state. Ameliorative conditions, whether under the laws of the sending or receiving state, shall be to the benefit of the transferee.

A scheme for transfer of offenders can be said to rely in part on the assumption that a given state will recognize the criminal judgment of the Tribunal. The manner in which this Article is drafted does not necessarily make such an assumption and leaves open the possibility that such a procedure is in the nature of an administrative transfer which derives from the sovereign powers of a state to enter into international agreements. The possibility of interpreting this Article in this manner allows needed flexibility for those states which would not other~,vise be able to recognize the validity of a foreign penal judgment. *See also* Epp, *7he European Convention on Transfer of Prisoners, in* BASSIOUNI, 2 ICL 253.

The general conditions for transfers are found in the EUROPEAN CONVENTION ON THE TRANSFER OF SENTENCED PERSONS, Europ. T.S. No. 112 (1983); MULLER-RAPPARD & BASSIOUNI, 1 EUROPEAN INTER-STATE COOPERATION chapter 3. Acceptance of the responsibility to enforce a sanction partially transfers competence over the sentence from the Tribunal and vests it with the Administering Party, subject to the supervision of the Court.

CHAPTER 9. BASIC PRINCIPLES OF FAIRNESS

Article XLIV. Rights of the Individual

1.   In all surrender proceedings and other forms of legal assistance and cooperation, the subject of said proceedings shall have the right to appear in person before the appropriate judicial organs of the state in which these proceedings are conducted to oppose the request or contemplated action of the Tribunal, to be represented by counsel, to be heard before an ordinary tribunal, and to appeal before a reviewing court.

Commentary

This provision was included in recognition of the desirability of acknowledging that the procedures under this Convention are of importance and interest to the State-Parties in the prosecution or extradition of accused persons, but not to the exclusion of basic human rights to which an accused is entitled. It is intended to establish that individuals subjected to such procedures have a right to claim compliance with the provisions of this Convention, and to international human rights standards of such procedures. This provision is consonant with the EUROPEAN CONVENTION FOR THE PROTECTION OF HUMAN RIGHTS AND FUNDAMENTAL FREEDOMS, 4 Nov. 1950, 218 U.N.T.S. 221, Europ. T.S. No. 5 and ADDITIONAL PROTOCOLS 1-10 inclusive. *See* UNIVERSAL DECLARATION OF HUMAN RIGHTS, 10 December 1948, G.A. Res. 217A (III); INTERNATIONAL COVENANT ON CIVIL AND POLITICAL RIGHTS, 26 December 1966, G.A. Res. 2200A, 21 U.N. GAOR Supp. (No. 16)49, U.N. Doc. A/6316 (1966); OPTIONAL PROTOCOL TO THE INTERNATIONAL COVENANT ON CIVIL AND POLITICAL RIGHTS, 16 December 1966, G.A. Res. 2200A, 21 U.N. GAOR Supp. (No. 16) 59, U . N. Doc. A/6316 (1966); INTER-AMERICAN CONVENTION ON HUMAN RIGHTS, 22 November 1969, O.A.S. Official Records Ser. K/XVI/I.I, Doc. 65, Rev. 1, Corr. I (January 7, 1970).

CHAPTER 10. GENERAL TREATY PROVISIONS

Article XLV. Settlement of Disputes

Any dispute arising out of the interpretation, application, or implementation of this Convention, which has not been settled by negotiation or arbitration, shall, at the request of any party, be submitted the Court pursuant to Article XIX, paragraph 1.

Article XLVI. Reservations

1.   Any reservations a State-Party may wish to make to this Convention shall be subject to the provisions of the *Vienna Convention of the Law of Treaties.*

2.   No reservation to the applicability of any provision of this Convention can he made with respect to existing international obligations.

Article XLVII. Signature and Accessions

1.   This Convention is open for signature by all Member States of the United Nations.

2.   Accession shall be effected by the deposit of an instrument of accession with the Secretary-General of the United Nations.

Article XVIII. Ratification

1.   This Convention is subject to ratification by the signatory States in accordance with their national legal requirements.

2.   Instruments of ratification shall be deposited with the Secretary-General of the United Nations.

Article XLIX. Entry into Force

1.   This Convention shall enter into force on the thirtieth day after the deposit of the tenth instrument of ratification or accessions.

2.   After the date of entry into force of the Convention, the date of entry into force for subsequent ratifications and accessions by States shall be on the thirtieth day after the date of the deposit with the Secretary-General of that State's own instrument of ratification or accession.

Article L. Revision and Withdrawal

1.   A request for the revision of this Convention or withdrawal therefrom may be made at any time by any State-Party by means of a notification in writing addressed to the Secretary-General of the United Nations, with copies to all other State-Parties.

2.   A request for revision or withdrawal shall have effect after the passage of the sixth month after the notification has been received by the Secretary General of the United Nations.

3. A State-Party requesting revision or withdrawal shall remain obligated to carry out the provisions of the convention during the six month period stated in paragraph 2, and also with respect to the execution of sentences commenced before the notice.

Article LI. Changes in Annex Schedule of Offenses

The State-Parties may change the scheduled offenses in Annexes 2 and 3 without such a change being considered a revision or withdrawal whenever:

a. New offenses are added to Annex 2 and 3
b. Offenses scheduled in Annex 3 are moved to Annex 2

Any other change in the schedule of offenses in Annexes 2 and 3 shall be deemed a request for revision or withdrawal, and shall be subject to the provisions of Article XLIX.

Article LII. Annexes

1. Each State-Party shall attach a separate Annex 2 and 3 containing a schedule of the crimes or offenses it shall agree to submit to the jurisdiction of the Tribunal pursuant to Article XIX, paragraphs 2 and 3.
2. A State-Party agreeing to the *Ad Hoc* jurisdiction of the Tribunal pursuant to Article XIX paragraph 4 shall not be required to file a separate schedule, but shall inform the Tribunal of its *ad hoc* decision with respect to any crime or offense listed in Annex 1.

Article LIII. Notification

The Secretary-General of the United Nations shall inform all Member States of the following particulars:

a. date of entry into force of the present Convention;
b. signatures, ratifications, accessions and reservations;
c. notification of Revision and Withdrawal;
d. date of entry into force or effect with respect to a State-Party as to revision and withdrawal; and
e. Notification to all State-Parties of a State-Party's amendment to the schedule of offenses in Annexes 2 and 3.

Article LIV. Official Languages

This Convention, of which the Arabic, Chinese, English, French, Russian and Spanish texts are equally authentic, shall be deposited with the United Nation

Article LV. Transmittal

The Secretary-General of the United Nations shall transmit certified copies of this Convention to all State-Parties.

ANNEX 1

Proposed Schedule of Crimes which the State-Parties recognize as susceptible of being the subject of the Tribunal's jurisdiction in accordance with Article XIX

1. Aggression
2. War crimes
3. Unlawful use, production and stockpiling of certain prohibited weapons
4. Crimes against humanity
5. Genocide
6. *Apartheid*
7. Slavery and slave-related practices
8. Torture
9. Unlawful human experimentation
10. Piracy
11. Offenses against international maritime navigation
12. Unlawful seizure of aircraft, sabotage and related crimes
13. Attacks against internationally protected persons
14. Taking of hostages
15. Unlawful use of the mails (for terror-violence)
16. Drug offenses (international)
17. Destruction and/or theft of national treasures and cultural heritage
18. Environmental violations
19. Cutting of submarine cables
20. International traffic in obscene materials

21. Counterfeiting (currency)
22. Bribery of foreign public officials
23. Theft of nuclear materials
24. Mercenarism

ANNEX 2
Schedule of Crimes contained in Annex 1, which the State-Parties agree to submit to the Tribunal's exclusive jurisdiction in accordance with Article XIX, paragraph 2.
(To be negotiated by the State-Parties)

ANNEX 3
Proposed Schedule of Crimes contained in Annex 1 for which the Tribunal would have jurisdiction based on Concurrent and/or Transfer of Criminal Proceedings in accordance with Article XIX, paragraph 3[1]

2. War crimes
3. Unlawful use, production and stockpiling of certain prohibited weapons
4. Crimes against humanity
5. Genocide
6. *Apartheid*
7. Slavery and slave-related practices
10. Piracy
11. Offenses against international civil maritime navigation
12. Unlawful seizure of aircraft, sabotage and related crimes
13. Attacks against internationally protected persons
14. Taking of hostages (for terror-violence)
15. Unlawful use of the mails (for terror-violence)
16. Drug offenses (international)
17. Destruction and/or theft of national treasures and cultural heritage
19. Cutting of international submarine cables
21. Counterfeiting (currency)
23. Theft of nuclear materials

* * *

Unofficial Proposals on the Establishment of the ICC

1. Report on the Creation of an International Criminal Jurisdiction, by V.V. Pella to the Interparliamentary Union, XXII Conference, held in Berne and Geneva, 1924, *in L'Union Interparlementaire—Compte Rendue de la XXII Conference Tenue à Berne et à Genève en 1924, publié par le Bureau Interparliementaire*, 1925. *See also L'Union Interparlementaire—Compte Rendu de la XXII Conference Tenue à Washington et à Ottawa en 1925* (1925).

2. *Project d'une Cour Criminelle Internationale (Project for an International Criminal Court)*, adopted by the International Law Association at its 34th Conference in Vienna, August 1926, *The International Law Association, Report of the 34th Conference, Vienna, August 5-11, 1926* (1927).

3. *Project of the International Association of Penal Law, in* ACTES DU PREMIER CONGRÈS INTERNATIONAL DE DROIT PÉNAL, BRUXELLES, 26-29 JUNE 1926 (1927) and *Projet de Statut pour la Creation d'une Chambre Criminelle au Sein de la Cour Permanente de Justice Internationale*, presented by the International Association of Penal Law to the League of Nations in 1927, 5 REVUE INTERNATIONALE DE DROIT PÉNALE (1928).

---

[1]   The numbers used are those listed in Annex 1.

4. PROJECT FOR THE ESTABLISHMENT OF A CONVENTION FOR THE CREATION OF THE UNITED NATIONS TRIBUNAL FOR WAR CRIMES, established by the United Nations War Crimes Commission, 1944, *see* UNITED NATIONS WAR CRIMES COMMISSION (W. Wright ed. 1948).

5. *Project d'une Jurisdiction internationale de L'Union Interparlementaire—Compte rendu de la XXVII Conference Tenue à Rome en 1948* (1949).

6. *Draft Statute for an International Criminal Court, in* J. STONE & R. WOETZEL, TOWARD A FEASIBLE INTERNATIONAL CRIMINAL COURT (1970).

7. *Draft Statute for an International Criminal Court,* Foundation for the Establishment of an International Criminal Court (Wingspread Conference, September 1971).

8. *Draft Statute for an International Criminal Court, Work Paper,* Abidjan World Conference on World Peace through Law, August 26-31, 1973.

9. *Draft Statute for an International Commission of Criminal Inquiry, International Law Association, 60th Conference, Montreal, August 29-September 4, 1982, in* REPORT OF THE 60TH CONFERENCE OF THE INTERNATIONAL LAW ASSOCIATION (1983).

10. *Draft Statute for an International Criminal Tribunal,* presented by the International Institute of Higher Studies in Criminal Sciences to the Eighth United Nations Congress on the Prevention of Crime and the Treatment of Offenders (Havana, Cuba, August 27-September 7, 1990), A/Conf.144/NGO7 (ISISC), 31 July 1990. *Reprinted in* 15 NOVA L. REV. 374 (1991).

11. M. Cherif Bassiouni, *Draft Statute: International Criminal Tribunal,* 9 NOUVELLES ÉTUDES PÉNALES (1993).

12. M. Cherif Bassiouni, *Draft Statute: International Criminal Tribunal (Projet de Statut du Tribunal Penal International, Proyecto de Estatuto del Tribunal Penal Internacional),* 10 NOUVELLES ÉTUDES PÉNALES (1993), translated in French and Spanish, *Projet de Statut du Tribunal Penal International, Proyecto de Estatuto del Tribunal Penal Internacional,* 10 NOUVELLES ÉTUDES PÉNALES 1993.

13. *Draft Statute for an International Criminal Court (Siracusa-Draft),* prepared by a committee of experts and informally submitted to the 1995 *Ad Hoc* Committee on the Establishment of an International Criminal Court by the International Association of Penal Law, the International Institute of Higher Studies in Criminal Sciences and the Max Planck Institute for Foreign and International Criminal Law, July 31, 1995.

14. *1994 ILC Draft Statute for an International Criminal Court With Suggested Modifications (Updated Siracusa-Draft),* prepared by a committee of experts and informally submitted to the 1996 Preparatory Committee on the Establishment of an International Criminal Court by the International Association of Penal Law, the International Institute of Higher Studies in Criminal Sciences, the International Scientific and Professional Advisory Council, Parliamentarians for Global Action, the World Federalist Movement/Institute for Global Policy, the Max Planck Institute for Foreign and International Criminal Law, and the International Human Rights Law Institute, DePaul University, March 15, 1996.